The Slaughter of Cities

The Slaughter of Cities
Urban Renewal as Ethnic Cleansing

E. Michael Jones

ST. AUGUSTINE'S PRESS
South Bend, Indiana
2004

1 2 3 4 5 6   10 09 08 07 06 05 04

Library of Congress Cataloging in Publication Data
Jones, E. Michael.
    The slaughter of cities : urban renewal as ethnic cleansing / E. Michael
      Jones.
         p. cm.
    Includes bibliographical references and index.
    ISBN 1-58731-775-3 (hardcover : alk. paper)
    1. Urban renewal – United States – History. 2. Inner cities – United States
    – History. 3. Ethnic neighborhoods – United States – History.
    4. Community life – United States – History. 5. United States – Ethnic
    relations – History. I. Title.
HT175 .J65 2002
307.3'416'0973 – dc21   2002012097

∞ The paper used in this publication meets the minimum requirements of the American National Standard for Information Sciences – Permanence of Paper for Printed Materials, ANSI Z39.48-1984.

You will see bloodshed and poisoning and have accusations of defendants, the slaughter of cities and genocide and the heads of leaders up for auction, torched houses and cities in flames and enormous spaces of territory blazing with hostile fire. Behold the scarcely traceable foundations of the most eminent cities: anger destroyed them. Behold wastelands empty for thousands of miles: anger emptied them.

> Seneca
> *De Ira* 1.21–2

I must speak also of the earthly city . . . of that city which lusts to dominate the world and which, though nations bend to its yoke, is itself dominated by its passion for dominion.

> St. Augustine
> *City of God*

There is nothing so infuriates me as the disguised aggressions of a Quaker.

> Michael Novak
> *The Rise of the Unmeltable Ethnics*, p. 207

Down South you were black or white. You wasn't Irish or Polish or all of this.

> Southern Christian Leadership Conference worker Dorothy Tillman
> (from John McGreevy, *Parish Boundaries*, p. 197)

Where there are several distinct minorities in a country the dominant group can allow itself the luxury of treating some of them generously and can entrench itself and secure its dominance by playing one minority against another.

> Louis Wirth
> UC Archives

The precedent setting role of Philadelphia government should be documented very carefully.

> Dennis Clark
> Diary

The Foundation is a calculating political instrument; there's no question about it and therefore it has to be watched in a society like ours.

> Paul Ylvisaker
> Autobiographical Memoir for the Ford Foundation

Contents

Acronym Abbreviations

ABCD	Action for Boston Community Development
ABM	Anti-Ballistic Missile
ACLU	American Civil Liberties Union
ADA	Americans for Democratic Action
AFL	American Federation of Labor
AFSC	American Friends Service Committee
ADL	Anti-Defamation League
AJC	American Jewish Committee
B-BURG	Boston Banks Urban Renewal Group
BCCS	Boston College Citizen's Seminars
BHA	Boston Housing Authority
BPE	Better Philadelphia Exhibition
BRA	Boston Redevelopment Authority
CAD	Council against Discrimination
CCC	Citywide Coordinating Committee
CCCO	Chicago Coordinating Council of Community Organizations
CCCP	Citizens Council on City Planning
CCPGP	Catholics Concerned about Population and Government Policy
CFGC	Church Federation of Greater Chicago
CFR	Council on Foreign Relations
CHA	Chicago Housing Authority
CHD	Campaign for Human Development
CHR	Commission on Human Relations
CIA	Central Intelligence Agency
CIC	Catholic Interracial Council
CIO	Council of Industrial Organizations
CIRC	Catholic Intergroup Relations Council
CORE	Congress for Racial Equality
CPI	Committee of Public Information
CRD	Community Relations Division
CU	Catholic University
DDHC	Division of Defense Housing Coordination
DEA	Drug Enforcement Agency
DHC	Detroit Housing Commission
FBI	Federal Bureau of Investigation
FHA	Federal Housing Administration
FSH	Friends Suburban Housing
FUND	Fund for United Negro Development
FWA	Federal Works Agency
GBIA	Garfield Boulevard Improvement Association
GIU	Gang Intelligence Unit
HADV	Housing Association of the Delaware Valley
HOLC	Homeowners Loan Corporation
HOP	Housing Opportunities Program
HUAC	House Un-American Activities Committee
HUD	Housing Urban Development
IHR	Institute on Human Relations

IIT	Illinois Institute of Technology	PCPC	Philadelphia City Planning Commission
ILGWU	International Ladies Garment Workers Union	PHA	Philadelphia Housing Authority
IRA	Irish Republican Army	PHAssoc	Philadelphia Housing Association
JCMH	Joint Committee on Minority Housing	PMFHP	Philadelphia Metropolitan Fair Housing Program
JDL	Jewish Defense League	POAU	Protestants and Other Americans United (for the Separation of Church and State)
KKK	Ku Klux Klan		
KWRU	Kensington Welfare Rights Union		
MBS	Most Blessed Sacrament (Parish)	PRR	Pennsylvania Railroad
		RA	Redevelopment Authority
MHPCC	Metropolitan Housing and Planning Council of Chicago	SCLC	Southern Christian Leadership Conference
MOVE	black commune in Philadelphia in the '70s and '80s (not an acronym)	SDIA	South Deering Improvement Association
		SFA	Suburban Fair Housing
MPHP	Metropolitan Philadelphia Housing Program	SNCC	Student Non-Violent Coordinating Committee
NAACP	National Association for the Advancement of Colored People	STRESS	Stop the Robberies Enjoy Safe Streets
NATO	North Atlantic Treaty Organization	UAW	United Auto Workers
		UBMC	United Brokers Mortgage Company
NCC	National Council of Churches		
NCWC	National Catholic Welfare Conference	UCCA	Urban Community Conservation Act
NORC	National Opinion Research Center	UF	United Fund
		UNESCO	United Nations Education Scientific and Cultural Organization
NSC	National Security Council		
OEO	Office of Economic Opportunity		
OIC	Opportunities Industrialization Corps.	USHA	United States Housing Authority
		VA	Veterans Administration
OFF	Office of Facts and Figures	WASP	White Anglo-Saxon Protestant
OSS	Office of Strategic Services	WPB	War Production Board
OWI	Office of War Information	WTO	World Trade Organization
PCCA	Philadelphia Council for Community Advancement	YMCA	Young Men's Christian Association

Prologue

The Republican Convention and the Reality Tour

Si monumentum requiris, circumspice!

If, during the 2000 Republican National Convention, you wandered about the city of Philadelphia from one protest to the other looking for a coherent focus of the sort the World Trade Organization provided in Seattle, you wandered in vain. The protest was made up of the usual grab-bag of leftist causes, all in search of an event that would focus their efforts into one coherent action. The Republican Convention, however, was doing its best to deprive them of this cause by espousing the very same identity politics that motivated the protesters. What exactly were the protesters supposed to protest in Colin Powell advocating affirmative action? There was plenty of military imperialism to protest, but the war in Kosovo was a distant memory, and besides, wars are no longer scheduled to happen during political conventions. As a result, most of the protest was rage looking for a cause, and the inchoate thrashing which followed therefrom was largely the result of protest being co-opted by the dominant culture's main control mechanism, namely, sexual liberation. If the left dug far enough into the culture they hated, they inevitably found some connection with the forces of sexual management, which they would invariably defend. This meant that the protesters were *against* globalism but *for* global population control, because that was sexual, and once the issue became connected with sexual liberation, well, that was, as the young punk anarchist had told me, different.

What the overwhelming majority of the protesters ignored was the one thing that might have given their protest some coherence, namely, the city itself, whose state of devastation offers mute proof of the baneful effects that government policies have had on Philadelphia for the entire second half of the twentieth century. If cities could speak, Philadelphia might have borrowed a phrase from the architect Christopher Wrenn. *"Si causa requiris,"* Philadelphia might have told the protesters by way of paraphrase, *"circumspice."* If you need a monument to the folly and malice of government policy over the past fifty years, look around you.

As a matter of fact, one group did just that. The Kensington Welfare Rights Union created an impromptu tent village at the corner of 6th and Jefferson in the area far enough north of the renewed center city to show what has happened in the shadow of all of the new high-rise downtown buildings. They also organized a bus tour, known as the Reality Tour, of the area around the camp, a section of what was once working-class Philadelphia known as Kensington. What those who took the bus tour learned is what anyone who grew up in Philadelphia knew already, namely, that the city beyond the high-rise hotels and office towers of center city has been so devastated that the only analogue that makes any sense is war-torn areas of places like Mostar in Bosnia. The analogy to Bosnia is especially apt because ethnic conflict led to the destruction of both cities, but ethnicity is not something that the KWRU discusses on its tour.

Philadelphia, 2000

Tamsin, our tour guide, allows the facts to speak for themselves, and to a certain extent they do, but only to a certain extent. Philadelphia now has 40,000 abandoned homes and 17,000 vacant lots. If you require a monument to what happened to Philadelphia, none would be more imposing than the abandoned Schmidt's brewery building at Second and Girard. Schmidt's used to provide the beer for Philadelphia's saloons and bars when the area around Girard between 2nd and 5th Streets was a thriving German neighborhood and long after it was not. My grandfather attended school at St. Peter's at 5th and Girard, where St. John Neuman is buried and where, at the time, the language of instruction was German. When Schmidt's went out of business in 1982, 1,400 people lost their jobs. Now the building looks like the abandoned cliff-dweller villages of the Anazi in the Southwest, serving as a refuge for the city's homeless, who like cave dwellers in southern France, decorate their abodes by painting the walls. One of the tour guides informs those on the bus that graffiti is the only art form available to the homeless. When I ask which part of Kensington she is from, she tells me that she is from Seattle.

Kensington, in other words, has acquired an aura which draws young people from all across the nation to come and contemplate a devastation that is in many ways as mysterious as it is obvious. As in the Bible, the very stones cry out in Philadelphia. However, just what they are saying is not immediately clear. Tamsin, who is from that part of Kensington known as Connecticut, has studied history at the University of Pennsylvania and is well versed in the devastation that has visited Philadelphia. She talks about the abandoned factories on American Street, the heroin that gets sold on Elbow Alley, and the prostitution that flourishes at the corner of Front and Lehigh. But she seems less aware that Kensington was a place where people of a particular background used to live until they got moved out by forces which have yet to be explained. Cheri Honkala, the lady who is the driving force and media presence behind the KWRU, did not grow up in Kensington. She ended up there when she became homeless, because Kensington, which was once a thriving industrial blue-collar neighborhood, where it was said you could get a job in five minutes by walking down American Street, is simply the city neighborhood where the homeless congregate. And they congregate there because the natives have been driven out, leaving large numbers of vacant buildings.

Cheri is not on the bus tour, but Katie Engle, who is president of KWRU, is. Katie is considerably older than the average volunteer, and, unlike them, she actually comes from Kensington. On our first stop, at "Bushville," named in honor of the candidate who would eventually become the nation's president, Katie gives a long impassioned speech about HMOs and how the poor are being systematically deprived of health care. It is a theme which she returns to repeatedly. Katie is in her fifties and has had two heart attacks, so it is not surprising that health care is on her mind. When I ask her if she still has relatives in Kensington, she replies that she does, but that "they don't want to have anything to do with me because I'm poor." Katie, like Cheri, wants more government action. Yet the underlying theme of the Reality Tour is that government action created this mess in the first place.

During the '90s as part of the Democratic Party's recurrent efforts to revitalize the nation's cities, the Clinton Administration approved $80 million dollars for Philadelphia and declared Kensington's American Street part of an "Empowerment Zone," designating $17 million to rehabilitate it. The textile and hosiery mills left town during the '50s under the enabling gaze of the Eisenhower Administration. When the mill workers whose lives had been disrupted by workers imported from the South during World War II attempted to unionize, the people who owned the mills closed them down and moved them down South to capitalize on cheaper, non-union labor. When, twenty years later, the people down South tried the same thing, the mill owners moved again, this time across the border into Mexico. By now, the mills are probably all safe in China, or Nicaragua, or Vietnam, where Communist governments provide the infrastructure for capitalist exploitation of the working class. However, the Republican attempts to abandon the city pale in comparison to the destruction which the Democrats wrought by trying to rehabilitate the cities through schemes like urban renewal and "fair" housing laws. All one can say without the danger of being contradicted it that the destruction of Philadelphia was a bi-partisan effort.

Which is in many ways how the natives feel. Maureen is a red-headed Irish Catholic graduate of Little Flower High School who was not part of the Reality Tour. She is a recent refugee from Kensington, living in Northeast Philadelphia, at least temporarily, which is to say until the same forces which drove her out of Kensington drive her out of there too. Maureen did not want to leave Kensington. She felt she was forced out by the violence. Her story points up the fact that there are in effect two Kensingtons, the one composed of people who have been driven out, the other composed of the homeless who see it as the only place left to go. At certain points the two groups intersect, as in the case of Katie Engle. They manifest their alienation by two opposite extremes, both of which bespeak despair of the political process. On the one hand, there is the activism of the "homeless" faction in the mode of the civil-rights movement, featuring publicity stunts, parades without permits, etc., in the hopes of freeing up more federal money; on the other hand, the natives end up voting with their feet, like Maureen, or they manifest the same alienation from the political process by not voting at all. The KWRU announced that in the last mayoral election, only 17 percent of Kensington's registered voters went to the polls. Maureen says much the same thing. She and her husband don't vote.

If their convention was any indication of their priorities, the Republicans don't seem overly concerned about Maureen's vote. Like the Love Parade in Berlin and the Biker Rally in Sturgis, South Dakota, the Republican Convention was one more example of identity politics. Principles took a back seat to ethnicity as one Republican woman of color after another took the podium to give Cokie and Sam the impression that this was the real party of inclusion. The only exception to this rule was when Hispanics and men of color like Colin Powell took the podium to extol the virtues of military imperialism and affirmative action. The highpoint of this preliminary phase of the convention took place when Bush advisor Condoleeza Rice took the primetime stage to extol the virtues of military imperialism and her granddaddy, who went off to college and became a Presbyterian minister, when he ran out of money and heard that scholarships were available for that purpose.

In a convention that was scripted down to the last smile and semi-colon, there were no spontaneous outbursts and no deviations from the script, not by John McCain and George W. Bush, and so certainly not by Professor Rice, who informed the audience that the lesson she drew from her granddaddy's impromptu conversion to Presbyterianism, is that her family has remained "Presbyterian and college educated ever since." Now in a country which has nothing but versions of Protestantism to offer, this may be the best that we can expect. It is certainly better that a Dionysian Baptist like the former incumbent and his neo-pagan minions, but it is an ethnicity all the same, and it was not Maureen's ethnos.

At the convention they made it clear that the Republican Party is the Protestant party, and that Protestants come in two colors, black and white. This alliance of upper-class WASP and lower-class black was once known as the civil-rights movement. It was also, *mutatis mutandis,* the coalition which destroyed Philadelphia. Upper-class WASPs, large-ly Episcopalian and Quaker, united politically with the blacks they brought up from the South to work in their factories during World War II to defeat the group in the middle, namely, the largely Catholic ethnics who lived in neighborhoods like Kensington.

The Republicans used to run this city, but the Republicans who used to run Philadel-phia over fifty years ago were a different sort. They were white, they were Protestant, they were Masons, they also lived in neighborhoods like Kensington, but they were also wary of outsiders. Mayor Robert Lamberton became famous overnight in the early '40s when he turned down $19 million in federal housing funds, saying that it smacked of socialism.

It was the last time anyone in Philadelphia – Democrat or Republican – had any qualms about money from Washington, even if the money were used to destroy the city, which is how urban renewal money was used. The planners had an ethnic identity that went deeper than party affiliation. In 1947 Edmund Bacon, who, in 1964, would land on the cover of *Time* as urban planner extraordinaire, and Oscar Stonorow, a student of Walter Gropius who was also Bacon's brother-in-law, and Walter M. Phillips, a WASP aristocrat who would have enormous behind-the-scenes influence over the city in the coming years, put their heads together and came up with the Better Philadelphia Exhibit, their plan for the city's future. It covered almost an entire floor of one of the large downtown department stores, and its message could be grasped by even the most obtuse student of architecture: the future was Bauhaus and the enemy was the rowhouse, the traditional building block of housing in the city. Lest the especially dull-witted miss the latter part of the message, Messrs. Stonorow and Bacon constructed a full-scale model of 13th and Natrona, an inter-section in South Philadelphia, complete with dreary corner store and strategically placed trash can to show that vernacular architecture in the city of homes was an example of "everything that was wrong with Philadelphia," as the writer from *Architecture Digest* put it.

Lest anyone think this was a nonpartisan affair, the people who attended the Better Philadelphia Exhibit were given what seemed to be a blank piece of paper, which when placed under a black light at the exit of the exhibition informed them that they should vote for Barney Samuels, the man who, it turns out, was the last Republican mayor of Philadelphia. Edmund Bacon thought that his shameless campaigning for Samuels might mean the end of his career as a city planner in Philadelphia, but he was wrong. When it comes to city planning, ethnic blood runs thicker than political water. The Democratic reform team which came to power in 1951 was a coalition which included Catholics (in fact, it never could have come to power without their votes), but it was run by WASP blue-bloods like Joe Clark of Chestnut Hill and Dick Dilworth (who came from Pittsburgh) and Walter Phillips, the man who in many ways made the whole reform ticket possible by assembling the *dramatis personae*, including Bacon, and infusing them with his vision, which was a combination of WASP *noblesse oblige* and the Enlightenment's faith in things like urban planning.

On September 15, 1948, one year after the Better Philadelphia Exhibit and one year before the Democrats gained their first toehold in city government, the Philadelphia City Planning Commission under Phillips's aegis came up with its map of redevelopment areas and public housing sites. I say "came up with," not "published," because the contents of the map would remain secret for the next six years (although somehow these confidential documents ended up in the possession of Quakers in Chicago). Just why it had to remain secret became obvious when it became public. The largely Catholic ethnics who lived in the neighborhoods that were scheduled to be torn down were outraged and made their outrage known to their elected representatives. What followed was a war which eventually destroyed the reform coalition, which then broke down into its ethnic components over the dispute of whose neighborhood got torn down and where integrated public housing would be built.

The scale of the devastation which the Philadelphia City Planning Commission prepared for Philadelphia was simply breathtaking in scope. All of North Philadelphia from Diamond (the border would later be moved north to Lehigh) to Spring Garden Street and from Broad to 5th was scheduled to be torn down. The same fate awaited all of "East" Philadelphia from Vine Street north of Market to Tasker in the south, and from 8th Street to the Delaware River. All of what is traditionally known as South Philadelphia from South Street to Dickinson and from Broad to the famous 9th Street Market was also scheduled to be torn down, even though the best housing stock in South Philadelphia, owned by the Italian elite, doctors, lawyers, etc., was to be found along Broad Street.

The most shocking part of the map, however, lay in the gray-hatched patch off to the northeast well outside of the intensive-use central area where some of the city's oldest housing stock existed. That part of town was known as Bridesburg. It was, like Kensington, which lay to the south, industrial and residential combined, which was the pattern of industrial 19th-century Philadelphia. What Bridesburg did not have was run-down houses. What Bridesburg did have was ethnic homogeneity. It housed the overwhelming majority of the Polish population of Philadelphia. Ask those who know the history of urban renewal in Philadelphia today why Bridesburg was targeted for destruction, and you will get no answer. That is so for one simple reason: according to the criteria which the renewers themselves established, Bridesburg was not blighted, if by blight one means deteriorated housing stock. Bridesburg was a mixed-use neighborhood, but so was just about all of the rest of old Philadelphia. The trouble with Bridesburg lay not in its buildings.

When I asked one of the priests at St. John Cantius parish, which serves the Polish population there, why the planned destruction didn't happen, he couldn't come up with an answer either. But the answer in both instances has to do with ethnicity. Bridesburg survived because the Poles refused to move from the neighborhood. Unlike their Irish co-religionists, they were not seduced by the siren song of assimilation. The same thing can be seen in Polish neighborhoods like Hamtramck near Detroit. The Poles who were successful didn't move to the suburbs when they made money. Instead, they tore down the conventional housing stock and built a brick palace in its place.

Philadelphia, Bridesburg

Bridesburg was not blighted, but it was Polish. The Philadelphia Planning Commission, like the Philadelphia Housing authority, the agencies which plotted this destruction had no Poles on their boards or planning commissions. As a result, what went by the name of urban renewal was, in effect, one ethnic group, namely the WASPs from Germantown and Chestnut Hill, coming up with a plan for destroying the neighborhood of another ethnic group, without that group's consultation or permission, even when the obvious indicators of blight were missing. Taken as a whole the Planning Commission Map of 1948 was a recipe for ethnic cleansing on a massive scale. The Jews were to be moved from Philadelphia's "East Side" to make way for Society Hill, the residential enclave where the city's *Nomenklatura* were to be housed; the Italians were to be moved from large areas of South Philadelphia, the Irish from large areas of North Philadelphia. The fact that blacks were to be removed from areas around Temple University and the University of Pennsylvania would mean more ethnic cleansing for the Catholic ethnics as well, as wave after wave of displaced blacks would have to seek housing in adjacent, which is to say, Catholic and ethnic, areas. Each instance of urban renewal and redevelopment was like a rock dropped into a pool. The number of units of public housing which got built never equaled the number of units which got torn down, and as a result, more blacks got displaced than got housed by government efforts. As a result, Catholic ethnics were either removed directly, when their houses got torn down to make way for the projects, or indirectly by the waves of blacks who had to move to neighborhoods adjacent in price and geography when the houses they were living in were torn down and never replaced.

This book tells the story of housing policy and social engineering in four large cities in the period during and following World War II. Since housing was just one focus of social engineering, this book tells other related stories as well, all of which had an impact on these cities. There was a time when the Western World, and many Americans, believed in progress. As anyone who has seen the rebirth of cities in Europe after their destruction during the war can say, that progress is not a mark of American cities. This book is an attempt to explain why. The fundamental fact, however, is available to anyone who takes the time to go beyond the showcase buildings at the center of downtown Detroit or Philadelphia and look at the poverty and destruction that surround them in what were once thriving neighborhoods. If you require a monument to the folly of the social engineering that brought about that devastation, just look around.

E. Michael Jones
South Bend, April 2002

The Blanshard Boys Come to Philadelphia

In the summer of 1918, Paul and Brand Blanshard arrived in Philadelphia to participate in what would eventually prove to be an ill-fated social experiment. The Blanshard boys were born as twins to a Congregationalist minister in Fredricksburg, Ohio, in 1892. Paul, who would go on to become the more famous of the two, would say of his family that it "was afflicted with too much religion,"[1] but at an earlier age he seems not to have thought this, since he was ordained as a Congregationalist minister himself. In 1917, Paul abandoned his congregation in Florida and moved to New York City, where like John B. Watson and others of that generation, he abandoned the ministry and dedicated himself to the social sciences – as with John B. Watson again, under the tutelage of John Dewey.

Shortly after arriving in New York Paul ended up in an advanced seminar at Columbia University being taught by Dewey. His brother Brand, after taking a slightly different route – he received a Rhodes scholarship to Oxford in 1913 – ended up in the same course. Paul was hoping to get a Ph.D. in sociology. His brother Brand was to become a philosopher of some note, but both fell under the spell of John Dewey, the man who at the time was considered the Socrates of a particularly American brand of philosophy which went by the name of pragmatism. Also taking the same class was a Philadelphia businessman twenty years their senior by the name of Albert C. Barnes. Barnes, who had been born in Kensington in 1872, when it was a respectable working-class neighborhood whose textile mills had prospered during the American Civil War, was something of a *Wunderkind*, getting admitted to Central High School, the elite public school at the time, and then the University of Pennsylvania, where he finished his medical degree in record time.

Right around the turn of the century, Barnes began experimenting with silver compounds and eventually came up with a salve known as Argyrol, which would prevent the transmission of congenital syphilis when applied to the eyes of new-born children. Argyrol in short order made Barnes a very rich man, allowing him the luxury of building a granite mansion in Bala Cynwyd, one of Philadelphia's then-fashionable suburbs, which he promptly began to stock with modern art. In 1912 Barnes sent one of his agents to Paris with $20,000, and the man returned with a Renoir, a couple Van Goghs, a Matisse, and what would eventually become the basis for one of the most important collections of impressionist art in the world.[2] Had Barnes been possessed of a less abrasive personality he might have made a significant contribution to Philadelphia's already strong reputation as the center of the fine arts in America, a tradition which included artists like Thomas Eakins and institutions like the Pennsylvania Academy of Fine Arts. Barnes would eventually write a book which showed that he was no dilettante when it came to understanding the principles of fine art, but unfortunately the Philadelphia Museum of Art was run by people more dilettantish than knowledgeable, people who thought of art as something determined more by social standing than understanding, and so a conflict was inevitable. When Barnes died in an automobile accident in the summer of 1951, his collection of modern art was closed to the public and put under the trusteeship of Lincoln University, a Negro institution to the south of town.[3] Barnes seems to have chosen Lincoln as a way of deliberately scandalizing and antagonizing the pretensions of the Philadelphia high society which rejected him.

Barnes was a modernist in other ways as well. He was a financial backer of the *New Republic*, which had been founded in 1914 as the flagship of liberal internationalism under the guidance of Walter Lippmann, Herbert Croly, and John Dewey. Not surprisingly, Barnes became a devoted supporter of Dewey and his ideas, particularly after reading his book *Democracy and Education*. It was that infatuation with Dewey's ideas that led Barnes to enroll in Dewey's seminar at Columbia, inducing him to commute twice a week to New York.

Although by this time Barnes must have seemed far removed from the working-class Kensington of his boyhood, the old neighborhood must have still been on his mind. Or at least if not Kensington, then Bridesburg, the neighborhood just to the northeast of Kensington. Unlike the older Kensington, Bridesburg had become a center of Polish migration to the new world. Unlike the Scotch, English, and Irish residents of Kensington, the residents of Bridesburg spoke a language that effectively cut them off from the increasingly important instruments of mass communication and public education which facilitated Americanization. America was now at war with the central powers in Europe and in the midst of a propaganda war against ethnics, specifically Germans, at home. At the time Dewey held his seminar at Columbia, Walter Lippmann was working for George Creel at the Committee on Public Information, America's first propaganda ministry, trying to engineer the loyalty of the nation's ethnics away from their country of origin and toward supporting the war effort. Four years later Lippmann would distill his experiences with the CPI into one of the first books on information theory and psychological warfare, *Public Opinion*. Lippmann's point was frankly elitist. The ordinary citizen was incapable of making the judgments necessary to keep the government running in the scientific age, and so he should be fed "stereotypes" that made the right choices (i.e., those favored by the *New Republic*) easier for him. That meant that that every citizen had to be exposed to the dominant culture's media, which included newspapers, journals of opinion, and, most importantly, advertising, and that meant that ethnics would have to be "Americanized" in things like the Melting Pot Pageants which took place on July 4, 1918, at various parks throughout the country. As described in Lippmann's book, the various immigrant groups would climb into a large *papier maché* pot wearing their native costumes and singing their native songs only to emerge at the end of the ceremony wearing bowler hats and suits and singing the *Star-Spangled Banner*. No aspect of culture was going to be left unexamined under the new regime of Americanization, not even food. "What kind of American consciousness can grow in the atmosphere of sauerkraut and Limburger cheese?" Lippmann asked. "Or what can you expect of the Americanism of the man whose breath always reeks of garlic?"[4]

Not much, evidently. *The New Republic* never met a war it didn't like. In this its policies have a certain consistency stretching from World War I to the war in Kosovo. But even here their bellicosity had an ulterior motive. They loved war because they loved social engineering even better, and war, as John B. Watson, the father of behaviorism, said, was always the best excuse for social engineering. In a passage that would have an uncanny resonance with the study that Dewey was planning of the Poles in Bridesburg, Lippmann cites the effect that wartime propaganda had on Germany:

> . . . in the minds of most patriotic Protestant Germans, especially of the upper classes, the picture of Bismarck's victories included a long quarrel with the Roman Catholics. By a process of association, Belgian priests became priests, and hatred of Belgians a vent for all their hatreds. These German Protestants did what some Americans did when under the stress of war they created a compound object of hatred out of the enemy abroad and all their opponents at home.[5]

If the enemy abroad was, in other words, really only a transmuted version of the enemy at home, the real purpose of the war, especially from the point of view of the social engineers at the CPI, was the defeat of the domestic ethnic immigrants that populated neighborhoods like Bridesburg. World War I was creating in the minds of "native" Americans an enemy at home, and that enemy was the ethnic counterpart of the enemy abroad. The domestic equivalent of the draconian Versailles Peace Treaty would be the Palmer raids and the legal quotas on immigration, which at once stigmatized the largely Southern and Eastern European immigrants they were designed to exclude as being something less than fully American and an object of continuing suspicion. Two other sequelae of the war would be the simultaneous rise of the Ku Klux Klan, culminating in the campaign against Al Smith for President in 1928, and the rise of the Southern black sharecropper as the only source of untapped labor in the United States. Both these and other ills would flow from the decision to cut off immigration which followed shortly after the armistice. All of these issues would be revisited during the late '30s when the same people involved in the CPI during World War I (along with some new faces) got reorganized in the resurrection of psychological warfare which took place at the University of Chicago. That meant a renewed attack on ethnicity, one much more subtle than the one which prompted the Melting Pot Pageants of 1918, as well as new and more subtle attempts at social engineering and the manipulation of migration and housing policy for political ends.

Citing his former boss George Creel's book *How We Advertised America,* Lippmann goes on to say that "while the war continued it very largely succeeded, I believe, in creating something that might almost be called one public opinion all over America."[6] Unfortunately, at least from Lippmann's point of view, "Nothing like that exists in time of peace, and as a corollary there are whole sections, there are vast groups, ghettoes, enclaves and classes that hear only vaguely about much that is going on."[7] Which is to say, what Lippmann wants them to hear.

One of these "ghettoes" and "enclaves" was Bridesburg, and it was causing Albert C. Barnes a lot of concern. It was causing Dewey concern as well, so much so in fact that he took the opportunity presented by Barnes's attendance at the seminar to persuade him to finance a study of Polish immigrants and their "enculturation." Paul Blanshard would later characterize the whole project as "an amusing adventure" funded by "a respectable appearing elderly businessman" who "was a fanatical, almost unbalanced admirer of both John Dewey and Bertrand Russell. He wanted to use his money to advance their ideas in a practical way."[8] Swept away by those ideas and Dewey's prompting, Barnes

> suddenly . . . offered to take the whole seminar to Philadelphia for a summer of special study, concentrating on a district which was composed mostly of Polish immigrants. The suggested assignment was very vague. We were to apply the principles of John Dewey and Bertrand Russell to this area in any way we saw fit. He would rent a house for us and pay all the bills.[9]

Paul Blanshard never gets around to telling his readers why the experiment failed. He does say that Irwin Edman later wrote up a fictionalized account of the adventure in his book *Philosopher's Holiday*. The closest thing we have to a non-fiction report on the Barnes-funded research-program-cum-settlement-house is Brand Blanshard's dissertation *The Church and the Polish Immigrant*, a study of Polish immigrant mores from the point of view of the Protestant ruling class, as seen through the eyes of someone who had been anointed by that class to a position of intellectual importance by the fact of attending both Oxford (as a Rhodes scholar) and Harvard.

The first thing Brand Blanshard noticed after settling into Bridesburg was the influence of the Catholic Church. "The Church," he writes, "occupies in the Polish community a central place."[10] That religion should occupy the central role in a community is hardly novel; the same could be said about the influence of Unitarianism at Harvard. What Blanshard wants to impress on his reader is the difference between the two religions, something which is important enough to warrant repeated emphasis. "Those," he warns, "whose experience of Church influence has been confined to Protestant bodies will have exceedingly little idea of the extent of the Church's power in a Roman Catholic community."[11] That is so because, unlike the Protestant denominations, which solicit membership on an interest-group basis, the Catholic Church "particularly in a thoroughly Catholic community like that of the Poles is pervasive, continuous, aggressive and so ambitious as to demand the control of the whole of life."[12] The differences between Catholic and Protestant communities in the United States are based on radical differences in theology and as a result have far-reaching political consequences. Because of the claims which Catholicism makes on its Polish flock, it effectively denies the legitimacy of all competing ecclesial bodies. Blanshard complains that

> the direct and extra-ecclesiastical access to God which is commonly open to Protestants is impossible with [the Polish Catholic]. If he is to gain favor with the Deity at all, it must be through the recognized channels and in the approved manner of his Church. Unless his child receives the sacrament of baptism at the hands of the priest, it is cut off from all hope of heaven. If he is married by any other than Church authority he is living in adultery.[13]

As a result, the relationship between church and state, which Blanshard and Dewey see as typically "American," is called into question if not inverted. Instead of numerous denominational bodies, all of whom make essentially relativistic claims for themselves, all of which are therefore easily subsumed under government control, the Catholic Church makes absolute claims on its immigrant flock and, thereby, relativizes the claims of the American regime. From Dewey and the Blanshards' point of view, there are many different Protestant denominations in America, all of which are compatible with their democratic system of government. From the point of view of the Polish Immigrant, there is one true church, the same in Poland and the United States, which must find a *modus vivendi* with various forms of government, some better than others but all essentially subordinate to the true north on the compass established by the true faith, Catholicism. Viewing the same church-state relationship from his point of view, Blanshard concludes that the Roman Catholic Church's "influence is such as to create a many-sided and in some ways impassable barrier to the real democratization of the communities it controls."[14] The absolute claims which the Roman Catholic Church makes on Polish immigrants are, in other words, incompatible with the equally absolute claims which Dewey's form of Americanism makes on them. In a situation like this, something's got to give. Given both Blanshards' conviction that America was their country, and that their country was both Protestant and Enlightened, and their equally firm belief that human nature was a function of the environment and not of race ("Until you have thoroughly failed to see tradition being handed on from parents, teachers, priests, and uncle," Lippmann wrote, expressing their shared point of view and poking fun at the same time at the racialists of the Madison Grant–Lothrop Stoddard school, "it is a solecism of the worst order to ascribe political differences to the germ plasm."[15]) it was inevitable that the Blanshards under Dewey's tutelage would begin to think about social engineering as the cure for Polish lack of enlightenment in the new world.

Bridesburg was far from unique in this regard. The class of people which would look on it with suspicion in Philadelphia had their elite counterpart in other large cities with large immigrant populations. The Poles in Hamtramck and the Poletown neighborhood in Detroit were just as troublesome to the elites there as the Poles were to Dewey, Barnes, and the Blanshards in Philadelphia, for pretty much the same reason. The Poles may have been farmers in Europe, but when they came to America they became factory workers in the great industrial enterprises in America's industrial cities. Given the working conditions they found here, it was natural that they would become part of the workers' movement to unionize. The Poles had a natural advantage when it came to organizing for union activity because they were already organized as an ethnic and religious group. They even had their own "secret" language, one which defied espionage on the part of the government groups which attempted to break up their activities. During the Palmer raids of 1920 in Hamtramck and Poletown, government authorities seized what they suspected was socialist literature but were unable to read it because it was written in Polish. After seeing how many Poles voted for Socialist candidates in the 1918 and 1920 elections, Detroit auto manufacturer William Brush denounced them as an "alien threat" and an "enemy in our midst." The only solution to this threat, according to Brush, was "the total extermination of such monstrosities in human form."[16] During the labor unrest of the '30s, the Polish communities of Poletown and Hamtramck sided with their working class inhabitants as they engaged in sit-down strikes in Poletown's steel, auto, and cigar factories, causing "the old order in Detroit – the Protestants who controlled factories, the newspapers, the court system, and city hall" to view "these people as a threat." Their response to the threat was "to cut off immigration and to pressure immigrants into conforming to their standards."[17]

Like the CPI, the Ford Plants in the Detroit area sponsored their own version of the Melting Pot Pageant during the summer of 1918 as a way of Americanizing their fractious and recalcitrant ethnic workers. Of all of the European ethnic groups who created their colonies in the big industrial cities of the north, the Poles were least amenable to assimilation. In spite of their grudging participation in things like the Melting Pot Pageant, the Poles were "singularly uninterested in surrendering their 'foreign clothes and baggage.'"[18] As early as 1883, the *Detroit News* had written that the residents of Poletown "live and retain their customs to such an extent that the whole region more nearly resembles a fraction of Poland than a part of a city in the heart of America."[19] This cultural fact would eventually cause intra-religious conflict between the Poles and their more assimilationist-oriented Catholic co-religionists from Ireland. The conflict was exacerbated by the tendency among the Irish to the ecclesial version of upward mobility, which guaranteed that Irish priests would become bishops of just about every important diocese in the country at a time when there was virtually no pan-Catholic identity among the various immigrant groups. During the first half of the twentieth century, the Poles and the Irish viewed each other as members of mutually alien "races." This meant that Catholics were divided among themselves in ways in which their Protestant nativist opponents were not. According to the theory of the triple melting pot, country of origin is replaced by religion as the source of ethnicity during the third generation. Having been in the United States for more than three generations, the Protestants had attained a uniform animus against groups like the Poles. The Irish, on the other hand, still identified ethnicity with country of origin and were, in addition, more familiar with the English, whose language they spoke, than with their fellow Catholics from Southern and Eastern Europe. The Poles, as a result, were on their own when it came to the culture war in big cities like Detroit and Philadelphia, fighting oftentimes a two-front war against the Protestant factory owners on the one hand and an uncomprehending and often unsympathetic Irish hierarchy on the other. The conflict with the Irish hierarchy, mentioned in Brand Blanshard's treatise on the Poles in Bridesburg, eventually worsened to the point where it became the driving force behind the creation of the schismatic Polish National Church in the United States.

Divisions this deep and this bitter do not disappear overnight. Nor did the determination on the part of the Protestant industrialist ruling class to do something about what they perceived as a serious threat to the established order disappear either. The rhetoric changed, but the covert war against ethnicity, especially Polish ethnics as the least assimilationist-minded. continued.

During the '50s, Poletown in Detroit was one of the first victims of the dislocations caused by the building of the interstate highway system. Poletown suffered directly by having highways rammed through it, but it also suffered indirectly as well. When highways like the Chrysler Expressway were run through black neighborhoods in Detroit or when urban renewal showpieces like Gratiot (later Lafayette) Park got built, the dislocated black population invariably relocated along the Polish corridor up Chene Avenue toward Hamtramck. All urban-renewal projects, whether they targeted white ethnic neighborhoods or not, put pressure on those neighborhoods because they contained more often than not the only housing stock the displaced black population could afford. They were also desirable because they were invariably adjacent to already occupied black areas.

The pattern of ethnic animus which got expressed in the Palmer raids of the '20s and the union battles of the '30s did not end with urban renewal and highway projects of the '50s. In 1980, Detroit's black mayor, Coleman Young, a protégé of Henry Ford II, joined forces with Roger Smith, then chairman of General Motors, in building a Cadillac plant in Poletown which would necessitate tearing down 1,500 homes and fifteen churches and effectively destroy what was left of that community. The difference between Poletown and Bridesburg is as dramatic as the difference between a community which has survived and one which was destroyed, but what both communities shared was the fact that they were both Polish enclaves and as such an object of ongoing ethnic hostility throughout the course of the twentieth century. Bland Blanshard's dissertation is important because it explains in frank theological, philosophical, and political terms the *causus belli* in what would be a covert campaign of cultural warfare for the rest of the century.

Given Dewey's influence, it was also inevitable that Blanshard would take a long, hard look at the system of parochial education in Bridesburg as their first opening for social engineering. Given Dewey's influence and his concern about public education, it is also not surprising that the parochial schools in Polish Bridesburg come in for some fairly severe criticism. "It is a world," Blanshard writes, addressing his audience knowingly, "which is simply not our world, a world in which independent criticism and disinterested science is and must remain unknown, a world which still abounds with the primitive concepts and fancies of the middle ages."[20] It is a world, Blanshard continues, in which "the uses of rosaries and relics are a matter of common knowledge and are further evidence of the curiously mechanical character of Catholic magic."[21] As a result of being submerged in this bath of superstition, parochial school students find that

> the tide of modern thought sweeps by them almost totally unknown and unappraised. Persons who can in all soberness believe that omnipotence, omniscience and omnipresence could first translate itself into flesh and then transfer that flesh without one whit's alteration in the substance into a biscuit which the priest can carry about in his pocket and in eating which one actually eats the body and blood of God, is living in a half-forgotten world.[22]

As some indication of how benighted even the most intellectual Poles can be, Blanshard mentions pragmatism and the thought of John Dewey to a Polish monsignor who had the reputation of a man of learning in the community. To Blanshard's shock,

> The priest gave no indication of having ever heard of him. There is probably no more than a foggy notion among even the lights of Catholic thought of the significance of that system of ideas which has made a sweep of some of our leading universities and which forms America's most conspicuous claim to philosophic originality.[23]

As a student of John Dewey, Brand Blanshard was keenly aware of the role that public education played in the social engineering of America's children. Indeed,

"Americanization," as understood by people like Dewey and Lippmann, would be impossible without an ideologically homogeneous public school system, something that would be accomplished only after World War II by Harvard President James B. Conant under the guise of "consolidation." To bolster his case, Blanshard cites Theodore Roosevelt, a fervent opponent of what he termed "hyphenate-Americans." Roosevelt, like Blanshard, understands that the education question is ultimately a religious question, and that "the hostility" to public schools on the part of immigrants "is merely an illustration of the survival or the importation here of the utterly un-American and thoroughly old-world idea of the subordination of the layman to the priest. . . . The boy brought up in the parochial school is not only less qualified to be a good American citizen, but he is also at a distinct disadvantage in the race of life compared with the boy brought up in the public schools."[24]

The conclusion to be drawn here is simple: "After the child has remained in a Catholic school till the age of 12 or 13, his opportunities for receiving the pubic school influence has very largely gone."[25] Polish Catholics deprived of "the public school influence," then, quite simply can't become American citizens, at least as Brand Blanshard understands the term. They are condemned by their cultural environment to remain forever "hyphenate," divided in their loyalties and, in times of crisis, a fifth column. "The central point of criticism as regards the Church's intellectual influence," Brand Blanshard writes, "is not so much that the world that it still lives in is a world which has been outgrown, but that it offers the most systematic opposition to the approach of any influence that might modify it."[26] Dewey, Barnes, and the Blanshards are only interested in Bridesburg as social scientists because they are interested in using social science as a way of changing Bridesburg and other ethnic enclaves like it into something less threatening to their cultural hegemony. They were not alone in their concern. Within a year of the publication of Blanshard's book, the United States Congress passed the first laws limiting immigration by precisely this group of people.

The racist nativists might differ in their methods from the environmentalist nativists, but both groups were concerned about what they perceived as a common threat, namely, the threat of Catholic colonies in what they saw as an immutably Protestant and therefore enlightened country. Immigration restriction might stem the tide of alien hordes streaming into the country from Southern and Eastern Europe, but it did little to remedy the situation created by those already here. How was the ruling class in America going to bring about the assimilation of a group of people so separated from the dominant culture's organs of opinion management by what seemed to be the insuperable and mutually reinforcing barriers of culture, language, and, most importantly, religion, all marshaled together in a parochial school system which guarded the Polish immigrant "both from within and from without against intellectual influences that may disturb his medieval repose"?[27] "There can be little doubt," Blanshard continues, "that the tendency of these parochial schools keeping together as they do, people of one nationality and religion and preventing that free circulation of all nationalities and faiths together, which is the mark of the public schools, contributes to preserving the class consciousness of the children, both as Poles and as Catholics."[28]

This is a problem, of course, because the inevitable product of "class consciousness" and ethnic solidarity is political power. Blanshard tells us that "candidates for public office

. . . who wish to have the support of the Polish vote, which was usually cast in a block in the most unintelligent way, sometimes solicited the support of the priests and as the influence of these priests was immense, a slight indication of favor was considered of value."[29] Polish political power, already significant because of their cultural homogeneity is magnified further by the fact that the priests control other areas of life so rigidly:

> the influence of the Catholic priest who states the Church's attitude on any public question, regarding it as a moral issue is of vastly greater weight than that of a Protestant clergyman, who, treating it openly as political, expresses an opinion which he knows, however forcibly expressed, will be regarded as opinion only.[30]

Polish political power is also magnified by the other factors associated with urban living. Since the Poles and other Catholic immigrants live mainly in cities, they are more densely settled than their rural Protestant counterparts and, therefore, more politically powerful than their relatively low numbers would suggest.

All of these problems are magnified in Blanshard's eyes by the non-optional character of the Church's teaching. The priest can and does pontificate on morals when his Protestant counterpart can only proffer opinions. Nowhere is this difference more fraught with dire consequences than in the matter of sex. Not only does the educational system based on loyalty to the principle of divine authority inhibit the "emancipation of women,"[31] it also promulgates an absolute prohibition against divorce and an equally absolute prohibition "of any artificial means for limiting the size of families."[32] That means that since Protestants can and do use methods of birth control forbidden to the newer Catholic immigrants, they will be forever on the losing side of a demographic struggle. Blanshard was writing at a time when Darwin was becoming more important to the Protestant ruling class than Christianity. As a result, they became increasingly concerned about the issue of differential fertility and at the same time less inhibited by moral considerations about doing something about their concern. This concern soon surfaces in Blanshard's account of Bridesburg, which is seen as a symbol of all urban Catholic neighborhoods, mindlessly outprocreating the native stock because of the influence of priestly religion:

> Our Catholic immigrants are enormously prolific. It has become a platitude that the poorer the district which one visits the more numerous are the children and in the poorest of all, the streets literally swarm with them. It is precisely these districts, where the poorer Irish, Italian and Polish immigrants are located, in which the Catholic control is most complete. To say that these large families, who on a limited allowance and with no help find it impossible to keep their children in proper food, clothing or cleanliness, are to be excluded on pain of clerical condemnation from knowledge which would prevent the continued increase of such families, with their own breakdown as the frequent accompaniment, seems to the writer simply inhuman.[33]

Inhuman or not, Catholic fertility posed a potent political threat as well, because as good Darwinists the ruling class knew that political power was based on demographics, and that populations with high fertility inevitably replaced populations of low fertility over the long haul. Cut off from the Enlightened Protestant view on birth control, ethnic enclaves of pullulating Catholics like Bridesburg, if left to their own devices, would eventually wrest the reins of political control from the ruling class simply by outprocreating them. Once the situation got stated in those terms, it almost begged for social engineering of some sort as the only intervention that could prevent a catastrophe of enormous magnitude for progressive thinkers like John Dewey and his disciples.

All of these concerns, but especially the misgivings about Catholic fertility, would get restated twenty-nine years later when Brand's brother Paul would write his best-selling book, *American Freedom and Catholic Power*. In fact, Paul's bestseller is in many ways just a more explicit version of Brand's dissertation. Of the conflict between public and parochial education, Paul writes in 1949 pretty much what Brand wrote in 1920:

> Often the parochial and public schools are on opposite sides of the same street, dividing the children into competing and even hostile groups, conscious of their own differences and suspicious of each other's way of life. Even when both schools emphasize patriotism and community spirit, the fact that they exist as separate establishments tends to divide the community emotionally and culturally. The separatism is particularly harmful when, as so often happens, the Catholic group is largely an immigrant group that needs assimilation and Americanization more than any other part of the community.[34]

"The divisive pattern," Paul concludes, drawing presumably on his experiences in Philadelphia, "is most noticeable in the great Eastern and mid-Western centers of the country where Catholicism is strongest."[35]

Paul's experience in Bridesburg not only forced him to the conclusion that Catholicism was radically incompatible with American democracy, it also colored his attitude toward the nation's largest cities as well. These cities' Catholic ethnic enclaves had created all but unbeatable political machines which were increasingly robbing the rural, small-town, and increasingly suburban Protestant majority of its ability to structure the culture according to its norms. "Several of the most publicized political machines in American cities," Paul writes,

> have been essentially Catholic machines in the sense that their leaders and their most important members have been Roman Catholics. Tammany has been dominated for generations by Catholic politicians; James M. Curley's political machine in Boston has been a Catholic machine in a predominantly Catholic city; Frank Hague operated for many years in Jersey City a government which was essentially a clerical state.[36]

Like his brother, Paul Blanshard felt that the issue of sexuality was crucial. If the Protestant ruling class were to allow the Poles and other ethnics in Bridesburg and elsewhere to maintain their Catholic culturally separatist attitudes toward sex in general or birth control in particular, it was, in effect signing its own death warrant. The fertility differential between the two groups would ensure that over the long haul America would become a Catholic country. Blanshard even cites a Philadelphia priest to prove his point.

The Right Reverend John J. Bonner, diocesan superintendent of schools of Philadelphia, boasted in 1941 that the increase in the Catholic births in Philadelphia in the preceding decade had been more than fifty per cent higher than the increase in the total population, and that Philadelphia "will be fifty percent Catholic in a comparatively short time." . . . If the disparity in birth rates which he claimed should continue indefinitely, it would not be long before the United States became a Catholic country by default.[37]

"Today," Paul Blanshard continues, "several states still have ambiguous obscenity laws on their statute books which reactionary and Catholic-dominated courts could twist into prohibitions against contraceptive devices. . . . Two states where Catholic minorities are very powerful, Massachusetts and Connecticut, still interpret their statutes as forbidding doctors to give birth-control counsel to their parents."[38] If it were to survive in its capacity as the ruling class, the Protestants would have to face the Catholic fertility differential without evasion. Given their environmentalist views that meant some form of social engineering. Bridesburg was in desperate need of "Americanization," whether the Poles living there knew it or not, and that meant either changing the minds of their children when they were in school through things like sex education or, more drastically, breaking up the neighborhood to disperse the Poles to neighborhoods with no ethnic identity. Over the course of the rest of the century, the Melting Pot Pageant would return to enclaves like Bridesburg in increasingly sinister forms.

In spite of its unremittingly hostile and condescending tone throughout, Brand Blanshard ends his dissertation on a note of ambivalence about Bridesburg. The Catholic Church may be benighted, but it still keeps its minions morally in line. "If Catholic morality at times gives very dubious counsel as in its exaltation of the ascetic life, the type of living that it enjoins is, on the whole, a noble one. . . . The problem, therefore, is how to preserve the ideal and moral interest that the Church engenders while doing away with the obscurantism."[39]

At precisely the same time when Brand expressed his admiration of the Catholic Church's salutary influence on immigrant morals, Brother Paul was about to embark upon a life-long commitment to sexual liberation. "After our children were born," Paul wrote describing his arrangement with his first wife Julia, "we became utterly typical samples of the sexual revolution of the 1920s, unashamed and joyous in our defiance of orthodox sexual taboos." By the end of his life, Blanshard could play the role of prophet, claiming that "the world has caught up with us – or gone down the moral drain with us."[40]

As the ruling class's commitment to sexual morality began to wane, two things happened: first of all, their ambivalence toward Bridesburg disappeared. Once they adopted the sexual mores which Paul Blanshard adopted during the '20s, they didn't want to preserve any parts of it. In fact, the parts that Brand Blanshard wanted most to save in 1918 became the parts his brother and his followers were most avid to destroy at the century's mid-point. At the same time the ruling class's sexual morals disappeared, their moral restraint in the way they exercised political power disappeared as well. They became more and more likely to act on their convictions, and less and less constrained by moral scruples. "My interest in eugenics," Blanshard writes with disarming frankness, "was closely bound up with my interest in Catholicism and my increasing doubts about the validity of my earlier and rather naive socialism."[41] Just as Brand Blanshard's essentially Protestant dissertation morphed into his brother Paul's essentially secular bestseller *American Freedom and Catholic Power*, so the admiration of Church-fostered Polish morals which animated the group Brand represented gradually faded away as their commitment to sexual liberation increased.

Eventually Brand Blanshard's ambivalence was replaced by a determination to do something about what his class perceived as benighted sexual prohibitions and the ghettoes and ethnic enclaves which promoted them. If the problem was the fact that sexually backward Catholics lived in politically powerful ethnic ghettoes, the answer was still social engineering. The ethnic Catholic threat posed by neighborhoods like Bridesburg could be solved in either one of two ways. The ethnics could be Americanized by becoming sexually enlightened by exposure to sexual liberation or they could be Americanized by being moved out of their ethnic ghettoes. WASP concern about ethnic isolation combined with ethnic fertility eventuated in a culture war on two fronts. The answer to what Paul Blanshard called "the Catholic Problem" in the first instance was the Rockefeller-orchestrated plan to mainstream contraceptive use among Catholics and blacks; the answer in the second and related instance was urban renewal. Once fascism had been defeated in Europe, the social engineers could, as Lippmann predicted, devote their full attention to their domestic opponents. In the years following World War II, the campaign for contraception ran on parallel tracks side by side next to the plan to destroy ethnic neighborhoods. The one was always a function of the other, and both Paul and Brand Blanshard could explain the connection between the two campaigns in their books, both of which evoked fear of Catholic fertility, a fear which was based on their seminal and unhappy experience of trying to Americanize Polish Catholics in Bridesburg during World War I. "Is it possible," Brand asks, "to destroy an authority which has such markedly evil effects without destroying also the quantum of good which it produces in another field?"[42] By the time Bridesburg was targeted for destruction by the Philadelphia Housing Commission in 1948, the answer was obviously no. But by then the class for whom the Blanshards spoke didn't see any good in Bridesburg worth preserving, clearly not something associated with the sexual morality the priests taught in their parochial schools.

The Blanshards left Bridesburg convinced that being Catholic and being American were two mutually contradictory propositions. What grew in both as well as the ruling class they represented was a desire to engineer the offending characteristics of the Catholic Church out of existence. That meant engineering the offending ethnic community both psychically, through things like sex education, liberalized access to pornography, and decriminalization of contraception and abortion, and physically through the political manipulation of the real-estate market, the equally political manipulation of black migration from the South, "integration," highway construction, urban renewal, and forced busing. Having discussed the psychic engineering in *Libido Dominandi: Sexual Liberation and Political Control*,[43] I concentrate on the physical engineering in this study. "The Church," Brand wrote in 1920, "must become a community church whose leaders will consult the community need. The quasi-military hierarchy of Rome . . . must go. The community must be at liberty to choose its own leaders and to decide its own policy. . . . The type of education offered to those who are going into the Church must plainly be revised and radically revised."[44] Since no one in the WASP ruling class could affect the Catholic Church directly from within, that meant engineering the places where the Church had contact with the culture. That could mean funding a fifth column within the Church if necessary. Brand mentions the Polish National Church as a model: "what we have seen of the independent churches furnishes the clue. At least we find in these churches the worst element of danger removed."[45]

But, more importantly, it meant restricting the Catholic Church's ability to influence the culture, and this would come about by asserting state control over education, sexuality, and housing in more and more draconian forms. At this point, we can cite all of the Supreme Court cases that ratified their designs – *Griswold v. Connecticut, Lemon v. Kurtzman, Roe v. Wade* – and to that list we would now add *Berman v. Parker*, the decision legitimizing urban renewal. Just as the law in Connecticut prohibiting the sale of contraceptives had to go, so also the laws protecting property had to go for basically the same reasons. In the Blanshards' reaction to Bridesburg, we see the nucleus of the domestic political agenda which would occupy the ruling class for the rest of the century.

The influence of Paul Blanshard on the Supreme Court has already been documented. Hugo Black's son claimed that his father read all of Paul Blanshard's books. This is not to say that the Supreme Court created this country's housing policy by handing down *Berman v. Parker* any more than Paul Blanshard did so by writing *American Freedom and Catholic Power*. Both, however, contributed to how that policy would be applied, and both the Court and the Blanshards did that not by dint of any personal power or political genius but rather by the fact that they articulated in various ways the aspiration of the ethnic group they represented. The ruling class during the period around mid-century was ethnically homogeneous and in addition they held a shared group of religious conviction that allowed them to act in concert without necessarily becoming involved in conspiracies (although there were conspiracies as well). This group could act in concert because it shared certain beliefs and because the people comprising it constituted an ethnos which often shared family ties as well.

Housing policy beginning with the New Deal housing bill of 1937 was national in scope. But it was local in scope as well. If a city wanted to accept federal money, it had to create its own local housing authority, and these local housing authorities were invariably run by the local elites, and their policies were implemented as an expression of the local elites' ethnic prejudices, no matter how much these prejudices were disguised (or confirmed) by professional credentials from Ivy League schools. Housing policy was important to this class of people, a class of people who constituted what E. Digby Baltzell, another Philadelphian, termed "the White Anglo-Saxon Protestant Establishment." The "Establishment" was, according to Baltzell, "a national and associational upper class [which] replaced the local and communal gentry in America between the close of the Civil War and 1940."[46] Because Brand Blanshard had received a Rhodes scholarship he was *ipso facto* offered membership in the intellectual branch of this class, which meant, according to Baltzell, becoming part of "Rhodes' dream that 'between two and three thousand Nordic gentlemen in the prime of life and mathematically selected' should run the world."[47]

The ability of the WASP P establishment to run the world received a temporary setback during the years leading up to Pearl Harbor and America's entry into the war, caused by what amounted to an ethnic civil war over whether race or environment, nature or nurture, was more determinative of man's condition. The crucial issue was foreign policy, and with America's entry into the war the East Coast internationalist wing of the WASP ethnos took control of the United States government, and as a result the government became earnestly committed to the new social sciences and social engineering as well. The members of this group were, according to Baltzell,

> opposed to racism, Social Darwinism, imperialism and all forms of hereditary determinism; and all assumed the malleability of human nature which was capable of responding to improved social conditions; Dewey stated the aims of the new Science were much the same terms as the Social Gospel movement when he wrote that "there must be a change in objective arrangements and institutions; we must work on the environment, not merely in the hearts of men."[48]

The one thing the racialist isolationists and the behaviorist internationalists shared, however, was their distrust of Catholic ethnics. "I have been urging the Forum people," wrote Madison Grant, champion of the racial view of history, "to get some Protestant to take the position that the Catholic Church under Jewish leadership, the Jews and the Communist Labor Party are all international organizations and as such are hopelessly irreconcilable to the principles of nationalism upon which modern Christendom is founded."[49] Grant would eventually play an important role in framing the legislation restricting immigration which was finally passed by the Congress between 1921 and 1924. The role of the Catholic ethnic was in fact crucial to the identity of the ethnic group which opposed it, according to Baltzell, who claims that "the sense of caste which now prevails within the American upper class began to develop at the turn of the century in response to the flood of impoverished immigrants from Southern and Eastern Europe who came to these shores in ever increasing waves."[50]

In Philadelphia on the eve of World War II, this group was, again in Baltzell's words,

> a small community of Philadelphia families, predominantly of English and Welsh descent, Quaker turned Episcopalian in religion, educated at private schools and colleges like Harvard, Yale or Princeton, residents of fashionable neighborhoods, members of exclusive clubs, and listed in the Social Register – authoritatively dominated the business and cultural life of Philadelphia, as their ancestors had done since colonial days.[51]

One of the defining characteristics of this group was their anti-Catholicism, an attitude which found dramatic expression during the Philadelphia anti-Catholic riots of 1844 and which persisted under various guises into the next century. Baltzell notes the animus against Catholics among the otherwise tolerant Quakers in Philadelphia at the time of the riots:

> Although Philadelphia publicly mourned its dead and openly deplored its period of carnage, many among even the more substantial citizens were secretly exultant.

Quaker merchants, who spoke indignantly of the outrage in public, returned to their shops to express the sincere believe that "the Papists deserve all this and much more," and "it were well if every Popish church in the world were leveled to the ground."[52]

In his novel *The Quaker City*, George Lippard describes, "Fashionable dames going to the Opera, Merchants in broad-cloth returning from the counting-house, Bank Directors hurrying to their homes, godly preachers wending to their churches their faces full of sobriety and their hearts burning with enmity to the Pope of Rome."[53]

Arriving in Philadelphia as an impecunious Hungarian immigrant roughly one hundred years after the anti-Catholic riots of 1844, John Lukacs noticed that the more things changed the more they remained the same. The more progressive the Walter Phillips-ADA-Reform crowd became in Philadelphia, the more confirmed they became in their dislike of Catholic ethnics like Lukacs. The progressive crowd was no longer wending its way to church but its heart still burned with enmity toward the Pope of Rome. That enmity was couched now in the language of Bertrand Russell, Jean Paul Sartre, or Joseph Stalin, and the belief that "anti-Communism, especially in America, was simply dreadful, represented by backward, unrefined, crude people: moneybags, rednecks, Catholics."[54] Lukacs recounts being confronted by "these pervasive incarnations of liberal chic"[55] in various ways. In one instance it was Edmund Bacon, "a then celebrated city planner of Philadelphia [who] told me that his favorite painter was Klee; he also defended Alger Hiss at the time. . . . in 1933 he had proposed that City Hall be torn down and a modern parking garage be erected in its place."[56] In another it was the liberal professorate who formed "the clerisy of the New World, Darwinist and Einsteinian to the last man and, if not votaries, at least profoundly respectful of the Webbs and/or Trotsky, Freud and/or Marx; anti-conservative, anti-Catholic and anti-anti-Communist."[57]

When Cardinal Spellman attacked Blanshard's articles in the *Nation* at the 1947 commencement at Fordham University, as evidence of resurgent anti-Catholic bigotry, virtually the entire liberal WASP establishment from Eleanor Roosevelt to Archibald Macleish came to Blanshard's defense. John Dewey, according to Blanshard, came to the defense of *American Freedom and Catholic Power* with a "handsome endorsement," claiming that it was done with "exemplary scholarship, judgment and tact."[58] Dewey, again in Blanshard's words, "went out of his way to underscore the intellectual's case against Catholic policy," describing the church as "a powerful reactionary world organization" promoting "principles inimical to democracy."[59] Margaret Mead, harkening back to a theme that pervades both Brand Blanshard's dissertation and Paul Blanshard's bestseller, criticized "an immigrant community which is both foreign and Catholic attempt[ing] to keep its young people separate from the community . . . isolating them from the mainstream of American life."[60]

Even when this group quarreled among itself, its goals remained constant. The relationship between Bertrand Russell and Albert Barnes turned sour in 1940 when Barnes reneged on a deal to establish a lectureship at the Barnes Foundation after Russell's appointment at the City College was withdrawn because of his sexual liberationist views. Barnes died in 1951 one year after Russell had won the Nobel Prize. Returning in triumph to the town that had scorned him ten years earlier, Russell gave a speech at Columbia University in November 1950, declaring that it is a "dangerous error to think that the evils of communism can be combated by Catholicism."[61]

One year later Paul Blanshard wrote his sequel to *American Freedom and Catholic Power.* In *Communism, Democracy, and Catholic Power*, he re-states Russell's thesis in general as the thesis of the book and cites the above-quoted passage from Russell's speech explicitly. In 1951, the same year that the Blanshard sequel appeared in print, his book was being avidly discussed by the Walter Phillips-ADA-reform crowd, which had just taken over city hall in Philadelphia. Shortly thereafter Reform Mayor Joe Clark appointed Phillips head of the Philadelphia Housing Authority, and oftentimes violent opposition to the selection for public housing sites in ethnic neighborhoods would plague the city for the next decade.

As a group which believed in civic responsibility and the salutary effect of applied social science, it was natural that the WASP elite would take an interest in housing. In cities like Philadelphia, Chicago, Detroit, and Boston, the panels of experts in the housing field invariably had a definite ethnic cast. They became certified as experts either by going to the already mentioned Ivy League universities or by getting appointed to boards of the various cities' planning commissions, which were often descendants of local ruling-class initiatives that began with the city-beautiful movement or the settlement house movement around the time of World War I.

The Philadelphia Housing Association was one such group. It started off as a blue-blood organization complaining about back-yard privies and piggeries in South Philadelphia and recommending common-sense measures for local improvement of the housing situation, things like liens against absentee landlords to pay for repairs. All of that changed in 1937 with the New Deal housing act of that year, which established local housing authorities across the country with federal money and government authority. The various housing authorities were charged with creating master plans by staffs of "experts" of a certain ethnic (i.e., WASP) cast which was invariably not the ethnic cast of the neighborhoods which were targeted for destruction. Urban renewal as practiced in the case of *Berman v. Parker* meant that certain people were empowered to come up with a master plan for the cities, one that would now have the power of law, specifically eminent domain, behind it along with enormous amounts of federal money, which was made available to tear down neighborhoods where people from other ethnic groups lived. The experts could do this according to their own purportedly scientific but ultimately ethnocentric criteria of things like blight, hygiene, decay, etc. Taken together the WASP penchant for meddling in housing along with residual WASP anti-Catholicism meant bad news for places like Bridesburg and Poletown, especially when this group was empowered to act on its ethnic prejudices by federal money and a Supreme Court that was willing to abridge property rights in the interest of increased social engineering.

Herbert Gans noticed this destructive synergy when he worked on urban renewal in Boston's West End. Many writers cite Gans's book *The Urban Villagers*, but few cite the passages which tell the most uncomfortable truths about the urban-renewal enterprise, namely (1) that there was nothing objective about the criteria for selecting which neighborhoods got torn down and (2) the purpose of the renewal was not so much the creation of new structures (oftentimes the cleared lots would inexplicably remain vacant for years) as much as it was the destruction of older, invariably ethnic neighborhoods. According to Gans, who both lived in the West End and worked for the agency that tore it down and so knew their thinking from the inside, the federal reliance on the expertise of local housing authorities meant that neighborhoods were chosen for destruction for ethnic reasons. The purpose of renewal, in other words, was not construction but destruction. The prime purpose of urban renewal was social engineering, which meant, in effect, ethnic cleansing based on the prejudices of the local elites.

Keeping this in mind would eliminate much confusion from subsequent writings. June Manning Thomas, for instance, begins her recent study of urban renewal in Detroit with a series of questions:

> How could a city that for so long enjoyed prosperity turn into what exists today, given that so many people tried, for so many years, to improve it? For years, municipal politicians and staff fought the tide of decline, trying to recreate a viable and livable city. Their efforts to carry out "redevelopment" – a deliberate effort to rebuild decayed or declining areas – began as early as the 1940s and have continued to the present. Were their efforts completely in vain? Why were they not more successful?[62]

In light of the foregoing evidence, especially the testimony of Herbert Gans, whose book, if not that particular passage, Manning cites, the answer to all these questions is quite simple. Urban renewal did not fail, no matter what Detroit looks like today, because it was "based on a desire . . . to break up ethnic ghettoes." Given that as its purpose, urban renewal was a spectacular success. The parlous state of most of our older cities today is not evidence of failure; it is evidence of success. Thomas is confused because she never really understood the true purpose of urban renewal. Its purpose was destruction. Because she doesn't really understand the purpose of the project, Thomas comes up with the wrong answer to her question. "The lingering effects of racial antagonism and injustice," she writes, "are primary reasons that redevelopment failed to revitalize the modern city of Detroit."[63]

By viewing the urban-renewal story in Detroit through a racial lens, Thomas renders herself incapable of understanding the real dynamics of the struggle. For no matter how it seemed in the moment of confrontation when a black family moved into a white neighborhood, this was never a simple black-and-white struggle. It was a three-way battle in which the WASP ruling class made use of the black underclass to bring about the destruction of neighborhoods where the ethnic working class lived. Thomas hints at this struggle when she admits that "the categories 'Black' and 'White' hide great distinctions of class and ethnicity,"[64] but she can never bring herself to understand the implications of her own admission. The racial template which Thomas imposes on her material precludes any possibility of understanding it. So even when she comes up with an insight which challenges that black v. white template, for example her claim that "White liberal promoters of racial integration tended to come from highly educated upper class, and White opponents from lower class origins and circumstances,"[65] the insight never goes any further. Needless to say, it never gets to the heart of the matter, which was ethnic, not racial. Shorn of their ethnic and religious affiliations, the two groups of "white" people proposed by Thomas are invariably united in the end by their racial prejudice, and that uniting precludes any possibility of understanding the true dynamics of the culture war which destroyed cities like Detroit and Philadelphia.

The battle over housing was essentially an ethnic, not a racial, struggle, in which the blacks were brought up from the south to satisfy war manpower needs and destabilize ethnic neighborhoods which the WASP ruling class suspected of Fascist sympathies. Looked at from Thomas's bi-polar racialist point of view, the ethnic cleansing of Poletown comes across as a triumph of interracial cooperation, the black mayor of Detroit working hand-in-hand with the white chairman of the board of General Motors. Instead of the destruction of an ethnic neighborhood to build an extra-large parking lot, Thomas describes the Poletown incident as a model for private sector–government cooperation: "That [Detroit Mayor Coleman] Young," she writes, "and his talented staff, particularly CEDD Director Emmett Moten, were able to carry out the project without missing a step is testimony to both technical and political skills."[66]

It is also testimony to how a racial template can blind an otherwise intelligent observer to the true dynamics of what happened. Under the guise of opposing white racism, Coleman Young took the side of the ruling-class industrialists against the ethnic blue-collar population which had been a thorn in their side since the unionization battles of the 1920s and '30s. Instead of opposing white racism, Coleman Young simply did the bidding of one (albeit powerful) ethnic group in its decades long war with another ethnic group. The same story repeated itself *mutatis mutandis* in virtually all of the big cities of the North and is in essence the topic of this book. By framing the story in racial terms, Thomas ends up supporting more of the social engineering which destroyed Detroit in the first place. "Problems will persist," she writes, sounding a lot like Gunnar Myrdal, "as long as people have the freedom to express or act upon their prejudice, to seek homogeneity rather than heterogeneity, and to deny access to housing, employment, or community facilities for those who look different. Attacking both discrimination and prejudice, therefore, must become part of the race unity agenda."[67] Thomas then goes on to endorse the actions of "faith based organizations" in the Detroit area, after of course denouncing the actions of the Polish parishioners of St. Louis the King parish when they objected to having the Sojourner Truth housing project moved into their neighborhood as part of the government's attempt to engineer their Americanization.

In *Parish Boundaries*, Notre Dame professor John McGreevy proposes a more sophisticated interpretation of the housing struggles of the post-war period. Instead of a simple black-and-white struggle, McGreevy describes a Catholic-ethnic vs. black struggle, but one that is ultimately just as two-sided as Thomas's. McGreevy, for example, mentions the riot in Folcroft in September 1963 and the soul-searching this caused among progressive Catholics of the Catholic Interracial Council sort, but what he doesn't mention is the fact that the American Friends Service Committee bought Horace Baker's house in Folcroft and was hard at work destabilizing neighborhoods throughout the Philadelphia area. The AFSC was also instrumental in bringing Martin Luther King to Chicago in 1966 and urging him to march in neighborhoods like Cicero, which they had targeted for "integration" as early as 1951. To write about Folcroft without mentioning the behind-the-scenes machinations of the Quakers is a bit like doing a re-make of *King Kong* without the gorilla. Why, one wonders, are all those people running down the street? Are they nuts?

The standard answer is, of course, they were running down the street and throwing rocks through Horace Baker's windows because they were bigots. McGreevy, in spite of the nuance of his book, must accede in the final analysis to that interpretation because he hasn't given any evidence that other forces were at work destabilizing the neighborhoods. "To borrow from an older rhetoric," he writes, "acts of contrition are necessary."[68] Anyone who looks at the parlous state of cities like Detroit and Philadelphia would find it hard to disagree with McGreevy's call to repentance however we might disagree about the full list of those who are to be called to confess their sins. In describing another racial crisis, this one in Levittown, Pennsylvania, McGreevy cites "the pastor of a parish wracked by racial tension [who] believed that 'there are unknown groups behind this who are purposely stirring up the trouble.'"[69] Well, as a matter of fact, there were groups "behind this." The Quakers were also involved in moving black families into Levittown six years before they moved Horace Baker into Folcroft. In the meantime they participated in 200 other move-ins, none of which got the publicity of these two incidents. By citing the priest's fears without substantiating them as essentially well-founded, McGreevy does him a disservice. He also does a disservice to the Catholic ethnics who were on the receiving end of this covert and as yet unreported campaign of cultural and psychological warfare. It is the purpose of this book to document that campaign to the fullest extent possible. To write the history of neighborhood strife during this period of time without describing the efforts of people like Louis Wirth and his collaboration with the psychological warfare establishment during World War II, or the American Friends Service Committee and their work in both Philadelphia and Chicago, or Paul Ylvisaker and his creation of the Gray Areas grants for the Ford Foundation and their subsequent take-over by a quintessential establishment figure like McGeorge Bundy, or Leon Sullivan, one of the players created by the Ford Foundation, and his collaboration with Robert Weaver while head of the FHA, is to tell less than half of the story. It is to do a remake of *King Kong* without the gorilla. It is also a bad example of whiggish history, a genre depressingly familiar to anyone who has done any reading in the conventional accounts of the sexual revolution and the civil rights movement, where effects have no causes and actual people making actual decisions in actual rooms are replaced by broad historical forces and Enlightenment melodramas like the triumph of liberation over bondage and light over darkness.

To bring the story which began when the Blanshard boys arrived in Bridesburg full circle, Brand Blanshard finally exchanged the Congregationalism of his childhood for membership in the Society of Friends at a time when the Friends were taking concrete action to bring about the destruction of Philadelphia neighborhoods like Bridesburg and Kensington, the neighborhoods Blanshard found so repugnant when he stayed there as a guest of John Dewey and Albert C. Barnes during the summer of 1918. But the story doesn't end there either. Present at the meetings of the executive committee of Friends Suburban Housing during the early '60s, the group which moved Horace Baker into Folcroft, was a certain Paul Blanshard.[70] No one at the American Friends Service Committee archives could tell me if this was the famous Paul Blanshard because by now, a half a century after his best-selling attack on Catholicism appeared, no one knew who the famous Paul Blanshard was anymore. In the end, the Paul Blanshard at the meeting turned out not to be the famous Paul Blanshard, but his son. The fact that two generations of the Blanshard family could be involved in the destruction of one Catholic neighborhood gives some indication of the depth of their animus against the people who lived there and their religious beliefs. The transgenerational nature of this struggle gives some indication of its ethnic nature as well. This ethnic struggle may not go back as far as the one between the Croats and the Serbs, but it is every bit as destructive, as a comparison of certain sections of Philadelphia and Mostar would show.

In the end, Paul Blanshard may be forgotten, but his legacy remains in the destroyed city he and his son and his brother left behind. In the days following the Republican Convention in Philadelphia, news reports announced that the city's 40,000 abandoned houses were collapsing at twice the rate of the previous year. The John Street Administration in Philadelphia had budgeted, as a result, $150 million just to tear the houses down that were going to fall down anyway so that no one got hurt when they did. The rubble-strewn lots of North Philadelphia would remain as the Blanshards' unacknowledged legacy. The heaps of bricks now colonized by the summer's jungle-like infestation of junk trees testify to the powerful nature of forces which people like the Blanshards and Louis Wirth thought they could engineer. They thought of the people who lived in those houses as an ethnic fifth column which needed to be defeated in cultural battle, but in defeating them they destroyed the cities they sought to save.

Notes

1   Paul Blanshard, *Personal and Controversial: An Autobiography* (Boston: Beacon Press, 1973), p. 6.
2   John Lukacs, *Philadelphia: Patricians and Philistines 1900–1950* (New York: Farrar, Straus, Giroux, 1980), p. 266.
3   Ibid., p. 279.
4   Walter Lippmann, *Public Opinion* (New York; The Free Press, 1922, 1949), p. 57.
5   Ibid., p. 67.
6   Ibid., p. 31.
7   Ibid.
8   Blanshard, *Personal and Controversial*, p. 51
9   Ibid.
10 Brand Blanshard, *The Church and the Polish Immigrant* (no city of publication, no publisher, 1920, copy in Widener Library at Harvard University), p. 30.
11 Ibid., pp. 31–32.
12 Ibid., p. 32.
13 Ibid., p. 33.
14 Ibid., p. 30.
15 Lippmann, p. 61.
16 Jeanie Wylie, *Poletown: Community Betrayed* (Urbana, Ill.: University of Illinois Press, 1989), p. 2.
17 Ibid., p. 3.

18 Ibid., p. 4.

19 Ibid.

20 Brand Blanshard, *Church*, p. 42.

21 Ibid., p. 25.

22 Ibid., p. 42.

23 Ibid., p. 51.

24 Ibid., p. 48.

25 Ibid., p. 34.

26 Ibid., p. 44.

27 Ibid., p. 45.

28 Ibid., p. 47.

29 Ibid., p. 56.

30 Ibid.

31 Ibid., p. 58.

32 Ibid., p. 61.

33 Ibid.

34 Paul Blanshard, *American Freedom and Catholic Power* (Boston: Beacon Press, 1949), p. 60.

35 Ibid.

36 Ibid., p. 57.

37 Ibid., p. 284.

38 Ibid., p. 286.

39 Brand Blanshard, *Church*, p. 75.

40 Blanshard, *Personal*, p. 114.

41 Ibid., p. 223.

42 Brand Blanshard, *Church*, p. 76.

43 E. Michael Jones, *Libido Dominandi: Sexual Liberation and Political Control* (South Bend, Ind.: St. Augustine's Press, 2000).

44 Brand Blanshard, *Church*, p. 78.

45 Ibid., p. 76.

46 E. Digby Baltzell, *The Protestant Establishment: Aristocracy and Caste in America* (New York: Random House, 1964), p. xii.

47 Ibid., p. 137.

48 Ibid., p. 162.

49 Ibid., p. 96.

50 Ibid., p. 21.

51 Ibid., p. xii.

52 E. Digby Baltzell, *Puritan Boston and Quaker Philadelphia: Two Protestant Ethics and the Spirit of Class Authority and Leadership* (New York: The Free Press, 1979), p. 423.

53 Ibid.

54 John Lukacs, *Confessions of an Original Sinner* (South Bend, Ind.: St. Augustine's Press, 2000), p. 158.

55 Ibid., p. 159.

56 Ibid.

57 Ibid.

58 Blanshard, *Personal*, p. 52.

59 Ibid.

60 John T. McGreevy, "Thinking on One's Own: Catholicism in the American Intellectual Imagination, 1928–1960," *The Journal of American History* (June 1997): 119.

61 Paul Blanshard, *Communism, Democracy, and Catholic Power* (Boston: The Beacon Press, 1951), p. 6.

62 June Manning Thomas, *Redevelopment and Race* (Baltimore: The Johns Hopkins University Press, 1997), p. 1.

63 Ibid., p. 2.

64 Ibid., p. 208.

65 Ibid., p. 88.

66 Ibid., p. 163.

67 Ibid., p. 230.

68 John T. McGreevy, *Parish Boundaries: The Catholic Encounter with Race in the Twentieth Century Urban North* (Chicago: University of Chicago Press, 1996), p. 264.

69 Ibid., p. 105.

70 American Friends Service Committee Archives, CRD, Minutes of meeting of CRD NHPC 10/2/65.

The Richard Allen Homes

On September 12, 1939, less than two weeks after Hitler invaded Poland, an article announcing Philadelphia's first public-housing project appeared in the *Evening Bulletin*, one of that city's now-defunct daily papers. The public-housing project, which the *Bulletin* termed "the greatest mass-moving project in the history of the city,"[1] was to be built on a twenty-eight-acre site bordered by Fairmount on the south and Poplar on the north and 9th Street on the east and 12th Street on the west. The area was described as "one of the city's most congested band box sections."[2] The band-box house consisted of three rooms on top of each other; they were sometimes referred to as court houses, because they were built on alleys, not streets, and sometimes they were referred to as Father-Son-Holy Ghost houses, perhaps in deference to the piety of their often Irish Catholic inhabitants.

The pictures which accompanied the article gave the impression that the neighborhood's inhabitants were white since only white people were pictured. The reader also came away with the impression that most of the people living in the West Poplar neighborhood were looking forward to returning to new homes once the federal housing project was completed. The pictures of the homes to be torn down weren't especially effective in conveying a sense of dilapidation. For the most part the houses looked like the typical rowhouse that housed just about all of Philadelphia's middle and lower classes, in what had termed itself since the 1850s the "city of homes." In a tactic that would gain increasing importance in the generally biased press accounts in favor of urban renewal, the paper's photographers had to go around to the back of the houses to get pictures of blight.

The comments of those about to be moved from their homes occupied the psychic space between the extremes portrayed by the pictures, which is another way of describing their ambivalence in the presence of a reporter who was clearly trying to persuade them that the project which was going to evict them from their homes was a good idea. "They'll say they don't like it," opined the reporter, who clearly didn't want to leave it at that. "Yet strangely enough, most of them are inclined to accept their fate philosophically. In a negative reluctant fashion, they agree that it's probably for the best. That in the long run it will be a good thing for this city of homes to get rid of its slums."[3] Of course, once the issue gets framed in terms that broad, it's difficult to see how anyone could oppose the project. Generally it's difficult to find people who are in favor of preserving slums.

When the issue was framed in terms of the individual houses it took on a different color. Area resident William Clements, to give one example, paid $7,500 for his North Philadelphia home in 1924, a not-inconsiderable sum at the time. The price indicated that ten years before the project was announced the house he bought was not dilapidated nor in the middle of a slum. By the time the Philadelphia Housing Authority got around to making him an offer for the house in 1939, the assessed value of the house had dropped to $1,300. Clements eventually sold the house for twice that amount, but even in doing that took a loss of almost $5,000. The reporter gives no explanation for the precipitous drop in the value of Mr. Clements's house, probably because looking into that question might have undermined the premise of the article, namely, that building these homes was a good thing from which all concerned would benefit. Had he examined the situation more closely, he might have found that the drop in property value had been caused by the proposed public housing itself. The fact that the project was going to be located in that neighborhood automatically attached a stigma to its housing stock, which destroyed its value.

In addition to that, the decrease in value was also attributable to the Depression and the fact that a contraction in the money supply and the absence of employment had had catastrophic effects on demand in housing. Moreover, the Depression caused a general decline in the value of housing stock because, with less money available, people were less likely to make the repairs necessary to maintain the houses in their previous condition. But the second instance was common to all housing except the housing of the independently wealthy, and the first condition was a self-fulfilling prophecy. Taken together, neither condition made it objectively obvious that these houses, as opposed to others, had to fall to the wrecking ball. In a city which had existed for three hundred years without major catastrophes like the city-wide fire in Chicago or the San Francisco earthquake or Sherman's march to the sea, it was not difficult to find "obsolete" housing, especially since home-improvement loans and new housing starts had been effectively put on hold for ten years because of the stock-market crash of 1929. If the people who made the decisions about where federal housing projects were to be located had operated according to strictly objective criterion, they could have found other older and more-dilapidated neighborhoods in Philadelphia. In fact, the city's most notorious slums were well known at the time and located about two miles to the south along South and Lombard Streets.

Since the people who made this sort of decision prided themselves on being scientific, it is worth considering just what their criteria were. The housing stock in the West Poplar area was built for the most part in the mid-19th century, mostly for and by the Irish who had settled there to work in the textile mills of Kensington a mile or so to the north and east. Bauman writes that "the Richard Allen Homes replaced eight blocks of the neighborhood's most scabrous hovels and gang tenements. Of the structures cleared from the site, 68 percent lacked indoor toilets and almost half were without central heat."[4]

The fact that a certain percentage of the houses lacked indoor toilets is easily enough documented; however, Bauman overlooks the fact that band-box houses were designed for the bottom rung of the economic ladder, a fact that has become obscured by the fact that housing is no longer constructed for this group of people. The fact that this housing had deteriorated over time should not obscure the fact that during the '30s, the poor in Philadelphia occupied housing designed for poor people, not housing that the better off had abandoned. The fact that the residents of the West Poplar neighborhood were living in court houses meant that they were poor. But the same fact can be looked at in another way as well, namely, the fact that there were court houses in Philadelphia meant that the poor had a place to live. In areas like West Poplar, housing stock was a function of the street where it was built. Big streets had big houses on them, which would rent for $20 to $24 per month. Little streets or courts had the smaller band-box houses on them, which would rent for as little as $6 a month. If the housers termed band-box rowhouses obsolete, the people who lived in them, no matter how they felt about them otherwise, considered them affordable housing. What the construction of this federal housing project meant, although the *Bulletin* writer did not state it in these terms, was the destruction of twenty-eight acres of the most affordable housing in Philadelphia.

Bauman writes that "Of the 868 families displaced from the site, 88 percent were black and wretchedly poor."[5] That they were poor no one is going to dispute. It's safe to say that anyone who rents a house for $6 a month does so because he can't afford to pay more. During the Depression there were people who had trouble coming up with $6 a month for houses that the Philadelphia Housing Authority considered obsolete, but obsolete in this context is just another word for inexpensive. That means that the black people who lived in this area of North Philadelphia were poor, but they were not poor in the same way their children and grandchildren would be poor in the '50s and '70s. By then the entire white population had deserted North Philadelphia, creating an oversupply that even the huge waves of migration from the South could not fill. As a result, all of the housing depreciated in value as wave upon wave of new migrants occupied not only band-box houses built for the poor working class but decidedly middle class housing on big streets in addition to the mansions of the wealthy as well, until they fell down from neglect.

The real reason that the West Poplar neighborhood got chosen as the site of Philadelphia's first public-housing project was never explained in the article announcing its planned construction as an already decided *fait accompli,* but a perceptive reader could piece together a plausible explanation of the housing project's real purpose from other newspaper accounts as its construction spawned political controversy. By early 1942 it had become obvious that the white woman and children pictured in the original *Bulletin* article two years earlier would not be returning to the neighborhood, or if they were, they were not going to be living in the government housing everyone up until then had assumed was going to be built for them. Government housing – to formulate the rule that would explicate this field of endeavor for the next half century – served government purposes, and the main governmental purpose as of early 1942 was the war against fascism. "The occupants were told that they would be allowed to come back and occupy decent quarters," the *Bulletin* opined on January 31, 1942, but "Washington now says these homes are needed for defense workers."[6] As its story unfolded in the papers during early 1942, Philadelphia's first public-housing project started to sound like a maneuver that is known at the lower end of the retail trade as bait and switch.

On the eve of America's entry into the continuation of the first European war of the twentieth century, West Poplar was not a black neighborhood in the way North Philadelphia would become a black neighborhood in the '50s. It was not an integrated neighborhood, that chimera of social engineering that came into existence, at least in the heads of the social engineers, at around the same time. Saul Alinsky would go on to give the most accurate definition of integration in housing as the time between when the first black family moved in and when the last white family moved out. West Poplar was a mixed neighborhood where housing was determined by income. If one focused on the court houses that got torn down, the "neighborhood" was 88 percent black. If one focused on the West Poplar neighborhood as a whole, the percentage of black families dropped to 51.5 percent. If one focused on Girard Avenue, from Front to Broad, the main east-west thoroughfare in the neighborhood, the area was exclusively white. If one looked at the area from a Catholic perspective, the Richard Allen Homes were part of St. Malachy's Parish, which meant it was an Irish neighborhood, or at least an Irish neighborhood in transition.

Notes

1   Adolph Katz, "Old Houses Must Come Down to Make Way for the New: Housing Refugees Not Eager to Go . . . ," *The Evening Bulletin* (9/12/39), available at the Urban Archives of Temple University.
2   Ibid.
3   Ibid.
4   John F. Bauman, *Public Housing, Race, and Renewal: Urban Planning in Philadelphia, 1920–1974* (Philadelphia: Temple University Press, 1987), p. 48.
5   Ibid.
6   "A Housing Mistake," *The Evening Bulletin*, 1/31/42, Temple University Urban Archives.

Dennis Clark in Kensington

If the public housing projects at 9th and Poplar were intended for poor white people of the sort depicted in the *Bulletin* photos, Dennis Clark's family would have qualified. Clark was born on June 30, 1927, at St. Mary's Hospital at the corner of Front and Palmer Streets, roughly one mile east and two miles north of the Richard Allen Homes. When the construction of the Richard Allen Homes was announced, Clark was twelve years old. He would eventually go on to become an expert on housing, perhaps because of his experiences in Kensington as a child. "I lived in ten different locations before I was twelve years old," Clark wrote in a diary which he would keep for his whole adult life. "We kept moving because the rent man kept coming. We often couldn't pay the eight or twelve dollars a month rent so we'd have to move."[1] In the '50s, Clark remembered images of his father during the cold winters of the '30s, a man he described as "tough as nails"[2] and "theatrically combative"[3] yet reduced by economic want to rubbing his powerful workers' hands and crying because he couldn't find work. Clark could recall as well memories of "hopping to school along Gurney Street between the railroad and the looming drabness of Bromley's mill."[4]

Bromley's Mill symbolized for Clark the hegemony of the Protestant industrialist class over the immigrant laboring class in Philadelphia. Clark was Irish and Catholic and acutely aware of the position his ethnic group occupied in the city of Philadelphia. When he was ten years old, Ellen Devlin Clark took him aside and explained what it meant to be Irish, especially Irish in an American city like Philadelphia. "To be Irish," she explained, "means to fight, battle. That's how we have survived. Fight."[5] Years later, Clark would claim that he took this admonition "as instruction."[6] Once Clark internalized that description of his ethnic group, the only question which remained was "to choose the right conflicts and targets."[7] By the time Clark wrote this entry in his diary in 1991 he was near the end of his life, and for the previous twenty years he had chosen as his personal fight the conflict in Northern Ireland. But Clark got into that fight largely on the rebound from his disappointment over a fight that was closer to home, namely, the racial conflicts of the post-World War II period in Philadelphia. In this fight Clark would find himself on the side of some unlikely allies, namely, the Quakers whose reputation as partisans of pacifism did not preclude involvement in warfare of the psychological variety.

During the later Irish nationalist period of his life, Dennis Clark wrote a piece on the Quakers in one of Philadelphia's neo-ethnic Irish newspapers, claiming that every Irishman should say a prayer of thanks every time he passed a Quaker meetinghouse. Clark, as usual in matters dealing with the Irish in Philadelphia, took his paradigm for understanding Quaker-Irish relations from the nineteenth century, specifically the Quaker reaction to the potato famine, claiming that "During the famine, the Society of Friends in Philadelphia distinguished itself by its dedication to the relief of the suffering in Ireland."[8] Clark then went on to praise "the high principles of these families" claiming that many of the descendants of the earlier Quaker emigrants contributed heavily in the 1840s to the stricken Irish people. While Queen Victoria gave a niggardly sum to famine relief, the Philadelphia Quakers contributed over 4,000 pounds in 1846–47. . . . The merchant John Wanamaker headed the Famine Relief Committee and also contributed to the Friends' effort. To Irishmen whose families were dying of hunger before their eyes, the name "Philadelphia" must have seemed synonymous with "kindness."[9]

Digby Baltzell, sociologist from the University of Pennsylvania, inventor of the term "WASP" as the acronym for White Anglo Saxon Protestant and chronicler of the world from their point of view, had a different view of the relations between Irish Catholics and the already established Quaker ruling class in Philadelphia. Discussing the nativist riots of 1844, Baltzell described a disparity between public persona and private feeling that would characterize the Quakers for the next century. The Quakers felt privately that "it were well if every Popish church in the world were leveled to the ground."[10]

Clark knew Baltzell personally. He cited Batzell's claim that the riots of 1844 were anti-Irish and not anti-Catholic in his own history of the Irish in Philadelphia, and yet this passage and the notion that Quakers had some ambivalence toward Philadelphia's Irish Catholics never made it into any of Clark's writings. During the early '80s, Clark claimed in his diary that he had "refuted Digby Baltzell's idea that the history of the city of Philadelphia is the history of its Anglo Class."[11] Something Clark calls an "absurd idea,"[12] since there were at least three Philadelphias that needed to be chronicled: Proper Philadelphia, Pretzel Philadelphia (the Catholic ethnics), and Pigmented Philadelphia (the southern blacks who drove Pretzel Philadelphia into the suburbs). Although he had dedicated his intellectual life to chronicling at least the Irish part of Pretzel Philadelphia, Clark felt in the last decade of his life that ethnic Philadelphia "has yet to find its Digby Baltzell."[13] Part of Clark's ambivalence has to do with his own relationship with the Quakers and his own aspiration to be accepted by the ruling class in Philadelphia. Part of it had to do with his inability to understand just what the Quaker heritage meant. The fact that the Quakers received the Nobel Prize in 1947 for feeding starving refugees of war in Europe cemented their image as do-gooders in the public mind, but it also obscured their roots as revolutionaries during the English civil wars of the 17th century. Unlike Dennis Clark, Digby Baltzell was able to see the connection between the revolutionary struggles of the mid-17th century in England and the cultural revolution of the 1960s in America. Quakers achieved a role of cultural prominence far beyond their numbers in both revolutionary eras. "There is a haunting similarity," Baltzell wrote,

between the pattern of anarchy that followed the execution of England's king in January 1649 and the assassination of President Kennedy in November 1963. Once again the established church has disintegrated and a host of self-righteous seekers are loose upon the land. In this climate of opinion, it is understandable that the ideas and ideals of Quakerism are now more popular in America, especially among intellectuals and academics, than at any other time in our history. Since the close of the Second World War, for example, there has been both a reversal of the downward trend in numbers and a very real renaissance within the city, as symbolized by the award of the Nobel Peace Prize to the American Friends Service Committee. The Quaker ranks have been swelled by all sorts of refugees from the institutional churches and synagogues.[14]

The Quakers were a sect without a creed, whose liturgy entailed sitting in an empty room and waiting for the Holy Spirit to prompt them to speak. Since each member of the sect had equal access to the "inner light," the sect was composed of members who were all essentially personally infallible when it came to religious doctrine. This theological fact would have certain social and political consequences. Since the sect had no creed, which is to say, no first principles, consensus could only be achieved by intense application of peer pressure. In fact, peer pressure or "friendly persuasion" was the only principle that held the sect together. More than one observer has noticed the connection between the pietist sects of the 17th century and the rise of sensitivity training.[15] One observer noticed the connection first-hand while teaching at Haverford College, the orthodox Quaker college outside Philadelphia, during the 1950s.[16] Since sensitivity training was created as a form of psychological warfare,[17] it was no coincidence that Quakerism would thrive in an era dominated by that form of covert warfare. Unlike Digby Baltzell, Dennis Clark never seems to have noticed the revolutionary roots of Quakerism and their consequences for a revolutionary period like the 1960s. It was a misperception that would have far-reaching consequences both for him personally and for the "Pretzel Philadelphians" whose roots he shared.

Clark's Irish identity was bound up with his understanding of himself as an economic underdog in a society whose economic cycles had more and more to do with wars and the mills which supplied war materials, especially uniforms, to the government. But those economic and class differences were bound up with the ethnic struggles which the economic system created, struggles that often broke out into urban warfare of the type that would be more typical of the twentieth century.

On May 6, 1844, a meeting of Protestant laborers in Kensington, many of whom worked in that neighborhood's textile mills, eventually boiled over into a full-blown riot which lasted three days and eventuated in two Catholic Churches being burnt to the ground, the destruction of dozens of Catholic homes and sixteen deaths. The incident made such a deep impression on Philadelphia Catholics that roughly ten years later, when the Catholic Cathedral was being built near Logan Circle, the height of the stained glass windows was determined by how far a grown man could throw a brick. Clark, who wrote about the riots in one of his books on Philadelphia's Irish, took Digby Baltzell's lead in downplaying the religious element of the riot, portraying it as an essentially intra-Irish clash, in which other Catholics, e.g., the Germans, whose churches remained unmolested, had little involvement.

The anti-Catholic riots convinced both sides in the dispute that something had to be done about the increasing number of Catholic immigrants coming to Philadelphia, a tide that would increase to a flood when the effects of the contemporaneous potato famine began to be felt in Ireland. The Protestant establishment in Philadelphia clearly perceived the hordes of newly arrived Irish Catholics as a threat to the social order and acted accordingly by instituting various measures that would limit their political influence. Those measures ranged from the creation of a police force, whose vans were known as "Paddy

Wagons" because of the frequency with which they were used to transport Irishmen to the local police stations, to the Act of Consolidation of 1854, which brought huge amounts of farmland to the northeast and northwest within the city's boundaries as a way of diluting the political power of the newly arrived Irish immigrants. "The prospect of the old and eminent City of Philadelphia perhaps dominated by raucous Irish political blocs," Clark wrote, "was frightening to the city's older leaders, and even terrifying to those Protestant clergymen and laymen who saw Irish Catholicism as a massive threat to the moral and civic welfare of their city. Philadelphia County had more than sixty local councils of the Order of the United American Mechanics, a Know Nothing organization only too ready to campaign against the Irish Catholics."[18]

By 1850 there were 72,312 Irish born in Philadelphia. That meant that 18 percent of the total population was Irish. This coupled with the other Catholic immigrants constituted a considerable threat to a ruling class whose essential ethnic characteristic was the Protestant faith. The Irish settled in Southwark and Moyamensing in South Philadelphia. North of Center City, Kensington and Port Richmond were Irish neighborhoods. In 1850 they began to spread west toward Broad Street above Vine into the area of North Philadelphia that would become the 20th Ward.

Given a social situation this polarized and this explosive, it was in the interest of both parties – the Protestant and the Catholic – to find some *modus vivendi* that would preserve peace in the city. That *modus vivendi* involved the creation of Catholic ghettos, ethnic neighborhoods that would grant a significant measure of local autonomy and freedom of religious expression and at the same time contain the threat the Irish posed to the larger social order. Clark cites Ellis Paxson Oberholtzer of the University of Pennsylvania, a historian of the city and a partisan of the city's upper-class traditions, who wrote of the immigrants that they had "revolting and vicious habits. Being of the lower order of mankind, they were repellent to those who were further advanced in the social scale."[19]

The ethnic neighborhood solved the problem posed by large-scale Irish migration from the perspective of those on both sides of this cultural struggle. The ruling class was spared from having to deal with the "revolting and vicious habits" of "the lower order of mankind" directly, and the largely Irish Catholic immigrants could worship in peace and essentially organize their own local communities as they saw fit. In Philadelphia, that meant widespread home ownership. It also meant control of the instruments of local culture. It also meant that assimilation into American mores took place on a slower basis that many later reformers thought necessary.

Nowhere was this opposition to assimilation more apparent than in the Catholic resistance to participation in the public-school system. By the time Dennis Clark was a young adult in the late '40s, it was possible for Catholics to get sixteen years of education – from first grade to a bachelor's degree – without leaving their own church-controlled institutions, a situation that caused intellectual reformers from John Dewey to Margaret Mead and Paul Blanshard much consternation. The only thing that kept this Protestant/Catholic social schism from degenerating into open ethnic warfare or a socialist revolution based on ethnic antagonism was the creation of Catholic ghettos in the form of ethnic neighborhoods. "In the last third of the nineteenth century," Clark writes, the Philadelphia Irish concluded a compact with the rest of the urban society surrounding them. It was a Victorian compromise. Under it the Irish would largely remain within the institutional framework they had been constructing for themselves. They would avoid any attempt to overthrow or supplant the native Philadelphia institutions that dominated the city. The aristocratic clubs, schools, and elite family business connections that structured the leadership levels of the city's life went on unhindered.[20]

In foregoing any attempt to wrest control of city hall from the WASP establishment or engage in working-class revolutionary politics, the Irish and other Catholic immigrants were given control of their neighborhoods, and they consolidated this control by building and owning their own homes in them.

From the point of view of the Catholic leadership in Philadelphia, this meant in effect pursuing a course that discouraged assimilation and at the same time encouraged parish life. The parish was to become the self-contained local community, and in Philadelphia and other cities of the industrial north, the cultural autonomy of the local ethnic community, strengthened by home ownership, became the backbone of the Catholic Church's social arrangements with a country whose philosophical presuppositions and political institutions had been condemned by Pope Pius IX and Pope Leo XIII. In Philadelphia, as in few other cities in the United States and virtually no other city in Europe, home ownership in combination with parish life became a crucial element in support of local autonomy. According to Bauman's account, "By 1929 over 50 percent of Philadelphians owned or were buying their homes, up from 38.8 percent in 1920."[21] To the Irish in Philadelphia, as for just about all of other Catholic ethnic groups, owning a home meant owning a rowhouse. "It was the rowhouse," Clark writes, "that characterized its mass residential prospect."[22] The areas of highest Irish concentration – Southwark, Moyamensing, Grays Ferry, Kensington, and Port Richmond – were areas where the rowhouse predominated for one simple reason. The rowhouse was an inexpensive solution to the housing problem. The 16-by-31-foot brick structure, with two bedrooms and a bath on the second floor and a living room and a kitchen on the first, was based on the design of 18th century English townhouses, adjusted to the more modest circumstances of their American owners. Beginning in the 1860s, these houses could be bought new for $1,000 to $2,500 according to location. They could be rented for $8 to $15 a month, and they could be bought used for as little as $300. The proliferation of the rowhouse meant that in places like Philadelphia, the working class could own its own home in a way that it could not in Liverpool or even New York City for that matter. To the European visitor, Philadelphia's housing stock became one of its salient characteristics, a sign of the workers' prosperity and an indication of America's ability to share the wealth with its own people. "Half of Philadelphia," wrote one European visitor to the city in the 1860s,

> has been built in this way, and the workmen construct for themselves also houses, which make an extremely good appearance; they are healthy, airy, and provided with everything conducive to comfort and salubrity. . . . There is certainly not a city in the world where the working population lives with the comfort they enjoy

in Philadelphia, and we must add that they owe this superiority solely to themselves and their intelligent activity.[23]

Even if it were written seventy years before the arrival of the Richard Allen Homes, that fact puts subsequent descriptions of the housing stock of North Philadelphia in its proper context. The Philadelphia rowhouse meant economic security for that city's ethnic immigrants. The largely WASP housing establishment which staffed upper-class entities like the Philadelphia Housing Association knew this as well. In their early years people like PHAssoc head Bernard Newman offered prize money in contests sponsored to come up with new designs for the rowhouse. When the New Deal incorporated housing into its schemes for social engineering, that consensus was threatened. When Washington began to offer large sums of money to people who were ethnically committed to its foreign-policy initiatives against European fascism, the temptation to turn on the rowhouse and all it stood for became a temptation too great to resist.

The cultural meaning of the rowhouse combined with the anti-assimilationist emphasis on parish life which people like Bishop Neuman and Bishop Kenrick promoted, meant that for roughly one hundred years, the immigrant population in Philadelphia devoted most of its wealth and energy to creating local communities of remarkable stability, especially if one considers that most of the people who lived there were born someplace else. The stability of these communities contributed as well to the stability of the social and personal lives of those who lived there. The reputation of the Irish as brawling drunkards remained long after the social mores which begot these myths had disappeared. Daniel Patrick Moynihan, himself the product of a broken home, drew attention to the similarities between the Irish immigrants in 19th-century New York City and the black migrants from the South in the 20th because by the time he wanted to make his point the similarities were no longer apparent. According to Dennis Clark, "The attainment of a tidy row house on an orderly city street meant that the immigrant would have an actual stake in the urban community. It meant that the period of privation would be shortened, and that the hostility engendered by poverty and residential isolation would be tempered somewhat."[24] The situation in Philadelphia was a distinct improvement over the situation in Ireland. In Ireland, a two-story house was "a mark of notable affluence," whereas in Philadelphia, it "could be had by a thrifty workingman."[25]

If the Philadelphia ruling class found the Irish repugnant because of what they perceived as their moral failings, then they should have greeted the rise of home ownership as an unmixed blessing, but things are rarely so straightforward in life. The simple fact of the matter is that ghettoization in ethnic neighborhoods had a salutary effect on Irish morals, but with salutary morals came an unwanted, at least from the ruling class point of view, side-effect, namely political power. By the time the Blanshard brothers arrived in Bridesburg, the ruling class was becoming increasingly concerned about the ghettoes it had created for the city's Catholic immigrants, not because they were dens of vice and disease, but for precisely the opposite reason, because the people living there were thriving to the point where they were beginning to pose a political threat to the people in power. The compact which created the ethnic neighborhood in Philadelphia as a way of containing the Catholic threat would remain in place until the 1950s, when it was placed under two-fold assault because of the political power it generated. It was 1963 before an Irish

Catholic was elected mayor of Philadelphia. That meant that the walls of the ethnic ghetto had been broken, but with the wall broken conflict could ensue from both sides. The simple fact of the matter is that the election of a Catholic mayor coincided with an unprecedented assault on ethnic neighborhoods on the part of the Quakers, who were using their traditional allies, the blacks, as their shock troops in this assault. That assault on the neighborhoods led to the rise of aggressively ethnic politicians like Frank Rizzo, which in turn further enraged the Quaker/Episcopalian ruling class and spurred them on, this time with the support of the federal government, to ever bolder attacks on the strongholds of Catholic-ethnic political power in the city's neighborhoods.

Ghettoization was, it could be argued, a form of assimilation, but if so, it was a glacially slow form of assimilation, so slow that the more impatient reformers on both sides of the Catholic-Protestant cultural struggle must have seen it as virtually immobile. The social compact involving the ethnic neighborhood lasted for roughly 100 years, from the middle of the nineteenth century to the middle of the twentieth, and could have lasted longer, if the ruling class hadn't grown impatient with it and tried to replace it. Race was the excuse for replacing it. As Michael Lind has shown, the interaction between religion and ethnicity has created the most enduring configurations on the American political landscape. The fundamental religious differences between New England Puritans and Southern "Cavaliers" led not only to the Civil War between the North and the South, but also to the political conflicts which followed the war. In this regard, busing was in many ways a replay of that same struggle a century later in Boston, just as the early phase of the civil rights movement in the '50s and '60s was a replay of that struggle in the South. Roosevelt's New Deal brought southern agrarians and northern ethnics into common allegiance in the Democratic Party against the New England and midwestern Protestants, who were the backbone of the Republican Party. From the abolitionists to the civil-rights movement, Puritan New England was historically consistent in supporting the black underclass against its opponents in the South in the nineteenth century as well as against its Catholic ethnic opponents in the big cities of the north during the 20th century. Clark notes that in Philadelphia in the 19th century,

> The Irish Catholics had little sympathy for the Abolitionist cause. Although the *Catholic Herald* took a position against the extension of slavery to Kansas, the religious, political, and economic gulf between the average Irishman and the Yankee Abolitionist leaders was too great to bridge. The fervent Protestant evangelism and the Republican party identification of the antislavery leaders rankled the Catholic Democrats, and the link of the Abolitionists to British antislavery circles alienated Irishmen who could see such British moral reformers only as hypocrites blind to the near serfdom in Ireland.[26]

Dennis Clark remembered the Irish ghetto of Visitation Parish in Kensington with what one would have to characterize as mixed emotions. From the Catholic point of view which Clark learned as a young man, there were two Philadelphias – juridical Philadelphia, which was ruled by Protestants, and ethnic Philadelphia, according to which "the geography of the city was broken up into parishes."[27] If a Catholic introduced himself it was generally by way of parish, not section of the city: "So she would be a girl from

St. Anne's Parish or he's from the Ascension or Holy Name Parish. The neighborhood of the city we knew of as folk parody. Swampoodle was St. Columba's Parish."[28]

Each parish had its own ethnically based cultural life, which included local forms of entertainment which also had a definite ethnic flavor. Clark later characterized the minstrel shows he watched at Visitation Parish as "entirely racist."[29] But the rest of his explanation undercuts this assertion. Entertainment was ethnocentric, and blacks occupied just one ethnic niche in the city, all of which were essentially alien to each other. "Ethnic relations," he continues, "were such that we did not know blacks. Germans and Italians were to us an object of wonderful comedy. English people were often an object of contempt and as for the rest of the world, they appeared in the funny papers, nowhere else. It was a sort of self-contained psychology of ethnic self-assurance."[30] The alleged racism of the parish minstrel shows reveals itself upon closer inspection to be a suspicion of everything not Irish. That meant that the ethnocentric Irish were just as much at odds with their co-religionists from other European countries. What has come to be known as the race issue was at the time in fact an ethnic issue. From the Irish point of view, blacks were just one more alien group, like Germans, Poles, and Italians, who lived elsewhere and would be kept out of the neighborhood by force just as they would repel any other foreign ethnic group. That the situation did not remain this way is due to a number of factors virtually all of which are ethnic rather than racial. Blacks were immediately identifiable in a way that Germans were not; blacks were overwhelmingly Protestant in a country where religion was the ultimate basis of ethnic difference, but the biggest cause of animosity was the fact that black migration was being used against the Irish as a form of social engineering. It was this use of social engineering, especially after World War II, that turned the Irish into "white" people. The relations between the Irish and the Germans or between the Irish and the Poles, even within the Catholic Church, were far from irenic. But those conflicts subsided eventually when Catholicity replaced country of origin as a source of common ethnicity. That peaceful evolution was not allowed to take place in racial matters.

The earliest Catholic immigrants to this country clearly viewed the racial conflict as something not of their making. As a result, they all but unanimously embraced the idea of ghettoization both of themselves and every other non-ruling class group as the only solution to an intractable problem which they had inherited from the natives, simply by virtue of being immigrants. Baltimore's Bishop Michael Curley wrote to the Vatican, trying to make them understand "the keen race distinction which the Catholic Church in America has not made and cannot solve."[31] In 1922, Msgr. Luigi Giambastiani of Chicago's St. Philip Benizi Parish expressed a completely typical non-assimilationist, non-integrationist view of American life that was based not on racial but rather ethnic realities. "It is true that some idealists dream of an American millennium when all races will be found fused into one new American race," Giambastiani wrote, " – but in the meantime it is good that each one think of his own . . . Italians be united to your churches . . . give your offering to the Italian churches who need it . . . the Irish, Polish and Germans work for their own churches, do the same yourself. . . the Italian Church ought to be not only a symbol of glory for you, but a symbol of faith and race."[32]

Giambastiani's use of the term "race" is both instructive and typically Catholic. In Catholic parlance, race meant ethnos, and this understanding was common among virtually all of the Catholic ethnic groups and the cities they colonized. During the 1919 race riot in Chicago, Poles referred to "whites" as a separate group, distinct from Eastern Europeans. In Pennsylvania, the principal of a Catholic school explained that "our Polish and Lithuanian students expressed great surprise that their Catholic associates seemed to dislike them because of their race."[33] By urging ethnic "segregation," Msgr. Giambastiani was adopting what was from the Italian point of view at the time an essentially liberal and pluralistic solution to a problem thrust on him and his countrymen by an essentially hostile and alien culture. He was most certainly accommodating himself to a situation which was not Italian. Giambastiani made his peace with the American system of ethnic federalism as he found it because it seemed like the only plausible solution to an otherwise intractable problem. How else was it possible to achieve any type of social order in Father Giambastiani's Back of the Yards neighborhood in Chicago, where eleven Catholic churches – two Polish, one Lithuanian, one Italian, two German, one Slovak, one Croatian, two Irish, and one Bohemian – not counting Protestant denominations in other sections of the city, made one common community not only a cultural impossibility but a linguistic impossibility as well. John McGreevy notes that "the 1916 U.S. census survey revealed 2,230 Catholic parishes using only a foreign language in their services, while another 2,535 alternated between English and the parishioners' native tongue."[34]

Ethnic federalism was the only basis for a workable social order in the cities dominated by the new immigrants. The ethnic federalism of the large cities of the northern United States was completely compatible with the federalism which the founding fathers saw as the basis of the United States, even if the descendants of the founders did not always see it that way. Ethnic federalism was also completely compatible with the structure of the Catholic Church, which since the Council of Trent had been divided into the local geographical unit known as the parish. Acceptance of ethnic federalism was also, in effect, the official position of the Catholic Church in this country for the first half of the twentieth century. It remained in force until roughly 1958 when the United States bishops, reacting to the cultural pressure created by the civil-rights movement, issued its own statement on race based largely on the revisionist, integrationist thinking of Rev. John LaFarge and the various Catholic Interracial Councils he had founded. The Church changed its position on "segregation" not because of any internal dynamic but because the ruling class changed its attitude toward race and ethnicity, and they changed their position largely because of America's entry into the war in 1941 and their defeat of the America First, isolationist wing of the Protestant Republican Party in this country.

Dennis Clark would live under both regimes. He was born into the world of the ethnic parish as articulated by Msgr. Giambastiani, and he would later become a devotee of Father LaFarge. In fact, he would become Father LaFarge's successor as the head of the Catholic Interracial Council in New York in 1963. By then he had become so committed to the cause of integration that he could no longer examine it objectively. Like most Catholic liberals at the time, Dennis Clark made integration synonymous with social justice and then went on to judge the Church by this criterion. When the Church failed this test in Clark's eyes, he abandoned the Church and became an embittered opponent of religion whose main self-identification was Irish ethnicity. This transition from being an Irish Catholic to becoming an anti-Catholic Irishman was not without its ironies. Dennis Clark could see that the political realities behind the WASP/black abolitionist alliance were inimical to the interests of the Philadelphia Irish, but he never seems to have been able to transpose this lesson in history to the situation in twentieth century Philadelphia when the same alliance was driving Irish Catholics out of their neighborhoods. His commitment to Irish politics as a substitute for first religious fervor and then fervor for social justice in racial matters meant in effect abandoning the cause of his own ethnic group in Philadelphia by identifying them as a bunch of hopeless racists.

Since Dennis Clark held a position of leadership among Catholic intellectuals in Philadelphia during the crucial decade of the '60s, that meant the Church with its ethnic parishes would have to negotiate this change from the social paradigm of ethnic federalism to the opposed paradigm of "integration" without intellectual guidance. And that meant hard times for St. Malachy's Parish, the place where the Richard Allen Homes got built in the late '30s and early '40s.

Like the height of the windows at the Cathedral of Saints Peter and Paul on the Parkway, St. Malachy's Parish was in many ways one of the *sequelae* of the nativist riots. It was created out of the western part of St. Michael's Parish less than ten years after that parish got burned to the ground during the riots of 1844. It was named after the 12th-century bishop of Armagh as some indication of the nationality of its parishioners and as some indication that their numbers were increasing exponentially in North Philadelphia due to recent dislocations in Ireland. After the cornerstone to the church was laid in 1851, the parish community developed in ways that were typical of ethnic communities under the old dispensation. The woods surrounding the church were replaced with classic Philadelphia rowhouses, now owned by the Irish workers who found employment at the mills in Kensington. "These snug row houses," according to the parish historian, "created permanent neighborhoods and stable communities. There was great pride in home ownership; a privilege denied in Ireland."[35] By 1853 St. Malachy's was a large part of why Philadelphia was going to be known as "the city of homes."

In 1863 the same demographics which caused the western portion of St. Michael's Parish to split off into St. Malachy's caused the western part of St. Malachy's to split off into the Church of the Gesu, west of Broad Street. Because the Gesu was run by the Jesuits, it had its own college preparatory high school and a college in addition to the parochial school that St. Malachy's had. It was a sign that the Gesu was considered an upscale parish at the time. The college left the neighborhood in 1889. The high school is still there, although the parish is not, having been reconsolidated back into St. Malachy's because of racial migration in the 1990s.

Gesu might have considered itself a cut above St. Malachy's, but both parishes were thriving during the 1920s. When Eamon DeValera, the president of new Republic of Ireland, came to Philadelphia to speak to the Irish diaspora there, he spoke at the Met, an opera house on Broad Street, the boundary that linked these two parishes in this solidly Irish area. When Al Smith was nominated for president in 1928, the twentieth ward, which was the political name for St. Malachy's and Gesu, turned out the vote in force.

The good times in both parishes ended on December 22, 1930, when the Bank and Trust Company of Philadelphia failed. Between the end of 1930 and the time that Franklin Delano Roosevelt declared a bank holiday in 1933, a total of fifty banks would fail, dragging down with them local businesses and with them the jobs upon which the working class residents of St. Malachy's depended for a living. Deprived of their jobs the working class in Philadelphia was no longer able to make the mortgage payments on their modestly priced rowhouses. By 1932 there were 19,000 foreclosures in the city. In the ten years between the stock market crash and the arrival of the Richard Allen Homes in the parish, thirty-six of the sixty houses on North Van Pelt Street alone were repossessed. By 1934, both the public and private relief agencies in the city had exhausted their coffers, forcing the once-prosperous St. Malachy's Parish to operate its own relief agency, collecting food and clothing for their parishioners. Local charity was still largely an ethnic operation. When the Drueding Leather company, at one time the world's leading producer of chamois, opened an infirmary for its largely German-speaking employees from Lower Kensington in 1931, they invited the German-speaking Sisters of the Holy Redeemer to staff it.

Drueding Leather was in this regard the exception when it came to local factories. For the most part they were not owned by members of the same ethnic group that worked there. The division between capital and labor in Philadelphia bespoke ethnic division, and ethnic division invariably had a religious dimension as well. The immigrant workers who staffed the unions and agitated for higher wages were Catholic; their employers were anti-Union Protestants, who oftentimes used the economic dislocation caused by the depression to strengthen their position vis-à-vis the worker. One resident of St. Malachy's remembers her father walking to work at the Ford Plant at Broad and Lehigh. When he joined the union during the Depression, he lost his job and was then forced to seek work at the docks as a stevedore, when work was available, which was infrequently at best during the '30s.

The confrontation is instructive because it places the housing situation in St. Malachy's in a larger context. The Irish were in the forefront of the labor movement in Philadelphia and elsewhere. Two of the founders of the Knights of Labor were Robert McCauley and Joseph Kennedy, two Philadelphia Irishmen. These men depended on ethnic Irish churches like St. Malachy's as the basis of their organizational network. On the other side of the struggle, industrialists like Henry Ford were bitterly anti-union and made a practice of playing one ethnic group against the other in keeping the workers under control and wages low. One of the groups which Ford favored the most was southern blacks because of their docility and because they were willing to accept the jobs brokered by black ministers in Detroit on the conditions under which they were offered, namely, refusal to join unions.

The Second World War didn't change this situation. It merely intensified it. Demand for labor following the War Production Board's recapitalization of America's industrial plant insured that jobs were plentiful, which increased the power of the worker. But that recapitalization was done with the industrialists' interests in mind, often prompting them to move out of the big cities where unions were powerful. The war also justified draconian measures against strikes, the unions' main weapon in seeking higher wages and benefits. More than anything else, the war, as it had done twenty years earlier, increased migration from the South, and that increased migration meant that the government that wanted to win the war had to find a place for the workers to live when they got to places like

Philadelphia. Given the penchant for social engineering the East Coast internationalist elite favored (it was after all the Rockefellers who through their foundations had essentially created what came to be known as the social sciences at the University of Chicago), government involvement in housing under these auspices meant using housing as a form of social engineering. To committed Watsonians – and this is what the WASP elite had become by the late '30s – changing the environment meant changing man's behavior and that meant, of course, changing the man as well.

It is unlikely that anyone in St. Malachy's Parish knew about people like John B. Watson and his colleagues at the University of Chicago. If the topic had been brought up during the 1930s, it would probably have been dismissed in light of more pressing needs. People who are fighting for their economic existence don't have time to think strategically. They react to the forces that are pushing and shoving them as best they can, doing what they have to do to survive. That was, after all, the reason why they had left Ireland and come to Philadelphia. Confronted by the same face of grim economic necessity, it is not surprising that they would react to the same forces in the same way once again. Once the factories in the neighborhood began to close down, the people who had arrived in this area of Philadelphia for essentially economic reasons began to wonder whether it wasn't time to move again.

During the '30s, loss of employment was also coupled with continued black migration up from the South, and the destination of those black immigrants was almost invariably North Philadelphia, the once-Irish stronghold now weakened by ten years of economic adversity. Between 1930 and 1970, six and one half million black Americans would move from the rural South to the industrial North, the largest population movement in the nation's history. Any change of this magnitude brings with it a decline in morals, but the moral dimensions of this migration were magnified by the war and by the fact that the morals of the dislocated slaves from the South were nothing to brag about to begin with. Nicholas Lemann describes the situation in the South in the early '40s and the effect it would have on cities like Chicago:

> It is clear that whatever the cause of its differentness, black sharecropper society on the eve of the introduction of the mechanical cotton picker was the equivalent of big-city ghetto society today in many ways. It was the national center of illegitimate childbearing and of the female-headed family. It had the worst public education system in the country, the one whose students were most likely to leave school before finishing and most likely to be illiterate even if they did finish. It had an extremely high rate of violent crime: in 1933, the six states with the highest murder rates were all in the South, and most of the murders were black-on-black. Sexually transmitted disease and substance abuse were nationally known as special problems of the black rural South; home-brew whiskey was much more physically perilous than crack cocaine is today, if less addictive, and David Cohn reported that blacks were using cocaine in the towns of the Delta before World War II.[36]

The already weakened state of black morals in the South was aggravated by the removal of the sort of external control which the Jim Crow system provided there and by the increase of wages which gave an uprooted people more money than it had ever seen before while at the same time giving no social guidance about how it could be spent prudently. Lait and Mortimer trace the creation of the South Side ghetto and its mores to that simple fact:

> During the war, when the Chicago labor shortage was more severe than in most places because of the diversity of her plants and her unequaled transportation setup, it was not unique for a farmhand who had never owned $10 at one time to earn $200 a week with overtime. This started the Bronzeville boom, with its drinking and doping and the resultant laxities that blossomed into flagrant vice.[37]

A bad situation among the actual migrants of the South was made worse in the next generation as young people raised without even a vestigial sense of the social order of the South by parents who were busy working in the wartime economy sought to re-establish a caricature of the social order in the gangs that proliferated in black ghettos. The Blackstone Rangers, to name just one famous example, one which would eventually receive federal money to pursue criminal ends under the auspices of the War on Poverty, was the creation of children born during and after the war in Chicago to parents earning wartime wages with little time and no social institutions to pass on to the next generation. "Most of the people," according to Lait and Mortimer,

> had left behind them the influences which they had come to respect, in entirely different conditions. The problems attending migration from rural areas proved particularly acute with the youth. To get the swollen wages, the parents left their children largely to themselves, and they went wild. When the layoffs came the children had been up North long enough to refuse to accept the conditions of ordinary living, such as most Negroes in this country are accustomed to. Vice and crime were easy money. Politicians had discovered that they could remain in office indefinitely by buying the votes of entire large segments of the population.[38]

The main result of the moral dislocation caused by wartime migration was that

> Youth gangs, male and female, have gotten beyond control. In groups ranging from ages 11 to 18, and often in numbers up to 200, they terrorize the entire Black Belt and frequently invade white neighborhoods to pillage, rob, rape or beat up people of any race for the sheer pleasure of it.[39]

W.E.B. DuBois noticed something similar in Philadelphia following the dislocations which migration caused during World War I. "Among the lowest class of recent immigrants and other unfortunates," DuBois wrote in *The Philadelphia Negro*, "there is much sexual promiscuity and the absence of a real life. . . . Cohabitation of a more or less permanent character is a direct offshoot of the plantation life and is practiced considerably. . . ."[40] E. Franklin Frazier noticed much the same thing: if slavery were bad, the uprooting caused by reconstruction was worse in the toll that it took on family stability. Worse still was wartime migration to the anonymous big industrial cities of the north. When unwed mothers replicated the pattern of illegitimacy in the North with none of the social controls of the South in place, it was a foregone conclusion that illegitimacy would spread, and that all of the pathologies associated with illegitimacy – gangs, crime, drugs, etc. – would spread with it. Segregation was, in this regard, the defeated South's defense against what it perceived as "uncontrollable Black libido." Illegitimate childbearing, the short duration of romantic liaisons, and the constant domestic violence among the sharecroppers and poor blacks in town clearly demonstrated, according to Lemann, "that blacks were sexually uncontrollable. This made social segregation a necessity. Social segregation led to legal segregation in education, government, and the economy."[41]

If the Irish residents of St. Malachy's understood this fact intuitively, they lacked the political and economic power to deal with it effectively. Ghettoization of the Irish and other Catholic ethnics meant that they were granted some control over what happened in their neighborhoods in exchange for no control over the strategic forces that ran the city. That meant that the city could make decisions that would constantly impinge on what happened in the neighborhood by orchestrating forces that would affect them from without, but the residents of the neighborhoods could do nothing to stop those forces other than react in a violent and ad hoc and ultimately self-defeating manner when a black family moved into the neighborhood. Racial migration was by definition an interstate affair in the United States, and neighborhood councils had no power over interstate commerce, not even when it was orchestrated to their detriment.

Racial migration was promoted with strategic ends in mind, and the residents of St. Malachy's, even if they suspected the strategy behind the migration of blacks up from the South, were powerless to stop it. The simple facts of the matter indicate that they were not aware of that strategy either, and as a result they reacted as individuals to a campaign that was being orchestrated against them as a group. Just as they had during the potato famine, the residents of St. Malachy's reacted to the combination of political and economic pressure that confronted them by moving once again, this time north along 5th and Broad streets to places like Olney and West Oak Lane. In 1930 St. Malachy's Monsignor Fitzpatrick was transferred to Incarnation Parish in Olney, as an indication that the Irish population was shifting in the city and as an omen of things to come. In 1935, St. Malachy's celebrated the 85th anniversary of the founding of the parish, but as part of the celebration Father Martin felt constrained to note that the roof needed to be fixed, a sign that the economic forces arrayed against the parish were taking their toll. By the time the construction of the Richard Allen Homes was announced in 1939, St. Malachy's was a parish on the brink not only of change but of destruction as well. At this moment in history, the parish could have gone in either of two directions, and those directions were symbolized by the two positions the Catholic bishops had staked out on just what a parish community was. Had the bishops stood fast to the principle of ethnic federalism which the Church had made its own since the middle of the 19th century, St. Malachy's and Philadelphia and Chicago and Detroit might look very different today.

In this regard, the Richard Allen Homes were like a large rock dropped into a small pool. The effect on the community would radiate from it in ever larger ripples of both intended and unintended social effect. By 1939, St. Malachy's was a community which had suffered ten years of economic pounding. Nor were they in a position to maintain their homes as those homes had been maintained in the relatively prosperous '20s. But more important than that, they were incapable of understanding, much less countering, the effects of psychological warfare, because at this point in Philadelphia's history no one knew what such a thing was. Still less could they conceive that it would be waged against them. They were after all American citizens. And even if they were somewhat reluctant to go to war to pull England's chestnuts out of the fire, they still enlisted when the call came.

Notes

1   A complete copy of Dennis Clark's diary can be found at the Balch Institute for Ethnic Studies. An incomplete version can be found in the archives of the University of Notre Dame. The material in this note is taken from an interview which Deborah Kodish conducted with Clark on August 25, 1988. All subsequent references to the diary will refer to the date of the entry.
2   Clark, diary, 7/6/91.
3   Ibid.
4   Clark, diary, 12/18/52.
5   Clark, diary, 7/6/91.
6   Ibid.
7   Ibid.
8   Dennis Clark, "An Irish Tribute to Friends," probably from *The Irish Edition*, available at Notre Dame archives.
9   Dennis Clark, *The Irish in Philadelphia: Ten Generations of Urban Experience* (Philadelphia: Temple University10press, 1973), p. 29.
10 E. Digby Baltzell, *Puritan Boston and Quaker Philadelphia: Two Protestant Ethics and the Spirit of Class Authority and Leadership* (New York: The Free Press, 1979), p. 423.
11 Clark, diary, 6/12/81.
12 Ibid.
13 Clark, diary, 1/18/88.
14 Baltzell, *Puritan*, p. 455.
15 Michael Weber, *Psychotechniken: die neuen Verfuerhrer* (Stein am Rhein: Christiana Verlag, 1997). See also Thomas C. Oden, *Intensive Group Experience: The New Pietism*, 1972.
16 Morton A. Kaplan, "Letters," *Measure* (August/September 1995): 3.
17 Art Kleiner, *The Age of Heretics: Heroes, Outlaws and the Forerunners of Corporate Change* (New York: Currency Doubleday, 1996), p. 31.
18 Clark, *Irish in Philadelphia*, p. 118.
19 Ibid., p. 35.
20 Ibid., p. 126.
21 John F. Bauman, *Public Housing, Race, and Renewal: Urban Planning in Philadelphia. 1920–1974* (Philadelphia: Temple University Press, 1987), p. 16.
22 Clark, *Irish in Philadelphia*, p. 40.
23 Ibid., p. 55.
24 Ibid., p. 60.
25 Ibid., p. 54.
26 Ibid., p. 120.
27 Clark, diary, Kodish interview.
28 Ibid.
29 Ibid.

30 Ibid.

31 John T. McGreevy, *Parish Boundaries: The Catholic Encounter with Race in the Twentieth Century Urban North* (Chicago: University of Chicago Press, 1996), p. 8.

32 Ibid., p. 10.

33 Ibid., p. 31.

34 Ibid., p. 11.

35 Eileen Dougherty Troxell, *A History of the Community of Saint Malachy* (Philadselphia: no pub date), p. 15.

36 Nicholas Lemann, *The Promised Land* (New York: A. A. Knopf, 1991), p. 31.

37 Jack Lait and Lee Mortimer, *Chicago Confidential* (New York: Crown Publishers, 1950), p. 40.

38 Ibid., p. 41.

39 Ibid., p. 43.

40 W.E.B. DuBois, *The Philadelphia Negro* (New York: B. Blom, 1967), p. 32.

41 Lemann, p. 37.

John J. McCloy in North Philadelphia

Since John J. McCloy was born at 874 N. 20th Street, he was technically at least a member of the Gesu parish even if he wasn't a Catholic. McCloy was a descendent of the Scotch Presbyterians who had arrived in Philadelphia a century before the Catholic Irish, but the fact that he was technically a WASP did not change the fact that he was born literally as well as figuratively on the wrong side of the tracks. In the days before the upper-class suburban migration, the Philadelphia WASP establishment lived on the other side of the Chinese Wall, otherwise known as the railyards of the Pennsylvania railroad south of Market Street. McCloy's heritage reflected the other side involved in the nativist riots of 1844, the Scotch weavers who resented Irish Catholic interlopers into their trade. As such, his family had possibilities for advancement – if not to the top of the heap in Philadelphia, then certainly to the middle – denied to his Catholic neighbors on 20th Street. McCloy's father had a decent-paying job with a local insurance firm and might have advanced further if he hadn't died of a heart attack in 1901, leaving young Jack an orphan with difficult prospects, especially since the Penn Mutual Insurance company refused to pay out death benefits to the widow of one of its own employees.

But John McCloy's mother was not the sort of person to take even something like the death of her husband lying down. Trading on her ability as a hairdresser, she soon became the confidante of the Quaker-Episcopalian society matrons who lived in the area around Rittenhouse Square and parlayed those contacts into some real opportunities for her son. She was smart enough to realize that at that point in the nation's history, moving into the ruling class meant attending the right schools, and so she scraped together what she had earned and sent young John to the Peddie School in New Jersey. The Peddie School wasn't Choate, but it allowed young John to go on to Amherst, and a degree at Amherst allowed him to attend Harvard Law School, which was at the time the place where young men were groomed for assuming positions in service to the ruling-class elite – in just about every place in the country, it turns out, except Philadelphia. The period following the Civil War in this country saw the eclipse of local elites and their replacement by a national elite, which placed a premium on attendance at elite national schools like Harvard. In Philadelphia, a degree from the Harvard Law School, however, remained a necessary but not sufficient condition for admission to the upper class. The local Philadelphia elite had never got away from the necessity of blood ties, something which McCloy learned to his chagrin when he returned to Philadelphia looking for a job with one of the city's prestigious law firms. The Harvard degree would have entitled him to the job anyplace else. In Philadelphia it didn't even entitle him to serious consideration for the job, something which family friend George Pepper explained in his avuncular way.

"Now, listen John," he told the young Harvard law school grad who felt he had traveled far since his youth in North Philadelphia, "I know your family well. When your mother wanted to send you away to school, I was against it. I didn't think she could afford it. I was wrong about that, but I am not wrong about this. I know Philadelphians. It is a city of blood ties. You have got the grades, but they don't mean anything here. Family ties do. Even when I started out here, it was difficult and slow. It would be impossible for you. You were born north of the Chinese Wall, and they'll never take you seriously in this town. In New York, however, your grades will count for something."[1]

So McCloy went to New York instead, at precisely the moment when the East Coast establishment, under the tacit leadership of New York families like the Rockefellers, were coming into a position of national prominence and just as their Philadelphia equivalent were sinking into provincial insignificance. McCloy got a position with Cravath, Moore and Swaine, a law firm which was to become a national model for corporate law. McCloy arrived at Cravath just as that firm was becoming, in the words of *The New Yorker*, "a symbol of rapacious Capital."[2] As one of his first jobs at Cravath, McCloy arranged an insider stock deal which refinanced a railroad which was subsequently burdened with so much debt that it went bankrupt shortly thereafter. It was the kind of deal that would have been clearly illegal a few years later after the Securities Exchange Commission had been created in the aftermath of the crash of 1929 to prevent this sort of thing. He also hired William O. Douglas as a Cravath associate during the summer of 1925. Like McCloy, Douglas came from a family of modest means but made his way in the world as an enabler of ruling-class initiatives, from expanding eminent domain in *Berman v. Parker* to decriminalizing contraception and abortion in *Griswold v. Connecticut* and *Roe v. Wade* through his work on the Supreme Court. As a ruling-class law firm, Cravath maintained a consistent line on Catholic ethnic issues from the relatively innocuous – Paul Cravath raised money for Herbert Hoover when he ran against Al Smith – to the less benign. It was Cravath which defended Charles Curran *pro bono* during his battle with Catholic University in 1967. Having won that battle Curran then led the intra-Catholic opposition to *Humanae Vitae*, the Church's birth-control encyclical one year later.

All of this was far from John McCloy's mind in 1939. He had just won the biggest court case of his career, not something involving insider stock deals or Catholic theologians but a case involving German spies. On July 30, 1916, at 2:08 in the morning, a thousand tons of gasoline, munitions, and dynamite exploded at the rail terminal on Black Tom Island in New York City harbor not far from the Statue of Liberty. The suspicion that German sabotage had something to do with the explosion had all but faded from memory by the time McCloy got involved in the case in 1930, but in the space of the next nine years, McCloy not only revived the idea, but by 1939 he had actually succeeded in getting a conviction in the case that made his firm and his clients a lot of money. It had also succeeded in making McCloy a celebrity among the elite Wall Street firms and an expert on espionage.

The combination of those two factors had landed McCloy an even greater honor. After winning the Black Tom case in 1939, McCloy was invited to join the Council on Foreign Relations, one of the quintessential East Coast WASP establishment organizations. The CFR came into existence in the early '20s to keep the internationalist business trade apprised of political and economic developments which might affect their investments. The CFR had not only the support of the East Coast elite; it also had the financial backing of the Rockefeller Foundation. McCloy had made his first contact with the Rockefeller family when, while vacationing in Bar Harbor, Maine, and at the urging of his mother, he went up to the door of the Rockefellers' 110-room mansion in Seal Harbor and volunteered his services as a sailing instructor for John D. Rockefeller, Jr.'s sons. It was the unlikely beginning of a relationship with the Rockefeller family that would span seven decades. The Rockefellers saw in McCloy a man who identified completely with their interests and the interests of the class they represented and a man who could serve their interests by conceiving strategic initiatives. They saw in McCloy a man who could bring those initiatives to completion, and so they gave him one assignment after another from bringing about the merger of the Chase Manhattan Bank and acting as David Rockefeller's unofficial tutor in the world of politics and finance to running the Rockefeller Foundation's politically engaged form of philanthropy. The invitation to join the CFR meant that McCloy's role in the Black Tom case had impressed the people he had set out to impress when he took the job with Cravath. It meant, in the words of his biographer, that "McCloy was now a bona-fide member of the Establishment."[3] Taken together with his other accomplishments, especially his newly garnered expertise in intercept intelligence, it also meant that McCloy was about to be drafted into the inner circles of the Establishment's war machine. By the time the Black Tom case got handed down, Europe was at war once again, and the people who had invited McCloy to join the CFR and wanted to get the United States into the war on the side of England needed to make plans.

In order to get those plans rolling, the Rockefeller Foundation gave the Council for Foreign Relations an initial grant of $44,500 in December of 1939 to fund a joint "War and Peace Project" with the State Department. In April of 1940, the War and Peace Project produced a memo explaining how "to achieve military and economic supremacy for the United States within the non-German world."[4]

On April 2, 1940, a man by the name of William Stephenson entered the United States. Stephenson, a British citizen, had ostensibly come to this country on an official mission of the British Ministry of Supply. Britain was now in the middle of a war with Germany, a war which Winston Churchill, who would become prime minister on May 10, had concluded they simply could not win – without, that is, outside help – and the only place with enough sympathy and materiel to help Britain win the war was the United States. Stephenson was sent to the United States as a secret agent, whose job it was to get America into the war on the side of England.

To do this, Stephenson had to overcome considerable opposition. The Democrats had been excluded from the White House for the entire decade of the 1920s once the horrendous cost of the First World War became apparent to the American people. The Republicans, who benefited from the backlash against Wilson's foreign adventurism, were, however, divided into two camps: the conservative, isolationist faction which had the base of its power in the Midwest, and the Anglophile, East Coast WASP plutocrats, who as the description implied saw their ethnic heritage as English and their allegiance to a group that was similar to them in both income and ethnicity and race which transcended national borders. Their sympathies were with England in the war then raging in Europe. Perhaps because the elitist practice of American government differed so radically from its democratic theory, the WASP establishment spent much of its time and effort denying its own existence. The facts, however, spoke otherwise.

When he arrived in this country, Stephenson knew that President Roosevelt's sympathies lay with those of his ethnic group. He also knew that certain families had more clout than others. Which is why he ended up establishing his headquarters on the 38th floor of Rockefeller Center, prime office space for which he paid no rent. Stephenson knew as well that American history could be characterized not only by its source in English culture but by its desire to escape from that influence as well. That struggle did not end with the successful completion of the Revolutionary War. Emboldened by their victory over Napoleon, Britain tried to re-conquer their former American colonies during the War of 1812 and succeeded in burning both the Capitol and what came to be known as the White House to the ground.

This struggle did not end with the cessation of military activity in 1814. Throughout the nineteenth century, when the American system of protected manufactures brought about a spectacular rise in this nation's wealth, it lay dormant, but in the early twentieth century with the arrival of Irish Catholics and Southern and Eastern Europeans in great numbers, it reasserted itself, and the war was prosecuted by other means. At the heart of this intra-American struggle lay the question of whether America was to become an empire, on the British model, or remain a republic as conceived by the founding fathers, who warned against entangling European alliances. The Anglophile establishment got its first big break with the presidency of Woodrow Wilson, the professor who not only got America into World War I, but who also tried to rearrange the map of Europe according to his own preconceived ideas. Woodrow Wilson, according to Michael Hunt,

> was . . . certain of the universal relevance of Anglo-American political institutions and values. As a student of government, Wilson had long celebrated liberty as the flower of the Anglo-American tradition, its evolutionary advance the benchmark of progress, and constitution-making one of man's great accomplishments. The British parliamentary system was his institutional ideal, and the American Revolution stood for him as an epochal event that made "the rest of the world take heart to be free."[5]

Wilson, like Franklin Delano Roosevelt, was a Democrat. Being a conservative at this time meant being isolationist and being dedicated to the preservation of America as a republic. This Anglophobe tradition, based largely in the Midwest, had as its leaders people like George Norris, a Republican from Nebraska, and Robert LaFollette, Sr., a Republican from Wisconsin. But then as now the Republican Party was divided and the party's Anglophile eastern wing, representing the country's plutocrats, wanted war with Germany even if it wasn't on Wilson's terms. This group, according to Hunt, was

> self-consciously Anglo in their ethnic orientation and without exception Protestant (usually Anglican or Presbyterian).The emergent twentieth century variant of this type was usually a Northerner or Easterner and increasingly from Northeastern cities. His formal education at private schools and Ivy League colleges and law schools was supplemented by an informal education in foreign affairs promoted by trips to England and the Continent. He practiced corporate law until gaining public office, usually by appointment. His soundness on foreign-policy question

was insured by the values inculcated in elite social circles, in exclusive schools and in establishment clubs and organizations of which the [Rockefeller sponsored] Council on Foreign Relations (established in 1921) was the most important.[6]

Woodrow Wilson's legacy was the income tax, the hated Versailles Treaty, and an increasing penchant for social engineering of the sort which the *New Republic* under Lippmann, Dewey, and Croly applauded. Wounded by their association with the stock market crash and the subsequent Depression, the Republican isolationists were swept from the White House but regrouped when it became apparent that Roosevelt, like his predecessor Wilson, was determined to lead the United States once more into a European war. Like Woodrow Wilson, Franklin Roosevelt had a hard time separating ethnicity and value. If the Anglo-Americans were the repository of freedom and democratic institutions, then Germans must be bad. Hunt tells us that for Wilson

> it was not enough to defeat Germany. He wanted also to defeat those banes of humankind that Germany stood for – imperialism, militarism, and autocracy. A victorious war would be for him only the prelude to global reform. And enlightened peace would redeem the bloody sacrifices of the war and break the grim cycle of suspicion, hatred and conflict.[7]

Things didn't turn out as Wilson planned. The ascendancy of the "Anglo-America" internationalist faction created a crisis of major proportions for this country. Perhaps frightened by the arrival of immigrants from Southern and Eastern Europe, the eastern Anglophile establishment attempted to change the idea of what it meant to be an American. Now the prime designation was racial and/or ethnic rather than intellectual assent to a series of propositions, foremost among which was the idea that all men were created equal. Americans were now not so much those who accepted a set of propositions and agreed to live according to them: Americans were people of a certain stock, namely white, Protestant Anglo-Saxon. Once this decision was made, ethnic interest replaced citizenship as the primary tie of allegiance. National solidarity took a back seat to race and class. The Cabots and the Lodges and the Rockefellers identified more with people of their class in England than they did with, say, a Jew or an Italian in New York, which is to say their own newly arrived fellow citizens. This reordering of allegiance meant a transition from republic to empire would follow naturally if this group ever got its hands on the levers of power.

The last great battle came on the eve of World War II. Embittered by the cost of Wilson's War – $100 billion and over 100,000 lives – America turned isolationist in the '20s. The Anglophiles were out of power until the stock market crash of 1929 brought the Democrats back to the White House, and, like President Wilson before him, Franklin Delano Roosevelt was an Anglophile who orchestrated America's entrance into another war. His great opponent in this regard was Charles Lindbergh, head of the America First committee.

Throughout the 1930s Charles Lindbergh and the America Firsters, with many supporters in the Midwest, posed a significant threat to the Anglophile hegemony in foreign policy. That threat disappeared in a matter of minutes on December 7, 1941, when Japan attacked the U.S. fleet at Pearl Harbor and the United States entered the war against the Axis powers on the side of England. From that moment until the present, foreign policy was in the hands of the Anglophile establishment.

Thomas Mahl's book *Desperate Deception* shows that the defeat of the America Firsters wasn't just the result of superior debating skills. William Stephenson, a British millionaire, became head of an entity known as British Security Coordination in 1939. The BSC was an arm of British intelligence whose purpose was to get America into the war on the side of England. In order to do that, the BSC, in the words of Ernest Cuneo, the Roosevelt Administration liaison with BSC,

> ran espionage agents, tampered with the mails, tapped telephones, smuggled propaganda into the country, disrupted public gatherings, covertly subsidized newspapers, radios and organizations, perpetrated forgeries . . . violated the alien registration act, shanghaied sailors numerous times, and possibly murdered one or more persons in this country.[8]

BSC headquarters in New York occupied two full floors of the Rockefeller Center. The goal was clear. In the first of his seven wills, Cecil Rhodes, founder of the Rhodes Scholarship, called for the creation of a secret society whose aim (in Rhodes's words) is "the extension of British rule throughout the world . . . and the ultimate recovery of the United States of America as an integral part of the British Empire."[9]

Although the Rockefellers were Republican and Roosevelt was a Democrat, in foreign policy both acted on their common ethnic interests. On June 14, 1940, three months after Stephenson's arrival, Nelson Rockefeller wrote to Harry Hopkins to suggest the creation of an intelligence operation that would later, after its official establishment by executive order on August 16, 1940, be known as the Rockefeller Office. By the end of August, the Rockefeller Office was working on a "'voluntary program by which American businesses would eliminate all their Latin American representatives who were Germans or German agents."[10] The existence of the Rockefeller Office, otherwise known as the Office of the Coordinator of Commercial and Cultural Relations Between the American Republics, or later the Coordinator of Inter-American Affairs, came to light thirty years after the war had ended in 1976, and only then was it revealed that it had been an intelligence operation.

During the same year that the Rockefellers recruited John McCloy as an expert on intercept intelligence into the CFR, and during the same year that they funded the War and Peace Project in conjunction with the CFR and the State Department, the Rockefeller Foundation also funded a series of secret seminars at the University of Chicago which were to bring together the men it regarded as the leading communications theorists, a group which included Harold Lasswell and Hadley Cantril, two alumni of the Committee for Public Information, the U.S. government's psychological-warfare arm during World War I. The purpose of the seminars was to "find a 'democratic prophylaxis' that would immunize the United States' large immigrant population from the effects of Soviet and Axis propaganda."[11] The seminars were also created "to consolidate public opinion in the United States in favor of war against nazi Germany."[12] It was a classic instance of fighting fire with fire, and some of the participants did not like that fact. Donald Slesinger, former dean of the social sciences at the University of Chicago, felt that the Rockefeller-sponsored psychological warfare campaign was "willing, without thought, to sacrifice both truth and human individuality in order to bring about given mass responses to war stimuli . . . . We have thought in terms of fighting dictatorships-by-force through the establishment of dictatorship-by-manipulation."[13]

John McCloy was not afflicted with Professor Slesinger's scruples. He was an avid proponent of intercept intelligence, which included "second story" methods, i.e., break-ins in addition to the covert manipulation of public opinion in favor of entry into the war. Through his brother-in-law Lew Douglas, McCloy made contact with C. D. Jackson, Henry Luce's associate at *Time*. Under Jackson's direction, the CFR waged a covert and highly successful public relations war against Charles Lindbergh and America First, placing anti-Isolationism and anti-Hitler editorials in 1,100 different papers every week across the country.[14]

Nowhere do the workings of the East Coast WASP establishment become more apparent than in the turns John McCloy's life took following his departure from Philadelphia. Digby Baltzell has written about this establishment, as has Carroll Quigley. It was an ethnic group with close affinities to England. It was nominally Protestant but only in the ethnic negative sense of that term. McGeorge Bundy would later describe himself as "a committed but not convinced Episcopalian."[15] Because of its religious convictions, or lack thereof, it was also anglophilic and as a result avid to get into the war on the side of England, but it was also avid in its belief in science and the Enlightenment as the wellspring from which one would of necessity have to derive the solutions to the world's social and political problems. But more than all of the above, the Establishment was a "we"; it was an ethnic group which had a surprising unanimity of purpose, especially when confronted with an external threat to its interests. In addition to being in the CFR, McCloy was a member of the Century Group, which wanted America to become "top dog,"[16] in Harvard President James Conant's words. That meant, of course, working with England and becoming in effect co-administrators of the British Empire or some more sophisticated variation thereof. McCloy's brother-in-law put the case for empire in the following way when writing to Conant in October 1940: "Our endeavor and England's endeavor, it seems to me, should be aimed at the reconstruction of a world order in which . . . the United States must become the dominant power. . . . [I s]ee little hope in my lifetime if this remains undone."[17]

As McCloy's relationship with Lew Douglas indicates, the East Coast establishment was a group that was often united by blood ties. It was also a network which knew who could be relied upon to serve its interests. It was, in other words, more than just an ethnic group; it was the elite vanguard of an exceedingly powerful ethnic group which ruled the country and which was emerging as a result of the war as the world's premier power. The East Coast internationalist establishment was so powerful in fact that it was in no way an exaggeration to call it America's ruling class during World War II and the decades following the war. When it came to people who identified with the goals of this group and people who had the ability to get things done as well, John McCloy was on the short list of just about everyone in the establishment. Henry Lewis Stimson, for example, Roosevelt's new internationalist Secretary of War, was familiar with John McCloy's role in the Black Tom case and his consequent reputation as an expert on German intelligence. He was also aware of his skill on the tennis court. Given the homogeneous nature of this elite and McCloy's reputation for defending their interests, it is not surprising that he was soon called to Washington.

On September 16, 1940, Stimson told General Sherman Miles, chief of Army G-2 intelligence, to hire McCloy as a part-time consultant for the War Department. Once McCloy got to Washington he lost no time in agitating for the formation of a centralized intelligence agency. In order to immunize the 12 million German Americans living in the United States from Hitler's propaganda efforts, McCloy proposed what he was calling "Department X," a "well-organized bureau or department" whose job it was to protect ethnics from the "virus" emanating from their ancestral homelands.[18] "Democratic Prophylaxis" was the term current at the University of Chicago which signified the prosecution of psychological warfare against American citizens, and it was not reserved exclusively for deployment against German Americans. McCloy's brainchild, which eventually became the Office of Strategic Services during the war and the Central Intelligence Agency after the war, was an ethnocentric operation from the beginning. It was, in brief, WASPs worried about ethnics. As a result, McCloy's "Department X" assigned only one unit to "counter work in U.S. among Germans."[19] Another unit was assigned the task of running counterpropaganda in Germany, but more importantly "there were similar units for Italians, French, Czechs, Poles, and 'all other races' in the United States."[20] Some commentators have noticed the ethnic homogeneity of the nascent intelligence community in the United States and how it was recruited largely from Yale University and how a large segment of the Yale alumni were also members of the secret Skull and Bones society, but few have noticed the converse of this observation, namely, that the purpose of the newly created intelligence agency was spying on other Americans of the opposite ethnic persuasion. Both "Department X" and the Rockefeller-financed seminars at the University of Chicago were engaged in waging psychological warfare against "ethnic," which is to say largely Catholic, Americans. Since these people were also largely American citizens, McCloy's "Department X" was involved in Black (i.e., illegal) Operations from its inception. McCloy's arrival in Washington and the influence he wielded there meant that wartime intelligence and psychological warfare meant inter-ethnic warfare as well. That meant to a large extent that the rise of the intelligence, security state meant WASPs spying on Catholics, something that would have far-reaching consequences for the neighborhoods those people lived in, especially after the war.

After sketching out the broad outlines of what would become the national security state, McCloy then devoted his efforts to the war-time economy. "The warfare of today," he explained to Stimson, "is increasingly a question of industrial capacity to produce the ability to make, day after day, year after year, planes, ships, arms, and equipment. We must overtake and surpass in this connection an efficient, well-organized nation which is and has been devoting for a number of years the major part of its efforts to the job of preparing and fighting a war."[21] That meant retooling for war, but increasing industrial production also meant increasing black migration from farms in the South, where machines could now pick cotton, and relocating those people to factories in industrial cities in the North, which were suffering an acute manpower shortage. If we combine (1) McCloy's essentially amoral understanding of intercept intelligence and the need to apply it to suspect ethnic groups in the United States and (2) the need for black migration to solve war personnel needs we have *in nuce* the policy of covert ethnic warfare that would find expression in programs like government housing, urban renewal, the civil rights movement (and *sequelae* like busing) that would dominant the regime's social agenda for the rest of the 20th century.

McCloy had no scruples – moral, social, political, economic, or otherwise – when it came to putting his vision of the new America into practice. If winning the war against his ethnic opponents meant creating a socialist command economy, he was willing to pay the price.

"Business," he wrote, "is going on in the country as usual, and it cannot go on as usual if we are to build up our capacity to anything like German dimensions. . . . To triple or quadruple our present effort requires that radical things be done to our existing economy. Obviously the job demands industrial planning of a high order on the part of the Production Boss."[22] If it meant suspending the very constitutional freedoms he purported to defend, he was willing to do that too. "We have to restrain our liberties to preserve them," McCloy wrote at one point, "and in my judgment, we should be prepared to restrain them far more than the country now gives indication of being willing to accept."[23] If it meant using wire-tapping to break the unions, so be it. McCloy and Undersecretary of War Robert P. Patterson urged C. D. Jackson to create a special FBI unit that would use wire-tapping and other "second story" tactics against strike leaders in munitions plants. "The war effort," McCloy stated blandly, "will necessarily entail extensive centralization of power."[24] Ian Fleming, author of the James Bond novels, was so impressed with McCloy's devotion to the Anglo-American imperial cause that he urged William (Wild Bill) Donovan, eventual head of the OSS, to hire McCloy as his chief of staff.

As part of his involvement in the economic restructuring of the United States to win the war, McCloy wrote another memo (which Stimson then handed to Roosevelt) urging the creation of another $27 billion in production capacity. When the War Production Board finally got implemented, it was implemented with the good of both the war effort and McCloy's once and future establishment clients in mind. And that again meant bringing blacks, the most docile and untapped source of labor in the country, up from the South to the factories of the North to dilute the power that increased industrial demand for labor was giving to the northern ethnics and their unions. Bringing blacks north meant bringing their problems – the problems Nicholas Lemann mentioned in *The Promised Land* – up with them, and that meant that the government was going to have to engineer the behavior of both the black worker and his "ethnic" colleagues. That process of social engineering would continue long after the war against fascism had been won.

In order to win the war, McCloy set into motion forces which would soon take on a life of their own. Migration was one of those forces. It could be manipulated by certain strategic measures, but it would appear as if it operated independently of them. And once the migratory patterns were established, it did. During the 1940s, the black population of Chicago increased by 77 percent, from 278,000 to 492,000. In the 1950s, it grew by another 65 percent, to 813,000; at one point 2,200 black people were moving to Chicago every week. By 1960, Chicago had more than half a million more black residents than it had had twenty years earlier, and "black migrants from the South were still coming in tremendous numbers."[25] Eventually the word spread throughout the South that

> You could find a job in Chicago in a matter of hours. Being black and from Mississippi was the only credential you needed, because white people up there knew that black folks from Mississippi were used to working hard; anyway, because of the immigration restrictions passed in the 1920s, there wasn't anybody else in Chicago who was willing to start out at the bottom.[26]

With the advent of the mechanical cotton picker and chemical pesticides, migration was a policy which found ready acceptance in the South as the potential solution to the racial problems there. "All in all," Lemann writes, "the idea of getting the numbers of blacks and whites in the Delta a little closer to equilibrium began to seem attractive to whites on political as well as economic grounds. The best, the only, means to that end was black migration to the North. As Aaron Henry puts it, 'They wished we'd go back to Africa, but Chicago was close enough.'"[27]

Having set into motion the forces that would eventually destroy large sections of some of America's largest cities (and some might argue, in the case of Detroit, the city itself), McCloy then turned his attention to his next project, destroying German cities and their civilian inhabitants by fire-bombing. Flying to an Allied Conference in Cairo in November of 1943, McCloy wrote that "there is something of a very concrete nature to accomplish and it will mean taking part in an historical incident. How far away from 874 North 20th street [his childhood home in Philadelphia] it all is; yet it all ties back to there. . . ."[28]

Notes

1 Kai Bird, *The Chairman: John J. McCloy and the Making of the American Establishment* (New York: Simon & Schuster, 1992), p. 57.

2 Ibid., p. 63.

3 Ibid., p. 107.

4 Ibid., p. 109.

5 Michael Hunt, *Ideology and Foreign Policy* (New Haven and London: Yale University Press, 1987), p. 137.

6 Ibid.

7 Ibid, p. 134.

8 Thomas Mahl, *Desperate Deception: British Covert Operations in the United States 1939–1944* (Wasington, D.C.: Brassey's, 1998), p. 16.

9 Carroll Quigley, *Tragedy and Hope: A History of the World in Our Time* (New York: Macmillan, 1966).

10 Mahl, p. 17.

11 Christopher Simpson, *Science of Coercion: Communication Research and Psychological Warfare 1945–1960* (New York: Oxford University Press, 1994), p. 22.

12 Ibid.

13 Ibid, p. 23.

14 Bird, *Chairman*, p. 109.

15 Kai Bird, *The Color of Truth: McGeorge Bundy and William Bundy: Brothers in Arms: A Biography* (New York: Simon & Schuster, 1998), p. 134.
16 Bird, *Chairman*, p. 112.
17 Ibid.
18 Ibid., p. 118.
19 Ibid.
20 Ibid.
21 Ibid., p. 122.
22 Ibid.
23 Ibid., p. 136.
24 Ibid., p. 131.
25 Nicholas Lemann, *The Promised Land* (New York: A. A. Knopf, 1991), p. 70.
26 Ibid., p. 40.
27 Ibid., p. 49.
28 Bird, *Chairman*, p. 190.

Anna McGarry in North Philadelphia

Anna McGarry was one year older than John McCloy. Since they were born within a year of each other and lived within a mile of each other, it is conceivable that they might have passed each other on the streets of North Philadelphia in their youth. McCloy was born on 874 N. 20th Street. If he were a Catholic, McCloy would have been a member of the Gesu Parish, which split off from St. Malachy's in 1868 and was Anna McGarry's parish during most of her adult life. McCloy would eventually return to 874 N. 20th Street during the 1960s, when, as head of the Ford Foundation, he had decided to promote the Rev. Leon Sullivan, a black minister from North Philadelphia, as part of the Ford Foundation's Gray Areas program. There is no indication that he ever met Mrs. McGarry, not as a young man who lived in her neighborhood, and not in his capacity as chairman of the Ford Foundation as an enabler of politically motivated social change. By the time John McCloy re-visited his ancestral home during the early 1960s, North Philadelphia had become the most violent, crime-ridden neighborhood in Philadelphia, and it is unlikely that he would have been walking its streets and knocking on its doors without Rev. Sullivan's protecting presence.

If John McCloy had chosen to knock on Mrs. McGarry's door instead of the door of the anonymous black woman who was then living in the house where he grew up, there is no indication that either McCloy or McGarry would have perceived the other as an opponent in a cultural civil war, a war whose main casualty would be the city itself. McGarry was an ardent promoter of interracialism, and in the early '60s, in spite of the riots that would devastate the area surrounding Columbia (now Cecil B. Moore) Avenue a few blocks to the north, it appeared that the country was well on its way to solving one of its most perduring and intractable problems.

Anna McGarry was old enough to be Dennis Clark's mother, and in a certain sense she was. It was McGarry who embodied more than any one figure in Philadelphia, with the possible exception of Dennis Clark, the Catholic attempt to find a solution to the city's racial problems. Clark met McGarry while studying at St. Joseph's College, the Jesuit institution which got its start in Gesu Parish. It was also through McGarry that Clark learned about Jesuit John LaFarge's Catholic Interracial Council. McGarry, like LaFarge, was involved in bringing about one of the great paradigm shifts of Catholic polity in the United States, the change from the ethnic federalist understanding of parish and community that was regnant during the 19th century to the "integrationist" paradigm that would replace it during the 1960s. Cardinal McIntyre could still argue that ethnic churches were "natural groupings," where "kind lives with kind—Irish with Irish, Poles with Poles, Mexicans with Mexicans, Negroes with Negroes," but by the point he made his claim, the paradigm had changed, to the point where one historian would describe McIntyre's position, which is to say the traditional American Catholic position, as "utterly untenable."[1]

No one was more instrumental in bringing about that change than Father LaFarge, on the national level, and no one was more instrumental in bringing about that change in

Philadelphia than Anna McGarry. At around the same time that Philadelphia created its housing authority and set the wheels in motion which would lead to the construction of the Richard Allen Homes in St. Malachy's Parish, Anna McGarry began working with Father Edward Cunnie, pastor of St. Elizabeth's, the traditionally black parish in North Philadelphia, trying to ameliorate the racial animosity that was developing in the traditionally Irish parishes as the result of increased black migration into the neighborhood. At around the same time, Father James Maguire, a native of County Mayo in Ireland and a Jesuit priest living in the rectory of the same parish to which Anna McGarry belonged, came to his own conclusions about essentially the same phenomenon that was troubling Mrs. McGarry. Appalled that the property values of the hard-working Irish home owners in the neighborhood had plummeted 42 percent in the years between 1931 and 1937, Maguire founded the Gesu Parish Neighborhood Improvement Association as a way of stopping the area's decline and the concomitant Irish exodus from the parish. Maguire had worked as a missionary in Jamaica and dismissed charges that he was motivated by racial prejudice. He could claim this because his understanding of the racial situation in North Philadelphia was still based on the traditional ethnic parish paradigm of the American Catholic Church, which meant he believed that "our colored brethren are happier and more content in their own little neighborhoods."[2] That meant that when the black Protestant sharecroppers who had just arrived in the neighborhood expressed an interest in becoming Catholic and joining the parish—a not uncommon occurrence in these years—they were encouraged to take instruction at St. Elizabeth's, a church a few miles to the north which Maguire saw as the black equivalent of the ethnic parish. That the black residents of North Philadelphia didn't see things this way eventually led to misunderstandings, and the misunderstandings did little to ameliorate the tensions that migration and neighborhood change were already creating.

Eventually the situation attracted the attention of the black press, which took advantage of the war-time mood of the country and conflated Maguire's efforts to preserve the Irish ethnic community in North Philadelphia with Hitler's racial policies. During the Spring of 1941 reporters from *The Philadelphia Tribune*, the local black paper, confronted Maguire's Jesuit superior, Father Thomas Love, demanding that he take action against Maguire. Love, appealing to the paradigm of the parish as the religious embodiment of the ethnic community, took Maguire's side in the dispute. "We have nothing against Negroes," Love countered, "but we cannot stand by and see property which represents the life-savings of some of our oldest parishioners become almost valueless or go to ruin. I recognize that there is a conflict of rights here, but my interest is primarily in the question of preserving the unity of my parish."[3]

Once the story of the Jesuit-supported neighborhood-improvement association hit the papers, it was only a matter of time before the Jesuit who had dedicated his whole life to the cause of interracialism would hear about it, and only a matter of time after that before he would give his opinion on how the conflict should be resolved. The "only course," wrote Father LaFarge, "is for Father Love and Father Maguire to pull out of the Gesu Improvement Association and turn their attention towards integrating Negroes into the parish by zealous missionary and educational effort."[4]

This may or may not have been the "only course," but it was the course that got taken,

when the Cardinal Dougherty adopted the interracialist cause as the rule in his archdiocese. For years thereafter Dougherty's successors assumed that the parishes which had
been established by European ethnics could be used to evangelize the Protestant sharecroppers from the South. Once they were evangelized and converted to Catholicism, the
blacks, theoretically at least, would take over the parish plant which the ethnics had abandoned. John Cardinal Krol, the man who assumed Dougherty's job in 1960, created a system of interparish financial aid to facilitate the transition, but the transition never really
took place, except in a few isolated instances, primarily because the ethnics who left were
never replaced by stable black communities. What had once been stable communities
degenerated into way stations of essentially disposable housing stock as the first wave of
middle-class black settlers left as soon as they could afford something better. And since
racial transition would affect ever-increasing areas in Philadelphia during the period in
question, that meant that there was always a better house available somewhere else in a
neighborhood that would also succumb to the same pressure and become one more tran-
sient encampment until the housing stock deteriorated beyond repair. At that point the
housing at the lowest end of the real-estate market was abandoned and left standing empty
until it fell down. In abandoning the ethnic community in favor of "integration," the
Catholic Church abandoned a paradigm of community which had worked in the past and
put in its place one that subordinated community to issues like social justice. In the end,
the Church got neither, and in effect collaborated in the destruction of its most vibrant
parishes and the physical destruction of Philadelphia as well.

Anna McGarry never felt that she got anywhere with Cardinal Dougherty, the man
who succeeded St. Malachy's own Bishop Kendrick as ordinary of the Archdiocese of
Philadelphia in 1918, but she probably underestimated the effect of her own efforts, as
reformers often do. When Dougherty announced to thunderous applause that "any
Catholic who despises anyone for any reason, particularly on such baseless foundation as
race or color, is not a loyal Catholic,"[5] it was a clear indication that LaFarge and McGarry
had won the battle for the episcopal mind in Philadelphia, because, following the lead of
the interracialists, Dougherty had attached a moral charge to a phenomenon, the ethnic
parish and community, which its defenders considered an essentially neutral part of
nature. Dougherty's statement was not so much a refutation of the position of Father
Maguire as it was a *non sequitur*. In the years following the fateful decision to allow the
Irish to be driven out of North Philadelphia, the argument would invariably get framed in
moral terms that missed the point of what the other side was trying to say. In promoting
interracialism, the Catholics were reacting viscerally to the racist nativists who had
attacked the candidacy of Al Smith, but in doing so they were to find that the enemy of
their enemy wasn't necessarily their friend. The internationalists like McCloy and the people he served were every bit as anti-Catholic as the racist isolationists, and they were more
sophisticated to boot, and less likely to be troubled by constitutional scruples when it came
to dealing with their enemies. "The Negro is a child of God too," the Catholic interracialist would say with the air of uttering something indisputably true, but if true, the moralis-
tic approach was also beside the point. No matter what Madison Grant may have thought
on the matter, people like Father Maguire in Philadelphia and people like Father Lawler in
Chicago were not arguing that blacks were subhuman. In defending the integrity of the

parish, they were promoting cultural accommodation to a country that was not theirs by birth. They were not promoting a racialist biological worldview or any such thing. According to the traditional American Catholic understanding of the issue, race was more cultural than biological, and in either event not something that disqualified one from salvation or church membership. Race was synonymous with ethnos, and ethnos was a part of nature and to be treated as such when it came to the administration of parishes in the United States. This was the traditional Catholic point of view, and when the Catholics abandoned it, it was not without consequences for both Church and state.

The effect of racial migration on cities like Philadelphia, Detroit, and Chicago is obvious. Not so obvious is the essentially relativizing effect that interracialism had on the primary Catholic community, the parish. The subordination of community life to other extrinsic goals relativized it and made community seem a matter of choice, which in a culture like the United States in the 20th century, inevitably led to a kind of consumerism, as people chose their communities according to whim and ideological preference rather than having their communities chosen for them by where they lived. The parish became one more item to be chosen rather than a community of a certain kind of people who lived in a certain kind of place. This change corresponded to the devaluation of place that was being promoted by turnover in real estate at the same time. Instead of taking a stand against it, the Church simply accepted the migration of Catholics to the suburbs as something essentially beyond its control. This devaluation of community led directly to the de-facto consumerist congregationalism which characterizes community life in this country today. Both are a direct result of the American Catholic Church's failure to understand the real roots of community and its failure to understand the campaign of social engineering that was waged against them in the years following World War II. During those years, the beleaguered Catholic ethnics were demonized as racists by their own co-religionist intelligentsia with no mention whatsoever of the organized campaign of psychological warfare being waged against them. Dennis Clark, in this regard, provides us with the classic paradigm of the Catholic intellectual of the time, agitating for social change which he perceived as a moral imperative, and then abandoning the Church when she didn't conform to his paradigm of social justice, without once giving some indication that the program he supported might have been of political benefit to the opponents of Catholic ethnics, even when he sat on the councils of the organizations that plotted the destruction of their neighborhoods.

This paradigm shift would ultimately have significant consequences for Gesu Parish as well. When Anna McGarry died on January 3, 1978, the city was involved in the first confrontation with MOVE, a black religious sect which abjured modern hygiene in favor of more "African" arrangements like throwing garbage in the yard of their Powelton Village communal home. When the police tried to enforce code violations, a policeman died in the gun battle which ensued. It was only a bloody prelude to MOVE II when a number of blocks in West Philadelphia got burned to the ground during another police raid. In 1993 Anthony Cardinal Bevilacqua closed Anna McGarry's Gesu Parish and reassigned the territory to St. Malachy's, whence it had come in 1868. The huge abandoned Italian renaissance church which looms over the neighborhood where John McCloy was born is in many ways the legacy of her interracial work. She worked to bring about racial

Philadelphia, Catholic interracialism and the decline of the parish

harmony, which still exists over the cultural horizon, and brought about the destruction of her own parish instead.

Notes

1 McGreevy, *Parish Boundaries: The Catholic Encounter with Race in the Twentieth Century Urban North* (Chicago: University of Chicago Press, 1996), p. 220.
2 Ibid., p. 251.
3 Ibid., p. 252.
4 Ibid.
5 Ibid., p. 253.

Mayor Lamberton and the War

In November 1939, two months after what would eventually become the Richard Allen Homes had been announced in the paper, Robert E. Lamberton was elected mayor of Philadelphia. Since he had run in opposition to Roosevelt's New Deal, the outlook for public housing, which Lamberton termed an unproven experiment, did not look good. Opposition to public housing was not unheard of in Republican-dominated Philadelphia during the 1930s. Between 1932 and 1935, Lamberton's predecessor, J. Hampton Moore, had made the same case, drawing on the same traditions. "Philadelphia," Moore opined, "is a city of homes. A thousand cities and industries are appealing to the Federal Government for relief. Philadelphia is not among them."[1] Providing housing had never been one of the traditional roles which government performed in the United States, and it was certainly not part of the role which the founding fathers envisioned for the federal government, but all that changed when Franklin Delano Roosevelt took office in 1932 and the political benefits which could accrue from getting into the housing business became clear to him.

Rexford Tugwell would later claim that "on March 4, [1932,] we were confronted with a choice between an orderly revolution – a peaceful and rapid departure from the past concepts – and a violent and disorderly overthrow of the whole capitalist structure."[2] But it is difficult not to notice a certain political eagerness in response to the crisis as well. The crisis provided the opportunity for an unprecedented expansion of the power of the federal government, and in expanding that power the Democrats could create for themselves a coalition of constituencies which would guarantee that their hands would remain on the levers of power for a long time to come. It was Roosevelt's genius to take a number of groups spurned by the Republicans and to bring them together in a coalition that was now capable of defeating those Republicans. The WASP aristocracy had a constitutional aversion to Southerners and ethnics, and in 1932 the Democrats brought those two groups together for the first time. In order to keep them together, the New Deal used its new-found federal powers to give them what they wanted. That meant agricultural policies and development projects like the Tennessee Valley Authority and electrification for the South, and it meant urban development programs for the North. Eventually, the urban development programs for the North would get used against the very people they were supposed to benefit, but that would not become apparent to their supposed beneficiaries for a while. At the time it was clear that things like public housing were meant to benefit Democratic politicians and their supporters in the unions and trades, and this is one of the reasons that Republicans like Mayor Lamberton opposed them. Since they were intended to reward the Democrats who supported Roosevelt, a group which in Philadelphia was then in the process of building a political base from which they could mount an attack on the then-almost-eighty-year hegemony of the Republican Party there, it was a matter of simple self-interest. "Federal urban programs," Mollenkopf contends, "have provided a principal method – perhaps the key method – by which national Democratic political entrepreneurs have attempted to widen and organize their political support."[3] And they did this "by enacting new national programs which bolster their local constituencies."[4]

But a political engine as powerful as Roosevelt's New Deal expansion of federal power was not going to be stopped by a mayor, not even a mayor of one of the country's biggest and oldest cities, not even in that city itself. There were too many people who felt either that it made sense for the federal government to get involved in housing or felt that they could make a lot of money if it did, so as the federal government expanded its desire to give away federal money and reap the political benefits from that largesse, local entrepreneurs spent their time creating the instrumentalities that would receive that money.

On September 1, 1937, President Roosevelt signed the United States Housing Act into law. The object of the legislation was threefold: to obliterate growing slums in American cities and communities, to provide low-rent housing facilities for families whose incomes were so low that private enterprise could not supply them with modern sanitary dwellings, and to stop the creation of new slums. To loan monies for this purpose and supervise the program, Congress created the United States Housing Authority (USHA) with headquarters in Washington. In order to encourage local initiative, this federal agency was established as a large banking agency, but the actual program was planned and administered by local instrumentalities. As part of the trend toward centralized economies and state intervention that was already taking place in Great Britain, Sweden, and the Soviet Union, the United States created a permanent federal housing agency which would fund local agencies, which were now armed with a drastically expanded concept of eminent domain and therefore legally equipped to undertake massive slum clearance and rehousing. Furthermore, local authorities were empowered to receive and spend public dollars and to acquire bonded debt.[5]

By the time the Housing Act of 1937 finally got signed into law, the local agencies which were needed to receive the federal grants were already in place. On May 28, 1937, the Pennsylvania state legislature – in anticipation of the federal housing act – removed any legal obstacles to the establishment of local housing authorities in the state. Pennsylvania's "Little New Deal" governor, George Earle, gave top priority to slum clearance and, backed by a Democratic state legislature, successfully reversed a 1936 state supreme court decision killing the state's Housing Authority Act. On August 26, 1937, Philadelphia's City Council approved a resolution establishing a city-housing authority. On September 16, 1937, Philadelphia's mayor, S. Davis Wilson, appointed Dr. W. Harry Barnes, a local physician and surgeon with an interest in social problems, and John McShain, a prominent Catholic contractor, as members of the authority. Under the provisions of the state act, the Philadelphia Housing Authority was administered by a five-member board, two of whom were appointed by the mayor and two by the city controller. These in turn appointed the fifth member. The authority's main function was the clearance of slum areas and the construction on them of low-rental housing made available to families below certain income levels. These projects were financed through federal and private funds which were to be repaid through bonds issued by the authority.[6]

Although it was a political entity, the Philadelphia Housing Authority did not operate in a cultural vacuum. Its sphere of activity was determined largely by the plans and surveys of the City Planning Commission and the private but not-for-profit Philadelphia Housing Association, then run by managing director Bernard J. Newman. In cities like Philadelphia, Chicago, Detroit, and Boston, the panels of experts invariably had a definite ethnic caste. They became certified as experts either by going to the already mentioned WASP universities or by getting appointed to local housing boards, which were often descendants of local upper-class initiatives that began with the city-beautiful movement or the settlement-house movement around the time of World War I.

Empowered by the federal government and the state legislature, the local authorities began to make recommendations that sounded a lot like the sort of thing Mayor Moore rejected five years earlier. "The [Philadelphia Housing] Authority was saved considerable expense," opines the author of the official history of the PHA without any sense of irony, "by being able to avail itself of the plans and surveys of the City Planning Commission. . . . Surveys were also made available to the Authority by the Philadelphia Housing Association of which Dr. J. A. MacCallum its President and Bernard J. Newman, Managing Director."[7] Emboldened by their new mandate, the housers concluded that "the central slum area . . . extends from Girard Avenue to Washington Avenue, from the Schuylkill to the Delaware,"[8] which meant of course that all of center city was considered a slum, including Rittenhouse Square where the city's aristocracy had lived until the migration to the Main Line and Chestnut Hill began in the '20s. By the time Rittenhouse Square was designated part of the city's central slum area, that migration was in no way complete. In fact, remnants of the city's aristocracy continued living there for the rest of the century, supplemented by the other upscale arrivals from other ethnic groups. The PHA then got down to brass tacks, urging that some 39,000 "structurally substandard" homes be torn down and that 50,000 low-rent homes be built to replace them. Nine thousand nine hundred and forty three of those houses to be torn down were court and alley houses, otherwise known as band-box houses. That meant that these houses had "no provision for artificial light, no heat, usually no running water indoors, no rear yards and no bath or toilet facilities."[9] It also meant that they were inexpensive to rent or own.

The constitutionality of the government's entry into the housing market was challenged almost immediately, but on June 30, 1938, the Supreme Court of Pennsylvania handed down its decision in favor of the PHA. In *Dornan v. The Philadelphia Housing Authority, et al.,*[10] Judge Horace Stern upheld the arguments of the Authority by holding that slum clearance and the incident construction of low-rent housing is a public purpose and that "the power of eminent domain was properly conferred" when it was used to tear down the housing that had to be cleared for the projects to rise in their place. "The elimination of unsafe and dilapidated tenements," Judge Stern wrote, "is a legitimate object for the exercise of the police power."[11] He then launched into a panegyric on the benefits which would accrue if big government were to apply the principles of modern hygiene and science to the housing situation. "The veriest tyro in the study of social conditions," opined Mr. Justice Stern in the florid legal language of the time, "knows that the existence of slums is a menace to the health and happiness of the community in which they exist."[12] What followed was a curious mixture of classic American upper-class Yankee moralizing, faith in science, and heavy-handed condescension which assumed that only those in positions of power could help the denizens of "slums." Slums, according to Stern, are bad because "they exert a pernicious moral influence upon those unfortunate enough to be obliged to live in them and thereby engender those proclivities of youth to crime which have been characterized by many in high places as a disgrace to our civilization."[13] Since everyone could be presumed to be in favor of moral behavior, "it is now found necessary to resort to the more drastic and comprehensive method of demolishing such structures simultaneously and over more extended areas."[14] Urban renewal was, in other words, not only morally justified, it was morally mandated. But the state just couldn't tear down houses; it had to build new ones as well, or so Stern's logic went, because "For the state or a municipality to tear down objectionable houses without providing better ones in their stead would be merely to force those ejected into other slums or compel them to create new ones and the cardinal purpose of the legislation would thus be frustrated."[15] The decision had the air of unreality hovering about it which one had come to expect of Supreme Court decisions as the court system came more and more to rely on raw judicial power over legal reasoning.

Slums, in the case of Philadelphia, meant housing in St. Malachy's Parish which had been neglected for ten years because of widespread unemployment and a huge contraction in the economy. Had wages remained stable or had they increased during this period or had the labor market not been manipulated by imported labor which created an oversupply and drove wages down, the denizens of the "slums" might have kept their houses in better repair. The simple fact of the matter is that the court had no legal criterion whereby it could designate an area a slum. For this it relied on the opinions of people it designated as "experts," apparently assuming that ulterior motives would not taint their decisions. Judicial moralism meant that the economic conditions which created deterioration in housing would go unmentioned while at the same time justifying large-scale intervention into an area like property rights which were judicially clear. Underlying the whole decision was an unspoken faith in the tenets of behaviorism and social engineering. Intelligent people like Judge Stern had come down on the nurture side of the nature/nurture controversy. Man was a function of his environment. He was immoral because he lived in a run-down house.

The state opinion had much in common with *Berman v. Parker*, the federal Supreme Court decision which would get handed down sixteen years later. In both decisions, concerns about hygiene and morals and the social engineering of the behavior of the inhabitants of the housing to be constructed at government expense at some future date took precedence over the property rights of those who were being dispossessed to make that housing possible. By June 30, 1939, the USHA had earmarked a total of $32 million for slum clearance and low rent housing in Philadelphia. With local loans this raised the total available for the program to approximately $35 million.

Public housing, however, was only one part of the New Deal's entry into the housing business. The other half was represented by the Federal Housing Authority, whose purpose was to guarantee mortgages. Until this point mortgages rarely covered anything approaching the full value of the house for the full term of the mortgage. If one mortgage expired during a downturn in the economy when money was tight, the homeowner often lost his home because he couldn't get another mortgage to finance the rest of the purchase price. Federal reform of this issue was a good idea, but as in virtually every other instance of government involvement in housing the good that it did became the thin edge of the wedge of social engineering. Just as the USHA chose Bauhaus *Wohnmaschinen* (Walter Gropius's term for the house of the future; literally, "living machines") as its model urban dwelling for the poor, the FHA in 1939 asked each of its fifty regional offices to send in plans for six "typical American houses."[16] The photos and dimensions were initially used for a National Archives exhibit, but more subtly they became the paradigm of what kind of house the FHA would guarantee a mortgage. Since virtually all of the "typical American houses" were single bungalows or colonials on ample lots with driveways and garages, that meant that most of the mortgage money the FHA would provide went to the suburbs. It also meant that the Philadelphia rowhouse was decertified as typically American and that meant that the traditional housing in cities like Philadelphia and Baltimore was effectively eliminated from eligibility for loan guarantees.

Jackson's description of the situation in St. Louis is a paradigm for how the FHA operated throughout the country. "Of a sample of 241 new homes insured by FHA throughout metropolitan St. Louis between 1935 and 1939," he writes, "a full 220 or 91 percent were located in the suburbs. Moreover half of these home buyers (135 of 241) had lived in the city immediately prior to their new home purchase. That the FHA was helping to denude St. Louis of its middle-class residents is illustrated by an analysis of the HOLC Residential Survey Map. . . . [S]uburbanites were not being drawn from the slums or from rural areas, but from the second grade or 'B' areas – generally sound but aging housing in middle class neighborhoods of the central city."[17] The same differential applied to home-improvement loans. From the inception of the FHA until 1960, only $44 million went to the city, while three times that much or $112 million, went to the suburbs. "In the course of accomplishing its mission," Jackson concludes, "the HOLC developed real estate appraisal methods that discriminated against racial and ethnic minorities and against older, industrial cities."[18]

The FHA pursued a conscious policy of decentralization when it came to subsidizing new home construction, a trend that FHA officials liked to describe as if it were some inexorable natural phenomenon and not something they were deliberately engineering by their priorities. "Decentralization," one FHA official told the 1939 convention of the American Institute of Planners, "is taking place. It is not a policy, it is a reality – and it is [as] impossible for us to change this trend as it is to change the desire of birds to migrate to a more suitable location."[19] The rate of decentralization was further encouraged by the federal tax-code which permitted greater tax benefits for new construction than for the improvement of existing buildings, something which accelerated the rate at which economic activity is dispersed to new locations.

The FHA pursued its policy of dispersal with race in mind, but it consistently construed race as a function of class and not ethnicity. In other words, black people were assumed to be of a certain class. Neighborhood was determined by class, not by ethnicity, according to FHA criteria. Warning that "if a neighborhood is to retain stability, it is necessary that properties shall continue to be occupied by the same social and racial classes,"[20] the FHA encouraged restrictive covenants even after they were declared unconstitutional by the Supreme Court in *Shelley v. Kramer*. The net result of the combination of FHA policies for insuring mortgages and the USHA's policies for creating urban housing for the poor was social engineering on a scale unknown in this country before this time. According to Jackson's analysis, "the basic direction of federal policies toward housing has been the concentration of the poor in the central city and the dispersal of the affluent to the suburbs."[21] In Philadelphia, the net result was to take a city where poor people lived in small houses of the sort they could afford, creating as a result racially homogeneous streets in racially mixed neighborhoods, and, in its place, put federal policies created huge monoracial ghettos. Cities like Detroit became in effect one large ethnic neighborhood. As a result of these restrictions, 1 million people occupied a city that was built with twice that many people in mind. The resulting disequilibrium between supply and demand meant that the price of housing stock would plummet and then when no buyer could be found, housing would be abandoned. Social engineering may have led to the destruction of cities like Detroit and Philadelphia by way of misguided but essentially good intentions, but it created segregation as a matter of deliberate purpose, replacing mixed neighborhoods with sprawling ghettoes. "The result, if not the intent, of the public housing program of the United States," according to Jackson, "was to segregate the races, to concentrate the disadvantaged in inner cities, and to reinforce the image of suburbia as a place of refuge for the problems of race, crime, and poverty. By every measure, the Housing Act of 1937 was an important stimulus to deconcentration."[22] Bauman says much the same thing about Philadelphia:

> Many black Philadelphians lived on all-black streets, but these streets lay not more than a block or two away from white neighbors. Consequently, a study done at that time found black residents in all but a third of Philadelphia's 404 census tracts. After 1950, however, the tide of the postwar migration began to carve a new and odious residential configuration in Philadelphia – one that was unmistakenly segregated.[23]

Social engineering, in other words, created the very segregation it would purport to fight twenty years later.

Notes

1 John F. Bauman, *Public Housing, Race, and Renewal: Urban Planning in Philadelphia 1920–1974* (Philadelphia: Temple University Press, 1987), p. 29.
2 John H. Mollenkopf, *The Contested City* (Princeton, N.J.: Princeton University Press, 1983), p. 58.
3 Ibid., p. 48.
4 Ibid.
5 Bauman, p. 42.
6 Clearing Slums in Philadelphia, First Annual Report of the Philadelphia Housing Authority, 1939, p. 1, available from Philadelphia City Archives.
7 Ibid., p. 7.
8 Ibid., p. 5.
9 Ibid.
10 331 Pa. 209, 1938.
11 Ibid., p. 14.

12 Ibid.
13 Ibid.
14 Ibid., p. 15.
15 Ibid.
16 Kenneth T. Jackson, *Crabgrass Frontier: The Suburbanization of the United States* (New York: Oxford University Press, 1985), p. 208.
17 Ibid., p. 210.
18 Ibid., p. 215.
19 Ibid., p. 191.
20 Ibid., p. 208.
21 Ibid., p. 230.
22 Ibid., p. 219.
23 Bauman, p. 86.

Mayor Lamberton and the Housing Authority

As some indication of how politically sensitive public housing had become, Mayor Lamberton started making changes in the Philadelphia Housing Authority board shortly after taking office. On February 5, 1940, John McShain, who had been appointed on September 20, 1937, by Mayor S. Davis Wilson, resigned from the authority, and on April 4, 1940, Mayor Robert E. Lamberton appointed Raymond Rosen to fill his unexpired term. Philadelphia now had three public-housing projects underway. Glenwood and Tasker were being built on open sites, the latter over some twenty feet of garbage in South Philadelphia. The Poplar project (site of the Richard Allen Homes) was the most expensive of the three because it could only be built after expensive slum clearance.

As Mayor Robert E. Lamberton's first year in office wore on, he concluded that three projects were all that the city was going to have. On May 13, 1940, after a conference between members of the authority, officials of the USHA, and city officials, Mayor Lamberton issued a statement in which he announced his opposition to an extension of the public-housing program until the three projects under construction had been completed and occupied for a certain amount of time. He called public housing a great social experiment whose value had not yet been proven and indicated that he was against approval of the cooperation ordinance for the three new projects by the city council. "Slum areas," Lamberton contended, "exist because some people are so utterly shiftless that any place where they live becomes a slum, and others are so poor that they cannot afford to live anywhere else."[1] It was clear that Lamberton had not imbibed the environmentalist credo that motivated Judge Stern on the state supreme court. Instead of believing that bad housing created bad morals, the behaviorist/environmentalist view, Lamberton looked as if he held the exact opposite point of view. It looked as if he held the view that bad morals created bad housing.

Lamberton's retrogressive attitudes bespoke a split in the ethnic constituency that was the backbone of the Republican Party in Philadelphia at the time. Lamberton represented the brown-suited Protestant Republican Masons who still lived in neighborhoods like Kensington at a time when the ruling-class Protestants were moving out of the city and adopting attitudes then fashionable at the prestigious schools their children attended. The change mirrored a change in the country at large as "a national and associational upper class replaced the local and communal gentry in America between the close of the Civil War and 1940."[2]

The Philadelphians on the social register considered themselves a part of the "British-American, White-Anglo-Saxon-Protestant (WASP) establishment, consolidated through family alliances between Mayfair and Murray Hill."[3] It was a group that controlled considerable financial assets and felt that it "authoritatively ran the world as their ancestors had done since Queen Victoria's time."[4] In spite of the group's homogeneity, its identity bespoke class more than the national identity, antagonistic to England, that characterized the country from the time of its founding through the nineteenth century. The identity of the ruling class which emerged in the United States during the period between the Civil War and 1940 was at least to some extent negative. WASP-ethnic solidarity arose in reaction to the Catholic ethnics and Jews who flooded into Philadelphia at the end of the nineteenth and beginning of the twentieth centuries. "The sense of caste which now prevails within the American upper class," Baltzell, their Philadelphia chronicler writes, "began to develop at the turn of the century in response to the flood of impoverished immigrants from Southern and Eastern Europe who came to these shores in ever increasing waves."[5] The upper-class migration to the suburbs, which in Philadelphia was largely complete by 1930, was an expression of this ethnic solidarity as well as an expression that this ethnic group had abandoned the ties of nationality in favor of a way of living consciously modeled on the English country manner. By 1940 the split between city and suburb mirrored an ethnic split based on certain simple facts:

> 1) between 1900 and 1930, the majority of American people came to live in cities; 2) while old stock Protestants still dominated rural America, ethnic heterogeneity marked the city 3) the newer immigrants who came to America after 1880 were predominantly urban dwellers; 4) because of the shortage of labor during the First War as well as the closing of the gates to cheap labor from overseas immediately afterward, Negroes and poor whites from the South migrated to our large urban industrial areas in the North.[6]

By 1936 the Democrats had concluded the urban-ethnic revolution. Although Philadelphia was still run by Republicans, some of them were smart enough to see that support for New Deal initiatives meant their own political demise. Mayor Lamberton was one of these people. The Philadelphia ruling class, on the other hand, was not really of one mind with people like Lamberton and the Republican Masons from Kensington, who held what might be termed at the time the exoteric or classic version of the Protestant ethic, which found expression in Lamberton's views on the moral basis for slums. The ruling class which by 1940 had migrated to Chestnut Hill and the Main Line (which was outside the city) had converted to liberal environmentalism.[7]

That meant, of course, that the local elite saw the importance of the housing issue, especially in their struggle for control of the culture with the ethnics, who were now firmly in the camp of the Democratic Party. Lamberton, although a Republican, was defending a position which the rising generation of the city's ethnic elite found antiquated and ultimately not in their interests to defend because it conceded all of the opportunities for social engineering to the opposing party. The new paradigm for the national WASP elite was not the traditional Philadelphia families, but rather, as John McCloy found out, New York WASPs like the Rockefellers, a family which had virtually created the new social sciences at the University of Chicago and was putting that research to use as part of the country's increasing involvement in psychological warfare and (after the war) population control.

As a result Lamberton was in a bind. If he accepted the money, he allowed the Democrats an opportunity to build a base in the city which would eventually take control of the city from Republicans like him. If he didn't take the money, he ran the risk of alienating the upper-class devotees of science and the social gospel. In the end, those two groups coalesced when Joseph Sill Clark, a local aristocrat from Chestnut Hill, became a Democrat and wrested control of the city from the Republicans. Housing was the crucial issue in this equation. Lamberton, by objecting to the city's participation in the New Deal's housing program, denied the elite money that it wanted for its projects, but he also denied them the possibility of getting involved in social engineering. As in other instances involving social engineering, war would become the deciding factor which broke the back of the political opposition.

True to his word, Lamberton continued his opposition to public housing. On June 20, 1940, with thousands of angry union members and building-trades workers demonstrating outside city hall, the city council by a vote of 12 to 10 rejected a resolution approving the selection of new sites for additional housing projects in the city. Federal reaction followed shortly thereafter. On July 1, the USHA withdrew the $19 million which had been earmarked for Philadelphia and redistributed it among other housing authorities in Pennsylvania and other parts of the country. In doing so, the USHA upheld the principle that the low-rent housing program under the Wagner-Steagle Act was based on local initiative and cooperation and that only communities which took this initiative through their duly elected local representatives could obtain the financial aid of the federal government. In her history of Philadelphia, Margaret Kinehan claims that Lamberton turned down the $19 million because Joe Pew, head of Sun Oil and a local Republican Party kingmaker, told him to. Pew certainly hated Roosevelt and the New Deal, but the decision was based more on political self-interest. Both Pew and Lamberton realized that the purpose of federal housing money was the creation of Democratic cadres within this and other big cities. Pew's motivation was simple enough to understand. Philadelphia's Catholic ethnics had become part of the New Deal coalition. Like Lamberton's view, Pew's attitude was more classic Republican than East Coast Republican. Like Henry Ford in Detroit, Pew promoted black migration as a way of weakening the bargaining power of the unionized Catholic ethnics, in this case the Italians in Chester, just south of Philadelphia. Father John Macnamee, who became pastor of an all-black St. Malachy's Parish in 1982, remembers the pastor of his first assignment out of the seminary, a church in Chester, berate Pew for destroying Chester by bringing blacks up from the South to work at the Sun Shipyards there.

Because of the encroaching reach of the federal government into housing, Lamberton was under pressure from a number of sides. The local Republican establishment correctly saw public housing as the New Deal's attempt to create loyal Democrats by making an end run around the Republican administration and setting up local conduits for federal money. But they failed to realize that Roosevelt was at that very moment in the process of abandoning the New Deal in order to gain support for his foreign policy and the war against fascism. In standing by England in its hour of need, Roosevelt redeemed himself from the accusation that he was a traitor to his class. In fact, by scrapping the New Deal in favor of his war plans, Roosevelt essentially reversed the poles of the political equation he had established. He, in effect, abandoned his newly won ethnic constituency in favor of the bankers and industrialists he had alienated before. War was the philosopher's stone which made this political transformation possible, and it soon made itself felt in Philadelphia.

On June 13, 1940, just one week before the city council formally blocked the building of 3400 additional low-rent houses, Rear Admiral A.E. Watson, Commandant of the Fourth Naval District, asked the Philadelphia Housing Authority to make sixty dwellings in the Tasker Homes available to families of married enlisted men in the U.S. Navy.[8] On July 5th, one week after the president had approved the Defense Amendment to the United States Housing Act, Commandant Watson asked the Philadelphia Housing Authority to begin the development of a defense housing project of approximately 275 dwellings in the vicinity of the Navy Yard. On August 14, he increased his request from 275 to 1,000 dwellings and on August 21 he followed up his request to the PHA by asking Mayor Lamberton to use his influence to secure the approval of the city council for the development of this project.[9]

Soon the whole housing issue got subsumed into the war issue. In July of 1940, Roosevelt created the Office of Defense Housing Coordinator under the National Defense Housing Commission. In September 1940 Southern Democrats with Republican support blocked the $5 million annual subsidy for the United States Housing Authority. The New Deal was dead, but the Roosevelt Administration decided to use the war to resurrect it— in housing at least. In October 1940 Congress drafted and passed the Lanham Act, which assigned to the Federal Works Agency (FWA)—not the USHA—full discretion in spending the $150 million defense-housing appropriation. Roosevelt then appointed Charles F. Palmer, then head of the Atlanta, Georgia, Housing Authority, as defense-housing coordinator. The Lanham Act authorized the Federal Works Administration to provide housing for persons engaged in defense activities. By April 1941 this appropriation had been increased to $300 million.[10]

On October 7, 1940, Mayor Lamberton attended the ground-breaking ceremonies for the Richard Allen Homes, with thousands of people from the neighborhood attending. Sharing the tribunal with Lamberton was USHA Administrator Nathan Straus. Neither man attempted to disguise their opposing views on the project. But it was Lamberton who had most reason to be bitter. After having expended considerable political capital by turning down $19 million in federal money for public housing, even more money for housing was now flowing into the city for the benefit of his political opponents. Only now it was money for defense-worker housing. In December of 1940, Lanham Act money was being used to construct 500 dwellings, and in January of 1941, appropriations for 500 more dwellings were approved – all were destined for military personnel. Suspecting that defense-worker housing was simply public housing being smuggled in the back door, Lamberton tried to insist that the housing be temporary so that it could be torn down after the war, but again he was overridden by appeals to military necessity, even though the country was still not at war.

Lamberton's efforts to maintain the paradigm of home ownership in Philadelphia were being overwhelmed by the sheer amount of money pouring into the city to produce war materiel. On September 19, 1940, Coordinator of Defense Purchases Donald Nelson announced that Philadelphia's textile industry was going to be the beneficiary of a $22-million government order.[11] In the year following Lamberton's testy remarks at the groundbreaking ceremonies for Richard Allen Homes in October 1940, the government poured $131 million into Philadelphia, enabling the city's factory owners to expand their

Philadelphia, early 1940s, increased black migration

work forces by 27,000 workers. Given the realities of the wartime labor market, that meant bringing blacks up from the South to work in Philadelphia's factories. From 1940 to 1943 the black labor force expanded from 74,000 to 130,000, putting severe pressure on the housing market that had lain virtually dormant during the Depression. That meant increased pressure on Lamberton because of his refusal to accept public housing money. It also meant increased pressure on St. Malachy's and Gesu and all of the other parishes in the lower part of North Philadelphia.

Notes

1 Building Homes in Philadelphia: Report of the Philadelphia Housing Authority July 1, 1939–June 30, 1941, p. 37, at Philadelphia City Archives.
2 E. Digby Baltzell, *The Protestant Establishment: Aristocracy and Caste in America* (New York: Random House, 1964), p. xi.
3 Ibid., p. 11.
4 Ibid.
5 Ibid., p. 21.
6 Ibid., p. 229.
7 Ibid., p. 162.
8 Building Homes, p. 37.
9 Ibid.
10 Ibid.
11 Ibid., p. 56.

Walter M. Phillips
and the WASP Elite in Philadelphia

Like Robert E. Lamberton, Walter M. Phillips was caught in the middle of the WASP ruling class's shift from a local to a national elite. Since Phillips had attended Harvard as an undergrad and had graduated from Princeton Law School in the 1930s, he had the necessary credentials for membership in the national elite. But unlike John McCloy, another Philadelphian who had graduated from another elite law school, Phillips did not want to leave Philadelphia. Walter Phillips was an anomaly in more ways than one. He lived in Torresdale, a largely industrial area on the Delaware River, instead of to the west in Chestnut Hill or on the Main Line, where the rest of his class lived. Phillips was also an anachronism. He was a man who was rooted in Philadelphia at a time when being rooted in one place foreclosed just about any career of significance. Thatcher Longstreth, Philadelphia's last public WASP, was to find this out when he returned home after World War II, and found that advancement – whether as an employee of Time-Life or as a political protégé of Joe Pew – meant leaving Philadelphia. Walter Phillips found out something similar when he wrote to the Rockefeller Foundation in the spring of 1941.

Phillips was writing to the Rockefellers because he felt that Philadelphia was about to experience "a wave of civic rejuvenation,"[1] primarily because the war was creating a booming local economy.

> In the Defense Program the Philadelphia area is perhaps the largest ordnance center of the United States, the greatest shipbuilding locality and the most important shipping harbor. The textile mills, the numerous and varied manufacturing concerns, the chemical companies, the oil refineries reviving heavy industries such as Midvale's and Baldwin's, entirely new plants making airplane parts such as SKF and Bendix and the Frankford Arsenal are all humming or about to hum, The Navy Yard, New York Shipbuilding Co. Sun Shipbuilding Co. and Cramps Shipbuilding are working or about to work at tremendously expanded capacities to construct battleships, cruisers and merchant vessels, and the Port of Philadelphia, the second largest in the United States, is serving as the passageway to Europe, to date more goods having gone to England through Philadelphia than through any other port.[2]

The war boom, unfortunately had arrived in Philadelphia after "a decade of inactivity"[3] which was characterized by "a decade of little rebuilding within the City, a period of people moving out to the suburbs, a period of tremendous decline in real estate values, a period of civic slump. There have been practically no public works, nearly all government reform movements have been unsuccessful and a depression psychology has prevailed."[4]

The solution to this slump, according to Phillips, was urban planning. By focusing the efforts of the city, by mobilizing the city's elite, Phillips felt that Philadelphia could undo the damage done to the city over the past decade in its slow drift on a river of economic paralysis and political corruption. Like any good politician, Phillips approached the Rockefeller Foundation indirectly through his upper-class contacts in Philadelphia. The Rockefellers, however, were of a different opinion on the need to revitalize Philadelphia, or any other city for that matter, and in the mid-20th century it was New York WASP families like the Rockefellers and not the old-line Philadelphia families who were determining the national agenda. In early April of 1941 Phillips received a letter from Helen Hill Miller, a Philadelphian on the National Policy Committee and the National Press Committee in Washington, D.C. After some preliminary advice on whom to approach, Miller tried to deflate Phillips's expectations by explaining how the Rockefeller Foundation felt about big cities, citing the work of Douglas Brown of the Industrial Relations Section at Princeton. Brown served as the Rockefellers' advisor on urban issues, and what he had to say about cities like Philadelphia was not encouraging. In "The Problem of the City," Brown wondered

> whether we should keep investing more and more money on a type of community which may have outlived its usefulness. I do not mean that the city will ever go out of the picture, but there are serious questions as to whether many of our cites are not becoming top-heavy politically, socially and economically. With modern means of transportation and an increased interest in the amenities of life, perhaps we should be investing time, and money and energy in replanning areas far larger than the boundaries of a particular city. We are developing plans at Princeton for a Bureau of Urban research which draws together economics, local government, architecture, engineering, population research, etc. I am coming to be more and more convinced that their should be active cooperation between these various fields focused on community planning."[5]

Brown's animus against the cities soon found expression in "the greatest increment to manufacturing capital recorded in modern industrial history,"[6] namely, the War Production Board's total recapitalization of American industry. Between 1942 and 1944 the government spent $35.5 billion to rebuild the nation's factories, an amount equal to the entire 1939 value of the U.S. manufacturing plant. This recapitalization was done with the recommendations of people like Professor Brown and the Rockefellers in mind, and that meant with the interests of the industry owners in mind and not their largely urban workers. That meant abandoning central cities, where the percentage of union organization was relatively high, and relocating factories to the suburbs and the new Sunbelt cities of the Southwest. One review of WPB activities noted that "the larger factories were concentrated in a radius of 30 miles from the larger metropolitan areas."[7] As one of the most famous examples of this relocation, the WPB spent over $100 million to construct the Willow Run bomber complex seventeen miles outside of Detroit. The move away from the cities was calculated to weaken the power of the largely ethnic unions, something that became apparent as the planning unfolded. When in late 1940 United Auto Workers' president Walter Reuther came up with his own plan for organizing labor for the war effort and converting existing idle plants to aircraft production, the government rejected his plan. The Roosevelt Administration chose instead to go with former Sears Roebuck president Donald Nelson. By separating the WPB from all other federal agencies, FDR "devised a radical form of industrial mobilization that contained no seeds of reform" of the sort that characterized the New Deal, and was "implemented as to give no alarm to the nation's industrial interests."[8] By bringing the chairman of the Army-Navy Munitions Board into the WPB, Nelson completed the marriage of the military-industrial coalition. Although the man behind the changes was the same FDR who created the urban coalition at the heart of the New Deal, the War Production Board was essentially a repudiation of those programs. The WPB's executive committee located the new plants outside the nation's big cities, according to Mollenkopf, to keep them "beyond the reach of the unions, New Deal-leaning mayors, and the other constituencies which had fueled urban liberalism in the 1930s."[9] The WPB essentially determined the shape of post-war development as well, especially when the same industrial military coalition used the opportunity presented by the Eisenhower Administration to push through its interstate highway bill and further increase the decentralization Professor Brown found so desirable. The WPB, working for the interests of the industrialists

> created a massive reindustrialization program whose scale swamped anything attempted by the New Deal. This investment program had none of the New Deal's social reform characteristics. Instead, it emphasized industrial expansion outside the older central cities. Its housing element was designed to melt away rapidly after the war's end. It operated through the private sector rather than the public sector and reflected choices sought by dominant private institutions. Finally, this investment program set loose forces which were to shape and constrain all subsequent efforts at urban liberalism.[10]

There was nothing Walter Phillips could do to stop the decision to decentralize American industry, a decision which got made in Washington and the halls of the Rockefeller Foundation. But all of his subsequent decisions about revitalizing Philadelphia were contextualized by those decisions, constraining Phillips to act in a certain way toward forces he could not control. Phillips was a local patriot, but he was also a member of the local ruling elite in Philadelphia, with all of the prejudices against other ethnic groups which that affiliation entailed. Instead of joining the national elite, he decided to assemble a cadre of like-minded Philadelphians to work on revitalizing the city. Given Phillips's ethnic background and his education, that meant a certain type of organization, one which would function fairly smoothly as long as the members of the coalition which comprised it accepted the idea of *noblesse oblige* which was its foundation. In an essay he had written at Princeton in 1937, Phillips gives some indication of his understanding of the American political system and, as a result, some indication of the kind of organization he was interested in promoting in Philadelphia:

> our democracy does not depend on the constitution. It depends rather on the reasonableness and enlightenment of men; upon having numerous, educated, tolerant and thinking leaders; and upon having a relatively conservative and emotionally

steady people. Law school has convinced me that there are enough reasonable men in the law profession alone to see that things don't go really bad. So as long as the leading people from all over the country interchange ideas and convene, as for example, do young men at Harvard Law School and like centers; so long as such people go out and talk with the common people and the less educated local leaders, so long as they remain fairly objective and know the real needs of the country, democracy will survive.[11]

Beginning in the late '30s, Phillips began to assemble what he considered the "leading people" in Philadelphia, as a way of bringing about the wave of rejuvenation that was poised to break over the city. Those people would be organized according to Phillips' understanding of "our system":

> The great thing about our system which we call democracy is not that the masses themselves govern, but that the *clever few* who force themselves into positions of leadership and responsibility are in general sensitive and responsive to the wants of the people. The danger comes when that relationship breaks down [my emphasis].[12]

Anyone familiar with Phillips's frankly elitist vision could see danger just over the horizon in Philadelphia. Phillips was proposing his version of the Philadelphia ruling class at precisely the time when the ruling class there was running out of demographic steam and the ethnics were in exactly the opposite demographic position, poised to take over the reins of power according to their understanding of democracy. Phillips's vision was essentially ethnocentric, but since he was part of the ruling class which had governed the city up until that time and had his credentials from the universities which certified membership in the national elite, he did not see things that way. From Phillips's point of view, some people were unqualified for public office no matter how many votes they could get at the polls. That the people outside the ruling class might not see things that way seems not to have entered Phillips's mind at this stage of the game. That meant that Philadelphia was to be governed by "young men at Harvard Law School and like centers," because Phillips had "unusual faith in the English speaking people to govern themselves." Whether that faith extended to the Philadelphia's Polish population in Bridesburg remained to be seen; it did not, according to his own admission, extend to "Europe, Asia, South America, and our own neighbor Mexico."[13]

Phillips was not a deep thinker, certainly not as a grad student. When pressed by his own logic to explain the difference between Mexico and the United States, he fell back on essentially ethnic stereotypes – "There seems to be some inherent distinctions, but what they are I would not attempt to explain"[14] – of the sort that celebrated the Anglo-Saxon penchant for freedom, the genius of the Magna Carta, and the other cultural and historical milestones routinely cited by Whig historians. Faith in science and the Enlightenment was one of the most commonly held ethnic prejudices which Phillips shared with his group at the time. Phillips believed in the Enlightenment by nature and by nurture at a time when its stock was high among the "clever few" in Philadelphia. That meant that faith not only in people of like mind, but faith in their ability to make plans for the rest of the city, including "the common people and the less educated local leaders," which were objective and rational and not tainted by ethnic bias and not hampered by reverence to traditional ways. "Stability," according to Phillips, "consists not in fixedness but in a steady pace of change."[15]

That "the common people and [their] less educated local leaders" might have a different view of stability seems not to have occurred to Phillips. Phillips failure to see that the Catholic ethnic idea of stability was bound up, not with a "steady pace of change," but with things like family and parish life and the fact that both of those values found reinforcement in home ownership, would have serious consequences within the space of a decade when the cadre he assembled in the late '30s and early '40s, finally took power in the city in the early '50s and began to impose its views on the neighborhoods of Philadelphia through programs like urban renewal and public housing, violating – wittingly or not – the arrangement that the Irish had hammered out with the city's Protestant rulers during the 19th century. Phillips's attitude toward housing was crucial in this regard. By becoming involved in urban planning, Phillips was saying that the "clever few" had the right to determine what was going to happen in the neighborhoods which the ruling class had conceded to the Catholic ethnics. Had the WASP ruling class done this in the 19th century when the Irish were relative newcomers and relatively weak politically, it would have changed the entire make-up of Philadelphia and probably would have diverted the energies which the Irish devoted to their homes and parishes (with the social stability that went with it) into agitation for proletarian revolution of the sort that was haunting Europe in the early years of the 20th century. Once Phillips and his circle showed that they were serious about violating the integrity of local neighborhood communities, they got the equivalent of social rebellion, but now ameliorated by one hundred years of the social stability that parish and family life in locally controlled communities could create.

Phillips gives no indication in his writings that he is aware of the shortcomings of his elitist views, nor does he give any indication that in intruding into neighborhood affairs that he was violating a compact of some standing in Philadelphia political life. Nor does he give any indication that his "clever few" lacked the demographic muscle to pull off this change in policy. Phillips's ethnic background compounded by the Whiggish education he received at Harvard and Princeton made him oblivious to such considerations at precisely the time when his ethnic opponents were starting to chafe under WASP hegemony. Walter Phillips never considered his opinions ethnocentric. As long as the direction of change was in the hands of people like Phillips and his friends, the "wave of rejuvenation" was inevitable.

Others outside the charmed circle weren't so sure. John Lukacs, the distinguished professor and historian, met the "clever few" who constituted the Phillips crowd when he arrived in Philadelphia as a Hungarian immigrant in 1947, the moment when they were on the verge of seizing power in the city. When Lukacs tried to debate their arguments on their merits, he found himself dismissed condescendingly as "an anti-Communist, a Catholic and, philosophically at least, Rightist" and that, "in baseball terms, meant three strikes against me, to the effect that I was excluded from stepping up to the plate."[16]

> Their response to my arguments and, consequently, to me was dismissal at best and contempt at worst. Whether they were sure of themselves I do not know; I am inclined to doubt it. But they were certainly sure of the value of their ideas, like

shrewd investors who pride themselves on the value of their investments – or, rather, on the knowledge that in virtue of these investments they have shown themselves to be smarter and better than others. They preferred to think that because of the superiority of their opinions they were people of superior taste and judgment. . . .[17]

Growing up in Hungary, Lukacs was to learn, prepared one but little to be what the "clever few" in Philadelphia considered as a thinker. Instead of principles which could be debated in the light of logic and one's own knowledge of history, Lukacs was confronted by a class of people who based their judgments, in the Quaker fashion, on shared ethnic consensus as focused by the approval and disapproval of certain personalities. So, if one were enlightened one was "a votary of Bertrand Russell or Pandit Nehru," and that meant that, by the law of ethnic association that "one would (or should) be an admirer of Sartre and Picasso" as well.[18] What held this essentially ad-hoc congeries of shibboleth and totem together was notions of science, enlightenment, and progress and all of the other detritus of Whig history which got transmitted by what Lukacs called the modern clerisy, which is to say, the professors at the institutions of higher education this group controlled:

In 1948, especially in the better universities, this professorate was predominantly Liberal and Leftist, many of them Henry Wallace voters, in their case less because of chic than because of their intellectual constructions about the nature of the world and of mankind, to which they had arrived from their admiration of the eighteenth century, having left the remnants of seventeenth-century popular credulity disdainfully behind. Unlike the Upper Bohemians, they were not the avant-garde but the clerisy of the New World, Darwinist and Einsteinian to the last man and, if not votaries, at least profoundly respectful of the Webbs and/or Trotsky, Freud and/or Marx; anti-conservative, anti-Catholic and anti-anti-Communist.[19]

One of the most influential members of the New World clerisy when it came to modern architecture and urban planning was the German émigré and cultural Bolshevist Walter Gropius, who arrived to take up the reins of leadership at the Harvard School of Architecture at the same time that Walter Phillips was assembling the "clever few" in Philadelphia. Throughout the 1930s, Gropius would proselytize for his vision of worker housing – thirteen-story machines for living which would facilitate the new social arrangements that modern science was then making possible. This entailed the abolition of the family as well as the assumption into large communal cafeterias of much of what got done in the traditional home. Much of Gropius's vision got implemented in Communist bloc countries after World War II. His lieutenant and successor at Bauhaus Dessau, Ernst May, actually emigrated to Moscow in 1933 to put that vision into effect there. Gropius's vision also entailed a revision of the notion of private property that would be especially radical for Philadelphia, a place which in the 1930s still considered itself the "city of homes."

In late January of 1933 Gropius gave a speech at Leningard in which he praised the Soviet Union as "up until now the only country that has achieved the most important precondition of healthy urban renewal, namely, free land."[20] By "free land," Gropius meant the abrogation of the right to own property, which went into effect in Russia following the 1917 Communist Revolution. "All sensible urban planning," he continued, "must remain purely utopian as long as society permits its inhabitants to retain private property."[21] The Soviets, as history would show, were only too happy to implement Gropius's vision, not because he was a member of the Communist Party – he was not – but because as a cultural Bolshevist, Gropius had a profoundly secular idea of man and of the family and of the relations between the sexes, as well as a design for buildings that embodied those ideals. Bauhaus was the architectural expression of social engineering, something that Gropius's American disciples were smart enough to pick up on, as Catherine Bauer, one of the most influential proponents of public housing, did when she visited places like the Weissenhofsiedlung in the late 1920s on a tour of British and German housing projects. In her book *Modern Housing*, published in 1934, Bauer argued that the European experience had demonstrated that, to be successful, a housing movement must spring from the anger, militancy, and determination of the working class.[22]

In July of 1933, Gropius was back in the Soviet Union, again railing against what he now called "the immoral right of private property":

> Without the liberation of the land out of this private slavery, it is impossible to create a healthy, development-capable urban renewal that is economic in terms of society in general. Only the Soviet Union has fulfilled this most important requirement without reservation, and thereby opened the way for a truly modern urban planning.[23]

Four years after he made this speech, Gropius was chairman of the architecture department at Harvard. From then on he refrained from using phrases like the "immoral right of private ownership." Instead, he talked about things like "our belief in democratic government." "Planning," he said in the '50s in a speech aptly entitled "Faith in Planning," "grows from the ground up and not from the top down by force."[24] One wonders what Stalin would have thought of these sentiments and why Gropius didn't express them when he was in Leningrad in 1933.

Gropius would go on to become a devout disciple of "Faith in Planning," and during the '30s and '40s, the people at the Philadelphia Housing Association converted to the same religion. "Conversion" is the appropriate term because of both its religious connotation and the fact that the new faith was a radical departure from what the PHAssoc used to profess. From 1911, when he took over the PHAssoc two years after its founding, until 1930, Bernard Newman concerned himself with piggeries and outdoor privies in South Philadelphia – he considered himself a "certified sanitarian" – and promoting the privately financed rowhouse as the ideal solution to sheltering the low-income worker and his family. In 1913, the PHAssoc under Newman's leadership sponsored a contest for a block of workingman's rowhomes to be built on a city lot 404 feet by 306 feet. At around the same time, the Octavia Hill Society, one of the PHAssoc's predecessors, built 32 rowhouses for workers in Kensington and then rented them to workers for $8 to $10 a month.[25]

Newman was a fervent believer in private enterprise and the rowhouse as the solution to Philadelphia's housing problems – until, that is, he went to a meeting of the American planning fraternity in Baltimore in the mid-1930s. Dorothy Montgomery remembered Newman coming back from the meeting, like Saul arriving in Damascus, full of enthusiasm for the Bauhaus European approach to housing the working poor. "Well," Newman announced when he got back to Philadelphia, "I took a big step; I decided to be in favor of public housing."[26] The conference proved to be a watershed in housing history in the United States, as American housers abandoned the rowhouse, and all of the social arrangements that went with it, in favor of *Zeilenbau* ("the superblock") and the *Wohnmaschine* ("living machines") and all of the social arrangements that went with that German import, most notably large-scale government involvement in housing. In addition to promoting Bauhaus architecture, the Baltimore conference called for the creation of a permanent government housing agency, which, much like the USHA, would work with local communities. "The responsibility for securing adequate housing accommodations," concluded the report, "and for focusing to this end the various efforts to supply new low-cost dwellings, to maintain sanitary conditions in existing dwellings, and to clear slums and abate overcrowding, must rest on the local governments administering each area."[27]

The spirit of Walter Gropius would arrive in Philadelphia most tangibly in the person of Oscar Stonorov, a student of Gropius, member of Phillips's charmed circle, and co-designer with fellow Bauhaus devotee Catherine Bauer of the Carl Mackley Homes, a union-financed housing project for hosiery mill workers in Philadelphia's Juniata Park section. Stonorov's greatest (or most dubious) achievement, however, was the design of the Schuylkill Falls Housing Project, one of the greatest monuments to the failure of its ideas which the Philadelphia Housing Authority ever produced. One of the unique features of the thirteen-story twin high-rise buildings which dominated the banks of the Schuylkill River just east of the mouth of the Wissahickon Creek was their so-called "walkways in the sky," the PHA's term for the fact that all of the apartment's balconies were connected in one continuous path which went past each apartment's plate-glass windows, destroying whatever sense of privacy the inhabitants might have desired. What might have worked for Prussian student aristocrats was a complete failure for the sharecroppers just arrived in Philadelphia from their tarpaper shacks in the south. The sharecroppers soon lost control of their own children, who could use the "walkways in the sky" to terrorize their high-rise neighbors. The Schuylkill Falls Project was not only a disaster for the residents of East Falls, who opposed it from the start. It was a failure for its own intended inhabitants as well. The people it was built to house eventually refused to live there. The Schuylkill Falls Project was built in 1953; by 1976 it was 100 percent empty and would remain so for the next twenty years until it was dynamited in the mid-'90s. It was such an embarrassment for the Philadelphia Housing Authority that they even lied about its impending demolition in the mid-'90s.[28]

Johannes Hoeber was also part of Stonorov's team. Formerly the socialist mayor of Mannheim in Germany, Hoeber was jailed by the Nazis and then emigrated to Philadelphia in the '30s, where he met Phillips and became the reformers' expert on dealing with the unions and combating Communist subversion. His wife Elfriede became a research assistant at the PHAssoc. Eventually the combination of the times and Phillips's influence in bringing people of his own persuasion into the organization began to have its effect by creating a shift away from the PHAssoc's traditional preference for private housing of the rowhouse variety to the principles of Bauhaus and all the social and political baggage that brought with it from Germany.

Eastern European Ethnic Catholics like Lukacs, however, continued to remain skeptical of the enthusiasm the "charmed few" in the Phillips circle exhibited when it came to urban planning and other expressions of Central European cultural Bolshevism, newly transplanted to WASP universities:

> Soon after my arrival in the United States I was able to recognize these pervasive incarnations of liberal chic. I remember how a then celebrated city planner of Philadelphia told me that his favorite painter was Klee; he also defended Alger Hiss at the time. (Only a few months ago I read that he criticized – and rightly so – the erection of monstrous office buildings that would in 1988 tower above and obscure Philadelphia's famous French-Victorian City Hall; in 1933 he had proposed that City Hall be torn down and a modern parking garage be erected in its place.) I remember, too, how about 1948 at an upper-class liberal dinner party in Philadelphia I ventured to say that Roosevelt's view of Stalin had not been very realistic, and that I was harrumphed down by a high-powered social medico who, as I had gathered from his conversation, was a local snob of great assiduity and precision, qualities that I hope also marked his practice with his patients.[29]

The celebrated city planner mentioned by Lukacs was Edmund Bacon, one of the first people recruited by Phillips. Edmund Bacon was born in 1910. Ninety years later in May of 2000 he was feted as a local hero at a retrospective lecture in his honor at Philadelphia's Civic Center. "I haven't made up my mind whether I'm going to tell the truth or not," Bacon announced by way of introducing his talk. According to Henry Sawyer, "Ed Bacon always knew where his political bread was buttered."[30] If so, the trajectory which led Bacon to Philadelphia's most celebrated city planner and the cover of *Time* in 1964 was circuitous.

After graduating from Cornell in 1932, Bacon sailed to England and looked up Sir Raymond Unwin, the great English planner, who invited the brash young American student to his home for dinner and exclaimed after listening to him, "Young man, you ought to be a city planner."[31] Bacon then took $1,000 which he had just inherited from his grandfather and sailed to Shanghai by way of Egypt to cash in on the building boom occurring there in 1933. Two years later he was back in the United States, this time Flint, Michigan, working for Elio Saarinen and the WPA. When he came back from Washington with a $3.5 million grant to build public housing, he had established himself as a young man to be watched. Unfortunately, according to his account, one of the groups that had decided to watch him was the local real-estate board, which suddenly became concerned that public housing might put a crimp in the money they were making from selling and then repossessing tarpaper shacks to the local proletariat. They then proceeded to spread the rumor that Bacon was a Communist and succeeded as a result in running him out of town.[32]

"The Junior Chamber of Commerce in 1938," Bacon remembered, "gave me the distinguished service award as having made the greatest contribution of any citizen of Flint to its civic life of the year before. In 1939 they didn't make the award at all because they didn't want to remind themselves who they had given it to the year before."[33]

In 1939, Bacon returned to Philadelphia "out of sheer desperation."[34] He had no job, and he and his wife had to live with Bacon's family. Eventually, Bacon got a job with W. Pope Barney, the architectural firm which came up with the design for the new government housing projects in the city. His salary was $10 a week. Bacon's initial idea upon returning to the city was to get out again as quickly as possible "because I had decided I disliked Philadelphia very much, and it was very dull, and I wanted to go back to China."[35]

But then Bacon met Walter Phillips through Phillips's sister Louisa, and Phillips immediately recognized Bacon as one of the "clever few" and persuaded him to stay by getting him and Oscar Stonorov, who would soon become Bacon's brother-in-law, to design the new house Phillips wanted to be built in Torresdale. Eventually, Phillips used his connections to arrange an interview with Dr. McCallum, then head of the Philadelphia Housing Association. When PHAssoc executive director Bernard Newman died in October of 1941, Bacon succeeded him as that organization's executive director at around the same time that his wife was in the hospital getting ready to give birth to their first child. Which is to say just about six months after Walter Phillips made his first and unsuccessful attempt to interest the Rockefellers in funding city planning in Philadelphia. Not the kind of person to be discouraged by his rebuff at the hands of the Rockefellers, Phillips saw one hopeful sign on the horizon:

> The Philadelphia chapter of the American Institute of Architects and the City Policy committee was formed to raise $1,000 to induce the National Conference on Planning to come to Philadelphia this year. That has been accomplished and the conference is scheduled for May 12–14.[36]

Notes

1 "Philadelphia, Unprepared, Faces a vast City Planning Problem," 4/18/41, in Walter Phillips folder, ACC 527, Temple University Urban Archives.
2 Ibid.
3 Ibid.
4 Ibid.
5 Temple University Urban Archives, ACC 527, Walter Phillips folder, letter from Helen Hill Miller to Walter Phillips, 4/3/41.
6 John H. Mollenkopf, *The Contested City* (Princeton, N.J.: Princeton University Press, 1983), p. 103.
7 Ibid.
8 Ibid., p. 108.
9 Ibid.
10 Ibid., p. 109.
11 Temple University Urban Archives, Walter M. Phillips, Personal Correspondence, Box 53, 2/13/37.
12 Ibid.
13 Ibid.
14 Ibid.
15 Ibid.
16 John Lukacs, *Confessions of an Original Sinner* (South Bend, Ind.: St. Augustine's Press, 2000), p. 159.
17 Ibid.

18 Ibid.

19 Ibid., 161

20 E. Michael Jones, *Living Machines: Bauhaus as Sexual Ideology* (San Francisco: Ignatius Press, 1995), p. 57.

21 Ibid.

22 John F. Bauman, *Public Housing, Race, and Renewal: Urban Planning in Philadelphia, 1920–1974* (Philadelphia: Temple University Press, 1987), p. 25.

23 Walter Gropius, "Was erhoffen wir vom russischen Staedtebau?" BMS Germ 208.2 Gropius, Collected Papers, Archives, Harvard University (my translation).

24 Jones, *Living Machines*, p. 57.

25 Bauman, p. 7.

26 Ibid., p. 27.

27 Ibid.

28 During the summer of 1995 I held a press conference with the Schuylkill Falls Project in the background, calling it a monument to a failed regime. During the course of the conference I announced that the Philadelphia Housing Authority planned to blow up the building in the immediate future. The head of the PHA denied this to the *Philadelphia Inquirer*. In fact, she had been brought to the site of the conference by the *Inquirer* for that purpose. A few weeks later, the buildings were in fact blown up, with no mention of the denial in the *Inquirer*.

29 Lukacs, *Confessions*, p. 159.

30 "Henry W. Sawyer, III," Walter Phillips Oral History Project, Box 4, Temple University Urban Archives,

31 "Edmund Bacon," Walter M. Phillips, Oral History Project, Box 1, Temple University Urban Archives.

32 Interview with Edmund Bacon 5/15/00.

33 Ibid.

34 "Edmund Bacon."

35 Ibid.

36 "Philadelphia, Unprepared, Faces a vast city Planning Problem," Walter M. Phillips papers, 4/18/41, Temple University Urban Archives.

The Planning Conference

Even though America's relations with Germany left something to be desired in the fall of 1941, and even though the WASP establishment was avid to go to war with Germany to save England from conquest, the largely WASP practitioners of urban planning were enamored of the Bauhaus school of design and architecture and urban planning, not so much because it happened to be German, but because it was aggressively modern and international and, as everyone could see, the cutting-edge of Enlightenment thought when it came to design. The fact that the National Socialists didn't like Bauhaus was another reason for the school's popularity among enlightened social planners in the United States. Secure in his knowledge of Phillips's support, Edmund Bacon dedicated his efforts to bringing the 1941 National Conference on Planning to meet in Philadelphia. Bacon succeeded in securing the agreement of the Planning Conference's three-member organizations – the American Society of Planning Officials, the American Institute of Planners, and at that time the American Planning and Civic Association – provided he could meet their condition of raising a $1,000 subvention fund.

Raising the money was to prove more difficult than Bacon thought. Bacon first turned to Peter Widener, one of Philadelphia's leading philanthropists at the time and then chairman of the City Planning Commission, but found it was not easy to meet with him. Widener owned one of the area's great estates, a huge complex on Cheltenham Avenue which included its own race track, all of which would eventually be torn down to make way for an apartment complex. Bacon remembered trying to call Widener at his home and getting his butler instead, who informed Bacon that Widener was away. When Bacon asked when he would return, the butler informed him that, "Mr. Widener will return at his pleasure and convenience."[1] Bacon eventually got $50 from Mr. Widener. That and a conversation with fellow planner and Phillips's man Henry Beerits convinced Bacon that the old planning commission was no good, despite the fact that it had on it the most distinguished people in Philadelphia. Perhaps because of their experience with Widener, Bacon and Phillips decided that Philadelphia needed a new planning commission.

Bacon eventually raised the money and was on hand when Mayor Lamberton arrived at the Bellevue Stratford Hotel on May 12, 1941, to greet the delegates. Bacon had arranged to have as their keynote speaker a distinguished houser and planner from Virginia whose eloquence on the issue had impressed him at another planning conference. Bacon had urged him to be politic and expound on the rationality of city planning and how it was to the city's benefit, but the memory of Mayor Lamberton having turned down $19 million in federal housing money was still fresh in everyone's mind, especially in the mind of the speaker, who turned in mid-speech to the mayor, while pointing a finger, and accused him of being personally responsible for the existence of the city's slums because he had turned down the money. Bacon, watching the back of Lamberton's neck get redder and redder and seeing large amounts of smoke rise from the mayor's cigar, feared that the speaker had effectively ended whatever chances urban planning had in the city of Philadelphia, but he was wrong.[2] The mayor told Bacon that, while he was unhappy with the speaker, he would like to continue working with the Phillips group in the city planning movement. "In essence," Bacon said later, "that was the moment when we moved from being a totally peripheral group to being a central kind of group because Lamberton said as an outgrowth of that luncheon to us that he was a busy man, he was in accord with our ideas but he was too busy himself to prepare the steps necessary."[3]

Now that a city planning group was functioning under a mandate from the mayor, a burst of activity followed – "literally hundreds of luncheons and dinners at the Quaker Lady on Locust St.,"[4] according to Bacon, at which the nature of the planning commission was hammered out. Having been influenced by Robert Walker's argument that planning commissions endowed with legal powers were the least successful because they created such jealousies that the regular departments easily defeated their proposals, the Phila-del-phia planners chose to create a voluntary organization because "the ones that were successful were those which had such clear and strong ideas that the community supported them and therefore they became efficacious and effective."[5] The other model for what eventually became the Citizens' Council on City Planning was the City Policy Committee, Walter Phillips's committee of the "clever few" founded in 1939. "Walter," according to Bacon, "was influenced . . . through his experience with the charter campaign, the fusion ticket and all, which didn't work. That was in '38 and '39, and from that he concluded that the grass roots movement was necessary which also coincided exactly with my own experience in Flint."[6] The founding of the committee and the Urban Planning Conference coincided with an unusual amount of turmoil and turnover at the Philadelphia Housing Association. By the time Bernard Newman died in October of 1941 and Edmund Bacon replaced him, the PHAssoc had changed its direction from an organization which promoted the construction of privately financed rowhouses in Philadelphia into an organization that would be committed to the Bauhaus idea of social engineering. By the 1960s the PHAssoc would become a radical organization committed to promoting black power in the city through manipulation of the housing market.

When the construction of the West Poplar Project was announced in the *Bulletin* in 1939, along with pictures of the white families it was displacing, the most significant fact about it was that it had no name. In few other areas of life was the term *nomen est omen* so applicable as in the housing projects of this era. In an era of segregated housing, the name of the project was an indication of who was going to live there. In Chicago, the name of the Cabrini Homes was an indication that housing was intended for Italians. When the Chicago Housing Authority allowed blacks in instead, a riot ensued. In Detroit, parishioners in St. Louis the King Parish noticed that Sojourner Truth didn't have a Polish ring to it. That that project was named after the black feminist and abolitionist was some indication of who the government intended to have live there and, more importantly, some indication of the social engineering that was being planned for the essentially Polish neighborhood where it was going to be located.

In December of 1941, Robert Stephenson (the British agent known as Intrepid) finally succeeded in getting America into the war on the side of England, and Winston Churchill finally got a good night's sleep. One month later in January 1942, Philadelphia was expecting the influx of more than 100,000 war workers. Depending on how long the war lasted, Philadelphia could expect even more over the course of the next few years. In January 1942 Philadelphia Housing Authority chairman Raymond Rosen traveled to Washington and, in Bauman's words, "dangled the Allen deal before [USHA Secretary] Palmer and Keyserling."[7] Once the USHA money had been cut off by Congress in the fall of 1941, the only source of federal housing money was the Lanham Act, and that meant the public housing would now have to become defense-worker housing or go out of existence. Washington Rhodes, editor of the local black paper, *The Philadelphia Tribune*, blamed the switch on "some wise fellows who decided it would be an excellent thing to rob the underprivileged people of decent housing in the name of defense."[8]

Shortly after Raymond Rosen returned from Washington in early 1942, the Philadelphia Housing Authority announced that the West Poplar Project would be known as the Richard Allen Homes, after Philadelphia's own 18th-century African Methodist bishop. That meant that the inhabitants of the Richard Allen Homes were going to be black, and that meant, of course, that all of the white people pictured in the *Bulletin* article two years and some months before would not be able to return to the neighborhood. The government had got involved directly in determining where people were going to live.

But that was only the beginning of the controversy. Shortly after announcing the name of the housing project and hence the race of its prospective inhabitants, the Philadelphia Housing Authority announced that none of the former black residents of the neighborhood would be able to move back either. The Richard Allen Homes had been turned into war worker housing and the local paper noted that "Irritation over the decision to rent Richard Allen Homes to defense workers rather than to low income families now living in substandard dwellings is in some measure due to the fact that a promise was broken."[9] The occupants had been told "that they would be allowed to come back and occupy decent quarters," but "overnight all of this had changed."[10] The Richard Allen Homes had been caught up in the mobilization for war that had swept the country following the Japanese attack on Pearl Harbor. The Richard Allen Homes were to be used for war-worker housing, specifically black workers brought up to Philadelphia from the South to work in Philadelphia's bustling port and armaments industries.

Once the controversy became public it was difficult to discern whether the Richard Allen Homes were ever intended to be housing for the people in the neighborhood. It began to look as if they were intended as war-worker housing from their inception, even though this country was not at war at the time. Once the controversy became public, responsibility for that decision got tossed back and forth between local and federal authorities like the political hot potato that it in fact was. When the local authorities claimed that the decision had been forced on them by Washington, Washington let it be known that the local authorities knew all along what was going on.

Someone who evidently did know what was going on was the district's congressman, Michael Bradley, who traveled to Washington in early February to confer with U.S. housing administrator Leon H. Keyserling on how to save the Richard Allen Homes for underprivileged tenants it was originally intended to house. At the same time, "representatives of various Philadelphia agencies who are seeking to save the homes for the original tenants expressed confidence that they will not be turned over to defense workers, as has been proposed."[11]

The hope proved to be short-lived as the war effort in effect countermanded every other social priority. Baird Snyder III, the Washington bureaucrat responsible for the homes, tried to defuse the issue by racializing it. Since many of the people who were displaced by the project were black, Snyder tried to calm the situation by limiting the new residents to exclusively black defense workers. "In converting the project to war use," Snyder told the *Bulletin*, "I am asking the U.S. Housing Authority to the limit that is possible to have the project made available to Negro defense workers. The housing need seems most compelling among the Negroes and in meeting it this arrangement should be about as effective as the original plan."[12]

But the more the newspaper looked into the matter the more they began to discern that the real original plan was different from the original plan which was announced two years earlier. When the local authorities tried to blame the switch on Washington, Charles F. Palmer, the former head of the Atlanta, Georgia, housing authority, whom Franklin Delano Roosevelt had appointed as his defense housing coordinator, announced that the Philadelphians had been in on the planned switch all along. "When application was made for the priorities assistance to complete the Richard Allen homes," Palmer said in a telegram to Edmund Bacon, then head of the Philadelphia Housing Association, "it was understood that project would become available for defense workers, in which understanding this office concurred."[13] Eventually, the Philadelphia Housing Authority, the local government entity which was created to accept funds from the New Deal Housing Act of 1937 came up with an explanation of the bait-and-switch that came very close to what Palmer was saying in Washington.

"It is correct that the Philadelphia Housing Authority applied for priorities to complete the Richard Allen Homes as early as October 1941," said Roland R. Randall, PHA vice chairman. "It is also correct that we were told at that time that if these priorities were used Richard Allen Homes would have to be turned over to defense workers."[14]

One week later, Washington issued a categorical statement which pretty much laid the entire controversy to rest by *force majeure*. "The Philadelphia Housing Authority's decision to carry out the request of the US Government to make the Richard Allen Homes available in totality for defense workers has not been changed," said one Washington official. "How this request is to be executed is in the hands of Washington. The status of the entire project is that it is to be made available for defense workers."[15]

The controversy surrounding who was going to live in the Richard Allen Homes is instructive for a number of reasons. It mirrored, first of all, a change in the priorities of the Roosevelt administration as it abandoned the domestic New Deal in favor of its aggressive foreign-policy confrontation with fascism. This change meant that Roosevelt had to abandon his attempts at socialistic ameliorism and make peace with the East Coast internationalist establishment which had been alienated from him by them. By waging the war they wanted to see waged, Roosevelt was no longer a traitor to his class, and his policies reflected that reconciliation. Foremost among them was the creation of the War Production Board, which agreed not only to spend billions to recapitalize the entire industrial infrastructure of the country to win the war by outproducing the fascists, but more importantly agreed to recapitalize the country on the industrialists' terms, and not on the terms of the New Deal constituency of ethnic Northerners and agrarian Southerners which had put Roosevelt into office. That meant bringing the essentially ethnic unions into line in the northern industrial cities. The simplest way to do that was to bring black workers up from the South, thereby inflating the labor supply and undercutting the bargaining power of the unions. Henry Ford was a master of this technique in Detroit. Ford had a network of black ministers who operated their churches as de facto employment agencies. The one condition of employment for blacks was being non- (or better anti-) union.

The biggest impediment to bringing blacks up from the South on short notice was finding a place for them to live when they got there, and that meant commandeering public housing for their use. Entry into the war would mean, as Gunnar Myrdal mentioned in his book on race, social engineering, and the first place that the war-related social engineering would become evident was in the field of housing.

If social engineering was the real reason for the construction of the Richard Allen Homes, it was also the real reason for the regime's interest in race relations. Race became a pretext for changing the neighborhoods into political configurations more congenial to Washington's policies, in this instance the war in Europe. The Washington intelligence community considered the ethnic community a security risk. Race was a way of intervening in the internal affairs of these communities without creating the reaction which the CPI's heavy-handed tactics inspired during World War I.

Federal concern for integration also masked the fact that many neighborhoods in Philadelphia were already integrated and would have continued to be so. In both South Philadelphia and the lower sections of North Philadelphia, the streets tended to be segregated by race, but the neighborhood taken as a whole was often racially integrated. In general the neighborhoods were integrated if the housing stock was economically diverse. In South Philadelphia, the blacks lived in court houses and worked for the white people in the neighborhood who lived on bigger houses on bigger streets

In spite of what the Philadelphia Housing Association would say on the matter, the real issue was not housing stock, and it was not hygiene; the real issue was race, but race was only a pressing issue in Philadelphia during the 20th century because of war. And as America would learn, war and social engineering went hand-in-hand in the 20th century. In the 1930 edition of his famous book which first appeared when Europe dissolved into World War I, John B. Watson, one of the creators of WASP environmentalism, tried to allay any fears his readers might have concerning the social experimentation he was proposing. "First we all," he assured them, "we all must admit that social experimentation is going on at a very rapid rate at present – at an alarmingly rapid rate for comfortable, conventional souls. As an example of social experimentation . . . we have war."[16]

War invariably increased the demand for labor, and since the United States could not import cheap labor from Europe during the First World War and did not want to import it from there in the nativist period in reaction to the war during the 1920s, there was only one source of untapped labor in the United States and that was the pool of black sharecroppers in the South. Between 1916 and 1918, agents of the Pennsylvania and Erie Railroads as well as many other Philadelphia businesses eventually lured about 40,000 blacks to Philadelphia to work in its labor-starved factories. Those laborers moved into the cheapest housing the city had available, and that meant the courthouses of North and South Philadelphia.

By 1939, it was obvious that America was gearing up for war once again, and since the same constraints on cheap labor still applied, that meant that the city would have to import more rural blacks as factory workers if they wanted to win the war. If Philadelphia's housing establishment had simply been interested in eliminating the city's worst housing, then by their own definition of blight they should have concentrated on the Lombard/South Street area, where they had concentrated their efforts during the first years of the Philadelphia Housing Association by urging the removal of piggeries and outdoor privies. That they chose West Poplar indicates that considerations other than hygiene were involved in their decision. The most significant of the other considerations was race. West Poplar was a mixed neighborhood, but more significantly it was on the cusp of racial transition already established by the black migration to Philadelphia during World War I.

Although the author of the article in the *Evening Bulletin* didn't view it this way, the entry of the federal government into the housing construction business would have far-reaching consequences, none of which were apparent to the average citizen when the project was first announced. First there was a change in terms of what housing meant. The housers were modernists, which meant they took the lead of people like Le Corbusier and Walter Gropius in seeing the house as a "machine for living." According to Bauman:

> Increasingly in the late 1930s, such housers as James Ford and Elizabeth Wood (who until 1954 headed the Chicago Housing Authority) envisioned the neighborhood unit, or superblock, as the critical design model for public housing. A modern urban community form first propounded by the French architect Le Corbusier and incorporated into the Bauhaus community designs of Walter Gropius and Ernst May, these bold, large-scale, comprehensively planned freestanding superblock communities, the communitarians claimed, would exert a salutary impact on the residents of the project and the surrounding region.[17]

The size of the project also made the government's involvement in housing mandatory. Just as the rowhouse was a form of housing that could be built and financed largely by the people who would live in those houses, the housing project demanded government intervention. First of all it demanded a revision of the concept of eminent domain. In order to get into the housing business, the government had to undermine the property rights of the average citizen, a subversion that would be made into law with the Warren Court's 1954 *Berman v. Parker* decision. But the government's entry into housing meant other changes as well. It meant increasing the government's control over its citizens. It meant increasing involvement in social engineering. Initially all of this was justified as part of the war effort and as necessary to defeat fascism in Europe. However, since the federal government invariably worked through local housing authorities and these authorities invariably had a certain ethnic cast, global decisions involving foreign policy invariably got implemented on the local level according to the ethnic prejudices of the implementers.

If the controversy surrounding the conversion of the Richard Allen Homes proved nothing else, it showed that government involvement in housing was linked with larger related issues. In fact it would be virtually impossible to understand the government's involvement in housing without seeing it as part of its involvement in the issues of war and social engineering and race. Similarly, it is impossible to understand the government's policy on race without examining its wartime manpower needs and as a result its housing policies. Housing policy was always seen as a means to an end, and once the East Coast internationalist establishment defeated the isolationists when the Japanese attacked Pearl Harbor and America entered the war, they would use housing policy as one of their prime instruments for social engineering.

In this regard, the government's entry into the housing business was much like any other Enlightenment project. There was an intention behind it, but in the application of that intention, the complicated interface between war, race, and social engineering would also bring about unintended consequences. The government would build the housing, and the government would then determine who would live in the newly built housing. If it were designated as low-income housing, that meant inquiring into the financial details of the lives of would-be renters. But low-income housing also meant that one could not prosper in that particular situation. As soon as the renter's income exceeded a certain level, he had to leave. This meant that the only thing that made stability possible in a neighborhood was economic stagnation. It also meant that the cultural diversity of the previous neighborhood in terms of income would disappear in a very short time. By the time the dislocations of the war were over, especially the housing shortages which it created, housing projects like the one in the West Poplar neighborhood would degenerate into monocultures of poverty in ways that the "slums" they had replaced had never been. These failures were not intended, but the social engineering which set them in motion was certainly not unintended either.

Social engineering was part of the Bauhaus design from the beginning. One of the tenets of the modernists in housing was that "efficient or functional environments have positive behavioral consequences." As a result, "modern housing was to liberate the family from the cluttered, overstuffed, emotionally stifling Victorian residential environment; it was to provide housing for the 'machine age.'"[18]

Other aspects of government housing were equally invisible to the casual observer in 1939. Once the government got into the housing business, the housers never built as many units as they tore down. That meant that the government's entry into the housing business meant the net destruction of housing for the poor, because housing for the poor was ipso facto obsolete and according to housers' principles should be torn down. No one, in other words, would rent a house for $6 a month if he could afford a house for $20 a month. The fact that the court houses in the West Poplar neighborhood were occupied meant that they were fulfilling a need for the people who rented them. If they were not, they would not have been occupied. By tearing these units down, the Philadelphia Housing Authority destroyed twenty-eight acres of the most affordable housing in Philadelphia.

Public housing, in other words, drove people from homes they were willing to pay rent to occupy. Theoretically those people were supposed to be accommodated by the new government-built units, but things never worked out that way in practice, primarily because government would always be willing to commandeer the housing it constructed to achieve some social end, but also because the government never built enough units to replace the housing they tore down. That meant that in practice, government housing displaced people from houses they could afford and sent them into the neighborhoods which were closest in proximity and price to the neighborhoods they had just left. In other words, government housing invariably destabilized the neighborhoods around the neighborhoods they destroyed.

In May 1942 President Roosevelt told Congress that in order to defeat fascism in "total war" the United States would have to construct government housing. At around the same time, federal manpower commissioner Paul McNutt estimated that, nationally, the war had triggered a migration in which 1.6 million workers – many accompanied by families – traveled toward war-industry centers.[19] Like the rest of the Phillips crowd, Edmund Bacon was a supporter of the war. Like many of his ethnic group, Bacon would join the Navy, but as a houser he supported the war as well. Bacon recommended billeting war workers in boarding schools and dormitories, but the the main thrust of his argument was for the urgent construction of government-built war housing. In urging this program, Bacon, like his Bauhaus-inspired peers, reverted to the language of social engineering. "His reasons," according to Bauman,

> had a familiar ring; as during World War I, the new war intensified the Progressives' concern for bureaucratization and scientific efficiency. Bacon linked decent housing to both efficiency and internal security. Substandard housing posed the threat of impaired efficiency in output, and, much worse, it threatened "a massive breakdown in morale."[20]

By the time Mayor Lamberton unveiled a plaque honoring Bishop Richard Allen, founder of Negro Methodism, at the projects on September 27, 1942, the PHA under Raymond Rosen's direction had reached a compromise with local black leaders. No more than 200 defense workers, all black, would be housed in the Allen project. No matter what the racial make-up of the projects, and no matter how many of the black people there had come up from North and South Carolina within the past few weeks as opposed to the past few years, the precedent that government housing policies should be used to achieve governmental goals in social engineering had been established and the covenant the Irish in St. Malachy's Parish had made with the Protestant rulers of the city had been irrevocably broken. From now on the federal government could determine not only who your neighbors were going to be, they could also, under the vastly expanded understanding of eminent domain that urban renewal entailed, take your house away from you as well. The only thing that made this massive violation of the social order possible was war – that and the fact that the ruling class supported that war with all its Anglophilic heart.

Notes

1   Bacon, oral history, Temple University Urban Archives.
2   Ibid.
3   Ibid.
4   Ibid.
5   Ibid.

6   Ibid.

7   John F. Bauman, *Public Housing, Race, and Renewal: Urban Planning in Philadelphia, 1920–1974* (Philadelphia: Temple University Press, 1987), p. 68.

8   Ibid.

9   "End of Slums Sought for General Good," *The Evening Bulletin* (2/9/42), Richard Allen Homes, Temple University Urban Archives.

10 "A Housing Mistake," *The Evening Bulletin* (1/31/42), Richard Allen Homes, Temple University Urban Archives.

11 "Foes of Home Shift feel Confident," *The Evening Bulletin* (2/7/42), Richard Allen Homes, Temple University Urban Archives.

12 "Allen Unit to Open for Negro Tenants," *The Evening Bulletin* (1/28/42), Richard Allen Homes, Temple University Urban Archives.

13 "Allen Homes Shift due to Priorities," *The Evening Bulletin* (1/27/42), Richard Allen Homes, Temple University Urban Archives.

14 Ibid.

15 "US must decide on Allen Homes," *The Evening Bulletin*, (2/3/42), Richard Allen Homes, Temple University Urban Archives.

16 John B. Watson, *Behaviorism* (Chicago: University of Chicago Press, 1930, 1958), p. 41.

17 Bauman, p. 48.

18 E. Michael Jones, *Living Machines* (San Francisco: Ignatius Press, 1995), p. 84.

19 Bauman, p. 66.

20 Ibid.

The WASPs Go to War

Thacher Longstreth, a Quaker-Episcopalian hybrid in the classic Philadelphia ruling-class mode, describes at great length the efforts he made to join the Navy during the early years of World War II. Longstreth's family had taken a financial beating as a result of the stock-market crash of 1929. That and watching his mother drink herself to death – "My mother drank and was miserable and unhappy and died a wretched person."[1] – caused a fundamental transformation in his understanding of the Protestant Ethic,

> for what was the point of accumulating wealth in a world where fortunes could be wiped out overnight? Thus the Quaker maxim "Do well before you do good" underwent a modification in my case: It became "Do good, have fun, and don't hurt anyone along the way."[2]

Longstreth was big enough to play football at Princeton, but his eyes weren't good enough to see the ball when it was thrown to him. The ball as a result would often hit him on the helmet as he blinked uncomprehendingly with his hands raised in the other direction waiting for the pass he couldn't see. This meant that when Longstreth went to enlist, he was rejected almost as soon as he walked through the door of the draft board and classified 4-F. This meant that he could not take part in the great WASP crusade of his lifetime, the war against fascism, and that thought drove him to smuggle that era's hard contact lens somehow on his naked person into the draft physical eye test so that he could read the charts and pass the test and end up on a ship in the Pacific Ocean. Longstreth didn't have a clear idea of what would happen to him if he had been caught cheating on his physical exam, but even a death sentence seemed mild compared to the humiliation that he would suffer if he had been forced to spend the war years in Philadelphia. "If he didn't catch me," Longstreth wrote referring to his examiner at the draft board, "I'd get into the Navy for four years and become a hero and emerge from the war with medals and decorations. But if he caught me, I'd spend the rest of the war making artillery shells in some factory, humiliated at the thought of walking down the street while everyone who passed me wondered: Why isn't he in the war?"[3] The war convinced Longstreth's class that it was not, contrary to popular opinion, a bunch of effete upper-class sissies. It gave people of that ethnic group a renewed sense of purpose, and it was armed with that sense of purpose that this group returned after the war and decided to reform Philadelphia.

Ed Bacon enlisted in the Navy in December of 1943. Like Digby Baltzell, who envisioned a revitalized Protestant Establishment as the result of his wartime experiences, Ed Bacon arrived at his vision of a physically revitalized Philadelphia the same way. Bacon had become a good friend of Oscar Stonorov before the war. When Bacon was in the Pacific, Stonorov wrote to him about conversations he was having with Walter Phillips about an idea they had for something which eventually came to be known as the Better Philadelphia Exhibition, which was essentially a Bauhaus-inspired revision of the downtown area and the housing stock of the surrounding neighborhoods. That vision involved a large-scale model of how the revitalized city was going to look, and Bacon designed the model while on board the *U.S.S. Shoshone* between the invasions of Iwo Jima and Okinawa.

His stint in the army taught Bacon other things as well, something he described in a taped conversation with Phillips in 1975.

"I had learned to work with regular people although I was brought up in a relatively rarefied circles of Quaker middle upper class," Bacon told Phillips, "I never was brought up in your level of society, Walter, but nonetheless, it was in many ways probably more rarefied than yours because being overloaded with this tremendous religious preciousness and we only associated with the right people."[4]

Phillips was an Episcopalian, and although there was frequent cross-fertilization between Quakers and Episcopalians in the Philadelphia upper class, Bacon thought the traditions distinct enough to feel the need to explain the differences to Phillips. One of those differences was "a really terrible institution" which Bacon referred to as "the 'thee' institution."

> We had a whole group of people we called "thee" and if I called my brothers, sisters , or relatives "you" it would be an insult worse than it is possible to conceive of, worse than any of the newer words that the young people have made popular. And so all of our friends had to be instantly categorized either into the "thee" group or the "you" group and you never called a person who was not a Quaker "thee" and you never, never called a person who was a Quaker and one of the in group "you." which would be an insult of indescribable , . . . I don't know if it carries on today, but it was the total basis of my upbringing.[5]

What prompted Bacon's effusions about growing up Quaker was Phillips's not-so-slightly condescending question about his ability to work with lower-class politicians like Bernard (Barney) Samuels, successor to Robert E. Lamberton (who died in office). Barney Samuels's approach to urban planning was essentially a series of incredulous questions. "You mean you want to tell me what I can build at Second and Shunk?" Samuels said to Bacon. Bacon was smart enough to see that Phillips's reference to Barney Samuels's lower-class demeanor was really a reference to someone Phillips considered another low-class mayor, James H.J. Tate, the city's first Catholic mayor, and the man Phillips ran against in the 1963 mayoral primary. "You mean," Bacon responded mockingly to Phillips, "that working with one low class person, Samuels, I, therefore, was able to work with another low-class person, Tate. As contrasted with the two aristocrats?" Bacon's response gives some indication of how Phillips dealt with the class of what he considered his inferiors in Philadelphia. Rather than deal with the ethnic issue out in the open, Bacon made it clear that "Walter prefers the euphemism of educational advantages."[6]

It was the war, which meant living "for 13 months on the deck of the *U.S.S. Shoshone* with 400 sailors all in a single room" that gave Bacon skills to transcend the "fairly rarefied atmosphere" he was brought up in where he "wasn't really used to people like Bernard Samuels."[7] The war, rather than working in Philadelphia, gave Bacon these skills because when he worked with Samuels as mayor he was "quite protected by such aristocrats as Edward Hopkinson and yourself," i.e., Phillips.[8]

A thousand miles away from Bacon's ship in the Pacific, fellow Philadelphian Joseph Sill Clark was supporting the war effort by perfecting his tennis game on the grass courts of New Delhi. Like John McCloy, Joe Clark was a championship-caliber tennis player. Like Walter Phillips, Clark was a member of Philadelphia's ruling class, and like Phillips and unlike McCloy, Clark decided to cast his lot with Philadelphia after the war. Like Thacher Longstreth, Ed Bacon, Digby Baltzell, and other Philadelphia WASPs who joined the Navy, Clark's war experiences led him to envision new possibilities for political engagement in Philadelphia.

In 1943 Clark was in Calcutta recovering from a case of amoebic dysentery when he picked up a copy of *Life* and read an article on the mayoralty campaign in Philadelphia. One of the pictures accompanying the article showed local publishing magnate William Bullitt campaigning in a coonskin coat and derby hat, a get-up that struck Clark as "rather comical."[9] Bullitt was eventually beaten by Barney Samuels in the 1943 election, something which caused the aristocratic Clark to start thinking, "if that guy could get to be mayor of Philadelphia, certainly I can. So I made up my mind then and there that when I got back into civilian life, I would get back into politics and see if I couldn't get myself nominated and elected Mayor."[10] Clark had met Richardson Dilworth on the beaches of Southampton, Long Island, during the '20s, where "we learned the American way of life" in an atmosphere that was what he would later characterize as "plutocratic."[11] Clark met Phillips after the war, and both men began to assemble the team that would lead Clark to the mayor's office. Along the way, Phillips got Clark interested in housing enough to join the Citizen's Council on City Planning, the Committee of 70, and the Philadelphia Housing Association. "Those," he said later, "were the principal non-governmental organizations that I became interested in largely through [Phillips's] help and assistance."[12] Clark also became involved in the local chapter of the Americans for Democratic Action, the group of liberals who broke with Truman when they saw him as betraying Roosevelt's New Deal legacy.

Gradually, the reformers began to turn up the heat on the Republicans who ran the city. In 1949 Clark was elected city controller, at which point he brought Walter Phillips into the administration and both began examining the city's financial records. At that point a certain Mr. Foss committed suicide, and then their complete takeover of the city was only a matter of time. Housing played a crucial role in the political transformation of the city, according to Frank Hoeber, son of Johannes and Elfriede, and the war was instrumental in transforming housing.

War, as John B. Watson indicated, always favors social engineering, and World War II was no exception in this regard. In fact, it could be seen as paradigmatic. The East Coast Internationalist WASP establishment which ached to get involved in both world wars in this century, returned home after the successful completion of their second war energized by their success in whipping fascism so convincingly and felt that the lessons they had learned there could be applied to domestic problems. But if the WASPs returned united, the ethnics returned more alienated from their particular traditions than when they left. They may have left as Germans and Irishmen and Italians and Poles who felt they had no dog in a fight that involved the English, but they returned as Americans, identifying with American imperial goals. The largely Catholic ethnics were, in other words, divided and weakened at the same time that their opponents in the coming *Kulturkampf* were at the top of their game.

In addition to that, there was, in 1940, no pan-Catholic ethnic identity in the United States of the sort that the various Protestant sects had achieved during the much longer time they had been living in the country. The Irish still regarded the Poles an alien "race." The opposite was true of the various Protestant denominations which had fused together into what Digby Baltzell would call "The Protestant Establishment." The rejuvenated WASP establishment fresh from whipping fascism saw all ethnics as generically Catholic before the Catholics themselves did. They could wage their battle to assimilate the ethnics from a position of strength, whereas the ethnics were still only halfway to the pan-Catholic identity that the triple melting pot would eventually provide.

"I visualized the possibility of an ethnically mixed establishment," Digby Baltzell wrote in *The Protestant Establishment*, "which underlies the theory of American leadership developed in this book, during my own experiences in the wardrooms and officers clubs of the South Pacific."[13]

The ethnic conflict, however, which the war bumped from the headlines of the nation's papers, continued unabated. Detroit witnessed the biggest race riot in the nation's history in June 1943. Two months later, soldiers were riding Philadelphia's buses and trolleys because of a strike which the transport workers' union called when blacks were hired as bus drivers to take the place of the Irishmen who were off fighting in the war. And in October 1943 Philadelphia's Polish community held a protest meeting at Kaczynski Hall because there were rumors that black families were going to be moved into the Tacony Homes in the neighborhood. Ethnic identification had been weakened by the war, which led the ethnics to see themselves as generic Americans at a time when the ruling class began to view them as generically suspect Catholics. This was a decided disadvantage in a country where the real rules of engagement in cultural and ethnic conflict were kept a closely guarded secret.

Notes

1 Thacher Longstreth, *Main Line WASP: The Education of Thacher Longstreth* (New York: W.W. Norton, 1990), p. 44.

2 Ibid., p. 48.

3 Ibid., p. 102.

4 Bacon, oral history, Walter M. Phillips Oral History Project, Temple University Urban Archives.

5 Ibid.

6 Ibid.

7 Ibid.

8 Ibid.

9 Joseph S. Clark, oral history, Interview 3/18/75 Walter M. Phillips Oral History Project.

10 Ibid.

11 Ibid.

12 Ibid.

13 E. Digby Baltzell, *The Protestant Establishment: Aristocracy and Caste in America* (New York: Random House, 1964), p. 301.

Louis Wirth and the Ethnics

On April 10, 1941, which is to say, eight months before America would enter the war, Louis Wirth presented a scholarly paper on "The Present Position of Minorities in the United States" at a sociology symposium. "The newer European immigrants," Wirth wrote, "coming at the time of the greatest industrial expansion, are overwhelmingly concentrated in the larger industrial cities and retain to a much greater degree the compactness of their ethnic communities. In some cases their colonies in the cities of the US exceed their numbers in the largest cities of their respective mother countries."[1]

Louis Wirth was a sociologist from the University of Chicago, which is another way of saying that he was involved in psychological warfare, which, at this moment in the nation's history, meant keeping tabs on America's ethnics, which meant in common parlance, recent immigrants from Southern and Eastern Europe, but the Irish as well. As the inclusion of the Irish indicated, the common denominator among these suspect groups was not geographical; it was religious. Since virtually every group in the United States was an ethnic group, including the groups involved in spying on others, Wirth had to explain why some groups posed more of a threat to American security than others. To do this he had to get into religion:

> In the face of the numerical as well as economic, social and political dominance of the Protestant groups, the Catholic population may be regarded, and in certain communities thinks of itself, as a distinct minority, especially since in some communities Catholicism is also associated with Irish, Italian, Polish or certain other ethnic or national origin. Whereas the internal division and lack of cohesion of the Protestant denominations detracts from their capacity to play the role of a dominant group effectively, the relative internal unity and concentration of settlement of the Catholic groups in the urban centers increases their capacity to act collectively and to develop an appropriate group consciousness.[2]

Although there is no indication that he read it, Wirth's analysis of the ethnic situation is virtually identical with Brand Blanshard's analysis of Bridesburg, which, it should be remembered, was written during World War I, when the intelligence community of that era had similar concerns. The unspoken assumption behind Wirth's analysis, a view which would find expression in Brand's brother Paul's book when it came out in the late '40s, is that Catholics had a congenital weakness for fascism. In fact both Blanshard and Bertrand Russell would claim that Catholicism and fascism were politically indistinguishable. This was of special concern to the intelligence community because, in Wirth's words, "the totalitarian nations of Europe have substantial representation of their subjects or former subjects"[3] in the United States, "a fact worth emphasizing in the light of their extended conception of nationality."[4] Once again war was creating ethnophobia in the intelligence community, which was worried about "the descendants of these foreign born residents early 1940s, the war and "subversives," triple melting pot

who presumably are at least in part subject to the ideologies of their respective mother countries."[5] Once again the intelligence community was trying to disrupt communications among subject peoples, whose populations had increased significantly in the intervening twenty years. The numbers, according to Wirth, were impressive:

> Of our total foreign white stock of 38,727,593, more than one-sixth is German and nearly one-eighth is Italian. If we note further that the Italians have the highest percentage of any of the major immigrant groups unable to speak English (15.7 percent in 1930) we have further reason to fear their exclusive susceptibility to news and propaganda purveyed by their foreign language press, which in part has been subsidized by agencies of the mother country's government.[6]

But the ethnic facts became even more worrisome once one considered the fact that most of those ethnics belonged to one religious denomination. The change in ethnic make-up of the country has brought with it, according to Wirth, "a corresponding shift in religious affiliation of the American population," making the "nation now a little over one third Roman Catholic." As if that weren't bad enough, many of these people dominate "certain highly skilled occupations in essential defense industries." In fact, "some of the key skilled jobs are virtually monopolized by certain groups *whose national origin makes them suspect*"[7] [my emphasis].

Wirth never gets around to explaining the criteria whereby he established which nations are *ipso facto* suspect, but his inclusion of Ireland and Poland in the list indicates that it wasn't just countries at war with the United States. In fact the only thing which the Irish and the Polish, who viewed each other generally as members of mutually alien races at the time, had in common other than American citizenship was the fact that they were Catholic. It was a commonality which existed only in the eyes of the people who considered them a threat, certainly not in the minds of the Poles and the Irish themselves. The tension between the Polish laity and their priests, on the one hand, and a largely uncomprehending Irish hierarchy in the American Catholic Church, on the other, was so intense that it was the driving force behind the formation of the schismatic Polish National Church. The theory of the triple melting pot states that religion supersedes country of origin as the source of ethnicity in the United States after the third generation. If so, then Catholics in America had no ethnic identity at the time Wirth was writing about them. The only identity they had was in the eyes of the class which perceived them as a threat. The Catholic ethnics were particularly vulnerable in this regard; they were regarded as a group by the people who wanted to attack them, but they couldn't look beyond the bounds of national origin to prepare a pan-Catholic defense, assuming that they were even aware of what was going on at the time. Since psychological warfare demanded stealth to insure its effectiveness, it was clear that they weren't going to find out what was going on for a long time, certainly not when the war was going on and the normal channels of communication had been shut down in the name of national security. So at the same time that the Catholic ethnics were being called upon to assert their patriotism and fight in a European war – often, as in the case of Italy and Germany, against their countries of origin – the psychological warfare establishment had targeted them as a fifth column and, therefore, as fair game for the panoply of whatever black operations the intelligence community thought they deserved.

Wirth's designation of Catholic ethnics as "groups whose national origin makes them suspect" was not only an example of pure ethnic prejudice; it was also a clear violation of the bond of citizenship which, officially at least, was supposed to unite all Americans regardless of race, creed, color, and national origin. Wirth and the people he worked for in the intelligence establishment were involved in nothing less than a clandestine redefinition of what it meant to be an American, and more than that they were also allowed a free hand in creating operations that would amount to a covert attack on certain citizens simply because their country of origin had made them "suspect." As subsequent events would show, the manipulation of housing for political ends would form the foundation of that attack.

John J. McCloy, who presided over the creation of the OSS and the CIA in Washington, had the same animus against what Teddy Roosevelt called hyphenate-Americans but was if anything less scrupulous when it came to constitutional guarantees than Wirth was. McCloy, according to Bird, was "prepared to have the government do things in the name of national security that might offend certain 'constitutional' sensibilities."[8] McCloy insisted that "Department X," his name for the government's newly created central intelligence agency, establish counter-propaganda units for Italians, French, Czechs, Poles, and "all other races" in the United States. Neither McCloy nor anyone else in the intelligence community seems to have been troubled by the fact that most of these people were American citizens. Similarly, "none of these men questioned the propriety of having a government agency secretly plant propaganda in newspapers read by American citizens. McCloy was not insensible to such civil-liberty concerns, he just discounted them in the present emergency."[9] It soon became clear to the people working with McCloy that he considered the law a hindrance to the effective application of psychological warfare. As a result he was pushing his boss Stimson "to the edge of illegalities,"[10] using the war as justification. "The war effort will necessarily entail extensive centralization of power," he wrote, "We have to restrain our liberties to preserve them, and in my judgment, we should be prepared to restrain them far more than the country now gives indication of being willing to accept."[11] This was particularly true, he believed, for Americans of Japanese and German ancestry. When the war against fascism became the Cold War, the same arguments were used time and again to justify more centralization of power, including "a broad range a covert activities carried out in the name of the national-security state."[12]

As part of this undeclared war on ethnicity, Wirth goes on to propose the paradigm of change that will become normative in the period following the war, namely, "the shift from a caste-like relationship to a class relationship."[13] The solution, in other words, to the threat ethnic communities posed was to break them up by inducing in them a desire to move up the economic ladder into the middle-class, where the organs of the dominant culture – public education, advertising, and the mass media – and not foreign-language newspapers and customs associated with religion and family and country of origin determined the group's norms. "Whatever we may think about the desirability or undesirability of a class-structured society," Wirth continued, "it can at least be said that the latter offers more hope for eventual equality of opportunity on the basis of individual merit. While the status of the person as a member of a minority is ascribed to him on the basis of attributes over which he has no control, the dominant ideology of America still is to confer status on the basis of earned, as distinguished from inherited or categorically ascribed, characteristics."[14]

In other words the notion of class is more congenial to social engineering because it is easier to manipulate according to economic force and mass-media propaganda techniques. The identification with class rather than ethnos, which Wirth got from his younger days as a Communist, was the classical Marxist solution to what Stalin called the nationalities problem in the Soviet Union, and thanks to the efforts of people like Louis Wirth, it would become the American solution as well. Wirth was convinced that the substitution of class for ethnos as the engine of assimilation would work because it had been so effective in his own life.

Louis Wirth was born in Gemuenden, a town near Koblenz in Germany on August 28, 1897, to a family of Jewish cattle merchants who had lived in the area, in fact in the same house, for four centuries. Wirth, the adult sociologist, would later go on to scorn Gemuenden as a paradigmatic example of narrow, provincial small-town life. There is some indication that he felt the same way while growing up because when a relative who had emigrated to the United States offered to bring Louis over to further his education, Wirth leaped at the chance. After excelling in the public-school system in Omaha, Nebraska, Wirth won a scholarship to the University of Chicago, where he quickly became a politically engaged academic by joining the many Marxist student organizations which were active on campus during World War I. Wirth's daughter claims that his attachment to Marxism "seems never to have been very deep,"[15] and then she conveniently leaves out the references to Lenin and Stalin in his mature writings which would contradict that statement. His attachment to Stalin's solution to the nationalities question in the Soviet Union is one example of this selective omission. Wirth's conception of the nationalities issue was formed during the days of the united front, when socialist, Communist, and Democratic New Deal policies on certain issues were indistinguishable. One of those issues was their attitude toward fascism and the attraction to fascism, which, in the minds of people like Wirth and Stalin, certain ethnic groups shared. Wirth, who died in 1952, was considered an expert in the field of sociology on the topic of ethnicity and never changed his essentially Marxist views of the relationship between ethnos and class, but he did adapt them to changing circumstances.

Like many Jews of his generation, Wirth assimilated with an alacrity which must have caused consternation to his relatives in Germany. In 1923 he married Mary Bolton, a Baptist from Kentucky, who had also gone to the University of Chicago, to become a social worker. "In marrying her," Wirth's daughter writes,

> Wirth was the first member of his family to marry a non-Jew. . . . Wirth's assimilationist inclinations and principles, like those of his wife, partly derived from their common reaction against dogmatism and provincial ethnocentrism. Their two daughters were to be encouraged in agnosticism with audible atheistic overtones, at the same time that they were to acquire a "generalized minority" ethnic identification.[16]

In 1926, Wirth received an appointment as an assistant professor at the University of Tulane in the department of sociology. It was his first introduction to the race situation in the South, but it was also an introduction to another group that would occupy his thinking as a sociologist, namely, Roman Catholics, and the influence they had over the local culture, specifically education. After word got around that Wirth's speeches to various local groups were "pro-birth control," his contract for the 1930 academic year was not renewed. Instead, Wirth received a fellowship from the Social Science Research Council for a chance to study in Europe, just as fascism was on the rise in Germany. Between 1932 and 1937, all of Wirth's relatives would leave Germany, and most of them would emigrate to the United States. While in Europe Wirth received an offer for an associate professorship from the University of Chicago and so could take up his position there just as Franklin D. Roosevelt was taking his in Washington. Wirth began his professional career in earnest with the threat of fascism fresh in his mind, but with the equally potent threat which Catholicism posed to his academic career as well, something which probably linked the two phenomena in his mind. At least this is the impression that his writings give. Catholics, he found out first-hand, did not like what he had to say and were willing to use their political clout to prevent him from saying it in not only religious institutions but public institutions where they wielded local political power. Like Wilhelm Reich, another German Jewish Marxist immigrant, Wirth saw the Catholic Church in America in a different light from the way his WASP contemporaries did. As a result of growing up in an essentially Protestant country, they had long seen the Catholic Church, because of what had happened in England, as malign but essentially marginalized. Wirth's view was much closer to Reich's sense that the Catholic Church was the main competitor to Marxism for the mind of modern man, primarily because both systems were more all-encompassing than the essentially *laissez-faire* English ideology.

Given his Marxist politics, his repudiation of traditional religious belief, and his assimilationist attitude toward ethnicity, it is not surprising that Wirth would be drawn to the internationalist cause during the days preceding World War II. Like his New York counterpart, Robert Moses, Wirth saw ethnicity as retrograde and something which was to be replaced by faith in things rational and enlightened. The irony, of course, is that in espousing the Enlightenment, Wirth was also espousing what one might call internationalist ethnocentrism, which is to say, the views of the dominant ethnic group in the United States at that time, the WASP East Coast establishment, as defined by the interests of the Rockefeller family, which had created the University of Chicago, Wirth's employer, and the modern social sciences along with it. By identifying with the cause of the Rockefeller family and the ethnic interests they represented, Wirth became a paradigm of the assimilation he would impose on his fellow Americans. This meant not repudiating ethnicity in the interest of class – although that's what Wirth claimed he did – but rather exchanging one ethnic identification for another. Wirth was a paradigmatic example of what Digby Baltzell urged in his 1963 book *The Protestant Establishment*, the Jew who rose to a position of acceptance in the WASP ruling class by internalizing their cause and using the latest scientific advances (in the social sciences) to do their bidding. By doing what he did, Wirth endowed ethnicity with something less than ultimate value. Ethnos was, as Lenin and Stalin believed, subordinate to class. In the United States, membership in "the middle class" would serve the same purpose that absorption into the proletariat would serve in the Soviet Union. Assimilation would function as an instrument of control. Just as the Communist Party was the official explicator of the interests of the working class in the Soviet Union (and therefore the instrument which controlled them), the regime represented by the combination of advertising, behaviorism, and psychological warfare that went by the name of communications theory in America would become the official explicator of the interests of the middle class in the United States. In both instances, class replaced ethnos as a form of political control. Unlike the nativists and people like Henry Ford, the East Coast WASP elite was perfectly willing to adopt Jews into their class if the adoptee was willing to espouse the same Enlightenment environmentalist philosophy they espoused and, an issue which would gain more importance over time, if he was willing to endorse the same contraceptive sexual practices.

Wirth's attitude toward ethnicity would exert a profound influence on his activities during the war while working for the OSS and the OWI, activities which involved monitoring the dismantling of the America First offices in Chicago and then monitoring ethnic newspapers there too. "I can think of no more important task on the domestic front," Wirth wrote to Clyde Hart, his boss at the Office of War Information on September 23, 1943, "than close and continuing analysis of the minority press, not only as it reflects attitudes but as it reflects emerging organizations, activities and orientations to the changing events of the war and our diplomacy."[17] In addition to running the OWI, Hart was the head of the National Opinion Research Council, also located at the University of Chicago. To Fullerton Fulton, president of the OSS Foreign Nationalities Branch, Wirth wrote a note explaining the importance of knowing "the current relations between the Slovaks and Hungarians in the United States (leaders, different groups and the broad masses); the Hungarians and the Rumanians; the Czechs and the Poles; the Bulgarians, Slovenes, Serbs, and Croats."[18] This is important because of the "problems of war-cooperation and loyalty then arise."[19] Wirth goes on to assure Fullerton that "we are not policemen," which means "we are not concerned with sedition, secret meetings, sabotage and betrayal." "That," Wirth adds, "is the province of the F.B.I."[20]

Wirth made no bones about his suspicion of the groups that were traditionally known as "ethnic," i.e., the recent immigrants from Southern and Eastern Europe. Like Stalin, his mentor on the nationalities issue, Wirth considered ethnics as a fifth column which could not be trusted to serve the interests of the ruling class. Those interests became national-security issues once that elite succeeded in maneuvering America into war.[21] In this he shared the political views of the psychological-warfare establishment as well as the ethnic prejudices which undergirded them. The purpose of psychological warfare as it was resurrected at the University of Chicago in the late '30s was ultimately ethnic. The WASP elite used their advanced communications techniques to prevent ethnic groups in America from communicating with their countries of origin but also to disrupt communications among the members of those groups in the United States as well. "At heart modern psychological warfare has been a tool for managing empire," writes Christopher Simpson, "It's primary utility has been its ability to suppress or distort unauthorized communication among subject peoples, including domestic U.S. dissenters who channeled the wisdom or morality of imperial policies."[22]

As war approached, the Rockefeller Foundation clearly favored efforts designed to find a "democratic prophylaxis"[23] that would immunize the United States' large immigrant population from the effects of Soviet and Axis propaganda. In 1939, the foundation organized a series of secret seminars with men it regarded as leading communication scholars to enlist them in a effort to consolidate public opinion in the United States in favor of war against Nazi Germany – a controversial proposition opposed by many conservatives, religious leaders , and liberals at the time.

According to Harold Lasswell, a CPI alumnus and participant at the secret conferences at the University of Chicago, the WASP elite ("those who have the money to support research," as Lasswell put it) "should systematically manipulate mass sentiment in order to preserve democracy from threats posed by authoritarian societies such as Nazi Germany or the Soviet Union."[24] Once the threat of fascism became too great to ignore, sociology at the University of Chicago became another word for psychological warfare, and the target for this warfare on the domestic front became Catholic ethnics.

But Wirth's interest in sociology as a form of domestic espionage had a different ethnic component as well. Wirth was a member of B'nai B'rith, and would eventually get elected to the executive board of the Anti-Defamation League in 1947, when he was heavily involved with the Chicago Housing Authority in their battles over integrated housing in the city. During the 1930s, the American Jewish Committee brought two British agents (or social scientists) to the country – Sir Solly Zuckerman and Sir Eric Rowle – to help them create their own domestic intelligence agency. The ADL set up its domestic political intelligence operation, which would work in collaboration with Division Five of the FBI, the group Wirth felt was responsible for "secret meetings, sedition and betrayal," at around the same time. What all of these Jewish groups had in common was a desire to be engines of assimilation. Claiming to be an ethnic organization, the American Jewish Committee was in fact an ethnic-assimilationist organization which, in the immediate post-war period, "did not shrink from sacrificing fellow Jews on the altar of anti-Communism." by "offering their files on alleged Jewish subversives to government agencies."[25]

All of these groups were interested in psychological warfare. All of them got interested in real estate as well, especially when public housing became a tool of social engineering by being caught up into the war effort. Philip Klutznick, the man who created Park Forest, the first post-World War II suburb in Chicago, would eventually go on to become president of B'nai B'rith. Both Wirth and Klutznick were on the board of governors of the Metropolitan Housing and Planning Council of Chicago during its stormiest years, which to say between 1944, when they started to engineer Chicago's ethnic neighborhoods, and 1954, when the ethnic counter-attack succeeded in getting Elizabeth Wood fired as the head of the Chicago Housing Authority. When B'nai B'rith co-sponsored the Chicago Housing Rally on February 15, 1950, Wirth was one of the speakers, along with Wood and Samuel Freifeld, director of the Discriminations Department of the Chicago Branch of the ADL. But trouble began brewing in Chicago long before that.

In April of 1943, a riot broke out outside the newly constructed Frances Cabrini Homes in Chicago. As the name indicates, the housing project was intended primarily for poor Italians. When the CHA engaged in the same bait-and-switch tactics the PHA had engaged in Philadelphia by diverting the Richard Allen units to black defense workers, violence ensued and gunshots were fired into an apartment occupied by blacks. Ultimately war aims triumphed in Chicago as they had in Philadelphia. That meant that the 380 Italian families dispossessed by the project were not able to return to the neighborhood. "Bitterness," Hirsch writes, "turned to hatred as blacks proved the primary beneficiaries of the project's change in status. The *Defender* hailed the rapid integration of the area and proclaimed, over optimistically that Little Hell was become a 'Seventh Heaven' for blacks."[26] Something similar would happen in Detroit.

Wirth's attitude toward ethnicity would exert a profound influence on his attitude toward housing. As the Cabrini riots showed, the main challenge to social engineering during the period beginning with America's entry into the war was the engineering of a *modus vivendi* between suspect ethnics, who controlled the neighborhoods of the large industrial cities of the north, and much needed black defense workers from the South. In the mind of people like Louis Wirth, race and social engineering were two sides of the same coin. Since social engineering believed that man was a function of his environment, housing, along with education, would become a crucial area of cultural contestation once the social engineers had the levers of political power securely within their grasp.

Notes

1   Louis Wirth, "The Present Position of Minorities in the United States," Symposium 4/10/41, Louis Wirth papers, University of Chicago archives, box LI, folder #10.

2   Ibid.

3   Ibid.

4   Ibid.

5   Ibid.

6   Ibid.

7   Ibid.

8   Kai Bird, *The Chairman: John J. McCloy and the Making of the American Establishment* (New York: Simon & Schuster, 1992), p. 95.

9   Ibid., p. 119.

10   Ibid., p. 120.

11   Ibid., p. 131.

12   Ibid., p. 128.

13   Louis Wirth, "The Present Position of Minorities in the United States."

14   Ibid.

15   Louis Wirth, *Louis Wirth on Cities and Social Life* (Chicago: University of Chicago Press, 1964), p. 336.

16   Ibid., p. 337.

17   Letter, Wirth to Clyde Hart, 9/23/43 Louis Wirth Papers, Box XXVIII, Folder 10 Office of War Information, Archives, University of Chicago.

18   Letter to Fullerton Fulton, Louis Wirth Papers, Box XXVIII, Folder 10 Office of War Information, Archives, University of Chicago.

19   Ibid.

20   Ibid.

21   Cf. Robert Stinnett, *Day of Deceit: The Truth about FDR and Pearl Harbor* (New York: Simon & Schuster, 2001).

22 Christopher Simpson, *Science of Coercion: Communication Research and Psychological Warfare 1945–1960* (New York: Oxford University Press, 1996), p. 8.

23 Ibid., p. 22.

24 Ibid.

25 Norman Finkelstein, *The Holocaust Industry: Reflections on the Exploitation of Jewish Suffering* (London: Verso, 2000), p. 15.

26 Arnold R. Hirsch, *Making the Second Ghetto: Race and Housing in Chicago 1940–1960* (Cambridge: Cambridge University Press, 1983), p. 45.

Louis Wirth Meets Gunnar Myrdal

In early March 1939, Wirth received a letter from a Swedish diplomat by the name of Gunnar Myrdal, thanking Wirth for their recent meeting in Chicago. Myrdal had been recruited by the Carnegie Foundation two years earlier to "review the most serious race problem in the country."[1] The Carnegie Foundation chose a Swede to do the study because they wanted someone from "a nonimperialistic country with no background of domination of one race over another" who "would approach the situation with an entirely fresh mind."[2] The fact that Myrdal and his wife Alva had distinguished themselves as committed socialists and feminists by that time certainly did nothing to lower their standing in the eyes of the Carnegie Foundation either. Carnegie, while certainly not the biggest of the foundations based on the fortunes which the robber barons had amassed during the late 19th and early 20th century, was arguably the most left-wing. At the time Myrdal was recruited, it was run by Alger Hiss, who would eventually go on to be convicted of perjury in one of the most famous espionage trials of the century. Hiss, documents released after the fall of the Soviet Union in 1991 would reveal, was a Communist agent who had access to Roosevelt at Yalta when the fate of eastern Europe was decided for the post-war period. He was also a man who symbolized one side of the political struggle at mid-century in America as effectively as Senator Joseph McCarthy of Wisconsin symbolized the other. Like the opposing ranks in psychological warfare during the war, Cold War politics in the period immediately following had an ethnic component as well. The WASP elite considered Hiss one of their own, every bit as much as Irish Catholics from Boston identified with McCarthy. When William Bundy, brother of McGeorge, contributed $500 to the Hiss legal defense fund, McCarthy subpoenaed him to appear before his Senate committee, precipitating a crisis at the State Department which eventuated in McCarthy's demise, when the WASPs successfully mounted their counterattack against what they perceived as the Catholic-led insurgents.

Louis Wirth was not just a one-time consultant on the project that eventually produced the book known as *The American Dilemma*. He would go on to write at least eight chapters of it and have a profound influence over the way the clueless Swede framed the race issue in it. In fact, given the historical circumstances surrounding the writing of the book, it is safe to say that *The American Dilemma* was essentially ghost written by the American intelligence community with Myrdal as their front man, something the book's chronology makes apparent. The Carnegie people contacted Myrdal in August of 1937. After turning them down once, Myrdal finally decided to become involved in a study on a topic of which he had had no experience. In fact, his ignorance is one of the reasons he got chosen for the job. The first memorandum on the planning of the research to be undertaken was then submitted to the Carnegie Foundation on January 28, 1939. The Nazis invaded Poland eight months later. In April of 1940, they invaded Denmark and Norway, and it is at this point that Myrdal, always the Swedish patriot, decided to break off research on blacks in America and return home. At this point, he left the project, to use his words, "in the capable hands of Samuel A. Stouffer,"[3] a man whom he identifies as a sociologist at the University of Chicago. What Myrdal does not tell us is that in handing the project over to Stouffer, he was placing it in the hands of the American psychological warfare establishment as well.

After being dissolved after World War I, the group of people who made up the Committee of Public Information under Frank Creel, America's first psychological-warfare establishment, were reassembled during the late '30s under the aegis of the Rockefeller Foundation during a group of seminars at the University of Chicago. The big foundations – Carnegie, Ford and Rockefeller – all contributed to the creation of communication science/psychological warfare in the pre-World War II period. Indeed, since the government contributed no funding at all in this period, what goes by the name of psychological warfare/communications theory was solely a creation of the foundations and operated with their interests in mind. That meant getting America into the war by defeating the America First crowd, but it also meant at first monitoring and then disrupting communications between groups of "ethnic" Americans who still had strong ties to their European countries of origin. Ethnic in this instance meant of course primarily Germans and Italians, but it also meant virtually every other nationality group from Southern and Eastern Europe and, with the exception of the Irish, virtually none of the ethnic groups from Northern and Western Europe.

Since Myrdal's book *The American Dilemma* originated at the instigation of the Carnegie Corporation and ended up in the hands of Louis Wirth and Samuel Stouffer, it was probably a project of the psychological-warfare establishment from its inception. Christopher Simpson makes clear that the arsenal of the psychological-warfare establishment included black operations, i.e., the "clandestine targeting of the U.S. population, in addition to that of foreign countries, for psychological operations."[4] What Simpson doesn't specify is which groups got targeted, a gap which can be filled by investigating Louis Wirth's wartime activities. In his paper, "Problems and Orientations of Race Research in the United States," Wirth praises Myrdal's *American Dilemma* as giving "fresh impetus to the social-psychological approach to the wider issues of racial and cultural relations" as "no other work of social science in America" has done.[5] Myrdal's book is a clear repudiation of the earlier racist/biological school of thought in America, the one which grew out of nativism and isolationism and spawned things like immigration quotas and IQ tests. According to Wirth, the purpose of Myrdal's book on race,

> derived from the democratic value system to establish the scientific untenability of a policy seeking to perpetuate a caste-like society. The more the assumed traditional beliefs in biologically rooted and ineradicable racial and ethnic differences could be shown to be either unfounded or such differences as existed could be demonstrated to be the product of different historical and cultural conditions, the more indefensible became the position of those who opposed a policy of greater equality of opportunity for minorities. Fortunately, in this instance, the products of scientific research served as an effective instrument in the pursuit of democratic values.[6]

Wirth is being more than a little disingenuous here. Since the book was written with those goals in mind by people in the intelligence community like Louis Wirth and Samuel Stouffer, it is hardly coincidence that it supports their agenda. As early as 1940, Wirth was perfectly clear in sketching out the connection between a peaceful settlement of the racial situation and America's emerging role as the preeminent power in the world. Internationalism in foreign policy and anti-racialism in domestic policy were, from Wirth's point of view, two sides of the same coin.

"To us today," Wirth wrote in 1940, "it appears as if the day of sovereign states is over." If the war were going to bring about the end of the nation state, that "new world order" would necessitate the creation of "a form of world government going far beyond the tenuous structure represented by the League of Nations":[7]

> What we have known as sovereign nations in the past may have to be transformed into cultural provinces in the future. The line of demarcation between affairs domestic and foreign will become considerably blurred and men the world over will be each other's keepers to an extent hitherto undreamt of. In short, what is required is that the world which has been created and shrunk by modern technology, by propaganda, and by the bonds of interdependence and mutual vulnerability that have been molded by the free flow of goods, of men and of ideas will have to take on the institutional and legal cast of a cosmos.[8]

That means "the disappearance of such special privileges as tariffs and trade barriers."[9] It also means that when the war is over, America "will not be able suddenly to disband our armed forces and to relapse into an isolationist slumber."[10] It means, in short, the creation of the American Imperium. The main domestic impediment to America's position as leader of the "emerging new order," however, is its still unresolved racial issue. The new international order will require a new domestic order, "for only insofar as no nation will be able to maintain racial, caste and class barriers within will it be inclined to keep the peace without."[11]

Accomplishing this will not be easy – "the translation of this vision into concrete reality, into constitutions, laws, forms of administration, and police power will encounter many serious obstacles from all sides – but there is no going back to isolationist slumber; there is no alternative to racial integration" because we cannot attempt "to sell something to them [the rest of the world] which we have not been able to sell to ourselves."[12] What Wirth fails to mention is that achieving this goal meant waging war on the ethnic communities in the United States which made up virtually all of its big cities. Wirth also fails to mention that this war is going to be waged not on foreigners, but on fellow citizens, people he already views with suspicion because of their religious and ethnic cohesion.

The only way that America could obliterate the last remnants of the race-based caste system which the isolationists created and assume its role as leader of the world is by the steady application of social engineering to America's less-enlightened communities. In *Brown v. Board of Education of Topeka, Kansas*, the Supreme Court's epoch-making race decision, Gunnar Myrdal's book, *The American Dilemma*, is cited as a crucial intellectual influence and as the decision's scientific underpinning. That decision, in conjunction with *Berman v. Parker*, handed down six months later, meant that the court, as the WASP establishment's representatives, had given its official stamp of approval to Wirth's theories of ethnicity.

The American Dilemma is a huge book, over 1,000 pages in length. Its message is simple though: human nature is changeable, and it will be changed by social engineering. The immediate impetus for social engineering was brought on by the war with fascism and enabled by the defeat of the isolationists, whose policy was based on outmoded ideas of race. But its effects will continue after the war. In fact, the main thrust of it will take place after the war. Americans, so the Swede Myrdal warns, better get used to social engineering. The race issue is, in this regard, the thin end of a very large wedge that will soon have enormous repercussions on where people would live and where their children would go to school. America, according to Myrdal, needs to solve its race problem before it can assume its role as leader of the coalition against fascism and then leader of the new internationalist world order following fascism's defeat. Myrdal's vision of the future is both frank and chilling:

> From the point of view of social science, this means, among other things, that social engineering will increasingly be demanded. *Many things that for a long period have been predominantly a matter of individual adjustment will become more and more determined by political decision and public regulation.* We are entering an era where fact-finding and scientific theories of causal relations will be seen as instrumental in planning controlled social change. The peace will bring nothing but problems, one mounting upon another, and consequently, new urgent tasks for social engineering. The American social scientist, because of the New Deal and the War, is already acquiring familiarity with planning and practical action. He will never again be given the opportunity to build up so "disinterested" social science[13] (My emphasis).

"Social engineering of the coming epoch," Myrdal continues, "will be nothing but the drawing of practical conclusions from the teaching of social science that 'human nature' is changeable and that human deficiencies and unhappiness are, in large degree, preventable. . . . We have today in social science a greater trust in the improvability of man and society than we have ever had since the Enlightenment."[14]

The suspicion that Myrdal was merely a front for the psychological-warfare establishment becomes unavoidable when one considers the people he contacted almost immediately after he began his research. It becomes inescapable when one considers who took over writing the book when Myrdal left the country. After he left the United States for Sweden in 1940, it was these people who literally wrote his book for him. One of them was Louis Wirth, like Samuel Stouffer a University of Chicago sociologist and as such another member of the psychological warfare establishment. Louis Wirth was a seminal thinker for the OSS and the OWI during the war, and it was in this capacity that he came up with the policy that would eventually inform both *Berman* and *Brown*. The policy he proposed would come to be known as "integration," but in reality the policy he articulated was what Lenin and Stalin would have called the Soviet solution to the nationalities question.

These two issues – the behavior of blacks from the South and "ethnics" from the

North as it impacted the war effort – were really two sides of the same coin, what Lenin and Stalin would have called America's nationalities problem. Since the Carnegie Corporation had proposed Myrdal's study in 1937, the nationalities issue had been on the establishment's mind for some time before America's entry into the war. But the issue was given new urgency by America's entry into the war. Suddenly, the country which had lately suffered huge unemployment was now faced with a labor shortage. Total mobilization required unprecedented numbers of men to staff the armed forces, but more importantly it required even more men to staff the factories that would build the armaments that those men needed to defeat fascism. America had traditionally solved its labor problems by unlimited immigration, but that source of labor ended in the early 1920s when nativists put immigration quotas in place. Now that the war was on, that group of people wasn't available anyway. That meant that there were only two sources of untapped labor in the United States: women and blacks from the South.

As part of his clipping file, Wirth kept an article citing fellow psychological warrior Samuel A. Stouffer's claim that more than 400,000 blacks migrated to the North during 1939–40. That migration, as of early 1942 when the article was written, promised to be just the tip of the migration iceberg, because since the government had taken action curbing the unions' ability to strike, "manpower [was] the greatest hazard."[15] Wirth and Stouffer and the people they worked for lost no time answering the question, "where will American industry get the manpower that will be absolutely essential, 10 or 12 months from now, for a productive task of simply colossal dimensions."[16] The answer is simple: "In the opinion of some best-qualified observers they can be found only among two classes of America's population, among women and among the American Negroes. . . . America's rearmament can only hit its ultimate supreme stride if both women and Negroes are employed on a very large scale."[17] More than any other factor, war manpower needs explain the internationalist establishment's interest in the race issue, and their subsequent involvement in the social engineering of the housing issue. This engineering was necessary from their point of view because "the Negroes' attitude toward the national crisis can become an exceedingly grave problem unless government leaders swiftly gain some comprehension of the situation."[18]

The United States could not win the war if blacks continued as sharecroppers down South. The South was not an important area either politically or economically as far as the internationalists were concerned. ("The white South," Myrdal wrote, "is itself a minority and a national problem."[19]) It was important only as a source of much-needed labor, at a time when most white southerners concurred because they no longer needed them to chop or harvest cotton and considered migration a simple solution to their biggest social problem. The foundations which did the thinking for the internationalist ruling class quickly realized that that flow of labor into the factories of the industrial North was impeded less by the system of political segregation in the South than by what they would eventually term the de-facto housing segregation in the North, which meant, in effect, the existence of residential patterns based on ethnic neighborhoods. The logistics problem facing Wirth and his colleagues in the psychological-warfare establishment was not so much how to move the black up from the South – the wage differential and the railroads would accomplish that – but rather where to put him when he got there. Northern cities like Chicago,

Detroit, and Philadelphia were essentially an assemblage of neighborhoods arranged as ethnic fiefdoms, dominated at that time by the most recent arrivals from Southern and Eastern Europe as well as the Irish and the Germans.

As Wirth makes clear in his sociological writings, any group that has this kind of cohesiveness and population density had political power, and the question in his mind was precisely whether this political power was going to be used in the interests of the WASP ruling elite, who needed these people to fight a war that had nothing approaching majority support among ethnics of the sort Wirth viewed with suspicion. This group of "ethnic" Americans posed a problem for the psychological-warfare establishment because it posed a problem to the ethnic group that made up that establishment. This group of people constituted a Gestalt – ethnic, Catholic, unionized, and urban – whose mutual and reinforcing affiliations effectively removed them from the influence of instruments of mass communication which the psychological-warfare establishment saw as critical in controlling them. If one added the demographic increase this group enjoyed – as Catholics they were forbidden to use contraceptives – it is easy enough to see that their increase in political power posed a threat to WASP hegemony over the culture at precisely the moment when the WASP elite was engaged in a life-and-death struggle with fascism. It was Wirth's job to bring them under control, lest they jeopardize the war effort.

The people in Chicago "whose national origin" made them "suspect," continued living in their ethnic neighborhoods after the war ended, but with fascism defeated, the same group of people who was concerned about their loyalty before the war could now devote their efforts to engineering them now full time. As Wirth had indicated in various passages in *The American Dilemma*, social engineering would be focused on race and housing. "Integration" as defined by Louis Wirth and ratified by the Supreme Court in *Berman* and *Brown* meant first and foremost solving America's nationality problem, and that meant bringing the ethnic neighborhood under control. Once the war was over and the danger of German and Italian fascism receded, the same groups who were living in the same impenetrable ethnic neighborhoods in Chicago began to be identified more by their religion than by their country of origin. Even as early as 1941, Wirth was concerned about "a corresponding shift in religious affiliation of the American population" which had created a "nation now a little over one-third Roman Catholic."[20] In the parlance of psychological warfare, ethnic would increasingly come to mean Catholic, especially in the period following the war. And in the ethnically balkanized cities of the North, it was this group of people who presented the greatest obstacle to Wirth's concept of "integration," much more so than the challenge posed by de-jure segregation in the politically and economically insignificant South.

The nationalities problem required, as a result, two forms of social engineering tailored to suit the two groups who needed it most. The strategy of the psychological-warfare establishment involved manipulating the two subjugated groups – Protestant blacks and ethnic Catholics – in the interests of a group of people who felt that America could not become leader of the world in the new internationalist order unless it solved its nationalities problem. One attribute which both the blacks, who had to be moved up from the cotton fields of the South to the factories of the North, and the "ethnics," the largely Catholic immigrants from Southern and Eastern Europe, who had developed neighborhoods that were still functioning largely outside the media/propaganda machine created to control the population at large, shared was their retrograde attitude toward religion, something which was significant from the point of view of the social engineers because it affected their attitude toward sex and therefore had an impact on their fertility. "The strength of church and religion in America," Myrdal writes, "presents another inhibition. Specifically, the fundamentalistic Protestant religion in some of the regions where fertility is highest in the South, and the Catholic Church in the big Northern cities are against discussions of population policy."[21]

Although the immediate problem was the war, employment, and housing, the long-term problem was demographic. Both blacks and Catholics were outbreeding the "native" Protestant population, a fact that concerned Myrdal every bit as much as it concerned Madison Grant, the theoretician of the now-defeated Nativists:

> The increase for the whites was fastest during the last century when they gradually became able to control deaths but had not as yet brought births under control. The whites are, however, now in the second phase of this dynamic sequence: the white birth rate is falling so fast that it is catching up with the relatively stable death rate. The population expansion of the whites is now slowing down, absolutely and relatively. Many of the Western nations, including America and all those other peoples on the highest level of industrial civilization, will probably start to shrink in population numbers within a few decades. The colored nations, on the other hand, are just entering the first stage where expansion is likely to be pushed by an increasingly improved control over death, and it is unlikely that the increase in birth control will keep pace with the improvement of the control over death. The whites will, therefore, from now on become a progressively smaller portion of the total world population.[22]

The racist, nativist Madison Grant-inspired wing of American politics, which was defeated at Pearl Harbor, was also concerned about differential fertility but attempted to solve the problem in the same way Hitler did by things like coercive sterilization. In fact, Hitler got the idea for his racial laws from Madison Grant, as Grant himself used to brag.[23] As a result of the bad name these methods had acquired, new methods were needed, methods consistent with an internationalist foreign policy and a domestic policy based on environmentalist social engineering. Because of Hitler's racial theories, the form of social engineering proposed for blacks had to be eugenic in a way that was not Hitlerian. It also had to be compatible with the American system, which put a premium on education and self-interest.

> The main international implication is, instead, that America, for its international prestige, power, and future security, needs to demonstrate to the world that American Negroes can be satisfactorily integrated into its democracy. In a sense, this War marks the end of American isolation. America has had security behind two protecting oceans. When now this isolation has been definitely broken, the historians will begin to see how it has always greatly determined the development of America.[24] . . .

Moreover, in this War the principle of democracy had to be applied more explicitly to race. Fascism and nazism are based on a racial superiority dogma – not unlike the old hackneyed American caste theory – and they came to power by means of racial persecution and oppression. In fighting fascism and nazism, America had to stand before the whole world in favor of racial tolerance and cooperation and of racial equality. It had to denounce German racialism as a reversion to barbarism.[25]

According to Myrdal (or more probably Princeton demographer Frank Notestein, who is listed as an advisor to the book), "The most direct way of meeting the problem, not taking account of the value premises in the American Creed, would be to sterilize them. The fact that most whites would want to decrease the Negro population – particularly the lower class Negroes – would strengthen the argument for sterilization of destitute Negroes."[26]

Hitler and the war against fascism had made this option unusable. As a result, the social engineers had to come up with a policy which would guarantee the same results, which Grant and the nativists wanted but without the same association with nativism, racism, and, now, fascism. "If we forget about the means, for the moment," Myrdal writes,

> and consider only the quantitative goal for Negro population policy, there is no doubt that *the overwhelming majority of white Americans desire that there be as few Negroes as possible in America.* If the Negroes could be eliminated from America, or greatly decreased in numbers, this would meet the whites' approval – *provided that it could be accomplished by means which are also approved*[27] (my emphasis).

The American Dilemma as a result zeroed in on education as the solution to its dilemma, and its emphasis on education eventually bore fruit in the Supreme Court's *Brown* decision in 1954. Myrdal makes the role of education as a form of social engineering clear in *Dilemma*:

> As we have already seen, the whites' desire to decrease the Negro population becomes, even in regard to birth control, entirely overshadowed by quite other valuations centered on the health and happiness of individual parents and children, which are all backed by the American Creed shared by the Negroes. The full possibilities of these latter valuations in permitting a birth control policy in America have not yet been realized. Under their sanction birth control facilities could be extended relatively more to Negroes than to whites, since Negroes are more concentrated in the lower income and education classes and since they now know less about modern techniques of birth control. On this score there would probably be no conflict of policy between Negroes and whites.[28]

Myrdal's idea of combining eugenics and public education would eventually find expression in the school-based clinics established in Chicago's (and other cities') public schools to distribute contraceptives to its pupils. By the end of the century, black resistance to contraception had been worn down by public education, media propaganda, and the War on Poverty, but at the time Myrdal wrote it was still formidable. In fact it was the biggest internal obstacle to engineering the black race at that time. "A more serious difficulty," Myrdal continues, "is that of educating Southern Negroes to the advantages of birth control. Negroes, on the whole, have all the prejudices against it that other poor, ignorant, superstitious people have."[29] Assimilation of blacks meant first of all education, and that could not take place if blacks were confined to ghetto schools. The sheer density of population would create a culture of its own which would be typically black and, given the views of this "poor, ignorant, superstitious people" on matters sexual, that would mean continued resistance to birth control, which would mean that the black/white differential in fertility would continue unabated and continue to be seen as a threat by the not-so-fertile ruling class whites and as a result would continue to reinforce prejudice and segregationist attitudes on their part as well, contributing to further balkanization and isolation of the already non-mainstream ethnic population. The only way to break this vicious circle was to intervene directly and simultaneously in the area of both education and housing, policies which were placed in effect after the war and which were contested before the Supreme Court in 1954.[30]

Notes

1 Gunnar, Myrdal, *An American Dilemma: The Negro Problem and Modern Democracy* (New York: Harper and Row, 1962), p. lx.
2 Ibid.
3 Ibid., p. liv.
4 Christopher Simpson, *Science of Coercion: Communication Research and Psychologoical Warfare 1945–1960* (New York: Oxford University Press, 1994), p. 13.
5 Louis Wirth, "Problems and Orientations of Race Research in the United States," Box LIII, folder 1, Louis Wirth Papers, Archives, University of Chicago.
6 Ibid.
7 Louis Wirth, "Prerequisites for Peace," 1940, Louis Wirth Papers, Archives, University of Chicago.
8 Ibid.
9 Ibid.
10 Ibid.
11 Ibid.
12 Ibid.
13 Myrdal, p. 1022.
14 Ibid., p. 1024.
15 "U.S. Must Call Negro Workers, Stowe Asserts," Louis Wirth papers, Box LXVII, folder 6.
16 Ibid.
17 Ibid.
18 Ibid.
19 Myrdal, p. 1010.
20 Louis Wirth, "The Present Position of Minorities in the United States," Box LI #10.
21 Myrdal, p. 167.
22 Ibid., p. 1017.
23 Mary Meehan, "How Eugenics Birthed Population Control," *The Human Life Review* (Fall 1998): 81.

24 Myrdal, p. 1016.
25 Ibid., p. 1004.
26 Ibid., p. 176.
27 Ibid., p. 167.
28 Ibid., p. 176.
29 Ibid., p. 180.
30 Ibid., p. 627.

Environmentalism and the Ethnic Neighborhood

Given the now-dominant assumption that man was a function of his environment, the main obstacle to the successful integration of blacks into the northern urban work force was the urban ethnic neighborhood, and since schools were a function of neighborhood, housing became the crucial issue in the battle over integration in the post-War period. Myrdal warns against the person who "in his private dealings with people to whom he does not feel akin, has dangerous traditions derived from exploitation of new immigrants."[1] According to Myrdal, the social paradox in the North is exactly this, "that almost everybody is against discrimination in general but, at the same time, almost everybody practices discrimination in his own personal affairs."[2] In order to break out of this impasse, social engineering is needed. Attitudes have to be changed. Prejudice has to be uprooted. Once again the war was used as the cover which would allow large scale social engineering and widespread disruption of traditional living arrangements and the traditional rights associated with them. "The War," Myrdal writes, "will force this change forward step by step. After the War, in the great crisis of demobilization and liquidation, mass unemployment will be a main problem. Large-scale public intervention will be a necessity. In this endeavor no national administration will dare to allow unemployment to be too much concentrated upon the Negro."[3]

Given the environmentalist assumptions of the engineers, it is not surprising that housing would provide the first arena for social engineering after the war. "It seems of urgent importance that residential segregation and all the connected problems of black housing become the object of scientific research with more practical vision than hitherto. The general structure of this complex problem is clear-cut and ready for social engineering," Myrdal wrote. "The strategic time for this planning work is now."[4]

> After the War a great increase in private and public building is likely, since housing construction has been moribund for several years, and popular needs seemed about to cause a building boom when the War started and diverted the construction industries' efforts into the field of defense housing. Also, the War will leave in its wake a tremendous need for public works and private investment to prevent a new and more devastating world depression. To be maximally useful this housing boom should be planned in advance.[5]

The housing boom in question here took place largely in the suburbs, places like Levittown on Long Island, which got built in 1947, and Park Forest, which got built outside Chicago one year later. All of the relevant studies stress the social-engineering aspects of the suburbs, an attitude which William Levitt himself expressed when he said, "No man who owns his own house and lot can be a Communist. He has too much to do."[6]

Another word for the social engineering which the suburbs accomplished was

"Americanization." In his history of the interstate highway system, Arnold Rose gives his version of how this happened:

> During the decade following World War II, most Americans, including state road engineers, believed that immigrants to the nations' cities were busily and eagerly going about the business of becoming "Americanized." Serious scholars of American culture and history reinforced the popular impression which learned publications identify a "triple melting pot" in which the barriers of ethnicity, if not race, collapsed into three generally comparable religious traditions. As part of this vast changeover, researchers pointed out that the children of immigrants from Italy, Ireland and Russia intersected one another in the suburbs and along the cool green rim of every city. Many Americans, again including state road engineers, believed that Americanization and movement to the suburbs accompanied one another in a nearly effortless fashion. Above all, the trolley and then the automobile, by facilitating the process of outward movement, were valuable adjuncts to certain and beneficial change. State road engineers, with their passion for traffic service and cheap land in crowded neighborhoods near downtown, could thus readily imagine that they were only giving another nudge to inevitable progress.[7]

William O. Whyte, one of the early chroniclers of the first post-World War II suburbs, saw pretty much the same thing. The suburbs "have become the second great melting pot,"[8] he wrote in *The Organization Man*. When the residents of Park Forest and Levittown moved into their new homes, they exchanged their ethnic identification with their new identification of themselves as "middle class." "This expansion of the lower limits of the middle class," Whyte continues, "is happening in towns and cities as well, but it is so pronounced in the new suburbs *that it almost seems as if they were made for that function*"[9] [my emphasis]. Even furniture played a role in this transformation. "Home furnishings," Whyte writes, "are another symbol of emancipation. Merchants are often surprised at how quickly their former customers in city stores discard old preferences when they arrive in suburbia. "They won't touch 'Polish Renaissance' any more," the manager of a chain store in Levittown, Pennsylvania told me."[10]

The suburb as engine of assimilation was described by Myrdal a full ten years before William O. Whyte wrote his book. The discrepancy in time is easy enough to understand. Whyte was describing the suburban phenomenon empirically after it had happened. Myrdal was describing the intention behind the plan the foundations had concocted to solve the nationalities problem before the plan had been put into effect. In both *a priori* and *a posterior* accounts, the role class plays in assimilation is crucial. Neighborhoods have always had a dual identity in America. They functioned as an index of ethnicity but they also functioned as an index of class. The two indices were in fact related because certain ethnic groups traditionally occupied the upper-class neighborhoods (the WASP) and the lower-class neighborhoods (the blacks) and the neighborhoods in between (the ethnics).

The key maneuver in engineering the ethnics out of their neighborhoods was, as Wirth already knew, getting them to identify more with class than with ethnicity. A move to the suburbs was desirable in this regard for a number of reasons. First of all, it was *ipso facto* a move up into the middle class. Secondly, blacks were excluded from middle-class status primarily because they were excluded from suburban housing. This meant that the crime that invariably accompanied black migration could be used as the stick to chase ethnics out of their neighborhoods. Moving to the suburbs meant a move into a world safe from the dangers and insecurities which racial succession had created in the vulnerable ethnic neighborhoods in the cities. "All the various national groups of immigrants have," Myrdal tells us, "for reasons of economy and ethnic cohesion, formed 'colonies' in the poorer sections of Northern American cities."[11] Blacks from the South were no exception to this rule. In fact the tendency to ethnic cohesion is "particularly true of Southern-born Negroes who have been brought up in a strict ethnic isolation enforced by the Jim Crow laws and the racial etiquette in the South."[12] A group which was less dogmatically environmentalist in its thinking might have said that it was "natural" for ethnic groups to want to live together in large American cities, but Myrdal was speaking for a group which disbelieved in the concept of nature –human, social, or otherwise. At the very least, the WASP foundations saw ethnicity as a problem which called for engineering in light of other priorities. And what they wanted to bring about most by their engineering was assimilation or "Americanization," and they wanted to bring this about for various reasons, the most obvious of which was control:

> For when the members of a national group become so "assimilated" that they no longer regard members of their ancestral group as closer than persons of the dominant group in the society – when they feel themselves to be more American than Italian, Polish, or Czech – they tend to disregard ethnic affiliation in seeking a residence and to pay more attention to their personal needs and their ability to pay rent.[13]

The assimilated are by that very fact more amenable to the suggestions of advertising and the other communications instruments of the dominant culture, which function as a form of social control in the interests of the ruling class. In addition to the lure of middle-class status – the carrot of assimilation, so to speak – the ethnic neighborhood is also vulnerable to the stick of racial succession. "When white residents of a neighborhood," Myrdal tells us, "see that they cannot remove the few Negro intruders and also see more Negro families moving in, they conjure up certain stereotypes of how bad Negro neighbors are and move out of the neighborhood with almost panic speed."[14]

Integration, which we have adumbrated here in terms used by the psychological-warfare establishment, was one large black operation waged against the residents of certain neighborhoods in Chicago and elsewhere. "It must be stressed," Myrdal (or Wirth) writes in *The American Dilemma*, "that if white people insist on segregation – and if society is assumed not to tolerate a socially costly sub-standard housing for Negroes – *the logical conclusion is that, in a planned and orderly way, either areas now inhabited by whites or vacant land must be made available for Negroes.*"[15]

Since vacant land meant new housing in the suburbs, it meant housing that blacks for the most part could not afford, but it also meant housing they could not get even if they could afford it because the FHA and the banks it controlled would not give mortgages to blacks who wanted to live there. The Federal Housing Administration, which would not insure new home mortgages for blacks, according to Goddard, created thousands of new settlements like Levittown across the country by "encouraging banks to lend on millions of new low-risk suburban homes while openly refusing to stake money on older city properties."[16] One FHA manual cautioned: "Crowded neighborhoods lessen desirability" and that "older properties in a neighborhood have a tendency to accelerate the transition to lower class occupancy."[17]

The fact that virtually all of the nation's new housing was built in the white, de-ethnicized suburbs during this period of time meant that the only real area of expansion for black housing was housing already inhabited by "whites," which is to say ethnics living in the cities. By forcing the emptying of ethnic neighborhoods, Wirth's system killed two birds with one stone: it opened up new areas for black migration and at the same time it broke up the suspect ethnic neighborhoods by driving their inhabitants to the suburbs, where they were assimilated. Solving the race problem in housing meant breaking up those neighborhoods and making them available to racial minorities who were not welcome in the neighborhood precisely because of their ethnicity.

At some point in the period under discussion, it became obvious that "integration" was nothing more than an unattainable ideal or a meaningless fiction. The system of social engineering that was erected in this country after the war needed that fiction as justification for a housing policy which was ultimately segregationist in intent. The system involved allowing ethnic neighborhoods, "areas now inhabited by whites" to "be made available for Negroes." The dispossessed white ethnics would then be driven to the suburbs where they were "Americanized" according to class – each suburb would be segmented according to price – and absorbed into the mainstream of American life, which is to say, subjected to the controls imposed by media culture and the car.

"This War," Myrdal wrote, echoing Wirth's view, "is crucial for the future of the Negro, and the Negro problem is crucial in the War. There is bound to be a redefinition of the Negro's status in America as a result of this War."[18]

Throughout this discussion, I have been citing Myrdal whenever I have quoted from *The American Dilemma*. In questions of ethnicity however, it would probably make more sense to cite Wirth as the source of the ideas than it would to cite Myrdal. In the same way, the best gloss on the blueprint which the foundations, the psychological-warfare establishment, and the urban planners had for postwar housing developments would be Wirth's writings during the early to mid-'40s, when the strategic plans for post-war social engineering were cast. His writings give the rationale behind the development of the post-war housing boom, which was based on driving Catholics out of their ethnic neighborhoods into the suburbs and replacing them with docile black workers from the South.

Wirth at one point refers to ethnicity as "reminders of a dark past."[19] Taking the Nazis as his model of everything wrong with ethnicity, he tries to formulate the United States policy as the antithesis of that policy. The Nazis, he writes "are openly trying to turn the clock of history back to where such a state of affairs would be the general condition of mankind for all but the 'master race.'"[20] Whereas most forward-looking men are ashamed of the survival of such archaic conditions, "the Nazis are boastfully attempting to resurrect them as part of an alleged 'New Order.'"[21] We, on the other had, writes Wirth, speaking for the WASP elite, "in the future . . . can hope to be even freer from the crystallization of any part of our population into permanent minority status."[22] That means in the America which Wirth visualizes for the future, there will be no ethnic division because there will be no ethnic groups to divide up the population. All will be Americans. That means in particular that in that same future that "it would probably be too much to expect that the totalitarian doctrines of racism, of religious intolerance and of political dominance will leave us free to pursue uninterruptedly our policy of uncoerced assimilation of minorities."[23] If we eliminate all of the double negatives, Wirth seems to be saying that the social engineers are planning to embark on a policy of coerced assimilation of minorities.

That suspicion is reinforced by a close reading of another paper Wirth did around the same time on minority groups. "As the war approaches a climax and the nature of the peace to follow becomes a matter of public discussion," he writes,

> the minorities question again moves into the center of world attention. . . . Unless the minorities problem, especially on the continent of Europe, are more adequately solved than they were upon the conclusion of World War I, the prospects for an enduring peace are ominous. The influence which the United States will exert toward the solution of these problems abroad is contingent upon what transpires on the domestic scene in the molding of a national conscience and policy toward American minorities, for it is unlikely that our leaders in their participation in the making of the peace will be able to advocate a more enlightened course for others than we able to pursue ourselves.[24]

The record of minority groups left to their own devices, according to Wirth, is not good. Here Wirth is talking not just about the Germans and Italians, with whom the United States was at war, but specifically the Poles, who were ostensibly our allies. "The none too generous treatment accorded by the newly emancipated Poles between the two World Wars to the Ukrainian, White Russian, Lithuanian, Jewish and other minorities allotted to the Polish state offers another case of the lack of moderation characteristic of militant minorities once they arrive at a position of power."[25] There may be some residual atavistic Jewish anti-Polish animus at work here, but a more likely explanation of the animus comes from the situation in Chicago, not Europe. The Poles were perhaps the most tenacious of all the ethnic groups that Wirth wanted to integrate. They were behind the protest against the Sojourner Truth housing project in Detroit in 1942 and over the course of the next forty years would oftentimes have to be literally driven out of their neighborhoods by fire, the arsons surrounding the demolition of Poletown for the building of a GM plant in Detroit being just such an example. "If a group should by accident of history and geography find itself united on a great range of cultural characteristics and fairly densely concentrated in a compact area so that the contrast between its status and that of its neighbors stands out sharply, the emergence of that group as a minority is almost inevitable."[26] The foregoing description had much more relevance to Chicago in the mid-'40s than it did to Poland in the period between the wars. The same danger existed in Chicago in the period following the war.

If ethnicity was bad "from a military point of view . . . because it weakens national loyalties and solidarity,"[27] then the attitudes of the people inhabiting Chicago's ethnic neighborhoods were going to be just as inimical to America's interests during the Cold War as they were during the war against fascism. In the case of Poland, the change of wars was fraught with even greater significance, because after the war Poland was officially a Communist country, and people like Wirth had little or no way of knowing where the sympathies of Chicago's Poles lay.

If the continuing existence of ethnic enclaves constituted bad news from Wirth's point of view, there was good news too, and as usual in moments like this Wirth adverts to the future in general and the future of social engineering in particular: "if science has demonstrated anything, it has shown conclusively that these traits are subject to human intervention, that they can be changed. The possibility of the ultimate assimilability of ethnic groups is thus beyond doubt."[28] But even if this is true, Americans still need models to show how it is to be done, and it is in coming up with models for solving our nationalities problem that Wirth is forced to show his political hand. "In recent years," Wirth writes,

> the Russian experiment is regarded by many as not only at least as enlightened as our own, but as much more relevant to the minority problems of Europe and the backward nations of the world. It is generally agreed among students of the problem that the Soviet nationalities and minorities policy represents one of the most outstanding achievements of the revolution and the period of reconstruction and that it holds great promise for the settlement of minority problems in the coming peace. . . . The Soviet Government under Lenin's leadership and with Stalin as Commissar for Nationalities, proceeded immediately after the Bolshevik revolution to inaugurate a policy which accords with the best scientific knowledge and the most *enlightened moral principles*[29] (my emphasis).

And what did Wirth have in mind when he praised Stalin's handling of the nationalities question in the mid-'40s? The answer depends on which Stalin Wirth is talking about. If it's the Stalin of the early period, or if he is referring to Stalin's writings, Wirth is talking about assimilation. If Wirth is talking about Stalin's deeds in the mid-'40s, however, he is talking about something more sinister, namely, ethnic cleansing. According to Pohl, Stalin's regime, which Wirth proposes as the model for solving America's nationalities problem, "pursued ethnic cleansing as part of its overall security policy."[30] In 1937 Stalin deported Soviet Koreans to central Asia. In 1941, he deported the Volga Germans to Siberia, and in 1943 he deported the Kalmyks from their home just west of Astrakhan to Kazakstan. The 1937 deportation of the Koreans had been kept secret, but the deportation of the Volga Germans and the Kalmyks were announced in official Soviet ukases when their ethnic soviet republics were abolished by Stalin. Since Wirth was working as one of the leading theoreticians of our military-intelligence establishment at the time, it is unlikely that he was unaware what was going on.

In a secret speech before the Supreme Soviet in 1956, Nikita Khrushchev described the practical application of "the enlightened moral principles" undergirding Stalin's nationalities policy:

> All the more monstrous are the acts whose initiator was Stalin and which are crude violations of the nationality policy of the Soviet State. We refer to the mass

deportations from their native places of whole nations, together with all Communists and Komsomols without any exception; this deportation action was not dictated by any military considerations.

Thus, already at the end of 1943, when there occurred a permanent break-through at the fronts of the great patriotic war in favor of the Soviet Union, a deci-sion was taken and executed concerning the deportation of all the Karachai from the lands on which they lived. In the same period at the end of December 1943, the same lot befell the whole population of the Autonomous Kalmyk Republic. In March 1944 all the Chechen and Ingush people were deported and the Chechen-Ingush Autonomous Republic was liquidated.

In April 1944, all Balkars were deported to faraway places from the territory of the Kabaidine-Balkar Autonomous Republic and the Republic itself was renamed Autonomous Kabardine Republic. The Ukrainians avoided meeting this fate only because there were too many of them and there was no place to which to deport them. Otherwise, he would have deported them also.[31]

Khrushchev's reference to the Ukrainians elicited "laughter and animation in the hall,"[32] we are told. His speech indicates that even Stalin had limitations placed on his power. Even he couldn't deport the Ukrainians. The same constraints were *a fortiori* true in the United States. But as in the Soviet Union, when a political group in the United States lacked demographic mass and political power, as did the Japanese on the west coast, it was deported and interned in camps. Since there were literally millions of "ethnics" with flourishing communities and corresponding political power in the United States, they fell into the same category as the Ukrainians in the Soviet Union: "There were too many of them, and there was no place to which to deport them" if deportation meant internment camps. In addition to that, they were needed for the war effort and so other means were necessary to insure that they did not function as a fifth column. Deportation was impos-sible, but ethnic cleansing can take numerous forms, and it can be adapted to any number of different circumstances.

Since the Japanese lacked the demographic clout of the Ukrainians in the Soviet Union and the Germans and Italians in the United States, they were subjected to an offi-cially sanctioned governmental policy of ethnic cleansing and deported to internment camps spread out through the desert areas of the western United States. The architect of that deportation was another member of the intelligence community, John J. McCloy. Reacting to a January 4, 1942, column in which syndicated Hearst columnist Damon Runyon reported (falsely) that a radio transmitter had been discovered in a Japanese boarding house, Congressman Leland M. Ford wrote to McCloy's boss, Secretary of War Stimson, demanding that "all Japanese, whether citizens or not, be placed in inland con-centration camps."[33] McCloy then went to work drafting Executive Order 9066, which Franklin Roosevelt signed into law on February 19, committing America, as Stalin had committed the Soviet Union at around the same time, to an official policy of ethnic cleans-ing. McCloy was still defending what the ACLU in 1981 called "the greatest deprivation of civil liberties by government in this country since slavery"[34] at war's end. When four German saboteurs were arrested on June 3, 1942, burying uniforms and explosives on the beach of Long Island, McCloy saw to it that they were electrocuted on August 8, a month after their trial had begun and only six weeks after the first of them had been caught. McCloy would have been in favor of putting German Americans in concentration camps but, like Stalin when confronted with the Ukrainian situation, "he recognized that this was impractical, given the large numbers and the widespread integration of the German ethnic minority in American society."[35] When the president of McCloy's alma mater raised the issue of Japanese internment with McCloy, McCloy claimed that the camps not only contributed "in solving the Japanese problem in this country," they also "afford a means of sampling opinion and studying their customs and habits in a way we have never before had possible. We could find out what they are thinking about and we might very well influence their thinking in the right direction before they are again distributed into communities."[36] Ethnic cleansing, in other words, was justified by the contribution it might make to the social sciences, which could then be put to use for social engineering of the Japanese and other ethnic populations after the war.

What concerns us here are the similarities between the Soviet and American solutions to the nationalities question during World War II. Both Wirth and McCloy in the United States and Stalin in the Soviet Union considered certain ethnic groups as traitors simply because of their ethnic background; both Wirth and Stalin felt that certain groups of people would have to be moved; both Wirth and Stalin felt that the labor of these groups was nonetheless essential for the war effort and that that transplanted labor would contribute to the economic development of the regions to which they were moved; both Wirth and Stalin felt that class was more important than ethnicity (for Stalin the class ideal was the proletariat; for Wirth the middle class). Both Wirth and Stalin were committed to engineering suspect ethnic groups for economic and political gain. "We may thus summarize the whole Soviet position on nationality as follows," writes Robert Conquest. "Communist theory present the national question as secondary and ephemeral. National interests are to be sacrificed where necessary to the interest of the proletarian revolution. These are normally to be identified with the interest of large Communist nations."[37] The same could be said, *mutatis mutandis*, of America's solution to the nationalities issue under Wirth's leadership. Class in both instances takes precedence over ethnos, but in America the role of assimilator was assumed by the middle class not the proletariat. Most importantly, Wirth, like Stalin, believed that certain ethnic groups were ipso facto traitors:

> For all the internationalist rhetoric of the preceding decades, it was obvious that Stalin no longer believed – or never had done – in the new 'Soviet man' whose loyalty was to the 'supra-national' USSR rather than to his ethnic nation. Stalin presumably feared that the Soviet Germans' loyalty would be to the practically unknown country of their distant forbears, now ruled by an abominable regime, and not to their adopted country in which they had lived for many generations; though as a realist he was no doubt aware how abominable his own regime was, after the collectivization holocaust, to a nation of hard-working farmers. The Volga Germans were therefore regarded as a 'fifth column' of 'spies and saboteurs' (though there is no evidence of any having ever been discovered) and exiled to remote areas beyond the Urals, where the local inhabitants, suitably 'prepared' by the authorities, treated the deportees as traitors.[38]

Wirth said virtually the same thing about minorities in the U.S.

> That the totalitarian nations of Europe have substantial representation of their sub-
> jects or former subjects here is a fact worth emphasizing in the light of their
> extended conception of nationality. If to this group be added the descendants of
> these foreign born residents who presumably are at least in part subject to the ide-
> ologies of their respective mother countries, we get an impressive segment of our
> total population.[39]

According to Pohl, "The Stalin regime embraced the ethnic prejudices of the former
Tsars. Despite their Georgian origins, Stalin and Beria behaved like Russian chauvin-
ists."[40] The same could be said of Wirth, the assimilated Jew, who adopted the prejudices
of the WASP ruling class, in particular their feelings toward Catholic ethnics, as part of
his own personal assimilation process. Like Stalin, Wirth also saw a financial benefit to
ethnic cleansing. Just as the black sharecroppers from the South would provide the labor
force to win the war and create prosperity afterward, so The Volga Germans would bring
their agricultural know-how to the empty Asian sectors of the Soviet Union:

> The deportations also provided a secondary benefit to the USSR. They provided
> the Soviet government with a supply of labor to develop the economy of Siberia,
> Kazakhstan, Central Asia, and other sparsely populated areas. The Stalin regime
> assigned the exiles in special settlements to agricultural work, animal husbandry,
> fishing, lumber preparation, mining, construction, and industrial work. Exiled
> national minorities greatly assisted the economic development of Siberia,
> Kazakhstan, and Central Asia.[41]

The Soviet deportations would continue up till 1949, the entire period during which
Wirth was active in both intelligence work and housing policy in Chicago. With Stalin as
his model, the man who was the brains behind our nationalities policy became a promoter of ethnic cleansing – American-style, which is to say a program promoting "integration" in housing where class replaced ethnicity as the criterion of where one lived. When
Ferd Kramer, president of Metropolitan Housing and Planning Council of Chicago, issued
the rationale for the choice of public housing sites in the city on August 23, 1948, one of
the reasons he gave in support of pubic housing projects was that "It will open new neighborhoods to occupancy by the non-white families."[42] Louis Wirth was listed as being on
the MHPCC board of directors at that time, along with Park Forest developer Philip
Klutznick.

The ethnic groups which could not be trusted would have to be moved, but ethnic
groups as large as the Germans, the Italians, the Poles, and the Irish, which could not be
rounded up like the Japanese and interned in camps in the desert, would have to be moved
by other means. In the American system, the suburbs were the engine of ethnic assimilation into the "middle class." Otherwise Wirth agreed with Stalin on basic principles. "The
strategic time for this planning work is now," Myrdal (or Wirth) wrote in *The American
Dilemma*:

> After the war a great increase in private and public building is likely, since hous-
> ing construction has been moribund for several years, and popular needs seemed

about to cause a building boom when the War started and diverted the construction industries' efforts into the field of defense housing. Also, the War will leave in its wake a tremendous need for public works and private investment to prevent a new and more devastating world depression. To be maximally useful this housing boom should be planned in advance.[42]

Notes

1 Gunner Myrdal, *An American Dilemma: The Negro Problem and Modern Democracy* (New York: Harper & Row, 1962), p. 1010.

2 Ibid.

3 Ibid.

4 Ibid., p. 627.

5 Ibid.

6 Kenneth T. Jackson, *Crabgrass Frontier: The Suburbanization of the United States* (New York: Oxford University Press, 1985), p. 231.

7 Mark H. Rose, *Interstate: Express Highway Politics 1939–1989* (Knoxville: University of Tennessee Press, 1979), p. 116.

8 William H. Whyte, Jr., *The Organization Man* (New York: Simon & Schuster, 1956), p. 300.

9 Ibid., p. 299.

10 Ibid., p. 301.

11 Myrdal, p. 620.

12 Ibid., p. 619.

13 Ibid., p. 620.

14 Ibid., p. 623.

15 Ibid., p. 627.

16 Stephen B. Goddard, *Getting There: The Epic Struggle between Road and Rail in the American Century* (New York: Basic Books, 1994), p. 200.

17 Ibid.

18 Myrdal, p. 997.

19 Louis Wirth, Morale and Minority Groups, Louis Wirth Papers, University of Chicago Archives. LI, #10.

20 Ibid.

21 Ibid.

22 Ibid.

23 Ibid.

24 Louis Wirth, "Minority Groups," Louis Wirth Papers, University of Chicago Archives.

25 Louis Wirth, "Negroes in the South," Louis Wirth Papers, University of Chicago Archives.

26 Ibid.

27 Ibid.

28 Ibid.

29 Ibid.

30 Otto J. Pohl, *Ethnic Cleansing in the USSR 1937–1949* (Westport, Conn.: Greenwood Press, 1999), p. 137.

31 Robert Conquest, *The Nation Killers: The Soviet Deportation of Nationalities* (New York: The Macmillan Company, 1960), p. 144.

32 Ibid.

33 Kai Bird, *The Chairman: John J. McCloy and the Making of the American Establishment* (New York: Simon & Schuster, 1992), p. 147.

34 Ibid., p. 154.

35 Ibid., p. 163.

36 Ibid., p. 165.

37 Conquest, p. 133.

38 Bohdan Nahaylo and Victor Swoboda. *Soviet Disunion: A History of the Nationalities Problem in the USSR* (New York: The Free Press, 1990), p. 90.

39 Louis Wirth, "The Present Position of Minorities in the United States," Louis Wirth papers, University of Chicago archives.

40 Pohl, p. 3.

41 Ibid., p. 4.

42 Statement of the MHPC 8/23/48 presented by Ferd Kramer, President to the Housing Committee of the City Council. Louis Wirth Papers, University of Chicago archives, Box XXVII, folder 1.

43 Myrdal, p. 627.

The War Comes to Detroit

In May of 1941, one month after Louis Wirth gave his paper outlining the threat that Catholic ethnics posed to the internal security of the United States, the Division of Defense Housing Coordination under Charles F. Palmer, issued a report on the housing situation in Detroit which recommended the construction of 11,000 housing units (1,000 of which were to be financed by the government) as the first step in accommodating the workers who were streaming into town to fill the 84,000 newly created jobs in the metropolitan area. Between April of 1940 and the summer of 1945, more than 250,000 people, largely from the South, poured into the Detroit area. Many of them ended up working at the Ford Motor Company's newly constructed Willow Run bomber plant some 15 miles west of the city. The in-migration was so sudden and so intense – 100,000 new residents arrived in the period between April 1940 and September 1941 alone – that it immediately precipitated a housing crisis. Between April 1940 and July 1941, the vacancy rate for the city dropped steadily from 3.5 percent to 0.9 percent, requiring the occupation of virtually uninhabitable structures and the doubling up of families.[1]

The competition for housing inevitably created ethnic conflict, and those conflicts were aggravated by racial and religious differences. The blacks who arrived from the South accounted for the most dramatic increase in population while at the same time, because of their visibility, they were the most limited in terms of the housing options available to them. The Southern whites who came north as part of the same migration brought with them segregationist attitudes, which the Detroit's Catholic ethnics began to adopt as part of the assimilation process that the war was fostering. In addition to those divisions, there was a split in the Protestant attitude according to class. Lower-class Protestants, especially from the South, became anti-black because of direct competition for jobs and housing. Upper-class Protestants, on the other hand, were pro-black because they were not in direct competition but also because education at eastern universities had allowed them membership in national elites, and the national elites, taking their heritage from Yankee universities had, along with a congenital dislike of the Irish and other Catholic ethnics, a history of support for abolition. The Ku Klux Klan also began to take on a new configuration because of the war's promotion of patriotism, becoming as a result less anti-Catholic and more anti-black.

The arrival of the war also meant an exponential increase in federal power, and that meant a corresponding increase in the power the WASP elite could exercise over other sections of the country when they went to Washington to staff the war effort's newly created agencies. That change would upset the balance of power between the local and federal agencies involved in government housing. Since the DDHC was under the jurisdiction of the Federal Works Agency, it bypassed all of the local controls that the local housing authorities had over federal funds under the New Deal Housing Bill of 1937. That meant that once war was declared, the federal government could effectively build what it wanted

Detroit, late 1930s, early public housing

where it wanted it, overriding local objections in a way it could not have done before. The difference between public housing under these two very different auspices would soon become apparent in Detroit, especially if one compared the relatively peaceful occupation of the Thomas Brewster Homes in 1938 with the riots that surrounded the occupation of the Sojourner Truth Housing project four years later. In 1938 the Detroit Housing Commission moved 701 black families into the Brewster Homes without incident, giving some indication that Detroiters had no objection to government housing for blacks as long as the racial make-up of the neighborhood was respected. The riots which ensued four years later when the DHC tried to move black families into the Sojourner Truth Homes at Nevada and Fenelon made the same point in a different, more dramatic way. What had changed in the meantime was America's entry into the war and the commitment of the federal government (and ruling class) to using housing, as Myrdal had indicated it would now be used, as a form of social engineering.

Local geography played a role in the racial conflict that social engineering would create as well. Even government housing projects which respected neighborhood racial make-up would have destabilizing consequences for the areas surrounding them because, as the case in virtually every city where they got built would show, projects never created as many housing units as they destroyed. That meant that even when the federal government's agencies respected the neighborhood's racial make up, the people it displaced inevitably sought housing in neighboring communities, and in Detroit that meant blacks coming into conflict with Poles and Italians.

Gratiot (later renamed Lafayette) Park, Detroit's premier showcase urban-renewal project, displaced both industrial infrastructure (warehouses and factories) and black residences. Both displacements would have adverse consequences for the ethnic communities in the immediate vicinity. Because the city had torn down the warehouses in Gratiot Park, it then needed to tear down the residences in Corktown, an originally Irish neighborhood, in order to build new warehouses and transportation terminals. The black residents who got displaced to make way for the Mies van der Rohe *Wohnmaschinen* ("living machines") that would house the city's governing elite (much as Society Hill Towers would accomplish the same end in Philadelphia) would then seek housing in the next adjacent neighborhoods, which meant that they were driven up the Polish corridor along Chene Avenue into previously Polish neighborhoods. Housing projects like the Sojourner Truth Homes, located north and east of a largely Polish community like Hamtramck, amounted to an attempt to outflank those traditional ethnic boundaries and would create pressure on Polish neighborhoods from two sides instead of one. America's entry into the war meant that the federal government could set up these racial enclaves pretty much where it wanted to. It meant that no neighborhood was safe from subversion. It meant the end of local control over federal housing money as well as the locally autonomous ethnic community. It meant, in other words, a complete abrogation of the articles of peace which allowed the various nationalities to live in harmony with each other. It meant as well the fulfillment of Louis Wirth's prediction that the government could no longer tolerate uncoerced assimilation. "This conception of Americanization," Wirth wrote,

> as a slow, gradual, uncoerced, reciprocal interpenetration of immigrant and native groups and their cultures has had to be subjected to serious reconsideration in the

light of the Nazi and Fascist policy to retain control over their nationals in foreign countries and to use them as spearheads of penetration and conquest abroad. In the face of the propaganda and organizational campaigns of the totalitarian nations even the most liberal wings of the Americanization movement have been forced to ask whether our traditional tolerant attitude toward the immigrant could be maintained without seriously undermining national solidarity.[2]

The WASP elite had been worried about Catholic demographic increase and the political power which went with it for some time. The war allowed them to act on their fears with impunity.

As of 1940, the power over who got to live where, when the government footed the bill, was fairly evenly divided between the local and the federal government. The New Deal Housing Bill of 1937, in order to get passed, had to give local communities veto power over where government housing got built. If the local community didn't want it, they could simply choose not to bring into being the local housing authority, which was the conduit for federal funds. And most small communities did just that. However, once the local housing authority got created, as the case in Philadelphia showed, it invariably attracted those who would benefit from the federal money, and they in turn acted as the local lobby for federal initiatives. The war would simply accelerate this process by increasing the amount of money available and by simultaneously removing local objections in the name of national security. Once the precedent had been established, the same procedural steamroller would be extended by invoking the Cold War and the crusade against communism or the civil-rights movement or any other federally favored social-engineering initiative which had the net result of abrogating property rights. As of 1940, the Poles and other Catholic ethnic groups were powerful locally because of representation on city council; the blacks, however, had the WASP elite and the federal agencies they controlled behind them. As the war increased the power of the federal government to intervene in local affairs, it increased the power local blacks had over housing policy as well.

Unlike the "hillbillies" who brought their segregationist attitudes toward blacks north with them, the Poles had no particular racial animus against blacks in 1940. Government policy would change that within the course of a few months. Much of this came about because of the racial solidarity which the melting-pot mentality brought about. Exposed to the ideas of the white Southern migrants, second-generation Poles "Americanized" in a way that Louis Wirth would have found annoying by adopting the racial stereotypes which had dominated the country from its inception and which had in fact been written into its constitution. Assimilation meant that the Irish, the Poles, and the Italians began to identify themselves as "white" in a way that would have been incomprehensible to their immigrant parents. During the 1919 race riot, Chicago's Poles could refer to "whites" as a race distinct from Eastern Europeans, because in the parlance of the time "race" was often a synonym for ethnicity. The Irish, the Poles, and the Germans all considered themselves members of distinct races, and they were so viewed by the "Anglo-Saxon" race which ran the country.[3]

Unfortunately, the largely Catholic ethnics who were in the process of becoming "white" as part of becoming Americans, failed to understand the revolution which the WASP elite had accomplished by taking power when the war broke out. The immigrants were adopting the categories of Madison Grant and the racialists at the very time these concepts were considered superseded by the environmentalist ideas of the social engineers who ran the foundations, the intelligence establishment, and as a result the higher levels of the federal government.

The racial template which got placed over ethnic conflict in Detroit and other industrial cities of the North would obscure the real dynamics of the struggle, which was ethnic and religious rather than racial. Black in-migrants, as a result, were thrown into direct competition, not with the WASP elite which was orchestrating events, but rather the ethnics – specifically the Poles and to a lesser extent, the Italians – who lived in the neighborhoods immediately adjacent to the black ghettoes that were now filled to the bursting point with people hoping to benefit from the new employment opportunities the war economy provided. This led to some tragic misunderstandings, as blacks possessing their own nativist prejudices started accusing Poles of racism. The Poles who had been born in Europe were generally oblivious to racial concerns. Their children, the Poles who had been born in America, thought that the adoption of racial attitudes was part of the Americanization process. Poles in general wanted to know why they were being singled out as responsible for a situation which antedated their arrival in this country by hundreds of years, and blacks, facing Poles in direct competition for jobs and housing, wanted to know why "too many blacks had been fired to make jobs for 'other racial groups, some of whom can hardly speak our language and owe no allegiance to our flag.'"[4]

The same racial fictions would pervade the nation's housing conflicts for the next thirty years, creating a no-win situation for the ethnics. When ethnics considered themselves Poles, Italians, etc., they were berated as being un-American and a potential fifth column. When they adopted the American racial paradigm and considered themselves "white," however, they were condemned as racists. It was in the interest of the WASP ruling-class elite to portray the ethnic conflicts their federal policies created as racial, because in doing so the real purpose of the programs became invisible to the naked political eye, allowing the WASP elite to pursue a campaign of ethnic cleansing and social engineering under the cover of altruism. "Astonishingly," Capeci writes, "blacks rarely singled out old Americans, the most ideological supremacist, as their nemesis, perhaps because few blacks came into regular contact with them and found identifying difficult. Only the Ku Klux Klan presented blacks with a predominantly old-American target."[5]

As late as the 1980s, during the Poletown incident in Detroit, Coleman Young could do the bidding of the Detroit elite, which was indisputably white, by destroying an ethnic neighborhood to create a GM plant while at the same time portraying the Poles who objected to the destruction of their houses and neighborhood as "racist." The term "race" obscured what was essentially an ethnic/religious conflict based on an ethnic/religious alliance. Since according to the doctrine of the triple melting pot, religion – Protestant, Catholic, Jew – and not country of origin would be the ultimate criterion of ethnicity in America, the Yankee-black alliance should come as no surprise, because both Yankees and blacks were Protestant. Black Protestants and white WASPs found common cause in their opposition to the ethnic Catholics in the middle. The rank-and-file black worker from the South wanted access to the housing stock in these ethnic neighborhoods, and the WASP elite, which had always viewed Catholics with suspicion, wanted those neighborhoods broken up and their inhabitants "Americanized." The Catholic ethnics, on the other hand, largely unaware of the forces arrayed against them, were still plagued by the differences of national origin which had not yet been erased by the triple melting pot. Soon a class schism which paralleled the Protestant class schism would develop within the Catholic Church as upwardly mobile, oftentimes Irish, assimilationist-bent "liberal" Catholics would join upper class WASP converts like Father John LaFarge in the Catholic Interracial Council and plot the "integration," which is to say, the destruction, of the neighborhoods of their less-enlightened, less-assimilated fellow Catholics. In Detroit, that meant that "liberal" bishops like John Dearden and Thomas Gumbleton would adopt the racial categories which the WASP elite had hammered out in Gunnar Myrdal's book and apply them to the detriment of the average Catholic ethnic and the average Catholic parish throughout the archdiocese. But that would not happen until the '60s. The initial Catholic reaction was the sort that the social engineers feared.

Notes

1   Domenic J. Capeci, Jr., *Race Relations in Wartime Detroit* (Philadelphia: Temple University Press, 1984), p. 33.
2   Louis Wirth, "Morale and Minority Groups," LI, #10, Wirth Papers, University of Chicago Archives.
3   John T. McGreevy, *Parish Boundaries: The Catholic Encounter with Race in the Twentieth Century Urban North* (Chicago: University of Chicago Press, 1996), p. 30.
4   Capeci, p. 63.
5   Ibid.

The Mysterious George Edwards

When Edward J. Jeffries became mayor of Detroit in 1939, it was his job to placate the various ethnic groups which got him elected while at the same time finding a solution to the city's housing problem that would offend none of them and, more importantly, offend none of the powers in Washington that were now looking upon Detroit and its industrial infrastructure as the "arsenal for democracy." Jeffries, according to Dominic Capeci "rewarded faithful blacks, ethnics, and whites, though not identically."[1] As a politician he rewarded them according to their clout, and in local politics the Catholic ethnics were much more powerful than the newly arrived blacks from the South, while in Washington the exact opposite was true. During the early months of 1941, A. Phillip Randolph threatened to lead a march of black workers on Washington in June, causing the president to create the Fair Employment Practices Committee in order to keep the much-needed black workers within the New Deal Coalition and on the job producing weapons.

To help him solve this increasingly contentious problem, Mayor Jeffries made an appointment that was at once both controversial and mysterious, by appointing George Edwards as the head of the Detroit Housing Commission in early 1940. Born in Texas on August 6, 1914, Edwards was the son of a lawyer who was both a socialist and actively involved in challenging that state's racial policies. In 1933, at the age of nineteen, Edwards enrolled as a student at Harvard University.[2] Two years later, in December of 1935, Edwards was active enough politically to attend the Socialist Party's political convention and worried about the split taking place in its ranks in a letter to his father. Edward's involvement in socialist politics came at the time of that party's united front against fascism with the Communist Party, a fact which his political opponents held against him. Local publisher Floyd McGriff claimed that Edwards had "cut his eye-teeth on Karl Marx" and "advocated overthrowing the nation's social order, sabotaging munitions factories, creating bi-racial housing and disseminating graphic sexual information."[3]

Edwards arrived in Detroit in November 1936 to take a job as labor organizer with the United Auto Workers, just as they were about to organize a series of violent sit-down strikes under Walter Reuther which would revolutionize the auto industry. Edwards's critics, according to his biographer, "claimed that he was sent by unnamed socialists to infiltrate and radicalize the autoworkers' union."[4] If his purpose in coming to Detroit was to infiltrate, Edwards succeeded beyond all expectation. After supporting Jeffries for mayor in 1939, Edwards found himself a few months later named the head of the Detroit Housing Commission. In a story entitled "Dallas Intellectual to Guide Detroit's Housing Program," *The Detroit News* wondered aloud how a twenty-six-year-old "son of a labor and Socialist lawyer in Dallas,"[5] who had arrived in the city barely three years before with no experience in public life could now be appointed to the head an agency with a $10 million annual budget and plans to build between $60 and $80 million in government housing over the next few years. The answer to this question seems to lie in his political as well as his ethnic connections. Edwards had gone to Harvard when the WASP elite was deeply enamored of the socialist cause and enamored as well of things like urban planning and the command economy. When Harvard went to Washington to prepare for war, Edwards had entrée there as well. Edwards would go on to become a good friend of Eleanor Roosevelt and William O. Douglas, and would become, with them, one of the founding members of the Americans for Democratic Action in 1947.

Consumed with the business of running Detroit during the most rapid industrial expansion in its history, Mayor Jeffries in effect delegated the increasingly contentious housing issue to Edwards, and it was up to Edwards to find a way to placate all of the local parties and the people in Washington as well. That also meant that Edwards could put his thumb on the scale when he wanted events tipped in a particular direction. And that meant, given his ethnic and educational background and his access if not membership in the national elite, that Edwards would come down on the federal racialist side of the housing fight that was looming in Detroit as America lurched toward war.

In January 1941, Edwards abandoned the Socialist Party of his father and his youth and became a Democrat, apparently so that he could run for city council in the upcoming fall election. The ease with which Edwards changed parties belies the constancy of his core beliefs, which did not change when he dropped the socialist label and would not change appreciably for the rest of his political career. He was constitutionally attached to the black cause in a way that was more ethnic than political. Like the rest of the WASP ruling-class elite, he shared certain core beliefs and cared not whether they were made into policy by Socialists or Democrats. One of those beliefs, one which he shared with Eleanor Roosevelt and other members of what was to become the ADA, was an aversion to Catholics. The aversion was deep-seated and ethnic but based even in the '40s on what people like Edwards considered the Church's medieval attitude toward sexuality.

Edwards married Peg McConnell of Detroit on April 10, 1939, something which caused rancor in his wife's family because of his radical beliefs.[6] On February 26, 1941, Edwards wrote to his father, announcing the birth of his son Andy, after sixteen hours of labor and "a major operation."[7] Andy, Edwards assured his father, "was not the result of a mistake in contraception. His conception resulted from an excess of love and the willing-ness to take a rather long chance."[8] To calm his father's fears about the effect another birth might have on his daughter-in-law's health, Edwards goes on to say that "we have been and will continue to practice the most complete and satisfactory form of contraception recommended by our doctors, and I think we need have no fears on that score. . . . In any case we had planned him within a fairly short number of months and were both completely satisfied that Nature took a hand and thereby proved the Catholic method of birth control as untrustworthy as the rest of that religion."[9] Edwards closes his letter by saying that he has to leave for a "hasty Washington trip."[10]

Edwards attitude toward Catholicism would play a crucial role in the see-saw battle over the Sojourner Truth housing project, which would consume his efforts during his tenure as head of the DHC. While Mayor Jeffries saw the housing issue in essentially local political terms, Edwards construed it in more global terms. The East Coast WASP inter-nationalist establishment, which was now running Washington and gearing up for war, saw blacks from the South as essential to the war effort. They also considered Catholic ethnics at best indifferent to the war effort and at worst a potential if not actual fifth column. The crucial issue in this context was housing because the ethnics controlled the neighborhoods of cities like Detroit and saw black migration as a threat to their very existence and the way of life those neighborhoods made possible. It was up to people like Edwards, as agents of the national WASP elite, to used local housing agencies to engineer the consent of Detroit's recalcitrant Catholic ethnics by framing the social engineering of their neighborhoods as a moral, social-justice issue, something like Prohibition, another WASP moral crusade whose purpose was also the weakening of the ethnic community.

Edwards represented the national elite point of view in a way that the more pragmatic Jeffries did not. Understanding the strategic role of housing in the struggle against fascism meant working to assure that Sojourner Truth would be used to house black defense workers, but it also meant placing those black defense workers in ethnic neighborhoods. Metropolitan Detroit, like Chicago, was unlike Manhattan in that it had virtually unlimited possibilities for housing sites in 1940, since at that time the great suburban expansion had not taken place, and there were large numbers of suitable lots both within the city and in the largely vacant suburbs as well. If the goal were simply to house black defense workers, plenty of noncontroversial sites were available. But the purpose of government housing, as both Louis Wirth and Gunnar Myrdal had stated, was more than just giving people a roof over their heads. The purpose was social engineering as well, and that meant mixing the races as a way of homogenizing the country and undermining ethnic loyalty, and the quickest way to do that was to break up ethnic enclaves. Washington's desire to use Sojourner Truth as a form of social engineering (while having Jeffries pay the political price for this decision) first became apparent when federal officials rejected the DHC's first choice for the location of the new defense-worker housing project, an undeveloped site at the northwest corner of Dequindre Road and Modern Avenue. Under pressure from Washington, the DHC chose instead a twenty-acre tract at Nevada and Fenelon in St. Louis the King Parish, a decision which was bound to destabilize the neighborhood. This was true for the Polish residents of the neighborhood, but also for the black homeowners of nearby Conant Gardens, who also objected to public housing because they thought the project would drive the price of their houses down. The federal government further complicated the matter – and further signaled its intentions – when the FHA refused to insure mortgages in the area near the proposed projects, indicating that it was destined to become an all-black ghetto.[11] Over the summer of 1941, the Polish residents of the neighborhood realized that they were being targeted for ethnic cleansing and began to mobilize their counter-attack.

Like his counterpart at Gesu Parish in Philadelphia, Rev. Constantine Dzink was concerned about the effect that racial migration would have on his flock at St. Louis the King Parish in Detroit. Like Gesu, which was predominantly Irish in the 1930s, St. Louis the King was an ethnic parish. According to McGreevy:

> St. Louis the King was a protoype of the tightly bound parish community. In the 1940 parish census, Father Djiuk [*sic*] estimated that only 2 percent of parishioners missed mass on a given Sunday. The 224 children in the elementary school received instructions from an order of Polish nuns. At four of the five packed

Sunday masses in a church that seated over six hundred people, Djiuk gave the homily in Polish, since, as he put it, "the Poles generally like to hear Polish spoken, even those who are born here and whose parents were born here. And I like to have them keep up with their Polish."[12]

Since, in addition to being a baptized Catholic, residency within certain geographical boundaries was the requirement for membership in a particular parish, any change in the conditions of residency had an effect on parish life, and since things like mortgage payments and home ownership affected residency, Rev. Dzink considered them his business as pastor. Like Father Maguire in Gesu Parish, Rev. Dzink was instrumental in creating a local neighborhood improvement association which held regular weekly meetings at St. Louis the King Parish, where its members could listen to invited guest speakers and plan strategy, and, if necessary, organize protests.

By August of 1941, Dzink was worried about the effect the proposed and as-yet-unnamed project would have on real-estate values, and as a result, parish life. He wrote to Defense Housing Coordinator Charles F. Palmer in Washington, worrying that an influx of "primitive southern Niggers"[13] would reduce property values, threaten the safety of white girls, and ultimately "ruin the neighborhood."[14] "This," Dzink continued, "would mean utter ruin for many people who have mortgaged their homes to the FHA. . . . May I feel that I have found a friend in you, Mr. Palmer, and that the many sleepless nights that I have spent in trying to ward off this future danger to my parish and citizens will not prove in vain."[15]

The discussion never got off the ground because the Polish Catholics in the neighborhood had fundamentally different attitudes toward community, race, religion, and morals than their Protestant interlocutors in Washington. The Poles valued community support in an alien culture, and that support and the ethnic solidarity upon which it was based were linked to the Catholic Church, which had specified that religious communities were not the result of free association, as Protestant denominations had become, but rather of living in a particular place. Moving out of the neighborhood for the Poles of St. Louis the King Parish meant not upward mobility, not a better more expensive house and the status that went with it, but rather the destruction of the community upon which they all depended for support. They had, as a result, no desire to move to neighborhoods where this support was lacking. "These national neighborhoods," Saul Alinsky wrote at a later date, when the government was well on its way to dismantling them, "served a significant function in providing a harbor, both economic and cultural, from which the newcomers could occasionally sally forth into the strange American seas about them. After the immigrants and their children had germinated for some time in this cultural cocoon absorbing American information and attitudes in their minds and American money in their pockets, they would emerge and take wing into the non-national American society."[16] Alinsky's half-affectionate, half-patronizing account of the ethnic neighborhood gives an air of inevitablity to something that might not have happened if the government had not decided to make it happen. Poles still lived in Bridesburg and Hamtramck forty-two years after Alinsky predicted that they were emerging from their "cultural cocoon." They would still be living in Poletown if they hadn't been driven out by government force.

The crucial issue at the heart of the Sojourner Truth conflict in Detroit was whose notion of community was going to prevail. The ethnics had one idea; the WASP ruling class had another and was willing to use the power of the government, augmented by the war emergency, to enforce its idea on anyone who disagreed. Part of the government's idea was that race was more important than religion in determining how the local community was organized. As Brand Blanshard had noticed twenty years earlier in Bridesburg, the urban ethnic community was particularly resistant to Americanization because it was, in effect, based on the Catholic faith. What the politicians called a ward was, from the religious point of view, a parish, which is to say a geographically based administrative unit of the Catholic Church. When asked where they lived, Catholic ethnics would more often than not give the name of their parish rather than the name of their neighborhoods. When Irish Catholics from Visitation Parish in Chicago came across strangers in the neighborhood whom they suspected of being Communists, or Jews, or, worst of all, University of Chicago students, they would ask them what parish they belonged to, and if they didn't get a satisfactory answer, would beat them up. Alinsky, who was familiar with the situation in Chicago, notes the intimate connection between religion and neighborhood in the national neighborhood:

> A preponderant number of immigrants, particularly from Slavic nations, were Catholic in religious faith and the role of the Roman Catholic church was that of being a central anchor of security to these immigrants. It was the one familiar part of their life and experience which was the same here as it had been in their native home. In the national churches even their priests spoke their language and practiced the old world customs and traditions.[17]

The same thing was true of St. Louis the King Parish in Detroit, and this lends poignant irony to Rev. Dzink's letters. In addition to the tone problems that go with using words like "nigger" when writing to public officials in Washington, Dzink's reference to the vibrancy of the local Polish parish was precisely the sort of thing that someone connected with the intelligence community would see as suspect, because people like Louis Wirth and Clyde Hart had been briefing them on the situation. No matter how cogent or impassioned his arguments were, Rev. Dzink was writing to Commissioner Palmer at the very moment that the government was beginning to view housing as a form of social engineering necessary to the war effort. That meant that they would look with disfavor, not favor, on Dzink's arguments about the stability of the Polish community. It was precisely this stability, which would have to give place to "integration" as the engine of Americanization and assimilation, that bothered Palmer, Wirth, and Hart.

The mainline Protestant denominations which constituted the WASP elite saw race in increasingly moral terms, something that must have seemed alien to Poles, who looked upon blacks as an ethnic group like any other, which, according to the American system of ethnic federalism in effect until this time, should occupy its own ethnic community. Just as Father Maguire urged the blacks in North Philadelphia to join St. Elizabeth's as their own ethnic parish, so Rev. Dzink was willing to "take up collections for the blacks in his church"[18] so that they could find housing someplace else. The key feature of the housing issue according to Dzink was neighborhood stability. The key issue for the middle-class "American," on the other hand, was upward mobility, and the key issue for the professional housers whose funds came from Washington was social engineering, first to win the war and then to accomplish other ends. According to the middle-class understanding of housing then being promoted by the FHA and other government agencies, one house was just a stepping-stone to a better house. By denying blacks access to their neighborhood, the Poles were denying them opportunity for advancement and full participation in American life. Poles, on the other hand, generally preferred community over advancement. Dzink, for his part, could not understand why his parish was being singled out, and Palmer, initiated into the real reason for the choice, simply could not tell him. To do so would let the social-engineering cat out of the federal-housing bag. Capeci makes many good points about the Polish notion of community and how it differed from the mainstream American view:

> Polish aversion reflected an ethnic concept of home ownership and neighborhood that few government officials or native-born citizens understood. Coming from Eastern European agrarian societies where owning land connoted status, Poles placed the highest priority on purchasing their own houses. Doing so gave families not only prestige but shelter, a way-station for oncoming relatives, and a much-needed source of income from boarders: Polish Detroiters built homes on the far end of lots so street-front rooms could be added as funds became available. More important, proprietorship meant greater control over the neighborhood – an area determined spatially and held together by the local church. To Poles, the parish in which they lived defined their social turf; its customs, friendships, "accepted patterns of behavior," institutions, markets, and streets all provided the "context for life." From this perspective, the Sojourner Truth area represented more than a geographic setting. Poles expressed ethnocentrism and concerns over property values, school enrollments, and community development exactly because they believed that black occupancy would – in Father Contantine Dzink's words – "ruin the neighborhood" or, more precisely, destroy their way of life. Instead of welcoming new neighbors, they mobilized, as had other ethnics in similar settings elsewhere, to protect their economic and emotional investment from outsiders.[19]

But by ignoring the federal government's commitment to social engineering, Capeci makes the conflict sound inevitable when it was not. If Washington had been simply interested in housing black defense workers, they could have accepted the DHC's first recommendation and avoided a lot of unnecessary strife. That they didn't meant that housing had other ulterior goals in mind for the community where it got built, goals which could not be discussed openly, hence the futility of the discussion. Community meant homogeneity to Dzink. What Palmer didn't say in response is that the very homogeneity which the Poles valued had become one of the reasons the neighborhood had been targeted for integration by the intelligence community, which now had its agents in St. Louis the King Parish spying on its parishioners. As Louis Wirth could have told Rev. Dzink, St. Louis the King Parish was considered a threat precisely because it was a strong, supportive religiously homogeneous ethnic community where sermons were delivered regularly in a foreign language. In doing so the Poles evaded the ban on unauthorized communication which the intelligence community felt it needed to establish in order to control them.

By the summer of 1941 the intelligence community was more than just theoretically interested in the ethnic neighborhood. The Office of War Information, which would send Louis Wirth to Detroit to write a report on the 1943 riots, sent an investigator to snoop around St. Louis the King Parish. He concluded that the dispute over the housing project "could better be called a Polish-Black conflict, or a European vs. Black conflict than a white-black conflict."[20] The fact that the government continued to portray it as a racial conflict bespoke their disingenuous attempt to engineer a certain outcome out of it. If it were simply an ethnic conflict, there was no moral charge capable of being attached to it, and that was precisely why the Catholics viewed it more instrumentally than the WASP housers who wanted a certain outcome from it. In an interview with auxiliary bishop Stephen Woznicki, the man responsible for Detroit's 35 Polish Catholic parishes, researchers, which is to say other OWI agents, learned that "he likes to have Catholic people live in Catholic communities. These Catholic communities of single-family homes must include a Catholic church, a Catholic school, and facilities for recreation that meet Catholic standards. The bishop added that these are his specifications for the Poles."[21] Catholic liberals, on the other hand, tended to see the conflict the way the WASP elite saw it, betraying in the process their own prejudices against their co-religionists. Catholic liberals saw the conflict as racial and therefore an issue of social justice rather than ethnic and merely instrumental, with the integrity of the local community as the higher good. Rev. John LaFarge wrote disparagingly about the "painful evidence about the Polish Clergy,"[22] to a fellow priest, disapprovingly noting that "knowing how some of the foreign clergy behave in these neighborhood questions I should be by no means surprised if some of them took an equally unjustified attitude."[23] LaFarge, who was a convert to Catholicism, still viewed some of his fellow Catholic priests as "foreign." As a result, he identified more with the WASP ruling elite he had abandoned on race issues.

Unlike Cardinal Dougherty of Philadelphia, Detroit's Cardinal Mooney overcame his Irish ethnic prejudices and sided with the Poles against the Yankee-black attempt to engineer their neighborhood, concluding that "any declaration of mine which might have a general apologetic value for the Church among the negroes would most certainly have a disastrously disturbing effect on the more than 200,000 Polish Catholics who are a large part of my direct responsibility."[24]

Given the support which the local ordinary gave to his fellow Polish Catholics, it is likely that Rev. Dzink would have prevailed in getting the housing project moved to a more ethnically compatible location, if he could have relied on the local politicians to run their own housing authority. But this is precisely what he could not rely on because of the preparations for war which the Roosevelt Administration was making in Washington. In August of 1941, FWA and USHA representatives decided to proceed with plans to develop the Nevada-Fenelon site without disclosing which racial group was going to live there, all the while assuring their black supporters on the city council that they were recommending the site for black occupancy. In September of 1941, the USHA asked the Detroit Housing Commission to name the city's first defense-housing project. Following the lead of Edwards, the DHC endorsed the suggestion of the commission's only black member, Rev. Horace A. White, pastor of the Plymouth Congregational Church, and called the project the Sojourner Truth Homes, thereby making it apparent that it was intended for black defense workers. Six weeks later, George Schermer, who would move on to Philadelphia to head that city's Commission on Human Relations and engineer neighborhoods there in the '50s and '60s with the help of Dennis Clark, began registering prospective tenants while federal officials were still saying that the question of which race would occupy the homes was still open. At the same time the FHA stopped insuring loans in the neighborhood, something which convinced its residents that they had been targeted for economic extinction. If the housers were attempting to evade the notice of the ethnics, they not only failed, they increased the force of the backlash once the full extent of their duplicity became known.

Notes

1 Dominic J. Capeci, Jr., *Race Relations in Wartime Detroit* (Philadelphia: Temple University Press, 1984), p. 18.
2 Mary M. Stolberg, *Bridging the River of Hatred: The Pioneering Efforts of Detroit Police Commissioner George Edwards* (Detroit: Wayne State University Press, 1998), p. 38.
3 Ibid., p. 75.
4 Ibid., p. 47.
5 Ibid., p. 65.
6 Ibid., p. 63.
7 George Edwards in a letter to his father, Feb. 26, 1941, George Clifton Edwards, Sr. Papers, Walter Reuther Library, Wayne State U. Box 13
8 Ibid.
9 Ibid.
10 Ibid.
11 Capeci, p. 80.
12 John T. McGreevy, *Parish Boundaries: The Catholic Encounter with Race in the Twentieth Century Urban North* (Chicago: University of Chicago Press, 1996), p. 74.
13 Capeci, p. 78.
14 Ibid.
15 McGreevy, p. 74.
16 Saul Alinsky, "The Urban Immigrant," presented at the University of Note Dame, symposium on Roman Catholicism and the American Way of Life, Feb 13, 1959, University of Illinois at Chicago archives, Alinsky papers, box 81.
17 Ibid.
18 McGreevy, p. 74.
19 Capeci, p. 147.
20 McGreevy, p. 74.
21 Ibid., p. 75.
22 Ibid.
23 Ibid.
24 Ibid. p. 76.

The Sojourner Truth Housing Project Riots

In November of 1941, George Edwards, the quondam socialist, won a seat on city council as a newly minted New Deal Democrat. In January of 1942 he left his position as head of the DHC feeling that he had steered the housing project through the shoals of local ethnic politics to where it could do the federal government's war effort the most good. He was wrong. In spite of the attack on Pearl Harbor and American's entry into the war in December of 1941, Edwards's successor, Charles Edgecomb, an Irish Catholic with little sympathy for white "do-gooders" and "those sons of bitches" they worked with in the black community, was determined to undo Edwards's decision. On January 15, 1942, Edgecomb and other members of the DHC board met with Blair Snyder and Charles Palmer and other Washington housing officials. Siding with one of the Polish members of the DHC, and against Rev. White, Edgecomb claimed that a riot would occur if the government attempted to move blacks into the Sojourner Truth Homes. Faced with local opposition, Snyder and Palmer backed down and agreed to place only white families in the Sojourner Truth Homes and to build another project altogether for black war workers. Reflecting the local political balance of power, Snyder later told Rev. White that he would rather have difficulty with blacks than with Poles, for "Negroes did not constitute a serious political threat."[1]

Perhaps not in Detroit, but Snyder miscalculated by underestimating the power which black organizations like the NAACP and the Urban League were amassing under the patronage of the federal government. Upon hearing that the DHC had reversed its decision, its race relations advisor Robert R. Taylor threatened to resign and take the rest of the black-housing establishment with him. One of those people was Robert C. Weaver, who would become head of the FHA in the 1960s and use his influence there to destabilize neighborhoods in Boston and Philadelphia by sharing FHA repossession lists with local black activists. Both the government housing policies and the *dramatis personae* who would implement them were assembled during the war, and this group of people saw the Sojourner Truth case as crucial to their future plans.

Council members who wanted black occupancy and their supporters began to talk about a "Catholic conspiracy"[2] behind the government's change of heart and redoubled their efforts to get the reversal reversed. Local ethnics had nothing but local support, but the Yankee-black alliance could draw on people like Eleanor Roosevelt, who wrote a letter to Cardinal Spellman of New York, blaming the Catholic Church for the racial turmoil in Detroit, adding darkly that the same sort of thing happened in Buffalo when public housing got blocked by Catholic opposition there too. Mrs. Roosevelt knew where Spellman and the people he represented were vulnerable. Catholics, who were always sensitive to their status as hyphenate-Americans and the accusation that, in following the pope, they had divided loyalties, could not afford to appear unpatriotic with the nation at war, and the WASP elite exploited their weakness in this regard, as did the black press, which began to adopt the nativist rhetoric of an earlier era, failing to notice its similarities with in the Madison Grant school of thought, which disliked blacks as much as they disliked Catholics. "The Negro," Catholic ethnics were told if they took the time to read the black press, "was part of this country before the ancestors of these people ever heard of America."[3] Like Louis Wirth, the black press saw a connection between domestic and foreign policy. America could not claim to be champions of freedom with the race problem unsolved, and it was now going to be solved by killing two birds with one stone, by simultaneously housing black defense workers and weakening communities "which were suspect because of their origin."

In the midst of crisis created by government authorities first taking one position and then reversing themselves under pressure, George Edwards wrote to his father from his new vantage point as a member of Detroit's city council, which was now "crowded with protestants and protesters – white and black – each wanting to threaten the dire consequences of failing to do as he wishes."[4] Edwards promised his father to stand firm in favor of black occupancy for the projects but concluded that "There are no answers to the problem."[5] He then goes on to state the issue in terms which ignore the arguments of people like Rev. Dzink in favor of community stability and which would ensure that no answers will be found: "The Negroes have all logic, decency, civilization and ethics on their side. The whites have the simple argument, 'We don't want Niggers living near us' and probably a majority of Detroit citizens on theirs."[6] As a representative of the people of Detroit (there were no local councilmanic seats), Edwards's duty should have been clear to him, but Edwards was involved in a redefinition of the role of local government and morals according to the environmentalist principles of the WASP elite, notions which would largely get implemented by court decisions in the post-war period. The new idea of government Edwards adumbrates in his comments on the Sojourner Truth controversy placed the will of the people he was chosen to represent under a series of constraints which effectively abrogated it in the interests of the national elites, to whom he owed his primary allegiance. "I don't know how the Sojourner Truth issue will turn out," he concludes, watching the federal authorities change their mind one more time, "but I intend to stand my ground."[7]

On February 5, Rev. Dzink and two other Catholic priests persuaded Councilmen Charles E. Dorias, James Garlick, Eugene I. Van Antwerp, and William G. Rogell, a former Detroit Tigers infielder who described himself as "a Catholic first, last and always,"[8] to wire Palmer and ask him to delay black occupancy until another site could be found. The opposing faction then went to Auxiliary Bishop Woznicki, asking him to intervene, but Woznicki refused, because, according to Capeci, "he shared his priest's nationalism and conservative views."[9] The Church stood firm in spite of accusations of a "Catholic conspiracy." Dzink also managed to get the support of city council, but when Palmer and the DHC finally decided to stay with their original decision to move blacks into the project Edgecomb resorted to delaying tactics, denying on February 17 that he had received any written instructions. On the same day, the Wayne County prosecutor's office issued a warrant for real-estate dealer Joseph Buffa, accusing him of inciting a riot through his local paper, the *Seven Mile-Fenelon Homeowner's News.* Palmer arrived in town the next day to affirm in person that Edgecomb was to move the black defense workers into the project. Buffa's indictment bolstered black morale. As a matter of fact, Capeci indicates that it might have been done with precisely that effect in mind. "Some Justice Department officials," he writes, "might have initiated investigations and charges simply as the means to bolster black spirits, check racial violence, demonstrate federal authority, and ease the way for black occupancy."[10]

On Saturday, February 28, Edgecomb arrived at the Sojourner Truth Homes with a contingent of policemen accompanied by the first black families to be moved into the homes, only to be confronted by a group of protesters who barred their way. As that confrontation stood at impasse, other protesters drove through the neighborhood beeping their horns and announcing from a sound truck that the long-awaited move-in was about to take place. When the police commissioner finally got to the site, the crowd had swelled to between two and three hundred supporters, necessitating a call for police reinforcements. The police, however, seemed to sympathize more with the protesters than the people they were called to assist. A black mob in support of the move-in soon formed as well, and verbal altercations escalated to the point where the black mob drove the white mob three blocks down the street, whereupon the white mob, supported by police reinforcements, drove the black mob back again. Sensing that the move-in might lead to bloodshed "and possible death," Edgecomb called it off, but by then the mob had grown to 1000 people divided along racial lines facing each other angrily at Nevada and Ryan Avenues.

One reason for the stand-off was that no local politician thought the move-in was worth the political effort. It was certainly not worth dying for, and so everyone concerned tried to come up with some compromise solution acceptable to all the parties concerned. And they might have, were it not for the insistence of the federal housing authorities. From March 3 to March 5, Mayor Jeffries met with John D. Blandford, an administrator with the National Housing Agency. Since Blandford was under pressure from Washington to come up with sites for 15,000 units, costing $60 million, within the next 60 days, he could not waste time on Sojourner Truth. After his meeting with Jeffries and the NAACP officials which followed, Blandford announced that blacks would be moved in. In the meantime, the discontent over the government's housing policies had spread to predominantly Polish Hamtramck. When local authorities moved 300 white families into the Colonel Hamtramck Homes, the Hamtramck black Taxpayers and Housing Committee protested the decision. When the housing commission got funding to build a separate project for thirty-six black families, "Catholic priest and parishioners blocked construction of those homes."[11]

By now, the intelligence establishment was worried about the effect of these protests on civilian morale and whether it was going to affect the war effort. During April of 1942, Archibald Macleish of the Office of Facts and Figures warned the War Production Board of "the extreme seriousness of the problem" and noted that "a satisfactory solution of the Detroit housing crisis would have a tremendous effect upon Negro morale."[12] The intelligence establishment, as a result, took quick action lest the protest spread to other cities. Once the intelligence community portrayed the fight over who was going to live in the Sojourner Truth Homes as a national-security issue, this time with the nation at war, the outcome was a foregone conclusion. Macleish was a friend of Harvey Bundy, who like John J. McCloy had been recruited by Secretary of War Stimson to serve in Washington.

Like Bundy and Stimson, Macleish was a Skull and Bones man (class of '15) at Yale. Like McCloy, he was a graduate of Harvard Law School. He was also a mentor to Harvey Bundy's two sons, William and McGeorge, both of whom were also involved in intelligence operations during the war. The nexus of relationships shows the ethnic homogeneity of the intelligence community and how that community was willing to portray its own ethnic interests as national-security issues. Having become part of that community often by admission to secret societies like Skull and Bones, they learned to operate in a clandestine world that moved freely from government office to private foundation in ways often outside the law. In addition to their penchant for stealth, the one thing they shared was an inability to get elected to public office – hence their reliance on appointment to government agencies. "For the Bundy brothers," Bird writes, "Skull and Bones was always some kind of touchstone; it taught the future keepers of national secrets a code of absolute discretion."[13] For a time both of Harvey Bundy's sons would work under Macleish at the Office of Facts and Figures (OFF), a newly created intelligence and propaganda agency housed in the Library of Congress.

William Bundy would go from wartime work at Bletchley Park on the enigma code machine, to work in the CIA after the war. His brother McGeorge went from the Office of Facts and Figures to Harvard, where he coordinated covert funding of military projects. With the support of John McCloy, he then moved from the White House to become director of the Ford Foundation, where he expanded funding of the Gray Areas work, which was disrupting neighborhoods in places like Philadelphia under the leadership of people like Leon Sullivan. Shortly after he took over at Ford, Bundy expanded Ford funding to include support for Martin Luther King's Southern Christian Leadership Conference, which was assaulting ethnic neighborhoods in Chicago at the time. Many commentators have professed to be puzzled over McGeorge Bundy's funding of "liberal" racial causes while at the same time being a hawk in Vietnam, without seeing the ethnic consistency behind those actions. WASP domestic policy was forged during the early years of World War II, and racial integration, as Wirth explained in detail, was a necessary complement to WASP foreign policy. People like Macleish, Bundy, and McCloy would apply this policy with remarkable consistency, both in and out of government, over the coming decades.

Both the Office of War Information and the Office of Facts and Figures had their agents in St. Louis the King Parish, monitoring the activities of the neighborhood-improvement association and sending their reports back to Macleish in Washington and to Wirth's boss, Clyde Hart at the OWI. Given the ethnic prejudices of the intelligence community, it is not surprising that none of the agents sent to spy on the ethnics gave a favorable rendition of their position. One OWI investigator recommended that the government consider every opportunity "to dramatize its good intention toward Negroes"[14] in Detroit. "A firm stand" in behalf of black interests, this agent continued, should have been taken "before, not after" friction developed. One OFF agent claimed that if the situation were not defused by "some high official, preferably the President,"[15] all hell would break loose in every northern city where blacks and ethnics came in contact.

By April 15, the concerns of the intelligence community finally reached the housing people, and Blandford instructed the Detroit Housing Commission to move the black families into the Sojourner Truth Homes, "as soon as feasible,"[16] taking whatever measures were appropriate. Once again the federal government decided to end the debate over which paradigm of community would prevail in Detroit by *force majeure*. Shortly after midnight on April 28, two battalions of state troopers occupied the Sojourner Truth project, while other units secured the surrounding area. Over the next three weeks, 168 black families moved into the project under their watchful eyes. Confronted with overwhelming military force, resistance to black occupancy collapsed. Aiding that collapse was the infiltration of the community by undercover agents:

> In order to monitor white movement in the neighborhoods beyond the project, an intelligence or S-2 unit of five troopers operated as undercover agents and filed daily reports. The operatives infiltrated the ranks of protesters to identify agitators, their followers, and their plans; they noted the concentration points of hecklers, enabling guard units to be strengthened in those areas. In short, they knew "the pulse of the situation" as it unfolded in the white community. Above all, their sleuthing revealed the disintegration of the white protest: Buffa and most residents became very careful about what they said and did in the face of military might and possible prison terms.[17]

It was a civics lesson which cities across the northern tier of the country would all learn in similar fashion. Dzink and his Polish supporters had, in good American fashion, convinced their elected representatives of the justice of their cause, only to have the federal government countermand their efforts with a combination of black intelligence operations directed against American citizens and overwhelming military force. The government's actions in the Sojourner Truth case would also establish a precedent in both housing and racial matters for the post-war period. Whenever blacks claimed discrimination, they could be sure of the federal government's concern. Whenever the Catholic ethnics would claim that their neighborhoods were being targeted for destruction, they were written off as racists suffering from paranoid delusion. No matter how much clout the ethnics could muster locally, it could always be countered by some judge, appealing to higher moral principles. The same was true of Poles in Detroit, where "vested powers might have considered Polish Detroiters and neighborhood brokers expendable."[18] One year later when the worst race riot in the history of the country broke out in Detroit, the Poles again were blamed, but with the experience of Sojourner Truth behind them, Detroit's residents were skeptical. "After the street battles of 1943," Capeci writes, "Conant Gardens residents remembered 'something funny' about the 1942 housing controversy, something phoney that seemed to come from outside the neighborhood."[19]

Residents of Chicago would soon notice the same thing.

Notes

1   Domenic J. Capeci, Jr., *Race Relations in Wartime Detroit* (Philadelphia: Temple University Press, 1984), p. 82.
2   Ibid., p. 89.
3   John T. McGreevy, *Parish Boundaries: The Catholic Encounter with Race in the Twentieth Century Urban North* (Chicago: University of Chicago Press, 1996), p. 76.
4   George Edwards, letter to his father, 2/9/42, Wayne State University Archives.

5   Ibid.
6   Ibid.
7   Ibid.
8   Ibid., p. 90.
9   Ibid., p. 89.
10 Ibid., p. 159.
11 Ibid., p. 140.
12 Ibid., p. 135.
13 Kai Bird, *The Color of Truth: McGeorge Bundy and William Bundy: Brothers in Arms: A Biography* (New York: Simon & Schuster, 1998), p. 61.
14 Capeci, p. 158.
15 Ibid., p. 162.
16 Ibid., p. 134.
17 Ibid., p. 138.
18 Ibid., p. 151.
19 Ibid., p. 169.

Wirth on the Detroit Riot

One year and one day after the state troopers marched into Sojourner Truth, Mayor Jeffries tried to put an end to the disturbances by persuading the city council to prohibit the use of public housing to alter the racial make-up of existing neighborhoods. True to his word to his father, George Edwards was the lone voice on city council opposing the measure. The Detroit Housing Commission then went on to approve the same recommendation, again with only one dissenting vote. Hamtramck had passed the same regulation a year earlier. Taken together the regulations sent a clear message to Washington. Plagued by the disorders that Washington's meddling in local affairs had created, city councils in cities like Detroit and later Chicago and Philadelphia would attempt to reassert the authority which the federal government claimed was theirs in the federal housing bill of 1937, which stated that all federal funds had to be administered by local housing authorities. Cities like Detroit would learn over time, however, that federal money always had strings attached and that if they were interested in federal money they would have to get used to the social engineering that went with it.

The city's countermove against federal interference came too late, however, to stop the violence it was intended to forestall. Less than two months later, on June 20, 1943, on a hot Sunday afternoon, a group of blacks led by a newly arrived migrant from Brookhaven, Mississippi, began assaulting whites who had gone to Belle Isle in the middle of the Detroit River for a Sunday picnic. Stealing the white families' food and overturning their picnic tables, the black mob eventually created an equally violent reaction on the part of the city's white residents, one that was led by the large numbers of men in uniform from the city. Before nightfall on June 20, some fifty white sailors organized a counter-attack that clashed with the black mob on the bridge leading to Belle Isle. Before long, rumors were circulating through the black community that whites had thrown a pregnant black woman into the Detroit River, and that drove more blacks into the streets looking to avenge an action which had never occurred.

Before the riot burned itself out, thirty-five people would be dead, and 1,200 troops would be needed to restore order. Just as the mayhem was winding down on the evening of June 22, a twenty-six-year-old black defense worker shouted "Heil Hitler!" and was shot in the back by a state trooper as he ran into the St. Antoine YMCA.[1]

In the aftermath of the riot, various people tried to pin the blame on the groups they felt were responsible. One of them was Louis Wirth, who had been sent to Detroit to write a report on the riot for Clyde Hart, his boss at the Office for War Information. Wirth would eventually go back to Chicago to apply what he had learned in Detroit to the situation there.

Wirth feared that the rioting which had shaken Detroit would soon spread. In fact, there was every indication that it was already beginning to happen in Chicago. In April of 1943, blacks began moving across the Grand Avenue border which separated the black from the Italian community in that part of Chicago. Recent black arrivals from the South were so desperate to find a place to live that they began occupying the area's vacant and dilapidated structures. Before long, real estate agents began evicting the area's Italian residents in favor of newly arrived blacks who were willing to pay much more for their quarters than the Italians were. Practices like these quite predictably created a reaction among the Italians, who began to talk about murder and arson as a way of protecting what they considered their neighborhood.[2]

Fueling the same ethnic animosity at the same time was the opening of the Frances Cabrini Homes in April of 1943. Like the Richard Allen Homes in Philadelphia, the Cabrini Homes were planned before the war to accommodate the people living in the neighborhood. Like the Richard Allen Homes, they became, as a result of pressure from Washington, a pawn in the war effort and were converted to war-worker housing, which meant that housing intended for Italians, as the name of the project indicated, was turned over to recently arrived black migrants from the South instead. That meant that the Italians who had been promised new housing were permanently run out of the neighborhood.

The results were predictable. In April of 1943, fourteen months after the Sojourner Truth riot in Detroit and two months before the big riot there in June 1943, 300 blacks and whites clashed over who was going to live in the Frances Cabrini Homes in an exchange that included gunshots being fired into the apartment of one of the newly arrived blacks. The vector of transmission did not travel from Detroit to Chicago or from Chicago to Detroit; it traveled instead to both cities from Washington, which with the arrival of war was the prime agent for using housing as a form of social engineering. Wirth must have known as much since he was instrumental as an agent of the OWI in creating Washington's wartime housing policies, but modesty or other considerations apparently kept him from mentioning this in public. Instead, he hinted darkly that the racial violence in Detroit was the result of a conspiracy.

Five days after the Detroit riot began, on June 25, 1943, Louis Wirth addressed a Conference on Racial Problems sponsored by Chicago Industrial Union Council (the local branch of the CIO), and used the occasion to denounce the "recent mob violence attacks in which many were killed and hundreds maimed and injured"[3] claiming that this racial unrest "has culminated in a reign of terror in the city of Detroit."[4] He then quickly got to the point:

> These terrorist outbreaks constitute a conspiracy which is not only directed against the Negro but against the very fundamental principles of our Government and the Four Freedoms. No American can view this as the concern of only the discriminated against minority groups. It is the concern of all the American people. We condemn these disgraceful outbreaks of racial conflict as instigated by our country's enemies.[5]

In private correspondence Wirth was much more circumspect. In fact, in private correspondence in his capacity as an intelligence agent of the United States government, Wirth said the exact opposite of what he said in public. In a letter to his OWI boss Clyde Hart written four days after he gave his speech to the Chicago CIO conference on racial problems, Wirth claimed that "I do not attribute the situation here to any recent Axis or

Axis-inspired propaganda."[6] Wirth felt that the situation in Chicago was considerably less dangerous than the situation in Detroit, which he saw as "a direct offshoot of the type of Ku Klux [Klan], colored shirt or other form of race bigotry"[7] but again not inspired by Axis propaganda. "I do not mean to say we do not have race bigotry here too," he continued referring to the situation in Chicago. "There are some organizations that cultivate it. But I do not think it amounts to much in this situation relative to the other factors I have mentioned"[8]

The "other factors" which Wirth enumerated in his letter to Hart are all traceable to Washington's policy of bringing black workers up from the South to work in war industry factories. Housing, for example, ranked as factor number one in creating racial tension in Chicago, followed by employment, relations between white merchants and black customers, recreational facilities, and policing tactics.

The same was true for Detroit. There was no conspiracy, at least none behind the race riot. The source of racial tension was the federal government's employment and housing policies and the huge internal migration and consequent social dislocation which it had created in its wake. Since Wirth was one of the main architects of that policy, it is understandable that he was reluctant to criticize it in public or private. In his OWI correspondence, though, he was more concerned with particulars. "I have had a number of conferences with both newspaper men and others who have been to Detroit recently and during the riot,"[9] Wirth wrote to Hart on July 24. As in his earlier private correspondence there is no talk of conspiracy, just complaints about management practices at the Ford plant, which provoked Wirth's ire by following his orders. It seems that "the management provoked trouble by deliberately interpreting the upgrading regulations literally and putting a husky Negro into the position of foreman over some white girls."[10] "The people that know say this was done to provoke trouble," Wirth continued, lapsing into the paranoid style he had used in his CIO speech. "This seems to me an interesting instance of what can happen to a good principle when it is applied by vicious persons who want to destroy the principle."[11] Or perhaps what can happen when a bad principle is applied by people who are just following orders.

Just as the absence of evidence did not stop Wirth from claiming that a conspiracy caused the riots, so it did not stop him from using the opportunity the riots provided to urge Chicago's city fathers to take measures to stop this phantom conspiracy. "We urge the Mayor of the City of Chicago," Wirth told his CIO audience, "to immediately set up a broad commission of representative citizens who shall investigate the basic causes of racial friction and propose recommendations for the elimination of these causes toward the aim of preventing any racial outbreaks in the city of Chicago."[12] Largely at the urging of Louis Wirth, Chicago was the first of what would eventually be the thirty-two cities which created various local commissions on human relations to deal with the racial conflicts the war had created. Chicago went a step further. It was also the first city in the nation to "establish a human relations committee supported by public funds."[13] The purpose of the Chicago Commission on Human Relations was not so much to create racial harmony as it was to engineer consent for integration because without wartime migration and government-mandated "integration" of public housing, there would have been no racial tension to defuse. In fact, far from defusing violence, the CHR precipitated it by becoming the psychological-warfare arm of the systematic assault that the Chicago Housing Authority was orchestrating on the city's ethnic neighborhoods.

The creation of the Chicago Commission on Human Relations, like its counterparts in Philadelphia and elsewhere, meant that now local governments could engage in psychological warfare against ethnics in a way that had been previously limited to agents of the federal government. When Philadelphia got its new city charter in 1951 Clarence Pickett and other area Quakers saw to it that Philadelphia, like Chicago, had its own government-funded CHR. When they needed a director, they hired George Schermer, the man who was in charge of tenant placement at the Detroit Housing Authority when its policies created the Sojourner Truth housing riots in 1942. Schermer, in a move that would become predictable, then hired Dennis Clark, a liberal Catholic and local head of the Catholic Interracial Council to act as his agent in engineering the consent of Catholic ethnics in the "integration" of their neighborhoods. After provoking the neighborhood to mob violence by one of their move-ins, CHR representatives would then often call on the local parish priest to calm the crowds down again, thereby gaining in addition to an immediate benefit the long-term benefit of driving a wedge between pastor and parishioners.

The local government's use of the commission on human relations as an instrument of social engineering got justified in the name of the war emergency, and it happened in Chicago before it happened anywhere else. "The war years," according to Hirsch, "saw the first attempts in Chicago to expand and harness governmental powers under the guise of 'urban planning' in order to reshape the local environment and control the process of succession."[14] After the war was over, the same social engineering took on a life of its own, and again psychological warfare, including the techniques of "sensitivity training," developed by Kurt Lewin under the auspices of the Office of Naval Research, got turned against recalcitrant ethnics. After the Fernwood riots broke out in Chicago in 1947, ninety of the protesters who got arrested were sentenced to "compulsory group therapy" as part of their rehabilitation.[15]

The purpose of the Chicago Commission on Human Relations can be gleaned from documents proposing the creation of the Institute on Human Relations which Louis Wirth established under the auspices of B'nai B'rith at Roosevelt College in 1945. "Chicago," writes Mrs. A. B. Counselbaum of the Anti-Defamation League to Wirth describing just what the IHR is supposed to accomplish,

> holds a good share in both disruptive movements. It is the classical site of restrictive covenants against the extension of Negro housing and the seat of numerous militant anti-Semitic organizations. It harbors all the nationality groups of which this nation is composed and has them live under such conditions that social disintegration, even crime, abounded. From there arises the necessity for an institution like Roosevelt College to be an active agent in intergroup education. Having a large Jewish and Negro student body and also, if not in sufficient numbers, students from other ethnic groups, Roosevelt College appears to be in a strategic position for the purpose.[16]

Since it was funded by a Jewish agency, the IHR at Roosevelt College could hardly be expected to engage in the social engineering of the area's Jews. But the IHR also seemed little concerned about the black population of the South Side of Chicago where Roosevelt College is located. Conspicuous by its absence from Mrs. Counselbaum's concerns were the criminal behavior and loose sexual morals of the newly arrived blacks from the South which were causing the residents of the South Side such concern at the time. The sort of social pathology that Lait and Mortimer noted and Nicholas Lemann noted fifty years later is nowhere mentioned in Mrs. Counselbaum's proposal. Instead, as the prime beneficiaries of the IHR's new program, she proposes "close cooperation with leading neighborhood and nationality organizations such as the Polish National Alliance, the West Side Community Committee, the Back-of-the-Yards Council, and similar groups."[17] This is necessary because "at present, precisely those groups are underrepresented who need a new type of education most."[18] In other words, it is the Poles and other ethnics from places like the Back of the Yards who "need a new type of education most" and not the blacks, because at this point in the history of liberal consciousness the southern blacks were perceived as much more docile than northern ethnics. Mrs. Counselbaum's plan became clear when she explained how "a scholarship fund should be created which would enable eligible boys and girls from these groups [the Polish National Alliance, et al] to enter the College."[19]

According to Counselbaum's analysis, it is the ethnics and not the blacks which pose a greater threat because "it so happens that these groups are the most disintegrated and their members, therefore, among the most troublesome in our population at large."[20] Disintegrated in this instance does not mean that the ethnic groups in question are falling apart. In fact, the term "disintegrated" in this context means the exact opposite. The ethnic groups in question are perceived as a threat precisely because they are not falling apart. They are perceived as a threat because they are so cohesive that they are immune to the suggestions of liberal cultural control. They are "troublesome" not because of family breakdown and the delinquency of the sort that was evident in the black migrants' neighborhoods, but because they were in a position to resist integration, which in this context is another word for assimilation. They were not integrated into the mainstream culture enough to satisfy people like Mrs. Counselbaum, whose idea of social progress has much in common with the Jewish settlement houses of an earlier era – with one exception. With the creation of the IHR at Roosevelt College, the same settlement-house principles will be applied not by Jews to newly arrived fellow Jews, but rather by Jews to other "troublesome" ethnic groups, i.e., Polish Catholics. With the creation of the Chicago's Commission on Human Relations, the same principles could be applied with the force of the state to back them up.

Because of the influence that Wirth and the rest of the psychological-warfare establishment had in orchestrating public opinion, the blame for the Detroit riot started to shift from the blacks who started it to the ethnics. Although Capeci finds no evidence that the Poles played any role in the 1943 Detroit riot, they began to take the rap for it in public opinion.[21] That meant, more often than not, that "Polish Catholics" were singled out for blame because it was they "who contested blacks for the Sojourner Truth Homes and several neighborhoods east of the ghetto, immediately north and south of Hamtramck – itself an 'anti-Negro' enclave" in spite of the fact that "except for minor skirmishes and a few arrests in Hamtramck, Poles did not stand out in the minds of onlookers as rioters."[22] The disparity between reality and perception is due to a large extent to the efforts of the psychological-warfare establishment, who made it their business to manage public perceptions in their own interests. That meant portraying ethnics as aggressors and blacks as victims, when in the 1943 Detroit riot the exact opposite was the case. That paradigm for understanding racial conflict was established as part of this country's wartime propaganda needs, and it would continue essentially unchanged after the war, as evidenced in June Manning Thomas's recent book. "In the race riot of 1943," Thomas writes, "White crowds attacked innocent Blacks, Blacks fought back, and battling mobs took over the streets."[23] Since those ethnic animosities both preceded the war and continued after it was over, the paradigm of ethnic vilification at the heart of this country's racial policy would continue as well.

What Louis Wirth, the sociologist, really wanted when he made his public case against unnamed conspirators before the CIO in June of 1943 was a change in the environment, and that meant above all else a change in housing. "We support," he told his CIO audience,

> immediate and practical plans for re-housing of slum dwellers in decent, federally financed as well as privately-financed housing developments. We urge that obstacles to war industry housing projects such as the Princeton Park Project, at 93rd and Wentworth be removed and work be started immediately, and that the state legislature be urged to adopt House Bill 563 to outlaw restrictive covenants.[24]

In this instance, there was no discrepancy between Wirth's private and public views. Nor did he have a difficult time convincing his boss at the OWI Clyde Hart that housing was important as the most effective form of social engineering that could be applied to the racial situation, a position Myrdal (or Wirth) had taken in *The American Dilemma*. "Our position," Hart wrote in response to Wirth's report on July 21, 1943,

> has been that the [race] problem is not one to be dealt with in the main by informational programs; it requires rather direct, sensible readjustments of the kind you suggest – in *housing*, recreation and health facilities, transportation employment practices, recruitment policies and programs, Army camp arrangements, policing, etc.[25] (my emphasis).

When Louis Wirth and Clyde Hart agreed on something, it was a pretty good indication that that something was going to end up being government policy. That is precisely what happened in housing in Chicago. Integration became housing policy in Chicago because Wirth and Hart believed that man was a function of his environment and because they believed that by changing man's environment that they could change man. Housing and, to a lesser extent, education, were simply other words for environment. Wirth and Hart felt that housing was the Archimedian point for social change. If social engineering could change housing patterns, it could change just about any repugnant attitude the people who lived in those houses possessed. That meant that it could eliminate "prejudice,"

Wirth and Hart's term for attachment to local community, ethnos, unenlightened religious beliefs, and the child-rearing practices which flowed therefrom, something both men made clear in a radio discussion of prejudice on May 2, 1948.

During the course of the discussion, Clyde Hart, now head of the National Opinion Research Center (NORC), one of the nation's first polling operations, claimed that "the prejudiced person is much more likely than others to have what may be called an 'authoritarian personality,' that is, he is more likely to believe very strongly in strict discipline and order. Such a person believes that the most important thing to teach his child is absolute obedience to his parents."[26]

Wirth then directed the discussion to the topic of housing projects, one of the major arenas of social engineering at the time, as a potential cure for the "authoritarian personality." Taking his cue from Wirth's claim that "studies of housing projects . . . show some evidence of what happens when people meet and become acquainted to one another,"[27] fellow sociologist Robert Merton opined that his studies indicate "the following facts":

> Whites who have not lived in a bi-racial community and who come into this mixed community – comprised of 50 percent Negroes and 50 percent whites – undergo an amazing transformation in the course of a few years. In due time they tend to take on the attitudes of other whites in the community who have previously had the experience of bi-racial living. At the end of a few years, four out of five whites are prepared to say, on the basis of experience, that the races in this community get along not only amicably but well.[28]

Wirth, who once contacted a psychiatrist to see if prejudice were a form of mental illness, then went on to claim that ethnic neighborhoods contribute to personality disorders by promoting prejudice. "What is wrong with this prejudice apparently is that it ruins us as integrated personalities, it cripples our lives, it inhibits our contacts, and it cuts us off from the world in which we live – the wider world of human beings."[29] Then as if recognizing that claims like that were a bit of a stretch, he came back to essentially economic arguments against ethnic communities. Prejudice is bad because "it does not allow us to utilize our human resources in this society where human resources are scarce, [i.e. the factories of the north] because we keep certain people, by virtue of our prejudices from equal opportunities. And, of course, it divides our nation making us less effective in the world at large as a symbol of the democratic ideal."[30]

Clyde Hart then stressed the importance of education, indicating that "every study that has been made of prejudice shows that there is a correlation between the degree of formal education – that is that amount of schooling the individual has had – and prejudice."[31] Hart's emphasis on education give some indication of why *Brown v. Board of Education* was an important ratification of the project the psychological-warfare crowd had staked out in *The American Dilemma*. "Unless we change the actual institutional and social conditions," Robert Merton said, continuing in the same vein, "we cannot hope appreciably to modify prejudice. . . . There is evidence that the less segregation we have, the less prejudice is likely to develop. Prejudice and segregation reinforce each other."[32] That meant essentially moving people out of homogeneous neighborhoods by the methods mentioned above. As in virtually every other area of social endeavor after the war, ethnic cleansing was also justified by an appeal to science, "in this case social science," which, Wirth opined,

> has begun to deal with the problem of prejudice and its associated problems of discrimination, segregation and hostility. It has made considerable advance in isolating the causes that breed prejudice and that are responsible for its contagious spread. It has progressed toward the definition of ways and means of controlling or minimizing its disastrous effects. We do not yet have all the answers, but we do know that prejudice is not inherited. It is acquired. And, if it is made by man, then it can be unmade by man.[33]

Since man is a function of his environment, changing the environment means changing the man. What Louis Wirth failed to mention in his summary of the environmentalist creed was that implementing this creed would mean the unmaking of the social order of Chicago, based as it was at the time on the coexistence – peaceful or not so peaceful – of ethnic neighborhoods. From his position on the board of the Metropolitan Housing and Planning Council, Wirth promoted integrated housing in Chicago. His policy of using housing projects to bust up potentially traitorous ethnic enclaves, however, had from its inauguration with the integration of the Airport Park Homes in 1946 caused the very turmoil which social engineering was supposed to defuse. Even the most sympathetic reading of his policy of integrating first government housing and then entire ethnic neighborhoods in Chicago would have to conclude that that policy backfired. In the short run it reinforced the very ethnic solidarity that it was supposed to dissipate.

What followed from Wirth's conception of human nature was in Arnold Hirsch's words, ten years of "chronic urban guerrilla warfare"[34] as the ethnics who were the target of Wirth's social engineering reacted in violent protest against it. Hirsch went on to say that the warfare was "really tied less to ideological currents than to the ebb and flow of populations"[35] without quite seeing that the ideology decreed the population movements in the first place – first of all, to win the war but after that to break down "prejudice," which is to say the ethnic neighborhood's sense of itself as a community. The most intense disputes occurred during the ten-year period beginning in May of 1944 when the first skirmishes began and ended in August 1954 when Elizabeth Wood was fired as the head of the Chicago Housing Authority. If one includes Martin Luther King's ill-fated march on Chicago's ethnic neighborhoods in the summer of 1966, the scope of the urban-guerrilla warfare roughly doubles in length to something that would have a greater impact on determining who lived where in Chicago than the Chicago fire.

As the CHA could tell from the tension map it posted on its wall, racial tension in Chicago during this period was invariably associated with housing policy. Incidents occurred when pioneers from the overcrowded Black Belt crossed neighborhood boundaries in search of new homes. The ethnics who lived on the other side of those boundaries invariably saw this as a threat to the very existence of their communities and reacted as if they were defending their homes from a foreign invasion. "From the whites' vantage point," Hirsch writes,

> the issue was one of community control. Given their view of such issues as "all or nothing" propositions, "integration" was a meaningless concept to them. Black

access to community facilities simply meant that they would soon "take over" the neighborhood and drive the whites out.[36]

That, of course, meant that the ethnics were not motivated by racial animosity – although policies like this certainly generated that – as much as they were motivated by self-preservation. No matter what the official explanation was, the people in the neighborhoods understood from lessons in the expensive school of experience that "integration" was another word for the extinction of their community, and those communities reacted accordingly. Beginning in January 1945, there was at least one attack a month on black residences in transitional areas, attacks which would continue unabated for the next two years. Twenty-nine of the attacks involved arson, causing at least three deaths.

If the CHR had wanted to eliminate racial friction, it could have done so by abandoning its policy of race-based social engineering, and it could have come to that conclusion by examining its own statistics of what was causing the friction in the first place. Of 485 racial incidents reported to the CHR from 1945 to 1950, 357, according to Hirsch, "were directly related to housing or residential property."[37] Similarly, 85.1 percent of all the incidents reported took place on the edge of black expansion into white neighborhoods. Contrary to Louis Wirth's claim that an Axis-fueled conspiracy was the driving force behind the disorders, ACLU agents spying on the ethnic neighborhoods in question found that "the riot was begun and carried out in the first two days almost exclusively by persons from the immediate vicinity."[38] There was, in other words, no long-range planning and no outside agitation. The riots resulted in a disproportionately large number of women being arrested because they were oftentimes the only ones home when the moving trucks arrived. According to Hirsch, "the participants in the 'contested area' riots were with few exceptions, residents of the territory involved. Of the total of 319 persons arrested for whom addresses were found 78.7 percent lived within one mile of their respective riot areas and 87.5 percent lived within 1½ miles; only 22 of the arrestees lived more than 3 miles away."[39]

Notes

1 Domenic J. Capeci, Jr., and Martha Wilkerson, *Layered Violence: The Detroit Rioters of 1943* (Jackson: University Press of Mississippi, 1991), p. 17.

2 Arnold R. Hirsch, *Making the Second Ghetto: Race and Housing in Chicago 1940–1960* (Cambridge: Cambridge University Press, 1983), p. 36.

3 Louis Wirth, "Proposals of Action for Special Conference on Racial Problems" called by Chicago Industrial Union Council, CIO, June 25, 1943, Box XXVIII, Folder 10, Office of War Information, Louis Wirth Papers, University of Chicago Archives.

4 Ibid.

5 Ibid.

6 Louis Wirth to Clyde Hart 6/29/43, UC Box 51, Folder 3, University of Chicago Archives.

7 Ibid.

8 Ibid.

9 Wirth to Hart 7/24/43, Box XXVIII, Folder 10, Office of War Information, Louis Wirth Papers, University of Chicago Archives.

10 Ibid.

11 Ibid.

12 Louis Wirth, "Proposals, " Box XXVIII, Folder 10, Office of War Information, Louis Wirth Papers, University of Chicago Archives.

13 Hirsch, p. 44.

14 Ibid., p. 36.

15 Ibid., p. 208.

16 Memorandum Concerning Institute of Human Relations at Roosevelt College from Mrs. A.B. Counselbaum to Louis Wirth, 11/23/45, Wirth papers University of Chicago, Box XIX, Folder 2.

17 Ibid.

18 Ibid.

19 Ibid.

20 Ibid.

21 Capeci, *Layered*, p. 25.

22 Ibid.

23 June Manning Thomas, *Redevelopment and Race* (Baltimore: The Johns Hopkins University Press, 1997), p. 17.

24 Wirth, "Proposals."

25 Clyde Hart to Louis Wirth, 7/21/43, Office of War Information folders, University of Chicago Archives.

26 "What Do We Know about Prejudice?" A Radio Discussion with Clyde W. Hart, director of the NORC, formerly with the Office of War Information, Eugene L. Hartley, Robert K. Merton, prof. of sociology Columbia U. and Louis Wirth, prof. of sociology U of Chicago, May 2, 1948, The National Broadcasting Company, Box LVI Folder 3, Louis Wirth archives of the University of Chicago.

27 Ibid.

28 Ibid.

29 Ibid.

30 Ibid.

31 Ibid.

32 Ibid.

33 Ibid.

34 Hirsch, p. 41.

35 Ibid.

36 Ibid., p. 63.

37 Ibid., p. 52.

38 Ibid., p. 73.

39 Ibid., p. 69.

The Airport Homes Riots, 1946

In January of 1946, the Chicago Housing Authority attempted to integrate the Airport Homes at 60th and Karlov and precipitated a riot that would inaugurate the post-war period. As the date of the riot indicates, winning the war was no longer the main consideration driving the government's housing policy. War in this regard was a pretext which allowed social engineering that could not have taken place without the excuse of war but which was desirable in and of itself and would continue after the war had allowed the housers to establish the precedent of engineering local communities for social ends. War migration necessitated the creation of public housing, but the fact that the CHA could choose sites with no political accountability meant that "communities situated considerable distances from areas of black concentration found their homogeneity threatened" by the CHA's social engineers.[1] The sense of local insecurity which this fostered made the reaction to racial succession that much more violent than it would have been otherwise.

At the end of the month when the Airport Homes riot took place, Louis Wirth gave a talk entitled "Housing as a Field of Sociological Research" to the American Sociological Society. The talk makes clear that Wirth (and by extension agencies like the CHR and the CHA and the MHPC) were less interested in defusing racial tension than they were willing to accept racial tension as the price of achieving certain social goals. Social engineering of the race issue would eventually come to mean combining the carrot and the stick. Once the war was over and housing started to get built to make up for the shortfall created by the Depression and the war, the ethnics could be lured to a generically white suburbia free of ethnic associations and "prejudice." If the carrot didn't work, the ethnic neighborhoods could be broken up by moving a few black families in, a move which inevitably caused panic and flight. In his paper, Wirth proposes to sociologists the following areas of study, without telling us how he is going to use that information once he gets it:

> the phenomena of invasion and succession of different population groups into specific areas of the city; the factors underlying the flight from the city and the emergence of suburban communities, and in turn the fate of those suburban communities as the central urban influences extend outward; the attitudes underlying the resistance to the invasion of strange racial and ethnic groups, the methods used to block this invasion and the alternative methods that might be used for building sound communities in which people of various economic strata and racial and ethnic characteristics can live together amicably, the relation of community institutions to housing and the relationship of place of work to place of residence, and the role of transportation in the general pattern of living.[2]

"These are problems," he continues, "with which in the past the human ecologist, the demographer, the student of the community organization and the city planner have been primarily concerned. A more definite focusing of sociological interest upon these issues would be of immense scientific as well as practical significance."[3]

Wirth never says so, but his wartime experience with the OWI makes clear that the "practical significance" of such sociological research finds its application in psychological warfare. Wirth's desire to engineer ethnic communities did not end when the war ended, as his 1948 radio broadcast on prejudice showed. Just why is Wirth interested in understanding "methods used to block this invasion," if not to neutralize such methods? It was he, after all, who told us in *The American Dilemma* that Americans could no longer afford the luxury of disinterested science. Wirth's message on housing is the same as his message on nationalities. Just as the days of *laissez-faire* assimilation are past, so too are the days long gone

> when individuals or families could solve their housing problems mainly on the basis of their own resources and their own decisions. . . . *Like other social movements of a reform or revolutionary nature,* [my emphasis] (the housing movement) has set itself the goal of achieving certain social objectives toward which there either exists a public apathy or against which there operates the organized resistance of the special interest groups. We shall not achieve an adequate solution of the housing problem nor shall we make satisfactory progress toward that goal without a better understanding of the collective behavior of those various groups within the housing movement.[4]

Like the social engineering which inspired it, the black migration to the North which the war necessitated took on a life of its own after the war was over. Throughout the '50s, thousands of blacks would arrive at Chicago's Central Station each week and then head south with their cardboard suitcases in hand looking for first lodging and then a job. That continued in-migration combined with the fertility of the people already here created a powerful engine of demographic change in the city which threatened to overwhelm not only the city's ethnic neighborhoods but the downtown business interests as well. The city of Chicago has since memorialized this migration with a statue of a newly arrived Mississippian complete with rope-tied cardboard suitcase near the site of the old Illinois Central terminal. The same business interests soon realized that they were every bit as threatened by the American version of the *Voelkerwanderung* (the great ethnic migration at the time of the fall of the Roman Empire) as the ethnics in their neighborhoods were and they began to make their own plans. Those plans, which stretched from the Blighted Areas Redevelopment Act of 1947 to the Urban Community Conservation Act of 1953, expanded government power while at the same time severely curtailing the average citizen's right to own and dispose of property.

Since the blacks who migrated to Chicago had no say whatsoever about where they were going to live, the ensuing battle, no matter how it looked during the various race riots over next decade, would not be a battle between blacks and whites. It would be a battle between the older European immigrants and the newer immigrants, which was another way of saying that it would be a battle between Protestants and Catholics. The defensive measures which the ethnics took against black migration were known as riots; the defensive measures the WASP business interests took against the same invasion were known as urban renewal. "The expansion of the ghetto and the deterioration of the central city," according to Hirsch,

> alarmed corporate property holders, but their response differed from that of individual homeowners or renters. Downtown businesses and institutions located in slum or transition areas turned not to violence or suburban flight but rather to the use of political and legal power. Locked in a desperate struggle for survival, the city's large institutions used their combined economic resources and political influence to produce a redevelopment and urban renewal program designed to guarantee their continued prosperity. Their response to the changing condition of the city was not a fundamentally different form of behavior; it was simply a different mode of reaction within a white consensus. If the white ethnic working class felt driven to the streets to protect its self-defined interests, Chicago's business and institutional interests resorted no less forcefully to the political arena.[5]

In October 1946, two months before the Airport Park riots, Henry Heald, head of the Illinois Institute of Technology and soon to be head of the Ford Foundation, unveiled the MHPC's four-point plan for revitalizing Chicago as the "only practical method of getting a real redevelopment program going."[6] Chicago's business interests had been wrestling with the idea of urban renewal since 1942. Six months before Heald's announcement, the presidents of Marshall Fields and the Chicago Title and Trust Company had approached the city to see if it would absorb the cost of clearing land for private developers, who would then purchase the property at a price "less than the cost of acquisition."[7]

The Loop interests realized that they would have to expand government's power to do what it wanted. That meant creating a non-black buffer around the downtown area and creating life-lines, i.e., limited access highways that would connect them to the upscale shoppers who were fleeing to the suburbs. "Chicago's business elite," according to Hirsch,

> clearly envisaged a postwar building boom on the city's periphery, the flight of the middle class, and the insulation of State Street from its "normal market." They subsequently tried to counter the forces promoting decentralization through the "complete rehabilitation of the center of the city." "The real purpose of redevelopment," one knowledgeable observer later noted, was "to reattract solvent population and investment to the dying areas of the city."[8]

The people the city's ruling elite displaced to create enclaves like the Michael Reese Hospital, the Illinois Institute of Technology (IIT), and the "renewed" University of Chicago would flow in wave upon wave into the immediately adjacent neighborhoods. That meant another threat to the city's already beleaguered neighborhoods, and that often meant riots as well, but the riots presented the ruling elite with certain benefits as well because it allowed them to distance themselves from the fray, which was invariably seen as a struggle between blacks and ethnics. By engaging in the ethnic cleansing of blacks from certain areas targeted for renewal, the Loop interests could blame their real opponents in the struggle over racial migration, namely, the ethnics, for the violence while at the same time creating the incidents which were driving the ethnics out of their neighborhoods.

Former federal housing official Philip Klutznick would play a crucial role in the development and implementation of these policies. Like Louis Wirth, Klutznick was both a member of B'nai B'rith (he would later go on to become its president) and a member of the MHPC, the urban planning think-tank that developed public policy on housing in Chicago. Wirth was chairman of the MHPC planning commission, and Klutznick was chairman of its public-housing committee. Klutznick would go on to become the man responsible for Park Forest, Chicago's first post-World War II suburb. In the many hats that Klutznick wore during his tenure as developer and advisor we can see the emergence of the vague outlines of the post-war system of "integrated" housing which entailed the curtailment of property rights and the all but universal abolition of community life. Klutznick played a crucial role at both ends of the equation. As the developer of Lake Meadows, Chicago's first post-war high-rise apartment building, he was instrumental in urban renewal. That meant, of course, displacing blacks by tearing down their homes. But as the man in charge of Park Forest, Chicago's premier post-war suburb, that also meant that Klutznick was building new homes for the white ethnics the blacks displaced. Klutznick was responsible for creating the engine of assimilation that would absorb the ethnics who were displaced from their neighborhoods by the blacks who had just been displaced from theirs to make room for downtown renewal.

As with every other instance of expanded political power during this period, in order to understand how the power would eventually get used, we have to understand the interests of the ethnic group which wielded it. In the case of Chicago that is fairly simple. The two movers and shakers for the downtown Loop interests were Milton C. Mumford, an assistant vice-president of Marshall Field and Company, and Holman D. Pettibone, president of the Chicago Title and Trust Company. Mumford and Pettibone authored the state housing bill. Like Wirth and Klutznick, but in a much more hands-on manner, they were the architects of Chicago's post-war housing plans. Both men were "almost stereotypically small town, Midwestern, and Protestant in origin."[9] There was in fact a "yawning chasm" between the representatives of Chicago's downtown interests and the interests of the ethnics that inhabited the neighborhoods between downtown and the suburbs that were bearing the brunt of racial migration. Hirsch notes the ethnic division at the heart of Chicago's housing wars:

> Where the protesting neighborhoods were largely working class, Catholic, and ethnic, the architects of the redevelopment program were overwhelmingly professional, Protestant and Jewish, and native American. Pettibone and Mumford were members of Congregational and Methodist churches, respectively, and were virtual models of upward and outward mobility in their professional and personal lives. Residence in the suburbs to them was both desirable and possible; it was certainly not a prospect to be dreaded, even if one was "pushed" there by changing inner-city realities. Pettibone, moreover, was a captain in the American Protective League during World War I, an organization that "snooped through German

neighborhoods looking for enemy agents," and, in the words of Edward F. Dunne, onetime mayor of Chicago and Illinois' only Catholic governor, "goaded and insulted persons whose only offense was the possession of a German name."[10]

As in Philadelphia, the experts the ruling elite hired to run their programs shared their ethnic affiliation and the prejudices that went with it. That meant "reforming zeal" was defined by their particular religious denomination. It also meant that reformers possessed credentials from prestigious WASP universities, which were also invariably associated with the same liberal religious denominations. Elizabeth Wood, the scourge of Chicago's ethnic neighborhoods during her tenure as the head of the Chicago Housing Authority, had been born in Japan to an Episcopal lay minister, educated at the University of Michigan, and taught at Vassar College. Homer Jack, one of the leading advocates of integrated housing in Chicago, was a minister for the Unitarian Church of suburban Evanston, a church which described its mission on its stationery as "63 years of religious liberalism on the North Shore." As members of similarly liberal organizations like B'nai B'rith and the Anti-Defamation League (ADL), Jews like Wirth and Klutznick had similar views and found allies at the University of Chicago in people like Julian Levi. Together they dominated boards like the Metropolitan Housing and Planning Council (MPHC) and the CHA, which then got to call in experts who shared their dislike of people with ethnic names, who were deliberately excluded from the deliberations that determined the fate of their neighborhoods. When the United Councils of the Polish Roman Catholic Union requested that the Polish community be represented on the board of the MHPC, the MHPC replied that it did not "recognize national groups as such, but only individuals or groups having an interest in housing."[11] One would think that people whose neighborhoods were threatened with destruction would have a very real interest in housing; however, for the MHPC, an interest in housing evidently meant an interest in housing occupied by other people. It excluded those who were concerned about the fate of their own house and those of their neighbors. Hirsch confuses the issue by claiming that "[h]aving become 'white,' ethnic interests merited no distinct consideration,"[12] when the opposite was in fact the case. Membership on the MHPC was restricted to certain preferred ethnic groups, i.e., WASPs and Jews, and off-limits to others, i.e., Polish Catholics. Once these ground rules had been established, the MHPC would then invariably choose experts who espoused the goals of the ethnic groups which hired them as consultants.

One of those experts was Reginald Isaacs, colleague and biographer of Walter Gropius at Harvard, devoted Bauhausler, head of Michael Reese Hospital's planning board, and author of the MHPC's study on conservation, which argued for the creation of a government-backed conservation authority which could make use of eminent domain to "force owners to maintain minimum standards with the threat of seizure if they do not comply."[13] These same sweeping powers, however, did not extend to the local groups which represented the people who were being dispossessed and displaced by Isaacs's urban-renewal projects. Those councils "should be merely advisory at best," with the task of comprehensive planning left in the hands of the "centralized authority." Isaacs felt this way because the people in the neighborhoods, "don't know themselves what is good for them much less for the city as a whole."[14]

Undeterred by the violence their decision to integrate Airport Park in 1946 had created, the CHA pursued the same policy in Fernwood Park in Roseland in August of 1947. Outraged by the fact that black veterans had been moved into the project, a mob of anywhere from 1,500 to 5,000 angry neighborhood residents surrounded the project for three successive nights in August, battling police and, when they were unable to break through the police lines, attacking blacks in cars passing through the neighborhood. In keeping with the spirit of the times, the crowd suspected that the assault on their neighborhood was being orchestrated by Communists, and some urged Senator Joe McCarthy to investigate the CHA as a Communist organization. Local alderman Reginald DuBois toyed with the idea of introducing a resolution in city council which would liquidate the CHA because it "persist[ed] in theories of housing which are shared by no other representative local governmental agencies . . . and are not in accord with those of a great majority of citizens."[15]

CHA chairman Robert R. Taylor responded to the charge by claiming that DuBois's resolution was "a smokescreen for a demand that the Authority enforce racial segregation."[16] The CHA could wreak such havoc in the city because it was outside the political process. It could choose housing sites without consulting the city council, whose members answered directly to the people in the neighborhoods who elected them to office. Mayor Edward J. Kelly supported the CHA, but in November of 1947, Kelly was voted out of office. After the Fernwood riots of 1947, no Chicago politician, including Kelly's successor Martin Kenelly and Kenelly's successor Richard Daley, could ignore the continuing and increasingly violent protests which CHA policies were creating in the city.

As a result, forces were set in motion which would eventually lead to the reabsorption of the CHA and the CHR back into the political process. On October 15, 1947, Alderman DuBois introduced a resolution calling for council approval of CHA policies. Two months later, Pettibone and Mumford orchestrated passage of the Redevelopment and Relocation acts of 1947, acts which Pettibone claimed were the model upon which the Federal Housing Act of 1949 was based. The 1947 act specified that redevelopment projects would be privately owned and, therefore, exempt from CHA restrictions. At around the same time, Pettibone and Mumford persuaded the Illinois state legislature to grant the Chicago City Council the right of approval over the sites selected for relocation projects.

Outraged by the reverses the CHA suffered over the course of 1947, Homer Jack, national president of the Unitarian Fellowship for Social Justice and Secretary of the Chicago Division of the American Civil Liberties Union, wrote a series of articles in *The Nation* on the Chicago housing situation in general and on the Fernwood riots in particular, which he describes as the "most serious racial disturbances since the widespread riots of 1919."[17] Careful to say that white veterans took no part in the riot, Jack criticizes the 168 police who had been sent to the Fernwood Homes on August 12 for not dispersing the crowds more quickly. Emboldened by their ability to assemble, yet frustrated by their inability to get into the projects by the police, the mob then took to the neighboring streets stopping cars and throwing stones through the windows of those carrying blacks. Two nights later the police force had increased to 365, but the mob had increased as well to 5,000 people, a force which allowed them to get close enough to the project to break windows with stones. Jack is quick to defend the CHA, absolving them of any role in causing the disturbance:

> Local Alderman Reginald Dubois . . . begged the Chicago Housing Authority and
> its director, Elizabeth Wood, to by-pass its non-discriminatory policy just this
> once. But the authority, mindful of its public trust and of state statutes forbidding
> it to discriminate, went right down its list of 25,000 applications. And of the eight-
> een veterans assigned apartments at Fernwood, eight happened to be Negroes.[18]

Jack is, of course, being disingenuous here. No one familiar with the writings of
Louis Wirth would say that blacks just "happened" to end up in the project's apartments.
However, even judging from Jack's own tendentious description of the situation, the local
politicians seemed less motivated by racial considerations and more interested in keeping
the peace than the CHA, which was attempting to pursue its policy of social engineering
under the cover of following objective procedures. Between DuBois and the ethnics on the
one hand and the CHA and the "reformers" on the other, stood Mayor Kenelly, whose job
it was to keep the peace and hold the city together. When Kenelly first turned to the CHA,
Jack and the housers suspected that he would pressure them to move the eighteen blacks
out of the project. This meant that the CHA's supporters had to exert counterpressure on
the mayor, which happened when they along with "Professor Louis Wirth of the
University of Chicago and the American Council on Race Relations act[ing] as their
spokesman,"[19] met with the mayor on the following Saturday afternoon. At that point,
according to Jack, "the Mayor indicated that he would back up the Chicago Housing
Authority and promised a public statement of policy."[20] Perhaps reacting again to pressure
from the other side, Kenelly never issued his promised policy statement, something which
Jack also dutifully notes.

As Louis Wirth had done four years earlier, Jack called upon the local authorities to
"investigate the possibility that the disturbances at the Fernwood project were the result of
organized activity and a conspiracy to deprive people of their civil rights."[21] Since the Axis
powers were no longer in a position to orchestrate this sort of thing, Jack pointed his finger instead at "a network of so-called neighborhood improvement associations"[22] as well
as area "churchmen," who "behave little differently from non-churchmen in these situations."[23]

Of course, Jack was referring to Catholics, whose role in protesting the CHA's housing policies was well known at the time. "It is comparatively easy," wrote one observer,
"for an experienced observer mingling with mobs of this type to determine Catholic affiliations. Sweaters with school names or crests on the back, Knights of Columbus lapel pins
and rings, scapulars or other medals seen through an open shirt are some fairly definite
physical symbols of Catholic faith."[24] According to Hirsch the "common denominator
among riot participants, aside from their geographical affinity, stemmed from the fact that
most appeared to be working class Catholics."[25] Fernwood, according to Hirsch, was the
least Catholic of all the riots, something which leads him to confirm "the central role
played by Catholics" in virtually every other disturbance, something that would prove to
be a source of deep embarrassment to the Catholic liberals on the Catholic Interracial
Council. "The church," according to Hirsch,

> and especially the Catholic Interracial Council, were greatly concerned over the
> prominence and notoriety Catholics earned through their violent actions. The radical

press, of course, quickly condemned church involvement in racial disorders. Catholic clergymen, *The Worker* declared, "lent their church in Englewood as a base of racist operations" to the mob at 56th and Peoria and were part of the "alarming rise of fascist activity in this city." But more respectable, and hence more troubling, criticisms were also heard. Homer Jack, a Unitarian minister and co-founder of CORE, similarly attacked Englewood's Catholics and Monsignor Byrnes for sanctioning block organizations designed to keep blacks out of the area and for not "lift[ing] a finger to stop the violence against the Negroes and other people."[26]

Lloyd Davis, speaking for the CIC, tried to defend Catholics but the fact that the CIC accepted all of the liberal premises when it came to the racial issue, left him with little ammunition. It also caused a rift between the CIC and the Council Against Discrimination, which gave voice to anti-Catholic feelings at several of its public meetings. Chicago's racial disturbances were being portrayed in liberal circles as one more manifestation of "the Catholic problem." Catholic liberals like Davis could express "deep disappointment" when the South Deering Methodist Church claimed that Trumbull Park's racial disturbances were caused by the area's Catholics, but his protests left the liberal Protestants unconvinced. It also left later commentators unconvinced. "If it was possible," Hirsch writes, "to take umbrage at the claim that the riots were exclusively a 'Catholic problem,' the CIC was still compelled to confront the fact that it was at very best a problem involving many Catholics."[27] The attempt to qualify the identification of the rioters as "working class" Catholics does nothing to diminish the Catholics' role in the disturbances. If looked at in the absence of material on social engineering, the facts of the matter indicate racial animus as the cause of the riots, even though Hirsch goes on to say that the ethnics were "not motivated simply by a blind, consuming, and uncontrollable racial hatred. . . ." If looked at in light of the evidence, the Catholic composition of the mobs gives evidence that these groups were being specifically targeted for ethnic cleansing.

By 1947, the Catholic conspiracy had replaced the Axis conspiracy as a major area of concern to the nation's liberals, the kind of people who subscribed to *The Nation*. *The Nation's* liberals were concerned about the influence Catholics were having on Hollywood: "The important issue here is not whether Selznick has a moral picture or an offensive picture, but whether a small segment of the population is to impose its standards on all the rest – whether one group has the right to decide for everyone what is right or wrong."[28] They were concerned about the Vatican's excommunication of the Yugoslavian officials who took part in the trial of Cardinal Stepinac, wondering about "the extent to which representatives of the Vatican are influencing American foreign policy – either as employees or officials of our Department of State or as propagandists."[29] They were concerned because

> through the centuries the papacy has always been on the side of reaction. Its very hierarchical system contradicts the concept of democracy; it is built from the above down. It has never modernized itself; on the contrary, it has grown more authoritarian. The waves of freedom that have battered mankind and swept over old privileges of various sorts have broken at the Vatican gardens. With the proclamation

in 1870 by the Council of Rome of the infallibility of the pope in matters of belief and morals, any chance of democratization from within is ended. Half a century later, in 1918, the new code of the Catholic Church, the *Corpus juris canonici* was adopted and the totalitarian papacy received its final touch. A careful study of the famous Encyclical "Immortale Dei" (1885), which has been used to prove the liberalism of the church, shows that even the "Socialist" Leo XIII had no faith in government of the people, by the people and for the people. There never was a Lincoln in the Vatican.[30]

The Nation's liberals were above all concerned about the sexual teachings of the Catholic Church. In fact, it was "The Roman Catholic sexual doctrines which have excited the most opposition in the United States."[31] The author of that statement was Paul Blanshard. His article on "The Sexual Code of the Roman Church" appeared in *The Nation*, sandwiched between two articles by Homer Jack, decrying the effect rampaging Catholic mobs were having on the CHA's integration efforts in Chicago. Paul Blanshard was, like Jack, a liberal Protestant minister who, in Blanshard's case, had abandoned the ministry in favor of socialism and sexual liberation. What he failed to abandon was the animus his ethnic group had always felt against Catholic immigrants. Blanshard had spent the summer of 1919 in a Polish neighborhood in Philadelphia with his brother Brand and would within the space of two decades become a famous author by championing the views Brand Blanshard had expressed about Polish Catholics some twenty years before. Of all the teachings of the Catholic Church on sex, the one which was drawing "the heaviest fire" from Blanshard and *The Nation* in 1947 was their position on birth control, something which "The aged [Pope] Pius [XI] [who] had just piloted the Vatican to a concordat with Mussolini and perhaps he felt that the future belonged to dictatorships in both the moral and the political field. . . announced in his famous encyclical 'Casti Connubii.'"[32] Birth control may have been "against nature," according to the aged pope, but, according to Blanshard,

> Since the days when Margaret Sanger first went to jail, birth control has become so respectable that almost all well-to-do people in the United States, Catholic and non-Catholic practice it to some extent. In fact, if the Catholic opposition, acting as a pressure group did not block legislative reform in many states, the idea of birth control as a human right would be almost universally accepted in this country.[33]

Blanshard knew quite well that the political power of "the Catholic opposition" was based in neighborhoods like Polish Bridesburg in Philadelphia, Hamtramck in Detroit, and all of the neighborhoods which Homer Jack complained about in Chicago. Of Irish Catholic Boston, Blanshard writes, that a referendum on birth control "was defeated, but by a margin of only about seven to five in spite of this campaign, and the liberals have now started a new drive for revision which will probably lead to a vote in the fall of 1948."[34] In *American Freedom and Catholic Power*, the book based on Blanshard's *Nation* articles which appeared two years later, we learn much the same thing about the urban neighborhood base of "Catholic Power."

several of the most publicized political machines in American cities have been essentially Catholic machines in the sense that their leaders and their most important members have been Roman Catholics. Tammany has been dominated for generations by Catholic politicians; James M. Curley's political machine in Boston has been a Catholic machine in a predominantly Catholic city; Frank Hague operated for many years in Jersey City a government which was essentially a clerical state.[35]

Blanshard did not create what he termed "a tremendous revival of anti-Catholic feeling in the United States in recent months"[36] single-handedly. As a journalist he simply articulated the palpable feelings of the ethnic group to which he belonged, the one which also happened to be the ethnos of the country's ruling class. That ethnic group responded with all but universal acclaim to Blanshard's book. McGeorge Bundy praised it from his position at Harvard. John Dewey and Albert Einstein followed suit. Their fears had been crystallized by another event in 1947, the Supreme Court's *Everson* decision, which allowed the state to absorb the cost of bus transportation for the nation's parochial school students. Cardinal Spellman of New York concurred in seeing *Everson* as the cause of resurgent anti-Catholic feeling. "Bigotry," he announced to the 1947 graduation class of Fordham University, "once again is eating its way into the vital organs of the greatest nation on the face of the earth, our beloved America. Once again a crusade is being preached against the Catholic church in the United States . . . now it is the growth and expansion of Catholic education which is claimed to be a constant threat to the supremacy of public education in the United States."[37]

In response to one of Eleanor Roosevelt's syndicated columns, Spellman asked the wife of the late president of the United States, "why . . . do you repeatedly plead causes that are anti-Catholic? . . . For, whatever you may say in the future, your record of anti-Catholicism stands for all to see . . . documents of discrimination unworthy of an American mother." Mrs. Roosevelt replied that she had "no intention of . . . attacking the Roman Catholic Church." She then went on to release a twisted version of what Spellman said to the press which constituted a subtle attack on the Catholic notion of priest and hierarchy as mediator: "I assure you," she wrote, "that I have no sense of being 'an unworthy American mother.' The final judgment, my dear Cardinal Spellman, of the worthiness of all human beings is in the hands of God."[38]

Both Paul Blanshard's book and Eleanor Roosevelt's letter as well as the *Everson* decision itself were symptomatic of some bigger conflict. "When the Supreme Court by a five to four vote last February allowed the state of New Jersey to charge the costs of parochial school transportation to the taxpayers," Blanshard informed the readers of *The Nation*, "the battle lines were drawn for a much larger conflict, of which the bus fight was only the preliminary skirmish."[39] At stake, according to Blanshard's teacher John Dewey, was "the encouragement of a powerful reactionary world organization in the most vital realm of democratic life with the resulting promulgation of principles inimical to democracy."[40] And this was an issue because of the rise of Catholic political power after the war. That power was based on two supports: Catholic demographic increase fueled by the Church's rejection of birth control and the compact and cohesive nature of Catholic ethnic neighborhoods in places like Boston, New York, Philadelphia, Detroit and Chicago and the other large industrial cities of the Northeast and Midwest. The sexual revolution, in particular the development of the birth-control pill, was the ruling class's response to the first threat. As Blanshard told *The Nation's* sexually liberated readership: "Catholic education is based upon the celibacy of its teaching nuns, and the whole educational system of the church might collapse if its teachers were allowed to live a normal [i.e., sexual] life."[41] The solution to the second threat was THE social engineering of ethnic neighborhoods that was taking place at that moment in places like Chicago, as described by Homer Jack in the same magazine. One week after Blanshard's article appeared, Jack described how ten blacks had died in a midnight tenement house fire on West Ohio Street in Chicago. According to "Chicago race-relations experts," the fire was set "in the middle of a 'tension area,' where Italian Americans and others were resisting the 'invasion' of Negroes."[42]

Catholic journals like *America* and *Commonweal* decried Blanshard's thesis, at least in part because it called into question their ability to assimilate. Cardinal Spellman called for a boycott of Blanshard's book, which provoked an anti-boycott, and both spurred sales. But the reaction among *Nation* readers to what Blanshard had to say was uniformly warm and enthusiastic. Letters to the editor in support of what Blanshard had to say often emphasized the dire threat the Catholic Church posed in places like Boston and Philadelphia. Catholics in cities posed an especially serious threat to the American way of life. One resident of a suburb of Boston wrote that "the Catholic Church is becoming aggressive in its attempts to dominate American life. Here in Boston medieval bigotry and superstition have stifled freedom, ruined the school system, and atrophied the public conscience."[43] A reader from western New York felt that Blanshard's articles were "timely and to the point," especially "in view of what is going on now in Philadelphia, where an official of the Roman Catholic Church 'demands' that a certain movie be withdrawn from public showing."[44] One writer touched on a theme which would become the thesis of Blanshard's next book, namely, the moral equivalence between Communism and Catholicism. "We are so preoccupied with the 'reds' that we have failed to realize the presence of a far more dangerous, subtle, and effective menace right here – the curse which wrecked and enslaved Spain, which helped precipitate World War II, and is doing its utmost to bring war again."[45]

Catholic liberals, unable to admit that Chicago's race riots were an essentially Catholic phenomenon, were also unable to admit its logical corollary as well, namely, that the CHA, the CHR, and the MHPC were pursuing their policies with Catholic neighborhoods in mind. The inability to admit that nativism wasn't really dead would have far-reaching consequences for the Catholic Church in America. Since race relations was almost by definition a project led by liberal intellectuals, it meant that the Catholic Church could not respond properly to the destruction of its parishes in big cities because it could not see what was actually happening. Instead of dealing with the manipulation of race, migration, and housing, the Catholic Church under the leadership of the Catholic Interracial Council, especially its Chicago branch, issued essentially true but irrelevant statements about the humanity of blacks – issues that no Catholic was prepared to contest – that simply internalized the categories which the WASP ruling class had codified in Myrdal's book. The country's postwar housing system – suburbs for deracinated white ethnics and projects for underclass blacks – was hammered out in 1947 with the "Catholic Problem" in the minds of those doing the hammering. Shortly after the period of "chronic urban guerrilla warfare" began in Chicago in the mid- to late '40s, most observers, from the spies employed by the ACLU to official race spokesmen like Louis Wirth and Homer Jack, recognized that the one thing the opponents to racial integration had in common was the fact that they were working-class Catholics. But no one was willing to draw the logical conclusion: that the neighborhoods were being engineered because Catholics lived there and because by living there those Catholics posed a serious political threat to liberal Protestant hegemony over American culture.

Notes

1 Arnold R. Hirsch, *Making the Second Ghetto: Race and Housing in Chicago, 1940–1960* (Cambridge: Cambridge University Press, 1983), p. 56.
2 Housing as a Field of Sociological Research by Louis Wirth American Sociological Society Dec. 30, 1946, Box LIII, folder 1, Wirth Archives, University of Chicago.
3 Ibid.
4 Ibid.
5 Ibid., p. 99.
6 Ibid., p. 104.
7 Ibid., p. 106.
8 Ibid., p. 268.
9 Ibid., p. 99.
10 Ibid., pp. 203–4.
11 Ibid., p. 197.
12 Ibid.
13 Ibid., p. 205.
14 Ibid.
15 Ibid., p. 220.
16 Ibid.
17 Homer A. Jack, "Chicago Has One More Chance," *The Nation* (September 13, 1947): 250.
18 Ibid.
19 Ibid.
20 Ibid.
21 Ibid.
22 Ibid.
23 Ibid.
24 William Gremly, "The Scandal of Cicero," *America* (August 25, 1951): 495
25 Hirsch, p. 85.
26 Ibid., p. 86.
27 Ibid., p. 87.
28 "Catholics and Hollywood," *The Nation* 164 (February 15, 1947): 185.
29 *The Nation*, Letters to the editor (January 18, 1947): 83.
30 "Del Vayo – the Vatican and Democracy," *The Nation* 165 (July 12, 1947): 45.
31 Paul Blanshard, "The Sexual Code of the Roman Church," *The Nation* (November 8, 1947): 496.
32 Ibid.

33 Ibid.

34 Ibid.

35 Paul Blanshard, *American Freedom and Catholic Power* (Boston: The Beacon Press, 1949), p. 57.

36 Paul Blanshard, "The Catholic Church and Education," *The Nation* (November 15, 1947); 525.

37 Ibid.

38 Paul Blanshard, *Communism, Democracy, and Catholic Power* (Boston: The Beacon Press, 1951), p. 308.

39 Paul Blanshard, "The Catholic Church and Education," P. 528.

40 John T. McGreevy, "Thinking on One's Own: Catholicism in the American Intellectual Imagination, 1928–1960," *The Journal of American History* (Juen 1997): 120.

41 Blanshard, "The Sexual Code," p. 496.

42 Homer A. Jack, "The New Chicago Fires," *The Nation* (November 22, 1947): 551.

43 Letters on the Catholic Series, *The Nation* (December 13, 1947): 659.

44 Ibid.

45 Ibid.

Oscar's Brainstorm

At some time between when Ed Bacon went off to war in the Pacific and the outbreak of the riots in Chicago, Walter Phillips found himself at the bar of the hotel where he was staying in Chicago attending a national planning conference there, discussing what could be done to advance the cause of urban planning in Philadelphia. With him were Oscar Stonorov and Robert Mitchell, originally from Chicago, but now working with the housers in Philadelphia. Eventually the three planners came up with an idea for an exhibit which would give Philadelphians a graphic sense of what their city would look like if it were redesigned with Bauhaus instead of the rowhouse as its basic architectural model in mind. Soon the men were dividing up the work necessary to make their vision a reality. Stonorov wrote to Bacon in the Pacific about the actual model of the city, which was to occupy a large part of one whole floor of Gimbel's, the downtown department store where the exhibit would be held. Phillips was dispatched to sell the idea to Edward Hopkinson, who would enlist the support of the downtown business interests, and Mitchell and Stonorov were to go to Arthur Kauffman to persuade him to let them use Gimbel's. Mitchell would attribute ultimate responsibility for the idea to Stonorov. "This was one of Oscar's brainstorms." Mitchell claimed, "he was always extremely enthusiastic about city planning and about the kind of work that was going on."[1]

Oscar's brainstorm occurred around the same time that urban planning was being reestablished under the protective covering of the war. "It was felt," Mitchell said later, "that Pennsylvania should prepare itself for what we expected would be a major national program of urban renewal for American cities."[2] Once the war was over, the major obstacle to that major national program being implemented in Philadelphia had been removed. Now it was up to people like Stonorov, Mitchell, and Phillips to see that Philadelphia didn't drop the ball again, as it had in 1941 when the mayor turned down $19 million in federal money. That meant portraying urban renewal in a positive light, and that meant orchestrating an unprecedented public-relations coup of the sort that would cause the inhabitants of the "city of homes" to re-think their attitudes.

It would also mean an unprecedented intrusion of government power into their lives, something that did not get mentioned at the exhibition, but which caused both Mitchell and Phillips some concern when they reviewed their efforts with the benefit of almost 30 years of hindsight. Phillips by then would admit openly that renewal was predicated on "the idea of having the legislature grant power to the city to take by eminent domain sizable areas in conditions of physical deterioration and social blight."[3] The City Planning Commission, which was dominated at the time by Phillips and his supporters, had the power to designate an area as blighted, but they had no power to act on their recommendations. That was done by the redevelopment authority in conjunction with City Council. It was precisely the commission's power to declare an area blighted which caused Mitchell a twinge of conscience, because in retrospect he could see that the designation of blight was destined to become a self-fulfilling prophesy. "I think we made a great mistake at that time," Mitchell told Phillips thirty years later,

> because a large amount of the areas that were considered blighted in Philadelphia were designated all at one time. The effect of this, of course, was that since they were called blighted it was expected that they would deteriorate unless some urgent public actions were taken within time, and a number of owners began to stop repairing their houses, paying taxes and so forth. This probably made the blight increase rather than relieve it. Later it was discovered that the designations for a number of these areas should be removed and areas should be designated only shortly in advance of the time that the Redevelopment Authority was prepared to take action.[4]

But by then, of course, it was too late to save the areas which had already been declared blighted. At the time of the Better Philadelphia Exhibition, which is to say in October of 1947, none of these dangers seemed evident to Mitchell or Bacon or Phillips or Stonorov. The general atmosphere surrounding the exhibition, according to Bacon, was "that we needed science to improve the cities. The feeling was that we were moving into the age of technology and that we needed technocrats to run things. The cities needed the support of science."[5] In a way that typified the era, Philadelphians were being offered a revolutionary new order in which the traditional property rights of certain groups were going to be curtailed in the interest of other groups, as managed by still other groups. Since this transaction would seem outrageous if it were described according to its actual ethnic outlines, it would have to be disguised beneath scientific trappings and appeals to the future, something they accomplished by adopting the style of other futuristic ventures. When the reporter from *Architectural Forum* arrived to do a story on the BPE, he was struck by how "the entrance to the exhibition, with ramps leading to a dimly illuminated area, is strikingly reminiscent of the Futurama at the World's Fair."[6] Drawn into its vision of the future by "publicity unprecedented in scope," the reporter felt that "The public could hardly help itself"[7] in resisting the vision of the New Philadelphia which Phillips's and the rest of his "clever few" presented to them. Eventually more than 385,000 Philadelphians would pass through the exhibit during the two months of its run on the fifth and sixth floors of Gimbel's. There they saw three dimensional models of how Philadelphia would look with Bauhaus high-rise buildings replacing its traditional buildings, as well as "a huge aerial photo map, movies, a diorama, murals, wall panels, cartoons, mechanical gadgets" and the "reproduction of an actual street corner," whose purpose was "to sock home what is wrong with Philadelphia and what, specifically, can be done about it."[8]

The life-sized model was based on an actual intersection in South Philadelphia, 13th and Latona. The location of the intersection was significant because South Philadelphia, the city's Italian section, had been "chosen for overhauling by the city's Redevelopment Authority."[9] In spite of the reporter's enthusiasm for urban planning under the direction of "a brash bluestocking named Walter M. Phillips, fresh out of Harvard Law School [it was actually Princeton Law School] and aching for reform,"[10] a number of disquieting facts start to intrude into the narrative, almost in spite of the writer's intention to praise the exhibit and everything progressive associated with it. Thirteenth and Latona, for example, is described as a "dingy object lesson of what is wrong with Philadelphia."[11] The area surrounding 13th and Latona, has been "chosen for overhauling by the city's Redevelopment Authority" because it "is typical of South Philadelphia's dingy [that word again], overcrowded neighborhoods. *Although not a slum* [my emphasis], it nevertheless lacks adequate shops, play space and new housing."[12] The neighborhood, in other words, is not run down; it is "dingy," the subjective term which is going to be used to justify tearing the neighborhood down and driving the people living there out of it. At another point in the same article, we read that the full-sized reconstruction of 13th and Latona, "complete even to a messy garbage can . . . recreates the atmosphere of drabness and monotony which blights many of Philadelphia's residential areas *more than actual disrepair*"[13] (my emphasis). In other words, the houses in South Philadelphia which the Redevelopment Authority wanted to tear down were not in disrepair and the area was not a slum, something which might lead the thoughtful observer to wonder why the Redevelopment Authority was planning to tear them down.

Discerning the answer to that question and discovering the intention which informed the BPE in general and the model of 13th and Latona in particular can be accomplished best by examining the artifact which dominates the corner's foreground, namely, the overflowing trash can. It was a device which got used frequently in the urban-renewal battles of the '50s. Ray Flynn, while mayor of Boston, remembers talking to a photographer from one of that city's newspapers which had campaigned avidly for the destruction and subsequent "renewal" of the West End. The photographer's assignment was to go to the West End, find a trash can, empty it on the sidewalk, and then take picture of the mess he had just made as evidence that the area was blighted. That picture subsequently propelled public opinion and therefore political action into destroying a neighborhood which its own residents did not want destroyed, and the photographer not only remembered the role he had played in that destruction, he was bothered enough to confess it to the "ethnic" mayor who would go on to use the last vacant lot in the renewed West End as the site for an apartment building to house its refugees.

Renewal, in other words, was based more on the manipulation of public opinion than the science and hygiene Bacon talked about. In fact, it was based on the deliberate and dishonest manipulation of fear of things like disease at a time when the inhabitants of these neighborhoods made a habit of things like scrubbing their front steps. Like Phillips and Mitchell, Ed Bacon viewed things differently with the benefit of hindsight. In 1975 he gave a speech at Temple University in which he admitted that the "scientific" criteria of blight could be pretty much skewed however the housers wanted to skew them. "They came up with a scoring system," Bacon related later, "that would scientifically establish the status of the decay of the housing stock. They would give a house a numerical value and then add up the numbers on a block and divide by the number of houses and come up with a number which they would use to create maps of black and gray and white that would specify if a neighborhood was blighted or not. This was the fundamental intellectual basis for the housing program."[14]

As an example of how the condition of one house could affect the status of an entire block, Bacon recounted visiting one of the properties his family owned in the city. Their house was completely derelict with rats running out of the cellar. It was the only rundown house on the block, but it dragged the value of all of the other houses on the block down with it, and since the ratings for blight were cumulative, it could have meant that the entire block would be designated as a slum by Phillips' Planning Commission and then torn down by the redevelopment authority. The designation of blight was, in other words, based not so much on objective criteria as on the feelings of certain people, who felt that certain places were "dingy" and so needed to be destroyed. It was also based on the fact that people in certain neighborhoods did not like people in other neighborhoods, and those people suddenly found themselves empowered by the federal government and the courts to act on their dislike. The housers may have been troubled by guilty conscience in their later years, but they could never bring themselves to form a coherent picture of what they had wrought in Philadelphia. When asked fifty-three years after the BPE if the process of which areas got designated as blighted might have been affected by political or ethnic considerations, Bacon exploded in angry denial. "We were doing good," he said, forgetting evidently the speech he gave at Temple twenty-five years earlier. "Everyone was trying to do good."[15]

When Rotello's claim in *October Cities* was brought up, namely, that the Crosstown Expressway, a ten-lane highway that did not get built along the Lombard/South Street corridor because of community opposition, was intended as a barrier between "professional" center city and "ethnic" South Philadelphia, Bacon explodes again, "I don't give a fucking damn about any book." Calming down a bit, Bacon went on to give his version of why the Crosstown Expressway was proposed.

> Lombard and South Streets were the worst slums in the city. It was just sensible to come up with some way to get across the city there from a traffic point of view by the clearance of the most decrepit houses and that the corridor west of Broad would be the South and Lombard street corridor. Mayor Dilworth came to me and said that we needed a regional plan for transportation for the whole area. I was in over my head on that one. So Dilworth called in Robert Mitchell who gave Dilworth the plan for SEPTA. The idea of a major expressway along South Street was Bob Mitchell's. Dilworth adopted a plan which called for an expressway. I proposed a boulevard, but I promised every mayor I served under that I would support their ideas. It is not true that the South Street Expressway was intended as a racial dividing line. If you're asking for my motivation, it was the last thing on my mind to construct a barrier. I planned along with it in my 1963 plan, but it was Mitchell's idea and not mine. I used my influence to help undermine the South Street Expressway.[16]

If Bacon were using his influence to undermine the Crosstown Expressway, it was not apparent to the people who gathered to hear him address a community hearing in the 1960s on the impact the expressway would have on the neighborhood. Sam Maitin, a local artist, remembers how Jared Ingersoll, WASP patrician and resident of Society Hill, stood up and said that he was having misgivings about the road. He had been for it in the beginning but now that he actually saw how wide it was going to be he thought it would act as a barrier to keep the people of South Philadelphia out of center city. Bacon denied this. "It's 11 lanes wide, Ed," Ingersoll persisted. "How could an old lady ever cross that street before the light would change. It's not possible." Bacon insisted that it was, and when pressed for his explanation of how it was possible, responded, "Because I have said it is."[17]

Ed Bacon was having another Quaker moment. Maitin characterized Bacon as an arrogant mendacious man, who stole all of Louie Kahn's ideas for the city (Louie Kahn said, "don't tear down the old neighborhoods") and then made sure that he couldn't get any work in Philadelphia. What Maitin failed to see is that arrogance and mendacity are not so much personal as ethnic characteristics which derived ultimately from the Quaker religion, whose belief in the "inner light" confers personal infallibility on its members. Quakerism is a sect which has neither dogma nor doctrine, whose liturgy is nothing more than long silences interrupted by personal testimony. Since they have no religious principles, Quakers are raised in a profoundly anti-intellectual atmosphere and are, as a result, not skilled at argumentation. "Anyone who has lived among Proper Philadelphians for any length of time," Digby Baltzell noted in his book comparing Quaker Philadelphia and Puritan Boston, "would have observed their lack of the kind of seriousness and deep concern exhibited by Proper Bostonians."[18] Baltzell quite rightly traces Philadelphia's lack of seriousness and their lack of intellectual accomplishment when compared to Boston to the Quaker sect whose religious beliefs were incapable of sustaining serious intellectual discourse. In addition to that the irrationality of those principles when it came to maintaining the social order quickly earned the sect a reputation for mendacity and hypocrisy, one that stretched all the way back to its founder. Ben Franklin tells the story of how William Penn and his co-religionists while on their voyage to America were threatened by an approaching ship which they feared was going to attack them. All of the Quakers but one retreated below deck. The one remaining was given a weapon to help defend the ship. When the attack proved to be a false alarm, the Quaker joined his co-religionists only to find himself upbraided by Penn for taking up arms, something which struck the man as hypocritical. "I being thy servant, why did thee not order me to come down? But thee was willing enough that I should stay and help to fight the ship when thee thought there was danger."[19]

Since Quakers wanted to control the lands of Pennsylvania in spite of their pacifism, they quickly became adept at war by proxy. As Baltzell noted in the same book, Quakers hated Catholics but declined to say so publicly in the aftermath of the 1844 riots. Instead they condemned the violence publicly while supporting its effects in private. Prohibited by their pacifism from bearing arms, Quakers became adept in getting others to do their fighting for them, twisting the language to rationalize the purchase of arms. When the Pennsylvania assembly was required by the Crown to appropriate money for weaponry to defend the colony, the Quakers found themselves in a bind. "They were unwilling," Franklin wrote,

> to offend government, on the one hand, by a direct refusal; and their friends, the body of the Quakers, on the other, by a compliance contrary to their principles; hence a variety of evasions to avoid complying, and modes of disguising the compliance when it became unavoidable. The common mode at least was to grant money under the phrase of its being "for the king's use," and never to inquire how it was applied.[20]

The Quakers made use of other equally dishonest evasions as well. Franklin noted with disdain that Quakers in the state assembly would not appropriate money for gunpowder for the colony's defense, but they would appropriate money for the purchase of "bread, flour, wheat, or *other grain*,"[21] knowing full well that by "other grain" everyone knew they meant gunpowder. Similarly, their religious principles would not allow them to buy a cannon, but they would allow them to purchase a "fire engine," their word for the same thing.

Since their religious principles demanded this sort of logic chopping and equivocation, the Quakers quickly became adept in what later generations would call "spin control" and "public relations," something which naturally lent itself to the practice of psychological warfare as a substitute for the conventional warfare their religious principles condemned. Since their religion prohibited the use of force in defense of community, the Quakers had to resort to more sophisticated means to maintain social order, means that were completely consistent with the methods of cultural warfare and social control which got implemented in the mid-20th century. They early on became adept at the psychological manipulation of peer pressure known as "friendly persuasion," something which would later become "sensitivity training," when 17th-century Pietism got weaponized by Kurt Lewin working for the Office of Naval Research. At around the same time, Ed Bacon was putting on the Better Philadelphia Exhibition, which was also the same year that the American Friends Service Committee won the Nobel Prize. The Quakers had no need to get the idea from the psychological-warfare establishment, because the military got the idea of psychological warfare from them. Quakers took their model for discourse on things like the Crosstown Expressway from their experience of liturgy at the Quaker meeting house. Discourse for Quakers like Ed Bacon meant giving personal testimony, which was to be accepted as one would accept this sort of thing at a Quaker meeting. Any attempt to reason with this testimony was perceived at community meetings as it would be if it occurred at their religious services, which is to say, as an act of impiety, and quite rightly (at least from the Quaker point of view) shouted down with angry denial.

Quakers were staunch supporters of abolition (although William Penn declined to free his slaves upon his death, as he had promised) when it came to the black population of the country, and just as staunch in their support of ethnic cleansing when it came to the Indian population. The Quakers employed German mercenaries from central Pennsylvania to drive the Catholics out of Maryland. All of these themes would re-emerge in the Philadelphia housing battles of the 1950s and '60s when Quakers turned the newly arrived black sharecroppers into another proxy army which would wage another campaign of ethnic cleansing against another domestic enemy – all under the guise of "doing good." The destruction of Philadelphia's ethnic neighborhoods was an essentially Quaker project rationalized in typically Quaker fashion, by people whose religion conferred on them personal infallibility. Quakers were the quintessential do-gooders, and since they were personally infallible, everything they did – from evicting Indian tribes from their lands in the 18th century to driving Italians from their neighborhoods in the 20th century – was *ipso facto* good. Because they constituted the ruling class in Philadelphia, their ethnic prejudices were considered normative, especially when it came to issues like housing, since they dominated things like the Philadelphia Housing Association simply by the fact that they constituted the ruling class. Rather than openly declaring war on Philadelphia's Catholics, the housers, in the Quaker tradition of combining warfare by proxy, psychological manipulation, and public relations, used the Better Philadelphia Exhibition to declare war on the rowhouse instead. In the end it would prove to be two different ways of doing the same thing.

Although they all claimed to be credentialed scientists, the housers in other cities were invariably drawn from the elite ethnic groups there and acted ultimately with their interests in mind, not objective "scientific" criteria. Herbert Gans, who lived in Boston's West End and worked for the agency that destroyed it, gives a clear picture of the ethnocentric and ultimately subjective norms that guided reformers in his classic book on urban renewal, *The Urban Villagers*:

> in most communities, the area's physical condition is a necessary but not sufficient criterion. What seems to happen is that neighborhoods come to be described as slums if they are inhabited by residents who, for a variety of reasons indulge in overt and visible behavior considered undesirable by the majority of the community. The community image of the area then gives rise to feelings that something should be done, and subsequently the area is proposed for renewal. Consequently the planning reports that are written to justify renewal dwell as much on social as on physical criteria, and are filled with data intended to show the prevalence of antisocial or pathological behavior in the area. The implication is that the area itself causes such behavior, and should therefore be redeveloped.[22]

The purpose of urban renewal was, in other words, to change behavior by changing buildings. The BPE focused on the rowhouse in waging its attack on the ethnic neighborhoods in Philadelphia because urban renewal was the only respectable way people who didn't like the Italians in South Philadelphia could attack the way those people lived. "The Professionals' evaluation of the behavior of slum residents," Gans continued, "is based on class-based standards that often confuse behavior which is only culturally different with pathological or antisocial acts. . . . these standards are used to tear down poor neighborhoods, while better housing for the residents is not made available."[23]

The deliberate destruction of affordable housing served a social purpose as well. The people who were driven from the neighborhoods were forced to better themselves; they were forced to become middle class. Gans, the social worker, told this part of the story from personal experience with other social workers. "The relocation staff's lack of interest in social criteria of housing choice was based partly on a desire – implicit in much of planning and housing ideology – *to break up ethnic ghettoes*, in the belief that this would encourage people like the West Enders to adopt middle class standards and behavior patterns" (my emphasis).[24] The ethnics, in other words, would have to move to the suburbs, with all the increased costs that entailed, because no other housing was available, while at the same time the well-to-do got to occupy their intrinsically more valuable location because it was closer to town.

Forty-two years after the West End was destroyed, an article on its destruction appeared in the *Wall Street Journal*, describing the crusade of Jim Capano, who, along with other Italians, was ethnically cleansed from the neighborhood. "What Boston did to its West End," the *Journal* reporter opined, "was called slum clearance at first, then urban renewal, and then a crime." In tacit recognition of that fact, Ray Flynn, Irish Catholic Mayor of Boston thirty years after the West End was destroyed, worked to get new housing constructed on the same site for the people who were displaced, but after the building was built, federal authorities once again stepped in and set aside most of the units for blacks. "Years ago, we were asked to pay the price of 'the new Boston,'" Mr. Capano would tell a City Council hearing. "Now we are asked to pay the price of segregation. When do we stop paying?" Capano's community organization sued the housing authority, alleging reverse discrimination, but lost the suit in 1998.[25]

What made this ethnic cleansing possible was the aura of science and progress with which the housers surrounded their projects. In order to understand how it worked and why it worked, one has to understand the *Zeitgeist*. The BPE took place one year before Alfred Kinsey, another master of manipulating the symbols of science for political ends, orchestrated what his biographer called the greatest public-relations coup in the history of the United States, the publicity surrounding the publication of his 1948 study of male sexuality. One of the things which made this possible at the time was the mass migration of the intelligence community into the mass media and foundation complex after the war. OWI's overseas director Edward Barrett wrote in 1953 that OWI alumni were now

> the publishers of *Time, Look, Fortune*, and several dailies, editors of such magazines as *Holiday, Coronet, Parade*, and the *Saturday Review*, editors of the *Denver Post, New Orleans Times-Picayune*, and others; the heads of the Viking Press, Harper & Brothers , and Farrar, Strauss and Young; two Hollywood Oscar winners, a two-time Pulitzer prize-winner, the board chairman of CBS and a dozen key network executives; President Eisenhower's chief speech writer; the editor of *Reader's Digest* international editions; at least six partners of large advertising agencies, and a dozen noted social scientists.[26]

The psychological-warfare crowd took their ethnic prejudices with them when they went into journalism and used the journals they controlled to promote the projects people like those in the Rockefeller Foundation, which was also instrumental in the creation of psychological warfare, were funding. Another reason was the migration of the intelligence community into the big foundations themselves, one of which, Rockefeller, would fund Kinsey, and another of which, Ford, would fund race-based change in ethnic neighborhoods. Another reason was the already mentioned ethnic homogeneity of the psychological-warfare crowd and their penchant for science and technology. Another was the virtual identity of social sciences, communications theory, and psychological warfare. The net result, according to Simpson, was that

> various leaders in the social sciences engaged one another in tacit alliances to promote their particular interpretations of society. Their wartime experiences contributed substantially to the construction of a remarkably tight circle of men and women who shared several important conceptions about mass communication research. They regard mass communication as a tool for social management and as a weapon in social conflict, and they expressed common assumptions concerning

the usefulness of qualitative research – particularly experiment and quasi-experimental effects research, opinion surveys, and quantitative content analysis – as a means of illuminating what communication "is" and improving its application to social management.[27]

The message of the BPE was that the people who could be relied upon to have something of value in the housing field were not the people who lived in the houses which were scheduled for destruction, but rather "professionals," which meant people with credentials, which meant people who attended WASP universities. The people who lived in the neighborhoods, according to Reginald Isaacs, who was busy dispensing credentials from Harvard University, didn't know what was good for their own neighborhoods, much less the city as a whole. Catholic ethnics were, as a result, disenfranchised from discussing the fate of their own neighborhoods. The BPE, while fostering this sense of the professionals' power at the same time dishonestly gave the Philadelphians who came to see it some sense that it was empowering them to make these very decisions. In a move which Ed Bacon consciously borrowed from Burnham's 1910 exhibit in Chicago, Philadelphia's school children were asked to make models of their neighborhoods and then say how they would change their neighborhoods, without being informed that the tacit assumption behind the question was that all of their neighborhoods needed to be changed. This sort of social engineering was necessary, according to the *Architectural Digest* article, in order to "gain favor with conservative citizenry which has little quarrel with the status quo."[28] And this was necessary because "[t]he anonymity of huge, one class housing projects, already in disrepute among planners themselves, would definitely not go down with Philadelphians."[29] But it did go down with Phillips's Citizens Council, which could "gloat over the mass base for planning this program should produce in a decade"[30] when the school children reached voting age. It also delighted the Philadelphia Board of Education because it gave them opportunity to "teach children how to integrate themselves into society"[31] or at least into the plans of those who wanted to commandeer the housing situation in Philadelphia for their own benefit. The city's public-school children, drawn into a covert manipulation of public opinion that probably eventuated in the destruction of many of their own homes, were described as being "for the first time actively involved in community life" and "filled" as a result "with a new importance."[32]

Bauman, in his history of housing in Philadelphia, describes the BPE as "extraordinarily successful," characterizing it as an event in which "More than 400,000 people paid a $1 fee to gaze at Philadelphia's grim past and behold its planned and magnificent future."[33] Bauman calls the BPE an event which "accomplished its purpose."[34] Years later, Edmund Bacon said much the same thing. Bacon remembered being "surrounded by the earnest and marvelously moving voices of the children about their dissatisfaction with the city and their neighborhoods and the kind of vision and urge that they had for making it better, and of course it wasn't very long before those children grew up and really started working in the neighborhoods and voting on the bond issues"[35] that would permit the government to tear down their houses. "We had the different idea," Bacon continued, "of having the children not study somebody else's plan, which was obsolete by the time they grew up, but to experience the process of planning themselves."[36]

Again, the Quaker meeting comes to mind. Everyone has an equal right to his own plan guided by his own "inner light." Instead of assuring the city's school children that "every man [was] his own priest," a notion Walt Whitman promoted in his poetry after rowing across the river from Camden to hear the Quaker revivalist Hicks, Bacon was promoting its 20th-century variant, "every man his own city planner." Both were equally disingenuous. After the initial glow wore off, the enthusiast would return to his normal life as the real plan – the one which had the blessings of the wealthy and powerful – got put into effect, to the detriment of those who had been duped into thinking they had a say in such things.

"People," Bacon concluded, "were deeply moved by it."[37]

Philadelphians would soon discover that they were going to be moved by it in more than one sense of the word. One of the major accomplishments of the BPE according to Bacon was the destruction of the rowhouse as the housing paradigm for the "city of homes." "At the time it was done," Bacon continued, "it was supposed to be an extremely radical concept."[28] But after the BPE, "overnight the whole pattern changed and almost all the buildings in the Northeast since then have been based on that."[39] Instead of a uniform façade of houses facing often tree-lined sidewalks, where the people could sit on their front steps and socialize with their neighbors, Bacon came up with "the idea of reversing the row house."[40] That meant "putting the garages in front"[41] thereby putting an end to the front step as an area of socializing and creating at the same stroke some of the ugliest housing ever created in the city of Philadelphia, some of which can still be seen in Northeast Philadelphia, the one area of the city that was created largely under the inspiration of the BPE.

The BPE was an all-out attack on the rowhouse and, by extension, the manner of living the rowhouse made possible. It was, by still further extension, an all-out covert attack in the Quaker manner on the largely ethnic Philadelphians who lived in those houses. The rowhouse, as foreign visitors to Philadelphia noticed in the 19th century, meant unprecedented cultural independence for the working class families in Philadelphia fortunate enough to own them. Bauhaus, as anyone who has visited the South Side of Chicago or any of the countries ruled by the Soviet Union after World War II could testify, meant social regimentation and government control of family life, leading ultimately to the destruction of family life and pathologies like alcoholism, illegitimacy, and drug addiction. This is also what it would come to mean in Philadelphia in projects like the Richard Allen Homes and Schuylkill Falls. The demise of the rowhouse in Philadelphia meant that pathologies which were associated with a government-dependency syndrome would increase in direct proportion to the number of Bauhaus-inspired buildings which got built there.

The real significance of the BPE can only be understood by understanding its position in the context of the times, a context which included not only the Kinsey report one year later but the founding of the Americans for Democratic Action six months earlier, the *Everson* Supreme Court decision around the same time, as well as the occupation of the first houses in Levittown and Paul Blanshard's articles on Catholic power which appeared in *The Nation* during the same month Philadelphians were streaming into the BPE to applaud the imminent destruction of their own homes and neighborhoods. Looking back on the era of the Supreme Court's *Everson* decision with fifty years of historical perspective, Tocqueville scholar Michael Ledeen finds "hilarious" references in the decisions to "America's [being] threatened by two forms of totalitarian tyranny – the Roman Catholic Church and the world Communist conspiracy. And of the two, the Roman Catholic Church is by far the more dangerous. That's the kind of stuff they were reading."[42] Hugo Black, in fact, got the idea of the Catholic conspiracy from his days in the Ku Klux Klan, when he defended a man who murdered a priest, but his suspicions were reaffirmed by reading Paul Blanshard (his son said that Black read everything Blanshard ever wrote) and eventually those ideas began to crop up in Supreme Court decisions.

Ledeen calls this "European thinking," but people like John Lukacs noticed the same thing when he wrote about Bacon and the Phillips crowd in Philadelphia from the perspective of a newly arrived Hungarian immigrant in 1947, and didn't find it particularly European. In fact, it had a kind of invincible liberal provinciality to it that extinguished all thought in favor of WASP ethnic prejudice about things progressive and enlightened. What Lukacs discovered was the Quaker simulacrum of discourse, namely, ethnically sanctioned prejudice which worked essentially by association, not reason. That meant that it would be impolite to bring up the fact that the same Ed Bacon who in 1988 wanted city hall preserved as a monument with no building higher than it in center city had proposed that the same building be torn down and a modern parking garage erected in its place in 1933. The Philadelphia Quaker-Episcopalian elite, Lukacs discovered at around the time of the BPE, could not think. It could only approve or disapprove, based on commonly shared ethnic prejudice.

Given the limitations of the Quaker mind – its absence of rational principle, its reliance on personal witness of the sort which brooked no opposition, its recourse to psychological manipulation rather than straightforward appeal to principle and then physical force if that failed, its simultaneous cultivation of the illusion of democratic principle coupled with its reliance on behind-the-scenes manipulation, its 300-year tradition of mendacity in defense of untenable religious principle – as well as their domination of the housing profession, urban renewal as practiced in Philadelphia could be nothing other than a psychological warfare campaign to implement ethnic prejudice. The Better Philadelphia Exhibition was the opening shot in that war.

Like Hugo Black, the Phillips crowd was reading Paul Blanshard, and like virtually everyone else in their class at that time they were concerned about the rise of "Catholic power." The rowhouse was significant because it was the architectural locus of "Catholic Power" in Philadelphia. The Phillips crowd probably noticed the references to Philadelphia, things like the fact that

> The Right Reverend John J. Bonner, diocesan superintendent of schools of Philadelphia, boasted in 1941 that the increase in the Catholic births in Philadelphia in the preceding decade had been more than fifty per cent higher than the increase in the total population, and that Philadelphia "will be fifty percent Catholic in a comparatively short time." . . . If the disparity in birth rates which he claimed should continue indefinitely, it would not be long before the United States became a Catholic country by default.[43]

In addition to the Catholic Church's ban on contraception, a ban which had added force because of the religious cohesion of the ethnic neighborhood, one of the main things which fueled this demographic increase in Philadelphia was the rowhouse. It was cheap enough for a worker to own. It was more spacious than an apartment, and instead of paying rent and being at the mercy of landlords, a man could own his home free and clear in the time it took him to pay off his mortgage. Since it was located in the city near public transportation, the rowhouse did not require the expense of owning a car. Since it was surrounded on both sides by other houses, it was cheap to heat. As a result, it allowed the working-class Catholic family to have a large family, and over a period of time, it allowed him to benefit from the political power which followed demographic increase, which is precisely what was causing Blanshard and the Phillips crowd concern. The attack on the rowhouse which the BPE orchestrated meant an attack on all of the cultural attributes that went with the rowhouse, a building which symbolized the cultural independence of the ethnic neighborhood based on religious cohesion and the economic independence of immigrant workers who could own their own homes. The attack on the rowhouse in Philadelphia was a covert attack on the Catholics who lived in them, orchestrated by a ruling class that knew, as good Darwinians, that demography was destiny and that they, because of their all but universal adoption of contraception, were on the losing end of the demographic equation. Urban renewal, like the sexual revolution which followed it eighteen years later, was the WASP ruling class's attempt to keep "the United States from becoming a Catholic country by default."

Notes

1 Robert Mitchell, Walter M. Phillips oral histories, Temple University Urban Archives.
2 Ibid.
3 Mitchell, oral history, Temple.
4 Ibid.
5 Interview with Edmund Bacon 5/15/00.
6 "Philadelphia Plans Again," reprinted from *Architectural Forum* December 1947, The Better Philadelphia Exhibition, Temple University Urban Archives.
7 Ibid.
8 Ibid.
9 Ibid.
10 Ibid.
11 Ibid.
12 Ibid.
13 Ibid.
14 Bacon, Interview.
15 Ibid.
16 Ibid.
17 Interview with Sam Maitin, 8/00.
18 E. Digby Baltzell, *Puritan Boston and Quaker Philadelphia: Two Protestant Ethics and the Spirit of Class Authority and Leadership* (New York: The Free Press, 1979), p. 451.

19 Benjamin Franklin, *Autobiography*, in *A Benjamin Franklin Reader*, ed. Nathan G. Goodman (New York: Thomas Y. Crowell Company, 1945), p. 149.

20 Ibid.

21 Ibid.

22 Herbert J. Gans, *The Urban Villagers: Group and Class in the Life of Italian Americans* (New York: The Free Press of Glencoe, 1962), p. 308.

23 Gans, p. 309.

24 Gans, p. 323.

25 Barry Newman, "West End Story: A Neighborhood Died, But One Bostonian Refuses to Let It Go," *The Wall Street Journal* (August 23, 2000).

26 Simpson, *Coercion*, p. 28–29.

27 Simpson, *Coercion*, p. 29.

28 "Philadelphia Plans Again."

29 Ibid.

30 Ibid.

31 Ibid.

32 Ibid.

33 John F Bauman, *Public Housing, Race, and Renewal: Urban Planning in Philadelphia, 1920–1974* (Philadelphia: Temple University Press, 1987), p. 100.

34 Ibid.

35 Bacon, oral history, Temple.

36 Ibid.

37 Ibid.

38 Ibid.

39 Ibid.

40 Ibid.

41 Ibid.

42 Kathryn Jean Lopez, "Tocqueville Is Our National Psychoanalyst."

43 Paul Blanshard, *American Freedom and Catholic Power* (Boston: The Beaco Press, 1949), pp. 284, 286.

Levittown Opens Its Doors

In October 1947, the same month that the Better Philadelphia Exhibition opened its doors, the same month that Homer Jack wrote about the housing riots in Chicago in *The Nation*, and the same month that Paul Blanshard broached "the Catholic problem" to the same readers, the first families began to move into a recently completed housing development on what was once 4,000 acres of potato farm in the Town of Hempstead, New York. Hempstead was on Long Island, known among other things as the setting for F. Scott Fitzgerald's novel *The Great Gatsby*, among the estates of the wealthy on the island's north shore and public works projects like Jones Beach on the south and truck farms in between. The name of the new development was Levittown, named after the corporation of Levitt and Sons, rather than some advertising formula based on evocations of the English countryside with lots of archaic e's tacked on to the end of each word.

The suburbs were not a new phenomenon in America, but Levittown was a new kind of suburb. It was not connected to a train line, and it was not built with the wealthy in mind. It bespoke the democratization of themes which the wealthy had appropriated in their flight from the increasingly ethnic cities in the period following World War I, when the WASP elite abandoned Philadelphia's Rittenhouse Square in favor of the Main Line and Chestnut Hill, both of which were connected to the center of the city by rail lines. Levittown was different; it was in many ways another version of worker housing of the sort that the federal government had erected during the war. But it was a hybrid as well. It was privately built but publicly subsidized war-worker housing. Now that the war was over, the government could devolve its government agencies into private agencies that would serve government purposes. Privatization would serve those interests more effectively than central planning as the debacle in public housing would soon show. The new suburbs were worker housing for the 16 million GIs returning from the war. The success of the war effort had convinced the technocrats in charge of government agencies that man could be engineered to an extent hitherto unimagined if they could control man's environment, and controlling housing, as Louis Wirth and his colleagues knew, was the key to controlling the environment. As Robert Merton, Wirth's colleague, announced in 1948, six months after Levittown had opened and a few months before Park Forest, Chicago's Levittown, would open as well, it was time to "change the actual institutional and social conditions," rather than just trying to persuade people to be nice to each other.

The connection between Levittown and war-worker housing becomes even more apparent when one becomes familiar with the corporate history of Levitt and Sons. In 1941 they were able work out the bugs involved in the mass production of homes, learning along the way things like how to pour hundreds of foundations in a single day, after they received a government grant to build 2,350 war-worker homes in Norfolk, Virginia. William Levitt's stint with the Seabees from 1943 to 1945 allowed them to further refine the techniques of mass production in housing. Putting what they learned during the war into practice after it was over, the Levitts built 2,250 homes in suburban Roslyn in 1946. From the time they completed the more expensive homes in Roslyn to when the first tenants moved into Levittown, the biggest private-housing project in American history, the Levitts refined the techniques of mass production as it applied to housing, doing essentially for the house what Henry Ford had done for the automobile by taking advantage of uniform techniques and materials and the vast economies of scale they provided.

As with war-worker housing, the Levitts could not have done what they did without massive government support. The main instrument of support for suburban development was the Federal Housing Authority. Created as part of the National Housing Act on June 27, 1934, to protect homeowners from losing their homes when their partially amortized loans had to be renewed during an economic downturn, the FHA soon began to use its financial clout as a tool in social engineering, as Gunnar Myrdal had predicted. "No agency of the United States government," Jackson writes, "has had a more pervasive and powerful impact on the American people over the past half-century than the FHA."[1] That influence derived from the sheer bulk of money it loaned – over $119 billion over the next forty years – as well as the guidelines that specified how that money was to be loaned. Taken together these aspects of FHA policy would largely determine how Americans were going to live for the rest of the century, and it would do so without all of the heavy-handedness of the urban housing authorities and the violent reaction they provoked. Beefed up by the Servicemen's Readjustment Act of 1944 (otherwise known as the GI Bill), the FHA, in combination with the Veteran's Administration, not only provided the wherewithal to help the 16 million soldiers who returned from World War II buy a home, it also determined to a large extent what kind of home he would buy and where it would be located. That meant, to a large extent, a house in the suburbs. "Decentralization is taking place," a senior FHA official told the 1939 convention of the American Institute of planners. "It is not a policy, it is a reality – and it is impossible for us to change this trend as it is to change the desire of birds to migrate to a more suitable location."[2] Devotees of the Enlightenment always like to describe their policies as if they were immutable natural processes because that absolves them of responsibility for them in the public mind. The simple fact of the matter is that the government created housing patterns from its housing policies just as inexorably as birds hatched from eggs. The federal government promoted change through its tax code as well, which encouraged businesses to abandon old buildings by providing greater tax benefits for the construction of new buildings. "The government," as a result, subsidized "an acceleration in the rate at which economic activity is dispersed to new locations."[3]

The FHA promoted the creation and spread of the suburbs in a number of different ways. In 1939, the same year as GM's Futurama exhibit at the New York World's Fair shared with visitors GM's vision of the highway system it wanted, the FHA made plans for the communities along those highways by asking each of its regional offices to send in plans for six "typical American houses,"[4] which then became the pattern for the standard suburban home. Typically and uniquely American housing like the Philadelphia rowhouse was excluded from consideration. Since all of the model homes promoted by the FHA National Archives Exhibit had driveways and garages, any home that did not make provision for the automobile was not going to be subsidized by the government. The rowhouse, because it did not and could not make sufficient provision for the automobile, was, therefore, decertified as an American home.

In an attempt to standardize such ideal homes, the Federal Housing Administration set up minimum requirements for lot size, setback from the street, separation from adjacent structures, and even for the width of the house itself. While such requirements did provide light and air for new structures they effectively eliminated whole categories of dwelling, such as the traditional 16-foot wide rowhouses of Baltimore, from eligibility for loan guarantees. Even apartment house owners were encouraged to look to suburbia: "Under the best conditions a rental development under the FHA program is a project set in what amounts to a privately owned and privately controlled park area."[5]

Reflecting the racist tradition of the United States, the Federal Housing Administration was extraordinarily concerned with "inharmonious racial or nationality groups."[6] It feared that an entire area could lose its investment value if rigid white-black separation was not maintained. Bluntly warning, "If a neighborhood is to retain stability, it is necessary that properties shall continue to be occupied by the same social and racial classes," the Underwriting Manual openly recommended "subdivision regulations and suitable restrictive covenants" that would be "superior to any mortgage."[7] Such covenants, which were legal provisions written into property deeds, were a common method of prohibiting black occupancy until the United States Supreme Court ruling in 1948 (*Shelley v. Kramer*) that they were "unenforceable as law and contrary to public policy." Even then, it was not until 1949 that the FHA announced that as of February 15, 1950, it would not insure mortgages on real estate subject to covenants.

The push for suburbanization began almost as soon as the FHA was brought into existence. Of 241 new homes insured by the FHA in metropolitan St. Louis between 1935 and 1939, 91 percent were built in the suburbs. Most of the people who bought those homes moved to them from St. Louis, a fact which prompts Jackson to claim that "the FHA was helping to denude St. Louis of its middle-class residents."[8] By 1960 the suburbs surrounding St. Louis would received five times the amount of mortgage money received by St. Louis itself. The suburbs also received roughly three times more home-improvement loans than the city, in spite of the obvious fact that the older homes in the city were more in need of repairs. The same policy applied to other cities, including the nation's capital, whose suburbs got seven times as much mortgage insurance as Washington during the same period of time. Much of this social engineering was accomplished by real estate agents using HOLC maps which "discriminated against racial *and ethnic* minorities and against older, industrial cities"[9] (my emphasis).

After claiming with some justification that "the basic direction of federal policies toward housing has been the concentration of the poor in the central city and the dispersal of the affluent to the suburbs," Jackson then goes on to say that "American housing policy was . . . devoid of social objectives."[10] Jackson's statement bespeaks more than anything else a misunderstanding of the actual social objectives the housing system sought to bring about. That system favored the construction of single homes over urban style apartment buildings. It favored detached single homes over rowhouses, which were the typical urban dwelling in places like Baltimore and Philadelphia. Beyond that it favored buying a new home over repairing an old one by the nature of its loan structure, and finally it favored all-white areas for its loans, and that again amounted to favoring suburban development. If an area was racially mixed, it was considered on its way down, and since loans were no longer guaranteed for that area, mortgage money dried up.[11] Local banks based their lending practices on HOLC maps, which in turn reflected the notion that racially mixed neighborhoods were risky investments, which guaranteed that the suburbs got the lion's share of the mortgage money, which, of course, encouraged the creation of more suburbs and the simultaneous demise of urban neighborhoods, whose middle class evaporated over the next three decades because of government policy. "Suburbanization," according to Jackson, "was an ideal government policy because it met the needs of both citizens and business interests and because it earned the politicians' votes."[12] Eventually over 35 million families would benefit from these policies between 1933 and 1978, but they would pay a price as well. That price was an unprecedented amount of social control.

The FHA was every bit as much a part of the federal government as the USHA, but they pursued diametrically opposed policies when it came to race. Whereas the USHA was adamant in pursuing an aggressive policy of integration in every project it funded in every city where they got built, the FHA pursued an equally aggressive policy of racial segregation, refusing to guarantee loans in areas where there was even a threat of racial mixing, no matter how high the quality of the housing stock. The superficial observer might conclude that, when it came to government housing policy, the left hand didn't know what the right hand was doing. But upon closer inspection, the two seemingly contradictory parts created a whole system with a very clear set of intentions about who was going to live where and why. The suburban ranch house and the urban housing project were, in effect, two sides of the same policy coin. Both were instruments of control. Although FHA and USHA policies were intended for different groups of people living under radically different conditions, each program functioned in tandem with the other.

By promoting integration, the USHA helped to channel the flood of blacks streaming up from the South into the ethnic neighborhoods of the North. By promoting segregation in the suburbs, the FHA provided the refugees from these neighborhoods a safe, i.e., all white, haven from the racial succession and social disorder the USHA policies were promoting in the city. It was, in effect, the real-estate version of good cop – bad cop. The largely Catholic ethnics who were caught in the middle were simultaneously threatened by the stick of racial succession which the USHA was orchestrating by "integrating" the neighborhoods where it built its housing projects, and enticed by the carrot of FHA-guaranteed low-interest loans for new houses in the suburbs in developments which the FHA could also guarantee were going to be all white and, therefore, free of the mayhem blacks were inflicting on neighborhoods in the city. Given this combination of subtlety and massive economic power behind government housing policy during these years, it is not surprising that many succumbed to its wiles. It even less surprising that many people believed that they were acting out of their own self-interest when they did. One of the hallmarks of psychological warfare is the engineering of consent. "When you work for developers, you hear that almost everything that goes on in development is based on fear and flight," says Walter Kulash. "It's based on fear of cities, fear of the people that are in cities, and flight from them."[13]

By 1960 Levittown had 82,000 residents, but not one of them was black. Racial segregation was necessary in the suburbs because without it, one of the main reasons for moving there was removed. Fear of racial succession probably drove more people into the suburbs than low-interest loans. Without either the low-interest carrot or the racial stick, the suburbs would have remained what they were before World War II, which is to say, the estates of the rich and the near rich. What they would not have become is the huge engine for assimilation which they became for the country's returning GIs. Without the fear of racial succession and the crime and disorder that went with it, ethnics would most probably have stayed in their neighborhoods, which meant that their assimilation would have been postponed indefinitely or that it would have happened on their terms and not the government's.

What years in uniform began, the suburbs completed. Army life had created a standardized life for millions of men, who returned to civilian life with their ethnic identities weakened (unless they were part of the WASP elite) and their sense of being Americans enhanced. The suburbs simply continued this process. Many of the early anecdotes about Levittown and Park Forest mention the ubiquitous mud and the privations as similar to army life. The returning soldiers were now living in a different kind of barracks, but the same inter-ethnic ambiance prevailed in both places. The war had prepared Catholic ethnics to be settled in camps far from their traditional neighborhoods; now after the war these same ethnics were being driven into settlements which would complete the job of Americanizing them by "integrating" them into communities with no ethnic character and no local culture other than that created for them by the corporations who created the developments.

Suburbs like Levittown were in many ways army life without the war. By creating the suburbs, the FHA also brought about the demise of residential neighborhoods in the cities "by stripping them of much of their middle-class constituency."[14] Being middle class would come to mean living in the suburbs, which was the opposite of lower class, which would come to mean "ethnic" and urban. The suburbs meant de-ethnicization. Their purpose, as Louis Wirth following Stalin's example could have explained, was to facilitate the choice of class (in this instance, the middle class) over ethnicity. Early chroniclers of the suburbs noticed this principle in action.

As one has come to expect in the sexual realm, "emancipation" in the area of housing was another word for control. "Ethnics," according to Hirsch, "sought stability rather than mobility. The trek to the suburbs, for them, would be a forced march made at great sacrifice; it would represent the end rather than the fulfillment of a dream."[15] The fact that many of them made the trek nonetheless shows how powerful the cultural engines driving that change really were.

In many ways the government was pursuing the same policies which had enabled Philadelphia to become "the city of homes" by encouraging widespread ownership and the domestic stability it fostered. But the similarities were deceptive. To begin with, rowhouses were financed by the people who lived in them often through their own ethnic benevolent associations. In that respect, the FHA was pursuing the exact opposite policy by creating the suburbs, which were the beneficiaries of over half of their loans during the '50s and '60s, because while millions of people got equity, they got it on the lender's terms and not their own. Because of government subsidy the cheapness of the house masked the fact that its new inhabitants had to have a car and the expense that went along with that form of transportation. Residents of the suburbs later realized that they had to join a health club to get exercise because the design of the suburb (as well as its distance from shopping) made walking impossible and cycling dangerous. Gradually, the more perceptive analysts of the new post-war suburbs began to see them as instruments of political control and social engineering:

> The ultimate outcome of the suburb's alienation from the city became visible only in the twentieth century, with the extension of the democratic ideal through the instrumentalities of manifolding and mass production. In the mass movement into suburban areas a new kind of community was produced, which caricatured both the historic city and the archetypal suburban refuge: a multitude of uniform, unidentifiable houses, lined up inflexibly, at uniform distances, on uniform roads, in a treeless communal waste, inhabited by people of the same class, the same income, the same age-group, witnessing the same television performances, eating the same tasteless pre-fabricated foods, from the same freezers, conforming in every and outward and inward respect to a common mold, manufactured in the central metropolis. Thus the ultimate effect of the suburban escape in our time is, ironically, a low-grade uniform environment from which escape is impossible.[16]

Just as the custodians of the first housing projects in Philadelphia would inspect each unit and berate certain tenants for their poor housekeeping skills, the Levitts micromanaged the residents of Levittown at the beginning as well, making sure that they mowed their lawns properly (charging them if they didn't), forbidding fences, and allowing outdoor clothes drying only on specially designed racks.

The officious meddling was in many ways the least malignant form of engineering because it was the most obvious. In many ways, the early reports on the suburbs are deceptive because they attribute to the suburbs the characteristics of the people who had just moved in, characteristics which they had obviously not learned in the suburbs. So early commentators commented on the fertility of suburban women, attributing it to the suburbs when it was the result of the way they had been raised before they got there, and to a large extent that was based on the teaching of the Catholic Church and the model of the ethnic neighborhood the suburb was designed to subvert. The same is true of suburban gregariousness. Many commentators attributed it to the suburbs when in fact the people were gregarious because they had, until very recently, not lived in the suburbs. The gregariousness of people who had just moved is more attributable to where they have been, not where they are. The constant turnover and the concomitant rootlessness which the suburbs fostered would soon take its toll, forcing the people who lived there to withdraw to their TV sets as the only social constant in their lives. Before long, it became apparent that the natural outcome of suburban living was isolation. Again this would become apparent only with time. Unlike William O. Whyte, Lewis Mumford did not mistake the behavior of the newly arrived suburbanites as somehow flowing from suburban living arrangements. When it came to gregariousness, in fact, Mumford correctly saw the exact opposite. Suburbs were engineered with isolation and alienation in mind. The technology of suburbia all but guaranteed that:

> The end product is an encapsulated life, spent more and more either in a motor car or within the cabin of darkness before a television set: soon, with a little more automation of traffic, mostly in a motor car, traveling even greater distances, under remote control, so that the one-time driver may occupy himself with a television set, having lost even the freedom of the steering wheel. Every part of this life, indeed, will come through official channels and be under supervision. Untouched by human hand at one end: untouched by human spirit at the other.[17]

Only after the nation had been herded into suburbs for over a decade were perceptive critics like Lewis Mumford able to see the type of person the housers were trying (and succeeding) to engineer. The suburbs fostered what Mumford called "compulsory mobility,"[18] which was more controlling than the compulsory stability of being forced to live within the medieval city's walls, because it limited the possibility of human interaction much more dramatically. And without the possibility of contact that is not managed for commercial or other purposes congenial to those who want to control him, man is reduced to the most vulnerable form of individual life and political impotence. The sprawling nature of the suburb was itself a form of control. "Sprawling isolation," according to Mumford, "has proved an even more effective method of keeping a population under control"[19] than enclosure and close supervision because it dramatically limits the possibility of human interaction and the unpredictable and uncontrollable flow of information that goes with it. Modern forms of social control depend on controlling the flow of information, not on constant supervision. By limiting the options to choosing a Ford over a Chevy or Coke over Pepsi, the people who control the flow of information channel behavior into certain acceptable patterns while at the same time promoting the illusion of freedom of choice.

By inhibiting direct contact, the suburb allows information to be "monopolized by central agents and conveyed through guarded channels, too costly to be utilized by small groups or private individuals."[20] As a result, "each member of Suburbia becomes imprisoned by the very separation that he has prized: he is fed through a narrow opening: a telephone line, a radio band, a television circuit."[21] Here Mumford is articulating, without being specific about it, one of the prime goals of psychological warfare, namely, the prohibition of unauthorized communication among subject peoples. Mumford goes on to say that "this is not . . . the result of a conscious conspiracy by a cunning minority"[22] but his disclaimer is less persuasive than the picture of social control he paints. If, one wonders, this system has not been put into effect by conscious design, how did it get there? Is it possible to have social control without social controllers?

The disclaimer is especially unpersuasive with the benefit of hindsight because now we know that the intelligence community was both expanding its operations, including its reliance on black operations, which is to say illegal operations or those carried out against U.S. Citizens, and simultaneously devolving them to private sector initiatives which the government funded clandestinely. Truman may have vetoed the New Deal's housing bill, but he had no qualms about expanding the government's involvement in black operations of the sort that got started during the war. In fact, largely at John McCloy's urging, Truman in 1947 "assigned the CIA responsibility for covert psychological operations,"[23] a mandate which was expanded in June 1948 when Truman approved George Kennan's NSC directive 10/2. Beginning in early 1948, the CIA had secretly begun subsidizing the election campaigns of anti-Communist politicians in France and Italy. Those campaigns proved so successful that the CIA sponsored a Congress of Cultural Freedom in Berlin in 1950 as well as a number of journals – *Der Monat* in Germany and *Encounter* in England – which in turn promoted the Congress and its credibility among European intellectuals and intellectual celebrities like Norman Mailer and Irving Kristol. McCloy justified this "psychological warfare offensive," by claiming to a group of U.S. ambassadors in Frankfurt that it "would make it possible for these groups to undertake projects considered desirable and necessary in an all-out psychological offensive but which might not be financially remunerative."[24] Rather than run its own psychological-warfare establishment in its entirety, the intelligence community was going to make it "financially remunerative" for others to run certain operations as subcontractors.

And if McCloy couldn't get government money to fund these operations, there were other options available to him. Toward the end of his tenure as high commissioner in Germany in the early '50s, McCloy wrote to the Ford Foundation mentioning *Der Monat* and asking them to "help to carry on certain operations which the future U.S. Embassy may find it difficult to continue, but which are of great significance to United States objectives in Germany."[25] The Ford Foundation, we are told, "obliged."[26] Other organizations were happy to oblige as well. One of the things one notices in the reports on the housing riots in Chicago is that the reports which were filed by spies working for the OWI and the OFF during the war years started getting filed by spies working for the American Civil Liberties Union and the American Friends Service Committee once the war was over. This was precisely the devolution of government policy by "private" agency which McCloy was urging at the Ford Foundation, which would in turn become a major benefactor of the American Friends Service Committee, which in turn became a major player in disrupting ethnic neighborhoods in cities like Philadelphia, Chicago, Oakland, California and elsewhere by promoting racial "integration."

McCloy did not confine his concerns to foreign policy nor did he limit himself to government agencies when he wanted to support initiatives he felt were worthwhile. McCloy was at this point chairman of the board of the Ford Foundation, and the Ford Foundation, more than the Rockefellers or any other similar institution, was the main funding agent of social and racial change in the nation's cities. The constants in this equation were ethnic; the variables were political and institutional. Here again the distinction between private and public funding is deceptive. The same people – people like John McCloy – had their hands on the levers of both sets of machinery, and at certain crucial points privately funded initiatives could mutate into government programs and vice versa. The big foundations' money was, as the Rockefellers had claimed, venture capital for controversial ideas. Once an idea was given respectability by foundation funding, as happened in the case of Alfred Kinsey, the government could come along and adopt the program and then fund it with federal money. The Great Society, to give an example of a program which was directly relevant to the cities and racial succession, was the Ford Foundation's Gray Areas program, adopted whole cloth by the federal government and then given federal funding.

Notes

1   Kenneth T. Jackson, *Crabgrass Frontier: The Suburbanization of the United States* (New York: Oxford University Press, 1985), p. 203.

2   Ibid., p. 190.

3   Ibid., p. 191.

4   Ibid., p. 208.

5   Ibid.

6   Ibid.

7   Ibid.

8   Ibid., p. 209.

9   Ibid., p. 215.

10 Ibid., p. 230.

11 Ibid., p. 206.

12 Ibid., p. 216.

13 Philip Langdon, *A Better Place to Live: Reshaping the American Suburb* (Amherst: University of Massachusetts Press, 1994), p. 73.

14 Jackson, p. 206.

15 Arnold R. Hirsch, *Making the Second Ghetto: Race and Housing in Chicago 1940–1960* (Cambridge: Cambridge University Press, 1983), p. 195.

16 Lewis Mumford, *The City in History: Its Origins, Its Transformations, and Its Prospects* (New York: Harcourt, Brace & World, Inc., 1961), p. 486.

17 Ibid., p. 512.

18 Ibid., p. 503.

19 Ibid., p. 512.

20 Ibid.

21 Ibid.

22 Ibid., p. 513.

23 Kai Bird, *The Chairman: McGeorge Bundy and William Bundy: Brothers in Arms: A Biography* (New York: Simon & Schuster, 1998) , p. 302.

24 Ibid., p. 357.

25 Ibid., p. 358.

26 Ibid.

Robert Moses and the Creation of the Car Culture

At around the same time that Harry Truman approved George Kennan's NSC 10/2 directive allowing the CIA to assume responsibility for covert psychological operations, at around the same time that those operations were put in effect to subsidize the election of anti-Communist politicians in France and Italy as well as to subsidize numerous front operations, Robert Moses, New York's public-works czar, received a visit from Yale classmate Senator Robert A. Taft. Taft decided to pay Moses a visit because he was considering sponsoring a bill which would allow the federal government to get involved in housing construction in an unprecedented way.[1] Since Moses had more experience in carrying out massive public works projects than anyone else in the country, it was understandable that Taft would turn to him for advice. Not so understandable was how this massive violation of the separation of powers squared with Taft's political philosophy. Taft was the standard bearer of conservatism at that point. His bill, the Federal Housing Act of 1949, would not only bring the phrase "urban renewal" into common parlance, it would also take control over what happened in terms of urban planning out of the hands of the elected representatives of the nation's largest cities (and by extension, out of the hands of the people who elected them) and put it into the hands of powerful local entrepreneurs like Robert Moses, who could control the flow of federal money for his own benefit.

What was true of housing was also true of roads. At around the same time that Senator Taft visited Moses, another acquaintance, Bertram D. Tallamy, took over control of what would eventually become the Interstate Highway System. Since Tallamy had taken lessons on the art of getting things done from Moses beginning in 1926, it was clear that Interstate Highway System, when it finally got written into law, was destined to become the lengthened shadow of the man who had already made a name for himself in New York among federal road builders by the highways and bridges he had constructed around Manhattan.

In 1932 Mackinac Island, the small cusp of limestone jutting up out of the westernmost end of Lake Huron between the upper and lower peninsulae of Michigan, and Long Island, New York, the place F. Scott Fitzgerald in 1926 called the "fresh, green breast of the new world" had one thing in common: neither was connected to the continental United States. In 1936 Long Island lost that distinction with the construction of the Triborough Bridge, which connected its green shores to the finger of land that heads southwest from Connecticut and eventuates in the Bronx. From that fateful moment to the present day, Long Island has been flooded by rivers of automobiles at perennial flood tide which have transformed its once verdant breast into what seems to be an unending succession of housing developments (Levittown arrived there in 1947), strip malls, and parking lots – the paradigm of what the nation has become by following its example. In a word, Long Island has become synonymous with sprawl.

Perhaps no one man has done more to re-shape the United States for the convenience of automobiles than Robert Moses, the man who wrecked New York City by trying to make it accessible to automobile traffic. Born in New Haven, Connecticut, in 1888, Moses was part of the proto-modern generation, the group that came up with just about all of the cultural artifacts associated with modernity – cubism, twelve-tone music, Bauhaus architecture – all were creations of people born in this decade, people who came into prominence in the cultural vacuum created after World War I. Robert Moses attended Yale University, where he was excluded from the clubs that were crucial to social advancement because he was, in the words of the yearbook, a "Hebrew."[2] If he were, it was news to his mother, who wanted nothing whatsoever to do with things Jewish, and enrolled the family instead in the ethical cultural society in New York. Moses' mother, like the devotees of the social gospel, which was also prominent at the time, compensated for her lack of piety by devoting herself to work at one of New York's settlement houses, whose purpose was the socialization in American mores of newly arrived Jews from Eastern Europe by the already arrived Jews who had arrived from Germany during the nineteenth century.

Moses completed his education by going to Oxford and writing his thesis on the British civil servant. His vision of the future seems to have solidified early on. It was a combination of the *noblesse oblige* of the English civil servant and the condescension of the Jewish Settlement house, but the glue which held those parts together was the Enlightenment belief in technology's ability to solve social problems. The rise of modernism was always tied with a vision of the future, perhaps because it hated the past so much it could have no other vision. By the late 1920s, the idea of the future was fixed in the culture's mind, and everyone knew what it would look like. It was Le Corbusier's Radiant City: high-rise buildings surrounded by lots of space, presumably green, elevated highways, people traveling in their own personal vehicles. It was a vision which came true, but not in the way it was envisioned; the dream became a nightmare. Those high rise buildings became the Robert Taylor Homes on the South Side of Chicago: tall cages with metal detectors at the entrance and steel mesh covering the balconies so that manhole covers and other heavy objects would not be dropped on unsuspecting children playing in the mud below. The only future we have now in popular culture is bad: *Robocop, Mimic, Terminator, Road Warrior, Escape from LA* – virtually every artifact of popular culture by the end of the 20th century saw the future as one failed technological promise after another, and one of the main reasons that vision went sour was Robert Moses and the impact he had on the nation's cultural capital, New York City. Moses believed in Enlightenment technology and the car in particular as the solution to the world's problems and as a result condemned New York in particular and the country in general to its own hell for generations to come. Hell bespeaks the ultimate in ipsation, and no other cultural artifact symbolizes ipsation for 20th century Americans better than the automobile. Its only rival is the television or its most recent variant, the internet as a vehicle for pornography.

Moses came of age during the Progressive Era, an age of reform dominated by people like Theodore Roosevelt and a sense of virility and purpose among Americans of that class. How he went from producing city-beautiful parks to ethnic cleansing in the Bronx is a cautionary tale that the county would do well to learn. Since we're talking about the nation's premier road builder, it seems especially apt to say that the road to Hell is paved with good intentions. In the case of Robert Moses, it was an especially long road.

Robert Moses' first project after doing his master's degree on the British civil service system at Oxford was the institution of civil-service reform in New York City, a project which failed spectacularly and left him without a job until he got a call from a friend of the family who asked if he were interested in serving under Al Smith, New York's newly elected governor. Moses was very interested. He quickly became a genius at writing self-serving legislation and ended up as a result parks commissioner for the state. It was at this point, during the 1920s, that Moses's vision took on concrete form in just about every sense of the word. Robert Moses envisioned a world emancipated from the crush of over-crowded cities, a world in which people swept along elevated highways in their own per-sonal automobiles savoring the best views the landscape had to offer. As early as 1914 he dreamed of covering the New York Central switching yards along the Hudson River with a combination park and elevated highway. Since Moses grew up riding horses up and down his street in New Haven, parks and roads were inextricably linked in his mind in a way inconceivable now. Hyde Park had carriage roads. So did the Bois de Bologne; Moses hated congestion and thought the railroad hopelessly bound up with the 19th century. His legacy was to create ever-more congestion in the attempt to alleviate it. This happened for a very simple reason: the automobile as a form of mass transportation is a self-defeating proposition. The more the culture builds roads and bridges and parking lots to accommo-date the automobile, the more it creates the very traffic it attempts to alleviate. The term for this mathematical formula is "traffic generation." Most people still don't know it exists, which is one reason why this country's roads look the way they do.

Robert Moses was by all accounts a remarkably intelligent man, but he wasn't smart enough to comprehend this one basic fact about reliance on the automobile as the basis of mass transportation. For just about the entire forty-four years during which he ruled New York City like a fourth unelected branch of government, Moses was promising that the next bridge or the next highway he built was going to be the solution to the city's traffic problems. Then after that road or bridge got built, a strange thing happened. Within a mat-ter of weeks, traffic would be jammed on the new bridge while at the same time traffic was just as heavy on the bridges which were to be alleviated of that same traffic. Moses's solution was predictable: build more roads and bridges. A strategy like this was bad enough for the relatively open spaces of Long Island, guaranteeing a low-density popula-tion that would, in turn, guarantee further dependency on the automobile, which in turn generated more low-density settlement in a vicious circle that would continue for genera-tions to come with no solution to the traffic problem in sight. This strategy was, however, nothing less than catastrophic for the densely populated boroughs of New York City. First of all, since Long Island was one big cul de sac without its own industrial base, the roads Moses built on it necessitated that all the traffic there would converge on Brooklyn and Manhattan in the morning and re-emerge and head eastward in the evening. Because of the size of the automobile, the huge numbers of commuters who shifted from rail traffic to their automobiles were condemned to be stuck in traffic for their entire working lives and, beyond that, condemned to fight each day for a never-adequate number of parking spaces.

The numbers tell the story. In 1914 there were 125,101 motor vehicles in New York City, by 1934, the year that construction on the Triborough Bridge began, that number had increased to 804,620.[3] By 1960, the Triborough Bridge alone was carrying 46 million cars per year. Since each lane could accommodate 1,500 cars an hour, that meant that the Bridge was operating at full capacity for 200 of the 365 days of the year if traffic were spread out evenly over a twenty-four-hour period, which never happened. That meant that the bridge was jammed most of the time. And that meant that that same bridge was funneling 46 million cars per year into streets and neighborhoods with no possible capacity for handling that number of vehicles.[4]

For a long time, the city planners claimed that the increase in traffic resulted from an increase in population, but the numbers show that this is false. In 1930, 301,000 people commuted to New York City on a daily basis; by 1950 that number had increased to 357,000, an increase of 19 percent.[5] That number fails to explain the increase in traffic because it fails to explain the change in commuting habits that occurred. During those 20 years, the number of rail commuters declined from 263,000 in 1930 to 239,000 in 1950, but during the same period of time the number of auto commuters increased from 38,050 in 1930 to 118,400.[6] The population/commuter increase of 19 percent was dwarfed by the 321 percent increase in auto commuters. The decline of rail commuters can be directly translated into congestion. One trainload of commuters switching to cars requires four acres of parking space in Manhattan or curbside parking stretching along one side of Fifth Avenue from Washington Square to 68th street, a distance of three miles.[7]

By building roads and bridges at the expense of mass transportation, Robert Moses brought hundreds of thousands of cars into a space that could never accommodate them. The result was wasted time, frustration, and the destruction of the city's infrastructure in a battle that could never be won. The only way Moses's vision for the auto could have worked is if it had been supplemented by rail transportation. By relieving the roads of the great masses of commuters, for most of whom the car was a significant financial burden, Moses could have preserved his parkways for the wealthy who could have used them as they were intended to be used.

But Moses deliberately thwarted the development of rail traffic, partially perhaps because the bridge and tunnel authorities he controlled received tribute every time an automobile crossed them, something which is not an isolated event in a city of 14 million built on islands and a peninsula. One highway lane could carry 1,500 cars an hour. One railroad line could bring 40,000 to 50,000 people per hour into the city, and when they arrived by train, they didn't have to find parking spaces.[8]

But Robert Moses hated trains, and by thwarting rail transportation, he created a highway system that was self-defeating from the day it carried traffic. A Scotsman by the name of F. Dodd McHugh tried to explain this to Moses during the planning stages of the Van Wyck Expressway, which was to link Idlewild (later renamed Kennedy) Airport with Manhattan.[9] For each day of its operation, the airport had to accommodate 40,000 employees and 30,000 air travelers. This meant that during peak periods 10,000 people per hour would be converging on the airport. Unfortunately, the peak carrying capacity of the Van Wyck Expressway under optimum conditions was 2,630 vehicles per hour, many of which contained one passenger. Given these statistics, it was clear that the airport traffic alone would overwhelm the Van Wyck Expressway, and added to that there was the commuter traffic which peaked in the morning and evening, prime arrival and departure times.

McHugh was of the opinion that the only possible solution was a rail link between

Manhattan and the airport. For an additional $1.875 million (out of a total cost of $30 million) Moses could have purchased the additional 50 feet of right of way that would have made a rail link possible,[10] but Moses chose not to, and as a result the Van Wyck Expressway was jammed weeks after it opened, and Manhattan remains one of the few major metropolitan centers in the world with no rail link to its major airports.

The stupidity behind Moses's vision turned tragic when Moses built roads through densely populated areas. Robert Caro claims that 250,000 people were driven from their homes by Moses's various projects. Tearing down the Third Avenue El in Sunset Park, a thriving Finnish neighborhood in Brooklyn, Moses erected in its place an elevated highway more than twice as wide in its place and set in motion the forces which brought about the destruction of that neighborhood. As if a solid mass in the sky like that weren't bad enough, Moses tore down every building on one side of Third Avenue to accommodate a truck thoroughfare at ground level. The stores on Third Avenue were the commercial heart of the neighborhood. With a stroke of Moses's pen, half of them were doomed, and the people who lived in the neighborhood were confronted with the task of crossing a ten-lane truck road, wider than a football field, every time they wanted to go to the stores which remained. Faced with this sort of assault the Finns started to move out, which meant that the remaining stores folded one by one, to be replaced by boarded-up, abandoned store fronts where prostitutes and drug dealers engaged in their activities. But beyond that, the road which killed the neighborhood for the convenience of the people who passed through it on their way back to the bedroom communities of Long Island, never worked anyway. The Gowanus Parkway was built without shoulders, so that one car breaking down insured a traffic jam, and with the opening of the Brooklyn-Battery Tunnel it was overwhelmed with traffic anyway. The neighborhood was sacrificed to a concept that didn't work and never could have worked, if anyone had taken the time to think it through.

The story of the Cross-Bronx Expressway is even worse. The devastation inflicted on the defenseless Jewish families there is comparable to the Nazi assault on the Warsaw ghetto in terms of the sheer physical ruin it brought about. By moving the proposed route of the Cross-Bronx Expressway two blocks south and running it through the northern end of Crotona Park, Moses could have spared 1,530 apartments from the wrecking ball.[11] The route would have been shorter; the expense less, and yet Moses refused to change his plan, forcing thousands of lower-income Jews with ninety days' notice, either onto the streets or into already-vacated, soon-to-be-demolished apartment buildings further along the proposed route.

Normally Moses preferred running roads through parks and, in building the bridge from Manhattan to Spuyten Duyvil, ruined the last marshland in New York City at the center of Van Courtlandt Park and the last stand of virgin forest by ignoring the most obvious route. When building the Northern Expressway in Long Island, Moses added a twenty-mile detour to that road to spare one robber baron's golf course. Taking all these facts into consideration, it is hard not to see something like personal spite as motivating Moses in his attitude toward the Jews of Fremont Park in the Bronx. They, unlike he, were not deracinated. They had not adopted the anglophilia of the Oxford grad. They, unlike Moses, were decidedly "ethnic," which is to say, possessing attitudes toward religion and custom which ignored the Enlightenment's values in favor of traditions passed down from generation to generation. They also lived in crowded ethnic neighborhoods which impeded the free flow of automobile traffic, and the automobile embodied the future. They were, to use a phrase that Moses used to cow anyone who opposed his will, "impeding progress," and so they had to go. The ethnic neighborhood embodied everything Moses considered retrograde and so, to use his term, he took a "meat ax" to the neighborhood and chopped it to death.[12]

Progress meant that white people dropped ethnic affiliation and bought cars and moved to the suburbs. It meant that the ambitious among them adopted these attitudes on their own, as a way of "bettering" themselves. It meant that the less ambitious would be forced out by other means. It meant that traditional neighborhoods were left to those too old, or too poor, or too "uneducated" to move out. Once a man bought a car in a traditional neighborhood like those in the large cities on the East Coast, that automobile became an agent of social change because cities and cars don't mix. Given the post-World War II push to sell cars – cars that were invariably portrayed as gliding alone on sinuous empty roads through the country or parked on a beach or perched atop mesas in the Mojave Desert – the car's owner would be forced to make a choice between his rowhouse or his car. And given the psychological pressures that were brought to bear on him through a combination of advertising and racial migration, many white men chose their cars over their rowhouses and neighborhoods, moving to a house in the suburbs where the main architectural feature of the façade was the garage door. Like the pig farmer in Westphalia, the commuter on Long Island could go to bed knowing that his car was safely under the same roof he was. The automobile industry, the oil companies, the FHA, and the federal government through the interstate highway system all collaborated in fostering the illusion that by pulling up stakes and moving out of the city, the average head of the average white family could absent himself from the dirt and disorder of the cities, dirt and disorder which were, along with other factors I have discussed elsewhere, increasingly the result of making the cities completely accessible to the car.

Lewis Mumford talked about the increasing encapsulation and isolation of life in the post-war period – people spending enormous amounts of their free time either staring through the windshield of an automobile or at the screen of a TV set in the darkened family room of some bedroom community, but no one in any position of power was taking Mumford seriously, certainly not someone like Robert Moses, who wielded all but absolute power over the construction of public works in New York City in the period immediately after World War II. The reason people like Mumford were ignored should be obvious by now. The automobile and the television are instruments of political control, instruments which decree that people will live in a certain way and, more importantly, will spend their money in a way congenial to those who wield that power.

To cite the most obvious example of how transportation policies affect income, when Robert Moses came to power, New York City had the best subway system in the world and it cost a nickel to ride on it. By the time he fell from power, it cost twenty times that amount to ride on one of the worst subway systems in the world. But the most significant fact about that period of time is the number of people who stopped riding the subway and switched to the car as their way to get to work. A car costs on average $6,000 a year to maintain, that fact coupled with the fact that houses in the suburbs invariably cost more than houses in ethnic neighborhoods in the city and the fact that wages stopped going up in this country in 1973 have forced millions of women into the job market so that families with two wage earners (and perhaps the kids working at child labor mills like fast food restaurants) can earn what dad alone could do on his wage before, which is to say raise a family with mom at home to run the household. The cost of a car and a house in the suburbs is enough to drive mom out of the home, and with mom out of the home the kids come home after school and watch MTV. With mom out of the home, the vampire TV culture has a free hand in forming the minds of the young, telling them how to spend their money in the best interests of the people who advertise on MTV.

Beyond the financial aspect of social control, there is another simple fact. The automobile and television and suburban housing all foster isolation. During Moses's long reign as public-works czar, the only people who opposed him successfully were those – as the in the case of the Tavern on the Green, where he wanted to build a parking lot in Central Park – who could unite with each other locally. It was a woman who took her children to play in Central Park who inadvertently found the blueprints for the parking lot which Moses was planning to build there and alerted her neighbors to what was going to happen. That set the chain of events in motion which stopped the parking lot from being built. If that mother had been at work and her child in a daycare center, that part of Central Park would be under asphalt today.

Suburbs, like Levittown, which empty out every morning, are little more than barracks for helots. They are not a locus of political power in the way that Al Smith's neighborhood at the foot of the Brooklyn Bridge was because power is a function of interaction. The automobile and the settlements based on its roads impede interaction between people. The television added to that mix impedes it further, fostering, instead of social interaction, identification with the financial powers that pay for the advertising which supports its programs. This leads to a situation in which children in this environment know the names of the N' Sync but not the names of other children living on the same block.

By 1946, even the normally obsequious *New York Times* was beginning to have doubts about the wisdom of Robert Moses's road-building master plan for New York, and letters to the editor suggesting that cars be banned from Manhattan were common. By 1956 with thousands of families evicted from their homes, the Bronx looking like London after the Blitz, and traffic even more backed up than before, it should have been obvious to even the most obtuse observer that the car as mass transit wasn't working and would never work. But it was precisely in 1956 that New York's problem became the nation's problem with the passage of the Moses-inspired Interstate Highway Act. Bertram D. Tallamy, who replaced F. V. du Pont as chief administrative officer of the Interstate Highway System during the 1950s and 1960s, would later claim "that the principles on which the system was built were principles that Robert Moses taught him in a series of such private lectures in 1926."[13]

Just as Moses's system of roads at the expense of rail guaranteed sprawl on Long Island, the Interstate Highway System guaranteed the same destructive development in virtually every city across the country. Strip malls sprang up at highway exits like mushrooms after a rain. The malls were occupied by national chains which undercut the prices of local merchants and drove them out of business. Federally sponsored wrecking expeditions known as urban renewal gave federal money to cities and towns so that these towns could tear down their own buildings and widen their roads so that, as in the case South Bend, Indiana, and numerous other cities, drivers could speed by the vacant lots that dotted the devastated town centers with minimal inconvenience.

As local retail died, the money began to drain from the local economy and end up in places like Bentonville, Arkansas. Once billions got concentrated into so few hands, it could be used to finance the campaigns of politicians who would defend the system in order to have the money to get re-elected. Taken together this gigantic centralization of power accompanied – in fact, constituted – the rise of the American Empire, an empire which fattened itself at the expense of the majority of its own people. Gradually, the manufacturing jobs that were the economic backbone of cities in the industrial north would be replaced by service jobs where not even two wage earners could support a family. As a result, families started to crack under the strain. Unable to create their own cultural space, families in which mom had to leave home for her job as a greeter at Sam's Club gradually succumbed to the seductions of television culture. The wood frame houses that were the staple of domestic life in places like Detroit and other cities in the Midwest began to collapse after decades of neglect. The average wooden house in the Midwest, a house which was built, say, in the 1920s, had to survive the Depression, the war, racial migration, and the post-war autoboom, all of which drained money away from repairs. Many simply did not survive, and gradually neighborhoods thinned out as the houses there burned down and were abandoned and then razed to provide a parking lot or another used-car lot or more urban taiga.

In his magnum opus against sprawl, *The Geography of Nowhere*, James Howard Kunstler documents the conspiracy to destroy commuter rail lines throughout the country, thereby forcing people into the car. "In 1925," he writes, "with the acquisition of the Yellow Coach company, the General Motors Corporation undertook a systematic campaign to put streetcar lines out of business all over America." Which is precisely what it did, ripping up lines in San Jose, Stockton, and Fresno, California. "By 1950," according to Kunstler, "GM had converted more than 100 electric streetcar lines to gasoline powered buses."[14] GM was convicted of criminal conspiracy in 1949 and eventually fined the grand sum of $5,000.

Conservatives of the free-market stripe in the meantime were either asleep at the switch or avidly defending this transfer of money out of the pockets of the average citizen and into the coffers of the Highwaymen, by claiming, as true devotees of the English Ideology, that it all just happened: "even though nobody really planned it. It just worked out that way through the myriad individual decisions of hundreds of millions of people." This is how B. Bruce Briggs claims it happened. In his book *The War against the Automobile*. Bill Kauffman writing in *The Family in America* counters by saying, "The Invisible Hand didn't build the Interstate."[15]

Any situation this extreme was bound to cause a reaction, and in New York City the reaction came with the election of John Lindsay in 1968. Lindsay appointed Thomas Hoving as parks commissioner, and from then on it was safe to criticize the "Moses approach" of sending in the bulldozers first and asking questions later. But by then the landscape of New York City had been changed – set in concrete – for what seemed like generations to come. The first three decades of the 20th century provided a golden opportunity for Long Island, an opportunity that was lost, perhaps forever.

For the rest of the country, the situation was not as acute and so the reaction was later in coming. In fact, in many parts of the country, the reaction never arrived. The sprawl around most mid-sized cities continues unabated. Farmland disappears at the rate of eight acres an hour in Indiana, ten acres an hour in Michigan. Walmarts continue to proliferate. In 1996 alone South Bend, Indiana, received the dubious benefit of having three Walmarts being built in its outlying regions.[16]

Elsewhere, it seems that the dime has dropped. Doug Farr of Farr Associates in Chicago says that retrofitting newly gentrified neighborhoods is a "no-brainer," which is another way of say that he sees it happening in lots of places across the country. Central Station, a handsome set of townhouses just south of the loop in Chicago, is an example. More challenging from his point of view is "in-fill" development in less desirable neighborhoods where half of the buildings are gone. Like many New Urbanists, Farr does not see the car as the main problem; rather roads are the problem. "In Vancouver," he says, "they have a saying: 'Congestion is our friend.'" If, in other words, the urbanists get to determine that streets get built on a human scale with human priorities in mind, the car problem will take care of itself.

In its September 28, 1997, Sunday supplement, the *Boston Globe* announced that "across the country cities are currently enjoying a remarkable rebirth as young families begin to flock back to the urban lifestyle."[17] At the Congress for a New Urbanism's annual conference that year in San Francisco, Peter Katz, one of the founders of that movement, announced that "the writing is clearly on the wall."[18] People are no longer interested in the suburban house with a big garage door and a lawn on an overly wide cul-de-sac in an isolated single-family subdivision where it takes a half an hour to drive to a "convenience store" for a quart of milk, and even longer now that the streets are clogged with traffic.

Instead of all that, "today's consumer," according to Robert Gibbs, a consultant from Birmingham, Michigan, "is looking for a 1940s Main Street Lifestyle."[19] Echoing Gibbs, *New Urban News*, the CNU's newsletter, promotes an "urban design . . . based on U.S. town and city pattern before automobile-dominate planning became the standard after World War II."[20] In this regard, the new urbanism isn't really new. It's an attempt to return to ideas of city planning that prevailed during the '20s across the country. The difference is that what was then a consensus based on shared values is now a program promoted by reformers who have to get the public's ear in order to repair, according to Professor Rybczynski, "the urban fabric, which was torn apart by a whole set of principles loosely termed modernist."[21]

Notes

1   Robert A. Caro, *The Power Broker: Robert Moses and the Fall of New York* (New York: Vintage Books, 1975), p. 707.
2   Ibid., p. 38.
3   Ibid., p. 544.
4   Ibid., p. 715.

5 Ibid., p. 916.

6 Ibid., p. 917.

7 Ibid.

8 Ibid., p. 901.

9 Ibid., p. 904.

10 Ibid., p. 907.

11 Ibid., p. 882.

12 Ibid., p. 837ff.

13 Ibid., p. 11.

14 James Howard Kunstler, *The Geography of Nowhere: The Rise and Decline of America's Man-Made Landscape* (New York: Simon & Schuster, 1993), p. 91ff.

15 Bill Kauffman, "Doesn't Anybody Stay in One Place Anymore?" *Family in America* 11, No. 4 (April 1997): 7.

16 The mayor of South Bend lives in a classic midwestern urban neighborhood; he owns a number of houses in that neighborhood, which, since he is a carpenter, he restores. Before he was mayor, he worked on restoring houses in neighborhoods throughout the city, and yet when asked why he changed the zoning to allow two Walmarts in, he shrugs and says the city needs the tax base.

17 Anthony Flint, "Rebuilding the City," *The Boston Globe Magazine* (September 28, 1997), p. 15.

18 Ibid.

19 Ibid.

20 Robert Steuteville, "Year of Growth for New Urbanism," *New Urban News* 3, No. 5 (September/October 1998): 3.

21 Ibid.

Louis Wirth and the Chicago Housing Authority

On March 31, 1948, the Chicago City Council gave unanimous endorsement to the nondiscriminatory housing policy of the Chicago Housing authority and extended that policy to all other city departments. Less than a month later, on May 3, the Supreme Court handed down *Shelley v. Parker*, in which it claimed that racially restrictive covenants violated the Fourteenth Amendment to the Constitution because they constituted a denial of the rights and freedom of black citizens. The housers in Chicago now felt that they had a mandate from both local and federal governments and lost no time trying to capitalize on the situation. On April 23, 1948, in anticipation of a favorable ruling from the Supreme Court, Louis Wirth stated in a "Memorandum on . . . Race Restrictive Housing Covenants" that the "invalidation of judicial enforcement of racial covenants will remove one of the threats that face minorities in urban redevelopment."[1] This was significant because blacks in Chicago were hemmed in by communities which were "still covered by racial covenants." With that barrier now removed, the CHA could proceed with moving black families out of the areas they had traditionally occupied and into the surrounding communities. Still enamored of the environmentalist credo that claimed that man was a function of his environment, Wirth felt that "further delay, or failure to solve this basic problem of more-space-for-living for Negro citizens will bring about untold continuance and increase of social ills in the manifold forms of crime, delinquency, disease and indefensible deaths in the overcrowded public areas."[2] Hirsch has maintained that restrictive covenants were a sign of neighborhood weakness and not strength, and as a result they did little or nothing to impede racial succession to the South, where the covenants predominated, while to the West they were not necessary.[3] This fact mattered little to the Chicago Housing Authority, which felt emboldened by the Supreme Court's decision. On June 25, 1948, the Chicago Housing Authority announced the recommendation of four relocation sites. This meant moving black families out of traditionally black areas into neighborhoods which saw their arrival as a threat to their existence.

Nelson Algren captured that sense of impending doom in his novel on Chicago's ethnic neighborhoods, *The Man with the Golden Arm*. No one could have documented the case at the time, but novelists are bound not by access to documentation but rather by the limitations of their imagination, and in this respect Algren, who lived in Chicago, was prescient enough to see that an entire way of life was being threatened at the dawn of the post-World War II new order. The new order was symbolized best by the Safari, a "bar" with indirect lighting, mood music, and table cloths but no drinks on the house. The old order was portrayed in distinctly ethnic terms by Sophie, who remembers

> years when eveything was so well arranged. When people who did right were rewarded and those who did wrong were punished. When everyone, in the long run, got exactly what was coming to him, no more or no less. God weighed virtue and sin then to the fraction of the ounce, like Majurcek the Grocer weighing sugar.[4]

The old order was theological because it was ethnic. The new order was technological because it was not ethnic, a connection which Algren touched on repeatedly if inchoately.

> On the day that the double-tiered causeway is merged with the expressway that merges with the coast to coast thruway making right-hand turns every mile into a hundred solid miles of mile-high skyscrapers, each rising a mile hop-high to the sky out a mile dream-deep in the earth, my own name will not be brought up.[5]

Algren was as prescient about his own literary reputation as he was about Chicago's ethnic neighborhoods. Within a few years, he would become the American literary equivalent of the Soviet officials who got cropped from official photos. Leslie Fiedler would go on to write Algren off as a "museum piece – the last of the Proletarian writers."[6] Norman Podhoretz, whose book *Making It* was a paradigm of Jewish craving for assimilation, "couldn't fathom why [Algren] finds bums so much more interesting and stirring than other people."[7] For years Podhoretz edited *Commentary*, a publication of the American Jewish Committee, which around this time began "offering their files on alleged Jewish subversives to government agencies"[8] because they feared that "any organized opposition of American Jews against the new foreign policy and strategic approach could isolate them in the eyes of the non-Jewish majority and endanger their postwar achievements on the domestic scene."[9]

All of the big forces Algren criticized led the little people who were the unwitting recipients of the social engineering those forces orchestrated to question the notion of the traditional ethnic community as something obsolete. "Why don't we move out of the neighborhood?" one of Algren's characters asks. "The spades are movin in and it's getting smokier every day."[10] According to Rotello's reading of *The Man with the Golden Arm*, Algren articulated the feelings in the neighborhood, in this case the largely Polish near northwest side that was being displaced by a highway at a time when

> many whites were moving out of Chicago proper to the nation's fastest-growing suburban area, pursuing opportunities for jobs, affordable homes, better schools, a restricted choice of neighbors. For many white ethnics, the move to the suburbs meant moving from the hyphenated immigrant-ethnic sphere into the large community of the American middle classes; especially during the prosperous 1950s and early 1960s, they could imagine themselves acquiring a stake in a perfectible America.[11]

Perhaps fearful of more losses on the left to groups like the newly formed ADA, Harry Truman signed the Housing Act of 1949 into law, authorizing the construction across the nation of 135,000 low-rent homes a year for six years. The purpose of the bill was "the realization as soon as feasible of the goal of a decent home and a suitable living environment for every American family" (from the Declaration of National Housing Policy of the Housing Act of 1949), but as in the housing bill of 1937, all of the decisions about particulars were left in the hands of the local housing authorities. While that sounded admirable on paper, in practice it meant that the ethnic groups which controlled the local housing authorities now had federal money to tear down the houses of ethnic groups they feared and disliked. It meant that certain ethnic groups got to determine what happened in the neighborhoods of other, less-favored ethnic groups. Groups like the Polish Roman Catholic Union were barred from membership in the MCPC not because they represented ethnic interests but because they – unlike Klutznick and Wirth and Pettibone and Mumford – represented the wrong ethnic interests.

Emboldened by support from Washington, the Chicago Housing Authority in conjunction with the city's housing and redevelopment coordinator announced its recommendation for four relocation housing sites for the people who were going to be displaced by the city's urban renewal projects in the downtown area. Freed from the restrictions that the now-unconstitutional racial covenants had placed on them before, the announcement of the new sites represented "a complete reversal" of the CHA's previous policy. Now every square inch of the twenty square miles of vacant land within the city limits was available for potential development according to the ground rules established by people like Louis Wirth. That meant, in Wirth's words, that "public policy should not establish or facilitate segregation."[12] It also meant "that the provision of the sites for relocation housing is a city wide responsibility, and that its purpose is the facilitation of slum clearance, from which the city as a whole will benefit."[13] That meant that the sites would be chosen as much for their social engineering of the people who already lived there as for the housing of those who were about to move in. The term "city wide responsibility" meant that no one could object if an unwanted project were scheduled to be built in his neighborhood. It also meant that the experts would determine whose neighborhoods the projects got built in without input from the residents themselves.

If anyone had any doubts about the intentions of the planners, those doubts should have been laid to rest when Ferd Kramer, President of the Metropolitan Housing and Planning Council of Chicago, addressed city council on August 23, 1948, on the topic of location sites for redevelopment and relocation housing sites. Kramer assured the council that the MHPC had "combed the city for suitable locations for these housing projects."[14] The MHPC, like the Philadelphia Housing Authority, was "a voluntary citizen body dedicated to the goal of good housing and neighborhood conditions throughout the metropolitan area."[15] As such, Kramer continued, it had "no political connections of any kind." In fact, Kramer assured the city council, "On our board we have as many points of view as are represented in this council chamber today." Kramer, of course, neglected to tell the city council that the Polish Roman Catholic Union had been turned down when it applied for membership on the MHPC. He also neglected to tell them why because it was essential to convey the impression that the MHPC was functioning in conformity with "a democratic community," where decisions are reached by "give and take," and "progress comes slowly and action only through compromise."[16]

Preliminaries aside, Kramer got to the heart of the matter. The MHPC was "urging immediate approval of the relocation sites which the CHA has recommended." Kramer then went into a long list of why they were urging this approval. Reason number six may have given the council pause. In it Kramer admits that one of the reasons the MHPC accepted the CHA list of sites was because "It will open new neighborhoods to occupancy by the non-white families who have for so long received the short end of the housing."[17] Kramer concluded by telling the council that "It will be impossible to please everyone in the matter of relocation housing sites."[18]

The council, which was given veto power over the CHA in 1949 by the state legislature in Springfield, eventually rejected five of the seven sites. The two which got approved were in slum areas where the local aldermen wanted the projects built. It was, in many ways, a civics lesson about democracy in action, but if so it was not a lesson the CHA wanted to learn. The CHA continued to press for sites that would open new neighborhoods to black occupancy and as a result continued to cause social unrest in the city. The central-city business interests were determined to rid the downtown area of blacks; the suburbs were determined to keep them out, a plan which the federal government backed up by its mortgage policies. Adding those two policies together meant that the blacks were forced out of traditionally black neighborhoods by urban-renewal projects and into the neighborhoods between the downtown areas and the suburbs by the federal government's mortgage policies. That meant doom for the unlucky ethnic neighborhoods in between the downtown and the suburbs. By "scattering thousands of other blacks across the face of the city," urban renewal in Hirsch's view, "accelerated the pace of racial succession and helped trigger a scramble for survival among several outlying neighborhoods."[19] The result was "virtual guerilla war" which erupted into actual hostilities whenever any of the city's myriad racial boundaries got crossed.

In July of 1949 Roscoe Johnson crossed the 71st Street border of the Park Manor neighborhood when he bought a two-flat at 7153 St. Lawrence. Before long the word got out and by July 25, 1949, a mob of 2,000 whites had assembled in front of his house. Within months of that riot, two of the city's major banks concluded that the neighborhood was going black and decided as a result to lend mortgage money to the black migrants, who shortly drove the white people out of the neighborhood. Hirsch concludes, "This change of policy on the part of large lending institutions accelerated the process of succession" and then cites one resident who claimed that "it has become easier to move out of Park Manor than it has to stay," and another who said, "We cannot get mortgages in the area and all day real estate men call us up and want to know if we would like to sell, and of course it is always to Negroes."[20]

The Catholic ethnics were, of course, caught in the middle of a squeeze play orchestrated by the federal government and the most powerful groups in Chicago, and in the early days of the struggle had no alternative but to stand and fight. The suburbs with their cheap VA and FHA mortgages would change that, providing a safety valve for the social planners' soon-to-fail social-engineering schemes as well as a lucrative market for real estate agents and bankers selling mortgages. In the meantime, the Catholic ethnics who participated in the riots whenever a black family crossed one of the city's ethnic fault lines were engaged in an intellectual struggle on two fronts: first of all defining who the enemy was and secondly defining their own identity in the process. The first task was the easier of the two, since the enemy was often simply defined in racial terms. But the ethnics whose neighborhoods were threatened began before long to see the hand of unseen manipulators behind the black families who happened to show up in their neighborhoods. Some claimed the Communists were behind the move-ins. Others were more specific. Louis

Dinnocenzo told his followers that they were involved in a battle over the existence of the small community's right to govern itself. "The nation," he announced, was "astounded that a community so small has dared to fight . . . against such organizations as the NAACP, the Urban League, the CIO Packinghouse Union, the Anti-Defamation Council [*sic*], the B'nai B'rith, the Catholic Interracial Council, and several human relations groups."[21] Given the constraints placed on the flow of information and the penchant of the "integrating" groups to act clandestinely, it was a remarkably accurate list. Missing from it was the American Friends Service Committee and its funding agent, the Ford Foundation. With those links missing, the South Deering Improvement Association couldn't really understand the magnitude of the forces arrayed against them. Had they known they might have been intimidated or they might have waged a more effective campaign. As it was, they were compelled to use physical force to counter the psychological and cultural intimidation that was being wielded against them to drive them out of their homes. Few were as articulate as Mr. Dinnocenzo in describing their enemies. For the most part, the people in the ethnic neighborhoods felt that they were being besieged by "unseen forces they could not control." Those forces were identified as "Jews," "small niggers," and rapacious real-estate agents.[22] The result was paranoia. The incidents which provoked the riots in this period were not orchestrated, but the people who rioted knew that forces which they could not control were at work in their neighborhoods. That in fact created the hypersensitivity which allowed sometimes innocuous incidents to explode into violent confrontations.

In addition to not knowing precisely who the enemy was, the ethnics didn't know precisely who they themselves were either. Abandoned by Catholic intellectuals who could have explained their true ethnic identity, the Catholic ethnics began to identify themselves as "white." None of the protests against racial migration took place in a "pure" ethnic neighborhoood because there was no such thing in Chicago. The closest approximation to a "pure" ethnic riot was the Englewood riot in Visitation Parish at 56th and Peoria, where 51 percent of those arrested had Irish names. But even here the real ethnic designation was Catholic, something which was not considered an ethnic designation at the time.

On November 8, 1949, a woman from the neighborhood noticed a number of blacks in the living room of Aaron Bindman, who lived at 5643 S. Peoria. Almost immediately rumors began to spread through the neighborhood that some "dirty Jew had sold [his house] to a nigger for $20,000 to move 'niggers' into the neighborhood." That Bindman was also a Communist added to the fears of the people in the neighborhood, but the fact that a riot eventuated from something that would on other occasions hardly have been worth noticing is some indication of how sensitive the situation had become. Because the reach of the Chicago Housing Authority now extended to anywhere and everywhere in Chicago, no one could know whether the arrival of blacks meant the dissolution of the neighborhood was imminent, something the Irish who lived in Visitation Parish did not view with indifference.

Founded in 1886 as an Irish ethnic parish, Visitation by the late 1940s had a imposing cluster of buildings on 55th Street, which housed a convent for 60 Domincan nuns, a grammar school for 1,847 children, a high school for 1,062 girls and a rectory which held the five priests who said the twelve masses that were held in the imposing church each Sunday. The parish also had its own summer camp for parishioners as well. Visitation

Parish had a natural boundary on the south, the railroad tracks between 58th and 59th Streets. When the black migrants from the South began pouring into the South Side of Chicago, that boundary began to sag. Having witnessed three solid years of racial strife, the parishioners at Visitation Parish were on edge to begin with, and the people in Aaron Bindman's home pushed them over the edge into a riot that raged for days. They might have also been pushed over the edge if they had known that the ACLU had its agents in the parish spying on the "traditionally Irish" parishioners, whose "Celtic trust in the Most High" found physical expression in the imposing campus of buildings at 55th and Peoria.[23]

As in just about every other instance of racial conflict in the Chicago area during this period of time, the parish priests sided with their parishioners and as a result found themselves at odds with chancery officials and the intelligentsia. During the late '40s, Visitation's Monsignor Byrne encouraged the creation of the Garfield Boulevard Improvement Association, whose avowed purpose was to "keep Negroes out" of the neighborhood and would allow the use of the parish hall for GBIA meetings. If a black family moved into the neighborhood, block captains would go door to door collecting dollar bills to buy them out of their rental leases. Byrnes, as other pastors in other cities did, would also announce from the pulpit when houses were for sale in the neighborhood and encourage people to maintain their homes as a way of keeping property values up. In nearby St. Ambrose Parish, Pastor F.J. Quinn took an even more direct approach to the problem of racial migration, announcing from the pulpit that "The niggers have taken over Corpus Christi Church, Holy Angels and St. Ann's and they are now trying to take over this church; but if it's left to me, they will not . . . Our forefather from Ireland came over here and prepared the way for us in this church, and the Niggers are not going to run us out."[24]

Cardinal Stritch warned Quinn to "keep strictly to Catholic doctrine" in his homilies, but his efforts to rein in people like Quinn were largely ignored by people like Homer Jack, who continued to accuse the church of racism. "Despite requests, some by liberal Catholics," Jack wrote, "neither the local parish nor Cardinal Stritch, so far as is known, has in any way condemned the violence."[25] Jack was supported in his accusations by the Catholic Interracial Council, which concluded in a memo written around this same time that "the mobs are entirely white, many of them Catholics . . . it seems that it has come to the point where Catholics believe our church condones and approves segregation."[26]

Stritch, who was from the South, had a Southerner's awareness of the problems the former sharecroppers were bringing with them up from Mississippi. In a homily in one of the new churches suburban expansion made necessary for the archdiocese, Stritch announced to the faithful that he feared three things in particular for his flock. One was the materialism that pushed Catholics into buying automobiles, one was "the road," i.e., the Eisenhower Expressway, and one was "jungle rhythms" in the new music and the effect they were having on the passions of the young.[27] While Stritch was able to articulate his personal fears, he was unable to formulate a strategy that could resolve the disparate views on racial migration within the Catholic Church. On the one hand, people like Father Quinn could articulate the claims of the local community, and, on the other, groups like the Catholic Interracial Council could articulate the Church's opposition to racist ideology and practice and the claim that the black migrants were also children of God. But no one, least of all Cardinal Stritch, could say how these two competing truths were supposed to be integrated into one coherent policy for the archdiocese. In this Stritch was like Cardinal Dougherty of Philadelphia, who chose integration and assimilation by default by not deliberately opposing the government's efforts to integrate the neighborhoods.

Six and a half years after the Englewood riots, when the Trumbull Park riots had taken center stage in the mind of Chicagoans as the latest battle in the ongoing racial war in Chicago, Cardinal Stritch finally issued a statement condemning the violence. In addition to being blamed for the behavior of Catholics in the Trumbull Park area, Stritch was also being blamed for the behavior of members of the Polish National Catholic Church, over which, as he made clear in his statement, he had no jurisdiction. "Anything which is in violation of people's rights is wrong," he announced in June of 1956. "We have no word of sympathy or mitigation for the use of violence or discrimination by those who are practicing it."[28] Stritch's announcement was met with skepticism by *The Defender*, Chicago's black newspaper, which gave the impression that the cardinal's statement was an example of too little, too late. "Although many of the rioters and the agitators in the disturbances have been identified as Catholic," *The Defender* opined, giving voice to a long-standing complaint in the black community, "this is the first time the Church has taken any official position on the matter."[29] As a Southerner, Stritch clearly understood that "the transition from the plantation lands of Mississippi to urban life is a shock to the individual." But in claiming that the "ultimate goal is full integration into the total life of the city," he failed to specify which part of the city was to bear the brunt of social dislocation during this "transition period."[30] The omission was particularly glaring because it was precisely thriving ethnic parishes like Visitation which were in danger of being taken over by the newly arriving sharecroppers from Mississippi.

At least part of the problem lay in the overlapping layers of identification involved in the struggle. The ethnics whose neighborhoods had been targeted for "integration" were overwhelmingly Catholic but had not yet coalesced into an ethnic group based on religion as opposed to country of origin. The triple melting pot had not yet done its work on them. This identification was also hampered by the fact that the Catholic hierarchy was ambivalent about wholeheartedly espousing the cause of its own people. While some pastors clearly represented the ethnic interests of their parishioners, some priests had adopted the antithetical position of the Catholic Interracial Council. Bishops like Cardinal Stritch found themselves in the middle of this fight and unable to come up with a position of their own that articulated the fact that (1) yes, the blacks from the South were children of God, but (2) they were not Catholics for the most part and (3) even if they were, it was not clear that, given the huge cultural differences between the two groups, they could be integrated into pan-ethnic parishes any more than the Germans and the Irish could have been integrated into one pan-ethnic parish twenty years earlier. Also missing from the equation was any recognition that the black sharecroppers were being pushed into Bohemian, Irish, and Polish ethnic parishes with completely incommensurate social mores by the social engineers at the Chicago Housing Authority, a group with its own hidden agenda in the matter of racial migration. The bishops also found themselves in a bind primarily because it was not clear to them that the ethnic parish was something more than a transitional arrangement. If it were transitional, then what was the point of doing the ecclesial equivalent of going to the barricades for it. If the ethnic parish were transitional, then there was no reason why a bishop should fight something that was inevitably going to disappear anyway. When asked why he let the premier Catholic parish in Philadelphia be overrun by racial migration, John Cardinal Krol of Philadelphia simply said, "You can't tell people where to live."

Faced with a Church that seemed indifferent or, over the course of time, often hostile to their interests, the Catholic ethnics who were half-way through the transitional process known as the triple melting pot identified themselves increasingly as "white," rather than Catholic, an identity which they conferred on themselves more in reaction to the race of the southern invaders than because of any ideological commitment to the racial theories of Madison Grant or Houston Stewart Chamberlain. Part of the anomalous nature of the protest came from the position the ethnics occupied on the spectrum of assimilation. No one ethnic group – if we construe ethnicity as based on country of origin – dominated any of the protests. The Irish came closest in the Englewood riot of 1949, where 51.2 percent of those arrested had Irish names. At Trumbull Park no group based on country of origin could claim more than 25 percent of those arrested. However, the Irish, Slavs, Italians, and Poles taken together comprised 68 percent of those arrested. These people were traditionally Catholic, and the Church could have claimed them as her own and thereby exerted some influence over their behavior, but this is precisely what the Catholic Church was unwilling or unable to do at this particular moment, perhaps because the bishop feared guilt by association. The more avid the Catholic desire for acceptance by the ruling class, the greater the fear of being accused of racism.

Half-way along the spectrum of assimilation, the ethnics still manifested some of their older prejudices. South Deering's Poles often complained about Louis Dinnocenzo, the "dago" who was in charge of the South Deering Improvement Association. Abandoned by the Catholic intelligentsia and the Catholic bishops, these Catholics began to identify themselves as "white" instead, in what could be seen as a pathetic attempt to ingratiate themselves as Americans in a country which had been taken over by a political faction, the environmentalists, who held them in contempt for espousing the wrong ideology of assimilation. Deprived of any positive ethnic identity by the Catholic intellectuals, the ethnics in the beleaguered parishes could only identify themselves by their common enemy, namely, the black migrants, while the shadowy unseen forces that were manipulating that migration remained invisible to them.

This essentially negative definition of themselves as a group outraged the black community, which saw in their public statements nothing but the crudest form of racism, articulated now, not by nativists or Southern whites, but by people who could hardly speak English. Walter White, executive secretary of the NAACP, compared the Cicero crowd to southern lynch mobs and felt that he had never encountered as much "implacable hatred as I found in Cicero." "Some of those with whom I talked," he added, had "such thick Bohemian, German, Polish, or Greek accents that it was not always easy to know what they were saying."[31] St. Clair Drake, the University of Chicago sociologist, who was kept from buying a house near the university by the university, complained about what he read in the neighborhood press, where Southern and Eastern Europeans talked about the glories their cultures had created while the blacks were still "swinging in trees" and "eating each other."[32] Eventually Chandler Owen and A. L. Foster of the Urban League proposed deporting the rioters of European stock back to Southern and Eastern Europe because so many of the rioters were "first generation Americans who do not fully appreciate the concept of democracy."[33]

The ethnics caught up in the racial struggles of the post-war period in Chicago were in the unenviable position of people who had the rules changed on them in mid-game. The Poles who settled Calumet Park as Sobieski Park had created their neighborhood enclaves under certain assumptions, all of which got changed when the environmentalist East Coast WASP internationalist establishment took power in 1941. Not only hadn't they been informed of the rule change, they were doubly vulnerable because compared to their opponents who were further along on the scale of assimilation, they didn't have a clear sense of themselves as Poles or Catholics or Americans or "white" people. They also feared the sexual mores of the invading black hordes but could not articulate this fear in polite language. As a result, each attempt to explain their position drove them further beyond the pale of acceptable public discourse. More often than not, the only people who were articulating their position were the ACLU and AFSC agents sent into their neighborhoods to spy on them. One AFSC spy reported that fear of intermarriage "caused the intensity of feelings" in Trumbull Park.[34] Black attempts to use the community swimming pool were similarly seen in a sexual light. The ACLU agent who was paid to infiltrate bars in South Deering reported that the real motivation behind *Brown v. Board of Education*, the Supreme Court's landmark 1954 decision mandating desegregation of Southern schools, was to move "niggers into every neighborhood" to intermarry and thereby send the "whole white race . . . downhill."[35] Deprived of their ethnic designation as Catholic by a Church that was either hostile (as in the case of Catholic intellectuals) or indifferent (as in the case of the bishops and their chancery officials), Chicago ethnics, attempting to be good Americans, chose to become "white" instead, a transformation that not only guaranteed that they would lose their battle in the court of public opinion, but one which also guaranteed that they would go out of existence as well, through the very assimilation process being proposed by their enemies. While hardly taking their side in the struggle, Hirsch can't help but note the irony in their position. "The ethnics' defensive yet militant espousal of their 'whiteness,'" he writes,

> . . . and the demand for privilege on that basis, was a flawed defense in the context of post-World War II race relations. First, their assertion of what they held in common with the majority society, and the acceptance of that assertion, led, by the 1950s, to their "invisibility." . . . Second, the immigrants and their children displayed the poor judgment of becoming militantly white at the precise moment prerogatives of color were coming into question. As the more mobile and well-to-do fled to the suburbs, those still tied to the city were left to face a rapidly expanding ghetto and an increasingly hostile government with anachronistic racial slogans as their primary defense. What could ring more hollow in 1955 than the South Deering Bulletin's proud assertion that a "real American white ha[d] been evolved" out of the various nationalities?[36]

The ethnics simply could not articulate their position, even when it was to their advantage. In their attacks on Jews as outsiders, they failed to bring up the fact that the Jewish store owners on Halsted Street were left unmolested because they were considered part of the local community and not outside agitators, like the largely Marxist University of Chicago students. This fact was duly noted by ACLU spies in the neighborhood but, of course, not publicized by the ACLU in its official statements because the fact was not useful in the cultural war being waged against the ethnics. The fact that their position was based largely on the rights of the small community was left largely unarticulated because their racial attitudes provided their enemies with such a handsome and irresistible target.

As soon as the ethnics made race the main issue of contention, they disqualfied themselves from having a vote in the court of polite opinion. They also deformed their own identity in the process. No matter what sort of victories they might achieve on the local level, this misidentification became the source of the problem, and once the issue of the local community got cast in racial terms, this would insure that the apologia for their cause would not make it out of the parish or out of the neighborhood. The ethnics proclaimed themselves white, while their enemies saw them as Catholic. More than that, their enemies saw them as racist Catholics, which is to say the worst of both worlds. They had the racial attitudes of the now-defeated isolationists combined with the un-American, sexually benighted views of the Roman Catholic Church. Since the Church intelligentsia remained silent on the issue, or more frequently espoused the position of the Catholic Interracial Council as the only defensible position, Catholic ethnics were rendered defenseless and intellectually disarmed in the psychological warfare campaign being waged against them.

On January 11, 1950, two months after the meeting in Aaron Bindman's house brought the largely Irish residents in the area around 56th and Peoria out into the streets in protest, the commissioners of the Chicago Housing Authority formally adopted a resolution stating that "in the selection and admission of families to the projects now and to be operated by the Authority, families shall not be segregated or otherwise discriminated against on grounds of race, color, creed, national origin, or ancestry."[37] In order to generate public support for the CHA and in order to counter the adverse publicity which integration efforts had received as a result of the Englewood Riots, Samuel D. Freifeld, director of B'nai B'rith's Anti-Defamation League announced two weeks later that B'nai B'rith as well as the Chicago Council Against Racial and Religious Discrimination would hold a Chicago Housing Rally at the Congress Hotel on February 15. In addition to Mr. Freifeld himself, Saul Alinsky, Elizabeth Wood, and Waitstill Sharp, one of the people invited to speak was Louis Wirth.

Six months later, Wirth gave another speech on racial tensions. This one was given to UNESCO and went into a depth which the rally format did not allow. By September of 1950, the battle with fascism had been long won, but Wirth was still involved in battling his fellow Chicagoans over the integration of ethnic neighborhoods. Wirth was still complaining, but this time the enemy's identity was more religious than ethnic. In his speech on "Domestic Ethnic and Racial Tensions and American Foreign Policy," delivered on September 8, 1950, Wirth continued to see racial integration as the cornerstone of America's foreign policy:

> As long as we continued to pursue a policy of isolationism in foreign affairs, we could, with a certain amount of reason say that it was no other nation's business

how we treated racial minorities in the United States. But the abandonment of isolationism in foreign affairs necessarily involves an abandonment of the same principle so far as our domestic racial minorities are concerned.[38]

Wirth continued to complain about "hyphenate Americans," those who were "tied to
the mother country by an umbilical hyphen three thousand miles long," who "settled
together to lead a more or less separate communal life, associated with organizations of
their own or were affiliated with religious bodies distinctive from the dominant Protestant
denominations characteristic of the earlier settlers."[39]

Lest his listeners not know who this group was, Wirth went on to say that

> A complication has recently been introduced into American political affairs as in
> those of other nations, by the international relations of the Roman Catholic
> Church, the Communist movement, and the emergence of the United Nations. The
> fact that a number of ethnic groups in America are also predominantly members
> of the Catholic Church and that the church as an important political factor in the
> world may pursue objectives which cannot always be reconciled with American
> foreign policy has occasioned considerable domestic controversy concerning the
> balance of loyalties between the appeals of the church and those of the state.[40]

As his authority for this statement, Wirth cites Paul Blanshard's book, *American
Freedom and Catholic Power.* Wirth's citation of Blanshard as an authority does more than
link him to the growing group of people who were beginning to express concern about
"the Catholic Problem." It also shows the disparity in ethnic identification at the heart of
the culture wars of the time. At the very moment that the ethnics, thinking that they were
being good Americans by doing so, began identifying themselves as "white," their enemies on the other side of the cultural fault lines were identifying them as Catholics. Wirth,
in this regard, was right, and the ethnics, even if they applied the label to themselves, were
wrong. Race is not an adequate indication of ethnicity in America. Even in the case of the
majority of America's blacks, where race because of historical circumstances certainly is
an ethnic indicator, race is less an indicator of behavior than religion. The same was *a fortiori* true of "ethnics." The fact that they considered themselves "white" was purely negative. It was a reaction to the race of the invaders from the South, and it was a reaction by
default to the fact that the Catholic intelligentsia was embarrassed by their lack of education and assimilation, and as a result denied them the ethnic status that was truly descriptive, namely, Catholic. Wirth, who was nothing if not perceptive in ethnic matters, simply
applied to the ethnics the true category which they out of ignorance and which the intellectuals out of embarrassment refused to apply to them, namely, the designation of
Catholic. Because the ethnics didn't know who they were, they could not understand who
their real enemies were. They could also not formulate anything approaching a coherent
strategy in dealing with their enemies. In conferring on this group its true identity, Wirth,
on the other hand, could also explain why it was dangerous to the WASP establishment.
Like Blanshard, Wirth was worried about Catholic ethnics because of

> Their importance as forces in maintaining the separate identity and solidarity of
> the minority group on a local scale is often appreciable and may be enhanced by

the federation of local unions, lodges, clubs and associations into nation-wide bodies which are capable of exercising effective control over great numbers and can maintain the group's capacity for collective action and can cultivate group sentiments and attitudes toward national issues to an extent where they approximate political blocs.[41]

Since "substantial groups of immigrants are unable to speak English," Wirth concludes that "we have further likelihood that the minority groups will be exposed and perhaps susceptible to news and propaganda purveyed by the foreign language press and conversely inaccessible to the media of communication of the nation at large."[42] The nativists' animus toward immigrants only makes a bad situation worse because their prejudice "thus helps to perpetuate the minority status of immigrant and other distinguishable sections of the population by ascribing characteristics to them as groups and thus inhibiting the individuation of the members."[43]

Individuation, it might be said, is what happened to Louis Wirth when he abandoned his own ethnic background in favor of class and upward mobility. It might have happened to the rest of America's ethnics over the course of time, but the war with fascism meant that nature could not be left to run its course unaided, if in fact deracination was the course of nature. Wirth makes this clear in the same paper:

This conception of Americanization as a slow, gradual, uncoerced, reciprocal interpenetration of immigrant and native groups and their cultures has had to be subjected to serious reconsideration in the light of the Nazi and Fascist policy to retain control over their nationals in foreign countries and to use them as spearheads of penetration and conquest abroad. In the face of the propaganda and organizational campaigns of the totalitarian nations even the most liberal wings of the Americanization movement have been forced to ask whether our traditional tolerant attitude toward the immigrant could be maintained without seriously undermining national solidarity.[44]

The war years also saw the first attempts in Chicago to expand and harness governmental powers under the guise of "urban planning" in order to reshape the local environment and control the process of succession. According to Hirsch's history of housing in Chicago, the MHPC under Wirth's direction turned Chicago into the model for the national housing bill of 1947. The roots of that policy in Wirth's wartime work for the OWI is evident in the already cited letter Clyde Hart wrote to Wirth thanking him for his evaluation of the race riots in Detroit, and urging at Wirth's suggestion "direct, sensible readjustments of the kind you suggest – in housing" right around the same time that Stalin, Wirth's model in ethnic matters, was preparing to deport the Kalmyks to Kazakstan.

Ethnic cleansing under the guise of integration is precisely what Wirth prescribed for Chicago in the period following World War II, and rioting was the result. The rioting also resulted in a vicious circle in the mind of the planners. According to the mind of the urban planner, that rioting indicated the presence of prejudice, which indicated the necessity of more social engineering and more integration as the cure. That mindset succeeded in bequeathing to Chicago close to ten years of all but unbroken civil unrest as the professional planners and social engineers attempted to break open ethnic neighborhoods either by "integration," which invariably failed, or its more plausible alternative, panic and racial succession which drove the ethnic into the arms of the "Americanizers" in the suburbs. The immediate ethnic reaction was rage, and it was on this rage that the social engineer's first assault on the ethnic neighborhood ran aground.

Notes

1 "Memorandum on Race Restrictive Covenants," Louis Wirth Papers, Box XXVII Folder 1, University of Chicago Archives.
2 Ibid.
3 Arnold R. Hirsch, *Making the Second Ghetto: Race and Housing in Chicago 1940–1960* (Cambridge: Cambridge University Press, 1983), p. 217.
4 Carlo Rotella, *October Cities: The Redevelopment of Urban Literature* (Berkeley: University of California Press, 1998), p. 73.
5 Ibid., p. 92.
6 Ibid., p. 59.
7 Ibid.
8 Norman Finkelstein, *The Holocaust Industry: Reflections on the Exploitation of Jewish Suffering* (London: Verso, 2000), p. 14.
9 Ibid., p. 15.
10 Rotella, p. 78.
11 Ibid., p. 42.
12 Press release to all member of City Council 7/16/48, Wirth papers, Box XXVII Folder 1, University of Chicago Archives.
13 Ibid.
14 Statement of the MHPC 8/23/48 presented by Ferd Kramer, President to the Housing Committee of the City Council, Wirth papers, Box XXVII Folder 1, University of Chicago Archives.
15 Ibid.
16 Ibid.
17 Ibid.
18 Ibid.
19 Hirsch, p. 134.
20 Ibid., p. 59.
21 Ibid., p. 199.
22 Ibid., p. 200.
23 Ibid., p. 78.
24 John T. McGreevy, *Parish Boundaries: The Catholic Encounter with Race in the Twentieth Century Urban North* (Chicago: University of Chicago Press, 1996), p. 93.
25 Ibid., p. 96.
26 Ibid., p. 93.
27 Interview with Father McKenna.
28 "Cardinal Stritch Assails Trumbull Park Violence," *Chicago Defender* (June 14, 1956), in American Friends Service Committee papers, University of Illinois at Chicago archives.
29 Ibid.
30 Ibid.
31 Hirsch, p. 79.

32 Ibid., p. 80.
33 Ibid.
34 Ibid., p. 195.
35 Ibid.
36 Ibid., p. 198.
37 AFSC Report Progress Report on Trumbull Park Homes March 1959, AFSC papers, University of Illinois at Chicago archives.
38 "Domestic Ethnic and Racial Tensions and American Foreign Policy," Louis Wirth for Unesco 9/8/50, Box LXVII, folder 6, Wirth Papers, University of Chicago.
39 Ibid.
40 Ibid.
41 Wirth, "Morale and Minority Groups," Wirth papers, UIC archives.
42 Ibid.
43 Ibid.
44 Ibid.

Joe Clark and the Reform in Philadelphia

Not everyone was happy with the Better Philadelphia Exhibit, not even everyone in Walter Phillips' circle. One person who was extremely unhappy was Joseph Sill Clark, the patrician from Chestnut Hill who came back from the war with political ambitions. What made Joe Clark "mad as a wet hen"[1] at Walter Phillips was not the BPE's manipulation of school children but rather its flagrantly manipulative political conclusion. As each visitor passed the last display, an attendant handed him what looked like a blank piece of paper. What they really got, in fact, when it was passed under an ultraviolet light, was a message from Mayor Samuels taking credit for the exhibit and thereby asking those who liked what they saw to cast their vote for him in the upcoming election. What annoyed Joe Clark most was that the ploy worked. It contributed to the defeat of Clark's co-reformer Dick Dilworth in that year's election.

But in spite of making "[Mayor] Barney [Samuels] look great," the BPE didn't prevent Clark from becoming city controller, and when he did the Reform Democrats took their first step to keeping the Republicans out of the mayor's office for the rest of the century. Even if Barney Samuels could use the BPE to say "Look what I've done, and see how we Republicans are going to rebuild the City of Philadelphia,"[2] he couldn't overcome the fact that Philadelphia's Republicans were saddled with the legacy of Mayor Lamberton in the eyes of the progressives, and so not in a position to collaborate with the federal government's urban renewal program in the way that the Democrats were under the guidance of people like Jim Finnegan and Michael Bradley. The Republicans had turned down government money once; they might turn it down again. Cities, even politically backward cities like Philadelphia, were now edging toward having the majority of their voters firmly in the Democratic camp. Normally, that meant a Catholic mayor, but not in Philadelphia, not until 1963 anyway. Digby Baltzell inadvertently put his finger on the situation in Philadelphia when, in describing his vision of the "Protestant Establishment," he claimed that "the final protector of freedom . . . may very well be a unified establishment from within which the leaders of at least two parties are chosen."[3]

That was, in reality, the situation in Philadelphia, and it provided the ethnic backdrop for the Clark-Dilworth reform. In 1950 Philadelphia was still run by "a small community of Philadelphia families, predominantly of English and Welsh descent, Quaker turned Episcopalian in religion," who were "educated at private schools and colleges like Harvard, Yale or Princeton," and were "residents of fashionable neighborhoods, members of exclusive clubs, and listed in the Social Register."[4] This group, which included Walter Phillips and Joseph Sill Clark, still "authoritatively dominated the business and cultural life of Philadelphia, as their ancestors had done since colonial days."[5]

It was, as a result, somewhat misleading to talk about the "reform" in Philadelphia as if it were some break with the past. It would be more accurate to describe it as the ruling class changing party affiliation or the ruling class coming up with a different idea of how to run the city, this time according to the progressive social theories of cultural bolshevists recently expelled from Germany and now teaching at Harvard. The election of Joe Clark and Dick Dilworth, no matter what their party affiliation, did not change the fact that the ruling class had one of its own in the mayor's office. But the change in party did change the way they got there. Now the Catholics were part of the Democratic coalition which elected WASP bluebloods like Clark and Dilworth, who now knew that they could not get elected without Catholic ethnic support. This made for an uneasy political alliance which would eventually break down along ethnic lines in 1963, but even when it did, the crack-up of the coalition was still carefully couched in euphemistic terms like "reform," which meant WASP and "machine," which meant Catholic (largely Irish) ethnic.

But all that was in the future. For now it looked as if the ideology of "reform" – a mish-mash of big government liberalism, coupled with support of the unions, WASP *noblesse oblige*, urban planning, public health measures, and a new city charter basing employment on civil service criteria rather than patronage – might paper over ethnic divisions. The hope was the standard left-wing hope that powerful ideology might actually make ethnic difference disappear, as it had in the Soviet Union, or at least as people like Louis Wirth said it had.

It was this hope which fueled the creation of Americans for Democratic Action. In Philadelphia the ADA was seen as the melting pot in action. Ideology triumphantly united Jews from liberal unions like the International Ladies Garment Workers Union and the Amalgamated Clothing Workers, with WASPs from Chestnut Hill and Italians from South Philadelphia – unless, of course, those Italians identified themselves as Catholics, in which case they would not join the ADA. Membership in the Philadelphia chapter of the ADA was equally divided between WASPs and Jews, with Catholics finishing a distant third. Catholic membership peaked in 1955, when the Reform reached its high point in Philadelphia, at 9 percent. By 1968, Catholic membership had plummeted to one-third of that figure largely because the Phillips crowd pulled out of the Reform when the first Catholic was elected mayor in 1964 but also because of the increasingly anti-Catholic tone that began to suffuse the increasingly contentious battles over government funding of birth control during that era.[6]

In March of 1947, Hubert Humphrey wrote that there was "no enthusiasm for Truman out here" and suggested either Supreme Court Justice William O. Douglas or General Dwight D. Eisenhower as an alternative candidate for the upcoming election.[7] If the Democrats stayed with Truman, "we not only face defeat in November," according to Humphrey, "we face a possible disintegration of the whole social Democratic bloc in this country."[8] Truman had earned the ire of the liberals by purging the party of its New Deal operatives, but also by opposing their housing bill "under pressure from real estate interests." But the real issue was redefining New Deal liberalism as the vital center of the American political tradition. The ADA was founded to protect the interests of WASP progressivism from the Communists on the left but also from the influence of the Catholics on the right. What bothered the Jewish and WASP progressives who made up the ADA's core constituency the most was the fact that "The President," according to one of the ADA founders, "takes his orders from the rotten, corrupt reactionary Democratic machines."[9] He was referring, of course, to places like Boston and politicians like Mayor Michael

Curley, who was on his way to jail at the time. "Machine" would soon become a code word for Catholic in ADA circles, especially in Philadelphia.

At around the same time that Hubert Humphrey was expressing his misgivings about Harry Truman, the "Organizing Committee of the Philadelphia Chapter of the ADA" announced that their first meeting would be held on March 22, 1947, as a way of kicking off a membership drive from which they hoped to enroll one hundred charter members. One of the main constituencies of the new Philadelphia ADA was the area's union locals, which, if Marxism were an accurate predictor of political affiliation, should have been united enough to come up with a common program. But the unions were not united. In fact, they were split along ethnic lines as well. The Teamsters and building-trades unions wanted to support the "machine" candidate because their members were predominantly Catholic, whereas the ILGWU and the Amalgamated Clothing Workers wanted to support the "reform" Democratic candidate because their members were predominantly Jewish. Eventually "the politically active AFL," as ADA executive director Harry Ferleger put it, "moved into the ADA"[10] and as a result the ADA took on their interests as union interests.

The ADA also attracted social register types like Richardson Dilworth, the reform candidate for mayor in 1947, as well as Lawrence M. C. Smith, whose wife owned the Houston estate, a huge chunk of property in and around Chestnut Hill which included houses which could be rented to impecunious WASPs in order to maintain the ethnic character of the neighborhood. The Philadelphia ADA could give the impression that it was a broad-based coalition because of the incongruity of union members sitting down at the same table with WASP patricians, but ethnically the Philadelphia ADA was pretty much what Digby Baltzell would go on to urge in his book, *The Protestant Establishment*, namely, the WASP ruling class rewarding capable Jews with patronage and admission into their clubs. This alliance imposed some constraints on ruling-class behavior. If the businessmen on the board opposed minimum-wage legislation, the labor leaders would threaten to leave, but this did not in any way threaten the chain of command. "Most of the policy ideas originated with the independent liberal group," said one member, "but we always made it a point to clear it with the labor people before a new policy was recommended."[11] As economic issues faded in significance in the '60s in comparison with social-sexual issues, the reality of the ADA as an essentially ethnic coalition of Jews and WASPs united against the "machine" Catholics became more apparent.

One of the upper-class Jews who joined the ADA was Emily Sunstein, a woman whose fundraising and organizing prowess earned her the title "Mrs. ADA."[12] Sunstein supported Walter Phillips's ill-fated 1963 mayoral campaign on personal grounds out of loyalty to Phillips, who was by dint of his organizing if not Mr. ADA then Mr. Reform. She also supported him by construing the issue as one of principle. Principle in this instance had a distinctly ethnic cast. It was construed as resistance to the "machine," which meant Catholic politicians like Jim Tate and Bill Green, but also people like Eugene McCarthy, whose invitation to the 1968 Roosevelt Day Dinner Sunstein opposed. Sunstein would go on to write a book on Mary Shelley, which gave some indication of her broader political views. Mary Shelley, we are told in her book, "was born in the eighth year of the French Revolution when hopes for a just, free new order were succumbing to reaction."[13] Sunstein fails to mention that the main thing driving the reaction was the number of people

– from the king to the revolutionaries themselves – who were murdered in bringing about the "just, free new order" that has inspired revolutionaries ever since. The same idea could still inspire the ADA in Philadelphia even after they got over their disenchantment with communism. In the post-war period, the communality of wives rather than the communality of property became more of an inspiration for the area's revolutionaries. "Women," Sunstein tells us in a passage that would have direct relevance to the birth-control battles in Pennsylvania in the 1960s, "were hostages to their anatomy" because "contraceptive devices were primitive and unreliable until the 1870s."[14]

One of Sunstein's mentors on organizational techniques was Johannes Hoeber, like Walter Gropius another refugee from Nazi Germany where he had been an assistant to the socialist mayor of Mannheim. Hoeber's wife Elfriede became intimately involved in housing issues in Philadelphia shortly after she arrived here and both she and her husband were inducted into the Walter Phillips group. Elfriede Hoeber, among other things, edited *Issues*, the newsletter of the Philadelphia Housing Association. When the Democrats held their national convention in Philadelphia in 1948, the local ADA opened an office nearby to sway the outcome. Their biggest triumph came when Hubert Humphrey gave his now-famous civil-rights speech. Humphrey was torn, as most politicians are, about whether he would benefit from the speech politically or not, even in the last hours before he was to give it and was apparently tipped toward civil rights by the influence of the ADA. Humphrey spent some of the time during which he agonized over supporting civil rights or not with Hoeber at his home washing dishes with Hoeber's daughter and promising them that he would invite the whole family to the White House when he became president.

The ADA may have been "united by its belief in the expansion of Rooseveltian liberalism, by its acceptance of American foreign policy, and by the firm conviction that Communist infiltration should be vigorously resisted"[15] but that did not prevent its critics from the isolationist Midwest from seeing it as every bit as bad as the communism it opposed. In February of 1950, Senator Homer Capehart of Indiana told the Senate that the ADA was part of "an international conspiracy to socialize America."[16] A few months earlier John Flynn, formerly of America First, referred to the ADA as "the spearhead and central planning and propaganda machine of the National Socialist Economic Planners in this country"[17] in his book *The Road Ahead*.

As in the horror movies that Hollywood would produce in the early '50s, the sense that subversion was afoot was much clearer than the identity of the subversives, who were invariably identified (or misidentified) as Communists, even when they were associated with plutocratic institutions like the Rockefeller Foundation. On October 24, 1949, GOP city chairman William F. Meade denounced the "Dilworth ADA" as "his own private hot-house of Reds" and announced on the radio that "I am going to prove the Communist infiltration of the ADA Dilworth campaign in Philadelphia."[18] Like Senator Joe McCarthy, the Catholic Republican from Wisconsin, Meade was going to "name names and cite the record." One of those names was Mollie Yard, a woman Meade identified as "a member of the orginal board of directors of Dilworth's ADA" as well as a member of the American League of Peace and Democracy, something Meade identified, with the help of the congressional committee on un-American activities as "the largest of the Communist front movements in the United States."[19] Meade also identified Yard as a member of the Washington Book Shop, which was also cited as a Communist front organization.

Walter Phillips must have been listening to the radio on the 24th because he responded the next day condemning Meade's "action in calling Mollie Yard a Communist."[20] Phillips knew this because he had rented his Torresdale estate to Yard and her husband. It was during this period that Phillips learned that Yard was "emphatically not a Communist." In fact she was their "bitterest enemy," and spent her time in the organizations that Meade mentioned, fighting communist attempts to control them. "When she failed in those attempts," Phillips continued, "she withdrew." Phillips, who concluded his attack on Meade by claiming that "I am a Republican and have been so registered all my life," stated that "we never had any infiltration from Communists into the Citizen's Council on City Planning" because "Mollie could spot a Communist in quick order."[21]

Phillips claim is plausible if one considers that Johannes Hoeber was brought into the Phillips circle and ADA for precisely the same qualities he attributed to Yard. It was also plausible in light of the ADA membership form, a copy of which he appended to his letter, which specified:

> We believe that all forms of totalitarianism, including Communism are incompatible with these objectives [i.e., democratic planning, enlargement of fundamental liberties and international cooperation]. In our crusade for an expanding democracy and against Fascism and reaction we welcome as members of the ADA only those whose devotion to the principles of political freedom is unqualified.[22]

Phillips's claim is plausible, however, largely in light of the crude terms in which Meade stated his case. If Meade had been more precise he might had made a better case with Philadelphia's voters because Mollie Yard was a revolutionary. She was, in the parlance of Wilhelm Reich, whose *Mass Psychology of Fascism* had just appeared in English translation in the United States, a sexual revolutionary who would go on to become the head of the National Organization of Women. Meade was handicapped by the crudeness of his political categories and the fact that Yard's revolutionary activity would become apparent only after there was no longer any political liability associated with it. Conservatives like Meade made the mistake of painting their foes as Communists at precisely the point when the Left was abandoning communism in favor of a more sophisticated form of revolutionary activity, a cultural revolution that was more Reichian than Marxian in its focus.

In effect, the class struggle of the '30s was being superseded by the ethnic struggle of the '50s, but it was still being portrayed in the political terms of a bygone era. Communism had no domestic following of any political significance in America after the mass conversion to liberalism typified by the founding of the ADA in 1947. Yet, communism, perhaps because the foreign threat was still real, still dominated the political debate and obscured the deeper ethnic meaning behind it. Joe McCarthy and Alger Hiss corresponded to the two poles of the ethnic struggle that got portrayed as the struggle against communism. The WASP elite stood by Hiss in spite of all of the evidence against him because he was one of their ethnic group. When Joe McCarthy threatened to subpoena

William Bundy to find out why he had contributed $400 to Hiss's legal defense fund, he started the chain of events in motion that eventually led to his censure at the hands of the Senate. The WASP state department closed ranks behind Bundy and persuaded President Eisenhower to go along with them. Because of the people who supported him, Joe McCarthy was perceived as part of "the Catholic problem" by those who opposed him. As one of McCarthy's recent biographers has noted, the split over McCarthy in terms of public opinion mirrored fairly precisely the split over abortion twenty years later because the cultural divide on both issues was defined by the same ethnic configuration. And it was directly over this cultural fault line that the shaky edifice of Philadelphia reform was built. The Jews and WASPs who made up the bulk of the Philadelphia ADA, and therefore the leading edge of that coalition, were outraged by Meade's charge because they, like Paul Blanshard, whose book *Communism, Democracy, and Catholic Power* was being discussed by the Phillips crowd at this time, were involved in a two-front war against both Catholics and Communists at the time.

One year after Meade denounced the Philadelphia ADA as Dick Dilworth's "own private hothouse of Reds," Bertrand Russell returned in triumph to New York City, the place which had barred him from teaching there because of his sexual practices and views. In November of 1950, shortly after winning the Nobel Prize, Russell declared in a lecture at Columbia University that it is a "dangerous error to think that the evils of communism can be combated by Catholicism."[23] He then went on to describe Catholicism and communism as virtually identical systems of thought, both of which espouse:

> Adherence to a rigid and static system of doctrine, of which part is doubtful and part demonstrably false; persecution as a means of enforcing orthodoxy; a belief that salvation is only to be found within the church and that the True Faith must be spread throughout the world, by force, if necessary; that the priesthood, which alone has the right to interpret the Scripture has enormous power.[24]

The equivalence of communism and Catholicism was not apparent to Chairman Meade at the time. He made the mistake of attacking the ADA at precisely the moment when the ADA broke with the Communists, and as a result of the imprecision of his political analysis, he got into trouble. Yard, with Joe Clark as her lawyer, sued Meade for libel, asking for $25,000 in damages. On July 26, 1950, Meade agreed to an out-of-court settlement according to which he agreed to pay her $1,000 and issue a public retraction in which he stated that "there was no evidence to justify the charge" that Yard was a Communist.[25]

Meade's charge bespoke a serious error in political intelligence. Worse than the libel suit and the retraction it forced him to make, the charge that the ADA was all a bunch of Communists revealed that the Republicans didn't really know who their opponent was in the upcoming war over who would control Philadelphia. As a result, the reformers, capitalizing on the ignorance of their political opponents, began to take over the city government. The change began in the very campaign which Meade hoped to influence by his accusation. In November of 1949, Joe Clark was elected city controller. Within hours of being elected, on November 10, Clark announced that his first act upon taking office on January 2, 1950, would be to appoint "white knight"[26] Walter M. Phillips to the

Philadelphia Housing Authority, replacing Republican appointee William Reinhardt, who represented the city's real-estate interests. Mrs. Hoeber characterized Phillips's housing philosophy as "sincere human sympathy and a sense of common interest with his fellow citizens, combined with a thorough knowledge of the processes of good government."[27] This meant specifically that

> Politics has no place in the management of the housing program, in the selection of tenants, in the employment of administrative personnel, in *the selection of sites* [my emphasis] or in the business dealings of the authority such as purchasing, insurance, construction contracts and banking.[28]

What Phillips meant by "politics" was clear to Hoeber and her readers. It meant that they, i.e., the professional housers, would now get to choose the housing sites and who would live in the projects once they got built, without the interference of city council and the people who elected them to office. "Politics" meant, in short, the political process in a representative democracy, something credentialed planners found inconvenient at best. Phillips, according to Hoeber, was "fully backed by Mr. Clark, who has publicly stated that housing is one of his foremost concerns and that he wants the administration of housing removed from politics,"[29] i.e., put into the hands of WASP planners.

At this point no one knew exactly what those plans were, since the housers had kept them a closely guarded secret. But the planners, who "were not under the direct control of the mayor," knew. Less than a year after the Philadelphia City Planning Commission helped bring about the Better Philadelphia Exhibit, they came up with the map of what their version of "Better Philadelphia" was going to look like. Bauman states blandly that the map, which "certified 16 areas for development" was created "with housing as much as slum clearance in mind."[30] He goes on to claim that the areas scheduled for demolition, "with few exceptions," involved the demolition of "aging, largely black wards that originally had been developed in the nineteenth century as the city's industrialized streetcar suburbs."[31]

Bauman's description belies the scale of devastation which the Philadelphia City Planning Commission was preparing for Philadelphia, a plan which was nothing less than breathtaking in scope. All of North Philadelphia from Diamond (the border would later be moved north to Lehigh) to Spring Garden Streets and from Broad to 5th was scheduled to be torn down. The area around Temple University was in fact leveled in what was probably Philadelphia's worst example of the bulldozer approach to urban renewal. The same fate awaited all of "East" Philadelphia from Vine Street north of Market to Tasker in the south and from 8th Street to the Delaware River. All of what is traditionally known as South Philadelphia from South Street to Dickinson and from Broad to the famous 9th St. Italian Market was also scheduled to be torn down, even though the best housing stock in South Philadelphia, owned by the Italian elite – doctors, lawyers , etc. – was to be found along Broad Street.

According to Bauman, in order to come up with the Philadelphia City Planning Commission map of September 15, 1948, "the RA and the planning commission collaborated from the outset on an area survey using the Public Health Association's Neighborhood Environmental Standards."[32] This meant counting sinks, toilets, and outdoor privies, adding them up and then dividing them by the number of houses on the block and coming up with the number which determined the fate of the neighborhood. It was precisely this quasi-scientific approach which Bacon criticized in his 1975 speech at Temple University as in no way reflective of the actual condition of the neighborhood. But even these rules didn't apply to the "few exceptions" to the intensive-use central area scheduled for redevelopment.

The most shocking part of the map, however, and one of the "few exceptions"[33] mentioned by Bauman, lay in the gray hatched patch off to the northeast well outside of the intensive-use central area where some of the city's oldest housing stock existed. That part of town was known as Bridesburg. It was, like Kensington, which lay to the south, industrial and residential combined, which was the pattern of industrial 19th-century Philadelphia. What Bridesburg did not have was run-down houses, something that can be ascertained by walking through the neighborhood today. The houses in St. John Cantius Parish are the same houses that were there in 1948. They are still occupied and still in good condition. Given the assault on ethnic neighborhoods which characterized the post-war period in Philadelphia, a safe rule of thumb for housing stock is that anything which existed in 1948 was probably in better condition then than it is now. Since there is no blight in Bridesburg now, there was *a fortiori* no blight when the same houses were scheduled for demolition in 1948. Why then did the Philadelphia City Planning Commission want them torn down?

Ask those who know the history of urban renewal in Philadelphia today why Bridesburg was targeted for destruction, and you will get no answer. Ed Bacon remembers the PCPC map vaguely but cannot recall that Bridesburg was scheduled for redevelopment, much less why. Frank Hoeber, son of Johannes and Elfriede and an authority on both the reform and its redevelopment plans, draws a similar blank. When I asked him why Bridesburg was scheduled for demolition according to the 1948 PCPC map, he has no answer. "That's wild," Hoeber says. "Crazy."

It was crazy for one simple reason: according to the criteria which the renewers themselves established, Bridesburg was not blighted, if by blight one means deteriorated housing stock. Bridesburg was a mixed-use neighborhood, but so was just about all of the rest of old Philadelphia. In a world without automobiles, workers had to live near the factories where they worked. In one of the nation's oldest manufacturing centers, one where the factories antedated even the street-car lines, that often meant walking to work, something which necessitated the proximity of housing and industry. The tallow plant on Aramingo Avenue may not have been an especially pleasing olfactory experience, but its existence did not justify the destruction of the houses of the residents who suffered most from its smell. If renewal were simply interested in hygiene and pollution, the renewers could have arranged for the removal of the tallow plant to a site downwind from Philadelphia's residential neighborhoods. The fact that it didn't indicates that other considerations led to Bridesburg's designation as blighted. As in the placement of low-income housing, so in redevelopment, its twin, blight was always an excuse for social engineering. The absence of blight makes the presence of social engineering as the prime motivating factor almost a certainty.

Which brings us to Bridesburg's most salient characteristic, which was not the condition of its buildings but rather the ethnic homogeneity of its inhabitants. As Brand Blanshard had noted in his doctoral dissertation, Bridesburg housed the overwhelming majority of the Polish population of Philadelphia, the one ethnic group which was notorious for its peasant Catholicism and its resistance to assimilation. The connection between the Blanshard family and housing in Philadelphia is more uncanny than fortuitous. Brand and Paul lived in Bridesburg during World War I. Paul Blanshard mentioned Philadelphia in his best-seller on the "Catholic problem," and was read avidly by the people on the Philadelphia City Planning Commission, which eventually decreed Bridesburg worthy of "redevelopment." Paul's son, Paul Blanshard, Jr., eventually became a Quaker and was on the board of Friends Suburban Housing during the '60s when the American Friends Service Committee was actively involved in the clandestine manipulation of race and housing in and around Philadelphia.

The fact that they never succeeded in destroying Bridesburg was not, as the PCPC map indicates, from lack of trying. When I asked one of the priests at St. John Cantius parish, which serves the Polish population there, why the planned destruction didn't happen, he couldn't come up with an answer either. But the answer in both instances – both why Bridesburg was singled out for destruction and why that destruction never took place – has to do with ethnicity. Bridesburg survived because the Poles refused to move from the neighborhood. The same thing can be seen in a Polish neighborhood like Hamtramck near Detroit. The Poles who were successful didn't move to the suburbs when they made money. Instead, they tore down the conventional housing stock and built brick palaces in their place.

In the PCPC map of September 15, 1948, we get a glimpse of what Joe Clark and Walter Phillips meant when they said that "politics had no place in housing." It meant that people who lacked credentials would have their houses torn down by people who had them. It meant that WASP planners from Chestnut Hill with no interference from the neighborhood's duly elected representative to city council got to decide whose house got left standing and whose house got torn down. The ethnic homogeneity of the WASP housing establishment in the city meant that decisions like this were made according to ethnocentric criteria that almost guaranteed that the ethnic groups who were not represented would suffer. If one looks for a Polish name on the PCPC board, the Philadelphia Housing Association Board, the Philadelphia Housing Authority board, or the Redevelopment Authority Board, one looks in vain. As a result, what went by the name of urban renewal was, in effect, one ethnic group, namely the WASPs from Germantown and Chestnut Hill, coming up with a plan for destroying the neighborhood of another ethnic group, even when the obvious indicators of blight were missing.

Late 1949 was a heady time for the Philadelphia Housing Association. Two years after the Better Philadelphia Exhibition, PHAssoc president Phillips was appointed to the Philadelphia Housing Authority, and the PHAssoc celebrated its fortieth anniversary. Dorothy Schoell Montgomery gave a speech at the fortieth anniversary dinner indicating what the next ten years promised to bring. When the congratulatory speeches died down, however, Walter Phillips was to learn that getting what he called "politics" out of housing was easier said than done, especially since Phillips and Clark and the PHA were in effect injecting their own version of politics into that very arena in the name of removing it.

By May of 1950, five months into his term on the board of the housing authority, Phillips was already embroiled in a fight with the city council over who was to have ultimate authority over site selection in the city. In what would become a replay of the same story in Chicago, where Reginald DuBois, South Deering's councilman, called for an investigation of the CHA's Elizabeth Wood, Phillips was protesting councilmanic approval of sites as a covert device for defeating integration of the neighborhoods. According to Phillips, Philadelphia's city council wanted "the power to kill every project that the Authority approves,"[34] which is precisely what the city council got in Chicago. The issue in both cities was the same, namely, who would have the final say about where public housing got built. The Philadelphia City Council wanted public housing confined to the black sections of town; Phillips, on the other hand, "favored a selection of sites by neighborhoods in such a way that integration of racial occupancy could be accomplished with the most community acceptance."[35] Phillips then added that "the degree of integration, however, will be determined by the Philadelphia Housing Authority, giving full weight to such important factors as the character of the neighborhood, the maintenance of established values and the orderly process of assimilation."[36] It was going to be more social engineering, in other words, with Phillips at the controls.

Four months later on August 8, the Joint Committee on Site Selection of the Philadelphia Housing Association and the Citizens Council on City Planning came to the conclusion that "Site selection should be a positive process, not a negative one. Sites should not be selected primarily because public housing will not be opposed by people living in the vicinity."[37] After the double negatives were eliminated from their memo, it seemed that both the PHA and the CCCP were saying that the negative feelings of the people living in neighborhoods targeted for public housing should not be a factor in site selection. With this evidently in mind, Ed Bacon, three months later on November 14, wrote to Walter E. Alessandroni, executive director of the Philadelphia Housing Authority, recommending the Schuylkill Falls site "as a good location for low rent housing"[38] in spite of the fact that the residents of East Falls and Manayunk were dead set against it. Bacon's brother-in-law, Oscar Stonorov, was the architect of the Schuylkill Falls project, which was made up of low-rise buildings on Ridge Avenue near the Schuylkill River and twin fifteen-story towers farther up the hill away from the river. The rationale for forcing the Schuylkill Falls project on the unhappy residents of East Falls was the same environmentalist credo articulated by the Pennsylvania Supreme Court in the1930s. The credo was the same one which Mayor Lamberton had rejected when he turned down federal funds in the early '40s. It was the Watsonian/Bauhaus environmentalism favored by Louis Wirth, Gunnar Myrdal, and the social-engineering/psychological warfare establishment, which claimed that bad housing created bad morals. "From these depressed areas," the Philadelphia Housing Authority claimed,

> come high crime and juvenile delinquency rates, low morale, high fire and disease rates, low standards of education and an increasing lack of hope on the part of their inhabitants. The slum is a very real sense has contributed to creating slums

of the mind and heart. The cost to the taxpayer and to the city, the costs to human lives in a democratic society is tremendous. The costs over the next twenty years could be devastating.[39]

The costs *were* devastating, but not as devastating as the effect the buildings themselves had on the social pathologies they were designed to cure. The initial PHA reports on the projects reminded one of reports on progress in meeting the latest five-year plan then being issued by similar government agencies in the Soviet Union. The PHA annual report for 1955 reported on an Easter Parade and Brownie Troop Square Dance being held at the Wilson Park Homes and the Chef's Club and 4H program at the Tasker Homes. Apparently sensitive to the criticism that the projects were breeding grounds for crime and illegitimacy, the brochure informed Philadelphians that "over 90 percent of the families have both husband and wife and regularly employed wage earner" living in their units. The housers didn't leave it at that either. They sent their social workers into the residents homes and came up with a list of 53 families "whose housekeeping was unacceptable to the housing authority." Of those families, evidently 43 finally shaped up, because 10 shipped out after they were deemed "apparently hopeless in attitude and results."[40] A teacher in a nearby elementary school said, "On the first day . . . we can tell which are more of the children from the housing development. They are better dressed, seem as if they had a better night's sleep, pay more attention and learn better."[41]

Since the projects which got built in Philadelphia in the early '50s were often used to house returning Korean War veterans, the accounts were probably true. There was no one social class predominately in the projects when the first residents moved in. Before long the social-engineering aspects of the projects became intolerable, and those who could quickly moved out, leaving behind those who couldn't move and a concentration of pathology that no other neighborhood in the city had thus far created.

The Raymond Rosen Homes were right in the middle of the North Philadelphia ghetto. That meant that the few white families would have no contact with the surrounding community. Schuylkill Falls meant the same thing for the black families. The projects, which were built to integrate the neighborhoods, had, in other words, the exact opposite effect, singling out their residents as alien invaders and driving them back to their buildings where they were confronted by the inhuman nature of Bauhaus building design.

Schuylkill Falls, in this regard, was worse than all of the other PHA elevator buildings in the rest of the city because of the peculiarities of its design. In 1986, thirty-three years after Schuylkill Falls opened its doors, *Philadelphia* magazine did an article on their by-then-vacant twin towers. Schuylkill Falls "was considered both architecturally and socially innovative" when built because of the long common balconies, "streets in the sky," on each floor of the apartment buildings and series of individual elevators that provided access to three or four apartments on each floor and eliminated long internal corridors." As the projects gradually came to be occupied more and more by weakened and vulnerable one-parent families, the lack of privacy that the "streets in the sky" made mandatory soon proved fatal, first to family life and then to life in general. The weakened family was always losing its children to peer pressure and gangs. The design of the building simply accelerated this process by depriving those families of whatever control over the domestic sphere the rowhouse provided. "The concept of high rise housing projects," *Philadelphia* magazine continues, "eventually proved to be flawed and Schuylkill Falls was one of the first in the city to be close down, most because its design innovations exacerbated the crime and vandalism problems: The many elevators and open balconies could not be controlled or secured."[42]

The PHA could have avoided this problem if they had listened to the consultants they had assigned to evaluate the project's design. In July of 1951, Lancelot F. Sims, Jr., an architect called in to evaluate the situation, mentioned the lack of cross-ventilation in the low-rise rowhouses as a source of potential problem, but felt "this deficiency can be ameliorated by planting sufficient trees to shade the western face of all row house units."[43] Not so simple were the problems which Stonorov's design of the twin high-rise towers caused. "I told Mr. Stonorov," Sims wrote, "that I was very worried about privacy for the living rooms facing on the outside balconies. I suggest that he move the stairs on either end of the building in toward the end so that each stair would have two dwelling units on one side of it. This arrangement will greatly decrease traffic passing in front of the living room windows."[44] Stonorov ignored Sims's suggestion, with predictable results. Decent people found the lack of privacy unbearable and fled the building. Soon the indecent people fled as well. By 1976, the two high-rise towers at Schuylkill Falls were 100 percent vacant, although the rowhouses on Ridge Avenue continued to be occupied.

The verdict of failure which got handed down on Bauhaus-design based social engineering was not limited to Schuylkill Falls, which was perceived as the worst case scenario because of its design peculiarities. "The saga of Schuylkill Falls," *Philadelphia* magazine continued, "will probably be repeated with every high rise housing project in the city, as a sad story of an outdated social concept and the 'haunted' buildings left behind."[45] The Raymond Rosen Homes opened in July 1954. By the time the 1,122 units in eight elevator buildings covering thirty-one acres at 22nd and Diamond were fully occupied in November, two-thirds of the residents were either veterans of World War II or Korea. One generation after the first families had moved into Philadelphia's first post-World War II public housing, the other projects without the "streets in the sky" still had people in them, but the name project had already become synonymous with crime and degradation.

Maida Odom described the condition in the Raymond Rosen Homes in November of 1980, twenty-six years after they had opened. By then housing authority social workers had stopped upbraiding the people "whose housekeeping was unacceptable to the housing authority." As a result, the halls now smelled of urine. Eleven years later, Building no. 4 at the Raymond Rosen Homes was on the verge of collapse and was declared a dangerous hazard by the city's Department of Licenses and Inspections, after the building's facade had buckled, showering the sidewalk below with loose bricks.[46] Surveying the state of the projects in his district, State Senator Chaka Fattah concluded that the high-rise buildings were "not conducive to a quality life-style for families."[47]

That was putting it mildly. During 1979, residents of the Raymond Rosen Homes reported one killing, three rapes, six aggravated assaults, thirty-eight burglaries, nine armed robberies, and twenty-two thefts, which was in its way a dramatic improvement over 1978, when the same residents reported three killings, ten rapes, twenty-one aggravated assaults, seventy-three burglaries, twenty-four armed robberies and thirty-two thefts.[48]

The urban planners may have nourished illusions about the effect their designs were going to have on the people who lived in their buildings, but it took twenty-five years of bad experience to dispel those illusions before a consensus would emerge that Bauhaus elevator buildings were part of the problem and not the solution to the social ills that the Better Philadelphia Exhibition claimed they would cure in 1947. But by the time the irrefutable evidence was in, it was too late to save the neighborhoods that had been sacrificed on the altar of social planning. The residents of those neighborhoods could have told the planners what they thought if the planners were willing to listen, but the planners were the experts and the people who lived there were not. When city housing coordinator William L. Rafsky addressed a local meeting on public housing in April 19, 1956, asking, "Do we or do we not want housing units," the audience bellowed "No" in response. But there was no indication that anyone in authority was listening.[49]

Notes

1 Interview With Joseph S. Clark, 3/18/75 Walter M. Phillips oral hisory project, Temple University Urban Archives.

2 Ibid.

3 E. Digby Baltzell, *The Protestant Establishment: Aristocracy and Caste in America* (New York: Random House, 1964), p. 293.

4 Ibid., p. xii.

5 Ibid.

6 Hal Libros, *Hard-Core Liberals: A Sociological Analysis of the Philadelphia Americans for Democratic Action* (Cambridge, Mass.: Schenkman Publishing Company, 1975), p. 44.

7 Steven M. Gillon, *Politics and Vision: The ADA and American Liberalism, 1947–1985* (New York: Oxford University Press, 1987), p. 39.

8 Ibid.

9 Ibid., p. 40.

10 Libros, p. 23.

11 Ibid., p. 27.

12 Ibid., p. 101.

13 Emily W. Sunstein, *Mary Shelley: Romance and Reality* (Boston: Little, Brown & Co., 1989), p. 5.

14 Ibid., p. 12.

15 Libros, p. 26.

16 Gillon, p. 77.

17 Ibid.

18 Radio Speech by William F. Meade, Oct 24, 1949, Walter Phillips papers, Box 1 Communist Charges, Replies 1956–1962, Temple University Urban Archives.

19 Ibid.

20 Statement in Reply to Mr. Meade offered by Walter M. Phillips, October 25, 1949, Phillips papers, Temple University Urban Archives.

21 Ibid.

22 Ibid.

23 Paul Blanshard, *Communism, Democracy, and Catholic Power* (Boston: The Beacon Press, 1951), p. 6.

24 Ibid.

25 Retraction appeared in *The Philadelphia Bulletin*, July 26, 1950, in Phillips papers, Temple University Archives.

26 John F. Bauman, *Public Housing, Race, and Renewal: Urban Planning in Philadelphia, 1920–1974* (Philadelphia: Temple University Press, 1987), p. 103.

27 *Issues* [the newsletter of the Philadelphia Housing Association], 7, nos. 11–12, (November–December 1949): 6. Temple University Urban Archives.

28 Ibid.

29 Ibid.

30 Bauman, p. 105.

31 Ibid.

32 Ibid., p. 99.

33 Ibid., p. 105.

34 W. M. P.'s Record on Racial Policies of Philadelphia Housing Authority, 5/8/50, Phillips papers, Temple University Urban Archives.

35 Ibid.

36 Ibid.

37 Joint Committee on Site Selection of the Philadelphia Housing Association and the Citizens Council on City Planning 8/8/50, Phillips papers, Temple University Urban Archives.

38 Letter from Edmund N. Bacon, Executive Director, City Planning Commission, to Walter E. Alessandroni, Executive Director, Philadelphia Housing Authority, 11/14/50, Phillips papers, Temple University Urban Archives.

39 Report of Philadelphia Housing Authority, 1955.

40 Ibid.

41 Ibid.

42 *Philadelphia* magazine (11/86).

43 Memo from Lancelot F. Sims, Jr. 7/20/51, Phillips Papers, Temple University Urban Archives.

44 Ibid.

45 *Philadelphia* magazine (11/86).

46 Vanessa Williams, "Housing Officials See Obstacles to Replacing the High Rise Project," *Philadelphia Inquirer* (January 14, 1991).

47 Ibid.

48 Maida Odom, "Views from the Project," *Philadelphia Inquirer, Today Magazine* (November 23, 1980).

49 Bauman, p. 163.

The Cicero Conspiracy

Six months after Louis Wirth gave his speach to UNESCO in the Spring of 1951, Camille DeRose, a resident of Cicero, Illinois, sold the twenty-unit apartment building she owned at 6132–42 W. 19th Street on the edge of Berwyn, an adjacent suburb, to a black by the name of Harvey Clark, Jr. Those who knew DeRose speculate that she sold the building to Clark to spite her neighbors. On July 10, 1951, the Clark family moved its furniture into the building but did not attempt to stay there. Sensitized to the racial dimensions of any move-in by five years of continuous racial violence, someone in the neighborhood noticed that Clark was not white and on July 10 a mob gathered outside the building. At the time of the riot, Cicero was an incorporated town of about 67,000, just west of Chicago, which had the dubious distinction of being Al Capone's base of operations during Prohibition. In an article deploring the riots, the liberal Protestant *Christian Century* claimed that the town had maintained its independence "for the purpose of serving as a base from which hoodlums can operate against the surrounding city with a high degree of immunity. . . Cicero has been known as a municipality where bad politics flourished. From that to mob rule is a short step."[1]

Cicero's fifty-man police force was probably more sympathetic to the crowd than the people attempting to move in and so did nothing to disperse them, nor did they push the mob back far enough from the building to prevent it from breaking Clark's apartment windows with stones. Writing in *Commentary*, Charles Abrams complains that the police did nothing when two University of Chicago students and a man on whom the mob found a B'nai B'rith card were beaten. The police told a reporter from the *Chicago Daily News* that it was acceptable to beat up certain people, "because they were communists." When asked how he knew they were communists, the policeman answered, "because they were Jews."[2]

By the time the crowd swelled to over 2,000 people on July 13, the Cicero police had lost the ability to control the situation, and the National Guard was called in to restore order. Up until the Cicero riot, the Chicago CHR had persuaded the Chicago papers not to give coverage to racial incidents. This was still their policy in 1951; however, what had changed in the meantime was the advent of television, whose reports forced the newspapers to abandon the CHR policy. Clark tried to move into the apartment again on June 18 but was unsuccessful. On June 26, 1951, U.S. district Judge John P. Barnes issued a preliminary injunction restraining Cicero officials from interfering with Clark's entry into the apartment. On July 10, 1951, under protection of the injunction, Clark moved into the apartment. A crowd gathered around the building. Once again the Cicero police did nothing to disperse it. At night the crowd grew to between two and three thousand persons and began breaking windows in the building. Sensing that the situation was getting out of hand, the Clarks left before the real violence began. They were never able to return. On July 11, 1951, the rioting continued, and the mob grew to about 6,000 persons, which this time succeeded in gaining entry to Clark's apartment, dragging his furniture and belongings onto the sidewalk and burning them. On September 19, 1951, the Cook County Grand Jury assigned to investigate the riot returned indictments against Camille DeRose, George Leighton, an attorney for NAACP, and two other people, charging them with, among other offenses, conspiracy to sell to blacks to depreciate the value of the property of white persons. Three months later, the forces supporting integration, backed by the ACLU, counterattacked by bringing indictments against Henry Sandusky, President of Cicero, and others for depriving Harvey Clark of his civil rights. On June 4, 1952, Sandusky and all of his co-defendants were convicted in a rebuke to the local government and "the open encouragement that in many instances police gave the rioters in their vandalism."[3]

Like every other "ethnic" neighborhood in and around Chicago where violence occurred in the late '40s and early '50s, Cicero was a mix of nationalities – in this case mostly Czech and Polish – but, therefore, predominantly Catholic – a fact which the press soon emphasized. The community was united against the black invaders, but it was not clear at this point whether they possessed any identity that was more than negative. The negative identity was racial. Joseph Beauharnais of the White Circle League passed out handbills and buttons reading "GO GO Keep Cicero White"[4] during the riot and at the police court hearings, but with limited success because the people of Cicero had already been mobilized. Most of them belonged to Our Lady of the Mount Parish in Cicero, which was the "center of Czech social and cultural traditions in the community."[5] One generation earlier, Czech xenophobia in the neighborhood was focused on a different group of aliens. The parishioners of Our Lady of the Mount then held a less-publicized protest when the first German Catholic family moved into the neighborhood and attempted to attend services at the church. American life was so raw, so alien, and so lacking in any rooted traditions that it could not in and of itself accommodate the various groups that had settled there during the last great wave of European immigration during the period from the 1880s to the 1920s. The only way that socialization – or, for that matter, civilization – was possible was through the establishment of transitional colonies based on the various European languages. Those colonies would change in character with the passage of time as subsequent generations became more familiar with the mores of the dominant Protestant culture, but they could only serve their purpose, even as agents of assimilation, if they remained more or less segregated from other language-based communities of the same sort. At one point that meant excluding German Catholics. At another point, as the various nationality groups began to take on a religious identity according to the theory of the triple melting pot,[6] it meant excluding Protestants. In the early '50s, the same group that once excluded German Catholics in order to maintain its identity, now felt the need to exclude black Protestants.

Those who accused the Czechs and Poles of intolerance had lost sight of a simple sociological fact. A community which excludes no one is not a community. The "Czech housewives" who were now being scrutinized by ACLU and the AFSC agents in Cicero were caught in the middle of a redefinition of community according to which ethnicity was no longer considered to be a criterion of relevance. No one was maintaining that blacks had a right to live in neighborhoods whose houses were beyond their financial means; however, no one who was promoting the cause of integration was willing to discuss the fact that ethnic homogeneity was the only thing that maintained real-estate values either, no one, that is, other than the people in Cicero who brought suit against the building's former owner and were subsequently discredited in the court of public opinion. According to the new housing system being imposed on them surreptitiously by social engineers like Louis Wirth, the residents of Chicago's beleaguered neighborhoods were supposed to accept class, which is to say, income level, as the sole criterion of who got to live where, when everyone knew that the ethnic stability of the old neighborhood system was the only thing that guaranteed the economic stability of the housing stock. Change in ethnos meant change in price. Ethnicity was also a way of keeping the price of housing low for certain groups by eliminating competition from other groups for the same housing stock. If price was a function of supply and demand, the ethnic neighborhood limited demand by excluding from consideration anyone who did not belong to that ethnic group. It also stabilized demand by providing a steady but limited group of buyers for that area. Opening any neighborhood to any group of buyers destroyed that stability. In the case of gentrification, it drove prices up by opening the market to people who had, on the average, more money than those who lived in the neighborhood. In the case of racial migration, it did the opposite, driving the price down, initially at least, by causing panic selling, or, as in the case of Detroit, by turning the entire city into one large ethnic neighborhood, in which one ethnic group, namely the blacks, occupied a city intended for twice as many inhabitants, with concomitant loss of property value.

The ethnic neighborhood was, as Saul Alinsky noted, a transitional arrangement, but at the heart of the dispute lay the question of just how long the transition was going to last and whether it was something that should be left alone to follow its own rules and natural trajectory or whether it was something whose "nature" could be controlled by science – in this instance, social science – as a way of achieving certain political goals. As Hirsch notes, the racial disturbances in Chicago in the post-war period all took place in neighborhoods that were ethnically mixed, if country of origin and language were taken as the basis for ethnicity. This meant that the Poles and the Bohemians in Cicero, like the Irish and the Germans in Englewood, had achieved a *modus vivendi* that would have been impossible a generation earlier. At that point, there were essentially two options when it came to the question of the emerging ethnicity of the groups protesting "integration": They could identify themselves according to race or religion. The people of Cicero were no longer Czech or Polish in the way that previous generations there had been Czech and Polish, and as a result they could identify themselves as either white or Catholic.

The choice, rarely conscious, on the part of those who made it, was complicated by all sorts of factors. To begin with, the very process of assimilation which people like Louis Wirth were orchestrating against them drove the ethnics in places like Cicero to identify themselves as "white," because white was an essentially American designation, and the ethnics thought of themselves as being good Americans when they applied this designation to themselves. Of course, people like Louis Wirth had repudiated race as a category of political significance, and so the ethnics were condemned for adopting the very process of assimilation they thought they were supposed to be following. As in Chicago, so in Cicero: The natives identified themselves as white, while their enemies identified them as Catholic, and this was in large measure because the Catholic intelligentsia, having committed themselves to a program of assimilation, were embarrassed by their behavior and vilified them as racists rather than helped them explicate an idea of a Catholic community that included both love of neighbor and provisions for self-defense, in particular against psychological warfare, joined the dominant culture, as Gremly's article in *America* makes clear. During this period not one Catholic apologist rose above the parish level to articulate the position of the ethnics in any journal of opinion in language more sophisticated than the crude prose of the neighborhood-improvement association newsletters. Instead of trying to articulate the Catholic idea of parish and community and how this was the context for any attempt to deal with racial migration or racial justice, the Catholic intelligentsia seemed bent on assimilating more than explicating and, as a result, they seemed equally determined to distance themselves from the Catholic ethnics in cities like Chicago as an embarrassing anachronism.

William Gremly, member of the Chicago Catholic Interracial Council, arrived in Cicero on the evening of July 12 and was immediately struck by how easily the rioters could be identified as Catholics because they were wearing "sweaters with school names or crests on the back, Knights of Columbus lapel pins and rings, scapulars or other medals seen through an open shirt" and other "physical symbols of the Catholic faith."[7] After going into detail about how "the particular area in which Clark desired to live is heavily Catholic," including a comparison with "the all too similar. . . Peoria Street incident of November, 1949, which took place in a Chicago area estimated to be over 90 percent Catholic," Gremly then launches into a long peroration on how both disturbances bespeak "the failure of Catholic leaders, spiritual and secular, in this and other communities to prevent such attitudes and such outbursts of hatred among Catholic youth."[8] This "shameful glaring failure," according to Gremly, "lies at the doors of the Catholic churches and schools in Cicero and Berwyn and for that matter in the entire Chicago area."[9] Gremly mentions the local point of view, one taken by one of the Catholic priests in one of the local parishes – "that the people of Cicero were only 'defending' their homes" – only to dismiss it as "a degrading mockery of Catholic principles of justice and decency."[10]

Writing one month later in *Commonweal*, the classic organ of American Catholic assimilationist liberalism, the Rev. David M. Cantwell, also a member of the Chicago Catholic Interracial Council, took much the same tack, in slightly less vehement prose. Cantwell saw Cicero as an example, not of something intrinsically evil, but rather of ethnic ideals gone bad. "The town," he writes, "is an enviable picture of order and peace. Czech housewives are second to none in the care of their homes."[11] However, Cicero's ethnics, according to Cantwell, have taken something good, home ownership, and turned it into an idol:

> The home-making virtues of those people have been oversown by cockle, by national exclusiveness, by middle-class materialism, by the drying up of human compassion and sympathy for other families in need. They have acquired homes, but then made them the golden calf to be worshipped and possessed at all costs. They have arrived at middle-class suburban utopia. The story of Dives repeats itself. . . . The god worshipped in Cicero is the unencumbered deed and . . . the town's real churches are its savings and loan associations.[12]

Gremly's article appeared in the Jesuit magazine *America*, Cantwell's in

Commonweal. At the time that pretty much exhausted the possibilities for discussing an issue in the Catholic press on a national level. The fact is significant because neither Gremly nor Cantwell is willing to discuss the fact that as of that moment in history and for the foreseeable future as well, there was no such thing as an integrated neighborhood. The local pastors portrayed the issue as one of self-preservation because no community in Chicago until that time had survived racial succession. Once black families got established in an ethnic neighborhood, the neighborhood was condemned to change, sometimes virtually overnight, and change brought with it the destruction of the ethnic community, which more often than not did not regroup in the suburbs. Racial change brought about as well the loss of the value of the house, which plummeted because of panic selling, often encouraged by mortgage bankers and block-busting real-estate dealers. So, no matter what Gremly and Cantwell wrote in *America* and *Commonweal*, the plain facts of racial life in Chicago indicate that it *was* a matter of life or death for the community whether blacks moved in or not. Those communities which kept them out survived; those which did not, perished. Integration was at best a chimera in the minds of social engineers or at worst an excuse to destroy the communities which they found inconvenient and obsolete.

Gremly makes much of one teenager saying, "I don't want those jigs sitting in the same pew with me," without mentioning the fact that her parents probably felt the same way about German Catholics and that that attitude changed with time. Gremly also fails to mention the fact that the blacks were doubly alien to the community because most of them weren't Catholics. Instead Gremly lets one of the girls in the crowd answer for him. She assured the young man that he had nothing to fear, because "those niggers don't join the Church anyhow."[13] Integration was an issue which could have been addressed without calling for a wholesale condemnation of the Catholic parishes in the area, but that is precisely what Gremly felt called upon to do, claiming, "There is probably little or nothing that can be said in defense of this failure of the Catholic institutions of the community. Somewhere at its roots are the attitudes of Catholic teachers and priests, stamping such attitudes with social approval and condoning the hateful actions that inevitably flow from them in a riot situation."[14] The parish priest who talked about his parishioners defending their homes was indicative of "the failure to apply Catholic dogma and principles directly to this one social problem of our time" and that meant that "until Catholic leaders, clerical and lay, cleanse themselves of their bigoted attitudes or timidity in the face of this challenge to our most cherished principles, nothing can be done."[15]

Well, almost nothing. One month after the Cicero riots began, Cantwell and other members of the Chicago Catholic Interracial Council met with Tom Colgan of the American Friends Service Committee (AFSC) and out of that meeting the "Cicero Project" was born. Charles Abrams concluded his article on the riots in Cicero by assuring *Commentary*'s readers that "There was, of course, no conscious 'plot'"[16] behind the incident which began when DeRose sold her apartment building to Clark. But while there was no plot behind the incident, the incident did in fact create a plot, one which would eventually get funding from the Marshall Field Foundation from August of 1951 until March of 1952. The plot involved, in the words of a confidential memo to AFSC members in Chicago and Philadelphia, a plan "to move a Negro family into a house in Cicero"[17] and was known in AFSC documents as "the Cicero Project."

The organization of the Cicero Project was undertaken by Tom Colgan, a Philadelphian who had been raised as a Catholic in that city's Fairmount section and had converted to Quakerism because of his animus against the war. Colgan's reasons for collaborating with the Catholics were more than personal. After gathering intelligence on the Cicero area, the Quakers quickly came to the conclusion that the only possibility they had to contact and therefore influence public opinion in Cicero was through the Catholic Church. Following initial meetings between Quakers and Catholics, the working committee for the Cicero Project chose David McNamara of the CIC as its director. The purpose of the Cicero Project was the manipulation of Catholics, something the Quakers could only do with the collaboration of other Catholics who were of like mind on the racial issue. "McNamara's job," according to black leader Bayard Rustin, who was present at the organizational meetings of the Cicero Project one month after its inception, "is to establish contact with Catholic parishes."[18] McNamara was then given "orientation with the AFSC and its thinking"[19] and sent off into Cicero to get the lay of the land. Before long, McNamara, in the words of a confidential AFSC memo, "found that no other human relations organization had contacts in the town of Cicero except the Catholic groups."[20] As a result, McNamara, as a Catholic but also as an agent of the Quakers, began to approach the local clergy to help them "to assess the moral implications of the riot."[21] McNamara, unfortunately, got nowhere with the local Catholic clergy, who expressed "general hostility . . . to any effort to break down the rigid pattern within the community."[22]

As a result of local intransigence, the people involved in the Cicero Project resolved to create the West Suburban Catholic Interracial Council as a way of giving the impression that the desire to move black families into Cicero had local support. "Numerically," one AFSC document stated, "Catholics constitute the largest denominational group in the west suburban area. For this reason alone," they conclude, giving some idea of who was manipulating whom, "the existence of the [West Suburban Catholic Interracial] Council is worthwhile."[23] The impression was, however, largely a PR-driven illusion, as AFSC documents showed. In addition to meeting with Catholic clergy, McNamara met with members of the Cicero Civic Commission, which "carries on some respectable 'front' activities," but is, "like any typical property owners group, organized to keep Negroes out of a community." McNamara "made several attempts – all unsuccessful – to dent this organization."[24] He then discovered that the officers of the Commission were influential members of the local "Rotary, Lions, Kiwanis, American Legion, VFW Business Men's association, sectional improvement clubs, women's clubs, taxpayers' organizations" and that these organizations were not open to his arguments either. The same was true of the Cicero newspapers, which "finally proved to be impregnable"[25] as well. The same was true of town officials Berkos and Sandusky. McNamara met with them and urged them to form a "Cicero Commission on Human Relations as an official agency of the town government,"[26] giving some indication that the role of the various local CHRs was to engineer racial change, something that was probably apparent to the officials in Cicero as a result of their experience with the Chicago CHR.

Having failed to change local public opinion by "friendly persuasion," the Quakers and their Catholic co-conspirators decided to change it in the manner that Louis Wirth had suggested to Clyde Hart in the aftermath of the 1943 Detroit riots. Since, as subsequent events would show in detail, the Quakers had been collaborating with Louis Wirth, it is not surprising that they would also come to the conclusion that the solution of the problem in Cicero required not more discussion but "rather direct, sensible readjustments of the kind you suggest – in *housing*." One year after the inception of the Cicero Project, Dave McNamara and Tom Colgan met to discuss "whether to contact Dick Bennet at this time about the possibility of getting foundation money for purchase of a house in Cicero."[27] The confidential memo then stated the following "reasons for this plan":

1) to break the segregated character of Cicero
2) to utilize the symbolic value of the move both locally and internationally
3) to demonstrate the futility of violence
4) to activate dormant social leadership
5) to create a good example of a Negro resident who will care for his property and be a good neighbor.[28]

Having stated the ends they hoped to achieve, McNamara then discussed the means to achieve that end, all of which involved some engineering of the community by manipulating the local Catholics. "Should they," McNamara wondered, referring to black families he hoped to move into Cicero, "be Catholics?"[29] The Catholic Church, according to McNamara, was easier to manipulate in this respect than the more autonomous Protestant communities "because it is required by Canon Law to accept parishioners regardless of race."[30] McNamara then goes on to wonder whether the migrant families should have children, or whether the "risk of violence or name-calling may be too great."[31] He then wonders "should we locate the house near a church"? If they located the house near a Catholic Church, "which would be obliged to accept any parishioner," the local pastor could also be dragged into the conflict "as a deterrent to violence."[32] McNamara then wonders whether they should "identify the plan with the CIC or AFSC, or both or neither? Should [AFSC agents] Cassels and McNamara work it out as free agents? Should we get the white family who would live in the house and let them get the Negro family?"[33]

Cicero, according to the same memo, is crucial because it "lies directly in the path of Negro Population movement westward through Chicago. The fact that Cicero has its own government, has the suburban characteristic of exclusiveness and has a widely known anti-Negro reputation will retard the natural movement."[34] Bayard Rustin said much the same thing. "It is obvious that Cicero must become integrated," he wrote. "Otherwise mob violence and anarchism will be seen to be the dominant power in dealing with community tension."[35] Cicero, in other words, had become a symbol of local resistance, both to the Quakers and the social engineers and to the other ethnics in Chicago who were facing the same threat of extinction. Hirsch notes that:

Just as the rioters at Fernwood were aware of the "redemption" of the Airport Homes, the people of Trumbull Park frequently pointed to the Cicero riot of 1951 as evidence that violence paid. South Deering residents admired the "guts" of Cicero's fighters, talked of importing a few of them "to show us how to get rid of these damn niggers," and openly hoped Trumbull Park would become "another Cicero."[36]

According to McNamara, "The crucial test of the success of this project will be the community reaction to another attempt by Negroes to move into Cicero. Furthermore, not until a significant number of Negro families do live peacefully in Cicero will our educational program have any practical meaning."[37]

Those documents also give some indication of how and why the Quakers got into the field of housing. Shortly after the end of World War II, the AFSC Social-Industrial Committee expressed concern over housing conditions for Chicago's black population. AFSC concern increased when the social unrest caused by the CHA's housing policies began in earnest in 1946, when the first of a series of major disturbances occurred at Airport Park. After the Fernwood riots of 1947, the AFSC began conferring with the CHA, the Chicago Welfare Council, and the Commission on Human Relations about whether they could take a specific course of action in the area of housing in Chicago. Energized by getting the Nobel Prize in 1947, the AFSC began to apply "the technique of top level conference"[38] which had proven so effective in the area of employment, to the area of housing. It was at this point that they ran into a brick wall in Chicago's ethnic neighborhoods. In order to apply the technique of "friendly persuasion" to intransigent ethnics, the Quakers had to be able to talk to them first, but preliminary investigation showed that "no other human relations organization had contacts in the town of Cicero except the Catholic groups."[39] In order to approach the local powers in Cicero, the Quakers had to find Catholics who were willing to talk to them, and that meant that the Quakers had to make use of Catholic groups which shared their attitudes on race and social engineering, and that meant collaboration with the Catholic Interracial Council.

The Catholic Interracial Council was the creation of Father John LaFarge, S.J., a WASP blueblood convert to Catholicism who became sensitized to the racial issue when he was assigned as pastor to a black parish in rural Maryland in the 1900s. LaFarge was ahead of his time on racial matters, but that also meant that he failed to share the civil rights' movement's enthusiasm for social engineering, especially in the sexual arena. In his tendentious biography of LaFarge, David W. Southern faults him for "Catholic narrowness," because he found the "aggressive atheists" in the civil-rights movement "distasteful."[40] Southern quotes approvingly the strictures of Harvard social psychologist Gordon W. Allport, who was offended when LaFarge accused those who shunned theism and embraced contraception as being guilty of "ethical anarchy."[41]

Because he opposed the sexual engineering of the black population, LaFarge found himself criticized by his own organization. This was especially true in Chicago. The Chicago CIC had always considered itself the premier branch of Father LaFarge's organization. In fact they often considered themselves more advanced on racial matters than Father LaFarge himself, who was often criticized because of his retrograde ideas about contraception, secularism, and collaborating with atheists. As a result of the zeal with which certain Catholics embraced the racial apostolate, the race issue always ran the danger of becoming a two-edged sword, and the reformers were always in danger of losing sight of just which institutions they were being called to reform. Were they called to bring the light of Catholic teaching to the racial situation in America? Or was the Catholic Church itself the source of the problem and in need of reform? The reports of people like William Gremly and Father Cantwell seemed to indicate that, if not the

Church itself, then certainly certain Catholic churches in the Chicago area, were in need of reform.

Bolstered by what they read in journals like *America* and *Commonweal*, the reformers in the Catholic Interracial Council became an agent for engineering the lives of their fellow Catholics. R. Sargent Shriver, president of the Catholic Interracial Council, claimed that "the apostle of interracial justice among highly prejudiced fellow citizens resembles . . . the missionary conversing with a foreign people accustomed to ancient tribal customs and taboos."[42] Shriver, who was John F. Kennedy's brother-in-law and managed the Kennedy-controlled Merchandise Mart in Chicago, felt that "The false idols will fall only when people have become sufficiently enlightened to wish to remove them themselves."[43] The Catholic Interracial Council was, especially in Chicago, the primary agent of enlightenment for Catholics on racial issues. As one of the best examples of "this missionary approach," Hirsch cites the Cicero Project as well as, again without irony, "an AFSC proposal for civilizing Trumbull Park."[44] This involved "underwriting" a "'Catholic, Eastern European descent, working-class' family to live in South Deering for two years, during which they would work to change local racial attitudes."[45]

Shriver's involvement in the Chicago CIC and later in the federal government as the head of the Office of Economic Opportunity gives some indication of how far the government was willing to go to change the attitudes of those who impeded progress on the racial and socially related sexual fronts in the culture wars of the '60s. On December 13, 1965, William Bentley Ball, acting in the name of the American Catholic Bishops, threatened to take the OEO to court because it was using the War on Poverty as a front for the dissemination of contraception in black neighborhoods. Shriver, ever the apostle of enlightenment, responded by saying that he would not stop funding OEO birth-control clinics because he was under pressure from Dr. Alan Guttmacher and Planned Parenthood to expand that funding to include sterilization and abortion.[46] Shriver's promotion of birth control would have been an affront to Father LaFarge, but by the time Shriver had found himself working for the OEO, LaFarge had been dead for two years, and his successors seemed determined to carry his racial beliefs to their logical contradiction by involving his name in the cause of a sexual engineering he found morally repugnant.

But all that was in the future. For the moment, the CIC began its trajectory into becoming a fifth column on other issues by collaborating with the Quakers in trying to find foundation money to buy a house in Cicero. As the power of the federal government increased, the Chicago organizations with a city-wide orientation – groups like the Commission on Human Relations, the CHA, and private citizens' groups such as the Catholic Interracial Council – began to gain the upper hand over agencies that were firmly rooted in local soil. Just as the housing authority and the CHR had to fight recalcitrant local "improvement associations," the CIC had to deal with an "uncooperative and hostile clergy" at the parish level. The outcome of that struggle seemed to be a foregone conclusion, but events in Chicago would show that that wasn't so.

Notes

1   Chicago Council against Racial and Religious Discrimination Documents, AFSC papers, AFSC 70 #1 UIC Archives.

2   Charles Abrams, "The Time Bomb that Exploded in Cicero," *Commentary* (November, 1951), AFSC 70 #1.

3   William Gremly, "The Scandal of Cicero," *America* (August 25, 1951): 495. AFSC 70 #1 Chicago Council against Racial and Religious Discrimination Documents, UIC Archives.

4   Information Service Central Department of Research and Survey National Council of the Churches of Christ in the United States of America October 13, 1951, AFSC 70 #1 Chicago Council Against Racial and Religious Discrimination Documents, UIC Archives.

5   William Gremly, "The Scandal of Cicero," p. 495.

6   Cf. Digby Baltzell, *The Protestant Establishment: Aristocracy and Cast in America* (New York: Random House, 1964), p. 390 n.4.

7   Ibid.

8   Ibid.

9   Ibid.

10 Ibid.

11 Rev. David M. Cantwell, "Postscript on the Cicero Riot," *Commonweal* (September 14, 1951): 543.

12 Ibid.

13 William Gremley, "The Scandal of Cicero," p. 495.

14 Ibid.

15 Ibid.

16 Charles Abrams, "The Time Bomb that Exploded in Cicero."

17 Confidential Memorandum 8/7/52, Report to the Marshall Field Foundation, The Cicero Project, AFSC Papers, Box 88 #8, UIC Archives.

18 Rustin memo 9/11/51, AFSC papers, Box 88 #7, UIC Archives.

19 Confidential Memorandum from J. Cassels 8/1/52, AFSC paper, Box 88 #8, UIC Archives.

20 Ibid.

21 Ibid.

22 Ibid.

23 The Cicero Project: Report to the Marshall Field Foundation (Confidential – not for general circulation), AFSC 70 #1 Chicago Council against Racial and Religious Discrimiantion Documents, UIC Archives.

24 Ibid.

25 Ibid.

26 Ibid.

27 Confidential Memorandum 8/6/52, AFSC papers, Box 88 #8, UIC Archives.

28 Confidential Memorandum 8/7/52, AFSC papers, Box 88 #8, UIC Archives.

29 Ibid.

30 Ibid.

31 Ibid.

32 Ibid.

33 Ibid.

34 The Cicero Project, Chicago Council against Racial and Religious Discrimination Documents, AFSC papers, Box 70 #1, UIC Archives.

35 Report to the Marshall Field foundation 11/30/51 Confidential – not for general circulation, AFSC papers, Box 88 #7, UIC Archives.

36 Arnold R. Hirsch, *Making the Second Ghetto: Race and Housing in Chicago 1940–1960* (Cambridge: Cambridge University PRess, 1983), p. 232.

37 The Cicero Project, AFSC 70 #1, UIC Archives.
38 Origins of the Housing Opportunities Program in Chicago 1945–51, AFSC 86 #16, UIC Archives.
39 The Cicero Project, AFSC 88 #8, UIC Archives.
40 David W. Southern, *Jobn LaFarge and the Limits of Catholic Interracialism, 1911–1963* (Baton Rouge: Louisiana State University Press, 1996), p. 299.
41 Ibid.
42 Hirsch, p. 208.
43 Ibid.
44 Ibid.
45 Ibid.
46 E. Michael Jones, *John Cardinal Krol and the Cultural Revolution* (South Bend, Ind.: Fidelity Press, 1995), p. 298.

Klutznick and the Quakers

The Cicero Riots during the summer of 1951 didn't cause the Quakers to become involved in housing in the Chicago area. The American Friends Service Committee, energized by receiving the Nobel Prize in 1947, had already decided to get into housing as the logical extension of their pacifism during World War II and their social activism during the '30s, when they collaborated with the Rockefellers in establishing birth-control clinics for coal miners in West Virginia and sugar refinery workers in Puerto Rico. In 1947, James G. Fleming of the AFSC wrote that "there are present murmurings that in Philadelphia the real estate and finance interests have the same ideas of redeveloping South Philadelphia so that a large area in each direction from city hall will become a totally white, 'quality community.'"[1] After a tour of the country, Fleming saw a similar pattern emerging in "St. Louis, Indianapolis and of course, the Chicago area."[2] The housing shortage created by the Depression as well as the mass dislocation of population created by the employment needs of the war industries had created "crowdedness, lack of housing, jobs and manufactured tensions by Ku Klux types groups" which lent themselves to "the kind of incitement to intergroup strife which Gerald Smith, the KKK and other hate groups are capable of."[3]

In order to prevent this, the Quakers created the Housing Opportunities Program, with programs in Chicago ("Violence as a method of enforcing segregation," they wrote, "has a shocking degree of acceptance in Chicago and the involvement of our regional office there in the field of housing has been frequently faced with crisis situations."[4]), Philadelphia, and Richmond, California, because "the area of housing represents the worst area of American life as far as putting democratic belief into practice goes."[5]

Needless to say, the Quaker idea of democracy differed from that of the people living in the areas which were targeted for their ministrations. The Quaker idea of democracy involved using foundation money to move blacks into previously all-white neighborhoods, without of course telling the people in these neighborhoods that they were involved in doing this. "We have helped make the moving in of Negro families to three of the previously all-white public housing projects, similar to Trumbull Park, a more peaceful event by working with the present residents and community," they wrote describing their Housing Opportunity Program.[6] Whether the residents of those felt that the Quakers made their communities "more peaceful" is doubtful. But the people in the communities the Quakers decided to engineer were not consulted on such matters.

Their idea of democracy was based not on what the people who lived in those neighborhoods wanted, but rather what the Supreme Court, which in 1954 would hand down both *Brown v. Board of Education of Topeka, Kansas* and *Berman v. Parker*, thought best for the local community. Segregation was bad, not because it was undemocratic, but because "rigid housing segregation patterns tend to make inoperative in many areas the Supreme Court decision concerning school integration."[7]

At around the same time the riots were raging in Cicero, James Cassels became head of the AFSC's Chicago Housing Opportunities Program and began, in that capacity, to meet with various influential people in the Chicago area to influence their thinking on housing by applying "friendly persuasion" in the Quaker manner. On April 19, 1952, he met with Julia Abrahamson, also a Quaker, who described efforts to integrate the Hyde Park-Kenwood area around the University of Chicago. Cassels learned from Abrahamson what Quakers had been learning all along, namely, that integration was at that point a hopeful gleam in the eye of utopian city planners and social engineers. Abrahamson informed Cassels that she knew "of no communities in which there has been a considerable Negro immigration that haven't become Negro communities eventually."[8] This meant that the Quaker pursuit of "integration" in ethnic neighborhoods of the north was either quixotic pursuit of the chimera, or it was done with the deliberate destruction of those neighborhoods as its goal. Abrahamson, nonetheless, supported Cassels's efforts and suggested that HOP should have eight or ten members, half of whom should be Friends.

On April 29, 1952, Cassels met with Ferd Kramer, head of the Metropolitan Housing and Planning Council and head of the Planning Committee of Michael Reese Hospital, who told him that those projects would cause "considerable relocation of families."[9] Cassels does not say where these displaced families were supposed to find shelter in an already overcrowded city. Kramer's solution was to integrate the entire metropolitan area, claiming that the "real answer to race problem in housing is to open all areas of Chicago and suburbs to Negroes."[10] This "would mean there would be no places for whites to flee and whites in all neighborhoods would realize they could remain the majority residents."[11] Kramer indicates to Cassels that he got the idea from Louis Wirth, who was considered the brains behind Chicago's housing policies. Wirth's "solution" ignored, however, some simple facts. Since Chicago's blacks had as a group limited financial resources, certain neighborhoods would remain forever out of their reach financially. Racial migration also followed strict patterns based on contiguity. That meant that all of the pressure for "integration" which followed from forced relocation would be brought to bear on the neighborhoods nearest the traditionally black areas, which would, as a result of that pressure, never become integrated. If the black population could be magically dispersed throughout the entire Chicago area, integration might have worked. But the forces of racial migration themselves militated against this solution.

In addition, any powerful organization in the path of racial migration could simply buy its way out of racial inundation by getting the city to engage in urban renewal for its benefit. This is precisely the tack that the University of Chicago would take during the latter years of the 1950s, buying up a strip of land between 60th and 61st Streets and turning it into the racial equivalent of the DMZ in Korea. This practice, of course, also increased the pressure on the ethnic neighborhoods in the path of racial migration by increasing demand. The only recourse in those neighborhoods became, as a result of these policies, physical resistance, which, of course, also accelerated racial succession in the neighborhoods that lacked the will to resist. Everything, in short, which Cassels learned through his conversations indicated that integration had not taken place in spite of ten solid years of effort and that all of the forces which advocated it, in reality prevented it from happening.

On June 9, 1952, Cassels met with Theodore Robinson, chairman of the housing committee of the Chicago branch of the NAACP, who had just invited Cassels to become a member of that committee. If Robinson brought up the topic of integration, Cassels does not mention it in his memo. Instead, Cassels says that the purpose of their program was "helping colored families move into 'new areas,'"[12] a goal that could be characterized more by the term colonization than by integration. Cassels's experience with Robinson was consistent with other Quaker encounters with black organizations, which saw the Quakers as their allies in acquiring new real estate but were always frank about their priorities as well. Integration was always a justification for moving into "new areas," but it was never the goal of black organizations.

Shortly after his meeting with Robinson, Cassels met with Max Woolpy, a real-estate agent who lived in Hyde Park and was experiencing the effects of racial migration first-hand. Woolpy told Cassels that he liked the community and had "lots of friends there,"[13] but the crime which invariably accompanied racial change was causing him and his friends to consider leaving the neighborhoods. Woolpy mentioned in particular a recent kidnapping as standing out in the minds of the neighborhood's residents. Woolpy did not blame the newly arrived blacks for the crime, but he did feel that the neighborhood's racial mixture did now "enable [a] colored criminal element to work the area more easily."[14] Eventually the University of Chicago would take charge of racial migration in the Hyde Park-Kenwood area and manage it in its own self-interest. But the pattern which Woolpy as a Realtor noticed in other neighborhoods remained basically the same – racial migration in the name of integration, followed by increased crime, followed by whites leaving the neighborhood, followed by resegregation along racial lines. If Cassels were looking for empirical evidence that integration was possible, he was not getting it from the people he talked to in Chicago. "Similar things are beginning to happen in Roseland," Woolpy told him, "since Negroes have moved into that area."[15]

Because he was familiar with real-estate practices in the Chicago area, Woolpy was also aware that the policy of integration which was universally acclaimed by government officials and their agents was not universally applied. He mentioned Park Forest, Chicago's first post-World War II suburb, which opened in 1948, one year after Levittown had opened in Long Island – and clearly based on that model – as an instance of where the integration rule did not apply, and thought out loud to Cassels that "it would be important to know the reasons why Klutznick, Manilow, financial interests and FHA decided Park Forest should not allow Negroes"[16] into that subdivision. Woolpy speculated that there were "economic reasons" for this decision, especially since the social reasons for keeping it segregated were non-existent. Since Park Forest had been created out of virgin cornfields 30 miles southwest of Chicago virtually *ab ovo*, there were no residents already in place with ethnic turf to defend. As a result, Park Forest, according to Woolpy, "would have been [the] ideal situation for a mixed community."[17] That it was still 100 percent white after being in existence for over four years must have got Cassels thinking.

Perceptive observers noticed that the purpose of the suburbs was to create a new man as much as it was to create a new habitat. Given the environmentalists' thinking in vogue at the time, the former was clearly seen as a function of the latter. In fact so much so that the purpose of any new living arrangement subsidized by the federal government would necessarily entail the rearrangement – psychically, politically, socially, and eventually morally – of the people who lived there.

Thus, one of the best early analyses of the suburbs is not a book about the suburbs but rather about the type of person the suburbs were supposed to create, a new species which William O. Whyte called "the organization man," to give the title of his 1956 bestseller of the same name. Whyte focused much of his attention on Park Forest, which according to the intentions of its developers, was to "provide a sort of captive market – a constantly replenished, nonsatiable reservoir of 30,000 people"[18] who would circulate from Park Forest to other suburban enclaves across the country. Those suburban enclaves were created to house the former soldiers who were to make up the deracinated national professional class, the people who had no local ties but worked for national corporations and were seen by their employers as interchangeable parts which could be switched from one plant or office to another. This meant that "the first wave of colonists was heavy with academic and professional people,"[19] in other words people who relied more on credentials than family or local ties for their livelihood. Park Forest, Whyte tells us, "had an extraordinary affinity for Ph.D.s," as well as "trainees for the big corporations, research chemists with the AEC, captains and majors with the Fifth Army, airline pilots, FBI men."[20] Park Forest provided, in effect, housing for "a cross section of almost every kind of organization man in America."[21]

What all of the organization men had in common was a positive feeling toward assimilation. The people who flocked to Park Forest did so because it meant upward mobility, and that meant the passage from the ethnic neighborhood to the middle class. Whyte even indicates that the suburbs were created to facilitate this transition: "This expansion of the lower limits of the middle class is happening in towns and cities as well, but it is so pronounced in the new suburbs *that it almost seems as if they were made for that function"* [22] (my emphasis). The suburbs, according to Whyte, "have become the second great melting pot."[23] They have been built to replace "the close knit society of the padrone"[24] – in other words, the ethnic neighborhood – which was destroyed by "the influx of Negroes into the houses they left behind,"[25] something which Whyte describes as "a specter they do not for a moment forget."[26] Whyte, in other words, admits that the largely Catholic population of the suburbs has been driven there by ethnic cleansing, but then goes on to claim that the action was purely voluntary. "Suburbia is the dream,"[27] he continues, conceding that "for older people . . . such [i.e. ethnic] neighborhoods can be ideal."[28] Ignoring the coercion involved in the move which he himself has described, Whyte concludes that "the neighbor who puts the 'For Sale' sign up as he prepares to move to suburbia does so with a feeling that he has made it."[29] Making it for the "organization man," in other words, means loss of ethnic identity and affiliation. The Organization Man is de-ethnicized man. He is deliberately shorn of ethnic ties as a way of making him a more pliant and useful employee of national corporations, but also as a way of making him a docile consumer of goods like the automobile and the television which will complete the process of alienation, isolation, and control. Driven from his ethnic neighborhood by race-driven ethnic cleansing, he flees out of fear to the suburb, which has been designed to complete the process of de-ethnicization by psychological and technological means. "As the newcomers to the middle class enter suburbia," Whyte tells us, "they must discard old values" and adopt instead "sensitivity to those of the organization man."[30]

As of 1952, that meant changing political parties as well, from Democrat to Republican, because "people from big, urban Democratic wards tend to become Republican" when they move to the suburbs.[31] Whyte's observation also reveals the political armature that will inform housing policy for the rest of the 20th century. Republican policies like Eisenhower's Interstate Highway bill and Reagan's dismantling of what was left of the war on poverty, tended to favor the suburbs and see cities as hotbeds of Democratic patronage and welfarism. Democratic policies, on the other hand, went from supporting New Deal-based urban political entrepreneurs to supporting black urban political entrepreneurs under the Carter and Clinton Administrations. Both sets of policies have been equally destructive of urban life. Both sets of policies were also a variant of the heads-I-win-tails-you-lose ploy for the Catholic ethnics that made up the bulk of the northern cities' neighborhoods. Taken together the FHA's policies promoting segregation in the suburbs and the USHA's policies promoting integration in the cities created an engine whose purpose was assimilation of "ethnic," largely Catholic, minorities but whose effect was the promotion of sprawl and the destruction of those cities' housing stock. "The values of Park Forest," Whyte concludes in one of his more prescient moments, "are harbingers of the way it's going to be."[32]

The main form of control which the suburbs created was isolation and de-ethnicization, but this was not the only technique of control the suburbs spawned. In fact, over the next half century, marketing would collaborate with design and psychology to come up with even more sophisticated ways of engineering the consent of suburbanites and controlling their habits with the controllers' interests in mind. After spending some time in Park Forest, Whyte concluded that he could "come up with an unsettlingly accurate diagnosis of who is in the gang [i.e., popular socially] and who isn't"[33] simply by knowing which house a person lived in. People in the center of the courts got lots of "social traffic,"[34] whereas those off by themselves did not.

Whyte seems to be saying that man is much more a function of his physical environment than people had hitherto realized, and that the living arrangements at Park Forest were providing valuable information in this regard. At one point he tells us that "even Park Foresters, in a characteristically modern burst of civic pride, sometimes refer to their community as a 'social laboratory.'"[35] If so, the Park Foresters were the guinea pigs in an experiment in design which seemed to confirm everything environmentalists like Louis Wirth had been saying. Man was a function of his physical environment; his happiness could be engineered, or so it seemed at the time, probably because none of the people who lived in Park Forest had grown up there or lived there long enough to resent the engineering of their lives. Herbert Gans, who would spend time in Levittown, New Jersey, found a very different attitude among that community's teenagers, one which fueled things like the neo-tribal hippie movement of the late '60s. "The comparison of physical layout and neighborliness," Whyte writes, "will show that it is possible deliberately to plan a layout which will produce a close-knit social group."[36] In fact, "the social patterns show rather clearly that a couple's behavior is influenced not only by which court they join but what particular part of the court they are assigned to."[37] "The location of your home in relation to the others not only determines your closest friend, it also virtually determines how popular you will be. The more central one's location, the more social contacts one has."[38] The right design, in other words, can create happy people:

> it would appear that certain kinds of physical layouts can virtually produce the "happy" group. To some the moral would seem simplicity itself. Planners can argue that if they can find what it is that creates cohesiveness it would follow that by deliberately building these features into the new housing they could at once eliminate the loneliness of modern life.[39]

It turns out that the urban planners were thinking along precisely the same lines. This was the case because of the havoc their housing projects were wreaking in places like Chicago:

> Not all planners go along with this line of thought, but some are enthusiastic. At several meetings of planners I talked to about suburbia, I have noticed that the most persistent discussion is on this point. Planners involved with urban redevelopment are particularly interested. *Concerned as they are with the way housing projects break up old family and neighborhood ties*, they see in the tight-knit group of suburbia a development of great promise[40] (my emphasis).

Whyte hastens to assure us that the architects who discovered this "development of great promise" "were not trying to be social engineers – they just wanted a good basic design that would please people and make money for the developers."[41]

Whyte's disclaimer notwithstanding, the principle is clear. Design in the minds of both urban and suburban planners was a form of social engineering that would or would not get implemented depending on whether it could make money for the developers. If it were applied with the happiness of the residents in mind, it was done only in a secondary sense to make the suburbanites "happy" with the arrangements the developers created for them and, most importantly, willing to pay for them as well. If it is true that "the more central one's location, the more social contacts one has," then the subsequent development of things like the typical suburban street hierarchy, with feeder roads leading to arterials and everyone living on cul-de-sacs gives some indication that the architects and the social engineers were more interested in control by isolation than fostering social contact. Writing forty years after Whyte, Philip Langdon, with the insight that goes with hindsight, claims that "America has devoted most of the past fifty years to building neighborhoods that foster just such individualistic impotence."[42] If, as Langdon argues, good streets are like good conversations," which is to say,

> means of making connections – as many kinds of connections as possible. We might insist on creating streets that connect pedestrians to local stores and institutions. We might demand streets that help people make contact with the other members of their community. We might require streets that nurture residents' pride and involvement in their neighborhood. . . . We must make it clear to them that we need streets that help connect people to the larger society, by making access to other neighborhoods plentiful.[43]

We might if we understood what was really going on, but controlling the flow of information has contributed to the fact that that did not happen. If what Langdon says about street plans and social connection is true, then the suburban street hierarchy was designed to prevent all of the social interactions which the urban grid enables. Street hierarchy was designed to isolate each suburban community into what the developers called "pods,"[44] and each pod was based on "market segmentation," a concept, Langdon tells us, "that has been widely accepted in the building industry since the 1970s."[45] Twenty years after Whyte praised the suburbs as the engine which allowed millions of lower-class ethnics entrance into the middle class, Langdon explains how "market segmentation" has turned that entrance into something like an ever-receding horizon toward which the hapless housing consumer is driven by class envy and psychological pressure orchestrated by the developers' marketing strategists. Park Forest as the exemplar of the generic middle-class suburb ceased to exist during the '70s when it was replaced by "pods" based on thinner and thinner financially based segments of the housing market. Just as Levitt was to housing what Ford was to the Model T automobile, so the newer "pod" suburbs did to the housing market what General Motors did to the automobile, dividing what was essentially the same car into different psychological categories based on income. Market segmentation in housing provided the ultimate antithesis of the ethnic neighborhood that was destroyed to create it. People lived in an ethnic neighborhood because of their common background regardless often of what they earned and regardless of the housing stock. Hamtramck is still a case in point, where houses vary widely in quality because ethnicity and not price is the common denominator for the community, a factor which naturally leads to community stability. Market segmentation produces the opposite social configuration:

> The family's income had risen, and they felt they should not stay among townhouse dwellers any more. They should be in a neighborhood with a higher economic status, in a single-family house, now that they could afford it. The townhouse subdivision was severely limited – it had no mix of houses, little mixture of incomes, and little ambiguity about its level of prestige. It was a pigeonhole, and the family escaped it as soon as the pigeonhole no longer fit. In American suburbs, moving out is the common pattern, propelled by the narrowness of any one subdivision.[46]

According to Langdon,

> The great boon of market segmentation is that people ostensibly get to live among people who are much like themselves. When the housing is of a single kind, in a narrow price range, appealing to a small slice of the market, one result is a concentration of people of the same age group, the same economic status, and other similarities. Most people find comfort in living among people who are like themselves.[47]

The pod suburb, however, is built on the exact opposite principle of the ethnic neighborhood. Here there is no ethnic homogeneity and instead of stability, the operant principle is high turnover because people know that the only reason they live there is because they have been unable to buy a more expensive house. Their goal in life is to move up, which is another way of saying that they aspire to be burdened by ever-more-onerous mortgage payments in a world which insures that no one will ever be satisfied by living where he lives because the house which is the outward sign of what a man has achieved in life is also simultaneously the sign of what he has not achieved. In the later pod suburbs, race eventually became a non-issue because of the rigorous enforcement of market segmentation. It was in many ways Louis Wirth's and Stalin's ideal come true, except for the fact that segmentation meant that the term "class," as in middle class, had become meaningless. Middle class, as the antithesis of ethnicity, came to mean a series of market segment based suburban pods which were churned by real-estate salesmen who made a steady stream of commissions based on a system which rewarded constant motion and punished stability.

The pod street system encouraged a new form of segregation, one that was based on income rather than ethnicity. Just as the urban grid made it clear that ethnic neighborhoods were based on free association and promoted interaction among the people who formed that group, suburban street hierarchy makes it clear that suburbs are based on control by forces which hide behind the façade of technological neutrality. A house in Pod A may be a few yards away from a house in Pod B, but the roads in those pods do not connect them directly. In order to get anywhere in the suburbs one must drive, and in order to traverse the short distance between houses in different pods one must first follow the ever-curving feeder roads out of the first pod to the arterial which leads to the entrance to the second pod and back down the same hierarchy of streets again. The result is atomized communities:

> As early as 1972 sociologist Gerald Suttles noticed that suburban areas laid out with features such as segregation from cross-traffic – a key trait of pod-style development – "seem to be among our most atomized communities and the least able to develop a corporate body of representatives and a native identity apart from the one developers have given them."[48]

The purpose of the suburban street labyrinth is to guarantee segregation according to market segment. "At Boca Pointe," Langdon tells us, "no through streets allow one pod to come into contact with another. The developer does not want anything potentially discordant to intervene and break the golden spell."[49] Just as the urban grid enables social contact, the one-entrance suburban pod facilitates control. The more "suburban" the suburb, the more it conforms to this pattern of control. "In the purest enclave developments there is only one entrance for each pod, and this entrance takes on tremendous importance, becoming both a symbol of the residents' social standing and a prelude to the village's interior. Builders lavish attention on entrances."[50]

The suburban paradigm comes full circle with the creation of the gated community, which is the ultimate expression of flight and fear, which drives suburban psychology, but also the ultimate expression of the suburb as a form of control. Driven by fear, the inhabitants of the gated community surround themselves with a medieval wall, yet live in suburban houses within that wall that guarantee isolation. At the same time the houses, what Langdon calls "see-through houses"[51] because of the amount of window space, provide isolation but no privacy:

> To builders these defects are no secret. Builders accept the deficiencies because they make for effective marketing. In fact, builders joke about them. They call a dwelling that has visually impressive but hard-to-live-with features a "twenty-minute house," by which the builders mean a house designed to be so striking that it will be remembered by people who spend twenty minutes in it during a harried house-hunting expedition.[52]

Just as the gated community is a parody of the medieval town based not on ethnos and belief but rather on fear, envy, and ultimately control, the suburban mall is a parody of the medieval marketplace, where the free exchange of goods is short-circuited by psychological manipulation disguised as freedom of choice. Like the suburb, the mall is based on engineering behavior. Judith Coady, who set out to study community life in malls, discovered that there was no community life there to be studied. Instead she found people shuffling around in a trance-like state she described as "the mall walk"[53] as part of the behavior which mall psychologists engineered in the people who come to the mall looking for social interaction. "It's primarily a slower walk to the rhythm of music in the mall," she said. "The eyes are unfocused. Generally speaking, there's a kind of glaze on the eyes and a benign stare on the face. The mall brings it on."[54]

Abolishing the grid in the suburbs also allows the concentration of traffic on arterials which creates for them a captive audience of people in automobiles who are then subjected to the marketing devices of down-scale retail outlets. The arterial becomes, Kulash says, a "sellscape,"[55] which most people find ugly and depressing, which in turn reinforces their impression that the public sphere is something which should be avoided. This consumerist free-for-all also convinces the suburbanite of the need for more regulations in the development where he lives and so tends once again to place more control at the hands of homeowners' associations which specify the minutiae of life. "In almost every case," Langdon writes, "the homeowners' association is pre-organized by the developer before the houses go on the market. It is the developer who draws up the by-laws and the standards of the homeowners' association."[56] And he draws them up in his interest and not that of the owners.

It is impossible to discuss the forces driving this concentration of power without going too far afield. Suffice it to say that the same forces which promoted sexual liberation as a form of control (forces I discussed in *Libido Dominandi*)[57] were at work in engineering housing as a form of control as well. In both cases the dialectic was the same. From the consumer's point of view, what seemed like liberation, in this instance from the artificially created racial crisis in the cities, turned out to be a form of control. As in sexual liberation, the moment self-control based on the internalization of morals (as articulated by the church in the ethnic neighborhood) was abolished in favor of "liberation," external controls took their place. For the most part these controls were built into the technology that created suburban infrastructure and remained invisible to the unsuspecting, but as the "liberation" increased so did the clamor for controls, something which soon manifested itself in the draconian regulations put out by homeowners' associations, in which, as Plato predicted, tyranny inevitably followed the "democracy" of unfettered desire. "If you could trust that people would use good judgment," said one resident of Burke Center, a sort of Yankee residential theme park on Nantucket Island, "you wouldn't need controls. But they don't."[58] In an earlier age, Nantucket's homogeneous design arose from its ethnic and ultimately religious homogeneity. Once the principle of ethnic unity was driven out of the social sphere by federal edict, there was no natural order to community anymore, and so order had to be imposed by purely arbitrary force. As the urban planners lost whatever prestige they might have had in the late '40s, largely because of the disastrous consequences their plans had, the vacuum for planning was filled by private industry, especially in the suburbs, which used the weapons the planners had forged as tools for engineering more and more money and control out of the people who lived in its developments. The suburbs' most perceptive critics realize that America was a freer more creative place when most of its people lived in traditional communities, but many of even these people are handicapped by framing their arguments in terms of faulty design, as if a technologically advanced nation of 280 million people and incalculable wealth were unable to come up with anything more appealing in terms of design than the average strip mall.

The issue is design, of course, but not in the way that, say, the new urbanists understand it. "The cultivation of needs," writes E. F. Schumacher, "is the antithesis of wisdom. It is also the antithesis of freedom and peace. Every increase of needs tends to increase one's dependence on outside forces over which one cannot have control, and therefore increases existential fear."[59] The Marquis de Sade said the same thing from a radically different perspective in his revolutionary rant *The Philosophy of the Bedroom*:

> for the state of the moral man is one of tranquillity and peace, the state of an immoral man is one of perpetual unrest that pushes him to, and identifies him with, the necessary insurrection in which the republican must always keep the government of which he is a member.[60]

The system which is based on the systematic manipulation of appetite, in other words, naturally creates fear, and fear is an emotion which leads naturally to systems of control. So, the purpose of the system – its design, so to speak – has always been control. The issue is not so much the design of the buildings and the roads but rather the designs of the people who created this system, people like Robert Moses and Philip Klutznick.

On October 6, 1952, Cassels met with the Rev. Hugo Lienberger, who felt that the reason Park Forest was all white lay in the fact that "the homeowners in Park Forest really have the balance of power, and they will be most opposed to a Negro family moving into the community" because "the majority of them moved there to escape from the Negroes in Chicago."[61] In typical fashion, Cassels ignores a valuable piece of information in his haste to bring about certain social goals. Park Forest was designed as an all-white community, precisely as a place of refuge from the racial succession that was driving whites out of their ethnic neighborhoods in Chicago. By late 1952, it is clear that Cassels has resolved to take his technique of "friendly persuasion" to the top by arranging a meeting with Philip Klutznick, the man in charge of Park Forest. Cassels was prepared to answer the economic and social objections of those who wanted to defend the segregated status of Park Forest, but, in typically Quaker fashion, he added, "our main argument was a moral one."[62]

Like Louis Wirth, Philip Klutznick was a member of B'nai B'rith. Like Wirth he was also well connected to the housing and planning establishment in Chicago. Like Louis Wirth, he had also been formerly employed by the federal government, not as an agent of the OWI, but as a federal public-housing commissioner. It was because of his experience and expertise in this area that he had been hired by a group of influential backers which incorporated itself as American Community Builders, and it was as their agent that he defined the character of this new suburban community which would in many ways be more of a template for similar communities than Levittown.

The target population for Park Forest was young people with (1) children, (2) expectations of transfer, (3) taste for good living, (4) not too much money. It was the group which William O. Whyte would later characterize as "organization men," based largely on research he did at Park Forest itself. The FHA encouraged this cohort, many of whom were veterans and, as a result, used to the regimentation of living in barracks, with low-interest mortgages with twenty-five- and often thirty-year terms which insured low monthly payments. The FHA also encouraged banks to lend millions of dollars to subsidize the low-risk suburban homes while at the same time it was refusing to lend money on older city properties. One FHA manual cautioned: "Crowded neighborhoods lessen desirability" and "older properties in a neighborhood have a tendency to accelerate the transition to lower class occupancy."[63] When things like this get written in FHA manuals, they become self-fulfilling prophecies. Or, stated another way, they become some indication of the government's intention in creating enclaves like Park Forest. Part of that intention decreed that Park Forest should be all-white, a decree which should have caused considerable embarrassment since the federal government had committed itself, by this time, to a policy of encouraging complete integration. The exception to the rule of integration in places like Park Forest bespoke not so much a double standard as commitment to the system of social engineering through housing that got erected in the aftermath of World War II, the greatest triumph of social engineering to date. By promoting integration in the doctrinaire fashion in which they did, the Quakers showed that, in spite of using the decisions of the Supreme Court as the moral equivalent of true north, they really didn't understand how the system, which was based on driving ethnics into "strategic hamlets" where they could be Americanized, worked.

On January 29, 1953, James Cassels finally got his meeting with Philip Klutznick. The meeting did not go well. Cassels had reason to feel encouraged going into the meeting because the day before he had met with Klutznick's lieutenants, Frank Horn and Henry Dietsch, President of Park Forest. During that meeting Dietsch assured Cassels that "integration would best take place right now" because "that would spike anyone's chances of a whispering campaign on a 'keep Park Forest white' slogan."[64] Dietsch also assured Cassels that "the longer integration is postponed the stronger and better organized the homesteaders would become, and they are main source of organized opposition at present."[65] With that type of assurance from those in charge of the community, Cassels must have felt that the integration of Park Forest would be a comparatively easy task compared to the sort of thing the Quakers and their Catholic allies on the Catholic Interracial Council faced in places like Cicero. If so he was mistaken.

With Klutznick present at the January 29 meeting, Horne now claimed that he had to get the assurance of the village board, the church, and the school board before he would collaborate with Cassels on integrating Park Forest. Cassels was taken by surprise by what must have seemed an about-face from the position taken just twenty-four hours before. "I suggested," Cassels wrote later, "we all knew the village board would take no action on this as a board, so he was setting up impossible conditions."[66]

At this point Klutznick brought up the fact that "over 30 percent of present residents of Park Forest are Catholic."[67] Klutznick's statement has the air of a *non sequitur* about it. Either that or it is an indication that he is trying to tell Cassels something in a round about way which he cannot state directly. In this it was similar to his inability to explain to Cassels why Park Forest had to remain segregated. Cassels knew that the Quakers and the Jews were allies in the housing struggles in post-war Chicago. On August 24, at a meeting of the Quaker-inspired Cicero Project, the minutes mention the fact that A. Abbott Rosen of the ADL was negotiating with the Polish American Congress and the Polish National Alliance, the latter group being the one which held the mortgage for Camille DeRose's apartment building. The minutes go on to stress that

> The effectiveness of the joint committee or any other Chicago agency is severely limited by its identification as an outsider in the community of Cicero. Native leadership must be developed. This process has been started with the West Suburban Catholic Interracial Council, which is, however, limited by its religious character (although the limitation is not so serious due to the large Catholic population of Cicero.)[68]

The Quakers were collaborating with Jews on engineering Catholics with the help of the CIC. On September 5, Ralph Rose wrote to Richard Bennett of the AFSC in Philadelphia, proposing "the very real possibility of a helpful sharing of experience in relation to the Cicero problem with the American Jewish Committee," a collaboration which involved "the preparation of a pamphlet illustrating good Negro housing, which will offset the usual pictorial emphasis on slums."[69]

Cassels was well aware of what was going on in the Cicero Project. He was also aware that as a member and soon to be head of a liberal Jewish organization, Klutznick shared his views on integration. Klutznick was clearly aware of Quaker efforts in this area, because at one point, after the meeting had deteriorated, he told Cassels that he had only met with him as a favor to Clarence Pickett. Cassels apparently precipitated the hasty close of the meeting when he misread Klutznick's statement about Park Forest's Catholic population. Instead of taking it as Klutznick intended it, Cassels took it as a sign that he should use his connections with the Chicago Interracial Council to "round up" Catholic support for integration. That was apparently not what Klutznick wanted to hear, and after hearing it "Mr. K" announced that "he didn't want to see me again just to talk about this subject. His board doesn't think he should have spent as much time on the subject as he did, and he only did it because of his respect for the Friends Service Committee and Clarence Pickett. And it has been a tough problem for him all along, and he feels guilty in the situation."[70] Klutznick then announced that he would be resigning from American Community Builders in a few months to accept the international presidency of B'nai B'rith. That position would entail "traveling all over the world" and he "didn't want to leave the corporation with this problem on its hands."[71]

Undeterred by his rebuff at the hands of Philip Klutznick, Cassels contacted FHA Commissioner Walter Greene a few days later, asking him "If American Community Builders and Park Forest Homes were to adopt an open-occupancy policy in Park Forest, would the Federal Housing Administration's willingness or ability to insure mortgages on proposed construction in Park Forest be influenced in any way?"[72] Greene, of course, responded on February 6 by claiming, "The FHA is willing to insure eligible mortgages on open occupancy projects in any area."[73] What else was he supposed to say? Was he supposed to put the de-facto approval of segregation at Park Forest in writing, and thereby lose his job? When word got back to Klutznick that Cassels had written to the FHA about mortgage policy at Park Forest, Klutznick was furious. "I do not have to tell you," he wrote to Cassels on February 9, "that the subject matter with which we are dealing is delicate at best."[74] It was delicate because neither Klutznick nor Greene could afford to admit the truth to a naive do-gooder like Cassels. Klutznick had tried to explain the situation obliquely – that Park Forest had to be white to attract Catholic ethnics – by adverting to the percentage of Catholics living there, but Cassels, who was too obtuse to take the hint, took Klutznick's statement as calling for more social engineering, something Cassels thought he could pull off by making use of his connections – through the Cicero Project – with the Catholic Interracial Council. The last thing Klutznick needed was having the Quakers play him off against the FHA as being in favor of segregation. Hence, Klutznick was "somewhat surprised, therefore, to find you writing direct to the FHA on this matter. The least that you could have done was to have contacted me before you did so. Frankly, I would have discouraged you from writing such letter as it pertains to Park Forest."[75] This was not surprising because as administrator of Park Forest, Klutznick had "a responsibility for some extremely valuable properties and what is equivalent to a trust relationship with some consequential interests."[76]

Klutznick never got around to explaining just who those "consequential interests" were, nor is it likely that he would have explained this sort of thing to a naif like Cassels, but his decision to cut him off from further contact upset Frank Horne, Klutznick's administrative assistant, who informed Klutznick that "the content of the remainder of my conversation with Jim was directed at tactics and strategy regarding the marshaling of significant public opinion in Park Forest, especially elements of the Catholic Church."[77] Cassels wrote to Horne that he was planning to contact the Catholic pastor at Park Forest "through Father Dan Cantwell [of the Catholic Interracial Council] here in Chicago."[78]

This is precisely what Klutznick did not want to happen. He did not want to integrate Park Forest, not because of any animosity toward blacks, or because he was less liberal than Cassels on racial matters, but because by integrating Park Forest he would destroy its very reason for existing as a catch basin and assimilation camp for Catholic ethnics fleeing the racial migration out of Chicago, which Klutznick was creating through urban-renewal projects like Park Meadows, the high-rise apartment building he helped build for Metropolitan Life. With blacks in Park Forest, the Catholic ethnics would have no reason to move there, and with no reason to move they would stay in their neighborhoods and fight integration, which would impede the ability of the Loop interests, Michael Reese Hospital, and institutions like the University of Chicago to deflect migration away from areas that affected their self-interest and further survival. If Jim Cassels was too stupid to figure this out on his own, Philip Klutznick wasn't going to jeopardize his "trust relationship with some consequential interests" by spelling it out to him. Nor was he going to allow Cassels to play some FHA official's letter against him and thereby jeopardize Park Forest and the model it was to become for the suburban paradigm. Klutznick had the job he had because he understood the system that was being created in Chicago. He was not going to jeopardize either the job or the system because Cassels, the Quaker do-gooder, didn't understand it, or understood only part of it.

Again undeterred by Klutznick's rebuff, Cassels continued to meet with agents of influence and continued to exert on them his version of "friendly persuasion," with mixed results. On February 12 Cassels met with Rev. Gerson S. Engelman, pastor of Park Forest's United Protestant Church. If Cassels thought he was going to get a sympathetic hearing, he was wrong. As soon as he mentioned the Chicago Human Relations Commission, Engelman "spouted off" about "how immoral they have been acting" because they were "trying to bring Negroes into Park Forest and then once they get them in they will try to prosecute anyone who objects."[79] If Cassels missed the point of what Park Forest was all about in his conversation with Philip Klutznick, Engelman restated the point when he mentioned that integration wouldn't work because "too many home owners have moved to Park Forest to escape the Negro invasion in Chicago."[80] Cassels's meeting one day later with Father Coogan, Park Forest's Catholic priest, didn't fare much better. Coogan assured Cassels that "if Negro Catholic families moved into Park Forest they would be welcome in his school and church,"[81] but he also informed Cassels that he would not encourage a move like that by attending a meeting which Cassels was hoping to hold to promote it.

Eventually word of the meeting which Cassels was proposing got back to Klutznick, who called Cassels on February 17. Klutznick informed Cassels that he would not attend such a meeting and that he would also not discuss the topic further with Cassels. Any communication between the two from that point on would have to go through Don Morris, the man in charge of public relations. Klutznick then banged down the phone without giving Cassels a chance to reply. Cassels for his part was nonplused but again undeterred, concluding that "Mr. K was [just] pretending to be angry" because "he had decided negotiations would be broken off and this was the best time to do it."[82]

One month later, Cassels was still trying to find people sympathetic to the cause of integration at Park Forest. On March 11, he met with Phyllis Davidow, then in the process of going through a divorce, to persuade her to sell her house to a black family. Mrs. Davidow was, however, put off by the suggestion, explaining to Cassels that she "wouldn't do such a thing to her neighbors" because "if she picked up the phone and told the people on either side of her house that it would be sold to a Negro family there would be a panic in Park Forest within a couple of hours."[83] Mrs. Davidow then went on to say that "even though she didn't go to temple that it certainly would be bad for a Jewish family to be the first to sell to Negroes in Park Forest. Much better for it to be a Catholic family."[84] Cassels then played his trump card by claiming that it was "the moral position" to sell her house to any qualified buyer, but Davidow in turn trumped his ace by claiming that "she had different values than those [Cassels] represented."[85] With "friendly persuasion" getting such meager results from Protestants, Catholics, and Jews, it is not surprising that the Quakers later turned to the sort of direct action which Louis Wirth had advocated from the beginning.

In his twenty-one-month evaluation of the Housing Opportunity Program, Cassels tries to put the best face on what must have been a disappointing two years of work. From May of 1952, when Cassels began his work until January 25, 1954, when he wrote his report:

> A major effort was made to encourage the president of the corporation that is building Park Forest to rent and sell to Negro families. Park Forest, a planned community some thirty miles from the center of Chicago is the symbol of the builder-sponsored FHA-insured housing development sprouting up all over the Chicago area. The fact that the president of the corporation had had several good contacts with the Service Committee in the past, and is a high official of a liberal service organization [B'nai B'rith], the community is brand new, has a liberal village government, well educated population, is quite isolated and hence in no danger of becoming a predominantly Negro community – all this favored integration.[86]

But in spite of such favorable prospects, "the corporation would not rent to the Negro family."[87] Cassels then goes on to speculate why his efforts have met with such little success, his best opinion being that "the corporation has promised the mortgage lenders and the homeowners association that they would not be the first to rent or sell to Negroes in Park Forest."[88] Having failed to persuade the corporation to rent to blacks, Cassels then tried to persuade individuals to sell their houses "to a Negro family and Negro families financially able and desirous of living there," but he failed here as well. The best he could do was show a black family a house in all-white Merrionette Manor, a deal which also fell through when the homeowners' association persuaded that family to buy a house elsewhere, after, of course, a mob showed up in front of the house in question indicating "no public support for the Negro family."[89] After two years of effort, the only success which Cassels can report is the fact that he "helped a Negro rent space in a loop office building."[90]

Cassels could have written the almost two years of futile effect off as a learning experience, but there is no indication that he learned anything from the experience, certainly not the lesson that just about everyone, including the blacks, were trying to teach him. The head of the board of realtors refused to meet with Cassels, claiming that he would not "have a criminal in his office,"[91] causing Cassels to explain that he had gone to prison during World War II for refusing to go into the army, but had subsequently received a presidential pardon.

His reception at the hands of black realtors was even more instructive. After meeting with them a number of times, Cassels was forced to come to the conclusion that black realtors were no more interested in integration than Philip Klutznick was. They wanted, instead, "the ability to buy and sell anywhere."[92] The black realtors, in fact, were in favor of "the gradual extension of the Negro segregated area" because that was "the most profitable area of operation" for them.[93] "We have received absolutely no help from Negro realtors to whom we have gone asking for aid in finding families for Park Forest, Glencoe, Winnetka or Merrionette Manor,"[94] Cassels concluded sadly.

Notes

1 Memo on Study of West Coast needs by G. James Fleming, archives of the American Friends Service Committee, AFSC.race.47.
2 Ibid.
3 Ibid.
4 Housing Opportunities Program, AFSC Report to Executive Committee 12/30/54, AFSC papers, UIC Archives.
5 Ibid.
6 Ibid.
7 Ibid.
8 Confidential Memorandum J. Cassels, visit with Julia Abrahamson 4/19/52, AFSC papers, Box 88, #9, UIC Archives.
9 Confidential Memorandum, J. Cassels, visit with Ferd Kramer, head of Metropolitan Housing and Planning Council, head of Planning Committee of Michael Reese Hospital, 4/29/52, AFSC papers, Box 88, #9, UIC Archives.
10 Ibid.
11 Ibid.
12 Confidential Memorandum, J. Cassels, conversation with Theodore Robinson, 6/9/52, AFSC papers, Box 88, #9, UIC Archives.
13 Confidential Memorandum, J. Cassels, visit with Max Woolpy, 6/9/52, AFSC papers, Box 88, #9, UIC Archives.
14 Ibid.
15 Ibid.
16 Ibid.
17 Ibid.
18 William H. Whyte, Jr., *The Organization Man* (New York: Simon & Schuster, 1956), p. 282.
19 Ibid., p. 283.
20 Ibid.
21 Ibid.
22 Ibid., p. 299.
23 Ibid., p. 300.
24 Ibid., p. 306.
25 Ibid.
26 Ibid.
27 Ibid.
28 Ibid.
29 Ibid.
30 Ibid., p. 300.
31 Ibid.
32 Ibid., p. 281.

33 Ibid., p. 331.
34 Ibid., p. 330.
35 Ibid., p. 331.
36 Ibid., p. 335.
37 Ibid., p. 336.
38 Ibid., p. 346.
39 Ibid., p. 348.
40 Ibid., p. 349.
41 Ibid., p. 331.
42 Philip Langdon, *A Better Place to Live: Reshaping the American Suburb* (Amherst: University of Massachusetts Press, 1994), p. 19.
43 Ibid., p. 61.
44 Ibid., p. 65.
45 Ibid., p. 63.
46 Ibid., p. 76.
47 Ibid., p. 73.
48 Ibid., p. 76.
49 Ibid., p. 67.
50 Ibid., p. 68.
51 Ibid., p. 69.
52 Ibid., p. 71.
53 Ibid., p. 21.
54 Ibid.
55 Ibid., p. 36.
56 Ibid., p. 90.
57 E. Michael Jones, *Libido Dominandi: Sexual Liberation and Political Control* (South Bend, Ind.: St. Augustine's Press, 2000).
58 Langdon, p. 96.
59 Ibid., p. 153.
60 Marquis de Sade, *Justine, Philosophy of the Bedroom, and Other Writings* (New York: Grove Press, 1965), p. 315.
61 Confidential Memorandum, visit J. Cassels with Rev. Hugo Lienberger, 10/6/52, AFSC papers, Box 88 #9, UIC Archives.
62 Ibid.
63 Jackson, p. 207.
64 Confidential Memorandum from J. Cassels, subject Park Forest Lunch with Frank Horn and Henry Dietsch, President of Park Forest, 1/28/53, AFSC papers, Box 86, #14, UIC archives.
65 Ibid.
66 Confidential Memorandum, J. Cassels meeting with Horne and Klutznick, 1/29/53, AFSC papers, Box 86, #14, UIC Archives.
67 Ibid.
68 Report to the Marshall Field foundation, 11/30/51 (confidential – not for general circulation), AFSC papers, Box 88, #7, UIC Archives.
69 Ibid.
70 Confidential Memorandum, J. Cassels meeting with Horne and Klutznick, 1/29/53.
71 Ibid.

72 James Cassels to Commissioner Walter Greene FHA, 2/4/53, AFSC papers, Box 86, #14, UIC Archives.

73 Walter L. Greene to James Cassels, 2/6/53, AFSC papers, Box 86, #14, UIC Archives.

74 Klutznick to Cassels 2/9/53, AFSC papers, Box 86, #14, UIC Archives.

75 Ibid.

76 Ibid.

77 Frank S. Horne, Assistant to the Administrator to Philip M. Klutznick, 2/6/53, AFSC papers, Box 86, #14, UIC Archives.

78 Cassels to Horne 2/11/53, AFSC papers, Box 86, #14, UIC Archives.

79 Confidential Memorandum, J. Cassells, visit with Rev. Gerson S. Engelman, Pastor United Protestant Church, 2/12/53, AFSC papers, Box 86, #14, UIC Archives.

80 Ibid.

81 Confidential Memorandum J. Cassels, Park Forest Conversation with Community Leaders 2/13/ 15, and 16, '53, AFSC papers, Box 86, #14, UIC Archives.

82 Confidential Memorandum, J. Cassels, phone conversation with Phil Klutznick 2/17/53, AFSC papers, Box 86, #14, UIC Archives.

83 Confidential Memorandum, meeting with Phyllis Davidow 3/11/53, AFSC papers, Box 86, #14, UIC Archives.

84 Ibid.

85 Ibid.

86 Summary of Chicago Housing Opportunities Program after 21 Months, 1/25/54, AFSC papers, Box 86 #16, UIC Archives.

87 Ibid.

88 Ibid.

89 Ibid.

90 Ibid.

91 Ibid.

92 Ibid.

93 Ibid.

94 Ibid.

The Death of Louis Wirth

On May 10, 1952, eight months into the Cicero Project, and two years before *Brown v. Board of Education of Topeka, Kansas* got handed down, Louis Wirth died suddenly of a coronary thrombosis after making a speech to a conference on community relations in Buffalo, New York. Throughout his career, Wirth's animus against "ethnics" remained constant. What changed were the labels he applied to them. In the early '40s he considered this group of people crypto-fascist traitors and fifth columnists in the war against fascism. In the early '50s he considered the same group, which in the meantime had fought against Hitler and fascism, as having divided loyalties because of their religion. As a man intimately involved in the crucial nexus of foundations, psychological warfare, and housing policy, Wirth turned the Chicago housing program into a national paradigm. With Stalin as his model, he made urban renewal a euphemism for ethnic cleansing. His policies then went on to be codified as official government policy in both the *Berman* and *Brown* Supreme Court decisions, two years after he died in 1954. In that same year, both Elizabeth Wood and Walter Phillips, of the Chicago and Philadelphia Housing Authorities respectively, were forced out of office by the ethnics whose neighborhoods were targeted for destruction. Unfortunately, this was not the end of the story. If it were, cities like Philadelphia would look different today. The response of the social engineers was, unfortunately, more social engineering, this time under the guise of the civil rights movement as Martin Luther King returned to Chicago in 1966 to complete the unfinished legacy of Louis Wirth. The ethnic neighborhood had been granted a reprieve in 1954, but the actions of the Supreme Court indicated that it was only temporary.

At the time of his death Wirth was involved in the last stages of a Rockefeller Foundation-financed study of the influence of black in-migration and the changing racial composition of local communities upon real-estate values. The study was part of the program in race relations at the University of Chicago, a program which had also been brought into being by Rockefeller money, this time in collaboration with the Carnegie Foundation. Wirth's study was considered as having "unusually strategic value at the present time because not only in Chicago but in many other cities throughout the country which have experienced large scale Negro in-migration the issue of property values has repeatedly arisen."[1]

In the same month that Louis Wirth died, James Cassels took over the American Friends Service Committee's Housing Opportunity Program in Chicago. Cassels had already discussed Wirth's study of real-estate prices in changing neighborhoods with E. F. Schietinger, the University of Chicago professor who was doing the bulk of the work on Wirth's project and who would finish it after Wirth's death. Schietinger, according to a memo Cassels wrote for the AFSC was "comparing real estate values in stable white community of Chicago's north side with those in Kenwood, Woodlawn and Park Manor into which Negroes have recently moved."[2] He had at that point reached no conclusions and would reach none, at least he told Cassels, until the end of the summer. But he did know that there was no such thing as integration. According to Cassels, Schietinger "said he didn't know of any private interracial housing projects or any communities into which Negroes moved in considerable numbers that weren't eventually predominantly Negro communities."[3] Schietinger's statement about the non-existence of integration had a definite bearing on Quaker policies at the time. Quaker documents abound with similar statements. In the late '50s, another Quaker attended a meeting of the NAACP during which the blacks assured her that they were not interested in integration either. They were only interested in collaborating with the Quakers because they were interested in taking over new neighborhoods. Leon Sullivan of Philadelphia would assure the Quakers of the same thing during the mid-'60s. At some point then, one has to draw certain conclusions. Either the Quakers couldn't read their own memos, or they chose not to believe what they read there, or they pursued the policy of integration knowing that it would lead to the destruction of the neighborhoods they claimed to be integrating.

Wirth's death dealt a blow to the racial-integration community because it was clear that whatever results his study might come up with, they would lose their prestige by not being associated with his name. On April 29, 1952, Waitstill Sharp of the Chicago Council Against Racial and Religious Discrimination wrote to the American Friends Service Committee, thanking them for a grant of $2,500, which was to be used to publish Wirth's soon-to-be-completed study. Sharp was especially grateful to the AFSC because the $2,500 would now allow his committee to send Wirth's study to "every official city and state commission on human relations and all private agency civic unity councils."[4] On May 9, Richard K. Bennett of the AFSC in Philadelphia responded to Sharp's letter by enclosing a check for $2,500 and at the same time expressing condolences over Wirth's death a few days before, something he considered "a considerable blow to the total work of community relations in which we are all interested."[5] This was, of course, the same Dick Bennett mentioned in correspondence surrounding the Cicero Project as being the man who might be able to get money from an as-yet-unnamed foundation to buy a house for a black family in Cicero. What Bennett did not mention to Sharp was the fact that the money he was sending him did not belong to the American Friends Service Committee. When it came to money, the AFSC was strictly a go-between, and in the instance of Louis Wirth's book, the money came from the Ford Foundation, something which Bennett made clear in a confidential letter to fellow Quaker John Willard. In his letter of April 22, 1952, Bennett assured Willard that he had received verbal assurance by telephone that the Ford Foundation was willing to put up the money for the Wirth project. He then cautioned Willard not to mention the actual source of the money because the AFSC enjoyed an exclusive relationship with the Ford Foundation as their agent of social change in racial and housing matters. "We approach this whole matter," Bennett informed Willard,

> with a great deal of caution because we are in a very awkward and possibly a vulnerable position. As you probably know, no other groups in the United States operating in the field of community relations have received grants from the Ford Foundation other than the AFSC. We do not want to be in a position of being thought of as the only approach to the Ford Foundation for this field of work.

Because there were six projects on which we had information that desperately needed funds and because we knew that the Ford Foundation would not be making grants to organizations in this field until such time as a sub-foundation is set up for this purpose by them, we went out on a limb and asked for six small grants to be transmitted through us to several organizations. Three of these grants were made and three rejected. It is extremely important that no publicity be given to this matter. As this is in a sense a grant to the Chicago Council, I hope that you can take steps to tell them that money will soon be available in the amount of $2500 without necessarily telling them the source. If you approve, we would plan to send a check when we receive the funds direct to them with a rather carefully worded letter indicating to them the source of the funds, the reason why the Ford people did it this way, and the absolute necessity for not publicizing this matter. I do not like to sound so cloak and dagger about this, but I am afraid that if word gets around to a number of organizations that the AFSC has the "open sesame" to the Ford Foundation we will be swamped by requests from some people and burdened with the antagonism of others.[6]

At the time Bennett received the grant money to pass on to Sharp, Henry Heald, president of the Illinois Institute of Technology, was head of the Ford Foundation. As president of IIT, Heald was intimately involved with urban renewal in Chicago, collaborating with Reg Isaacs and Mies van der Rohe, who gave the South Side campus just north of the projects its distinctively modern feel. It was also around this time that John McCloy was transferring many of the government's intelligence operations to private agencies, and the Ford Foundation, the richest of all the big foundations in the United States, was McCloy's favorite source for funding operations that the government would not or could not cover. McCloy would eventually become dissatisfied with what he perceived as Heald's timidity and lack of imagination, replacing him with the more adventurous establishment figure McGeorge Bundy in 1965. In the time between when Heald sent Bennett the money for the publication of the Wirth study and when Mac Bundy took over in 1965, the Ford Foundation would become the major player in shaping domestic race and housing policy under the direction of Paul Ylvisaker, who created what he called the Gray Areas [gray being neither black nor white] program after leaving his job as Joe Clark's assistant in Philadelphia.

By the time Bundy arrived at Ford, all of the Gray Areas programs had migrated into the federal government under Lyndon Johnson's War on Poverty. Bennett's letter is full of such caution because he wanted to keep his source of funding a secret but also because it exposed the inner workings of the government-foundation–activist-agency engine of social engineering that was crucial to remaking America's cities as the WASP ruling class wanted them remade in the period following World War II. The last thing the Quakers wanted was publicity because general awareness that certain groups were orchestrating events from behind the scenes destroyed the illusion that things were just happening all by themselves because people were choosing to make them happen that way by the collective weight of their individual decisions, a crucial tenet of Whig ideology in America. In its abhorrence of publicity, Ford was like foundation colleagues at the Rockefeller and

Carnegie foundations, who were coming under the increasing scrutiny of Congress. Joe McCarthy's hearings were followed in 1954 by the Reece Commission hearings which looked specifically into the Rockefellers' use of its foundation money for political advocacy.

On July 30, 1953, Mr. and Mrs. Donald Howard and their two children, ages three and four respectively, moved into an apartment in the CHA-run Trumbull Park housing project, located between 105th Street and 109th Strett and Ogelsby Avenue and Bensley Avenue in South Deering, an all-white but mixed-ethnic neighborhood on Chicago's South Side. The move-in was without incident because all of the preliminary arrangements were made by Mrs. Howard, whose complexion was very light. By August 5, however, word got out that the Howards were blacks and as CHA commission members toured the area in the until-then-uneventful aftermath of the move-in, they noticed that a crowd had gathered in front of the Howards' apartment and called the police. By the time the police arrived, a crowd of around 50 people had begun breaking windows in the Howards' building. By August 9, the crowd had swelled to 1,500 and police had been assigned to a permanent detail in the projects and would remain there for the next few years, escorting black families from their apartments to the local bus stop or taxi stand when they wanted to go shopping and back again when they returned.

Unlike the riots in Cicero and Englewood, which were ignited by accidents, the Chicago Housing Authority brought on the riots in Trumbull Park by deliberately moving black families into a housing project which had been all white since its construction in 1938. The official explanation of the Trumbull Park riots is that the move-in of the Howard family happened by accident. "Miss Elizabeth Wood, the executive secretary of the Chicago Housing Authority," according the Commission on Human Relations, which by 1953 was functioning as the CHA's propaganda arm, "has pointed out that because this introduction of the first Negro family was not planned but happened by accident, the usual preparations were not made."[7] Even if this were the case with the Howard family, the CHA decided to exploit its "mistake" to its own advantage. Undeterred by the violence which the July move-in had caused, the CHA moved three more black families into Trumbull Park on August 13, as a crowd of 200 local residents showered them and their police escorts with a barrage of rocks. Over the next few weeks, the situation at Trumbull Park took on the dimensions of a protracted siege. In addition to rocks and bottles, the locals began firing what the CHA termed "aerial bombs," their word for roman candles, at the project buildings. During this period of siege, the police also reported thirty instances of arson.

The unrest and the arson would last for years. Four years after the Howard family moved into Trumbull Park, a riot broke out in nearby Calumet Park on July 29, 1957, and quickly spread to Trumbull Park, which by that time had taken on significance in that area of Chicago as the symbol of the government's attempts to engineer its citizens and of the ethnics' determination to resist those efforts. The mob attacked a black resident who happened to be walking through the projects at the time, pelting him with stones, an assault which required hospital treatment. They then broke into the apartment of a black family whose three small children were sleeping in an upstairs bedroom while their parents were talking with another black family in the project. The mob then broke all of the windows in the apartment, destroyed the apartment's furniture, and then set the apartment on fire. By the time the police arrived, the entire project was awash in similar incidents. During the summer of 1953, when Trumbull Park exploded, five other police districts in the area – Grand Crossing, Gresham, Englewood, Burnside, and Marquette – were all forced to deal with similar racially based unrest.

After "accidentally" moving the Howard family into Trumbull Park on a weekend, the CHA decided to avoid further conflict by moving black families in during the week when most of the community's men were at work. In October 1953, the CHA attempted a daylight move-in of a number of black families, only to find, in the words of a CHR report, that several local women "literally hurled themselves first at a truck loaded with the newcomers' furniture and later at a new car driven by the head of one Negro family."[8] To honor the role that local women played in their attempt to keep more black families from moving into Trumbull Park, a lawyer for the SDIA sang "Mother Machree" in honor of three women arrested that day.[9]

In a memorandum on the violence at Trumbull Park prepared by the Church Federation of Greater Chicago, the CFGC's Department of Citizenship, Education and Action, apparently unaware that Elizabeth Wood was maintaining that moving the Howard family into Trumbull Park was accidental, claimed that the CHA had to move black families into the project. In fact, "the fundamental fact that must be underscored for all citizens is that the Chicago Housing Authority has no choice in this matter. It must obey the law."[10] The CFGC was here referring to the desegregation regs the CHA passed in 1950. On January 11, 1950, the commissioners of CHA formally adopted a resolution stating that "in the selection and admission of families to the projects now and to be operated by the Authority, families shall not be segregated or otherwise discriminated against on grounds of race, color, creed national origin, or ancestry."[11]

In their zeal to support the integration policies of the CHA, Chicago's pro-integration forces rushed into print without checking on the consistency of their respective justifications. After giving a fairly convincing explanation of the causes of black migration based on labor needs in Chicago and the increasing mechanization of farming in the South, the CHR went on to claim that these forces were beyond human control. "Thus," the Commission on Human Relations concludes, "impersonal social and economic forces have created the changes in Chicago's population. . . . Therefore, not by anyone's plan or intervention but by the cooperation of the economic law of supply and demand has Chicago's Negro population expanded. The job looking for the man and the man looking for the job have come together in Chicago."[12] The CFGC is slightly less disingenuous in describing the cause of racial unrest in Chicago. There is no question that migration from the South is the cause of the housing shortage and the housing shortage is the cause of racial unrest, but the CFGC also notes that "the principal reason" for this increased demand in Chicago "is that in the main the slum clearance and public improvement programs of the last few years are displacing low-income Negro families."[13] So it wasn't just "impersonal social and economic forces" after all. Whether it was or it wasn't, and whether the Howards ended up in Trumbull Park by accident or not, the battle lines were clearly drawn after ten years of increasingly intrusive social engineering, and neither the ethnics nor the social engineers were planning to back down. "It is known to agencies close to this problem," the CFGC informed its readers, "that in some sections of the city, the Trumbull Park affair is being watched closely by those who will use the same tactics to prevent Negroes from living in their own communities."[14]

What they failed to say is that it was being watched just as closely by the agencies who were trying to "integrate" the neighborhood. As in Cicero and Englewood, the ACLU and the AFSC sent spies into South Deering to find out what was being planned in the neighborhood's steel mills and taverns. Hirsch notes that "when the ACLU sought to infiltrate the area to get inside information as to who was behind the recurring violence, they placed a young Polish-speaking male in one of the steel mills and had him regularly make the rounds of area taverns with his co-workers."[15] McGreevy notes, "Eavesdroppers hired by the ACLU reported that steelworkers in the local bars believed that the parish priest placed the 'blame for the whole trouble' on the African American families."[16] Hirsch further notes that the ACLU was interested in identifying the ethnicity of members of the inner circle of South Deering Improvement Association, noting that the activists in the SDIA had names like "Nahirney, Santucci, Salvatore, Lalich, Mitovich, Bogdanovich, Kral, Kelly, Dorio, Robish, Michalik, Jarmusz, Landini, Diclemente, Barnowski, and Sickick."[17]

The AFSC was also involved in the Trumbull Park disturbances. In fact, the Quakers knew that the move-in was going to happen months in advance, giving the lie to Elizabeth Wood's claim that it happened by accident. On January 7, 1953, at around the same time that he was trying to arrange a meeting with Philip Klutznick to talk about integrating Park Forest, James Cassels, now eight months into his tenure as director of the AFSC's Housing Opportunity Program in Chicago, met with Nick and Laurel Pastor, two Chicago-area Quakers, "to discuss protective covenants of Merrionette Manor and consider possibilities of Negroes moving into the area."[18] In the course of the ensuing conversation, which was attended by "a few of their personal friends" who had been invited to take part in "a very informal discussion," Cassels announced, seven months before it actually happened, "that the Chicago Housing Authority Trumbull Park Project would be getting Negro residents in the not too distant future."[19]

It is not surprising, therefore, that the ethnics in South Deering remained unconvinced when the CHR explained patiently to them that the disturbances in their neighborhood were the result of "impersonal social and economic forces." Louis B. Dinnocenzo, head of the South Deering Improvement Association, could not have been aware of what the Quakers were doing in Chicago at the time, but he was also not naive enough to believe the CHR's explanation of Trumbull Park as happening "not by anyone's plan or intervention but by the cooperation of the economic law of supply and demand." At the height of the Trumbull Park struggle, Dinnocenzo brushed aside allegations that he was "anti-Negro." Dinnocenzo felt that he was being accused of racism "because I am fighting the enforced housing of Negro families here."[20] Dinnocenzo countered the accusation by claiming that "I work with hundreds of Negroes in my job. They'll all tell you we get along and I treat them justly."[21] But his strongest argument was based on the fact that he ultimately didn't hold blacks responsible for the assault on the South Deering community. The Negroes, according to Dinnocenzo, were "being used as tools by the Communists and by the Human Relations Commission to force a situation upon a people."[22]

As in Englewood and Cicero, the population of South Deering was overwhelmingly Catholic, but as in both previous instances, the Catholic Church gave no support to the protesters above the parish level. In fact, in 1956, Cardinal Stritch finally broke silence on the matter and condemned the violence surrounding Trumbull Park, an implicit rebuke to St. Kevin's Parish, two blocks away from Trumbull Park, whose parishioners were active in the protests. Many of the ushers at St. Kevin's were also members of the South Deering Improvement Association. With no ethnic homogeneity in the traditional sense of that term and no support from the chancery of the Chicago Archdiocese, the beleaguered ethnics in South Deering had no choice but to see their "whiteness" as the only source of unity in a community threatened by black invaders. Abandoned by the Catholic intelligentsia and the chancery the CIC controlled, Chicago's Catholic ethnics became "white" by default, and as a result they were found guilty of racism in the court of public opinion.

If they had been tried in a regular court, there would have been plenty of evidence to convict them. The local papers complained about being subjected to the "savage, lustful, immoral standards of the southern Negro"[23] thrust upon them. The *South Deering Bulletin* referred to blacks as "hyper-sexed, immoral, and dangerous,"[24] and therefore a threat to the community which the ethnics perceived not only as their own but created by them out of something approaching the wilderness. Hirsch notes what he terms South Deering's character as an "ethnic amalgam,"[25] claiming that "nowhere was a single ethnic group fighting for its own homogeneous neighborhood or nationality."[26] But his claim ignores the "triple melting pot" and the fact that the Italians and the Croats and the Poles of South Deering were in the process of becoming an American ethnic group based not on race, as they often mistakenly claimed, but on religion. The Slavs and Poles who told the pastor at St. Kevin's, "We built this church. It's our church and the Niggers can't come here,"[27] clearly identified themselves as Catholics. They had an ethnic identity as American Catholics, and clearly saw St. Kevin's as the center of that community and the source of its unity, but Hirsch ignores this evidence in favor of racial categories which simply obscure the real dimensions of the ethnic struggle that was actually taking place. Deprived of their own ethnic identity as Catholics, the ethnics could be demonized as racist. Portrayed as having no cause of their own to defend, they were seen by default as being motivated by simple hatred. Housing politics in places like Chicago and Detroit were inexplicable when reduced to racial lines because the "white" people in the equation were on two different sides of the struggle, which was invariably a three-way battle in which the Jews and the WASPs sided with the newly arrived black migrants as a way of confronting and curtailing the political power of the equally "white" Catholic ethnics. The fact that the ethnics often identified themselves as "white" simply adds a note of tragicomedy to the entire story.

The Catholics could provide no defense because they were divided internally, between the liberal Catholic Interracial Council, which denounced the violence and took the Quaker line on integration, and the people of St. Kevin's Parish, two blocks away from the Trumbull Park housing project, who saw the move-ins as an assault on their community. The division was best symbolized when a sixty-four-year-old woman parishioner slugged a Catholic Interracial Council member escorting Trumbull Park residents to their homes. The Catholic Interracial Council played up the fact that "our Christian faith is of its nature universal"[28] and as such "it knows not the distinctions of race, color or nationhood"[29] and as a result "discrimination based on the accidental fact of race or color . . . cannot be reconciled with the truth that God has created all men with equal rights and dignity."[30] This was the formulation that eventually made it into the CIC-inspired statement on "Discrimination and Christian Conscience" issued by the Catholic Bishops of the United States on November 14, 1958. The position of the bishops was in many ways, however, extraneous from the point of view of those resisting the forced integration of their communities. No pastor in any Catholic parish on the South Side of Chicago would deny that "God has created all men with equal rights and dignity."[31]

The racial doctrines which the American nativists espoused by way of Darwin and Madison Grant never found theoretical purchase on the Catholic mind in the United States, certainly not as much purchase as they found among the WASP ruling class. But admitting that blacks were children of God did not address the crux of the issue as the ethnics construed it, an issue which revolved around the historical nature of the ethnic parish in America and the rights of the local community to control its own destiny free of the clandestine machinations of social engineers. McGreevy cites the case of the Catholic priest who was asked why he ignored "church teaching" on "integration" by proposing an ethnic parish for blacks. "What teaching?" the priest responded. "The hierarchy knows very well what's going on out here. There's always been this sort of situation in the Church. There's always been a Polish Church and a Mexican Church. Nationality Churches. This is the same thing. As a matter of fact, when this parish was set up the colored requested it themselves."[32]

The question of race took precedence over the question of who controlled the local community because the American Catholic bishops had already abandoned the idea of the ethnic parish. By not explaining the history of that accommodation to American life with the same force with which they denounced discrimination, they were silent accomplices to the charges, then being leveled against the ethnics, that those who still believed in the ethnic parish were in fact racists. The bishops' failure to address the racial problem as a parish problem would have long-term effects as well because by accepting "integration" as the only Christian possibility, they undermined the very notion of what a parish community was. According to the new "integrationist" dispensation, anything that was what it was was guilty of not being something other than what it was. Catholics would be made to feel guilty if large numbers of black Protestants did not attend their services on Sunday mornings, when in fact the all-white nature of their congregations in later years was largely the result of the fact that they had all been driven into the suburbs by forces intent on destroying their ethnic neighborhoods.

Because the Chicago archdiocese refused to address the racial disturbances as a community issue first and a racial issue second, Chicago's ethnics found themselves in an intellectually untenable situation. They identified themselves as "white" while their enemies identified them as "Catholic." Hirsch is, of course, right when he claims that "in virtually every case (the Fernwood riot is again the lone exception), the central role played by Catholics is apparent."[33] At another point, he takes the opposite point of view without seeing or resolving the contradiction. "When the Howards 'accidentally' integrated the Trumbull Park Homes," he writes, they thus found a community welded together by an intense race consciousness. The *South Deering Bulletin* submerged nationality and stated the case plainly: "White people built this area [and] we want no part of this race mixing. . . Race pride has come to the fore as a new set of values." Throughout the Trumbull Park disorders, each apparent "attack" on the community was viewed as a racial affront that called for an appropriate "white" response. Additionally, the array of organized civil rights forces operating in the area led members of the defensive-minded community to repeatedly call for the creation of a "white" organization to represent their interests in much the same way the NAACP and others advanced those of blacks. Significantly, this deep concern for "white," not "ethnic," rights was often heard in taverns where Polish remained the primary language. Nor was the common denominator of color peculiar to Trumbull Park. The disturbances in Cicero, Park Manor and Englewood were, above all, viewed as the results of black incursions into "white" areas. Airport Homes protectors denounced the blacks' insistence on "living with white people," and the spokesman for the Fernwood Park opposition firmly asserted that "we live in a white community and we intend to keep it white."[34]

Because of the workings of the triple melting pot, the Serbs, Croats, Italians, and Poles of South Deering were clearly on their way to becoming something else. The unanswered question here is whether the ethnics of South Deering (with the exception of the Serbs) were white or Catholic. Hirsch takes the liberal position by default, holding both possibilities against them. They were, in other words, not an ethnic group defending itself against another ethnic group, whose migration was orchestrated by still another ethnic group. They were not even racist Catholics. They were Catholic racists, a formula which reversed the true ethnic nature of their group and demonized them at the same time. They were motivated by a completely blind and gratuitous hatred based on obsolete and historically tainted intellectual theories. In defining them in this way, Hirsch ignores the fact that people like Homer Jack, Louis Wirth, Paul Blanshard, and the rest of the social-engineering establishment had targeted these neighborhoods for change precisely because they were Catholic, depriving them of any right to defend their own communities. The inhabitants of these neighborhoods, in other words, were "racist" by default. They ended up espousing behavior based on a philosophy which few if any understood because the Catholic Church, in many ways the real reason they were being attacked, had cut them off without any intellectual support. Ironically, the ethnics espoused the same ideology of race that had been used against them in the 1920s, a fact noted with mordant irony by many of their opponents. A further irony, of course, is the fact that the ethnics thought they were becoming American by describing themselves as "white," unaware that the racialism that was used against them in the '20s had gone out of style, partially because of the fact that they had adopted it.

The Catholic Interracial Council itself was in many ways hamstrung in dealing with the situation. They were being whipsawed in their own way. By espousing the "integrationist" line of the liberal Protestant denominations which were using it to attack the Catholic Church, they were cut off from their co-religionists and often perceived as a fifth column. But at the same time they were still perceived as Catholic by their ostensible allies in the struggle for racial equality and perceived as having, as a result, dual loyalties. Homer Jack, a Unitarian minister and co-founder of CORE, similarly attacked Englewood's Catholics and Monsignor Byrnes for sanctioning block organizations designed to keep blacks out of the area and for not "lift[ing] a finger to stop the violence against the Negroes and other people."[35] Lloyd Davis of the Catholic Interracial Council found that no matter what the liberal Catholics did they were still perceived as Catholics and, therefore, part of the problem. Indeed, as Hirsch indicates, the idea that the "Catholic Problem" was at the heart of the racial disturbances was never far from the minds of the CIC's ostensible allies in that struggle. Davis was acutely aware of these suspicions and was defensive in the face of anti-Catholic slights. "Davis," according to Hirsch, "took exception to 'the rather ruthless attack . . . made upon the Roman Catholic Church' and felt that such endeavors 'will not help us to solve the problem.'"[36] "I am greatly disturbed," he continued, "by what appears to be a failure on the part of some CAD leadership to admit that Catholics have done anything positive in regard to this recent disturbance." The Council Against Discrimination newsletter failed to carry CIC statements or that of any other Catholic organization "a long with statements of the Protestant and Jewish Faiths." This seemingly anti-Catholic attitude "has been also noted at several public meetings sponsored by the Council Against Discrimination," Davis added, "and is proving to be most distressing." The defensiveness and acute sensitivity to the charge that racial disorders were a "Catholic problem" were characteristic responses. Liberal Catholic organizations such as the CIC were forced to be defensive because of the patently obvious roles played by Catholics in Chicago's racial disorders.[37]

Chicago's ethnics were identified as aggressors in the racial struggles of the '50s, but the charge stuck precisely because they were denied any ethnic identity of their own. With no ethnic identity of their own, they had no ethnic interests to defend. As a result, the only principle of unity they possessed was negative, which is to say, racial animus, and irrational racial animus at that. Since it accepted the categories of its liberal Protestant comrades in arms, the CIC was forced to recognize "the validity of many of the charges made against their co-religionists by organizing local chapters of the CIC in knee-jerk fashion in riot-torn areas."[38] No matter how hard it tried, the CIC could never take control of the integrationist agenda in Chicago, not in general and not even for Catholics. It was condemned to forever seek the approval of people who would use them as a fifth column to gain entree to Catholic organizations, as the Quakers were doing in Cicero, but who never treated them as equal partners with an ability to shape strategy and ultimate goals. The CIC was in the unenviable position of being a useful tool that was otherwise held in suspicion, if not contempt. "If it was possible to take umbrage at the claim that the riots were exclusively a 'Catholic problem,'" Hirsch writes, dredging up Paul Blanshard's term, one which remained in the back of the minds of the CIC's collaborators, "the CIC was still compelled to confront the fact that it was at very best a problem involving many Catholics."[39] The CIC was hated by the ethnic Catholics in parishes like St. Kevin's and held in scarcely concealed contempt by people like Homer Jack and the Quakers, who used them to infiltrate Catholic institutions that would have been otherwise impregnable.

On July 16, 1954, halfway between the time the Supreme Court handed down *Brown v. Board of Education* and when it would hand down *Berman v. Parker*, Louis Dinnocenzo, head of the South Deering Improvement Association, met with Mayor Kenelly, James Downs, then housing coordinator for the city, and Chicago's police commissioner to discuss the riots that had taken place in the aftermath of the Chicago Housing Authority's attempt to integrate the Trumbull Park Homes. What resulted from this meeting and another in early August was an agreement whereby the SDIA agreed to stop its protest in exchange for the CHA's promise that the number of black families in Trumbull Park would not exceed its current number. The terms of the agreement seem to indicate that it was not racism that motivated the SDIA protesters as much as the fear that racial succession was being used to drive them from their own neighborhood. When the threat of ethnic cleansing was removed, the rioting may not have stopped completely – the situation was too tense for that, and would remain so for years into the future – but it decreased significantly.

The Quakers, who had been agitating for racial change for years in the Chicago area, were clearly upset by the deal, which gives some indication that their goal for the neighborhood was not peaceful solutions. "During the past year," one AFSC staffer wrote,

> AFSC staff members have overheard conversations or have been directly told by South Deering residents that "no more Negro families will be placed in the project and the SDIA thinks it can sit back and wait for all the ones who are still here to leave. They feel they've won the fight so they don't need to raise Cain anymore."[40]

The Quakers were convinced that CHA was reneging on its stated policies of the recent past. Then, as if to confirm their fears, as part of the same deal, Elizabeth Wood, the social-engineering head of the CHA, was fired. A similar fate awaited Walter Phillips, Wood's counterpart on the Philadelphia Housing Authority, as the ethnics there, backed by their representatives in city council, won out in that city too. The victory, however, was short lived. *Brown v. Board of Education* had unleashed forces that could not be controlled by city councilmen or the people they represented. It called into being what would come to be known as the civil-rights movement, a movement which had the backing of the most powerful forces in the country and against which city councilmen and their ethnic constituents were no match.

Three years after the beginning of the Trumbull Park riots and two years after Elizabeth Wood's ouster as part of the same deal which established quotas at the project and, as a result, brought relative peace to the neighborhoods, the Quakers were still licking their wounds and planning their next move. On July 17, 1956, Ed Holmgren, director of the AFSC's Housing Opportunity Program, wrote to Martin Luther King, Jr., explaining how the AFSC "has for three years grappled with the tense Trumbull Park Homes situation in Chicago."[41] He then got quickly to the point. The Quakers were planning a meeting at a suburban forest camp, with "The Trumbull Park Mission," a group of three Friends from the Chicago area and three Friends from the Philadelphia area who arrived in Chicago on the third anniversary of the move-in at Trumbull Park to discuss "this perplexing problem."[42] Holmgren was writing to King in the hope that he would agree "to spend a few hours at this camp and share your Montgomery experience in helping to develop new insight to a similar problem."[43] There would be no pressure and no experts at the meeting, just "a group of sensitive and concerned individuals with a wide background in general community affairs. It might be added that this is somewhat typical of the way Friendly concerns are expressed."[44]

It would be ten years before Martin Luther King would take the Quakers up on their offer. In the meantime, faced with the prospect of civil war on the issue of racial migration, Chicago's political powers took the situation into their own hands and arranged a separate peace on the racial front. Elizabeth Wood was replaced by General Kean, who inaugurated a new policy of site selection for housing projects at the CHA, one which necessitated the approval of the aldermen in charge of the wards where the proposed sites were to be located. Needless to say, the Quakers and their allies considered local approval of housing sites a defeat for "democracy," but by the mid-'50s the Quakers had exhausted whatever purchase "friendly persuasion" had had on the minds of Chicago officials. Alvin Rose, General Kean's successor, was even more attentive to the community's reaction to site selection. After addressing an open meeting of the Planning and Housing Committee of the City Club of Chicago on January 17, 1958, Rose was asked if the CHA would consider building public housing uptown. Rose responded by pointing out, in the words of an AFSC informer sent to monitor the meeting, "that the coming in of those public-housing projects would create another problem – namely, that CHA could not guarantee that the projects would be all-white, that Negroes would have to come in."[45] Rather than change the racial make-up of the neighborhood, policy under Alvin Rose specified that it was better to move the housing to an area where the make-up of the residents was more compatible to the make-up of the neighborhood. "We are not going to use public housing as a wedge,"[46] he claimed, thereby tacitly admitting that that is how CHA policy was applied by his predecessor, Elizabeth Wood. "Our role must be one of the friend to the community."[47] The Quakers were outraged by Rose's claim, but the policy that "elected officials will tell us where public housing is wanted"[48] had in fact become CHA policy after Wood's ouster.

The city's ultimate solution to the problem of racial migration was "intensive centralization."[49] Which is to say the erection of high-rise Bauhaus-style *Wohnmaschinen* on a massive scale beginning with the erection of the Robert Taylor Homes just south of IIT in the years from 1960 to 1962 and marching south with the same kind of building for the next two miles. Eventually some 27,000 Chicago blacks were re-settled on the quarter-mile-wide strip between the railroad tracks to the east and the Dan Ryan Expressway to the west. There the blacks from Mississippi and their descendants for the next two or three generations settled into welfare dependency as wards of the state that had brought them north as cheap labor but didn't know what to do with them when the jobs that were supposed to employ them left town. The inherent weaknesses in the black family might have fared no better had they been left to develop in bungalows surrounded by trees and grass, but after a while it became clear that the Bauhaus formula for dealing with living arrangements according to materialist principles exacerbated the problems the sharecroppers brought north with them.

The anonymity of fifteen-story high-rise buildings gave the people who had been living under the Jim Crow form of social control in the south the sense that anything was possible, and this did little to foster moral behavior or social order. By the end of the 20th century, the Robert Taylor Homes and its high-rise neighbors to the south were still standing, but the perceptive observer might have noted as he passed by in his car on the Dan Ryan Expressway that most of the apartments, even those not burnt out, were vacant and boarded over. Reg Isaacs's great social experiment was awaiting the day when the last welfare mother would move out of the last apartment in the last high-rise building. Then, like Schuylkill Falls in Philadelphia and Pruett-Igoe in St. Louis, the Robert Taylor Homes would be imploded to make way for something new. If that something new entailed a repudiation of government-sponsored social engineering, there would be at least some consolation to draw from this costly experiment in social control. But all signs indicate that this was not to be. Instead, Chicago, recognizing that the land on which the projects were built had become too valuable for public housing because of its proximity to downtown, decided to engage in another form of social engineering, this time the reverse of what they had done in the '50s. According to the new plan the white folk, who were by now sick of spending hours in their cars as they commuted from far-flung suburbs like Barrington Lakes, were going to be allowed to return to the city to purchase neo-rowhouses of the sort recently erected at Central Station for prices beginning at $550,000. The black folk on welfare would then be sent to the older suburbs where they would rent the houses that were originally built for the displaced white ethnics as Section 8 homes. As the French say, the more things change, the more they remain the same. The only thing that hasn't changed in this futile experiment in political control is the government's penchant for social engineering.

Notes

1   Louis Wirth to Joseph H. Willits, Director, The Rockefeller Foundation, 4/28/52, Wirth Papers, Box XXIX folder 7, University of Chicago Archives.
2   Confidential Memorandum, J. Cassels visit with E. F. Schietinger, University of Chicago, 4/17/52, Box 88, folder #9, AFSC papers, UIC Archives.
3   Ibid.
4   Waitstill H. Sharp to AFSC Philadelphia Office, 4/30/52, AFSC papers, Box 88, folder 8, UIC Archives.
5   Richard K. Bennett, AFSC Philadelphia, to Waitstill H. Sharp, 5/9/52, AFSC papers, Box 88, folder 8, UIC Archives.
6   Richard K. Bennett, AFSC Philadelphia, to John Willard AFSC Chicago 4/22/52 confidential, AFSC papers, Box 88, folder 8, UIC Archives.
7   Trumbull Park Racial Disturbances: A Memorandum prepared by the Department of Citizenship Education and Action, the Church Federation of Greater Chicago, 10/2/53, AFSC Papers, Box 50, Folder 1, UIC Archives.
8   Arnold R. Hirsch, *Making the Second Ghetto: Race and Housing in Chicago 1940–1960* (Cambridge: Cambridge University Press, 1983), p. 76.
9   Ibid., p. 78.
10 Trumbull Park Racial Disturbances.
11 AFSC Progress Report on Trumbull Park Homes March 1959, AFSC Papers, Box 62, folder 14, UIC Archives.
12 Trumbull Park Racial Disturbances.
13 Ibid.

14 Ibid.

15 Hirsch, p. 79.

16 John T. McGreevy, *Parish Boundaries: The Catholic Encounter with Race in the Twentieth Century Urban North* (Chicago: University of Chicago Press, 1996), p. 100.

17 Hirsch, p. 204.

18 Confidential Memorandum, Meeting at Nick and Laurel Paster's House, 9820 Merrion, 1/7/53, AFSC papers, Box 86 #14, UIC Archives.

19 Ibid.

20 Remarks of Louis P. Dinnocenzo, "Trumbull Park Homes Still Resembles a Besieged Fortress," *Daily Calumet*, 1/22/54, AFSC papers, Box 62, folder 14, UIC Archives.

21 Ibid.

22 Ibid.

23 Hirsch, p. 186.

24 Ibid.

25 Ibid.

26 Ibid.

27 Ibid.

28 "Discrimination and Christian Conscience: A Statement Issued by the Catholic Bishops of the United States," November 14, 1958, *Pastoral Letters of the United States Catholic Bishops 1941–1961* (Washington D.C.: National Conference of Catholic Bishops, 1983), p. 202.

29 Ibid.

30 "Discrimination and Christian Conscience," p. 203.

31 Ibid.

32 McGreevy, p. 101.

33 Hirsch, p. 85.

34 Ibid., p. 187.

35 McGreevy, p. 86.

36 Hirsch, p. 87.

37 Ibid.

38 Ibid.

39 Ibid.

40 AFSC Report, Progress Report on Trumbull Park Homes, March 1959, AFSC papers, Box 62, folder 14, UIC Archives.

41 Ed Holmgren, Director, Housing Opportunities Program AFSC to Martin Luther King. 7/17/56, AFSC papers, Box 50, folder 1, UIC Archives.

42 Ibid.

43 Ibid.

44 Ibid.

45 "Alvin E. Rose addressed open meeting of the Planning and Housing Committee of the City Club of Chicago on January 17, 1958," AFSC papers, Box 62, folder 14, UIC Archives.

46 Ibid.

47 Ibid.

48 Ibid.

49 Hirsch, p. 242.

Dennis Clark at the Housing Authority

*Public housing must do many things by law and administrative ruling which
tend to depress the morale of residents.*

PHA guidelines for integrating housing projects

On November 19, 1953, Bernard Orr of the Philadelphia Housing Authority called Dennis
Clark, an employee of the authority, into his office for a little talk. Orr, it seems, was worried about Drayton Bryant, another employee of the agency who was then assistant to the
executive director of the PHA. Orr "felt convinced" that Bryant was "somewhat more than
a Marxian," he felt with a certain amount of certitude that he was "in short a Communist"
who needed to be watched. Orr, perhaps hearing that Clark was looking for another job,
was "in a spot," because he felt that if Clark left, no one at the agency would be able to
keep Bryant in line.[1]

Orr felt this way because of Clark's "background," his euphemistic way of referring
to the fact that Clark was a Catholic and could, therefore, be depended upon as being anti-
Communist. "My Catholicism, Jesuit training, etc.," Clark confided to his diary, "were to
keep Bryant wary."[2] Clark had described Bryant in a diary entry of March 7 of the same
year as "a fighting liberal,"[3] which was a compliment as far as Clark was concerned, but
at the same time "an exploiter of knowledge, not a scholar,"[4] who "believes that anthropology, as he has eclectically seen it, has demolished religion."[5] Clark was obviously flat-
tered by Orr's attention, especially when Orr told Clark that Bryant had "been damned
careful with you around."[6] Modesty prevented Clark from disagreeing. "It is true," he concurred, "that I watched Bryant keenly and easily picked off his relativist naturalistic arguments."[7] He then conceded that he "thought Bryant's past highly suspicious," but more
than that, he felt that Bryant's political views were potential "dynamite" for the cause of
public housing in Philadelphia. If "Senator McCarthy's traveling road show"[8] ever decided to investigate public housing, the Republicans could find plenty to talk about at their
hearings, something that Clark, as a liberal, feared. "The Republicans would gleefully discredit housing with a sensational case,"[9] he concluded.

Orr was right of course but wrong as well. In many ways his suspicions were a replay
of the Molly Yard-Meehan incident four years earlier. Bryant was a subversive; he was
working with the Quakers. On January 24, 1952, he sent Tom Colgan, then in charge of
AFSC housing efforts in Chicago, a copy of the PHA's "Outline of Procedure for
Integration of Existing Housing Projects," a confidential document, which was presumably not supposed to be shared with other Philadelphians, much less with people from
Chicago.[10] On the other hand, there is some indication in the document itself that the
Philadelphia Housing Authority was playing a double game when it came to confidential-
ity, since the document itself stipulated that "The policy statement of the Authority should
be circulated among special groups likely to give support to the Authority position."[11]

Confidentiality was defined in terms of the cultural warfare going on at the time, not according to the prerogatives of government agencies acting in the interests of all of the city's citizens. That meant that the document could be (and, in fact, was) shared with Quakers, but that it should be kept out of the hands of Catholic ethnics because it could easily provide evidence that the integration was first of all planned, as opposed to something that just happened – the official explanation – and that it was something that was being planned with specific outcomes to benefit specific interests in mind. That meant, in short, it was okay to share this confidential Philadelphia Housing Authority document with Quakers from Chicago but not with Catholics from Philadelphia.

Just why the PHA wanted their plans to integrate the projects in Philadelphia kept confidential was easy enough to understand. The official explanation of the integrators, as espoused by the Chicago CHR, the psychological-warfare arm of the Chicago Housing Authority, was that "impersonal social and economic forces have created the changes in Chicago's population. . . . Therefore, not by anyone's plan or intervention but by the cooperation of the economic law of supply and demand has Chicago's Negro population expanded."[12] Racial succession, according to the official explanation, was supposed to be a quasi-natural process, like the movement of glaciers, and not something orchestrated by specific groups for specific political ends, but that is how it was portrayed in the PHA document Bryant passed on to Colgan. The PHA's outline "recommended that a period of not less than three months be spent in preparation for integrating all existing housing projects."[13] Those preparations included preparing a pamphlet "on the positive values of fair housing practices to the entire community,"[14] making use of sensitivity training/psychological warfare techniques by hiring "a skilled discussion leader" from the "Temple University Institute of Group Dynamics," getting "articles to weaken stereotyping, fears and mis-apprehension of the uninformed" placed in newspapers, especially about the "positive contributions of the Negro community"[15] in improving housing in West Philadelphia and Germantown, two "integrated" neighborhoods which were on their way to becoming all black.

Part of the preparation for integration also meant carefully selecting the first black families to move in as unrepresentative of the black families which were to follow. "This means that the Supervisor of Applications is required to use considerable judgment in selecting Negro families which will contribute the least to prevalent stereotyped thinking."[16] That meant that "the first few Negro families accepted for occupancy in now all white projects should have only pre-school children so that school problems are not immediately added to those of housing."[17] However, this fact, unlike the other recommendations, which involved an elaborate public-relations campaign, was to be kept secret. "No element of selectivity," the PHA guidelines warned, "should appear in any public document."[18] The general impression to be given, according to the guidelines, was that it was all happening, if not naturally, then at least impartially according to the strict application of color-blind bureaucratic rules.

According to the official CHR explanation in Chicago, the CHA just went down its list, and some of the applicants just happened to be black. According to the PHA guidelines, which got passed on to the Quakers in Chicago eighteen months before, the CHA moved black families into Trumbull Park (and about six months before Jim Cassells told fellow Quakers in Chicago that the CHA was going to move them in there), it was "also recommended that about one-third of the vacancies in the now all-white projects be leased to Negro families."[19] The PHA guidelines also "recommended that the policy be announced for all projects simultaneously,"[20] something which was probably intended to forestall the serial crises that had been plaguing Chicago since 1946. Piecemeal integration allowed the forces opposing segregation to deal with the move-ins one neighborhood at a time. Simultaneous integration would limit participation from those outside the neighborhood. The PHA guidelines also called for placing "appropriate articles for the Negro press to encourage application,"[21] which indicates that even the demand side of the racial migration equation had to be, if not orchestrated, at least encouraged.

The timing of the new guidelines in Philadelphia corresponded to the greatest change in local government in Philadelphia's recent history. In November 1951 Joseph Sill Clark, a Chestnut Hill patrician, was elected mayor on the Democratic ticket, and the long reign of the Republicans in the city came to an end. Philadelphia in 1950 was still run by "a kind of Business-Biblical Americanism of the Old Protectionist Dispensation,"[22] to use John Lukacs's words, whose candidates were "real-estate men and Masons, brownish men with owlish faces."[23] Joe Clark and Dick Dilworth were determined to convince their fellow Philadelphians that they were not "politicians out of the '20s."[24] They were, instead, the New Deal arriving in town twenty years after it had arrived everywhere else, and both of those facts put together meant the repudiation of the racially based nativist thinking of the '20s and its replacement with the Louis Wirth-style environmentalism which brought with it enlightened attitudes toward race and lucrative federal housing money as well.

"We must make it certain," Clark announced in his inaugural address in January 1952, "that every citizen, regardless of race, religion or national origin, can have an equal opportunity to share, without discrimination, in all of the manifold activities of a great modern city."[25] It sounded innocuous enough, especially in light of subsequent repetition at similar events as a nationalities policy based on integration became political orthodoxy in the coming years. But then Clark indicated that he was going to take concrete measures by "appointing a commission on Human Relations of men and women dedicated to this end."[26]

The Philadelphia Commission on Human Relations had been in existence since March 12, 1948, when it was created by a city council ordinance. It was the brainchild of the ADA crowd, including Abe Freedman, Murray Schusterman, Maurice B. Fagan, Dorothy Montgomery, and Judge Gerald Flood, who was the first chairman of the Commission on Human Relations. But it was also heavily influenced by the Quakers, in particular Frank Loescher, long-time Quaker activist in Philadelphia, and Clarence Pickett, fresh from accepting the Nobel Peace Prize for the AFSC in 1947. It was also heavily supported by Philadelphia's black clergymen, including Luther Cunningham, Rev. Bill Gray, and Charles Shorter, then director of the Philadelphia NAACP. In 1951 the original five-member board was replaced under the terms of the City Charter of 1951 with a nine-member board, all of whom were appointed by the mayor with "the duty of enforcing all statutes and ordinances prohibiting discrimination in any area when such jurisdiction was not specifically vested in another governmental agency."[27]

The board was, in other words, a function of the people on it, something which Clark underscored when he brought in George Schermer as its director in the spring of 1952. Schermer had distinguished himself in liberal circles as the director of occupant placement at the Sojourner Truth Housing Project in Detroit ten years earlier. Now he would pursue the same tough-minded course in Philadelphia, with pretty much the same results. If the test of effective integration was the absence of controversy, then Schermer failed the test in both Detroit and Philadelphia. The integration of the Sojourner Truth Housing Project required the presence of thousands of federal troops and the involvement of the psychological-warfare establishment in Washington before local resistance was quelled. The same fate, on a lesser scale, awaited the CHR's integration efforts in Philadelphia.

Joe Clark concluded his inaugural address in January 1952 by assuring Philadelphians that he would put "an end to government from smoke-filled rooms."[28] Given the monumental political dimensions of the transition that was taking place at the time, most people probably thought that he was referring to the city's now defeated Republicans. No one knew at the time that Clark would soon be applying it with equal relish to the Catholic "Machine" wing of his own party. The reform in Philadelphia in 1952 was based on an alliance that would eventually come apart at its ethnic seams. No WASP could get elected without the Catholic vote, but the housing policies which WASPs like Clark implemented soon after taking office would alienate precisely that segment of the population. When the WASPs in the early '60s realized that a Catholic was finally going to become mayor of Philadelphia, they took their ball and went home, which is to say they dropped out of formal participation in local politics and became agents of the federal government's culture war against the ethnics. The same policies which put Catholic ethnics and their local political representatives on a collision course with the Chicago Housing Authority in that city would shake the Reform alliance apart in Philadelphia.

The conflict was not long in coming. In order to receive a $9 million federal loan to build a 742-unit project on land at the corner of 26th and Snyder in South Philadelphia, the Philadelphia City Council first had to re-zone the area from industrial to residential use. The rezoning alone was so controversial to the area's Italian and Irish residents that 300 hundred of them, led by local priests and politicians, packed the city-hall gallery in protest. When the city council on March 4, 1952, went ahead and re-zoned the area over their protests, they insured that the protests would continue for the next twenty years. It was some indication of how deep feeling for neighborhood went in certain sections of Philadelphia. The beginning of the Clark reform administration in Philadelphia was in many ways similar to the beginning of World War I. A series of impressive initial victories was followed by protracted trench warfare during which the entire area was devastated.

One month after the administration's first zoning battle, Ed Bacon and other "young people," including Walter Phillips, set up a luncheon with James Sims, president of the Pennsylvania Railroad, during which Bacon presented a plan to tear down the Chinese Wall of PRR tracks that ran the length of Market Street between the Schuylkill River and city hall and replace them with a settlement of Bauhaus buildings, later known as Penn Center. When one of the WASP establishment lawyers told John McCloy, fresh from Harvard Law School, that he was from the wrong side of the tracks, it was these very railroad tracks that he had in mind. Penn Center, the cluster of dreary Bauhaus buildings which replaced it, would become the showplace of urban renewal in Philadelphia and, after Bacon appeared on the cover of *Time* in 1964, a model for other cities to emulate as well. Bacon remembers Mayor Clark as also being at the meeting, but Clark was so worried about the possible negative political side-effects stemming from the project that he refused to sit at the same table with Bacon. "I don't know why he was so scared," Bacon said later.[29] He needn't have worried. Penn Center and the revitalization of center city would become so tame in comparison with the Clark administration's attempts to integrate the city's ethnic neighborhoods that it would in effect absorb all of the city's energy after the PHA got bogged down in the mid-'50s in a trench war it couldn't win.

Two months after the tumultuous city-council meeting on the re-zoning of Wilson Park, on May 26, the Philadelphia Housing Authority announced that it was adopting "a policy of housing for all projects without discrimination or segregation for reasons of race, color, creed, religion or national origin," a policy which "was determined to be desirable and correct to carry out the responsibilities of the Housing Authority."[30] The decision came two years after the PHA had invited "a wide variety of organizations concerned with the progress of the program to form an Advisory Committee."[31] The "wide variety" of organizations read like the list of usual liberal suspects when it came to housing matters in Philadelphia. It included the Citizens Council on City Planning, the Philadelphia Housing Association, the Philadelphia District of the Health and Welfare Council, and the Fellowship Council, but no Catholic or ethnic organizations. The Italians and the Irish from South Philadelphia had, of course, just demonstrated their interest in housing matters in the city, but they had, unfortunately, demonstrated the wrong kind of interest. The individuals representing the organizations that were invited were the same people who had given Philadelphia its Commission on Human Relations, people like Maurice Fagan, Dorothy Montgomery, and Sadie M. Alexander. The only Catholic on the board was Anna McGarry, whose integrationist sympathies were well-known. Once again the people in Chestnut Hill and Germantown banded together as "experts" to determine the fate of Catholic neighborhoods like Roxborough, Manayunk, Olney and South Philadelphia, and once again the people in those neighborhoods protested what they perceived as outside interference.

On August 14, 1952, eight months into the Clark Administration, Clark appointee Walter M. Phillips, in his capacity as acting chairman of the Philadelphia Housing Authority, announced "arrangements determined upon in the Mayor's office yesterday relating to the integration program at Abbotsford Homes and Bartram Village."[32] Phillips's assistant Walter E. Alessandroni wrote to Robert J. Callaghan at the Commission on Human Relations to ask for the CHR's assistance in the move. The CHR was responsible for engineering the consent of the people in the neighborhood. Since the Abbotsford Homes were in a largely Catholic area, the PHA asked the CHR to use Anna McGarry as their agent there. In order to spur him on, Alessandroni sent Callaghan a pamphlet entitled "Integration of Racial Minorities in Public Housing Projects: A Guide for Local Housing Authorities on How to Do it," prepared by Edward Rutledge of the Racial Relations Office at the New York Public Housing Administration. "Experience," according to Rutledge, "has taught us there is only one way to integrate: DO IT!"[33]

And so on the evening of August 1, 1952, the PHA just did it, bringing a black couple by the name of Bernardino and their two small children to the Abbotsford Homes to move in. The results were predictable. The locals protested until the police were called in. The protest continued until the police and a rainstorm dispersed the crowd. The attempted move-in created such an angry response among the neighborhood's residents because it was perceived, as a later survey indicated, as the thin end of the wedge of social engineering. The white tenants at the Abbotsford Homes felt that the Philadelphia Housing Authority had surrendered to pressure from the NAACP, that the Bernardinos were "paid blockbusters," and that the projects were a "test case," where integration, if successful there, would be used to engineer the rest of the neighborhood.[34] Abbotsford residents also mentioned the prospect of "black and white intimacy,"[35] a reference to the sexual morals of the blacks and the impact the ethnics feared it would have on their community. The manipulation of race by the PHA, in other words, was perceived as a threat to the continued existence of the community. Since the people wanted the community to continue as they, and not the mandarins at the city's various housing associations saw fit, they decided to act in the community version of self-defense. The responses to the survey indicate that the residents of the Abbotsford Homes felt that race, in other words, was being used as an excuse to restructure the way they lived and wanted to go on living. Any animus toward black families needed to be understood in that context. The ethnics in the Abbotsord neighborhood felt that certain forces were orchestrating events from behind the scenes and, as the guidelines which Drayton Bryant sent to Tom Colgan indicated, they were right.

Since he was a friend of Anna McGarry and often had described his work as following in her footsteps, and since he was an employee of the Philadelphia Housing Authority at the same time, Dennis Clark was doubtless aware of what was going on in Abbotsford during August of 1952. He doesn't mention it in his diary, though, probably because he had other things on his mind at the time, namely, his impending marriage to Josepha O'Callaghan, a recent graduate of Hunter College in New York City. Clark had met his wife-to-be at a ceilidh in New York in February of 1949. As the battle over the integration of the Abbotsford Project raged in the streets of Philadelphia, Dennis Clark, who would become intimately involved with racial matters there over the next decade, documented instead the milestones of his courtship in his diary in anticipation of his marriage in September. Clark had got engaged shortly after graduating from St. Joseph's College, the local Jesuit institution, in the summer of 1951. In recounting the events leading up to his marriage, Clark admits that "the discovery of such a delightful creature was somewhat facilitated by my very intentional limitation of social contacts almost entirely to Irish Catholic college graduates who were fairly intellectual in outlook."[36]

Like the Catholic ethnics in Chicago but unlike the ruling class in Philadelphia at that time, Dennis Clark occupied a position of some ethnological ambiguity. The ruling-class WASPs had been in Philadelphia long enough to have a clear sense of their identity. They knew who they were, and they knew who their enemies were, and this sense of identity and purpose had only been strengthened by the successful conclusion of the recent war, something which they perceived as their war. Catholic ethnics like Dennis Clark were in a completely different situation. As an Irishman who had been drawn into a war to defend England and Anglo-American international interests, he came back from the war with his ethnic identity diminished. As a Catholic Irishman in Philadelphia with a politically activist bent, he was forced to chose between the Republican "conservative" Masonic nativist party or the liberal-WASP elite environmentalist urban-renewal, soon-to-be-sexual-revolutionary Democratic Party. Early on in his political life, he was faced with the fact that neither the "reform" ADA Democrats nor the old-line Masonic Republicans represented his interests as either a Catholic or an ethnic, and so he had to make certain accommodations to that fact. The main accommodation he made was by becoming a liberal on racial matters. This is not to deny that there was an element of sincere conviction on his part, but even conceding that, there were also certain career advantages to that position as well. Clark made his career in the city of Philadelphia as the man who was an expert on race and housing and the intersection of those two issues as points of conflict in ethnic neighborhoods. He made his career by essentially adopting the Quaker point of view on racial matters and by working for Quaker institutions like the PHA and the CHR in engineering the integration, if not the destruction, of ethnic and oftentimes Irish neighborhoods. After leaving the CHR, he spent a disastrous interlude as head of the Catholic Interracial Council in New York. When he came back to Philadelphia he worked first for Ford Foundation initiatives, which were also anti-ethnic, and finally he ended his career as an agent of the Fels Foundation, a largely Jewish agency.

"Working for the Fels Fund," Clark wrote, reflecting on his position there in the mid-'80s, "an organization in which the Board is dominated by Jews keenly sensitive of their Jewish identity, I have been constrained in my own Christian identity, since I am the subordinate and must discretely respect the mores of that group. This has meant that Christian holidays have been moderated in my view. Thus Good Friday, holy week and Easter are not to be too broadly heralded in my little work world."[37]

The irony, of course, is that during this time Clark became more and more of an Irish nationalist at a time when he was always serving the interests of other more dominant ethnic groups in the city, groups which often used Clark to work against the interests of Philadelphia's Irish. Clark's later aggressive Irish ethnic identity can be seen in many ways as a compensation for the jobs he took as an agent of other ethnic groups in the city. Those agencies would have seen an aggressive Catholicism as a threat to their interests, and as a result Clark probably also saw it as a potential threat to his career, and so Clark cultivated his persona as the Irish nationalist instead at a time when it was becoming, according to the principle of the triple melting pot, more and more of an anachronism.

In fact the persona of the politically aggressive secular Irishman which Clark cultivated later in his life had no precedent in his family's history. The Clarks were Irish and Catholic and persecuted in equal measure for being both. In an ironic commentary on Clark's fear of showing up at the Fels Fund offices with ashes on his forehead, Clark wrote some thirty years before about his grandfather Willie Clark, then a resident of St. Michael's Parish in Fishtown. When Willie Clark showed up at the public school he attended on Ash Wednesday in 1875, he was told by his teacher to leave the room and go to the public fountain in the schoolyard and wash the ashes off his forehead. Willie refused and was suspended for his refusal.[38] The incident fueled Clark's animus against the ruling class in Philadelphia, but the incident also served as a warning to those who wanted to get along with the ruling class and share in the benefits they were willing to grant to those who did their bidding. Clark's description of the incident makes clear that his grandfather was punished because he was a Catholic for a public manifestation of Catholic piety and not because he was an Irishman. Willie Clark was a Catholic because he was an Irishman. It was one unit of ethnic culture in Philadelphia, but gradually over the years Clark began a strategy of separating the two – the Irish and the Catholic – with his career advancement in mind. His later aggressive Irishness served as compensation for his increasingly tepid and finally non-existent Catholicism. It may also have arisen in compensation for the fact that Clark made his career by working against the interests of actual Irish ethnics in the city's neighborhoods. Toward the end of this life, Clark's role as an agent for Quaker and then Jewish interests in the city clearly made him uncomfortable in a way which he had difficulty admitting to himself even in the privacy of his own diary.

"I long," Clark wrote in 1985, "to shake off the constraints of working for the conservative Fels fund so that I could throw my energy into fighting nuclear arms, ecological crimes, Nicaraguan victimization and censorship."[39] The sentiments are clear enough, even if they involve Clark lying to himself in his own diary. Clark was acutely aware of ethnic realities in the city of Philadelphia, something which makes him just as acutely aware that he was serving the interests of people other than those he aggressively identified as his own. In order to compensate for his shortcomings in his own eyes, Clark engaged in various forms of self-deception. He cast the issue in political terms – Fels is "conservative" – rather than the actual ethnic terms he has used to describe the situation elsewhere. Clark then deflected this self-loathing away from its true source by fantasizing alternative work, helping other ethnic groups, e.g., Nicaraguans far away from the actual source of conflict in his own life, namely, in the ethnic neighborhoods of Philadelphia.

But all of this was still in the future. If in the early '50s Clark was more honest with himself; he was still confused about his identity. He was Irish and Catholic as well as an intellectual and an activist, and it was oftentimes unclear to him how these parts fit together. Taking inventory of this life mid-way through his engagement, Clark makes up a list of the "outstanding provisions" which had been bestowed upon him by "a generous and merciful deity."[40] The top three entries on his list of "good fortunes" all have to do with the Catholic faith. Clark is grateful for "1) birth and education and a home fast in the rudiments and strengths of Catholic belief and practice," followed by gratitude for "2) formal education past the college level under Catholic auspices, where little heavy burden of costs was incurred because of the school system of Cardinal Dougherty (his monument) and due to the government's investment in citizen-soldier education," followed by gratitude for "3) character development among friends who were treasures of virtue and shrewd intellect," followed by gratitude for meeting his future wife.[41] It is only after mentioning his wife that Clark gets around to mentioning "Irishry" because the two of them had recently attended a "ceilidh," during which he "savoured completely of the atmosphere of half-mystic Celticism."[42]

Irishry, at this point in Clark's life, possesses an intermediary function, connecting the doctrines of the Catholic Church, on the one hand, which he perceived as "somewhat isolated and its resources partly inaccessible," to the "alien culture," with which it was at war.[43] Irishry was not so much an end in itself as an enculturation of Catholicism for Clark at this point in his life. It was also a repository of myth and custom that gave meaning to and ennobled lives that were often drab and sometimes made desperate by the exigencies of life under an oftentimes ruthless economic system. Irishry made life bearable in a place like Philadelphia where "continuity, formal virtue, tradition, depth of homely wisdom, seasoned and virulent speech, good face-to-face relationships – all these were disorganized or eradicated by maudlin, unimaginative, urban-industrial patterns, undistinguished and insipid."[44]

Being Irish was, in the final analysis, a way of being Catholic, and not the other way around. Nor could it work the other way around. The same was true, often *a fortiori*, for the other more-recently-arrived, less-assimilated ethnic groups. In their rush to assimilate, the American (often Irish) bishops failed to note the importance of the intermediary structure of ethnicity as the prime vehicle for the transmission of the faith. At this point in the Church's history in the United States, no one was simply Catholic without some ethnic qualifier to the term. When the bishops abandoned the ethnic parish as an outdated anachronism, they affected the transmission of the faith in ways that they did not and still do not understand. Dennis Clark understood that fact in an almost inchoate fashion in the early '50s. The Catholic Church was "at war and in an alien society, stifled by the two most deadly gases, subtle secular ridicule and sterile indifference. The life of the people was not identified with its liturgical living. They were formed by corporations and rude material needs. The next best source of the craved lore and spiritual fare I knew was in the coffers of Irishry."[45]

Ethnicity could, however, only function as the implementation of a religion; it could not, Clark was to learn the hard way, function as a substitute for religion. At this point in his life, Clark did not need a substitute for religion because he was willing to defend the religion that he had, even its sexual teachings, the first thing that got thrown overboard when the winds of renewal swept through the Church following the Vatican Council of the 1960s. In 1951, Clark could write that he was

> furious at elders and others who habitually cavil at *Casti Connubii* [Pius XI's encyclical on marriage] and courtship. It is a broad campaign of concerted slander detracting sadly from both institutions. Like their views on religion, politics, entertainment, etc., the pratings are gross, abhorrent, coarse and ill-spirited. How sad it is. It is like the widely held view on Negroes. Just gross stupidity. My heart goes out to Camilla, our office secretary, who wants a nice home for her children so much and fears the consequences of trying to live in a white neighborhood. These things must be inspired by something satanic to be so widely held and so subtly instilled. They are direct repudiations of collective responsibility and are grievously current in public mores and private little minds.[46]

At this point in his life, Clark's views on racial matters were contextualized by Catholic faith and morals. Soon that would change. By the end of the 1960s, the exact opposite would be the case in Clark's life as it would be in the lives of many Catholic liberals who took the civil-rights movement as the criterion of whether the Catholic Church was worthy of support and not vice versa. However, on the Feast of St. Frumentius in 1953, Clark, ever the liberal on racial matters, is at least willing to entertain the notion that there were pathologies in the black community which needed to be addressed for what they were and not merely as a figment of the sexual obsessions of fearful white racists.

"God help our Negroes," Clark writes, "with their black cults of devilment, narcotics, murder, violence and emotion. Their neighborhoods are full of a lawlessness that they laugh at. I have only had three as friends and it is a terrible task to bridge the gap across suspicion and bewilderment that separates man's soul in a white skin from man's soul in a black skin."[47] By the 1960s Clark had nothing but ridicule and contempt for the ethnics who felt that their neighborhoods were threatened by racial migration, and, at least until 1962, when he left Philadelphia to work for the CIC in New York, he worked for the CHR to engineer those ethnic, oftentimes, Irish neighborhoods, knowing full well that black neighborhoods were "full of lawlessness" and that integration was another word for creating another black neighborhood.

In August 1955 Clark co-authored a pamphlet on panic in changing neighborhoods, in which he mentions Germantown and West Philadelphia in a slightly different light from the propaganda campaign promoted by the PHA. "Time and again," Clark writes in a pamphlet which, it should be remembered, was supposed to reassure the ethnics and prevent panic, "rashes of 'For Sale' signs have appeared along whole blocks of homes in Germantown or among the rows of West Philadelphia. Within a year, it will be a foregone conclusion that the block will soon be all Negro."[48]

The Catholic Church was the only institution which gave Clark an Archimedean point on racial matters. In the early '50s, in fact, race was just one issue in an intellectual universe dominated by Catholic thought and Catholic thinkers. Largely under the influence of John Mulloy, a St. Joseph's College graduate twelve years Clark's senior who would later go on to become the main promoter of Christopher Dawson's thought in the United States, Clark read Aristotle, Plato, Christopher Dawson, R. H. Tawney's *Religion and the Rise of Capitalism*, as well as the works of Jacques Maritain, and Thomas Merton's *Seven Storey Mountain* during 1949 and discussed them with Mulloy in Mulloy's great-books discussion group. By 1952 Clark's reading had expanded to include "brilliant writers" like "Claudel, Maritain, Cocteau, Graham Greene, Eliot, Auden, Berdyaev, Chesterton, Heinrich Rommen, Sturzo, [and] Karl Adam."[49] Having read Catholic writers like this under the guidance of John Mulloy, Clark felt that he was able to refute people like "Gide, Lasky, Russell, Dewey, Hemingway, Thomas Mann, etc and the philosophical errata that they represent."[50]

Clark also read widely in the Catholic press – including, *the Dublin Review, Thought, Review of Politics, America, Commonweal, The Catholic Mind, Cross Currents, Worship, Integrity, Social Order* – with the same single-mindedness of purpose. Clark felt that these Catholic periodicals had been "of tremendous assistance"[51] because the intellectual battlefield of the early '50s had grown more complicated that it had been during the '30s and '40s when Catholics were contending with communism as the enemy. In the period following the war, the "criticism of Christ's Church has been oblique and disjointed, lacking the sweep and consistency of the Communist ethic. The increase in communications media has dispersed effort and thought, so that instead of facing integrated onslaughts, we face fusillades of piecemeal carping."[52]

Since Clark's intellectual identity was clearly tied to the Catholic Church at this point, his understanding of race was tied to the Catholic understanding of that issue as one among many, in no way central to the Catholic Church's understanding of itself. With time, that would change. On November 17, 1952, Clark noted that his circle of acquaintances was changing. John Mulloy and other Catholic intellectuals in the Dawsonian mode had been replaced by a more activist crowd, by "John McDermott and Mrs. McGarry,"[53] people, in other words, whose primary interest was in racial matters and achieving specific results rather than more contemplative Dawsonian views of history from the Catholic point of view. One week later, Clark, who felt earlier that he tended to dilettantism, now felt convinced "of the need for concentration of effort," and concluded that "housing seems to be the most prominent field."[54]

But even here it is safe to say that he can only conceive of taking on this "apostolate" as a Catholic whose intellectual program is firmly rooted in Catholic principle, something which in late 1952 gave Clark a sense of "precious security"[55] of the sort he found in François Mauriac, who spoke for Clark when she said, "I belong to that race of people who, born in Catholicism, realize in earliest manhood that they will never be able to escape from it, will never be able to leave it or reenter it. They were within it, are within it for ever and ever. They are inundated with light and they know that it is true."[56]

Mauriac's thoughts were touching but, unfortunately, in Clark's case they would prove to be untrue. Clark eventually abandoned the Catholic faith in spite of such an ardent beginning as a Catholic intellectual, and race provided him with the excuse he needed to leave the Church. Once he lost his faith in the Church, largely because of what he perceived as its failure in racial matters, he sank into mutually contradictory nationalisms because there was no place else to go. Clark became an Irish nationalist who also supported black nationalism because by that point in his life the Catholic Church had lost its function as a supranational as well as a supernatural institution. Once that happened, ethnic nationalism was all that was left, but promoting ethnic nationalism in a multi-ethnic society was a contradiction in terms which was, by then, beyond his powers to resolve.

In the early '50s Clark was determined to become an intellectual who would make a difference in the lives of people in Philadelphia, beginning with his fellow Catholics. He attempted to form a credit union at his parish, with minimal success in overcoming the "initial coolness"[57] of his fellow parishioners. At this point in his life, Clark felt that the key to these social endeavors lay in a deeper understanding of Catholic thought, but he felt oftentimes inadequate, "bogged down," in his "work on a Catholic view of urban and community planning problems" because of "want of more cogent thought and further reading."[58]

Clark was drawn to urban planning because the forces which promoted it in Philadelphia had just taken over that city's government, because it was in vogue when Clark came of age as a young intellectual activist, but also because as a Catholic, Clark recognized that "American Catholics are deeply involved in the complex urban areas of our country"[59] and that as a result of the "strong networks of parish structure submerged and functioning in the mainstream of American life,"[60] Catholics were bound to be affected by any drastic change in the urban environment. In an article, one of his first, which appeared in *Social Order* the same month he got married, Clark tried to assess urban renewal from a Catholic perspective, aware that "the contrasting emphasis of Catholicism" is the antithesis "of liberal secularism."[61] That means that "the distractions and depersonalization of modern life must be conquered from within the soul."[62] It means that Catholics versed in papal encyclicals understand the "social disorganization emanating from the mythical and absurdly ubiquitous 'laws' of supply and demand."[63] It means that "Catholics should readily welcome rational undertakings free of the capricious irregularities fostered by a false and happily waning individualism,"[64] even if individualism was far from on the wane. It means that "refined materialism and moral decay" were the source of the problem. It means, conversely,

> that nothing can be gained without holiness. All the organizational ingenuity and intellectual effort in this world cannot prosper without the beneficence of grace. The whole papal program is predicated upon an intense moral struggle with terrible intimacy within the hearts of individual men. To proceed toward reconstruction means initially to proceed no further than one's own personal conscience. Only after a sufficient climate of selflessness, dedication and exalted purpose has been created within the individual can social charity be fittingly exercised. This is the sine qua non of Christian action.[65]

It means that in any honest attempt at urban planning the Catholics "who built the functionally integrated and aesthetically wholesome cities of the Middle Ages may yet have their counterpart among the faithful of the future who will master the new environment with the tools of the spirit."[66]

But even granting all of this, an air of unreality pervades Clark's article. He seems unwilling to become "Irish" enough to descend from those undeniably true and noble Catholic principles to the fact that urban renewal in Philadelphia had the cast of ethnic struggle about it. "Parishes entangled in the confusions of our cities," he says at one point, adverting to the conflicts urban renewal were causing, "may occasionally evidence reluctance it the face of demolitions or relocations, but a wider cooperative attitude is definitely in existence."[67] Clark never gets around to telling us where this wider cooperative attitude existed in reality. It certainly didn't exist in the neighborhoods of Philadelphia or Chicago, where the Catholics considered themselves under a state of siege at the hands of urban planners who seemed determined to drive them out of the neighborhood.

Clark was many things at this point in his life – he was Catholic, he was Irish, he was an intellectual, and he was an activist – but he was never one thing, and all of the disparate elements that made up his cultural life remained in suspension alongside each other without ever bonding into one coherent world-view. As he grew older he became more Irish and less Catholic, but he never became Irish enough to see the situation in Philadelphia from their ethnic point of view. His Irish studies deal invariably with some part of Irishry distant from his current situation, either in time, dealing with the Irish in Philadelphia in the 19th but not the 20th century, or in place, dealing with contemporary problems in the '70s and '80s in Ireland but not in Philadelphia. If he had sat down in a moment of honest self-assessment and said this is what I am, what should I do? he might have been able to unify the various facets of his personality, but no matter how much he agonized in his diary, Clark had difficulty combining sufficient reflection with full consent of the will.

As a result his Catholicism would lead him in one direction and his ethnicity in another. His ethnicity was submerged for the first twenty years of his adult life by the racial apostolate, which he could never see as just another form of ethnicity. Race, for Clark, and in this he was like most of his generation of Catholic activists, was invariably seen as a moral issue and not an ethnic issue. The blacks were not just one more ethnic group drawn to the city, as the Irish had been, by the political manipulation of economic forces. They had moral claims which trumped the moral claims exerted by other ethnic groups. In racial matters, Clark, as he did in the issue of urban planning, espoused Catholic principles but adopted as their implementation strategy the essentially ethnic views of the Quaker-Episcopalian ruling class in Philadelphia. And he adopted these views for a simple reason, something which becomes apparent from reading his diaries. He adopted the ethnic views of the ruling class in Philadelphia because he worked for them.

"We American Catholics," he wrote in his article in *Social Order*, "are too used to working with molds that are created for us by others according to secular specifications. We must set some practical, realizable specifications of our own, if we are to give evidence of the sincerity and realism of our social objectives."[68]

Clark spent his entire working life working in molds created for him "by others according to secular specifications." In 1953 the first of his six children was born, the others following, except for the last, in quick succession. Clark as a result became obsessed in his diary entries with finding a job. During the summer of 1953, Clark began to get some appreciation of how strong the wind was once he had stepped out of the boat of bachelorhood into the storms of adult life. The Housing Council and ethics discussion groups he founded had been foundering because he hadn't been able to bring out a newsletter, and that chore was made more difficult by the fact that he didn't possess a typewriter. As a result, he was left to ponder "the complexity and tortuous hardness of the liberal mind"[69] pretty much on his own, in his spare time when he got home from his job at the Philadelphia Housing Authority. "I have not been able to change my job," he confides to his diary, shortly before the birth of his daughter, "after seeking one with the National Conference of Christians and Jews and another as Information writer at City Hall."[70] The worrying about a new job was to become a constant refrain in diary entries over the next decade or so. After announcing that he had composed two Gaelic songs for his newborn daughter, and savoring "visions of reclining in my old age while a soft-haired daughter fills the air with shimmering harp concertos by Ravel and Debussy,"[71] he concludes the reverie by returning to economic reality with an abrupt thump: "No new job yet, damn it."[72]

Finding a job meant working for the ADA Reform crowd in Philadelphia, and doing that meant compromising Catholic principles. More importantly it also meant engineering his fellow Catholic ethnics in the interests of the WASP ruling class, something he could never admit to himself. At one point during the time he kept his diary, Clark toyed with the idea of returning to his roots in Kensington as a local politician, an idea which was even more Utopian than "fighting nuclear arms. ecological crimes, Nicaraguan victimization and censorship"[73] because at least no one knew him in Nicaragua, which was not the case in Kensington, where he was well known as an agent of the forces who wanted to integrate the neighborhood. This was not the case in 1953, but in 1953 Kensington was not hiring housing specialists. The only people who were doing that were the people who were interested in engineering the neighborhood in their own interests and not the interests of the natives.

And so faced with the choice, Clark decided to represent the interests of the people who could pay him the salary he wanted. That decision probably more than any other insured that there would be no Catholic version of urban planning in Philadelphia. "Catholics are interested in beneficial planning," Clark wrote in 1952. "We realize our plight."[74] Catholics made up the majority of the neighborhoods in question in Philadelphia at the time and yet they controlled none of the institutions that were determining the fate of those neighborhoods, a fact which necessitated cooperation, but which also raised the question in Clark's mind, "To what extent can we cooperate with our secular neighbors in community planning?"[75] Clark was probably voicing personal concerns here as well, because the question of what contribution he could make to the city of Philadelphia was constrained by religious and ethnic considerations, but it was also one based on all the religious and moral values which Clark had internalized from being raised in the Catholic Church. "The alternative," he concludes, "is to ride along with our continually worsening society, caught in its demoralization and its inhuman attitudes waiting for retribution to fall upon it for its pride and selfishness, as well as its tragic perversion of the talent and ingenuity God has bestowed upon us."[76] The abstract tone of the passage belies the fact that this was precisely the decision which Clark himself faced as a young man who wanted to succeed in a city where upward mobility was defined by people who were involved in ethnic warfare with Clark's people. It was a group which was nothing if not sly and sophisticated and one which brought about the same "perversion of the talent and ingenuity which God had bestowed" on Dennis Clark as well.

Notes

1. Dennis Clark, Diary, 11/19/53, CCRK 1 Diary folder 1948–63 Notre Dame Archives.
2. Ibid.
3. Clark, Diary, 3/7/53.
4. Ibid.
5. Ibid.
6. Clark, Diary, 11/19/53.
7. Ibid.
8. Ibid.
9. Ibid.
10. Letter from Drayton S. Byrant assistant to Executive Director of the Philadelphia Housing Authority (Walter Phillips) to Tom Colgan AFSC, Chicago 1/24/52, AFSC Papers, Box 62, folder 14, UIC Archives.
11. Ibid.
12. "Information on New Migration," The Commission on Human Relations, AFSC Papers, Box 50, folder 1, UIC Archives.
13. "Outline of Procedure for Integration of Existing Housing Projects," AFSC Papers, Box 62, folder 14, UIC Archives.
14. Ibid.
15. Ibid.
16. Ibid.
17. Ibid.

18 Ibid.

19 Ibid.

20 Ibid.

21 Ibid.

22 John Lukacs, *Philadelphia: Patricians and Philistines, 1900–1950* (New York: Farrar, Straus, Giroux, 1980), p. 311.

23 Ibid.

24 Ibid.

25 Joseph Sill Clark Inaugural Address Jan 1952, 1/52, Box 16, Walter M. Phillips Papers, Temple University Urban Archives.

26 Ibid.

27 Commission on Human Relations, Fair Employment Practices Commission.

28 Joseph Sill Clark Inaugural Address Jan 1952, 1/52, Box 16, Walter M. Phillips Papers, Temple University Urban Archives.

29 Interview with Edmund Bacon, 5/15/00.

30 Report of the Philadelphia Housing Authority, July 1, 1950 to June 30, 1952, Philadelphia Housing Authority Papers, City of Philadelphia Archives.

31 Ibid.

32 Letter Walter E. Alesandroni to Robert J. Callaghan, Commission on Human Relations, 8/14/52, Box 30, Racial Questions, 1950-2, Walter M. Phillips Papers, Temple University Urban Archives.

33 Ibid.

34 John F. Bauman, *Public Housing, Race, and Renewal: Urban Planning in Philadelhpia, 1920–1974* (Philadelphia: Temple University Press, 1987), p. 129.

35 Ibid.

36 Clark, Diary, 8/7/52.

37 Clark, Diary, 3/26/84.

38 Clark, Diary, 2/12/54.

39 Clark, Diary, 12/24/85.

40 Clark, Diary, 1/5/52.

41 Ibid.

42 Ibid.

43 Clark, Diary, 12/19/51.

44 Ibid.

45 Ibid.

46 Clark, Diary, 8/28/52.

47 Clark, Diary, 11/19/53.

48 John McDermott and Dennis Clark, "Helping the Panicked Neighborhood," reprinted from *Interracial Review* (August 1955): 2.

49 Clark, Diary, 11/3/52.

50 Ibid.

51 Ibid.

52 Ibid.

53 Clark, Diary, 11/17/52.

54 Clark, Diary, 11/25/52.

55 Clark, Diary, 11/30/52.

56 Ibid.

57 Clark, Diary, 11/30/51.

58 Ibid.

59 J. Dennis Clark, "Human Community Planning," *Social Order* (September 1952): 311.

60 Ibid.

61 Ibid., p. 312.

62 Ibid.

63 Ibid., p. 311.

64 Ibid.

65 Ibid., p. 312.

66 Ibid., p. 314.

67 Ibid.

68 Ibid., p. 316.

69 Clark, Diary, 5/9/53.

70 Clark, Diary, 8/1/53.

71 Clark, Diary, 9/20/53.

72 Ibid.

73 Clark, Diary, 12/24/85.

74 Clark, "Planning," p. 314.

75 Ibid., p. 316.

76 Ibid.

Coleman Young Testifies before HUAC

In 1952 a young community activist from Detroit by the name of Coleman Young was called to Washington to testify before the House Committee on Un-American Activities. Far from being intimidated by the attempt to portray him as a Communist infiltrator, Young made use of the occasion to lecture his interrogators on the proper pronunciation of the word, "Negro." Not one to hide his light under a bushel, Young had recordings made of his testimony and then had them circulated among the black community in Detroit, making himself a minor celebrity in the process. Young would later parlay his local fame into a political career that traveled the same trajectory his own life had when Young's family had moved from Alabama to Detroit as part of the great northern migration created by the personnel needs of the war. His father was a tailor who established his shop in Black Bottom, Detroit's historic black ghetto.

One of the first lessons Young learned as a child was that his residence was a function of the forces which orchestrated population movements for political purposes. Shortly after the Young family settled into Detroit, they were forced to uproot once again, this time with 3,000 other black families, because the city fathers had decided to renew the downtown area by building Gratiot (later Lafayette) Park, the modernist residential enclave (designed by Mies van der Rohe) that, like Society Hill in Philadelphia, was to house the city's administrative elite. Those parts of the neighborhood which did not get destroyed by Lafayette Park were destroyed by the large gash through the city known as I-75. Young would enter political life in 1959 by capitalizing on black resentment at the dislocation caused by the highway and urban-renewal projects that would ultimately slice and dice that city into a series of incoherent fragments. Because of urban renewal and the highway building that went with it, Young and his demographic cohort of uprooted southern sharecroppers and their descendants would be thrown into a path that would take them northwest along streets like Chene and Joseph Campo in a line of march that would put them into direct ethnic conflict with Detroit's Polish population, the one ethnic group which was least disposed to fold its tents and fade away into assimilation in the suburbs.

Young himself was raised a Catholic, but abandoned the faith of his youth, he claimed, when he could not attend the Catholic high school of his choice because of racial discrimination. Whether that was the real reason he abandoned the Catholic faith or not is beside the point. Young was nothing if not politically astute and being politically astute he realized that being a Catholic black was an anomaly which had no political future in a place like Detroit, a place where the overwhelmingly Protestant black population was pitted in a struggle for *Lebensraum* with the overwhelmingly Catholic ethnic population in a game whose rules were written by the local WASP establishment, which in this instance meant the automobile industry.

As similar projects were now doing in Chicago, I-75 and the Lafayette Park development sent waves of angry displaced blacks washing over the adjacent ethnic neighborhoods with all of the social conflict that brought with it. Both I-75 and Lafayette Park were part of Detroit's Master Plan, and The Master Plan was another creation of the Warren Court and the febrile brain of William O. Douglas. The Master Plan was something akin to "redeeming social value," another concept of the Warren Court, which in this instance spawned a whole generation of pornographic films on the model of *I Am Curious: Yellow*, a Swedish import which interspersed soft-core porn with redeeming, socially valuable footage of Martin Luther King.

The idea of the Master Plan as a justification for the unprecedented expansion of state power was first codified in *Berman v. Parker*, a landmark Supreme Court decision in the erosion of property rights in the United States. In 1950 the Planning Commission of the District of Columbia, after years of preparation, finally published a comprehensive plan for renewal of what it termed the blighted areas of Washington, D.C. As it would in large cities across the northeastern and midwestern section of the United States, this plan entailed the demolition of large sections of the city. One of these sections, known as Area B, contained a building located at 712 Fourth Street, SW. This building, owned by a certain Max R. Morris, who eventually died before the plan would get put into effect, was not a residential property; it was not slum housing, and no one on the planning commission was maintaining that it was in any way run down and deserving because of its condition to be torn down. Max Morris's building housed a department store, and the executors for his estate, Samuel Berman (whose name would be appended to the case contesting the ruling) and Solomon H. Feldman, felt that the renewed residential area which was scheduled to arise from the ashes of blight could be served by this department store as well. Berman and Feldman contended further that since the agency which was to build the new housing project was a private agency and that the land was to be developed for private not public use, that the condemnation of their building meant that their property was taken contrary to two mandates of the Fifth Amendment: (1) "no person shall . . . be deprived of . . . property without due process of law" and (2) "nor shall private property be taken for public use, without just compensation."

The case, ultimately known as *Berman v. Parker*, was argued on October 19, 1954 and decided on November 24, 1954, with Justice William O. Douglas writing the majority opinion for the court, which came down on the side of the Washington, D.C. Planning Commission and against the claims of Messrs. Berman and Feldman. Douglas felt that this unprecedented expansion of the idea of eminent domain was justified because, in his words,

> Miserable and disreputable housing conditions may do more than spread disease and crime and immorality. They may also suffocate the spirit by reducing the people who live there to the status of cattle. They may indeed make living an almost insufferable burden. They may also be an ugly sore, a blight on the community which robs it of charm, which makes it a place from which men turn. The misery of housing may despoil a community as an open sewer may ruin a river.[1]

Of course, Mr. Morris's building was neither a house nor was it run down. The plaintiffs, Douglas continues, "maintain that since their building does not imperil health or safety nor contribute to the making of a slum or a blighted area, it cannot be swept into a redevelopment plan by the mere dictum of the Planning Commission or the use commission."[2] Douglas dismisses these inconvenient facts by essentially saying that the people on the board of the planning commission were "experts," and that

> The experts concluded that if the community were to be healthy, if it were not to revert again to a blighted or slum area, as though possessed of a congenital disease, the area must be planned as a whole. It was not enough, they believed, to remove existing buildings that were unsanitary or unsightly. It was important to redesign the whole area so as to eliminate the conditions that cause slums – the overcrowding of dwellings, the lack of parks, the lack of adequate streets and alleys, the absence of recreational areas, the lack of light and air, the presence of outmoded street patterns. It was believed that the piecemeal approach, the removal of individual structures that were offensive, would only be a palliative. The entire area needed redesigning so that a balanced integrated plan could be developed for the region, including not only new homes but also schools churches parks streets and shopping centers. In this way it was hoped that the cycle of decay of the area could be controlled and the birth of future slums prevented.[3]

Planning had a special meaning for the housing professionals at the time. Planning meant the repudiation of the *laissez-faire* policies which the New Dealers considered the cause of the stock market crash of 1929. Planning was the antidote to the topsy-like chaotic growth of cities which had taken place during the period of industrial expansion following the Civil War. It was also, although it didn't seem so at the time, the last attempt of the WASP east coast elite to reassert its control over a country that seemed poised to head in a less-congenial direction under the pressure of ethnic, which is to say, Catholic demographics in the big cities of the northeast and Midwest, cities which were more often than not the beneficiaries of urban renewal and "planning." The East Coast WASP elite had just whipped the Fascists, and now they were going to roll up their sleeves again and renew the cities according to the same principles which, under the guidance of people like former Ford executive Robert McNamara and the Whiz Kids, had won the war. This was a group of people who were ethnically and nominally Protestant but who had long since abandoned faith in Christ as a guide to policy and replaced it with faith in all of the scientific ideologies of the Enlightenment, isms that were enjoying their heyday in the post-war period. Along with Darwinism and Freudianism, there was hygiene and social science, all of the things mentioned obliquely by Douglas in his opinion. Along with the other progressive isms, the WASP ruling class believed in urban planning. The 1947 Better Philadelphia exhibit was a classic example of this fusion of WASP ethnic solidarity based on its ideological understanding of progress, science, and engineering, both physical and social. Bauhaus high-rise apartments for the revitalized administrative elites, who were to staff the government offices and corporations, would rise from the rubble of obsolete 19th century rowhouses, while at the same time wide high-speed roads leading to the suburbs would whisk them to the new shopping malls and bring their suburban-dwelling counterparts back to the center of town for cultural events like concerts and plays. As justification for the death of the rowhouse, which symbolized "everything that was wrong with Philadelphia," the urban-planning fraternity emphasized hygiene and public health concerns, which necessitated "planning," which meant that a Master Plan for the entire city would have to take precedence over the property rights of the individuals who were unfortunate enough to own property in places like Area B.

In handing down *Berman v. Parker*, William O. Douglas, who was appointed to the court by Franklin Delano Roosevelt in his attempt to pack the court with New Deal sympathizers, was simply giving expression to the philosophical and ideological terms which lay at the heart of the political struggle the New Deal had been waging with the Republican Isolationist wing of that same ethnic group. In addition to being the antithesis of *laissez-faire* economics, "planning" was a code word for the antithesis of limited government as well. The WASP ruling class had just undergone a civil war. That civil war was fought during the '30s over the United States' entry into the war in Europe, and it ended when the Japanese attacked Pearl Harbor on December 7, 1941. With that blow, America First was defeated. But the entry into War meant that everything associated with America First was defeated as well. Pearl Harbor signaled as well the defeat of racial theory. It signaled the defeat of isolationism based on the idea that America was a predominantly white, Protestant country, which, the nativists argued, had no business getting involved in foreign wars.

The battle over nature v. nurture had been a long-standing fight. In the '20s Margaret Mead cooked the books in favor of nurture in her hymn to blue-lagoon anthropology by writing *Coming of Age in Samoa*. If teenagers were raised in a laid-back culture with loose sexual morals, there was no *Sturm und Drang* associated with puberty, at least according to Mead's reading of Samoan society. Morals caused sexual hang-ups. That was the bad news. But the good news was that morals were a function of culture, which is to say, environment, and now the internationalists were convinced that culture could be engineered to come up with results that would make everyone happy.

Following Pearl Harbor, the nurture people were in the saddle. Under the new regime, racial characteristics had no consequences in terms of behavior. That along with nationalism was Hitler's view. The new regime in the United States would now pursue a course which was of necessity the opposite of that point of view, a course that was both internationalist in terms of foreign policy and behaviorist/environmentalist in the domestic sphere. Following Pearl Harbor, there was no such thing as human nature anymore. Now there was only man and his environment. And the people who ruled the country in the aftermath of Pearl Harbor were convinced that he who controlled the environment controlled the man, an idea which finds expression in *Berman v. Parker*.

To give some idea of the opposite point of view in terms of housing policy, Mayor Robert E. Lamberton, a representative of the pre-New Deal, Republican old guard in Philadelphia, caused a stir in 1940 when he turned down $19 million in federal, which is to say, New Deal money. On May 13, 1940, after a conference between members of the Philadelphia Housing Authority, officials of the USHA, and city officials, Mayor Lamberton issued a statement in which he announced his opposition to an extension of the public-housing program until the three projects under construction had been completed and occupied for a space of time. Lamberton not only viewed public housing as a social experiment which needed to be evaluated before the city should sink more money into it, he also held radically pre-New Deal, anti-environmentalist views on why slums existed in the first place. "Slum areas," according to Lamberton, "exist because some people are so utterly shiftless that any place where they live becomes a slum, and others are so poor that they cannot afford to live anywhere else." Lamberton's diagnosis of the housing situation was an embarrassing throwback to an outdated era, at least from the New Dealers' point of view. It was based to a large extent on the Protestant Ethic notion that prosperity was a reward for virtue and poverty a punishment for vice. But there was something less crude and, as a result, more intolerable to the progressives behind that notion as well. Lamberton was claiming in his politician way that morality had something to do with the state of housing stock, an intolerable affront to a group of people who felt that technology and hygiene had superseded moral considerations, and whose notion of housing was thoroughly materialistic. Houses were, to use Walter Gropius's term, *Wohnmaschinen*, and the moral state of its inhabitants had nothing to do with the physical condition of their dwellings. In fact, judging from Justice Douglas's effusions, the exact opposite was true. Unlike Mayor Lamberton, William O. Douglas held that morality was a function of housing. It was impossible to be a moral person in a rundown house. By tearing down blighted housing as specified in the "master plan" of the various federally mandated housing authorities, the government was promoting moral behavior.

On June 20, 1940, thousands of building-trades workers and supporters of public housing demonstrated at Philadelphia's city hal. But city council, in spite of the pressure, rejected, by a vote of 12 to 10, a resolution approving the selection of new sites for additional housing projects, thereby forfeiting $19 million in federal money when the USHA withdrew funds earmarked for Philadelphia on July 1 and redistributed them to other, more-amenable housing authorities across the country. Mayor Lamberton died in office shortly after giving his theory about the connection between slum areas and shiftlessness. The Republican nativists continued for another decade but were swept from office by Democrats in 1951 who were avid for New Deal money for the cities, and in particular for the housing money which started to pour out of Washington in earnest in 1947, creating *Berman v. Parker* as its test case.

In his book *The Tempting of America*, Robert Bork sees the activist Warren court in the period immediately following the war as an agent of social change. In the case of housing this was not true. The agents of change had already been active for at least thirteen years before the *Berman* decision. All the court, in this instance in the person of William O. Douglas, did was ratify the designs of the regime which had taken power when its domestic enemies were defeated in 1941. If this regime had any faith at all, it had, to use Bauhaus émigré and Harvard professor Walter Gropius's phrase, "Faith in Planning." And it was this reliance on "planning," i.e., the ideas of experts, which William O. Douglas ratified in *Berman v. Parker*. In doing this, the Court expanded the concept of eminent domain to its present state, a state one would have to characterize as infinite elasticity. The fact that Mr. Morris's building was in good repair and in no way deserving to be torn down was in fact no match for "The Master Plan," which had been drawn up by experts completely outside of the political process. "Property," Douglas writes,

> may of course be taken for this redevelopment which, standing by itself, is innocuous and unoffending. But we have said enough to indicate that it is the need of the area as a whole which congress and its agencies are evaluating. If owner after

owner were permitted to resist these development programs on the ground that this particular property was not being used against public interest, integrated plans for redevelopment would suffer greatly.[4]

The Berman case is significant because it concerned property destined for demolition in Washington D.C., which is anomalous as far as American cites go. Unlike every other city in the United States, Washington is governed directly by the U.S. Congress, none of whose members were elected to office by people in Washington. In this respect, Washington is a paradigm for the erosion of local government which has characterized all of post-New Deal developments in housing in the United States. The Supreme Court took this anomaly and made a precedent out of it. In the other cities, it was the people's representatives, the city councilmen, who eventually, if not permanently, defeated urban renewal, which was a project dominated by "experts," largely East Coast WASP technocrats with degrees from universities like Harvard and Princeton, which empowered them to rearrange America's oldest cities with their ethnic interests in mind. In Detroit, which abolished local councilmanic representation in favor of an at-large council during the 1920s, the devastation was greater than in cities like Chicago, where the people's representatives did battle with the "experts" and to a large extent defeated them. In cities like Philadelphia, Chicago, Detroit, and Boston, the panels of experts invariably had a definite ethnic cast. They became certified as experts either by going to the already mentioned ethnic universities or by getting appointed to boards like the D.C. Planning Commission, which were often descendants of local ruling class initiatives that began with the city beautiful movement or the settlement-house movement around the time of World War I.

Berman v. Parker was part and parcel of the Warren Court's creation of new, largely sexual, "rights," like the right to privacy as a replacement for traditional rights like the right to be safe from unjust seizure of property. William O. Douglas, the man who denied Mr. Morris the right to own property in face of the powerful individuals who benefited from urban renewal money, was also the man who found a right to privacy for those interested in purchasing pornography (*Roth*, 1957), contraceptives (*Griswold*, 1965), and abortion (*Roe*, 1973). In this trajectory we see the substitution of sexual "rights" for real rights, previously guaranteed by the Fifth Amendment. The government was now in the business of creating new rights based on gratifying its citizens' illicit appetites while at the same time undermining their real right to own property as guaranteed in the Constitution. The new rights, specifically the right of privacy, were in Bork's view "clearly the fruit of judicial activism."[5] According to Bork, "Justice Douglas was unabashedly an activist judge. Responding to a question about the role of precedent, Douglas characteristically replied: 'I once said, to the consternation of a group of lawyers, that I'd rather create a precedent than find one. Because the creation of a precedent in terms of the modern setting means the adjustment of the Constitution to the needs of the time.'"[6] Or the needs of certain powerful groups and individuals. The so-called "needs of the time" would eventually be called upon, as I have demonstrated elsewhere, to justify the erection of a powerful new form of social control.[7]

This same emphasis on the triumph of environment over race found its way into another more famous decision handed down by the same court six months earlier, namely, *Brown v. Board of Education of Topeka, Kansas* (347 US 483), a decision which was first argued on December 9, 1952, then reargued on December 8, 1953, and finally decided on May 1, 1954. The assumptions governing urban renewal are essentially the same as those governing the government's racial policies. In each instance, environment is the key issue; environment determines behavior. Unlike Mayor Lamberton, who felt that shiftless people created rundown houses, the federal government in both *Berman* and *Brown* became officially committed to the proposition that bad environment creates bad people. In order to look out for the public good, in other words, the state must use its police power to engage in social engineering, which by changing the environment would change people's hearts. "Education," Chief Justice Earl Warren wrote in *Brown*,

> is the very foundation of good citizenship. Today it is a principal instrument preparing him for later professional training and in helping him to adjust normally to his environment. In these days, it is doubtful that any child may reasonably be expected to succeed in life if he is denied the opportunity of an education. Such an opportunity, where the state has undertaken to provide it, is a right which must be made available to all on equal terms.[8]

"Today," Warren concluded, "education is perhaps the most important function of state and local governments."

By the time both *Brown* and *Berman* got handed down, which is to say 1954, the people of Detroit, Philadelphia, and Chicago might have come up with another explanation of the primary function of local government because each of these cities had been by that time subjected to at least ten full years of social engineering at the hands of "experts" who were determined to force "integration" through the agency of those three cities' respective housing authorities onto their ethnic neighborhoods. Local government of the sort that was conspicuously absent in the District of Columbia was the only bulwark against the ravages of urban renewal and other federally mandated forms of social engineering during the housing battles of the late '40s and early '50s. In promoting what it termed "integration" in both education and housing, the federal government was engaged in social engineering on a massive scale. It was deeply involved in promoting both racial succession in previously stable communities and the unjust seizure of property. Education was necessary to change the minds of the young, but in order the change education, the regime had to change housing patterns first, since school districts were geographical entities. The confluence of *Berman* and *Brown* would eventually lead to the busing battles of the '70s, but in this instance we get ahead of our story.

Notes

1 *Berman v. Parker* (75 S.Ct. 98).
2 Ibid.
3 Ibid.
4 Ibid.
5 Robert H Bork, *The Tempting of America* (New York: The Free Press, 1990), p. 56.
6 Ibid., p. 73.
7 E. Michael Jones, *Libido Dominandi: Sexual Liberation and Political Control* (South Bend, Ind.: St. Augustine's Press, 2000).
8 *Brown, et al. v. Board of Education of Topeka, et al.* (347 US 483).

Dennis Clark and the
Commission on Human Relations

By the time Dennis Clark's first child was born, the Clark-Dilworth reform regime's hous-ing policies had created an uproar across the entire city by proposing public housing and sites in outlying areas which no one considered blighted. Once the Philadelphia Housing Authority expanded its idea of renewal to include neighborhoods like Northeast Philadelphia, Roxborough, and Southwest Philadelphia, it became clear to the residents of those neighborhoods that the goal in mind was social engineering, not better hygiene or removal of blight. Throughout 1953 the Philadelphia Housing Authority pressured city council for approval of public housing sites in those neighborhoods. "The result," accord-ing to Dennis Clark, "was a furor of resistance that shook City Hall and caused Council to recoil from the effort to extend the renewal process beyond the inner city."[1] Because the Clark-Dilworth administration sided with the WASPs at the Philadelphia Housing Association, the coalition which brought Clark and Dilworth to power began to crack along ethnic lines. The Catholic politicians as well as the locally elected city councilmen began to realize that the Clark-Dilworth administration's housing policies were political suicide, and as a result they began to pull out of the coalition.

At least part of the problem revolved around what Dennis Clark called "ethnic griev-ances,"[2] based on the fact that "the Irish Catholics in the Democratic party were never fully at ease with the Anglo-Protestant and Jewish reformers."[3] But Clark fails to see that the antagonism between the ethnic groups was largely exacerbated by the policies the rul-ing clique had chosen to pursue. The Clark-Dilworth administration came to power hop-ing to bring the federal contracts to Philadelphia which Mayor Lamberton had turned down in 1941. But all of the federal programs involved tearing down someone's house or neighborhood, something that was bound to cause a political backlash. The Schuylkill Expressway, to give just one instance, was a WASP project with the WASP goal of link-ing up center city with the suburbs and thereby solidifying that group's political power over the community. In building it, the WASPs had to destroy large sections of Fairmount Park on the west bank of the Schuylkill River, something which outraged John B. Kelly, the Irish Catholic kingmaker in Philadelphia, who considered himself, because he was a championship rower, the park's protector. The same was true, *a fortiori*, for the Crosstown Expressway, a road which would have displaced thousands of center city residents and cre-ated a moat of traffic separating ethnic South Philadelphia from up-scale Society Hill and center city. The Crosstown Expressway became so controversial in fact that it never got built, largely because a trans-ethnic coalition which included the last remnant of the city's patrician WASP establishment opposed it. The Delaware Expressway started to march through South Philadelphia during the '60s when James Tate was the city's first Catholic mayor, Tate had to listen to the neighborhood's residents in planning the route simply as a matter of political survival.

Before long the highway and urban renewal policies of the Clark-Dilworth years began to take their toll. Jim Finnegan, the key link between the WASP patricians and the Catholic ethnics, resigned to take a job in Harrisburg and was replaced by William Green, who could not play the same role precisely because the reform had sown the seeds of its own destruction by pursuing policies antithetical to Catholic interests. Between 1955 and 1965, government spending in the city rose 81 percent, while individual earnings in the city rose only 37.2 percent, an impressive gain by anyone's reckoning, but nowhere near enough to cover the increased costs of government. In this era, there was only one place to turn for money, and that was to the federal government, whose nationalities policies were destined to make short work of the coalition in Philadelphia.

"The reform," according to Clark, "had never really been conversant with the ethnic constituencies in the electorate."[4] He mentions Richardson Dilworth referring to the Italians of South Philadelphia as "greasers" during a campaign stop there as an example of WASP cluelessness, when in fact the WASP reformers were locked into policies that put them on a collision course with the city's ethnics. Housing policies lay at the heart of that conflict. Clark and Dilworth had come to power to bring federal policies to Philadelphia. They did so because they believed that policies like federally mandated integration were both intellectually sound and morally upright but also because all of those policies brought huge amounts of money into the city. In order to qualify for the money, the city had to destroy certain neighborhoods. Even when those neighborhoods, as they often were, were black, the ethnics suffered the consequences because the displaced blacks then invariably sought housing in their neighborhoods, setting off racial conflict, which the city administration then felt that it had to engineer according to the WASP environmentalist standard, which meant invariably siding with the blacks.

Most commentators talk about urban renewal as an essentially altruistic experiment which ran aground on the shoals of racism. Few see it as a social experiment which contained the seeds of its own political destruction, even when their own evidence points them in that direction. "By the mid-1960s," Clark concludes, "the planning strategists and reformers had done their utmost to confront the most difficult community problems of the inner city through urban renewal, but had to confess that the task was beyond their capacity."[5] Clark again fails to take into account the mendacity of the urban renewers and their penchant for using technical terms as a cover for social engineering and ethnic cleansing. The absence of blight in the neighborhoods targeted for integration by the PHA in 1953 plus the fact that many of the neighborhoods' residents were refugees from racial migration in the city's older sections guaranteed a political reaction that was destined to doom the project. The seeds of this destruction lay within the confines of the program itself, because, as Clark himself concedes, "Slum clearance had promoted antagonistic internal migration, frustrated black hopes and demonstrated massive racist resistance, while actually worsening the plight of the most jeopardized poor and elderly. The increasing loss of jobs to the suburbs and other areas further undercut neighborhood stability as mobile families moved out and poorer families increased."[6] When they realized that they lacked the clout to orchestrate social engineering on a city-wide scale, the reformers withdrew to enclaves like center city and Temple and Penn. "A half generation of planning, rebuilding and controversy," he concludes, "had produced a new city image, a rebuilt center city, but a wide disruption of what was perhaps the greatest single social resource of the city, its working class neighborhoods."[7]

In order to take control of a rapidly deteriorating situation, Joe Clark in January of 1954 appointed William Rafsky to the newly created post of city housing coordinator. Rafsky, who began working for Clark in 1945, came to the Clark-Dilworth ADA reform crowd administration from the Jewish garment unions, which were traditionally liberal and in that respect unlike building and trade unions in Philadelphia such as the roofers' union, which were traditionally Catholic. Like Philip Klutznick in Chicago and Jerome Rappaport in Boston, Rafsky was a member of B'nai B'rith and so probably shared information with other members in similar lines of work, since that was the purpose of the organization. He was the patrician Clark's man of the people, and it was his job to deal with the various housing factions which had grown up in the wake of World War II, nourished by federal money with the prospect of more to come, and mobilize them in opposition to growing ethnic Catholic opposition.

Rafsky's bio reads like most bios. It celebrates a procession of personal triumph and benefit for the city, whose real-estate value increased from $3 billion to $4 billion under his tenure. Under Rafsky's guidance, we also read that "Philadelphia gained fame around the world for its success in modernizing and improving its housing, its industrial pace and its facilities for living."[8] The reality, as one has come to expect, was slightly different. Rafsky's tenure in Philadelphia outlasted the crisis which the Clark-Dilworth administration precipitated by decades. Rafsky had, in effect, a window of two years to bring about what the administration wanted. What they wanted was, however, different from what they got, and the political forces which influenced what they got would affect the city for decades to come.

As in Chicago, the Philadelphia housing establishment was dominated by "liberal environmentalists,"[9] to use Hirsch's term, who were determined to use housing as a form of social engineering for the city. In both Philadelphia and Chicago, that meant scattering public-housing sites across the city, including the all-white neighborhoods that were in the process of forming around the fringe as the result of racial migration into the traditional ethnic neighborhoods of North and West Philadelphia. Philadelphia was even more inclined to do this because of "Philadelphia's Quaker tradition and the strength of its housing reform, planning, and fellowship organizations,"[10] something which Bauman mentions but does not explicate in any detail. That meant, as we have indicated earlier, a commitment to psychological warfare, ethnic cleansing, and war by proxy, as the subtext to all of the usually extolled virtues having to do with tolerance and the Friends' involvement in the abolition movement.

Since Dennis Clark was working for the Philadelphia Housing Authority at the time, he gradually got drawn into those battles. Shortly after Rafsky was appointed housing coordinator for the city, Clark conceded that his two-year collaboration with John McDermott and Anna McGarry "to widen the interest of Catholics in housing affairs" had "met with practically no success."[11] The city, however, was at the same time abuzz with activity which filled Clark with misgivings. One month later, Clark took note of the demolition of the Mercantile Library, a building where he spent many pleasurable hours, to make way for a three-story parking garage. "The clouds of thought," he concluded sadly, "have been replaced by clouds of engine exhaust. Sanitation and progress have won a crude victory."[12]

Clark's ambivalence continued unabated during this period of time, perhaps because he was unable to apply any sophisticated Catholic analysis to what was happening. The closest thing he possessed to a philosophy of applied Catholic thought was the thinking on social justice in racial matters that he was getting from his association with the Catholic Interracial Council, and that was hardly sophisticated. In November of 1954, Clark wrote an article on the racial situation in Philadelphia entitled, "The Anatomy of Anger" for *The Catholic Worker*, in which he claimed that the thing which drove "the thriving energy of this body of anger" was "white skin. The surrounding neighborhood was rather heavily Italian and Irish."[13] Which is to say, Catholic. Clark was unable to take Catholic thought on his own and apply it in some sophisticated fashion to the racial strife in Philadelphia, and so he was left to make sense out of it by the ideas he picked up in CIC circles from people like Ed Marciniak, who arrived in Philadelphia to give a lecture at the Grail Center in southwest Philadelphia, an area plagued at the time by racial migration. Marciniak, who was a member of the CIC in Chicago, tried to put the current crisis in historical perspective. What Clark took from what he termed a "very good evening," and a "stimulating . . . talk on the Catholic Social Movement in this century" was a sense that "the greatest reason for the lack of new leadership is because Catholic leaders, educators etc. have underestimated the power of the environment our young people face when they leave school,"[14] which was, of course, precisely Clark's situation at the time.

Clark, as always, was worried about a job. He had one at the time but wanted a better one. In April of 1954 he got what he wanted – sort of – a job as press director with the Philadelphia Fellowship Commission. Clark was, if not exactly underwhelmed by the prospect, less than enthusiastic. It didn't pay much more than his previous job with the PHA, even if it did provide "a broader field for learning."[15] What it did not do was provide any room to operate as a Catholic, nor did it give him a chance to work with any of the Catholic organizations that he was trying to get off the ground to deal with the issues that were facing the city at the time, a time when the conflict between the Catholic ethnics and the social engineers was heating up to Chicago-like proportions. As in Chicago, something had to give, and, as in Chicago, Walter Phillips lost his job on the Philadelphia Housing Authority, during the same month, July of 1954, that Elizabeth Wood lost her job as head of the housing authority in Chicago.

If Joe Clark thought that personnel changes – bringing Rafsky in and letting Phillips go – were going to solve the city's racial problems, he was wrong, and he was wrong because by the mid-'50s the city had committed itself to a course of action that guaranteed strife. Urban-renewal projects in Philadelphia like the Temple University and North Allen projects, projects which Temple University used to gain control of the racial migration in their neighborhood as the University of Chicago was doing at the same time, displaced thousands of black families, most of whom would not and could not be accommodated by public housing. As a result, these displaced black families poured into the next neighborhood, putting pressure on the Catholic ethnics to fight or flee or, as was usually the case, to do both sequentially.

Ten years after the fact, New York officials announced that 40 percent of the families displaced by urban renewal between 1954 and 1963 moved into another slum area. That figure disguised the fact that contiguity was the rule in racial migration. Black families, feeling beleaguered anyway, sought the support of other black families and did not like being racial pioneers in the suburbs. They preferred to move a block at a time, and that fact coupled with the pressure that urban renewal created by tearing down homes, put pressure on the next demarcation point in the line of racial migration.

In August 1954, one month after Walter Phillips lost his job at the Philadelphia Housing Authority, a black family bought a run-down storefront residence near 22nd and Lehigh, thereby crossing the line of racial demarcation as it then existed in North Philadelphia, and setting off a riot. As in Chicago, the pro-growth coalition of downtown interests that was benefiting from urban-renewal money was also becoming increasingly annoyed at the resistance their policies were creating. As the resistance increased, the City Planning Commission began to turn its attention more to efforts to stabilize the downtown area by coming up with that creation of *Berman v. Parker*, also handed down in 1954, the comprehensive plan. According to Rotella, "The plan [for Philadelphia] envisioned a Center City designed to attract the more cosmopolitan element of the growing service sector's largely white professional workforce, people who would live conveniently near to the office towers in which they worked, the universities in which they taught and the upscale businesses they would own and support."[16] It was, in other words, the same plan as the one foreseen by Detroit and Chicago.

The racial situation was complicated by the fact that beginning in 1955 industry began to pull out of Philadelphia. The city's textile mills, which had sewn the uniforms for union soldiers during the Civil War and contributed significantly to the wealth of the city, began to pull out of Philadelphia and move south because air conditioning made manufacturing there possible but, most importantly, because wages were lower in the South and because the labor force there was not unionized. The same thing was true of Chicago for the same reasons: "Chicago's manufacturing base was starting to move from the city to the suburbs," as well as "to the South and West of the nation (and to other parts of the world), where operation costs were lower and labor more easily managed."[17] Between 1955, when the textile mills pulled out of town, and 1975, Philadelphia would lose three out of four of its manufacturing jobs. Those jobs would eventually migrate from the southern United States to sweatshops in Central America and Asia, driving down wages and fueling discontent with globalization at the turn of the century. That movement began in earnest in the '50s, when industry pulled out of unionized northern industrial cities as a way of bringing the ethnic workforce's demand for higher wages under control. Deindustrialization along with integration of housing as well as the creation of the suburbs were all parts of the same strategy which in Mollenkopf's words, "dismantled the mosaic of blue collar ethnic segmentation which developed within the occupational and residential order of the older industrial cities."[18]

By the mid-'50s, Philadelphia's blue-collar ethnics were competing with blacks for an ever-decreasing pool of jobs as well as, thanks to urban renewal, an ever-decreasing pool of affordable housing. The dislocations caused by urban renewal threw wave upon wave of black migrants into ethnic neighborhoods already beleaguered by financial insecurity and pressures that encouraged whites to move out of the neighborhood into other residential settings more congenial to control.

In 1950 the Philadelphia Housing Authority, along with the Philadelphia Housing Association and the Citizens' Committee on City Planning pooled their resources and created the Joint Committee on Site Selection to choose sites for public-housing projects in the city. The JCSS board was made up of "architect-planners such as Oscar Stonorov, Ray Lawson, John Grisdale, Henry S. Churchill, and prominent downtown lawyer-businessmen such as John Bodine and William Ludlow. Dorothy Montgomery and Elfriede Hoeber represented the PHAssoc; Robert Mitchell spoke for city planning. Frank O. Walther of Philadelphia's prominent Girard Trust Corn Exchange Bank chaired the body," and as was to be expected of such a body, their "site selection policy in 1954 reflected an enduring environmentalist passion for social engineering."[19] As such it was on a collision course with the feeling in Philadelphia's blue-collar Catholic ethnic neighborhoods.

Dennis Clark, as usual, found himself in the middle of that conflict. One year after taking a job with the Fellowship Commission, Clark was still working with the Catholics in his spare time. In March of 1955, he and his wife and John McDermott talked to students at LaSalle College and their prospective wives about "family budget problems." This, in turn, was part of his "idea of an urban community experiment that John and Josie and I feel is necessary for our personal development apostolate, family life, friendship, group, parish work and neighborhood."[20] Clark understood his organization as different from the contemporaneous Catholic Family Movement, which was rural in its orientation, and hoped that he and his new organization could "bring vitality to the great mediocre parishes that sprawl beyond the city's slum core" because "this is where most of our Catholics are and will remain for some time."[21] At present, "they continue to be estranged, individualistic, hearing masses in dumb show fashion, seldom hearing an epistle read at all, working out their problems without strength of association and religious direction."[22]

At the same time that Clark was trying to get his apostolate for urban Catholics off the ground in his spare time, he was becoming disenchanted with his job, wondering whether it was either right or prudent to cooperate with non-Catholics in civic work, "but especially in my own work at the Fellowship Commission."[23] Clark never gets around to saying just why collaboration with non-Catholics suddenly seems no longer possible, at least not in any detail. He does mention that the "areas of activity" which his colleagues at the Fellowship Commission are promoting are "unacceptable even repugnant," even though "they profess bland cooperative motives on limited issues, like race relations."[24]

Clark provides some clues to his disenchantment with the Fellowship Commission in an article he co-authored with John McDermott around that time, one that was published in August of 1955 in the Catholic Interracial Council's *Interracial Review*, and was later published in pamphlet form under the title, "Helping the Panicked Neighborhood." In it, Clark, drawing on his experience at the PHA and the Fellowship Commission, says that the city, after recognizing that it had "a definite stake in the 'changing neighborhood' situation" because "rapid population turnover disrupts organization patterns and institutions and undermines community stability," turned to the Commission on Human Relations, which, in turn, "worked out . . . bit by bit an experimental approach to the problem."[25] Recognizing that "sudden and rapid flights of white neighborhoods are easily brought about," the Fellowship Commission and the Commission on Human Relations developed "an informal 'warning system'" so that "the agencies can know of Negro move-ins, often before they occur, thus gaining time in which to work against panic."[26] Clark and McDermott go on to say that the FC and CHR often talk to the neighbors of move-ins to help them "examine their position and, in effect, examine their conscience and the attitudes they have adopted."[27] They also assure them that "Negroes are moving into many areas," because "this helps to break down objections that one locale is being victimized or 'worked over.'"[28] The FC and CHR agents, which by now should be understood as Clark and McDermott, then go on to mention "good well-cared-for interracial neighborhoods" as well as "facts and figures . . . that disprove the property loss theory,"[29] facts and figures the Quakers got from Louis Wirth's study, after it had been disseminated by a grant from the Ford Foundation. "Fortunately," the authors tell us, "Philadelphia has enough areas integrated on a stable and healthy basis to provide good illustrations of successful democratic living with steady property values."[30] Just what those areas are, Clark and McDermott never get around to telling us. Evidently Germantown and West Philadelphia were not included in those areas because the same pamphlet confides that "within a year, it will be a foregone conclusion that the blocks [in those areas] will soon be all Negro."[31]

If we combine Clark's privately expressed misgivings over the activities of the Fellowship Commission and the CHR along with his publicly expressed explanation of what those organizations claimed to be doing, a different picture emerges. The FC and the CHR, according to his account, knew about move-ins in advance. Their agents could enter the neighborhood at precisely that moment to help engineer the consent of reluctant neighbors by having them "examine their conscience." They could also assure them that "Negroes are moving into many areas," something which they also presumably knew about in advance. The FC and the CHR, in other words, were not so much working to defuse panic as they were working to move black families into ethnic neighborhoods and then to engineer the consent of those affected in favor of the move-ins. This is probably what Clark means when, in his diary, he refers to FC involvement in "areas of activity" which are "unacceptable even repugnant." The fact that he never gets more specific is an indication that he can't face the specifics of what he is involved in himself, not even in the privacy of his own diary. Clark, in other words, can't admit that he is being paid to engage in the social engineering of his own people by secular liberals like Drayton Bryant, who may be, for all he knows, Communists as well.

Clark never resolved this issue intellectually. As it would throughout his life, the course of events resolved it for him. At the end of May 1955, Clark received an eviction notice. He was living with his young family in Southwest Philadelphia at the time in St. Francis de Sales Parish and therefore near the Grail Center, which brought in speakers like Ed Marciniak. "As a housing specialist," he writes in his diary on June 2, 1955, "this is amusing to me."[32] Two weeks later he made settlement on a house at 618 W. Sedgewick Street in the city's Germantown section. The move was significant for a number of reasons. First of all, Clark moved from a Catholic to a Quaker neighborhood and as a result from the working class to the middle class. Once he settled into his new house, Clark took stock of his life at the age of twenty eight. He took cognizance of the changing sexual mores. Kinsey's second book had appeared and in its wake *Playboy*, and Clark noticed a change in Philadelphia's streets, which are "glutted with temptation,"[33] causing Clark to "think that the challenge to purity is probably not greater than the challenge to patience, temperance, fortitude, understanding, charity, etc, But we feel the attack on purity physically. It registers sensibly, for every corner news stand is now a moral ambush."[34] Beyond that, the move to Germantown meant that Clark was no longer a working class ethnic. His new neighborhood "is a precinct of comfort and presents the danger that the children will grow up with that blight of the middle class, the limitation of knowing only the middle class."[35] That means that Clark was having misgivings about sending his children to "the big, mediocre diocesan high schools," where they would be "buffeted by the crowded gangs, easily alert to evade responsibility and really fruitful study" and subjected to "ordinary teachers in a place where rudeness rules the aggravated classes of recalcitrant insolent minors."[36] Moving to a Quaker neighborhood would influence his family's religious development over time by determining where the next generation of the Clark family would go to school.

Secondly, Clark bought the house from Johannes Hoeber, a crucial figure in ADA reform circles in Philadelphia, whose wife, Elfriede, was an equally crucial figure in the housing establishment in the city. For years, Elfriede Hoeber was the editor of *Issues*, the Philadelphia Housing Association newsletter. Clark, because of his connections, was now on the inside of housing issues in Philadelphia.

Four months after Dennis Clark moved to Germantown, the Fellowship Commission's Committee for Democracy in Housing called for an "extensive change in the character of public housing," mainly "smaller developments of a dispersed and non-institutional nature."[37] In October 1955 the PHA/CCCP Joint Policy Committee proclaimed that public housing sites and developments "should maximize their distribution in good neighborhoods consistent with the . . . objectives of sound planning."[38] Fearing that he was being maneuvered into an impossible political situation by the housing establishment, Rafsky tried to create his own site-selection committee in early 1955 to combat the forces of Quaker liberalism on the one hand and the "forces of particularism" in the ethnic neighborhoods in the other. The other major consideration was not to jeopardize federal funding.

Ed Bacon opened another front in this war by proposing urban renewal on a house by house, street-by-street basis. When he made the proposal formally at a meeting of Richardson Dilworth's cabinet, it was Rafsky who vetoed the idea. Bacon felt that the reason for the rejection was personal, but in retrospect it becomes clear that the issue was funding. The government would only fund massive comprehensive plans, because such plans had been annointed by the Supreme Court's *Berman v. Parker* decision as the only thing which justified such a massive violation of property rights hitherto guaranteed by the Constitution. Shorn of its Enlightenment-sanctioned "plan," which promoted hygiene and morals, the urban renewal program looked like a land-grab.

In April of 1956, Rafsky was facing a June deadline for federal funding when he finally unveiled his plans to build 2,850 low rent housing units on twenty-one "scattered sites" located mainly in outlying all-white neighborhoods like Olney, West Oak Lane, Manayunk, Roxborough, Rhawnhurst, Fern Rock, and Germantown. If, as Dennis Clark alleged, Rafsky deliberately held back the announcement of the sites to the last minute to avoid controversy, his strategy failed. The "scattered" nature of the sites convinced the city's ethnics that the PHA public-housing plan was a form of social engineering whose purpose was "to mold society to suit middle-class requirements without considering the economic and cultural preferences of the people being squeezed into the mold."[39] Anyone who said otherwise at the packed PHA meetings on the Parkway was shouted down, and that included Richardson Dilworth, the man who inherited the Reform coalition's internal contradictions when he succeeded Joe Clark (who was now in the U.S. Senate) as mayor. The city's social engineers had badly miscalculated the depth of feeling the city's ethnics harbored against their plans. The site selection indicated that housing policy was no longer driven by hygiene or morals or any of the other justifications that had been used in the past. "Public housing," according to Bauman, "now functioned as a powerful tool for engineering the goal of a better city. . . . Rafsky was obviously attempting to accomplish human relations goals as well as renewal goals in his public housing program."[40]

Once the depth and breadth of the opposition among the ethnic constituency became clear, Irish Democratic politicians abandoned Dilworth and crossed over to the other side of the issue. Sensing a political debacle of seismic proportions, Rafsky turned to those he felt he could count on for support, and Dennis Clark was one of those people. A little over a month before the site selection criteria were announced, Clark spoke to a community group on racially changing neighborhoods. What he encountered then did not bode well for the city's plans to engineer its neighborhoods. Clark found himself confronted by "Silence. Stonecold silence. The people were just intensely and silently aggravated by the movement of Negroes through the city. As I left I knew that they despised me because they believe I am 'against them.'"[41] Undeterred by his reception, Clark, at Rafsky's request, lobbied Philadelphia's priests for their support. In the end that didn't help either.

By the end of the summer of 1956, public outrage had only increased, and Rafsky was forced to capitulate, "cowed by the intensity of the opposition."[42] Both the PHA and the Fellowship Commission pronounced the site-selection debacle "a defeat for citywide human relations and for racial integration," which caused "a critical reevaluation"[43] of Philadelphia's plan to use public housing to engineer racial integration. That re-evaluation followed pretty much the same lines in Philadelphia that it took in Chicago, when people like Louis Dinnocenzo forced the resignation of Elizabeth Wood, and the city's aldermen took control of redevelopment and the site selection for public housing in the wake of her departure. In both instances, in order to safeguard the money flowing in from Washington and to placate the newly enraged ethnic interests, both cities' respective housing authorities embarked on a program of concentrating black settlement in high-rise buildings in already black areas. Rafsky's capitulation to political realities enraged Dorothy Montgomery at the Philadelphia Housing Association, who complained that Rafsky "makes policy for all the public agencies and the mayor listens to no one else."[44] However, the setback on housing sites did not end attempts to integrate the city's neighborhoods. And in this respect Dennis Clark's efforts were not in vain, certainly not as far as his career in Philadelphia housing circles was concerned.

Philadelphia, 1955, black indifference to integration

By the end of 1955, Clark, who was expecting the birth of another child in April of 1956, was once again praying that "all the saints will help me to get a better job."[45] Either the saints were impressed with the fervor of his prayer or the housing establishment was impressed with his work lobbying the city's priests in favor of Rafsky's scattered-site housing plans. Either way in early 1957, Dennis Clark finally landed another job, this time with the Commission on Human Relations, something he characterizes as "a definite improvement in working conditions."[46] On June 17, 1958, Clark was promoted to the position of supervisor, thereby earning $7,200 per annum, a sum which prompts him to exclaim, "Deo Gratias!"[47]

Clark was still a devout Catholic. In fact, five and a half months after taking the job at the CHR, he called "the new fasting regulations [which] now make it possible for me to attend Mass and receive Communion on lunch hour" a " great blessing,"[48] indicating that he attended Mass at that time with some frequency. Clark's financial good fortune, however, did not change his position as a man whose job put him on the fault lines of ethnic conflict in the city of Philadelphia. Nor did the defeat of Rafsky's site-selection plan change the housing establishment's determination to integrate the city's ethnic neighborhoods, even if it did cause Ed Bacon and newly appointed PHA head Albert M. Greenfield to turn their attention to renewing Society Hill and center city in lieu of getting their noses bloodied in one more bruising contract with the city's Catholics. Chastened by the opposition their plan aroused in 1956, the PHA quietly abandoned any attempt to locate public housing in white neighborhoods. However, that did not change the fact that the engine of racial migration was still in place, changing white neighborhoods to black neighborhoods in the same inexorable fashion.

As before, the city's blacks showed no interest in integrated neighborhoods and made no bones about saying just that to the white do-gooders who showed up at their gatherings. On March 29, 1958, Thelma W. Babbitt of the American Friends Service Committee attended an NAACP regional conference, and as was the AFSC custom wrote a report on her experiences which she shared with other concerned Quakers. Babbitt was "one of the very few white people who were in attendance at the conference,"[49] and perhaps, because of that fact, "was asked to lead the discussion on Housing."[50] What she heard shocked her liberal sensibilities, because for "the first time in a gathering such as this, I sense a very definite over-all belligerence that I've never seen before. . . . Reactions were very strong and evidenced by such questions as '. . . do they think they can get rid of us from the cities now that we have voting power. It's their fault. They left the city to us and now we're going to stay.'"[51] It turns out that terms like "discrimination" and "integration" meant different things to Quakers than they did to members of the NAACP. The latter, according to Babbitt, "claim they want 'no discrimination.' If this means all Negro, okay, but what they're interested in is a free choice in housing and no questions asked. They also want better schools but not necessarily integrated ones."[52] Once again Quakers were confronted with the fact that an "integrated neighborhood" was an oxymoron of their own making, and once again they chose to ignore what they learned. Or the perceptive observer is forced to other conclusions, namely, that the Quakers pursued policies which they claimed fostered integration knowing full well that what they really fostered was blacks taking over ethnic neighborhoods.

Dismayed by their defeat at the hands of the city's Catholic ethnics, the Quakers formed Friends Suburban Housing in 1957 as a way of integrating the suburbs. What happened in the city was still under the purview of the CHR, which pursued the same course of action Clark described in his pamphlet on panic in the neighborhoods, this time with Clark himself on the front lines. Clark's job was, in short, to go into neighborhoods like Kensington, where he had grown up, and persuade the largely Irish Catholic residents not to throw stones at the windows of the house where the black family had just moved in. Working for an essentially Quaker-inspired organization, his job was to integrate neighborhoods with a minimum of violence. Since there was no such thing as an integrated neighborhood in Philadelphia in 1960, this meant that Clark's job was to persuade the Irish to participate in the destruction of their own ethnic neighborhood. It is not clear that Clark ever saw his work in this light, but his involvement with the Commission on Human Relations ended in the early '60s when he went to New York to become head of Fr. LaFarge's racial council. When that venture failed less than a year after he took the job, Clark returned to Philadelphia but was no longer active in racial matters. What took their place was an interest in Irish ethnicity, but one well removed from the struggle over ethnic neighborhoods in Philadelphia in both time – he concentrated on Irish history in Philadelphia in the 19th century – and place – his political concerns focused on the struggles of the IRA in Ireland, especially in the wake of the Bloody Sunday massacre in Belfast in 1969.

Some indication of his standing in the Irish neighborhoods can be gleaned from a report of Clark's involvement with a move-in at 3115 C Street in late September 1960. When Clark and CHR member Groth tried to attend a meeting of the local residents led by Gerald Dougherty, he was "informed of the fact" in the words of the report, "that they were not welcome at the meeting."[53] Barred from the meeting, Clark then arranged to have police spies attend in his stead. The commission had informed the Juvenile Aid Division of the meeting and had agreed that plain clothes detectives would attend. By 8:00 P.M. of the following Monday, September 26, a crowd of 300 to 500 people had gathered outside 3115 C Street in spite of the fact that Ernest J. Harris had decided not to move into the building. Harris had contacted the CHR earlier that day and told Groth and Clark that "the burden on his family would be too great if he moved in,"[54] which caused Mr. Groth of the CHR to complain that Harris's decision would cause the CHR difficulties "because the community would feel that it had gained a 'victory.'"[55] In the heat of an incident like this, it is easy to lose sight of the big picture, but one is tempted nonetheless to ask just what Groth meant when he termed Harris's decision not to move into the neighborhood a victory for the Irish. Apparently Clark and the CHR were more concerned with intimidating the Irish who lived in the neighborhood than with the welfare of the black family they wanted moved in.

Eventually Clark persuaded the local Catholic priest to address and help disperse the mob, but Clark had to leave this predominantly Irish neighborhood under police escort. The CHR report gives some indication of how the Irish neighborhood felt about Clark's ministrations. "Commission representatives," the report concludes, "were escorted from the area in police cars because the police felt it would be dangerous for them in the area since they were known and identified as workers for the commission."[56]

Notes

1   Dennis J. Clark, The Urban Ordeal: Reform and Politics in Philadelphia 1947–1967, p. 29, Clark papers, Notre Dame Archives.

2   Clark, Ordeal, p. 30.

3   Ibid.

4   Ibid.

5   Ibid., p. 29.

6   Ibid.

7   Ibid.

8   William Rafsky, Temple University Urban Archives, Acc. 355, Box 1, File 1-1.

9   Hirsch, p. 173.

10 John F. Bauman, *Public Housing, Race, adn Renewal: Urban Planning in Philadelphia, 1920–1974* (Philadelphia: Temple University Press, 1987), p. 145.

11 Clark, Diary, 1/26/54.

12 Clark, Diary, 2/20/54.

13 Dennis Clark, "The Anatomy of Anger," *The Catholic Worker* (November 1954).

14 Clark, Diary, 11/17/54.

15 Clark, Diary, 4/12/54.

16 Carlo Rotella, *October Cities: The Redevelopment of Urban Literature* (Berkeley: University of California Press, 1998), p.164.

17 Ibid., p. 53.

18 John H. Mollenkopf, *The Contested City* (Princeton, N.J.: Princeton University Press, 1983), p. 13.

19 Bauman, p. 156.

20 Clark, Diary, 3/23/55.

21 Ibid.

22 Ibid.

23 Clark, Diary, 5/2/55.

24 Ibid.

25 John McDermott and Dennis Clark, "Helping the Panicked Neighborhood," reprinted from *Interracial Review* (August 1955), p. 2.

26 Ibid.

27 Ibid.

28 Ibid.

29 Ibid.

30 Ibid.

31 Ibid.

32 Clark, Diary, 6/2/55.

33 Clark, Diary, 6/30/55.

34 Ibid.

35 Ibid.

36 Ibid.

37 Bauman, p. 157.

38 Ibid.

39 Ibid., p. 163.

40 Ibid., p. 159.

41 Clark, Diary, 2/29/56.

42 Bauman, p. 165.

43 Ibid., p. 167.

44 Ibid., p. 178.

45 Clark, Diary, 11/1/55.

46 Clark, Diary, 3/20/57.

47 Clark, Diary, 6/17/58.

48 Clark, Diary, 7/16/57.

49 Report on NAACP regional conference, March 29, 1958, Thelma W. Babbitt, AFSC, Philadelphia, AFSC papers, Box 70, #1, UIC Archives.

50 Ibid.

51 Ibid.

52 Ibid.

53 11/4/60 Incident at 3115 C Street, September 1960, City of Philadelphia Commission on Human Relations, AFSC papers, Box 63, folder 1, UIC Archives.

54 Ibid.

55 Ibid.

56 Ibid.

Detroit's Master Plan

Lafayette Park and Corktown

By 1954, when *Berman v. Parker* was handed down by the Supreme Court, Detroit's Master Plan had already been in existence for seven years. Carl Almblad, senior city planner under Charles A. Blessing, director of the Detroit City Planning Commission, and that city's equivalent of Philadelphia's Ed Bacon and Boston's Ed Logue, mentioned the Master Plan repeatedly in a Residential Redevelopment City Plan Commission report for that year in a way that is both mantra-like and circular. The 1947 Master Plan, according to Almblad, "specifically pinpointed areas in need of redevelopment."[1] Those areas included Gratiot, Lafayette, Corktown, and Skid Row, and Almblad adds that they had been selected "on the basis of having fitted within the framework of the Master Plan."[2] That plan called for the eventual removal of 39,622 dwelling units during the first eighteen years of the renewal program and the further destruction of another 50,281 in the years following. All in all, 20 percent of the city's housing stock was scheduled to be torn down. If their goal were simply the destruction of housing stock, then Detroit's Master Plan would succeed beyond the planners' wildest expectations in the coming decades. However, it is doubtful that the ultimate disastrous outcome brought about by the confluence of housing and nationality and road policies in Detroit corresponded to anyone's explicit intentions. As was the case with more than one Enlightenment-based project over the past 200 years, the social engineers felt that they could tinker with fundamental social forces and tweak them until they got the desired results, only to discover as Dr. Frankenstein, ill-fated hero of Mary Shelley's novel had, that the experiment was by virtue of its design bound to careen out of control.

The destruction or "redevelopment" of Corktown was necessitated not by any blight in the neighborhood but by the exigencies of the Master Plan, which first required the destruction not only of large amounts of housing stock to renew the Gratiot and Lafayette areas but also the large-scale destruction of trucking terminals and warehouses. In order to replace what the planners destroyed in an area close enough to the center of town to ensure that industry would not flee to the suburbs completely, Corktown, an originally Irish but by 1954 an equally ethnic Mexican and Maltese neighborhood, was scheduled to be torn down so that the planners could rebuild the terminals which they had just torn down near the center of town. Needless to say, they couldn't tell the area's residents that without enraging them further, so the city planners then had to pretend that the area was blighted in order to justify their plan. Eventually the planners' mendacity would backfire on them and create the very opposition their dishonesty was supposed to circumvent. Corktown's residents were furious when they heard that their neighborhood had been designated as blighted because they knew designations like this were often self-fulfilling prophecies which prevented people from getting loans and making the normal improvements they would have done to their property there. Official designations of blight also drove housing prices down, which was, of course, in the interest of those entities which wanted to buy up property and not in the interest of the people who already owned homes in the neighborhood.

Dr. Frankenstein's equivalent in the social experiment which was to run amok in Detroit during the post-World War II period may have been Charles A. Blessing. If so, his assistant was Carl Almblad. Carl W. Almblad was born on August 16, 1924, in Chicago and spent his entire professional career as an urban planner. He pursued undergraduate studies in civil engineering at the Illinois Institute of Technology in the early '40s and received a B.S. in architecture from the University of Illinois in 1950 and an M.S. in urban planning from Wayne State University in 1961.[3] In 1950 he began work with the Chicago Plan Commission as a student intern and was later promoted to associate planner. His responsibilities included conducting redevelopment studies, housing and economic studies, and regional studies. Mr. Almblad left Chicago in 1953 to join the Detroit City Plan Commission, where he worked over the next several years as a senior, principal, and finally head city planner, responsible for urban renewal planning, master plan studies, coordination with neighborhood groups, model neighborhood plans and city wide historic and renewal studies. In 1971 he was appointed assistant director of the Detroit City Plan Commission.

Almblad arrived in Detroit as its senior city planner just as the Corktown controversy was heating up. After approving the Master Plan for Detroit on July 17, 1947, Detroit's Common Council adopted a resolution approving a Redevelopment Priority Schedule for residential and industrial sites, listing Corktown Industrial Redevelopment as Priority No. 2 after the Lafayette Project, which was already underway, destroying the trucking terminals and warehouses that were, according to the Master Plan, to be rebuilt in Corktown. One month later, the Detroit Common Council filed a request with the Division of Slum Clearance and Urban Redevelopment, requesting prior approval of preliminary planning expenditures. Less than a year later, in September of 1953, members of the Plan Commission met with Father Clement Kern, pastor of Most Holy Trinity Catholic Church, to discuss with him the impact which redevelopment would have on his parish. One month later Almblad and other members of the Plan Commission met with Miss Ethel Claes, the President of the Corktown Home Owners Association. Claes would fight a decades-long battle with the Plan Commission and eventually be responsible for saving what got saved. In the end, neither side got what it wanted out of the Corktown battle.

Given the type of beliefs Almblad was educated to hold on urban planning, it is doubtful that anything Miss Claes could have said would have changed his mind. It is also just as doubtful that he could have been honest with her about the intentions of the renewers, because anything they had to say about hygiene and blight was contextualized by their desire to use planning as a form of social engineering anyway.

On May 23, 1949, Almblad submitted a paper to one of his courses on city planning at the University of Illinois in partial fulfillment of the requirements for a B.S. in architecture. According to the young Almblad, "housing in practically every country on earth was effected [sic] by the last war."[4] Part of this revolution was brought about by shifts in population, part was brought about by the development of the new materials and construction methods that Levitt was applying in Long Island, but the thing which contextualized both was that fact that, in Almblad's words, "new theories of living were evolved" at around the same time.[5] The new theories were evidence for a "growing interest in reorganization of human living [which] has become universal in scope." This entailed a repudiation of "the overall grid system" as the model pattern for city development as well as a "trend . . . toward decentralization in the central districts" which is practiced now "almost every-where . . . except in the United States."[6] In Italy, Almblad tell us, "progressive groups of architects" have now come to "the same conclusions at the same time as the pioneers who began functionalism in Germany and Switzerland and other countries."[7] That means that there is now general "agreement that the destroyed villages, towns and cities shall be rebuilt with exclusive consideration being given to the functions they shall fulfill and the purpose they shall serve."[8]

After telling us that form will follow function, Almblad then tells us the exact oppo-site when it comes to the function of the family. "It has been decided," he tells us, but not by whom, "that due to the changed circumstances of town planning it will be necessary to sacrifice the individuality of the house."[9] No one, however, should lose sleep over this because "today this individuality has no logical reason for existing here. The production of housing is to be done en masse and to unify the whole plan repetition is necessary."[10] The 'here' which Almblad mentions refers, of course, to the United States, which is even more attuned to finding technical solutions to social problems than the tradition-bound Italians. "We Americans," Almblad continues, appointing himself as the technocratic spokesman for the nation, "are proud of our technical achievements."[11] In fact, "for every technical problem, we can find an answer," he says, again without specifying who "we" is. "Thus," Almblad concludes, giving some indication that majors in architecture did not have to take courses in logic, "it is that we see the housing shortage as a technical prob-lem." Technical problems, of course, demand technical solutions, and so "Utopia, just like the automobile, comes from the factory."[12]

The problem, according to Almblad, is that "the economic system of the United States has been producing slums for the past 150 years and will continue to do so" because "it is the essence of this system that it operate without a plan."[13] People like Almblad felt that "Faith in Planning," to use Walter Gropius's term, would create a "point of contact between the capitalist and the socialist" – in other words, a whole new social system based on a mystical, Hegelian convergence between the two systems which were currently on opposing sides of the Cold War. This new system would be based on shared enthusiasm for modernist design. Design, according to the Bauhaus concept, extended all the way from door handles to cities, in which case design was known as "planning," something which had much in common with the centrally planned economy of the Soviet Union, where, not coincidentally the planners were building Gropius style *Wohnmaschinen*. The fact that Gropius's Bauhaus design was common to both sides in the Cold War lent cre-dence to the planners' notion that they were on their way to discovering a third way which would synthesize the best parts of the capitalist and socialist systems. Gropius's Cambridge firm, with Reg Isaacs as his lieutenant, was busy building projects on the South Side of Chicago just as Ernst May, his former Bauhaus Dessau protégé, was build-ing the same kind of building on the outskirts of Moscow. Both sets of buildings had as their philosophical basis a profoundly deracinated – it would come to be known as the "International School" – environmentalist materialism, according to whose principles "it has become known," in Almblad's words, "that slums are not caused by the people who live in them."[14] As a result, "it is going to be necessary for the government to bring about relegislation and to do some planning."[15] Thus, the man who started off by claiming that form should follow function ends up by calling for massive social engineering, which means of course that function should follow form. "If this means substantial changes in our customs and laws and practices, then we must have these changes. It is not enough that planners be technicians; they must also be accomplished politicians."[16] Or put another way, it is not enough that planners simply build buildings, they need to coerce the people in those buildings into living a certain kind of life, one based on crudely materialist principles.

It would be comforting to think that Almblad's paper was nothing more than the callow thoughts of an undergraduate caught up in a social movement whose malevolent inner dynamic he was too obtuse to understand. He was, however, twenty-five years old when he wrote it and already a part of the urban-planning fraternity in Chicago at a time when they had the prestige of minor deities. Any student of his thought would, however, have to abandon this idea after reading his paper "Master Plan and Stratification" which he wrote eleven years later.

Eleven years after completing his undergraduate degree, Almblad was still struggling to articulate a coherent policy of urban planning. His notion of planning is based on the contradictory notion that form follows function on the one hand and a just as strong belief in social engineering on the other. As a result he feels that the planner is presented with a dilemma – "Should he provide for convenience or a variety of choice, for containment or for free movement"[17] without ever understanding that the basis of the dilemma, even more than its mutually contradictory foundation, is the idea that the planner must be a social engineer in the first place, i.e., that he must forever be engineering social outcomes rather than enabling people to live better according to their own criteria of the good. The dilemmas which the planning fraternity faced all arose from the planners' conclusion that environment determined behavior. Being in charge of design, as a result, turned them into gods, but as soon as they became gods, with full hegemony over good and evil, they were faced with decisions they could not resolve. As a result of placing the burden of social engineer on his own shoulders, the urban planner now had to decide whether "people move about the city because they have no roots or because there is a need to have a variety of experiences."[18] He also needed to decide whether "the cohesive group,"[19] his term for *ethnos*, meets "an emotional need or is it simply a sentimental thing from the past culture, which encourages undesirable segregation," since "the purpose of such units, or neighborhoods" is that "it provides a sense of belonging for an otherwise rootless society."[20]

Almblad then goes on to try to square the social circle by coming up with a small community which is not exclusive. If, for example, "a neighborhood were designed to encourage close relationships on a very localized level, it might result in such a court or other unit consisting of members of one class. But other courts, etc., in the neighborhood, might contain members of other classes. As a result, the neighborhood would not be a segregated unit."[21] Almblad cites Whyte's book *The Organization Man* as the source of this insight, and Whyte, in this regard, was talking about the social engineering of ethnics that was occurring in the suburbs at the time through the strategic placement of housing on courts and the social results which could be achieved as a result. Failing to see that social engineering is trying to achieve the impossible goal, Almblad then tries to decide which instrumentalities will bring this contradiction in terms about. "The design of streets within a neighborhood," he tells us, "should be considered for the social effect"[22] they exert on the people who live there. The statement itself is a true statement, but in stating his case as he does, Almblad makes it clear that he feels himself in no way bound by any sense of the common good of the people he sets out to engineer. All outcomes are equally good or bad, from the technocratic point of view. Terms like 'good' and 'evil' depend on the desires of the engineers, or, more accurately, the desires of those who pay the engineers to engineer other people. Thus, streets can be used "to encourage close or distant relations between people"[23] depending on what the social engineers want to encourage. According to Almblad, "a close relationship can be encouraged . . . by a narrow, intimately scaled street" or "conversely, a wide, open type street" can encourage "fast through traffic" which "makes contact across it very difficult." It all depends on who determines the "social goals of a plan" and why. "This is particularly true," he concludes, "with federal aid hastening the program. It also has ramifications when considering the displacement of minority population – and thus the forced mixing of classes – required for expressway construction."[24] If we pause for a moment to untangle the complicated syntax of the last sentence, Almblad seems to be telling us that part of the function that roads serve in the menu of social engineering is first to displace and then remix ethnic groups. As Coleman Young could have testified from personal experience, this was the function roads served in Detroit. And as the role that road construction played in social engineering became apparent through the implementation of Detroit's Master Plan in Corktown, opposition to that plan increased. In order to deal with that opposition, Almblad corresponded throughout the dispute over Corktown with the American Institute of Planners, located at 34 Brattle Street in Cambridge, Massachusetts.

Almblad's meeting with Ethel Claes in October 1953 seems to have done little to defuse the issue. In fact, if anything the situation was even more polarized one month later when 500 Corktown residents signed a petition which they filed at city hall on November 28, demanding a public hearing at which they could bring up their grievances. The petitioners were especially outraged at the fact that the plan commission had labeled Corktown a "slum." Since they didn't consider their neighborhood a slum, the petitioners were also not keen on moving. "This area is essentially one of home owners." one resident told the local paper. "Many of us have lived here more than 50 years. It would be impossible for us to find equivalent housing in an equivalent area."[25]

Meanwhile, instead of listening to what the people were telling the planners at the meetings the planners scheduled to listen to them, Almblad and the social engineers continued to collect data to prove to the residents of Corktown that they really did live in a slum and that they really would be happier elsewhere, in spite of what they said to the press and the petition they dropped off at city hall. Corktown, Almblad and his planners informed its residents, had 2,250 dwelling units, of which 3 percent were vacant. One-third of the dwellings were dilapidated or did not have a private bath. About 15 percent of the residences "had no running water or were dilapidated."[26] As we have already indicated, the designation of blight was always vague, often deliberately vague. Nowhere are we told exactly how many units did not have running water. Assuming it was less than the 15 percent which "had no running water or were dilapidated," we could estimate that, say, 5 percent were without running water, or it might be 10 percent. Even if we agree on a figure of, say, 10 percent, it is not immediately clear then why the other 90 percent of the residents had to lose their homes because 10 percent of the residents do not have running water. The only thing that mandates this outcome is the "Master Plan," which took on mystical significance for the planners, a significance which William O. Douglas accepted at face value and underscored in *Berman v. Parker*.

But if we look to the Master Plan for clarification, we quickly learn that the destruction of Corktown had nothing to do with the number of private baths then extant in that neighborhood. In the same memo which documents the number of private baths in Corktown, Almblad urges his readers to "talk with people of the area to get them oriented as much as possible. Find out what organization they have and be prepared to cope with it."[27] He even indicates that the residents might benefit from urban renewal "because the city will most likely pay them more for their property than they could get privately if it was to remain in its blighted condition. The city can afford to do this since the property will have a higher value as an integrated well-planned industrial district than it has at present and the city will be able to sell it for more."[28]

In private Memos to Head City Planner Francis Bennett, however, Almblad explained the real reason for the Plan Commission's interest in Corktown. The real objective of the study, according to this memo, is "to determine the types of industrial uses that would be acceptable and suitable for Corktown" and how "to establish plants in the area."[29] In other words, the real reason for redevelopment in Corktown is not the blighted nature of its housing stock but rather the area's desirability for industrial development. "According to Master Plan of Generalized Land Use," Almblad tells Bennett on June 3, 1953, which is to say six months before he met with Miss Claes and the Corktown residents association, "the Corktown area is designated for light industrial use."[30] Once the plan is set, the fate of the residents is an ancillary outcome which is to be engineered by psychological and political maneuvering. As an example of the precedent which Detroit plans to follow, Almblad mentions one week later the fact that the Montgomery (Alabama) Housing Authority had just received $1.396 million "for use in slum clearance and urban redevelopment project" because "new uses of the area proposed by the redevelopment plan for the project as primarily industrial."[31] As if to assure his co-workers that this is not just a brutal land grab, by which the powerful simply deny property rights to the less powerful, Almblad adds that "the 20 white and 222 Negro families now residing in the area will be offered rehousing in decent, safe and sanitary dwellings as required by Title I of the Housing Act of 1949"[32] and then underlines it for emphasis.

The *a priori* nature of the "Master Plan" insured that what masqueraded as democratic process and consultation would invariably turn out to be psychological warfare and the engineering of consent to already-agreed-upon goals, goals established by the planners and the behind-the-scenes ethnic interests who paid their salaries. It was this dishonesty, backed up by brute government force of the sort which the Supreme Court would ratify in the middle of the ongoing Corktown struggle, which more than anything else created hatred and ill-will. And as is so often the case, the ethnic groups which fell victim to the process more often than not blamed other ethnic groups, who were also victims of the same machinations, for their problems. And so in Detroit the malevolence of the white man began to take on mythic power in the minds of Detroit's black population, a fact which could be manipulated by up-and-coming politicians like Coleman Young for his personal benefit and the benefit of his political cronies.

In the meantime, the opposition to the Corktown project continued to grow. On January 7, 1954, Rev. John P. Mangrum, rector of St. Peter's Episcopal Church, wrote a letter to the *Detroit Times*, after reading that city council gave informal approval to clearing part of Corktown. "One thousand families," Mangrum claimed, "will be moved into the streets as if they were sacks of meal" and "the tragedy is that seemingly nobody in the whole city cares what happens" to "the frightened Americans in Corktown" who were engaged in a "heroic struggle to get an American chance to preserve their homes."[33] Mangrum felt that the city's aster plan was "crude and cruel" and "hatched from the same evil spoor that drifts from Moscow."[34] People like Almblad and Blessing may "not know it," but "they are behaving like an all-powerful state, crushing inconvenient subjects."[35] Speaking "as a priest of the Episcopal Church," Mangrum then waxes prophetic: "Destroy families, tear up homes, and supplant them with questionable business and development and the wrath of God will fall on our city. . . . Make no mistake about it. Woe unto anyone who harms one of these little ones! Better for him – be he mayor, councilman or planner – that a millstone were wrapped around his neck."[36] On April 22, 1954, Mangrum wrote directly to Charles Blessing, describing the Master Plan for Corktown as something "evil and bad," which must "be beaten completely." "The proposed 'redevelopment,'" he concluded, "is not progress, is not just, and is at base a cruel, cruel proposal."[37]

Blessing and Almblad, however, were unmoved by the pleas emanating from Corktown and continued to ignore the human casualties that their Master Plan was causing by diverting attention instead to "Principles Justifying Residential Redevelopment" which Almblad culled from Hoyt's *Industrial Redevelopment of Chicago,* which claimed that "1) that the area will yield more taxes after redevelopment and 2) that redevelopment will permit downtown workers to live closer to work, thus reducing transportation, congestion and costs."[38] All of this may have been true, but none of it benefited the residents of Corktown. As if remembering that, Almblad added that "Redevelopment of blighted residential areas with industry serves purpose in eliminating areas detrimental to health, safety, and morals."[39] As a result, the City Plan Commission recommended at its February 3, 1954, meeting that "this project area be approved."[40]

Less the Old Testament prophet than Rev. Mangrum, Father Clement Kern, pastor of Holy Trinity Parish at 1050 Porter, was no less opposed to the "redevelopment" of Corktown. Arguing in a way that should have made sense to social engineers in the school of Louis Wirth, Kern claimed that the neighborhood had provided a vehicle for assimilation for the Irish and was continuing to do the same thing for the Mexicans and Maltese who were living there in the early '50s. "Of course they want to move on – just as the Irish families did before them. But they need education first. We have six English classes in our night school. . . . When families arrive from Malta or Mexico or Texas, we teach them the

American way – then they are ready to move into new neighborhoods. . . . They don't stay here – and certainly we don't want them to. But they aren't ready to move someplace else until they have lived in Corktown."[41] Because of the socialization the neighborhood and the parish church provided, there was "very little juvenile delinquency"[42] in Corktown, a phenomenon created by the breakdown of family and neighborhood which was causing national concern at the time.

Jim Shanahan, who had been born in Corktown in 1871 to the generation which had settled the area after famine drove them from Cork in Ireland, was less sociological than Father Kern, calling the plan to redevelop the neighborhood "a crime, a dirty outrage, and a landgrab."[43] If the city's Plan Commission wanted to build factories and warehouses in Corktown, Shanahan wanted to know "Why don't they let us make our own deals with the buyers – we won't get half of what the property is worth from the city. If they have to tear it down why don't they build apartment houses so the people who live on the outskirts and who spend half their time on buses and the other half waiting for them, could have some decent homes and leave the people who live there alone."[44]

These and other questions finally got aired at the Corktown Redevelopment Conference which was held in May of 1954. During the conference, the residents of Corktown were repeatedly told that "the purpose of redevelopment . . . is not that of clearing land for a new use, but removing blight."[45] When the representative of the City Plan Commission was asked the same question again by the neighborhood's increasingly skeptical residents, he gave what was purported to be the same answer but this time in an expanded fashion which undercut the force of the original assertion. "The purpose," the anonymous planner reasserted, "is the removal of blight. However, it is again brought out that the master plan which was developed in the late '40s, indicates the area now under discussion as being recommended for light industrial use."[46]

Well, which is it? Removal of blight or industrial development? The answer to that question invariably returns to "the 1947 Master Plan," which "indicates light industrial areas for this section." But suppose the buildings which are scheduled to be torn down aren't in fact in disrepair? "If," the Plan Commission replied, "there were one or two small good structures located on the middle of a large tract, the redevelopment plan would probably remove them"[47] because, as Justice Douglas indicated in *Berman v. Parker*, the plan specified this, and if the planners did not follow the plan, then the plan would suffer. Or, as Douglas put it in *Berman*, "If owner after owner were permitted to resist these development programs on the ground that this particular property was not being used against public interest, integrated plans for redevelopment would suffer greatly."[48] This means that all development, even commercial or industrial development, must stop because "It would be unfortunate if any substantial commercial buildings were built until the overall plan for the area can be prepared."[49] At around the same time as the conference, Samuel Gottlieb, owner of a gas station at 1450 Howard, wrote to Almblad to ask if he should go ahead and make alterations of the premises. Almblad informed him on May 3, 1954, that he "Can't say yes or no" because "It will now be even 3–5 years before condemnations begin."[50] Redevelopment meant, in other words, the end of any activity in the affected area, even the type of activity the Master Plan specified as good for the area.

No matter what question the residents asked, the answer involved the Master Plan, which in effect killed whatever local initiative there was in the neighborhoods. Could they build a club in Corktown, the residents wondered? "The plan for the area would have to be studied first."[51] If their property is condemned, the residents wondered, "Is it going to be sold by the city to industry?" "Yes," the planners answered, "under the Master Plan it would be. Under redevelopment procedures, the area is condemned under the right of eminent domain and prepared for sale at a public auction for a specified land used determined by the master plan. There, first of all, must be the master plan to guide the redevelopment program."[52] But if this were the case, "shouldn't the sale of lands be left up to the individual," since "the individual [w]ould get more money" that way? No, "individual sales of parcels in the projected area" was a bad idea because "it would be difficult to implement the master plan for the area and also difficult to accumulate parcels of proper size."[53]

At this point one of residents pointed out the fact that "the planners' criteria for blight were dishonest because the designation "no running water" and "no baths" or "dilapidation" as a result of same, is based on the fact that there are many rooming houses where running water, baths, etc., are not provided in each individual unit. A central facility must be used. These then in the census are carried as dwellings with no running water or baths."[54]

No answer to this objection was forthcoming from the planners, who kept maintaining the fiction that current blight and future use were two completely separate issues, when in fact the alleged existence of the former was simply an excuse to implement the latter. "We would like to point out," the planners patiently reminded the incredulous natives, "that Slum Clearance's first and primary obligation is that of removal of blight." But then they undercut their own assertion by adding immediately "The new use is determined by a master plan which is a first requirement of the Federal Government."[55] The people of Corktown were first told that it was in their own interest to remove blight from Corktown even if it meant that they were going to be removed as part of the process. They were then informed that the Master Plan determined that Corktown had to be transformed into a warehouse and shipping district because "Without nearby shipping facilities our downtown central area would be strangled and would eventually die."[56] In other words, the residents of Corktown were supposed to give up their homes to make way for the warehouses and shipping terminals which the master planners had just torn down in Lafayette and Gratiot because "the new use is determined by an existing master plan which has been approved by our Council and which indicates this specific area to light industry."[57]

When one resident complained that "where trucking goes, the area becomes a mess," he was told in barely comprehensible bureaucratese that, like it or not, trucking was coming to Corktown because "we associate it more directly with the Central Business District in functional relationships." The area's residents were then informed, "If the area is accepted by the Common Council as one for redevelopment, they will then freeze building permits."[58] With that the meeting was over.

The residents of Corktown may have got nowhere with the planners, but they were starting to have an effect on public opinion. On July 20, 1954, the *Detroit Free Press* ran an editorial in their favor entitled "Let's Not Trade Corktown for Another Gaping Hole."[59] The hole in question referred to the urban renewal which had already taken place in the Gratiot and Lafayette sections, which left "a big hole," which "nobody has found a way to fill . . . with the new housing which was supposed to go there."[60] Instead of bringing new housing to the East Side, urban renewal created "just another littered jungle for vicious derelicts to prowl,"[61] and *The Detroit Free Press* was afraid that the same thing was going to happen to Corktown.

In order to prevent that, Ethel Claes gathered another 2,000 signatures from area homeowners attached to a petition, which assured the city fathers that the residents of Corktown "have no social disease, have committed no crimes and are not drinkers."[62] Claes also mentioned the obvious, namely, that the residents were being prevented from fighting blight by the city itself which refused to issue building permits and so brought about the very blight they claimed to oppose. The city, however, was unimpressed by their efforts. One month after Claes's efforts in October 1954, the City Council, the City Plan Commission and the Housing Commission declared that seventy acres of the area were blighted. On November 10, 1954, two weeks before the Supreme Court would hand down *Berman v. Parker* but a month after it had been argued, the Detroit City Council reaffirmed its decision to designate Corktown a blighted area, but perhaps a bit intimidated by what the paper called "the bitterly protesting Corktowners," assured them "that they would be granted another public hearing before actual condemnation is considered."[63] Deprived of their own representative because Detroit had abandoned local councilmanic seats, the people of Corktown lacked the political power enjoyed by the residents of Philadelphia and Chicago, who had just ousted Elizabeth Wood and Walter Phillips from their respective housing authorities and were enjoying one of the ephemeral triumphs in the long, losing war that local communities waged against the federal government and its ethnic interests in the period following World War II.

Notes

1 Residential Redevelopment City Plan Commission, Detroit 1954, Almblad papers, Box 5, folder 23, Wayne State University Archives.
2 Ibid.
3 Carl W. Almblad Collection, Wayne State University.
4 Term paper, 5/23/49, Almsblad Series I, Box 1, Folder 28, Wayne State Archives.
5 Ibid.
6 Ibid.
7 Ibid.
8 Ibid.
9 Ibid.
10 Ibid.
11 Ibid.
12 Ibid.
13 Ibid.
14 Ibid.
15 Ibid.
16 Ibid.

17 Soc 703 Ravitz Master Plan and Stratification, May 1960, Almblad Papers, Box 1, folder 28, Wayne State Archives.

18 Ibid.

19 Ibid.

20 Ibid.

21 Ibid.

22 Ibid.

23 Ibid.

24 Ibid.

25 "Corktown rises in Wrath at Plan for Slum Zoning," 11/28/53, Almblad papers Box 3, folder 47, Wayne State Archives.

26 "Preliminary Planning for Corktown Redevelopment Approved," Almblad papers, Box 3, folder 46, Wayne State Archives.

27 Ibid.

28 Ibid.

29 Memo Carl Almblad to Francis Bennett, Head City Planner June 3, 1953, Almblad papers, Box 3, folder 46, Wayne State Archives.

30 Ibid.

31 Ibid.

32 Ibid.

33 "Death of Corktown," *Detroit Times*, 1/7/54 letter to the editor from Rev. John P. Mangrum, Rector, St. Peter's Episcopal Church, Almblad papers, Box 3, Folder 47, Wayne State Archives.

34 Ibid.

35 Ibid.

36 Ibid.

37 Letter from Rev. John Mangrum to Charles Blessing, 4/22/54, Almblad papers, Box 3, folder 47, Wayne State Archives.

38 Notes on Hoyt's Industrial Redevelopment of Chicago June 1951, Almblad papers, Box 3, folder 47, Wayne State Archives.

39 Ibid.

40 Ibid.

41 Robert J. Murphy, "Corktown: A Vanishing Tradition," *Detroit Times,* 3/15/54, Almblad papers, Box 3, folder 47, Wayne State Archives.

42 Ibid.

43 Ibid.

44 Ibid.

45 Corktown Redevelopment Conference Minutes 5/54, Almblad papers, Box 3, folder 47, Wayne State Archives.

46 Ibid.

47 Ibid.

48 *Berman v. Parker*, 75 S.Ct. 98.

49 Ibid.

50 Almblad papers, Box 3, Folder 47, Wayne State Archives.

51 Corktown Redevelopment Conference Minutes, 5/54, Almblad papers, Box 3, folder 47, Wayne State Archives.

52 Ibid.

53 Ibid.

54 Ibid.

55 Ibid.

56 Ibid.

57 Ibid.

58 Ibid.

59 "Let's Not Trade Corktown for Another Gaping Hole," *The Detroit Free Press*, 7/20/54, Almblad papers, Box 3, folder 47, Wayne State Archives.

60 Ibid.

61 Ibid.

62 "Corktown Is ready for Survival Battle," *The Detroit Free Press*, Almblad papers, Box 3, Folder 47, Wayne State Archives.

63 "City Calls Corktown Blighted," *The Detroit Free Press*, 11/10/54, Almblad papers, Box 3, Folder 47, Wayne State Archives.

Paul Ylvisaker and the Gray Areas

At some point during the 1953–54 academic year at Swarthmore College, the Hicksite Quaker institution just outside Philadelphia, Paul Ylvisaker, a young professor of political science there, invited Robert Moses, then fresh from advising the Eisenhower Administration on how to structure its newly planned interstate-highway system, to give a lecture on urban planning. It was a bit like asking General Custer to lecture on Indians, but evidently Ylvisaker realized his mistake too late. After giving an enthusiastic introduction to the crowd which assembled at Swarthmore's Quaker Meeting House to hear Moses, Ylvisaker was forced to endure a lackluster talk and the subsequent embarrassment in front of his peers, both in academe and politics, since Ylvisaker was also Democratic chairman for the town of Swarthmore. As if to make up for the embarrassing performance of the speaker he invited, Ylvisaker launched into an attack in the Q & A period following, something which the man he invited must have found bewildering or annoying or both.

Someone who found Ylvisaker's attack neither bewildering nor annoying was Joseph Sill Clark, newly elected mayor of Philadelphia. Clark happened to be in the audience and was so impressed with Ylvisaker's intellectual throttling of Moses that his staff called Ylvisaker a few days later and offered him a job as Clark's executive secretary. When Ylvisaker, perhaps concerned about his qualifications, asked what the job description was, he was told, "It's to help fight the battle for my mind."[1]

Hearing that, Ylvisaker accepted the job. Clark's job description may have intrigued Ylvisaker because he had just been involved in fighting the battle for his own mind in the immediately preceding years. Ylvisaker had been born in 1921 in Minnesota as the son of a Lutheran minister of Norwegian extraction. As one might expect of someone whose father was also the head of Bethany Lutheran College, Ylvisaker was educated completely within the Lutheran parochial system as a young man. He attended Lutheran primary and high school and then Bethany, but he graduated from Mankato State. Later in life, Ylvisaker concluded that most people attended parochial schools for "democratically unhealthy reasons"[2] although he would also add irenically that he had "seen both the virtues and problematics of religious education and of public education."[3] Even conceding that there might be some merit to religious education, Ylvisaker chose to abandon the Lutheran faith of his father and of his youth, because he "needed to be 'released' at one time from the prejudices and parochialism of Lutheran dogma and to come to respect through wider association the myriad truths and percepts of truth that creation has given us."[4] Like William Godwin, another figure who was destined for the ministry but ended up espousing the Enlightenment instead, Paul Ylvisaker reacted to the denigration of reason which Luther bequeathed to his followers, by abandoning his faith instead. "The break from the church of my childhood, when it came," he wrote later, "was agonizing and traumatic."[5]

Ylvisaker then did graduate work at the University of Minnesota, and finally ended up as a graduate fellow at Harvard University in the '40s. As this trajectory indicates, the transition from religious schools to state schools was accompanied by a crisis of faith, one which was resolved fairly quickly, if not fairly painlessly. "When I found that my church could not easily be taken with me into life," Ylvisaker told a group of Episcopalians in 1965, "I concluded I would also have to leave my religion behind."[6] Ylvisaker had learned at Harvard that both religion and ethnicity were outmoded ways of thought which had been replaced by the Enlightenment's version of science. After Ylvisaker abandoned Christianity, he, in typical Enlightenment fashion, began to view society, and therefore, the city as one large aggregate of atoms bumping into each other. "Nuclear physics," he told a convention of Life Insurance advertisers in September of 1960,

> may have more to say about the structure of our society than sociology and polit-ical science – for our people are in constant motion like the particles of the atom. Like these particles, one can describe their behavior and location in mathematical terms and probabilities, but say nothing definitely about the individual particle.[7]

In another speech, Ylvisaker saw all of human history as one "long historic sweep . . . to release human energies and progression toward the exercise of free will."[8] Then strug-gling to make his vision clear to his audience, Ylvisaker once again fell back on imagery taken from science. "The analogy which insists its picture on my mind," he continued, "is that of the atomic pile; in our case, a social structure whose internal reactions are releas-ing its individual particles and by their release are creating human energy far beyond the capacity of earlier societies."[9] By subsidizing agents of change, institutions like the Ford Foundation could speed up that reaction, and, like the chain reaction caused by achieving critical mass in an atomic pile, "this quickening rate of change re-enforces the reaction which is liberating the individual: it wipes the slate of existing institutions habits and taboos clean for each new individual who comes along. He doesn't have to free himself from the old; the old is going, if it's not already gone."[10]

It's difficult at certain points to see just how literally Ylvisaker understood the analo-gies from science he so often applied to social behavior. It is clear though that the para-digm which he applied to society as a whole was largely derived from his own personal experiences, carefully transmuted into the imagery of nuclear physics. Ylvisaker was a human particle whose own atomic speed had been accelerated by coming into contact with the vast material resources of the ruling class, as he had at Harvard. As a result of this increased energy, he was effectively catapulted into a whole new orbit, far removed from the beliefs and values he associated with his boyhood in Lutheran Minnesota. Ylvisaker didn't "have to free himself from the old" neighborhood; all he had to do was abandon the faith of his fathers and the energy flow emanating from the culture's then dominant insti-tutions would accomplish the rest. Or so it must have seemed to him in retrospect, as he was swept along from one prestigious job to another – from Swarthmore College to work-ing for Joe Clark, to the Ford Foundation, to Harvard's School of Education, after an ill-fated attempt at hands-on urban planning in New Jersey.

Ylvisaker had made his first explicit contact with the Enlightenment when he read Kant in high school. When he got to Harvard, the universalist philosophy of Kant was expanded to include now the "global political theory"[11] then in favor in the politics department there, which in turn was reinforced by the "sense of global interdependence" he picked up during the year he spent in England on a Fulbright fellowship.[12] By the time John Nason, president of Swarthmore, wrote to Harvard's Department of Political Science in 1948 for recommendations for a tenure track position at the college, Ylvisaker had taken on an intellectual identity completely different from that of his father Sigurd. Ylvisaker, like John McCloy, for whom he would work at the Ford Foundation, was not born into the ruling class. Like McCloy, Ylvisaker went to Harvard, where he adopted the ruling class point of view as his own, and after he graduated he went to work promoting their interests. Ylvisaker felt that he was part of – perhaps an atom in – the great movement of history out of the darkness and into the light, up from bondage and into freedom – he believed, in short, in all of the clichés of Whig history. At any rate, he felt that his job was to be an advocate of "scientific politics,"[13] since he was living in "an era in which government, as heretofore industry has the advantage of continuous research and development."[14] "Scientific Politics" received its practical application to "the problems of the city" by "speeding the process by which newcomers to urban life adjust to this new and more impersonal environment."[15]

With an attitude like that, it's not difficult to see how Ylvisaker, who considered himself an expert in urban affairs, would come to view the small community in general and the ethnic neighborhood in particular. In a lecture to the city council of Indianapolis in January of 1963, Ylvisaker said that he liked the city because it allowed "widening residential and occupational choice"[16] which in turn was "a way of releasing individuals from the chains of ethnic, racial and other attachments not freely chosen."[17] Ylvisaker, in other words, clearly viewed the city as an escape from the small community, not something that was made up of small communities, known otherwise as neighborhoods. Ylvisaker was nothing if not astute in internalizing the desiderata of the WASP establishment. That meant seeing the local community as an obstacle to integration and the politicians who represented those people as a "machine," which had to be expunged so that the city could function rationally. That meant that racial discrimination was a barrier which had to be removed from civic life in order to save the city. "Until we solve the problem of racial discrimination, until we remove every political machine from local politics," he told a group of students in November of 1949, "we shall not have fully reaffirmed the meaning of Valley Forge."[18] Ylvisaker's understanding of the traditional American system was skewed by the ethnic prejudices of the people he served. Instead of attempting to preserve the small community, the big foundations and the interests they represented looked upon it as its enemy, a bastion of particularistic prejudice and obscurantism, standing in the way of Enlightenment and progress. In waging war on the small community, the big foundations invariably reduced the social order to some mechanism that was fueled by money – "A dollar is an instrument of freedom and choice," Ylvisaker said[19] – and so he worked to organize the nation's big cities along materialistic lines to benefit the wealthy families whose fortunes lay at the basis of big foundations like Ford and Rockefeller. The means of control Ylvisaker wanted to put in place may have been subtle – "More and more, we'll be turning away from controls to incentives"[20] – but the end will be political control in the interest of the big foundations effectively disguised as technological progress. "The production, distribution and consumption of these services," Ylvisaker wrote, " – on a mass, yet personalized and a quality yet equalitarian basis – will be the organizing theme of the future city."[21]

Twenty-four years later, Ylvisaker had a slightly less Manichean view of urban life, one which took more cognizance of ethnic realities. Ylvisaker claims that he admired the Clark-Dilworth Reformers "from the Swarthmore distance,"[22] but nonetheless identified with them and their goals. The "good guys . . . had won the mayoralty and now we were going to move."[23] By 1973, Ylvisaker was aware that the "we" he mentions had a definite ethnic identity, one that was not really compatible with the city of Philadelphia anymore because "the city was going increasingly towards blacks and Italians and so forth,"[24] something which Joe Clark, the Chestnut Hill aristocrat, resented. The resentment, it turns out, was mutual. "These guys," Ylvisaker continued, referring to the city's Catholic ethnics, "must have resented Joe deeply because it was a benign dictatorship in many ways which the charter enabled and I suppose that in a sense that it cost the less articulate, the less privileged in Philadelphia. It forced them in a direction and ultimately more demagogic leadership which I think [former Mayor Frank] Rizzo represents."[25]

Ylvisaker is referring here to the civil service provision of the charter, which eliminated large numbers of patronage jobs and awarded positions according to "merit," which usually meant the university credentials which Clark's ethnic group favored and which got Ylvisaker his job at Swarthmore and with Clark as well. Having "a Harvard degree didn't hurt at all with Joe,"[26] Ylvisaker told Walter Phillips, who probably agreed with both Ylvisaker and Clark on the matter, since he too had a Harvard degree and was part of the reform as well. Philadelphia's Catholic ethnics, on the other hand, had a different view of local government. To begin with, higher education for them meant going to LaSalle, Villanova, or St. Joseph's College, not Harvard, Princeton, or Yale, and to make a further point, most of them hadn't attended even those colleges. The Catholic ethnics scoured the Constitution in vain, trying to find the passage which specified that an Ivy League degree was a necessary condition for holding public office, and they – Jack Kelly, Jimmy Byrne, Bill Green, Sr., and Jim Tate – began to feel that by accepting the civil-service provisions specified by the new City Charter, they were agreeing to play a game with the deck stacked against them. Was it their job to bring Enlightenment, as defined by the politics department at Harvard, to the administration of the city of Philadelphia by hiring only credentialed "experts"? Or was the government supposed to represent the actual people in actual communities, no matter how unenlightened they were on matters of race and urban planning? Walter Phillips and Paul Ylvisaker had clear answers to those questions. So did Bill Green and Jim Tate. And the political conflicts of the coming decade would be the arena which would determine whose answers would prevail.

In just about all of its crucial aspects, Ylvisaker's urbanism was his own personal history writ large. He had abandoned the small religious ethnic community in favor of the "universal" rational global "community," which was about to take nature by the hand and liberate her from the mistakes of the past. Ylvisaker, of course, just ended up working for another ethnic community, but it probably did not seem that way to the boy who grew up in Lutheran Minnesota. Harvard had given him a ticket to the big leagues, an ethnic community which aspired to rule the world according to universalist rational principles. Soon he would be dispensing money in sums that would make this fantasy seem like reality.

Joe Clark seems to have viewed Philadelphia as a small community too, too small for his ambitions anyway. Shortly after getting elected mayor of that city, Clark began his campaign to become a senator from the state of Pennsylvania, and Paul Ylvisaker was the man who was his factotum in that campaign, which is to say that he was a man under considerable stress. So much stress in fact that he suffered a heart attack in December of 1954 and didn't even know it until it showed up during a subsequent medical examination. Part of the stress came from the fact that even after Ylvisaker accepted the job as Clark's executive secretary, he was still a faculty member at Swarthmore. Now his medical condition forced him to make some hard choices. Joe Clark wanted Ylvisaker to follow him to Washington, but Ylvisaker was afraid that either his health would fail or that, if it did not, he would become the young man who would be absorbed into the older man's more dominant personality. Either way, Ylvisaker had no desire to return to academic life at Swarthmore.

Fortunately for him, a third opportunity came along at the same time. At around the same time that Ylvisaker had his heart attack, Don Price and Dyke Brown of the Ford Foundation called "out of the blue," to say that they wanted to come down to Philadelphia to talk to him about "how we're spending our money in public affairs" at Ford.[27] They must have liked what they heard. Two weeks after meeting with Ylvisaker, they offered him a job. Ylvisaker was a man who never enjoyed robust health in life. In addition to suffering a coronary at the age of thirty four, he waged a life-long battle with diabetes, a disease which would eventually render him legally blind. Because of his infirmities, Ylvisaker decided to go to the Ford Foundation, he later stated, because of their health benefits.[28]

Ylvisaker joined the staff of the Ford Foundation on May 1, 1955, as an expert on urban and regional problems. He arrived to find an atmosphere he later characterized as "suspicious and paralyzed."[29] Ylvisaker arrived at Ford at a time of crisis for all of America's foundations. Rockefeller and Carnegie had just undergone a rigorous grilling at the hands of the Reece Commission, which had left the impression in many people's minds, in spite of all of media propaganda to the contrary, that the nation's biggest foundations were hotbeds of subversive activity, supporting people like Alfred Kinsey and Alger Hiss to destabilize morals domestically and hand over countries like China to the Communists on the international scene. At Ford, Barney Berelson's behavioral science program was being questioned, especially since he had become involved in a grant which involved bugging a jury, something which caused general outrage. "His equities were beginning to run out," Ylvisaker said of Berelson. "His magic was beginning to be questioned" at precisely the time when Ylvisaker arrived at Ford.[30]

The Ford Foundation at the time was under the direction of Henry Heald, the man who had used urban renewal to save IIT in Chicago from black migration. Heald had essentially a university president's view of the foundation as a bottomless money trough for penurious academics, but the foundation board was afraid that the massive amounts of money they could bring to bear on a sector as limited and poor as academe might simply cause inflation, and, as a result, they were eager to find other outlets for their philanthropy. The first group to benefit from this restlessness at the Ford Foundation was the nation's hospitals. Ford was so avid to find new channels for its philanthropy that two houses of prostitution got grants of $250,000 because they were nominally listed as hospitals.[31] Heald, as a result, was in trouble because he was perceived as "being socially behind the times and a few other things."[32]

The conflict at the Ford Foundation had other roots as well. Heald was an academic and as such naturally inclined to give money to academic institutions, which the more activist branch of the philanthropic establishment perceived as a waste of resources. They wanted results, and they wanted them more quickly than academics could provide them. Heald chafed under the prodding of the Ford trustees, who under the direction of John J. McCloy, "still thought of the Foundation as a quasi-extension of the U.S. government."[33] McCloy, as a result, also felt that Heald "was a little too prone to confine the benefactions of the Ford Foundation to conventional university academic areas."[34]

Part of Heald's problem was his association, by way of IIT, with urban renewal, because, by the time Ylvisaker arrived at Ford, urban renewal was in deep trouble in both Chicago, where Elizabeth Wood had been fired the year before, and Philadelphia, where Irish Catholic politicians like Bill Green would rein in the ambitions of the WASP planners in 1956. According to Ylvisaker's reading of the situation at Ford, Heald was in trouble because "the urban renewal projects which 'establishment' members (such as Bechtel and other Foundation trustees) were individually involved in were being stopped because of the social veto that blacks and other urban minorities had imposed."[35] Eventually, Heald would lose that fight when McCloy brought McGeorge Bundy in to head Ford as a more activist arm of the WASP establishment in the mid-'60s. The fact that Heald lasted until then was largely the result of Ylvisaker's efforts and his creation of the Gray Areas program, something that was just what McCloy had in mind as a "quasi-extension of the U.S. government."

Ylvisaker was acutely aware of the conflict and the fact that it was causing paralysis at the foundation. He was also aware that the real power at the foundation lay with the board of trustees and not with Heald, who had been hired to do their bidding. Just what those interests were Ylvisaker would later explain. "Since the family control of the corporation," according to Ylvisaker, "was the prime reason for the creation of [the Ford] foundation,"[36] it would follow that the foundation existed to pursue family interests, as broadly, which is to say as ethnically, construed as possible. That meant, of course, the manipulation of labor through migration. That meant involvement in the race issue because it meant recruiting cheap labor in the South and bringing it north to dilute the power of Catholic ethnics who were already living there and were heavily unionized. "The Ford Motor Company," Ylvisaker admitted in one of his more candid moments, "I think it's clear, has been as guilty as any major industrial firm of recruiting cheap labor from the South while having a surplus locally. I always used to feel slightly guilty about talking in Detroit about handling the migrant problems when you were up against that canvas of things."[37]

Handling the migrant problems is precisely what Ylvisaker did during his tenure at the Ford Foundation, and he did it with the interests of the Ford family and the representatives they chose to staff their foundation board in mind. That meant, broadly speaking, the WASP establishment, as symbolized by John J. McCloy, who was asked by Henry Ford II to join the board in 1953. "The Foundation," Ylvisaker later admitted, "is a calculating political instrument."[38] Philanthropy, according to Ylvisaker, was in reality, "the power structure up there . . . taking care of its own," something which might prompt "a liberal with a conspiratorial outlook" to say, "it proves what I've been saying" all along.[39] The Ford Foundation's "philanthropy," if that is the right word for their activity, was always a form of social engineering, pursued with certain political benefits in mind. Social engineering was the means; political hegemony for the *ethnos* which gave away the money was the goal. Ylvisaker arrived on the scene at Ford when a broad consensus among both liberals and conservatives still supported the idea of social engineering. "The conservatives," according to Ylvisaker,

> admit that social engineering has not [brought about] and need not bring about tyranny and disaster; that it has in fact helped keep us alive and prospering and opens more markets for business than it closes. The liberals concede that the system is too complex and has too many advantages for drastic changes to be effective; that the public interest isn't necessarily synonymous with governmental action.[40]

> This rapprochement between former foes has produced a powerful alliance, which so far has outvoted every coalition of discontents brought together to oppose it. It has provided a climate of pragmatism extraordinarily favorable to a melding of public and private interests and toward large-scale efforts at social engineering.[41]

This "revolutionary change in social outlook" was fostered by a Supreme Court decision which "forced fundamental changes in education and race relations" during the 1950s and then went on to remove "the verbotens from the earlier untouchables of social engineering and family planning"[42] in the 1960s. The result, at least from Ylvisaker's point of view, is "one of the liveliest and most creative periods in American history, at least with respect to domestic affairs," as well as "a golden age of American social and political development."[43]

Needless to say, the ethnics whose neighborhoods were socially engineered during this "golden age" probably viewed things differently. But their opinions were not sought out by Ylvisaker or anyone who received grants from the Ford Foundation. Since the policies of the Ford Foundation of the 1950s were simply extensions of the policies of the Ford Motor Company of the 1930s when it came to things like migration, the beneficiaries of their "philanthropy" were all selected with the same ethnic-based social engineering in mind. This meant supporting Catholics like Father Theodore Hesburgh of the University of Notre Dame, because Hesburgh was working at the time to undermine the Catholic Church's ban on contraceptives. "Ted Hesburgh," according to Ylvisaker, was a "genius"[44] who "used to come to my office occasionally"[45] and chat, knowing that "he'd get his big money from the fat cats in the Foundation,"[46] in spite of the fact that he was a Catholic priest. Ironically, "some members of the Catholic clergy who were non grata for being too liberal,"[47] but all of that changed when John F. Kennedy became president, and "made it legitimate for the Foundation to be heroic"[48] on population control issues. That also meant taking control of migration at both ends. Since the Rogers Act had effectively cut off European immigration in the 1920s, migration meant the movement of blacks up from the South into the decaying sections of the northern cities where they were put to work as cheap labor, undercutting the wages of the ethnics who had already established themselves there before them.

Given his enthusiasm for social engineering and the Supreme Court–backed consensus which supported it, Ylvisaker's only remaining question was "Where could we launch the first experiments?"[49] Ylvisaker's answer to that question was the Gray Areas project. Ylvisaker came up the term "gray areas," during a brainstorming session with Robert C. Weaver, whom he had just hired at Ford. Weaver had been involved in the integration struggles of World War II and had just worked on Averell Harriman's unsuccessful Senate campaign, and was, as a result, out of work and looking for a job. The "gray areas" referred to "that section of deteriorating real estate between downtown and the newer suburbs," which had "become symbolic of urban problems" and, as a result, "the focus of a variety of converging Foundation interests."[50]

In the vocabulary of the Enlightenment materialist, community has no lasting value. As with every other aggregation in the universe, it is a happenstance concatenation of human atoms which take on a particular configuration at particular time but which is always evolving into something else. The "gray areas" are no exception to this rule.

> Into this part of the city are drawn most of the low-income migrants from rural areas, attracted by the greater opportunities of he city but ill-prepared for the urban way of life which has suddenly become their lot. The homes they occupy are the left over and obsolescent stock of the community's housing supply; the neighborhoods, they inherit are usually stripped of leadership and stabilizing institutions by the exodus of mid- and upper-income groups to the suburbs; family ties and community organization are dissolved in the flow of personal mobility and neighborhood change.[51]

The city, according to Ylvisaker, was a "system" whose purpose was assimilation. Anything ethnic, as a result, had only instrumental provisional value, as a transitional stage to something else. The same thing was true of the ethnic neighborhood, which Ylvisaker viewed as:

> a continuous system that attracts the newcomer (once the Scotch, the Irish, the Jews, the Italians; now the Negroes, the Puerto Ricans, the mountain Whites, the Mexicans and the American Indians) and assimilates this newcomer into all that is up-to-date and sought after in urban culture. In the past, it has taken about three generations for a newly arrived group to climb the totem pole of urban culture – by current symbols, to get from central-city tenement to suburban ranchhouse, from menial employment to the university club for lunch, from the sheer necessities of ethnic-bloc voting to the relaxed assurance of nonpartisan elections.[52]

The only trouble with this system, "as any production expert could tell you,"[53] is that "it's dangerously slow, full of inefficiencies and in many respects primitive and barbaric.

The waste of manpower over the production timespan of three generations has been fantastic."[54] At this point, science steps in and takes this natural process by the hand and "liberates" it. "Why not," Ylvisaker asks, "put systems analysts to work on the social production system of the modern metropolis to look for the bottlenecks, to cut waste and to reduce time, to speed flow, and to increase social output? Why not make one of our national goals to do in one generation for the urban newcomer what until now has taken three?"[55]

Ylvisaker is clearly a man imprisoned by the inexorable logic of his own inadequate categories, all of which have been derived from his understanding of the Enlightenment and its mechanistic modes of thought. After establishing the ethnic neighborhood as nothing more than an engine for assimilation, in other words, a vehicle which transports the neighborhood's residents someplace else, he then decides that progress entails accelerating that process and achieving assimilation in one generation instead of three. Ylvisaker clearly feels that this involved the social engineering equivalent of breaking the four-minute mile, whereas the people who were the "beneficiaries" of his ministrations probably saw it as something like playing "The Minute Waltz" in forty-seven seconds. Ylvisaker, in other words, not only had faulty ideas based on a completely mechanistic misunderstanding of the small community, he had the power and the money to put that misunderstanding into effect in one city after another. The ethnic neighborhood had been declared an inefficient engine of assimilation and, therefore, condemned to die by someone who was completely outside the political process and, because of the money he could give away, more powerful than any of the local officials. Where the people who lived there saw community, Paul Ylvisaker saw only decay:

> The most familiar pattern of the "Gray Areas" on the American scene is the decay noticed first in the near-downtown sections, centered usually around the railroad station or other main hubs of the old transportation systems, and spreading blight-like toward the boundaries of the central city and suburban fringe. Slums, skid-rows, etc. form a dark inner ring; from there out, the "gray" grows lighter but moves more swiftly as obsolescence of housing and industrial plant accelerates.[56]

Social engineering is necessary because "the normal operations of the market will not clear the economic and physical problems of these areas." New remedies will have to be found. On the human side, the "normal" process of historical evolution has eased the problems of each successive group of immigrants to the city. But the process is a "long and primitive one that can and should be shortened and perfected for present and future newcomers." The "gray areas," Ylvisaker said at another point, is "that growing wasteland which starts at a moving point uncomfortably close to the central business district and extends to a moving point uncomfortably close to the better residential suburbs." The gray areas, in other words, were ethnic neighborhoods, then being contested by the black migration the foundations and the psychological warfare crowd had orchestrated to supply wartime factories with workers. This is precisely how it was defined in Chicago, where the downtown interests divided up the resources of the areas between the Loop and the suburbs between themselves. Chicago's downtown interests, a group which included the University of Chicago, Michael Reese Hospital, and IIT, used urban renewal to drive blacks out of their neighborhoods, knowing full well that would never make it into the suburbs and would land in the "gray areas" in between instead. This practice was justified, according to Ylvisaker, because that part of the city had already

> been abandoned two, three and in some cases four times before, by the successive waves of migrants who have come looking for the city only to be told that it was still a suburb or two ahead of them. Certainly, the City of the Gray Area . . . is being abandoned; *but that is its function* [my emphasis]. For this is not really a city; it is a social process wrapped up in an appropriately shabby form. It is a process of transition and aspiration and self-improvement – for the immigrant from abroad, for the rural uprooted, for a wide assortment of human beings who are at the bottom rung of their life's ambitions.[57]

Ylvisaker's theory amounts to a decertification of the gray areas neighborhood as a bona fide community. It was, instead, a transitional device in a system of assimilation, and one which didn't work all that well either. Reducing the ethnic neighborhood to one function in his system, Ylvisaker then complains that it doesn't even serve this function very well. And he does this without ever once considering that the small community might have other meanings to those who live there. Once again Ylvisaker shows himself the intellectual captive of Enlightenment mechanistic thinking. The ethnic community is obsolete, according to Ylvisaker, because in a Darwinian universe there is no such thing as a stable community. Instead of that stable community, Ylvisaker, the urban expert, describes what he calls the "Iron Law of Outward Movement," in imitation of one of his Enlightenment models, the Manchester School's "Iron Law of Wages."[58] The city of history, with its "immobile and class-bound population and glacial rate of technological change," cannot prevail against the "Iron Law of Outward Movement," which is determined to a large extent by the "psychology of the automobile, that mechanized symbol and means of our release from the slavery to the single place."[59]

In typically Whig fashion, Ylvisaker saw not the city of history when he looked at the small community, but rather a "creative evolution," which erected "one-way systems of technology and communication" and destroyed the "option of reverse motion" in the process.[60] It was the job of the Ford Foundation to aid this natural movement, to create out of the obsolete city of history a new city, "the city of accelerating change and unstable form," where the main problems will be "the ever-exaggerating ones of personal and civic adjustment to social mobility and of economic and administrative accommodation to rapid obsolescence and of function and physical plant. Almost certainly, this will be the era of the discardable building, the movable utility system and the landscape that can be changed overnight."[61] In other words, it is the job of the Ford Foundation to engineer the consent of a recalcitrant and backward population to the constant change that the industrialists find beneficial to their interests. Those "with romantic memories" of the city of history may not like it, but no one can revoke this "Iron Law of Outward Movement," because, "like the universe, we seem to racing perpetually into the space around us."[62]

Behind all the typical Enlightenment talk of "iron laws" and inexorable natural processes, one can still detect the unsavory odor of ethnic self-interest. Since even Ylvisaker seems to be admitting that assimilation takes place naturally in America, his efforts to accelerate it bespeak as well a desire to control it in the interests of the people he represents at the Ford Foundation. That means assimilation on their terms and not on the terms of those who are assimilating because "the culture of the Gray Areas . . . is not the culture that should be the image of urban America."[63]

At another point, Ylvisaker admits that the term "gray areas" came from his search for neutral language. If we break down gray into its component parts, we realize that those components are black and white. The "gray areas," as conceived by Ylvisaker and Weaver, were a euphemism, in other words, for the ethnic neighborhood, then being contested by black migration. Ylvisaker's goal was to take control of that migration at both ends, and manage it according to the ethnic interests of the Ford Foundation. In order to accomplish this, the Ford Foundation targeted seven cities – Chicago, Cleveland, Detroit, Philadelphia, Pittsburgh, St. Louis, and Milwaukee – which Ylvisaker described as "among the 14 largest in the United States,"[64] without stating that they were also the cities where the black-ethnic struggle was currently hanging in the balance. The Gray Areas Program was the Ford Foundation's way of insuring that the outcome of that battle would coincide with their interests, which were historically the interests of the Ford Motor Company and the Ford family.

When Ylvisaker would describe his understanding of the city in public talks, it took on the nature of an epiphany as if he had just made some great scientific discovery. "I came to [a] sudden perception of the city as the magnet and passage-point of great migrations," he recounted later, ". . . it was for me an intellectual breakthrough. I had the sense that we were dealing with people problems, not bricks and mortar and not power structure problems."[65] In private, however, the aura of disinterest disappeared. Ylvisaker had got involved in the Gray Areas Program so that he could take "an entrepreneurial role in public affairs."[66] That involved doing "my homework very carefully."[67] And doing his homework meant that Ylvisaker had "probed both the black power structure, the city hall, and *our* power structure"[68] [my emphasis] before he decided to make any grants.

The Ford Foundation first attempted to take control of the black-ethnic conflict in Philadelphia by establishing the Philadelphia Council for Community Advancement in 1960 by convening at the University of Pennsylvania "a meeting . . . of the brightest minds in Philadelphia – educators, planners, social workers and social scientists – for an orientation to our program and to consider planning a comprehensive design."[69] One Ford Foundation memo indicates that "not much happened" after the meeting, until, that is, "four young professors at Temple University decided to spend the summer of 1961 thinking," a statement that causes the perceptive reader to wonder what the professors had been doing in the time leading up to the summer of 1961.[70]

Inspired by the meeting, or perhaps inspired even more by the prospect of getting both front feet into the Ford funding trough, Herman Niebuhr, a social psychologist at Temple University, developed a plan for North Philadelphia, Philadelphia's prime "gray area," which was, according to just about anyone who was anyone in Philadelphia, "bold innovative, founded on a clearly stated theoretical basis and inclusive of concern for all aspects of human betterment."[71]

This, of course, meant that the program, once it was funded, ran almost immediately into trouble. When the PCCA professors announced that they were going to use the Ford money to study the situation in North Philadelphia, Cecil B. Moore, the flamboyant head of the local NAACP, perhaps outraged that he didn't get any of the money, denounced the entire program as unnecessary. What was needed, according to Moore, was not study but action. At that point, the perennially disorganized Temple University staff was forced to spend most of its efforts on damage control and public relations, while Moore threatened to lead his black constituents in a boycott of the Ford Motor Company. Before long, professorial incompetence and black intransigence created a stalemate that had Ylvisaker and the people at Ford looking for another way to get traction in North Philadelphia, Philadelphia's crucial "gray area."

One month after PCCA received $1.6 million from Ford Foundation, Ford rep Henry Saltzman wrote that Andrew Freeman called to say that the Urban League, a notorious promoter of birth control in the black community, was supporting the PCCA, perhaps in the hope that he might get some of the PCCA's money. Freeman, trying to play the role of go-between, met with Cecil Moore, and told Saltzman that Moore planned to "actively cooperate."[72]

Six months later, Saltzman was forced to admit that Cecil Moore was still not cooperating, although his opposition had abated somewhat because he had been distracted by other issues. As soon as those distractions were taken care of, Saltzman told the foundation to brace themselves for renewed attacks. By December, Moore's attacks from the outside were combining with the Temple professors' incompetence from the inside to threaten the further existence of the program. By August of 1964, Clarence Faust wrote that "PCCA has almost certainly failed to implement a program."[73] As a result, the Ford Foundation was "considering termination of its activities."[74]

Notes

1. Virginia M. Esposito, ed., *Conscience and Community: The Legacy of Paul Ylvisaker* (New York: Peter Lang, 1999), p. xx.
2. Ibid., p. xvii.
3. Ibid., p. xviii.
4. Ibid.
5. "The Responsibility of the Individual in his Community," by Paul N. Ylvisaker, The Robert L. DeWitt Lectureship, Friday November 19, 1965, Christ Church Cranbrook, Bloomfield Hills, Michigan, Saul Alinsky papers #568, UIC Archives.
6. Ibid.
7. "The Sixties : A Forecast" Life Insurance advertisers association, New York, 9/21/60, Ylvisaker papers, Box 5, Gray Areas, 1961, Harvard University Archives.
8. "Responsibility," Saul Alinsky papers #568, UIC Archives.
9. Ibid.
10. Ibid.
11. Esposito, p. xx.
12. Ibid.
13. "The Sixties: A Forecast," Ylvisaker papers, Box 5, Gray Areas, 1961, Harvard University Archives.
14. Ibid.
15. Ibid.

16 Esposito, p. 18.
17 Ibid.
18 Ibid., p. xxxv.
19 "Responsibility," Saul Alinsky papers #568, UIC Archives.
20 Ibid.
21 Ibid.
22 Walter M. Phillips interview with Ylvisaker, p. 14. Ylvisaker papers, Box 24, Harvard University Archives.
23 Ibid.
24 Ibid.
25 Interview, p. 23, Ylvisaker papers, Box 24, Harvard University Archives.
26 Ibid.
27 Oral History for Ford Foundation, conducted 9/27/73, Ylvisaker papers, Box 5, Harvard University Archives.
28 Ibid.
29 Esposito, p. xxi.
30 Oral history for Ford Foundation, conducted 9/27/73, Ylvisaker papers, Box 5, Harvard University Archives.
31 Ibid., p. 11.
32 Ibid., p. 13.
33 Kai Bird, *The Chairman: John J. McCloy and the Making of the American Establishment* (New York: Simon & Schuster, 1992), p. 519.
34 Ibid.
35 Oral History, p. 23.
36 Ibid., p. 45.
37 Ibid., p. 81.
38 Ibid., p. 47.
39 Ibid., pp. 46–47.
40 Esposito, p. 48.
41 Ibid.
42 Ibid.
43 Ibid., p. 47.
44 Oral History, p. 70.
45 Ibid.
46 Ibid.
47 Ibid.
48 Ibid.
49 Ibid., p. 24.
50 The Gray Areas, Gray Areas folder, January to June 1963, Paul Ylvisaker papers, Box 5, Harvard University Archives.
51 Ibid.
52 Esposito, p. 14.
53 Ibid.
54 Ibid.
55 Ibid.

56 The Gray Areas, Gray Areas folder, January to June 1963, Paul Ylvisaker papers, Box 5, Harvard University Archives.

57 Esposito, p. 95.

58 Ibid., p. 99.

59 Ibid.

60 Ibid.

61 Ibid., p. 100.

62 Ibid., p. 99.

63 The Gray Areas, Gray Areas folder, January to June 1963, Paul Ylvisaker papers, Box 5, Harvard University Archives.

64 Ibid.

65 Oral History, p. 58.

66 Ibid., p. 15.

67 Ibid.

68 Ibid.

69 Public Affairs and Education: Gray Areas Program Request for an Extension of the Great Cities – Gray Areas Program March 1962, Ylvisaker papers, Box 5, Harvard University Archives.

70 Ibid.

71 Ibid.

72 Memo from Henry Saltzman, 1/31/63, Gray Areas folder January to June 1963, Ylvisaker papers, Box 5, Harvard University Archives.

73 Report from Clarence Faust, 8/14/64, Gray Areas folder, Ylvisaker papers, Box 5, Harvard University Archives.

74 Ibid.

The Interstate Highway System

At the same time that Ethel Claes and the residents of Corktown were gearing up for battle, the forces that were about to devour that and other similar neighborhoods in other cities were poised on the brink of achieving their greatest victory. In addition to *Berman v. Parker* and *Brown v. Board of Education of Topeka, Kansas*, 1954 was the year which saw the triumphal conclusion to a plan to create a national network of limited-access highways orchestrated by a group of automobile, oil, rubber, and concrete magnates collectively known as the Highwaymen when the Eisenhower Administration finally convinced Congress to approve the Interstate Highway Bill. It was the culmination of a plan which had been years in the making, beginning in fact in 1920 when the United States census showed that, for the first time in its history, a majority of Americans lived in cities. Taking note of that fact, Alfred P. Sloan, then chairman of GM, decided to "reorder society . . . to alter the environment in which automobiles were sold."[1] That meant bringing the car to the city and that meant getting city dwellers, who were used to paying for their transportation needs in increments measured in pennies, to invest in automobiles, which would cost them thousands of dollars a year. As if recognizing that any rational person without coercion would never accept this sort of change, the Highwaymen decided to coerce the public at large "by getting intercity rail passengers out of trains and into cars."[2] During the early 1930s, GM tried to buy up the interurban rail lines from the electric utilities which ran them, and replace the trains with buses but without much success. What GM couldn't do directly at the beginning of the decade, they began to do indirectly by the end of the decade, through a man by the name of Roy Fitzgerald, whose dummy bus line gobbled up one financially troubled rail line after another. Fitzgerald would then rip up the rail lines and replace the trains with buses, sparing GM, Standard Oil, Firestone Tire and Rubber, and the rest of his corporate backers any unpleasant publicity. When Illinois Power and Light was forced to divest itself of its street-car lines in Bloomington, Quincy, Champaign-Urbana, Decatur, Danville, Kewanee, and LaSalle-Peru, Fitzgerald with the support of his unnamed backers moved quickly, and soon many residents of Illinois were faced with the prospect of riding the bus instead of the train, all in the name of progress, at the behest of people manipulating the transportation market for their own interests. Soon the buses would disappear as well, because "the real profits were going to be made from sales of cars after the destruction of mass transit opened the way for a huge public network of streets and highways."[3]

As part of its ongoing psychological-warfare campaign against the interests of the American people, GM sponsored its Futurama exhibit, a 35,738 square foot mock-up of GM's plan for America's future, at the 1939 New York World's Fair. Visitors to the Futurama exhibit were told that by 1960 they would be traveling along 14-lane expressways at speeds of 50, 75, and 100 miles per hour. They were also told that traffic would eventually penetrate this nation's cities – where it would never get snarled, where it would not foul the air, and where it would be "so routed as to displace outmoded business sections and undesirable slum areas."[4] Studebaker would go out of business three years after all of this was supposed to happen, but in 1939 Studebaker's president, Paul Hoffman, was as infected with the idea that the automobile was the vehicle of the future as anyone else. Even then, the automobile's enthusiasts seems to sense that it was incompatible with city life, but even if that were the case, their feeling was that it was so much the worse for cities. "Most of our cities," Hoffman wrote in the *Saturday Evening Post* in 1939, "are almost as antiquated, trafficwise, as if they had medieval walls, moats, drawbridges."[5] As a result, they were, Studebaker-wise, "the greatest untapped field of potential customers."[6]

Since his days at Harvard, where he took classes under Professor William Z. Ripley, Franklin Delano Roosevelt had always been fascinated by the road's ability to bring about dramatic increases in the value of the land immediately adjacent to it. While pondering a way to get America out of the Depression, President Roosevelt toyed with the idea of buying up a two-mile strip of land coast to coast and then financing the road he would build on it by proceeds accruing from increased land sales. During the '30s, Roosevelt even summoned Thomas MacDonald, probably the greatest road lobbyist in the country's history and eventually the man who would oversee the implementation of the Interstate Highway System, to the White House to discuss the idea. Roosevelt, who was worried about unemployment and was considering the coast-to-coast road as a huge public-works project, could never decide who should benefit from the road system and so the idea languished, until America got into the war.

On April 14, 1941, Roosevelt summoned MacDonald again, this time to be on the Interregion Highway Committee to plan for the construction of roads following the war. With people like MacDonald, and prominent socialists and planners like Rexford Tugwell on the committee, the committee's recommendations were in many ways a foregone conclusion. In January 1944 the committee issued its final report and, *mirabile dictu*, it recommended a combination of Tugwellian urban renewal and concomitant expansion of the central government's powers in combination with MacDonald's vision of what would make the Highwaymen happy. Roads, in other words, would solve the cities' problems and enrich the road lobby at the same time. It was something for everyone, or almost everyone. Rose tries to explain that unlikely premise in the following way:

> Urban revitalization occupied an equally lofty place in the imagination of committee members. Central urban places, as they pointed out, were "cramped, crowded, and depreciated." Industrialists, shopkeepers and homeowners had relocated to the suburbs, thus chopping urban tax bases, thus reducing money available for urban services. Construction of interregional expressways, or so went the reasoning, offered urban leaders a tool to reduce the size of trouble spots and stop others from materializing.[7]

It was a classic instance of big government getting in bed with big business and both then determining public policy to suit their interests. The war enabled this marriage of convenience for the same reason that it got Roosevelt to abandon the New Deal's social program. Roosevelt needed the support of the WASP ruling class to win the war, and he could only get that support by bartering away the interests of the urban Catholic ethnics who put him in office. Since the urban Catholic ethnics were overwhelmingly blue-collar workers in WASP-owned factories and because their penchant for unionization was a constant source of anxiety to the capitalist class, Roosevelt sought to placate the fears of the ruling class by re-tooling the nation's industries on terms favorable to the capitalists and not the workers. This meant suburbanization of the new plants as well as moving them to non-union areas like California and the Southwest, which is where the aviation industry relocated as a result of federal largesse.

It also meant moving plants in traditionally industrial areas far from the cities which housed the workforce that worked in them. Between 1942 and 1944 the U.S. government through the War Production Board spent $35.5 billion to recapitalize American industry for the war effort, an amount almost equal to the entire 1939 value of the U.S. manufacturing plant. In order to insure the support of the industrialists, Roosevelt organized this recapitalization on their terms. That mean hiring former Sears Roebuck executive Donald Nelson, and not Walter Reuther, to run the WPB. Reuther had a plan of his own, one that would have been more beneficial to the workers who staffed the plants. By creating the WPB as an independent agency under Nelson's direction, Roosevelt "devised a radical form of industrial mobilization" which gave "no alarm to the nation's industrial interests."[8] Since it was done with the nation's industrial interests in mind, that recapitalization also meant suburbanization of industry because relocating plants like Ford's brand new $100 million Willow Run Bomber plant thirty miles outside Detroit "placed their new facilities largely beyond the reach of the unions, New Deal-leaning mayors, and the other constituencies which had fueled urban liberalism in the 1930s."[9] Suburbanization in industry, like suburbanization in residence, was aimed at taming the political power of the largely urban ethnics.

The deal Roosevelt cut with the War Production Board to appeal to the interests of the industrialist class was virtually identical in scope with the deal he cut with the highway lobby to solve the cities' problems. In fact they were two sides of the same coin. Suburbanization was simply a new way of dealing with a group of people – urban ethnic Catholic unionized workers – that the ruling class had always found threatening and intractable. During the turbulent '30s, Henry Ford dealt with this threat by brute force, hiring his own private goon squad of gangsters and ex-prizefighters under Harry Barnett to keep the unions out of his plants. In 1946, Henry Ford II, shortly after taking over the company after its founder's death, decided to make peace with the unions, largely because the industrialists had a new and more effective form of control at their disposal, namely, the suburbanization of the plants and the concomitant suburbanization and "Americanization" of the Catholic ethnic workforce that was taking place there.

The unpleasant note of social control was never far from the thoughts of the Utopian road builders, who were now, as a result of the recommendations of the MacDonald/Tugwell committee, allied with the thinking of the utopian urban planners and social engineers. "During the decade following World War II," Rose writes,

> most Americans, including state road engineers, believed that immigrants to the nations' cities were busily and eagerly going about the business of becoming "Americanized." Serious scholars of American culture and history reinforced the

popular impression which learned publications identify as a "triple melting pot" in which the barriers of ethnicity, if not race, collapsed into three generally comparable religious traditions. As part of this vast changeover, researchers pointed out that the children of immigrants from Italy, Ireland and Russia intersected one another in the suburbs and along the cool green rim of every city. Many Americans, again including state road engineers, believed that Americanization and movement to the suburbs accompanied one another in a nearly effortless fashion. Above all, the trolley and then the automobile, by facilitating the process of outward movement, were valuable adjuncts to certain beneficial change. State road engineers, with their passion for traffic service and cheap land in crowded neighborhoods near downtown, could thus readily imagine that they were only giving another nudge to inevitable progress.[10]

The suburbanization of both industry and residence was orchestrated by the federal government, primarily through defense contracts in the former instance and FHA mortgage policy in the latter. "Federal defense spending during and after World War II," according to Mollenkopf,

> fostered "new" industries which chose an even more pronounced pattern of suburban location. Between 1950 and 1980, military spending accounted for one-quarter of the growth in federal spending. . . . Between 1932 and 1952, military spending accounted for over half the growth in federal spending. This spending created the electronics and aircraft industries as we know them today. As these industries abandoned central-city locations for new suburban plants, they spurred considerable suburban population growth.[11]

In short, "suburbanization and decentralization shifted the traditional, ethnic, blue collar labor force out of the older central cities and built up suburbs and new metropolitan areas"[12] where they were no longer identifiably ethnic. What the ethnics who followed the jobs to the suburbs gained in individual buying power, they lost in traditional political power by being dispersed according to class rather than concentrated according to ethnicity.

Road building was crucial to this dispersal and control. Cities were considered obsolete because the residential areas around the fringe of central business districts were now "almost untenable, occupied by the humblest citizens, they . . . form the city's slums – a blight near its very core!"[13] In his January 1944 report, Roads Commissioner MacDonald was proposing a system which would kill two, or three, birds with one stone. A national expressway network would relieve traffic, create jobs and serve as a framework for urban redevelopment all for a price that was roughly 60 percent of the budget for the United States government, and all that money would flow into the coffers of the people whose interests MacDonald represented. As an added benefit, one that would appeal to both big-business "conservatives" like MacDonald, representing the highway lobby, and Tugwell and the big-government social engineers, they would create a new instrument of social control which would benefit both constituencies. "If men were going to be put to work on roads after the war," they argued, *"they should construct a different social, urban and economic order, not just build highways* [my emphasis]."[14] MacDonald had always argued that roads were a form of social engineering. He just never used the term. Instead he said that national highways fostered a "broad Americanism"[15] which not only promoted under-standing – if the modern highway had existed in 1860 it would have prevented the Civil War. "The intersectional misunderstanding which gave rise to it," he claimed, "could not have reached the critical stage of war had it been possible, as it is now, for the Southern planter to spend his summer in Maine and the new England businessman to journey south-ward in his own car for golf at Pinehurst and a winter vacation in Florda."[16]

What the Interregion Highway Commission and the collaboration it enabled between forces represented by MacDonald on the one hand and Tugwell on the other made popu-lar was the emerging consensus that, somehow, expressways, far from destroying cities by tearing down buildings and clogging their streets with cars, would solve the cities' prob-lems. Engineer Lawrence I. Hewes told a meeting of business and political leaders at the Commonwealth Club of San Francisco on December 7, 1945, that "the modern express-way can help preserve the city" by "allowing convenient access now found only in subur-ban centers."[17] It was, therefore, "important to coordinate urban renewal and expressway building" because "expressway roads could penetrate areas" with "obsolete buildings and lowered property values."[18] Engineers and planners, as a result, would have "to work hand in hand to obtain the maximum benefit in cleaning up those blighted sections."[19]

In 1947, MacDonald was saying much the same thing, hoping that the Highwaymen could "insinuate themselves into the urban renewal field, retain control of highway build-ing and direct both toward a broader program of urban design."[20] Between the two of them, the urban planners and the Highwaymen dominated one way or another the future of the country's infrastructure and certainly urban infrastructure from 1950 onward. It all depended on which faction exercised the greatest leverage on the local scene. As the fed-eral government became more and more deeply committed to large road and urban renew-al projects, it created a huge pool of money that could be used to remodel American cities according to the predilections of the local political factions which got control of that money. Whole new regimes, like the Clark-Dilworth-ADA Democrats came to power to capitalize on this funding, and when it arrived they used it, as politicians are wont to do, in their own self-interest. The power might pass from the road lobby which was controlled by Republican interests, to the urban renewal lobby, which was controlled by Democrats, but both spelled disaster for the nation's large cities. It was also a situation of heads-I-win-tails-you-lose for the ethnics who lived in those cities.

Notes

1   Stephen B. Goddard, *Getting There: The Epic Struggle between Road and Rail in the American Century* (New York: Basic Books, 1994), p. 126.
2   Ibid.
3   Ibid., p. 132.
4   Mark H. Rose, *Interstate: Express Highway Politics 1939–1989* (Knoxville: University of Tennessee Press, 1979), p. 1.
5   Goddard, p. 170.

6   Ibid.

7   Rose, p. 20.

8   John H. Mollenkopf, *The Contested City* (Princeton, N.J.: Princeton University Press, 1983), p. 108.

9   Ibid.

10 Rose, p. 116.

11 Mollenkopf, p. 26.

12 Ibid., p. 38.

13 Rose, p. 13.

14 Ibid., p. 17.

15 Goddard, p. 103.

16 Ibid.

17 Rose, p. 61.

18 Ibid.

19 Ibid.

20 Ibid.

Margaret Collins Creates
Friends Suburban Housing

Shortly after Jim Cassells failed to persuade Phillip Klutznick to integrate Park Forest, Margaret H. Collins came up with a plan to do the same sort of thing in the suburbs of Philadelphia. The idea for Friends Suburban Housing, according to the organization's history, "originated in the mind of one woman."[1] The timing of the operation, however, makes it unlikely that Collins came up with the idea on her own. Like Cassells, Collins was a Quaker. Cassells described his failure to influence Klutznick in a memo he wrote in early 1954. The memo was confidential, but it was meant to be shared with other Quakers who were interested in housing. Collins was especially interested because she was "an expert in home remodeling and redecoration."[2] In addition to those skills, she had also been trained as a community organizer. In addition to that, her address alone showed an interest in real estate. She lived at "Arnecliffe Stable" [no numbers], Gulph Road and Merion Avenue, Bryn Mawr, one of the ruling class suburbs outside Philadelphia. In typical Quaker fashion, the lady from Arnecliffe Stable had decided that she was going to determine who would live next door to the recent refugees from C Street and 58th and Chester. She would do this in the name of democracy and conscience – also in typically Quaker fashion – which meant not consulting the consciences of the people who lived in the neighborhoods she decided to engineer.

The idea of manipulating residence as a form of social engineering had a long tradition with the Quakers. Collins would later claim that the idea for Friends Suburban Housing "arose out of a friendship [she had] with a Negro woman schoolteacher, whose personal qualities impressed her deeply."[3] But she also mentioned Quaker participation in the Underground Railway as contributing to the idea as well. During the late '30s, the Quakers had built Penn-Craft in western Pennsylvania, something which was billed at the time as an attempt to create jobs for out-of-work coal miners. Later the Quakers admitted that social engineering played a role there as well, since it was set up as "the first intentionally interracial housing development in the country."[4]

Quaker benevolence served as a cover for social engineering elsewhere as well. In Logan, West Virginia, the Quakers ran contraceptive clinics for the families of the men who worked in the Rockefeller-owned coal mines there. As a sign of their gratitude the Rockefellers were consistent supporters of Quaker ventures since that time, not just in the area of contraception, funding Quaker clinics in Puerto Rico, Mexico, and Hong Kong, but also in the area of "democratic" housing. In the American Friends Service Committee consolidated budget for the year 1962–63 (the fiscal year ending September 30, 1963), a total of $97,137 was allotted to their "Integrated Housing Program."[5] In the AFSC annual report for 1962, the Quakers explain just what this program entails:

In areas surrounding our cities, housing opportunities for minority group members have become increasingly restricted. To respond to this problem in their area, a group of citizens from Burlington County, New Jersey, organized four years ago with the requested aid of the AFSC. Educational and action programs have been designed to bring about more democratic living patterns.[6]

On November 17, 1965, Earle Edwards of the AFSC wrote to Dana S. Creel of the Rockefeller Brothers Fund for financial assistance for the fiscal year 1965–66. As part of their appeal to the Rockefellers, Edwards cited the AFSC's "on-going housing opportunities programs in [Philadelphia and] other Northern cities" whose budget by fiscal '65–'66 had grown to $276,300.[7]

Collins was not getting Rockefeller money in 1955; in fact, the whole idea behind Friends Suburban Housing was to create an organization that wouldn't need charity because it was a business. FSH was conceived as a real-estate agency with a social purpose behind it. One year after the idea sprang full-blown from Miss Collins's mind, Friends Suburban Housing, Inc. had its own real-estate office at 53 Cricket Avenue in Ardmore, a suburb close to, but not quite as tony as, Bryn Mawr, and was "prepared to transfer property in the suburbs with a view to encouraging integration."[8] The operation may have been small, but it had the backing of the ruling class in Philadelphia, especially its Quaker wing. S. Allen Bacon, cousin of city planner Ed Bacon, was on the board, as was Clarence Pickett and Frank S. Loescher. Miss Collins could also count on the assistance of George Schermer, head of the Philadelphia Commission on Human Relations. In addition to the CHR, FSH could also count on the support of the Philadelphia Housing Association and the Fellowship Commission. It also had the full support of the local Quaker establishment. "Where FSH has made a sale," one program participant stated, "it often relies on both the Committee on Race Relations of the Yearly Meeting and on the Community Relations Program of the AFSC for community work."[9] It also relied on the Quaker community in Philadelphia for its staff.

After attending an FSH meeting in December of 1955, Clarence H. (Mike) Yarrow, an executive with the American Friends Service Committee, agreed to serve as its chairman. In order to gain support for FSH, Yarrow "brought its concern before the Philadelphia Yearly Meeting in 1956,"[10] giving some indication that this was a clearly Quaker operation, not just something promoted by the "radicals" at the AFSC. "We urge all Friends," Yarrow later wrote in an article in *Friends Journal*, which probably summarized in written form the case he made before the Yearly Meeting, "to ponder the question of whether the privileges we enjoy in our suburban homes are open to our brothers of darker color."[11]

Yarrow would learn the unpleasant answer to that question before too long, but for the moment he was full of enthusiasm for the new project and took the opportunity to let his fellow Quakers know that "we would be particularly glad to know if you would welcome a responsible family from a minority group as a neighbor."[12] The answer to that question would become apparent soon enough, and when it did it would point out the fact that the term "suburban" in the title was much too broad. Friends Suburban Housing concentrated its efforts overwhelmingly in new post-World War II suburbs like Levittown. They did not sell houses in Bryn Mawr for a number of reasons, which would become apparent during the course of their operations. FSH invariably targeted new suburbs, which is to say, ones filling up with refugees from the Philadelphia ethnic neighborhoods which were emptying out because of racial succession.

As a result, the open-handed approach at the beginning of his appeal quickly shifts to the more familiar ground of psychological warfare, which makes use of the procedure which the area committees are supposed to follow in getting black families into areas which would prefer not to have them there. Yarrow's instructions follow the same contradictory line throughout. "The Friends Suburban Housing Committee," he writes, "wishes to work in neighborhoods where you know that some people are willing to give a welcome to the new family."[13] But since the Quakers did not live in the new suburbs which the FSH wanted to engineer, other plans had to be made. "Experience," he continues, contradicting what he just said about welcoming families, "has shown that it is not sound practice to poll or survey community sentiment prior to the introduction of new neighbors."[14] That is because "a certain amount of discomfort and tension"[15] were certain to follow their efforts. That discomfort and tension can be ameliorated, however, by having the Friends share with the disgruntled members of the community they have just violated, "what has been discovered in scientific studies" of "successful integration which have occurred in other suburbs as well as Philadelphia."[16] Since there had been no integration, successful or otherwise, in Philadelphia, the number of examples to be kept in mind would not have taxed the memory of committee members who were engineering the neighborhood.

As should be apparent by now, FSH was a project deeply rooted in Quaker theology, or the lack thereof. The Quaker idea of conscience did "not require that everybody agree with us before we make moves in accordance with our own conscience" as they set about creating "more democratic living patterns."[17] The Quakers never get around to defining what "democratic living patterns" entail, but it was clear from the context of the grant proposals that they submitted to the Rockefeller Foundations that it did not entail the consent of the people living in Philadelphia or its suburbs. The Quakers had taken it upon themselves to teach Philadelphians a lesson. "Diversified neighborhoods," the AFSC wrote in its 1961 pamphlet *Homes and Community*,

> have "built-in" lessons in democracy – lessons in the dignity of the individual and respect for his contributions to society. Such communities build citizens more secure in their knowledge of democracy and better able to share its responsibilities.[18]

The use of the word "democracy" is especially ironic, since the Quakers were operating what was first of all an essentially clandestine operation, and secondly one that would hardly have gained the approval of the majority of the residents of the area which received the benefit of their ministrations if they had been asked.

At certain moments facts like these seem to trouble the otherwise impervious Quaker conscience. "Is FSH," Yarrow wonders at one point, "justified in 'playing God' in this fashion?"[19] The answer to that question is, of course, "yes," because "FSH was founded on the premise that little progress can be made in intergroup relations by techniques of education and persuasion which do not involve concrete experience."[20] The people who bear the brunt of this "concrete experience" may not like it, but Quaker experience has shown that they will get over it soon enough, if they are presented with a "fait accompli." According to Yarrow, "The best way to integrate a plant is to go ahead and do it."[21] In other words, force it down the throats of the unsuspecting beneficiaries of social engineering. "Employees will react negatively if their opinion on integration of the workforce is asked; but, presented with a fait accompli, all but a very few will soon adjust to it."[22] In other words, don't ask. Just do it. The less-enlightened portion of mankind will be grateful for the change ultimately, even if in the meantime, "progress in intergroup relationships almost inevitably [is] accompanied by tension."[23] The recipients of Quaker social engineering will eventually be grateful because by engineering the small community in their own interests, the Quakers are "strengthening democracy":

> When we insist that any man who has the resources should have the freedom to buy a house of his own choosing in a community of his own choosing, we are not only aiding him to implement his right under the law but we are helping ourselves, *strengthening democracy*, giving expression to our religious convictions and making it possible for our whole society to benefit from the diversity in culture and heritage of which our country has been justly proud. We can rejoice in the relevant and significant, even though modest, role we are playing in the struggle for freedom – a struggle which can and must be won for all, if it is to be secure for any [my emphasis].[24]

When it comes to "democracy," housing, according to the AFSC's 1954 Housing Opportunities Program, "represents the worst area of American life as far as putting democratic belief into practice goes."[25] This is so because "rigid housing segregation patterns tend to make inoperative in many areas the Supreme Court decision concerning school integration."[26] The situation was especially bad in Chicago, where "violence as a method of enforcing segregation has a shocking degree of acceptance."[27] As their contribution to social peace in Chicago, the Quakers "have helped make the moving in of Negro families to three of the previously all-white public housing projects, similar to Trumbull Park, a more peaceful event, by working with the present residents and community."[28]

More peaceful than what, the Quakers don't specify. But they do make clear that "the 'restructuring' which FSH set out to effect is of a very basic nature," requiring, in Chicago at least, "an advisory committee, predominantly Quaker," as well as "social workers, a professor, an architect, a member of the Chicago Housing Authority, a member of the Chicago Land Clearance Commission, a member of a mortgage bankers firm."[29] The Quakers somehow sensed that their "long overdue [sic] . . . restructuring of intergroups relations in the housing field" might create "hostility, even to the point of violence,"[30] but they remained undeterred in disrupting the social fabric of cities like Philadelphia and Chicago because of their deeply held principles, which they felt free to impose on their unsuspecting fellow citizens. "As is the way of Friends, they did not welcome the thought of hostility. But neither – in the tradition which has led many Quakers to accept prison rather than desert principle – did they accept the 'solution' of the problem which involves letting nature take its course."[31]

In spite of having the backing of the establishment in Philadelphia, FSH got off to a slow start. FSH held its first formal organizational meeting on February 15, 1956, at the home of Thomas B. Harvey, a Philadelphia manufacturer and philanthropist who was a "perennial champion of liberal causes."[32] Harvey, not surprisingly, was a Quaker, as was just about everyone else at the meeting, since those who had been invited, were as Miss Collins put it, "weighty but liberal"[33] Friends from fourteen monthly meetings in the suburbs.

Four months later, at another meeting, this time at "Arnecliffe Stable," Miss Collins was pleased to announce that the FSH had its first listing. Needless to say, the listing was not in the vicinity of Arnecliffe Stable, but rather in Yeadon, one of the newest suburbs north of the city which served as a collecting point for Catholic ethnics driven out of their former neighborhoods by racial migration. Not surprisingly, "it was pointed out that we did not as yet know any families in the area whom we can count on to be friendly."[34] The fact that the Quakers didn't know anyone in Yeadon gives some indication that the Quakers were not involved in integrating suburbs like Swarthmore or Haverford, the neighborhoods where they lived, a fact which led to "a thorough discussion of the question as to whether we should go forward with the sale until such a time as we are confident of at least some support in the area."[35]

Eventually, it was not a fear of "serious repercussions" but simply the fact that FSH was seen by just about everyone as a realtor of last resort that hampered the organization's effectiveness. "Even people who should know better," the Quakers state in a moment of candor, "often list with somebody else first. When they come to us, it is usually a desperation measure."[36] As some indication of the type of people who were offering their homes for sale through FSH at the time, Jane Reinheimer, in a confidential memo, mentions the fact that a certain Margaret Whitney contacted FSH and expressed a willingness to sell her house through them, but in the same conversation she also made a point of telling Margaret Collins that she was a member of the Communist Party because she felt "that it might adversely affect public relations in the neighborhood."[37] Reinheimer also mentions "one other new fact," namely that Miss Whitney is sharing the house with another woman, and so is presumably a lesbian in addition to being a Communist. In the end, Collins and Reinheimer agreed not to represent Miss Whitney, for pretty much Miss Whitney's reasons, not because of the effect the sale might have on the community, but because "it might adversely affect public relations."[38] With clientele like this, the real-estate business was not booming at FSH in the early years of that organization's existence.

All that changed in 1957 when a recession hit the economy and caused many people who had bought their homes with VA mortgages into default. Those VA defaults provided FSH with a golden opportunity to make social gain at the expense of someone's financial loss. Five of the eighteen houses they sold between 1956 and October 15, 1958, were VA foreclosures. More importantly, it opened up to the Quakers and their agents the best avenue for integrating neighborhoods in Philadelphia. Once they got the repo lists from the FHA, which they would do after Robert Weaver went to Washington, they had first call on housing stock in transitional areas and could buy up houses at bargain-basement prices, something which translated into significant leverage in certain threatened communities. Friends Suburban Housing, however, was not involved in Philadelphia because "integration" in Philadelphia was accomplished by other agencies. It was being done by black real-estate firms like Tucker and Tucker, black political entrepreneurs like Leon Sullivan, and city agencies like the Commission on Human Relations.

In November 1957, Tom Colgan, while discussing the pros and cons of notifying the local police before a move-in, cited John McDermott, Dennis Clark's colleague at the CHR, who "advises me that it is routine in Philadelphia to discuss with police the move-in of a Negro family in an all-white area."[39] The facts of the matter were simple. The Quakers didn't need work on the integration of Philadelphia because they had created the CHR as an arm of the city government, and the CHR was doing the integrating for them. In March 1960, in one of their many memos, the Quakers noted that "the Philadelphia Commission on Human Relations" had just issued a "new kit of materials . . . *which is directed, as you know, at encouraging Negro families to pioneer in all-white areas.* As was anticipated, this new approach has drawn a storm of protests from local neighborhoods, some political powers and certainly from the real estate board here" [my emphasis].[40] Beginning in earnest in 1958, "the American Friends Service Committee undertook a full-time program aimed at changing the prevailing patterns of housing segregation in *selected areas of the Delaware Valley*" [my emphasis].[41]

In June of 1958, FSH moved Kenneth and Julia Mosby into Levittown. The Mosbys followed Bill and Daisy Myer by one year, the first black family in Levittown. In a confidential memo, the Quakers explained that "employees of the Concord Park management put the Mosbys in touch with the director of the AFSC Metropolitan Housing Program who had been working closely with civic groups in Levittown."[42] FSH found moving the Mosbys in easier than expected because "many persons had expressed regret and shame over the mob scenes which accompanied the previous move in."[43] After the Mosbys expressed interest in becoming pioneers in a white neighborhood, the FSH bought the house via the VA foreclosure list.

The reaction in Levittown was more turmoil, based not so much on hatred of this particular black family or any black family but on the fear that this was another "blockbusting attempt" of the sort which had driven them to Levittown in the first place. Aside from a number of "nuisance calls," nothing much happened. On Wednesday June 25, the Mosbys called the AFSC office after they moved in to give them their unlisted phone number. The AFSC, in turn, provided guards for the house, and it was on one of these details that Dick Taylor met his future wife.[44] The AFSC memo also notes that "there have also been few overt expressions of friendliness. Only two neighbors came to visit."[45] But this seems not to have concerned them. Their purpose was not to create a new community; their purpose was to change the nature of the community they found. One of the lessons the FSH gleaned from their experience in Levittown was precisely the effect they had on community formation there. "When the average white resident sees a Negro enter his neighborhood," they commented in retrospect, "he envisions the ruin of an environment which he has often sacrificed heavily to obtain for himself and his family."[46] Once the neighborhood is confronted with a "fait accompli," however, "open resistance rarely prevails long. Large scale panic selling will ensue only if there is sufficient waiting Negro market to buy the houses."[47] Before long the Quakers realized that the opposition to integration in the suburbs was hardly formidable. White suburbs were part of the system and would remain so, not because the whites were such fierce racists, but because for the most part, the blacks did not want to live there. Aside from a few intrepid pioneers, the great majority of blacks in Philadelphia did not want the risks associated being the first black on an all-white block, but beyond that they did not particularly want the isolation that went with that status either.

As a result, in March of 1959, the FSH was having trouble not with recalcitrant whites but with persuading blacks to move to suburbs like Levittown. "FSH," according to one of their memos, "has had a number of desirable properties available in Levittown, both through VA foreclosures and voluntary listings by owners, yet it has found only one Negro family to date willing to take advantage of them."[48] With the economy on the mend, FSH was now faced with a dwindling number of VA repossessions as their source of housing. By focusing on the dwindling VA mortgages, FSH ignored a more fundamental fact. Blacks did not like being pioneers in the suburbs; the standard migration pattern was one or two blocks across the racial dividing line in the next contiguous neighborhood, which emptied out and then filled up again with blacks. On March 18, 1960, Judy Howard congratulated FSH staff for moving another black family into Levittown, citing the "smooth teamwork between Friends Suburban Housing, the housing staff here, and probably most important, the township official and community authorities in this particular section of Levittown."[49] But the fact remains that in an age of huge racial migration, the FSH had moved just five families into Levittown over a period of as many years.

Integrating the suburbs, if that is what the Quakers' true intention was, was not going to work because migration patterns, even if they could be stimulated artificially, still had a life of their own based to a greater or lesser extent on the psychology of the people who did the moving. The system intended the suburbs for white people. If they were integrated, there would be no reason for beleaguered urban ethnics to move there.

As a result FSH was creating a lot of ill will without doing much of anything at all to change the system or accomplish their ostensible goals. When Irving Mandel sold his Levittown home to Bill and Daisy Myers in 1957, his act "brought latent anti-Semitism to the surface."[50] The same thing could be said of the Quakers, when they orchestrated the second move. At the end of 1957, Thelma Babbitt of the AFSC had a "heated discussion" of the sort Jim Cassells excelled at in Chicago with Rev. Daniel Stevick, pastor of the Episcopal Church in Balsington. Rev. Stevick, criticized

> the ability of an "outside group" like the Quakers – that is the AFSC – [to] actually bring about integration in a community where they were not prepared to deal with the consequences. He warned me I would probably find a cool reception among some of the ministers who rather resented the Quakers expecting other religious groups to pick up the pieces after the Quakers had stirred up the problems.[51]

Rather than seeing the criticism as worthy of merit, Babbitt tries to "psychologize" Stevick's response out of existence by claiming that she

> somehow had the feeling that Rev. Stevick was somewhat piqued because he wasn't taken into the confidence of those working to bring about integration, and I have a feeling, though I am not absolutely sure, that were we to involve him from the very first he would probably be extremely helpful.[52]

If the Quakers were concerned about their growing reputation as meddling do-good-ers who created turmoil and then left to leave others to straighten things out, they gave no indication that they were having pangs of conscience in any of their memos. The housing issue was a matter of conscience, and when it came to conscience each Quaker was endowed with the charism of infallibility. Problems arose then only when one infallible Quaker had to deal with another, which became the situation in Swarthmore during the summer of 1958 when Mike Yarrow was offered another job in Des Moines, Iowa, and decided to have FSH sell his Swarthmore home. "FSH was from the first," according to its official history, "an organization dominated by Quakers; but not one which enlisted the support of all Quakers."[53]

Mike Yarrow found that out first hand when he tried to sell his house in Swarthmore. Six days after announcing his intention to sell to his home to blacks through FSH, Yarrow was handed a petition signed by thirty-nine members of Swarthmore Friends Meeting informing him among other things that "The fundamental belief of a true Quaker requires that he examine his own conscience and try to live by its guidance."[54] What the petition did not explain is how to adjudicate a dispute between two Quakers, both of whom feel they are following their consciences. Yarrow might, according to the petition he got from the Swarthmore Friends Meeting, "believe it is your duty to sell your home to a Negro family. [However,] there are other Quakers who believe just as firmly that your duty requires you to consider the neighbors and friends in the community where you have lived for several years."[55]

Since all Quakers were *ipso facto* infallible when it came to deeply held convictions, the thirty-nine members of the Swarthmore Friends Meeting had to appeal to something greater than conscience (or racial integration) to exert "friendly persuasion" on Yarrow. And that greater good was ethnic solidarity. The Quakers, no matter what they said in their pamphlets, lived in an ethnic neighborhood, and they wanted to keep it ethnically homo-geneous, which was to say in the parlance of the times, "white." "The move that you are contemplating," they told Yarrow, "will cause unrest, anger and distress in the community that has been your home, and that you are leaving. Also it will probably again place the Society of Friends in an unfavorable and unfair position in the eyes of the public."[56] It's difficult to know just what actions the Quakers of Swarthmore were contemplating to keep the black family out of Yarrow's home. It's hard to imagine them throwing rocks and bot-tles, but evidently they were willing to consider actions dramatic enough to be visible to the public eye as a last resort.

In order to avoid that sort of embarrassment, "the Friends whose names appear at the end of this letter" begged Yarrow "to reconsider your plan to sell your house to a Negro family, and to withdraw from your apparent position of discrimination against white buy-ers."[57] In the Society of Friends, a sect which has no dogma, all issues are issues of con-science, and in the absence of principle, all issues of conscience must be resolved by peer pressure. And in the town of Swarthmore, the prime consideration driving peer pressure was property values. Blacks moving into the neighborhood would drive Quaker property values down. *"Regardless of the principles underlying the problem of integration,"* the petitioners informed Yarrow, "it is a cold, hard economic fact that property decreases in value when blacks move into a neighborhood. We feel that you are deliberately depreciating the value of your neighbor's real estate when you sell your home to colored people."[58] In typically Quaker fashion conscience turned out to be a front for self-interest. In a religion without dogma, principle, or liturgy, there was no other option.

In approaching Yarrow as they did, it became apparent that the Quakers were not following their own principles when it came to integration. It turns out that the Swarthmore Quakers weren't reading their own propaganda either, or if they had read it, didn't believe it. In the early '50s in Chicago, the Quakers had channeled Ford Foundation money to the University of Chicago to publish Louis Wirth's study proving that integration did not cause property values to go down. Two years after Yarrow was being subjected to "friendly persuasion" in Swarthmore, FSH was still saying the same thing. In a pamphlet entitled, "Property Values: A Report on the Effect of Non-White Entry into Residential areas," the FSH claimed that no less a luminary than George Schermer, head of Philadelphia's Commission on Human Relations, had proven that "that property values and community standards do not drop when Negroes move in."[59] In fact, "under certain conditions it may increase values."[60] Schermer never stated what those conditions were. Even if he had, it is doubtful that the Quakers in Swarthmore would have been moved by his arguments.

Thus, placed in a position between choosing principle which might decrease property value and Enlightened self-interest as expressed by Swarthmore's friendly persuaders, Yarrow chose the latter option. "At the end of the month," the FSH memo informs us, Yarrow "considered it unlikely that a Negro purchaser could be found without considerable further delay" and as a result, "accepted the offer of the family next door . . . for $22,000 an amount $500 above the appraised price."[61]

In the end what finally swayed Yarrow was precisely the appeal to ethnic solidarity which the Catholic ethnics were not allowed to make in defense of their own neighborhoods. In order to explain his un-Quakerly abandonment of principle, Yarrow later claimed "that both the age and price of the house militated against its purchase by Negroes."[62] Even if this were the case, it pointed up the hypocrisy of claiming that a class-based housing system was open to integration. In the end, proponents of integration like Yarrow knew that the only houses blacks could afford were in Catholic neighborhoods. As a result the residents of places like Swarthmore and Bryn Mawr could advocate integration knowing full well that their neighborhoods would never be affected by their activism and knowing full well that the only neighborhoods blacks were interested in were Catholic neighborhoods with affordable housing within migrating reach of the expanding ghetto.

Yarrow returned to the Philadelphia area in 1962 and was welcomed back to the FSH board just in time for the board to vote to change its name to the more religiously neutral name of Suburban Fair Housing, Inc. The change was ostensibly made in "order to indicate a broader base of support – Catholic, Protestant, Jewish and those with no religious affiliation,"[63] but, no matter what the Quakers called their organization, the simple fact remained that the SFH had no more broader support than the FSH among other denominations and virtually no support at all from the Catholics who were the prime beneficiaries of its policy of social engineering. The real reason for the change lay more with the intelligence which was coming from interviews with people like Rev. Stevick. The activities of the FSH were giving Quakers a bad name; putting the name Friend in the title also militated against the covert action that was more in keeping with the FSH mission, and in this respect FSH was on the verge of its most famous move-in, one which would have had very limited effect if it were known that the Quakers had orchestrated it.

During the summer of 1963, Mr. and Mrs. Horace Baker applied to the FSH for a house and after the FSH spent two or three months showing them houses, they finally selected a VA-foreclosure house in the newly built, heavily Catholic suburb of Folcroft. For some reason, the people at FSH failed to inform the police in that southwestern Philadelphia suburb, and what ensued as a result was a Chicago-style riot which was to have far-reaching consequences for the Catholics of the Archdiocese of Philadelphia. Folcroft was the Quakers' most successful psychological attack on the area's Catholics, and that success was in large measure due to the fact that, in spite of two small newspaper articles to the contrary, no one knew that the Quakers had orchestrated the move. John McGreevy mentions Folcroft in his book, but not the fact that the Quakers bought the house.

The inescapable conclusion which flows from leaving Quaker agents out of the Folcroft picture, therefore, is that the residents of Folcroft did what they did because they were racists. And that explanation would bear consequences among the area's Catholics for a long time to come. Catholics – usually at the urging of liberals like Dennis Clark, who almost certainly knew of the Quaker involvement in the move-in – would be educated to view themselves as racists, when their main fault was the fact that they lacked inside information on the activities of the area's Quakers, something which Dennis Clark did have by virtue of attending their meetings.

Notes

1   "Friends Suburban Housing: An Approach to Breaking Racial Barriers in the Philadelphia Suburbs" by George and Eunice Greer, *Friends Journal*, March 1959, Friends Suburban Housing Committee: Project Section, Community Relations Files, American Friends Service Committee Archives.

2   Ibid.

3   Ibid.

4   Ibid.

5   American Friends Service Committee, Rockefeller Brothers Fund papers #5, Rockefeller Archives.

6   Ibid.

7   Ibid.

8   "White Suburbia," C. H. Yarrow, Chairman Friends Suburban Housing Committee, in *Friends Journal*, 9/8/56, Friends Suburban Housing Committee: Project Section, Community Relations Files, 1956, American Friends Service Committee Archives.

9   Memo: Relationship between Community Relations Program AFSC and FSH, Friends Suburban Housing Committee: Project Section, Community Relations Files, 1958, American Friends Service Committee Archives.

10   "White Suburbia."

11   Ibid.

12   Ibid.

13   Ibid.

14   Ibid.

15 Ibid.

16 Ibid.

17 Ibid.

18 American Friends Service Committee, Rockefeller Brothers Fund papers #5, Rockefeller Archives.

19 "Friends Suburban Housing: An Approach to Breaking Racial Barriers in the Philadelphia Suburbs" by George and Eunice Greer, *Friends Journal*, March 1959, Friends Suburban Housing Committee: Project Section, Community Relations Files, American Friends Service Committee Archives.

20 Ibid.

21 Ibid.

22 Ibid.

23 Ibid.

24 Suburban Fair Housing, Inc., Friends Suburban Housing Committee: Project Section, Community Relations Files 1958, American Friends Service Committee Archives.

25 AFSC Report to Executive Committee 12/30/54, AFSC papers, Box 70 #1, UIC Archives.

26 Ibid.

27 Ibid.

28 Ibid.

29 Ibid.

30 George Greer and Eunice Greer, "Friends Suburban Housing: An Approach to Breaking Racial Barriers in the Philadelphia Suburbs," *Friends Journal* (March 1959).

31 Ibid.

32 Ibid.

33 Ibid.

34 Meeting at the home of Margaret Collins, Bryn Mawr, June 18, 1956, Friends Suburban Housing Committee: Project Section, Community Relations Files 1958, AFSC Archives.

35 Ibid.

36 "Friends Suburban Housing.".

37 Confidential memo from Jane Reinheimer [Motz] 7/6/56, Friends Suburban Housing Committee: Project Section, Community Relations Files, 1956, AFSC Archives.

38 Ibid.

39 Memo from Tom Colgan 11/8/57, Friends Suburban Housing Committee: Project Section, Community Relations Files, 1957, AFSC Archives.

40 Judy Howard to Jane Weston AFSC 3/18/60, AFSC papers, Box 70 #1, UIC Archives.

41 First Annual Report of the American Friends Service Committee Metropolitan Philadelphia Housing Opportunities Program October 1959, AFSC papers, Box 70 #1, UIC Archives.

42 Case #2 confidential, Memo Relationship between Community Relations Program AFSC and FSH, Friends Suburban Housing Committee: Project Section, Community Relations Files 1958, AFSC Archives.

43 Ibid.

44 Interview with Richard Taylor.

45 Case #2.

46 "Friends Suburban Housing."

47 Ibid.

48 Ibid.

49 Judy Howard to Jane Weston AFSC 3/18/60, AFSC papers, UIC Archives.

50 "That Which Is Hurtful to Thee. . ." by Thomas E. Colgan, AFSC papers, Box 70, #1, UIC Archives.

51 Memo from Thelma Babbitt to Barbara Moffett AFSC Philadelphia 12/17/57 interview with the Rev. Daniel Stevick, Episcopal Church, Balsington, PA, AFSC papers, Box 70, #1, UIC Archives.

52 Ibid.

53 "Friends Suburban Housing."

54 Case #4, Friends Suburban Housing Committee: Project Section, Community Relations Files 1958.

55 Ibid.

56 Ibid.

57 Ibid.

58 Ibid.

59 "Property Values: A Report on the Effect of Nonwhite entry into Residential areas," compiled by FSH, Jan 1960, Friends Suburban Housing Committee: Project Section, Community Relations Files 1960, AFSC Archives.

60 Ibid.

61 "Case #4."

62 Ibid.

63 Suburban Fair Housing, Inc.

Msgr. Egan Tangles with Robert Moses

On July 27, 1957, a riot broke out in Calumet Park and quickly spread to the Trumbull Park Homes, perhaps because that evening marked the fourth anniversary of Donald Howard's family's move into the project. According to an AFSC report on the incident which appeared in March 1959, the mob then

> attacked a Negro resident who was walking through the grounds. He escaped across the prairie after being severely stoned, requiring hospital treatment. The mob then broke into the home of a Negro family, whose three small children were sleeping in an upstairs bedroom while the parents were in a home further down the block, talking with a Negro resident who had been attacked earlier on his way to work. The mob broke all the windows, destroyed most of the downstairs furniture, including a new television set and radio-phonograph. They turned on the gas jets, blew out the flames and set fire to the living room curtains. Police, who were called by neighbors, didn't respond until much later. The entire area was aflame with incidents of mob violence against Negro bus drivers, workers in neighboring steel mills, autoists passing through the community.[1]

The AFSC was concerned because the violence was driving the black families out of Trumbull Park. In spite of the fact that "white tenants, including those who were not previously sympathetic to their Negro neighbors, unanimously condemned mob action,"[2] the AFSC was concerned by "the subsequent exodus of Negro families, who felt no confidence in the desire or ability of the city's law enforcement agencies to protect their persons or property."[3] Nine families, according to the same report, moved out of the project during the four months immediately following the riots. The Quakers were quick to sniff out conspiracies, probably because they were involved in one themselves. One of their informants noted that "the lawyer who was hired by the East Side Civic League to defend the residents of the East Side who were arrested was Patrick Allman who is one of the leaders of the South Deering Improvement Association."[4]

The strategy of the University of Chicago was less clandestine but more cynical. Early on in the protracted conflict over racial migration, the Chicago Woodlawn Businessmen's Association issued "a virtual declaration of war against outlying white neighborhoods" by opining that in the interest of racial peace, "the ghetto should be permitted to expand solely into neighborhoods 'immediately adjacent to it.'"[5] Given this decision, the University of Chicago could espouse open occupancy for Hyde Park knowing that it would never happen because the destruction of affordable housing in the neighborhood in the name of urban renewal insured that virtually no black family could afford a home there. It also ensured that those who were displaced would be forced to find housing in the "immediately adjacent" neighborhoods, creating opposition among the less hypocritical Catholic ethnics that would make them look bad in the court of public opinion.

On March 29, 1958, Thelma Babbitt of the Philadelphia branch of the AFSC attended a regional NAACP meeting, where she was shocked to learn that the blacks in attendance were not interested in integration. In a memo which circulated in Quaker circles around the same time that Msgr. John Egan was battling the University of Chicago's final plan, Babbitt expressed surprise at the "over-all belligerence"[6] of those attending the meeting, describing it as "something I've never seen before."[7] What the people in attendance wanted was "no discrimination." "If this means all Negro, okay," she continued, "but what they're interested in is a free choice in housing and no questions asked. They also want better schools but not necessarily integrated ones."[8] Babbitt's memo, in many ways, explains the intention behind subsequent Quaker efforts in housing. When they redoubled their housing efforts when Cushing Dolbeare took over the PHAssoc in the mid-'60s, integration was not what they had in mind, even though this was the rationale they still mentioned in public. They were interested in taking over neighborhoods for black occupancy, something that the inhabitants of those neighborhoods saw as synonymous with their destruction.

A general sense of asymmetry pervades the intelligence gathering on the South Side during the 1950s. Quaker informants regularly attended SDIA meetings, and reports on what they heard found their way not only to Quaker headquarters in Chicago but to Philadelphia as well, where the sect pondered how to put the full force of its resources to bear on the problem. No Polish steel-mill workers attended Quaker meetings, however, not the public meetings that were their religious services nor the private meetings in which they tried to come up with a strategy for the social engineering of neighborhoods like South Deering. What was true of the South Deering Improvement Association, which at least suspected that their neighborhood had been targeted for destruction, was *a fortiori* true of representatives of the Archdiocese of Chicago, who didn't have a clue that this sort of espionage and black operation was going on.

At one point during a conversation which took place a few months before his death, Msgr. John Egan, Cardinal Stritch's assistant on racial matters in Chicago, mentioned Ed Marciniak as an authority on racial issues without knowing that Marciniak was part of the Quaker-organized, Marshall Fields–funded Cicero Project. As a member of the Chicago CIC at the time, Marciniak collaborated with the Quakers in planning how to move black families into Cicero in the wake of the riots there in 1951.

As a result of the fact that Chicago Catholics were divided between the proponents of enlightenment at the CIC and "uncooperative and hostile clergy,"[9] whose sympathies were "firmly rooted in local soil,"[10] Egan could come up with no coherent strategy which would allow the Catholic Church to take control of racial migration on its terms and not the terms of its enemies. Instead of coming up with a coherent strategy for Catholics, Egan compounded the issue by involving himself in ecumenical ventures which further diluted his efforts and further insured that whatever came out in the end would be "liberal" by default. Given handicaps like this, it was a foregone conclusion that Catholic ethnics would lose the battle for the public mind, or that they would be "frequently compared to the German people under Hitler."[11] The only person who could have combated these stereotypes effectively was Cardinal Stritch, but his views were essentially the same as Egan's on the matter of race, which is to say suspended between the CIC and the local soil options which were being advocated by pastors on the South Side, and as a result damned as a villain by both sides in the dispute.

The Catholics were the largest religious group in Chicago. According to the triple melting pot, that meant that they were also the largest ethnic group as well. They were also the group most affected by the racial migration that the WASPs and the Jews were orchestrating for their own benefit. They were also the least effective group in dealing with racial migration because they were the most divided. Egan found this out when he submitted his article attacking urban renewal, "Trojan Horse in Our Cities," for publication, not to *Ave Maria*, where it would eventually get published but to *America*, the Jesuit weekly which was his first choice. What Egan didn't know at the time he submitted the article was that, shortly after receiving it, *America* editor Thurston Davis, s.j., then forwarded it to Robert Moses for his comments and, by implication, his approval.

Needless to say, Moses didn't like the article. On March 27, Moses wrote to Davis attacking Egan's piece as "so bitter, dogmatic, so biased, so factually wrong in many instances and so reminiscent of the sensational press that I am astonished at your printing it."[12] Moses went on to say that he knew "no case, so far as concerns park, arterial, housing power and other public works for which I have any direct responsibility, which could justify the strictures of the Egan piece."[13] Moses had evidently forgotten the fact that he was currently engaged in driving less-than-prosperous Jews out of the Bronx to make way for the Cross-Bronx expressway, an exercise in ethnic cleansing that made the University of Chicago's final plan look like a Sunday School picnic by comparison. Moses concluded his diatribe against Egan by sniffing that "I have too much constructive work to do to engage in unnecessary controversy with those I have had reason to believe were my friends."[14]

After receiving a copy of Moses's letter, Egan responded by telling Davis that "I would be less than honest if I didn't say that I was disappointed in the decision."[15] Egan goes on to sympathize with Davis by indicating that he knows the decision not to run his piece attacking urban renewal "was forced upon you."[16] By whom, Egan doesn't say. But Moses gives a clue in his own rebuttal of Egan's thesis. "So far as New York is concerned," Moses tells Davis half-mockingly, "I suggest that you ask Cardinal Spellman, Father McGinley of Fordham, and any other leaders whether they agree with the conclusions in the Egan article."[17]

Moses was referring here to a deal he had worked out three years earlier in which he had used his sweeping powers as chairman of New York's Slum Clearance Committee to evict hundreds of families, many of them Catholic, from their homes to make way for Moses's Lincoln Center project, four square blocks of which would go to Fordham University.[18] When Spellman heard of the project, he urged Fordham President Laurence J. McGinley to take advantage of the opportunity Moses was dangling before him. For Spellman, the chance to get four square blocks of prime real estate was "the greatest thing that has happened to Fordham since my predecessor Archbishop Hayes built the University."[19] Given Moses's largesse to the Jesuits, Thurston Davis's decision to publish Egan's article attacking urban renewal in general and Robert Moses by name in particular would have seemed like an act of ingratitude, and the Jesuits had no desire to bite the hand that was feeding them. By the end of the '60s, the Jesuits showed how far they were willing to accommodate Church teaching to secular imperatives when they took the crucifixes off the walls at Fordham in order to qualify for money from McGeorge Bundy.

In spite of Moses's protestations about "the people he believed were [his] friends," Catholics bore the brunt of his urban-renewal efforts in New York City. Moses's manipulation of Spellman and McGinley was a way of making sure that there would be no official repercussions coming from the Church's highest level in the Archdiocese when Moses destroyed parish after parish to make room for his increasingly ambitious projects. Moses had leveled six square blocks of Holy Name Parish on the Upper West Side during the '50s, and after a delay of several years when the site lay empty, it was eventually filled in with expensive housing of the sort that the Catholics in the neighborhood, even if they had a mind to return, could not afford. By 1956 Moses had forced 3,000 parishioners out of Holy Name Parish, leaving those behind with "a large Church and large school at great expense."[20] Something similar happened to St. Michael's Parish, which was destroyed when "in the name of progress, three tubes fed traffic into the neighborhood but sucked out the parochial life-blood, the faithful parishioners, until what was left was an emaciated ghost."[21]

No matter how edifying (or disedifying) we find Jesuit gratitude to Robert Moses, the plain fact of the matter remains: Moses was trading favors with Fordham at the expense of the large percentage of American Catholics who lived on the wrong side of the tracks. Moses, for example, vigorously defended Fordham against the charge that their participation in the Lincoln Center land-grab violated the separation of church and state. But he also ignored the protests of the 7,000 families he displaced in order to make that present to Fordham a reality. The Archdiocese of New York, as a result, found itself faced with a dilemma, which arose from the fact that Fordham benefited from the project but "many of the displaced residents were Catholic."[22] The university profited at the expense of the parish, in this instance, St. Matthew's Parish on West 68th Street, which was destroyed to make way for a school of theology. Moses, ever the astute politician, was engaging in the age old divide-and-conquer strategy when it came to the Catholic Church in New York, an entity which could have become a significant opponent to urban renewal if it hadn't been bought off by favors to places like Fordham. "Don't let's spend too much time with an individual pastor who thinks his jurisdiction and membership may be somewhat reduced," is how Moses framed the issue. "There must be adjustments in the churches to keep pace with adjustments of the general population."[23]

While these adjustments may have benefited Fordham, they did not benefit Catholic parishes in New York, which were engaged in a never-ending struggle against the New York's never-ending inter-ethnic struggle for *Lebensraum* in Manhattan, a struggle that was fueled by Jewish and WASP worries about Catholic fertility. As part of its ongoing *Kulturkampf* against neighboring Catholic parishes in mid-town Manhattan, the Hudson Guild "distributed birth control literature to low-income families and advocated an Ethical Culture program with the motto 'deeds not creed.'"[24] In order to achieve the upper hand in that cultural battle, one of the guild's supporters advocated the "displacing of hundreds of poorer families, mostly Roman Catholic, with a more heterogeneous population of a higher social class."[25] When the Chelsea Community Council named a Catholic priest as its president, the Hudson Guild responded by claiming it was creating a Catholic "power center" in the neighborhood.[26] Father Henry Browne declared that "the American city has up to now been Catholic . . . it is not time to desert the city. We need not argue with the family that chooses the suburbs, but for those who choose to stay where our oldest parishes are, we can assist in the choice."[27]

Browne and his parishioners were, however, unfortunately unable to resist the developers, who bought up land in places like St. Joseph's Parish on East 87th Street and replaced the two and three story homes that Catholics lived in there with high rise buildings whose rent the Catholics could not afford. Deputy Mayor Paul O'Keefe warned Spellman that a "combination of luxury housing and large Jewish-sponsored, middle-income housing developments, particularly Coop City in the Bronx and Penn Station South in Chelsea"[28] were driving Catholics out of the city, but Spellman had been swayed away from condemning the ethnic cleansing that lay at the heart of urban renewal by Moses's generosity to Fordham. The Catholics as a result were driven to Queens and Staten Island.

The same thing was happening on the South Side of Chicago. "Predominantly Catholic communities," according to one IAF report, "which have nurtured and supported large parishes, have disappeared overnight, to be replaced by overwhelmingly Protestant and non-Catholic populations."[29] Msgr. Patrick Malloy, pastor of St. Leo's Parish, warned his parishioners not to move to the suburbs because "undesirables will be everywhere, not only here in our city but in the suburbs."[30] Instead of the flight into isolation in the suburbs, Malloy argued for the alternative to the restless policy of constant outward motion that was the government's housing policy by urging that the people who were being dispossessed "should be taken care of in the neighborhood in which they were born and raised."[31] Msgr. Egan found himself falling between two stools: unable to support Msgr. Malloy but also unable to get his critique of urban renewal published in America.

In his letter to Thurston Davis, Egan announces that he is "not finished with Mr. Moses."[32] But it was also clear that Egan was going to get no support from America in documenting the plight of Catholic ethnics in big cities. America, like much of the Catholic press in the United States, seemed reluctant to deal with the neighborhoods issue on its own terms. Instead, the neighborhood issue invariably got dealt with as the race issue, as William Gremly had done in the pages of America when he wrote about the riots in Cicero. The CIC line on race, soon to be adopted by the American bishops, overshadowed the parish/neighborhood issue, and as a result America and other journals which provided a forum for Catholic intellectuals did nothing "to save many of our people and our institutions from the dictatorial powers which people like Moses are arrogating to themselves."[33] According to Egan's estimate Robert Moses was "powerful" but "not unique." In fact he was simply an agent – albeit a uniquely powerful agent – of the same forces that were at work in Chicago. "His counterpart," he told Davis, "exists in many of the cities throughout the United States."[34] That meant, of course, that Catholic parishes were in trouble across the country because of the neighborhoods where they were located.

On May 21, 1958, Egan gave a speech entitled "Urban Renewal in Chicago" in which he attacked Robert Moses by name. "In employing the term ruthless renewal," Egan told the annual convention of the Association of Community Councils in Chicago, "I am not pointing a finger at an imaginary evil. We need but look to the city of New York where Robert Moses, who is a commissioner of nearly everything, has agreed that that city and the nation is to forego the beautiful and historic Washington Square."[35] Egan was especially annoyed because Moses had flown into Chicago the week before "to declare that all such matters should be left in the hands of the people who understand them"[36] and not in the hands of the people whose houses were going to be torn down. To counter Moses's influence, Egan proposed a set of principles which would have humanized the urban-renewal process, by making it "a servant to human needs, human aspirations and human dignity" and not a plan "for the privileged alone," which continued "to play box cars with some of our population."[37] Unfortunately, humanizing urban renewal was like coming up with Stalinism with a human face. It was an inherently self-contradictory process, primarily because the advocates of urban renewal could never be honest about its true intent.

If Egan had been hoping that the bishops would take up his cause and denounce urban renewal in general and Robert Moses in particular, he hoped in vain. The involvement of Cardinal Spellman as a beneficiary of Moses's schemes in New York insured that that would not happen. Instead of following Egan's lead on an issue that was of direct relevance to Catholics in big cities across the country, the American bishops entered the parish/neighborhood issue through the Catholic equivalent of the back door when they issued a statement on race and discrimination. The occasion for their statement was not the over ten years of social turmoil social engineering had brought to the big cites of the North and Midwest, but rather Orval Faubus's defiance of a court order mandating the desegregation of schools in Little Rock, Arkansas in 1957. The school had always been dear to the liberal environmentalists as a tool of social engineering but, since school attendance followed residence, it was always an epiphenomenal issue, especially for Catholics, who had their own school system which was based on the parish. By addressing the neighborhood issue as the race issue, the American bishops guaranteed not only more social turmoil but also the decline of the very institution, the parish, that was the basis of Catholic culture in the United States.

Notes

1 AFSC Report Progress Report on Trumbull Park Homes, March 1959, AFSC papers, Box 62, #14, UIC Archives.

2 Ibid.

3 Ibid.

4 A New Approach to Residential Segregation: The East Side Civic League, AFSC papers, Box 62, #14, UIC Archives.

5 Hirsch, p. 141.

6 Report on NAACP regional conference March 29, 1958, AFSC papers, Box 70, #1, UIC Archives.

7 Ibid.

8 Ibid.

9 Arnold R. Hirsch, *Making the Second Ghetto: Race and Housing in Chicago 1940–1960* (Cambridge: Cambridge University Press, 1983), p. 210.

10 Ibid.

11 Ibid., pp. 207–8.

12 Robert Moses to Thurston Davis, SJ 3/27/58, Alinsky papers, #81, UIC Archives.

13 Ibid.

14 Ibid.

15 John Egan to Thurston Davis 4/2/58, Alinsky papers, #81, UIC Archives.

16 Ibid.

17 Robert Moses to Thurston Davis, SJ 3/27/58, Alinsky papers, #81, UIC Archives.

18 Robert A. Caro, *The Power Broker: Robert Moses and the Fall of New York* (New York: Vintage Books, 1975), p. 471.

19 John T. McGreevy, *Parish Boundaries: The Catholic Encounter with Race in the Twentieth Century Urban North* (Chicago: University of Chicago Press, 1996), p. 127.

20 Ibid., p. 126.

21 Ibid.

22 Ibid., p. 127.

23 Ibid.

24 Ibid., p. 114.

25 Ibid., p. 115.

26 Ibid., p. 116.

27 Ibid., p. 117.

28 Ibid.

29 Ibid., p. 119.

30 Ibid., p. 121.

31 Ibid.

32 Egan to Thurston Davis 4/2/58.

33 Ibid.

34 Ibid.

35 "Urban Renewal in Chicago, "Speech on Urban Renewal, May 21, 1958 before the annual convention of the Association of Community Councils of Chicago, Alinsky papers, UIC Archives.

36 Ibid

37 Ibid.

John Egan and the Catholic Counterattack

Two years after Cardinal Stritch held his press conference denouncing the behavior of the rioters in South Deering, Msgr. John Egan, with Stritch's tacit support, attended a conference on urban renewal. He was the only Catholic priest in attendance. In fact, as far as he could tell, he "was the only clergyman present from any faith,"[1] something that Egan felt was some indication of the secular purpose at the heart of urban renewal. Egan noticed something that had been apparent to anyone involved in the housing movement for some time, namely, the destruction of neighborhoods was never determined by the people living in those neighborhoods. That destruction was determined by "experts," people who invariably were drawn from the same ethnic groups, which also dominated the universities which granted them credentials. That meant, according to Egan, that "no labor leaders"[2] were at the East Lansing meeting. In fact, "the middle class and the poor who compose the bulk of the population in our cities were absent."[3]

Since Egan was a Catholic priest, it is not surprising that he also noticed that the "vast sections of American cities" which were scheduled to "have their faces fundamentally changed or razed entirely" were also "the sections where most of our Catholic Churches and their parishioners are."[4] In fact, the population of the neighborhoods "where most of the humble people who dwell in our big cities are forced to reside" were deliberately excluded from those deliberations, in favor of "very practical men, government administrators, federal and municipal as well as people from private enterprise,"[5] including T. Mellon and Sons, the famous banking firm. The poor had been excluded, according to Egan, because, in the aftermath of the federal housing acts of 1949 and 1954, "urban renewal" had become "big business with big social and economic repercussions for construction and real estate."[6]

By 1958, it was becoming clear to Egan that urban renewal was having equally big repercussions "for institutions like the Catholic Church which have been built with big city America as their base":

> For Catholics, and especially for hard-pressed bishops, who are trying to hold their diocese together in an age of gigantic population upheaval, and city and suburban change, the example of the pastor who woke up one morning to find a superhighway had been built between his church and his school is less than a consolation. Nor is the pastor who found that all the homes in the vicinity of his parish were torn down five years ago so that land could lie idle in any prettier position.[7]

In this regard, Egan was echoing the fears of his ordinary, Cardinal Stritch, who took the opportunity of visiting one of the newly opened suburban parishes in the late '50s to announce that he feared the effect of highways, materialism, and "jungle rhythms" on Catholic culture in Chicago. Egan was later to say that he mounted his attack on urban renewal with the full support of his bishop, who felt "it is high time to ask ourselves whether [urban renewal] is doing what we want it to do,"[8] especially since by 1958 it was apparent that "land clearance invariably replaces homes for low income people with homes for higher income people."[9] Egan would not go so far then to say that that was the intention of urban renewal, nor would he say so later in his life. But other people were coming to that conclusion, especially in the project which was the trip wire which set off archdiocesan concerns at the time, namely, the University of Chicago's involvement in ethnic cleansing as a way of taking control of racial migration in the Hyde Park neighborhood.

The University of Chicago began having problems associated with racial succession beginning in 1944 as soon as the massive war-induced migration up from the South to staff Chicago's industries created a sufficiently large pool of workers with no homes but plenty of money (especially in comparison with what they had been accustomed to earning as sharecroppers down South). By the summer of 1944, the university noted with increasing concern that the Woodlawn neighborhood to the south of the campus was becoming a threat that was perceived entirely in racial terms. In 1946, the university began to notice black families moving into the western areas of Hyde Park. Eventually the number of blacks living in Hyde Park would more than triple during the 1940s. As time went on it became apparent that much of this migration was caused by the city's redevelopment planning, something which invariably destroyed more housing than it created. Liberal icon Robert Maynard Hutchins, then president of the university, took to expressing the fears of the university community in verse at the time:

> The Chancellor and the President gazed out across the park,
> They laughed like anything to see that things were looking dark.
> Our neighborhood once blossomed like the lily [but]
> Just seven coons with seven kids could knock our program silly.[10]

It wasn't great verse, but Hutchins's poem pointed up a number of things that the university would never admit in public. Like the various "improvement associations" that sprang up in ethnic neighborhoods across Chicago, the university claimed to be restoring the neighborhood when they were actually trying to find ways to keeps blacks out of it. Like the various improvement associations, the University of Chicago perceived its plight "almost entirely in racial terms," but unlike some of the more candid newsletters emanating from the neighborhoods, the university founded by the Rockefellers could never admit that in any of its public pronouncements. "I abhor discrimination," University of Chicago Chancellor Kimpton said at the time, "and I am appalled by . . . incidents of [racial] violence."[11]

Publicly, Chancellor Kimpton denied that community deterioration was a "racial problem." Privately, the goals he stressed for the renewal of Hyde Park were clearly racial in nature. Kimpton explicitly sought an economically upgraded and predominantly white neighborhood. He viewed upper-income housing as "an effective screening tool"[12] and as a means of "cutting down [the] number of Negroes"[13] residing in the area. He was also prepared to take more direct action.

As a result, the university chose the two courses of action open to those with influence and money but unable to admit their racial bias. They began to buy up real estate, and they got involved in "urban planning" of the sort that Msgr. Egan was witnessing at the East Lansing convention. That involved, among other things, buying up all of the property on the strip of land immediately south of the campus between 60th and 61st Streets and Cottage Grove and Dorchester Avenues, and tearing it down so that that strip could "serve as a buffer between the University and the deteriorating neighborhood to the south."[14] In the mid-'40s, the University of Chicago was hampered in its efforts by the fact that the 1947 Blighted Areas Redevelopment Act only allowed clearance and reconstruction in existing slum areas. Since the area around the University of Chicago hardly qualified as a slum by even the most liberal definition of the term, significant action had to be postponed.

That particular problem got solved in 1953 with the passage of the Urban Community Conservation Act of 1953. Now an entity like the University of Chicago could use eminent domain, as well as government power and money, for the newly created public purpose of "slum prevention," a concept broad enough to justify the confiscation of any piece of property or land. Enabled by the UCCA of 1953, the University of Chicago could engage in the ethnic cleansing of the blacks in Hyde Park–Kenwood on a scale that was guaranteed to cause problems in the immediately adjacent Catholic ethnic neighborhoods that were the catch basins for this forced migration. "Many of the people being forced out of slum areas were moving to conservation areas,"[15] one observer noted. That meant that the people who got displaced "were causing new overcrowding and problems in the vast middle belt of the city,"[16] which is to say in the Catholic neighborhoods, something that meant problems for parishes like St. Leo's.

Enabled by liberal interpretations of eminent domain coming from the courts, the University of Chicago stepped up its campaign to use the government to drive blacks out of the neighborhood. As the battle heated up during the later '50s, Msgr. Egan found himself in the middle of the struggle, fighting in many ways a war on two fronts. On the one hand, there were the pastors in parishes on the South side who were most affected by the migration which urban renewal's displacement of blacks was causing. "Father Pat Malloy at St. Leo's," according to Egan, "wanted to get people to keep up their houses, paint them but that was just a way of saying that they should keep blacks out of their neighborhoods."[17] Malloy and many other pastors were upset when Egan joined the Cardinal's Commission on Conservation because being on the commission meant that Egan opposed efforts to keep blacks out of the neighborhood. According to Egan, "there was no support for these pastors from chancery but not too much opposition either."[18]

When it came to the situation created by the University of Chicago, Egan found himself in the unenviable position of opposing both the university and the pastors who were opposing the black migration caused by the university's actions. By 1958, Egan clearly understood that the university's final plan was "a fraud" because "its purpose was to drive people out of the neighborhood."[19]

During the spring of 1958, Egan said as much in community meetings; he also wrote articles to the same effect in the diocesan newspaper, *The New World*. When Egan complained to Julian Levi of the University of Chicago that too many good homes were being destroyed and that there was no provision being made for the lower- and middle-income families being displaced, Levi responded by saying that the only reason Egan was complaining was because of the effect it was having on Catholic parishes. Egan would later say that he was "deeply hurt"[20] by Levi's response and that the effect renewal was having on the nearby parishes was not the main reason for his concern.

Part of Egan's hurt came from his surprise at Levi's response. He hadn't brought up the effect on the Catholic parishes in the conversation. Levi had, which is some indication that the effect of black migration on Catholics in Chicago was something that was clearly on Levi's mind at the time. Yet, when questioned explicitly about the effect the university's policies were having on Catholic parishes, Levi refused to answer the question, ruling it instead "out of bounds," claiming that he was "not about to cut up this town with anybody."[21]

But that, shorn of the Catholic references, was precisely Egan's point. Egan claimed that the university was trying to save itself at the expense of the rest of Chicago. In this he agreed with the Catholic Slavs in South Deering, who stated in their bulletin that the university was trying to create a "buffer zone," that would allow them to "save their own hides" at the expense of South Side communities with less clout. This is also Hirsch's verdict: "The quick resort to political and legal measures and the willingness to expand public power for private ends set the Loop interests and the Hyde Park community apart from the ethnic, working-class, and heavily Catholic neighborhoods that witnessed the worst postwar violence."[22] The result of the university's policies was "that whites in other communities were left to face the possibility of a substantial and sudden in-migration of low-income black families."[23] But whenever Church representatives mentioned this fact they were accused of being narrow, parochial, and racist. In trying to distance itself from these claims, the Catholic Church ended up alienating a large segment of its own members, who, abandoned by the Catholic intellectuals who adopted the Catholic Interracial Council line on the matter, began to identify themselves as "white" instead of Catholic.

In an article entitled "White People Must Control Their Own Communities," which appeared in the *South Deering Bulletin* on July 31, 1958, that neighborhood's largely Slavic Catholic residents, who had been involved in pitched battles since 1953 when Elizabeth Wood tried to integrate the Trumbull Park Homes, announced that "We are proud to be the only community in Chicago which has successfully repelled the Negro invasions. We still own our own homes in our own community and will still maintain the lowest crime rate in Chicago. . . . We may be called bigoted and intolerant but we would rather this than have to disappear into the suburbs as have the people of those communities who accepted integration. They accepted it and then had to sell their homes and run for their lives."[24]

Hirsch claims that the University of Chicago battle had an ethnic component as well. The residents of Hyde Park were largely well-educated Jews who invariably considered themselves liberal on racial matters and would have been appalled to be lumped together with "other whites" like the people in South Deering. That aversion points up the futility of viewing the issue as racial but, in addition to that, the necessity of viewing it as ethnic.

The *South Deering Bulletin* went on to mention the Jews in the Fillmore area as recent victims of the city's decision to force blacks into the neighborhoods and suggested "to our

Jewish friends in the Manors that they contact the Rabbis who lived in the Fillmore area and ascertain what happens when acceptance and welcome is given to a horde of people who haven't learned to live like human beings."[25]

The discussion in the *South Deering Bulletin* bounced back and forth between ethnos and race, at one point describing a number of "fine neighborhoods" where "the only white people left are those who were unable to sell."[26] Vowing to "fight to the end, whatever it may be,"[27] the *South Deering Bulletin* specifically mentioned the NAACP, which "wants all of the South Side and will not be satisfied until they devour it."[28] But in the end, the SDIA felt that the struggle was "well worth the five year fight we have waged" because it saved "our homes and our community."[29] Even here, however, the racial message is clearly defensive and conditional. This is not a campaign based on a racial theory. It is an ad hoc campaign of people who want to defend their community against a group which they define in racial terms. The terms of engagement, however, are not immutably tied to race. "If the day ever comes when the Negroes prove that they can be an asset to a community, instead of a plague," the SDIA concludes, "we may change our attitude."[30] The trauma which the Chicago Housing Authority had inflicted on these communities was, however, deep and lasting, and because the social engineers manipulated racial migration, blacks, not the engineers, got blamed for the trauma. "What they," the SDIA wrote referring to the black and not the social engineers, "have done to other communities in the past five years plainly indicate that our attitude will not be changed for a Long, Long Time."

Those more familiar with the causes of the strife saw things differently. "The post-World War II triumph of liberal environmentalism," according to Hirsch,

> thus added to the anxiety of people who sensed the breakdown of traditional neighborhood insularity in the face of political and social forces beyond their control. The intrusion of government into the day-to-day life of Chicago's neighborhoods in an unprecedented fashion, the overwhelming nature of racial change in the postwar city, and the growth of strong ideological currents, which would soon culminate in the "civil rights revolution," all contributed to a second strong reaction by the city's ethnics.[31]

The Slavs in South Deering were well aware of the ethnic nature of the struggle, even if they consistently portrayed it in racial terms, but Msgr. Egan, as Cardinal Stritch's representative, refused to join the battle on those terms. When his thoughts were finally published in *Ave Maria Magazine* in May of 1958 under the title "Trojan Horse in our Cities," Egan spoke "as someone who has lived most of his adult life in the rectories of big city Catholic parishes"[32] and as a result knew that the community life of ethnic neighborhoods in big cities was "as strong as good and as vital as that which the small town affords,"[33] but he did not frame the issue in specifically ethnic or Catholic terms. He did not issue a call to arms addressed to an ethnic "We," calling for a united ethnic/religious front, even though the fact that his article appeared in a Catholic magazine allowed his opponents to dismiss it as such without reading it. Egan framed his argument in secular terms, claiming that it destroyed the human community, not just Catholic parishes:

> When the superhighway is rammed through such a neighborhood, it takes with it more than the buildings it demolishes for its right of way. It abolishes a human

community and a way of life which has much to be said for it. No churchman, be he of whatever faith, be he a pastor or a Bishop, can look at this destruction of healthy social cells with equanimity.[34]

However, since this battle was being prosecuted on covert but very definite religious and ethnic lines, an argument appealing to the common good could find no purchase on the public mind. The University of Chicago's final plan was not something that could have been rectified by experts coming up with a better design; it was covert ethnic warfare from its inception, something which could never be honest about its intentions. That fact points up Egan's dilemma. He was damned in the circles he wanted to influence for doing the very things which he avoided doing. Egan had a sense of himself as an American and a Chicagoan which prevented him from using the Church as an ethnic rallying point of the sort that would have saved the Slavs in South Deering from appearing to be racists, but the fact that he raised any protest at all led people like Julian Levi to claim that all he was doing was promoting Catholic interests and worrying about how the effects of the University of Chicago's final plan were going to wreak havoc in Catholic parishes. His failure to take the ethnic line, on the other hand, alienated him from the priests in Chicago whose parishes were threatened with racially orchestrated extinction. It also caused him to lose whatever influence the Catholic Church might have had with the local improvement associations.

Egan finally testified before city council against the University of Chicago's plan, reminding them that "you are not voting on a plan to build something; you are voting . . . to tear something down."[35] By backing the Hyde Park initiative, the University of Chicago was cynically pushing its racial problems onto the rest of the city by using liberally acceptable euphemisms like "urban renewal" as a cover for what amounted to ethnic cleansing. When Egan's testimony before city council failed to prevent the University of Chicago from implementing its final plan for the Hyde Park neighborhood, Egan drew certain conclusions. Largely as a result of conversations with Saul Alinsky, he became convinced that Catholics couldn't go it alone if they wanted to have an effect on public life in Chicago. "After we failed before City Council," Egan said later, "we got together with a number of people for breakfast including Rabbi Hirsch, and I said my mistake was try- ing to go it alone, just Roman Catholics."[36] From then on, Egan was determined "to work with Protestants and Jews," and as one of his accomplishments in this regard he mentioned the Interfaith Council on Catholic Affairs which he helped create in 1983 under Cardinal Bernardin.

Egan went on to found things like the Campaign for Human Development and as a result developed the reputation for being a liberal in conservative (the heir to ethnic) Catholic circles, without much conservative thought on the fact that this appellation meant, more than anything else, a form of assimilation. To the extent that Egan saw him- self as a liberal, he adopted the missionary attitude toward his fellow Catholics, a less-vir- ulent version of the attitude that Sargent Shriver, then head of the Chicago Interracial Council, manifested when he said that "the apostle of interracial justice among highly prejudiced fellow citizens resembles . . . the missionary conversing with a foreign people accustomed to ancient tribal customs and taboos."[37] "The false idols will fall," Shriver continued, "only when people have become sufficiently enlightened to wish to remove them themselves."[38] So Shriver's task as head of the CIC was to bring "enlightenment" on racial matters to his fellow Catholics, a project which invariably construed enlightenment in terms favorable to those who were planning the destruction of Catholic parishes and neighborhoods at the time.

Egan didn't go that far. Yet he was handicapped by the same mentality. He viewed himself as an American when all the while his opponents viewed him as the representative of a foreign power. He refused to see the conflict in ethnic terms, when those were precisely the terms on which his opponents were waging that war. "It may be that the University of Chicago had an anti-Catholic bias,"[39] he conceded a few months before his death, but this idea didn't occur to him at the time, nor did he plan his strategy in opposing the university's final plan with ethnic considerations in mind. "They said we were worried that urban renewal would drive blacks into our parishes," he continued, "but that never occurred to us as the reason we opposed what they were doing."[40]

In addition to ignoring the ethnic dimensions to the struggle surrounding the implementation of the University of Chicago's final plan, Egan was unaware that other groups were working to engineer the consent of recalcitrant Catholic interests. The ACLU sent its own Polish-speaking undercover agent to sit in bars and talk to steel-mill workers from South Deering. The American Friends Service Committee proposed "underwriting" a "Catholic, Eastern European descent, working-class" family to live in South Deering for two years, during which they would work to change local racial attitudes.[41] But Egan was unaware of any effort on the part of any other ethnic groups to engineer Catholic neighborhoods.

He did not know, for instance, that the Quakers had been involved in the Hyde Park neighborhood association from the beginning. The 57th Street Meeting of Friends was instrumental in the creation of the Hyde Park–Kenwood Community Conference in 1949 not because the Quakers were interested in blight but because they wanted to engineer racial succession in ways they considered congruent with their interests. Egan did not know that the Quakers had been involved in attempting to move black families into Cicero, nor did he know that the CIC was involved in helping them to do that by engineering Catholic opposition. He did not know that the Ford Foundation funded the Hyde Park "demonstration grant," nor, if he did, is there any indication that he would have seen their Gray Areas Program as something inimical to Catholic ethnic interests. The University of Chicago's final plan necessitated a massive public-housing program, which Julian Levi was determined not to allow into the Hyde Park neighborhood. Levi claimed that public housing of the sort that the people of South Deering were supposed to embrace was "something harmful to the [Hyde Park] neighborhood which the people did not want anyway." Tacit acceptance of Levi's double standard on the part of Chicago's city council meant, according to Hirsch, "that whites in other communities were left to face the possibility of a substantial and sudden in-migration of low-income black families."[42]

By the mid-'50s, Quaker involvement in the housing situation on the South Side of Chicago had become a sect-wide project. When David K. Fison, the pastor the Methodists sent to integrate their church on the South Side of Chicago, was evicted from the house he was renting in the Spring of 1957, he received a note of sympathy from Clarence Pickett, assuring him of "our concern and prayers for you in these trying times" as well as the fervent hope that he would also receive "the same kind of backing from some of our own Quaker members of the Chicago community."[43] As a sign of Quaker approval, Fison was invited to Philadelphia one month later in June of 1957 "to consult with you from time to time regarding the problems in Trumbull Park" because "we are grateful for your leadership in this field."[44]

The Quakers also pursued a black minister by the name of Martin Luther King, Jr. with equal avidity, albeit with less success, hoping he could bring his expertise on "non-violent techniques" to a workshop during the summer of 1957 in the Chicago area that would train "30 Negro families at Trumbull Park."[45] King begged off, but the Quakers continued to hold seminars on Trumbull Park in his absence. In May of 1957 Judy Wioll gave a paper in Philadelphia entitled, "A Group Work in a Community Center in a Changing Neighborhood," which described the community of South Deering as "a steel workers community, predominantly settled by Polish, Italian and Yugoslavian families"[46] which had been under the Quaker microscope since South Chicago Community Center opened its branch in Trumbull Park in 1954. Wioll opined that during "the early days of Trumbull Park the South Deering homeowners were distrustful and antagonistic toward the residents of the project because of its high rate of one-parent families, families on relief and high rate of delinquency."[47] She concluded her report by saying that the staff of the center were virtually unanimous in their belief that a "direct attack on the racial problem only arouses antagonism and resistance."[48]

The indirect attack on the community which the Quakers initiated instead involved infiltrating the local improvement association. Quaker involvement in this and other black operations was necessary because the AFSC was "concerned that the CHA is turning its back on integration, not only at Trumbull Park, but in public housing as a whole."[49] Since, as the *South Deering Bulletin* made clear, the prime concern of the ethnics was not racial but rather the preservation of the community, the spying which the Quakers and ACLU engaged in probably increased the paranoia in the South Deering community, and as a result it probably increased the violence as well.

Notes

1   Msgr. John J. Egan, "Trojan Horse in Our Cities," *Ave Maria*, 5/10/58, p. 10, in Alinsky papers, Box 81, UIC Archives.
2   Ibid.
3   Ibid.
4   Ibid.
5   Ibid.
6   Ibid.
7   Ibid.
8   Ibid.
9   Ibid.
10 Arnold R. Hirsch, *Making the Second Ghetto: Race and Housing in Chicago 1940–1960* (Cambridge: Cambridge University Press, 1983), p. 146.
11 Ibid., p. 182.
12 Ibid., p. 153.

13 Ibid.

14 Ibid., p. 148.

15 Ibid., p. 149.

16 Ibid.

17 Interview with Msgr. Egan, 7/18/00.

18 Ibid.

19 Ibid.

20 Ibid.

21 Hirsch, p. 206.

22 Ibid., p. 173.

23 Ibid., p. 172.

24 "White People Must Control Their Own Communities," *South Deering Bulletin* (7/31/58), AFSC papers, Box 62, #14, UIC Archives.

25 Ibid.

26 Ibid.

27 Ibid.

28 Ibid.

29 Ibid.

30 Ibid.

31 Hirsch, pp. 173–74.

32 "Trojan Horse."

33 Ibid.

34 Ibid.

35 Hirsch, p. 164.

36 Interview with Msgr. Egan, 7/18/00.

37 Hirsch, p. 208.

38 Ibid.

39 Interview with Msgr. Egan, 7/18/00.

40 Ibid.

41 Hirsch, p. 208.

42 Ibid., p. 172.

43 Clarence Pickett to David K. Fison, 5/24/57, UIC American Friends Service Committee 67-87, AFSC papers, Box 50, #1, UIC Archives.

44 Lewis M. Hoskins to David Fison, 6/4/57, UIC American Friends Service Committee 67-87, AFSC papers, Box 50, #1, UIC Archives.

45 Ed Holmgren to Martin Luther King, Jr., 7/12/57, UIC American Friends Service Committee 67-87, AFSC papers, Box 50, #1, UIC Archives.

46 AFSC memo from Judy Wioll, 5/24/57, UIC American Friends Service Committee 67-87, AFSC papers, Box 50, #1, UIC Archives.

47 Ibid.

48 Ibid.

49 AFSC Report, Progress Report on Trumbull Park Homes, March 1959.

The Bishops Issue a Statement on Race

I have just returned from a Chicago Conference on interracial justice where we made
up a good report and I framed the leading resolution, a plea for the prayers of Catholics
in these days of the Little Rock Integration troubles.

Dennis Clark, Diary, 9/2/58

David Southern claims that "the Little Rock crisis in the fall of 1957 put more pressure on
the bishops to act,"[1] but it's difficult to understand why a crisis in the public-school system in an essentially Protestant area of the country would prompt them to act when the
housing riots in largely Catholic Chicago did not, nor did Msgr. Egan's attack on urban
renewal, which was yet another way of dealing with the same issue. The fact that the bishops took Little Rock as their impetus to deal with racial discrimination was in large measure due to the influence that the Catholic Interracial Council had among members of the
growing episcopal bureaucracy in Washington.

The American bishops' statement on race and discrimination was largely the work of
Father John F. Cronin, a Sulpician priest who was also associate director of the Social
Action Department of the National Catholic Welfare Conference. Unlike Father LaFarge,
Cronin considered the Little Rock incident a big deal, and he effectively conveyed his
sense of urgency to the American bishops when he returned from Europe, where he had
been embarrassed by press reports of the governor of Arkansas blocking the doors of one
of that state's schools. After drafting a statement on his own for the bishops to sign, Cronin
engaged in a "bitter struggle" to get their support.[2] Cardinal Mooney of Detroit and
Cardinal McIntyre of Los Angeles opposed the Cronin statement as divisive, while
Cardinal O'Boyle of Washington supported it. The bishops had reached an impasse when
two things happened. In October Pope Pius XII ordered the bishops to issue a statement,
largely at the urging of Father LaFarge. In 1956 LaFarge had urged Pius XII to remove "all
uncertainty" as to where the church stood on segregation by issuing a statement supporting Archbishop Rummell of New Orleans, who had just excommunicated Catholics for
supporting it. Pope Pius XII died the day after he sent the cable ordering the bishops to
issue a statement. Because the message lacked the official papal seal, Apostolic Delegate
Amleto Cicognani ordered it suppressed, and the bishops might have remained at that
impasse had not Cardinal O'Boyle persuaded the ever-influential Cardinal Spellman to
back his proposal. With Spellman on board, the document was approved and issued by the
bishops on November 8, 1958.

The bishops' statement was in large measure an exercise in irrelevance. After promising "to cut through the maze of secondary or less essential issues and to come to the
heart of the problem,"[3] the bishops endorsed a number of propositions which were irrelevant to the real issue, which, as far as Catholics were concerned, was being played out in
the parishes of Chicago and Philadelphia and not in front of schools in Little Rock,

Arkansas. "The heart of the race question," according to "Discrimination and Christian Conscience," "is moral and religious."[4] The bishops followed up this statement with the assertion that "All men . . . are brothered [*sic*] in Jesus Christ."[5] The statement is, of course, true, and it would only be disputed by a polygenist or a Darwinist of the sort one might find on the faculty of Harvard University or the planning commissions of big cities like Philadelphia and Chicago, but emphatically not in those cities' ethnic parishes, where the issue was not whether a black person was a child of God, but rather whether he had the right to destroy Catholic communities of long standing by moving into Catholic parishes and displacing the local population. "Our Christian faith," the faithful were told, "is of its nature universal. It knows not the distinctions of race, color, or nationhood."[6] That statement is, as it stands, false. The Catholic Church, by its nature, is universal. Race, in the American sense of the term as referring to skin color, had no meaning in Catholic parlance. However, "nationhood," if by that we mean *ethnos*, certainly did. The church's understanding of *ethnos* had always been cultural and never biological. That meant that seminarians studied in Rome from the various colleges – based on nationality and language – and never just as atomistic individuals. The existence of the North American College in Rome should have been some indication to Father Cronin that the Catholic Church did, in fact, "know . . . nationhood" and that it did not try to abolish it in order to preserve its charism of universality. By lumping "race, color and nationhood" together, the document confuses what it should have distinguished.

To make matters worse, the document then throws the idea of "class distinction" into the same murky stew of ideas. "Among all races and national groups," the document continues, "class distinctions are inevitably made on the basis of like-mindedness of a community of interests. Such distinctions are normal and constitute a universal social phenomenon," but they are bad when "a factor such as race, by and of itself, should be made a cause of discrimination and a basis for unequal treatment in our mutual relations."[7] First of all, class distinctions are different from ethnic identity, which is also different from the "like-mindedness of a community of interests" which binds together stamp collectors and NASCAR fans. The United States government was orchestrating racial conflict at the time in order to drive Catholics into choosing class distinction over ethnos as the basis of how they identified themselves. Secondly, the "local soil" pastors on the South Side of Chicago were never using "a factor such as race, by and of itself." By articulating the paradigm of the ethnic parish as the alternative to black migration into and subsequent destruction of their communities, these pastors were framing the issue, even if in inchoate fashion, as an ethnic issue and not a racial issue, because the Catholic Church, especially in the United States, had traditionally framed the issue on these terms. Did the Germans have the right to take over an Italian parish? If not, why then did largely Protestant blacks have the right to drive the Irish or the Poles out of their parishes? The Catholic Church had traditionally stated that each ethnic group had a right to organize its own parish, not that they had a right to take over the parishes of other groups.

The bishops attempt to root their argument in the natural law, but even here the argument gets muddied by misapplying it to race, a category of American origin which has no referent in classical thought. "Reason alone," the bishops tell us, taught philosophers through the ages respect for the sacred dignity of each human being and the fundamental rights of man. Every man has an equal right to life, to justice before the law, to marry and rear a family under human conditions and to an equitable opportunity to use the goods of this earth for his needs and those of his family.[8]

Since the bishops can't really move from those principles to the principle that people of a certain ethnic group have the right to live in certain neighborhoods, much less that they have the right to drive other ethnic groups out of those neighborhoods, the bishops' statement has to step outside the traditional parameters of natural law in the Catholic understanding of that term to "the principle – embodied in our Declaration of Independence – that all men are created equal in the sight of God."[9] Having imported this principle by fiat, the bishops then go on to conclude that "discrimination based on the accidental fact of race or color, and as such injurious to human rights regardless of personal qualities or achievements, cannot be reconciled with the truth that God has created all men with equal rights and equal dignity."[10]

Again, all of this may or may not be true, but all of it is irrelevant to the situation in Chicago, which revolved not around the rights of individuals before God but rather the rights of ethnic groups to maintain their local communities and parishes:

Today we are told that Negroes, Indians and some Spanish-speaking Americans differ too much in culture and achievements to be assimilated in our schools, factories, and neighborhoods. Some decades back the same charge was made against the immigrant Irish, Jewish, Italian, Polish, Hungarian, German, Russian.[11]

The bishops' statement here ignores the fact that the Catholic Church made precisely "the same charge." By organizing its parishes according to ethnic group, it was only admitting the obvious, namely, that someone whose native tongue was, say, Hungarian or Polish, might have difficulty getting along in an English-speaking Protestant culture, and so, therefore, needed the support of people facing the same problems. The ethnic parish was an engine of assimilation when Hungarians arrived in Chicago, and it could have been an engine of assimilation as well for blacks who arrived there from Mississippi if the CIC hadn't consistently and deliberately misconstrued what had been Catholic praxis in this country from the time Catholics started living here in significant numbers. If the ethnic parish was a form of segregation, why hadn't the Catholic Church condemned it when it was used to segregate Poles and Italians? The answer to that question is that the Church didn't consider the ethnic parish as wrong. And if it wasn't wrong for Poles, why was it wrong for blacks? Ultimately the CIC could not go beyond the peculiar American understanding of race. As a result, the claims of one ethnic group were elevated above the claims of every other ethnic group in a philosophical muddle of ideas that bespoke less a desire to know the truth and act in justice than a desire to absorb the contradictory categories which the dominant culture imposed on Catholics as the price of assimilation.

Even if Father LaFarge wasn't instrumental in getting it passed, the bishops' statement on discrimination was his crowning achievement. Congratulations poured in to Father LaFarge from eight United States Senators as well as from black leaders like Roy Wilkins and A. Philip Randolph as if he had written it himself. LaFarge's triumph, however, could not disguise the fact that at this point of his life, five years from his death, he was losing control of his own organization. If the New York Catholic Interracial Council had the position of *primus inter pares* because of its association with Father LaFarge, that position was being constantly challenged by the Chicago CIC, which had the reputation of being closer to the cutting edge of racial struggle. "Several young Turks of the movement," according to Southern, "such as Father Cantwell, Matthew Ahman, Lloyd Davis and Robert Sargent Shriver, all Chicagoans, believed that events had overwhelmed LaFarge and Hunton. The midwesterners also believed that their council was superior to New York's."[12]

Probably the one tenet which most convinced the Chicagoans that LaFarge was out of step with the times was his dogged opposition to birth control. LaFarge was opposed to birth control because he was a Catholic priest and understood it as being morally wrong, but he was against birth control for blacks because he was aware of the hold racial eugenics had on the American mind. When LaFarge heard a rumor (which turned out to be false),

> that the National Association of Colored Graduate Nurses planned to open birth control clinics, he addressed a letter to the secretary, instructing her to sever at once his connection with the association and "to make known this disassociation in any way possible." In addition, he berated the organization for taking a step that was sure to be "fatal to the Association's purposes," and in a final salvo he declared that birth control was "aimed directly at the freedom, progress and prosperity of the Negro race."[13]

These sentiments were bound to alienate LaFarge's support among his liberal fellow travelers on the racial issue. Harvard professor Gordon Allport attacked LaFarge because:

> By the time he had reached the end of his life, LaFarge's position on racial equality was not enough to ensure his bona fides as part of the liberal consensus on race. That consensus had been expanded to ensure support of birth control, something which LaFarge could not approve because he was old enough to remember the pre-World War II eugenic campaigns of Margaret Sanger and the Birth Control League, something the other liberals had forgotten or repressed. Harvard's Gordon Allport criticized LaFarge "for denigrating all secular liberals as purveyors of 'ethical anarchy'" because they favored birth control and divorce.[14]

LaFarge, who died on the same weekend in November 1963 that Jack Kennedy was murdered, had outlived his usefulness because the government, with Catholics like Kennedy providing protective cover, had decided that birth control was the solution to the "Negro problem" every bit as much as it had been proposed as the solution to the "Catholic problem" twenty years earlier. The "Negro Problem," which is to say their differential fertility vis-à-vis the WASPs and Jews who ran the machinery of social engineering at the time, was easier to solve, precisely because by the '60s a large number of them had been herded into government-subsidized housing projects. Unlike the Catholics, whose leaders opposed contraception and still had control over their own institutions, blacks had largely become wards of the state, and as a result, or so it was thought, easily amenable to the suggestions of social workers who could establish their birth-control clinics in ghetto neighborhoods, if not in the very projects themselves.

No one epitomized the link which the Kennedy Administration forged between Catholic liberalism on racial matters and the government's idea of social engineering as well as Sargent Shriver, Jack Kennedy's brother-in-law, the man who went from running Kennedy's Merchandise Mart in Chicago to running the War on Poverty for Lyndon Johnson. The crucial intermediary link in that chain of events was the fact that Shriver was also president of the CIC in Chicago during the '50s, when the Chicago CIC arrogated to itself the mantle of leadership on Catholic interracial matters. By 1963 Shriver was making invidious comparisons between the Church's "laissez faire" policy on race as compared to its dogmatic opposition to birth control and divorce, when it was clear from the liberal point of view that a Copernican revolution had already taken place reversing those two poles.

Cardinal O'Boyle, a liberal on racial matters, as evidenced by his support of the 1958 bishops statement on discrimination, was nonetheless adamantly opposed to the government's involvement in birth control on terms that Father LaFarge would have understood perfectly. Birth control was a weapon in the arsenal of the eugenics crowd. It had been that when Margaret Sanger was arguing for a "nation of thoroughbreds" with Rockefeller money, and it was still that when the government promoted birth control under the auspices of the War on Poverty. After working with Quakers in Chicago to engineer that city's Catholic neighborhoods, Shriver then went to Washington to become head of the Office of Economic Opportunity, where he worked to engineer the sexual behavior of blacks he had previously supported in his capacity as head of the Chicago CIC.

Notes

1   David W. Southern, *John LaFarge and the Limits of Catholic Interracialism, 1911–1963* (Baton Rouge: Louisiana State University Press, 1996), p. 314.
2   Ibid., p. 317.
3   "Discrimination and Christian Conscience: A Statement Issued by the Catholic Bishops of the United States, November 14, 1958," *Pastoral Letters of the Bishops of the United States, 1941–1961* (Washington, D.C.: National Conference of Catholic Bishops, 1983), p. 202.
4   Ibid.
5   Ibid.
6   Ibid.
7   Ibid., p. 203.
8   Ibid.
9   Ibid.
10 Ibid.
11 Ibid., p. 204.
12 Southern, p. 325.
13 Ibid., p. 364.
14 Ibid., p. 366.

Dennis Clark Becomes Head
of the Catholic Interracial Council

In December 1961, a little over a year after trying to integrate the Irish neighborhood in Kensington around C Street, Dennis Clark noted in his diary that he had "decided to resign my comfortable post with the Commission on Human Relations and perform some vocational acrobatics with the Catholic Interracial Council of New York as director."[1] Just why he would call his position at the CHR comfortable is anyone's guess. At another point in the same diary, he would claim that during this period of his life he was away from home for 300 nights in one year. In addition to the sheer time involved, there was also the stress of defusing potentially violent confrontations involving angry residents and the police. But there is evidence that other issues were involved as well. Clark still considered himself a Catholic and was also acutely aware that most of the people whose consent to integration he was paid to engineer were Catholics as well. For someone who was acutely aware of ethnic realities in Philadelphia, it must have been doubly painful to learn that he was "not welcome" at meetings the Irish were holding to plan how to deal with CHR incursions into his former neighborhood. Seven months before the incident on C Street, Clark was mulling over how to help "this huge, bumbling, television addicted Catholic population"[2] solve "the problems that are rioting on every flank"[3] at the same time he was working to destroy their neighborhoods. In other words, he was working to destroy the very social matrix that was the antidote to television's colonization of the people in Catholic neighborhoods at the same time he was expressing concern about the fate of Catholics living there.

Clark most probably resolved this contradiction in the way that Sargent Shriver and other members of the CIC did, by claiming that he was bringing enlightenment to his fellow Catholics, but the fact remains that he most probably did not feel "comfortable" at his job at the CHR because it would be impossible not to know the ethnic ramifications of what he was doing there. No matter how he tried to justify it to himself, Clark knew that he was working for what was essentially a Quaker operation; the CHR had been brought into existence by Quakers, and it was still run according to their ideas of right and wrong and in their interests. In addition to that, the Irish Catholics had told him in so many words that he was considered a traitor to his own people. Shortly after the C Street incident and just about one year before he decided to accept the post as head of the CIC in New York, Clark described his job with the CHR as having "been chased by a wild Italian with a razor, hung by a man with a gun, howled at by mobs, growled at by pugs, sneered at by cynics and oafs, [but] beloved by sincere people."[4] Clark was hoping at the time that his children would come to appreciate his role as an interracial peacekeeper, but his own description of the job militates against describing his work for the CHR as "comfortable."

In spite of describing his decision to quit the CHR and go to work for the CIC as "irrational," Clark decided to make the move anyway, because, in his words, "I owe my life one good gamble anyway. I have up to now steeped my personal choices in caution since college."[5] Clark knew that taking the position was a gamble because the CIC was in a financially precarious situation at the time because both the Grace Foundation and the Stillman Fund had created a deficit of $30,000 by withdrawing their grants. He knew it was risky for other reasons as well. In a discussion of racism in the North which appeared in *America* shortly after the Jesuit magazine had turned down Msgr. Egan's attack on urban renewal, Clark indicated that "the most responsible elements in community life are for eventual and complete desegregation."[6]

That, of course, did not mean that Catholics were for complete segregation. In fact, it was Clark's way of saying that they were not, and that that dichotomy had become a fundamental fact of his life. "What is conceded at the upper levels of urban society," Clark wrote in his book, *The Ghetto Game*, which appeared shortly after he took over as head of the CICNY, "is not even accorded a hearing at the local community level, where housing segregation is defended."[7] Clark, of course, was referring here to Catholics in places like Philadelphia, the people he was paid to engineer when he accepted his job with the CHR.

Clark was in many ways the classic graduate student for his entire life. He was smart enough to understand what his teachers wanted but not smart enough to see through what they wanted – not smart enough, in other words, to understand the basic contradictions he was expected to internalize on his way to success in academe and elsewhere. He was willing to defend the civil-rights movement as a moral crusade even after he clearly explained it in his own book as based on economic interests, specifically those of the industrialists who were interested in low wages, the sort who exploited his father and his Irish co-religionists. This, of course, was a more profound version of dualism than the usual graduate-school variety, but it was a dualism nonetheless, one whose consequences would become painfully apparent when Clark became the head of the CIC. Clark's understanding of racial justice was based upon knowledge which made it obvious that justice was not the main issue involved. The call for racial justice was, according to evidence he presented in his own books, a cover for ethnic injustice and economic exploitation. He understood this every bit as much as he understood the fact that he was being paid to engineer his own people, and yet he reacted with shock and dismay when a program that was bound to fail failed to gather significant Catholic support under his leadership.

Part of the answer to this riddle lies in Clark's idea of ethnicity. At the time he took over as head of the CIC, Clark was convinced that "the old white immigrant and ethnic enclaves are dissolving."[8] Clark gives every indication that they were dissolving for good. In spite of being a sociologist, he gives no indication that he is familiar with the theory of the triple melting pot, which maintains, among other things, that ethnicity, while changing from country of origin to religion, will remain a constant in American life. Clark seems to feel that the ethnics who abandoned their traditional neighborhoods could become generic Americans, which is to say, people without ethnicity. This, at this point in his life, seems to have been Clark's path. According to the triple melting pot, the dissolution of the old ethnic neighborhood meant the emergence of the new ethnic group based on their shared Catholicism, but Clark simply didn't see things that way. Catholicism would always remain associated in his mind with the old Studs Lonigan type of ethnicity he remembered as a child or with the carping, CIC, liberal, anti-ethnic attitudes he adopt-ed as an adult. There was no such thing as a Catholic ethnic group for Clark. Catholicism and ethnicity were antipodes and would remain so. When he was at his most Catholic he was at his least ethnic. The most extreme example of this was his interracial justice phase, which reached its culmination when he became head of the CIC, when he would spend his time haranguing his fellow Catholics for not being in the forefront of the civil-rights movement, which at this phase of its existence was moving to the North to destroy their neighborhoods.

Conversely, the period during which Clark was his most "ethnic," i.e. Irish, was also the period during which he was least Catholic, and in fact shaded over into the final peri-od of his life, when he ceased to belong to the Catholic Church. Once Clark realized that the Church was not going to follow his notion of racial justice to the point of self-immo-lation, he abandoned the Catholic faith and became a flaming Irish nationalist instead. Ethnicity at that point became a substitute for religion. At no point in his life did Clark understand the fundamental sociological fact that religion was the basis for ethnicity in the United States, even though that transformation was taking place before his very eyes with the destruction of the ethnic neighborhoods that he himself was engineering. All that Clark could see was that "this dissolution" of the ethnic neighborhood would "permit move-ment" that would allow "the Negro population . . . more flexibility within the central city framework."[9] All Clark could see was the negative side of the equation, namely, the fact that "the native white working class" abandonment of the ethnic neighborhood "has opened up a tolerable supply of housing to take the edge off the worst housing difficulties of non-whites."[10] "Public housing and urban renewal projects," he concludes blandly, "have assisted in this process."[11]

Two years before accepting the job at the CIC, Clark noted in his diary that "it is not possible to influence local policies without professional stature that commands the respect of the strategic elite."[12] Clark's work at the CHR, in other words, had made him aware of the existence of the "strategic elite" in Philadelphia. Instead of construing that elite as a political force at war with the city's Catholics and then making the necessary political cal-culations about how to deal with that fact, something that the Irish politicians must have been contemplating at the time, Clark felt that the best response was to get an advanced degree at Penn or Temple and thereby achieve the credentials that would gain the respect of those in the "strategic elite." It was an illusion that would cost Clark many years of hard and fruitless labor at Temple University, where he, as the forty-year-old grad student, who also happened to be the author of a number of books on the topics his classmates were studying, would somehow still consider himself inferior to those whose idea of "creden-tials" had more to do with enlightened attitudes toward birth control than it did with expertise in housing.

Clark's decision to take the job as head of the CIC also coincided with a change in strategy on the part of the city of Philadelphia. Bloodied by the PHA's failed attempt to integrate the city's neighborhoods in 1956 and worried by the defection of Irish Catholic politicians like Bill Green on the housing issue, Richardson Dilworth decided to withdraw from the politically impossible situation in the neighborhoods and concentrate his efforts on the considerably less threatening task of revitalizing center city. The change in policy was best symbolized by the departure of the doctrinaire Walter Phillips and the arrival of the more pragmatic real-estate magnate Albert M. Greenfield, whom Dilworth appointed to the City Planning Commission in 1956. Edmund Bacon soon discovered that Greenfield shared his interest in revitalizing downtown Philadelphia, and soon both were making plans.

In 1960, Philadelphia's City Planning Commission unveiled its "blueprint for the Philadelphia of tomorrow," which envisioned "a new kind of city, its beginning already in evidence, which is within the financial and physical means of Philadelphia's peoples to bring to full realization in the remaining decades of this century."[13] Falling back to center city after their defeat in the neighborhoods, the planners decided on a defensive strategy which entailed surrounding center city with a moat of highways that would keep out the Catholic ethnics and the blacks they had failed to integrate in the neighborhoods to the north and to the south. That involved completing the perimeter which they had begun when the city built the Schuylkill and Vine Street Expressways to the north and the west by adding the Delaware Expressway to the east and, most controversial of all, the Crosstown Expressway, a ten-lane traffic barrier, to the South. "Center City," according to Rotello, "would be a showpiece central place, a self-contained walled city for the next century."[14]

Ed Bacon disputes the idea that the Crosstown Expressway was intended to be a wall protecting center city from South Philadelphia. "Lombard and South Streets," he claimed "were the worst slums in the city. It was just sensible to come up with some way to get across the city there from a traffic point of view by the clearance of the most decrepit houses and that the corridor west [sic] of Broad would be the South and Lombard street corridor."[15] But Bacon is quick to add that the Crosstown Expressway was not his idea.

"Mayor Dilworth," he claimed, "came to me and said that we needed a regional plan for transportation for the whole area. I was in over my head on that one. So Dilworth called in Robert Mitchell who gave Dilworth the plan for Southeastern Pennsylvania Transit Authority. The idea of a major expressway along South Street was Bob Mitchell's. Dilworth adopted a plan which called for an expressway. I proposed a boulevard, but I promised every mayor I served under that I would support their ideas. It is not true that the South Street Expressway was intended as a racial dividing line. If you're asking for my motivation, it was the last thing on my mind to construct a barrier."[16] Bacon is adamant in maintaining that highways were not intended to be racial barriers, but he is also quick to add that the Crosstown was not his idea. He goes on to add that in spite of supporting it publicly that he "used my influence to help undermine the South Street Expressway,"[17] something not substantiated by other people's recollection of his involvement at the time.

Dilworth's role in urban renewal was less ideological that either Joe Clark's or Walter Phillips's doctrinaire attempts to use housing as a form of social engineering. Phillips noted in 1958 that the Delaware Express was going to destroy two Catholic schools, something that could have been avoided if the city were to relocate the route to the east of the Pennsylvania Railroad tracks near the northeastern border of the city. Dilworth was quoted as describing the expressway as "essential to the life of the city,"[18] but he was also more willing to compromise when it came to routing it.

In August of 1961, Dilworth announced that he had agreed to a new routing of the

Delaware Expressway in South Philadelphia away from Second Street, one of the area's Irish neighborhoods. Dilworth's willingness to compromise bespoke, however, more political reality than the intentions behind the road in the first place. If the route of the expressway could be moved to do less damage to the neighborhood after political pressure was brought to bear, why was it designed to go through and, therefore, destroy the neighborhood in the first place? What actually got built (or, in the case of the Crosstown Expressway, did not get built) was more an indication of political reality than it was of the intention of the planners, who always seemed to come up with plans which created maximal destruction in the neighborhoods they sought to "renew." Wearied by the political toll ideologically driven development was taking in the city, Dilworth turned with relief to center city, when in 1960 he invited the city's *prominenti* to City Hall and accounted the New Philadelphia Movement's plans to "revitalize" the commercial, financial, industrial, historical, and residential sections of center city.

Since Dennis Clark was, by then, an expert on cities in general (his *Cities in Crisis* had appeared in March of 1960) and on Philadelphia in particular, he must have been aware of what was going on at the time and perhaps left for New York because he knew that the city, by focusing on the less-controversial development in center city, would have less need of his services working in the neighborhoods for the CHR. Dennis Clark wasn't the only one preparing to get out of town in 1962. In February 1962 Richardson Dilworth resigned as mayor of Philadelphia, as the charter which Clark and Dilworth had bequeathed to the city as their legacy required him to do, in order to run for governor. According to the provisions of the same charter, City Council President James H. J. Tate then became acting mayor. When the Supreme Court shortly thereafter confirmed him as mayor in fact rather than just acting mayor, Tate became the first Irish Catholic mayor in the 300-year history of the city of Philadelphia, and when he did, the ADA faction, under Walter Phillips's leadership, pulled out of the Democratic coalition and began to contest the Catholics openly for control of the city. Digby Baltzell described the change from the WASP point of view:

> Whereas Philadelphia has been tolerant of Catholics from the very beginning (as long as they kept to themselves, which they did), it was the last of the older cities in America to elect a Catholic to the mayor's office. The first Irish-Catholic mayor in Philadelphia's history, James, H. J. Tate, was elected in 1964 after the great reform movement under Joseph S. Clark and Richardson Dilworth had lost its steam.[19]

The reform in Philadelphia didn't lose its steam; it broke apart along ethnic fault lines when the first Irish Catholic politician became mayor. By 1962, Philadelphia's establishment could no longer be tolerant of Catholics because Philadelphia had become, as Msgr. Bonner had predicted in Paul Blanshard's book a generation before, a Catholic city. On July 4, 1962, as part of the nation's celebration of independence from England, a Catholic mayor, a Catholic governor, and a Catholic president of the United States all gathered on one dais in front of Independence Hall in Philadelphia in a celebration that must have convinced Paul Blanshard's followers of the prophetic nature of his 1949 book. The Catholics were in control of Philadelphia, and, what is more, the control of other cities like it across the nation had put a Catholic in the White House for the first time in the nation's history. Now the WASPs who had put the Democrats in power in the city looked on helplessly as the Democratic Party fell under the control of the Catholic ethnics they had read about in Blanshard's books.

Contrary to what Baltzell said, the reform hadn't "lost its steam"; the reform coalition was torn apart over ethnic issues, and at the heart of the ethnic issue was the bigger issue of who was going to run Philadelphia and according to whose principles was it going to be run. Frank Hoeber, son of Johannes and Elfriede, admits that there "was a lot of enmity between reformers and the machine politicians,"[20] but refuses to assign ethnic designations to those labels. The conflict, according to Hoeber, was "professional vs. nonprofessional." It was "not ethnic. It was not a plot to get rid of Irish Catholics. It would be an historical injustice to say that it was Elites vs. Catholics, although it is true that it broke along those lines."[21] Hoeber admitted that it was also "true that Paul Blanshard was discussed"[22] by Phillips and his crowd, but refuses to admit that fact had any significance in the ADA pull out of the reform coalition when Tate became mayor of Philadelphia.

In this he was like the correspondent for the *Chestnut Hill Local*, who came out in support of Walter Phillips when he ran against Tate in the 1963 Democratic primary. She referred to Phillips's Democratic opponents as simply "the baddies."[23] She didn't have to refer to them as Irish Catholics, since everyone in Chestnut Hill knew that already. "We all wail," she continued, "when the baddies get a stranglehold on our city." Phillips, who is identified as "another . . . distinguished . . . Chestnut Hiller" was organizing a campaign to "blow the 'baddies' out of City Hall,"[24] and the *Chestnut Hill Local*, addressing Philadelphia's prestigious WASP neighborhood, was urging the same type of ethnic solidarity in opposing Tate that this group found repugnant when citizens from, say, Polish neighborhoods like Bridesburg practiced the same thing. The article in the *Chestnut Hill Local* was more than just an example of an ethnic double standard; it was an indication of the ethnic fault lines in the city, but also an indication that the WASPs could never bring themselves to address the ethnic enemy in open fashion, even though it was obvious who the "baddies" were in the Phillips/Tate battle. The sides in the struggle were camouflaged to prevent those involved on the WASP side of the struggle from thinking of themselves as motivated by either ethnic or religious bigotry.

When the Irish Catholic Jim Tate became mayor, however, the WASP/ADA faction abandoned the city they could no longer control. "My father jumped ship when Tate became mayor," Hoeber claimed. "Most of the professionals, all liberals, ran away from the administration when Tate became mayor."[25] The one exception to that rule was Ed Bacon, whose decision not to defect "surprised everyone in the reform movement,"[26] according to Hoeber. As a result, Bacon, along with anyone else who stayed on to work with the Tate administration, was subjected to ostracism from their WASP fellow ethnics and treated as pariahs. "The political," according to Hoeber, "was personal,"[27] meaning that there was a bond between the reformers, but that bond, Hoeber is quick to add, was not ethnic. "The issue was credentials,"[28] according to Hoeber, that and the way Jim Tate talked. Of course, the Catholics didn't have credentials, and they talked the way they did because they belonged to the same ethnic group. Ultimately, the argument would always get around to its irreducible ethnic components, but once it did, the ethnic element would be denied by the WASP reformers as soon as it got stated in those terms because to deal with ethnic facts would have reduced them to the level of their opponents. The ruling class, like the Enlightenment principles it espoused, had transcended ethnicity by the very fact of being the ruling class and espousing Enlightenment principles, or so they thought at least.

Shortly after Richardson Dilworth stepped down as mayor and precipitated the crisis which brought about the demise of the reform coalition in Philadelphia, Dennis Clark began his job at the CIC in New York City, without, that is, having moved his family there to live. That meant long hours on the train back and forth from New York. If he thought that the CIC was going to be a respite from the stress at the CHR in Philadelphia, Clark was mistaken. The stress, he soon realized, had only increased. The commute back and forth between New York and Philadelphia was taking five hours a day. As a result Clark rarely saw his children, and, if at all, not during the daylight hours. Clark, as a result, was suffering from "dyspepsia, tension" and a fatigue which left him "dead, dead tired with a hatchet of migraine pain splitting my skull."[29] Clark had always prided himself on his robust physique. His idea of training as a runner and boxer entailed unloading 50 pound bags of sugar from ships docked along Delaware Avenue, but after taking the CIC job in New York, he had to admit that "I am now rarely well." "If I ever get over this interracial council job," he wrote in his diary in April of 1962, barely four months into his job, "I do solemnly hope for a 9 to 5 job, a nice, quiet steady job. No ideological trauma three times a day. No night, midnight work, just sanity."[30]

In July of 1963, the Clarks finally sold their house in Germantown – albeit at a $10,000 loss – and bought a house in one of the new suburbs in Freeport on Long Island. It was a living situation that still required a significant commute, although not five hours a day. Eliminating the commute to Philadelphia, however, only made Clark more aware of how much he missed his friends there. Although his wife was from New York, there is no indication that she had maintained contact with her friends from her college days there almost ten years before.

On October 25, 1962, shortly after the Cuban Missile Crisis, Clark had to admit that the CIC was undergoing its own crisis as well. The issue was money. "The New York Council can run for about two months unless we get funds from somewhere,"[31] he wrote in his diary, but the funding issue disguised a deeper issue. In his final report, Clark joked that his tenure as head of the CIC had proved that he was no fund-raiser. He portrayed the issue as being a vicious circle. The CIC needed skilled full-time people to make its programs work, but it didn't have the people because it didn't have the money, and it didn't have the money because it didn't have the people. Clark complained that Catholics lacked proactive lay apostolates in the social arena; Catholics suffered instead from "budget crisis, haphazard planning, inefficiency and stultifying self-delusion."[32]

Eventually he would resign because of the CIC board's failure to hire a full-time fund-raiser. But the absence of money simply disguised other, more-basic problems, problems that became apparent when Clark's book *The Ghetto Game* was published in 1962 while he was head of the CIC. *The Ghetto Game* makes clear that Clark apprehends the basic intention behind racial migration in the United States. No matter how much he referred to the civil-rights movement as a moral imperative, the bottom line was really economic. To get specific, the crusade for racial equality was ultimately driven, in Clark's own analysis, by "the manpower needs of technical society" which "will not permit any quarantine of the large non-white group."[3] This was essentially Louis Wirth's position, and Clark probably picked it up in one of the many sociology courses he was taking at the time or from his work with the CHR and its affiliates in Philadelphia. The one thing that stood in the way of a quick resolution of the problem of satisfying "the manpower needs of a technical society," was the ethnic community, which constituted "an obstacle course"[34] of ethnic taboo that hindered social mobility and therefore, economic progress:

> Their concentration in ethnic pockets gave ample social expression to [the ethnic community's] willingness to reject intrusion and adhere to group loyalties. These groups became key factors in shaping the course of Negro movement through urban residential areas. In many places they rebuffed non-white entry into their areas or deflected it to other neighborhoods. At times they formed walls of resistance to non-white infiltration by moving away in concerted and disciplined fashion. The ethnic communities of the large cities have constituted an obstacle course through which the non-whites have had to move.[35]

"These immigrant communities," in other words, "served as barriers against Negro mobility," not just for blacks, but "for the rest of the population" as well. The ethnic community, as a result, had to be broken up to foster economic progress. The whole project of ethnic cleansing could be articulated, as Clark did in *The Ghetto Game*, in a series of linked propositions: "the movement to rebuild immediately presented the question of the disposition to be made of the ethnic communities. Cities cannot be rebuilt without moving people. People could not be moved without defying the ethnic taboos and racial codes of the past."[36]

The worst offenders in this regard were the Poles, who were "a highly individualistic people" who were very familiar with how to operate in a multi-ethnic society because of their experience in Poland where they lived in uneasy co-existence with "Lithuanians, Estonians, German speaking elements, Ukrainians, White Russians, Jews and various Balkan strains. . . . With such a legacy of intergroup difficulty, it is not surprising that Poles did not come to the polyglot American city with a bland attitude toward minority neighbors in the New World."[37]

Compounding "the furious quality of Polish nationalism" and adding significantly to the "formidable quality . . . of working class pugnacity in a Polish neighborhood" is the fact that Poles are "near the bottom of 'the social distance scale,'"[38] when it comes to their desire for assimilation. "People with real relations experience," Clark writes, probably referring to himself, "contend that Polish neighborhoods are particularly resistant to racial change and are likely to react violently to incursions by non-whites."[39] Clark, who is probably talking about Bridesburg here because he had dealings with that neighborhood in his work with the CHR, is only reflecting in sociological jargon the same facts that Brand Blanshard made clear forty some years earlier after his stay there. Since the Poles are at the bottom rung of the Catholic social ladder, the perks which induced upward mobility and, therefore, social conformity held little or no attraction to them, especially since they had a fairly supportive community already. As a result, the Poles will have to be "educated" to understand their inferior status before they will feel motivated to do anything about it. Clark, of course, states their position the exact opposite way, by claiming that Catholicism, of the sort proposed by the CIC, will "civilize" the Poles by raising their educational level. "Since the Poles are a predominantly Roman Catholic group," Clark writes, "the gradual but pervasive Catholic moral concern for the elimination of racial inequalities will have an effect as the educational level of people of Polish background rises."[40]

Poles, according to Clark, "are . . . determined to resist, with violence if necessary, any Negro invasion of the areas they inhabit. Political committeemen in Polish neighborhoods have vocally associated themselves with this attitude."[41] This is, of course, significant because as Clark learned from environmentalists like Louis Wirth and Robert Merton, the only way to change ethnic attitudes is by changing ethnic environments. If the environment remains in the hands of the ethnics, their attitudes will never change. If their attitudes never change, their neighborhoods will continue to remain barriers to the free flow of labor that the U.S. economy needs for increased profits. Hence, the need for integration, especially in the Polish neighborhood, which "is less of an accident and more of a group bastion than the neighborhoods of most other immigrants."[42] Hamtramck, therefore, is, according to Clark, a sign of unwelcome contradiction because this "Polish Principality . . . has for years been impenetrable by Negroes."[43]

Therefore, the urban renewers had to break up ethnic taboo and the neighborhoods that harbored them if progress was to be made in the cities. All of this became apparent, according to Clark, during World War II, when "the housing shortage and curtailment of private building . . . made the needs of urban communities starkly evident even to those who opposed federally sponsored action. The immense change induced by the war and the post-war migrations forced municipalities to evaluate their physical and social needs. In the post war years the concept of redevelopment took form."[44] With redevelopment came social engineering: "To redevelopment was added the expanded concept of broad-scale urban renewal, which included not just physical building, but social reorganization at various levels of life."[45]

Clark, in other words, understood that urban renewal involved social engineering of Catholic groups in general, and groups like the Poles in particular, for ends that were often cloaked in moral garments but were ultimately utilitarian and economic. Yet, even knowing all this and stating it *expressis verbis* in a book that was published the same year he became head of the CIC, he still expects his fellow Catholics to willingly embrace the engineering, as well as the destruction of their communities that accompanies it, because it is their moral duty to do so. Clark was quite capable of living in two completely different spheres and making statements from one sphere that contradicted the interests of the other. He was at one and the same time a Catholic ethnic and an anti-Catholic ethnic sociologist with no clue about how those two *personae* could be brought together into one coherent world view or that it was necessary to do so.

At one point, as if trying to say something that might have impressed his professors at Temple or Penn, Clark writes that "it has been well verified that residential proximity between persons of different races in an environment will without undue stress produce an improvement in intergroup attitudes"[46] without giving any indication that his role at the CHR was to do precisely that, and that in attempting to implement Louis Wirth's idea of social engineering he had unleashed all sorts of social unrest in his attempt to improve "intergroup relations." Because of his inability to integrate what he had learned on the streets with what he had learned from his sociology textbooks, Clark's books, which by and large describe accurately the story of what was happening in Philadelphia at the time, take on an air of unreality.

"The Roman Catholic Church," according to Clark, "is heavily urban."[47] Clark, it should be noticed, does not use the past tense here, but he soon reverts to it once he gets around to his vision of the future, which clearly indicates that that urban Catholic configuration is a thing of the past. "The residential segregation of the past" which "was maintained as a part of a patchwork of urban ethnic partitions . . . was sanctioned by a legacy of superstition and ignorance that is now being dissipated."[48] Clark, the sociologist, makes it appear as if the Enlightenment is about to triumph in the area of housing, without explaining just what the consequences of this "triumph" will be for the Catholic ethnics, also people like himself, who are the prime beneficiaries of this exercise in social engineering. Instead of seeing the engineering of the Catholic ethnic neighborhood as the death knell for a way of life, Clark sees it as symptomatic of "educational advances" which lead to "a greater homogeneity of the urban population."[49]

Clark's internalization of the imperatives of social engineering may have got him good grades in graduate school or a job with the CHR, but they were of no help when it came to running a Catholic organization, not even one as liberal as the CIC. In fact they put him in an uncomfortable bind as head of a Catholic organization because his own book makes clear that the movement for racial equality in the United States is another name for breaking up what were essentially Catholic communities. Once that becomes apparent, as it does after a close reading of *The Ghetto Game*, there is no reason why Catholics should support the efforts of either the CIC or the civil-rights movement. Either they recognize its malevolent intent vis-à-vis the Catholic ethnic neighborhood, in which case they should not only not support it financially but should actively oppose it, or they do not recognize its malevolent intent, in which case an organization like the Catholic Interracial Council comes off as ineffectual and a pale imitation of the civil-rights movement, which is a more effective way of achieving the same goals. Both interpretations can be gleaned from Clark's writings at the time. Neither was calculated to swell the coffers of the CIC.

Shortly after becoming director of the CIC in 1962, Clark also became editor of the *Interracial Review* and inaugurated his tenure there by writing an article entitled "The Peril of Pussyfooting," in which he denounced his fellow Catholic interracialists for being "content with rhetoric and resolutions, second guessing and mopping up" instead of risking "jail and jeopardy in the South and stigma in the North"[50] as their more Enlightened Protestant brothers were doing. At around the same time Clark told the board of the CICNY that it was shameful that Catholics were not represented in greater numbers in the voter registration drives in Mississippi, something which caused anger and alienation among board members.

Clark had apparently developed the habit of talking this way while working for the CHR and other organizations in Philadelphia, where it earned him the esteem of his Quaker superiors, who considered him a progressive Catholic and, therefore, someone to cultivate. The same sort of approach would turn deadly, however, when Clark became the head of a Catholic organization, where it would either convince Catholics that they could put their money to better use by supporting the SCLC or the NAACP, or the approach might convince the more perceptive Catholic donors that their money was being used by the CIC in ways detrimental to Catholic interests.

The latter conclusion is probably what prompted both the Stillman and Grace Foundations to cut off support to the CIC as Father LaFarge lost control of his own organization to young turks like Sargent Shriver from the Chicago branch, which according to Southern, set the tone for CIC activities during the '60s. In January of 1963 the CIC held its national convention in Chicago at the Edgewater Beach Hotel. As their keynote speaker, they invited Martin Luther King, Jr., who gave a rousing speech in which he cited Augustine and Aquinas in a way that made the Catholics in attendance feel that they were more than ever behind the times. It was as if Clark's pussyfooting article had come to life for those in attendance, making them feel that the Catholic Church was hopelessly behind the more progressive Protestant denominations when it came to promoting racial equality and, coincidentally or not, the destruction of backward Catholic ethnic neighborhoods throughout the big cities of the North. King would soon make a triumphal appearance in Detroit, where after being welcomed by the Catholic mayor and Aretha Franklin's father, he would talk about civil disobedience, with predictable consequences. The best that Clark could muster from the conference was a weak "I told you so," as a prelude to his resignation as head of the CIC, which he handed in on March 10.

Notes

1   Clark, Diary, 12/30/61.
2   Clark, Diary, 2/26/60.
3   Ibid.
4   Clark, Diary, 11/2/60.
5   Clark, Diary, 12/30/61.
6   Dennis Clark, "Racism in the North," *America* (March 27, 1959): 663
7   Dennis Clark, *The Ghetto Game: Racial Conflicts in the City* (New York: Sheed & Ward, 1962), pp. 231–32.
8   Ibid., p. 239.
9   Ibid.
10 Ibid.
11 Ibid.
12 Clark, Diary, 5/5/59.
13 Carlo Rotella, *October Cities: The Redevelopment of Urban Literature* (Berkeley: University of California Press, 1998), p. 130.
14 Ibid., p. 132.
15 Interview with Edmund Bacon, 5/15/00.
16 Ibid.
17 Ibid.
18 "2 Private Schools, Can Firm Oppose Expressway Route," Robert J. Eilser, *Bulletin*, 9/125/58, Walter Phillips papers, Box 16, Temple University Urban Archives.
19 E. Digby Baltzell, *Puritan Boston and Quaker Philadelphia: Two Protestant Ethics and the Spirit of Class Authority and Leadership* (New York: The Free Press, 1979), p. 431.

20 Interview with Frank W. Hoeber, 5/00.
21 Ibid.
22 Ibid.
23 Letter to the Chestnut Hill Local, Walter Phillips papers, Box 32, Mayoral Campaign 1963, Temple University Urban Archives.
24 Ibid.
25 Interview with Frank W. Hoeber, 5/00.
26 Ibid.
27 Ibid.
28 Ibid.
29 Clark, Diary, 4/24/62.
30 Ibid.
31 Clark, Diary, 10/25/62.
32 Ibid.
33 Clark, *Ghetto Game*, p. 14.
34 Ibid., p. 108.
35 Ibid.
36 Ibid., p. 7.
37 Ibid., p. 113.
38 Ibid., p. 115.
39 Ibid., p. 113.
40 Ibid., p. 115.
41 Ibid., p. 114.
42 Ibid.
43 Ibid.
44 Ibid., p. 161.
45 Ibid.
46 Ibid., p. 79.
47 Ibid., p. 200.
48 Ibid., p. 226.
49 Ibid.
50 David W. Southern, *John LaFarge and the Limits of Catholic Interracialism, 1911–1963* (Baton Rouge: Louisiana State University Press, 1996), p. 349.

Jerry Cavanagh Appoints
George Edwards Police Chief

In 1961, the same year that John F. Kennedy took office as the first Irish Catholic president of the United States, and in the same year that Dennis Clark decided to become director of Father LaFarge's Catholic Interracial Council in New York, a thirty-three-year-old Irish Catholic lawyer by the name of Jerome P. Cavanagh became mayor of Detroit. Within a year James H. J. Tate would become the first Irish Catholic mayor of Philadelphia. The '60s in America, in spite of whatever they would come to symbolize later, were the decade during which the Irish Catholics finally came into their own in American politics. Their day in the sun would be short and violent and come to a bloody end almost before it had time to begin. By the end of the decade virtually all of the liberal Irish Catholic politicians who had begun the decade as synonymous with its optimism would be dead or swept from office by either the blacks they had hoped to promote or the ethnics who had become outraged at the excesses of the civil-rights movement and all of the other instances of social engineering it had enabled. Coleman Young symbolized the former option in Detroit; Frank Rizzo symbolized the latter option in Philadelphia.

The rise and fall of Jerry Cavanagh as the charismatic liberal Irish Catholic politician in the Kennedy mold paralleled as well the rise and fall of Detroit as the liberals' model city. In many ways, the fate of politicians like Jerry Cavanagh was tied to the Irish ideal of assimilation. Had Jerry Cavanagh been as cynical as his successor Coleman Young in courting the favor of the ruling class in Detroit, he might have been able to make course corrections along the way, but Cavanagh had internalized the exoteric WASP view of the city instead. Cavanagh believed in urban planning and Bauhaus architecture. He was, in a word, a modernist in the most naive sense of the term, and he would soon pay the price for what he didn't know about the real, which is to say the ethnic, dynamics of urban planning. Like Jack and Bobby Kennedy, Jim Tate, Dennis Clark, and a whole generation of Irish Catholic liberals who thought that they had found the solution to the long reign of ethnic and racial struggle that had characterized so much of American history, Cavanagh was ultimately destroyed by what he supported and what he didn't know about what he supported.

"Detroit," Mayor Cavanagh told the Michigan Society of Architects on March 8, 1963, "is gaining increasing renown as a center of progressive architecture."[1] Cavanagh could say this without irony or exaggeration. As representative of the new Detroit, Cavanagh was featured in a flattering piece in *Look* magazine as typifying a new sort of political leader, one who could serve as a paradigm for the renewal of America's oldest cities. As examples of the progressive architecture he had in mind, Cavanagh cited Eero Saarinen's GM technical center and Mies van der Rohe's Lafayette Park, one large high-rise slab surrounded by a series of low-rise cubes which had already become yesterday's version of tomorrow by the time they got built in the mid-'60s.

But even more significant than any individual buildings, according to Cavanagh, was "Detroit's new role as a pilot city in urban design."[2] The political matrix for the triumph of this sort of urban design was even more challenging because it required a "cooperative effort of government and architects with the responsibility to the public foremost in mind."[3] And it was the Irish politician, in the role of cultural intermediary, who was going to bring this about. Cavanagh's election paralleled Tate's election as mayor in Philadelphia one year later because both were enabled by a split in the traditional Democratic coalition. The liberal establishment comprised of the liberal leaders of the UAW and the Democratic Party feared alienating the core of their support because of the race issue, and so supported the incumbent, Mayor Miriani. This, of course, enabled Cavanagh to appeal to the black Trade Union Leadership Council for its support, and ride the new demographics into office. During the 1950s, the percentage of blacks in Detroit increased from 16 percent to 29 percent. That demographic increase, coupled with further migration from the South and the problems of assimilation and culture that that created would dominate Detroit politics for the rest of the century. Cavanagh arrived as the balance tipped and was smart enough to exploit that fact politically.

But he was not smart enough to solve the problems that opportunity created, something which became clear during his 1963 speech to the Michigan Society of Architects. Nor was he smart enough to understand that the very solution he was proposing was destined to create more problems than it solved. "No city in this nation," Cavanagh crowed, "knows better where it has been and where it is going. No other city has done more to blueprint and implement a comprehensive urban renewal program."[4] That blueprint, according to Cavanagh, "will assure Detroit's future as the pilot city in urban design in America."[5] Taking a page from the book his fellow urban planners had written in Philadelphia, Detroit's master planner Charles Blessing, with Cavanagh's blessing, planned to construct

> a large three-dimensional study model of its entire 17 mile Riverfront, as well as the entire center city area extending to Grand Boulevard. This model will reveal, as perhaps nothing before has done, the significant three-dimensional design elements, both old and new, in Detroit's center city of a third of a million people. It will show the relationship of the park and recreational areas, the freeways, boulevards and other streets and access routes and the architecture which gives the final and dominant sense of form and order to the city, whether viewed by the pedestrian, the passenger in an automobile on the freeways or even from the air.[6]

As in Philadelphia, the design model being proposed was Le Corbusier's Radiant City: high-rise buildings surrounded by large lawns and connected by superhighways. The Ford Motor Company would do the same sort of thing, dividing east and west Dearborn by a suburban campus that was so large it effectively turned them into two separate towns. In a series of articles which had appeared in the *Detroit News* in 1956, Blessing revealed that his plan for "Detroit's 'City of Tomorrow,'" the title of the series, involved reconstructing "30 square miles of Detroit's inner city according to good planning and design concepts."[7] Cavanagh assured his audience "that the construction of some 50 to 75 major urban renewal projects in the center of any city offers a challenge to that city to achieve greatness and excellence in its building."[8] Cavanagh was right in seeing the demolition of "8000 acres of residential blight" as a challenge, but he failed to calculate the cost that challenge would mean for the city that undertook it.[9]

Blessing's plan involved two problems. The first was design. Like the Better Philadelphia Exhibit in 1947, the plan involved tearing down housing that was densely packed and replacing it with the modernist vision of large open spaces allowing lots of light and air. The only way that that plan could have accommodated the same population in the same neighborhood with large spaces in between the buildings was to construct a series of high-rise buildings like the Brewster Homes, which had been built in 1938, at around the same time that the federal government had begun constructing the Richard Allen Homes in Philadelphia. By 1963, however, the profile of the average project dweller had changed. The residents of the projects were no longer working poor, oftentimes returning soldiers, who needed a transition to conventional housing that was in the process of being built as the nation overcame its war-induced housing shortage. By the '60s the population in public housing had changed to the permanent class of welfare recipients, which would continue to occupy it for the rest of the century. Projects, in other words, concentrated social pathology, and the government's decision to get involved in birth control as the solution to this problem would only exacerbate it by accelerating the decline of the black family. As Philadelphia's planners were then learning in the expensive school of experience, projects based on the high-rise model that Bauhausler Oscar Stonorov created for the Schuylkill Falls project in Philadelphia simply concentrated the pathology even further, to the point where living in the projects became intolerable.

Because of his naive acceptance of the principles of Bauhaus design, Jerry Cavanagh placed himself in the unhappy situation of bringing about the very situation he hoped to avoid. By replacing densely built housing with high-rise buildings, he concentrated the pathology in settlements which, because of their design, could not hope to accommodate all of the people he needed to displace in order to build them. As a result, he created an angry army of uprooted, ultimately revolutionary-minded blacks, who with some justification began to see the local government as a conspiracy against their interests. The projects would become breeding grounds for resentment because of their physical design. But the neighborhoods they demolished would also send the equally resentful blacks the projects could not accommodate in wave after wave into the adjacent ethnic, oftentimes Polish, neighborhoods where they were met with fierce resistance by people who felt that their way of life was being threatened.

The Cavanagh/Blessing plan for Detroit as a "pilot city in urban design" was an unacknowledged recipe for social unrest because of the dislocations it necessitated. Compounding that fact was the further fact that Lafayette Park, the jewel in Detroit's urban-renewal crown, was intended for neither the blacks it displaced nor the ethnics whose neighborhoods would have to accommodate their displacement. It was intended for the city's modernist elite. Others have noticed this fact, in retrospect – "The designers' resulting plan was a marvel in urban design," Thomas writes, "but it would have meant demolishing the neighborhood"[10] – but no one seems to have noticed it at the time. As a result, each time the city took a step toward what they saw as the solution, they made the problem worse.

By the time Jerry Cavanagh gave his speech to the architects, Detroit had demolished 10,000 buildings, an effort which displaced 43,096 of the city's residents, 70 percent of whom were black. One year before Cavanagh gave his speech, one of Detroit's newspapers estimated that 160,000 blacks – in other words, one-third of the black population of Detroit – had been adversely affected by the urban-renewal programs which were ostensibly trying to ameliorate the housing problems which racial migration had caused. By the time Cavanagh gave his speech to the Michigan architects, the handwriting was on the wall, but he was unwilling or unable to read it. "No single governmental activity," a Detroit Urban League official claimed, "has done more to disperse, disorganize, and discourage neighborhood cohesion than has urban redevelopment."[11]

Rather than face the turmoil which social engineering was creating in the city head on, Cavanagh decided to press on with more social engineering as the solution. In addition to the thousands of structures which had been demolished before he took office, Cavanagh presided over the demolition of 25,927 more dwellings during the time between when he took office and the Detroit riots of 1967, which eventually drove him from office, giving graphic evidence that the policies of liberalism had failed. During that time only 15,494 new housing units were built. That meant that the government's efforts not only did not ameliorate the housing crisis the city inherited from World War II, it exacerbated it.

The fact that the houses that did get built during this time were beyond the financial means of the people who were displaced to build them further exacerbated the situation. This again was done by design, even if the ultimate outcome was not intentional, because the whole principle behind the integration scheme proposed by Louis Wirth was that class would replace ethnos as the main principle of social organization in this country. This meant that whites need not worry about black migration to exclusive neighborhoods because the price of the house insured that they the average black could not afford the housing there or, if they could, they would have the same social mores. Integration based on class meant "sheltering middle class Whites from lower class Blacks"[12] but it also guaranteed that the housing shortage among lower-class blacks would intensify the more the government got involved in urban renewal. It also meant that those lower-class blacks would become more and more concentrated in pockets of deep social resentment, and that the only escape valve for this resentment was the adjacent ethnic neighborhoods. These same lower-class blacks had no sense of the ethnic composition of these neighborhoods, and, thanks to the increasing drum beat of social discontent and civil disobedience that was being orchestrated by the civil-rights movement, they began to see the inhabitants of these neighborhoods as generic white people, whose representatives were people like Bull Connor of Birmingham, Alabama. As a result, the resentment against social engineering in the black community got turned not against the people who were orchestrating the social engineering that was driving them out of their neighborhoods but against the "white" people who resisted when the migration which the social engineering created threatened the existence of their neighborhoods and way of life.

Gratiot (later renamed Lafayette) Park was a greater monument to the folly of central planning than even the agricultural policies of the Soviet Union because it was based on the engineering of something more intractable, namely, human nature. In 1960, researchers discovered that the people who moved into the Mies van der Rohe village just northwest of downtown were "highly educated professionals" who saw Lafayette Park as "an experimental area," and living there as "something of a cause."[13] The planners' penchant for social engineering blinded them to the fact that only a small percentage of the population would have been happy in the housing they were constructing. The cultural and economic bar was so high that integration could take place, but the numbers of people who felt comfortable living the Bauhaus version of Brave New World were such a small percentage of the population that the experiment was doomed to failure from the beginning. Living in Lafayette Park required a commitment to modernity that was equally lacking in both the black sharecroppers the project displaced and the ethnics whose neighborhoods would have to absorb them. Bauhaus principles of design, tellingly known also as the "international school" of architecture, were intentionally based on notions of deracination – having buildings up on pillars, for instance – that would be alien to all but small group of committed ideologues who were willing to run their lives according to enlightened but essentially inhuman principles. Making that sort of design the model for a multi-ethnic, working-class city like Detroit was a bit like decreeing that everyone would have to wear size 9 shoes. What may have worked – for a while at least – for the sons and daughters of Prussian Junkers in student dormitories in Dessau would not work with people who had grown up on farms outside Jackson, Mississippi, or Lodz. People like that needed a much more organic form of community – in short an ethnic community – as well as a sense of design which flowed from those exigencies, and that was precisely what was denied them.

Jerry Cavanagh knew none of this at the time, and some might say that it was not the business of the mayor to be an expert in urban design, especially when all of the "experts" were in such unanimous agreement over what needed to be done. Eighteen months after Jerry Cavanagh gave his speech, Ed Bacon appeared on the cover of *Time* magazine, the ultimate ratification of the conventional wisdom of the times. According to that same conventional wisdom, Detroit's Charles Blessing and Philadelphia's Edmund Bacon "exemplified the best of the architecturally trained urban planners."[14] That Detroit would follow Philadelphia's example in urban planning was only natural since as a special edition of *Architectural Forum* had stated in 1964, "Philadelphia has what is generally accepted as the most rounded, well-coordinated renewal program in the U.S."[15] Two years later, Robert Weaver, who had just become secretary of the newly created Department of Housing and Urban Development concurred by calling Philadelphia, "a trailblazer in planning, in renewal, and, indeed, in most of our federal urban aid programs," a place, "where planning has worked."[16] Jerry Cavanagh, as a result, can hardly be faulted for believing that the same thing could work in Detroit, but ultimately it did not work, and he and his generation of Irish Catholic politicians would pay the price when everyone realized that it was not going to work.

Some people woke up, but usually too late to do anything about it. In 1962, Detroit Councilman Mel Ravitz sponsored an open-housing ordinance that went down to defeat. Ten years later he was having second thoughts on the whole enterprise of urban planning. In 1972 he addressed the American Society of Planning Officials at the convention they were holding in Detroit. What he had to say was not going to make them happy, but it was based on a number of semesters in the expensive school of experience. "America's urban regions," Ravitz said, "both central cities and urban fringes alike, have been shaped far more by cultural and social forces than by the skills and perceptions of their planners. . . . The unfortunate truth is that planners have counted for little in the development of our cities and suburbs compared with giant technological, political, economic, and social forces. Most of what has happened in and to our urban areas would probably have happened even if there had been no planners or planning agencies."[17] Ravitz's pessimistic determinism was in many ways the mirror image of Cavanagh's optimistic faith in planning ten years earlier. Instead of urban planners taking the lead in changing the city, the city was changed by forces over which the city had no control – "the automobile; the inequitable tax system, which punished low-income people trapped in central cities; and attitudes toward race and poverty" [18] – created the mess that Detroit now found itself in. According to Ravitz, the "attitudes of the White, middle-class majority about race and poverty – not the concepts of the planners – decide how the American urban region grows and changes,"[19] a charge that brought offended response from Walter Blucher, Detroit's planning director until 1934, who felt that Detroit's was "the best highway-street system of any major city in the country."[20]

What both Ravitz's pessimism and Cavanagh's optimism ignore is the fact that urban design as a form of social engineering was neither the solution to the problem nor irrelevant to the problem; it caused the problem because the displacements it necessarily created fueled both black resentment and the white response to black resentment. It also took on the nature of a vicious circle. Because the solution was, in effect, causing the problem, the more the liberals tried to solve the problem, the more they made it worse, and the more they made things worse, the more they returned to social engineering as the solution to the problem. Like most of his generation, Cavanagh never learned that lesson, even though the bill finally came due on his watch. As a result, Detroit "began the decade [of the '60s] as the nation's model city and ended it as the nation's most tragic example of urban disintegration."[21]

By the time Cavanagh became mayor, twenty years of social engineering had created a significant if inchoate reaction, certainly among the city's black population, who were growing increasingly restive at being pushed around by urban-renewal schemes that never brought significant improvements in the city's housing situation in spite of their promises to the contrary. Cavanagh knew this intuitively, but instead of dealing with social engineering as the source of the problem, he decided to deal with its symptoms by engineering the police department as well. He did this by bringing in George Edwards, the man who was responsible for the engineering of the Sojourner Truth housing project when he was head of the Detroit Housing Authority, into his administration as police commissioner.

The change in roles Edwards was to play was significant. Edwards had no experience in police work, but he was regarded as a liberal fixer by the establishment in the city because of his connection to establishment figures in Washington. Edwards had cultivated a relationship with William O. Douglas and William Brennan while on Michigan's Supreme Court, and they supported him when he became police commissioner and decided to remodel the police department according to the principles which the court was putting into practice through its *Escobedo* and *Miranda* decisions. Edwards in many ways never overcame his reputation as the mystery man and the fixer from afar that he gained after becoming head of the Detroit Housing Authority shortly after arriving in the city as a labor organizer. "Mr. Edwards," wrote one irate correspondent to the *Detroit News* when it was announced that Cavanagh had appointed him police commissioner, "ran for mayor in our city and was rejected. As soon as he lost that election, he was appointed by [Governor G. Mennen] Soapy Williams to be a judge. Now our mayor-elect picked him again for a public job, even though the people of Detroit turned him down. . . . Why can't new people be picked for these jobs."[22]

By choosing Edwards to become police commissioner, Cavanagh solidified his support among black voters and among the national liberal establishment as well by appointing someone who was going to take the classic sociological approach to law enforcement. Edwards believed that slums created crime, and in this he was the opposite of the tradition represented by former Mayor Lamberton of Philadelphia, who felt that criminals created slums. In an article which appeared in *The New Republic* in 1960, Edwards expounded on his liberal environmentalist philosophy by stating his two main assumptions about the problem of delinquency: "The first is that no child is born predestined to be a criminal."[23] In other words, there is nothing genetic or racial about crime. "The second is that we can cure a far higher percentage of our juvenile delinquents than we do."[24] In other words, the causes of crime are environmental, and government can solve that problem by changing the environment. The "cure" for delinquency was "rehabilitation rather than punishment,"[25] and rehabilitation meant changing the environment, which meant "we must bring light and space into the core of our cities by tearing down slums, replanning to include parks and recreation space, and rebuilding."[26] Of course, that was precisely what was fueling black resentment in Detroit at the time, but neither Edwards nor Cavanagh gave any indication that they knew this was happening. Resentment and anger do not by themselves lead to crime, but the blacks who came to Detroit from the South brought with them a deep suspicion of the law as something calculated to keep blacks down. That frame of mind was compounded by the fact that the police department regularly hired white southerners as police officers because it was felt that they understood the black better and so could deal with him better as well. That many of those white southerners were also members of the Ku Klux Klan did not help racial matters.

Coming to an understanding of the problem would have meant repudiating the principles of liberal environmentalism and social engineering, but at the time Edwards became police commissioner there was no real reason to do this. The great racial catastrophe in Detroit was five years over the horizon when Edwards took office. Beyond that, no federal administration in the history of the United States had been more friendly to the idea of social engineering than the Kennedy Administration. The fact that Kennedy was a Catholic purged the idea of all of its connections with its nativist, eugenic past. In addition, the Kennedy Administration was willing to put its money where its mouth was when it came to "helping" the cities, which meant, of course, that the temptation to get even more deeply involved in the social engineering that was causing the problem was all but irresistible. The road to more social engineering was a two-way street at the time. In 1964 Cavanagh was instrumental in the creation of HUD, which soon took on Robert Weaver as its head, and Weaver, imbued with the ideas of social engineering which he had acquired when he was associated with Paul Ylvisaker's Gray Areas Programs at the Ford Foundation, would make sure that federal money got back to like-minded people in the cities, which mean people like Cavanagh and Edwards in Detroit and Leon Sullivan in Philadelphia.

Unfortunately, by appointing Edwards police commissioner, Cavanagh lost the support of the police department and those who backed the Mayor Lamberton approach to the relationship between crime and the environment. Detroit would become the flagship of liberal environmentalism among American cities in the '60s, and when that ship ran aground on the shoals of social engineering, the crew would go down with it. The signs that both the city and the social philosophy with which Mayor Cavanagh chose to associate it were in trouble were visible on the horizon shortly after Cavanagh appointed Edwards police commissioner.

Shortly after all of the liberal and black kudos following Edwards's appointment died down, a morale crisis began to emerge in the police department. The issue was black crime and how to deal with it. Shortly after Cavanagh took office, crime increased dramatically in the city. Just as dramatic was the connection between crime and the city's black precincts. The statistics were clear. Blacks comprised 29 percent of the city's population but accounted for 65 percent of the arrests. The city's highest crime rates were in the neighborhoods with the largest percentage of the black population. And all of those statistics took a dramatic increase after Edwards became police commissioner.

Detroit was not alone in this regard. Less than one year into Edwards's tenure as police commissioner, FBI director J. Edgar Hoover released its Uniform Crime Reports in August 1962, which indicated that the national crime rate was at an all-time high. Hoover announced that between 1956 and 1961 "crime has outstripped the growth of population by five to one."[27] According to Hoover's statistics, Detroit's increase in crime was four times greater than the average increase in cities with populations of over 25,000 inhabitants. Crime for July 1962 had increased 21.8 percent over what it had been in July '61, before Edwards took office.

Faced with statistics that dramatic, both sides tried to come up with an explanation of what was going on. The liberals reached their conclusion more or less by the process of elimination. Since race could not be a factor influencing behavior, the only possible explanation was environment, since that was the only other option their essentially materialistic calculus allowed. The solution then was to change the environment, which, of course, liberals like Edwards had been doing for twenty years by 1963. The fact that those changes had met with little apparent success only encouraged them to redouble their efforts. The other side in this battle was not racial; it was moral, something which had also been banned from the liberal calculus of social forces. J. Edgar Hoover concluded his recitation of statistical evidence by concluding that "we shall see no abatement in widespread lawlessness as long as there is wholesale disrespect for law and order in our Nation. Indulgence and materialistic selfishness are eroding the tried and true American traditions of honesty, integrity and fair play."[28] Edwards's nemesis and counterpart in Los Angeles, William H. Parker, took a similar approach, blaming the rise in juvenile delinquency on the increase of working mothers.

Knowing that the statistics were disastrous to his policing approach, Edwards tried to explain the statistical increase away as an increase in people reporting crimes (which redounded to the credit of his policies) rather than an actual increase in crime. The city's black community came up with its own interpretation of the crime statistics, one which would persist for the rest of the century. It was not that blacks were largely responsible for crime in Detroit, but rather that the police department was racially biased in its methods.

Interestingly, both sides might have come up with a different explanation if they had looked more closely at the facts. Most of the increase in crime occurred in the city's 10th Precinct, which was also the area which had to absorb the bulk of the 175,000 people who had been displaced by urban-renewal projects. So, even an environmentalist could have come to the conclusion that the environment was causing crime, but that would have meant, of course, repudiating the social engineering that was causing the change in the environment in the first place, and that was something a *liberal* environmentalist was unprepared to do.

As a result, Edwards had to fall back on "do-gooder" principles that absolved people of certain groups of moral responsibility. The result was a morale crisis in the police department that arrived shortly after Edwards took office. During the spring of 1962, all of Detroit's major newspapers ran stories documenting the low morale in the police department. "The word," according to Edwards's account, "is out on the street. The police aren't working."[29]

Edwards's biographer takes his side in the issue by claiming that "citizens took their cue from the newspaper reports and began writing to Edwards detailing how they were witnessing increased crime in their neighborhoods,"[30] an assertion which avoids the real issue, namely, was crime increasing or not? The statistics indicated that it was, and the personal anecdotes that flowed in after the stories appeared in the paper seemed to support the statistics. That response soon got polarized on racial lines – "Whites claimed that there was a real increase; blacks claimed it was all a matter of reporting"[31] – but the issue would not go away, and Edwards had little success in persuading people that his interpretation of events was something other than self-serving. The fact that it continued unresolved with the police commissioner on the other side of the issue contributed in large measure to the morale problems that kept getting mentioned in the newspapers. Officers in the equally beleaguered 16th Precinct convinced one newspaper reporter "that they feel their hands are tied, that they cannot make a legitimate arrest without subjecting themselves to physical injury or a lawsuit and that their morale is shot."[32] John Millhouse, in his series of articles for the *Detroit News*, reported that a "sergeant, speaking off the record, predicted that law enforcement in Detroit would collapse and Edwards would be out of his job in six months."[33] In January of 1963, Councilman William G. Rogell attacked Edwards, claiming that his "main goal is to appease the Negro" and that as a result "we don't have police protection in this town anymore."[34]

Edwards's actions didn't help his case any. On June 10, 1962, Edwards decided to attend a Nation of Islam national protest rally that was being held in Detroit. Its main speaker was a man who used to go by the name of Detroit Red, before he became a black Muslim and took the name of Malcolm X. Malcolm X offered Edwards a place of honor on the stage, but Edwards chose to sit in the audience instead, where he listened as

Malcolm X "welcomed him to the meeting and praised him for trying to bring equal law enforcement to Detroit."[35] It is hard to imagine a more damning condemnation of his policies in the minds of Detroit policemen than praise coming from the mouth of Malcolm X.

On April 16, 1962, a group of policemen met at a Detroit pizza parlor and discussed ways in which they "could get rid of that little son of a bitch."[36] But Edwards found support, as he always had during his career in Detroit, on the national level. On May 21, 1962, an essentially favorable article on Edwards and the policing reforms he was trying to bring about in the city appeared in *U.S. News and World Report*. Two weeks after the article appeared, William O. Douglas came to Detroit to give a speech and in lieu of the customary cocktail party after the speech opted to ride around town with Edwards in a squad car as some indication that the establishment favored his efforts. Lest there be any doubt about the meaning of the gesture, Douglas later wrote to Edwards after he returned to Washington, assuring him that "it is a great job you are doing along the banks of the River of Hate – the most important one in America at this particular time. I was thrilled at your achievements. . . . Let me know if there are occasions when some people of Washington, DC can come out to help on a project."[37] Referring to the inhabitants of Detroit as living along "the banks of the River of Hate" hardly seemed calculated to win support among the population in general or among the police force in particular, but it did point up Douglas's and Edwards's attitude toward their fellow citizens at the time. They were engaged in the cultural version of a civil war, according to which ideological purity meant more than natal soil. Edwards could always count on the elite to support his career because he was doing their bidding in Detroit, but this did not solve the morale problem in the police department which arose when the policemen came to the conclusion that their commissioner was working against their interests and, in effect, making their lives more dangerous.

That fear became a reality in early 1963. At 2:30 A.M. on February 24, 1963, Sergeant Stanley Sech responded to a domestic disturbance call at 13475 Dequindre in northeast Detroit. Charles L. Washington, a thirty-four-year-old, became irate when he returned from work and found that his wife was not home. When he finally found her, a violent argument ensued during which he threatened her with a revolver and threw her out of the house. When Sech arrived, he found her standing barefoot in the snow and decided to resolve the conflict by first talking to Washington. After knocking three times on the front door, Sech's attempts at peacemaking were greeted by a shotgun blast through the house storm door. Sech died on the way to the hospital, and the other four officers on the scene were treated for injuries resulting from flying glass.

Sech's murder was immediately laid at the feet of Edwards, whose policy of "mollycoddling" the black criminal element was seen as not only misguided but life-threatening as well. On March 6, 1963, radio commentator Lou Gordon announced that Edwards's "noble experiment" had failed. "In addition to a considerably high crime rate," Gordon opined, "it is common knowledge that more and more streets in our city become less and less safe to walk on after dark. Police officers tell me they have great hesitation in making arrests, because inevitably they become the accused rather than the accuser."[38]

As if to prove Gordon prophetic, another police officer was murdered on March 24, again by a thirty-four-year-old black man, this time a drunken motorist who wrested the gun from forty-six-year old policeman, who was the father of three children, and then shot him through the heart and lungs. In one of the ironies of history, Edwards was scheduled to receive the American Jewish Committee's Amity Award for furthering racial harmony in Detroit the same night as Officer Adams's funeral. Edwards decided to attend both functions, and so was praised by the AJC for fostering racial harmony at one event and excoriated for being responsible for the death of two policemen at the next. Adams's Pastor, the Rev. Dr. E. T. Bernthal, claimed in his eulogy for the slain policeman that the murders of Officer Adams and Sergeant Sech were an indication that "crimes of violence are increasing" and that "our wives and children are afraid to walk the streets, people are afraid to visit their loved ones in hospitals, and we are terrified in our homes."[39] Bernthal then asked rhetorically, "Who is responsible for turning our city into a jungle of crime."[40] Then, as if to answer his own question, Bernthal laid the blame for Adams's death at the feet of "those who advocate the easy parole and soft approach to crime,"[41] a veiled reference to Edwards, who then returned "seething"[42] to the AJC Amity banquet where he announced that "the battle for freedom, order and equal treatment goes on and on."[43]

As if to make matters worse in the mind of the policemen whose lives were affected by his policies, Edwards spent the spring campaigning against capital punishment, with the result that Adams's slayer did not get the death penalty, and in fact as a result of a technicality had his life sentence reduced to 19–55 years. ("The [appeals] court," according to Stolberg, "ruled that the original trial was marred by the judge's failure to adequately instruct the jury on the issue of malice."[44])

The results of this sort of leadership were predictable. Demoralization in general led to edginess in moments of stress, which in turn meant increasing recourse to deadly force on the part of the police, which, of course, fueled the idea in the black community that the they were a bunch of trigger-happy racists. On May 16, 1963, Officer Doyal Johnson, responding to a domestic-disturbance call of the sort which resulted in the death of Sergeant Sech, decided to err on the side of safety (at least his own safety) by shooting suspect Kirby Brown in his own home.

Notes

1 Remarks by Mayor Jerome P. Cavanagh, before the Michigan Society of Architects, March 8, 1963, Almblad Papers, Box 2 folder 13, Wayne State Archives.
2 Ibid.
3 Ibid.
4 Ibid.
5 Ibid.
6 Ibid.
7 June Manning Thomas, *Redevelopment and Race* (Baltimore: The Johns Hopkins University Press, 1997), p. 112.
8 Remarks.
9 Ibid.
10 Ibid., p. 115.
11 Ibid., p. 63.
12 Ibid., p. 64.
13 Ibid.

14 Ibid., p. 111.
15 Ibid., p. 120.
16 Ibid.
17 Ibid., p. 143.
18 Ibid.
19 Ibid.
20 Ibid., p. 144.
21 Mary M. Stolberg, *Bridging the River of Hatred: The Pioneering Efforts of Detroit Police Commissioner George Edwards* (Detroit: Wayne State University Press, 1998), p. 11.
22 Ibid., p. 131.
23 Ibid., p. 185.
24 Ibid.
25 Ibid.
26 Ibid.
27 Ibid., p. 191.
28 Ibid.
29 Ibid., p. 163.
30 Ibid.
31 Ibid., p. 172.
32 Ibid., p. 164.
33 Ibid., p. 174.
34 Ibid., p. 240.
35 Ibid., p. 171.
36 Ibid., p. 163.
37 Ibid., p. 168.
38 Ibid., p. 241.
39 Ibid., p. 242.
40 Ibid.
41 Ibid.
42 Ibid., p. 244.
43 Ibid.
44 Ibid.

Martin Luther King Comes to Detroit

By the spring of '63, the Detroit police department was lurching from one crisis to another under Edwards's increasingly inept direction, when events from the national scene intervened. On April 12, 1963, Martin Luther King, Jr., was arrested in Birmingham, Alabama, while leading a Good Friday march aimed at overturning that city's segregation laws. After being placed in solitary confinement, King wrote his "Letter from a Birmingham Jail," which stirred the conscience of the nation and the world, including the politically involved black clergy in Detroit, who under the direction of the Rev. C. L. Franklin, pastor of New Bethel Baptist Church and chairman of the Detroit Council for Human Rights, invited Rev. King to Detroit to lead a freedom march there. King's letter was actually written by Michael Harrington, author of *The Other America* and another Irish Catholic involved in racial matters. The fact that King's cause could be articulated by Harrington and espoused just as passionately by Jerry Cavanagh, when he got word of the march, showed how completely the Irish political class supported the black cause, even though it would eventually bring about their eclipse politically.

George Edwards most certainly shared Jerry Cavanagh's enthusiasm for the march, especially since he was police commissioner of the city and could therefore position himself advantageously on the national level when the inevitable invidious comparisons between him and Bull Connor would get made. The Detroit Freedom March was a golden opportunity for the city of Detroit to do exactly the same thing. The comparison must have been on Edwards's mind because when he met King at the airport on the morning of the June 23 march, he announced a bit tendentiously to King, "you'll see no dogs and fire hoses here."[1]

That was certainly a true statement because the Cavanagh administration was not only not hostile, it went out of its way to welcome King with open arms, as if to show the rest of the nation that Detroit had the answer to the racial problems that were then plaguing the benighted south. On that cloudless Sunday 150,000 demonstrators, largely black, marched in a throng ten-lanes wide down Woodward Avenue to Cobo Hall, where 12,000 of them listened as Martin Luther King, Jr., gave a longer version of the "I have a dream" speech that would make him even more famous than his letter from jail when he gave it in front of 200,000 people in Washington, D.C, two months later.

With King's speech, liberal optimism reached its high water mark, and Detroit, by hosting King with such enthusiasm, became, as Jerry Cavanagh had predicted a few months earlier, a paradigm for liberal urban politics. Cavanagh and his police chief had proved their critics wrong. People like Mr. W. Jones had written into the local paper warning about what might happen "when you allow 100,000 niggers," who "are an emotional race anyway," to "get to such an emotional pitch."[2] The city's white citizens feared mayhem and, as Sam Goldwyn might have said, stayed away in droves, but all of their fears proved groundless thanks to Cavanagh's enlightened leadership and Edwards's equally enlightened police policies. Instead of leading to mayhem, the march was a triumph of peace and "crime took a holiday" that Sunday.

The euphoria surrounding the march, however, obscured its purpose, for no matter how hostile the reception in Birmingham had been, the purpose of the march was perfectly clear. King and his supporters wanted an end to laws supporting segregation. The march in Washington two months later would be similarly clear in purpose. King and his supporters wanted Congress to pass the civil-rights bill that was then being threatened with defeat by a filibuster under the direction of people like Senators James Eastland of Mississippi and Strom Thurmond of South Carolina. Since Washington was the nation's capital and the bill was then being debated in Congress, the purpose of the demonstration was clear as well.

But what exactly was the purpose of the demonstration in Detroit, where the Cavanagh administration had gone out of its way to welcome the very people Bull Connor had attacked? Was it simply to show that Detroit had solved its racial problems and could now be a shining light to the rest of the nation? Jerry Cavanagh thought so. "We wanted to show as clearly as possible by word and deed," he said later, "that whatever happened to Martin Luther King, Jr. and his adherents in Alabama" would not happen in Detroit.[3] The Freedom March on June 23 was also a triumph for Edwards and a vindication of the reforms he had undertaken in the police department. *The Detroit News* announced afterward that the march "represented the pinnacle of Edwards's efforts for racially unbiased policy."[4] Instead of a riot, "crime took a holiday."[5]

Martin Luther King had much the same thing to say. "I was both uplifted and consoled," he wrote Edwards afterward, "to be with a police force that proved to be a genuine protector and a friend indeed."[6] Edwards, if anything, was probably more "uplifted and consoled" by King's letter than King was by the march, which was an unmitigated public relations coup for Detroit. It showed, in Jerry Cavanagh's words, that Detroit was "ahead of the nation in respecting the rights of man."[7]

The phrase had an ominous ring to it, foretelling blood in the streets and revolutionary disorder, but no one pointed this out to Jerry Cavanagh at the time, because in the popular mind "revolution" had a reservedly positive meaning, something that was ominous as well. The optimism of the day, however, seemed to brush away any foreboding. All that Jerry Cavanagh could see at the end of June in 1963 was "evidence that the unsavory traditions of prejudice are being shaken to their roots."[8] The spirit of the times concurred. One day before the march, when the conclave chose a successor to Pope John XXIII in Rome, the *Detroit News* screamed, "Liberal Montini Elected Pope." One day after the March, President Kennedy reached the pinnacle of his popularity when he gave his *"Ich bin ein Berliner"* speech in front of 1.8 million adoring Germans. Everyone seemed willing to do something, but that only made more urgent the need to understand just what needed to be done, and that question haunted the scene of King's triumphal march in Detroit long after the crowds had gone home.

While the purpose of the march from George Edwards's and Jerry Cavanagh's point of was clear, the purpose of the march from Martin Luther King's point of view was more difficult to discern. King made it clear that there were racial problems that needed to be solved in Detroit, but the outpouring of good will in the city upon his arrival was in many ways more disconcerting that being attacked by police dogs in Birmingham. There were no laws prohibiting the mixing of races in Detroit. As a result, King's attempt to attack segregation in housing there left the city with no clear response. Just what was the city supposed to do in response to King's march? The NAACP had been leading demonstrations in Dearborn, protesting the fact that few blacks lived there although many of them worked at the Ford plant there. One day before the March, the NAACP led 400 marchers to Dearborn, where they encountered 2,000 countermarchers who told them to go back to Detroit, where they belonged.

King's tactics, in other words, were more suitable for the South or for Washington, where his goals were clear. Specific laws were to be overturned. A specific bill was to be passed. If it didn't happen, King would hold demonstrations until it did. When he arrived in Detroit for the Freedom March, King told the *Detroit News* that he was considering the possibility of "sit-ins on Capitol Hill and 'civil disobedience.'" When the paper asked him what that meant, King "did not elaborate."[9]

Over the course of the next few days, however, some things would become clear. King's "plan," according to the paper's reading of his speech at Cobo Hall, "is to negotiate for change and if the negotiations break down to stage massive demonstrations."[10] Those demonstrations could paralyze a city, as his actions in Birmingham had shown, and now King "was considering bringing all its forces to bear on another city – possibly in Mississippi – in an operation similar to the one at Birmingham."[11] The point, according to King, was to "create a situation so crisis-packed that a community has to do something."[12]

This threat to the public order was precisely what was bothering King's opponents at the time. Who was to say that his followers would maintain his "turn the other cheek" attitude when confronted with the forces that were being paid to maintain and, in this instance, restore order in the light of King's disruptions of it for political purposes? Who was to say that the whole thing wasn't going to get out of control? One of those who expressed this fear was President Kennedy, who asked King, shortly before King arrived in Detroit, to call off the march scheduled for August in Washington. King, of course, refused, and Kennedy then used his refusal as a veiled threat to Congress to get them to pass his civil-rights bill. The threat which Kennedy conveyed was by the time he conveyed it an open secret. On the day after the March, in an editorial tellingly titled "The Negro Revolution," *The Detroit News* opined that

> if Congress does not deal swiftly with the problem in legislative halls, it will be fought out on the streets of Birmingham and Jackson, of Brooklyn and Durham, of Savannah and Cambridge. There will be violence on the picket lines, hate in the schools. The club and the police dog will haunt America's image abroad.[13]

The violent riots which followed police reaction to sit-ins in Charleston, South Carolina, indicated to the *Detroit News* that "the demand by the Negro for equal opportunity suddenly burst all traditional barriers and threatened civil chaos."[14] Like a snake charmer, King continually threatened social disorder but always under the assumption that he could control it once it occurred. King's civil disobedience was like the peaceful use of atomic power. King kept assuring his audience that that power would be used for good and that the reaction, though potentially dangerous, would not get out of control – as long, that is, as the country acceded to his demands. If they did not, then King couldn't guarantee what might happen. King's strategy was, in other words, a form of extortion. Soon it would become, in the hands of less Christian proponents, extortion pure and simple. "Give us money or the cities will burn," is how Daniel Patrick Moynihan phrased the threat years later.

The congressmen who were expected to pass King's and Kennedy's bill did not like the threat that went with it. One congressman complained that Kennedy's use of King's threat was "provocative" and claimed that it would encourage more "mob action and public disorder."[15]

King would, of course, have been forced to admit that this was true. The only thing that gave the peaceful sit-in the force that it did was the unspoken threat that the next demonstration might not be peaceful if King's demands weren't met. In addition to mustering the threat, King also had to convey the sense that he was still in control of the forces of social disorder, which he could turn on and off iike a light switch for certain political results. It was, in other words, one more example of the Enlightenment taming natural forces to bring about liberation. In this regard, King was one more "modern Prometheus" in the line of Dr. Frankenstein and Ben Franklin, the man who stole the fire of electricity from the sky and used it to benefit mankind. King was going to do similar things. He was going to arouse black passion and use it as the 1960s version of electricity or atomic energy in order to bring about changes in the country's laws and, ultimately, "liberation." Freedom, as his audiences in Detroit and Washington would learn, was King's dream, and he was becoming more and more skilled in arousing the passions of his listeners to achieve that end. As the *Detroit News* noticed, King's dream of freedom at the end of his forty-eight-minute speech "brought a wild response from the overflow crowd."[16] The unanswered question after that talk was whether King would be able to control the passions he was so successful in arousing.

One of the things that kept King's strategy of threat and extortion under control was its focus. In other words, King needed a bill to pass or a law to overturn in order to first summon the forces of "civil disobedience" into existence. But King also needed that external control in order to know whether to increase the pressure in the face of intransigence, or to call it off completely in the aftermath of victory. When he got to cities like Detroit, however, King was faced with a different and in many ways much more bewildering situation than the one he faced in the South or Washington. "Segregation in the North," King said, "is more subtle and takes form in jobs, housing, and education."[17] King was, of course, correct here, so correct in fact that his statement masked an increasing sense of befuddlement on his part about the strategy he was hoping to pursue in the North. King urged Detroiters to support his efforts in the South with money and by "working to get rid of any segregation and discrimination in Detroit."[18]

Just what that meant was not clear, and after King left town it was up to his followers to help fill in the blanks he left when he left town. After King's departure, the NAACP and the Urban League "called for further programs and demonstrations to obtain equal rights."[19] Officials at Detroit's Council for Human Rights indicated, again ominously, "that they plan to adopt a moderated version of Dr. King's method of creating 'crisis packed situations' with demonstrations in order to gain their demands."[20] One of their demands centered on housing. James Del Rio, a real-estate broker and member of the CHR, announced that "some way must be found to break down the pattern of exclusively white neighborhoods, especially in the suburbs."[21]

King's speech, in other words, was taken as an endorsement of the turmoil that racial migration was already creating in ethnic neighborhoods throughout the city. The fact that Detroit was settled the way it was with certain ethnic groups living in certain neighborhoods was now taken as a sign that the city was "segregated," and King's triumphal march through the city gave Detroit's blacks the sense that they could now take that matter into their own hands. The mayor of the city and the city's police chief had, after all, endorsed King's efforts completely. The signs the marchers carried indicated that they were interested in implementing King's vision on a local level. "Time is running out," said one. "Let's move to Grosse Pointe," said another.[22] Of course, even the most naive observer of the local scene knew that blacks would never be able to move in significant numbers into a neighborhood like Grosse Pointe. For one reason, the FHA would never permit it. But the frustration of their efforts in the suburbs, which were reserved as catch basins for whites fleeing the cities, only redoubled their fury and the intensity of their assault on the vulnerable ethnic neighborhoods within the city's limits. It was these enclaves that would bear the brunt of the attack which King unleashed in his speech.

Once King left town, the continuation of what he started fell to those who stayed behind. They promised more of the same. But the message changed subtly as it passed from spokesman to spokesman. The Rev. James W. Bristah, executive secretary of the Methodist Board of Christian Social Concerns, claimed that Sunday's freedom walk indicated "that there is a social revolution going on in the city,"[23] which is precisely what those who opposed King felt as well. King's followers got his message, but in implementing it, there was no guarantee that they were going to keep it within the bounds he established. In fact there was no indication that they were not using the demonstrations as a form of social revolution. In another editorial, the *Detroit News* opined that "the national emergency generated by violent demonstrations throughout the country will make it easier to limit debate"[24] on the civil-rights bill, indicating that they thought limiting debate was a good thing. Arthur Johnson of the NAACP, referred, again ominously, to "other methods,"[25] including "selective buying or whatever steps are necessary to accomplish essential things."[26]

Johnson's formulation of tactics was reminiscent of Malcolm X's threat to achieve black ends "by any means necessary." Malcolm X was considered at the time beyond the pale of responsible leadership, but the fact that his formulations were creeping into the rhetoric of Dr. King's supporters indicated that the situation was more fluid and dangerous than its proponents were willing to admit. Since according to the principles of the natural law, "civil disobedience" was a form of insurrection anyway, why shouldn't King's followers take his rhetoric to the next logical step? The rise of Black Power later in the decade indicated precisely this progression. Who was to guarantee that the forces of social disorder which King aroused would remain under his control? Who could assure that once aroused these forces might not seek a leader more in tune with their passions? Someone like, say, Eldridge Cleaver, who would try to spread Marxist insurrection as the head of a criminal conspiracy known as the Black Panthers.

In many ways, the call to armed insurrection that the Black Panthers represented was the least pernicious threat they proposed. Who was to say that this movement for freedom from oppression had to be organized at all? Why couldn't each black simply take the situation into his own hands by engaging in criminal activity against his white oppressors? That was the option Cleaver defined in his book *Soul on Ice*, which appeared in the same year that Martin Luther King was murdered. Long before that time, Cleaver had "arrived at the conclusion that, as a matter of principle, it was of paramount importance for me to have an antagonistic, ruthless attitude toward white women."[27] The crime statistics in Detroit indicated that Cleaver was, if anything, a more representative leader of the 10th Precinct than Martin Luther King. Cleaver "wanted to send waves of consternation throughout the white race"[28] and so he became an "outlaw,"[29] by stepping "outside of the white man's law, which I repudiated with scorn and self-satisfaction"[30] and becoming "a law unto myself."[31] For Cleaver, "rape was an insurrectionary act."[32] Cleaver was "delighted" to be engaging in criminal activity. Defiling the white man's woman had a larger purpose. It allowed Cleaver to engage in "defying and trampling upon the white man's law, upon his system of values."[33]

If Eldridge Cleaver could become a law unto himself by the early '60s, why couldn't every other disgruntled black in the 10th Precinct do the same thing? What was there in Martin Luther King's theory of civil disobedience which prevented this transformation? Why should the average citizen of the 10th Precinct subject himself to the indignities of the sit-in, especially since Martin Luther King had been murdered for his pains in doing so, when he could bring about social change on a much more grass-roots level by raping white women or shoplifting or selling drugs?

In his speech at Cobo Hall in June of 1963, King told his audience "I still hear a voice saying, 'Love thy neighbor and put up thy sword,'"[34] but in the body of his speech he adverted to other things as well. "We see our brothers in Africa and Asia moving at jet-like speed to freedom and self-determination while we go at a horse-and-buggy pace to be able to get a cup of coffee where we want it,"[35] he said, referring to the guerrilla wars of liberation that were sweeping Asia and Africa at that time. King clearly felt solidarity with those guerrilla warriors. The result was a deeply incoherent, deeply conflicted appeal to the people whose passions King came to town to arouse. King's appeal is full of references to Christianity, but at the same time it also mentions the largely Marxist anticolonial guerrilla warfare going on in Africa and other parts of the Third World as the paradigm for civil-rights struggle in the United States. King mentioned the wars of liberation at the same time he continued to urge his followers not to have recourse to their methods. The question which remained is which of King's exhortations his followers would heed. Eldridge Cleaver ended the '60s by fleeing to Cuba where he became a Communist revolutionary. The clearest indication of how their writings affected the black masses in places like the Detroit is the exegetical principle that the information would be received according to the mode of the receiver. That did not bode well for the nation's big cities.

At around the same time that the riots broke out in Detroit, the British military historian B. H. Liddell-Hart was coming to a reassessment of irregular warfare. The man who, in effect, wrote the book on irregular warfare now felt in the light of bitter experience that

that sort of warfare invariably disintegrated into revolution in precisely the way that the civil-rights movement would disintegrate in America during the '60s. Guerrilla warfare had expanded exponentially in the period following World War II largely because the H-bomb in 1954 had created a stalemate in conventional warfare but also because of the influence Liddell-Hart's book on T. E. Lawrence's irregular-warfare campaign against the Turks during World War I had on Winston Churchill, who fomented guerrilla wars in both Europe and Asia because of his "instinctive pugnacity and complete intentness on beating Hitler – *regardless of what might happen afterwards*"[36] (my emphasis).

It was precisely what happened afterward which gave Liddell-Hart pause at the end of his life and caused him to reject his earlier endorsement of guerrilla warfare. Irregular warfare, he concluded, invariably got out of control, and once that happened it invariably caused more harm than good. The most successful guerrilla-war campaign in history, the one which gave us the name "guerrilla," was conducted in Spain against Napoleon's forces there after the regular Spanish army had been defeated. The success against Napoleon, however, "was followed by an epidemic of armed revolutions that continued in quick succession for half a century, and broke out again in this century."[37] Similarly, the franc-tireurs which were created in France to harass the German invaders of 1870 "turned into a boomerang."[38]

> They had been merely a nuisance to the invaders, but they had developed into the agency of the appalling fratricidal struggle known as the Commune. Moreover, the legacy of "illegitimate" action has been a continuing source of weakness in the subsequent history of France. . . . The disease has continued to spread. In conjunction with the an unrealistic view and treatment of external troubles, it has undermined the stability of France and thereby dangerously weakened the position of NATO.[39]

The trajectory which Liddell-Hart described culminated one year after *Strategy* was published, when the revolt of '68 broke out in Paris. Liddell-Hart then goes on to explain why irregular warfare invariably "boomerangs" on those who promote it by comparing it to the constraints under which regular warfare is prosecuted.

> Violence takes much deeper root in irregular warfare than it does in regular warfare. In the latter it is counteracted by obedience to constituted authority, whereas the former makes a virtue of defying authority and violating rules. It becomes very difficult to rebuild a country and a stable state on a foundation undermined by such experience.[40]

"The heaviest handicap of all, and the most lasting one," involved in promoting irregular warfare, according to Liddell-Hart,

> was of a moral kind. The armed resistance movement attracted many "bad hats." It gave them license to indulge their vices and work off their grudges under the cloak of patriotism, thus giving fresh point to Dr. Johnson's historic remark that "patriotism is the last refuge of a scoundrel." Worse still was its wider effect on

the younger generation as a whole. It taught them to defy authority and break the rules of civic morality in the fight against the occupying forces. This left a disrespect for "law and order" that inevitably continued after the invaders had gone.[41]

Urban areas, according to Liddell-Hart, were not particularly suitable for guerrilla operations. However, they did provide fertile ground for a subversive campaign, which could become revolutionary if it were combined with "an appeal to national resistance or desire for independence with an appeal to a socially and economically discontent population"[42] and could take advantage of "social discontent, racial ferment and nationalistic fervour."[43] Detroit, in other words, provided the ideal environment for the sort of subversive campaign that Liddell-Hart felt invariably degenerated into social disorder and anarchy.

The civil-rights movement was, in other words, a black operation (in both senses of the word) that got out of control. The suspicion that irregular warfare degenerated into social disorder in America during the '60s is reinforced by the fact that the Kennedy Administration decided to get deeply involved in promoting irregular warfare at precisely the same time that Jerome Cavanagh became mayor of Detroit. In May of 1961, according to Liddell-Hart,

> the new President, addressing Congress, announced that he was "directing the Secretary of Defense to expand rapidly and substantially, in co-operation with our allies, the orientation of existing forces for the conduct of non-nuclear war, paramilitary operations and sub-limited, or unconventional wars." The Secretary of Defense, Mr. McNamara, spoke of a "150 percent increase in the size of our antiguerrilla forces, while aid to foreign guerrilla forces operating against communist regimes was envisaged by the new administration.[44]

Paul Ylvisaker's Gray Areas Programs, adopted lock, stock, and barrel by the Kennedy Administration when it brought Robert Weaver to Washington, was the domestic equivalent of McNamara's dramatic involvement in guerrilla warfare. Just as those guerrilla tactics would backfire abroad and lead to the debacle of Vietnam, so their domestic equivalent would "boomerang" and lead to the very racial riots they were designed to forestall. The black population of cities like Detroit was caught in a emotional shear consisting of rising expectations fueled by leaders like Martin Luther King and Jerry Cavanagh combined with the frustrations that resulted from the policies of more and more intrusive social engineering that were actually forms of social control. Blacks were told that people like Mayor Cavanagh were on their side, but Cavanagh's uncritical belief in policies like urban renewal continued to tear down more and more black residences and contribute to greater and greater social dislocation in the black community. In addition to twenty years of disruptive urban renewal and ethnic cleansing, the federal government under Kennedy decided to get into the distribution of birth control as a way of blunting the black demographic threat at the same time it decided to promote guerrilla warfare. That black operation "boomeranged" too by contributing to the meltdown of the black family, which created an exponential increase in disorder in communities that were already weakened by the migration up from the South. As it always does, social engineering created the need for more and more draconian social engineering as the solution to the social chaos which it created in the first place.

The first indication of what Detroit could expect from King's arousal of black passion coupled with the government's attempt to engineer it occurred within days of the Freedom March. On July 4, 1963, George Edwards and his wife set sail for England with Supreme Court Justice Brennan to take part in an Anglo-American Judicial Exchange. Edwards left for a month in Europe confident that the changes he had instituted in Detroit's police department had been vindicated by the absence of violent incident at the Freedom March and Martin Luther King's explicit endorsement afterward. His confidence was to prove short-lived. One day after he left, two police officers spotted a hulking six-foot-tall, 193-pound prostitute by the name of Cynthia Scott swaggering around the intersection of John R. and Edmund Place with one arm around what appeared to be a john and the other hand waving a huge roll of dollar bills. Scott had been arrested a number of times before, and the police in the area had been inundated with complaints about prostitutes robbing their customers. When Officers Theodore Spicher and Robert Marshall attempted to put Scott in their squad car, however, she pulled a knife, slashed Spicher's hand, and ran away. When Spicher caught up with her, she turned on him again with the knife. When he tried to stop her, she turned and began to walk away, and he shot her in the back, killing her.

Edwards heard about the incident from Mildred Jeffrey, information director for the UAW, who called him in England and informed him that the incident was turning into a public-relations disaster which required his immediate return. Edwards eventually arrived home on July 28, over three weeks after the incident occurred, to find that the program of police reform which had been so triumphantly vindicated one month before now lay in ruins. The city's blacks were outraged that a police officer had shot a black woman in the back. The city's white population was convinced that Edwards had fatally undermined the authority of the police in the eyes of an increasingly unruly black population, an under-mining which necessitated the use of more and more deadly force, which in turn created more unrest and hatred of authority in the black community. It was a vicious circle, all of which, rightly or wrongly, was being laid at the feet of George Edwards, who at this point simply wanted to get out of town as quickly as possible to his job on the Court of Appeals in Cincinnati, which seemed to be his reward for engineering the Detroit police department. Edwards later conceded that "my decision to leave Detroit in the summer of 1963 was one of the worst mistakes of my life."[45] Praise from his handling of the Freedom March had left him "overconfident."[46] His absence during the Cynthia Scott crisis allowed the city's extremists to take control of the issue. Wilfred X of the Detroit Temple of Islam showed up at the funeral, where demonstrators carried signs demanding that "Killer Cops Must Go."[47]

When Edwards took office in early 1962, he set himself four goals, the first of which was "to prevent a riot like the one Detroit had experienced in 1943."[48] Roughly four years after the Cynthia Scott incident, Edwards watched helplessly from his sinecure in Cincinnati as that achievement slipped out of his grasp as well. In the early morning hours of July 22, 1967, police raided what was known as a "blind pig," an illegal drinking establishment. As the outnumbered policemen tried to herd the establishment's customers into police cars, a riot broke out, and for the next week the city burned out of control, and once again Detroit had to ask for federal troops to help quell one more riot. That riot eventually result-ed in the deaths of forty-three people, thirty three of whom were killed by officers of the law. Among its many effects, the riot ended Jerry Cavanagh's short career as the charismatic liberal Irish Catholic politician in the Kennedy mode.

It ended along with any sense of optimism the nation might have had in solving the race problem. In its place, panic followed. The flow of white residents out of the city and into the suburbs increased to a hemorrhage in the wake of the riot. From 1964 to 1966, an average of 22,000 whites left the city each year. That figure jumped to 47,000 in 1967 and jumped again to 80,000 in 1968. The net result of King's Freedom March in 1963 was the creation of the nation's most "segregated" city three decades later. That "segregation" was not based on laws but rather on the fears of whites who felt they were defenseless in the face of an increasingly lawless black population, and, when Coleman Young became mayor, an administration that refused to protect them if they were white.

In its post-mortem on the riot, the national advisory commission noted that the violence had begun in the 12th Street area, which "housed more than 21,000 persons per square mile, double the city's average density, because *urban renewal clearance of nearby project sites had caused an influx of Blacks into the area*"[49] (my emphasis). The official post-mortem would, however, not list urban renewal, social engineering, the expectations raised by the civil-rights movement, or disordered passion as the cause of the riot. Instead, they blamed it predictably on "white racism," something which fueled further migration out of the city on the part of the whites, further resentment on the part of blacks, and further decline for the city as a whole. The riots, coupled with an unsuccessful bid for a Senate seat in 1966, effectively ended Jerry Cavanagh's political career. Shortly after declining to run again for mayor in 1969, Cavanagh accepted an appointment as a professor at Wayne State University, the political equivalent of wanting to spend more time with his family. In June of 1969, Cavanagh appeared on *Meet the Press* and announced that the era of "progressive white mayors"[50] was over. People like Cavanagh had been outflanked by aggressively ethnic black nationalists on the left and equally aggressive "white law and order types" on the right.

Cavanagh's assessment of the situation proved prophetic. He was followed as mayor by both types in short succession. After declining to run in 1969, Cavanagh was succeeded by Wayne County Sheriff Roman Gribbs, whose STRESS (Stop the Robberies Enjoy Safe Streets) program tried to reimpose law and order on Detroit but succeeded only in antagonizing the now demographically powerful blacks in the city into bringing in Coleman Young as Gribbs's successor in 1973. Martin Luther King proved to be prophetic too, although probably not in the way he intended. The United States government passed its civil-rights bills; the inner-city ghettoes went up in flames. He was right on both counts. His reference to the connection between the guerrilla warfare in Africa and Asia and the civil-rights movement in the United States proved prophetic too. After Coleman Young became mayor, Detroit, as part of its attempt to make sense out of the social chaos which social engineering had brought to the city, "developed a quasi-official ideology that regards the pre-Young era as a time of white colonialism, ended by the 1967 insurrection and its aftermath."[51] The situation in Detroit, according to Ze'ev Chafets, who lived there as a boy before moving to Israel, "is very similar to postcolonial situations in the Third World. People always say, 'The Africans can't govern themselves,' and that's what they say about us too."[52]

George Edwards was long gone by the time the bill for social engineering came due in Detroit. He watched the riots from the safe distance of Cincinnati. By the time Jerry Cavanagh retired from public office, Edwards realized that a new wind was blowing in the land with the election of Richard Nixon and Spiro Agnew to the White House on a frankly pro–ethnic, anti–civil-rights platform. He continued to "offer a liberal voice"[53] on the court even though few in comparison with the heady days of 1963 were listening. But because he was a judge he could compel an audience's attention no matter how outdated his ideas sounded. This is precisely what he did by becoming involved in one last scheme of social engineering. Busing was completely consistent with his world view as a liberal environmentalist. It caused just as much social turmoil as the crusade to integrate housing had, but not in Detroit. A city which was 80 percent black could not achieve "racial balance" no matter how many children it put on buses. When Edwards died, on April 8, 1995, Detroit was the most racially homogeneous big city in the nation – a tribute in a perverse way to his commitment to social engineering and a tribute as well to the ineradicable nature of ethnicity in American life.

Notes

1 Mary M. Stolberg, *Bridging the River of Hatred: The Pioneering Efforts of Detroit Police Commissioner George Edwards* (Detroit: Wayne State University Press, 1998), p. 249.
2 Ibid., p. 248.
3 Ibid.
4 Ibid., p. 250.
5 Ibid.
6 Ibid., p. 251.
7 Ibid., p. 250.
8 Ibid.
9 Laurence Barrett, "Rebuff Kennedy on Plea to Curb Rights Protests," *Detroit News* (June 22, 1963).
10 Jack Crellin and John M. Carlisle, "Cry for Freedom Rings out to Throng," *Detroit News* (June 24, 1963): 4A.
11 Ibid.
12 Ibid.
13 "The Negro Revolution," Editorial, *Detroit News* (June 23, 1963).
14 Ibid.
15 Tom Joyce, "Kennedy Plan Stirs Congress to Rights Battle," *Detroit News* (June 20, 1963).
16 Jack Crellin and John M. Carlisle, "Cry for Freedom Rings out to Throng," *Detroit News* (June 24, 1963): 4A.
17 Ibid.
18 Laurence Barrett, "Rebuff Kennedy on Plea to Curb Rights Protests," *Detroit News* (June 22, 1963).
19 Michael Parks, "City Negroes Aim for Full Integration," *Detroit News* (June 25, 1963): 1.
20 Ibid.
21 Ibid.

22 "Greatest Freedom Walk: Leaders Hail City's Progress on Rights," *Detroit News* (June 23, 1963).

23 Crellin and Carlisle, p. 4A.

24 Tom Joyce, "Specter of Coming Civil Rights Filibuster Haunts Capitol Hill," *Detroit News* (June 22, 1963): 8A.

25 Jack Mann, "Negroes Here Pledge More Demonstrations," *Detroit Free Press* (June 25, 1963): 1.

26 Ibid.

27 Eldridge Cleaver, *Soul on Ice* (New York: McGraw Hill, Ramparts Books, 1968), p. 13.

28 Ibid., p. 14.

29 Ibid., p. 13.

30 Ibid.

31 Ibid.

32 Ibid.

33 Ibid.

34 "125,000 Walk Quietly in Record Rights Plea," *Detroit Free Press* (June 24, 1963).

35 Ibid.

36 B. H. Liddell-Hart, *Strategy* (New York: Praeger, 1967), p. 379.

37 Ibid., p. 380.

38 Ibid.

39 Ibid., p. 382.

40 Ibid., p. 380.

41 Ibid.

42 Ibid., p. 375.

43 Ibid.

44 Ibid., p. 376.

45 Mary M. Stolberg, *Bridging the River of Hatred: The Pioneering Efforts of Detroit Police Commissioner George Edwards* (Detroit: Wayne State University Press, 1998), p. 256.

46 Ibid.

47 Ibid., p. 254.

48 Ibid., p. 279.

49 June Manning Thomas, *Redevelopment and Race* (Baltimore: The Johns Hopkins University Press, 1997), p. 130.

50 Stolberg, p. 291.

51 Ze'ev Chafets, *Devil's Night and Other True Tales of Detroit* (New York: Random House, 1990), p. 177.

52 Ibid., p. 178.

53 Stolberg, p. 293.

Dennis Clark and the Ford Foundation

Dennis Clark returned to Philadelphia with his tail between his legs. His failure as head of the CIC prompted not a re-evaluation of his essentially self-contradictory and self-defeating political program but rather a crisis of faith. "For the first time," he wrote in his diary.

> I am now sorely tempted to throw over the lay apostolate as I have known it. Two books, a thousand speaking engagements, endless meetings and ten years since college have taken a toll. Why am I using what talents I have to stir others when my own children hardly see me? I desperately hope now to get some job that will free me to build that rapport, that dear confidence that tuition and interesting tradition for the children that will make a difference in their formation and education. The lay apostolate as I've practiced it simply will not permit this. Something has to give.[1]

As if things weren't bad enough, his wife had a miscarriage the night he resigned. All he could do was settle back to Philadelphia and bide his time while "fishing for something else."[2] That something else turned out to be the Ford Foundation's Philadelphia Council for Community Advancement, Inc., Paul Ylvisaker's first attempt to establish a ruling-class beachhead among the blacks of North Philadelphia. PCCA was the Gray Areas Program that would eventually lead to, and be replaced by, the funding of Leon Sullivan's Opportunities Industrialization Corps. "After a month of enforced idleness," Clark wrote in July of 1963, "I am back to work with a [Ford] Foundation sponsored effort to plan and reorganize social services in Philadelphia. The salary is $12,000 a year. I am to develop job training and advancement programs, largely for the young and the Negro population."[3] After his failure as head of the Catholic Interracial Council, Clark learned that for a Catholic liberal the only career move which made any sense was working for an anti-Catholic operation like the Ford Foundation or the CHR. If Clark had been interested in working with the Catholic strategists of his day he could have worked with Archbishop Krol, Cardinal O'Boyle of Washington, and William Bentley Ball, head of the Pennsylvania Catholic Conference, but Clark's work with the CIC precluded that, primarily because it created categories in his mind that would eventually take the place of Catholicism. Given the role that racial justice was assuming in Clark's mind, the only way he could work for what Clark called "strategic elites" was to go to work for the other side, which is what he did when he went to work for the Ford Foundation's PCCA.

In this regard, it is interesting to compare Clark's ill-fated career to the much more successful career of Paul Ylvisaker, who was in some sense his boss when he worked for the PCCA in Philadelphia. Clark and Ylvisaker were both born in the '20s, and both died in the early '90s (Ylvisaker in '92 and Clark in '93). Both Clark and Ylvisaker could be considered experts in urban affairs; both were involved in the struggle for racial equality;

both got their start in Philadelphia at around the same time; both were influenced by the ADA-Clark-Dilworth reform movement there; both were ambitious; both worked for the establishment, and both were paradigms of upwardly mobile assimilation because both abandoned the religion they were born into.

But with the mention of religion, their paths begin to diverge. The transition from Protestantism to the Enlightenment which Ylvisaker took was much less traumatic because in a sense it involved the inner trajectory of Protestantism in a way that the transition from Catholicism to the Enlightenment did not. In many ways, the difference between the two men was ethnic. Ylvisaker never had to switch ethnic groups. Clark, on the other hand, would have to do that if he chose to take the same route, but the fact remains that he could never make the break from his past the way Ylvisaker did. Ylvisaker had abandoned the Lutheran faith by the time he was a grad student at Harvard because he found it inconvenient.

Clark, by comparison, was agonizing over why the Second Vatican Council wasn't fulfilling its expectations in 1965. At the time when Ylvisaker had already abandoned the faith, Clark was defending *Casti Conubii* and attending daily Mass. Clark's loss of faith was less calculating and more complicated than Ylvisaker's. The differences point up the ethnic nature of the struggle at the time. By the time Clark abandoned the Catholic faith, he had fathered six children and had become so associated with the Catholic faith in the mind of the establishment that he could never be accepted by them as anything but a paid mercenary. He learned too late that he would never be accepted by the WASP elite on their terms in the way that, say, John McCloy, another Philadelphia boy from the wrong side of the tracks, or Paul Ylvisaker had been. McCloy and Ylvisaker were part of the inner circle that came up with the plan to destroy ethnic neighborhoods and were treated as confidants of the establishment in a way that Clark could only dream of.

Clark was faced with a choice that neither McCloy nor Ylvisaker had to make. If he espoused the real or esoteric meaning of social engineering, then he had to embrace explicitly his role as an agent working for the destruction of Catholic communities. If, on the other hand, he continued to espouse the exoteric rationale for urban renewal, then he would not be taken seriously by the "strategic elites" which were running the operation. They might hire him in a subordinate role, but they would not promote him to the type of position which Ylvisaker occupied, and which his expertise merited. Clark's desire to work for the "strategic elites," in other words, was frustrated by his fatal association with Catholicism, an association that he himself would sever but only after it could have no beneficial effect on his career. "The great attraction of the Philly job," Clark wrote, "is the proximity to school at Temple U"[4] where he hoped to get his Ph.D. Clark's faith in education is touching, but it is doubtful whether anyone who traveled in the circles frequented by McCloy and Ylvisaker would have been impressed that a forty-year-old Irish Catholic was getting a degree from Temple University. Harvard, where McCloy and Ylvisaker got their advanced degrees, was a prestigious school because it was the school of the ruling class; it was not, according to the vulgar understanding, a ruling-class school because it was prestigious. Clark was naive enough to believe the ADA-Reform crowd in Philadelphia when they insisted, in Hoeber's words, that "it was about credentials" when the subtext to credentials was always ethnic. In other words, no degree from Temple

University was going to redeem any Irish Catholic's ethnicity in the eyes of the ruling class.

After starting work at PCCA, Clark noticed that "the race relations field" had become "tumultuous"[5] over the summer of 1963. "Picketing, sit-ins, riots and progress under pressure"[6] had become part of the general consciousness at the time; however, Clark also noticed that "the Catholics are not part of the mainspring of militancy,"[7] something he feared might estrange blacks from the Church and vice versa. Clark felt oppressed by the civil-rights movement because of what he perceived as the lack of Catholic participation in it. At the same time that the liberal Protestant sects were enjoying (at least from their own perspective) their finest hour, all the Catholics could muster, in the absence of any lay apostolate, was rampant "individualism" and "fragmented, pathetic effort."[8] The civil-rights movement was giving Clark the Catholic version of a massive inferiority complex at a time when he was feeling especially vulnerable in terms of his own career. In the period of enforced idleness following his resignation from the CIC, Clark wrote a film script on the civil rights movement entitled "The Children's Choice," in which he referred to the red diaper babies who were then engaging in the activity that constituted the cutting edge of sexual liberation and, therefore, the rise of the feminist reaction as "destined to be the greatest shining hour of American democracy."[9] If Clark had actually gone to Mississippi during the summer of '63 or '64, he might have come away with a different opinion of what was going on, but already married with five young children, he would have to idolize civil rights workers like Stokely Carmichael from afar.

What Clark failed to notice upon his return to Philadelphia (in his diary at least) is that Walter Phillips, the WASP standard bearer, went down to overwhelming defeat at the hands of Jim Tate and the Catholic ethnics in the May 1963 democratic primary. Clark had arrived back in Philadelphia just as Walter Phillips's battle against Jim Tate in the democratic primary was reaching its climax and denouement. Phillips, known in crypto-ethnic parlance as the "reform" candidate, had been sparring with Irish Catholic "machine" politicians like Bill Green all spring. Dick Dilworth thought that Phillips's campaign was quixotic at best and divisive to the point of political suicide. Even Joe Clark, much more of a WASP-ethnic partisan than Dilworth, was initially cool to Phillips's bid but made it clear that he would support him "because his attitude and philosophy toward the government of Philadelphia are the same as mine."[10]

By early May, however, Clark's coolness had dissipated in the heat of the campaign. Claiming that he had no plans to work for the Phillips's campaign, Clark, nevertheless, came back to Philadelphia to attack what he termed "Bossism" in Pennsylvania politics. "For many years," Clark told the *Philadelphia Inquirer*, "our Commonwealth has been in the Jukes Family of American politics."[11] Clark's choice of words was instructive. His reference to R. L. Dugdale's classic in Darwinian eugenics, *The Jukes*, showed that Philadelphia's Catholic ethnics were clearly linked, in his mind at least, with the racial degenerates that he had read about as a young man. Clark's comment also indicated that the movement to get government involved in birth control in the 1960s had its roots in the eugenic movement of the earlier part of the 20th century. Clark's second wife, Noel, was local head of Planned Parenthood, and Clark was becoming more and more overt in calling for government-funded birth-control programs from the floor of the Senate at the time.

Instead of dealing with the eugenics issue directly, Tate referred to Clark as "low blow Joe,"[12] and Green made a point of not inviting him to the Philadelphia Democratic Party's Jefferson-Jackson day dinner on May 16.

By April of 1963, one month before the election, word of the fratricidal Democratic primary had reached the Kennedy Administration in Washington. As a result, Kennedy dispatched aides Larry O'Brien and Ken O'Donnell to talk demographic sense to the combatants. The numbers were plain enough for anyone to see. Kennedy carried the state of Pennsylvania in 1960 by 116,326 votes. In order to offset Republican strength in the state's rural sections, that meant piling up a lead of 331,000 votes in Philadelphia, and that meant he needed the support of the city's Catholic ethnics, and that meant he needed the cooperation of William Green, Sr., whom both O'Brien and O'Donnell regarded "as one of the most effective Democratic organization leaders in the country."[13] This may have sounded like common sense to O'Brien and O'Donnell (who also happened to have Irish names), but it did not sound that way to Walter Phillips, whose decision to oppose Jim Tate "was prompted in part by the pleas of party leaders from outside Philadelphia"[14] and who now construed the race as a "personal struggle" with Bill Green, who was "determined to see Phillips, head of the ADA chapter here, disposed of as a political threat."[15]

Once again the ethnic dimensions of the struggle were delivered in code words like "machine" and "ADA" or "reform." In spite of that, the situation was not without its ironies and complexities. Bill Green was working with Jim Tate to get redevelopment money for the city at the same he was fighting Walter Phillips, the man who used the PHA as a way of engineering the city's Catholic neighborhoods. The Kennedy Administration was involved in a similarly complicated strategy. Kennedy needed the urban ethnic vote to get elected, but he also needed the urban black vote that had traditionally been part of the Democratic coalition as well. That meant that Kennedy had promised to fight for a federal law against discrimination in housing during his 1960 campaign, something which was political poison to Bill Green, who had backed away from the Dilworth administration in 1956 on precisely this issue. Kennedy also had to placate the country's Protestants, who still feared that he was taking secret orders from the pope in Rome. He also had to placate less perfervid Protestants like Walter Phillips, who feared that Catholic ethnic interests were going to prevail over principle in racial matters.

Kennedy, who had, after all, attended Harvard and had surrounded himself with Harvard deans like McGeorge Bundy when he went to Washington, attempted to finesse this impasse by taking social engineering to the next level, and that meant turning public housing from temporary way stations for down-and-out veterans into on-site birth control clinics for blacks on welfare. Kennedy's decision to get involved in the '60s version of the eugenics movement was, considering the web of political forces surrounding him, understandable from a certain point of view. Birth control could easily be seen as the magic bullet that would solve all of his problems. It would allow him to look both anti-Catholic and undeniably progressive to the WASP establishment, which had been promoting the eugenic solution to the country's race problem since John D. Rockefeller began supporting Margaret Sanger in the '20s. It would also mean that he could offer government money to black political entrepreneurs who were willing to go along with the sexual engineering of their own people. That meant the support of people like Leon Sullivan and Andrew

Freeman of the Urban League. It also opened up an internal front among blacks by causing the NAACP leadership to turn against Cecil Moore because he opposed government-funded birth-control clinics for blacks as a form of genocide. In order to accomplish this, Kennedy needed blacks experienced in social engineering, and as a result he turned to Robert Weaver, who was then working for Ylvisaker's Gray Areas Program at the Ford Foundation, and brought him and eventually all of the Ford programs to Washington, where they were transformed into government programs of the sort which eventually became the War on Poverty. Kennedy's decision to get the government into the birth-control business entailed a massive betrayal of the Catholic ethnics who had put him in office, because among other things, it involved accelerating the forces that were destroying their neighborhoods, but Kennedy seems not to have been overly troubled by this fact, especially when he could buy off opposition by giving politicians like Bill Green and Jim Tate "redevelopment" money.

Walter Phillips eventually lost the Democratic primary by the three-to-one margin (Phillips polled just over 41,000 votes; Mayor Tate, who won the nomination for a full, four-year term, had 128,312 votes), something that must have convinced him, in case he hadn't figured it out already, that the WASPs no longer had the demographic clout to win elections in cities like Philadelphia. Rather than concede defeat gracefully and retire to their country clubs, the WASP elite decided to pursue their political goals by other means. War, von Clausewitz noted, is politics by other means, and in this instance, the WASP elite, with the support of the agencies they controlled in Washington, embarked upon a campaign of irregular warfare to defend themselves against the Catholic demographic threat which had now become the Catholic political threat, as Paul Blanshard, who by now was being invited to the White House to talk to the Catholic president, had always said it would. In his clipping file, Walter Phillips, who was, like most of his class, a contributor to Planned Parenthood, took note of the development of the birth-control pill by Dr. John Rock, its Catholic inventor and a Harvard professor, who claimed "at a luncheon meeting sponsored by the Planned Parenthood Federation's World Population Emergency Campaign," that "Catholic doctrine today is no obstacle to a massive program of government action on the population problem."[16] Rock said this because (1) the government was planning to get involved in "a massive program" at that very moment and (2) because the government needed to defuse Catholic opposition. Claiming that "many Catholic scholars are as concerned with the tragic consequences of overpopulation as non-Catholics," Rock called for "a scientific effort comparable to the wartime Manhattan Project."[17] As far as America's cities would be concerned, it would be just like that, only more destructive.

As some indication that the war over the neighborhoods in Philadelphia was far from over, Philadelphia sent 18,000 of its citizens – the largest delegation from any city in the country – to the civil-rights march in Washington in August of 1963, where Martin Luther King, Jr., would give his famous "I have a dream" speech. Leading the Southeastern Pennsylvania division of the Americans for Democratic Action was Walter M. Phillips, fresh from his defeat at the hands of Mayor Tate. By participating in the march, Phillips was telling the world not only that "the ADA are joining many others in saying to our elected officials that as to civil rights the Congress has failed to perform properly its legislative function under the US Constitution,"[18] he was also announcing – obliquely, albeit

Philadelphia, 1963, WASPs go down to electoral defeat

– that support for the war on the neighborhoods was now going to be more federal than local.

Notes

1 Clark, Diary, 10/25/62.
2 Clark, Diary, 3/23/63.
3 Clark, Diary, 7/7/63.
4 Clark, Diary, 7/7/63.
5 Clark, Diary, 8/4/63.
6 Ibid.
7 Ibid.
8 Ibid.
9 "The Children's Choice," film script (June 13, 1963). Clark, Diary, 9/13/63.
10 "Clark is Cool to ADA Bid for Mayor," *Philadelphia Inquirer*, 3/1/63, Walter Phillips papers, Mayoral Campaign 1963, Box 32, Temple University Urban Archives.
11 "Clark Plans No Role in Phillips Campaign; Will Battle 'Bossism,'" Jerome S. Cahill, *Philadelphia Inquirer*, 5/2/63, p. 8, Walter Phillips papers, Mayoral Campaign 1963, Box 32, Temple University Urban Archives.
12 "Tate Assails Senator Clark, Calls Him 'Low Blow Joe,'" *Philadelphia Bulletin*, 5/17/63, Walter Phillips papers, Mayoral Campaign 1963, Box 32, Temple University Urban Archives.
13 "Phillips Says Green Hurts Party Image," John G. McCullough, *Philadelphia Bulletin*, Walter Phillips papers, Mayoral Campaign 1963, Box 32, Temple University Urban Archives.
14 Ibid.
15 Ibid.
16 "Fertility Control Research Urged by Catholic Doctor," UPI, Walter Phillips papers, Mayoral Campaign 1963, Box 32, Temple University Urban Archives.
17 Ibid.
18 Robert A. Thomas, "Philadelphia to Send Biggest Contingent to Rights March," *Philadelphia Inquirer*, 8/28/63, p. 16, Walter Phillips Papers, Box 2, March on Washington, Participants, 1963, Temple University Urban Archives.

Paul Ylvisaker Discovers Leon Sullivan

Fortunately for the Ford Foundation's efforts to influence the situation in North Philadelphia after the demise of Philadelphia Council for Community Advancement, Paul Ylvisaker had discovered someone who had something approaching Cecil Moore's demographic clout combined with Andrew Freeman's amenability to social engineering. Ylvisaker had discovered the Rev. Leon Sullivan. Leon Sullivan was a 6' 5" former basketball player from West Virginia who was also the pastor at Zion Memorial Church in North Philadelphia. During Sullivan's tenure as pastor at Zion, membership would increase from 600 to 6,000, and Zion would become a major conduit for, first, foundation money and, then, federal money into the operations he created in the local community. According to Ylvisaker's account of their meeting in the early '60s, Sullivan was not talking to white people at the time. If not, then Ylvisaker's magical association with the Ford Foundation must have loosened Sullivan's tongue. Ylvisaker went to Sullivan to "eat crow" about the failure of PCCA and was swept away by the reverend's charismatic presence. Ylvisaker was also impressed by the fact that Sullivan was a minister and Ylvisaker's father was a minister as well. When Ylvisaker told Sullivan that he looked and acted like his father, Sullivan asked whether his father was "passing," i.e., a black pretending to be white.[1]

Knowing that what he termed the "bureaucrats" at the Ford Foundation were against Sullivan because Sullivan was involved in vocational training, Ylvisaker, "who just had the instinct that this guy was great," committed what he later termed "a Machiavellian act," by arranging to have Sullivan show up at the Ford Foundation board meeting just as the trustees were heading for the elevator.[2] Within a few moments, the Ford trustees had gathered at Sullivan's feet as if he were delivering "the Sermon on the Mount." Finally, Henry Ford II broke their awed silence by asking, "My God, how do we manufacture more of you?" It was a question for which Sullivan had a simple answer. "By giving me some money," he replied.[3]

Ylvisaker later stated that "from there on I had no trouble,"[4] but that was not the case. Shortly before the Sermon on the Mount at the elevator, Ylvisaker was mulling over the troubles at PCCA, feeling that "the outcome is still uncertain."[5] The main problem was the hostility of Cecil Moore, which had discredited the PCCA in the eyes of the black population of North Philadelphia. In order to dig himself out of that hole, Ylvisaker needed the support of what he termed "middle-ground Negro leadership,"[6] blacks, in other words, who were neither radical nor perceived as Uncle Toms – blacks, in other words, like Leon Sullivan, who were perceived by the residents of North Philadelphia as militant but were perceived by the board of the Ford Foundation as amenable to the social engineering of those same residents.

Sullivan, according to Ylvisaker's account, however, was "still wary, still waiting to see whether more than talk and tokenism are involved."[7] The opposite of talk in this context was money. Ylvisaker was anxious for Ford to give Sullivan money, but worried that the incompetents at PCCA, Ford's go-between, might screw up the transaction. Eventually Ylvisaker reached the point where he was willing to pull the plug on PCCA if they didn't fund "Reverend Sullivan's employment training program (Opportunities, Inc.) and without attempting to control or mastermind."[8] "If so," Ylvisaker continued, "PCCA will have opened the major door to acceptance in the North Philadelphia community. We have candidly said as much to PCCA officials and find agreement among them."[9]

The main source of opposition to Sullivan's project, however, was not the PCCA. It was the Ford Foundation itself, and the opposition was based on the evaluation of Sullivan's program which they themselves commissioned. On December 18, 1963, two weeks after Ylvisaker's memo expressed the hope that Sullivan would get funding, Michael Harris submitted his evaluation of Sullivan's Opportunities Industrialization Center. What he wrote was not calculated to make Ylvisaker happy. "I cannot think of a single feature of the proposal [which Sullivan had submitted]," Harris wrote, "that impresses me favorably."[10]

"It is quite obvious," Harris continued,

> that the people who have put this together know very little about the field in which they are attempting to work and have not displayed a slightest shred of evidence that they have made any attempt to understand it. They have done well in the things they know how to do, namely, to get financial and moral support from local businesses and organizations. There is not, I am afraid, a single aspect of the proposal that stands up.[11]

By reading between the lines of the proposal, it was obvious that Sullivan had used his impressive rhetorical skills to inspire a group of local followers (in subsequent years he would hire professional grant writers) to produce a document about a job-training program that promised to train young blacks to work in the electronics industry when no one in the program knew anything about vocational training or things like the fact that knowledge of electronics required knowledge of electricity as a prerequisite. Sullivan's proposal stated: "The existing or projected training programs have not been designed to meet the urgent employment needs of the most severely deprived inter[*sic*]-city population, without regard to age, race, or special need."[12] This alleged fact, in turn, caused Harris to wonder if Philadelphia was worth saving. "If this is really the case in Philadelphia, then that city is benighted beyond repair. But if it is the case, what evidence is there that in such a barren community people can be found who will design and conduct the programs that are required?"[13]

"The training program," Harris opined, "looks like something someone picked out of a book or dreamed up."[14] The simple fact of the matter, as Harris makes clear, is that the OIC simply could not possibly accomplish what their grant proposal said they were going to accomplish. The trainees "simply cannot become electronic technicians in a period of one year,"[15] unless, of course, they had substantial training already. But "if they have had substantial training before coming to this institution," Harris wonders, "why wouldn't it be better to continue their training rather than creating a new institution?"[16]

Why, in other words, should the Ford Foundation pay Leon Sullivan to provide vocational training at a cost of $532 per student when Dunwoody, another vocational school mentioned in the report, did the same job for less than half the cost and got no support from Ford? "There must be hundreds of vocational schools and some in Philadelphia who daily do what this institution purposes it will do, but which operate on a lower cost basis,"[17] Harris argued.

Pursuing the issue of cost, Harris reminded the foundation that there was nothing in the proposal which stated how the OIC was going to get funding after their first year of operation. This, of course, implied that the operation would become a permanent ward of the Ford Foundation, but "if the organization didn't continue for more than five years," Harris continued, "this would mean an expenditure of well over $3 million which would leave absolutely nothing permanent."[18] Which, of course, brings Harris back to his original point: why should the Ford Foundation support OICs "when so many good institutions doing a fine job are hard pressed for funds to continue . . . would it not be much sounder to improve these to meet the needs mentioned in the proposal?"[19]

The short answer to that question was "no," at least as far as the Ford Foundation was concerned. After listening to Mr. Harris demolish the pretense behind the proposal stone by stone, the Ford Foundation went ahead and granted Leon Sullivan over $200,000 in early 1964. Just why they did can be at least partially gleaned from a vehement memo rebutting Harris's claims (or if not rebutting, then attacking them) written by Christopher Edley one month later. As with Ylvisaker, Edley's case for funding OIC is not based on any sense that they can actually do what they say they will do in the proposal but rather on Sullivan's charismatic personality. Sullivan's "vast energy and unlimited faith"[20] outweigh the fact that both the foundation and PCCA "were disturbed by the discrepancies between OICs well-publicized plans and its present capacity to deliver."[21]

Having conceded Harris's case, Edley goes on to urge funding nonetheless, and it is at this point one begins to suspect that vocational training is not the real reason the Ford Foundation is interested in Rev. Sullivan. Edley is more interested in the continued survival of PCCA in North Philadelphia than vocational training. If PCCA could channel money from Ford to Sullivan, then "its place in the North Philadelphia community should become much more secure. PCCA would be seen – at long last – as it was intended; a down to earth instrumentality for community betterment, ready to work with the constructive elements of the community and not be far removed from them."[22]

In other words, PCCA needed Sullivan to give it credibility among the blacks in North Philadelphia. Ultimately the role of PCCA was purely instrumental. In December of 1964, the Ford Foundation pulled the plug on PCCA funding, and it went out of existence. In a post-mortem memo, one Ford staffer wrote that, "in complete candor, staff must report that PCCA has almost completely failed to achieve its objectives and is presently in the process of putting itself out of business."[23] PCCA's fatal mistake was to announce at its inception a survey instead of the expected action programs, something which "triggered an attack by the Executive Director of the NAACP which, when added to the general tension created by the civil rights protest movement in Philadelphia, forced PCCA staff to divert their energies from program development to public relations."[24] The only thing of merit which the PCCA accomplished, according to the same memo, was giving a grant to the OIC, an organization run by "one of Philadelphia's outstanding Negro leaders."[25]

Ford could pull the plug on PCCA because, in spite of what the internal memos described as its almost complete failure as a program, the PCCA had fulfilled its purpose by funding Leon Sullivan. In funding Sullivan, Ford accomplished a number of goals, none of which had anything to do with vocational training in electronics. First of all, they got to determine who the "responsible" black leaders in North Philadelphia were. That meant withholding approval from people like Cecil Moore, something that would inhibit his ability to raise money and, as a result, foment dissatisfaction at NAACP headquarters when he failed to pay his chapter dues. This, in turn, led to various internal attempts to have him removed, one of which was orchestrated by C. Delores Tucker, a lady who will become significant to this story for other reasons.

Without a charismatic black leader like Sullivan, Ford's sphere of influence in North Philadelphia was confined to a bunch of ineffectual professors from Temple University. With Sullivan, Ford had traction in the community and could influence the course of events there. That, of course, meant taking control of racial migration and skewing it to benefit the Ford Foundation's interests. Ylvisaker had made it clear from the moment of their inception that this was the real purpose of the Gray Areas Program. After bringing Bob Weaver on board, Ylvisaker would strategize with him about how to take control of the black-white contention then plaguing the nation's largest cities. Ylvisaker then went to Henry Heald and said, "Look, you know that we're interested in these problems of migration and the city, you know how tricky it is because you did IIT's renewal in the middle of the black ghetto." [26] Both Weaver and Ylvisaker felt that education was "the easiest way to get into those problems," [27] but that meant keeping Ford money out of the local school boards, which as in the case in Boston, were controlled by the local ethnics, and creating alternative institutions which they could control, things like Leon Sullivan's OIC. Sullivan got, in Ylvisaker's words, "the Good Housekeeping Seal of Approval" [28] when he got Ford money, something that would be quickly translated into the ability to get even more lucrative federal money. Ford, for its part, got credibility in exchange for its money.

But, in purchasing the services of Leon Sullivan, Ford got more than that. Sullivan became their paid consultant on racial migration at a time when Ford wanted to control both ends of the migration route. After persuading Heald of the soundness of his idea, Ylvisaker assembled a team of "between 58 and 60 people who were expert in the migration process, and we took out of each of the migrant streams somebody to work with me as consultant." [29] Bob Weaver, according to Ylvisaker, was "working on the blacks." In this respect, he was working hand-in-glove with Leon Sullivan, who was valuable to the Ford Foundation not because of his expertise in electronics, but because of his ability, in Ylvisaker's words, "to localize and identify a good deal of the migrant process," which was scientifically "almost predictable" because "sociological observations" have established that "the passage will affect certain people at certain ages." [30]

When the riots broke out in Watts in 1965, Sullivan refused to go there because he did not understand the mentality of the blacks living there because most of them came from what he termed "the deep, deep South, the bayous and Mississippi." [31] Sullivan, however could "deal with the more sophisticated migrants that were coming up from North Carolina, Georgia and so forth to Philadelphia," [32] and that meant his expertise was valuable to the Ford Foundation, because it was precisely this group of people that it wanted to control in Philadelphia. Under Ylvisaker's direction, Ford had funded programs in North Carolina under the direction of former governor Terry Sanford, because "we knew that tobacco was going to be mechanized and there was no reason why then we just couldn't case the plantations that were going to be affected"[33] and take control of the migration that would flow from those plantations to places like Philadelphia. Taking control of that migration stream was important for the Ford Foundation, just as it had been important for the Ford Motor Company to do the same thing in an earlier era, because once Congress passed the Rogers Act [in 1924], that "meant immigration had to turn to migration in order to get the cheap labor supply."[34]

When Ylvisaker went to Ford in 1955, North Philadelphia was still in the hands of Catholic ethnics, who were by and large unionized blue-collar workers. By the time Ylvisaker left Ford ten years later, North Philadelphia was well on its way to becoming the all-black ghetto it is today. By turning Leon Sullivan into the foundation equivalent of a "made man," Ylvisaker helped bring about that transformation. While claiming to be in the vocational-training business, Sullivan operated a large real-estate operation whose purpose was breaking down ethnic neighborhoods and moving black families into their recently vacated homes at discount prices. He did this with the collaboration of Robert Weaver, who went directly from Ford to Washington, where as head of the FHA he would share FHA and VA repossession lists with Sullivan and a select number of other favored black real-estate brokers in the city. The search for cheap labor would continue, in places like China and the tax-free zones of Nicaragua, but few are willing to count the cost this quest has levied on the nation.

The Ford Foundation, in the end, got the cheap labor supply it wanted. There was only one problem, namely, that the labor supply didn't labor. While many of the blacks who came up from North Carolina ended up taking menial jobs, the overwhelming majority became either welfare wards of the state or part of the bloated bureaucracy that took care of them. By setting up a migration pattern that replaced ethnic workers with black welfare recipients, the Ford Foundation eventually drove the city to the brink of bankruptcy. It also established a policy of "slash and burn" housing which resulted in the effective destruction of the rowhouse as a viable form of housing in Philadelphia. By the time the Republican Party held its convention in Philadelphia in the year 2000, Philadelphia had 40,000 abandoned houses, in spite of the fact that urban renewal had already torn down huge numbers of houses in North Philadelphia already. Those houses would then collapse at an even faster rate than normal because of that year's heavy rains.

By the time of Leon Sullivan's death in March of 2001, Philadelphia's second black mayor, John Street, announced that he needed $1.6 billion dollars just to tear those houses down and erect a few new ones in their place. One discordant note in the eulogies which were embarrassingly lavish in their praise of Sullivan concerned Progress Plaza, Sullivan's North Philadelphia shopping center which was supposed to be a base for black entrepreneurs to spread through the city. At the time of Sullivan's death, the neighborhood surrounding Progress Plaza was still all black and still poor, but all of the stores were now owned by Koreans.

On June 25, 1965, Leon Sullivan wrote to Henry T. Heald, announcing that the OIC had just received a federal grant of $1,756,163. Sullivan was quick to thank Heald because "had it not been for the support of the Ford Foundation to our efforts a year and one half ago, we would not possibly have been able to develop the kind of program that now can attract and secure the support just received."[35] Thanks to Ford's $200,000 grant, the OIC was "being looked upon as a model, for massive adult training and retraining programs in the country."[36] Sullivan went out of his way to praise Paul Ylvisaker, "whose confidence in our work and whose constant encouragement gave us the heart to continue when we might have stopped."[37] Without Ylvisaker, Sullivan admitted "frankly," "I hardly think that OIC would be the success that it has become."[38] Sullivan also made sure that a copy of the letter to Heald got sent to John J. McCloy.

The migration of Ford program personnel to Washington began in earnest in the early '60s when President Kennedy invited Robert Weaver to join the FHA. What followed was a wholesale take-over. Ford programs became government programs. The Gray Areas Program became the War on Poverty. Ylvisaker served on President Kennedy's Task Force on the Cities and was the chairman of President Johnson's Task Force on the City. Ylvisaker's 1967 report on the riots of that year formed the heart of the 1968 Kerner Commission report on the same topic. The seamless transition from foundation grant to government program when "the Ford Foundation was golden"[39] during the early '60s was "just one of those perfect sequences."[40]

Perfect, at least from his perspective. This unprecedented expansion of federal power combined with the moral righteousness which the civil-rights movement emanated was lethal to anyone interested in preserving the integrity of the local community. That meant that city councilmen in places like Philadelphia and Chicago now had even less leverage in opposing what was going on in the neighborhoods than when they were contending with people like Elizabeth Wood and Walter Phillips. In addition to the Gray Areas/War on Poverty programs, the federal government was also funding other initiatives which Ylvisaker had developed at Ford, including Head Start, VISTA, and children's educational television. As one of the side benefits which accrued from trying to control the migration stream from North Carolina to Philadelphia, Ylvisaker met John Ehle, a professor at Chapel Hill who had just written a book on the student revolt in North Carolina. Through Ehle, Ylvisaker made contact with Kenneth Kenniston, and Marian Wright Edelman, and Allard Lowenstein, who as of the mid-'60s was in the process of making the transition from being a civil-rights organizer to being a student rebellion organizer under the auspices of the Ford Foundation. Like Sullivan, Lowenstein was anathema to the Ford "bureaucrats." Ylvisaker thought that Lowenstein was "just great" because of how he "moved round the country for us and began meeting in dormitories in the incipient time."[41] Clarence Faust, however, told Ylvisaker that he couldn't have Lowenstein as a consultant "[b]ecause I have made a check and he is a . . ." Ylvisaker wouldn't say what Faust called Lowenstein – "I won't quote him, but the implication was that he's too dangerous for the Ford Foundation – radical."

Ylvisaker fails to add that Lowenstein was homosexual, who was eventually murdered by one of the students he tried to "organize" as he moved around the country meeting in dormitories. In each instance, the Ford Foundation deliberately bypassed any institution which was under local political control and established alternative institutions, like Sullivan's OIC. These organizations, given legitimacy by Ford funding, which certified that they were working in the interest of the WASP establishment, eventually passed to the federal government, which funded them even more lavishly than Ford had done, with grants that were administered often by Ford alumni. Any local institution still under local control – something like the Boston School Board and Louise Day Hicks – became fair game for this sort of hostile takeover. In his Oral History, Ylvisaker emphasized the fact that he wanted "to by-pass [local school boards] because they were still committed to segregated schools."[42] Local school boards under local control were, in Ylvisaker's eyes, "capable of taking money and making damn sure nothing got done with it."[43] Ylvisaker made sure that something got done with the money. His career at Ford was "a trajectory of coming at a time to start ahead of its time a concern with urban and social problems, building up through a sort of learning curve of my own to the point where everything went right for about two or three years, and what we had generated and conceived and negotiated suddenly flowered. Then it went to the Feds and suddenly we became a threat in a sense."[44] Foundation money was, as the Rockefellers had proven in the case of Kinsey, venture capital for subversive ideas. Once the idea or program was given what Ylvisaker called the Good Housekeeping Seal of Approval the federal government would go on to fund it with tax dollars.

Shortly after arranging the "Sermon on the Mount" at the elevator, Ylvisaker invited Ford board chairman John J. McCloy to Philadelphia for a closer look at Leon Sullivan. Interestingly, Ylvisaker mistakenly identifies McCloy as "an Irish Catholic boy out of Philadelphia out of a working class family or something,"[45] when in fact McCloy had been baptized a Presbyterian. McCloy came from the wrong Protestant sect (in Philadelphia, at least), and he lived on the wrong side of the tracks, but Ylvisaker did get one thing right. He knew McCloy had been born in North Philadelphia, and he knew that bringing him back there with Leon Sullivan now as his guide would evoke powerful emotions. Eventually the three men arrived at 874 N. 20th Street, at which point Leon Sullivan knocked on the door and after a moment's discussion, he and a "little black lady" led McCloy up to the bedroom where he had been born and where he had spent his childhood. Ylvisaker clearly felt that McCloy had been moved by the encounter, but he gives no indication of the thoughts that had passed through his mind. McCloy might have thought about how far he had traveled since the days when he walked the streets of Philadelphia. He might have pondered as well the change in the neighborhood – both in the housing stock and the race of the neighborhood's inhabitants – since the time when he was a boy. He might also have pondered how effectively racial migration could change the nature of a city and how profound its effect is on the people who live there. No one, least of all Paul Ylvisaker, knew what was going through John McCloy's mind at the time.

Less than one year after the encounter though, in the spring of 1965, McCloy had decided that it was time for Henry Heald to go as head of the Ford Foundation. On November 7, 1965, McCloy phoned McGeorge Bundy, then looking for a way to bail out of the Johnson White House, and asked him if he would like to become the new head of the Ford Foundation. After some initial hemming and hawing, Bundy agreed. Twelve days later, on November 19, Bundy met with Lyndon Johnson and told him that he had decided to accept the Ford post. Both agreed, one day later, that Bundy would leave the White House in February 1966. The conventional explanation for Bundy's departure revolves around his disenchantment with the Johnson Administration's prosecution of the war in Vietnam. Ylvisaker to some extent concurs with the conventional explanation, but only to some extent. When prompted by the question, Ylvisaker claimed that Bundy came to Ford because "he had to clean himself up from Vietnam."[46] But Ylvisaker's actual experiences with Bundy indicate that he had something more positive in mind, something other than just running away from the Vietnam nightmare. Bundy was, in fact, attracted to Ford because of Ylvisaker's Gray Areas Programs. Shortly after arriving at Ford in the spring of '66, Bundy showed up in Ylvisaker's office and told him, "Paul, the only shop that survives as having any relevance is yours."[47] According to Ylvisaker, "Mac [Bundy] had decided that what I had built up in the Foundation in that program was where it was at."[48]

If Bundy liked Ylvisaker's programs, he evidently didn't like the idea of having Ylvisaker run them. Bundy, according to Ylvisaker, "had to make a decision: would he let me run the empire or he had to take it over himself."[49] After some temporizing and vacillation, Bundy decided to get rid of Ylvisaker and run the programs he liked by himself. Ylvisaker would later claim that his departure from Ford was "just a cold analysis of a leader of an institution who has got a lot of feudal barons, and suddenly Ylvisaker emerged as a baron, and you know, do you want to go through all the business of having to deal with the baron, or do you deal with it yourself?"[50] but that doesn't change the fact that Ylvisaker never really understood how Bundy got the job in the first place, much less why Bundy got rid of him after telling him how much he liked Ylvisaker's programs. He knew that McCloy engineered Bundy's appointment by leaking the story to the *New York Times*, but he never knew why. "I think," Ylvisaker said, "it would be interesting to get the complete story on that appointment, you know, how it happened."[51]

Ylvisaker would later fault Bundy for "not doing his homework"[52] and, as a result, involving the foundation in a number of controversial projects, like supporting the black side in what would turn out to be an incredibly divisive Jewish vs. black battle over control over the New York City school system. That debacle and the similarly controversial voter registration campaign in Cleveland led Ylvisaker to believe that "after I departed there was a gap where some of their homework wasn't being done that carefully."[53]

Unlike Bundy, Ylvisaker "had probed both the black power structure, the city hall, and our power structure"[54] before he acted. Bundy arrived at Ford when it was the premier engine of social change – certainly in racial matters – in the United States. Ylvisaker is perplexed because "this was a time when, suddenly we were going to do great things, cure social poverty and all the rest of it, and the black thing was paramount; the blacks were riding high." When Bundy showed up in Ylvisaker's office and "clearly indicated that this was where he could see his presidential thrust and move it,"[55] Ylvisaker was surprised that he wasn't ultimately included as part of the team.

But there is another way of looking at Ylvisaker's veiled references to Bundy's recklessness. Bundy's arrival could just as well mean that McCloy thought that Heald and Ylvisaker were being too timid in pursuing Foundation goals. McCloy had always felt that Heald "was a little too prone to confine the benefactions of the Ford Foundation to conventional university academic areas."[56] There is every indication that Bundy liked what Ylvisaker was doing, but felt that he wasn't going far enough, something that can be seen from the type of grants he made. The Cleveland voter registration campaign was a direct assault on the ethnic neighborhoods there, with the added panache of having Catholic nuns work for the Ford Foundation against their fellow Catholics. Similarly, in spite of his fame as a civil rights leader and Nobel Prize winner, Martin Luther King (and his Southern Christian Leadership Conference) had never received any money from Ford during Ylvisaker's tenure there. Ford issued its first grant to the SCLC in 1967, one year after Bundy arrived and six months after Ylvisaker resigned. Bundy realized that "the black thing was paramount."[57] He also realized that the black migration which Ford had set out to control as the goal of their Gray Areas Program "could," in Ylvisaker's words, "be his baby."[58] As a result, Bundy "moved fast and hard, and I think it was very apparent from the very beginning that this was where he was going."[59]

John J. McCloy had always thought of the Ford Foundation as "a quasi-extension of the U.S. government."[60] With the government taking over so many of Ford's former programs, however, it was important to push the foundation further into the forefront of social change, and that is evidently why McCloy felt that it was necessary to bring McGeorge Bundy in to replace Henry Heald and, eventually, Paul Ylvisaker as well – not because they were heading in the wrong direction, but because they weren't heading in the right direction fast enough to suit McCloy. If the Foundation remained timid, they ran the danger of losing control of the increasingly nationalistic, increasingly ethnocentric black-power movement and having "responsible" leaders like Leon Sullivan supplanted by people like Stokely Carmichael and H. Rap Brown and the Black Panthers.

In this respect, the fact that Ford finally got around to giving money to the Southern Christian Leadership Conference one year after Bundy arrived at Ford is some indication of the direction they wanted events to take. After years of running voter registration drives and sit-ins in the South and coming up empty at Ford, the SCLC finally hit gold when Martin Luther King led them in an assault on Chicago's ethnic neighborhoods in the summer of 1966. Whether something like this would have been funded by Heald and Ylvisaker is a moot point. Only the facts remain: Ford did not fund the SCLC during its Southern campaign when the foundation was under the leadership of Heald and Ylvisaker. It did, however, fund them as soon as King, acting under the direction of the Quakers, who had been trying to engineer places like Cicero since 1951, started marching through ethnic neighborhoods in Chicago. That Bundy would have done this after firing Ylvisaker is perfectly consistent with Ylvisaker's feeling that Bundy wasn't doing his homework and perfectly consistent as well with the sense McCloy had that Heald, and by extension, Ylvisaker, were not pursuing the real goals of the civil-rights movement, namely, Ford's migration strategy, aggressively enough.

Bundy remains an enigma to his biographer because he was a "conservative" in Vietnam and a "liberal" when it comes to racial matters. "We," Bird writes describing the attitude of his generation of Vietnam protesters, "probably would have been surprised to learn how much of this money Bundy was funneling to black-power advocates, in the civil rights movement, environmentalists and public-interest law groups around the country."[61] What Bird fails to see is the ethnic if not political consistency in policy behind acts like murdering Ngo Dinh Diem and rewarding Martin Luther King for marching in Chicago's ethnic neighborhoods. The explanation for both acts is the Bundy's understanding of the centrality of the "Catholic Problem" to his generation and his ethnic group. Bird fails to see the connection because he failed to note that McGeorge Bundy was an avid supporter of Paul Blanshard's book when it appeared in the late 1940s.

Notes

1 Paul Ylvisaker, Oral History for Ford Foundation, conducted 9/27/73, p. 49, Ylvisaker papers, Box 5, Harvard University Archives.
2 Ibid.
3 Ibid., p. 50.
4 Ibid.
5 Paul Ylvisaker, Philadelphia Council for Community Advancement, 12/4/63, Ylvisaker papers, Box 5, Harvard University Archives.
6 Ibid.
7 Ibid.
8 Ibid.
9 Ibid.
10 Memo from Michael Harris to Edward Meade on Sullivan and Opportunities Industrialization Inc. Proposal 12/18/63, Ylvisaker papers, Box 5, Gray Areas, Harvard University Archives.
11 Ibid.
12 Ibid.
13 Ibid.
14 Ibid.
15 Ibid.
16 Ibid.
17 Ibid.
18 Ibid.
19 Ibid.
20 Memo Christopher F. Edley, 1/2/64, memo 2/24/64, Ylvisaker papers, Box 5, Gray Areas, Harvard University Archives.
21 Ibid.
22 Ibid.
23 PCCA, Review Paper Public Affairs: the Gray Areas Program confidential 9/64, Ylvisaker papers, Box 5, Gray Areas, Harvard University Archives.
24 Ibid.
25 Ibid.
26 Ylvisaker, Oral History, p. 25.
27 Ibid.
28 Ibid., p. 28.
29 Ibid., p. 59.
30 Ibid., p. 61.
31 Ibid.
32 Ibid.
33 Ibid., p. 63.
34 Ibid.
35 Letter from Leon Sullivan to Henry T. Heald 6/25/65, Ylvisaker papers, Box 5, Harvard University Archives.

36 Ibid.
37 Ibid.
38 Ibid.
39 Ylvisaker, Oral History, p. 28.
40 Ibid.
41 Ibid., p. 38.
42 Ibid., p. 31.
43 Ibid.
44 Ibid., p. 40.
45 ibid., p. 50.
46 Ibid., p. 43.
47 Ibid., p. 40.
48 Ibid.
49 Ibid., p. 41.
50 Ibid.
51 Ibid., p. 43.
52 ibid., p. 16.
53 Ibid.
54 Ibid., p. 15.
55 Ibid., p. 44.
56 Kai Bird, *The Chairman: John J. McCloy and the Making of the American Establishment* (New York: Simon & Schuster, 1992), p. 519.
57 Ylvisaker, Oral History, p. 44.
58 Ibid.
59 Ibid.
60 Bird, *Chairman*, P. 519.
61 Kai Bird, *The Color of Truth: McGeorge Bundy and William Bundy: Brothers in Arms: A Biography* (New York: Simon & Schuster, 1998), p. 14.

Folcroft and Leon Sullivan's Real Estate Campaign

Shortly after returning from the march on Washington where Martin Luther King gave his "I have a dream speech," Charlotte Meacham, one of the Philadelphia Quakers involved in housing, received a phone call at 11:30 in the evening. Friends Suburban Housing had bought a house in Folcroft, a new suburb full of refugees from racial succession in southwest Philadelphia for Horace Baker and his family and had moved him into the neighborhood without making the normal preparations and taking the normal precautions. As a result a Chicago-style mob formed outside of Baker's new house. By 11:30 on the Friday night after the move in, AFSC operative Dick Taylor was calling Meacham to tell her that most of the state police who had been stationed in Folcroft to protect Baker were being withdrawn "for turnpike duty."[1]

That meant that the mob which had swollen by then to almost 1,000 people was going to have to be contained by the twenty-three state cops who were left on the scene. Perhaps convinced that any action on their part would only make the situation worse, the State Police stood by as the crowd threw rocks and eggs through Baker's windows. By the time Taylor called Meacham, the crowd was yelling "attack, attack" and had thrown a firebomb into the back room, setting it on fire. Black groups were gathering in nearby Darby and planning to march on Folcroft to defend the Baker family. The potential for mayhem which the clash of those two mobs would have almost certainly brought about convinced the NAACP to pull the firebrand Cecil Moore out of the situation and to send in his stead Phil Savage, who was more experienced in defusing tense situations as a result of his work in Levittown and Cambridge, Maryland.

Taylor's response to the crisis was to rally as many "ministers and Friends" he could find on short notice and position them in their full regalia, cassock and white surplice, between Baker's house and the "white mob." Taylor had been successful in getting clergymen from as far away as Harrisburg and Washington, but his luck did not extend to the area's Catholic clergy. "About the only denomination not represented," Meacham wrote in her memo, "was the Catholics, alas."[2] This was significant because "Folcroft is only a short distance from Eastwick and its residents are drawn from the same South Philadelphia group, heavily Catholic."[3] Meacham felt that Taylor and Savage had "averted a race riot in Philadelphia" at least partially because they had worked with Black radio station in Philadelphia, WDAS, which had "broadcast appeals every 30 minutes from everybody from Savage through [disk jockeys] Georgie Woods and Lord Fauntleroy not to march on Folcroft."[4]

The riot at Folcroft, however, left Charlotte Meacham with a feeling of foreboding for the future because she was aware that the move-in there was only the beginning of a much larger assault on Philadelphia's ethnic neighborhoods. If Folcroft indicated the typical reaction they might expect, Philadelphia would soon be engulfed in civil war.

One month before the Folcroft incident, Miss Meacham had met with Leon Sullivan.

According to Meacham, Sullivan "began the interview by saying, 'Alright, Mrs. [*sic*] Meacham, we're going to level with you. We're going to give you the whole picture. I've been down and talked to Dr. Weaver and he had said that he can't publicly come out and back this but that he'll see to it that I get lists of homes with FHA/VA mortgages as well as the FHA/VA reclaim lists."[5]

Dr. Weaver was Robert Weaver, then head of the Federal Housing Authority in Washington. The goal of Sullivan's campaign was to place 500 black families in white neighborhoods throughout Philadelphia and its suburbs. Sullivan was "leveling" with Miss Meacham because he was aware that the Quakers had already established a program of putting black families in white neighborhoods and wanted to coordinate their efforts. If an outside observer had to judge the intention behind these actions in the sobering light of experience, he could only say that there was as of 1963 no such thing as an integrated neighborhood and that bringing black families into white neighborhoods meant one thing, namely, the dispersal of white residents to farther-flung suburbs. An added benefit was that Leon Sullivan's supporters could now get good houses at fire-sale prices. This conspiracy, as Sullivan's testimony makes clear, involved not only the Quakers and black groups like the OIC and the Urban League. It also involved the FHA in Washington.

It also involved the big foundations. In the same interview during which Rev. Sullivan "leveled" with her, Miss Meacham learned that "Stuart Wallace . . . said that he had been encouraged by Roy McCorkel to go after a $2 million grant from Ford, on the basis of his experiences as a salesman with Milgram and Eastwick, to expand Friends Suburban Housing in the Philadelphia area."[6] On November 23, 1964, Barbara Moffett wrote that "The FHA is hunting for a national private agency of sufficient 'weight' and experience in the housing field to enable it to feel secure in venturing forth into this 'pilot.'"[7] Eventually, the AFSC would become a de-facto arm of the federal government when their metropolitan housing committee became a subcontractor receiving federal funds.

Sullivan announced his buying campaign and the fact that Robert Weaver was going to share VA and FHA repo lists with him in August of 1963, four full months before the Ford Foundation gave him its first grant. Since Harris's internal memo evaluating the OICs gave it virtually no chance of succeeding as vocational training, Ford's decision to go ahead and fund Sullivan must have been based on other considerations. Since Weaver had left the Ford Foundation to work in Washington, he was still in close contact with Paul Ylvisaker, who could have learned about Sullivan's "buying campaign" from him or from Sullivan directly. Either way, Sullivan's involvement in the destabilization of ethnic neighborhoods throughout Philadelphia was probably more attractive to the Ford Foundation than his nonexistent credentials as an expert in vocational training.

The Quakers were also interested in Sullivan's "selective buying campaign,"[8] which was going "to send 500 eligible black couples out to buy housing in all white areas of the Philadelphia metropolitan area."[9] These families, Sullivan told Meacham, were

> 1) between the ages of 25 -50; 2) gainfully employed; 3) at least one child so we can crack the school situation at the same time, 4) good educational record, 5) enough money for equity in a home, 6) no police record. We're going to weed these people out, give them counseling, concentrate on the Northeast area. They

are all going to apply within a months' time. They're going to apply for new construction. They'll have money in the bank. October, November, and December will be the months of preparation, March is the month we want them to move. All these are cold months and there won't be lots of people out. We're going to get out a simple brochure with around 50 words and a couple of pictures. We're going to have a committee of three, myself (Sullivan) and a Jewish and a Catholic co-chairman. We're going to go after the archdiocese blessing. We're going to go after the Mortgage and Loan Associations, but if they won't come along, there's an institution that we can use.[10]

Meacham felt that Sullivan's "buying campaign" "could be the most exciting thing happening in the Untied States in the housing field"[11] during the fall and winter of 1963–64, but she also had misgivings about it. If 400 black ministers started buying up real estate in Philadelphia's ethnic neighborhoods and doing with it what Friends Suburban Housing had done in Folcroft, the potential for violence was enormous.

But Charlotte Meacham was concerned for other reasons as well. Sullivan clearly, if obliquely, indicated to her that he was not particularly interested in the suburbs when he said that the focus of the "buying campaign" was going to be the Northeast, an all white area still within the city's boundaries. Meacham's concern, in other words, was based on two fundamental facts: (1) blacks were not interested in living in the suburbs and (2) blacks were not interested in integration. That meant that Sullivan and the black ministers he was coordinating wanted complete control of the neighborhoods in between, and that led to conflicts with the Quakers, especially in their dealings with the Urban League in Washington. Thus, if the Quakers wanted to collaborate with Leon Sullivan, they would have to collaborate without agreement on two of their fundamental principles in the area of housing.

Given the forces arrayed against them, it's not surprising that one ethnic neighborhood after another succumbed to destabilization. To begin with, Sullivan and the Quakers had the element of surprise on their side. No one outside the circle of conspirators knew that what looked like normal economic activity was really an attempt to wrest control of Philadelphia's neighborhoods out of the hands of Catholic ethnics and into the hands of Sullivan's black supporters. Sullivan's hand was further strengthened because he had the federal government, in the person of Robert Weaver, on his side as well. As a result of getting the repo lists from Weaver, Sullivan knew which houses were going up for sale before even the people in the neighborhoods did. The fact that so many black families could be moved in so quickly was certain to increase the insecurity of people already worried about neighborhood change and push that insecurity over the edge into panic selling, which would drive the prices of the houses down, further enabling Sullivan's campaign. Sullivan concluded his meeting with Meacham convinced that he couldn't fail because he had all the bases covered. "We'll take care of the Catholics, and the Jews won't be any trouble," he assured her.

On October 21, 1963, roughly six weeks after the Folcroft incident, Charlotte Meacham wrote a "strictly confidential" memo to Barbara Moffett, also of the AFSC, in which she discussed a meeting in Washington with the director of the Urban League, where she had to explain to Mrs. Secundy, the director's assistant, "what Folcroft had been all about."[12] The Quakers were intimately involved in the destabilization of Folcroft. Horace Baker's wife was the sister of Susan Webb Lewis, a former staff member of the AFSC mid-Atlantic region. Unfortunately, the Bakers had moved in with no inkling of the resistance awaiting them, unaware in fact that the house had been vandalized before they moved in. Charlotte Meacham claimed that faulty coordination had botched the move-in in Folcroft but then went on to say that Folcroft was only one of over 200 such move-ins which had taken place in the Philadelphia area over the past six years, almost all of which had attracted no publicity at all. Meacham attributed the "completely inept"[13] handling of Folcroft to an over-confidence that was completely out of place when it came to the "inner ring"[14] that Sullivan and his friends were planning to integrate.

In addition to filling Secundy in on Folcroft, Meacham had to assuage her feelings of being treated like a second-class citizen at the hands of the Washington area Quakers. Both Urban League executive secretary Walter Lewis and Lucille Secundy, his assistant, were upset by their contacts with Neighbors Inc. and the AFSC because they felt they were being told "their place."[15] The feeling of antipathy, it turns out, was mutual. Margery Ware of Neighbors, Inc., a Quaker operation, "felt extremely negative toward any participation in the suburbs by the Urban League" because their incompetence in the area of housing "raised the possibility of their blundering into a move-in situation which would then become uncontrollable."[16] Lewis and Secundy, however, were eager to get involved in housing because "the word had come down through their staff meeting that morning that there would be increased and stepped up activity in the housing field and that this had come from the direction of their National Office."[17]

Eventually Meacham persuaded the Quakers at Neighbors Inc. and the blacks at the Urban League to kiss and make up because there was "plenty for everybody to do."[18] The new modus operandi involved having the AFSC check with Secundy "in the areas where move-ins are imminent to see if any of her suburban resources could be useful, this might take a good deal of pressure off this situation."[19]

The AFSC contingent, however, left the meeting still unconvinced that the Urban League was competent in housing affairs and unable to disguise the increasing competition between these groups for the federal money which they knew was increasingly available to destabilize neighborhoods in the "inner ring" of cities like Philadelphia and Chicago. Upon learning that Meacham felt dismayed by this attitude, Ware expressed willingness to "play along" with the Urban League, but indicated that this was really only preliminary to the "second step," which was to "encircle them."[20] The reference is a bit unclear, but in context it seems to refer once again to the inner ring of urban neighborhoods that the Urban League and Leon Sullivan were so avid to occupy. Ware's idea of common strategy was encirclement of those neighborhoods. The Quakers would work on occupying the suburbs and the blacks would work from the other direction by moving out of their enclaves into the ethnic neighborhoods in between them and the suburbs. That way the Quakers could keep groups like the Urban League out of the suburbs and from bungling move-ins there. Meacham felt that "the League people" had been "most open to cooperation in such an instance."[21]

Roughly one year later, on November 26, 1965, Barbara Krassner met with Andy Freeman and Carrie Bash of the Urban League in Philadelphia. Freeman began the meeting by describing what he called a "new action emphasis" for the Urban League, one which involved forging a "coalition of 600,000 Negroes [and] 350,00 Jews and other liberals [into] an effective political force"[22] in the Philadelphia area. But then putting the big picture aside, Freeman turned to the issue of housing. Freeman "asked if any of our [i.e., AFSC] efforts would be expended in Eastwich [sic] which provides good housing, although it's poorly situated geographically."[23] With the federal government on their side, the Quakers and the Urban League could now pick and choose which neighborhoods they wanted to occupy with impunity. The city and its suburbs had become a virtual real estate catalogue which they could browse through at their leisure, disrupting one neighborhood after another with the threat of racial transition.

Once the Quakers moved a black family into the neighborhood, the neighborhood began to change, and once the neighborhood began to change, the whites stayed as long as it took them to sell their homes and get out. Then the neighborhood became segregated again, this time all black. Given this fact, the question of intention becomes moot. In the light of their actions there was no practical distinction between integration and destabilization. The latter may or may not have been their ultimate goal, but it was most certainly a necessary prelude to achieving the former. Destabilization of the neighborhoods was necessary in order to integrate it. More often than not, destabilization was the only consequence in a process that stopped only when the neighborhood reached ethnic homogeneity and, therefore, equilibrium once again with people of another color.

This idea that destabilizing neighborhoods required a division of labor finds support in the grants that the Urban League subsequently received. On May 10, 1966, shortly after McGeorge Bundy took over as its director, the Ford Foundation announced the funding of what would turn out to be one of its most controversial projects, a $1.5 million grant to the Urban League, "to show how persuasion, guidance, consumer and community education and community organization can provide better housing opportunities for Negro families and other minority groups."[24] The fact that Bundy made this grant to the Urban League to disrupt ethnic neighborhoods in Cleveland, with plans to expand it "in up to seven other cities" was some indication that Paul Ylvisaker was right in contending that after he left, the foundation under Bundy's direction "didn't do its homework."[25] The disruption which followed and the bad light it cast on the Ford Foundation was proof that Ware and Meyers were correct in their assessment of the Urban League's competence in the area of housing.

Whatever their long-term goals, the Quakers were most interested over the short term in preventing people from discovering what they were doing. Shortly after the Bakers were moved into Folcroft, Meacham reported in one of her confidential memos that "a reporter from WCAU had called to ask about the rioting in Folcroft over the Horace Baker family's attempt to move into 2002 Heather Drive."[26] Meacham was also worried because someone from the state "was on the scent that the house had been sold by Friends Suburban Housing"[27] as well. The AFSC response was to deny any involvement and then manage the spin by getting its people on friendly venues like "Taylor Grant's program" on WFLN, the WASP classical-music station.

On September 9, 1963, Dennis Clark wrote in his diary that "there was a bad racial uproar in the suburb of Folcroft when a Negro entered a heavily Catholic village to occupy

Philadelphia, late 1950s, Clark recommends that the Quakers concentrate on inner city

a house."[28] After describing the fruitless attempt of "a group of Negroes" to meet with Archbishop Krol, Clark gives his take on the Folcroft incident. Clark is happy that "the wall has been broken after ten years of do nothing," but then he adds, enigmatically, "My hand in all this must remain obscure."[29]

Clark might have been referring to the non-meeting between the archbishop and the disgruntled black Catholics, but he might have been referring as well to the Baker move-in in Folcroft. One month before the Folcroft incident, Leon Sullivan told Charlotte Meacham, "We'll take care of getting the Catholics, and the Jews won't be any trouble."[30] Getting the Catholics involved working with the Catholic Interracial Council, since no other Catholic group would work with Sullivan, and that entailed, sooner or later, in one way or another, working with Dennis Clark. Given the history of the CIC's secret collaboration with the Quakers in Cicero in 1951, it is not far-fetched to believe that the Philadelphia CIC would collaborate with the Quakers and Leon Sullivan on a similar project.

When Clark was working for the Philadelphia Commission on Human Relations, he met with Judy Howard Wicoff of the AFSC's Community Relations Division on a regular basis. On October 31, 1958, she discussed with Clark how "to get busy immediately to develop teams of young Negro couples to visit suburban developments, ostensibly looking for homes to buy, and to, therefore, obtain documented records of instances of discrimination within this market."[31] Clark, however, suggested that the Quakers, in collaboration with the NAACP, whose "constituents . . . could be called upon to do some of this work,"[32] should focus their attention on "two of the largest all-white developments within the city limits."[33] Clark also promised to "bring Tom Colgan of FSH up to date"[34] on how to produce test cases.

At an earlier meeting which included George Schermer, Clark's boss at the CHR, and Clark, Wicoff learned what Quakers had been learning ever since they got involved in the housing issue, when George Schermer informed her that "there is no groundswell of demand for suburban housing from Negro community"[35] because there was "too much adequate housing open to them at fringe of the city."[36] Clark, in other words, was promoting the destruction of ethnic neighborhoods both directly – by urging the Quakers to concentrate their efforts there instead of in the suburbs – and indirectly because blacks were not interested in housing in the suburbs. By urging them to move, Clark was, in effect, urging them to move into ethnic neighborhoods in the city.

In addition to his profession activity in collaboration with the Quakers, Clark also mentioned Friends Suburban Housing a number of times in his book *The Ghetto Game*.

"Friends Suburban Housing . . . ," he writes, "has been one of the most active non-discrimination groups set up on a business basis."[37] At another point in the same book, he explains that "some families may enter an all-white area through the programs of such groups as Friends Suburban Housing,"[38] which "bring[s] together a willing white seller, usually a person of altruistic convictions, and a qualified minority buyer."[39] At another point, Clark explains that Friends Suburban Housing is not only "the most experienced and successful private group making open occupancy sales of houses in a city-wide program."[40] He goes on to add that FSH also "arranged some of the sales to Negro families in Levittown, Pennsylvania after the stormy entry into that community of the first Negro family."[41] Clark goes on to stress "the religious motivation of those participating in these efforts" because it "provides some assurance to the suspicious general white public that the groups are not aiming to exploit the issue of racial change."[42]

What Clark should have said is that the issue of racial change would be exploited to the detriment of the area's Catholics precisely because of religious motivation. Since Clark was working with, if not for, the Quakers when he was at the CHR, and since he knew about the role FSH played in moving black families into Levittown, it is unlikely that he was unaware of their involvement in moving Horace Baker into Folcroft, no matter what he says or does not say in his diary. This is also the opinion of Jack Malinowski, a one-time Catholic professor at St. Joseph's University who converted to Quakerism as a result of his involvement in the antiwar movement during the '60s. Malinowski is convinced that Clark was fully informed of what the Quakers were doing to promote changes in the housing market at the time.

It is surprising, therefore, to note that in Clark's most famous article, "Philadelphia: Still Closed," which appeared in *Commonweal* on May 1, 1964, there is no mention of Quaker involvement in Folcroft even thought the Folcroft incident is discussed there *in extenso*. Clark mentions the fact that the area was "heavily Catholic"[43]; he mentions the fact that Father John I. Kane's response was inadequate; he mentions the fact that Miles Mahoney read the bishops' 1958 statement on discrimination in St. Gabriel's Parish and that when he did most of the parishioners walked out. He mentions everything, in short, that makes the local Catholics look like racists, but nothing that would indicate that the area had been targeted for destabilization by the American Friends Service Committee. As a result, he contributed to the demoralization of Catholics in general but most especially to the Catholic intelligentsia. "Catholics moving in articulate circles," Clark announced making oblique reference to himself, "have been the butt of honest criticism for years about the local 'church of silence' situation."[44] Like the other "university types" who "typically wrung their spirits in disgust at the lack of official Catholic leadership in race relations over the years,"[45] Clark was embarrassed by the behavior of the Catholic ethnics in Philadelphia, but not embarrassed enough to come to their defense and admit that they were responding to unnamed groups who were manipulating the racial situation from behind the scenes for their own religious and political ends.

Clark knew this but somehow couldn't bring himself to say it in public. Just why he suppressed the truth about Folcroft is a matter for conjecture because Clark can't bring himself to admit that fact, not even in the privacy of his diary. When Archbishop Krol left Philadelphia to attend the Vatican Council without meeting with the black leaders, who had "begun drifting out of the [interracial] council and joining CORE and SNCC,"[46] Clark described his action as "notorious, scandalous, unpardonable, outrageous and daily a source of choking cynicism and alienation" and promised to make life for Krol and "the smug zombies" in his chancery "a rain of harassment."[47] Feeling slighted by the Church he appointed himself to reform on racial matters, Clark chose a policy of revenge as preferable to being ignored. The revenge would be overt, as the ads he signed in local papers and the *Commonweal* article indicated, and it would be covert as well, but if he hoped these efforts would translate into immediate benefits to his career, he was mistaken.

In November 1963, at about the same time that Paul Ylvisaker arranged the "Sermon on the Mount" meeting between Leon Sullivan and the Ford Foundation trustees at the elevator of the building where they were holding their board meeting, Clark noticed "a dragon's tangle of intrigue above and around me"[48] at PCCA. The dissension at work was so bad that Clark worried that it "may kill this Ford Foundation effort to renew the social services of the inner city."[49] Before he had time to develop further his analysis of what was going on at PCCA, tragedy struck from an unexpected corner. President John Kennedy was murdered – "apparently with insane lonely malevolence by a twisted rifleman in Dallas,"[50] he noted in his diary.

> Death came after Kennedy rose to contend with a meandering foolish nation and was baffled by a fractious, willful and wretched parliament packed with arrogant pygmies who sneer at history. . . . To the Irish Catholics, Kennedy was Cuchullain reborn, the golden boy, the hero champion. His death is like that of another man like him in gifts and ardent views, Michael Collins. Both were caught in the spasms of history and killed as the curtain rose on a new turbulence and opportunity. The assassination is the most terrible since Sarajevo. Trotsky and Gandhi were old men. Kennedy died with promise shining in the air about him.[51]

As if to underline the momentous nature of that weekend, Father LaFarge died three days later. Clark attended his funeral in New York at St. Ignatius and listened as Cardinal Cushing eulogized LaFarge in the Latin that he claimed he couldn't understand when he attended the Vatican Council. *Semper agens, semper quietus* could have been LaFarge's epitaph, as Cushing indicated, but in many ways it was the exact opposite description of the civil-rights movement, whose noise and inability to accomplish anything other than the destruction of the social order had led to the eclipse of LaFarge's influence in the Catholic Church and in his own organization as well, the one which Clark himself had led for a few ill-fated months before LaFarge's death. Clark regretted not meeting LaFarge when his "energy and sustained purpose"[52] had been undiminished by age, but it is unlikely that Clark could appreciate LaFarge's good points anymore than, say, Sargent Shriver could have.

By the time of his death, LaFarge's uniquely Catholic perspective on the racial issue, including his adamant opposition to birth control as a form of racial eugenics, had become an embarrassment to the progressive forces that had taken over the organization he founded. By the time he died, LaFarge came to symbolize not a Catholic solution to the racial issue but rather a racial version of Martin Luther, someone who "stood for interracial justice against all manner of opposition in the Church."[53] LaFarge's death was painful for Clark because it brought home to him the fact that he "did not succeed"[54] in carrying LaFarge's legacy forward. Months after LaFarge's death, Clark was still trying to overlook the deep philosophical contradictions he brought to the job as CIC director and portray his failure there as caused by the fact that the board would not hire a full-time fund-raiser. Nevertheless, "the realization of not having been able to enhance the achievement set out over the years by Father LaFarge and others is not easy to accept."[55]

In the wake of those tragedies, Clark agonized over "the radicalism of the right wing, the huge population, the want to waste, the crisis in work life" all of which "portend grave struggles,"[56] but he never really disagreed with the conventional explanation of Kennedy's death.

In this he differed from his colleague at Penn, E. Digby Baltzell, who saw a connection between Kennedy's death and the revolutionary activities of the Quakers. "There is a haunting similarity," Baltzell wrote,

> between the pattern of anarchy that followed the execution of England's king in January 1649 and the assassination of President Kennedy in November 1963. Once again the established church has disintegrated and a host of self-righteous seekers are loose upon the land. In this climate of opinion, it is understandable that the ideas and ideals of Quakerism are now more popular in America, especially among intellectuals and academics, than at any other time in our history. Since the close of the Second World War, for example, there has been both a reversal of the downward trend in numbers and a very real renaissance within the city, as symbolized by the award of the Nobel Peace Prize to the American Friends Service Committee. The Quaker ranks have been swelled by all sorts of refugees from the institutional churches and synagogues.[57]

Even though he had first-hand knowledge of their revolutionary activities, activities which threatened the communities of his own ethnic group, Clark failed to view Quakers with the suspicion that Baltzell, the WASP chronicler, did. In spite of that fact, Clark did see a connection between the assassination of Kennedy and the subsequent decline of Irish political power in the United States. "The tragedy of the Kennedy assassinations," Clark wrote later in *The Irish in Philadelphia,* "signaled the decline of the Irish as controlling political arbiters in Philadelphia, as in numerous other areas."[58] It also signaled the beginning of Clark's middle-age malaise.

Dennis Clark was thirty-six years old in 1963. He would live for another thirty years, which meant that he was at the midpoint of his life – *nel mezzo del camin di nostra vita,* as Dante put it – and about to enter a dark wood, from which – at least from the perspective of the Catholic faith – he would never emerge. At the heart of this conflict lay Clark's understanding of Church, race, and ethnos and the permutations they had undergone in his lifetime as part of a war whose existence would remain oddly mysterious to a man to intimately involved in its battles. Clark was raised in the ethnic Catholic Church of the pre-World War II era, but he could never really decide whether the ethnic solidarity that that community provided was good or bad. The Catholicism Clark knew in Visitation Parish as a boy

> animated and assisted the Irish in a multitude of subtle ways. It provided the Irish with a certain clan spirituality and with a complex vehicle that suited their active pursuit of social status and attainment. This Catholicism is changing. The hardy, accepted fidelity of the past is being subjected to pressures of intellectual and class movement that are altering it. Traditions of clergy dominance and catechetical simplicity are everywhere being challenged. The college bred sons and grandsons of Irish Catholic families are making reassessment of their religious attitudes and behavior.[59]

Next to black migration, "the second powerful force changing the Philadelphia Irish," according to Clark, "was the Second Vatican Council of the Catholic Church."[60] Manifesting an ambivalence that is typical of this period in his life, Clark blamed the Second Vatican Council for the changes that destroyed ethnic Catholicism, but at the same time, as a Catholic liberal, he faults the Church for not going far enough in making other changes, specifically in the area of race:

> The expunging of the folk quality, the hardy camaraderie of "our own kind," was divesting Catholics of one of the most familiar and amenable features of their religion. This religious transition with its social implications diminished a principal factor in the ethnic cult of local Irishry. It was one more factor in the sequence of neighborhood change, class mobility, decreased immigration, and assimilation influences that were curtailing the animation of the city's Irish community.[61]

Clark's view of the council is best summarized by his account of the decline of Irish political power in the face of the black migration he helped to promote. The Church, according to Clark, is "surrounded by Protestant denominations that in many ways embody reforms now espoused by Catholics."[62] As a result, she "is having an attack of nerves in the face of experiments and energy for change induced by the council."[63] Clark, in other words, is unable to see that (1) the Church is not surrounded by Protestant denominations; (2) that the Council was called to oppose modernity, not to implement it; (3) that the crisis which afflicted the Church arrived at the Church at the same time as the council and that the council was in many ways called to deal with that crisis; (4) that the interracial work he engaged in was in many ways part of that attack; (5) that the first victim of the "reform" which followed the council was the passing of the ethnic Catholicism which he mourns in his writings on the Irish in America.

Because he took his Catholicism seriously, Clark became involved in what he saw as the struggle for racial justice, but the inadequate way in which the Church framed that issue, through instruments like the Catholic Interracial Council, led him to believe in the end that the Catholic Church was not the solution to that issue but rather the source of the problem. Clark came to this conclusion while working for the institutions in Philadelphia which had been created by the enemies of the Catholic Church, there to engineer Catholic ethnic neighborhoods out of existence, but he never admitted that fact to himself. Instead, as part of the desire for social acceptance among the Irish which he could describe as a sociologist but not eradicate from his own personality, Clark began to blame his own people for the war that was being waged against them.

By the mid-1960s, Clark, after feeling that he had been rebuffed by Archbishop Krol, became part of the guerrilla-warfare campaign that was waging war on Catholic neighborhoods with the help of the federal government. By the time he started attending AFSC meetings with Paul Blanshard, Jr., on how to "integrate" Catholic ethnic neighborhoods, Clark's tenuous hold on Catholicism was being replaced by an increasingly virulent Irish nationalism. But with the dawn of Irish nationalism in his life came the realization that his interracial work was in many ways instrumental in causing the decline of Irish political power in cities like Philadelphia. In an article which appeared in *Hibernia* in March of 1967, Clark notes that "The Negro onset is the quietus of Irish municipal power."[64] That realization, no matter how disturbing it must have been, was ironically a function of his rapidly disappearing Catholicism. Without a universal, trans-ethnic referee like the Catholic Church to set the rules, there is no such thing as interracial justice. There is only ethnic struggle with one side winning and the other side losing power. That is precisely Clark's mature analysis of the struggle for racial justice to which he dedicated so much of his youthful energy. The Irish were eclipsed in political power in places like Philadelphia following the death of John Kennedy. "Tate's accession" to the office of mayor in Philadelphia, Clark wrote in his book on the Irish in America,

> coincided with a period of intense urban crisis. The Irish community ebbed as an organized group in the 1960s as two major forces greatly changed it. The first was the vast increase of the Black population. In 1940 there were 250,000 nonwhites, or 13.1 percent of the city's population; in 1970, there were 653,000, or 33.6 percent. Following World War II the Black population expanded and displaced the Irish from many inner-city parishes. There was grim resentment as the Irish left the old neighborhoods and the parishes they had built. The attempt to temper by such organizations as the Catholic Interracial Council was largely unavailing. Such local leaders as Judge Gerald Flood, Robert V. Callaghan, Mrs. Anna McGarry, and John A. McDermott strove mightily, in the best tradition of liberal social action, to assuage the anti-Black feeling, but church leaders were generally too short-sighted or prejudiced to comprehend the requirements of the new urban situation. As the Irish neighborhoods dispersed, the old ethnic ties became difficult to maintain.[65]

Once again, Clark can only face the situation by deflecting the blame onto "short-sighted" Church leaders. Rather than acknowledging his own role in bringing about the "quietus of Irish municipal power," Clark chooses more impersonal formulations. "Irish neighborhoods dispersed,"[66] Clark wrote, without adverting to the role he played in bringing about that dispersal. Since he could not not know what he was doing once hostilities broke out in the open and at the same time could not admit what he was doing was having adverse consequences on the Irish Catholic ethnic community, his psychic ambivalence became so acute it began to manifest itself in physical symptoms, something which was exacerbated by the uncertainty surrounding his job at PCCA.

By the beginning of 1964, Clark found himself increasingly boxed in in terms of how he could operate. His problems with the Church continued, as did his problems at PCCA, where he was "working in the tragi-comic proposal writing business" as operations there careened "wildly from crisis to crisis."[67]

By 1964 the Ford Foundation had already decided to fund Leon Sullivan's OIC as their organization in North Philadelphia. As a result PCCA's days were numbered. The chaos which the Temple staff could not control didn't help matters any, but in many ways that was coincidental to the program's fate. Clark's role as a grant-writing cog in a very large machine made any overview impossible. All he could see was that "deadlines, disorganization and distemper plague this outfit daily," something that would have been material for "high comedy except for the fact that the North Philadelphia target area screams for some, any, even minimal aid to the welfare wearing and sullen poor who rove the neighborhoods in hordes."[68]

The sense of futility at PCCA, where Clark was essentially working for an organization that had been slated to fail, caused him to focus on personal problems and to view himself, at the beginning of 1964 as "approaching 40 without any real career, heavily mortgaged, scarred by experience of my romanticism and with my idealism flickering in the strong gusts."[69] Clark felt that he had been treading water for the past year and a half: "My gamble to get to New York failed and cost me a lot of spirit. I lack some grand goal now, though if I pass my history course at Temple this semester, I can see the study of history being a catalyst for me."[70]

On February 19, 1964, Clark, as head of the delegation from the Catholic Intergroup Relations Council, met with Archbishop Krol, Bishop Graham, and Bishop McDevitt for two hours at the chancery offices in downtown Philadelphia. Krol, who had already told CIRC president Mitch Thomas, that he "would not be able to take a personal interest" in their work, struck Clark as "a logician, austere, but genial by virtue of office, a dignified person; a hard-minded conservative type,"[71] terms which were not complimentary in Clark's lexicon. Clark left the meeting feeling that the "episcopal response to our concerns" was "quite formal and almost entirely negative."[72] The bishops, according to Clark, saw "the issues according to their preoccupation with formal Catholic systems and orbits."[73] He and the rest of the CIRC, on the other hand, saw "the issues in terms of the civic arena, public action, individual initiative." The bishops saw "the great racial change as a problem," but only from an institutional point of view, which is to say, how it was going to affect their schools and seminaries. While they were in general agreement with Clark's group on racial equality as a goal, they disagreed on how to bring that about. When it came to means, the bishops, according to Clark, "urged a hands-off policy if simple persuasion failed to induce needed actions." Needless to say, the group which saw the civil disobedience of the civil-rights movement as a shining example to be emulated by Catholics came away from the meeting feeling "morose."[74]

Rather than pursue dialogue further, Clark and the CIRC chose to air their grievances with the Church by taking out an ad in the local paper. Clark chose to criticize the bishops in public not only because he "felt that all other avenues had been explored," but also because "laymen must meet such public scandals as that of the Bishops' local inertia and the collusion of the poor Folcroft pastor with the anti-Negro factions head on. Silence compounds the damage in a time of ubiquitous publicity media."[75] Clark was also worried because "some Negroes had stated their intention of leaving the Church because of the inertia on the part of the Archdiocese."[76] By making their grievances public Clark and his group of disgruntled black Catholics effectively burned whatever bridges they had to the hierarchy in Philadelphia, something that Clark ruefully grants when he admits in his diary that "the price we pay for the criticism is to shock a good many people not confident enough to bait bishops, and to close the archdiocesan channels that were slowly, creakily opening to us."[77]

The ad in the paper, coupled with Clark's article "Philadelphia: Still Closed," effectively ended whatever intellectual leverage Clark had on the mind of the hierarchy in

Philadelphia. He claimed later that the appearance of the article was instrumental in the formation of the archdiocesan commission on human relations. "Such a move might have been in the works before my impertinent article of May 1 in *Commonweal*, but perhaps the article helped to nudge things along."[78] But the main effect was that he had become *persona not grata* in the archdiocese, which meant the end of his speaking engagements, something he professed to be happy about.

By late June of 1964, it was clear to Clark that PCCA was "now dying" because "Mayor Tate does not want to accord it a larger role in the City-dominated 'war on poverty' programs."[79] PCCA, according to Clark, had "never been able to overcome its early injurious history."[80] That included the fact that the Temple University staff "alienated practically everybody by captious and cavalier criticism" compounded by the fact that the Negro community considered the project "a white man's handout" as part of a larger strategy of "welfare colonialism."[81] Clark claimed that the Ford Foundation insisted on "stronger board commitment and unity with the city" from a fifty-four-member board which "represented the vested interests that would be shaken up if community social development were changed and speeded up."[82] When the changes were not forthcoming, the Ford Foundation made it clear that PCCA would "fold."

By December of '63, Paul Ylvisaker was admitting that PCCA was having problems and was looking to Leon Sullivan to solve them. By mid-'64, the Ford Foundation staff was reporting "in complete candor" that "PCCA has almost completely failed to achieve its objectives and is presently in the process of putting itself out of business."[83]

In their own post-mortem the Ford Foundation staff made it clear that PCCA's biggest accomplishments were (1) launching Leon Sullivan and (2) getting Title II of the Economic Opportunity Act of 1964 passed in Congress. In spite of those accomplishments, PCCA expired because it never survived Cecil Moore's attack. Judging from their internal memos, Ford's decision to let PCCA die had nothing to do with the changes in the board membership which Clark mentioned. The request for change, if it were made at all, was simply a pretext used to justify a decision that had already been made. The Ford Foundation clearly felt that Sullivan was an asset that made PCCA's further existence unnecessary, and Sullivan's value to Ford had less to do with his ability to provide vocational training than with the "selective buying" campaign to break up ethnic neighborhoods that he was now orchestrating with the cooperation of Robert Weaver in Washington.

On November 19, 1964, Clark quit his job with PCCA and went to work at the Center for Community Studies at Temple University, where he headed "a job training project that includes a study of dialect (Negro dialect) as it affects employment."[84] The failure of PCCA, following so closely on the heels of Clark's failure as head of the Catholic Interracial Council, all but guaranteed more morose introspection as Clark took stock of his life at the beginning of 1965. "This new year finds us perplexed as usual," Clark wrote in his diary. "The youthful surfeit of zeal that we poured into Catholic activities has waned notably. The growing children need more attention, conversation and guidance. Halfway through the normal life span, I still do not have anything resembling a settled career. I do not, and cannot, write as much as I used to."[85]

Part of the problem was religious. Clark was undergoing his mid-life crisis at a time when he felt that all the eternal verities of the religion that was supposed to guide him through crises like these were being questioned. "My ideological grounds," Clark wrote at the beginning of the year during which the Vatican Council would end, "are shifting like sands."[86] As far as Clark could see, "The ecumenical council has not at all clarified the movement of the Church with respect to the vast forces that are shaping modern life – technology, science and immensities of population and politics."[87] Nor did it explain how what Clark was now expected to believe squared with the Catholicism he had learned as a child. Clark now felt that those beliefs – "the rationale of my early training and thinking – rigorist piety, a lay apostolate schema, association with the social action veterans of the '30s" – were "inadequate."[88] In trying to think his way out of his dilemma, Clark unfortunately put the cart before the horse. He felt that he had to "solve the personal puzzle of vocational direction for myself"[89] before he could come up with a consistent philosophical understanding of his situation – something he described tellingly as "enlarging my own ideological pretension" – when in fact the opposite was true. Clark needed a consistent worldview more desperately than he needed a job. Clark was a middle-aged grad student at the time who was unable to square his faith with his reason. This made him personally vulnerable at a time when his religion and his ethnic group were under sustained attack by the same forces he was seeking both credentials and a job from. If Clark had been better able to extricate his liberal ideology from his understanding of the Catholic faith, he might have quit grad school – since he was already the author of a number of books anyway – and sought employment elsewhere, perhaps with the very people he had so recently engineered. But behind Clark's ideology lay the deeper, less articulated issue of assimilation. Clark quite simply felt that he needed credentials from the "strategic elites" both because he wanted to work for them and because, as a liberal, he felt that they had an understanding of the pressing issues of the day – race, in particular – superior to that of the Catholic Church.

Clark resolved his crisis of faith (in 1965, at least) by concluding, in "the turbulent world of computers and revolutions," that "the Gospel remains. Christ persists. No other teaching approaches that Testament."[90] However, he also concluded that "organized religion is part of the problem of mortality with which we struggle."[91] Clark's ideas on "organized religion" were something that a Quaker might hold without danger to his faith, but that view was not a tenable notion for a Catholic, who professes as part of his faith his belief in "the holy Catholic Church." If the Vatican Council was supposed to clarify things like that for Clark, it was not succeeding. In fact, the council, which "will terminate formally soon," left Clark feeling "bemused"[92] because "the liberalization of the Church, started boldly, then becoming halting and confused it moved erratically."[93] The only sense Clark could derive from the changes brought about by the council was that he now lived in "a different world" from the one he lived in "when Josie and I married only 15 years ago."[94]

> Stern virtues, a patronizing élan to lift one above the non-Irish, the non-Catholic. Strong habits of piety. Now the scene has changed. It is all at once less rigorous, yet more perilous. We search for the center of gravity amid new forces. It is not only that our own youth's strength is tempered. The minds and spirits we made have been diffused, as if athletes arrived upon a field, but found that the game had

been changed to another kind of sport altogether. Whatever refractions the codes of new character building may bring, it is patent that character there must be, and politeness for the trouble with the boys is a rude animality bereft of politeness. They had better achieve some before much more times passes.[95]

As part of the crisis which the cultural revolution was causing in his life, Clark began to question his education under the Jesuits at St. Joseph's College. The same education which had allowed him to pick apart suspected Communist Drayton Bryant's materialist arguments in the early '50s was now seen as "hyper-rational" and, as such, rendered him incapable of understanding "the depth of history, emotion and experience pertinent to this racial problem."[96] The occasion for the brooding was "massive riots by Negroes in the last fortnight in Detroit." Clark now saw his Jesuit training not only as useless in making any contribution to solving the racial problem in the United States; he now saw it as in some way causing the problem. Because of his hyper-rationality, Clark saw himself as contributing "to the trend that has reached such a deadly stage today."[97]

The only good news that he had to impart to his diary at the beginning of 1965 was that his wife Josepha was pregnant again. It was her seventh pregnancy, and they jokingly referred to what would be their sixth child as "the child of our old age."[98] Brigid Maire was born on St. Patrick's Day, and her name as well as her birth date were an omen of the ethnic direction his life would take after her birth.

If Dennis Clark was expecting congratulations from his colleagues at Temple University, he was in for disappointment. "The snide people at Temple University mostly recoil at the mention of a sixth child,"[99] Clark noted bitterly in his diary. "They are highly contemptuous. They are quite right not to believe in reproduction. I hope they practice what they preach and do not extend themselves. We shall overcome."[100]

Clark's use of the Catholic ethnic "we" as well as his truculence vis-à-vis secular society were, however, on the wane. The intellectual and spiritual conflicts involved in "working for an MA in history in classes full of 20 year old graduate students" were making him physically ill. "My stomach has been giving ulcer signals because my job is vexing beyond belief,"[101] but he saw no way out of his dilemma. In many ways, he saw himself as sharing the same fate as the Catholic Church at the time. "Like the Church, I need a renewal of internal functions, but while I flounder around trying for it, the great waves of time and opportunity roar past."[102]

As he indicated in his diary, Clark would miss his opportunity, and he would miss it so completely that he would never know that it had passed. The attitude of Clark's colleagues at Temple was not fortuitous. At the same time that the Clarks welcomed their sixth child into the world, the ruling class and its sociological arm had decided that the only solution to the race problem was birth control, and they were in the process of making the necessary changes in the legal and social order to bring that about. The main impetus for this change in Philadelphia was the riots which shook that city in August of 1964.

Notes

1 Charlotte Meacham, Folcroft Move-in Delmar Village, 9/1/63 confidential, AFSC CRD Housing Program Administration Reports, 1963, American Friends Service Committee Archives.

2　Ibid.

3　Ibid.

4　Ibid.

5　Charlotte Meacham memo of Chicago Executive Committee Meeting 8/6/63, AFSC CRD Housing Program Administration Reports, 1963, American Friends Service Committee Archives.

6　Ibid.

7　Barbara Moffett memo 11/23/64, AFSC, CRD Housing Program, 1964, American Friends Service Committee Archives.

8　Charlotte Meacham memo of Chicago Executive Committee Meeting 8/6/63, AFSC CRD Housing Program Administration Reports, 1963, American Friends Service Committee Archives.

9　Ibid.

10　Ibid.

11　Ibid.

12　Charlotte Meacham to Barbara Moffett visit to Washington 10/21/63 strictly confidential, AFSC CRD Housing Program Administration Reports, 1963, American Friends Service Committee Archives.

13　Charlotte Meacham 9/1/63 confidential Folcroft Move-in Delmar Village.

14　Ibid.

15　Charlotte Meacham to Barbara Moffett visit to Washington 10/21/63 strictly confidential.

16　Ibid.

17　Ibid.

18　Ibid.

19　Ibid.

20　Ibid.

21　Ibid.

22　Logs, Barbara Krassner, 11/26/65, AFSC CRD Housing Program Administration Reports, 1965, American Friends Service Committee Archives.

23　Ibid.

24　Kai Bird, *The Color of Truth: McGeorge Bundy and William Bundy: Brothers in Arms: A Biography* (New York: Simon & Schuster), 1998), p. 379.

25　Paul Ylvisaker, Oral History for Ford Foundation, conducted 9/27/73, p. 49, Ylvisaker papers, Box 5, Harvard University Archives. p. 16.

26　Charlotte Meacham 9/1/63 confidential Folcroft Move-in Delmar Village.

27　Ibid.

28　Clark, Diary, 9/9/63.

29　Ibid.

30　Charlotte Meacham memo of Chicago Executive Committee Meeting 8/6/63.

31　Memo form Judy Howard Wicoff 10/31/58, AFSC CRD Housing 1958, American Friends Service Committee Archives.

32　Ibid.

33　Ibid.

34　Ibid.

35　Memo from Judy Howard Wicoff 10/24/58, AFSC CRD Housing 1958, American Friends Service Committee Archives.

36　Ibid.

37 Dennis Clark, *The Ghetto Game: Racial Conflicts in the City* (New York: Sheed & Ward, 1962), p. 102.

38 Ibid., p. 39.

39 Ibid.

40 Ibid., p. 187.

41 Ibid., p. 188.

42 Ibid.

43 Dennis Clark, "Philadelphia: Still Closed," *Commonweal* (May 1, 1964).

44 Ibid.

45 Ibid.

46 Ibid.

47 Clark, Diary, 9/28/63.

48 Clark, Diary, 11/9/63.

49 Ibid.

50 Clark, Diary, 11/24/63.

51 Ibid.

52 Clark, Diary, 11/27/63.

53 Ibid.

54 Ibid.

55 Ibid.

56 Clark, Diary, 11/24/63.

57 E. Digby Baltzell, *Puritan Boston and Quaker Philadelphia: Two Protestant Ethics and the Spirit of Class Authority and Leadership* (New York: The Free Press, 1979), p. 455.

58 Dennis Clark, *The Irish in Philadelphia: Ten Generations of Urban Experience* (Philadelphia: Temple University Press, 1973), p. 159.

59 Dennis Clark, "Post Kennedy Irish – The American Decline," *Hibernia* (March 1967): 7.

60 Clark, *Irish in Philadelphia*, p. 161.

61 Ibid., p. 162.

62 Clark, "Post Kennedy Irish," p. 7.

63 Ibid.

64 Ibid.

65 Clark, *Irish in Philadelphia*, p. 161.

66 Ibid.

67 Clark, Diary, 1/10/64.

68 Ibid.

69 Clark, Diary, 1/12/64.

70 Ibid.

71 Clark, Diary, 2/22/64.

72 Ibid.

73 Ibid.

74 Ibid.

75 Clark, Diary, 3/23/64.

76 Ibid.

77 Ibid.

78 Clark, Diary, 5/16/64.

79 Clark, Diary, 6/25/64.

80 Ibid.
81 Ibid.
82 Ibid.
83 Review Paper Public Affairs: The Gray Areas Program, confidential 9/64, Ylvisaker papers, Harvard University Archives.
84 Clark, Diary, 11/19/64.
85 Clark, Diary, 1/5/65.
86 Ibid.
87 Ibid.
88 Ibid.
89 Ibid.
90 Clark, Diary, 10/21/65.
91 Ibid.
92 Ibid.
93 Ibid.
94 Ibid.
95 Clark, Diary, Easter, 1967.
96 Clark, Diary, 8/30/67.
97 Ibid.
98 Clark, Diary, 11/19/64.
99 Clark, Diary, 3/17/65.
100 Ibid.
101 Clark, Diary, 1/5/65.
102 Ibid.

The Riot and the Birth Control Clinics

On the evening of Friday, August 28, 1964, a black woman by the name of Odessa Bradford got into an argument with her husband Rush in the middle of the intersection at 22nd and Columbia Avenues. Both Mr. and Mrs. Bradford were intoxicated, and when a police officer arrived and asked Mrs. Bradford to move her car, a struggle ensued which quickly escalated into a full-scale riot that would last for the entire weekend in spite of the futile efforts of thousands of policemen to quell it. Dennis Clark described the incident in his diary as Philadelphia reaping the racial whirlwind as "the tense nerves of the urban underdog population uncooled in a huge madcap spasm of riot, looting and vengeful vandalism."[1]

Clark, unlike most pundits, saw a connection between the riot and urban renewal. What Clark pointed out years later is that at the same time Bacon had his picture placed on the cover of *Time*, the black residents in the area around Temple University, a university whose campus was eight blocks east of where the riots began, had halted the university's expansion by demonstrations that were a prelude to the riot. Eleven years after his fifteen minutes of fame, Bacon would return to Temple University and give a speech in which, in Clark's words, he "compared the displacements in North Philadelphia to the policies pursued by the United States herding about various populations in Viet Nam."[2]

Clark clearly indicates that the riots were one of the *sequelae* of social engineering in North Philadelphia. The mob was finding in plundering and violence a cathartic release from the intolerable sense of cognitive dissonance that had afflicted North Philadelphia ever since it had become one of the main recipients of urban renewal and the more virulent forms of social engineering which would follow. The cognitive dissonance revolved around the conflict between freedom and control. Every program which promised freedom turned out to be a form of control, and the 1964 riot was an expression of frustration and discontent on the part of people who lacked the sophistication needed to name what was really happening.

Just when it looked as if things might calm down that fateful Friday night, Abyssinia Hayes, a community figure who operated out of a combination dry cleaning shop and "African-Asian Cultural Center" at 23rd and Columbia, started jumping up and down screaming, "We want freedom," and the rioting and looting started again. The residents of North Philadelphia had watched the civil-rights demonstrations in the South, that was their ancestral home, on television. As part of the public relations campaign that accompanied that movement, they had been caught in the conflicting shear of expectations. The civil rights movement raised expectations, but the programs that sought to channel those expectations involved increasingly draconian and increasingly intrusive forms of social control. One manifestation of "freedom" in North Philadelphia was urban renewal, which meant that the blacks who were drawn up from the South to the rowhouses of North Philadelphia were now going to be driven unceremoniously from their homes so that Temple University could expand the racial *cordon sanitaire* around its campus. Urban renewal, the blacks of North Philadelphia had discovered, meant more and more social control, and it arrived at the same time they were told to expect more and more freedom.

Since the city's black population was, if anything, less capable of understanding what was going on than the area's Catholics, they reacted violently when the frustration level they experienced became intolerable. Looting was in many ways the fulfillment of the campaign of civil disobedience being urged on them by people like Martin Luther King, Jr. In North Philadelphia, they could be civilly disobedient on their own terms, without the firehoses and police dogs, and even pick up a new television or a box of disposable diapers in the process. Rioting, in other words, was the logical outcome of the civil disobedience King proposed, with concrete benefits thrown in. When Cecil Moore, whose name would eventually replace Columbia Avenue as the name for the street which bore the brunt of the looting, arrived to urge the looters to return to their homes, they responded by holding up arms full of booty recently liberated from the stores of Jewish merchants along Columbia Avenue and taunted him saying, "See this, Cecil? See this? What are you going to do about this?"

The answer was, of course, nothing. But just because Cecil Moore could do nothing, that didn't mean that the ruling class was going to stand by idly as well. Just as social engineering led to the riots, so too the riots led to more social engineering, this time a form much more insidious and destructive to the black community than the urban renewal that had torn down their homes. "The North Philadelphia riot," according to Bauman, "forced the city to rethink its urban renewal and housing priorities."[3] The riot of August 1964 did more than that. It convinced the Philadelphia WASP ruling class that they had to take social engineering to a new level by turning the city's housing projects into birth control clinics. The change in attitude had already taken place on the national level during the first two years of the Kennedy Administration. Kennedy brought Robert Weaver to Washington in order to "retool public housing policy and transform housing projects into welfare centers for the poor."[4] The Kennedy Administration got the idea, as well as Dr. Weaver himself, from the Ford Foundation, where it had incubated as part of Paul Ylvisaker's Gray Areas Programs. Since, according to a 1963 Kennedy administrative memo, public-housing families "very often bring their behavioral problems with them and cause difficulties for management and other families,"[5] it was only logical that "public housing can provide the necessary physical environment in which efforts at guidance, counseling and education can more readily be made effective."[6] That meant, in plain English, birth control, which would defuse the explosive situation in the ghetto by blunting the black demographic surge.

The riots in North Philadelphia, in other words, did not create the idea of transforming housing projects into welfare centers, i.e., birth-control clinics, for the poor, but it did lend new urgency to the implementation of that idea, especially among the progressive types who made up the housing establishment in Philadelphia. The bitter site controversy of 1956 had balkanized the city. After 1956, according to Bauman, "white peripheral neighborhoods no longer shared the downtown's ecstatic vision of a 'Better Philadelphia.'"[7] The 1964 riots had an equally profound impact on the city's WASP housers. Now they knew not only that they couldn't count on the support of the white neighborhoods, they couldn't count on the ran-and-file blacks as allies anymore either. They now viewed them as just one more group to engineer. "The 1964 riot," according to Bauman, "forced the PHA[ssoc] to reexamine its historically progressive view of housing and renewal."[8] It also propelled them into the sexual revolution on the side of birth-control clinics for the poor. Under the new dispensation which came into existence after the '64 riots, the focus of urban renewal shifted once again, this time from center city back to the North Philadelphia ghetto, which was now known euphemistically as "the model city," the regime's term for what was to become "a vast staging ground for dispensing social welfare services to the poor,"[9] all of which revolved around birth control.

The change in government policy on birth control corresponded to a change in command at the Philadelphia Housing Association. At around the same time that Marie McGuire wrote a memo to Robert Weaver explaining how public housing constituted "a major resource" in the War on Poverty because it could now function as a "welfare center,"[10] health problems forced Dorothy Montgomery to retire as managing director of the PHAssoc. Bauman finds "symbolic meaning in Montgomery's retirement"[11] as well as the end of an era. Montgomery's vision of the housing project as a way station for the deserving poor was eventually defeated by the brutality and violence of the ghetto, which places like Schuylkill Falls and the Raymond Rosen Homes had brought about. Instead of admitting their complicity in bringing about this debacle, the PHAssoc decided to wade deeper into the waters of social revolution by making Cushing Dolbeare, who was Montgomery's assistant, Montgomery's successor as managing director of the PHAssoc. Dolbeare, who came to the PHAssoc in 1956 after five years as the associate executive director of the Citizens Planning and Housing Association of Baltimore, was married to the city planner Louis Dolbeare and described herself as a "militant liberal."[12] Dolbeare was also a Quaker; in fact, she was in the words of one AFSC staffer, a "weighty Quake," which is to say, a militant Quaker, a seeming oxymoron that would take on a very real meaning as the war on the neighborhoods in Philadelphia escalated under her tenure as managing director of the Philadelphia Housing Association. Under Dolbeare's tenure the fitful discussions which Charlotte Meacham had conducted with the Urban League were formalized into an alliance known as the Joint Committee on Minority Housing, and then blossomed into full-blown cultural warfare in 1965 when the JCMH, under Dolbeare's direction, joined forces with the NAACP, the Fellowship Commission, the Congress for Racial Equality, the Commission on Human Relations, and the Fair Housing Committee of the Delaware Valley to "plan and carry out a coordinated attack on racial segregation and discrimination in housing."[13]

As a Quaker, Dolbeare could count on the support of the American Friends Service Committee, which had become a beneficiary of federal funds when it formed the Metropolitan Philadelphia Housing Program, an organization which they listed as "a Pilot Project of the American Friends Service Committee"[14] on their letterhead. The MPHP received funding as a result of their plan "to encourage minority group families to take advantage of FHA and VA foreclosure properties."[15] In order to do this they needed to work with black real-estate brokers, and that brought them in contact with C. Delores Tucker, who with her husband William, ran the Tucker and Tucker real-estate agency as well as Penn National Investments, a corporation they used to buy up and resell properties in changing neighborhoods in Philadelphia. C. Delores Tucker attended an MPHP (or CRD) meeting on January 22, 1965, at which she announced that "Tucker and Tucker had applied to become management brokers but had not yet received a reply."[16] Tucker would eventually become a key figure in Cushing Dolbeare's "coordinated attack" on Philadelphia's ethnic neighborhoods.

For now the plan was to have MPHP staff "encourage minority group buyers in Philadelphia to buy houses in the Northeast"[17] while a the same time finding "brokers in the area who would be willing to show the houses."[18] As some indication of how the local government collaborated in this "attack," the Quakers announced that "the community relations work would be handled in cooperation with the Philadelphia Commission on Human Relations."[19]

Dennis Clark, unlike Father LaFarge, had no strong views on publicly funded birth control in general and no views on the use of birth control as a form of racial control at all. Since they had six children, the Clarks evidently did not use birth control themselves, but when the issue came up in '67, his response is oddly distant. "The Catholics," he writes as if referring to some group to which he does not belong, "are still railing on birth control and lay autonomy"[20] at the World Conference of the Lay Apostolate in Rome. Unaware of the role that the Rockefellers were playing in orchestrating this exercise in "lay autonomy," Clark portrayed it according to the usual intellectual template he applied to such incidents. The uproar over birth control was one more instance of "the great transition from a juridical system built on folk fidelity to a democratized Church built upon contemporary engagement and understanding."[21] It was one more instance of courageous laymen, like Clark, trying to bring the Catholic Church kicking and screaming into the 20th century. In this, the protest over birth control was completely in line with Clark's understanding of the purpose of the Second Vatican Council.

One of those courageous laymen trying to create a "democratized" Church as well as a member of Clark's clique was Dr. Edward E. Cahill, a sociologist on the staff of the University of Pennsylvania's human-resources program. Cahill was also co-chairman for Pennsylvanians for Freedom of Choice in Family Planning, a local group which was, according to the paper, "seeking liberalized birth control programs."[22] Cahill was also head of the local chapter of an organization known as Catholics Concerned about Population and Government Policy, whose national headquarters was the sociology department at the University of Notre Dame, where it was run by William D'Antonio, chairman of the sociology department there. Most of the membership of the Philadelphia branch of the CCPGP, which was formed in 1966 when the birth-control battle was at its height, was made of "Catholic intellectuals and from faculty members of Catholic colleges and universities in the area,"[23] people like Dennis Clark, in other words. Throughout the period leading up to the issuance of *Humanae Vitae* in the summer of '68, D'Antonio's name could be found on full-page Planned Parenthood ads at the time arguing something along the lines of "Bishops Oppose Birth Control, Millions Starve." The Notre Dame sociology department became a beachhead for the Rockefellers in the Catholic Church, shortly after the Population Council sponsored a series of secret meetings there from 1963 to 1965 on changing the Church's position on birth control. In the spring of 1965, the group of Catholic theologians invited to the Rockefeller-sponsored conferences issued a statement, as

Hesburgh assistant George Shuster promised they would, announcing that they no longer found the Church's teaching on birth control persuasive.[24]

The Population Council was working behind the scenes in other areas as well. Through the Notre Dame Conference Notre Dame sociologist Donald Barrett made contact with the Population Council, to whom he applied for a grant. The Population Council, in another instance of the same interlock we have already seen, then forwarded the application to the Ford Foundation, which granted Barrett $500,000 in the mid-'60s. The story becomes more complicated when Barrett, with Hesburgh's help, got appointed to Pope Paul VI's birth-control commission. Now someone who was receiving money from the foundation establishment at the very time it was trying to change American laws and Catholic teaching on contraception was voting on the commission Paul VI had established to decide whether the Church should change its position on the same topic. It was a flagrant case of conflict of interest, but no one seems to have noticed at the time. The same can be said of Pat and Patti Crowley, directors of the Catholic Family Movement at the time. The Crowleys had also been appointed to the birth-control commission because of their connection to Notre Dame, while at the same time getting money from the Rockefellers to undermine the Church's teaching on contraception. According to Robert McClory, their biographer, just as the Church was about to issue *Humanae Vitae*, "the Crowleys, *with a grant from the Rockefeller Foundation* [my emphasis], made plans for an international forum on the Christian Family in the World to be held in Italy during the summer of '68."[25]

During the crucial months of early 1966, D'Antonio came to Philadelphia at the invitation of Planned Parenthood to give the impression that Catholics were divided on the issue of birth control. As part of the same disinformation campaign, Cahill invited the Jesuit Dexter Hanley to speak at St. Joseph's College, Clark's alma mater, in 1967. Ever since he became aware of the state's desire to get involved in birth control, Pennsylvania Catholic Conference director William Bentley Ball had warned that this sort of government involvement was intrinsically coercive. When Ball was scheduled to testify before the Gruening hearings in the summer of '65, he found that Hanley had been scheduled to testify in his place, and Hanley testified then, just as he would argue at St. Joseph's College in '67 that there was no coercion involved. In fact, Hanley argued "that any Catholic who is sincerely concerned about coercion in government birth control programs has a moral duty to participate in such programs. Conversely, he suggested if coercion does develop 'it will be partly the fault of Catholics who refuse to take part.'"[26] This was essentially the line that the Rockefellers wanted their agents in the Catholic Church to take, and Hanley most probably picked it up when he attended the Rockefeller-sponsored conferences at Notre Dame.

The collaboration of Catholics like Cahill and D'Antonio was essential to the Rockefeller's birth-control strategy – which was also the birth-control strategy of the ruling class in Philadelphia – precisely because the Catholic Church had always opposed government birth-control programs as a form of racial eugenics. At recently as 1959, Cardinal O'Hara, Krol's predecessor, addressed the eugenic dimension directly when he said that "birth control programs were aimed largely at two groups with the highest birth rates – Catholics and Negroes."[27] If statements like that were allowed to go uncontradicted, a potentially unbeatable coalition of blacks and Catholics, led by people like Cardinal Krol and Cecil Moore, could have derailed the government's plans permanently by exposing its essentially eugenic intent. Hence, it was important from the point of view of the Rockefeller and Ford Foundations and their Philadelphia supporters to open up an internal front in the Church by subsidizing people like D'Antonio and Cahill.

Clark, who was nothing if not well-informed about racial/Catholic issues, never mentions Cardinal O'Hara's fears, even though he was working for the CHR when O'Hara made his statement, and friends with Cahill when the statement got repeated in an article on Cahill and his work in the local paper in 1967. Clark was, in other words, aware of the charge, but he chose to ignore it. Why he chose to do so is a matter for speculation, but it is probably related to his image of himself as a progressive Catholic, an image which came into being largely because of his involvement in racial issues. All of the members of the "strategic elite" which Clark had come to admire as leaders in the racial struggles of the '50s and '60s had decided that birth control was the answer to the racial problem in the cities, and Clark, who did not practice birth control himself, decided not to contest their strategy.

In fact, if his diary is any indication of what was on his mind at the time, Clark decided not even to think about it. The idea of the middle-aged Irish Catholic, father of six, standing up at a sociology seminar at Temple University or a meeting of the AFSC's housing committee and denouncing government-funded birth control as a form of genocide was more than Clark's assimilationist-oriented constitution could bear. So he remained silent on the issue, and concentrated instead on talking about his malaise. "How tepid I feel amid it all," he wrote in his diary describing his reaction to the turmoil of the mid-'60s. And then tellingly he adds, "I can't express – despite my speaking and writing – what I really feel. . . ."[28]

Similarly, Clark misread the Curran tenure battle at Catholic University in the spring of '67 in the same way. Instead of seeing it as one more attempt to subvert the Church's teaching on contraception so that the government could get involved in using birth control as a form of social engineering, Clark saw it in typical fashion as one more instance of a misunderstood promethean – someone like himself, in other words – standing up to the bishop-gods by bringing liberation to benighted rank-and-file Catholics.

Curran's real motivation in the tenure battle would become clear one year after it was resolved in his favor, when used his position at CU to orchestrate opposition to Paul VI's birth-control encyclical *Humanae Vitae*. "Winning such issues as that at Catholic University where total faculty student strike forced reinstatement of a fired theologian," Clark opined, giving some indication of where his sympathies lay, "will not alter the power distribution."[29] In light of the "large scale episcopal vs. anti-episcopal disjunction" that "is dawning" as "a major theme of US Catholic history," all that Clark can hope is that the Catholics who are looking for this "new dynamic" will "not find it on the right."[30] Clark's mind was so imbued with liberal categories of thought, especially on racial matters, that he failed to see the major conflict of his day – the battle over government funded birth control – even though (or perhaps simply because) it was the liberals who were trying to use concern about race as a front for applying the eugenic solution to the very people they claimed to be concerned about.

Leadership in this fight would, therefore, pass on to someone else. As Clark gazed at his navel worrying about whether he was going to pass the German language requirement for his Ph.D. in history at Temple, another Irishman from another neighborhood in Philadelphia announced that the state was not going to get into the birth-control business. The only reason anyone took his statement seriously was that the man who made it happened to be chairman of the house budget committee and in a position to hold up the entire state budget until the state backed down on its plan to rewrite its social work regs so that social workers could approach clients on welfare and ask whether they might like to get on birth control. The man's name was Martin Mullen. He was state representative from the 189th district, an area which included Most Blessed Sacrament Parish in southwest Philadelphia, where he had been a parishioner all his life.

Notes

1   Dennis Clark, Diary, 9/5/64.

2   Clark, Diary, 1/18/88.

3   John F. Bauman, *Public Housing, Race, and Renewal: Urban Planning in Philadelphia, 1920–1974* (Philadelphia: Temple University Press, 1987), p. 189.

4   Ibid., p. 182.

5   Ibid., p. 186.

6   Ibid.

7   Ibid., p. 198.

8   Ibid.

9   Ibid., p. 190.

10 Ibid., p. 192.

11 Ibid., p. 197.

12 Ibid.

13 Ibid., p. 198.

14 Memo 1/22/65, AFSC CRD, Housing, 1965, American Friends Service Committee Archives

15 Proposed Plan to encourage minority group families to take advantage of FHA and VA foreclosure Properties, AFSC CRD, Housing, 1965, American Friends Service Committee Archives.

16 Memo 1/22/65, AFSC CRD, Housing, 1965, AFSC Archives.

17 Proposed Plan.

18 Ibid.

19 Ibid.

20 Clark, Diary, 10/21/67.

21 Ibid.

22 Gary Brooten, "Catholics Put up Sternest Opposition to Public Family Planning Programs," *Philadelphia Bulletin*, (September 7, 1967). Cited in AFSC Family Planning Services for Medically Indigent Families in Philadelphia, AFSC 1970, AFSC Archives.

23 Ibid.

24 E. Michael Jones, *John Cardinal Krol and the Cultural Revolution* (South Bend, Ind.: Fidelity Press, 1995), pp. 254ff.

25 Robert McClory, *Turning Point: The Inside Story of the Papal Birth Control Commission, and How Humanae Vitae Changed the Life of Patty Crowley and the Future of the Church* (New York: Crossroad, 1995).

26 Brooten.

27 Ibid.
28 Clark, Diary, 10/21/67.
29 Clark, Diary, 4/30/67.
30 Ibid.

Sargent Shriver and Government-Funded Birth Control

On December 13, 1965, at 3:45 P.M. Sargent Shriver met with William Bentley Ball, head of the Pennsylvania Catholic Conference and in this instance a personal emissary from Cardinal O'Boyle, who was very upset about the government's plans to get into the birth-control business. Ball got immediately to the point. There was, he said, strong support among the bishops for the antipoverty program but deep dissatisfaction over the use of the program to promote birth control. Ball then challenged the legal authority of the birth-control funding directly. There was, Ball said, no legal authority to use the program to fund birth control in terms of statutory interpretation and construction. Shriver, in other words, was acting illegally and had been acting so all along. Implicit in the statement was the threat that Ball, acting on behalf of the bishops, might take the OEO to court if Shriver did not prove amenable to less contentious means of persuasion.

Shriver responded by dismissing the threat from the Church and making it clear that he felt he faced an even more potent threat from the left. As a result he "could not venture to defer even for a moment the approval of pending applications."[1] Shriver made it clear that the OEO would approve any birth-control project that had been recommended by a local antipoverty council. Because of the inaction of the NCWC at the program's inception, a precedent had been set, and Shriver could not now go back on that precedent without indicating that he had been acting illegally all along. Shriver continued by saying that he was anxious to "make a good record" by funding as many applications "of every sort possible" prior to the end of the year.[2]

When asked by Ball if he could hold off until February 1, Shriver replied in the negative, and then indicated that he was "under pressure" from Dr. Guttmacher of Planned Parenthood and others, who wanted funding for projects which involved financing for abortion and sterilization. In addition to that, Shriver informed Ball that he was under pressure from Paul Blanshard's organization, Protestants and Other Americans United, to defund any project sponsored by the Catholic Church. POAU felt that any involvement of the Church in welfare activity supported by the government was a violation of the separation of church and state. Shriver refused to accede to POAU's demands and tried throughout the interview with Ball to portray himself as a man who was trying to tread the reasonable middle ground on the issue. But it was just as evident that he was defining the middle in terms of the political forces being brought to bear on him at the time, and in the absence of a strong policy on the part of the NCWC he was being pushed considerably to the left of what the catholic bishops found acceptable.

As a final attempt to sway Shriver, Ball brought up the fact that the Congress had refused to adopt Senator Joe Clark's birth-control amendment that September, and that this reflected Congress's intention to exclude birth control from the poverty program, but

Shriver was not only unmoved, he also went on the offensive by warning Ball that the more the Church raised a fuss over the birth-control issue, the more unlikely it would be that her agencies would be included in poverty projects. On that not-so-veiled threat, the meeting ended.

Ball left the meeting convinced of two things: first of all, after talking to Shriver and his assistant, Ball was convinced that the authorization for birth control was lacking, and secondly, that Shriver and the OEO would continue to fund birth-control programs because reversing themselves on the matter would expose them to greater legal and political jeopardy than continuing would. As a result, Ball drew a number of conclusions. Most significantly, he concluded that further attempts at persuasion were pointless and that the bishops should look into the possibility of litigation as a way of making their point. Given the Congress's veto of the Clark amendment, this approach stood a good chance of success.

Beyond that, Ball concluded that the bishops missed a golden opportunity in the beginning of 1964, but that even with that as the case, they had no choice but to take a stand on the OEO birth-control programs because "if no resistance is offered to the OEO programs, Planned Parenthood should soon be 'in business' at public expense throughout the U.S.A."[3] Once programs like that got rolling they would only increase in scope to include abortion, sterilization, and "birth rationing," the idea that everyone should be made sterile unless otherwise permitted by the government to have children. It was an idea that was making its way through the media through the efforts of people like William Shockley, who received the Nobel Prize for inventing the transistor and then promptly used that as a platform for increasingly strident calls to racial eugenics. As before, the Church was outgunned on just about every front, but Congress's reaction to Ball's testimony and O'Boyle's sermon gave reason for hope.

The hope proved to be short-lived. Less than a week after Ball's meeting with Shriver in Washington, his and Krol's attentions were diverted away from the national scene back to Pennsylvania when the state's Department of Welfare announced that it was reversing its 1959 policy of only responding to queries by clients about birth control. As of December 1965, the social worker could initiate discussion of birth control. Archbishop John Krol of Philadelphia reacted almost immediately, denouncing the proposed change in a statement that was picked up by the AP wire as "a dangerous experiment with the lives of the poor."[4]

"These activities," Krol continued, speaking on behalf of Pennsylvania's bishops, "are not the business of the state, and they are serious threats to civil liberties."[5]

The State had decided that birth control was the solution to the black problem and all of the ruling class institutions – from Planned Parenthood to the Philadelphia Yearly Meeting – agreed. Also in agreement were virtually all of the "leaders" of the black community, from the Urban League to Rev. Bill Gray, Sr., pastor of Bright Hope Baptist Church in Philadelphia, which became home to Planned Parenthood's first birth-control clinic in Philadelphia. The one exception in this regard was Cecil Moore, who described the idea of birth control for blacks as another form of genocide and thereby earned the ire of more "progressive" black spokesmen in Philadelphia.

The only institution of any stature which opposed this eugenic social engineering of the nation's black population was the Catholic Church, and the only part of the Catholic Church which had any political traction in places like Pennsylvania was in the beleaguered ethnic neighborhoods, like Most Blessed Sacrament Parish in Southwest Philadelphia, which still had enough ethnic coherence and, therefore, political clout to send their own representative to Harrisburg. The ethnic neighborhood which had borne the brunt of racially based ethnic assault was in the end the only institution willing to defend the black population from the eugenic social engineering which the WASP ruling class was preparing for it. There was something Christ-like in the altruism involved here, and like Christ the people who followed him in southwest Philadelphia would get crucified for their benevolence.

Notes

1   William Ball to Cardinal O'Boyle 12/14/65, Krol papers, Box 29, Archives of the Archdiocese of Philadelphia.
2   Ibid.
3   Ibid.
4   "Archbishop Says Birth Control Plan 'Dangerous,'" AP (December 18, 1965).
5   Ibid.

Martin Mullen and the Birth Control Regs

In December of 1965, shortly after Pennsylvania Welfare Secretary Arlin M. Adams, with the backing of Governor Scranton, instituted its birth-control program for families on relief, Martin Mullen, the state representative from Most Blessed Sacrament Parish in southwest Philadelphia, announced that the budget was not going to get out of his committee until the welfare department returned to its 1959 regs, which prohibited social workers from bringing up the issue of contraception with their clients. Supporting Mullen, Bill Ball gave the position of the Pennsylvania Catholic Conference and Archbishop Krol, when he announced that the issue was "not basically a religious problem."[1] It certainly wasn't, according to Ball's reading, a "problem affecting Catholics," because Catholics "do not form a large percent of the people on public assistance."[2] It was rather "a problem affecting the dignity and rights of the privacy of the poor of all faiths or no faith. It points in the direction of family management and birth rationing by the state."[3]

When Norval D. Reece, who was black and also executive director of the Philadelphia branch of the ADA, countered by claiming that there was "no coercion involved"[4] in the state's plan, it was clear that poor blacks could not depend on WASP-appointed black "leaders" to defend them against the eugenic intentions of the state. The only exception to that rule was Cecil Moore, who opposed the birth-control programs as black genocide, and as a result was suspended from his post as local head of the NAACP by blacks more amenable to the eugenic plans of the ruling class. In one of the unremarked ironies in the history of this period, the only people who came to the defense of the black welfare recipients targeted for eugenic social engineering by the state were Catholic ethnics like Martin Mullen, the very people whose neighborhoods had been the target of weaponized black migration.

When it came to state-sponsored eugenics, Philadelphia's poor blacks could certainly not count on support from the leadership of the Democratic party because the leaders of that party, in a rare moment of bi-partisan cooperation, supported government involvement in birth control every bit as much as the Republicans. On June 16, 1966, Democratic legislative leaders put pressure on Mullen to "drop his effort to put the subject to a recorded vote in the House."[5] Those leaders informed the *Bulletin's* Richard Frank that "they would much prefer to have the entire matter quietly buried."[6] Among those hoping to attend the issue's funeral was Milton Shapp, soon to be Democratic governor of the State of Pennsylvania, and as a result a man on a collision course with Mullen. Shapp, who rose to political prominence in Pennsylvania as head of the American Jewish Committee there when it orchestrated the *Schemp* anti-school prayer Supreme Court decision, took the opportunity at this critical juncture to go "on record in opposition to Mullen's efforts in support of the state policy of offering birth control information."[7] Politically there was no opposition to eugenic welfare programs at all; the only opposition was ethnic, and that meant Catholic.

Philadelphia, 1966, Martin Mullen takes a position on birth control

If there was any question about why the liberals hated the ethnic neighborhoods, Martin Mullen was the answer. Mullen was born in 1921 and raised in West Philadelphia, attending Most Blessed Sacrament grade school and West Catholic High. He served with distinction in the air force in the Pacific during World War II, and in the summer of 1966 he had suddenly become the most important man in the state of Pennsylvania.

Mullen had been elected by Catholics from a Catholic district, and he was now giving the state a lesson in Catholic social teaching and representative democracy by refusing to release the state budget from his committee in the Pennsylvania House of Representatives. Martin Mullen was Paul Blanshard's worst nightmare come true, and the rage of the people who read Blanshard's books and, like him, believed in contraception as the benchmark of social progress was palpable throughout the state, but most acutely among liberal circles in Philadelphia.

KYW TV and radio, the NBC affiliate in Philadelphia, ran an editorial denouncing him on June 15, 1966. Mullen, the people at KYW announced, "has told us he personally does not believe in birth control."[8] From the liberal point of view, it was hard to imagine a more damning instance of self-incrimination. The enlightened folk at KYW, on the other hand, "believe the birth control program should be continued," primarily because "the Federal government encourages it through the anti-poverty program."[9] But there was more to it than that. The folks at KYW also "believe birth control is a personal matter, to be decided individually on the basis of private beliefs and religious convictions."[10] This, to a mind of even ordinary powers, should have meant supporting what Mullen was proposing. But that was not the case. In the parlance of the day, the attitude toward contraception was ultimately what determined whether what one held was a "personal belief" or not. If one opposed government funding of contraception, that was *ipso facto* a "personal belief." KYW's position in particular and liberal position in general is difficult to discern otherwise, since it was arguing, in effect, that contraception was such a personal matter that it should be funded by the government. If it was a personal, religious matter, then that on the face of it was good reason the government should not get involved. That was in effect the position of the Catholic Church, but since it was expressed by Catholics, it became in the parlance of the time a "personal, religious belief."

Other denominations did not labor under this constraint. When the Rt. Rev. Robert L. DeWitt, Episcopal bishop of Pennsylvania, signed a full page ad in the *Philadelphia Inquirer* on June 29 urging government funding of contraceptive services, no one objected that he was imposing his "personal, religious beliefs" on the Commonwealth of Pennsylvania. That was because *support* for contraception was not a "personal religious belief," only *opposition* to it was, especially if expressed by Catholics. KYW concluded its appeal by urging "approval of the necessary appropriations so that all of our citizens – rich or poor – can decide for themselves whether or not they want to practice birth control."[11] Evidently, the citizens of Pennsylvania were incapable of making a decision on this weighty matter unless the government funded the programs for them. Such was the logic of the day. Birth control had taken on a mantra-like quality. The more it got chanted, the less it possessed any meaning. It became a conjuring device, a shibboleth for separating those worthy of entering the brave new welfare state from those who were not.

But it was not having an effect on the one person who counted most in the matter at the moment, Martin Mullen, who continued to hold firm in his insistence that the regs be changed as the fiscal showdown came closer day by day. In late June, Governor William Scranton said that the entire welfare program depended on getting state funding, and that if the funding were not approved the entire program would go down the drain. Meanwhile, the head of Philadelphia's Planned Parenthood was claiming that support for birth control was "in the same public interest category as fluoridization [*sic*] of drinking water and the use of insecticides for mosquito control which 'have been programmed despite great opposition by segments of the community.'"[12] The fact that Planned Parenthood would become the main financial beneficiary of government involvement in birth control moved no one to mention conflict of interest. The only people who had ulterior motives in this discussion were the Catholics.

On July 26, Mullen was still standing firm. "If they buy this provision," he told the *Philadelphia Inquirer*, referring to a reversal of the DPW birth control regs, "we can get the whole budget out of the way tonight. The rest of it will fall in line."[13] The provision in question was the following statement: "No part of any funds appropriated hereunder shall be expended for the support of any birth control program adopted after 1959 by any department of the Commonwealth."[14]

One day later, the Liberal-Protestant alliance launched its counterattack against the Catholics. At a public hearing on federal aid to city programs, a group of twenty church and civic organizations asked the Philadelphia Board of Education to cut off all federally funded education programs being conducted at Catholic parochial schools because such services offered by parochial schools violated the Constitution and encouraged segregation.[15] The counterattack was sponsored by the Greater Philadelphia Council of Churches, the Episcopal Diocese of Pennsylvania, representatives of the Lutherans, Methodists, Baptists, and the United Church of Christ, as well as the American Civil Liberties Union, the Philadelphia Home and School Council, the Philadelphia Teachers Association, and a number of Jewish community-action groups. Given the make-up of the group, it is not surprising that Archbishop Krol would refer to them as "our so-called ecumenical friends."

With ecumenism like this, the Church had no need to look around for anti-Catholic bigotry. The alliance was, *mutatis mutandis*, a lot like the alliance which Bismarck had put together against the Catholic Church in Germany one hundred years before. Both the mainline Protestants and the liberals found common ground in their newly discovered zeal for sexual liberation. The neonativism of the 1960s would have a distinctly sexual tinge to it. As the letters to Krol indicated, one was suspected of being less than 100 percent American if one did not support the government-funded distribution of contraceptives. In addition to being labeled un-American, by opposing Planned Parenthood's eugenical excursions into North Philadelphia, the Church was also being publicly tarred as supporting segregation.

On July 26, a group of Protestant clergymen led by Bishop Robert L. DeWitt of the Episcopal Diocese of Pennsylvania sent a telegram to all of the Democrats of the Pennsylvania House of Representatives, asking them to pressure Mullen into backing down. "This tactic, if successful," DeWitt wrote of Mullen's refusal to let the appropriations bill out of committee, "would make the moral standards of one religious group public policy even though most citizens of the Commonwealth dissent from that position."[16] Neither DeWitt nor Richmond P. Miller, associate secretary of the Philadelphia Yearly Meeting of the Religious Society of Friends, who also signed the statement, seems to have noticed any irony in their statement. Weren't they trying "to make the moral standards of one religious group public policy" as well? The conclusion seemed inescapable. Yet no one was willing to draw it because, in the parlance of the times, imposing one's views had become synonymous with opposing sexual liberation.

To say that no one noticed the irony may be overreaching, for the House Democrats along with Mullen remained firm. Two days later they were still standing firm when Democratic gubernatorial candidate Milton Shapp attempted to undermine fellow Democrat Mullen's position. Ball was outraged at the stab in the back and wrote to Krol that "Shapp's wire openly flaunts our concerns and gives an indication of what might be expected from the Pennsylvania president of American Jewish Congress if elected governor."[17]

On the same day as the Shapp telegram, Mullen and the Democratic caucus were attacked from another quarter within the party as well. On August 27, Senator Joseph S. Clark called a press conference to announce that the Senate Subcommittee on Employment, Manpower and Poverty, which Clark chaired, had just approved a bill submitted on February 28 by Sen. Joseph Tydings of Maryland which would make federal grants available to both public and nonprofit private agencies engaged in providing birth control. This meant that both city and state agencies, as well as groups like Planned Parenthood, could collect government money to dispense contraceptives. The timing of the announcement, released on the eve of the Pennsylvania house vote, seemed calculated to cut even more ground out from underneath Mullen's position, by urging him to back down. Not only did it undermine Mullen's standing within the party, coming on the heels of the Shapp statement, it also made clear that the federal government would provide what the state legislature had deemed illegal. For the especially dimwitted, the *Philadelphia Bulletin* explained that Clark's actions

> meant, in Pennsylvania, that the action of State Sen. Martin P. Mullen (D PA) in restricting family planning services of the Welfare Department to married couples living together would be circumvented. Such people could seek help from another agency, not controlled by the Welfare Department.[18]

When asked whether the bills he proposed would provide funding for sterilizations, Clark responded by saying, "I don't think I'd better comment on that."[19]

One year before the stand-off on birth control *The Sunday Bulletin* ran an article by Hugh E. Flaherty, later legislative aide to Governor Raymond P. Shafer, on how "a quiet revolution in the attitude of Congress and the Federal Government toward establishing birth-control programs is reaching Philadelphia and other major urban areas."[20]

"Millions of federal dollars," according to Flaherty, "now are being made available for birth-control programs through medical research programs, the war on poverty and health care programs. . . . For the first time in Philadelphia's history, federal funds are available to local hospitals through the Philadelphia Department of Public Health for maternity and infant care programs that include giving patients birth control information and contraceptive devices. . . . The significance of the Clark amendment is that for the first time the Senate has been bold enough to state clearly it is permitting the use of federal monies for birth control in a broad, domestic, social welfare program."[21]

If Clark's announcement was intended to demoralize Rep. Mullen, it did not succeed. Mullen and the Democratic Caucus continued to stand firm. By July 30, Governor Scranton realized that he did not have the clout to override Mullen, and so he called Ball in to cut a deal. Scranton led off with a concession – he would remove the power of initiation and references to Planned Parenthood from the regs – but he quickly followed that up with a threat. If Mullen's amendment cutting off funds passed, the secretary of public welfare would ignore it as unconstitutional and go on using welfare funds to support it until told by the courts to cease. Ball replied by saying that he could not believe that any governor would flaunt Pennsylvania's statutes on fornication and adultery so flagrantly or that he would defy the expressed will of the legislature in such a flagrant manner. Ball left the meeting with the idea of calling a press conference as the best response to Scranton's challenge. Ball concluded his account of the meeting with Governor Scranton by telling Krol that he was in "one very hard fight" but that "so far we have kept the initiative." Ball also mentioned in closing the chairman of the House appropriations committee: "Mr. Mullen," he said, "is a truly courageous man."[22]

By August 2, the battle was over, and with the exception of a few minor concessions, the Catholics had won. In face of Mullen's intransigence, the state backed down and decided to revert to the 1959 regs. At 12:30 A.M. on the morning of August 1, the Democratic caucus accepted an agreement drafted by Ball which rolled back the Planned Parenthood position on everything except the termination of a strictly medical program limited to married women on relief. "Pennsylvania," Ball announced to Krol,

> now becomes the first state in which Planned Parenthood has suffered a reversal. Two months ago, they were looking forward to expansion of the December 17th program to include the other unmarrieds, "voluntary " sterilization and their own sex education program. Now these hopes are dashed. They have been severely set back, and will have great trouble even in trying to get back to the December 17th program.[23]

"Representative Mullen," Ball continued, "carried though this fight with no strong assistance from any other member of the legislature. He has been the soul of courage and deserves the greatest praise for the magnificent battle he has waged. . . . For the first time anywhere, great numbers of people have been focused on such matters as the privacy issue, the nature and aims of Planned Parenthood, persuasion by initiation, whether Pennsylvania has a population explosion, the sterilization and abortion issues."[24]

The Catholics had won the birth-control battle of 1966, but the outrage which resulted when the forces of Enlightenment found themselves defeated by the ethnics insured that the cultural war surrounding the birth-control issue would continue unabated, and that it would spill over into other areas of concern to these same groups, areas like housing. In March of 1966, just as the Mullen's role in the battle over the state's involvement in birth

Philadelphia, 1966, Scranton concedes

control was becoming a feature of daily report in the area's newspapers, the Quakers expanded their housing program to include southwest Philadelphia, where Mullen's congressional district was located.

Notes

1 "Mullen Battles Birth Control Plan, Promises Fight to Withhold Funds," *The Evening Bulletin* (December 19, 1965).
2 Ibid.
3 Ibid.
4 Ibid.
5 Richard Frank, "Democratic Leaders Press Mullen to Drop Birth Control Fund Fight," *The Evening Bulletin* (June 17, 1966).
6 Ibid.
7 Ibid.
8 KYW TV and Radio editorial June 15, 1966, Krol papers, Birth Control, Box 29, Archives of the Archdiocese of Philadelphia.
9 Ibid.
10 Ibid.
11 Ibid.
12 "Parenthood Unit Asks State to Give Birth Control Funds," *The Evening Bulletin* (June 28, 1966).
13 Saul Kohler, "Budget Periled as Democrats Vote to Bar Birth Control Funds," *The Philadelphia Inquirer* (July 26, 1966).
14 Ibid.
15 John C. Corr, "U.S. Funds Opposed for Catholic Schools," *The Philadelphia Inquirer* (July 28, 1966).
16 "Scranton Bars Halt in Birth Control Policy," *The Evening Bulletin* (July 27, 1966).
17 Ball to Krol 7/28/66, Krol papers, Box 29, Archives of the Archdiocese of Philadelphia.
18 David M. Cleary, "Sen. Clark Tells of Backing for Birth Control," *The Evening Bulletin* (August 28, 1966).
19 Ibid.
20 Hugh E. Flaherty, "U.S. Making Millions Available for Birth Control," *The Sunday Bulletin* (August 15, 1965).
21 Ibid.
22 Conference with governor Scranton Memo Ball to Krol, 7/30/66, Krol papers, Box 29, Archives of the Archdiocese of Philadelphia.
23 E. Michael Jones, *John Cardinal Krol and the Cultural Revolution* (South Bend, Ind.: Fidelity Press, 1995), p. 299.
24 Ibid.

The Quakers Move on West Philadelphia

On March 10, 1966, AFSC housing operative Barbara R. Krassner reported on the activities of Mr. and Mrs. Robert Murphy of the Upper Main Line Fair Housing Council, who on their own initiative had contacted eight ministers of large black churches in West Philadelphia where they arranged to speak to the congregations on housing opportunities. The Murphys were hoping to persuade the blacks in these congregations to buy houses in the suburbs, but after a few meetings with their targeted audience they discovered what Quakers who had been involved in housing since 1951 in Cicero had already discovered, namely, that the average black was not interested in moving to the suburbs. On April 10, 1966, the Murphys addressed the congregation of the Vine Memorial Church. After making their presentation, the response was typical. "Why should we move," one young man asked, "and be the only Negro family in an all-white neighborhood?"[1]

Even the minister who invited them to speak had the same response, initially at least. On April 7, the Murphys spoke with Rev. Carr, who expressed an interest in buying a house on the Main Line. Mrs. Carr, however, did not want to move, causing ambivalence on the part of her husband, who first said, "I don't want to go to a lily-white neighborhood where I'm not wanted"[2] but then added that "I really do want a house on the Main Line."[3] In his ambivalence Rev. Carr was atypical because most black ministers discouraged their congregants from leaving the neighborhood out of the fear that they would lose them as church members and because most blacks did not want to move to the suburbs, something the Quakers were discussing openly at their housing meetings.

At a February 19, 1966, meeting of Project Free, another housing initiative the Quakers were co-sponsoring with various black organization, Gayrud Wilmore explained candidly that (1) Project Free was "working in the real absence of any kind of mandate from either Negroes or whites."[4] As a result, they had to work on promoting "a climate that made the suburbanization of the Negroes important."[5] (2) that integration is a value that "has not yet been recognized in the Negro community and so we need to work in the Negro community."[6] The Quakers, in other words, needed to "get the Negro to come after the suburbs"[7] because he wasn't interested in going there on his own. "We have a need for transplantation of ghetto Negroes to suburbia in large numbers," Wilmore concluded. "Our obligation is to shake up Negroes."[8]

In spite of the general recognition that blacks did not want to move to the suburbs, the Murphys expanded their efforts in West Philadelphia to include black churches at 57th and Sommer Streets, 53rd and Chestnut Streets, 51st and Baring Streets, and 67th and Race Streets. Inciting the blacks in these congregations to move, combined with their reticence to move to the suburbs, meant that the net result of Quaker efforts in West Philadelphia was to encourage migration into the adjacent white neighborhoods, which meant into Martin Mullen's Most Blessed Sacrament Parish, which began to experience severe stress due to racial migration beginning in the summer of 1966. Ten years later, the Irish would be gone, dispersed to the suburbs, and shortly after that Martin Mullen would be out of a job. The defeat of Martin Mullen and the silencing of Catholic opposition to the eugenic social engineering of the city's black population would be accomplished by racial migration, a racial migration that was being promoted by the Quakers, who were also avid partisans in the cultural warfare promoting sexual liberation.

The Quakers had become concerned with the issue of government funded birth control in 1964, which is to say at around the same time that the government decided to get involved in the issue. In November 1966, three months after Martin Mullen forced the Pennsylvania welfare department to return to its noncoercive regs of 1959, a delegation of Philadelphia's Quakers met with Planned Parenthood of Southeastern Pennsylvania "to ascertain whether at that point there might be some useful contribution which the AFSC could make to family planning development in Philadelphia."[9] Not surprisingly, given the decision that the regime had already made to engage in the sexual engineering of the city's black population, the joint Quaker/Planned Parenthood committee decided that "it would be particularly helpful if the AFSC were to make a study of the availability of family-planning services for medically indigent families in the city and to form an estimate as to the extent of the unmet need for such services."[10] The Quakers, who had been instrumental in creating the housing situation in Philadelphia, including public housing, were now going to collaborate on the re-engineering of that housing to include birth control and ultimately abortion. The collaboration actually goes further back than that. The Quakers ran birth-control clinics for the Rockefellers in both Puerto Rico and West Virginia in the 1930s.[11] Clarence Pickett, who was instrumental in setting up those programs, became a member of Southeastern Pennsylvania Planned Parenthood in 1958.

Given their history, it is, therefore, not surprising that the AFSC would arrive at the conclusion "that all families without regard to economic status, should have equal access to reliable family planning services and that family planning services should be offered as an essential component of all programs of comprehensive health care."[12] That meant birth control clinics in the projects. "In 1967," the Quakers continue, "when the study was begun, publicly supported medical facilities for low income families were not providing birth control services."[13] This meant that the families on welfare "were experiencing de facto discrimination in not having family planning services available to them."[14] Thus was the rhetoric of the civil-rights movement turned against the very population it was supposed to benefit. Blacks were now victims of discrimination because they were having too many children. Joyce Ladner's book *Tomorrow's Children* indicated that blacks did not use birth control because they found it repugnant, but that was just an indication that their consent had to be engineered to different outcomes.

None of this, as already indicated, was surprising. What was surprising was the detail to which the Quakers targeted the opposition. That meant indicating in an appendix to their document that "most of the opposition to public programs in birth control is still the 'Catholic opposition,'"[15] and that the leader of the Catholic opposition in Pennsylvania was Martin Mullen, "who directed the long political fight to kill the [state-funded birth-control] program, [and] denounced this as an attempt to use taxpayer's money to encourage 'adultery, fornication and prostitution.'"[16]

In addition to identifying Martin Mullen as the villain in the birth-control battle and agitating for racial migration in the areas immediately adjacent to his West Philadelphia Congressional district, the Quakers also tried to engineer Catholic assent to racial change directly in a series of meetings they arranged over the summer of 1966. On July 7, 1966, when Mullen's standoff on the state budget had reached the breaking point, Barbara Krassner met with John Stokes for a six-hour meeting at which they discussed a grassroots approach to local clergymen, "particularly in the Roman Catholic situation."[17]

The Quakers were involved once again in a massive campaign of either friendly persuasion or psychological warfare, depending on your point of view, whose purpose was to persuade Philadelphia Catholics to abandon their defense of their neighborhoods because those neighborhoods and their elected representatives were the last obstacle to total acceptance of sexual liberation in general and the social engineering of the city's blacks through welfare-directed birth-control clinics in particular. Stokes, according to Krassner's account, "began to try to give us a broader picture of what was presently happening in the Roman Catholic archdiocese and how we might more creatively function there."[18] Since the Quakers had already learned that they got nowhere when they talked to priests, "creatively functioning" among Catholics meant dealing with people sympathetic to the cause of racial justice and that meant inviting people like Dennis Clark into the discussion.

Clark had received his master's degree in history from Temple in May of 1966. In June, when the public-relations campaign against Martin Mullen had reached its height, Clark gave no indication in his diary that he is aware of it happening. Instead he was hard at work on another book, whose "formula is the same as for *Cities in Crisis*," which is to say, "Historical and social treatment of a problem, then a Christian commentary upon it."[19] Clark, however, evinces little enthusiasm for his books, which he concedes "are not at all popular, Christian or not."[20] By October 1966 Clark was enrolled in "grim labors" trying to balance a Ph.D. program in history at Temple, attending class three nights a week, and "working hard by day," and trying to control the physical symptoms of his malaise, which now include "migraine headaches twice a week," something he terms a "disgusting weakness."[21]

Clark's malaise was becoming obvious to other people as well. On August 23, 1966, Stokes and Krassner invited him to a meeting at the Essex Hotel "regarding the Roman Catholic Archdiocese."[22] Krassner found the meeting "very disconcerting,"[23] primarily because it was apparent that "both Dennis Clark and Miles Mahoney had given up completely"[24] in their attempt to move the Catholics toward acceptance of racial integration. Mitch Thomas, on the other hand, a black Catholic, felt that "we need to build up an issue if we are to force the archbishop's hand at all."[25] Thomas then suggested involving either the archdiocese or the cardinal in a situation in which it "would be proven" that they had engaged in "discrimination against a Roman Catholic Negro."[26] Krassner came away from the meeting with the sense that the Catholic interracialists were "paralized" [sic]. [27] Her only suggestion was "that we attempt to use the *National Catholic Reporter* as a wedge"[28] to divide the bishop from his flock. A tone of impatience began to creep into Krassner's description of Clark and his malaise, which probably indicates that the Quakers now felt that they would have to take the situation into their own hands if they wanted to see results.

In essential agreement with this line of thinking, John Stokes "felt that we must make very clear to the Roman Catholic archdiocese, as well as others that we are not now talking about resolutions or workshops with the religious community." In other words, the time for talking with Catholics was over. The Quakers were no longer going to be satisfied with anything short of the Catholic "church's direct intervention in the field of housing." Stokes felt that the Church could now be pushed on this issue because it was now being pushed on the issue of contraception. To underline his case, Stokes "pointed to the recent full-page advertisement in Philadelphia newspapers by the several Roman Catholic Archbishops of Pennsylvania regarding contraception."

Stokes seems to be saying here that if the Catholic bishops can be roused from their normal lethargy enough to run a full-page ad in the local paper opposing contraception, they might be motivated to oppose segregation in housing as well. This reasoning bespoke more Quaker than Catholic moral thinking, since the Quakers had turned the racial issue into a moral imperative of the sort the Catholics usually reserved for sexual issues, but it also indicated that birth control and housing were, from the Quaker point of view, two sides of the same coin, and the name of the coin was social engineering. That meant that they were open to using sexual liberation as a way of engineering the housing situation and that they were also open to manipulating the housing situation as a way of engineering changes in Catholics' sexual attitudes. Martin Mullen would soon feel the effects of both approaches.

Notes

1   Krassner logs, Vine Memorial Church 4/10/66, AFSC CRD housing 1966, AFSC Archives.
2   Log, Barbara R. Krassner, 4/7/66.
3   Ibid.
4   Project Free, 2/19/66, AFSC CRD housing 1966, AFSC Archives.
5   Ibid.
6   Ibid.
7   Ibid.
8   Ibid.
9   ISD Family Planning program 1970 U.S. Phila. Study Finance Funds and Foundations Lovett Dewees Fund, AFSC Family Planning Services for Medically Indigent Families in Philadelphia AFSC 1970, AFSC Archives.
10 Ibid.
11 Ibid.
12 Ibid.
13 Ibid.
14 Ibid.
15 AFSC Family Planning Services for Medically Indigent Families in Philadelphia AFSC 1970, AFSC Archives.
16 Appendix G, AFSC Family Planning Services for Medically Indigent Families in Philadelphia AFSC 1970, AFSC Archives.
17 Barbara Krassner logs, Log Week of July 5, 1966, Meeting with Bill Cameron and John Stokes (would you believe 6 hours), 7/7/66, AFSC CRD Housing, 1966.
18 Ibid.
19 Clark, Diary, 6/6/66.

20 Ibid.
21 Clark, Diary, 10/23/66.
22 Log, Barbara Krassner, beginning 8/2/66, August 23, 1966 Meeting at the Essex Hotel regarding the Roman Catholic Archdiocese, AFSC CRD Housing, 1966, AFSC Archives.
23 Ibid.
24 Ibid.
25 Ibid.
26 Ibid.
27 Ibid.
28 Ibid.

Martin Luther King and the Blackstone Rangers

On July 10, 1966, when Martin Mullen's battle with the Pennsylvania department of welfare over their new birth-control regulations had reached its crisis point, Martin Luther King announced to 30,000 sweltering Chicagoans at a rally sponsored by the Chicago Freedom Movement that Chicago was now an "open city." King's Chicago rally took place just two weeks later in the year than the triumphal march in Detroit, three years earlier, but the climate had changed, in just about every sense of the word. Perhaps with the Detroit march in their minds as the sort of reception they could expect from a northern city with a large black population, King's Southern Christian Leadership Conference planned on attracting 100,000 people. When less than a third of that number showed up they blamed the discrepancy on the weather, which, it must be admitted, was more conducive to spending a day at the beaches along Lake Michigan than baking in the sun and listening to speeches, no matter how inspiring. The official temperature that day was recorded at 98°F., which meant that it must have been even hotter in the stadium where the rally took place.

Sheltered by a black umbrella from the blazing sun which beat down on his audience, King gave a speech as different from the early version of the I-have-a-dream speech which he gave in Detroit in 1963 as the weather in Chicago was from those halcyon days three years ago. "Freedom," he bellowed, "is never voluntarily granted by the oppressor; it must be demanded by the oppressed."[1] Instead of talking about his dream of a nation where black and white could live together in ethnic harmony, King harangued the overwhelmingly black crowd about engaging in what amounted to low-grade irregular warfare in a campaign that was aimed at fomenting social disorder until the city acceded to his demands. The initial stages of that campaign involved withdrawing money from banks and savings-and-loan associations which discriminated against blacks. It also involved boycotting companies which refused to employ the quotas of black workers which King established for them.

King had arrived in Chicago to create social disorder. Social disorder was an integral part of his program. He proposed creating it always under the assumption that he could bring it under control and use for his own political purposes. He also claimed that he believed in nonviolence, but he was never clear in explaining how the disorder he promoted was going to stop at the boundaries he had established, especially since the passions he evoked were so elemental and so difficult to control once aroused. When those passions were at their height in mid-August, King announced that it was "irrational" to blame the violence which he had fomented on the civil-rights marchers who had created it. Civil-rights marchers, according to King, were not *agents provocateurs*. Rather, they were "like a psychiatrist" because "they were bringing latent hostility to the surface so that this hostility can be faced and cured."[2] King, in other words, was the physician who had discovered the cure for the "cancer of hate."[3] By the time he left Chicago in the fall of 1966, many wondered whether the cure wasn't worse than the disease, or if the hate hadn't been created by the campaign to expose it. The fundamental question would remain long after King was gone, especially with regard to his ill-fated campaign of marching through Chicago's ethnic neighborhoods. Was the cancer of hate there in the first place, or did he simply create social disorder by threatening the stability of local communities by joining up with the forces that had been disrupting neighborhood life in Chicago since World War II when Louis Wirth formulated the country's nationalities policy for the OSS?

By spreading social disorder, King, according to his own reckoning, was releasing social pressure which might otherwise rupture society's pipes, a theory generally known as "plumbing psychology." King's social theories were based, in other words, on his personal morality, according to which King's obsessive womanizing was a way to relieve stress. When a friend raised the subject of what Garrow calls "his compulsive sexual athleticism," King answered, "I'm away from home 25 to 27 days a month. Fucking's a form of anxiety reduction."[4] King's politics were based on his psychology, and both fused into an essentially Reichian view about the source of evil in both the soul and the *polis*. The source of evil, according to the spirit of the times which King imbibed by being an especially receptive medium, was repression, specifically the repression of passion. Unleashing passion brought about liberation. King was going to achieve that end in Chicago even if it threatened to create widespread social disorder. Liberation of passion to the point of social disorder was, in effect, King's program in a nutshell. In a pointed message directed at the mayor of Chicago, he said that he was willing to fill up the jails in order to end the slums. That meant he wanted an end to "discriminatory real-estate practices,"[5] which meant that King intended to wade into the muddy waters of Chicago's housing policy, an area which had been rife with civil unrest for twenty years before King arrived.

One of the axioms of public life is that actions speak louder than words. King was willing to demonstrate the truth of this axiom in a number of ways – by encouraging demonstrations which brought the city to the brink of anarchy – but also by use of symbolic gesture of the sort which immediately followed the rally. Leading his supporters out of Soldier Field, he marched with them to the LaSalle Street entrance to Chicago's city hall, where, in imitation of his German namesake, he attached his 95 theses on race to the metal door with adhesive tape. He then turned to the crowd which had followed him there and announced that by this gesture he was marking the symbolic beginning of an American reformation.

The symbolism was significant because the Chicago Freedom Movement was a movement that was Protestant to its core, reminiscent of Luther's movement in Germany, but even more reminiscent of the Anabaptist takeover of Muenster at the hands of Johan von Leyden. But it was more than that. The taping of the theses to the door of city hall indicated that the Chicago Freedom Movement was a Protestant crusade that was going to unite all of the city's mainstream liberal denominations against the city's Catholic mayor. In the eyes of the insurgents led by Martin Luther King, Richard Daley represented the Catholic population of Chicago, a population which had been targeted to be driven out of their neighborhoods and into the suburbs by Louis Wirth. King's arrival in town was only the latest chapter in a twenty-year-long story of ethnic cleansing that was being waged in large cities across the country. King could count on the support of the Church Federation of Greater Chicago, which included the city's liberal Protestant clergy, people like Rev. Donald Benedict, the head of CFGC who had served two terms in prison for draft evasion, as well as people like the Rev. Homer Jack, who had written about the Chicago situation in the pages of *The Nation* twenty years earlier.

King could also count on the support of the national equivalent of the CFGC. That meant people like Robert W. Spike, who was not from Chicago. Spike was head of the racial-justice bureau for the National Council of Churches in New York City. He, more than anyone else, had guaranteed white Protestant participation in the August 1963 march on Washington. He had also been instrumental in orchestrating the opposition to the Moynihan report, Daniel Patrick Moynihan's attempt to get the government to strengthen the black family. Moynihan later attributed the demise of his proposal to Protestant opposition to it, opposition that was orchestrated by Robert W. Spike. At that time the clerical left opposed government programs which attempted to strengthen the black family as too Catholic. It also opposed them because the left knew that the government was getting into the contraception business as part of its efforts to take control of a racial situation that was rapidly spinning out of control.

When civil unrest reached the breaking point in Chicago in August of 1966, forcing Daley to negotiate, Spike was part of the negotiating team. Spike had converted to sexual liberationist views while a pastor in Greenwich Village in the early '50s, a job which allowed him to meet Allen Ginsberg and Jack Kerouac at bars like the White Horse and the San Remo. Being in an environment like Greenwich Village also encouraged him to engage in homosexual activity. Eventually, Spike would be murdered by a man he picked up in Columbus, Ohio, but not before exerting enormous influence in bringing the mainline Protestant denominations at the NCC into the civil-rights struggle and also making sure that that struggle was consistent if not coterminous with the struggle for sexual liberation. With the lone exception of the Catholic Interracial Council, which had been collaborating with the Quakers against Catholic interests in Chicago since the Cicero riots of 1951, King's Freedom Crusade during the summer of 1966 was a pan-Protestant crusade against Catholics, in a city represented by an Irish Catholic mayor who attended daily Mass, and who, unlike Jerry Cavanagh in Detroit, symbolized everything bad about that ethnic group's participation in urban politics from the liberal Protestant point of view. The Church Federation of Chicago felt about Richard Daley the way that Walter Phillips and the ADA felt about Jim Tate in Philadelphia. King had arrived in Chicago to lend his prestige to a campaign against the city's Catholic ethnics that was already twenty years old by the time he arrived.

King could also count on the support of the American Friends Service Committee. In fact, the main reason that King came to Chicago was because the Quakers asked him to come there to continue the campaign they had been waging against ethnic neighborhoods since the Cicero riots of 1951. According to Garrow, King came to Chicago because Jim Bevel of the Southern Christian Leadership Conference knew Bernard Lafayette, who was urban affairs director for the local office of the American Friends Service Committee. Lafayette had invited Bevel to give a series of workshops on King's campaign against segregation in the south. During one of those workshops, Bevel came to agree with

Lafayette's suggestion that "Chicago was an ideal target for SCLC's expansion into the north."[6] After coming to Chicago to become program director of Chicago's West Side Christian Parish, Bevel "enthusiastically endorsed efforts by Lafayette and his AFSC colleagues to make discriminatory housing practices a top item on Chicago's civil rights Agenda."[7]

Missing from this explanation is the fact that (1) the Quakers had been active in housing in Chicago since 1951 and (2) that they had been actively pursing King's participation in their movement for over ten years. The alliance between the AFSC and the SCLC in Chicago was based on more than just the fortuitous meeting of two people. The Quakers had been pursuing King since the riots in Trumbull Park, which is to say, since the period following the time when King had just made a name for himself by leading the bus boycott in Montgomery, Alabama.

By 1966 it was clear that both organizations had something to gain by collaborating. The AFSC would gain a charismatic leader, one who had a strong following in Chicago's black community, but the SCLC would gain something that it lacked as well, namely, a tightly focused organization that understood the housing situation in Chicago, because by 1966 they had spent the past fifteen years trying to destabilize it in their interests. Early accounts of the Chicago Freedom Summer made it clear that the SCLC knew nothing about the realities of ethnic neighborhoods in northern cities. "Down South," Southern Christian Leadership Conference Worker Dorothy Tillman said, "you were black or white. You wasn't Irish or Polish or all of this."[8] What the SCLC attempted to do was transpose the moral mandate they felt they had to end integration in the South, to the cities of the North where segregation existed only by tenuous analogy. Ethnicity, not skin color, determined residence in cities like Chicago. If Chicago's ethnics became "white" during the struggles over the social engineering of housing in the '40s and '50s, it was only because they defined themselves as the negative of the threat, which they perceived as black hordes streaming into and then taking over their neighborhoods, not because of any racially based theory or racially based laws.

Mayor Daley was quick to capitalize on SCLC ignorance of Chicago. When King announced that he intended to end slums in Chicago, Daley announced that Chicago already had a slum-clearance program staffed by people who knew more about the city than he did. "What the hell is [King] doing here anyway?"[9] Daley's staff wanted to know. "Does he think we don't care about slums? Why Chicago, instead of Atlanta or Harlem? King has no knowledge of Chicago."[10] When King announced that the SCLC planned to march in Gage Park, Daley countered by saying that King was "very sincere" but lacked "all the facts on the local situation" because "after all, he is a resident of another city."[11] When Daley suggested in April 1966 that King go home to Georgia, seven black committeemen seconded his suggestion.

The truth of Daley's charge finds corroboration in many of the SCLC's own memos. After King announced to the SCLC board that "the movement had to" move north in order to "transform itself from a southern to a countrywide effort,"[12] Andrew Young had to confess that "we don't have a program yet for the North."[13] Young conceded that the SCLC would have to rely on local groups for assistance because the movement's opponents in cities like Chicago were "more sophisticated and subtle" because in the North they could not "count on a Bull Connor or a Jim Clark"[14] to overreact and give them sympathetic world-wide publicity. On September 1, 1965, King announced that "Chicago . . . could well become the metropolis where a meaningful nonviolent movement could arouse the conscience of this nation to deal realistically with the northern ghetto,"[15] but when pressed for specifics Al Raby had to admit that "we don't have specifics yet."[16] The SCLC was still "laying the groundwork for a massive push in this city to bring the issue of northern ghettos to national attention."[17] That meant that the SCLC had to "broaden our interest in not just schools but housing."[18]

Raby stated the issue glibly enough, but there is little indication that he thought through the ramifications that followed from moving the movement north in any thoroughgoing sense. "Constitutional rights," he said, "was the subject of the fight in the South. In the North, human rights is more the question. So here, the concept of civil disobedience is different. There are fewer unjust laws. Also, nonviolence falls on more sympathetic ears in the North."[19]

But if Raby felt that some transpositions were necessary before the SCLC could bring the movement north, there were those who felt that the similarities overwhelmed the differences, and those people, by and large, carried the day. According to Jim Bevel, "the real estate dealers in Chicago are the equivalent to Wallace and Jim Clark in the South. These are the cats who are most vulnerable to an attack because this is one thing that everybody can see and understand – that is, you don't even need to philosophize about housing in Chicago, you can show that on television."[20] Bevel's impatience probably corresponded to the feelings of the majority at the SCLC. But the unwillingness to think through the differences between the situations in the North and the South would cause problems further down the road. In the South, the SCLC could frame clear demands, and focus their campaign on achieving those demands. In the South, they wanted laws taken off the books, something a legislature could do.

In the North, the situation was far from that clear. King and the SCLC wanted an end to what they perceived as discrimination in housing, but the discrimination was not based on a law that could be changed, nor did the SCLC, basing its program on a black/white racial dichotomy, have any understanding of the ethnic realities which lay at the heart of residential patterns in northern cities. As a result of not taking these realities into account during their planning phase, the SCLC was quickly faced with an impasse once the demonstrations began because, at least in the popular mind, they were marching through communities as foreigners demanding that the people living there give up their homes. When the SCLC finally arrived in Gage Park, they were greeted by an overwhelming show of anger on the part of the people who lived there. Some of the residents carried signs; some of them explained how they felt directly. "I worked all my life for a house out here," said one old man, "and no nigger is going to get it!"[21]

The misperception of what the SCLC wanted – if it was, in fact, a misperception – was not limited to ethnics with limited education. According to an editorial in the *Chicago Tribune*, the message of the "paid professional agitators" who made up the march was "give up your homes and get out so that we can take over."[22] The white ethnics were clearly reacting to the threat of racial succession which had plagued Chicago for over twenty years by the summer of 1966. The fact that they saw the march this way was largely the result of the efforts of groups like the American Friends Service Committee, which had been orchestrating the subversion of neighborhoods since the Cicero riots of 1951. In seeing the SCLC as the same sort of threat, the ethnics in Marquette Park and Gage Park were essentially correct because the main reason the SCLC had chosen Chicago as the beginning of their northern campaign is because they knew they could count on the Quaker infrastructure that was already in place there.

Since the SCLC knew next to nothing about the situation in Chicago, they would have to rely on those who did; they had neither the inclination nor the time nor the discipline to research the situation themselves. That meant the fact that the Quakers had a housing program already up and running was one of the main inducements in getting King to come to Chicago. That also meant that the Quakers were running the show in Chicago, something they were not shy about mentioning in their own memos, which in turn got reissued as fund-raising appeals. In a document entitled "Chicago: The 'Movement' in the Urban North," the Quakers brag that:

> The American Friends Service Committee played an active role in every phase of the Chicago Freedom Movement. The Executive Secretary of AFSC's Chicago Region Office sat on the policy-making committee of the Movement. In addition, four staff members of the Community Relations Programs in Chicago assisted in strategy, planning background research in the housing situation, the direction of the actions centers.[23]

The Quakers make equally clear that King's Chicago Freedom Movement was essentially nothing more than a continuation of the AFSC 1951 Housing Opportunities Program:

> This program, begun in 1951 at the time of riots in Cicero over open housing, is one of the longest running in the AFSC. Its goal is to establish an open housing market where race, creed, and national origin play no role in obtaining housing. Beginning in 1960, a major effort was directed at opening the suburbs to nonwhite home seekers through a process which included education, organization of local support and demonstration of successful move-ins. We have sought also to change patterns of residence through a fair housing listing service for white sellers and nonwhite buyers and renters, and to change people's attitudes on this sensitive issue. *The program has played an important part in the move of some 150 Negro families in the last three years to previously restricted communities*[24] [my emphasis].

The Chicago Freedom Movement was, in other words, a combination of northern and southern strategies. It combined King's penchant for public protest with the Quaker penchant for clandestine destruction of neighborhoods by manipulating the buying and selling of properties that they had been so successful in orchestrating in both Chicago and Philadelphia. Common to both Quaker and SCLC strategy was the desire to "arouse concern to the point of bringing about change."[25] The AFSC, according to their own documents, "has played a major part in helping to bring about this focus on open housing as a basic issue in achieving [the Chicago Freedom Movement's idea of] a just society"[26] for two reasons: first of all, because "the AFSC for years has been the only private agency with full-time staff devoted to working for an open housing market in city and suburban areas"[27] and, secondly, because the SCLC was ignorant of the situation in the North. "The AFSC," the Quakers wrote with barely concealed pride in their accomplishments, "through its Urban Affairs and Housing Opportunities Program has had a close relationship with the SCLC led by Dr. King even before SCLC decided to work in Chicago a year ago. Since the coming of SCLC to Chicago, our relationship has been even closer . . . through the experience of AFSC programs on which SCLC workers, *unfamiliar with Northern problems,* drew for their information and guidance"[28] [my emphasis].

As part of their plan, the Quakers targeted "ten neighborhoods *within the city* of Chicago"[29] [my emphasis]. "These areas were characterized by a lower-middle-income population of average schooling, and by the availability of homes and apartments within the financial reach of many Negroes living in the west side ghettoes."[30] By limiting themselves to neighborhoods within the city, the Quakers were declaring war on the ethnics, and that meant Chicago's Catholics. In order to survive, the SCLC had to move north, but in order to move north, into completely unfamiliar territory, the SCLC had to rely on the Quakers to set their strategic goals, and when the SCLC acquiesced to that, they became part of the war that the Quakers had been waging on Catholic neighborhoods since shortly after World War II.

King had to move north for a number of reasons. As early as 1944, the North, according to Gunnar Myrdal (or Louis Wirth) was "getting prepared for a fundamental redefinition of the Negro's status in America."[31] That redefinition was necessary because "America, for its international prestige, power, and future security, needs to demonstrate to the world that American Negroes can be satisfactorily integrated into its democracy."[32] As a result, America, or at least those Americans Myrdal represented, "cannot well afford any longer to let the white Southerners have their own way with the Negroes as completely as they have had."[33] Nor could they let the Catholic ethnics in places like Chicago have their way. Because of the internal migration policies they created to win the war, the East Coast internationalist establishment changed the focus of racial tension from "the white South," which it construed as "a minority and a national problem,"[34] to the North, where it was inextricably linked to "the Catholic problem." If King did not decide to move north, he would have become associated with an area that the ruling class had always considered a backwater and repository of backward if not seditious ideas. Once he chose to move North, however, King, of necessity, became involved in "the Catholic problem," because Catholic ethnics in cities like Chicago were the main barrier to "integration," once the South had been defeated by the passage of the Civil Rights Bill of 1964.

If he didn't know this early on, his decision to collaborate with the Quakers meant that he would discover it before long. King also had to move north if he wanted significant funding. The establishment saw him as a valuable tool in dealing with their main domestic enemy at the time, namely, the Catholics, which as of 1965 provided the only opposition to the ruling class's desire to get the government involved in birth control. As if to reassure the SCLC leadership that they had made the right decision in deciding to move north in September of 1965, Nelson Rockefeller gave them $25,000 one month later. King had to move north because, as Willie Sutton once said in another context, that was where the money was.

As if in recognition of the fact that dealing with the Catholics was now an inevitability, King met with Cardinal Cody shortly after arriving in Chicago. On February 2, less than a month after moving into the apartment which the Quakers had rented for him at 1550 South Hamelin Avenue in the heart of the Lawndale ghetto, King met with Cody to discuss the movement's goals. Cody had come to Chicago from New Orleans, where he had gained the reputation of being an integrationist. Perhaps because of that fact, King came away from his meeting convinced that Cody was in substantial agreement with what King intended to do. That agreement would soon disintegrate as Cody became more aware of how the situation in Chicago differed from the situation in the South, where the Catholic Church was a distinct minority, and not an explicit target of racial attack. Cody may have been helped to change his mind about King because of an FBI briefing. At any rate, he later professed himself "not impressed" by King and said that he intended to be "most circumspect" in dealing with him.[35] As King's campaign unfolded, Cody would begin to suspect that he had not been circumspect enough.

As part of the preparatory barrage that was to soften up the ten ethnic neighborhoods which the Quakers had targeted for social disruption, King spent time talking to the local press. The problem, according to King, was "internal colonialism."[36] His goal was to bring about the unconditional surrender of forces dedicated to the creation and maintenance of slums and ultimately to make slums a moral and financial liability upon the whole community. In order to get "the kind of comprehensive legislation which would meet the problems of slum life across this nation . . . on the federal level," King warned the city that it may be necessary to engage in acts of civil disobedience. This disruption of the social order was necessary, according to King, because "often an individual has to break a particular law to obey a higher law, that of brotherhood and justice."[37] In order to accomplish this, King said that one of his objectives was "to mobilize slum tenants into an army of 'nonviolent demonstrators.'"[38] If the power structure in Chicago didn't agree to implement King's proposals "in a hurry," King told a group of reporters who hurried to jot down his words, then they could look forward to "a darker night of social disruption"[39] in their city. In case that threat was too vague for them, King filled in the dots even further by claiming that the "system of internal colonialism" which flourished in Chicago's slums was "not unlike the exploitation of the Congo by Belgium."[40]

At this point even the most obtuse observer could see that King was once again referring to the wars of liberation that were sweeping the former European colonies in Africa and Asia at the time. Even such an obtuse observer could read King's imagery and conclude that he was bringing to bear the equivalent of the irregular warfare that lay at the heart of those anticolonial struggles on what he perceived as the "power structure" in Chicago.

In spite of his protestations of nonviolence, King was engaged in warfare in Chicago during the summer of 1966. The fact that most people did not recognize it as such at the time was attributable not so much to King's intentions, whose bellicosity can be gathered from the imagery he used to describe them, but rather to the changed nature of warfare. The H-bomb had transformed the nature of war, as Liddell-Hart had noted, but the

Communist revolution of 1917 had changed it just as profoundly, a fact noted by Liddell-Hart's contemporary and countryman, Major-General J. F. C. Fuller. The rise of Marxism had created a situation in which war and revolution had become "interchangeable terms."[41] That meant a corresponding de-emphasis on conventional arms as an instrument of war and an equally strong re-emphasis on using psychological means to extort political concessions. Subversive warfare, if carried out successfully, could result in victory through demoralization without the necessity of firing a shot. Liddell-Hart said that purely strategic campaigns where victory was accomplished without battle were known if not common throughout history. The techniques which led to them became even more important in an age marked by atomic stalemate which created a proliferation of guerrilla or irregular warfare units throughout the world. This type of unit specialized "in transforming an international or imperialist conflict into a civil war"[42] – that is, into a war in which the enemy destroys himself. The aim in these conflicts is to make them "the 'midwife' of revolution, by unceasing political and psychological attack: by systematic propaganda, the fomenting of strikes, mass fraternization and by stimulating mutiny and desertion."[43]

King may or may not have been a Communist – the Chicago police certainly thought he was – but his freedom movement was certainly a campaign of subversive warfare fought not so much for communist ends as it was fought in the manner which the H-bomb and the communist revolution of 1917 had transformed the concept of how warfare got waged. Reserves, according to this concept of war, "are to be found . . . in his discontented proletariat, in the liberation movements of his colonies and minorities and in the conflicts between his non-proletarian factions."[44] The weapons in a war like this are "liberty," or, as in the case of the Chicago Freedom Movement, "freedom," as well as related concepts like "free speech, peace, disarmament, colonialism, the colour-bar, world brotherhood and anything which will stir up popular emotionalism and undermine national discipline and social order."[45] Central to this form of warfare is the concept of the *Lumpenproletariat*, which is to say, a group which is so dysfunctional or deviant that it lacks the discipline of a regular military force, but because of that very deviance can be used effectively as a source of social disorder, creating demoralization among the group that needs to be destabilized.

King never used the term, *Lumpenproletariat,* in his speeches, because to do so would have been indiscreet, but as in the symbolism surrounding the posting of his ninety-five theses on the door of Chicago's city hall showed, actions spoke louder than words. One of the first groups King met with after arriving in Chicago in January of 1966 was the Blackstone Rangers, one of the most violent and "revolutionary"[46] gangs on the South Side of Chicago.

The Blackstone Rangers had come into existence sometime between 1961 and 1963, as gangs like that normally do, in reaction to, and as protection against, another gang in the neighborhood around 57th and Blackstone Avenues known as the Devil's Disciples. What began as self-defense soon blossomed into criminal activity. By the time Rev. King showed up at their doorstep, the Blackstone Rangers had been charged with "murder, robbery, rape, knifings, extortion of South Side Merchants, traffic in narcotics, extortion and intimidation of young children, forced gang membership, and a general history of outright violence."[47]

King was aware that they were involved in criminal activity – it would have been impossible not to know this at the time – but in public statements King and the SCLC tried to play down the violent nature of the crimes they were involved in perpetrating by claiming that "sure, they stole things, no denying that, and they fought" but "they didn't mess with narcotics, rape or prostitution."[48] The Rangers, in other words, "take pride in their street battles"[49] with other gangs in the same neighborhood. Unlike gangs from an earlier era, the Blackstone Rangers had become "politicized." Unlike earlier gangs, which were "involved more specifically in group criminal violence," the Blackstone Rangers had become "more involved in group political violence."[50]

Why then did Martin Luther King want to meet with people like this? There are two reasons given, according to the standard explanation of his meeting with them: (1) he wanted to convert them to the cause of non-violence and (2) he wanted to use them as protection when the SCLC marched in white neighborhoods. Both explanations are ultimately unpersuasive. If King were looking for candidates for non-violent resistance to the type of provocation that would take place in places like Marquette Park and Gage Park, he could not have found a group of less likely candidates than people by his own admission who "take pride in their street battles." According to Oates, some 200 gang members eventually "agreed to give nonviolence a chance and turn out for the demonstrations 'as soon as Brother Martin gives the word.'"[51] They did this because they "respected him enormously."[52] Oates's account is no more plausible than any of the other accounts of King's recruitment of gang members as converts to nonviolence. The simplest explanation is that King recruited the gangs to be part of his efforts during the summer of '66 because he knew they were violent and because he knew that they were already involved in criminal behavior of the sort that would destabilize the areas that he wanted destabilized.

King's philosophy of non-violence was similar to the views held by the Quakers, who in many ways wrote the book on the political uses of "non-violence." Like King, AFSC staffer Bernard Lafayette had also made contact with the Blackstone Rangers. He too was hoping to use the Rangers as marshals in the marches King and the Quakers were planning to hold in Gage Park. Unlike King, however, Lafayette was willing to admit – to other Quakers, at least – that neither "the Black Stone Rangers [n]or any of the other young people have adopted nonviolence as a way of life."[53] The Quakers, like King, were still willing to work with the Rangers, precisely because of this fact. The Quaker use of the Blackstone Rangers was perfectly consistent with their theory of nonviolence, which included using other groups to wage war by proxy in order to bring about ethnic cleansing. The Quakers used precisely this technique in getting Lutheran mercenaries from central Pennsylvania to drive the Catholics out of Maryland. Now instead of Lutherans from Pennsylvania, they were using Baptists from Mississippi to drive a different group of Catholics out of a different territory.

Gangs like the Blackstone Rangers and the Vice Lords and the Cobras and the Devil's Disciples were, in other words, a classic instance of the *Lumpenproletariat,* and they were utilized precisely in that fashion by the people who wanted to destabilize Chicago's ethnic Catholic neighborhoods.

The suspicion that King and the Quakers were using Chicago's South Side gangs to destabilize the neighborhoods there through criminal activity is borne out by the course of subsequent events. Less than one year after King's July 10 Soldier Field rally, the Blackstone Rangers received a grant of $957,000 from the Office of Economic Opportunity to engage in vocational training of the sort Leon Sullivan was promoting in Philadelphia.[54] According to a later account of the grant, "the purpose of the program was to utilize the existing gang structures – the Blackstone Rangers and the Devil's Disciples – as a means of encouraging youth in the gangs as well as nongang youth to become involved in a pre-employment orientation, motivational project."[55] The instructors in this program, known as "Center Chiefs," were not professionals but rather "gang leaders who were supposed to be under the supervision of professionals."[56] The vice president of the Blackstone Rangers, Jeff Fort, became a Center Chief, for which he received $6,000 a year, in spite of the fact that he could neither read nor write and had been arrested numerous times.

The man ultimately responsible for making that grant was Sargent Shriver, formerly of the Chicago Catholic Interracial Council, later appointed head of the Office of Economic Opportunity by his brother-in-law John F. Kennedy. If King could claim that he was from out of town and, therefore, unaware that the Rangers were involved in criminal activity, that excuse was unavailable to Sargent Shriver, who was from Chicago and had been head of an organization there that was known for its expertise in racial matters. The grant to the Rangers was clearly in the tradition of what the Ford Foundation had done by subsidizing an equally dubious venture in vocational training by giving Leon Sullivan $250,000, knowing that he could never deliver what he promised. By giving the Blackstone Rangers money, Shriver was only ratifying the move King had made in 1966 when he went to the gangs; he took the same principle involved in both King's endorsement of the Rangers and the Ford Foundation's endorsement of Sullivan to the next logical level. Shriver was subsidizing the Rangers, in other words, not simply to create a beachhead within a group that needed to be brought under control, but because they were involved in criminal activity and that criminal activity could be politically useful. The fact that Marion Barry was involved in the same sort of government subsidy of criminal activity in poverty programs in Washington, D.C., showed that the grant to the Rangers was far from an anomaly. It was impossible for people like Shriver not to know that the Rangers were involved in criminal activity. Since he subsidized them knowing this, he was using government money to subsidize crime.

When the Chicago Police Department heard about the grant, disbelief quickly turned to outrage. "The police department," one Chicago cop remembers at the time the grant was announced, "was breaking its ass trying to keep order in the city, and here Shriver is giving OEO funds to the people they are trying to put in jail. We were stunned. It was man bites dog. The OEO was subsidizing criminal activity."

The disbelief spread throughout the Chicago Police Department, causing the Gang Intelligence Unit to do its own investigation of the federally funded Blackstone Rangers. During the time they received money from the OEO, the GIU detectives made "extensive visits to the training centers"[57] and discovered that "no actual training [was] taking place."[58] In place of training, however, the GIU detectives found evidence of gambling and falsification of time sheets and evidence that marijuana was being smoked on the premises.

In other words, government money was being used, not for vocational training, but criminal activity.

By September 1967, three months into the grant, the outrage spread from the police department to the population at large when Jeff Fort and Eugene "Bull" Hairston, the Rangers' president, were arrested for soliciting three juveniles to murder a drug dealer named Leo McClure. Eventually the scandal led to Senate subcommittee hearings in July 1968, chaired by John McClellan of Arkansas. During those hearings, former Blackstone Rangers Warlord George Rose testified that the Blackstone Rangers were "involved in the sale of narcotics,"[59] that trainees in the program were forced to give kickbacks of anywhere from $5 to $25 a week to the people running it. Rose also testified that "the Rangers, from the start, had no interest in job training" and that the program "was used only to increase the gang's membership and its treasury."[60]

Rose also testified that the First Presbyterian Church, which housed the program, was used for the sale of narcotics as well a place to store guns and to engage in sexual activity. Government money was also used to finance a trip to Michigan, where the Rangers bought guns, and it was used to finance a trip to a Black Power conference in Philadelphia, where the Rangers plotted the murder of certain "nonmilitant"[61] civil rights leaders. In addition to that, the Rangers used Sargent Shriver's grant to force children in the neighborhood to drop out of school and join the gang. Those who refused to go along were beaten or shot in the arm or forced off the streets or killed. They also engaged in the systematic extortion of money to the tune of $5,000 to $8,000 a week from neighborhood merchants.

When Hairston was convicted and sent to prison in May of 1968, Jeff Fort assumed his duties as president of the Rangers. When Martin Luther King was murdered, Fort extended the extortion ring to virtually all of the businesses in the area by forcing them to buy signs which were supposed to protect them from the rioting which King's death was sure to occasion. When nothing happened, the Rangers were given credit in the press for keeping the peace in the neighborhood. When Fort was subpoenaed to appear before the McClellan committee at around the same time, he showed up but refused to be seated or to answer questions on the advice of his white lawyer, Marshall Patner, who further advised Fort to walk out on the hearings, an action which eventually earned him a contempt of Congress conviction.

In spite of all of his other troubles, Fort didn't have to worry about paying legal bills. Patner, it turns out, was being "paid by the Kettering Foundation to provide legal counsel for Rangers in general and Jeff Fort in particular,"[62] counsel, it should be noted, which quickly landed Fort in jail. Shortly after his federal windfall, Jeff Fort found himself caught in the cross-fire between the OEO, which had decided to use him as a revolutionary leader of black *Lumpenproletariat* whose role was to create social disorder through criminal activity on the South Side of Chicago, and the Chicago Police Department, which was trying to hold things together in spite of the federal government's efforts to tear them apart.

The most interesting part of Rose's testimony before the McClellan committee concerned the role of the Protestant churches in fostering the Rangers' criminal activities.

Rose testified that the idea behind the grant came from Rev. John Fry, pastor of the First Presbyterian Church where the Rangers ostensibly ran their program. The real movers and shakers behind this criminal conspiracy, according to Rose, were John Fry, Charles Lapaglia and Anne Schwalbach, all of whom were white, and all of whom were, again according to Rose's testimony, "attempting to control and direct the gang through [their] influence over Jeff Fort."[63] Rev. Fry, according to Rose, had written the OEO grant proposal for the Rangers. Rev. Fry was also the source of the idea that the Rangers get involved in extortion. Al Garrison, a twenty-five-year-old Chicago machinist, corroborated Rose when he testified that "white men run the gang."[64] According to Garrison, the white men gave the gang members "a new kind of dope that makes them want to kill people. They just go crazy when they take it." "The whites," Garrison concluded, "are just using those boys."[65]

Part of the Protestant/OEO strategy in using these gangs also involved subsidizing groups that could not and would not get along with each other. The Blackstone Rangers, for example, would not make a coalition with the Black Panthers, nor would they make a coalition with the Devil's Disciples, who also received money from the OEO. The revolutionary attitude of the gangs continued long after the federal government bent to public pressure and, ultimately, with the arrival of the Nixon Administration, stopped funding them. During the '70s the Blackstone Rangers changed their name to the El Rukns after they received a $1-million grant from Moammar Kaddafi of Libya to continue their irregular warfare in Chicago.

The local police were left pretty much to fend for themselves to figure out what was going on as best they could. "It was so new," one Chicago policeman recounted, trying to give voice to the confusion and bewilderment they felt at the time when faced with this sort of technique. "We didn't know what they were up to." The Chicago police could have learned the technique known as "gang and counter-gang" because it was described by Frank Kitson in his 1961 book of that name. Kitson had used the technique in helping the British take control of the mau-mau uprising in Kenya, and when the Kennedy Administration decided to get involved in promoting guerrilla warfare, in the same year that Kitson's book appeared, his theories started circulating through the intelligence community.

The Chicago police were handicapped by not knowing what was going on but also by feeling that Communists, rather than Quakers and Presbyterians, were behind Martin Luther King and the black gangs. Captain Edward Buckney, the black captain of the Gang Intelligence Unit at the time, had some sense of this when he blamed "overzealous clergymen"[66] for the rapid growth of gangs during the last two years of the '60s. Buckney criticized Rev. Fry publicly during the McClellan hearings.

The same sort of thing was going on in Philadelphia at the time, where Bishop Robert De Witt, head of the Episcopal Diocese of Pennsylvania, was promoting a less virulent form of criminal activity by supporting a man by the name of Muhammed Kenyatta, who would appear in local churches and attempt to extort money from their congregations. Bishop De Witt was also Martin Mullen's most vocal opponent in his attempts to keep the government out of the birth-control business.

In 1968, Buckney disclosed that ten people had been killed in the Woodlawn neighborhood, a rise in crime he laid at the feet of increased gang activity in the area. Increased gang activity, in other words, could be laid at the feet of "overzealous clergymen,"[67] who were involved in a campaign of increasing crime as a way of driving the Catholic ethnics out of the neighborhood. The OEO grants were related in purpose to George Edwards's attempts to reform the police department in Detroit in keeping with the Supreme Court's *Miranda* and *Escabedo* decisions. In each instance, the government was subsidizing the criminal activity of a *Lumpenproletariat* whose purpose was to create social disorder so that the people who were living where the government didn't want them to live would move to where it did want them to live.

Martin Luther King's July 10 rally was not unique. It was the first in a series of daily rallies that would last for the rest of the summer. Marie Pappalardo, a Quaker operative in Chicago who documented the Freedom Movement's activities that summer for the AFSC, attended one of those daily rallies or mass meetings in August when the tension in the city was getting to the breaking point. She remembered the powerful effect that listening to "1500 people all stomping and clapping in time with the music and singing freedom songs"[67] had on the passions of the people attending the meeting.

It was at this meeting that King gave his explanation of himself as the psychiatrist whose role was to bring out the hatred. King was determined to evoke passions and confident he could control them once he did. Pappalardo, however, began to notice tensions between the Quakers and the SCLC staff, which seemed more intent on singing and marching than working and organizing, tasks they left to the Quakers. No matter how annoying the Quaker staff might find the SCLC penchant for singing and clapping, it provided the Quakers with an opportunity to take control of the movement and use King's celebrity status as a way of achieving goals they had set years before.

Notes

1   Charles Johnson and Bob Adelman, *King: The Photobiography of Martin Luther King, Jr.* (New York: Bob Adelman Books, 2000), p. 238.
2   Chicago Debriefing 7/29/66 Maria Pappalardo to Barbara Moffett, Charlotte Meacham, etc., AFSC CRD Housing, 1966, AFSC Archives.
3   Ibid.
4   David J. Garrow, *Bearing the Cross: Martin Luther King, Jr., and the Southern Christian Leadership Conference* (New York: William Morrow and Company, Inc., 1986), p. 375.
5   Michael Eric Dyson, *I May Not Get There with You: The True Martin Luther King, Jr.* (New York: Free Press, 2000), p. 407.
6   Garrow, p. 432.
7   Ibid.
8   John T. McGreevy, *Parish Boundaries: The Catholic Encounter with Race in the Twentieth Century Urban North* (Chicago, University of Chicago Press, 1996), p. 197.
9   Stephen B. Oates, *Let the Trumpet Sound: The Life of Martin Luther King, Jr.* (New York: Harper & Row, 1982), p. 388.
10 Ibid.
11 Garrow, p. 493.
12 Ibid., 437.

13 Ibid.

14 Ibid.

15 Ibid., p. 444.

16 Ibid., p. 447.

17 Ibid.

18 Ibid., pp. 447–48.

19 Ibid., p. 449.

20 Ibid., p. 432.

21 Oates, p. 413.

22 Garrow, p. 500.

23 Chicago: The "Movement" in the Urban North, AFSC Community Relations Division, Housing, 1966, AFSC Archives.

24 Ibid.

25 Ibid.

26 Ibid.

27 Ibid.

28 Ibid.

29 Final Dispatch on Chicago by Kale Williams, Bernard LaFayette, William Moyer, Maria Pappalardo 11/22/66, AFSC Community Relations Division, Housing, 1966, AFSC Archives.

30 Ibid.

31 Gunnar Myrdal, *An American Dilemma: The Negro Problem and Modern Democracy* (New York: Harper & Row, 1962), p. 1010.

32 Ibid., p. 1016.

33 Ibid., p. 1014.

34 Ibid., p. 1010.

35 Oates, p. 391.

36 Ibid., p. 390.

37 David L. Lewis, *King: A Critical Biography* (New York: Praeger, 1970), p. 316.

38 Ibid.

39 Ibid.

40 Oates, p. 389.

41 Ibid., p. 390.

42 Major-General J F.C. Fuller, *The Conduct of War 1789–1961* (New Brunswick, N.J.: Rutgers University Press, 1961), p. 204.

43 Ibid.

44 Ibid.

45 Ibid.

46 Ibid., p. 211.

47 James Alan McPherson, "The Blackstone Rangers," in *Observations of Deviance,* ed. Jack D. Douglas (Washington, D.C.: University Press of America, 1970), p. 170.

48 Ibid., p. 171.

49 Dyson, p. 392.

50 Ibid.

51 McPherson, p. 170.

52 Oates, p. 393.

53 Ibid.

54 Chicago Report by Marie Pappalardo, Final Dispatch on Chicago by Kale Williams, Bernard LaFayette, William Moyer, Maria Pappalardo 11/22/66, p. 11, AFSC CRD, 1966, AFSC Archives.

55 McPherson, p. 172.

56 Ibid.

57 Ibid., p. 173.

58 Ibid., p. 176.

59 Ibid., p. 175.

60 Ibid., p. 176.

61 Ibid.

62 Ibid.

63 Ibid., p. 191.

64 Ibid., p. 176.

65 Ibid., p. 183.

66 Ibid.

67 Ibid., p. 186.

68 Pappalardo log, Thursday, August 18, 1966, AFSC CRD Housing 1966, AFSC Archives.

The Ethnic Cleansing of
Most Blessed Sacrament Parish

> Where there are several distinct minorities in a country the dominant
> group can allow itself the luxury of treating some of them generously and can
> entrench itself and secure its dominance by playing one minority against
> another.
>
> Louis Wirth
> UC Archives

In 1980, when Rev. John Noons arrived at Most Blessed Sacrament Parish at 56th and
Chester on Philadelphia's southwest side to begin his duties as pastor there, the transformation of the neighborhood from an all-white Irish Catholic to an all-black Baptist was
complete. "As near as I can figure out, it happened over the summer of 1966,"[1] he said
almost thirty years after the fact. Most Blessed Sacrament had the distinction during the
days before 1966 of having the largest Catholic grade school in the world. Its cathedral-
like church, four-story rectory, convent, and grade school buildings towered over the
eight-square blocks of cramped row houses which housed the Irish Catholics who supported MBS out of all proportion to their incomes. And what they could not supply with
money, they supplied with the lives of their children. MBS led the diocese in providing
vocations to the religious life. It was, as a result, the most outstanding example of Catholic
parish life in the city at that time, and, in addition to supporting the Church, the neighborhood was so densely populated that they could send their own representative to
Harrisburg, a man by the name of Martin Mullen, who was powerful enough as head of
the House Ways and Means Committee to hold up the state budget when the state decided it wanted to get into the birth-control business.

All of that would change over the course of time, and the changes began in earnest
over the summer of 1966. During the same months that Martin Mullen held up the state
budget, the demographic foundation of his political office began to erode in a dramatic
way. Up until the summer of 1966, the enrollment at MBS parochial school remained
steady at around 3,500 pupils. Then over the summer of 1966, while Mullen held the
Quakers and Episcopalians at bay over birth control, the enrollment of the world's largest
Catholic grade school suddenly dropped by 600 pupils. That meant that almost as many
families moved out of the neighborhood during that three-month period. That migration
would continue for the next decade. It was over by 1980, when Noons arrived as pastor.
The neighborhood was completely black by then.

Prior to the summer of 1966, many black families had moved into the neighborhood
and were living in harmony with the Irish families there. Those black families were driv-
en out of the neighborhoods along with the Irish following the arrival of the new migrants

of 1966, a group which seemed bent on not getting along with the people they would eventually displace. Cardinal Krol, according to Noons, tried to portray the ethnic cleansing of MBS as an opportunity. The physical plant left behind by the Irish could be used to evangelize the blacks. The main engine in this effort was the Catholic school, which did take in black children from the neighborhood in great numbers, but the catechesis they learned in school never stuck. As soon as they left the school, they reverted to the black gang culture that dominated the neighborhood of essentially one-parent families. Children, who had been abandoned by their fathers had a hard time believing in God, according to Noons.

Krol tried to mitigate the damage the migration was causing by creating a life-support system for the newly black parishes, which taxed the archdiocese's wealthier parishes, but that didn't work either. The numbers militated against it. The newcomers were by and large not Catholic, and so there was no way that they could fill up the parishes the ethnics left behind. During the 1990s, West Philadelphia's nine black parishes averaged 2,500 worshippers on any one Sunday, a group which contributed weekly a grand total of $10,000 to the collection plates of their vastly overextended churches. Nowhere was the contrast more dramatic than at MBS, where a Church which was built for 12,000 worshippers and was filled eight times on each Sunday attracted 258 worshippers on any one Sunday in the mid-'90s. Other than using the schools to evangelize, there was no strategy in dealing with migration, Noons claimed, "You were left to figure it out yourself."

What Noons did figure out is that the change from 1952, when, as an older priest told him, there was no such thing as a poor parish, to the time forty years later when virtually the entire heart of the church of 1952 – the parishes in North and West Philadelphia – were on life support took place suddenly and had, as far as he could tell, two causes: gangs and blockbusting. Throughout the decade following the summer of 1966, blockbusting realtors were able to spread panic with impunity throughout the neighborhood. Leaflets asking the residents "Are you willing to sell your home?" would appear stuffed in mailboxes or stuck under the windshields of cars parked on the streets. None of the city agencies whose job it was to prevent this sort of thing could seem to do anything about it; however, when one of the priests at MBS would announce after Mass that a house was for sale on Conestoga Street, hoping that someone from the neighborhood might buy it, he was threatened with prosecution by the city's district attorney.

Faced with this sort of pressure the families would crack one by one and move. Each story was different, but blockbusting and gang violence were common to all of them. One old white woman was subjected to constant verbal harassment by the blacks who moved in following the summer of 1966, but in spite of it all, she refused to move. Finally, she came home one night and found a butcher knife lying on her bed. Concluding, probably correctly, that her life was being threatened if she stayed in the neighborhood, she finally moved. Father Joseph Meehan, who arrived at the parish when the warfare surrounding the ethnic cleansing there was at its height, remembers one white woman who brought her six children back to the parish in the '70s to take part in parish programs. She had moved as a result of the same pressures to a house in Yeadon, the neighboring suburb. The blockbusting had driven the price of the house she owned in MBS down so dramatically that when she was forced to sell it she had to move into a house which she could not afford. The mortgage payments were so onerous that she had no money to buy furniture for the new house, a fact which earned her the reputation of being poor white trash in the eyes of her new neighbors. This woman had no contact with the community into which she was forced to move, a fact which was obvious when she brought her children back to MBS for the social contact that didn't exist in their new neighborhood.

By the time Noons arrived as pastor of MBS, there were 100,000 alumni of MBS still living, dispersed largely throughout Delaware County. The group got together on a regular basis at events like West Philly Night on the beach in Sea Isle, New Jersey, where they reminisced about the ethnic cleansing of their neighborhood in a raucous but ultimately melancholy manner reminiscent of Serbs remembering the battle of Kosovo Pole. "Where are we from?" the crowd chanted. "MBS." "Why did we leave?" "Because of the niggers," it answers. Noons bemoans the fact that these alumni will not support the parish financially, but why should they? They no longer live there, much as they might want to, and they have other parishes to support now, even if those lack the sense of community possessed by the one they left. Noons is quick to add that the blacks who arrived beginning in 1966 were not the same as the blacks who were already living there when they arrived. "The people who beat up the neighborhood," he claims, "are not the original people." Something new was afoot in MBS in 1966.

Something new was afoot at the American Friends Service Committee in 1966 as well. On October 2, 1965, the executive committee of the AFSC's CRD housing board met to discuss their new program, the Philadelphia Metropolitan Fair Housing Program (PMFHP) "which is expected to begin in early November."[2] The purpose of the PMFHP was "to increase the pace of housing integration in the Philadelphia metropolitan area . . . by relating minority buyers to the FHA and VA repossessed houses."[3] The Quakers, in other words, were now getting federal money to expand the program which Leon Sullivan had worked out with Robert Weaver in Washington. Instead of going through the laborious process of finding someone in a neighborhood who was interested in selling his house to a black family, the AFSC's PMFHP program had first crack at any house in the neighborhood where the resident defaulted on his loan. The AFSC or any one of its front groups could then buy the house, move a black family in, and then cause panic in the neighborhood and drive the rest of the white residents out to houses in the suburbs, and no one would know what was going on.

At the same meeting, Philadelphia Housing Association Executive Director Cushing Dolbeare "shared with the committee a 'preview' of a long-range program which the Philadelphia Housing Association and the Urban League are planning to foster desegregation throughout the Philadelphia metropolitan area."[4] The money for that long-range program came from the Ford Foundation. The Quaker scribe who recorded the minutes to that meeting doesn't go into the details of that plan, but he does add significantly that "Cushing felt that timing with the new AFSC 18 month program will be important."[5]

Dolbeare was both a vice-president of Americans for Democratic Action and a Quaker who came to the Philadelphia Housing Association in 1956 and stayed until 1971, when she left to take an assignment from the American Friends Service Committee. Her role as both a member of the AFSC housing board and head of the Philadelphia Housing Association is significant because it shows the networking that in effect determined housing policy in Philadelphia and because it showed that the overwhelming majority of

Philadelphians had no input whatsoever in formulating the policies that often meant life or death for the communities they lived in.

Just as in 1919 when the Philadelphia Housing Association came into existence and in 1948 when it collaborated on the urban-renewal map that decreed that Bridesburg was going to be torn down, there was no Catholic ethnic representation on the board of either organization. (Dennis Clark was on the AFSC board but for the reasons we have already discussed.) This is not to say that membership wasn't expanded during the organization's by-then fifty-year history, but the groups that got included were organizations like the Urban League and the NAACP and CORE, in other words black organizations that were just as avid to destroy ethnic neighborhoods as the Quakers. In Philadelphia as in Chicago, the only people who got certified as experts in housing were, in other words, those who shared the ruling class animus against ethnic neighborhoods.

What also changed during that period of time was the ruling class commitment to the moral order. During the course of the 20th century, the WASP ruling class adopted contraception as part of its idea of marital virtue. Over the course of the next half-century, this would eventually come to mean that people who did not contracept were not virtuous people. This meant that Catholics and blacks were not virtuous, and that meant that the housers were justified in making use of means not normally applied to decent people in dealing with them. The WASP slide into sexual degeneracy not only caused them to demonize their ethnic opponents in the culture war that would rage in Philadelphia after World War II, it fueled their fear of differential fertility, and with the specter of Philadelphia becoming a Catholic city, the Quakers were determined to act in a way that would prevent that from happening.

The sexual degeneracy of the ruling class in 1969 meant that they were willing to engage in tactics that their grandparents and parents would have found morally repugnant. As a result, the same ruling class which had created a comparatively benevolent and paternalistic agenda for the Philadelphia Housing Association during the days of the city beautiful movement had become involved in all-out irregular warfare and ethnic cleansing by the late '60s. In addition to that, the PHAssoc also now had the money and power of the federal government to back up its schemes. In addition they had the money and prestige of WASP agencies like the Ford Foundation to support them in their campaign to engineer Philadelphia's ethnic neighborhoods. The ethnics, for their part, didn't have a clue about the Quaker networking that was determining the fate of their neighborhoods, nor did they understand the strategic linkage between things like abortion and integration as integral parts of a cultural offensive who purpose was to blunt the Catholic demographic surge which had taken place during the '60s.

Dolbeare later claimed that when she became head of the Philadelphia Housing Association there was no distinct break in the continuity of what the organization had been doing under the leadership of Dorothy Montgomery, but during her tenure as director, which began in 1965, the Philadelphia Housing Association's public statements took on a political tinge that had been missing in earlier years and one which reflected the political concerns of the group that ran it at the time. In 1969 Dolbeare declared that the PHAssoc was going to function as "an initiator of social change in housing and as a supporter of needed social change or action in other related areas, such as education, opposition to

ABM [the antiballistic missile system] and disproportionate emphasis on military spending, opposition to police suppression and the like."[6]

During the first phase of the ethnic cleansing that emptied out Most Blessed Sacrament Parish, Dolbeare changed the name of the Philadelphia Housing Association to the Housing Association of the Delaware Valley when the association joined with the Fair Housing Committee of the Delaware Valley, which was in turn a coalition uniting the Urban League, the NAACP, the Fellowship Commission, the Congress of Racial Equality, and the Commission on Human Relations during her tenure there. Beginning in 1965, Dolbeare hoped to "plan and carry out a coordinated attack on racial segregation and discrimination in housing."[7] With each year her efforts to engineer "social change" in the neighborhoods became more and more overt. When Philadelphia Housing Authority Director Frank Steinberg protested the increasingly intrusive methods Dolbeare was promoting as head of the HADV, claiming that the HADV "agitators" wanted "to push them [the blacks] into Roxborough"[8] over the opposition of the neighborhood's residents and the consensus in the rest of the city as well, Dolbeare asked Mayor Tate "to act immediately to remove Frank Steinberg as chairman"[9] and eventually succeeded in forcing Steinberg out of office.

In October 1969, the HADV added the war in Vietnam to its list of causes, announcing that its offices would be closed to allow its staff to participate in a nation-wide protest against the war. Just what the War in Vietnam had to do with housing in Philadelphia was not immediately clear, but it became clear as soon as one came to see that the Quakers were involved in housing from the late '40s onward not because they were interested in improving the city's housing stock but because it enabled them to get involved in social engineering. By the time Dolbeare became head of the PHAssoc, the PHAssoc did not fund active programs. However, because of her connection with the Quakers, Dolbeare was in contact with groups that were involved in active programs of the sort Friends Suburban Housing or the Ford Foundation's AFSC/Urban League program ran and could coordinate her work accordingly. By the time she moved on to become director of an AFSC project in Washington in 1971, Dolbeare had simply updated the work of the PHAssoc and attached current political concerns to the social engineering the Quakers had been practicing since they decided to make housing one of their apostolates shortly after World War II.

Dolbeare later said that the HADV denounced the ABM because it was using up money that could be better spent on housing.[10] Using a housing association as a platform from which to denounce an anti-ballistic missile system was simply a tacit admission on the part of the Quakers who determined housing policy in Philadelphia that their involvement in housing had always been a means to an end. The main difference between their involvement in Cicero in 1951 and their involvement in using housing to attack the Nixon administration's foreign policy in the late '60s was the fact that their need to be circumspect about what they wanted to achieve had diminished because of so many years of success.

By 1970, the Quakers felt that they had been vindicated with the tribunal of history, and this meant they could be less circumspect about using things like housing to get what they wanted. One of the things Quakers wanted desperately in the late '60s was a loosening of sexual prohibitions. Since by 1970 no one was going to prevent Quakers or anyone else from engaging in whatever sexual practices they found gratifying, no matter how perverse, that meant the Quakers were interested in using sex as a form of social engineering, something that needed a change in the laws. Specifically they were interested in broadening the right to kill inconvenient offspring and, even more specifically, in the right to use the state's welfare agencies to intervene in the reproductive habits of troublesome ethnic groups.

In 1970 the Quakers released a slim book entitled *Who Shall Live? Man's Control over Birth and Death: A Report Prepared for the American Friends Service Committee*, which was the result of a decision which the Family Planning Committee of the AFSC reached in December 1966 "to explore the issues involved in abortion."[11] That meeting in turn flowed from the November 1966 meeting that the AFSC had had with Planned Parenthood, and that meeting resulted from the setback the Quaker and Episcopalian forces for sexual liberation and eugenics in Philadelphia had suffered at the hands of Martin Mullen, when the governor capitulated to his demands and backed away from state-promoted birth control in August of the same year. As a result of their meeting with Planned Parenthood, the Quakers decided to "make a study of the availability of family planning services for medically indigent families in the city and to form an estimate as to the extent of the unmet need for such services."[12] *Who Shall Live?* was the fruit of this labor.

Who Shall Live? is a graphic example of moral theology in the Quaker mode. It begins by announcing that "for 300 years members of the Society of Friends (Quakers) have been seekers after the truth"[13] and concludes by admitting that they have been so far unsuccessful in their efforts. Where once people like Fox and Penn "thought of himself as created only a few thousand years ago,"[14] the enlightened Quakers who wrote birth-control tracts in the 1960s "now know he is part of an evolutionary process that has been going on for billions of years. In that process he has arrived at a stage of knowledge and technology whereby he himself has the power, at least in part, to determine the direction in which he will evolve in the future."[15]

Having decided that their religious forebears were wrong on just about everything because they didn't understand science, the 1970 Quakers then give some sense of their own grasp of science as it applies to population issues. Looking at the world from outer space in 1968, the Quakers found it "incredible that 3.5 billion people should be living on that small spinning planet."[16] Taking their cue from Paul Ehrlich's 1968 book *The Population Bomb*, the Quakers concluded quite logically that if the planet cannot sustain 3.5 billion people in 1968, then it certainly couldn't sustain 6 billion people in the year 2000. Unless drastic population-control measures are introduced immediately, dire consequences will follow. "Lamont C. Cole, who is a Professor of Ecology warns that we may one day find ourselves short of breathable air," the Quakers announced breathlessly.[17]

With the foundation of their argument firmly anchored in junk science and a historical relativism that undermined their present position as much as it undermined the past they hoped to transcend, the Quakers moved on to the theological phase of their argument. "The most basic belief of Friends," they wrote, is that "every human being has the capacity to respond to the spirit of God, the 'Light Within.' It follows, therefore, that every human being is worthy of respect and reverence and that every human personality is sacred."[18] Quakers are especially concerned about "reverence for life," and that "is the reason for the traditional attitudes of Friends against the taking of human life in war and in capital punishment."[19]

If you thought that Quaker opposition to taking human life in war and capital punishment would lead them to oppose abortion, you are not thinking like a Quaker. If you thought that because "every human being has the capacity to respond to the spirit of God, the 'Light Within,'" that therefore each family should be allowed to decide how many children it should bring into the world, you were wrong again. Thinking like a Quaker meant that while it was wrong to take human life in war and in capital punishment, it was okay to take it in abortion. Reliance on a slim reed like the "inner light" as its source of guidance meant that Quaker theology was invariably a ratification of the *Zeitgeist*, which is to say the ratification of the views of the ruling class – whenever they constituted the ruling class – attained by orchestrated peer pressure. The ruling class decided in the early '60s that it needed abortion and contraception to control America's increasingly unruly black population, and, *mirabile dictu*, the "inner light" informed Philadelphia's Quakers the same thing a few months later.

The Quakers also felt this way because they had been reading Garrett Hardin, a scientist, who wrote in a magazine called *Science*, in an essay entitled "The Tragedy of the Commons." According to Hardin, "the only way we can preserve and nurture other more precious freedoms is by relinquishing the freedom to breed, and that very soon."[20] In order to save the human race from almost certain destruction (famine was going to wipe out India beginning in 1976), Hardin called for "mutual coercion mutually agreed upon,"[21] something the Quakers cite approvingly, probably because it could be used as a working definition of Quakerism.

In typical Quaker fashion, the authors of *Who Shall Live?* assure their readers that "at the center of our position is a profound respect and reverence for human life."[22] Quakers go even further. They feel especial reverence for the life "of the potential human being who should never have been conceived,"[23] and they express this reverence by urging the state to legalize, and eventually to pay for, abortion.

They, of course, never get around to telling us how they know that this life "should never have been conceived." The only possible answer to that question is that they learned it by direct revelation from the mind of God, which fits nicely in with the rest of Quaker theology. "There is nothing that so infuriates me as the disguised aggressions of a Quaker,"[24] Michael Novak wrote at around the same time that the Quakers issued their documents on abortion and birth control. *Who Shall Live?* wouldn't have been a real Quaker document without a disguised call to disguised aggression. First there is the call to exterminate inconvenient offspring, all done in the name of the Quakers' "profound respect and reverence for human life." The disguised aggression doesn't stop there though. The Quakers are also determined to deal with anyone who opposed their program. "The opposition to family planning programs," they announce vaguely, "on the part of certain governments, religious groups and special interests continues to be a deterrent to birth control."[25] But the charges soon become more specific as the document proceeds. According to the Quakers,

The Roman Catholic church currently holds that a new life begins at conception and therefore forbids destruction of that embryo or fetus except in cases of indirect abortion when a method is used to effect a cure of a disease or condition of the mother likely to be fatal, which incidentally causes the death of the unborn child.[26]

The call to action gets even more specific in their pamphlet on "Family Planning Services for Medically Indigent Families in Philadelphia," also issued in 1970, in which they announce in an appendix that "Rep. Martin P. Mullen (D. Phila.) . . . directed the long political fight to kill the [birth control] program,"[27] which the Quakers wanted instituted in Pennsylvania.

The Quakers opposed Mullen because "we believe that it is wrong as well as ineffective to use either law or the fear of consequences to enforce moral standards."[28] The Quakers failed to mention that this is precisely what they had been doing in housing for the previous two decades in cities like Philadelphia and Chicago. They had been using both the law and the fear of consequences as well as city agencies like the Commission on Human Relations to impose their will on neighborhoods throughout Philadelphia and Chicago, and now, if it hadn't occurred to them before, they realized that their success in manipulating racial migration could have an impact on the Catholic Church's opposition to abortion and birth control.

Martin Mullen, the man they identify as the being responsible for "the long political fight to kill the program," had to be elected to his office by people who lived in a certain neighborhood. If those people were no longer there to elect him, he could no longer oppose the Quakers' desire to change the laws on abortion and birth control. The idea that Mullen was holding up progress on abortion coincided with Cushing Dolbeare's radicalization of the PHAssoc and the creation of an especially virulent and refined form of the housing destabilization program which the Quakers had been working on for twenty years. Now the AFSC was an officially recognized grantee, receiving federal funds to "integrate" neighborhoods in Philadelphia through privileged access to FHA and VA repo lists. If housing could be used as a forum to denounce an anti-ballistic missile system, it could be used for other ends as well. It could be used to fight anything the Quakers thought worth fighting about, and by the late '60s, they clearly felt that birth control was not only an issue worth fighting about, they just as clearly identified the man with whom they would be fighting.

On June 29, 1966, Mrs. Hertha Reinemann, chairman of the Family Relations Committee of the Philadelphia Yearly Meeting of Religious Society of Friends joined Bishop DeWitt of the Episcopal Church and virtually every other Protestant denomination in the city of Philadelphia in signing a full-page ad in the *Philadelphia Inquirer* calling for government funding of birth control.[29] In 1970 the Quakers all but listed Martin Mullen's address and phone number in the document that sketched out the brave new sexual world they were proposing. In one of the tragic sidelights to this campaign, Dolbeare noticed that by the end of the '60s there were large numbers of abandoned houses in North Philadelphia, and was at a loss to explain why, even as she was engineering the takeover and evacuation of even more Philadelphia neighborhoods.

The same Quaker scribe who attended the meeting in which Dolbeare announced her concerted attack on the city's ethnic neighborhoods also noted that C. Delores Tucker, who by now had her broker's license, was at the meeting and "expressed excitement at the thought of a three-way approach involving the Urban League, the Philadelphia Housing Association, and the AFSC"[30] in ostensibly ending segregation in housing in Philadelphia's neighborhoods. Tucker was most probably more enthusiastic than most at the meeting because she as a real-estate agent stood to benefit directly from real-estate commissions in the neighborhoods targeted for change by the Quakers.

C. Delores Tucker was one of thirteen children born to a black preacher who moved to Philadelphia from the Caribbean. As a teenager, she had got involved with the ADA reform crowd in Philadelphia when she volunteered to work for Joe Clark's mayoral campaign. From that time onward, the ruling class had found her useful in representing their interests in the black community, and her career progressed accordingly. On April 19, 1967, Tucker, who by then had become first vice-president of the Philadelphia branch of the NAACP, held a press conference attacking Cecil Moore, claiming that he was "raping"[31] the NAACP till by not sending his yearly quota of $5,000 to the national office. According to Tucker, Moore hadn't paid his dues in three years and had "outlived his usefulness"[32] to the black community in Philadelphia, a fact which Tucker was hoping would drive him out of office.

Not someone to take a challenge like this lying down, Moore held his own press conference a day later and denounced Tucker and her husband as "part-time Negroes"[33] and slum landlords, citing a list of twenty-seven Philadelphia real-estate brokers compiled by former city Licenses and Inspections Commissioner Inspector Richard Buford. According to Moore, Tucker was attacking him because she was on Mayor James H. J. "Tate's payroll."[34] The charge that Tucker was on Tate's payroll is implausible, but there was some truth to the rest of his claim. Tucker had accumulated large amounts of Philadelphia real estate through Tucker and Tucker, the firm she owned jointly with her husband and through Penn National Investments, the firm which bought up properties in changing neighborhoods at fire-sale prices and then resold them to black families moving in at a handsome profit. Tucker, however, got to be a slum landlord not because of her association with Mayor Tate but because of her association with the American Friends Service Committee, which as of 1966 was involved in a major push to change the character of real estate in the city of Philadelphia.

The Quakers, as part of the Philadelphia establishment, were interested in getting rid of Moore for a number of reasons. He was the main opponent to the Ford Foundation's attempt to engage in social engineering in North Philadelphia during the early '60s. It was Moore's denunciation of Paul Ylvisaker's PCCA program that led to its demise, and that forced Ford to back Leon Sullivan as an alternative to both Temple University's ineptitude and Moore's grassroots opposition. The Philadelphia establishment was also interested in getting rid of Moore as a spokesman for the black community because, unlike Tucker, he disagreed with the Quakers and the Episcopalians on birth control, especially government-funded birth control for black welfare recipients, the crucial social issue in the state of Pennsylvania during the summer of 1966. Planned Parenthood, which began collaborating with the Quakers on the issue of birth control for blacks in November of 1966, was clearly upset by the charges of "black genocide" raised by Moore and other "irresponsible" black leaders, so much so that they commissioned a study from the consulting firm of

Bowne Burin, Barnes, Rock & Carleson Inc., to figure out what to do about it.[35] In September 1969, that firm conceded that "the specter of black genocide by the white community, most interviewees agree, is being raised by a small but articulate group of black militants and represents a minority view in the black community."[36] The same firm suggested that Planned Parenthood could ameliorate its image in the black community as an agent of genocide by "1) informing the leaders and members of the black community with respect to PPSP's role in helping solve the problem of population control"[37] and "2) expanded employment of individuals within the black community as employees and volunteers by PPSP."[38] In other words, by buying them off just as they had bought off their leaders.

Planned Parenthood's mailing list at the time of the survey consisted mainly of residents of Chestnut Hill and the Main Line, a fact completely consistent with the Rockefeller's earlier support of Planned Parenthood's "Negro Project," as a way of driving the black birth rate down. The only way this sort of overt eugenic intervention into black fertility could work is if the people who were identified as running it in the public eye were black. Planned Parenthood as one of the prime agents of ruling class population policy in Philadelphia needed black leaders like C. Delores Tucker, and not people like Cecil Moore, if they hoped to be successful in engineering the threat which black fertility posed to their interests.

As a result of her willingness to collaborate with the Philadelphia ruling class on its projects in the black community, Tucker's career took off during the late '60s. By the end of the decade she was co-chairman of the city's Fellowship Commission, which began opening "field offices" in ethnic neighborhoods "to ease race tension."[39]

Tucker was on hand to cut the ribbon at the opening of one of these centers at the corner of 46th and Lancaster Avenues on May 4, 1969. The purpose of the center, which, it turns out, used to house "a former Catholic athletic club which was founded in October 1895,"[40] was "to hear complaints and provide legal services for residents who charge they have been aggrieved."[41] After the hostile takeover of the building was orchestrated by the Fellowship Commission, the walls of what used to be the Shanahan Athletic Club were now decorated with posters announcing "I celebrate myself and I sing myself,"[42] lines which were originally written by a Quaker poet from Camden by the name of Walt Whitman.

After cutting the ribbon at the Fellowship Commission's latest beachhead in West Philadelphia, Tucker announced that other field offices were going to be opened in "Germantown, South Philadelphia, North Philadelphia, Kensington, Manayunk and Roxborough."[43] With the exception of Germantown, which was once a Quaker stronghold, by the '60s mostly black, all of the other areas targeted to receive Whitmanesque grievances from the city's black population were in Catholic ethnic neighborhoods.

Tucker played her own role in fueling that sense of grievance in the black community. Two months after cutting the ribbon at the former Shanahan Athletic Club, Tucker predicted a "burning summer"[44] because the Nixon administration had cut back funding for Job Corps and Youth Corps programs in Philadelphia. These programs evidently funded gangs in Philadelphia, much as Sargent Shriver's OEO money had funded the Blackstone Rangers in Chicago. We know this because Tucker announced that, deprived of federal money, these gangs would have to revert to crime, so desperate was their situation without the prospect of federal funds flowing into the gang coffers from Washington. "Gang members," Mrs. Tucker announced, "have nothing to lose by stealing. At least in jail they have bread and a place to sleep."[45]

After practically urging Philadelphia's blacks to riot, Tucker got around to the real reason for her animus against the Nixon Administration. It seems that she and her husband, identified as co-owner of Tucker and Tucker Real Estate Co. of 5912 Old York Road, had gone to Washington not so much to go to bat for Philadelphia's gangs as "to protest a new law effective July 1 whereby the VA will not finance repossessed homes that had a VA mortgage."[46]

So it turns out that Mrs. Tucker wasn't motivated by pure altruism after all. The Nixon Administration as part of its strategy to mobilize the backlash against social engineering now growing among the nation's largely Catholic ethnics, had pulled the plug on the program Robert Weaver had set up with the Quakers to destabilize Catholic neighborhoods in Philadelphia, and C. Delores Tucker, whose firm was going to be directly affected by this change was mad, so mad, in fact, that she spilled the beans in a rather indiscreet way in her newspaper interview. "The government," she told the *Bulletin*'s Margaret Eisen, "is yielding to a conservative element to keep Negroes from moving into certain areas."[47] The purpose, in other words, of the otherwise innocuous sounding VA regs was fostering racial change in urban neighborhoods. Since those neighborhoods only changed in one direction, that meant using federal leverage to break up "white," i.e., ethnic, i.e., Catholic neighborhoods.

Mrs. Tucker never got around to telling Eisen which areas she had in mind, but that could be deduced from the fact that Eisen described Tucker as "vice-president of the Philadelphia Fellowship Commission" and the fact that two months earlier the same paper announced that the Fellowship Commission would be setting up Quaker-inspired grievance centers in West Philadelphia, South Philadelphia, North Philadelphia , Kensington, Manayunk, and Roxborough.

Tucker may not have made much headway with the Nixon Administration, but her star was rising in the Democratic Party in Pennsylvania. In June of 1970, she was appointed vice-chairman of the state committee, a post she used to engineer the party into the new configuration disenfranchising the urban Catholic machines that would emerge when the 1972 convention nominated George McGovern as it presidential candidate. Tucker was instrumental in getting people like June Hayes, "a 30-year old woman with a 12-year old son, product of North Philadelphia's ghetto and a former school dropout"[48] appointed to serve on the Democratic State Committee's platform committee in September of 1970. "Mrs. Hayes," according to a report in the Bulletin, "was recommended for appointment to the 44-member platform committee last month by Mrs. C. Delores Tucker, vice chairman of the Democratic State Committee. She is one of the committee's four black and seven women representatives and a member of what she jokingly termed the committee's 'radical left.'"[49] The primary reason behind packing the platform committee with women of color was to distract the average observer from noticing that they were chosen for their political views, specifically on abortion, views which were incidental to their skin color.

The man behind the change was Milton J. Shapp, who in September of 1970 was the Democratic candidate in the race for governor of Pennsylvania. Shapp had made a name for himself in Pennsylvania as the head of the American Jewish Committee and the man behind the *Schempp v. Abington* Supreme Court decision striking down school prayer. He had also made a fortune for himself in electronics by producing a box which improved TV reception. Combining the personal fortune he accumulated with his penchant for social change, he embarked on a career in politics as a Democrat, and in Pennsylvania that meant finessing the Catholic vote. That meant being duplicitous on the issue of abortion. In the October 22, 1970, issue of *The Catholic Standard and Times*, Philadelphia's diocesan newspaper, Shapp announced that he opposed abortion in no uncertain terms. "I welcome this opportunity," he told Philadelphia's Catholics, "to set the record straight on this issue. I am against abortion. My commitment personally and as Governor is and will be to the preservation and protection of all life, and children not yet born are fully entitled to the full protection of the state. We need a sound, clear, unequivocal law in Pennsylvania to insure this protection."

The perceptive reader who read further down the column might have noticed something unsettling when Shapp announced in the same interview that he was planning to appoint a "commission of all women"[50] to study the idea of abortion. If Shapp were so opposed to abortion, why was he appointing a commission to study it? The idea behind the commission revealed Shapp's true intentions on the issue of abortion. Shapp campaigned for governor fully intending to legalize abortion, but he knew he could not do this without alienating Pennsylvania's Catholics. So instead of stating his position clearly, Shapp decided on subterfuge. He would appoint a commission of women "from all faiths and all races and all economic backgrounds" who would be chosen for membership on the commission by people like C. Delores Tucker because they supported abortion. Then once the committee he had packed with his own people came out for legalized abortion, Shapp could simply claim that he had to bow to the will of the people.

Since the average Philadelphia Catholic was by birthright a Democrat, he probably read as far as Shapp stating "I am against abortion," and decided there was no reason to change the way he had voted since the New Deal. As a result largely of the reflex Catholic support for Democratic candidates from cities like Philadelphia, Milton Shapp was elected governor of Pennsylvania in November 1970 and almost immediately set about working against the interests and beliefs of the Catholics who had elected him to office.

One of his first actions in this regard and a sign of things to come was his announcement, one month after the election, that he had appointed C. Delores Tucker as Secretary of the Commonwealth. The announcement was accompanied in virtually all of the press accounts reporting it with all of the usual oohing and aahing over the fact that Tucker was both black and female. Not one to keep her light under a bushel basket, Tucker showed up at Cheyney State College, an all black college south of Philadelphia, a few days later, and announced in her first public appearance since being named by Shapp to her post, "I stand before you as the first black woman in the cabinet of the state of Pennsylvania. And that's power."[51]

Then, as if to give some indication of the thinkers which had helped form her mind,

Tucker quoted Malcolm X. "For us," she said presumably referring to all of the citizens of Pennsylvania she had been chosen to represent, "it's either bullets or ballots."[52] In addition to a list of qualifications that included graduating from Girls' High School in 1946, Tucker was described as "real estate broker in a firm on Old York Road headed by her husband William L. Tucker," as well as "being selected as one of the Best Dressed Women of the Year by *Ebony Magazine*."[53]

Milton Shapp was nothing if not a calculating politician, and C. Delores Tucker was chosen with a number of goals in mind, all of which revolved around the key issues of real estate and abortion. Shapp would eventually fire Tucker for incompetence and corruption, but by the time that happened, the Democratic Party had achieved one of its major modern transformations, by marginalizing the influence of urban Catholic ethnics, an accomplishment which took place on the national level when George McGovern became the party's presidential nominee in 1972. That same displacement took place on the state level when Shapp became governor. If there were a joke surrounding the appointment of Ms. Hayes, "a 30-year old woman with a 12-year old son, product of North Philadelphia's ghetto and a former school dropout" to serve on the Democratic State Committee's platform committee in September of 1970, the joke was on the Irish Catholics who were being displaced from positions of influence in the Democratic Party.

Notes

1   Interview with Rev. John Noons, pastor of Most Blessed Sacrament Parish, 3/27/93.
2   Minutes of meeting of CRD NHPC 10/2/65, AFSC CRD Housing, 1965, AFSC Archives.
3   Ibid.
4   Ibid.
5   Ibid.
6   John F. Bauman, *Public Housing, Race, and Renewal: Urban Planning in Philadelphia, 1920–1974* (Philadelphia: Temple University Press, 1987), p. 199.
7   Ibid., p. 198.
8   Ibid., p. 202.
9   Ibid.
10 Interview with Cushing Dolbeare, 7/01.
11 *Who Shall Live? Man's Control over Birth and Death: A Report Prepared for the American Friends Service Committee* (New York: Hill and Wang, 1970), p. vii.
12 AFSC Family Planning Services for Medically Indigent families in Philadelphia AFSC 1970, AFSC Archives.
13 *Who Shall Live*, p. vii.
14 Ibid.
15 Ibid.
16 Ibid., p. 1.
17 Ibid., p. 7.
18 Ibid., p. 39.
19 Ibid., p. 40.
20 Ibid., p. 63.
21 Ibid., p. 62.

22 Ibid., p. 65.

23 Ibid.

24 Michael Novak, *The Rise of the Unmeltable Ethnics: Politics and Culture in the '70s* (New York: Macmillan Company, 1971), p. 207.

25 *Who Shall Live*, p. 12.

26 Ibid., p. 95.

27 AFSC Family Planning Services for Medically Indigent Families in Philadelphia AFSC 1970.

28 *Who Shall Live*, p. 60.

29 "An Important Message to the People of Pennsylvania concerning Family Planning," full page ad in *The Philadelphia Inquirer* (June 29, 1966.)

30 Minutes of meeting of CRD NHPC 10/2/65, AFSC CRD Housing, 1965, AFSC Archives.

31 Orrin Evans, "Savage Says Moore 'Rapes' NAACP Till," *The Evening Bulletin*, 4/19/67, Tucker folder, Temple University Urban Archives.

32 Ibid.

33 Orrin Evans , "Moore Says His Critics Are 'Part-Time Negroes," *The Evening Bulletin*, 4/20/67, Tucker folder, Temple University Urban Archives.

34 Ibid.

35 Report on a Fund-Raising Study for the Planned Parenthood Association of Southeastern Pennsylvania Inc Prepared and submitted by Bowne Burin, Barnes, Rock & Carleson Inc. September 1969, Planned Parenthood ACC 315, 319, 413, 683, Box 3, Temple University Urban Archives.

36 Ibid.

37 Ibid.

38 Ibid.

39 Orrin Evans, "Fellowship Group Sets Up Office to Ease Race Tension," *The Evening Bulletin*, 5/5/69, in Tucker papers, Temple University Urban Archives.

40 Ibid.

41 Ibid.

42 Ibid.

43 Ibid.

44 Margaret Eisen, "Civil Rights Aide Says Conditions in N. Phila. Ghetto Rival Depression," *The Evening Bulletin*, 7/26/69, p. 18, Tucker folder, Temple University Urban Archives.

45 Ibid.

46 Ibid.

47 Ibid.

48 Paula Herbut, "Democratic Unit Listens to Voice of the Ghetto," *The Evening Bulletin*, 9/6/70, Tucker folder, Temple University Urban Archives.

49 Ibid.

50 Ibid.

51 "Mrs. Tucker Speaks to Cheyney Students," *The Philadelphia Inquirer* (December 27, 1970).

52 Ibid.

53 Ibid.

Martin Luther King and the Ethnic Neighborhoods

On the evening of the July 10, 1966, rally following King's posting of his ninety-five theses on the doors of city hall, AFSC staffer Bernard Lafayette addressed the movement's regular mass meeting and announced that it was now going to focus its attention on real estate practices in Gage Park, a predominantly Polish neighborhood near 55th and Western, which is to say west of the ghetto and in the migration path the Quakers had established as a result of their work in Cicero in the '50s. Lafayette's plan resulted from the convergence of a number of forces. First of all, the Quakers had been working on the SCLC since January, trying to bring them around to their point of view that Cicero could become Selma if they could persuade the public that real-estate agents at the Halvorsen Agency in Gage Park were the equivalent of Jim Clark or Bull Connor. "At the beginning of the year," AFSC staffer Bill Moyer said, "most of the staff saw little relationship between slums and the closed housing market,"[1] but friendly persuasion had changed all that in the seven intervening months. Beyond that, the SCLC had announced its intention to do something in a major way at the July 10 rally, and now they had to follow up with something that produced results. Jim Bevel's tenant-organizing campaign had produced only meager results after six months' efforts. The SCLC, in other words, had been in Chicago for six months and had nothing to show for it. If the movement didn't do something significant by the end of the summer, it would be ridiculed as ineffective. Since the SCLC seemed incapable of understanding either the size or complexity of Chicago's social structure, that meant going with Lafayette's plan or having no plan at all.

King, at this point in time, was also beginning to feel pressure from competition to his left. SNCC and CORE were making inroads into King's constituency in Chicago by promoting Black Power, a less Christian version of the irregular warfare that King was promoting. If King did nothing, he would lose the left wing of his movement to this faction. If he acted, however, he could still portray himself as (1) a man who got results, to his black constituents, and (2) a man who could control the passions he evoked, to his white backers. In other words, King had to be able to both promote and control social disorder or he would lose control of his movement. There was no necessary connection between what King needed to do and what the Quakers wanted to do. In fact, as time would show, the Quakers essentially backed King into a no-win situation, but King, who was only in Chicago periodically, could come up with no plan of his own because, as Mayor Daley indicated, he was from out of town. He lacked both the time and the will to come up with his own plan, and his staff couldn't help him either. So King and the SCLC adopted the Quaker plan because the Chicago situation was too complex for their Southern strategy to succeed and because the march of events forced them to move lest they lose both their black and white backing.

The march of events intervened unexpectedly at this point in other ways as well. The same heat wave which had kept attendance at the Freedom Rally low intensified over the next two days, driving temperatures over 100° by July 12. When police arrived on the west side to turn off fire hydrants turned on by youths hoping to escape the heat, a confrontation ensued and out of that confrontation a riot. King tried to deal with the rioting by inviting neighborhood residents to a local church and asking them to air their grievances and thereby "relieve the tension."[2]

The gangs which King had hoped to recruit to his nonviolent crusade had been instead "at the forefront of the disorders,"[3] and many of them had been arrested. King then used his prestige to get them released and then invited them to come and speak at his tension-relieving sessions. The sessions, however, were relieving little tension. In fact, they may have been intensifying it. When the six gang members King had got released claimed at one of these sessions that they had been beaten by the police, their colleagues swore to avenge them. When one man from the neighborhood criticized the gang members for destroying their own neighborhood, the gang members left the hall in spite of King's entreaties and engaged in another night of breaking windows and general mayhem.

After a brief lull, the rioting broke out again even more virulently during the night of July 14. This time in addition to the usual looting, snipers had positioned themselves in the high-rise projects and were shooting at police and firemen sent to put out the fires the looters had started. King and his staff spent the night driving from one incident to another, trying to persuade the rioters to go home and stop fighting – but without much success. By dawn two people were dead, 56 had been injured, and 282 arrested, and Illinois Governor Otto Kerner had ordered 4,000 National Guard troops to Chicago, where they began patrolling the area in Jeeps full of soldiers with bayonets fixed on rifles carrying live ammunition.

King spent much of his time trying to gain control over events by gaining control over the gangs that were the main engine of destruction during the riot. King met with the leaders of the Vice Lords, the Cobras, and the Roman Saints in his apartment, trying to persuade them the demonstrations he was planning to lead in Gage Park were more "sensible and effective"[4] than the rioting that they had just engaged in. At least this is the conventional account of the riots. Missing from these accounts is the fact that King benefited strategically more from gang participation in the riots than he would have if they had stayed home. With gangs marauding in the streets of Chicago, King could position himself between the gangs and the police as the only force which could guarantee order in the city. He would benefit, in other words, more from violence than nonviolence because by giving the impression that he controlled the gangs who were wreaking that violence, he could blackmail the city into granting his concessions while at the same time benefiting from the violence he publicly deplored.

Mayor Daley, however, thwarted King's efforts when he blamed the riots on King and the SCLC (an accusation he later retracted under pressure) and when he mentioned the fact that the SCLC had been showing films of the 1965 Watts Los Angeles riots at their gatherings as one of the precipitating factors. Ever since his arrival in town in January, King had succeeded in politicizing the facts of everyday life in Chicago and that meant politicizing the actions of the gangs as well. What was once construed as antisocial behavior

had been transformed into discontent at an unjust situation. The gangs had simply internalized King's message and were now acting on it according to their lights. That much is
clear. But there was an even more sinister aspect to what was going on.

King was clearly attempting to manipulate the situation to his advantage by playing a
version of good cop–bad cop. The city could deal with King or the city could deal with
the Vice Lords and the Blackstone Rangers. That was the choice. King gave the impression that he was attempting to convert the gangs to his version of nonviolence when a just
as plausible explanation of what was going on was that his rhetoric had inflamed and
politicized the already tumultuous passions of the gangs to the point where even the procedures of normal law enforcement had begun to be construed as an intolerable affront to
their political autonomy. It was King, after all, who made the comparison between
Chicago and the Congo in the papers. If the Vice Lords acted on this bit of information in
their way, it would be disingenuous to say that King's framing of the issue had nothing to
do with their actions. It would be equally disingenuous to say that King's publicly professed allegiance to the tenets of nonviolence in any way dissuaded others from violence.

King spent his time arousing passions, and when the situation got out of control he
rushed in to calm things down. He was both the arsonist and the fire department when it
came to civil unrest in Chicago, and he profited from both sides of that political equation.
His rhetoric gave the criminal element in the black community the impression that their
actions were somehow redeemed by some overarching political purpose. By asking the
gangs to join him in the marches he proposed in Chicago's ethnic neighborhoods, King
was accomplishing two things at once. He was bringing the gangs under his control, but
he was also as a result positioning himself to use them as a threat against the recalcitrant
ethnics, who had been driven into the suburbs in huge numbers precisely because of the
threat of uncontrolled violence these gangs manifested.

In this regard, King's call to "civil disobedience" both incited violence and attracted
all of the "bad hats" Liddell-Hart had warned against as the first people attracted to a campaign of irregular warfare, and the group most likely to cause that warfare to boomerang
out of control. King was an expert in both fanning the flames of passion and making sure
that the heat got applied where he found it beneficial. King's talk about Chicago as the
Congo undermined the legitimacy of Chicago's elected government and made law
enforcement more difficult by politicizing just about every confrontation between blacks
and the police. But once the conflagration started, King would be in the forefront of those
trying to calm it down. The real question though was whether he could play the modern
Prometheus and steal the fire of passion from the sky without getting burnt by it himself.
King's strategy of arousing passion and then taking control of it constituted the political
equivalent of a chain reaction which was always threatening to get out of control, and ultimately that is precisely what would happen. But in the meantime King benefited enormously from the double game he was playing with the gangs. In the aftermath of the riots,
the *New York Times* correspondent who had been covering the riots attributed the return of
peace to Chicago not so much to the 4,000 troops Governor Kerner had sent in to restore
order as "to King's influence with the Negro gangs."[5]

King was, as a result, forever walking a tightrope between losing influence among
blacks to the more militant black-power crowd and losing influence among establishment

whites who felt he was no longer in control of the movement. As a result, King had to stage events to give the sense that he was somehow still in control of them in order to maintain his precarious hold on a movement that was always heading in the direction of uncontrolled civil disorder. The incubation period between a King speech and a riot had decreased dramatically in the time since he had spoken in Detroit. By asking the gangs to march with him, King secured some tenuous hold on their behavior, but the price he paid for that was that it forced him to act in a precipitous manner in a campaign that was doomed to failure by its very inception.

In order to maintain his position of leadership, King paradoxically had to follow the Quakers into a battle that they had been waging without success for over fifteen years. "The logistics of the marches," according to Quaker documents, "and in fact of many phases of Operation Open City, were handled through the action centers,"[6] and the action centers were run by Quakers. Bert Ransom ran the South Side Action Center, and Gerry Davis, also a member of the AFSC, ran the West Side Action Center, which he then handed over to SCLC staffer Billy Hollins when he moved to start another center in Chicago Heights. According to the same memo, "the Action Center Directors were also responsible for mapping out the logistics of the marches. For instance, if the target community for a specific weekend was geographically close to the South Side Center, Bert Ransom would make sure the community had been tested. . . . Bert would also visit the community to map out the best route of march and to detail the best streets of access from the South Side Center, including parking facilities."[7] King, in other words, was the leader of the marches in name only. He was essentially working for a Quaker operation.

Two weeks after the riots in Chicago had necessitated the deployment of 4,000 National Guard troops, King announced that the time for "creative tension"[8] had arrived. The movement was moving into Gage Park, a Polish neighborhood near 55th Street. King, who would not take part in the demonstration, announced that a group of protesters were planning to drive to a preassigned spot in Gage Park and then march to the Halvorsen Real Estate Agency there, where they would hold a prayer vigil for the entire night.

In announcing his plans, King made a number of mistakes. For one thing, he had been in Chicago seven full months before he mounted his campaign. That meant that the opposition was completely familiar with what he was planning to do and understood the ramifications of the campaign in many ways better than King himself did. King also made the mistake of choosing, as the focus of his attack, real-estate agents, a group which had no real power in the situation. Real-estate agents were precisely that – they were agents, which is to say an intermediary between two parties, one of which wanted to buy a property and another which wanted to sell. If the agent attempted to impose conditions on the sale, either one or the other or both parties could simply change agents if they felt the conditions were not to their liking. This was precisely the position the agents took during King's campaign. "We cannot persuade property owners to change their attitudes about whom they want to sell their property to," the real-estate agents argued. "We are the ones that are easy to blame . . . but the problem is not ours. The realtor is an agent; we must represent our clients. And therefore, because our clients are opposed to the open occupancy law, we must oppose the law if we are to honestly represent our clients."[9] Change could take place only if public attitudes shifted, and "realtors cannot take the lead in this."[10]

Chicago, 1966, mob counters protesters at Gage Park

That, of course, shifted the burden to the people who owned the houses, which is pre-cisely the direction the protests took once they got nowhere with the realtors. Once King and his followers started marching through the neighborhoods, the message changed to "give up your homes and get out so that we can take over," something which outraged the ethnics in the neighborhoods even more than protests at real-estate offices. Before long, it became apparent that neither the SCLC, nor the Agenda committee, nor the CCCO had done its homework.

The problem was simple enough, if anyone had taken the time to think it through. The Chicago Freedom Movement had adopted the Quaker strategy of neighborhood subver-sion, but they were now doing it out in the open, with disastrous results. It was as if ter-rorists were announcing which building they were going to blow up in advance of actual-ly blowing it up. It was, in other words, an example of the worst of both worlds. King's gift for moving masses of people had now been grafted onto a Quaker campaign of manip-ulating the real-estate market for political ends that only worked when no one knew it was occurring. This unthinking combination of the movement's northern and southern strate-gies was a formula for disaster.

Beyond that, no one seems to have noticed other discrepancies between what the SCLC had succeeded in doing in the South and what they were doomed to fail to do in the North. The SCLC had succeeded in registering black voters in the South, and they could have done the same thing in Chicago. Citizens have a right to vote. If they are excluded from voting, their rights are being denied and redress is in order. However, no one has the right to own a house. And therefore, *a fortiori*, no one has the right to own a house in a particular neighborhood. By claiming that they did, the SCLC simply aggravated the fears of the ethnics, many of whom had had to move because of racial migration already. The SCLC convinced the ethnics that they had come to take their houses away, just as blacks, at least from the ethnics' point of view, had taken so many houses away during the period following World War II. In pursuing this ill-fated combination of northern and southern strategies, the Chicago Freedom Movement mounted a frontal assault on their enemy's strongest position – never a good idea – and they also managed to concentrate their ene-my's forces against them, two of the cardinal strategic errors that inevitably lead to disaster.

On Friday afternoon, fifty protesters arrived outside the Gage Park office of the Halvorsen Realty Company, fully intending to stay there until Saturday morning. Once darkness fell, the demonstrators realized that they had miscalculated when a mob of 1,000 angry counter-demonstrators surrounded them and began taunting them and pelting them with missiles of various sorts. When it became clear that the police were incapable of pro-tecting the demonstrators, they persuaded them to break off their protest, which the pro-testers did, retreating to their cars under a hail of rocks and bottles.

The protesters responded to Friday's failure by redoubling their efforts. This time instead of fifty demonstrators, they marched 500 into the neighborhood itself, creating another hostile mob which again unleashed another barrage of rocks and bottles, which this time hit both Al Raby and Jesse Jackson. The march, like similar marches in the South, had a component of psychological warfare added to it as well. The conventional accounts mention the fact that an "interracial picnic" in a local park preceded the march. Missing from those accounts was the fact that the interracial picnic involved interracial couples as well, invariably a white woman and a black male. The purpose was to demoralize the locals by proclaiming, "see we can sleep with your women; you have been defeated," a message which was accentuated by the fact that some of the women pretended to be pregnant by wearing pillows under their dresses.

Whatever its intended effect, the tactic backfired, primarily because the Poles of Gage Park still did not consider themselves white, certainly not in the sense that the people in the South did. As a result, they did not see the blacks as sleeping with *their* women. Instead, they saw a horde of black "outsiders" consorting with a group of equally suspect "white" outsiders, who might have been Protestants or Jews or misguided Irishmen. The fact that they were white did not lead the natives to assume that they were Poles. As a result the main effect of this attempt at psychological warfare backfired. Instead of demoralizing the community, it united it against the outside agitators who were perceived as alien invaders no matter what their skin color.

The same thing happened when Martin Luther King arrived back in town to lead the march against the Lithuanians in Marquette Park. King stepped out of his car and was almost immediately hit on the head with a rock, a blow which dropped him to his knees. The SCLC protesters were now in the unfortunate position of redoubling their efforts to win a campaign that had already failed when they attempted it in Gage Park. The Lithuanians in Marquette Park not only knew what to expect; they were fighting on their own territory, with the added psychological advantage of knowing that they were defending their own homes. The result was the same sort of disaster which had occurred at Gage Park. After the protesters parked their cars and marched off into the neighborhood to protest the fact that the people who lived there lived there, the Lithuanians located the easily identifiable cars of the outsiders who had just driven into the neighborhood and then dropped lighted flares in their gas tanks. The ensuing fires further demoralized the protesters by attacking them from the rear and cutting off, at least symbolically, their ability to retreat. No army, not even a nonviolent army, can fight when its back is threatened. It instinctively has to turn around. All in all, fifteen automobiles were torched before the police brought the area under control. One policeman's clearest memory of the Marquette Park march was Al Raby running for his life down 71st Street.

The police, in other words, were the only thing between the quixotic demonstrators and injury or death. The Vice Lords, the Cobras, and the Blackstone Rangers, whom King had persuaded to come along as "marshals," were as intimidated by the rage of the crowd as Al Raby and so found the transition to nonviolence easier than expected. As a result of their sudden conversion, they provided no protection for the SCLC demonstrators. Instead of writing the police a letter of thanks for saving their lives, the Quakers complained about the fact that the police fraternized with the people from their neighborhood. The police, in other words, were more sympathetic to the people of Chicago they were paid to protect, than the people from New York and Alabama who had provoked the violence by their march. "It was obvious," sniffed AFSC executive director Kale Williams, "that some officers were torn between their duty and their identity with their friends and neighbors in the crowd."[11] Williams also complained about "friendly exchanges"[12] between the police and "obvious breakers of the law" to Police Superintendent Orlando W. Wilson, who must have found it odd to hear a Quaker complain about police being "friendly."

The best the SCLC could rescue from the march was a sense of itself as an aggrieved victim, a perception which spread through the media accounts and persists as a result in historical accounts of the march. Martin Luther King would later say that he "had expected some hostility, but not of this enormity."[13] In spite of the fact that he had been engaging in protests for over ten years, King had to admit that Chicago was different; he had "never seen anything so hostile and so hateful" in the South "as I've seen here today."[14] But King failed to recognize that he had changed the rules of the game. If he had come to Chicago to run a voter-registration campaign, his reception might have been less hostile. If he had gone down south to promote the type of racial succession that had been driving people out of their homes since the end of World War II, he might have received a different kind of reception there too.

But the mistakes associated with the ill-fated marches involved more than cuts and bruises and the loss of some automobiles. King's marches and the disorder they were spreading were beginning to alienate the average Chicago resident, but more importantly they were beginning to unite the city's Catholics. Shortly after the riots in Marquette Park, Father John Egan, the man who had written the article criticizing the University of Chicago's scheme to drive blacks out of Hyde Park, gave the AFSC's Kale Williams a call and told him that Archbishop Cody felt that St. Gaul's Catholic Church, the parish church for Marquette Park, had been unfairly singled out for criticism. Egan went on to tell Williams that if "this continued much longer," Cody would "publicly and officially pull out of the civil rights movement"[15] that was sponsoring the marches.

The prospect of Cody abandoning the Catholic Interracial Council and aligning himself with the ethnic parishes which were under assault sent a wave of panic through the Chicago Freedom Movement, and understandably so. The Quakers had been cultivating the CIC as a Catholic fifth column for fifteen years, and now when they needed Catholic support the most, it looked as if Cody were becoming aware that the CIC might not be representing Catholic interests in the matter. As a result of Egan's call, "everybody" at the AFSC "began madly scurrying around trying to set up meetings between Bishop Cody and Dr. King and Al Raby, between the pastor of St. Gaul's Church and Dr. King and in general attempting to straighten out the situation."[16]

The Quakers clearly did not want to lose the leverage with Cody which John McDermott and the CIC provided for them, but by mid-August they had pursued their ill-conceived plan of marching through Chicago's ethnic neighborhoods with such stubborn determination that a break was inevitable. On August 12, Archbishop Cody announced that he had had enough. He called publicly for an end to the demonstrations. There is every indication that the Quakers had been planning for this eventuality and were ready to go ahead without Cody as part of their coalition. In a press release in their files dated September 1966, the Quakers attacked Cody and the Catholics openly, deploring

> the fact that at no time has the Archbishop publicly or privately censured those Catholics who were responsible for the un-Christian and criminal behavior in the communities visited in recent weeks. We would request that the Archbishop begin fulfilling his responsibilities immediately by leading his fellow Christians in a march with the leaders of the Chicago civil rights movement, and by educating the mis-guided Catholics in his diocese.[17]

It is not clear whether the Quakers ever released this statement. If they had, its effect on Chicago's "mis-guided Catholics" would have been clear, and probably not what the Quakers had wished for.

Two days after Cody pulled out of the coalition, Jesse Jackson led a march in Bogan that was even more disastrous than the marches in Marquette and Gage Parks. The marches were becoming predictable, and that meant, according to a report the Quakers filed on the march that "the white crowd were [sic] evidently quite prepared for us."[18] As some sign of the fact that they knew what to expect, the counter-demonstrators in Bogan were holding signs which had been professionally printed. "On the whole," the Quaker correspondent wrote, "they seemed to have organized quite well to give us a proper reception."[19]

The SCLC marchers, by repeating the same mistake again and again, were beginning to fragment their own coalition. The Catholic archdiocese was the first major defection, but as the marches continued during August other fault lines began to appear. After the ill-fated march on Bogan, the Quakers began to look on Jesse Jackson as a publicity hound who was constantly putting himself "in the forefront of the picture" by "speaking at various places," but "in order to do this of course he is neglecting his organizing duties."[20]

During a meeting of the agenda committee, which was two-thirds of the way over before King and Andrew Young arrived, John McDermott and Bernard Lafayette complained about the way the coalition's organization was being run, with McDermott opining that "sitting around and singing is great but it doesn't get any work done."[21] McDermott's remark struck a chord with Maria Pappalardo of the AFSC, who felt what he said was "certainly in line with the opinion of their work that I have heard among AFSC people."[22] A consensus was emerging that the "SCLC is not doing the job it's supposed to be doing; they are not out organizing and they hang around the office too much."[23] SCLC shiftlessness was threatening the very nature of the coalition. It was one thing for Archbishop Cody to drop out, but a split between the AFSC and the SCLC was a fatal split which would have doomed the movement.

On Wednesday July 26, Maria Pappalardo entered a coffee shop on Chicago's southwest side in order to get out of the rain and have a cup of coffee when she discovered that Al Raby, Bill Moyer, Al Pitcher, Bernard Lafayette, and Dick Murray were "holding a meeting" in one of the coffee-shop booths. The subject of the meeting was the growing split between the SCLC and the AFSC over the direction the Summer of Freedom was taking (or not taking) as the demonstrations ran into increasing opposition. It was during this meeting that Pappalardo discovered for the first time what she termed "the Lafayette Plan," her term for the Quaker strategy for destabilizing neighborhoods on Chicago's southwest side. The plan got expressed as part of the dissatisfaction the Quakers were feeling with the SCLC and the increasingly disastrous results of the marches through the neighborhoods. Lafayette complained that "Bevel and the others [at the SCLC] are still using the strategy of the South and that this strategy simply does not work in Chicago."[24] It wasn't working because "in the South there is a real sense of community. Everybody knows everybody else"[25] that was lacking in the North. As a result the peer pressure and shame that public demonstrations generated in communities like that had no purchase on the tightly knit ethnic communities of Chicago, which were in many ways worlds unto themselves. As a result of collaborating with King on his campaign of public demonstration, Bill Moyer felt that the Quakers were neglecting the much more effective strategy of clandestine move-ins, which had leveled off over the past few years. Worse than that, the public demonstrations were making the Catholics, who were the main target of the move-ins, aware that something was afoot and, therefore, more resistant to moving.

To make matters worse, King struck Lafayette "and many of the others" presumably at the AFSC as "out of touch with the community level events and sentiment."[26] As the Freedom Summer campaign of 1966 went from bad to worse, King began to feel under pressure to produce some tangible result for what was an enormous expenditure of resources, and since "he is feeling pressure himself [he] is exerting pressure on the movement to have more direct action, more mass meetings, more demonstrations, a more dramatic phase of the Union to End Slums in Chicago."[27]

In other words, the more he failed to achieve his goal, the more King redoubled his efforts along the same lines which caused the failure in the first place. Lafayette, on the other hand, had become convinced that what had succeeded in the South was not going to succeed in the North and "pointed to the fact that the South and the North are two different sets of situations" as evidence for his conclusion. "Things are faster and easier in the South and in this line and things are more complex and will therefore proceed slower in the urban north." King and Raby, in other words, favored "concentrating on hot areas, mass movement and dramatic confrontations."[28] The Lafayette Plan, on the other hand, favored the clandestine Quaker approach based on move-ins, and Lafayette was now convinced that King's southern strategy was jeopardizing whatever gains the Quakers had already made in the Chicago area. King's tactics ran the danger of making Catholics aware of the clandestine campaign that had already driven so many of them out of their neighborhoods. If they knew what was going on, they could stop it as effectively as they were in stopping King's kamikaze-style marches. Unless the AFSC and SCLC differences got resolved, it was clear that the movement was about to fall apart.

Unaware of the tensions that were developing in the civil rights camp, Mayor Daley rescued Martin Luther King and his followers from the consequences of their own misguided actions by agreeing to sit down with him and negotiate on August 17. In doing this, Daley was ignoring his own advice. When a group of community leaders came to him to complain about the disruption the protesters had brought to their neighborhood, Daley advised them to "ignore the marchers and they'll go away," which is precisely what he was not doing.

The main reason that Daley ignored his own advice is that Al Raby was threatening to march in Cicero, "the impregnable suburban enclave of Slavic exclusivism."[29] The formulation was more than a little risible. If there were ever an oxymoron in the history of American housing policy, it was "Slavic exclusivism." In general a neighborhood that was Slavic was not exclusive, and vice versa. Beyond that, no black in his right mind would want to live in a suburb, much less a Slavic suburb, which threatened life and limb. By stating the situation in its naked ethnic dimensions, the commentator de-mystified it as well. "White exclusivism" made sense, but "Slavic exclusivism" did not, because for the most part the only people who wanted to live in Slavic neighborhoods were Slavs.

In focusing on Cicero, however, King and Raby brought the civil-rights movement back to its roots in Louis Wirth's campaign against the ethnics and the Quaker-CIC-

Marshal Fields Cicero Project, but with a new twist. Now they were going to add the Southern civil-rights strategy of frontal assault to an area already known for its violence when move-ins were clandestine or accidental. Cicero had no attraction for Chicago's black population, but it had taken on a symbolism for the Quakers and the rest of the liberal environmentalist establishment since it had successfully resisted integration in 1951. It symbolized ethnic resistance to the forces of social engineering, and that was why Al Raby was proposing to march there. Success in Cicero promised large financial rewards from foundations like the Ford and Marshall Fields Foundations, which had funded the first Cicero project in the early '50s.

But Raby and King had other reasons as well. Cicero promised to make Marquette Park look like a Sunday-school picnic by comparison. The Nazis and the Klan had been organizing in Cicero. The potential for violence and death was very real. So in the end the threat to march in Cicero was a test of who was willing to risk the greater violence to achieve its ends. According to the Quakers who were monitoring the civil-rights meetings at time, Al Sansom said it was "time to turn Cicero into Selma and make the whole movement a national thing right now."[30] In other words, the mayhem resulting from a march into Cicero plays well in the press and brings more sympathy and money to the movement.

Confronted with the threat, the commissioners on the Chicago Commission on Human Relations agreed to set up a meeting between the mayor, the civil-rights leaders, and the Chicago Real Estate Board. Daley decided to accept their recommendation and agreed to a "summit meeting" with the civil-rights movement, but just to make sure that Chicago would be spared further disorder, Daley got an injunction limiting further demonstrations within city limits on August 19. Since the injunction only covered Chicago, the threat to march on Cicero, which was outside city limits, took on greater significance for both sides.

At 10:00 PM on Friday August 19, Mayor Daley went to television to explain the terms of the injunction to the people of Chicago. Robert W. Spike and the rest of the SCLC/AFSC team of negotiators were furious when they heard about the injunction and what they considered the city's double-dealing in the matter. They now contemplated defying the injunction and marching in South Deering, home of the Trumbull Park disturbances twelve years before, but it was clear that their maneuvering room was becoming more and more constricted. Any serious expansion of demonstrations would violate the injunction and would shift the issue from nondiscrimination in housing to "law and order," a shift that would not be in the movement's favor.

On the morning of Saturday, August 20, the Agenda Committee met to come up with a reaction to the injunction. King gave some indication of the constraints the movement now faced, by claiming that "we do not have the federal courts, the Supreme Court in particular, behind us as we did in the South."[31] Apparently, the disorder the demonstrations were causing in the North in general and in Chicago in particular was giving the normally supportive Black/Douglas faction on the Supreme Court pause. King "pointed out that in recent months Justice Hugo Black has been down on the demonstration cases."[32] The Supreme Court had created the civil-rights movement by handing down *Brown v. Board of Education* in 1954, but now there was some indication that they felt it had gone far enough, at least according to King, who felt that Hugo Black was "no longer with us." As a result King was "not very hopeful that this injunction will rapidly move through the state and federal courts and on up to the Supreme Court." Nor did King feel "sure of a favorable decision" once "it reaches the Supreme Court."[33] That meant that Cicero became more important than ever.

The only trouble with the Cicero strategy was the fact that the SCLC simply lacked the political equivalent of force to bring it off. Once again the movement was pursuing a strategy of attacking ever-more-secure positions with an ever-dwindling amount of force. In addition to that, the injunction had narrowed the possible scope of their attack so much that it contained no element of surprise whatsoever. Had Daley allowed the marchers to follow through on their threat to march in Cicero, he might have brought about the complete destruction of the movement in Chicago. "Even sympathetic observers," according to one account, "were beginning to believe that Martin was heading for a Donnybrook in Chicago."[34] Andy Young was "openly worried" because "we haven't been able to put on enough pressure yet. In Birmingham and Selma we almost needed martial law before we got anywhere."[35] On the other hand, the violence which was sure to occur in Cicero could have been laid at Daley's feet in the mind of the public, and most certainly would have in any media account of what happened. Both sides, as a result, were unsure of how far to push the envelope.

After considering its options, the SCLC decided to press the threat of confrontation as far as it would go. "The Movement," according to one account, "finally concluded that, if success could come only through the peril of supreme social crisis, it must euchre out city hall with a final dangerous play, the Cicero march."[36] On Thursday night, King announced to the mass meeting being held at New Liberty Baptist Church that "no one is going to turn me around at this point." After the mob roared back its approval, King continued by saying that "we can walk in outer space, but we can't walk in the streets of Cicero without the National Guard."[37] King as usual whipped the mob into a frenzy to the point where they were ready to march out the door to Cicero that very night. The SCLC further inflamed the crowd by constantly reminding the black community that Jerome Huey, a black youth, had been murdered there in May. The march was portrayed as something that would avenge this martyr's death.

That frenzy was, as King predicted, causing concern among the people responsible for preserving order. The black man whose attempted move in had set off a riot in Cicero in 1951 appeared on CBS Television and announced "I'm scared to death. I don't know what will happen."[38] Joining him in expressing concern, the sheriff of Cook County opined that the march was suicidal. Governor Kerner put the state police and National Guard on alert. City Hall, Archbishop Cody, and other Progressive whites begged King to call the march off. King was becoming delusional. Ignoring the warnings of an impending bloodbath, he was claiming that "not only are we going to walk to Cicero, we're going to work in Cicero, we're going to live in Cicero."[39] The fact that someone might die in Cicero eventually brought Daley to the point where he felt he had to agree to King's demands and come up with an agreement that provided closure to that summer's chain of increasingly disruptive events.

After two and a half hours of wrangling on August 26, both sides announced that they had reached what would come to be known as the "Summit Agreement." According to its terms, Chicago's Commission on Human Rights would require real-estate brokers to post a summary of the city's open-housing policy, and the city itself would redouble efforts to enforce it and to encourage state housing legislation; the Chicago Real Estate Board, which had been lobbying against such a bill, would no longer do so (though it refused to drop a legal battle it was waging against Chicago's own fair-housing ordinance).

King hailed the agreement as "the most significant program ever conceived to make open housing a reality in the metropolitan area,"[40] but the euphoria following it was short-lived when King's supporters realized that the agreement mentioned no specific timetable to achieve its goals. Mayor Daley was equally effusive, calling the summit agreement "a great day" for Chicago. Daley had more reason to be effusive than King. He knew that since King was from out of town, the implementation of the agreement would take place in his absence, long after the revolutionary passions he had evoked to get the agreement had cooled down, a fact which was causing visible consternation among King's support-ers. Lafayette was upset because he felt the agreement was unenforceable. Writing on September 2, Maria Pappalardo claimed that "those people on a negotiating committee bill felt King really did not have the expertise and experience to really understand the real estate system and its relationship to open housing."[41] As a result, "Jesse Jackson is upset with [the agreement]; Bernard [Lafayette] is upset with it," and "there is a major dissent with the agreement and with what it really accomplished."[42]

Many of the people Pappalardo was talking to felt that King was "running scared"[43] and signed the agreement as a graceful way of getting out of town. Monroe Sharp stated, "We reject the terms of the agreement that Martin Luther King made. The rank and file Negro is a new breed of cat who rejects this."[44] On Wednesday, August 31, King was booed at the New Liberty Baptist Church when he tried to explain the agreement to the people ready to march out the door on Cicero a week before. It was a new experience for King; he had never been heckled by his own people before. The passions which he aroused found no resolution in the agreement he secured.

On September 4, in defiance of his leadership, a rump group composed largely of CORE and SNCC workers managed to round up 200 people and send themto Cicero, accompanied by 2,700 National Guard troops and 700 police who were more or less suc-cessful in keeping the much larger crowd of counter-demonstrators from killing them. When it became apparent that the march was going nowhere, the demonstrators beat a retreat under a steady barrage of rocks and bottles. The CCCO later termed the march "a pathetic little show of petulance,"[45] which resulted in thirty-nine arrests, fourteen serious injuries, but no deaths, an outcome which might have been different if King had led a larg-er force into Cicero. King was clearly shaken by his experience in Chicago. Except for Operation Breadbasket, "almost everybody involved in the Chicago Freedom Movement wrote it off as a failure."[46] That failure left King depressed and feeling that "he didn't know where he was going from here."[47] Three months after the conclusion of the agree-ment, the Quakers came to the conclusion that "the agreement is being ignored" because "it appears that little has been done to implement the agreement."[48] The Quakers in their usual passive/aggressive fashion laid the blame for this defeat at the feet of the SCLC, whose "long term commitment to Chicago was doubted by many both within and outside the Movement."[49]

Bernard Lafayette was just as pessimistic in his own assessment of that summer's activities. On December 4, 1966, Lafayette wrote his own post mortem concluding that "we now see that it is very difficult to implement this summer's demands, given the political economic and social patterns of Metropolitan Chicago."[50] Lafayette found that he had become the scapegoat for the debacle: "I have yet to find the person who is more criticized than myself about what happened this summer."[51] But on the positive side, Lafayette could say that he learned something about how teen-age gangs can be brought into the struggle. The events in Chicago during the summer of 1966 dispelled "the myth that teen-age gang members cannot practice nonviolence."[52] Lafayette gave no indication of what he planned to do with this new bit of information, but gangs would play a crucial role in the ethnic cleansing of Most Blessed Sacrament Parish in southwest Philadelphia, beginning in the same summer as King's abortive attempt to change housing patterns in Chicago.

Ultimately, the only consolation the Quakers could derive from what was a very expensive lesson in the school of experience was the fact that "the format of a Movement which was tested in Chicago in 1966 may spread to other areas."[53] On August 18, Maria Pappalardo reported that Julius Griffin, fresh from a "Black Power meeting in New York," announced that "everyone there had their eyes on Chicago."[54]

One of those New Yorkers was evidently McGeorge Bundy, who had taken over the reins of the Ford Foundation at around the same time that Martin Luther King had made his first contact with Chicago's gangs. Bundy came to Ford at John McCloy's bidding. When he arrived there, one of the first things he did was meet with Paul Ylvisaker and tell him that his Gray Areas Programs were "the only shop that survives [at the Ford Foundation] as having any relevance."[55] That fact, combined with the fact that Bundy eventually got rid of Ylvisaker at Ford, indicates that Bundy came to Ford to take over the Gray Areas Programs and take them to the next level.

In spite of King's fame, which began in the '50s after he organized the bus boycott in Montgomery, and in spite of the fact that Ford virtually ran the civil-rights movement, King and the SCLC did not receive their first grant from the Ford Foundation until 1967, which is to say after King's assault on Chicago and after Mac Bundy arrived at Ford. The terms of that grant indicate that Bundy planned to export the sort of social disorder which King visited on Chicago to fifteen other cities of the North. It also indicated that the real interest of people like Bundy and McCloy was the cities of the North where the blacks were in confrontation with Catholic ethnics, as they were in Chicago. One of Bundy's grants went to Cleveland, where it led to a debacle similar to the one King had brought about in Chicago. It was the fallout from the Cleveland grant which prompted Ylvisaker to say that Bundy hadn't done his homework. But that was just another way of saying that Bundy had decided on a much more aggressive attack on ethnic neighborhoods than Ylvisaker was comfortable with mounting, which may be one of the reasons why McCloy felt that Bundy was needed at Ford and why Bundy felt that Ylvisaker had to go shortly after he arrived.

In spite of presiding over what was generally perceived as a dismal failure in the eyes of the people involved in it, King had proved himself in Bundy's eyes by what he did in

Chicago, and Bundy planned to reward him with a $230,000 grant. This was not going to be another grant to train teenagers in electronics. It was instead given to the SCLC "for sessions to train ten black ministers from each of fifteen cities in community organizing and nonviolent tactics."[56] "Nonviolent tactics" had by now become a synonym for irregular warfare. In other words, Bundy, who had been Kennedy's chief of staff when Kennedy got the government involved in guerrilla warfare, wanted to set up cadres in fifteen cities in the north with large ethnic and black populations which could create the same sort of social disorder which King had created in Chicago during the summer of 1966. When King met with the Ford people in New York to negotiate the grant, he promised them "that the project would generate a nationwide cadre of activists whom SCLC could call upon in future protests"[57] and it was on precisely those terms and for those ends that Ford gave King and the SCLC the grant.

Notes

1 David J. Garrow, *Bearing the Cross: Martin Luther King, Jr., and the Southern Christian Leadership Conference* (New York: William Morrow and Company, 1986), p. 493.

2 Stephen B. Oates, *Let the Trumpet Sound: The Life of Martin Luther King, Jr.* (New York: Harper & Row), 1982), p. 408.

3 Ibid., p. 410.

4 Ibid.

5 Ibid.

6 Chicago Report by Marie Pappalardo, Final Dispatch on Chicago by Kale Williams, Bernard LaFayette, William Moyer, Maria Pappalardo 11/22/66, p. 11, AFSC CRD, 1966, AFSC Archives..

7 Ibid.

8 Oates, p. 411.

9 Garrow, p. 504

10 Ibid.

11 Ibid., p. 499.

12 Ibid.

13 Ibid. p. 500.

14 Ibid.

15 Chicago Debriefing 7/29/66 Maria Pappalardo to Barbara Moffett, Charlotte Meacham, etc., meeting of the agenda committee, AFSC CRD Housing, 1966, AFSC Papers.

16 Ibid.

17 No title notice, September 1966, AFSC CRD Housing, 1966, AFSC Papers.

18 Chicago Debriefing 7/29/66 Maria Pappalardo to Barbara Moffett, Charlotte Meacham, etc.

19 Ibid.

20 Ibid.

21 Ibid.

22 Ibid.

23 Ibid.

24 Ibid.

25 Ibid.

26 Ibid.

27 Ibid.

28 Chicago Debriefing 7/29/66 Maria Pappalardo to Barbara Moffett, Charlotte Meacham, etc.

29 David L. Lewis, *King: A Critical Biography* (New York: Praeger, 1970), p. 340.

30 Chicago: The "Movement" in the Urban North, AFSC CRD Housing, 1966, AFSC Archives.

31 Chicago Debriefing 7/29/66 Maria Pappalardo to Barbara Moffett, Charlotte Meacham, etc.

32 Ibid.

33 Ibid.

34 Lewis, p. 343.

35 Ibid.

36 Ibid.

37 Ibid., p. 344.

38 Oates, p. 414.

39 Ibid.

40 Ibid.

41 Chicago Logs, 9/2/66, Maria Pappalardo, AFSC CRD Housing 1966, AFSC Archives.

42 Ibid.

43 Lewis, p. 348.

44 Ibid.

45 Garrow, p. 529.

46 Oates, p. 417.

47 Ibid., p. 419.

48 Chicago Report by Marie Pappalardo, AFSC CRD Housing, 1966, AFSC Archives.

49 Ibid.

50 Chicago: The "Movement" in the Urban North.

51 Ibid.

52 Appeal for Support of Urban Community Relations Work, September 1966, AFSC CRD Housing, 1966, AFSC Archives.

53 Final Dispatch on Chicago by Kale Williams, Bernard LaFayette, William Moyer, Maria Pappalardo 11/22/66.

54 Chicago Debriefing 7/29/66 Maria Pappalardo to Barbara Moffett, Charlotte Meacham, etc.

55 Oral History for Ford Foundation, conducted 9/27/73, Ylvisaker papers, Box 5, Harvard University Archives.

56 Garrow, p. 581.

57 Ibid.

Ed Logue and the Ford Foundation

At 6:02 PM on April 4, 1968, James Earl Ray shot Martin Luther King, who was standing at the time on a balcony of the Lorraine Motel in Memphis, Tennessee. King died on the balcony of his motel room and, with him, whatever hope for racial reconciliation the country had associated with his name. King was a master at manipulating black passions, but his rhetoric was also imbued with the language of the Christian gospels, which, no matter how unsuccessfully in any particular instance, acted in general as a brake on the full implementation of that passion. Now that brake was gone, and the nation braced itself for a repeat of the riots which had occurred in Detroit and Newark during the summer of 1967, except that this time no one expected the riots to hold off until the summer. The danger in the wake of King's death is that they would happen within hours, and it was up to those who were responsible for preserving order in the nation's largest cities to see that that didn't happen.

Kevin White had taken office as mayor of Boston barely ninety days before King was shot. He heard the news while watching *Gone with the Wind* at a local movie theater. After some hesitation, White decided to return to his office, where reports of the first disturbances were now crackling over the police radio. Shortly after 9:00 PM White got word from his police superintendent that a black mob had surrounded a bus full of whites on Blue Hill Road, in a neighborhood that was once Jewish but now in the throes of racial change. Any one of these incidents could have become the spark that set off a city-wide conflagration, and it was up to White to figure out which spark that was going to be and what he was going to do to put it out.

After spending the night partially listening to police reports and partially in fitful sleep, White got a call a little after 9:00 AM concerning the incident which looked as if it might provide the spark White feared. James Brown, the rhythm-and-blues singer who would later term himself "the Godfather of Soul" after his career had stalled, was scheduled to give a concert that night at Boston Garden, but the Garden, fearing violence because of the mood among the city's blacks, canceled the concert, which in turn conjured visions in the mayor's minds of disappointed and disgruntled James Brown fans igniting a riot in the center of town that would send the recent attempt to rehabilitate it after the suburban exodus of the '50s up in smoke. White got the concert re-scheduled, but, understanding the power that television had to anesthetize large segments of the population, he arranged to have it televised over WGBH, Boston's public television channel as well. The decision to televise the concert created contractual conflicts for Brown, who had already signed an exclusive TV contract with another outlet. Brown's refusal to perform on TV threatened to jeopardize the whole deal, until at the last minute his legal scruples were anesthetized by a promise from Mayor White of a fee of $60,000.

The riot which the city feared never materialized, but in the aftermath of the James Brown concert Kevin White was forced to come up with $60,000 which the city did not have. That meant turning to the people who had money in Boston, and that meant turning to an exclusive club of WASP Brahmins which met on a regular basis in one of Boston's banks. It was known as "The Vault."

John Collins, White's predecessor, had met with the Vault every other Thursday at 4:00 PM in the boardroom of the Boston Safe Deposit and Trust Company. White's reluctance to meet with the same group of people arose from the fact that the Vault, in many ways the most influential representatives of Boston's WASP establishment, had supported Collins's handpicked successor in the mayoral race of 1967 when Collins had declined to run for re-election. That man's name was Ed Logue, a Philadelphia native who had made a name for himself while directing one of the country's most dramatic urban-renewal schemes in New Haven, Connecticut. Logue was the Vault's candidate because he supported the Vault's policies and interests, and, in Boston, that meant urban renewal, which meant pursuing high-profile, high-dollar projects in the central business district, while at the same time ignoring and sometimes even cannibalizing the city's ethnic neighborhoods to make it happen.

During the 1950s, Boston's suburban population increased by 50 percent. Just about all of the suburban growth spurt was caused by the construction of Route 128, the first stage in the area's projected freeway system. The new road attracted new development like a magnet. In a little over two years – between March of 1954 and June of 1956 – sixty-eight new plants comprising 4.5 million square feet of space were built along Route 128. By 1963, the number of plants had grown to 400, many of them start-up companies based on developments in electronics, which were in turn based on discoveries made at laboratories funded by the federal government at places like MIT. The move, which was financed by old-line Brahmin banks and arranged largely by development companies like Cabot, Cabot and Forbes, created an economic boom in line with the principles established by the War Production Board, which is to say the suburbs profited at the expense of the cities and the people who lived there.

In Boston, as in other cities like it, that meant at the expense of the Catholic ethnic working-class population of the city. During the same period in which suburban employment grew by 22 percent, Boston's employment dropped by 7.7 percent. That drop would affect the central business district, which, as in Chicago, soon came up with a plan to recoup its losses, but it affected even more severely the "inner ring of old, dense, ethnic neighborhoods,"[1] which could not come up with a plan to deal with the new situation the migration of jobs from the city created. That meant that neighborhoods like Roxbury/North Dorchester, the South End, Charlestown, and South Boston would be forced to finance the revitalization of the central business district at their own expense, all the while being robbed of the political power that was being eroded by the disappearance of good jobs to the suburbs. "About half the city's population decline" during the '50s, "came from these four neighborhoods,"[2] according to Mollenkopf. That population decline was hastened by black migration from the South, "which hastened the whites' departure and raised fears of declining property values"[3]:

> According to Boston's 1950 General Plan, 1,100 of Boston's 16,000 acres of residential land were severely substandard and deserving of clearance. These acres

were concentrated in the South End, Roxbury, Charlestown, and South Boston. Remarking on the West End, which became the city's first slum clearance project, the 1950 Plan observed that "such an environment undoubtedly impairs the mental and physical health of its inhabitants."[4]

In order to understand the forces that were changing the configuration of every large city in the United States at the time, and in order to ensure that those changes did not jeopardize their interests, the same WASP establishment which made up the Vault created a more exoteric forum to debate the same issues from the same point of view. Founded by the dean of Boston College's School of Business Administration in 1954, this group, which came to be known as the Boston College Citizen Seminars, would meet every other month for the next decade in order to debate policies of crucial interest to the city of Boston. The fact that these seminars were funded by the Ford Foundation gives some indication of the interests they would come to represent, as well as how seamlessly they would flow into Boston's implementation of the Ford Foundation's Gray Areas Programs during the 1960s. The purpose of the seminars was to create consensus among the city's WASP establishment and then "unite the forces we represent in a program of action."[5]

One of the action programs the BC Citizen Seminars united around was urban renewal, and one of the first people they recruited to their cause was "Whispering Johnny" Hynes, Michael Curley's successor as mayor of Boston. Mayor Hynes's nickname came from his low-key approach to volatile issues and his amenability to the groups which Curley so successfully antagonized. Hynes, not surprisingly, became an advocate of urban renewal, feeling that "the only way the decay and blight may be uprooted" was "by a complete physical change in the affected neighborhood or area."[6] The participation of the Ford Foundation, whose program would later be taken over by the federal government, coupled with federal funding, coupled with the ethnic homogeneity of the WASP business class and the housing "experts" who represented their interests insured that what was perceived as successful in one city would get replicated in others.

In the case of Boston's elite, Pittsburgh's Allegheny Conference provided the model whereby a city with a "Democratic mayor" recognized that collaborating with "Republican businessmen" was "good politics," especially when it meant that "petty differences must be cleaned out with the slums."[7] Reference to "petty differences" was the Ford Foundation's way of talking about ethnic interests, as represented by "machine" politicians who needed to be enlightened by "experts" about tearing down neighborhoods which needed "complete physical change" no matter whether the people who lived there thought that change was necessary or not. Philadelphia sent representatives to the BC seminars, as did New Haven, Connecticut, which was then being renewed by Ed Logue, a Philadelphian who would soon end up in Boston.

By the time Logue stepped down as head of the Boston Redevelopment Authority in 1967, the organization he directed had presided over the destruction of 9,718 low-rent units in the city. As in every other place where urban renewal was implemented, that housing was replaced by fewer units than it destroyed – in this case, 3,500 new units, leaving a shortfall of some 6,000 dwellings, and displacing in the process 22,000 people, who, as in cities like Detroit, were often black and determined to find housing in the next ethnic neighborhood. Urban renewal, in other words, exacerbated the very problem it was supposed to solve. Boston was no exception to this rule. Boston's business elite loved urban renewal in general and Logue in particular because both converted what they considered obsolete housing for people in need of socialization and assimilation into economic power for them and their friends. During his tenure as head of the BRA, Logue brought $500 million in office-building investment into Boston's central business district. But he did so at a price, and, as was so often the case, the bill would come due after he had left the scene. The social costs for that expansion of downtown business interests at the expense of the ethnic neighborhoods would come due ironically on the watch of Kevin White, the man who defeated Logue in his run for mayor in 1967.

But during the heyday of the BC seminars, no one was counting those costs. Needless to say, "persons who represent the highest level of economic power in the community" agreed wholeheartedly with Hynes and, hearing tales about the "sparkling leadership of Robert Moses"[8] and what he was accomplishing in New York City, they soon began to agitate for the wholesale destruction of housing in areas which the suburban exodus had left behind but which, because of their location and proximity to downtown, were intrinsically valuable pieces of real estate.

One of these neighborhoods was known as the West End, a decidedly ethnic and predominantly Italian neighborhood too close to downtown for its own good. (Italians accounted for 46 percent of the West End in the 1950s, while Poles, Jews, and Irish made up 11 percent, 10 percent, and 5 percent respectively.)[9] In 1950 in response to the federal housing bill of the year before, the Boston Housing Authority applied for preliminary-planning funds to study possible "redevelopment" of the West End, South End, and Roxbury. The study began in 1951, and in April 1953, the BHA announced that it had decided to proceed with the West End. By 1956, two years after the seminars at Boston College began, Boston received a Model Cities grant of $11 million from the Eisenhower Administration to promote "urban renewal" there. One year later, Mayor Hynes and Boston's city council approved the project. Then in October of 1957, the Boston Housing Authority surrendered its authority over the project to the newly constituted Boston Redevelopment Authority, which began holding hearings on the demolition of the neighborhood almost immediately. In spite of overwhelming opposition to the project from the West End's residents, the BRA decided to proceed because it felt that the project had gone too far to stop. In January of 1958, the city and the federal government signed the contracts which enabled the condemnation and clearing of the land. In April of 1958, the city announced its plans to demolish the neighborhood, and by November of the same year 1,200 of the neighborhood's 2,700 houses had been razed.

By the summer of 1960, all of the housing was gone; the only thing left standing was a museum housing Yankee artifacts and a Catholic Church, which now had no parishioners to serve. As the neighborhood emptied out, arson and vandalism increased, driving those reluctant to leave away more quickly. In the end, what was supposed to take three years took only eighteen months. By the summer of 1960, the ethnic cleansing of the neighborhood was complete. In January of 1962, the first residents began to move into the new high-rise apartment buildings which the displaced residents could not afford. The West Enders were handicapped by their lack of political sophistication but also by their patriotism.

Like the Poles in Detroit, they had not read *Berman v. Parker* and felt, as a result, that their property could not be taken away from them in a democratic country like the United States. That sort of thing could happen only in Russia, under rulers like Lenin and Stalin, not under people like Mayor Hynes. Gradually, however, they began to realize that their property was simply too valuable not to be taken away from them because of its location.

When Arthur Fiedler conducted the Boston Pops for public celebrations on the banks of the Charles River, the West End was in the background. "If as they say in real estate," said Raymond Flynn, who would eventually go on to become mayor of Boston, "everything is location, location, location,"[10] then the West End was a prime piece of real estate. "It was three blocks from the State House. It had the kind of location that money can't buy."[11]

Having ignored the West End during the suburban build out following the decrees and incentives established by the War Production Board, the WASP establishment suddenly decided that it wanted this valuable piece of property back, and, in the wake of *Berman v. Parker*, they now had the legal tools to confiscate large tracts of privately owned property, if it could be termed blighted and if a plan could be concocted to remedy that blight. The rest of the operation was simple because in the wake of the federal housing bills, the money from the federal government to clear the land of buildings was already there. "The Vault," according to Ray Flynn, "wanted this to happen. The old Yankee bankers supported this, and so they did a number of things to make it happen."[12]

One of the things the Yankee establishment did was create a propaganda campaign based out of the city's premier Boston newspaper, the *Boston Globe*. Connections between the *Globe* and the Vault were easy enough to trace. Ralph Lowell, often referred to as "Mr. Boston," was chairman and president of Boston Safe, where Vault meetings were held, a member of Harvard's board of overseers, on the board of the *Globe* and an officer of forty-four other local corporations as well. He was just one of many figures on interlocking boards whose sense of public concern and ethnic self-interest were usually synonymous, and, because of his connections, Lowell was capable of putting those concerns into action. During the '60s, Tom Winship brought about a journalistic revolution in Boston by shifting the *Globe* away from being a paper which supported Catholic interests in Boston to one which actively opposed them. Winship got his start in journalism at the *Washington Post*, covering redevelopment in that city, and it was with urban renewal that the same change began to take place in Boston. By the end of the 1960s, *The Globe* would espouse every suburban WASP cause, including campaigning for liberalization of Massachusetts's birth-control laws and, most importantly, forced busing, as part of its campaign to align the paper's policies with the people who had left the city and who now, with the help of the federal government, were trying to bring the city's remaining ethnic Catholics under control. The new editors at the *Globe* were "abolitionists," and as such supported the civil-rights movement, which they, like their Yankee forbears, saw in essentially moral terms. Most of the pro-busing editorials were written by Anne C. Wyman, a Boston Brahmin from the Cabot family, who described her editorial stance as "the Cotton Mather" position, "If it's right, it's right. Once you embark on the course, there's no turning back."[13]

Boston's Catholics, however, had a difficult time seeing how the paper's positions favoring abortion, birth control, pornography, homosexual rights, and, finally, busing were "right," much less infallibly so, and eventually the *Globe* began to take on the air of an occupying propaganda ministry in the eyes of the city's ethnic Catholics. Irish youths from Southie would regularly steal copies of the *Globe* and destroy them. The Massachusetts Council of the Knights of Columbus would condemn the *Globe* for its "irreligious attitude toward all things Catholic."[14]

Winship's editorial policies reflected a change of significant magnitude from the days when Cardinal Cushing's nephew had a job in the *Globe*'s newsroom, and the beginning of the change took place over urban renewal. *The Globe* consistently backed Ed Logue's attacks on ethnic interests in the city. *The Globe* would go on to back Ed Logue in his run for mayor against Kevin White. Ray Flynn would face the same antagonism to Catholic interests from the *Globe* when he became mayor. But he remembered other incidents as well. At one point during his administration, a photographer from the *Globe* announced that he wanted to make a confession. *The Globe* had sent him to the West End, where his assignment was to empty a trashcan onto the sidewalk and take a picture of it. The paper then ran the picture as proof of how blighted the neighborhood was.[15] It was a move right out of the urban-renewal handbook. The organizers of the Better Philadelphia Exhibition in 1947 had done the same thing in three-dimensional form by placing an overflowing trashcan right at the center of their full-scale mock-up of 13th and Natrona. It was their way of showing that the rowhouse symbolized "everything that was wrong with Philadelphia."

In order to make the destruction of Boston's West End more palatable to the people living there, the Boston Housing Authority announced, as their counterparts had done when the Richard Allen Homes were announced in Philadelphia, that the residents would get a chance to get better housing. Over the course of time, that formula got changed and what got built instead were luxury apartments, which the area's residents, who were used to paying $35 a month for six-room apartments, could not afford. The man who engineered the change and the man who primarily benefited from it was Jerome Lyle Rappaport, a New Yorker who had graduated from Harvard in 1949 and chose to remain in Boston, where he led "Youth for Hynes" during the campaign that put Hynes in the mayor's office. The city sold the land to Rappaport at a fraction of its real value. That price was kept unrealistically low because Rappaport was the only man who bid on it, something that many people felt that Hynes had arranged so that his former campaign organizer could benefit from the project financially.

Finally, after pulling strings to get the land, Rappaport got the John Hancock Life Insurance Company to back the high-rise apartment buildings, which he was planning to call Charles River Park. Rappaport's ties with the mayor convinced the residents of the West End that redevelopment was really a "politically motivated plot to take the West End for private profit with government help."[16]

If so, the plot succeeded admirably. Charles River Park became one more dreary Bauhaus settlement for the city's *Nomenklatura*, just as Lafayette Park had become the same sort of settlement for Detroit's elite, and Society Hill Towers had become the same version of the same thing in Philadelphia. It was an object lesson in the type of person the city was willing to promote and, equally, in the sort of people the city was willing to punish because they had not learned their lessons in assimilation well enough.

The demolition of the West End would become a paradigm for the new politics of assimilation that came into being as government involvement in social engineering expanded during the period following World War II. Just as Johnny Hynes was the paradigm of the new more amenable Irishman and a replacement for the antagonistic, frankly ethnic approach of Michael Curley, so Jerome Rappaport was a paradigm of the new Jew, someone who had gone to Harvard, someone who knew how to manipulate the levers of federal power, and someone, most importantly, who was willing to broker his own people's interests to the city's WASP establishment in a way that the Jewish version of Michael Curley – people like Julius Ansel and Samuel "Chief" Levine – were not. In the final analysis, all of Boston's social controversies, from urban renewal in the '50s to busing in the '70s, revolved around the issue of assimilation and the WASPs' use of class and assimilation to divide the ethnic groups they wanted weakened.

Irish Catholics like Judge Arthur Garrity, the man who came up with the busing decision, found that upward mobility was dependent on internalizing WASP values and carrying them out against the interest of other Irish Catholics. Irish Catholics like Ray Flynn discovered the converse of the same truth by not carrying out those wishes. Irish Catholic politicians like Flynn and Louise Day Hicks, who represented the interests of the overwhelming majority of Irish Catholics living in the city, were marginalized by the instruments of public opinion which the WASP establishment controlled, and, as a result, they were prevented from rising to higher offices because of the role media spin played in getting elected. Nowhere was the collaboration between the ethnics, especially the Irish, and the WASP power brokers more intense than in Boston, because nowhere in the country had Irish Catholic politicians amassed such political power. The establishment had to deal with them, and they dealt with them primarily by rewarding the people who were most avid to assimilate, who in turn reciprocated by coming up with schemes like urban renewal and busing which would have been too transparent in their anti-ethnic animus if the WASP elite had chosen to run them themselves.

One of the most significant changes that took place when the BRA took over authority for the West End project from the BHA was the appointment of Monsignor Francis J. Lally to serve as chairman of the BRA board. Lally's appointment to the BRA signaled a number of things. It indicated that the BRA needed to deal with the resistance of Catholic ethnics in what was fast becoming a public-relations debacle for urban renewal. It also indicated the full support of Cardinal Cushing and the archdiocese for policies that were clearing Catholics out of the city and forcing the Church to abandon parishes of long standing. Just why the Church would agree to something like this was puzzling to the West End's Catholic population. It created a feeling on the part of many Catholics in the archdiocese that the Church was willing to barter away their interests to gain favors from the powerful. The fact that one Catholic Church in the West End was saved from demolition while the houses of that church's parishioners were not fueled this feeling, and it fueled the resentment that the WASP strategy of *divide et impera* was bound to cause among Catholics.

Lally was the editor of the archdiocesan newspaper, *The Boston Pilot*, and he used his position to denounce his fellow Catholics and upbraid them for their intolerance on a regular basis. "Lally's appointment" to the BRA, according to Kennedy, "was widely regarded as an attempt to put a human face on urban redevelopment."[17] It would have been more accurate to see his appointment as an attempt to put a Catholic face on it, because the Catholics had amassed such political power in Boston that renewal schemes would have been impossible without the Church's cooperation. It would be both unfair and inaccurate to claim that the Church, like the rest of urban renewal's proponents, was completely cynical about projects like the West End and saw in them only an attempt to appropriate valuable property from politically powerless ethnics. But it would also be naive to say that political considerations didn't play a role in the Church's deliberations. Like Whispering Johnny Hynes and Jerome Rappaport, church leadership supported assimilation, and in Boston at this time Church leadership meant Richard Cardinal Cushing, a man whose ability to protect Catholic interests was compromised by his need to borrow money from the WASP establishment which ran Boston's banks.

When Richard J. Cushing became cardinal archbishop of Boston on September 28, 1944, he inherited a see that epitomized everything Paul Blanshard had in mind when he warned Americans about the rise of Catholic power. In spite of the fact that Cushing quarreled with Blanshard publicly, he embarked upon a course that promoted assimilation in the typically Irish manner. That meant backing the Kennedy family, Boston's own paradigm of Catholic political achievement and assimilation. When a Jesuit by the name of Leonard Feeney began preaching to the city's intellectual elite during the '40s, a number of "surprising conversions" followed in places like Harvard University, following Feeney's no-compromise definition of the Catholic Church as necessary for salvation. Feeney's ideas were a threat, however, to the Catholic dream of assimilation, and when the Kennedys objected to his teachings, Cushing obliged by excommunicating Feeney. Suddenly the man believed that *"extra ecclesiam nulla salus,"* found himself *"extra ecclesiam"* for his pains. When the Vatican ratified Cushing's decision in 1953, it also ratified Cushing's beliefs on assimilation as well, as epitomized by the man from Boston who would become the nation's first Catholic president.

The downside of all this from a Catholic point of view is that Boston became not only the paradigm of Catholic political achievement; it became, as well, the paradigm of Catholic assimilation, as personified by the Kennedy family. That meant that Cushing was completely unprepared for any of the assaults on the Church that the Kennedys would collaborate on, and that included most significantly the attempts to subvert Catholic sexual principles during the 1960s. Cushing was a friend of Dr. John Rock, the Catholic doctor who invented the birth-control pill with Rockefeller money. Similarly, when Charles Curran became embroiled in a tenure battle which grew out of his subversion of Catholic sexual morals at Catholic University in the spring of 1967, Cushing failed utterly to see the big picture and portrayed it as a disagreement over teacher qualifications which he as a bishop lacked any qualification to judge even though he, as bishop, was one of the university's trustees.

Cushing was, in many ways, the typical American bishop because he was the typical American Irishman, since the Irish dominated the Catholic clergy in the United States and gave it their indelible if peculiar stamp. Just as an Italian cardinal during the Renaissance modeled himself, consciously or not, on the Italian princes of his day, so Cushing was a bishop in the mode of the Irish Catholic politician. He was certainly no intellectual. After attending the first few sessions of the Second Vatican Council and realizing that its deliberations were in Latin, he returned home, claiming he could no more follow what was going on than if the council fathers had been speaking Eskimo or Chinese.

Cushing was not only not an intellectual, he also felt inadequate in making intellectual judgments of the sort he had to make during the Curran crisis in 1967. The fact that he did not feel shy in coming down so hard on Father Feeney while essentially ignoring Father Curran, who posed a much greater threat to the Church, showed that he was more concerned with assimilation than Catholic doctrine. Curran's protest against *Humanae Vitae* one year later in 1968 was part of an orchestrated campaign on the part of the Rockefeller interests to change Catholic teaching on birth control and drive down the Catholic birth rat. In this way they would weaken Catholic political power. But Cushing essentially ignored the threat because it bespoke a desire to be accepted by American culture in a way that Feeney's ideas about membership in the Catholic Church twenty years earlier did not.

As far as Boston and the rest of the country were concerned, Cardinal Cushing in 1944 represented a new kind of bishop. He was a bishop in the flamboyant mode of Michael Curley, a man who knew how to influence public opinion like a politician and calm fears like a politician. Cushing was perfectly capable of donning an Indian headdress or any other kind of hat, no matter how incongruous, and posing for newspaper photographers. He could ride a roller coaster with a bevy of squealing nuns behind him, their veils flapping in the wind, in a calculated attempt to give Americans the impression that if he, a cardinal, could be one of them, then they had nothing to fear from ordinary Catholics. Cushing was, in other words, the consummate Irish politician from the city which gave American its first Irish Catholic politician as president.

Like politicians of the more conventional sort, Cushing raised large sums of money, but never enough to keep ahead of his ever-increasing expenditures, and so by the time the cultural revolution broke out in earnest, which is to say 1967, the same time that Kevin White got elected mayor of Boston, Cushing found himself in the uncomfortable position of being $80 million in debt and beholden to the same group of bankers that Kevin White needed to talk to when he needed to pay off James Brown. In other words, the Vault. "Boston's bankers," according to Lukas

> had come to terms with the Irish. It was the resourceful Ephron Catlin who persuaded Cushing to adopt a technique the First had employed to bail out Hollywood's troubled movie industry. The bank would loan money to the movie companies, then take its cut directly from the box office. Catlin proposed that its loans to the Archdiocese be recovered straight from the parish collection plates. "Cushing loved it," Catlin recalls. "For years he'd been looking for a way to get his hands on more of the parish money, although I don't think he liked it when I compared him to Sam Goldwyn." But soon even the First could no longer keep the Archdiocese afloat on its sea of debt. The Cardinal called on several New York banks, who refused him more credit. By 1967, his debt had reached an unprecedented $80 million. During his last decade, Cushing's obsession with money affected every diocesan activity, including efforts to grapple with the city's growing racial polarization.[18]

Cushing soon found that his desire to be liked coupled with his need for money would jeopardize his ability to defend Catholic interests in the archdiocese of Boston, especially when those interests came in conflict with the WASP ruling class which controlled the city's banks. As in cities like Philadelphia and Chicago, the WASP establishment never really abandoned its animus against Catholics, but it did express that animus in ways that Catholics who had grown up under the old nativism found bewildering. Two campaigns against the Catholic Church that were especially bewildering for someone of Cushing's generation were the racial campaign and the sexual campaign. The first was bewildering because race, as defined by American parlance, was simply not a category of any significance in Catholic thought. When the American bishops did finally issue a statement in 1958, that statement was based on the public-school desegregation crisis in Little Rock, Arkansas, an event of no particular significance to America's Catholic population, the overwhelming majority of which neither lived in the South nor sent its children to public schools. While trying to base its position on the natural-law tradition, the CIC-inspired statement on discrimination ended up making an assertion that was essentially beside the point when it came to the assault then being conducted against Catholic parishes in the large metropolises of the North. The bishops' 1958 statement was routinely trotted out in instances of local crisis, like the Folcroft riot in 1963 outside Philadelphia, and it invariably infuriated the ethnics who had it read to them and saw in it an attempt to use the moral power of the Catholic Church to achieve ends that were at best irrelevant and at worst directly detrimental to the parishes they lived in. The people from the West End were equally bewildered. They accepted "the moral norms and sacred symbols of the Catholic religion,"[19] and as a result felt that it was the duty of the Church to come to the defense of those norms and the people who practiced them. Instead, the Church stood back and allowed the destruction of the neighborhood and the area's Polish church without protest. In fact, and this was especially bewildering, Msgr. Lally, one of the archdiocese's priests, was on the board approving those decisions.

Because of the political power the Irish Catholics had amassed in Boston, the WASP establishment had to treat them differently than they did in a city like Philadelphia. This was especially true when it came to urban renewal. Downtown business interests were pretty much the same in Boston, Philadelphia, Chicago, and Detroit. The opposite side of the same coin became just as apparent in the demolition of the West End. Just as the demolition was being carried out by ethnic deputies who had successfully internalized the imperatives of the ruling class, it was carried out against the interests of ethnics who had not internalized those imperatives. The West End, according to Flynn, was "not blighted" at the time the BHA decided to tear it down. It was, in his words, "a typical neighborhood in which people would grow up to become priests and nuns."[20] Herbert Gans, who was not Catholic, had much the same thing to say about the neighborhood's retrograde attitudes, especially in sexual matters, explaining that "in the West End, children come because marriage and God bring them. This does not mean that West Enders believe children to be caused by God, but that the Catholic Church opposes birth control, and that this is God's will."[21] Gans, who worked with the social workers who were engaged in the social engineering of the neighborhood at the time and so knew what was going on from the inside, so to speak, makes it perfectly clear that the ethnics' unenlightened attitude toward things like birth control and other forms of assimilation had a lot more to do with the destruction of the neighborhood than the condition of its buildings. "The area's physical condition," according to Gans, was "a necessary but not sufficient criterion" for the demolition of the West End:

> What seems to happen is that neighborhoods come to be described as slums if they are inhabited by residents who, for a variety of reasons indulge in overt and visible behavior considered undesirable by the majority of the community. The community image of the area then gives rise to feelings that something should be done, and subsequently the area is proposed for renewal. Consequently the planning reports that are written to justify renewal dwell as much on social as on physical criteria, and are filled with data intended to show the prevalence of antisocial or pathological behavior in the area. The implication is that the area itself causes such behavior, and should therefore be redeveloped.[22]

The real reason the West End or any other neighborhood like it got torn down was ethnic prejudice coupled with lack of political power – not run-down buildings. The social engineers, as a result, could never admit the real reasons behind their projects – not even to themselves, Gans would assert – and that fact necessitated psychological warfare to engineer the consent of the victims or, if that failed, at least the assent of the majority of the rest of the city. Boston's North End was just as dilapidated (or just as undilapidated) as the West End, but the North End's residents, according to Gans, were "socially and politically strong enough to discourage any official or politician from suggesting them for clearance or large-scale rehabilitation,"[23] probably because the neighborhood, being more ethnically homogeneous, was more cohesive. As in Detroit, all of Boston's neighborhoods had been weakened when Boston's city councilmen stopped being elected from geographical districts and were elected at-large instead. This reduced the neighborhoods' ability to defend themselves against attack. The attack, when it came, was based on the social workers' deeply internalized views on assimilation. According to Gans, the source of the social workers' attitude toward the people of the West End was an "evaluation of the behavior of slum residents based on class-based standards that often confuse behavior which is only culturally different with pathological or antisocial acts."[24]

Gans here misses the point which had been driving assimilation ever since "ethnics" started arriving in large numbers during the later part of the 19th century. From the point of view of assimilation, ethnicity was itself a pathological and antisocial condition. This was clearly the view of the nativists, and it was, with some modification, the view of Louis Wirth, whose books and papers the sociologists had to read in order to get their degrees. The fact that these "professionals" would never admit this openly did not diminish the force of the idea. In fact, that they repressed it under layers of "scientific" rationalization made it all the more powerful. By the time he gets to the end of his book, Gans is forced to admit that the main purpose of the relocation staff's work in the West End was "a desire," which Gans also found permeating "much of planning and housing ideology," to "break up ethnic ghettoes, in the belief that this would encourage people like the West Enders to adopt middle class standards and behavior patterns."[25] In other words, the social workers who engaged in the ethnic cleansing of the West End were motivated by the same desire which motivated Louis Wirth when he conceived of the use of social engineering through housing as the prime form which assimilation would take in this country. In the social workers assigned to the West End, the story of social engineering comes full circle – textbook theories which Wirth got from reading Stalin got put into practice by sociologists who read Wirth as part of their training and then used his ideas on assimilation as a way of justifying what was essentially ethnic cleansing .

The West End, however, would prove to be a pyrrhic victory for the urban-renewal crowd. Rappaport and the WASP establishment that backed him got what they wanted, but in getting it they were so brutal that they made resistance a certainty in the next neighborhood where they would try this sort of thing. In cleansing the West End of its ethnic inhabitants, the BRA "brutally displaced people, disrupted neighborhoods and destroyed pleasing buildings" in a way that "quickly gained national notoriety" and "symbolized all that was wrong with the city planning of the 1950s because it bulldozed the homes of poor people and replaced them with an enclave for the wealthy."[26]

If the excesses of the bulldozer approach in the West End created bad publicity for the BRA in other cities across the nation, it created even greater animosity in Boston's remaining ethnic neighborhoods, which now perceived urban renewal as a form of ethnic cleansing, even if the term was unknown at the time. Urban renewal allowed the rich to appropriate valuable real estate from the poor with government assistance. The debacle surrounding the West End did not change the Boston ruling class's attitude toward social engineering. If anything it made them more determined to carry it on with more attention to subtlety of method rather than *force majeure*. In the aftermath of the West End, that meant bringing Ed Logue to town. Logue needed to enlist the Ford Foundation in supporting his efforts at more sophisticated forms of engineering the consent of the city's remaining but increasingly recalcitrant ethnic population. One of the ironies of the great suburban move out to Route 128 which Cabot, Cabot and Forbes, the premier WASP real-estate firm, had orchestrated in the early '50s, is that it left some very valuable Boston real estate in the hands of the ethnics who got left behind. It was Logue's job to re-engineer this real estate in the interests of the WASPs who now wanted it back.

In 1960 Logue met with Paul Ylvisaker of the Ford Foundation and, after telling him that he was going to Boston to take over the BRA there, asked Ylvisaker if he "could get Ford help."[27] The result of Logue's request was Action for Boston Community Development (ABCD), a Ford Foundation–funded program whose purpose was to help Logue manage "the human side of physical renewal."[28] In August of 1962, the Ford Foundation approved a three-year Gray Areas grant of $1.9 million to Action for Boston Community Development. Ford made the grant, according to one of its own memos, because "Mayor John F. Collins, the Development Administrator, Mr. Edward J. Logue and other community leaders" realized "that the city's ambitious urban renewal program would be incomplete if human needs other than housing were not considered."[29]

The purpose of Ford money in Boston was, as in Philadelphia, to allow agents congenial to Ford's philosophy of social change in the interests of the nation's ruling class to take control of racial migration in the nation's big cities. Ford money, in other words, had "to obtain for itself an independent base for action to avoid becoming entirely related to the physical planning program."[30] As in Philadelphia, the Ford Foundation wanted political entrepreneurs on the ground in Boston who could manage things like racial succession and housing policy in their interests outside of the normal political channels, which were too often controlled by "ethnic" politicians who felt their main duty was to represent the people who elected them to office.

According to one account, Logue claimed that he "conceived what became the nation's first antipoverty program in New Haven" and then "sold the idea to Paul Ylvisaker at the Ford Foundation."[31] Logue's attempt to take credit for the War on Poverty is understandable, if unlikely, especially given what we know about Ylvisaker's efforts and McCloy's ability to influence both Ford policies and the policies of the federal government. It also obscures what was in effect the division of labor between the BRA and the ABCD, something which becomes clear when ABCD's projects get analyzed. In 1961, ABCD, at Logue's urging, conducted a neighborhood profile of the South End which disclosed that

> the income gap between the South End and the rest of Boston was wide and getting wider, that it had a disproportionately large AFDC case load, that 37.5 percent of its males between sixteen and sixty-five years of age were not in the labor force, that 78 percent of the households lacked an automobile, and that it had 28.9 percent of Boston's tuberculosis cases.[32]

Logue's motivation in commissioning a study which portrayed failure to own an automobile and tuberculosis as equally pathological conditions was just as obvious as the Ford Foundation's interest in funding it. By painting a picture of widespread social decay, Logue and the BRA took the first step toward justifying the physical intervention that would eventually lead to the destruction of the neighborhood, just as it had already led to the destruction of the West End. ABCD was, in other words, the peacetime equivalent of the World War II–era Office of Facts and Figures. ABCD was, in short, the psychological-warfare arm for the Boston Redevelopment Authority, which would create the "scientific" rationalization for its interventions. According to Mollenkopf, neither the BRA nor ABCD "could . . . acknowledge to those about to be displaced, or perhaps even to themselves that they were engaging in highly regressive social engineering."[33] As a result, "renewal entrepreneurs resolved this bind largely by denying it."[34] Before long the neighborhood profile behind the South End Urban Renewal Plan, which was adopted in late 1965, began to have predictable effects. The South End was devastated in ways that reminded its residents of the saturation bombing campaign against Germany's cities during World War II.

In January 1963, five months after Ford gave $1.9 million to ABCD, Clifford J. Campbell, Deputy Commissioner of Chicago's Department of City Planning, who also functioned as a consultant to the Ford Foundation in helping evaluate the effectiveness of their Gray Areas Programs, met with Mayor Collins in Boston to discuss ABCD. Collins's reaction was essentially negative. He perceived, with some justification, the Ford Foundation's initiative as a way of creating locally independent political operatives, who could then be deployed against the city administration in the same way that they were being used in Philadelphia and Chicago. In fact, in the same memo, Campbell tells Ylvisaker that it is common knowledge that ABCD is the Boston version of PCCA and that the ABCD staff Campbell talked to "were aware of the situation that has developed in the City of Philadelphia subsequent to the grant by the Ford Foundation"[35] there. Collins warned Campbell that "he would not permit the private social agencies to assume a controlling interest in the ABCD project,"[36] which was precisely the reason Ford was interested in creating ABCD in the first place.

Campbell also met with Ed Logue, "Boston's top man in the field of planning and urban renewal," who shared with Campbell "his positive position with reference to the urban renewal program being shaped up for the city of Boston."[37] Logue, according to Campbell, felt that "ABCD should accommodate itself to and maybe become *the tool for urban renewal*"[38] (my emphasis), whereas others were of the opposite point of view. The fact that ABCD and BRA often worked at cross purposes does little to disguise the fact that one of the main reasons that Logue came to Boston was because Paul Ylvisaker agreed to make the former a tool of the latter program. That becomes clear in an evaluation of ABCD done by Ford in September 1964. Ford got involved in ABCD through its Gray Areas Program because "urban renewal programs . . . were running into growing resistance – particularly from the Negro community which began opposing the relocation process."[39] Dealing with the "human side" of urban renewal meant, in other words, more vigorous engineering of consent by making contact with the Boston equivalent of local racial entrepreneurs like Philadelphia's Leon Sullivan, who could be counted on to orchestrate consent through community groups. "The Collins and Logue approach," according to Kennedy, "from the beginning was to treat neighborhoods much more carefully than the West End had been treated under the previous administration. The BRA tried to include community groups in planning neighborhoods."[40]

One of the neighborhoods the BRA was now interested in most was Charlestown. Engineering consent in heavily Irish Catholic Charlestown meant dealing with the Catholic Church, and that meant making use of Msgr. Lally once again. Lally moved into the rectory of St. Catherine's Church in Charlestown and used his position there, as well as his position as editor of the *Pilot*, to browbeat Charlestown's Catholic population into accepting Ed Logue's plan for "renewing" the neighborhood, a plan which initially called for demolishing 60 percent of Charlestown's housing stock. Selling the destruction of Charlestown to its own residents would prove to be a daunting task. Any illusions about the real intent behind urban renewal in the minds of Charlestown's residents had been removed with the destruction of the West End. Logue and the BRA were desperately in need of a breakthrough, but the BRA's plans had been effectively blocked by the actions of Logue's predecessors, a group that included Msgr. Lally.

Logue's attempts to engineer the consent of Charlestown's Catholics in the destruction of their own neighborhood did not stop with Msgr. Lally. In 1961, Logue used Ford's ABCD money to hire a Lithuanian Catholic by the name of Joe Vilimas to come to Boston and try to create some support for urban renewal among Charlestown's reluctant Irish Catholics. Vilimas had come to Boston from Chicago, where he worked for Saul Alinsky's Woodlawn Organization. Alinsky knew that the Catholic Church had a heavy financial stake in ethnic neighborhoods like Chicago's Woodlawn section, and he persuaded Chicago's Cardinal Meyer to fund his efforts to stabilize the neighborhood and prevent or at least slow down the Irish exodus to the suburbs. Meyer, as a result, ordered the Woodlawn neighborhood's nine pastors to provide $10,000 per parish to fund Alinsky's efforts, with dubious results. Police on Chicago's "Red Squad" felt that Meyer had been duped and that Alinsky was actually a double agent who took money from the Church and then used that money to sabotage the very neighborhoods he was claiming to save. The fact that Vilimas, an Alinsky agent, was getting money from the Ford Foundation to engineer consent for the demolition of Catholic Charlestown, lends credence to that charge, as does the fact that it was Alinsky's Woodlawn Organization which was the umbrella organization through which Sargent Shriver and the OEO gave over $900,000 to the Blackstone Rangers.

Vilimas and Lally then enlisted three other Charlestown pastors in the fight to "redevelop" Charlestown. But, by that time, actions spoke louder than words. Nothing Lally or Vilimas could say would be as persuasive as what the BRA had already done in the West End. On January 7, 1963, the BRA held a meeting to discuss its plans which attracted thousands of angry townies, who shouted down the plan. The residents of Charlestown liked their community better than any plans for upward mobility which the destruction of their neighborhood might enable. After listening to Logue present his plans, one ex-longshoreman resident stood up at the meeting and told Logue that no matter how it looked to outsiders, Charlestown was "my home. I fought for it, and that's all I want. So you can stick your money up your ass!"[41]

Logue tried to engineer the townies' consent once again in March of 1965. Cardinal Cushing endorsed his efforts by claiming that Logue's plan for Charlestown, which now involved tearing down only 11 percent of the neighborhood and removing the hated "El" tracks as well, held out "the most hopeful promise of the permanent rehabilitation of that beloved part of our great city."[42] As part of his continued efforts to engineer the consent of his fellow Catholics, Msgr. Lally had created a Boston branch of the Catholic Interracial Council in the same month that Ed Logue scheduled his meeting. By scaling back his demands and prodding Cushing and Lally into a full-court press on the issue, Logue eventually won approval for his plan for Charlestown, but the victory came at a steep price. By identifying Boston's Catholic clergy with urban renewal, Logue created a split among Catholics and created as well a situation in which the rank and file would be less likely to follow Catholic leadership in later campaigns. Anticlericalism soon surfaced in claims that the Fathers Lally, Flaherty, and Shea were "selling the people of Charlestown for 30 pieces of silver."[43] By bringing the Catholic Interracial Council into the picture, Msgr. Lally signed on to an agenda that eventually alienated him from Cushing, who began to see in their demands something left wing and subversive, and eventually something he wanted suppressed. By backing imprudent policies at odds with not only their flocks but also with the Catholic notion of the parish as a local community, the Catholic hierarchy was effectively undermining its own authority in the eyes of the faithful, who felt they had been abandoned in favor of a moral agenda concocted by Protestants from the suburbs.

The Charlestown fight also soon paled in comparison to the other fights which the BRA was becoming involved in. In September 1962 the BRA had declared thirty of the fifty homes in the North Harvard Street area of Allston blighted, and with city-council approval began tearing them down to make way for a 300-unit apartment building, which just happened to be adjacent to the Harvard Business School. By December of 1963

Harvard students had joined in the protest and, after several families refused to move, a pitched battle between demonstrators and police took place in August of 1965. The battle constituted a public-relations disaster for Collins, Logue, and the BRA at a time when they had got their much-diminished Charlestown plan through at the price of widespread public resentment.

By 1965, urban renewal as a tool of social engineering was in deep trouble in Boston. By the summer of 1966, the BRA's plans for the North Harvard Street project were doomed. It was clear in 1965 that urban renewal had had its day in Boston, and was now in its death throes, having expired largely as a result of its own wretched excesses. Logue's tenure as head of BRA was coming to an end as he contemplated an establishment-backed run for mayor that would eventually founder on the lack of support among the overwhelming majority of the city's ethnics, who finally saw urban renewal as something antithetical not only to their interests but to their continued existence in the city.

Logue had come to Boston claiming that he understood the importance of the social dimension in planning and the need to incorporate community participation and social planning into the process of rebuilding the city, but the project of urban renewal was so intrinsically dishonest that no amount of "planning with people" could eliminate the fact that urban renewal was not in the interest of the neighborhoods where it got practiced. In order to engineer the consent of the neighborhoods he was planning to "renew," Logue had to create a social-service agency with an agenda nearly as ambitious in its own realm as the BRA was in its domain. By 1965, it had become clear that "planning with people" meant nothing more than a more sophisticated form of social engineering and psychological warfare applied against the very people who were supposedly its beneficiaries.

The establishment, in other words, had overreached badly on urban renewal, and now it needed another way of changing the environment in order to change the man. Since there were essentially only two arenas for changing the environment – codified in the two 1954 Supreme Court decisions, *Berman v. Parker* and *Brown v. Board of Education* – that meant that a failure in housing policy would force the liberal environmentalists to concentrate their efforts in education. And this is pretty much what happened in 1965, when urban renewal ran out of steam and forced busing took its place.

Notes

1   John H. Mollenkopf, *The Contested City* (Princeton, N.J.: Princeton University Press, 1983), p. 144.
2   Ibid.
3   Ibid.
4   Ibid.
5   Ibid., p. 156.
6   Ibid., p. 157.
7   Ibid., p. 158.
8   Ibid.
9   Lawrence W. Kennedy, *Planning the City upon a Hill: Boston since 1630* (Amherst: The University of Massachusetts Press, 1992), p. 164.
10 Interview with Ray Flynn 6/9/00.

11 Ibid.

12 Ibid.

13 J. Anthony Lukas, *Common Ground: A Turbulent Decade in the Lives of Three American Families* (New York: Alfred A. Knopf, 1985), p. 503.

14 Ibid.

15 Interview with Ray Flynn 6/9/00.

16 Herbert J. Gans, *The Urban Villagers: Group and Class in the Life of Italian Americans* (New York: The Free Press of Glencoe, 1962), p. 291.

17 Kennedy, p. 161.

18 Lukas, p. 382.

19 Gans, p. 111.

20 Interview with Ray Flynn 6/9/00.

21 Gans, p. 54.

22 Ibid., p. 308.

23 Ibid.

24 Ibid.

25 Ibid., p. 323.

26 Kennedy, p. 162.

27 Ibid., p. 189.

28 Ibid.

29 Review Paper Public Affairs: The Gray Areas Program confidential 9/64, Ylvisaker papers, Box 5, Harvard University Archives.

30 Ibid.

31 Kennedy, p. 188.

32 Mollenkopf, p. 173.

33 Ibid., p. 175.

34 Ibid.

35 Campbell to Ylvisaker on visit to Boston 1/22/63, 2/5/63, Gray Areas folders, Ylvisaker papers, Box 5, Harvard University Archives.

36 Ibid.

37 Ibid.

38 Ibid.

39 Review Paper Public Affairs: The Gray Areas Program confidential 9/64, Ylvisaker papers, Box 5, Harvard University Archives.

40 Kennedy, p. 186.

41 Lukas, p. 154.

42 Ibid., p. 356.

43 Ibid.

Dennis Clark Becomes an Irishman

Dennis Clark was invited to the October 2, 1965, meeting at which Cushing Dolbeare announced her plans for the assault on the city's neighborhoods because he was on the AFSC Community Relations Division steering committee, but he did not attend. By the late '60s, Clark, as Barbara Krassner had noted, had become burned out on racial issues. In their stead he became involved in Irish issues in the wake of the 1969 Bloody Sunday attack on Belfast's Catholics. At least that's what he said. "Once more," Clark wrote in *The Irish in Philadelphia*, "the generation gap was bridged. Once more the bond between Irishmen defied time and distance to affirm a common interest, an interest that had been sustained in Philadelphia for three hundred years."[1]

Missing from Clark's glowing account of revived Irish nationalism is any mention of the plight that Irishmen in Philadelphia were experiencing in places like Most Blessed Sacrament Parish at the hands of Clark's friends the Quakers and their black proxy troops. Clark was unable to make the connection between his own actions and the plight of the Irish in Philadelphia largely because by 1969 he had disconnected himself from the Catholic Church. Unable to connect ethnos and religion in any coherent fashion, Clark abandoned the Catholic Church when it failed to meet his standards of interracial justice. As a result of abandoning the Catholic Church, he could not perceive the plight of his fellow Philadelphia Irishmen because he thought of them as Catholics and not Irish, especially when their communities were associated with parishes involved in racial conflict, as they invariably were in Philadelphia.

By 1969, Clark felt that the Catholic Church had failed in its mission. In a journal entry dated January 3, 1969, as part of his annual stocktaking around the new year, Clark wrote that he planned to retain "formal membership in the Church," but "there is no expectation" among Clark's fellow activist Catholics "that the Church can be a vehicle for social programs. Thus, the vision is to be sought elsewhere."[2] As early as 1967, Clark and Ed Cahill agreed that "we were mistaken in youth. We thought the Church an agency for social action. It is not,"[3] or at least not on the terms that Clark set out for it. The really "immense failure" which Clark lays at the Church's feet is her inability

> to construct a self-controlling community that lives with respect for its relationship to its surroundings. Our struggles over decentralization, metropolitan planning and urban renewal should not mask this broader fact from us. . . . At the level just above the family, that is the local community, we have not been able, after 340 years of effort, to develop a viable form of human settlement that is stable and in balance with our resources and human abilities. From the chaos of the exploitative frontier we have proceeded to the rapacity of the technological career.[4]

Clark concludes that "The old ethnic and religious coalitions fail," but he never gives any indication of the role he might have played in undermining the viability of

Philadelphia's ethnic communities. All that Clark can manage are platitudes about how "a new formulation of values is underway" and that "everything from genetics to moon flights are [*sic*] changing our definitions of man."[5]

The ethnic backlash which brought Nixon and Agnew to the White House in 1968 was largely a Catholic phenomenon, something noted by Norman Podhoretz, who is not Catholic, and denied by Michael Novak, who is. "Just as the black assertion," according to Podhoretz, "set the climate for the '60s, I think you'll find a comparable Catholic, white-ethnic assertion in the '70s. You have 40 million Catholics in the United States. They've never been organized as a political bloc around their resentments. You have an enormously potent force here, in this Catholic minority. It could result in the re-constitution of the Democratic Party as a relatively permanent majority. A Democratic Kevin Phillips could work this out."[6] ("Podhoretz," according to Novak, "stresses the Catholic assertion; I would stress its ethnic character."[7])

Podhoretz's reference to Kevin Phillips's book on the new Republican majority indicates that at around 1970 the triple melting pot was doing its work and that all of the various ethnic groups from Europe which were, in Louis Wirth's formulation, "suspect because of their origin" had now fused into one uniquely American ethnic group that was having trouble emerging into the sunlight of American politics because of a problem in classification. It was variously identified as "white" or "ethnic," but its real identity was Catholic. Like Yugoslavia, the United States was an empire based on an ideology whose population was divided between three major ethnic groups based on three religions. In the aftermath of the protest that was orchestrated against *Humanae Vitae* in 1968, Catholic ethnic identity was masked by the fact that a significant fifth column had been created among the Catholic intelligentsia, and by the fact that this intelligentsia was determined to assimilate on the terms proposed by the ruling class.

That meant acceptance of sexual liberation in general, including the use of contraception and abortion, and the eugenic engineering of the black population in particular. As a result of the fact that the intelligentsia most avid to assimilate controlled the Catholic media, publishing houses, universities, as well as many of the religious orders and many of the chancery offices, including the bishops' own national organization in Washington, that emerging identification of the new ethnic group as Catholic never took place in any convincing fashion. In fact, it was the intention of the WASP-subsidized fifth column within the Catholic Church to decertify the ethnics as insufficiently Catholic, making them thereby "white" and, as a result, somehow morally suspect. "One thinks," sniffed Theodore Hesburgh, "of the Catholic-educated who stoned nuns and priests in Chicago because they were marching for integrated neighborhoods and blacks. . . ."[8] Hesburgh, who served as an agent of Rockefeller interests during the time he was president of the University of Notre Dame, went out of his way to distance himself from "Catholic ethnics," who, according to his account, sent Hesburgh hate mail "every time I put in a good word for blacks or Chicanos."[9] The only solace Hesburgh can derive from the social backwardness of benighted "Catholic ethnics" in places like Philadelphia and Chicago is the effect that education at assimilationist-minded institutions like Notre Dame is having on their children, who, "thank God, largely do not share these ugly prejudices of their elders."

In failing to see that Catholicism was the new ethnicity he was praising, Michael

Clark as an Irishman more than as a Catholic

Novak was similar in outlook to Dennis Clark. Decapitated by the defection of its intelligentsia, the Catholic Church was not only not capable of coming up with a solution to the problem of racial migration, it was not even able to define the problem. Since the Catholic Interracial Council dominated the discussion of the race issue among the Catholic intelligentsia, all of Catholic education from seminary training on down to parochial schools defined the problem that was tearing apart Catholic parishes in city after city in the North as white racism. Deprived of any independent thinking on the race issue by this *trahison des clercs*, the Catholics by default adopted the categories of their oppressors and began to view themselves as villains in the story of the destruction of their urban parishes. Like the Indian children who watched cowboy movies, they cheered when the cavalry arrived and began gunning down their own people.

Notes

1 Dennis Clark, *The Irish in Philadelphia: Ten Generations of Urban Experience* (Philadelphia: Temple University Press, 1973), p. 163.
2 Dennis Clark, Diary, 1/3/69.
3 Clark, Diary, Christmastime 1967.
4 Clark, Diary, 1/3/69.
5 Ibid.
6 Michael Novak, *The Rise of the Unmeltable Ethnics: Politics and Culture in the '70s* (New York: the Macmillan Company, 1971), p. 9.
7 Ibid.
8 Ibid., p. 11.
9 Ibid.

Busing as the Alternative to Urban Renewal

One month after Ed Logue's much-diminished plan to "renew" Charlestown passed in the face of fierce ethnic opposition, and in spite of the full support of the Catholic hierarchy, the Advisory Committee on Racial Imbalance and Education which had been appointed by the State Education Commissioner, announced that Boston's schools were racially "imbalanced." "Racial imbalance," the committee concluded, "represents a serious conflict with the American creed of equal opportunity. It does serious educational damage to Negro children, impairing their confidence, distorting their self-image and lowering their motivation. It does moral damage by encouraging prejudice within children regardless of their color. . . . Separation from others breeds ignorance of others, and ignorance breeds fear and prejudice."[1]

The Advisory Committee recommended legislation to compel school systems to eliminate such imbalance. Four months later, on August 16, 1965, which is to say at the same time that the battle against urban renewal in Boston reached its climax, the Massachusetts state legislature passed what came to be known as the Racial Imbalance Act of 1965. Sponsored by a WASP, a Jew, and a Catholic (in this instance, a Jesuit priest, Robert Drinan, s.j.) the bill defined racial imbalance as schools having student bodies which were more than 50 percent black, a stroke which eliminated the need for racial redress in every suburban community in the state.

Suburban schools lacked enough black students to be racially "imbalanced," and as a result were exempted from the draconian methods which applied in the final analysis to only three of the state's cities: Boston, Springfield, and Cambridge. If the people who sponsored the bill were supposed to give some indication of its intent, it looked on first glance like the triple melting pot in action. Closer inspection of the pan-ethnic nature of the bill's sponsors, especially the support of Rev. Drinan, who would go on to be a fervent backer of the ruling class's eugenics program when he got elected to Congress, indicated that its main purpose was to put pressure on the predominantly Catholic Boston school board and the neighborhoods where Catholics had some control over community-based schools.

Levine and Harmon describe the Racial Imbalance Act of 1965 as "from the start a tool designed for use only in working-class inner-city neighborhoods."[2] The bill's sponsors, again according to Levine and Harmon, "represented, in essence an invincible cross-section of traditional northeast power structure."[3] Father Drinan was "a priest who spoke out for liberalized abortion laws had many friendships with progressive Jewish leaders in Boston's western suburbs."[4] Those Jewish leaders would "later help elect the outspoken Jesuit to the U.S. Congress."[5] Like Father Hesburgh, Father Drinan could be counted on to work against the interests of Catholic ethnics.

Lukas describes the Racial Imbalance Act of 1965 as a piece legislation which nakedly betrayed its class bias. In a sense, this was true. Rev. Drinan represented the interests of certain Catholics – the ones most avid to assimilate – against other less-influential Catholics, those either unwilling or unable to go along with the WASP agenda. But the bill also betrayed naked ethnic bias as well. It was calculated to put pressure on the last bastions of Catholic political power in the state. That threat became explicit even before the bill was passed. In June of 1965, Governor John Volpe introduced his own bill, one which allowed the State Board of Education to withhold state funds from any local school board which had not adopted a plan to eliminate "racial imbalance."

As on the issue of urban renewal, the Catholic Church had been co-opted into taking a position inimical to its own interests. Cushing had been drafted to become a member of the Kiernan Commission, which in April of 1965, announced that Boston's public schools constituted "a serious conflict with the American creed of equal opportunity."[6] As always, Cushing's views on the matter were essentially the views of Msgr. Lally, who fulminated from his perch as editor of the *Pilot* that Boston's Catholics "must pay for our wickedness as a people and do justice in the fullest sense to the Negro child"[7] by acceding once again to another form of social engineering.

Eventually Lally and Boston's branch of the Catholic Interracial Council pressured Cushing into establishing a Human Rights Commission, much as Cardinal Krol reacting to the same sort of pressure had established the Cardinal's Commission on Human Relations in Philadelphia. But the auspices under which the commission got created all but insured that it would construe the issues which came before it to the detriment of Catholic interests. Eventually, the CIC went too far and alienated Cushing by becoming involved in anti-war activities, something that jeopardized Catholic participation in the anti-Communist crusade, one of the pillars of Catholic assimilation for Cushing's generation.

Discussion of the Racial Imbalance Act of 1965 generally ignores the fact that the Ford Foundation, through its ABCD program, was just as heavily involved in trying to influence public education in Boston as it was in trying to influence housing policy. The Ford Foundation deliberately tried to keep its money out of the hands of the Boston School Board because they felt their policies were inimical to Ford Foundation interests. When Clifford Campbell came to Boston to evaluate ABCD for Ford, he spent much of his time meeting with local educators, as much time as he spent meeting with Logue and the housing establishment, and later carefully sketched out the lay of the land for the benefit of Paul Ylvisaker. Filling Ylvisaker in on the situation in Boston meant dealing with the ethnic facts of life, which in Boston meant the religious facts of life. Albert J. Garland, Campbell informed Ylvisaker, was "a former professor at the University of Notre Dame" and as such "represented part of the 'overstructure' in Catholic circles as distinguished from the 'Yankee power structure.'"[8]

Campbell later identified "Charles I. Schottland, ABCD President, Marx C. Wheeler, Treasurer, Theodore Chase, Assistant treasurer and the President of UCS, F. Douglas Cochrane, ABCD Clerk and of course our project director, Joe Slavet" as representing the "'Yankee Power Structure' in part at least, for the Boston project."[9]

The problem with the Boston School system, from Ford's perspective, was that it was decidedly under the influence of the "Catholic overstructure" and as a result not in tune with the Ford Foundation's goals. Ford wanted to take control of the nationalities issue in

Boston in both housing and education, but it was hindered in accomplishing its goals because WASP influence on the school board was negligible since most of the WASPs had migrated to suburban school districts. Since it would have been pointless to try to persuade the WASPs to move back into the city, the best way to remedy this situation was to increase the power of the black population in the city's educational establishment, since people like Mrs. Cass, who sometimes "wore the NAACP hat and at other times she had on her ABCD hat"[10] could be counted on to represent WASP interests.

In his memo to Ylvisaker, Campbell carefully analyzes how the integration issue can be used against the school board to foster Ford's interests in Boston. In spite of their efforts to distance themselves from school board policies, Campbell felt that "ABCD was identified with the schools and their problems . . . when Boston's school integration fight broke."[11] That meant that "some of the lightning which should have been focused on the School Committee was directed at ABCD." Ford's strategy, in other words, was to focus the lightning which racial unrest was causing – which, in fact, Ford was causing – on the school board as a way of bringing about change in Ford's interest.

Without the support of the hierarchy, that meant that the Catholics on the school board would have to bear the brunt of these attacks alone. Taking his cue from the Kennedy family, Cardinal Cushing had abandoned the plight of the white ethnic Catholic in favor of concern about racial injustice. This view was again predictable given Cushing's views on assimilation. If most of the Catholic ethnics were destined to migrate to the suburbs and become middle class, as the Irish seemed to be doing, what was the point of fighting a rear-guard action to save institutions that were destined to go out of existence anyway?

Cushing's views on assimilation not only became a self-fulfilling prophecy, they also all but guaranteed the rise of politicians like Louise Day Hicks, who represented in many ways the return of the Catholic repressed. She represented the Catholic who was supposed to have disappeared into the suburbs as one more assimilationist success story but had chosen to remain in the neighborhood instead. The fact that Hicks hadn't migrated to the suburbs with the more successful Irish and the fact that she intended to defend the interests of the ethnics who had remained behind meant that a confrontation was looming on the horizon. By the time she made her unsuccessful bid for mayor in 1967, the same year that Ed Logue, representing the opposite end of the ethnic spectrum also would go down to defeat, black rioting in places like Watts, Newark, Detroit and, closer to home, Roxbury, had created a social agenda which catered to black needs and heaped at best "benign neglect" on ethnic neighborhoods like South Boston and Charlestown. At worst, the same people who were concerned about the plight of blacks construed these places as part of the problem.

In November of 1967, Ed Logue, the Vault's candidate for mayor, went down to defeat at the hands of Kevin White, who got elected by tearing enough of the ethnic vote away from Louise Day Hicks, something he accomplished by not scaring the WASPs as much as Mrs. Hicks did. Now White, short on cash, had to go hat in hand to the very people who had funded his opponent in the recent election and ask for money to pay off James Brown, a guy who saw in Martin Luther King's death a chance to make a quick buck.

Eventually, James Brown would only get $15,000 of the $60,000 Kevin White had promised him. But once the idea of going to the Vault got lodged in White's mind he decided that this source of money could be put to better and more ambitious purposes than just funding greedy soul singers. Less than two weeks after the riot had been averted, White appeared before the Vault in person and asked for a much larger chunk of money, ostensibly to help Boston get through the long, hot summer of 1968, during which it looked as if violence loomed just over the horizon. In doing so, White put himself in the classical bind of American politicians, who need votes to get elected, but who need money to get the votes. In trying to solve that equation, they all too often end up bartering votes for money and selling their own constituents out to the monied interests.

In Boston these terms had a definite ethnic quality to them. Earlier than any other major city in the country, Boston's Irish Catholics took over the administration of the city, thereby setting up a long-term conflict with the WASP establishment which ran the state government. Ten full years before the Blanshard brothers arrived in Bridesburg to worry about whether Polish Catholics could become fully American, Boston's Archbishop O'Connell announced that "the Puritan has passed" but that "the Catholic remains."[12] In fact the Catholics had taken over Boston: "The city where a century ago he came unwanted he has made his own!" It was the sort of thing that Paul Blanshard would report on in *The Nation* as symptomatic of "the Catholic problem," and it had happened in Boston forty years before Blanshard wrote his book and almost sixty years before equally Irish Philadelphia would elect its first Irish-Catholic mayor. By the time Paul Blanshard's articles appeared in *The Nation* – in the same year in fact – Boston was so unabashedly Hiberno-Catholic that it re-elected Michael Curley as its mayor from his prison cell, where he was serving time for mail fraud and other charges which the majority of Boston's voters felt had been trumped up against their candidate by a WASP establishment determined to get rid of him.

If in Philadelphia, the ethnic dimensions of the struggle got camouflaged behind terms like "machine" and "reform," in Boston, the issues were more out in the open. "There was a feeling in Boston," wrote someone who participated in the early discussion of urban renewal in the city during the '50s, "that the city was in the hands of supercrooks. Nobody had ever seen an honest Irishman."[13] Irish-WASP animosity in Boston got expressed in many ways, both overt and covert. One of the covert expressions of this animus was the WASP-black alliance that came to be known during the '60s as the civil rights movement. In fact, the idea of a WASP-black alliance was, in many ways, a Yankee invention. In the nineteenth century, it was known as abolitionism, and Boston was its headquarters. The same spirit that found southern blacks an irresistible object of Yankee philanthropy, found the Irish Catholics equally repugnant, probably because when the feelings got framed blacks were still largely living down South, whereas the Irish had been pouring into Boston for some time and making their presence known in ways that the WASP natives did not like. Louisa May Alcott's mother, wife of the Transcendentalist and abolitionist Bronson Alcott, felt that it made more sense, from her ethnic and religious point of view to assist Boston's blacks, rather than "building up the Catholic faith on Protestant charity"[14] by giving to the equally penurious if more numerous "God-invoking Irish who choke you with benedictions and crush you with curses."[15]

Philanthropy in Boston took its cue from Mrs. Alcott, and at no time in its history did this happen more vehemently than in the wake of Martin Luther King's death. The money which Kevin White eventually received from the Vault came to be known as the Mayor's Special Fund. It was administered by Barney Frank, later the homosexual congressman from Massachusetts, largely to keep the lid on, which is another way of saying that it was used to pay off black political entrepreneurs who modeled themselves on the late Martin Luther King, but who modified King's message from "pass this bill, or the cities will burn," to "fund my program or the cities will burn." The Special Fund, in other words, "paid a small cadre of black informants and operatives,"[16] but it was not really all that different from the other outpourings of upper-class charity which sprang up in the wake of King's death with the same purpose in mind.

One of those private initiatives was known as the Fund for United Negro Development or FUND. It was the brainchild of Harvey Cox, the liberal Harvard theologian, and Ralph Hoagland, a Bostonian who had made a fortune from a chain of cut-rate drug stores known as Consumer Value Stores, or CVS. FUND soon became Boston's fashionable charity in the wake of King's murder, and through it the WASP elite in Boston began funding something called the Black United Front, a coalition of black organizations which formed under Stokely Carmichael's direction after King's death. The change in course which black activism would take could be roughly calibrated by comparing Stokely Carmichael's rhetoric to that of Martin Luther King.

With King out of the way, the Christian emphasis on brotherly love and reconciliation all but disappeared and the guerrilla warfare aspect, which was always latent in the civil-rights movement, came to the fore. That meant that philanthropy was once again involved in the promotion of criminal activity. According to Lukas, "Much of Boston's establishment – black as well as white – regarded the United Front's leaders as either crooks who would take the money and run off to Brazil or revolutionaries who would buy guns and bombs."[17]

FUND got involved in supporting the United Front less than a year after the OEO began funding the Blackstone Rangers. UF's reputation caused Boston's WASP establishment some consternation, but not enough to stop giving the United Front its money. This was the case because "Boston's Yankees had conducted political guerrilla warfare on their Irish adversaries down the hill at City Hall"[18] unabated from the period following the Civil War to the period following World War II. The only thing which had changed in the period following World War II was the dramatic increase in Boston's black population, which had nearly tripled in the twenty years between World War II and the '60s. The overwhelming majority of the blacks who arrived in Boston in the period following World War II were the "Cotton Belt Southerners" who came for the wartime military jobs and brought with them the same socialization problems they brought with them to Chicago and Philadelphia – in other words, more money in a month than they had earned in a year down south coupled with what seemed like the complete removal of the onerous system of social control that had grown up in the years following the South's defeat at the hands of the North. Mrs. Henry Cabot Lodge gave to FUND, as did representatives from the Lowell, Weld, Saltonstall, and Bradford families as well as Senator Edward Kennedy, and FUND, in turn, turned the money over to the Black United Front, which in turn channeled $1 million of the establishment's money to small black businesses, most of which went belly up within the next four years, leaving some to wonder where the money had really gone.

Boston, post-King philanthropy seeks to keep the lid on

In January 1968 newly elected Mayor Kevin White mentioned "continuing ethnic divisions"[19] as "the most disturbing of the city's problems."[20] What White didn't mention was how Boston's upper-class philanthropy was fueling those divisions. As in Chicago, the main "beneficiaries" of the establishment's decision to fund dubious if not criminal activity were the "ethnics" who lived in the neighborhoods immediately adjacent to black neighborhoods. In Boston, because of the peculiarities of that city's ethnic and political power base, that meant that the Jews in Roxbury would be the first to suffer from a campaign of government-sponsored ethnic cleansing. As in Chicago, black crime, now politically sanctioned by the city's wealthiest families as part of the black struggle for liberation, put pressure on ethnics to leave, which in turn had the added benefit of freeing up the valuable chunks of real estate the WASP establishment had left behind in its rush to the suburbs.

Notes

1 J. Anthony Lukas, *Common Ground: A Turbulent Decade in the Lives of Three American Families* (New York: Alfred A. Knopf, 1985), p. 130.
2 Hillel Levine and Lawrence Harmon, *The Death of an American Jewish Community: A Tragedy of Good Intentions* (New York: The Free Press, 1992), p. 218.
3 Ibid.
4 Ibid.
5 Ibid.
6 Lukas, p. 386.
7 Ibid.
8 Campbell to Ylvisaker on visit to Boston 1/22/63, The Gray Areas folder, January to June 1963, Ylvisaker papers, Box 5, Harvard University Archives.
9 Ibid.
10 Ibid.
11 Review Paper Public Affairs : the Gray Areas Program confidential 9/64, The Gray Areas folder, January to June 1963, Ylvisaker papers, Box 5, Harvard University Archives.
12 Lukas, p. 376.
13 Lawrence W. Kennedy, *Planning the City upon a Hill: Boston since 1630* (Amherst: The University of Massachusetts Press, 1992), p. 161.
14 Lukas, p. 342.
15 Ibid.
16 Ibid., p. 37.
17 Ibid., p. 40.
18 John H. Mollenkopf, *The Contested City* (Princeton, N.J.: Princeton University Press, 1983), p. 143.
19 Lukas, p. 199.
20 Ibid.

Msgr. Sawher Becomes Pastor of Assumption Grotto

Msgr. Clifford Sawher became pastor of Assumption Grotto two years after the '67 riots and four years before Coleman Young became mayor of Detroit. During the twenty-five years he was pastor, Sawher would watch the number of families at Assumption Grotto drop from 4,400 to 600, while he was faced with the unenviable task of raising money to support the same plant, the same expenses, and the same financial demands from the bishop. When he wrote his autobiography, Msgr. Sawher did not set out to write an account of the destruction of Detroit. He did not even set out to write an account of the destruction (and resurrection) of Assumption Grotto Parish, where he was pastor from 1969 to 1994. He set out to write an account of his priesthood, but because he was a pastor when he was, he became involved in a huge cultural battle that involved the destruction of the residential areas of Detroit and every other large northern city with a large Catholic population. It was a cultural battle that made Bismarck's *Kulturkampf* against the Catholic Church in Germany in the 1870s look like a Sunday-school picnic by comparison. Sawher describes this campaign of ethnic cleansing from what might be termed the worm's-eye point of view, meaning that Catholics in parishes like Assumption Grotto were the worms that were about to be stepped on by the big feet of federal government, in particular the Department of Housing and Urban Development, big industry – in this case the auto industry – and people like Coleman Young, erstwhile mayor of Detroit, who directed the local army of black proxy soldiers in this war.

Assumption Grotto is the second oldest parish in Detroit, which is significant in a city which had a Catholic presence before the United States was a country. When Msgr. Sawher became its pastor, Assumption Grotto was an ethnic parish which was predominantly Italian but contained as well one thousand Polish families, one thousand German families as well as pockets of Belgians and French. It was in many ways a typical example of the triple melting pot, which was creating one American Catholic *ethnos* out of immigrants from all over Europe. It was also full of the people whom Louis Wirth, the University of Chicago sociologist who created our nationalities policy by imitating Stalin's example in the Soviet Union, considered "suspect because of their origin."

Assumption Grotto was a microcosm of Detroit, which as late as 1960 was the home of 1.67 million people, 70 percent of whom were white ethnics – "Poles and Italians," Ze'ev Chafets wrote in *Devil's Night*, who "lived in neat little box-like homes along quiet streets on the east side."[1] The people who lived in those box-like homes on Detroit's east side belonged to communities which were based on churches like Assumption Grotto. "With nearly 4400 families or units," Sawher writes, giving his view of the same east side of Detroit, "we were like a small city."[2] Detroit, according to Chafets was "less a big city than a federation of ethnic villages bound together by auto plants, a place with more basements and bowling alleys than any other metropolis in the country."[3]

This situation changed dramatically after the 1967 riots. Within six years, the white population dropped precipitously. In an ironic commentary on the intentions of the destroyers, Detroit became one large ethnic neighborhood, now virtually all black, run by blacks (and some would say, under Coleman Young, for blacks) who constituted half the population of the city. The best analogy for what happened in Detroit is the de-colonization of Africa which happened anywhere from five to ten years before. "Detroit," according to Chafets, "has even developed a quasi-official ideology that regards the pre-Young era as a time of white colonialism, ended by the 1967 insurrection and its aftermath."[4] Detroit is best understood, in other words, not as an American city, but as part of the postcolonial Third World. The main result of the insurrection from Coleman Young's point of view was that it legitimated what Chafets called Young's "ongoing war of liberation"[5] against the surrounding white communities. If that is the case for the suburbs, then it is *a fortiori* the case for the white enclaves which remained in the city after the insurrection of 1967, and that meant places like Assumption Grotto Parish.

"Since the great migration of people from Detroit to the suburbs," Sawher writes, "our need for money remained the same, practically, while our income gradually decreased."[6] It was a burden which would have broken a weaker man. And, although he doesn't put it that way, it's clear that it did just that to many of Detroit's priests.

Sawher is not without his faults, and it is a tribute to his honesty that he was able to face up to many of them in this book and admit that he made mistakes. He regrets the fact that he supported no-fault divorce. He was, he claimed, instrumental in getting the church to loosen up the annulment process by persuading then Cardinal Dearden to take his notion that "if the love which this involves was absent from the beginning of marriage, the marriage should be null and void"[7] to the Vatican Council and promoting it there.

Sawher was exposed to first-hand contact with the age's pathogens. He went to Catholic University where then-Father Eugene Kennedy taught him the arcana of Rogerian therapy. Soon Carl Rogers wrought in Kennedy what he wrought in the Immaculate Heart nuns of Los Angeles, when Kennedy left the priesthood. Given the psychological warfare that was being waged against them at the time, it is no wonder so many priests succumbed to sex, drugs (or alcohol) and Carl Rogers during this period. The stress was enough to drive a strong man to drink. The fact that Sawher didn't succumb to these pressures was in large measure traceable not only to the natural gifts he possessed but to his faith, which saw him through a battle of Homeric proportions, although it must not have seemed that way when it was occurring. But then great spiritual battles seldom do.

As the account of the riots surrounding the occupation of the Sojourner Truth Housing Project shows, ethnic parishes had been targeted for social engineering beginning in World War II. The reason Detroit was devastated by the '67 riots and not by the '43 riots, which left thirty-five people dead, was in large measure due to the changes which had taken place in the Catholic Church in the interim. The main difference between 1942 and 1969 was the Second Vatican Council. The social engineering which got smuggled into the Church under its name had a devastating effect on religious life. But the biggest difference was the effect that the Council had on bishops, in particular on the bishop of Detroit. The irony, of course, is that the very Council which was supposed to rehabilitate the role of bishop in the church had the exact opposite effect, weakening them so that they could no longer defend the Catholic Church against the sophisticated attacks mounted against her and her people. Sawher noticed the change in John Cardinal Dearden, his ordinary in Detroit:

> Whereas he was always a traditional conservative person before the Council, now he was a liberal, and would become the leader of the liberal bishops of the United States. Gradually, the priests working downtown became divided between liberals and conservatives.[9]

The differences are even more apparent if we compare Dearden to his predecessor Archbishop Mooney. Mooney was an Irish bishop when the Irish and the Poles in the Catholic Church in this country considered themselves members of two separate races. The antagonism between Irish bishops and Polish clergy was the driving force behind the creation and spread of the Polish National Church in this country, but when the Church came under attack as federal agents tried to force the unwanted Sojourner Truth Housing Project down the throats of St. Louis the King Parish, Mooney supported his Polish auxiliary, and the Church presented a united front to the local politicians, who ultimately supported their cause until they were forced to capitulate to superior force (including troops) at the hands of the federal government.

The Second Vatican Council gave the Church in Detroit a completely unrealistic notion of the forces arrayed against her. At the very moment when the liberal regime in the United States was gearing up what was probably the most sophisticated campaign of psychological warfare ever waged against the Catholic Church, the Catholic faithful were being told through various Zeitgeist-inspired interpreters of *Gaudium et Spes* that they had nothing to fear from the modern world. Being progressive meant intellectual disarmament in this war. As a result the city with the most liberal bishop in the country ended up having the most devastated Catholic neighborhoods in the country as well.

Msgr. Sawher saw all this from the point of view of a soldier in the trenches of a cultural war that was, at the time it was happening, still undeclared. War is the only word that captures the devastation Detroit was experiencing at the time. One day Msgr. Sawher decided to go to a nursing home he chaplained by a different route. What he saw shocked him. "It was," he wrote,

> the first time I witnessed the destruction that had occurred by fire. I had not traveled down that street for some time. However, if I thought that was bad, this is what I wrote when I traveled down Kercheval, "Building after building was sacked, burned, destroyed, but standing and ugly." I was going to St. John's Hospital which is why I went down Kercheval. When I got to the hospital, I met a young lady from the Parish, and I told her about what I had just witnessed. She said she could cry over the devastation that had occurred where she had lived on Westphalia. We wondered if the mayor of Detroit had ever seen this destruction that was going on in our once-proud city of Detroit? It was no wonder people were leaving by the thousands each month. What could any of us do to prevent further destruction? . . . I was amazed at how many people began to tell me about their experiences. We were in a war zone. Detroit had become a battle zone. Through it all, I realized that I had to do all I could to make Assumption Grotto an oasis, a fertile area of living in the midst of the desert of destruction around us.[10]

In 1976 the fifth column which Carl Rogers's psychology had created within the Catholic clergy by enabling sexual deviance came out into the open at a conference at Detroit's Cobo Hall, sponsored by Cardinal Dearden and the American bishops called Call to Action. Right around this time – a month or so before Call to Action – Sawher noticed that the culture wars had created a beachhead within his parish boundaries. Coleman Young, it seems, "had made a remark that he would see to it that the 'lily-white' neighborhood out on the northeast side would change. We had heard about the tactics that had been used in the city in other areas, and we knew the same would happen to us. We just did not know when or how it would come about."[11]

Two years later, Sawher discovered that HUD agents were infiltrating the neighborhood, working hand-in-glove with real-estate agents who were involved in blockbusting.

> In the July 10th [1977] copy of the Grotto News, I reported to the people of the parish what had been told to me, and which was confirmed: HUD representatives were canvassing the neighborhoods of Grotto Parish, looking for houses to buy. In the week of August 21st I met with the Mayor's Director of Human Rights and with area leaders and block club leaders. We protested vigorously to the Human Rights Department against the unscrupulous efforts of the many realtors in the northeast area who were telling people that they might better sell now, for the value of their property was going to tumble. . . . While this worked, and many realtors were furious, the damage had been done. Fear had taken over many parishioners as well as non-parishioners. It was the beginning of what would eventually amount to the loss of 3500 families from Grotto over the next ten years. I knew I could not stem the tide completely, but perhaps I could do something to slow it down.[12]

As in every other large city where the same sort of thing took place, the terms black and white disguised rather than revealed the real sides in this cultural war. Chafets notes, "interestingly," that 45 percent of the money which funded Coleman Young's political machine came from the "white" suburbs. He goes on to add that Young was supported by the "white industrial establishment indebted to him for keeping the lid on."[13] Young was also a sexual revolutionary who had to defend himself against a paternity suit in his last years in office and (therefore) on this earth.

Sawher writes about Assumption Grotto's resistance to abortion alongside his attempts to keep the beleaguered parish afloat without any sense that the two issues might be related, when in fact abortion is one of the issues that breaks the black/white racial dichotomy into its true components. What the Catholics of Assumption Grotto faced was a war on two fronts, not just against the black foot soldiers who were moving into their neighborhoods but against the much-less-visible "industrial establishment" which was using the blacks as warriors in their war by proxy against the Catholics. It was upper-class white Protestants uniting with lower class black Protestants against the Catholic ethnic middle class in the middle.

Six years into his priesthood, in the mid-'50s, Sawher noticed that "the move of the black people from the inner city" was beginning and that "the direction" it was taking "was west and northwest."[14] He also noticed that the movement of blacks into Catholic neighborhoods was being driven by the construction of the same highway, the Lodge Freeway, "which divided Precious Blood [Parish] in half and weakened it considerably."[15] That meant that Assumption Grotto was not on the main route of ethnic cleansing in Detroit, but it meant that Immaculate Conception Parish was. When it was announced that GM was going to build a plant there in 1980, June Manning Thomas praised the ethnic cleansing of Poletown as a "testimony to both technical and political skills," of "[Coleman] Young and his talented staff, particularly CEDD Director Emmett Moten."[16]

Those skills included shepherding a "quick take" eminent-domain bill through the state legislature in Lansing, which abrogated even further property rights that had been weakened by *Berman v. Parker*, the 1954 Supreme Court decision approving urban renewal. "The project," Thomas goes on to tell us, "in no way jeopardized the support of Young's loyal constituency"[17] precisely because it appealed to the WASP/black alliance which lay at the heart of Young's political machine. As part of the Poletown deal, Young was able to steal land from the ethnics and give it to General Motors while at the same time shouting down anyone who disagreed as a racist. The Poletown deal revealed the true players behind what was called the civil rights movement in all of the Catholic ethnic urban strongholds of the North, which was an ethnic struggle based on religious affiliation.

In January of 1984, Sawher asked his parishioners to write to Young and the city council, "asking them to help us overcome the increasing crime rate in our neighborhood – the arson and looting taking place."[18] The net result of this letter-writing campaign was that the arson and looting increased. "We knew we would get no help from the mayor who had called our neighborhood 'that lily white north east area,'"[19] Sawher concluded. When Cardinal Czoka announced around the same time that he was closing 43 of the 114 churches in the city, Coleman Young "made it clear" – privately, of course – "that he was not sorry to see the churches close" because "Catholics are mostly white, and they've left the city. And a lot of the churches that are still here have erected racial barriers. Why should the church subsidize prejudice?"[20]

As a result the situation in Assumption Grotto Parish worsened. "The next six or seven years," Sawher wrote, "would be very trying. . . . Businesses on Gratiot, as throughout the whole city, began to close and unfortunately the store fronts soon became junk yards. The city was becoming a jungle" although "Coleman Young. . . did not like that expression."[21]

Ethnic cleansing benefited both parts of the WASP/black alliance. GM got prime real estate for a song. The benefit of ethnic cleansing from Coleman Young's point of view was equally clear. By driving the Catholics out of Detroit, Young could provide blacks who kept him in office with cheap, if not free, housing. His black constituents, in turn, showed their gratitude by making Young in effect mayor for life. Coleman Young was carried out of the mayor's office in a box, the only possible way he could have been removed.

One of the benefits of ethnic cleansing, as events in places like Yugoslavia have shown, is free housing. The situation in Detroit was no different. The effects were no different either. Msgr. Sawher soon noticed that people who were given houses as political plunder didn't have a good record when it came to maintaining them. As a result Coleman Young's ethnic-cleansing–based housing policies in Detroit were a lot like slash-and-burn farming. The people who were given housing would run one neighborhood into the ground and then move on to the next set of houses in the next ethnically cleansed enclave, leaving massive destruction in their wake. The blacks who replaced the Catholic ethnics in Assumption Grotto's neighborhoods, according to Msgr. Sawher,

> did not have either the money or the know-how to keep up their property. They were handed a piece of real estate and a house, but they did not now what to do with it. Many had lived in housing projects where everything was taken care of. No one taught them what to do, how to maintain a home and property. They were victims in a different sense than we were. Houses were selling for a pittance. Burglary was rampant. Fires were increasing. As a result of this, many families decided that there was no reason to stay. No one could stop the carnage that was taking place. Beautiful streets became lined with burned-out homes. The streets were littered with the material taken out of burned-out houses. Store fronts became dumping grounds. It was sad. We had to keep our heads and do what we could to make Grotto an oasis in the midst of the plundering. I wanted people to see that not everything was going to rack and ruin. I had to keep in my mind thoughts in the psalm-prayer of morning prayers for Wednesday, Week II, "Through your Son you taught us, Father, not to be fearful of tomorrow, but to commit our lives to your care. Do not withhold your Spirit from us but help us find a life of peace after these days of trouble." Trouble is what we were going to have and in abundance.[22]

In addition to free land for General Motors, the ruling class got other benefits from supporting Coleman Young's campaign of ethnic cleansing in Detroit. Destroying the Church's parish infrastructure disrupted its ability to influence the social order on moral issues. As a result, the Church was hampered in its efforts to oppose abortion, which meant demographic power by default to the ruling class, which stopped having large families in the 1920s. Msgr. Sawher continued the battle against abortion, while simultaneously trying to save his parish from destruction. At some points in his narrative he almost sees a connection between the two struggles:

> As though the subject of abortion wasn't bad enough, it also happened that on that particular Sunday we experienced the lowest offertory collection in the history of the parish. I thought, at the time, that it would be made up because some of the parishioners went downtown, but that was a not to be a fulfilled hope. Although I did not realize it at the time, this trend was going to continue and would, in such a few short years, result in our having to close the school. It seems impossible that things could disintegrate so rapidly.[23]

But it is at hopeless moments like this that providence intervenes in unexpected ways. Precisely because Sawher, who "while trying to keep solvent" was "also still involved in the battle of the abortion issue,"[24] heard about a priest who had been arrested while protesting at an area clinic. Sawher went to Father Eduard Perrone's trial and by doing so set up a chain of events whereby Perrone eventually ended up succeeding him as pastor of Assumption Grotto, an event which brought about a revival of the parish. Eventually,

Perrone would go on to organize the Call to Holiness conferences to protest the twentieth anniversary of Call to Action in Detroit.

The resurrection of Assumption Grotto was, however, a pyrrhic victory for the Church in Detroit. The refugees from ethnic cleansing who fled Assumption Grotto to the suburbs were replaced by refugees from suburban parishes who could no longer tolerate moral anarchy, bad theology, and the debased liturgies that got celebrated there. Assumption Grotto survived and went on to thrive but only because the sense of parish as a geographical community died when Detroit's neighborhoods died. This turn of events "turned out to be a wonderful turn of events for Grotto," Msgr. Sawher concluded, "but it was, nevertheless, sad that people could not feel comfortable in the parish where they lived."[25] The rise of what one might call "neo-ethnic" parishes like Assumption Grotto under Father Perrone was a function of the crisis of faith afflicting the Catholic Church in Detroit. The fact that many Catholics were unable "to find peace and go to Mass in their own neighborhoods" meant the further demise of the idea of local community that the ethnic parish once embodied. The Catholic Church was gradually being transformed from a collection of geographical parishes into a collection of affinity groups based on liturgy and doctrine – the Catholic variant of high church–low church. The destruction of the parish as the local community which the CIC and racial migration helped bring about a system of parish life based on the liberal/conservative dichotomy, another way of expressing the scale of assimilation among Catholics following Vatican II. Sawher characterizes those Catholics unwilling to assimilate on the sexual issues "Magisterial Catholics" and finds that they flock to Assumption Grotto because they "are not always welcome in their own parishes."[26]

The Catholic Church still teaches that a parish is a geographical unit and that the Church is divided up according to these units of geography and not according to lifestyle preferences which turn the Church into one more product-based consumer group, like Harley-Davidson motorcycle owners. The CIC response to racial migration contributed to the erosion of the parish as the basis for the local community by portraying it as guilty of racism simply because it excluded certain groups of people. No group can exist without exclusion, because exclusion is what creates the group in the first place. The parish, as a result of this assault, abandoned geography and ethnicity and took refuge in patterning itself on class- and interest-based affinity groups, a move that would have far-reaching consequences for both the Church and the state.

Notes

1   Ze'ev Chafets, *Devil's Night: And Other True Tales of Detroit* (New York: Random House, 1990), p. 18.
2   Monsignor Clifford F. Sawher, *An Autobiography of a Grateful Priest* (Detroit: Assumption Grotto Press, 2001), p. 191.
3   Chafets, p. 18.
4   Ibid., p. 177.
5   Ibid., p. 178.
6   Sawher, p. 403.

7   Ibid., p. 213.

8   Ibid., p. 213.

9   Ibid., p. 376.

10 Ibid., p. 279.

11 Ibid., p. 286.

12 Chafets, p. 192.

13 Sawher, p. 168.

14 Ibid.

15 June Manning Thomas, *Redevelopment and Race* (Baltimore: The Johns Hopkins University Press, 1997), p. 163.

16 Ibid., p. 164.

17 Sawher, p. 344.

18 Ibid.

19 Chafets, p. 188.

20 Sawher, p. 358.

21 Ibid., p. 359.

22 Ibid., p. 345.

23 Ibid., p. 361.

24 Ibid., p. 504.

25 Ibid., p. 594.

Robert Weaver and B-BURG

Less than one month after Kevin White defeated Ed Logue in Boston's mayoral race of 1967, Ford Foundation operative Robert Weaver, now head of HUD in Washington, arrived in Boston to announce the largest housing-rehabilitation program in the nation's history. Weaver, as the highest-ranking black in the Johnson Administration, was under pressure to do something to prevent a repeat of the riots which had taken place during the summer of 1967.

His solution for Boston was known as B-BURG, or Boston Banks Urban Renewal Group, a program which freed up $29 million in FHA loan money so that Boston's under-privileged could buy their own homes. What Weaver failed to tell the public when he announced the official beginning of the program in May 1968 is that that mortgage money would only go to blacks, and it would only go to blacks who agreed to buy houses in the area B-BURG had redlined for change, an area that coincided exclusively with up-till-then overwhelmingly Jewish Roxbury. B-BURG was, in other words, a government-sponsored ethnic cleansing scheme that for once targeted someone other than Catholic ethnics.

Why it targeted Jews could be deduced from a number of facts peculiar to the situation in Boston. First of all, the Irish in Boston were perceived as too tough to push around and willing to shed blood in the streets before they would move out of their neighborhood. The Jews, on the other hand, were perceived as generally liberal, which is to say, certainly sympathetic to, if not in the forefront of, the civil-rights movement. In a place like Roxbury, this impression was largely an illusion, because the main Jewish support for the civil-rights movement came from the suburbs, i.e., from Jews who were bent on assimilation and wanted to prove their bona fides by supporting WASP causes. B-BURG meant in effect that more-assimilated Jews would sacrifice the neighborhood of their less assimilated fellow Jews as an offering to the ruling class they aspired to join, even if it meant that some of those less-assimilated Jews happened to be their own parents.

The Jewish organizations, groups like the AJC and the ADL, were so unremittingly assimilationist in their orientation that they simply ignored the plight of the Jews who got left behind in the great move out to the suburbs. Hillel Levine and Lawrence Harmon even claim that those organizations were informed about the redlining that eventually led to the ethnic cleansing of the neighborhood. In a report on the demise of Roxbury written years after it had occurred, the *Boston Globe* reported that the existence of the B-BURG line, while not widely publicized, was "known to FHA officials, Boston Redevelopment Authority officials, and leaders in both the black *and Jewish communities*"[1] (my emphasis).

The intra-ethnic class issue in Boston housing was even more pronounced among the city's Jews than among the city's Catholics. The intra-ethnic conflict was between those who moved to the suburbs and those who remained in the city. As with the Catholics, the main issue behind the housing issue was assimilation. The Jews who were avid to assimilate, which meant moving to the suburbs, were also willing to sell out their less fortunate brethren as an offering to the ruling class. They were also willing to spy on their own people and share the information with the ruling class. When Rabbi Marvin Antelman founded a New England Chapter of Meir Kahane's Jewish Defense League, he found that he was being spied on by local agents of the Anti-Defamation League. The ADL routinely spied on other Americans over issues like housing, but now they were spying on fellow Jews "whose agenda seemed no more ominous than protecting a group of elderly residents,"[2] something which showed the rabid commitment of mainstream Jewish organizations to assimilation. Just as Ted Kennedy's failure to defend Catholic neighborhoods led to the rise of politicians like Louise Day Hicks and Ray Flynn, so the failure of Jewish leadership in Boston to come to the defense of Roxbury led to the rise of Meir Kahane and the Jewish Defense League, which sent its own version of the local militia to patrol Roxbury's streets in the wake of B-BURG and protect the aged Jews there from being attacked by black criminals.

The second reason B-BURG targeted Roxbury was essentially financial. Most of the Jews who lived there owned their own homes, having long since paid off their mortgages. This meant that Roxbury was the real-estate equivalent of a "dead zone" that was in need of "motion" in the form of the real-estate turnover that made money for the banks. The idea of constant motion as the ideal of an enlightened – or as the Marquis de Sade would say, revolutionary – society had collateral benefits by also turning Boston's lower-class blacks – who were "forced every three or four years to uproot themselves either because of a federal program for urban renewal or because of the fact that the decay in the community"[3] had made life there intolerable – into a permanent revolutionary cadre. Boston's blacks became, as a result, willy nilly part of the *Lumpenproletariat* whose antisocial mores helped drive ethnics – both Jews and Catholics – out of the neighborhoods they controlled.

The prospect of $29 million in mortgage money ignited a feeding frenzy among Boston's real-estate agents, who rushed in and applied the crudest form of blockbusting tactics to coerce the Jews into selling. The real-estate agents wanted to get a slice of the pie before the federal mortgage money ran out, and so they became, witting or not, agents of ethnic cleansing. "We weren't subtle about it," one blockbusting real-estate agent recounted years later.

> You'd say, how would you like it if they raped your daughter, and you've got a mulatto grandchild? I remember one particular family where this little girl was about 12 years old and blonde, she was a very pretty little kid. And I used that on them, and it did sway them. They sure as hell sold! I even used it once on a son, the little boy would get raped. Whatever worked, I would try to use.[4]

The financial incentives used to lure real-estate agents into the ethnic cleansing of Roxbury should not obscure the fact that the operation was done not with economic but rather political goals in mind of the sort we have already mentioned. The FHA functioned as the intermediary between political goals and economic benefits, orchestrating the latter with the former in mind. By dealing with local entrepreneurs, the FHA could achieve its political goals while bypassing the traditional political structure in the city. Roxbury, was according to Levine and Harmon, the "perfect operating environment for the FHA,"[5] because it allowed them to deal directly with the banking and construction community rather than city officials, who were elected by people actually living in Boston.

Once it became apparent that the neighborhood had been targeted for ethnic cleansing, there was no need to exaggerate the natives' fear of crime. The reality was intimidating enough. As in Detroit's Poletown, when it became apparent that the neighborhood had been abandoned, criminals moved in and engaged in crime with impunity. A welfare mothers' protest in June 1967 escalated into a full-scale riot, but, according to the spin put on it by the *Globe* and other local newspapers, the rioting only proved that blacks were oppressed and, therefore, justified in taking the law into their own hands, which they then proceeded to do on an individual basis. Slowly a transformation took place in certain elements of Boston's black population, a change that could be termed the Eldridge Cleaver effect, whereby criminal activity, including rape and assault, was now construed as an insurrectionary act and, therefore, morally justified. The main effect of the black-power movement in Boston, according to Levine and Harmon, was that now "many young black hoodlums fancied themselves as Freedom Fighters."[6] That meant that "an assault on an elderly pensioner" could now be portrayed as "an attack on capitalism itself."[7]

As in Detroit's Poletown, arson became a common form of intimidation in Roxbury. On the morning of May 27, 1970, two of the synagogues which had not yet moved out of the neighborhood – Chevra Shas and Agudun Israel – were set on fire within minutes of each other. Gradually, the victims of crime in Roxbury began to feel that there was a political force orchestrating what seemed to be random violent acts. The situation in Boston under Kevin White was different politically than the situation in Detroit under Coleman Young. White's "most solid political support" came from precisely "those black and Jewish neighborhoods most adversely affected by blockbusters in pursuit of the Boston Banks Urban Renewal Group largesse."[8] In other words, B-BURG was not in White's political interest, but it was in the political interest of Robert Weaver and the Ford Foundation and the Vault, all of whom had supported in one way or another Logue's candidacy for mayor. When White defeated Logue, Logue's backers in Boston were forced to pursue the same policies by different means. That meant using federal money and foundation money to circumvent local political control.

Roxbury's aged Jews were being punished, as a result, because of their reputation for liberalism on racial matters – or at least their children's attempts to continue this reputation. When slogans like "Move Jew" were painted on the walls of vandalized houses in Roxbury, liberal Rabbis like Balfour Brickner, who would later become a prominent defender of abortion and other aspects of the WASP eugenic movement, were determined to ignore the racial element implicit in such attacks. "Suburban Jews . . . were busy forging civil rights alliances with blacks of equal stature and accomplishment" whose burdens were borne "by poorer Jews for whom issues of basic safety outweighed ideology."[9]

The class divisions among Jews in Boston mirrored in an uncanny way the same class divisions the WASP ruling class was exploiting among the Irish. "The feelings of abandonment," according to Levine and Harmon, "in both Irish and Jewish neighborhoods, quickly turned into bitterness at one's own."[10] When Teddy Kennedy tried to talk to a crowd of Irish Catholics about busing in the fall of 1974 he was booed off the stage, pelted with tomatoes and eggs, and eventually driven at full run to the safety of his office in the new federal building off of City Hall Plaza. Similarly working class Jews whose neighborhoods were being handed over to blacks by Jewish organizations in collusion with the

Boston, late 1960s, busing into Roxbury as precursor to an attack on Roxbury's housing

federal government began joining the Jewish Defense League. Both groups were saying in an inchoate way that assimilation was being exacted at too high a price. Both groups were repudiating the policies of Ed Logue, who felt that "there was something un-American about returning to where you had already been"[11] and as a result was "confident that residents of Roxbury and other urban renewal areas would, in time, understand that they were involved in a historic national experiment upon which the progress of America depended."[12] What Boston's irate Jews and Irish Catholics could not have known at the time is that by rejecting Logue at the polls, they got his policies foisted on them by collusion between the Ford Foundation and the federal government.

In a sequence of events that reversed the order of events in South Boston and Charlestown, the attack on Roxbury's housing was preceded by an attack on Roxbury's schools. In the Spring of 1965, at around the same time that the committee created by the state's education commissioner announced that racial imbalance was a problem in Boston's schools, the Solomon Lewenberg Junior High School in Roxbury had 1,200 students, 10 percent of whom were black. One year later minority enrollment increased to 22 percent and enrollment dropped to 1,100. Those numbers would accelerate over the next few years. Each time the minority population increased by a certain percentage, a corresponding number of white students would drop out of the school. And when the school's Jewish students departed, the school's order and discipline departed with them.

By 1968, the overall student body at the Lewenberg school had shrunk to 754 students, of whom only 32 percent were white. Once classes re-opened for the '68–'69 school year, it became obvious that the teachers had lost control of the school. Black students ran through the halls of the school unhindered, shouting black-power slogans they had learned during the previous summer. As in the related instance of black crime, ideology did much to fuel antisocial behavior. Every time a white teacher disciplined a black student it was construed as a racist incident, causing increasing demoralization among the teaching staff at the school.

Lewenberg Junior High School was to busing what the West End was to urban renewal. It was a sign to the city's ethnic neighborhoods that the social engineering that portrayed itself as social justice may or may not have deliberately intended the destruction of neighborhood communities as its primary goal, but it certainly brought that destruction about as its primary effect.

The rest of Boston's ethnic communities as a result felt forewarned on busing by Lewenberg just as they felt forewarned on urban renewal by the West End. What they could not have known at the time was that the two campaigns were related, and that the Ford Foundation was once again a crucial link between them. In an internal memo on the Gray Areas Programs covering the period from January to June 1963, the foundation's leadership announced that "the schools are an obvious place to begin work on the problems of the Gray Areas."[13]

Along with reviving urban renewal by paying attention to its "human" dimension, the "integration" of the public schools was an integral part of Ford's ABCD grant to Boston from the beginning, but from Ford's perspective that meant weakening the control which the locally elected school board had over the schools. In July of 1963, Henry Saltzman, whom Paul Ylvisaker claimed had a "fatal attraction" to Saul Alinsky and his methods, told Ylvisaker, "I do not think we should get ourselves into the position of helping the Boston school system make up for its lack of growth over the past decade."[14] Growth, in this instance, meant increasing Ford control over the schools at the expense of local control over the schools. When Ylvisaker was asked years later if he wanted to "by-pass" local school boards "because they were still committed to segregated schools," he responded in the affirmative, adding that those local school boards "were capable of taking money and making damn sure nothing got done with it."[15]

Ylvisaker, on the other hand, knew what he wanted to do with Ford money. That money was spent to implement policies which were consonant, as he would later admit, with what the Ford family had always done, namely, manipulating migration for political effects beneficial to their economic interests. "The Ford Motor Company," Ylvisaker admitted in an interview conducted after he had left the foundation, "has been as guilty as any major industrial firm of recruiting cheap labor from the South while having a surplus locally. I always used to feel slightly guilty about talking in Detroit about handling the migrant problems when you were up against that canvas of things."[16]

Taking control of migration was shorthand for the attack on ethnic interests that the Ford Foundation was orchestrating in Boston and every other city where Ford's Gray Areas foundations had been set up, and that meant the manipulation of both housing and schooling in their interests. It also meant that the government would follow Ford's lead on matters like urban policy, because cities, in foundation parlance, were just another word for the place where housing and schools served as conduits for racial migration. Ylvisaker served on President Kennedy's task force on the city and was chairman of President Johnson's task force on the city, which, Ylvisaker bragged twenty years after the fact, had been adopted pretty much whole cloth into the Kerner commission's recommendations following the riots of the '60s. As part of its efforts to take control of migration in Boston and steer it in the direction of its own interests, Ford also funded a research project at Harvard and MIT by Edward Banfield and Martin Myerson, which articulated Ford's vision of the New Boston. Part of that vision entailed plans for the city's public schools which got published as a full-page ad in Boston's papers, entitled "What Price Public Schools?" after Banfield and Myerson's book, *Boston: The Job Ahead*, was published in 1963.

The attempt to "integrate" the Lewenberg school beginning in 1966 was not only part of Ford's educational plan for the city, it was also "a dress rehearsal for the desegregation crisis that would rock Boston in the middle 1970s."[17] Once again Mattapan's and Roxbury's Jews made an attractive first target because the WASP establishment knew from experience that their "Irish, Polish, and Italian neighborhoods preferred blood in their streets to blacks in their classrooms."[18] Boston's Catholic ethnics became convinced that integration was inimical to their interests precisely because of what happened at Lewenberg, where "the decline in standards of learning and behavior"[19] had been dramatic.

In the meantime, things were changing at Ford. In the early months of 1966, John J. McCloy tapped McGeorge Bundy to become head of the Ford Foundation; Ylvisaker left one year later and eventually became dean of Harvard's School of Education, where he almost got dragged into the busing debacle in 1974. Sensing both the magnitude of the disruption that busing posed for Boston as well as Ylvisaker's links with the establishment, Kevin White went to Derek Bok, then president of Harvard University, and asked him to release Ylvisaker to work on resolving the busing issue. Ylvisaker, however, refused to get involved in the issue. Bundy's initial endorsement of Ylvisaker's Gray Areas Programs as "the only shop that survives as having any relevance," followed by Ylvisaker's departure in December of 1966, and subsequent claim that Ford subsequently made grants under Bundy without "doing its homework" give some indication that Bundy took the same principles that Ylvisaker articulated and applied them in a manner that Ylvisaker found reckless.

One example of that recklessness which Ylvisaker mentions specifically was Ford's involvement in the New York City school decentralization fight of 1968, a battle which pitted largely Jewish teachers against largely black parents in the Ocean Hill-Brownsville section of Brooklyn. United Federation of Teachers President Albert Shanker accused his opponents of blatant anti-Semitism, and people like Norman Podhoretz accused Ford of funding this black anti-Semitism as a way of playing one ethnic group off against another in an attempt to gain control of the situation. The Ford-funded Ocean Hill-Brownsville debacle led to the biggest surge of membership increase for Meir Kahane's Jewish Defense League, the same group which would arrive in Roxbury to defend that neighborhood's aged Jewish residents against the black crime that became pandemic as soon as it appeared that the neighborhood was targeted for racial change.

Notes

1   Hillel Levine and Lawrence Harmon, *The Death of an American Jewish Community: A Tragedy of Good Intentions* (New York: The Free Press, 1992), p. 323.
2   Ibid., p. 262.
3   Ibid., p. 300.
4   Ibid., p. 4.
5   Ibid., p. 115.
6   Ibid., p. 89.
7   Ibid.
8   Ibid., p. 269.
9   Ibid., p. 258.
10 Ibid.
11 Ibid., p. 94.
12 Ibid.
13 Education and Public Affairs: The Schools and Urban "Gray Areas," Gray Areas folder January to June 1963, Ylvisaker papers, Box 5, Harvard University Archives.
14 Henry Saltzman to Paul Ylvisaker, 7/2/63, Gray Areas folder January to June 1963, Ylvisaker papers, Box 5, Harvard University Archives.
15 Oral history for Ford Foundation, conducted 9/27/73, p. 31, Ylvisaker Papers, Box 5, Harvard University Archives.
16 Oral history, p. 81.
17 Levine, p. 217.
18 Ibid., p. 218.
19 Ibid.

The Dirty Annies and Gang Warfare
in Most Blessed Sacrament Parish

By the time Father Joseph Meehan arrived at Most Blessed Sacrament during the summer of 1971, the situation in the neighborhood had reached the point of all-out irregular warfare waged by the neighborhood's gangs, warfare which resulted in people on both sides getting killed. On April 9, 1971, a fourteen-year-old black youth by the name of Russell Peed died after being hit over the head with a broomstick. One month later, twenty-year-old Tyrone Dunbar was stabbed to death. As it had in the past, *The Philadelphia Inquirer* continued its one-sided coverage of gang warfare in Southwest Philadelphia by focusing its attention on a white gang known as the Dirty Annies. Before the school year ended, 500 students at the predominantly black John Bartram High School poured out of classes one afternoon and roamed through the neighborhood determined to avenge the killings. After starting a number of fights, the Bartram students were eventually brought under control by the police, but the situation remained tense until school closed for the summer.

Throughout the spring and summer of 1971, the *Philadelphia Inquirer* consistently portrayed the situation as if there were no black gangs in the neighborhood. According to the newspaper reports, there was just a white gang in the neighborhood, the Dirty Annies, which engaged in unprovoked attacks on black individuals. The *Inquirer* then used the incidents to further inflame black animosity against the Irish Catholics, who had been living there for most of the century. The Peed family, according the *Inquirer* account, had just moved to the MBS neighborhood from the Tasker projects in South Philadelphia "to avoid racial conflict."[1]

Leon Dunbar, Tyrone's brother, took the occasion of his brother's funeral, which was held at Bethany Baptist Church at 58th and Warrington, a building which used to house the synagogue of Congregation Beth Am, to call on his fellow mourners to "do whatever is necessary."[2] Lest the assembled mourners find his exhortation too vague, Dunbar told the congregation at Bethany Baptist, "If you kill, do it because you have to, not because you're doing it for kicks or you want to,"[3] which the *Inquirer* dutifully relayed to its readers. Walter Palmer, someone identified as a "militant organizer" also attending the funeral, told the crowd not to cooperate with the police. "You're mistaken if you think the police are going to protect the black community," Palmer said to shouts of approval from the crowd of mourners, "We have to protect ourselves."[4]

Joe Alulis would have agreed with Palmer's assessment of police protection in the neighborhood, but Alulis was white, had lived in the neighborhood all his life, and was now finding himself on the receiving end of the violence, perpetrated by the nameless black gangs. On a Friday evening in the fall of 1971, Alulis was walking with his twelve-year-old sister from their home near 53rd and Kingsessing to a pizzeria neat 56th and Chester, when a black gang began shouting at them from across the street. Alulis had decided to ignore the gang when he noticed that they had crossed the street and were walking in his direction from behind. The next thing he knew one of the gang members was beating him over the head with a section of lead pipe.

As a bit of added symbolism, Alulis noted that the assault took place in front of Most Blessed Sacrament Church. It might have proved fatal if a number 13 trolley car hadn't pulled up in the middle of the beating and scared his assailants away. Two years later, Alulis's family, which had lived for Joe's whole life in MBS Parish, moved out of the neighborhood. By that point, the violence had become intolerable and the deterioration of the neighborhood inescapable. Rats began appearing in the alleys where Alulis used to catch fireflies as a boy. Cars were abandoned on the streets, where they turned into rusted, often burned-out, hulks. Across the street one of Alulis's new black neighbors opened an after-hours speakeasy, where the unbridled liquor consumption round the clock led to altercations which often resulted in gunfire.[5]

None of this, of course, made it into any articles on the neighborhood which appeared in *The Philadelphia Inquirer*. Instead, Most Blessed Sacrament Parish, which until the summer of 1966 had prospered for most of the century as the largest Catholic parish in the world, was suddenly portrayed as the source of the social tension and disorder in southwest Philadelphia. In an article tellingly titled, "Schools Are Blamed for Racial Tension," John Ricchini, vice president of the Southwest Coordinating Committee of the Philadelphia's Human Relations Commission, "was especially critical of Most Blessed Sacrament Parish . . . because it has done little about the 'Dirty Annies,' a white street gang in the area."[6] The Dirty Annies, by their own admission, had formed the gang out of self-defense – "If we don't stick together, we're going to get killed."[7] – but the paper was determined to identify them as aggressors because they were Catholic. Most of the Dirty Annies, according the *Inquirer*, "are Catholic from working class families."[8] As such, "they reflect all of the bigotry and prejudice of their community."[9]

The fact that the Irish Catholics of MBS had lived in peace with each other and the neighborhood's first black families before the invasion that began during the summer of 1966 did not figure in *Inquirer* accounts of the neighborhood, which invariably tried to portray Most Blessed Sacrament Parish as the source of violence in the neighborhood. The *Inquirer* carefully chose MBS's spokesmen in order to insure that the suspicion of white racism was magnified. Margaret Prendergast, who is identified as "speaking for the parents of Most Blessed Sacrament School,"[10] claimed that "we have done really everything to integrate"[11] the school but to no avail. The only decent Christian response, in other words, was to move out of the neighborhood. Anything else would be construed as white racism. The *Inquirer* contributed to establishing the paradigm for the city's neighborhoods. The only people who were guilty of racism were the people who stayed in their traditional ethnic neighborhoods. Since these people were invariably Catholic, Catholic ethnics who refused to leave the city were invariably portrayed as racists.

Paralyzed by its lack of understanding of the nature of the assault that was waged against her, the Catholic Church resorted to her own form of social engineering. The Christian Brothers at West Catholic arranged sensitivity training sessions for equal numbers of black and white students in the area – with predictable results. The Church's cluelessness emboldened the blacks who were engaged in the assault and demoralized the

Catholic ethnics, who were blamed for the turmoil they were powerless to understand. The same *Inquirer* article which quoted Margaret Prendergast also quoted Brother Mark Lowery, then vice-principal of West Catholic High School, as saying that "the Catholic Church has not involved itself in the social aspects of a changing neighborhood," Brother Lowery was also quoted as saying that "[a]ny active white Catholic who has tried to do something about this situation has been turned off by the church. There are no young priests, none who can really relate to the white kids."[12]

Lowery later denied having made the statement the *Inquirer* attributed to him, further bolstering the case that the *Inquirer* was not a impartial observer in the events occurring in Most Blessed Sacrament Parish during 1971. The paper was actively involved in fomenting discontent among the neighborhood's blacks and laying the blame for that discontent at the feet of the neighborhood's Catholics, something which increased the cycle of violence in the neighborhood and, therefore, contributed to driving the Catholics out of their neighborhood.

The *Inquirer*'s reports on MBS conform to the ruling class's use of black gangs against Catholic ethnics in other cities as well. It also corresponded to the *Boston Globe's* one-sided coverage of the busing issue in Boston. In Chicago, Rev. Fry used the resources of the Presbyterian Church and the federal government to fund the criminal activity of the Blackstone Rangers. In Philadelphia, Bishop Robert DeWitt used the resources of the Episcopal Church to support Muhammed Kenyatta. The Quakers played along by giving Kenyatta a building in Chester after he occupied it. In each instance, the WASP establishment promoted both black criminality and black grievance as a way of destabilizing Catholic neighborhoods. When the ethnics reacted to that crime, the WASP establishment used organs of influence like the *Inquirer* to blame the increasing social disorder on white racism. The media campaign against MBS gradually merged with the media campaign against Martin Mullen, especially after Mullen held up the state budget, preventing the state government's entry into the birth-control business. The animus against MBS was fueled by the knowledge that Martin Mullen came from that congressional district and the fact that by the late '60s and early '70s he was seen as the major roadblock on the road to sexual liberation in the state of Pennsylvania. Mullen represented everything the WASP elite hated about Catholic ethnics, and the neighborhood around MBS bore the brunt of that hatred in an unrelenting media campaign whose purpose was to portray the Catholics there as violent racists as the first step in driving them out of the neighborhood and into the suburbs, where their votes would be diluted enough to ensure that they would never be able to elect someone like Mullen to public office again.

Following his arrival at MBS during the summer of 1967, Father Joe Meehan watched the situation helplessly spiral out of control from the vantage point of the MBS rectory:

> As I met the parishioners, I heard the common greeting: "Welcome to the parish, Father. It's a shame what's happening, isn't it? Too bad you weren't here when . . ." And then the litany began: when the neighborhood was wall to wall Catholic; when we had Masses almost every hour in both the upstairs and downstairs church and both were bulging – people standing in the aisles and even in the street; when they had about four funerals a week and marriages had to be arranged about a year

> ahead of time; when twenty-five priests came at Christmas to hear confessions, when our school was probably the biggest Catholic elementary school in the world.[13]

Meehan soon concluded that he had been trained for the MBS of 1964 and not the MBS of 1971, which was "a world of smashing glass, barking guard dogs, [and] multiple locks."[14] Meehan became plagued by fear. To begin with, there was the fear of physical injury which was real enough. But before long, Meehan became convinced that he was witnessing a war, in fact, "children at war":

> the front steps of the Church, the schoolyard, the playgrounds, the neighboring streets saw many young children at war. The evenings found them marching in attack, and running in retreat. Even the daytime had its threatening moments: once when I was crossing the street, I was barraged by light bulbs thrown from a third-floor window. A man standing nearby explained simple: "Looks like someone just doesn't want you around here."[15]

Meehan intuitively understood that a war was taking place in his parish, but his training as a priest did not give him the intellectual tools to interpret and understand that war, much less the ability to formulate his own strategy in dealing with it. Seminary training was either dominated by the clichés of the Catholic Interracial Council or silent on the issue of race. As a result, priests were not only not instructed in measures to counter irregular warfare, they were incapable of recognizing it when it was happening. If anything, Catholic priests were trained to view their own parishioners as racists, something which was a direct result of the secularization of higher education in the Catholic Church that was taking place at the same time the racial assault was emptying the parishes of the big cities of the North in the United States. Those who found that option repugnant had to come up with some understanding of what was going on on their own, something not likely given the responsibilities a priest needed to fulfill and the fact that the Quaker archives would not be open for their inspection for another twenty years. As a result, the priests who were most sensitive to the situation began to internalize the conflict and portray the anguish they felt as a noncombatant in an undeclared civil war as a vocation crisis. Confronted with "this unfamiliar land of urban ministry in a changing parish . . . filled with violence and racial battles among the youth," Meehan began to ask, "like Moses, Who am I?"[16]

"Where then," Meehan began to wonder, "was the new mission, the new ministry" he had been trained to expect? For that matter, where was the old ministry? Where were the "crowded masses, sick calls, confessions, novenas, parish societies" that had characterized MBS during the '50s? The magnitude of the crisis caused Meehan to reflect not on ways of dealing with ethnic cleansing but on whether he had a vocation to the priesthood. Meehan, in other words, internalized the crisis, and instead of wondering why he wasn't getting reinforcements in a culture war, he began to feel that he was a bad priest or an inadequate one. The strife in the parish was, if not his fault, he thought, then indicative of his inadequacies as a priest. A better priest could have made both sides to love each other. A better priest could have squared the racial circle. He could have created an inclusive community. When that didn't happen, Meehan saw it as his failure. All that Meehan could see is that people were moving out of the parish as a result of the racial violence and that as a result, everything was "diminishing":

> Along with other urban ministers, I had to ask: What do I do today? And tomorrow? Is it hospitals and communion calls and waiting? Is it rejuvenating traditional parish societies and events? Or is the ministry to be community organizer and people's advocate? Is it sacramental, non-sacramental, parish priest or social worker? Is one the other? Anguish, loneliness. Am I losing my faith? What is this? Do I have a "vocation crisis"?[17]

The psychological-warfare campaign being waged against the Catholic Church was having its effect on people like Father Meehan, who was becoming demoralized not so much because of the fear of external threats like getting hurt in the street as from "the fear of internal isolation – isolation that came, I think, from two sources: from being in the middle between the races, and from the collapsing of previous images of myself and my role as priest."[18]

Father Meehan felt demoralized because he knew intuitively that he was functioning in a war zone but unable to describe it as such. As a result "emotionally and traditionally I was anticipating order and peace," but "there was no peace."[19] The Catholics were led to believe that they could solve the problem by abandoning their "racism," but since that allegation was simply a pretext, a ploy in a wider war, everything they did to make things better made things worse. The less-intelligent belligerents in this culture war viewed Catholic efforts at peacemaking in the neighborhood as weakness; the Catholics' more-intelligent enemies viewed their efforts as stupidity, and both wings of the opposition were encouraged by Catholic befuddlement to redouble their efforts to expel the Catholic ethnics from their neighborhoods.

Notes

1   Joseph L. Lincoln, "2 Kingsessing Killings Spark Racial Strife," *The Sunday Bulletin* (May 16, 1971): 35.
2   Ibid.
3   Ibid.
4   Ibid.
5   Interview with Joseph Alulis, 3/93.
6   Elizabeth Duff, "Schools Are Blamed for Racial Tension," *The Philadelphia Inquirer*.
7   Thomas J. Madden, "White Gang Is Resentful of 'Takeover' in Area," *The Philadelphia Inquirer* (May 16, 1971).
8   Ibid.
9   Ibid.
10 Duff, "Schools are Blamed."
11 Ibid.
12 Acel Moore and Gerald McKelvey, "Blacks Developing a 'Siege Mentality,'" *The Philadelphia Inquirer* (May 16, 1971).
13 Joseph J. Meehan "Changing Priest and Changing Parish: The Land of Jacob's Ladder,"

Dimensions (1975): 131.

14 Ibid.
15 Ibid.
16 Ibid.
17 Ibid.
18 Ibid.
19 Ibid.

Judge Garrity Orders Busing in Boston

The years between 1968 and 1971 corresponded to the time when Roxbury was ethnically cleansed as the result of Robert Weaver's efforts as head of HUD. The ethnic cleansing of Most Blessed Sacrament Parish in Philadelphia also took place during roughly the same period of time – with a different set of local entrepreneurs, but under the same federal auspices. Those same years corresponded to the greatest drop in the ethnic population of Detroit as well. Given the dramatic changes that were taking place in America's urban neighborhoods, it was only a matter of time before someone noticed that something unusual was happening.

On September 13, 1971, Senator Philip Hart of Michigan convened hearings at the John F. Kennedy Federal Building in Boston to look into the possibility that "the government," in California Senator John Tunney's words, "is acting in collusion . . . with local lending institutions and real estate agencies in order to develop and maintain ghettoes."[1] Activists across the country were claiming that the government was actively involved in the destruction of neighborhood communities, and they were demanding as a result an official inquiry into neighborhood change. Nowhere was that change more dramatic than in Boston, and so Hart decided to start the inquiry there.

Like the Reece Commission's inquiry into the subversive activities of the Ford, Carnegie and Rockefeller Foundations some seventeen years before, this inquiry got nowhere because it entailed investigating both the local and national branches of the country's elite. If anyone got punished, it was generally ethnics who were unfortunate enough to carry out the program and get caught in the process with their hand in the federal till. In the same year that Hart opened his hearings, the Justice Department filed a civil suit against the Kenealy family and their real-estate agency for enriching themselves to the tune of $350,000 by manipulating the price of housing. Kenealy was able to do this because as an FHA inspector, he "had direct access to confidential information on upcoming house sales."[2]

Kenealy and his family, in other words, were doing the same thing in Boston that C. Delores Tucker and her family were doing in Philadelphia. The Tuckers did this with impunity. In fact, in the same year that the Kenealys were convicted, C. Delores Tucker was made Pennsylvania's Secretary of the Commonwealth. The difference was both ethnic and political. Milton Shapp needed Tucker because the WASP/black alliance to ethnically cleanse Philadelphia's neighborhoods was still in full swing, and Shapp's most potent political challenger came from one of those neighborhoods. The Kenealy family, on the other hand, was expendable and, beyond that, part of the wrong ethnic group.

Senator Hart's hearings raised some uncomfortable questions, but they did not arrive in time to save Matapan's Jewish population, which fell below 3,000 people in 1972. Six months after the Hart hearings, the *Boston Globe* belatedly concluded that Boston's "policy makers played a decisive role in accelerating the movement of the slums along

Blue Hill Avenue and toward Matapan Square"[3] and that leaders in both the black and Jewish communities were aware of these efforts as they were going on. Large numbers of blacks had essentially been given housing for free. With no down payments or equity to protect, they simply occupied the houses until they were evicted because "walking away had become a rational option."[4] The destruction of Roxbury and Matapan had become a rational option for the banks too because "when the loans were foreclosed, the banks collected more from FHA insurance than they'd paid at the point of the loan origination."[5]

By 1974, over half of the people who got their mortgages through B-BURG money would lose those homes through default. That meant an increase, once again, in the rootlessness of the already rootless black *Lumpenproletariat* in Boston and a concomitant increase in all of the social pathologies which accompanied that increase. That meant, of course, further pressure on the city's remaining ethnic population. Because the real actors in the ethnic cleansing of Roxbury remained invisible, the whole thing looked like the operation of some natural phenomenon, as if "a tidal wave"[6] had broken over the neighborhood, something of political benefit to the "federal tinkerers"[7] who made it happen for political purposes.

Those political purposes could be deduced from the times. The years 1968–1972 corresponded not only to the ethnic cleansing of Roxbury, they corresponded on a national level to the high point of the ethnic revival and the Nixon Administration's attempt to create a lasting political coalition out of the resentment against social engineering which was fueling it. The ethnic revival was one more recurrence of the same forces that propelled Joe McCarthy into the limelight twenty years earlier. In 1971, the frankly ethnic Frank Rizzo was elected mayor of Philadelphia, and, in spite of being a Democrat, threw his support behind Nixon's 1972 re-election campaign. Within months of getting re-elected Nixon put a hold on the FHA's housing subsidy program, something that elicited howls of protest from C. Delores Tucker. In 1971 Roman Gribbs was mayor of Detroit and half way through the ethnics' last stand in Detroit before Coleman Young came to power in 1974.

But in 1971, the counterattack against the ethnics became evident as well. In 1971 the Supreme Court handed down its *Swann v. Charlotte-Mecklenburg* decision, which ruled that district courts could take whatever measures they deemed necessary, including steps that were "administratively awkward, inconvenient and even bizarre,"[8] to integrate the nation's urban schools. Busing must have qualified as an "awkward, inconvenient and even bizarre" measure because it was explicitly mentioned as one of the remedies which judges who chose to administer their local school districts could pursue. With this probably in mind, J. Harold Flannery, a former Justice Department lawyer who was now director of the Harvard Center for Law and Education, told Nathaniel Jones, counsel for the NAACP's Special Contribution Fund, that Boston's School Committee was a "sitting duck"[9] for a lawsuit which claimed that the Boston public schools were deliberately segregated. At around the same time, the assault on the Lewenberg school was finding its logical fulfillment in the B-BURG–funded attack on Roxbury's housing, the rest of Boston noted with concern that the state legislators, who had been at war with Boston ever since it had come under the political control of Irish Catholics, began to play up the issue of racial imbalance in Boston's schools once again.

In September 1971, the State Board of Education concluded that the Boston School

Committee had "taken official action to increase and encourage racial isolation"[10] and ordered an immediate freeze on $200 million worth of new construction in Boston and withdrawal of $14 million in state aid. In June of 1972, the U.S. Department of Health, Education and Welfare concluded that the Boston School Committee had violated the 1964 Civil Rights Act. Supported by attorneys from the Harvard Center and the Boston law firm of Foley, Hoag and Eliot, the NAACP finally filed suit against the city, and the case, officially known as *Morgan v. Hennigan* began moving through the courts. Judges were usually assigned to cases like this by anonymous lottery, and in this instance the luck of the draw went to an Irish Catholic judge by the name of Arthur Garrity. Garrity's attitude toward assimilation can be judged by the fact that he got his start in politics by working on Jack Kennedy's successful run for the senate in 1952. After directing a brilliant campaign in Wisconsin after Kennedy's successful run for the presidency in 1960, Garrity was rewarded for his loyalty when Kennedy got him a seat on the federal bench. When Boston's legal establishment heard that Garrity was the judge on the busing case, many felt that it was more than the luck of the draw that got him the job. Upon hearing that Garrity had got the busing case, Garrity's colleague Charles Wyzanski exclaimed, "Boy, I'm glad I didn't get it. You need an Irish name, a Catholic to do it."[11]

Assigning the busing decision to Judge Garrity was a bit like assigning *Roe v. Wade*, the abortion decision which would get handed down one year before Garrity handed his decision down, to Justice Brennan, the Catholic on the Court. Brennan may or may not have written the decision, but it was obvious that for political purposes any decision legalizing abortion had to have a Catholic name affixed to it.

The same thing was true in Boston when it came to busing, for much the same reason. Busing was so obviously something inimical to the Catholic interests who controlled the school committee that any other ethnic group's attempt to mandate it would cause people to view it as the obviously anti-Catholic, anti-Irish measure that it in fact was. Garrity was, in this respect, the classic lace-curtain Irishman, Irish in a demonstrative way that stopped short of opposing ruling-class initiatives that might adversely affect his shanty Irish co-religionists. Garrity had moved out of the ethnic enclave that had nurtured him as a child. He was in many ways a classic American success story in the Irish Catholic mode, but now because of his combination of success and ethnic background Garrity was called to get involved in the social engineering of the community he had left behind. It was in many ways precisely for such reasons of state that Irishmen were appointed to the bench.

As Garrity agonized over *Morgan v. Hennigan* over the next few months, the racial situation continued to bubble away. In October 1973, the Massachusetts Supreme Court ordered the school committee to put into effect a de-segregation plan for the coming fall. That in turn touched off massive protests on Boston Commons, which in turn prompted local legislators like Ray Flynn to introduce legislation repealing the Racial Imbalance Act of 1965, which, *mirabile dictu*, actually succeeded, so divisive had the issue become and so great the threat of social disorder which stemmed from it. Betraying the ethnic bias which the state's WASP establishment harbored against Boston for virtually all of the 20th century, Massachusetts Governor Francis Sargent destroyed whatever chance there was for peace in Boston when he vetoed the repeal of the Racial Imbalance Act in May of 1974. "We have not come down a nine-year road," Sargent announced on the evening of May 10 on state-wide television," only to turn our backs on those who deserve their place in the sun, their right to a quality education."[12] Then, as if recognizing how dangerous the issue had become, Sargent took a step back from the brink of civil war by announcing that he would replace the old law with a new one which allowed for voluntary rather than mandatory methods. The governor came out for "freedom of choice," and his liberal supporters, who only supported this sort of freedom when it resulted in a dead fetus, were enraged.

One month later, fifteen months after the trial had ended, twenty-seven months after it had begun, and one day after Boston's schools had closed for the summer vacation, Judge Garrity handed down his decision on *Morgan v. Hennigan*. He found that the school committee had channeled black students into certain schools not because of housing patterns, as Mrs. Louise Day Hicks contended, but with "segregative intent."[13] Garrity concluded, in the name of the court, "that the defendants have knowingly carried out a systematic program of segregation affecting all of the city's students, teachers and school facilities and have intentionally brought about and maintained a dual school system. Therefore, the entire school system of Boston is unconstitutionally segregated."[14]

Garrity then handed the implementation of his de-segregation plan over to Charles Glenn, a thirty-five-year-old Episcopalian priest from Boston who had been active in the civil rights movement in the South. Like the representatives of Boston who felt it was their duty to punish the South for the sin of slavery during Reconstruction, Rev. Glenn felt it was his duty to impose draconian if not punitive conditions on what he felt were the equally racist inhabitants of South Boston. That meant mixing now-black Roxbury with defiantly Irish South Boston, and that meant trouble, but Glenn, who "displayed a passionate zeal on racial issues," was "implacable."[15] In an instance like this, it becomes impossible to distinguish zeal for justice from animus against the group which was committing the injustice in Rev. Glenn's eyes. That meant dealing "with those bigots on the School Committee"[16] by giving them the treatment they deserved. Someone who knew Glenn sketched out his frame of mind at the time by imagining him saying to his opponents, "We've had enough of you racists in South Boston; you're going to Roxbury; let's see how you like that."[17]

Needless to say, the people in South Boston didn't like it one bit. When the schools opened in September 1974, the first buses carrying black students to South Boston High School were greeted with a barrage of rocks, bottles, and obscene suggestions and gestures. When the first buses carrying black students pulled up to South Boston High School, a mob of angry whites shouted, "Niggers, go home." Within a matter of days, the rioting escalated to attacks on buses traveling down Day Boulevard, named in honor of Mrs. Hicks's father – and Governor Sargent called out the National Guard.

Cardinal Cushing was no longer head of the Catholic Church in Boston when the busing crisis broke in the fall of 1974, but his successor, Humberto Cardinal Medeiros, the son of New Bedford's Portuguese community, lacked Cushing's ability to charm the media and in the end had no better understanding of the forces that were driving busing and their animus to Catholic interests than Cushing had. Medeiros, as a result, first supported busing, then he opposed it in a move that was guaranteed to confuse Boston's Catholics and remove the Catholic Church as a player in the dispute. Taking a page from the book on urban renewal, the Citywide Coordinating Committee named Father Michael Grodin as its director to supervise desegregation. Garrity, according to Lukas, "hoped a priest's appointment to the post would help legitimize his order, much as Frank Lally had been used a decade earlier to sanctify urban renewal."[18] If so the attempt failed. Beyond that, the presence of a priest on the CCC drove a further wedge between the rank-and-file Catholics and their leadership in Boston, making them even more difficult to manage than if no priest had been appointed to the board.

Taken aback by the vehemence of Irish Catholic protest in South Boston, the state's political establishment tried to come up with a less-disruptive plan, but they were thwarted by Judge Garrity once again, who imposed an even more draconian plan on Boston in September 1975. Not trusting the Boston's School Committee's willingness to accede to his demands, Garrity threatened to hold them and the teacher's union in contempt and ended up running the school system by fiat from his office in the federal court building, ordering things like basketballs and whistles for the system's referees until 1983, when the court finally terminated its receivership over Boston's schools.

The result of this micromanagement and what was, in effect, rule by tribunal was the destruction of the Boston public school system. Eventually, Mayor White would estimate that by 1978, five years before Judge Garrity relinquished control of Boston's schools, the busing plan had cost Boston $100 million. The school budget alone for the year 1974–75 was $131 million, a budget which included the cost of hiring minority teachers and aides, whose purpose was to stem the violence in the schools which busing had created. By 1976, Boston was spending twice as much per pupil as Cleveland and $54 million more per annum than St. Louis, which had 10,000 more students in its schools. This meant increasing taxes – to $193.20 per $1,000 of assessed value by 1975 – thereby jeopardizing the downtown renewal that began the whole chain of events. It also necessitated layoffs, which were racially applied exclusively to white teachers in order to achieve "racial balance." That meant, of course, that only experienced teachers got fired, causing a further decline in discipline and morale, which in turn showed up in enrollment figures.[19]

By 1980, three years before the court gave up administering the school system, Boston had lost 33 percent of its public school students. By 1980, 45,000 white students had left the system, which meant usually that their parents moved out of the city. During the 1970s, Boston's white population declined by 25 percent. That decline was paralleled by a similar exodus on the part of blacks who could afford other educational alternatives. The net result was a school system that by 1985 had become overwhelmingly black and poor, in other words, more segregated than the period before which Judge Garrity launched his ill-fated scheme. Boston's students were also more segregated economically than before busing. In 1985, 93 percent of all Boston public schools students came from households which earned less that the $15,000 poverty wage. By 1982, support for busing among blacks had dwindled to 14 percent. By 1988, 40 percent of Boston's ninth-graders dropped out of school, and 43 of the city's 120 schools scored so poorly on standardized tests that they now qualified for special state aid.[20]

The figures, dramatic as they are, do little to convey the human cost which busing exacted from the lives of Boston's people, something which Michael MacDonald conveys

Boston, 1975, busing unites the opposition

in his book *All Souls*, which chronicles the effect busing had on one family. MacDonald, who was born in 1966, describes experiencing the tail end of social engineering in Boston – a period during which

> the people in the neighborhood who had jobs, usually at factories and plants that bordered the neighborhood, were losing them. This was while downtown cafes and wine bistros continued to pack in the crowds of yuppies who were taking over traditionally working-class neighborhoods like Charlestown and the North End. With the rents outside the projects going up, we knew Southie was next.[21]

"Ma," MacDonald writes, "wondered out loud why we were always fighting for the same piece-of-shit schools and cockroach infested apartments."[22] The answer is simple enough. Southie had become valuable real estate and the simplest way to remove its inhabitants was by fomenting ethnic warfare with an equally undesirable group of people, namely, the blacks from Roxbury. Divide and conquer. Kill two birds with one stone. Ma, ever prescient on such matters, saw the rich liberals as the instigators in this race war, "doing what Ma said they always do: chase everyone out by bringing in the blacks, and then chasing the blacks out when it's time to build high-rise condominiums."[23] "Southie's waterfront," once the source of manufacturing and shipping jobs for the Irish proletariat, MacDonald tells us, "was set to become 'the Seaport District' with plans underway for billions of dollars in development, luxury condos, and jobs that these Boston Public School kids . . . would not be educated for."[24]

Mollenkopf has similar things to say about real estate values in the South End:

> The South End is strategically located between three institutional foci. On the northeast, the South End is only a few minutes' walk from Boston's central business district, and close also to the Tufts New England Medical Center. Boston City Hospital and the Boston University Medical Center from the southeastern border. To the southwest lies Massachusetts Avenue, a major demarcation line between the traditional South End and largely black Lower Roxbury. To the northwest, just over a set of depressed railroad lines, lie the headquarters of the Christian Scientist Church, the massive Prudential Center complex, Copley Square with its Hancock Building and chic shopping district and the rest of the Back Bay. Though redlined in the 1950s, it did not take a real estate genius to see that with financing and rehabilitation loan funds, the South End's "faded elegance" had tremendous market potential.[25]

Forced busing was the culmination of the social engineering which preceded it. The same people who had promoted the ethnic cleansing of the West End were now planning to send MacDonald and his classmates "to Roxbury with the niggers," where they were going to "get a beating."[26]

Busing, however, backfired. It united the very people it was supposed to disperse and brought to power a whole group of politicians – including Louise Day Hicks and Ray Flynn – in its wake. "We were united," MacDonald wrote, and by 1978 it was clear that the frontal assault on ethnos had failed. Forced busing simply intensified ethnic identification on both sides in the war.

> The kids in the crowd all looked at each other as if we were family. This is great,
> I thought. I'd never had such an easy time as this making friends in Southie. The
> buses kept passing by, speeding now, and all I could see in the windows were the
> black hands with their middle fingers up at us."[27]

When the frontal assault on Southie and Charlestown and Roxbury failed, the psychological warfare to break down the communities intensified. Psychological warfare had been there all along. There were in Southie the same instruments that had been used to pacify the country at large. Like their black counterparts in Roxbury, the children in Southie were avid TV watchers, as were the adults. When MacDonald's mother got hit by a stray bullet, she attracted a crowd as she was being put into an ambulance, until, that is, everyone realized that she had been shot on the same night that *Dallas* would reveal who shot J.R. "Never mind who shot Helen," said one of the project dwellers with a TV attention span, "I gotta get home and find out who shot J.R."[28]

TV was also the medium whereby the Irish learned to imitate the sexual mores of the blacks by listening to their music. That group included MacDonald's sister Mary, who began "dressing too in platform shoes and doing the dances that only the black girls knew," dances like "the robot" which she picked up by watching "Soul Train" on television.[29] Mary would go on to have two children out of wedlock, something her father attributed to her imitation of the black sexual mores she learned about on TV. Sexual liberation was a way of breaking down the integrity of communities like this as a prelude to colonization and political control. As the violence increased, the same authorities which had fomented it in the first place, then decreed that race-based violence could be prosecuted as "hate crimes."

The same sort of thing happened in Grays Ferry, which was, *mutatis mutandis*, the Philadelphia version of the same story. In early 1997, a brawl outside the hall of a Catholic parish got transformed, largely through the efforts of the *Philadelphia Inquirer*, into a racial incident in which fifty white guys allegedly beat up a black woman by the name of Annette Williams. In protest local blacks under the leadership of Charles Reeves marched through Grays Ferry in what they termed a "peace march."

When the day for the Grays Ferry "peace march" came, the police and the media were out in force. The whites decided that as a counter-protest they would turn their backs on the marchers, which of course earned them the ire of the talking heads on the Wally Kennedy show, a local talk show. "How can they solve the problem, when they turn their back on the problem" said one lady. This time there was no one on the show to take the side of the whites in Grays Ferry. Shots of the march were shown, but significantly there was no sound, although it was clear from both the *Inquirer* photos and the video tapes that blacks were shouting at the whites. Just what they were saying never became clear from the reporter sent to cover the march for *AM Philadelphia*, who contented himself by assuring the viewer that there were "words, inflammatory words to be sure" but no violence. The only language that got reported in the *Inquirer* was that used by one white man who referred to the demonstrators as "f-ing animals," while a man near him picked up a broken bottle, presumably to be used as a weapon.

Missing from all of the news accounts of the Grays Ferry "peace march" was what the black demonstrators actually had to say. The reporters on the scene decided to characterize what was said as harsh words and leave it at that, probably because any uncensored version of what the marchers had to say might cast doubt on their claim to be part of a peace march. Phelam Dean owns Dean's Bar at 29th and Tasker. He has lived in the neighborhood for all of his seventy years and what he heard didn't sound particularly peaceful: "You white motherfuckers," he heard the demonstrators shout. "We killed Brinkman, and we're going to kill you too." The reference to the murder of Chris Brinkman was unmistakable, as was the evidence that the killing was racially motivated. But neither the police nor the media seemed to pick up on this point, probably because in contemporary political parlance, racism is only something that whites inflict on blacks. Others at the march stood by and heard themselves referred to as white trash and get told that the marchers were going to burn their houses down, and then they got blamed for racial hatred in the media accounts which suppressed the racial epithets the blacks were shouting at them. Again, no one seemed to notice the irony here of a march whose purpose was to protest "ethnic intimidation" and "terroristic threats."

The Irish in Southie similarly discovered that hate speech was a one-way street. "Seamus," MacDonald writes, describing his two younger brothers, "was 13 and Stevie was 12, and friends their age were being arrested for calling people 'niggers.'"[30] The irony, of course, is that the Irish had routinely engaged in beating each other up, as MacDonald's mother had done to another Irish mother in the same projects. Now the behavior that no one had noticed had been elevated by the same people responsible for fomenting it into a federal crime, an irony not lost on Ma, who opined that "if Chickie [the woman she had punched out] had been black I'd probably have been in Federal Court."

The most powerful weapon against Southie came into play after the campaign to introduce forced busing had failed. After forced busing came drugs. MacDonald gives a clear indication of the connection between drugs and ethnic cleansing. Boston Brahmin families had made their fortunes in the drug trade with China in the 19th century. The same people who tried to solve the balance of trade problem with the Chinese by getting them addicted to opium were now using drugs like cocaine to pacify the Irish. "There'd been drugs in the neighborhood back before busing," MacDonald writes, "but not nearly as much as we'd seen since then, with so many kids dropping out of school. The neighborhood was more fragmented now. We didn't have the fight in us that we had back in 1974."[31] MacDonald's mother saw the net result of Judge Garrity's social engineering, the creation of "a whole generation of dropouts and jailbirds in our neighborhood. . . . The buses were gone for the summer, and we were left with our frustrations and anger, with high school dropouts, alcoholism and drugs galore."[32]

MacDonald claims that the drugs were introduced into Southie by Whitey Bulger, brother of the politician who was defending Southie's residents against busing. Whitey, according to MacDonald, had been turned by the government while still in prison, "after he took LSD for the government in some kind of experiments about the drug."[33] Whether this is an urban legend or a reference to the MK-Ultra program never gets clarified, due to a large extent, to the memoir nature of the book. Whatever its source, MacDonald makes clear that Whitey has some connection with the government and that during the late '70s and early '80s, Whitey started bringing up "the finest cocaine from Florida" to sell in Southie, thereby (1) enriching himself and (2) defusing the sense of solidarity the neighborhood had achieved during the busing riots. MacDonald makes clear that understanding Whitey is essential to understanding the government's involvement in using drugs as a form of social control. According to Kevin Cullen of the *Boston Globe,* Whitey Bulger was "one of the FBI's most prized informants":

> One Boston Police detective said anonymously that he believed that there was more cocaine in Southie per capita than in any other neighborhood in the city. "For years the Bulger organization has told the people of South Boston they were keeping drugs out of their community," a DEA agent said. "The people of South Boston have been had." But none of that was news to me, or to all the others who'd seen their families decimated. What was news to me was that the FBI had sponsored the parade of caskets that passed through the streets of Southie.[34]

For a moment MacDonald is taken aback by the magnitude of the forces arrayed against his neighborhood. He is tempted to dismiss the connections between Bulger and the federal government as part of Ma's "talk of conspiracies." But the fact of the matter remained, "The people of South Boston have been had," not simply by a "local gangster" but by this local gangster's collaboration with "one of the most powerful agencies in American government."[35] The Hart Committee had already demonstrated that the federal government was involved in the deliberate destruction of ethnic neighborhoods in Boston. The only thing that changed between the time of those hearings and the campaign MacDonald described as the follow-up was the federal agency involved.

Given the forces arrayed against them, it's a miracle that anyone in Southie survived, and it is that miracle which brings us to the core of the ethnic issue, namely, the relationship between ethnos and religion. Hitler, good Darwinist that he was, tried to make ethnos synonymous with race. The liberals in this country have tried the same sort of thing with about as much success. More thoughtful observers, however, have noticed something different. In America, ethnos is synonymous with religion. Digby Baltzell, apologist and chronicler of the WASP establishment, noted that in America

> the one suburban Catholic church has replaced the Irish, Polish and Italian churches and institutions which characterize the downtown neighborhoods. In short, the Italian, Polish, Russian, or Irish American of the first and second generation minorities, has now given way to the Protestant-, Catholic- and Jewish-American sense of self-identity in our postwar suburban era. While the American electorate, for instance, would not elect an obvious Irish American to the White House in 1928, they were apparently less prejudiced about the dangers of a Catholic American being sent there in 1960.[36]

MacDonald maintains an ambivalence toward Catholicism throughout the book, but at certain crucial junctures he makes just as clear the fact that if there were no Catholicism there would be no Irish. This is nowhere more apparent than when his sister Kathy lapses into a coma after falling (or being pushed) from the project roof in a drugged delusionary stupor. After watching her deteriorate steadily in the hospital, hooked up to tubes and wires, MacDonald's grandfather, the *paterfamilias* by default in this broken family, decides to take matters into his own hands. He shows up at the hospital with his Rosary beads and a jug of "some holy water from Fatima," which he proceeds to slosh onto his granddaughter while simultaneously pulling out the IV tubes, reciting the rosary. Holding the nurses at bay, MacDonald's grandfather shouts at his sister, "Kathy, if you can hear me now, move your arm."[37]

What followed was, by any definition of the term, a miracle. Kathy moved her arm, and two days later, on Easter Sunday, she opened her eyes and shortly thereafter left the hospital. The incident could serve as a warning to those who would attempt to define ethnos on anything other than spiritual terms. It also gives some indication of why the Brahmin masters of deceit were so interested in weakening the Catholic Church during this period of time, for in weakening the Church they attacked the very root of what made this group a "we," since ethnos is based on religion.

The goal of busing and all of the other forms of social engineering that have been employed over the past fifty years is deracination as a form of control. In *All Souls*, the destruction of the "we" takes place when the MacDonald family, or what's left of it, finally can't take it anymore and moves to Colorado, where they spent their time, in MacDonald's words, "in an all-American world out west, where kids their age took buses for miles to hang out on fake street corners at the indoor shopping malls."[38] By moving to a trailer park in Colorado, Ma finally hands the ruling class its ethnic victory. Now, "these weren't just poor people; they were poor people living on the edge of a godforsaken highway. There was no pretending you were anywhere else, no pretending you weren't poor and no pride about being from the Federal Heights Trailer Park."[39] When the MacDonalds lost their "we," they lost the only valuable thing they ever had, which may explain why the author moved back to South Boston in the mid-'90s. Ma, true to her ethnic heritage, finally figures out why Colorado is such a godforsaken place. "Ma said Golden [Colorado] was full of Germans. 'That explains it.'"[40]

Notes

1 Hillel Levine and Lawrence Harmon, *The Death of an American Jewish Community: A Tragedy of Good Intentions* (New York: The Free Press, 1992), p. 280.
2 Ibid., p. 207.
3 Ibid., p. 323.
4 Ibid., p. 324.
5 Ibid.
6 Ibid., p. 337.
7 Ibid., p. 338.
8 J. Anthony Lukas, *Common Ground: A Turbulent Decade in the Lives of Three American Families* (New York: Alfred A. Knopf, 1985), p. 233.
9 Ibid., p. 236.
10 Ibid., p. 218.
11 Ibid., p. 231.
12 Ibid., p. 240.
13 Ibid., p. 238.
14 Ibid.

15 Ibid., p. 239.

16 Ibid., p. 240.

17 Ibid.

18 Ibid., p. 366.

19 David J. Peterson , "Race War 101; The Battle of Boston," *Culture Wars* (September 2001): 34ff.

20 Ibid.

21 Michael Patrick MacDonald, *All Souls: A Family Story from Southie* (Boston: Beacon Press, 1999), p. 200.

22 Ibid., p. 215.

23 Ibid., p. 111.

24 Ibid., p. 257.

25 John H. Mollenkopf, *The Contested City* (Princeton, N.J.: Princeton University Press, 1983), p. 171.

26 MacDonald, p. 75.

27 Ibid., p. 83.

28 Ibid., p. 157.

29 Ibid., p. 31.

30 Ibid., p. 219.

31 Ibid., p. 216.

32 Ibid., p. 102.

33 Ibid., p. 112.

34 Ibid., p. 222.

35 Ibid.

36 E. Digby Baltzell, *The Protestant Establishment: Aristocracy and Caste in America* (New York: Random House, 1964), pp. 52–53.

37 MacDonald, p. 171.

38 Ibid., p. 226.

39 Ibid.

40 Ibid.

Martin Mullen's Abortion Bill

If Father Meehan had seen the campaign of ethnic cleansing in southwest Philadelphia for what it really was, he might not have been able to stop it, but he might have been spared a good deal of mental anguish. If Meehan had been reading the papers more closely during the spring of '71, he would have understood why the ethnic cleansing of Most Blessed Sacrament had suddenly become an issue of priority to Philadelphia's ruling class. On April 27, 1971, Martin Mullen introduced a bill which would outlaw all abortions in the state of Pennsylvania. "This bill," according to Mullen, "prohibits abortion 100 percent under any circumstances. . . . This bill would make all abortions for any reason unlawful."[1]

Mullen's proposed bill was a potential disaster for fellow Democrat Milton Shapp, now governor of Pennsylvania, and his efforts to finesse the abortion issue past the state's Catholics, the majority of whom were Democrats. Those with any memory at all would remember that Shapp had declared opposition to abortion in Philadelphia's diocesan newspaper. Now it looked as if Martin Mullen were going to hold him to his word. As his first line of defense against Mullen's efforts, Shapp fell back on the fact that his "women's" commission on abortion hadn't made its report yet, something that left Mullen unimpressed. "As far as I'm concerned," Mullen told the *Bulletin*, which constantly referred to him as a "Roman Catholic" in every article it wrote on him, "it doesn't require any study."[2] By December of 1971, the *Bulletin* had upped the ante and was now referring to him as "the leading spokesman for Roman Catholic Church policies in the Legislature."[3]

Unlike Martin Mullen, who was always identified as Roman Catholic and often misidentified as a spokesman for the Roman Catholic Church, Milton Shapp was never identified as a liberal Jew in any article mentioning him, nor did any of Philadelphia's newspapers give any indication that a liberal Jewish organization like the American Jewish Committee had any ax to grind on the abortion issue. Shapp probably agreed that the abortion issue required no study, but for reasons other than those entertained by Martin Mullen. Shapp was determined to change the state's stance on abortion, most of all by funding it through the state's welfare department, because that was the nub of the issue as far as the ruling class was concerned. Shapp was the sort of assimilationist-minded Jew that Digby Baltzell in his book, *The Protestant Establishment*, was urging fellow WASPs to admit to the ruling class. Shapp, for his part, was eager to curry favor with the WASP establishment by adopting their stance on abortion, but he needed to finesse the political consequences, and in order to do that he needed C. Delores Tucker.

Her role in the abortion controversy began to emerge during Shapp's gubernatorial campaign. On September 14, 1970, the state's Democrats approved the creation of a commission that would study the question of abortion. The Democrats did this, it was duly noted, over the "strenuous objections"[4] of Martin Mullen. When Mullen announced before the Pennsylvania house that "the majority of the Democratic Party is opposed to abortion,"[5] house members applauded his statement. Shapp was involved in engineering a change in that consensus, but he couldn't do so directly and still expect to get the Catholic vote in November. Hence, he needed the commission, which he could pack so that its eventual support of abortion was a foregone conclusion, and he needed C. Delores Tucker first of all to pack the commission, and secondly, to defend it by making it look as if the only reason Mullen and his supporters were against abortion was because they were male and therefore, ipso facto, oppressors of women.

Shortly after Mullen made his statement, Tucker jumped into the dispute by coming to Shapp's support. "Our gubernatorial candidate [Milton Shapp] has taken a public stand to let the women decide the issue," Tucker said. "Mr. Shapp's position is known statewide. I think we ought to go along with this."[6] If Mr. Shapp's position was known in the state of Pennsylvania it was in spite of the statements he had made in places like the *Catholic Standard and Times* to deliberately mislead people into thinking he was against abortion. The newspapers dutifully supported the sexual liberationist side in the argument. "The male diehards," editorialized reporter Duke Kaminski in the middle of what was supposed to be a news article, "were not about to allow the women's lib to take control of the meetings."[7]

Mullen was upset by the fact that the state of Pennsylvania had paid for 4,000 to 5,000 abortions since 1968, in spite of the fact that abortion was illegal at the time. The state welfare department was claiming that the law, which prohibited "unlawful" abortions, wasn't clear and was using that ambiguity as a cover for expanding its influence over black welfare recipients. The so-called women's commission was an attempt to stall for time and to block any efforts to do anything threatening the status quo in the meantime, something that became clear as soon as Mullen introduced his bill. House Speaker Herbert Fineman, one of Shapp's closest aids, denounced Mullen's bill as "unrealistic,"[8] and made the role of the women's commission in blocking this sort of legislation clear when he added that he didn't "foresee any action on abortion legislation until Governor Shapp's proposed women's commission studies the law and makes a report."[9] Fineman, who would eventually go to jail on corruption charges, was playing bad cop in this scenario. "I favor the right of abortion,"[10] he told the paper. Fineman gave the impression that Shapp hadn't yet made up his mind on the issue and was waiting to hear what the women's commission which he had packed with pro-abortion "left-wingers," as Ms. Hayes put, had to say on the matter.

Mullen, however, remained undeterred in his opposition. By December of 1971, which is to say, one year after Shapp had been elected governor and a little over a year after Shapp rewarded Tucker for her role in the abortion controversy by making her Secretary of the Commonwealth, Mullen announced that he was ready to hold up the state budget once again, as he had done in 1966. On December 21, Mullen announced to state public-welfare officials that if they did not stop funding abortions, he would not approve their budget for the coming year. "I don't think the department has the authority to make such a decision,"[11] Mullen told the *Bulletin*. "This is very offensive to a lot of people and if you don't do what we think is right, we have the votes to stop it."[12] In response to Mullen's threat, Rep. Charles F. Mebus, a Republican from Montgomery County just outside Philadelphia claimed that "the question of abortions is a matter of religious freedom in my mind."[13]

As if to show that great minds continued to run in the same circles, Duke Kaminski, the *Bulletin's* reporter, kept reiterating the fact that Mullen was a Catholic, thereby turning

abortion into a sectarian religious issue, even though Mullen, whose bill would eventually pass by an 80 percent majority, kept explaining that abortion was not a religious issue
and that he had the support of the majority of the upstate Protestants on the matter. *The
Evening Bulletin* kept hammering away at Mullen, claiming that abortion was a Catholic
issue even in sentences like the following, which contradicted that assertion: "Mullen, a
Roman Catholic, maintained that religion isn't involved in his decision to submit the bill
and that a substantial number of Protestants as well as Catholics are sponsoring the measure."[14]

The situation had changed significantly since 1966 in a number of ways. To begin
with, the state's Republicans were the direct heirs of the WASP eugenic tradition, and they
hadn't changed their mind about the black threat that was driving the welfare department's
push to abort the offspring of welfare recipients. The most significant change since 1966
was that a covertly pro-abortion Democrat was now governor of the state and determined
to use that office to change the state's stance on abortion. That meant that Mullen's stance
threatened the unity of the party. That meant as well that the state-wide Democratic coalition was about to split apart on the same ethnic lines as those which fractured the reform
Democratic coalition in Philadelphia. The same thing that had happened to the
Philadelphia Democratic Party in 1963 when Jim Tate became mayor was now happening
on the state level for the opposite reasons. The ADA/AJC faction in the party was determined to push policies that they knew Catholics could not support. Since they were not
about to back down on pushing those policies, they needed to marginalize, which is to say,
to destroy the Catholic opposition, and that meant dealing with Martin Mullen.

Five months after Mullen announced his abortion bill and less than a year after
C. Delores Tucker had been appointed Secretary of the Commonwealth, "the women's
lib," as Duke Kaminski might have said, took a severe hit when Tucker, their champion,
was implicated in a housing scandal. At around the same time that Tucker was putting single mothers from North Philadelphia like June Hayes on the state Democratic Party's platform committee, another black single mother from North Philadelphia by the name of
Frances Fitzgerald bought a three-story rowhouse at 3329 N. 19th Street through the
Tucker and Tucker real estate agency for $9,200. The previous owner of the house was a
corporation known as Penn National Investments. The president of Penn National
Investments was William L. Tucker, husband of C. Delores Tucker. Penn National
Investments had bought the house for $2,750 on October 31, 1962, which is to say when
prices in the neighborhood were still depressed from the white exodus out of North
Philadelphia. The racial dividing line in North Philadelphia in 1954 was Lehigh Avenue,
which was 2700 north. As it moved inexorably north during the late '50s and early '60s,
real-estate values plummeted and people like Mr. and Mrs. Tucker profited by snatching
up the houses the white ethnics left behind and then selling them to blacks at prices like
the 400 and some percent mark-up they charged to Ms. Fitzgerald.

Two weeks after moving into her new house, Frances Fitzgerald received a visit from
the one of the city's agents of the Licenses and Inspection Bureau, who informed her that
her new house was guilty of several serious housing-code violations, including a back wall
which seemed in danger of imminent collapse. Fitzgerald was shocked by the notice.
Since her house had been approved for an FHA mortgage, she felt that either they or the

real-estate agent should have informed her, and so in protest, she stopped paying her $68 monthly mortgage payment to United Brokers, a mortgage company also owned by Mr. and Mrs. Tucker. The Tuckers were aware of the condition of the house's back wall because they had received a notice from the city to that effect on June 3, 1969, when the house, which was then owned by Penn National Investments, was vacant. United Brokers was in the process of foreclosing on the house and evicting Ms. Fitzgerald when the wall collapsed and the story broke.

The story is interesting for what it says about how the real-estate market in Philadelphia got used for political purposes. The FHA, the *Inquirer* discovered, made a practice "of approving houses found defective by other government agencies."[15] Frances Fitzgerald purchased her home under the FHA's 235 program, "which means that the federal government makes part of her monthly mortgage payment."[16]

If the *Inquirer* had pursued the connection between the Tuckers and the FHA further to include the involvement of the Quakers and the fact that they had introduced the Tuckers to the FHA in the early '60s and were part of the effort to destabilize neighborhoods with FHA cooperation, they could have broken a much more significant story about a much more significant conspiracy, but they did not pursue this angle, nor did they pursue the fact that what had happened in North Philadelphia ten years earlier was happening in West Philadelphia at the same time they broke the story.

Tucker's attempt to talk her way out of an embarrassing situation had created some tantalizing leads. In disclaiming any involvement with Penn National Investments, she claimed that PNI, which came into existence on September 14, 1959, with an office at 2102 W. Diamond Street, was formed by her husband and "some professional men of Philadelphia to try to do something about bringing good housing to our people."[17] It would have been interesting to know who those professional men were, but the line of inquiry got dropped.

The same was true of Tucker's involvement with United Brokers Mortgage Company. UBMC "went into business in the early 1960s," in order to provide mortgages "to areas that had been banned by many of the other mortgage companies" in order to bring blacks into "certain areas" where blacks "were not able to buy . . . because of many discriminatory practices."[18] In other words, the Tuckers had been set up in business to capitalize on racial migration, and it was in their interest and the interest of those who supported them to promote it. The Quakers were instrumental in introducing the Tuckers to the FHA, but Quaker involvement never got mentioned in any of the *Inquirer* articles. To do so would have taken the story out of the realm of individual interests and exposed the political and ethnic interests behind them. To follow that trail meant cognitive dissonance between the *Inquirer*'s housing stories and their West Philadelphia-MBS-gang stories, which were closely related to their Martin Mullen stories. The *Inquirer*'s West Philadelphia story was about how racist whites from MBS were attacking and murdering the blacks who wanted to move into the neighborhood. It was not about the people who were profiting, either politically or financially, from sending those people into the neighborhood. And so a story in which "The *Inquirer* disclosed widespread abuses in FHA mortgage programs, ranging from the sale of substandard houses at huge markups by real estate speculators to FHA approval of defective houses for mortgage insurance"[19] got focused on North

Philadelphia, where the promotion of racial migration for political ends was a dead issue and ignored in West Philadelphia, where it was going on at the time the story broke.

Needless to say, the revelation that the woman who had been hired by the Shapp administration as a representative of the downtrodden was in reality a slum landlord who made enormous profits off her own people by selling them defective homes at huge mark ups did not help the Shapp administration in its struggle for control over the Democratic Party. Tucker's role in the housing scandal was a huge embarrassment, and she tried to control the damage by dissociating herself from the real-estate firm that bore her name. Shortly after the wall collapsed, Tucker announced to the *Inquirer*, "I don't know anything about real estate. I haven't been involved in it for at least seven years. I haven't shown a property in 15 years."[20]

C. Delores Tucker could have mentioned that fact in December of 1970, when Milton Shapp named her Secretary of the Commonwealth and all of the newspaper accounts on her nomination listed her as co-owner of Tucker and Tucker, but it probably slipped her mind at the time that she was not involved in real estate anymore. Apparently it also slipped her mind when she failed to list either Tucker and Tucker or Penn National Investments or the assets of her spouse on the financial disclosure form which the Shapp administration required all of its cabinet members to file. Tucker did disclose that she owned fifteen shares of stock in United Brokers Mortgage Company, the company which held the mortgage on the 19th Street property and was in the process of foreclosing when the wall collapsed. After failing to disclose her connections with the above-mentioned firms and then denying that she had any connection with those firms when the wall collapsed, Tucker, for good measure perhaps, then announced that she had "ceased all my activities with the real estate company because of the possible conflict of interest."[21]

Tucker's statements merely compounded the embarrassment she was causing the Shapp administration at the time. Milton Shapp had cause enough to fire her in 1971 if he had a mind to. Eventually he would fire her for using her public office for private gain on September 21, 1977, when she refused to curtail her lucrative career as a public speaker, a career which earned her $65,000 in speaking fees over a twenty-eight-month period, all of which was done on government time with government employees writing her speeches for her. Some of her biggest fees came from the NAACP, a group she was hired to oversee in her capacity as Secretary to the Commonwealth.[22]

When Tucker launched her unsuccessful bid to become Senator in the Democratic primary of 1980, she was listed along with her husband William as one of "Philadelphia's 10 'Most Wanted' Tax Delinquents,"[23] so evidently she still had ties to the real estate business after all. Shapp didn't fire her in 1971 because she was still more of an asset than a liability to him, and she was valuable to him because of the threat Martin Mullen posed. Tucker was useful to Shapp not so much because she was his administration's most visible woman of color and could, therefore, denounce Mullen's efforts to protect the unborn as racially motivated male chauvinism, but even more than that because she was intimately involved in the manipulation of racial migration and the housing market that would eventually drive Martin Mullen from office.

Mullen, who was probably the most guileless politician in the history of the state of Pennsylvania, didn't help matters any by his unguarded comments to the press. After inviting

Bulletin reporter Nancy Greenberg into his home at 5332 Glenmore Street, Mullen announced, after she noticed people showing up and dropping off rent payments, that he owned a number of houses in the neighborhood. In fact, to cite his exact words, he announced "We'd be doomed if I hadn't bought up most of the houses in the immediate neighborhood,"[24] an admission that people who had been manipulating the housing market for political ends for over two decades and who had identified Mullen as the main opponent to their program of sexual engineering must have found intriguing. Eventually, Martin Mullen ended up buying 80 houses in the neighborhood surrounding Most Blessed Sacrament Parish as part of his losing battle to defend it against racial migration.

Notes

1   Forrest L. Black, "Mullen Introduces Law to Outlaw All Abortions," *The Evening Bulletin* (April 28, 1971).
2   Ibid.
3   Forrest L. Black, "Mullen Fights 'Subsidies' for Abortions," *The Evening Bulletin* (December 1, 1971). See also Forrest L. Black "Pressure by Mullen Forces Showdown on 2 Abortion Bills," *The Evening Bulletin* (June 15, 1972).
4   Duke Kaminski, "Democrats OK Abortion Reform Study," *The Evening Bulletin* (September 15, 1970).
5   Ibid.
6   Ibid.
7   Ibid.
8   Forrest L. Black, "Mullen Claims He Has Enough Votes to Pass Bill Outlawing Abortions," *The Evening Bulletin* (May 9, 1971).
9   Ibid.
10 Ibid.
11 Duke Kaminski, "Fund Cutoff Threatened over Welfare Abortions," *The Evening Bulletin* (December 21, 1971).
12 Ibid.
13 Ibid.
14 Black, "Mullen Introduces Law to Outlaw All Abortions."
15 Donald L. Barlett and James B. Steele, "Wall Collapses on Tucker Home," *The Philadelphia Inquirer* (September 5, 1971).
16 Ibid.
17 "Mrs. Tucker Denies All Ties with Husband's Businesses," *The Evening Bulletin* (September 5, 1971).
18 Ibid.
19 Barlett and Steele, "Wall Collapses."
20 "Mrs. Tucker Denies All Ties with Husband's Businesses."
21 Ibid.
22 Gayle Becker, "Delores Tucker Joins Radio," *The Evening Bulletin* (December 17, 1977).
23 David Runkel, "Phila's 10 'Most Wanted' Tax Delinquents Revealed," *The Philadelphia Inquirer* (March 18, 1980).
24 Nancy Greenberg, "Marty Mullen on Abortion: 'God has told me what I must do," *The Sunday Bulletin* (January 7, 1973).

Frank Rizzo and the Ethnic Revival

Two months after the Tucker housing scandal hit the newspapers, Frank Rizzo was elected mayor of Philadelphia as part of the ethnic revival that was sweeping the country. In one of his first actions, Rizzo stopped construction at the Whitman Park housing projects, an attempt to engineer integration in South Philadelphia that the residents had been resisting for years. Whitman Park was originally designed to be a 440-unit high-rise building when it was first proposed in 1956. It was going to be, in other words, the South Philadelphia version of Schuylkill Falls. Eventually it was transformed into a public housing project made up of homes similar in style but superior in quality to the homes already in existence in the neighborhood.

At this point, the area's residents demanded that they be allowed to buy the 120 townhouses the Philadelphia Housing Authority was building there, but the people in the neighborhood were denied the opportunity to bid on the houses, something that led them to believe that social engineering and not housing was the ultimate purpose of the project. Whitman Park, according to John Bauman, "became a symbolic contest pitting black public housing tenants against Rizzo and white Philadelphians resisting government-ordered racial integration."[1]

Rizzo's decision to stop construction was a victory for the ethnics of South Philadelphia, but it proved to be short-lived. In 1976 Judge Raymond Broderick, the Republican who ran against Milton Shapp for governor, ruled that "by failing to build the Whitman park complex, Philadelphia violated the Fifth, Thirteenth, and Fourteenth amendments to the Constitution, and ordered the project constructed forthwith."[2] The Catholic ethnics, in other words, were frozen out of the political process. In the 1970 governor's race they were allowed to choose between two candidates, both of whom opposed their interests. When they finally did elect someone who was willing to act on their complaints, as Mayor Frank Rizzo was, his decision was overruled by the court, in this instance the candidate who lost in the 1970 gubernatorial election.

The same thing was happening on the national level. One year after Rizzo was elected as mayor of Philadelphia, Richard Nixon was elected to a second term in the White House. As one of his first acts in his second term, Nixon suspended all federal housing subsidy programs in January 1973. Nixon's "urban counterstrategy"[3] paradoxically gave him considerable support in major urban areas across the country because the ethnics there now realized that housing policy was being pursued as a way of destroying their political power. Nixon, according to Mollenkopf, "combined an appeal to the white, Catholic, blue collar ethnics of the northern suburbs with an appeal to the middle class whites of the newer southern and southwestern cities. From the first group he won enough votes to reduce the traditional Democratic majorities in the large, old central cities, and from the second he won absolute majorities."[4]

Unfortunately, as far as the nation's cities were concerned, it was once more a situation of heads-I-win-tails-you-lose. As with Eisenhower's strategy to counteract the effect of Roosevelt's New Deal programs, Nixon's urban counterstrategy meant starving the Democrats into submission by once again supporting growth in the suburbs and the south-west. As such, Nixon's policy, no matter how much it did to benefit Catholic ethnics, still favored their continued migration into the suburbs and their continued assimilation there, with all of its concomitant loss of political power. The War Production Board had laid down the pattern in the early '40s, and that pattern did not change, no matter how much people like Nixon tried to make it attractive to the ethnics in order to gain their political support against the WASP establishment and their black allies. No matter how sincere he was in wanting to aid the ethnics, Nixon simply accelerated their exodus from the cities by the fact that the only way he could reward them was by sending money to the suburbs. His assistance to ethnics still in the cities was purely negative. All he could do there was deprive their enemies of federal money, as in the FHA preferences that Robert Weaver had established. He could not or would not change the basic orientation of the whole system. "Conservative national political entrepreneurs," according Mollenkopf,

> adapted the Democratic urban strategy to their own political ends by developing an antiurban thrust within the delivery system. War Production Board investment patterns laid down the basic physical capital investment, which made possible the growth of suburbs and new metropolitan areas after the war. The interstate high-way system, the pattern of FHA-assisted housing construction, and the CDBG allocation formula, not to mention the incidence of defense procurements, rein-forced this pattern of growth. In contrast to the emphasis which urban liberal Democrats developed, conservative Republican political entrepreneurs used fed-eral urban programs to favor growth in conservative constituencies.[5]

But "conservative" in this sense did not mean ethnic. In many ways, it meant the exact opposite of ethnic because conservatism was a form of assimilation which ethnics adopt-ed when they arrived in the suburbs. The rise of conservatism was predicated on many things, and the abandonment of ethnicity was one of them.

No matter how much it reinforced the pattern of suburbanization established by the War Production Board, Nixon's actions constituted a clear and present danger to the gov-ernment programs which proliferated in the wake of the civil-rights movement, and so his actions were considered a serious threat by the people who had used that movement as one of the main weapons in their arsenal of social engineering. Nixon, as a result, would soon pay the price for his audacity in standing athwart initiatives the ruling class considered important.

The Senate's failure to entertain the evidence the house committee brought before it in the Clinton Impeachment trial showed that criminal activity is no impediment to hold-ing office as long as the office holder is doing the bidding of the ruling class. Nixon's forced resignation proved the converse of the same principle. Nixon had offended John D. Rockefeller by withdrawing his support from Rockefeller's Goals 2000 program when Nixon discovered that support of Goals 2000 meant support of abortion. When the Supreme Court handed down *Roe v. Wade* shortly after Nixon discontinued federal hous-ing subsidies, Nixon must have known that his opposition to Rockefeller's Goals 2000 program would have other ramifications. Nixon was willing to support contraception but not abortion. He was also willing to support Catholic initiatives like aid to parochial schools, and to pull the plug on the federal programs which had been driving Catholic ethnics out of their neighborhoods.

Shortly after Nixon was elected to his second term in office, Martin Mullen forced the issue on abortion in the state of Pennsylvania. On June 22, 1972, HB-800, Martin Mullen's bill banning abortion, passed both houses by huge margins, setting up a confrontation with the governor, which forced Shapp to veto the bill and thereby expose his true views on abortion to the state's voters. Having his cover blown on a hot button issue like abortion was serious enough, but Shapp's veto also exposed him as a liar to the state's Catholic voters, and in doing so set up the possibility of a negative reaction at the polls, a possibility which became a reality when Mullen warned that if Shapp vetoed his bill he was going to run for governor. "Don't get me wrong," Mullen told a reporter for the *Bulletin*, "I don't want to be governor, but if Mr. Shapp kills the bill and the Legislature doesn't come with two-thirds majority to overturn him, I'll have to take my case to the people. This is my life. I want the damned bill to become law. Why? Because I don't want to see any more innocent children getting killed."[6] Once again, the paper dragged the religious issue into the abortion story by describing Mullen as "a proud but not a professional catholic." And once again Mullen insisted, that "the issue was not religious but moral."[7]

"Hell," Mullen said, "I got more support from Protestants and others than from Catholics. If it were a Catholic issue, I wouldn't get anywhere because we're a minority in the Legislature. I'm supporting a doctrine all Pennsylvanians can support – all decent Pennsylvanians that is."[8]

In the meantime, Mullen was hearing a lot from indecent Pennsylvanians, who were besieging him with obscene phone calls at three in the morning as well as writing him "crazy letters,"[9] some of which contained death threats. When the reporter reminded Mullen that Shapp's "women's" commission had come out in favor of liberalized abortion laws, Mullen dismissed it as "a stacked deck of cards."[10] Mullen reminded the reporter that Shapp had stacked the committee with "people from the Planned Parenthood organization" making the committee's ultimate verdict a foregone conclusion. "I knew how they were going to vote," Mullen told Mr. Knight, "as soon as I saw their names."[11]

When asked if he felt that "the state should legislate morality," Mullen responded by claiming that "that's what we're elected for – to set standards. And if people don't like my judgment of what's right, they can always damn well kick me out."[12] Mullen then went on to explain to the reporter his sense of the ramifications of what it meant to be a moral being, which is to say a rational creature created by God with the ability to choose or reject the good as his final end. That meant, according to Mullen's view, that "you're born into this life with a purpose. I believe in an afterlife. If you don't do what is right for the good of mankind, when you face your Maker, he's going to be dissatisfied."[13]

The possibility that the Catholics might unite as an ethnic voting bloc was Milton Shapp's as well as the Democratic Party's worse nightmare. In fact, it couldn't have made the Republicans very happy either, because both parties were based on the principle of dividing ethnic groups according to class interest. The Republicans in the Pennsylvania state legislature consistently opposed Mullen's attempts to defend the traditional legal defenses around sexual morality, in spite of the fact that they would later become champions of what Dan Quayle called "family values." When Mullen attempted to recriminalize adultery the leader in opposing his efforts was Faith Ryan Whittlesley, then a freshman legislator from Delaware County, but later a fixture in the Reagan administration, where she served as ambassador to Switzerland. Mullen argued that "in this age of permissiveness, something has to be done about abandoning things of traditional value which have stood the test of time"[14] and eventually convinced the Pennsylvania House to support him in recriminalizing adultery (but not fornication) by a vote of 97 to 86. He did this over the strenuous opposition of Mrs. Whittlesley who ridiculed Mullen's efforts as "not a vote to strengthen the family," but "a vote for hypocrisy."[15]

Philadelphia's reform Democrats had always feared the Catholics as an ethnic threat, and now Milton Shapp had made that threat a reality by his stance on abortion, which lacked support not only in the Catholic wards of the state's big cities but in the state's predominantly Protestant rural counties as well. On January 3, 1974, Martin Mullen held a press conference in Philadelphia at which he announced that he was running for the Democratic nomination for governor of the state in the May primary and that he was basing his candidacy on "the whole morality question."[16]

What followed his announcement was a campaign to discredit Mullen unprecedented in its bias and viciousness, waged by the press who was supposed to be reporting on it. Mullen was ridiculed for the clothes he wore, and when he invited the reporters into his home they ridiculed his wife and his only son. Three weeks after he announced his campaign, Jon Katz of the *Inquirer* ridiculed Mullen's legislative battles as "a catalogue of rear-guard reaction to social change."[17] Mullen, according to Katz, has fought "the sexual revolution, liberalized divorce laws, pornography, fornication and abortion, as well as legal restrictions barring governmental aid to parochial schools"[18] – all, thank God, in vain, thanks in large measure to propagandists for social engineering like Katz. Taking its cue from the Better Philadelphia Exhibit, Philadelphia's fourth estate did everything possible to associate Mullen with the image of the rowhouse, which had become synonymous in the public mind with being a loser, in other words, someone who was so dysfunctional he couldn't manage to move out of the old neighborhood.

Sandy Grady referred to Mullen as "the Barry Goldwater of the row houses."[19] The punch-line to Grady's description was: "In your heart, you know he'll lose." The claim that Martin Mullen was a rowhouse loser extended to editorializing by photo. When the *Bulletin* wanted to give a sympathetic treatment to Republican gubernatorial candidate Drew Lewis, who happened to be running at the same time Mullen was running for the Democratic nomination, they posed him in a preppy crew-neck sweater perched on a split-rail fence with a cow in the foreground. When they wanted to do the opposite to Mullen they sent their photographer to his Glenmore street rowhouse, where he photographed the entire Mullen family sitting unsmiling and uncomfortable on their living room sofa, in a parody of Grant Wood's American Gothic.

The press's other ploy to discredit Mullen in the eyes of Pennsylvania's voters was based on the ruling class's chief fear associated with Mullen, namely, the one which grew out of the recognition of his Catholicism. The press relentlessly portrayed the Mullen campaign as a Catholic conspiracy of the sort that should remind the voters of Pennsylvania of Thomas Nast's crocodiles in mitres crawling up onto American shores. One month before the primary election David Runkel of the *Bulletin* was referring to Mullen as "Pope Martin"[20] and "Monsignor Mullen"[21] as he traveled with him to the western part of the state, where "a Roman Catholic priest last week introduced Mullen to a placard-carrying crowd in a school gymnasium as 'our candidate for governor.'"[22]

After listening to Bishop A. M. Watson of Erie compare Mullen's and Shapp's records on issues like abortion and pornography, one Knight of Columbus in attendance came away with an impression which he shared with Runkel. "We certainly got out of it," he declared, "that the entire Catholic population should be behind him."[23] If a black Baptist had told the same reporter after leaving a rally at New Bethel Baptist Church in Chicago, that the entire black population should "be behind" Martin Luther King, or Harold Washington, or Coleman Young, who created a political empire in Detroit based on the mobilization of churchgoers there, no one would have thought it was remarkable or threatening. It was only threatening when Catholics did it, and that was so because, as Leo Pfeffer had said, Catholics were different.

First of all, there were a lot of them. There were 4.1 million Catholics in the state of Pennsylvania. Forty percent of the state's Democrats were Catholic. Mullen, according to Runkel, said "he expects to get nearly all the Catholic vote."[24] But the Mullen threat went beyond that because during his campaign he had persuaded 30,000 Catholic Republicans in the five county area to change their registration so that they could vote for him (and against Shapp) in the primary. Mullen's campaign had Catholics uniting on ethnic lines and abandoning the two-party system that divided them according to class. The Mullen campaign brought up issues of ethnicity and morality which both parties wanted to suppress, hence the campaign in the press. "My candidacy," said Mullen, "is a referendum on abortion."[25] Since the country had never had a referendum on the issue, and the whole purpose of having the courts settle the case was to deny that possibility, that fact was bad enough, but the WASP ruling class knew that Mullen's candidacy was more than that as well. Abortion was the one part of the assimilation process which most Catholics would not swallow. The WASP ruling class had to have abortion and the sexual engineering that went with it to blunt Catholic demographic power. But in doing that they ran the risk of uniting the very people they hoped to divide. Mullen's candidacy seemed to be doing just that.

"The new ethnic politics," Michael Novak wrote in *The Rise of the Unmeltable Ethnics*, "is a direct challenge to the WASP conception of America."[26] If so, the challenge turned out to be a lot like the Susquehanna River that Martin Mullen had to cross on his way from Philadelphia to Harrisburg. It was a mile wide and 18 inches deep. Michael Novak's book, in fact, was as deep as it got. Novak at least had some appreciation of the strategic significance behind the programs the WASP ruling class promoted in the name of what people like Ed Bacon would term disinterested benevolence. "Educated partisans of a rational, modern, mobile culture support 'change,'" according to Novak, "because change is in their own self-interest. The breakdown of families and neighborhoods clears the way for sweeping programs, of the mobile way of life of experts and for the dreams of utopians."[27]

Novak rightly attributed the ethnic revival of the early '70s to "disillusionment with the universalist too thickly rational culture of profession elites" which he identified as quintessentially WASP and typical of "upper class Quakers," who "think and feel in a way that I cannot think and feel."[28] When Quakers or Yankees talk about "humanism" or "progress," it invariably means "moral pressure" exerted on ethnics "to abandon their own traditions, their faith, their associations, in order to reap higher rewards in the culture of the national corporations."[29] But when they do, they oftentimes discover that they have become the victims of an undeclared form of covert warfare being waged against them. In other words, Catholic ethnics, by adopting the values of the ruling class, collaborated in their own destruction. In this regard Novak cites the case of "a young Italian lawyer" who returned from Mississippi where he had been working for the civil-rights movement only to find that the planning commission of "his home city was running an expressway through the traditional homes of his family."[30]

According to Novak, the assimilation the Italian lawyer was expected to undergo really entailed the adoption of a "new religion," one which exalted as its *summum bonum* "power over others, enlightenment, an atomic (rather than a communitarian) sensibility, a contempt for mystery, ritual, transcendence, soul, absurdity, and tragedy."[31] In dealing with their Catholic ethnic employees, the WASP ruling class "perfected a system for mastering them," which entailed learning to "balance nationalities" against each other, a system which reached perfection in places like Detroit, where as Novak noted, two out of every three people were either Polish or black.[32]

Novak, in effect, put his finger on the strategy which would later come to be known as multiculturalism, namely, "by judiciously mixing many nationalities, the employer could keep them divided and incapable of concerted actions on their own behalf."[33] By determining what were going to be the default settings of the culture, the WASP elite could determine strategic outcomes in a way that the dominated ethnic groups could not. "American democracy," according to Novak's theory "operates as a shield for WASP hegemony and to reinforce a WASP sense of reality, stories and symbols."[34] That meant the creation of a "rationalized social order," which could only function efficiently if "local pockets of tradition, 'prejudice' and ignorance are made to give way to atomistic conceptions of self, sociality and happiness."[35] The point of Americanization was not just assimilation; it was domination and control based on the systematic destruction of anything that allowed the ethnic to function as something other than a naked atomistic individual:

> If one deprives people of their affective bonds to family, culture and value, then one can reconstruct them afresh. While they are confused and without identity, one can manipulate them more freely, telling them what they ought to be. One takes their souls and gives them bread and circuses. For a while – until they awaken – they are grateful.[36]

The ethnic revival of the '70s was supposed to be that awakening. At least that is the impression one gets from reading Novak's book. If so, it was followed by an even more profound slumber than the one which proceeded it, as the ethnics succumbed to ever more intrusive and pernicious forms of social engineering. "The crises in our cities," Novak concluded correctly, "are a direct effect of government policies."[37]

If so, the leaders of the ethnic revival were having a hard time translating theory into practice. One indication of the superficiality of the ethnic revival in Philadelphia is the fact that Frank Rizzo didn't support Martin Mullen in his gubernatorial campaign, nor did Jim Tate, who in fact supported Shapp in the primary. Mullen felt betrayed by Tate's action and denounced "people like Tate who call themselves Christians and yet supported Shapp."[38] Part of the problem was the inter-ethnic rivalry which Novak touched on in his book. The triple melting pot was, in many ways, not finished with its work in Philadelphia. Frank Rizzo was an Italian, and Jim Tate was an Irishman, and both of them may have been Democrats, but they did not identify themselves as Catholics in either the ethnic or political sense of the word, even though their enemies did.

They also did not think strategically, as their enemies did. WASPs like Joe Clark supported abortion, contraception, and sexual liberation in general because they knew that their ethnic group would never have big families. Therefore, anything that hindered other people from having big families was to their advantage. Similarly, anything that promoted racial succession and crime and turnover in ethnic neighborhoods was to his advantage as well. All that people like Joe Clark had to do was promote forces that increased social disorder and then let nature, or fallen nature, take its course.

Ethnics like Rizzo and Tate were also handicapped by their limited understanding of the situation. Priding themselves on the fact that they were practical men who knew how to get things done, they missed the strategic implications of the war that was being waged against them. Abortion for them was a moral issue or it was a religious issue, but seeing it that way blinded them to the fact that it was also a political issue that threatened their political power in a subtle but direct fashion.

As a result they did not come to Mullen's aid, and as a result Mullen lost the primary in May of 1974. After losing to Shapp in the primary in May, Mullen delayed until August before he endorsed him for the November elections. On September 10, Mullen held a press conference in which he said that Governor Shapp had "done an excellent job" as governor "outside of morality issues."[39] Mullen felt that out of party loyalty, he had to support "all the candidates on the Democratic ticket."[40]

In gratitude for his support, Shapp's henchman Herb Fineman stripped Mullen of his chairmanship of the House Appropriations Committee on December 27, 1974. "Mr. Mullen's dismissal is hardly lamentable," one of the Philadelphia papers sniffed, "however, the process by which he was removed should be cause for concern."[41] In spite of his failed run for the governor's office, Mullen was re-elected to his district by an over 2 to 1 margin. His Republican opponent could marshal only 4,330 votes to Mullen's 9,349. That meant that Mullen was not vulnerable to Republican opposition, but he was vulnerable to opposition from within the Democratic Party, especially if that vote could be mobilized along racial lines.

Four years after Mullen lost his bid to become governor, the *Inquirer* was still hounding him, this time by sending reporter Maralyn Lois Polak to interview him. Polak began by criticizing Mullen for wearing plaid pants and a striped shirt. The interview went downhill from there. At one point, Polak leeringly asked Mullen if he liked sex, to which he disarmingly responded "Well, sure, I'm married."[42] Mullen then turned the tables on the interviewer by bringing up the fact that he was being criticized for his religion by papers like the *Inquirer* who had turned his political demise into a journalistic crusade. "All you have to do is read that paper of yours," Mullen told Polak, "and see how they belittle people."[43] By 1978, Mullen was still in office, but his constituency was being eroded by racial migration. Polak's article was timed to make him look bad in the November '78 elections. When the racial make-up finally tipped, the Democrats ran a straight-up racial campaign against him, and he was out of a job.

On January 3, 1978, ten months before the *Inquirer* published Polak's hatchet job on Mullen, Anna McGarry, Philadelphia's tireless Catholic crusader for interracial justice, died. She was still living at Gesu Parish in North Philadelphia, even though the Irish had long since fled the parish, which was now in the heart of the black ghetto. Dennis Clark took melancholy note of her passing in his diary. He had been mourning the demise of Catholicism in Philadelphia and his own life for going on ten years by the time McGarry died. "The Culture of the old Catholic, large family" had been a bulwark against the "erratic nihilism of the mass society."[44] Now, Catholicism was afflicted with the same problems:

> We hear of old friends defecting from the Church. The low morale, the confusion, the floundering and cynicism have replaced the elan, purpose and plans of a decade ago. I believe so many were disillusioned to find that Catholicism was no refuge, no sanctuary from the political instincts and institutional stupidity existing elsewhere.[45]

With the death of Mrs. McGarry, Clark was forced to bury his dream of interracial justice as well. "The Catholics are in stumbling disarray," he noted years earlier. "The blacks want scant liaison with the white world."[46] When the Irish Catholic neighborhood died, the dream of interracial justice which inspired people like Anna McGarry and Dennis Clark died with it. "We are hungry for a new communion,"[47] Clark sighed, still unwilling to face up to his responsibilities for the communion he destroyed.

Notes

1   John F. Bauman, *Public Housing, Race, and Renewal: Urban Planning in Philadelphia, 1920–1974* (Philadelphia: Temple University Press, 1987), p. 202.
2   Ibid.
3   John H. Mollenkopf, *The Contested City* (Princeton, N.J.: Princeton University Press, 1983), p. 123.
4   Ibid.
5   Ibid., p. 136.
6   Hans Knight, "Mullen Vows to Run for Governor If Shapp Vetoes Abortion Measure," *The Evening Bulletin*, 11/25/72, Mullen folder, Temple University Archives.
7   Ibid.
8   Ibid.
9   Ibid.
10 Ibid.
11 Ibid.

12 Ibid.

13 Ibid.

14 Forrest L. Black, "Mullen Loses Again Over Adultery Issue," *The Evening Bulletin*, 5/23/77, Martin Mullen folder, Temple University Urban Archives.

15 Ibid.

16 "Mullen to Stump State for Gubernatorial Nod," *The Evening Bulletin* (January 3, 1974).

17 Jon Katz, "The Glorious Quest of Martin Mullen, a Lonely Crusader," *The Philadelphia Inquirer* (January 27, 1974).

18 Ibid.

19 Sandy Grady, "'Nice Man' Mullen Has High Hopes," *The Evening Bulletin*, 4/28/74, Mullen folder, Temple University Urban Archives.

20 David Runkel, "Churches Aid Mullen 'Crusade' in Primary Battle with Shapp," *The Evening Bulletin* (April 23, 1974).

21 Ibid.

22 Ibid.

23 Ibid.

24 Ibid.

25 Ibid.

26 Michael Novak, *The Rise of the Unmeltable Ethnics: Politics and Culture in the '70s* (New York: The Macmillan Company, 1971), p. 270.

27 Ibid., p. 7.

28 Ibid., p. 32.

29 Ibid., p. 61.

30 Ibid., p. 65.

31 Ibid., p. 67.

32 Ibid., pp. 79–80.

33 Ibid., p. 80.

34 Ibid., p. 231.

35 Ibid., p. 224.

36 Ibid., p. 229.

37 Ibid., p. 240.

38 John Corr, "Mullen Warns Shapp He Must Revise Position on Issues," *The Philadelphia Inquirer* (May 22, 1974).

39 David Runkel, "Mullen Endorses Shapp," *The Evening Bulletin* (September 10, 1974).

40 Ibid.

41 "Time for an Airing," editorial, 12/28/74, Mullen folder, Temple University Urban Archives.

42 Maralyn Lois Polak, "Martin Mullen: He's Never Met a Bad Woman," *The Philadelphia Inquirer* (October 22, 1978).

43 Ibid.

44 Clark, Diary, 1/3/78.

45 Clark, Diary, 9/16/68.

46 Clark, Diary, 12/12/70.

47 Clark, Diary, 1/3/69.

Turmoil in the Clark Family

In September of 1975, Dennis Clark's oldest daughter announced that she was moving in with her boyfriend and that both of them planned to live together without the benefit of the sacrament in Bethlehem, Pennsylvania, something that strikes Clark as "a distinctly unromantic place."[1] Clark tries to relate the news matter-of-factly, but he is clearly upset by the prospect, something he attributes to "the superstition of the blood tie of the Celt in me."[2] Clark believes "in families," because in a world of "freezing cynicism and depersonalized callousness" there is no "other leaf" to "protect us. Where else are we to be born, bound and buried. What other image is there in which we can see and know ourselves, blood of the blood and bone of the bone."[3]

In one of the few instances where Clark links the sexual microcosm to the political macrocosm in his diary, Clark senses some connection between his daughter cohabiting and the plight of the Irish in Boston, then at the height of the battle over forced busing. The busing battle in Boston "testifies to the persistent American failure to deal adequately with minority group aspirations,"[4] but it also indicates Clark's first awareness of the Irish under assault in America, not just in the 19th century but in his day, something that his commitment to racial integration blinded him to in Philadelphia. Irishmen without family ties, the same sort of ties his daughter rejected by moving in with her boyfriend, soon make "the terrified discovery that in this world of freezing malevolence the soul itself may be frozen."[5] The Irish have been "deserted by institutions grown too huge and complex in a mass society"; they have been "denied humane communities amid an urbanized misery that succeeded rural desolation," and as a result their "spirit cringes."[6]

Man alone is simply too vulnerable to survive in a predatory world. As a result he needs both oikos (household) and ethnos (nation) for protection. Clark was successful in keeping his own family together, but his diary entries of the 1970s indicate that he was not as successful in transmitting that information on to the next generation of Clarks. With his faith weakened, he felt inadequate in transmitting morals, especially sexual morals, to his children, who were being assaulted by the predations of youth culture – sex, drugs, and rock 'n roll at the time. Clark fell back on ethnos as a substitute for religion, but he failed to see how ethnos was a function of religion, especially by way of morals, as conduit of ethnic culture from one generation to the next. "The basic human gambit against history," according to Clark, is the one in which "the clan fights the stranger; each man in his clan and the clan against the world."[7]

Clark's ideal of the *clan na gael* is a far cry from the ideal of the Catholic interracialism he espoused during the '50s. It is, in many ways, its opposite, which is to say, a much more realistic assessment of the dynamic of human history, certainly history in the United States during the period of covert ethnic struggle which followed World War II, but it was still inadequate because missing from it was the spiritual core at the heart of ethnos. Each clan had its gods; nor would they have survived without them. Certainly, it would be foolish to think that the Irish could have survived from Cromwell to the potato famine to the great migration to the United States without the support of the Catholic Church, but this is precisely what Clark is proposing, namely, an Irish ethnos purged of the Catholic Church.

No matter how plausible it seemed to Clark, no matter how much that construct satisfied his psychic needs, it did not seem plausible to the next generation, which took its mores from a combination of the dominant culture and the Quaker ruling-class schools they attended at their father's suggestion. Seven years before Conna Clark moved in with her boyfriend, Clark and his wife talked about "how Conna and Brendan must see us as peculiar in our attachment to Catholicism"[8] when in fact, the opposite was the case. Peculiar is a word best applied to Clark's increasingly ethnocentric ideology and his abandonment of Catholicism, about which at this point all he can say is that it "was a big force in the '50s" and that his "earliest emotional life had been strongly influenced by the old clutter of religiosity."[9] His oldest daughter evidently picked up the idea that the Catholic faith was "old clutter," and yet Clark seems surprised when, in obedience to the dictates of the dominant culture, she decides to flaunt her disregard of matrimony before him.

Two years after leaving for Bethlehem, Conna and Michael Gaston were back in Philadelphia, this time to get married at St. Madeleine Sophie Church by Father Jack McNamee, soon to become pastor of St. Malachy's Parish in North Philadelphia, one of the first Irish parishes in the city. In his homily, Father McNamee bade the congregation to be mindful of the example of Fidel Castro as a paradigm of "human interdependence."[10] Clark explicated McNamee's example by saying that "When told his sister sees him as a monster, Fidel said, 'My sisters and brothers are the oppressed of the world.'"[11]

Father McNamee evidently should have chosen other examples to launch the couple onto married life. Two years later, Conna filed for divorce, and again Clark was at a loss to explain what was going on in the mind of the next generation. After thinking about it and coming up with "no clear reason" for the "fragility of social bonds – or character – in these times," Clark decides to be nonjudgmental and reserve his "censure these days for the sons of bitches in power who have sold out to the oil companies."[12] Two months later, Clark announces that "Conna is roosting with someone she describes as 'your basic, balding, middle-aged Jew'" and wonders how long this "weak-minded meandering" will last.[13] In the absence of any better anodyne, Clark tries to console himself with the fact that she has a professional-sounding job running the Art Museum bookshop. Two years later, the balding middle-aged Jew whose name we never got to know is gone, and Conna strikes her father as "anxious about her future" and "adrift as divorcee."[14]

By this time the younger children have also been afflicted by the same cultural malaise. At around the same time that Conna moved in with her first boyfriend, Clark's wife made her "annual trip to the third floor" of their house and discovered that Brian and Ciaran were growing marijuana plants under special lights in their closet.[15] When Clark hears about gang rapes at Penn State fraternity houses, he wonders if they involve the fraternity there which his son Patrick just joined. By 1980 Clark was worried about all of his children because none of them seemed established in life. Clark and his wife discussed "trying to coax them out of working class (or worse) status by encouraging further study by our subsidizing it";[16] however, his wife claimed "that won't work till they make up their own minds."[17] All of the children "are dead set against white collar jobs,"[18] something that must have been particularly galling to Clark, who was the first in his family to rise out of the working class. To see them subside back into it must have been troubling enough, but his fears were magnified by the knowledge that the days of working-class blue-collar life in Philadelphia were over. The manufacturing jobs had all been exported to cheaper labor markets or the suburbs, and the city, deprived of its tax base, could simply not provide enough jobs to maintain the infrastructure that had been the legacy of the last three generations.

But more troubling than that, from Clark's point of view, was the fact that his children "have little commitment to ideas and the power of ideas to shape and illuminate life."[19] Clark finds this "sad" because life is "nasty and brutish without the radiance of thought, poetry, imagination, and ideas. That is the one single thing I would most be concerned about for these youngsters. The rest is superficial."[20]

At another point Clark worries about the fact that "our children make no signs of having ideas of social justice or any activism in that direction," something he considers an "extraordinary deficiency" and a dramatic "contrast to our own early adult years."[21] In this instance, the lack is easier to diagnose. Ideas are not things of intrinsic value. There are good ideas and bad ideas. Since Clark himself no longer believed in the ideals of his youth, it's difficult to understand why his children should. As children often do, Clark's family was able to see through his objections and understand the real issue at hand, even if they were unable to articulate it. Clark's ideals, especially in racial matters, had proven to be so unrealistic that even he no longer believed them. By blaming the Catholic Church for the failure of his essentially Quaker-inspired racial apostolate and distancing himself from it as a result, Clark cut his children off from the only coherent set of values available to them, and without this system of belief as the intellectual underpinning to everything else in their intellectual life – which was certainly the case in Clark's early life – nothing made sense to them other than simply getting along, which is what Clark did, after all, in spite of his ideas. Clark also ignores the fact that the Catholic Church was the institution which made interracial justice possible in the first place. Without the universal principles of the Catholic Church to inform him, Clark lapsed into ethnocentrism every bit as much as the blacks did, and when they did there was nothing more to talk about. After that, everything was an issue of competing ethnic power.

By 1982, Clark had given up the illusion that he had some consistent world view. "I am," he confided to his diary at the beginning of 1982 as part of his annual self-assessment, "an incoherent socialist, anarchist democrat."[22] It is small wonder then that his children's lives mirrored that incoherence. Conna was remarried but fighting with her new husband. Pat was broke in Houston; Brendan was unable to get a computer job; Ciaran was still seeking direction, and all of them were surrounded by a "sea of troubles."[23] The only exception to all of the bad news was the fact that his son Brian had a child at the end of the year, but even this happened "somewhat out of sequence,"[24] which is to say out of wedlock.

Normally an ethnic group is the vehicle which makes the transmission of values from one generation to another possible, but Clark made the mistake of misidentifying his ethnic group, confusing the group he really belonged to with the group he wanted to belong to in Ireland. In addition, he deliberately chose ethnos in a way that excluded religion, which meant that the ethnic group he wanted to belong to had no real values to transmit and the ones it did have were so irrelevant and so insubstantial that his children's generation ignored them completely.

In a 1984 diary entry Clark waxes "terribly sentimental about the children."[25] At least part of what makes him "teary" is his failure to transmit to them the values he holds dear, which at this point consisted largely of Celtic myth and culture. "I do regret that they have no sense of the ancient thing," he continued, "the old, old Irish feel of beauty and all those wonderful songs we have sung over long evenings, but they would not learn the songs and do not sing them."[26] The realization leaves Clark "sad," but the indifferent reaction of the Clark children to his cultural offer is not surprising. They were after all Americans and not Irishmen. They were the fourth generation of the Clark family in America and as such, should have been completely assimilated as American Catholics, but this ethnic identification is precisely what Clark denied his own children by his defection from the Catholic faith. As a result, they were typically deracinated examples of the "Me" generation, set adrift on sea of cultural danger in a lifeboat fitted out with what meager moral and religious stores they could glean from twelve years spent at Quaker schools.

By the time he had reached the end of his life, Clark had become convinced that ethnos was a part of nature. He didn't use terms drawn from scholastic philosophy anymore, but in 1976 he did state in a talk to the City Policy Committee that "ethnicity" had not been abolished by the melting pot. Instead, it would remain "a continuing feature of our political life in Eastern cities like Philadelphia"[27] because "politics in America is related to pieces of geography, some of which are populated as legislative or electoral districts with ethnic groups" whose "presence must work its way into political recognition sooner or later."[28]

Two years later, Clark appeared on a television panel and described Philadelphia Mayor Frank Rizzo as "an ethnic leader par excellence."[29] He earned this title in Clark's mind by appointing only Italians to most city posts and not rejecting his colleague Buddy Cianfrani when that worthy ended up in jail. But then Clark's description of Rizzo began to reflect his own ambivalence about ethnicity in Philadelphia, the same sort of reservation he confided to his diary thirty years earlier. Frank Rizzo was a master of orchestrating "group feeling," but he was plagued by the "social disabilities so many white ethnics share," including being "monumentally crude and ignorant" as well as "terribly insecure and afraid of his own limitations" and using, as a result "bombast to prop himself up."[30] According to Clark, "the ethnic ghetto" was Frank Rizzo's world and his only world, and Rizzo was "confused and hapless outside of it."[31]

One year before his death, Clark gave a speech on the meaning of ethnos to the Balch Institute for Ethnic Studies. The break-up of Yugoslavia into its ethnic components had convinced Clark that "this identity is as basic for human behavior as the need for air or the urge to procreate. Ethnic identity is as inevitable for us as our genetic code or our ability to speak."[32] Although he didn't portray it as such, Clark's speech on "ethnic cleansing" as "history's revenge" was a complete repudiation of his earlier views on "integration." Clark's work for the commission on human relations was predicated on the fact that assimilation in America meant the abolition of ethnos. Like participants in the melting pot pageants of 1918, ethnic Philadelphians were supposed to descend into the crucible of assimilation and emerge as simply "Americans," which is to say rootless consumers in one large pan-national quasi-ethnic group of the sort that Hitler proposed for Germany and Mussolini for Italy. Now Clark was saying that "ethnicity has to do with the intimate life and being of people, the very basis of human consciousness and powerful human drives. It is for this reason that ethnic identity is important, universal."[33] Ethnos, in other words, was part of nature. "Ethnicity," according to Clark, constitutes "the bonds of people" which defends them against the perversions of individualism "by giving us loyalty to one another and to the human values and decency, history perceives among us. It is one of the wellsprings of human bonding along with family, religion, and social ideals."[34]

If this is the case, one is tempted to ask why shouldn't people be allowed to live in ethnic neighborhoods? Especially since the neighborhood as an intermediary form of geography corresponds so neatly with ethnos as the intermediary social structure, half way between the family and the state. Clark never raised questions like that in his talk, probably because in raising the issue of the ethnic neighborhood, he would also have to deal with the role he played in destroying it in Philadelphia.

He didn't raise other issues as well. If ethnos is a permanent part of nature, then what ethnic group did Clark belong to? Or better still what ethnic group did Clark's children belong to? Clark didn't deal with this issue because, like the first question, it would have forced him to face uncomfortable issues in his own life. Ethnos may be a permanent part of nature, but it can be suppressed and perverted in precisely the way that the dominant culture perverted it in the period following World War II. It can be perverted into consumer groups, or social classes, or into the vague feeling of rootlessness that plagued his own children and the rest of their generation, the people who in many ways were the prime "beneficiaries" of Clark's efforts to integrate Philadelphia. Ethnos may be a permanent part of nature, but it can't exist on its own, independent of religion and ideals, which is precisely how Clark was hoping it would exist when he disconnected Irishry from the Catholic faith in his own life. Clark failed to see the connection between ethnos and religion because of his own loss of faith, and his loss of faith led not only to loss of faith on the part of his children but, ironically, loss of the very ethnic identity he hoped would become a substitute for faith in his own life.

The one exception to this rule was Brigid, Clark's youngest daughter. Of all the Clarks' children, Brigid was raised most under the sway of secularism and, by default, most under the sway of Quaker schooling as well, something that would cause a good deal of confusion in her life. Brigid spent all twelve years of grade school and high school at Abington Friends school, something that now and again gave Clark pause. After describing the rest of his children as "inert," and Brigid as the exception, Clark quickly adds the hope that "she avoids Quakerly febrile limp wrists as a result of all her years at Abington Friends."[35] Brigid would avoid limp wrists at Abington Friends, but in a way which Clark did not anticipate at the time.

Notes

1   Clark, Diary, 9/8/75.
2   Ibid.

3   Ibid.
4   Clark, Diary, 3/13/75 Clark mss. rejected by NYT.
5   Ibid.
6   Ibid.
7   Ibid.
8   Clark, Diary, 12/17/68.
9   Ibid.
10   Clark, Diary, 6/12/77.
11   Ibid.
12   Clark, Diary, 6/27/79.
13   Clark, Diary, 8/19/79.
14   Clark, Diary, 8/31/81.
15   Clark, Diary, 11/16/75.
16   Clark, Diary, 12/26/80.
17   Ibid.
18   Ibid.
19   Ibid.
20   Ibid.
21   Clark, Diary, 11/23/81.
22   Clark, Diary, 1/16/82.
23   Clark, Diary, 9/19/82.
24   Clark, Diary, 12/10/82.
25   Clark, Diary, 3/17/84.
26   Ibid.
27   Remarks of Dennis Clark to the City Policy Committee 12/7/76, Diary.
28   Ibid.
29   Clark, Diary, 6/9/78.
30   Ibid.
31   Ibid.
32   Clark, Ethnic Cleansing: History's Revenge, Diary, 8/20/92.
33   Ibid.
34   Ibid.
35   Clark, Diary, 11/23/81.

The Ethnic Cleansing of Poletown

Two out of three persons in Detroit are either black or Polish.

Michael Novak, *The Rise of the Unmeltable Ethnics*

Nineteen Seventy Nine was not a good year for the automobile industry. Detroit had spent the '70s ignoring the handwriting on the wall. That handwriting included the 1973 Arab oil boycott that had given Europe auto-free Sundays and its first taste of gasoline rationing since World War II. In spite of omens like this, Detroit's auto industry had continued to produce the higher-margin, gas-guzzling cars that had become its trademark.

Then suddenly two things happened at once. A recession hit the American economy, and Americans awoke to the fact that they could buy cheaper, more energy-efficient cars from the Japanese and higher quality cars from the Germans. As a result the automobile industry went into a state of shock. Chrysler teetered on the brink of bankruptcy and was only saved when the government intervened and guaranteed $1.5 billion in loans. Ford Motor Company lost $1 billion on its North American operations during 1979. Even General Motors was affected. In spite of posting a record after-tax profit of $1.3 billion during the first quarter of 1979, GM would go on to post a loss of $763 million by the end of the following year. It was the first time since 1921 that GM had lost money. Within the course of the next two years, car production fell by 32 percent, and GM laid off 14 percent of its workforce.

The automobile industry reacted to the crisis in various ways. Following the strategy they had been following since World War II, they first tried to balance the books on the backs of their workers by simultaneously extorting wage concessions from the unions and threatening to move plants farther from where Detroit's unionized workers lived. In 1980, this meant not the suburbs, but Mexico, where GM, after investing hundreds of millions in the construction of two new engine and two new assembly plants, was planning to pay its workers less than $1 an hour. Not wanting to be left out of the opportunity to cut labor costs that the downturn enabled, Ford indicated in 1980 that it was investing $42 million in a Mexican car-assembly plant.

The automobile industry had other ideas in mind as well. Since local governments sought automobile plants avidly because of the tax revenues they brought with them, the automobile industry had grown especially adept at extorting tax and infrastructure concessions from potential site locations by playing off one locality against another. While head of Chrysler, Lee Iacocca explained how the Big Three in Detroit would "pit Ohio versus Michigan" or "Canada versus the U.S."[1] Ford, Chrysler, and GM had all become masters at extorting "outright grants and subsidies in Spain, in Mexico, in Brazil – all kinds of grants."[2] The crisis in the automobile industry also coincided with the 1980 presidential election, and taking its cue from presidential candidate Ronald Reagan's neo-capitalist attack on statism, the auto industry, which had been fattening at the public trough since 1954, sought to portray itself as a group of beleaguered entrepreneurs whose troubles derived from being overburdened by excessive taxation and government regulation. In order to make its threat to move out of state in search of a "better business climate" stick, GM began intimidating both the local workforce and the local government by laying off large numbers of unionized blue-collar and non-unionized white-collar workers.

All of this naturally spelled trouble for the city of Detroit because its tax revenues were tied so closely to the auto industry. In addition to the decrease in revenue which resulted from layoffs and plant closings in the auto industry, other major retail and manu-facturing firms began to go down as recession turned into a full-blown depression for the Detroit area by 1980. In 1980 the Uniroyal Tire Company shut down its riverfront plant, adding 5,000 people to the rolls of Detroit's unemployed. In 1979, Warner-Lambert had already put 2,000 people out of work when it closed its Parke-Davis pharmaceutical plant. Most significant of all, Hudson's, Detroit's premier retail outlet, made plans to lay off employees as a prelude to closing its downtown store. Hudson's eventually closed its landmark downtown store in 1983 and the building would remain vacant for more than a decade until it was dynamited in the late '90s in one violent and dramatic gesture which testified to the folly of suburban expansion which Hudson's had been pursuing since 1954.

In January of 1980, Chrysler announced that it was planning to close its Dodge Main plant in Poletown by the spring in order to streamline its operation and make itself more attractive to the people from whom it needed to borrow $1.5 billion dollars to survive. Given all of the closings and layoffs that were going on at the time, the closing of one more plant didn't seem especially significant, but its significance would increase with time. The closing of the Dodge Main plant in Poletown would provide a set of conditions that would bring together all of the themes involved in urban renewal over the past forty years – the ethnic cleansing, the use of race as a cover for economic exploitation, the erosion of prop-erty rights by the promiscuous expansion of the concept of eminent domain – and take them all to their logical, brutal conclusion when the city of Detroit announced that it was going to take the land surrounding Dodge Main and turn it over to GM so that they could build a new assembly plant there. The Coleman Young administration felt that its back was to the wall, and that as a result, it had to do something dramatic to keep the auto industry from emigrating one factory at a time to Mexico. In order to get his point across, Young met with GM chairman Thomas A. Murphy and challenged him to stay involved in the local economy. The terms of the challenge gave Murphy the impression that he was being offered an opportunity where he couldn't lose money by taking it. This willingness, in turn, put pressure on Coleman Young to deliver what he promised, no matter what the political consequences. Or, better put, no matter what hardships got inflicted on political-ly vulnerable groups.

In June of 1980 General Motors and the city of Detroit held a press conference to announce a joint venture which was their response to both the recession and the crisis in the automobile industry. After all of their threats, GM announced that it was not moving after all, but rather was investing in Detroit or investing in the destruction of Detroit, since the city graciously announced at the same time that it would collaborate in the condem-nation and purchase of a 485-acre plot of land within the city limits. That plot included the old Dodge Main plant in Poletown, but it also included a huge section of Poletown as well. Like most ethnic neighborhoods in Detroit, Poletown was no longer purely Polish, but there were still enough Poles there to insure that the name wasn't a misnomer. Like most neighborhoods in Detroit, Poletown had already been weakened by having a highway run through it. But none of this gave any indication of the magnitude of the operation Coleman Young was to embark upon.

Before the largest urban land assemblage and clearance project in the history of the United States was completed, 1,400 homes, 144 businesses, and 16 churches would have to be razed, and 3,438 of Poletown's 4,200 residents would have to be relocated, at a cost to the city of $300 million. In return for its investment, the city had to grant GM a twelve-year 50 percent tax abatement, in addition to "all necessary air, water, and waste permits, rezoning of the land, city expenditures to provide the plant with adequate access to rail lines, highways, water, utilities, and sewage removal, and city-funded upgrading of the ingress and egress roads to the plant, including more street lights, in order to provide 'adequate security'"[3] – all in order to construct a plant that could easily have been built on the old Dodge Main site.

Most of the neighborhood that got destroyed – including Immaculate Conception Church, where the last pitched battle between the aged Polish women who chained themselves to the church's altar and the city's SWAT team was fought in June of 1981 – got destroyed in order to provide space, not for the plant but for the plant's parking lot. When the Poletown residents whose homes were scheduled to be bulldozed reminded GM of this fact, GM executives responded by saying that the parking garages which would have eliminated the need to destroy the neighborhood posed a security risk because they might harbor urban guerrilla snipers who could then fire on GM executives as they sat at their desks behind the new building's plate glass windows. Two years after the plant opened in 1985, GM managers were complaining that "its Poletown-style plants were too big."[4] "If we had to do it over," J.T. Battenburg III, manager of the Buick-Oldsmobile-Cadillac Plant in Flint told *Automotive News*, "we would build them smaller."[5]

By then, the news provided little consolation to the residents of Poletown because by then Poletown had lost most of its residents, most of whom were dispersed to the suburbs where they languished for a few years in an alien environment until they died. Some did not languish because they died in their homes due to the unbearable stress associated with a neighborhood that was being vandalized and burnt to the ground by arsonists, which the police always seemed unable to catch, even before the bulldozers arrived to finish the job. The Poletown story provides an important chapter in the history of urban renewal because the magnitude of its brutality and irrationality explode all of the conventional explanations of why this sort of thing was taking place.

Like the interstate highway system, the demolition of Poletown took place not because it was rational but because it could benefit the individuals and groups who were powerful enough to manipulate the political process in their own self-interest. The fact that certain wealthy players benefited financially from this transaction should not obscure the fact that they were allowed to do so because of strategic considerations that transcended economics. In this regard, Poletown was like the interstate highway system, which got constructed because GM and the rest of the highwaymen would benefit financially from its construction, but also because this project was consistent with the plan of social engineering which the government had embarked on years before.

Poletown was in many ways the *reductio ad absurdum* of that trend. By 1980, thirty-eight years after the battle over the Sojourner Truth housing project, no one could seriously maintain that Detroit's Polish population posed a threat to national security or any of the government's myriad projects, but the system of social engineering, ethnic cleansing, and race-based psychological warfare had been in place for so long, it operated almost on its own. The necessary precedents had already been established to clear the way legally, but even more importantly they were in place psychologically, providing the justification for what by any objective account was an instance of the rich and the powerful robbing the poor of their property.

Poletown was chosen for destruction because of all the reasons we have already mentioned. It had a significant ethnic population in a town where ethnic had become a synonym for racist in the minds of the city's mayor. By 1980, the same ethnic cleansing which had driven most of Detroit's Catholic population into the suburbs left those who remained behind defenseless against a city which had defined them as the enemy. Poletown was also known as a bastion of union activity at a time when the auto industry and Detroit's city government were actively engaged in trying to wring wage concessions from the unions and, by extension, blame them for the auto industry's financial woes. In 1918 Poletown voted Socialist, and the ruling class in Detroit felt that socialism and being foreign born were synonymous. Auto manufacturer William Brush referred to the residents of Poletown as an "alien threat" and an "enemy in our midst" and proposed as a result "the total extermination of such monstrosities in human form."[6] When the local version of the Palmer Raids took place in Detroit in 1920, government agents found that they could not read the literature they confiscated because it was written in Polish. Poles were also in the forefront of the labor unrest which swept through the city during the 1930s. In fact, Detroit's earliest and most contentious sit-down strikes all took place first in Poletown's steel, auto, and cigar factories.

Detroit's industrial class was, as a result, in the forefront not only of the management side of the labor dispute but also in the forefront of the social engineering of assimilation as an ancillary battle in the same war. The WASP ruling class in Detroit was in the forefront of the nativist attack on both immigration and in coming up with strategies for Americanizing the immigrants who were already here. Those strategies included Ford Motor Company staging its own version of the melting pot pageant in 1918, a ritual whereby immigrants would climb into a fifteen-foot-wide melting pot in their native costumes only to emerge later wearing suits and bowlers as the local band played the Star-Spangled Banner.

The Committee for Public Information, America's propaganda ministry during World War I, was so impressed with Ford's foray into psychological warfare that it staged its own version of the Melting Pot Pageant in ethnic communities across the country during the summer of 1918. As early as 1883, the *Detroit News* had written that the residents of Poletown "live and retain their customs to such an extent that the whole region more nearly resembles a fraction of Poland than a part of a city in the heart of America."[7]

One hundred years later, the ruling class in Detroit still felt the same way about ethnics, who were now known as "whites," as a way of tarring them with the brush of racism and delegitimizing whatever claims they might make in protest against government policy.

The most significant change over those one hundred years was the rise of black political power in the city. Henry Ford made a practice of insuring that migration to Detroit always insured that there would be a labor surplus in the area. He also made a practice of playing off one ethnic group against another to insure that the workers would not be able to unite and demand higher wages.

Ford's greatest success in this regard involved his importation of black workers from the South, first of all, because the fact that they got recruited through the city's black churches insured that they would be anti-union, since that was a condition of employment Ford worked out with the black ministers, but it was also his most lasting success because eventually black migration would drive the ethnics out of the city, and thereby place city government in the hands of the one ethnic group in the city which had been most congenial to the auto industry's anti-union attitude. As Paul Ylvisaker indicated, the policies of the Ford Foundation were simply the ethnic policies of the Ford Motor Company expanded and extrapolated for application to the situation in big cities across the country. The Ford Foundation ran the civil-rights movement in the United States, and in effect the civil rights movement was the WASP-black alliance which Henry Ford conceived as a way of defusing the threat which Catholic ethnic commitment to unions posed to the industrialists' economic interests.

The Poles, in particular, were aggressively pro-union. During the wave of strikes which took place in 1937, "Chrysler was unable to splinter community support at Dodge Main because of the strong ethnic allegiance of the people in Hamtramck and Poletown."[8] In April of 1937 alone, 245,000 workers joined the UAW, and many of them worked at Poletown's Chrysler, Briggs, and Hudson Motor plants. The land grab in Poletown in 1980 was simply the logical conclusion of a war which the ruling class in Detroit had been waging against union-ethnic-Catholic interests for almost a century.

The only thing which made this injustice even remotely plausible in the public mind was Coleman Young's manipulation of race. Blacks had become the nation's officially designated oppressed minority, even when they had taken over the government of a major city like Detroit. According to the canons of official public logic, that meant that if blacks supported a project, then it was officially certified as just in the public mind. This meant, of course, that all that GM and the rest of the ruling class in Detroit had to do in order to get approval for any of their projects in the mind of the public was to get that city's black mayor to play the race card in supporting it, and in doing that they defused any possible opposition to whatever they did, no matter how flagrant the injustice involved.

This is precisely what they did in the instance of Poletown, and it was precisely why the ruling class was interested in supporting a race-baiting mayor like Coleman Young. Young was a genius at having his cake and eating it too. He could claim to be a black revolutionary in the mode of, say, Jomo Kenyatta or any of the other black nationalists who were instrumental in driving the European colonists out of Africa during the 1960s, and he could do this while simultaneously licking the boots of the WASP ruling class in Detroit, which had brought blacks to work in the factories there precisely to undermine the position of ethnic Catholics like the Poles, who were much more troublesome because of their ethnic coherence and their penchant for unionization. Poletown had always been a stronghold of union activity, and the destruction of the neighborhood to build a GM plant with the collaboration of a black mayor was in addition to one more incident in a long history of economic aggression and injustice also an instance of symbolic revenge.

Detroit's first black mayor was, in many ways, an earlier, more virulent version of Philadelphia's first black mayor, Wilson Goode. When the ruling class in Philadelphia realized that the demographic turnover they had engineered in Philadelphia had reached critical mass, they decided to find a black candidate for mayor who was amenable to their interests. That man was Wilson Goode, and he had shown that he could be counted on to do their bidding by working for PCCA, the Ford Foundation's first attempt to orchestrate racial change in North Philadelphia in its own interests. Coleman Young was less of a cipher than Wilson Goode, but he was a product of the same political forces, including the Ford family's penchant for orchestrating ethnic conflict in the interest of economic control. The same desire which prompted Henry Ford to rely on black ministers to insure that he could get reliably non-union black workers for his factories inspired the Ford Foundation's involvement in the civil-rights movement, and it also paved the way for Coleman Young's rise to power in Detroit.

Following the riots of 1967, Henry Ford II decided that something needed to be done to safeguard downtown interests. The '67 riots had put an end to the career of Mayor Jerry Cavanagh because they showed that the liberal-ameliorist-integrationist approach that Cavanagh had associated himself with when he marched down Woodward Street with Martin Luther King in June of 1963 could not contain the passions which King's appeal aroused. After the riots, the establishment in Detroit concluded that it would have to eliminate the Catholic middle-man and deal with the city's blacks directly through a leader who was undeniably, even aggressively, black but also equally amenable to their interests in a way that the union-ethnic-Catholics were not.

The Detroit News formulated the issue in its own way. The riots made the city's "historically powerful" aware that they needed a forum which could "put rich power together with street power."[9] That forum was the Detroit Renaissance, and the man who ran it was Henry Ford II. *The Detroit News* left no doubt as to where this new group's sympathies lay. "Detroit Renaissance," they opined, "is a businessman's dream."[10] The coalition the ruling class formed in 1971 in Detroit "builds things. It makes things happen. Discussions are matter-of-fact. Henry Ford II, Max Fisher, builder-developer A. Alfred Taubman and its president Robert McCabe run the show. No substitutes are allowed."[11] Detroit Renaissance was, in other words, Detroit's version of the Vault in Boston or the Walter Phillips/ADA clique in Philadelphia, both of which had been modeled on David Lawrence's Allegheny Conference in Pittsburgh. Detroit Renaissance was also open to blacks, but it was not open to blacks "who don't understand business."[12]

Like Martin Luther King, Coleman Young also had a dream. His was completely congruent with the "businessman's dream" which lay at the heart of the Detroit Renaissance. Young would soon show the Detroit establishment that he was a black who understood business, and especially the role which a mayor of Detroit could play in fostering the interests of business by large tax-abatement giveaways.

By the 1973 election, the voting population of Detroit had become totally polarized along racial lines. John Nichols, the city's police chief, ran a campaign based on a promise to restore law and order that got him 91 percent of the city's white vote. Coleman

Young ran an equally raced-based campaign which won him 92 percent of the city's black vote. The crucial change in the city since the time when a white Catholic liberal like Jerry Cavanagh could run a campaign based on an appeal to all races was racial migration. The whites had migrated in such large numbers to the suburbs, largely because of the 1967 riot, that they were simply reduced to the status of a minority which could not win elections anymore. That meant that in order to control the political process in the city, people like Henry Ford II could ignore the white vote entirely and concentrate all their efforts in electing a black mayor who was amenable to their interests. A man, in other words, like Coleman Young.

In the wake of the 1967 riots, Detroit department-store magnate Joseph L. Hudson, Jr. created a group called New Detroit, Inc., which tried to stabilize and take control of the situation in Detroit by funding a number of community, government, and organizational projects. The man Hudson appointed to run New Detroit, Inc., was Lawrence Doss, who soon became friends with Coleman Young and took the opportunity to introduce Young to Henry Ford II. It didn't take long before both realized, in the words of Henry Ford II, that "we saw eye-to-eye on a lot of things."[13] Ford was busy organizing his own response to the 1967 riots, a much larger operation known as Detroit Renaissance, Inc. To show that he was not going to abandon Detroit and that he was still in control of the situation, Ford personally persuaded the head of each major corporation associated with the automobile industry in Detroit to invest in the Renaissance Center, a cluster of steel and glass cylinders on the banks of the Detroit River which would dominate the skyline for miles around.

The Ren Cen was a classic expression of architectural ambivalence. It was built to show confidence in downtown Detroit when everyone seemed to be threatening to leave as a result of racial fear. As some critics have noted, the building itself gives expression to that fear by placing its first floor high above street level on a ziggurat of air-conditioning equipment which makes access from the street, from which black people might enter, virtually impossible. In other words, corporate Detroit's presence downtown is visually inescapable but physically inaccessible, and in this respect, the building with all of its space-ship brutalism is the physical correlative of the ruling class's urban policies there. The space-ship building destroys everything in its immediate vicinity when it lands, but its tenure never seems secure. It has no connection with its surroundings. It is not rooted in local culture or vernacular architecture or anything approximating local materials. In fact, it looks as if it might take off and fly off to another planet – or Mexico – if things do not develop according to its liking.

In order to get the Ren Cen project off the ground, Henry Ford II had to bring together the largest private investment group ever assembled for an American real-estate venture. Financing involved a $200 million loan from a consortium of banks and insurance companies as well as at least $300 million from the Ford Motor Company. The groundbreaking for the Ren Cen took place on May 22, 1973, shortly before Young was elected mayor.

Given the type of financial clout Henry Ford could command, it is not surprising that an enterprising politician like Coleman Young would want to do business with him. Young, according to one source, "wanted to work with powerful actors,"[14] and in Detroit that meant the auto industry in general and Henry Ford II in particular. The powerful actors, in turn, knew that they had something to gain from this political arrangement as well. Once

Ford gave his approval to Young, the support of the entire Detroit establishment quickly swung over to his side. That meant the support of "financier Max Fisher, UAW president Leonard Woodcock, Joe Hudson, Jr. (of department store fame), Republican Governor William Milliken, as well as local clergy and academics."[15]

Before long, it became apparent that while Young needed the blacks within the city to pull the levers on voting day, the bulk of his financial support did not come from the city. It came from the suburbs, something Ze'ev Chavets noted in his book *Devil's Night*. After announcing that "Interestingly, almost 45 percent of the mayor's cash flowed in from out of town, most of it from the suburbs," Chavets notes that "Young had no ready explanation for why so many hostile white suburbanites gave him money."[16] Part of Chavets's perplexity stems from the fact that he uses race in essentially the same way that Young uses the term without realizing how this terminology acts as a cover for the real terms of the drama, which were ethnic and not racial.

Chavets inadvertently stumbled across the true terms of the equation in a discussion of the fact that Young was raised a Catholic. Shortly before his interview with Young, Chavets notes that Cardinal Szoka was forced to close 43 of the 114 Catholic Churches in the city of Detroit, "the largest shutdown in the history of the American church,"[17] Chavets noted. If Young was upset, he didn't let his emotions show. In fact, he applauded the closings as "good sense" on Szoka's part because "Catholics are mostly white, and they've left the city," and those who are "still here have erected racial barriers."[18] By keeping those churches open, Szoka was, at least in Young's view, subsidizing prejudice. As if somehow unpersuaded by Young's argument, Chavets goes on to opine that the "ethnic whites who have remained in the city" are "mostly Catholic," and that "the church itself has never been an active enemy of the mayor."[19] The Catholic Church, however, is "funded and led independently" and as a result "one of the few institutions" in the city which "he doesn't dominate."[20] In other words, no matter how supine it had become under Cardinal Dearden, the Catholic Church was still a threat to Young's total control of the city.

After almost realizing that the term "white people" covers two distinct ethnic categories in Detroit, Chavets lapses once again into the racial model whose main purpose is the obfuscation of the true dynamics of political life in the city. Young, according to Chavets, has become "perhaps the most powerful and independent black politician in the United States," because he is "supported by a white industrial establishment indebted to him for keeping the lid on" and "covered by a press frequently charmed and bludgeoned into averting its gaze."[21]

Looking at the political landscape from the perspective of the Poletown incident, Jean Wylie comes up with a slightly different explanation. "The ruling elite," according to Wylie, found in Young "the perfect solution to the racial and class tension that culminated in the 1967 riots: they had a radical black mayor to front for their profit-making ventures in the city."[22] Race, in other words, was the concept which made the ruling coalition in Detroit possible because the term "white" disguised the fact that the ruling class was using black politicians like Young to drive the Catholic ethnics out of the city and, thereby, control the city government in their interests, interests which Coleman Young was avid to serve.

Ruling-class support of racial interests was clearly an instance of *quid pro quo*. Race disguised the real ethnic battle at the heart of the destruction of Detroit. It gave the ruling class the appearance of being interested in social justice, when all the while the black politicians it supported reciprocated by in effect giving away the city's assets, even when it meant, as it would in Poletown, taking private property from its poor ethnic owners. Even the pro-Coleman Young Thomas makes the same point, namely, that "the city's corporate leaders were prime beneficiaries of the city's pro-development mentality, since this gave them almost unqualified support for whatever projects they wanted to build."[23]

Graphic illustration of this policy appeared in an article in *National Geographic* in 1979, the year of the downturn in the auto industry and the year the Poletown plot was hatched. As part of an article entitled "Detroit Outgrows Its Past," *NG* featured a picture of Coleman Young standing beside Henry Ford II shaking hands with David Rockefeller over a caption which read, "Detroit's struggle for self-respect includes allies that might have seemed unlikely a decade ago."[24]

The alliance between black political entrepreneurs and the ruling class was not only not unlikely before the picture was published, it was by then a political fact of life that had come to be known as the civil-rights movement. The only thing that had changed in the intervening decade was the demographics of the city. White migration out of the city had eliminated the need of Irish Catholic politicians like Jerry Cavanagh. The ruling class could now eliminate the ethnic middleman and get political and financial concession directly from the black political entrepreneurs they had been promoting since World War II, and political entrepreneurs like Coleman Young were only too happy to reciprocate. In 1979 alone, Young had handed over $14.2 million in tax abatements to the interests represented by Ford and Rockefeller. Chrysler alone received $3.1 million.

That meant that in order to maintain his grasp on power, Coleman Young was willing to pass up on almost $15 million in taxes, some of which would return to him personally in the form of political contributions, at a time when the city of Detroit was on the verge of one of its most dramatic drops in revenue in the city's entire history. Young's largesse to his corporate masters coupled with the shortfall in revenue caused by the recession was bound to cause trouble, and it did just that. By the early 1980s, the city of Detroit tottered on the verge of bankruptcy, but the political and demographic realities which swept Young in to office all but determined how that financial crisis would be resolved. Given Young's allegiance to his black supporters in the city and his WASP backers in the suburbs, it was a foregone conclusion that Young would have to balance the books on the backs of the people least likely to afford it, and that meant the city's ethnic population, and that meant the city's Polish population.

By the time the financial crisis hit Detroit in 1980, the city was in a bind, even if it was largely a bind of its own making. The combination of decreasing tax revenue coupled with the increased demand on services which unemployment invariably accompanied in its wake, soon brought Detroit, which had been losing productive, tax-paying citizens on a massive scale since the 1967 riots, to the brink of bankruptcy. Coleman Young, who had been in power for six years by the time the economic crisis broke, was then faced with coming up with a plan to prevent the city from falling into receivership to the state of Michigan. Race again would play a crucial role in obscuring the real outline of the situation in Detroit. Instead of seeing the revenue shortfall as the result of Young's largesse in granting tax breaks to large corporations, and instead of seeing the automobile industry's problem as the result of bad management and ignoring the handwriting on the wall, the city's voters were told a different story. The auto industry's financial problems were the result of high taxes, over-regulation, and unionized labor. Similarly, the city's financial crisis was portrayed in racial terms as an attempt on the part of white politicians in Lansing to take away the black political gains Young and Company had wrung from a racist society during the civil rights struggles of the '60s.

Rather than admit that the city's financial woes were the result of his own mismanagement and imprudent largesse to both corporate interests and black interests in affirmative action contracts, Young convened his praetorian guard of loyal black pastors and framed the issue in the following way, "Are we willing to see that the city's destiny remains in our hands? Or will we do what thousands of bigots hope we do – vote no and let the state take us over?"[25] The term "we" here referred, it should be obvious, not to the citizens of Detroit, all of whom Young was elected to serve. At the heart of Young's rescue plan for the city was a tax increase that had been engineered by the city's corporate elite to insure that they would not have to pay for the havoc their mismanagement was wreaking in the local economy.

In order to insure that Young's version of the crisis prevailed and that the hapless citizens of Detroit would vote to take more money out of their own already diminished wallets, Detroit's ruling class gave Young $427,000 to spend on the public relations campaign leading up to the city-wide referendum on whether to raise the income tax. More than half the money was contributed by the city's largest corporations and banks. GM contributed $40,000; the UAW donated $37,500; Ford Motor Company gave $20,000 and Michigan Bell, American Natural Resources, Detroit Edition, and the National Bank of Detroit each contributed $16,000. As a result, Detroit's voters trooped to the polls and loyally decided to "balance the city budget on the shoulders of those least able to afford it."[26] Funded by the city's business community elite, Young had persuaded the citizens of Detroit to raise their own taxes, cut their own services, and, in addition to that, he forced the unions to give concessions to the people who had created the crisis in the first place. All in all, it was an impressive performance in political persuasion, and the only thing which made it possible was Young's masterful manipulation of the race card and funding from the city's WASP industrial elite.

Anyone familiar with the forces which Young manipulated to get into the mayor's office and which he continued to manipulate in order to stay there could have seen that he could move in one direction only once the tax increase got approved. Young had tightened his grip on power in Detroit by playing the race card. This meant driving the whites out of the city and then rewarding his supporters with the spoils that remained behind when they left. The main benefit which the average black person received as a result of this policy was cheap, and in some instances, free housing. Young's decision not to enforce the laws in certain neighborhoods resulted in white migration which dramatically reduced the cost of housing in the city by, in effect, doubling the supply of housing while at the same time decreasing the demand by half. During Coleman Young's tenure as mayor, a city which was built for 2 million inhabitants, suddenly had its population cut in half, resulting in a population of 1 million competing for housing constructed to meet a population of twice that size. American's racial mythology allowed Young to portray what was essentially an exercise in ethnic cleansing as "white flight," thereby blaming the victim.

The same logic would get used in Poletown, where people who owned homes in the neighborhood and had lived there all their lives were portrayed as racists because they were reluctant to allow those homes to be torn down so that GM could build an oversized parking lot. In public pronouncements, Young professed to be mystified by opposition to his deal with GM. When GM chairman Roger Smith and Young met at the Poletown plant site in January 1982 to celebrate the raising of the new plant's first structural column, Young portrayed himself as the victim of "vicious and unreasonable assault" for his role in bringing off the deal, and opined that opposition to the project was "like shooting Santa Claus."[27] In his 1984 state-of-the-city address, Young described the Poletown deal as his "most significant accomplishment," a view which June Manning Thomas echoes in her book, especially in her description of the role that Emmett Moten, Detroit's black city planner, played in bringing off the deal. Moten was "the aggressive African American" who, as part of Young's "talented staff," "put together the Poletown deal" "without missing a step," something Thomas feels is attributable to his "technical and political skills."[28]

The residents of Poletown, needless to say, had a different take on the whole story. They felt that "Moten's main talent during the Poletown debate was obfuscation."[29] As part of the preparation they needed to make to vote on the Poletown issue, Detroit's city council would ask Moten plain questions only to find that he and other city officials "generally played fast and loose with the figures, causing even the city council members to complain that they weren't being given adequate information to make a decision."[30] Councilwoman Maryann Mahaffey termed Moten's testimony before the council "a crock of shit."[31]

Representatives from the neighborhood would go to Moten to complain about the gratuitous cruelty involved in taking a huge parcel of land, especially when only a small fraction of that land was needed for the actual plant, but their pleas elicited only a shrug from Moten, whose genius in city planning was reduced to representing the interests of General Motors, no matter how extravagant their demands were or how illogical they were from the point of view of any rational canon of urban planning. "This is the site that fits the criteria," Moten would tell the people from Poletown who were about to lose their homes. "We have a crisis that has been engendered by General Motors coming to us and threatening to leave. We have to do something."[32] As was the case with the black mayor, the injustice of the situation was obscured in the mind of the public which had absorbed the categories of racial mythology forged during the civil-rights movement. The fact that the urban planner was black and the people being ethnically cleansed white meant that injustice could not be taking place. It was a bit like claiming that if Jewish guards ran the concentration camp, whatever happened there was okay.

After a while the combination of vague expressions of concern combined with bureaucratic evasiveness, truckling to powerful interests and callous disregard of the human cost the Poletown project was going to exact eventuated in the creation of a new word, the verb "to motenize." "It's a pathetic sight," one official complained, "to see aged couples hugging each other, sobbing on the sidewalks, looking at their homes perhaps for the last time before being Motenized."[33]

Coleman Young's behavior in crushing resistance in Poletown showed the iron fist beneath the velvet glove known as assimilation in the United States. The ethnic community had always been perceived as a threat. The people who chose community over upward mobility were always a reproach to the system. As a general rule, those ethnics who refused to go for the carrot of FHA mortgages were subjected to the stick of racial migration as a way of driving them into enclaves more in conformity with America's dominant culture. That meant places where people spent less time on the front porch or other places socializing with people like themselves and more time in front of the TV or behind the steering wheel of a car, in part because they had nothing in common with their new neighbors and, therefore, no reason to socialize. The destruction of Poletown may or may not have been done with this end in mind. (Young's papers are not available for study.) But it was allowed to happen because the government had been pursuing social engineering that involved weakening the local community for forty years. When a group of opportunistic politicians in Detroit decided to steal the land and houses from Poletown's remaining ethnic residents, there wasn't enough political power left in the community to prevent it.

One of the main reasons that Poletown was unable to defend itself was because the erosion of property rights which began with *Berman v. Parker* in 1954 received a dramatic impetus when the Michigan State Legislature, largely at the urging of General Motors, passed what it termed "quick take" legislation enabling the Poletown land grab. The Michigan legislature passed its new condemnation law on March 18, 1980, and on April 4, Republican Governor William Milliken signed the Uniform Condemnation Act into law. The rapidity with which the law passed and the alacrity with which it got applied to the situation in Poletown led some observers to wonder if the law wasn't "adopted to make things easier for General Motors in its current project."[34]

The new law ostensibly streamlined the state's condemnation policies, but it did more than that. It construed employment, as in employment at a GM plant, as a public benefit and therefore, in effect, conferred on General Motors the right of eminent domain. It also permitted the state, which acted as GM's agent, to take control of private property without having to wait for the resolution of legal challenges. Since the state could proceed to tear down houses while the appeals proceeded, the new law automatically made any appeal moot. The house would be gone by the time the courts got around to ruling on the matter.

Notes

1 Jeanie Wylie, *Poletown: Community Betrayed* (Urbana: University of Illinois Press, 1989), p. 36.
2 Ibid.
3 Ibid., p. 52.
4 Ibid., p. 215.
5 Ibid.
6 Ibid., p. 2.
7 Ibid., p. 4.
8 Ibid., p. 11.
9 Ibid., p. 40.
10 Ibid.
11 Ibid.

12 Ibid., p. 41.

13 Ibid., p. 39.

14 June Manning Thomas, *Redevelopment and Race* (Baltimore: The Johns Hopkins University Press, 1997), p. 183.

15 Wylie, p. 39.

16 Ze'ev Chafets, *Devil's Night and Other True Tales of Detroit* (New York: Random House, 1990), p. 206.

17 Ibid., p. 187.

18 Ibid., p. 188.

19 Ibid.

20 Ibid.

21 Ibid., p. 192.

22 Wylie, p. 39.

23 Thomas, p. 201.

24 Wylie, p. 40.

25 Ibid., p. 45.

26 Ibid.

27 Ibid., p. 201.

28 Thomas, p. 163.

29 Wylie, p. 56.

30 Ibid.

31 Ibid.

32 Ibid., p. 60.

33 Ibid., p. 63.

34 Ibid., p. 56.

Dennis Clark and the Wreckage of Kensington

> Growing up as he did with an Irish identity . . . in a predominantly Irish-American neighborhood, he never lost touch with his roots.
> *Irish American Magazine* on Dennis Clark

> Old Polish Popy John Paul came to the city yesterday.
> No more Popes! No more Popes!
> Dennis Clark, Diary, 10/4/79

At around the same time that the Poletown story was heading toward its climax in Detroit, Dennis Clark noted sadly in his diary that Dorothy Day had just died, thus ending "an era of social protest and reform that started in the 1930s."[1] Clark remembered attending *Catholic Worker* meetings on Mott Street in New York City, and his involvement with the *Catholic Worker* paralleled in a minor way his greater involvement in New York's Catholic Interracial Council. During the months immediately preceding Dorothy Day's death in the fall of 1980, Clark took busloads of people "on a tour of the industrial wreckage in Kensington."[2] Clark grew up in Kensington and was certainly familiar enough with its history, but he gives no indication – in his diary at least – of what he told the people on the bus perhaps because the complexity of his feelings was too daunting.

Clark felt that Philadelphia's infrastructure was "built on exploited 19th century labor."[3] That labor included his father's and his grandfather's generation, a group of people who were ruthlessly exploited economically by a ruling class in the city that was "militantly antilabor and instinctively repressive to the immigrants who were the basis of their wealth in this city."[4] America's traditional answer to the charge of economic exploitation that has been pandemic throughout its history was that the third generation would finally achieve acceptance and middle-class status with all that went with it. That turned out not to be the case in Philadelphia largely because the animus among the ruling class to Clark's ethnic group proved to be so deep-seated that the ruling class chose to destroy the city rather than let it fall into Clark's people's hands.

During what many might construe as Philadelphia's golden age, the reform years from 1952 to 1962, Philadelphia's labor force shrank by 8 percent, much of that occurring when Philadelphia's establishment closed its textile mills and moved them down south during the mid-'50s. Philadelphia's elite no longer considered themselves Philadelphians in any abiding sense of the word. They passed their wealth on to a generation which had attended national ruling-class schools like Harvard, Yale and Princeton and which seemed bent not on maintaining family businesses but rather fitting themselves into the world of national corporations, corporations which had no allegiance to any one city, and ultimately, as time would show, no allegiance to the United States either.

The jobs that migrated first to the non-unionized enclaves in the South would soon migrate farther south, to Mexico and Central America, as soon as the people in the South demanded decent wages as well. In the process, America began to lose the skilled labor force that was one of its most valuable industrial assets, and America began to lose it first in places like Philadelphia, a fact Clark duly noted. The dramatic drop in jobs, "right in the middle of the Reform period," created a "subversion of the technological tradition that had enriched this city as an industrial metropolis" and ultimately "impoverished the resource base of this city."[5]

Once the human infrastructure of skilled craftsmen which had built the city had passed from the scene without passing those skills on to the next generation, the physical infrastructure began to fall apart because no one knew how to keep it going. As a result, "the gas lines are blowing up, the water lines are deteriorating, the railroad is falling apart and there is nobody with a pick and shovel down in a hole repairing."[6] By 1987, when Clark began meditating on the failure of the Clark/Dilworth/ADA Reform in earnest, there were 8,000 vacant lots in North Philadelphia and over 10,000 vacant houses, numbers that had risen steadily after the 1980 census and would rise even more dramatically by the time the 20th century came to a close.

Philadelphia's ruling class had created a complex system of law, policy, custom, and inertia which was literally destroying the city, and not even someone as intimately connected with it as Dennis Clark could come up with coherent picture of what was happening, much less a program to stop the decay. "The people who were the leadership caste of Philadelphia," according to Clark, "benefited from the labor of tens of thousands of sweated workers,"[7] and yet they felt no obligation to preserve the public wealth those workers created for future generations. The wanton wastefulness of the system left Clark full of rage, even to the point of causing him to repudiate his commitment to racial justice, or at least see the manipulation of race the ruling class brought about, with his help, in a different light. Clark's rage is understandable. Clark's father and grandfather had helped build Philadelphia into a great industrial city, and by the end of his life, he could sit back and watch all that under-remunerated effort fall into ruin, largely because of the elite's racial policies – policies, it should be noted, he helped implement. Thus, the rage Clark felt was largely rage at himself, which had to be projected onto another group.

By the 1980s, Clark, the racial idealist of the '50s and '60s, had come to a different point of view on race. "The real problem," he confided to his diary, came about when Philadelphia's elite "trapped us with all of these people from the South who did not know how to live in an urban environment."[8] As Clark settled into the sinecure at the Fels Institute that would be his last and most remunerative job, he gradually withdrew from the struggles he had been involved in as a younger man. That and the fact that both the Catholic and racial scene in Philadelphia changed because of the course of events which he helped orchestrate caused him to come to other reevaluations as well.

On May 2, 1975, Clark attended a conference at Temple University on urban renewal. One of the speakers at the conference was Ed Bacon, who astonished those present by comparing the city's urban-renewal practices to the military's campaign of defoliation and strategic hamlets in Viet Nam. Bacon had just seen *Hearts and Minds*, a documentary film which showed "rampaging U.S. technology ravaging human structures."[9] After seeing it, Bacon was struck with the similarities between what the U.S. military had done to the people of Viet Nam and what he as "chief architect-planner of the rebuilding of center city, Society Hill, etc, for 20 years"[10] had done to the people of Philadelphia. Bacon's admission that "the urban clearance system" and "the redevelopment schemes in the city" were similar to the "techniques that had decimated Viet Nam" constituted an "extraordinary recantation" in Clark's eyes.[11] (Twenty-five years later, Bacon had no recollection of what he had said at Temple and bristled at the suggestion that urban renewal had anything to do with things like the devastation in Viet Nam. In May of 2000, he began the speech accompanying the celebration of his nintieth birthday at Philadelphia's Civic Center by announcing that he hadn't decided whether he was going to tell the truth or not.)

Since Clark, as an employee of the Commission on Human Relations, was involved in the human engineering that accompanied those efforts, it probably brought about some examination of conscience on his part as well. Just how much, we'll never know because a diary is nothing more that a record of what one can admit to oneself. The things one cannot or will not admit do not get recorded there. So in response to Bacon's "extraordinary recantation," Clark makes what we might call an ordinary recantation by pointing up three failures of what he called with some irony the "urban 'renewal' system." First there was a "leadership failure," a failure of "professional education to integrate the parts of the problem and see the human dimension." But beyond that, there was, more importantly, a "failure of political vision and sympathy," in other words, a failure "to understand that, like war and slavery the industrial city, though it has great benefits, takes an outrageous human toll constantly as the price of its bourgeois lifestyle."[12]

All of this was pretty tame compared to what Ed Bacon admitted, but listening to Bacon stirred up old memories. Clark remembers having "several very vigorous conversations" with Bacon when Bacon was Planning Commission director, "about the eventual racial composition of certain neighborhoods that were in development in the 1950s, including Society Hill, the area of East Poplar and North Philadelphia."[13] After admitting that the racial make-up of Philadelphia's neighborhoods was a topic of discussion among those commissioned by the city's ruling class to engineer them, Clark suddenly goes blank, giving no indication of whether he was arguing for the black or the ethnic side of the equation. But in many ways the details are irrelevant, and filled in by the inexorable course of history anyway. Social engineers like Clark and Bacon were being paid by the ruling class to tinker with the racial make-up of neighborhoods where the experiment got out of control anyway. By the beginning of the 21st century, places like North Philadelphia had been so devastated that city planners were now suggesting building a golf course there because it was so empty. A golf course in North Philadelphia corresponded to no one's plans for the region in the 1950s, but the simple fact of the matter is that those who felt called to tinker with the neighborhood set in motion forces which ultimately destroyed it. Ed Bacon gave some indication – in 1975, at least – that he played a role in that destruction. Dennis Clark was never that forthright, certainly not in his diary, because the one person to whom he had the most difficulty admitting failure was himself.

Just why it was harder for Dennis Clark to admit failure than Ed Bacon is not all that difficult to understand. Ed Bacon was a Quaker, working for the Quakers to engineer other people's neighborhoods. Dennis Clark was an Irish Catholic, working for the Quakers engineering the neighborhoods of his own people, a fact that must have become more and more painful to him as the dream of a racially integrated city faded away into all-out, no-holds-barred ethnic conflict of the sort he would soon see in Yugoslavia in the '90s. With the benefit of 20 years of hindsight, Clark was finally able to see that "the great deeds of physical reconstruction" had as, at least, one side-effect, an "underside of human grief and displacement" that came about because of "the destruction of community structure." That structure was "informal" but nonetheless important because it ensured "the city's stability over the generations."[14]

Peering into the abyss which North Philadelphia had become, at least to some extent because of his efforts, Clark steps back from a momentary spell of vertigo and goes on to say that the "path through this thicket of racism, discrimination and discontent in this city"[15] that he helped beat was successful after all. "It was an impressive record, I thought," he wrote. "There was no other city that I know of that had such an established nationwide reputation for attempting to deal with the problems such as Philadelphia had."[16] And there was no other city in the nation, with the possible exception of Detroit, which suffered similar devastation as a result of those efforts. The monuments which got erected downtown only pointed out the emptiness north of town more glaringly. "The precedent setting role of Philadelphia government," Clark writes without a trace of irony, "should be documented very carefully."[17]

At other moments Clark wasn't so sure of Philadelphia's achievements. Two years before this death he watched Arthur Miller's play *Clara* on television. It was "about a man who misled his . . . daughter by an imprudent or too blatant idealism about race."[18] Miller's play touched a nerve. "Blatant idealism about race" had become "a personal theme" for Clark because none of his children shared his "younger views on racial issues."[19] Having seen race used as a weapon against people like their father, the next generation of Clarks were "more cautious, even retrogressive."[20] The twin failures of racial integration and urban renewal were having a similar effect on Clark, although he didn't like to admit it. Clark's failure as head of the Catholic Interracial Council caused him to question both his commitment to Catholicism and his commitment to racial justice. In the period of soul-searching which followed that failure, Clark began to look upon ethnicity as a substitute for both.

Clark had spent most of his working life bringing "all of these people from the South who did not know how to live in an urban environment" into Kensington and other neighborhoods like it throughout the city, hastening the exodus of those skilled workers who were the heirs of his father's and grandfather's generation out of the city. But he can never quite bring himself to admit his culpability in the thousands of pages of introspection that make up his diary, and that is because behind the rage there was a more fundamental feeling driving it, and that was his servility. Once the altruism associated with the Catholic faith disappeared from Clark's life, all that was left were the baser emotions of rage and servility. Once the universalism associated with Catholic doctrine evaporated, all that was left was ethnic chauvinism. Behind the façade of the bantering Irishman that Clark cultivated lay a deep-seated ambivalence based on a simple fact of life: Clark hated the Philadelphia ruling class with an Irish chauvinist's traditional ancestral hatred of the English, but coupled with that fact was the knowledge that he had spent his life doing the bidding of the class of people he hated. That in turn created a feeling of self-loathing that was intolerable and so had to be projected away from himself, something which Clark accomplished by attaching it to the Catholic Church.

Clark's animus against the Catholic Church was surely connected with his disappointments on the racial front and can be dated to his unhappy tenure as head of the New York Catholic Interracial Council from 1962 to 1963. But the undeniable truth of that matter should not blind us to the fact that Clark's growing anti-Catholicism and his growing ethnocentrism were two sides of the same coin, and both served as a psychological escape mechanism that not only let him off the hook but also allowed him to have his cake and eat it too. Dennis Clark, the professional Irishman, could bluster all he wanted and still remain a subordinate in good standing in a way that would have been impossible if Clark had been as serious about his Catholicism. His ethnocentrism, no matter how ugly it got when he supported IRA terrorism, never got in the way of his career as his Catholicism might have, because by the time he became involved in working for Philadelphia's ruling class, their quarrel was no longer with the Irish, it was with Catholics who happened to be Irish, people like Martin Mullen, whose religious-based opposition to the WASP implementation of the sexual revolution in Philadelphia posed a serious threat to their interests at the time. Compared to Mullen, who was Catholic first and Irish incidentally, Clark's Irish blustering could be treated with smiling, if not eye-rolling, condescension.

As some indication of Clark's servile side, a side he deliberately repressed in his diary entries, Clark wrote an article on the Quakers, at some time between when Martin Mullen was defeated in the gubernatorial primary and when the last Polish lady was dragged wailing from the basement of Immaculate Conception Church in Poletown. In that article he opined that "no Irish-American in Philadelphia should pass a Friend's Meeting House without thanking God that there were such people and such a tradition as that of the Friends."[21] Clark was referring to the role the Quakers played in helping relieve the Irish during the potato famine. It was a role they would continue in the next century when they organized what the Germans called the "*Quakerspeise*" after World War I.

But in praising the Quakers in such embarrassingly fulsome terms, Clark could have been talking about himself and his own career as well. Clark had worked for the Quaker establishment in Philadelphia in one capacity or another for his entire adult life, and his trustworthiness in carrying out their interests had convinced the establishment in Philadelphia that Clark could be trusted as their factotum. That he ended his career working for Jews at the Fels Fund doesn't really change the trajectory and dynamics of his career. Like Wilson Goode, who proved his mettle to the establishment by working for the Ford Foundation's Philadelphia Council for Community Advancement project, Clark proved his mettle to the same group of people by working for the same Ford Foundation-funded project, but more importantly, he showed he could be trusted by internalizing Quaker values – in particular, the Quaker view on race.

When *New York Times* writer John Cogley died in April of 1976, Clark noted his deconversion from Catholicism and his subsequent conversion to Episcopalianism in later years as "the ultimate defalcation."[22] Clark's choice of words is interesting. To defalcate means to misappropriate money. To use that term to describe Cogley's opportunistic conversion must have meant that the move had some association with money in Clark's mind. Perhaps it reminded him of the generous salary he was earning as director of the Fels Fund at the time. Whatever the reason, Clark is appalled by Cogley's conversion, probably because of the Episcopal Church's connection to England, the *radix malorum* for the type of ethnic Irishman that Clark considered himself at the time. "Better," he confided to his diary, "Zen boobism than that, or the jumping Hari Krishna."[23]

Clark's comments about Cogley give some indication of his own "defalcation." The period between the early '70s and his death was one long gradual slide into unbelief. Clark's mind was still imbued with the liturgical calendar, but he would return to his diary each year to complain more and more about Catholicism. Easter Mass in 1975 was "too long, too much up and down, too hard to follow in confusing missal."[24] One year later he is struck by how "diminished" Easter seems to him and his family now. The "carousel of ceremony that we indulged in when the children were small is all but vanished."[25]

In its place, Clark now values the writings of Hans Küng, "one of the few churchmen with any sense."[26] Küng, according to Clark is a "splendid man," not so much because of any genius in his own right, but because he continues "smiting away at the nonsensical pomposity of the Vatican."[27] Clark's wife had gone to the University of Pennsylvania to hear a lecture by Küng in 1966 and from that moment onward Küng became Clark's guide to things Catholic, which meant of course that his connection to the Catholic faith became progressively more tenuous with time.

In October 1979, Clark cited Küng approvingly in connection with Pope John Paul II's visit to Philadelphia. Clark, with Küng as his mentor, now believed that women should be ordained priests, because, "God knows, so many priests have been old women."[28] Küng, according to Clark, "is right" in feeling that "the Vatican has blown it badly in the U.S. visit of John Paul with his Eastern European attitudes sticking out all over."[29]

At a certain point along his trajectory into disbelief, Clark, with Küng as his guide, claimed to be a follower of Jesus – "Jesus, the protagonist of the weak, is eternal whether you agree with his paternity in Deity or not"[30] – even if disaffected with his Church, but that position proved untenable before long, and by the mid-'80s, after he heard about the battle over removing Charles Curran from Catholic University and Archbishop Raymond Hunthausen from the Seattle archdiocese, Clark was dismissing the "whole arcane artifice of Mediterranean clerical comedy overlain upon Semitic legendary" as "cuckoo," especially "when there are serious things to be dealt with."[31] In 1983 Clark dismissed Christmas as "Hebrew fairy tales and consumer mania."[32] Clark had apparently attended Mass that Christmas but, not surprisingly given his views, found that "the religious ritual" was "less and less substantial."[33]

Three months later, on March 8, 1984, Clark met with James Fisher, then a graduate student doing his dissertation on "radical Catholics." Clark found the interview with Fisher "most recollective," but mostly in the negative sense, because it led him "to reflect on the naiveté and sincerity of our hearts then, the dreadful conservatism of the Churchmen we knew and the incredible lack of social mission of our fellow Catholics."[34] More than that, the interview forced Clark to face up to the fact that his connection with the Catholic apostolates of his youth was now "ancient history."[35]

Two years before his death, Clark spent a few days with the Oswalds, another Catholic family involved in the apostolates in the '50s, in Pearl River, New York, "discussing ourselves and themselves as Catholic radical romantics of the 1950s"[36]:

Their Marycrest community moved around the crackpot intellectual theories of Ed Willock and Carol Jackson. There were intensely voluble members, and Willock and his wife and 12 children formed a hurricane of pathology at the center. Our own scheme for an urban version of an intentional Christian liaison was more tepid and less tumultuous, but inflated with the same "higher Christian" idealism. As for myself, I sought an alternative to the bleak, suffering 1930s, the obscene stupidity of army life, the gross indignities of urban sterility, the flaccid rituals of ghetto religion. Josie was skeptical, temperate. I was agitated for social justice. Diversions and a growing family responsibility redeemed us from our early hectic course.[37]

At other points, Clark is more ambivalent about his loss of faith, especially when he considers the effect it had on his children. "The experiences of the '60s," including "our own broadening education and the peculiar inertia of Catholic structures," Clark wrote, trying to explain the phenomenon to himself, "led us to abandon the hyper-Catholicism that was our ethic and code in early years of family life."[38]

Clark portrays this slide into unbelief as "liberation,"[39] but even in the act of saying that he has no regrets, a certain ambivalence intrudes. Clark found that liberation and deracination were two different words for the same thing. Having abandoned the Catholicism of his youth, Clark now finds that "we do not have any integrated cultural ethic to replace that old one we so innocently toiled and struggled for."[40] Clark and his wife "owe . . . much of our ability to deal with life to the old discipline and the rules under which we were raised. Patience, fortitude, perseverance, honesty, humility were the chords by which we were trained."[41]

Clark's loss of faith had a complex effect on his life. It made him both more timid and more aggressive. Clark's disparaging remarks about Episcopalianism and Cogley's opportunistic conversion disguised the fact that he had by that time in his life adopted pretty much the same attitude toward Quakerism, Philadelphia's peculiar version of the religion of the ruling class. In November 1971, the same month that Frank Rizzo was elected mayor of Philadelphia, Clark announced in his diary that his three youngest children were now attending Abington Friends School. Quakerism is not a religion that puts great emphasis on liturgy, attendance at services, or formal conversion. There is no indication that Clark attended Quaker meetings, but by the early '70s, he had entrusted the education of his children to the Quakers, and in the absence of any strong direction from home, that meant the religious education of this children as well, at least by default.

In 1981, when his daughter Brigid was attending high school at Abington Friends, Clark made an attempt to talk to her about proofs for the existence of God with Hans Küng as his guide. Needless to say, the experiment didn't get very far, nor was it repeated. In the place of the Catholic education which Clark had abandoned, his youngest daughter was raised as a Quaker, an Irish nationalist Quaker.

In a memoir she wrote around the time she was still in high school, Brigid Clark said that "the most important part of my education came from my parents."[42] She then goes on to give some indication of what type of education she got from them.

"When they were toilet training me," Brigid said of her parents, "I was told that I was not to say doo-doo like all my little friends. I was to say 'Cromwell.' To this day, the name

Cromwell brings to mind shit, and when I have kids they're going to inherit this cosmic truth, along with the latest – that they do not 'vomit,' they Thatcher."[43]

This sort of nationalist bluster coupled with the fact that Brigid was attending a school run by the Anglophile establishment in Philadelphia would lead to a severe case of cognitive dissonance later on. At this point in her life, Brigid just repeated what she had learned from her parents with the same bantering Irish humor with which it was conveyed to her. Clark had imbibed too much theology and philosophy from the Jesuits to take Quaker theology seriously, but the fact that he sent his children to the Quakers to be educated indicated that he did take them seriously as the group which ran the ruling-class schools in Philadelphia. His choice in schools, in other words, was motivated not so much by any objective standards of excellence but by the same desire for religiously based upward mobility which he found repugnant in John Cogley.

Brigid's aggressively ethnic toilet training corresponded to a period of stress in Clark's life. Clark was still at Temple when the toilet training took place, where the birth of his sixth child was greeted with embarrassment, if not derision. He was still smarting from his failure as head of the CIC and hadn't really found a steady job since returning to Philadelphia with his tail between his legs. At the end of 1970, Clark was feeling pressure to "radicalize myself at age 43,"[44] he but also felt that if he succumbed to the pressure that he would be "producing material for a classic lampoon."[45] By early 1971, Clark felt that he had reached the end of the road. "The old major interest of Catholic social action and race relations have gone into a status in which any inputs on my part would be marginal," he wrote in his diary. That left "the family, writing, Irishry, [and] historical study . . . but the latter will, I fear, suffer eclipse unless I get to teach and use it."[46]

One month later, Clark got the job at the Fels Fund that would be the best paying job of his career, the job that would carry him until retirement seventeen years later. Nine months after getting the job, he enrolled his three youngest children at Abington Friends School. It is at this point that both the complaints about Catholicism and the rabid Irish nationalism begin to crop up in his diary entries with just about equal frequency. The one was, in many ways, a function of the other. As the *Kulturkampf* against the Catholic Church in Philadelphia heated up during the '70s, partially as a result of Frank Rizzo becoming mayor but mainly as a result of Martin Mullen's battles against sexual engineering, Clark was feeling pressure to conform to the secular *Zeitgeist*, especially in his capacity as director of the Fels Fund. Looking back at both his job and the erosion of his faith that had taken place over the past decade, Clark confided in his diary on Good Friday of 1984, that the one might have been a function of the other. Clark never mentions Martin Mullen, but the campaign against Mullen forms the background against which his apostasy played itself out. "Working for the Fels Fund," Clark wrote,

> an organization in which the Board is dominated by Jews keenly sensitive of their Jewish identity, I have been constrained in my own Christian identity, since I am the subordinate and must discretely respect the mores of that group. This has meant that Christian holidays have been moderated in my view. Thus Good Friday, holy week and Easter are not to be too broadly heralded in my little work world.[47]

Both the trajectory of Irish assimilation and the tragedy associated with it can be taken from incidents in Clark's diary. Dennis Clark's capitulation to peer pressure at the Fels Fund forms the ironic counterpoint to the anecdote in which he describes his grandfather Willie Clark being sent out to the schoolyard to wash the ashes off his forehead on Ash Wednesday roughly one hundred years before.

In a sense, everything had changed, but nothing had changed. The old ethnic antagonisms remained; the only thing that changed was the sophistication whereby they were applied and the destructiveness that resulted from their ever-more-scientific application. The WASP ruling-class was quite capable of bringing new allies, like the Jews and certain blacks into the ruling class coalition, but they were also quite capable of destroying the city before they would let it fall into the hands of their enemies. There would be no coalition with Philadelphia's Catholics, and Dennis Clark, who was not stupid, realized that before long. He also realized that if he wanted to play the role of the well-paid "subordinate," he would have to go along with that arrangement.

In many ways, Clark's truculent Irish nationalism was born out of that realization. Irish nationalism posed no threat to the ruling class in Philadelphia, but it did allow Clark to posture in front of the mirror of his own mind as a pugnacious crusader for social justice, even when the people he supported engaged in social injustice. In October of 1978, Clark is "hard at it" attending meetings on the Northern Ireland issue. "*Delenda est Britannia*," he writes at the end of his diary entry.[48] Less than a year later, on August 26, 1979, he applauded the IRA after they "blew Lord 'Dicky' Mountbatten to the hobs of hell . . . within sight of where we had stood on Sligo bay two weeks ago."[49] Clark bids "good riddance" to Lord Mountbatten and "all his ilk," and claims that he would have been willing to "put the fire to that charge," because of "how fully and foully 'Dicky' had served King and empire."[50]

On September 30, 1981, Clark attended a luncheon at Philadelphia's Union League, one of that city's bastions for the ruling-class establishment there. Clark is appalled that "the age of Reagan has brought out the economic Neanderthals in full cry"[51] but not appalled enough to dispute the issue in public. Instead he consoles himself in silence with fantasies of himself as a latter-day Molly Maguire. "Nourish yourself at the table of the Union League," Clark told himself while keeping his peace during the discussion that followed the talk. "Eat all you can for you remember that these men would not feed you or your father in the 1930s. Eat and plot against them."[52]

Clark never gets around to saying which plots got hatched as a result of his lunch at the Union League, but he must have found the fantasy of himself as the Irish revolutionary consoling and at the same time involving no personal risk to his career. Irish nationalism allowed Dennis Clark to get a free meal and then go back to his office at the Fels Fund, where he worked for the Jewish wing of the establishment in Philadelphia, earning $43,000 a year, all the while thinking of himself as a courageous freedom fighter. Of course, during the '50s and '60s Clark worked for the same establishment breaking up Irish neighborhoods in the city, but that thought seems not to have occurred to him, either during or after lunch at the Union League.

On November 1, 1985, Clark gave a speech to Philadelphia's St. Andrew's Society, something he characterizes as "the most proper group of Presbyterian worthies in town."[53] After his speech, the Presbyterians "complained at table of the lower orders breeding," but there is no indication in his diary entry that he in any way disagreed with them. In fact, every indication in his diary indicates that Dennis Clark had made his own separate peace in the eugenic war on the poor which Martin Mullen was battling from his precarious post as state representative in Southwest Philadelphia.

On October 16, 1984, at the height of that year's presidential campaign, Clark criticizes Cardinal O'Connor of New York for harping "on the abortion issue." The attempt to pass legislation against abortion, in Clark's view, "flies in the face of the social complexity of it."[54] Eight years later, Clark mentions in passing that his wife has been working "on Lynn Yeakel's campaign."[55] Yeakel's rabidly pro-abortion platform had attracted the support of feminists across the country, including Anna Quindlen, the *New York Times* writer whose family came from Most Blessed Sacrament Parish. The Clarks could support her because "Irishry" had become their source of "ultimate concern" by then, and there was no "Irish" position on abortion. In fact, the attraction of the neo-Irish ethnic position of the '80s and '90s was that it avoided the hot-button issues in the United States in favor of issues which most Americans could view with equanimity if not indifference. Ethnicity, as Clark defined it in his later years, became a way to avoid the conflicts that had given meaning to his life during the '50s and '60s. It was a way of being involved, where involvement carried no social cost, certainly not one that would have jeopardized his career in Philadelphia.

In one of the rare moments of true candor in his diary, Clark admitted that fact. If the diary is any indication of what conversation was like at the Clark home, apparently Clark discussed their slide into secularism frequently with his wife. The disparity between their early fervor and their later unbelief was too great not to be noticed, and since it was in many ways the fundamental fact of life of their later years, both Clark and his wife tried to come up with explanations justifying it. "At dinner last evening," Clark notes in his diary,

> Josie spoke about our young married days in which we were reacting against the soulless world of the secular society with its anomies, harshness, lack of support for the values we held – family, children, a circle of friends to aid and join one another. We turned to the Catholic ideological revival of such movements as the Catholic Worker, Friendship House, the Grail, the Catholic Interracial movement. There we found patterns of optimism and the shared desire for coherence amid the urban dissonance and anonymity. We got little of that succor from our dry parish churches. Liturgical renewal, a nostalgic imitation of rural peasant customs from Europe, intellectual schemes for community, models for educating children in the wonder of nature and life.[56]

But then something happened – or did not happen. "The renewal" which was supposed to flow from Vatican II, "did not expand. The religion remained mainly bureaucratic and staid. The greater society overwhelmed the aspiring movements of change."[57] Clark intuits in some general way that the Catholic Church was subjected to some cultural offensive, which he defines only in the vaguest terms, even though he was intimately involved in prosecuting it in Philadelphia, and that the Church was "overwhelmed" by that offensive, or at least overwhelmed because it did not rise to the challenge that offensive provided.

As a result, the Clarks made their separate peace with a hostile secular world. "We came to terms with the crudity of work life and domestic labors as we moved to middle age. Other things, family and study, took the place of youthful aspiration. There was ethical rigor beyond religion we knew, and *the intimidations of society divested us of plans for community networks based on those early enthusiasms*. We were tutored more and more about the breadth of the world and the empty spectacle of its follies[5] (my emphasis).

Clark, in other words, began his adult life with a plan for the strengthening of his ethnic group, which as a young man he perceived as more Catholic than Irish, but he was deterred from bringing that plan to fruition because of "the intimidations of society." Clark discusses the issue many times and in many different ways, but nowhere in his diary does he explain the causes of its failure with such clarity. Clark was torn for most of his young adult life between the conflicting claims of career and vocation.

By 1971 Clark solved the conflict by abandoning the Catholic faith, something that convinced him that the vocation he thought he had as a younger man was nothing but a youthful illusion and which allowed him to serve the interests of the city's ruling class. In lieu of his real ethnic identification, which according to the theory of the triple melting pot was American Catholic, Clark adopted a mythic Celtic ethnic identity which allowed him fantasies of often-violent activism which, at the same time, never jeopardized his career. During that career, Clark served the interests of the ruling class in Philadelphia, a group which was then actively engaged in driving other Irish Catholics out of their neighborhoods. That also involved driving Martin Mullen from office and hence removing him as a threat to their eugenic plans.

This decision did not affect Clark's life in any dramatic way because, as he himself noted, Catholic faith and morals had formed the character of both Clark and his wife so completely that that character remained long after the religion which supported it disappeared. The same thing was not true of Clark's children. Their characters were being formed not during Clark's early years but during the years when he was undergoing his crisis of faith and when the campaign of *Kulturkampf* being waged against the Catholic Church in Philadelphia was at its height. As a result the erosion of belief began to show up in the character of Clark's children in ways that it did not show up in the lives of either Clark or his wife. "The erosion of the old Catholic cult of our youth," Clark wrote one year before his death, was "not a spiritual crisis so much as a cultural shedding that animated a new life"[59] for Clark and his wife, but it was perceived as a spiritual crisis by his children, something he did not perceive, and a moral crisis, something he did perceive by noticing the changes in their behavior as they reached adolescence.

Notes

1   Clark, Diary, 12/14/80.
2   Clark, Diary, 5/10/82.
3   Clark, Diary, 1/18/88.
4   Ibid.
5   Ibid.
6   Ibid.

7 Ibid.
8 Ibid.
9 Clark, Diary, 5/2/75.
10 Ibid.
11 Ibid.
12 Ibid.
13 Clark, Diary, Interview with Dennis Clark, 12/7/76.
14 Clark, Diary, 1/18/88.
15 Clark, Diary, 12/7/76.
16 Ibid.
17 Ibid.
18 Clark, Diary, 2/6/91.
19 Ibid.
20 Ibid.
21 Dennis Clark, "An Irish Tribute to Friends," probably from *The Irish Edition*, Clark papers, Notre Dame Archives.
22 Clark, Diary, 4/10/76.
23 Ibid.
24 Clark, Diary, 3/31/75 Easter.
25 Clark, Diary, 4/10/76.
26 Ibid.
27 Ibid.
28 Clark, Diary, 11/30/79.
29 Ibid.
30 Clark, Diary, 3/27/85.
31 Clark, Diary, 11/10/86.
32 Clark, Diary, 12/27/83.
33 Ibid.
34 Clark, Diary, 3/8/84.
35 Ibid.
36 Clark, Diary, 6/13/91.
37 Ibid.
38 Clark, Diary, 3/12/86.
39 Ibid.
40 Ibid.
41 Ibid.
42 Brigid Maire Clark, Clark papers, Notre Dame archives.
43 Ibid.
44 Clark, Diary, 12/12/70.
45 Ibid.
46 Ibid.
47 Clark, Diary, Good Friday, 1984.
48 Clark, Diary, 10/20/78.
49 Clark, Diary, 8/26/79.
50 Ibid.
51 Clark, Diary, 9/30/81.

52 Ibid.
53 Clark, Diary, 11/1/85.
54 Clark, Diary, 10/16/84.
55 Clark, Diary, 4/30/92.
56 Clark, Diary, 2/10/91.
57 Ibid.
58 Ibid.
59 Clark, Diary, 12/30/92.

The Death of Poletown

On March 13, 1981, one year after the "quick-take" bill passed the Michigan legislature, it was ratified by the Michigan Supreme Court, although not unanimously. In fact there was fairly vehement dissent on the bench. Justice Ryan claimed to see "the unmistakable guiding and sustaining, indeed controlling, hand of General Motors Corp."[1] behind the legislature's efforts. The "quick-take" law raised fundamental questions for the dissenting jurists on the Michigan Supreme Court. The bill was not in the public interest. In fact, it was passed "solely [as] a result of conditions laid down by General Motors, which were designed to further its private pecuniary interests."[2] The new bill meant that "the power of eminent domain, for all practical purposes," was "in the hands of the private corporation."[3]

The legislature, in other words, had collaborated in the further erosion of property rights. The right to ownership was now conditional; it could be revoked if a powerful entity like General Motors wanted the property. The state instead of protecting the rights of the weak decided to augment the power of the already powerful, blurring in the process the distinction between the private and public spheres so dramatically that Justice Ryan was "left to wonder who the sovereign is."[4] The Court had "subordinated a constitutional right to private corporate interests" and in doing so, had "altered the law of eminent domain in this state" so significantly that, in Ryan's view, it "seriously jeopardizes the security of all private property ownership."[5]

The fact that Chief Justice Ryan's views did not prevail meant that the Michigan Supreme Court ratified both the economic and racial status quo in Detroit. Thomas, who praises Coleman Young's "political skills" as "essential to the success of the project," is forced to admit that "racial factors played an important role in Young's ability to proceed."[6] This was so primarily because "the project in no way jeopardized the support of Young's loyal constituency,"[7] which is to say, Detroit's blacks and the WASP corporate establishment.

But it was true for other reasons as well, all racial. Thomas, who did have privileged access to Young's papers to write her book, feels that Young in many ways had to punish the Polish community in order to retain his standing in the black community and, therefore, his grasp on the reins of power in Detroit. Thomas feels that Young might have alienated his political base had he "acceded to PNC [Poletown Neighborhood Council] demands."[8] The blacks who had been ethnically cleansed from various neighborhoods beginning with Coleman Young's own Black Bottom neighborhood, creating the angry rootless population that figured largely in the city's 1967 riots would wonder "why this neighborhood was more precious than their all-Black neighborhoods had been."[9] In order to take control of the political forces which resulted from the injustices flowing from urban renewal, Young had to perpetrate his own form of injustice to placate the racial feelings that lay at the source of his political power.

The only way that the Poletown land grab could work, in other words, was by using race to justify it. Race distracted everyone's attention from the fact that the largest corporation in the United States was using the city of Detroit to steal property from poor ethnics. The only way that could work was by having Detroit's black mayor play the race card. Playing the race card in Detroit would also figure in Young's strategy in dealing with the economic crisis in other ways as well. In order to keep the city out of receivership, Young had to raise taxes, but in order to persuade the citizens of Detroit to pay higher taxes largely because of Young's policies and the automobile industry's incompetence, he had to first divide the city's voters according to race and play one group off against the other. To his loyal black constituents, he would portray the possible bankruptcy as a failure of the black insurgency which he had orchestrated at the tail end of the civil rights movement. Young got black support for a tax increase by portraying it as the only thing that would preserve the black political gains so recently wrung from the whites from falling back into the hands of racist upstate politicians.

But Young needed financial support to bring off this coup, and for that he had to turn to the city's ruling class, something he had been doing in one way or another since he took office. Unlike Jerry Cavanagh, Young never felt that he had been elected to serve all of the people of Detroit. He had been elected by a certain group of people for certain reasons, and his continued existence in office meant giving these people the impression that he was representing their interests. That meant appealing to race in ways both blatant and subtle. In this respect race served as the basis for Young's demagoguery but also as a way to obscure the real dynamics of the situation, which were a complicated interaction between the centripetal forces of ethnos, which concentrated loyalty, and the centrifugal forces of class, which dispensed it. In order to secure, the financial support necessary to fund the public-relations campaign that was necessary to persuade Detroit's voters to raise their own taxes, Young needed money from Detroit's wealthy corporations, but he could only get that in the current political and economic climate by promising them something in return. That meant large tax abatements for Detroit's major corporations, just as it meant affirmative-action patronage jobs for Detroit's blacks. Race was the only thing which made this transfer of payments from the pockets of the poor into the pockets of the rich in any way politically defensible.

Young secured his hold on power by adopting the strategy which the ruling class in Detroit had always used to maintain its hold on power, namely, by playing ethnic groups off against one another. Young secured his hold on the black population in the city by driving the ethnics out of the city and dividing whatever spoils which remained among his black supporters, who were organized, as they had been in Henry Ford's day, by a loyal cadre of black ministers.

Poletown, in this scenario, became a way to turn the economic crisis into a success story and a way to pay back his corporate supporters for their support in the bankruptcy struggle. In order to bring this off, Young brought in Felix Rohatyn, a consultant who was winning acclaim in the Democratic Party at the time by telling them that they should grant more concessions to big business. Rohatyn felt that public services needed to be reduced and that more public money needed to be made available to the private sector, a message which corresponded exactly to Young's predicament in Detroit and which figured largely in how he was planning to get out of it.

Like the residents of the West End in Boston, the residents of Poletown whose houses would be torn down to make way for the plant were the last to know it was going to happen. Poletown residents Tom Olechowski and Richard Hodas became aware of General Motors plan accidentally when they read an article on it in the June 23, 1980 issue of the *Detroit Free Press*. By then, the project was "an accomplished fact,"[10] according to Hodas and the only question remaining was how GM and the city were going to engineer the consent of the people whose houses they were going to destroy.

Finding out about the plan so late in the game meant that the neighborhood's residents were forced to play catch up long after the city had made its moves. By 1980 Poletown had become so culturally impoverished by the city's predatory policies toward ethnic neighborhoods that they had difficulty initially even finding a lawyer to represent them. General Motors had Detroit's most prestigious law firm smoothing the way for the takeover of the neighborhood, and when the law, as in the state's condemnation law, stood in the way, they had the power to have the law changed. The residents of Poletown, on the other hand, found that most of Detroit's attorneys were unwilling to represent them because it meant taking on both General Motors and city hall, and they feared being blacklisted for their efforts. In the meantime, General Motors proved adamant in holding the city to the letter of their agreement, which meant that everything on a parcel of land of the size usually slated for a plant built on virgin land in a place like Oklahoma had to be cleared away from the site within two years.

That meant forcing all of the condemned properties on the market at once with no legal recourse in site, which in turn meant that the city could pick them up at fire-sale prices, thereby saving money, which it needed to hand over to GM in the form of infrastructure improvements. One man who had paid $50,000 for a grocery store in 1947 received $34,000 for the same property in 1980, in spite of inflation, the general increase in real-estate prices during that period, and the fact that he had spent thousands of dollars improving the store and the living quarters upstairs in the meantime.

As some indication of the weakness of the ethnic community in 1980 as a result of forty years of government policy waged against it, Wylie claims that "not a single institution in the city of Detroit rallied on behalf of the Poletown residents."[11] That included the one institution that could have stopped the destruction of Poletown if it had wanted to, namely, the Catholic Church. Poletown was one more sad chapter in a story of Polish-Irish tension within the Catholic Church in the United States. The sides in this conflict were represented by John Cardinal Dearden, Detroit's Irish bishop, on the one hand, and Father Joseph Karasiewicz, the Polish pastor of Immaculate Conception Church in Poletown on the other. Dearden was known as "Iron John" before he became Detroit's ordinary. After that he distinguished himself by gaining the reputation of being the most liberal bishop in the United States, a reputation which seemed confirmed in 1976 when the archdiocese of Detroit, under his auspices, sponsored a conference at Cobo Hall, known as Call to Action.

What began as a Catholic celebration of the 200th anniversary of America's independence from Britain, soon degenerated into the Catholic version of the estates general, as the fifth column of disaffected clerics which the Rockefeller interests had promoted within the Church, largely through sexual liberation, demanded that the Church change its beliefs to conform to their revolutionary praxis. Needless to say, next to sexual liberation, race played a major role in those clerics' demands. Just as the civil rights movement provided the model for feminists and homosexuals, it also provided the model for those clerics who wanted to change the Catholic Church from within.

"Change," like the related word "liberal," however, meant something very specific in the context of ethnic politics and the urban parishes which still made up the bulk of the Catholic Church in the United States. "Liberal" meant "assimilation." It meant adopting the categories of the dominant culture on issues of concern to the people who ran that culture. It meant, therefore, adopting WASP sexual mores, which meant birth control and abortion, because the WASP ruling class had always been concerned about Catholic fertility and the demographic and political threat it posed. That meant that the city with the most liberal Catholic bishop would also be the city with the most devastated neighborhoods, because the ruling class had upped the ante on what assimilation meant. It now meant the adoption of practices which the Catholic Church had always termed sinful. Since no bishop could espouse such beliefs, the consent of those who were about to be either assimilated or destroyed had to be engineered on other grounds, and, once again, race played the crucial role in allowing that to happen. Ever since the nation's bishops had adopted the Catholic Interracial Council view of race in their 1958 statement on discrimination, the Church had been committed officially to an explanation of events that not only obscured the real outline of what was happening, it also committed the Catholic Church to a course that involved a moral commitment to commit suicide when it came to the existence of ethnic parishes which were threatened by government-manipulated racial migration. In order to be moral, the ethnic parish had to cease discrimination, but in failing to fight the overwhelming nature of black migration into its boundaries, the parish ceased to exist. So the parish had a moral commitment to go out of existence. No one, not even the people at the Catholic Interracial Council, would have phrased it in those terms, but no one could explain how the inner dynamic the bishops proposed in their 1958 statement could lead anywhere else either. Taking this logic even further than his boss, Detroit's Auxiliary Bishop Thomas Gumbleton condemned his own school system as racist and set about shutting down one school after another.

Caught between the bishops who allowed themselves to be guided on racial matters by people like Sargent Shriver, who funded both birth control clinics and black gangs which drove ethnics out of their neighborhoods and the people who were being driven out of their parishes by those tactics were the pastors of the parish churches and neighborhoods which had been targeted for destruction. That meant people like Father Lawler in Chicago and Father Karasiewicz in Poletown in Detroit, priests who were fated to witness the destruction of the communities they had been called by God to defend. In their avidity to assimilate, the Catholic Church's largely Irish bishops had forgotten that the Church was based on units of geography known as parishes, and that these parishes comprised real communities, and that, according to the principle of the just war, communities had a right to defend themselves from aggression.

The American system of assimilation, as Louis Wirth had noted early on, was very similar to the system of assimilation which Stalin had erected in the Soviet Union in the wake of the 1917 revolution there. It entailed persuading the person who was to be assimilated to abandon ethnic identification in favor of class identification. Upward mobility would provide the solvent which would dissolve the old ethnic ties in the city and allow the new configuration to re-form according to class in the suburbs, and among America's Catholics this system worked nowhere better than among the Irish and nowhere worse than among the Poles. Wirth's model of assimilation based on Stalinism was the antithesis of the triple melting pot, and it worked especially well among the Irish whose fatal attraction in America was acceptance by the class which secretly despised them.

In the instance of Poletown it was easy to be fooled by the conflicting systems – the Wirth class-based system on the one hand and the triple melting pot on the other – because two of the major players on the ruling-class side of the equation were Irish Catholics. Thomas Murphy was CEO of GM when the Poletown land grab was approved, and he was what might be termed a devout Catholic by an impartial observer, since he attended daily Mass and communion. He also was close friends with Cardinal Dearden and put his private plane at Dearden's disposal. Dearden, like most American bishops, saw himself as the CEO of another large corporation and so was naturally, by bonds of religion, ethnicity, and class, inclined to see things the way Murphy saw them.

That meant, in general, favoring class-based assimilation, otherwise known as upward mobility, over ethnos. During Dearden's tenure, the ethnic parish had come to be viewed as an embarrassing anachronism, something destined to go out of existence anyway, and therefore, something not worth defending. In addition to that, the ethnic parish was doubly suspect because of the fact that it was ethnic, and therefore "white" and therefore, *ipso facto* guilty of racial discrimination. Gumbleton's policy toward Detroit's Catholic schools bespoke this attitude as did the editorial policy at the *Michigan Catholic*, the archdiocesan newspaper, which frowned upon and therefore suppressed any mention of the ethnic parish within its pages. Confronted with the loss of Immaculate Conception Parish, Auxiliary Bishop Thomas Gumbleton waxed philosophical or botanical: "The overall good of the city is achieved by cutting away a certain part. When you're trying to make something grow, you prune."[12]

Father Karasiewicz, in short, was running a dubious enterprise by being pastor of Immaculate Conception Parish. The ethnic parish may have once had a purpose in life, but it was clear in the post-civil rights movement era in Detroit that that was no longer the case. The ethnic parish was like one of the many mansions that dotted the formerly well-to-do neighborhoods of big cities like Detroit. It may have been something fine at one point in its history, but historical circumstances had reduced it to a flophouse or, worse, a crack house in the meantime, and it was time to get rid of it before it caused any more problems. It was time for the Catholic Church to cut its losses. It was certainly not time for the church to mount the barricades in a battle to save something that was going to go out of existence anyway.

Dearden's willingness to come to this conclusion was aided no doubt by the fact that the city, in order to buy off his opposition to the Poletown project, was offering him much more relatively for the Church's properties in the doomed neighborhoods than anyone else was getting. The archdiocese's willingness to fight for the preservation of Immaculate Conception Parish was considerably diminished by the fact that the city was offering the

Church $1.3 million to let them tear it down. In addition, the Church was also going to receive $1.09 million for St. John's Church. Almost $2.5 million was considerably more than the archdiocese got for its churches when they got abandoned in the course of racial succession, a fate that is apparent at St. Stanislaus, a formerly Polish church across I-94 from the Poletown plant that was taken over by the black migrants. It is doubtful that the people who bought that magnificent cathedral-like structure and redubbed it the Church of the Promise [sic] Land came up with anything approaching a million dollars for the purchase price.

No matter how prudent Dearden thought he was in cutting the deal with the city for Poletown's churches, the residents of the community were outraged and felt betrayed by the Church they had supported all their lives. On February 26, 1981, a group of forty Poletown residents, both black and white, protested in front of the chancery offices, accusing Dearden of being a Judas who sold them out for thirty pieces of silver. Intra-Catholic ethnic antagonism played a role in the protest as well. One protester carried a sign asking, "Cardinal Dearden, Why do you hate Polish People?"[13]

Throughout the battle, Dearden tried to maintain a position of neutrality in the fight over the neighborhood. He didn't campaign for the plant, but he also did not support the neighborhood. In fact, he felt that the best role the church could play in the matter was to offer counseling and help the residents of the parishes scheduled for demolition to find quarters in another neighborhood. The parishioners who were being displaced, however, felt betrayed. Once again it was the same conflict between the Irish Catholics who had made it, and the Polish Catholics who had not. The first group was avid to move to the suburbs; the second group would move out of their ethnic enclaves only under the threat of physical force. Neighborhoods meant two different things to those two different groups of people. For the former, it was a way station toward upward mobility; for the latter group, community meant not so much upward mobility as mutual support in a hostile culture. "Home and church," said one member of the latter group, "that's what's important."[14] GM's plant was going to take both away, and the Church refused to support them in their struggle. Hence, their feeling of betrayal.

Abandoned by any group of significance in Detroit, the residents of Poletown soon found that they could not count on even the rudimentary protections which government was supposed to provide. Knowing that the neighborhood was doomed even if it was still standing, vandals entered the neighborhood during the spring of 1981 and stripped houses with impunity of whatever they considered valuable, often while the people were still living in the houses. Once it became apparent that police protection had been withdrawn from the neighborhood, arsonists began arriving in the neighborhood, burning it down one house at a time. Some even accused the city of being responsible for the arson, which by the time Coleman Young had been mayor for a few years had become a local tradition, especially on the night before Halloween, a night which in local parlance came to be known as "Devil's night."

In addition to Coleman Young's "technical and political skills," the main tool used to get Catholics out of parishes like Assumption Grotto and Poletown was arson. In fact, the only reason Assumption Grotto wasn't devastated more by fire was because the arsonists were so busy in Poletown, and the fire department was so busy there not responding to the calls of the people whose houses were being burnt to the ground. "Epidemics of arson began breaking out in Poletown," Jean Wylie writes, "adding fire to the combined power of the corporate state."[15]

Once GM announced that it was going to build its plant in Poletown, the arson rate there doubled. Residents of Poletown began complaining, Wylie wrote, "that they were being subjected to psychological warfare."[16] According to Sgt. Robert McClary, an arson investigator, "The city hires a contractor; they hire subcontractors. Sometimes subcontractors, knowing full well that juveniles will be blamed, hire agents and send them in. With enough money you can do anything."[17]

McClary noticed that arson increased dramatically when GM announced it was building in New Center Area as well – something that was not lost on the residents of Detroit who began to see a connection between arson and city policy. "As soon as I saw that story, I knew we'd had it," one resident told Wylie, "It was right after that when the arson started. You can't tell me this isn't being deliberately ignored . . . or even worse . . . by the people downtown."[18] The fires continued to escalate. When the plant was announced in 1980, Poletown suffered thirty-three fires. In the first six months of 1981, there were over a hundred. Virtually no one Wylie talked to believed that the fires were random. All of them felt that the government, as an agent of GM, was behind the fires – if not setting them, then at least behind not putting them out. "Make no mistake," Chuck Moss told Wylie,

> the city government is indeed a conscious destroyer. When that cancerous "abandoned" rat-filled, junkie-infested house on your block is owned by the city, and your land is mapped out for a casino or a politically favored big corporation, the decay of your neighborhood is no coincidence. The city [Coleman Young] is destroying is summarized in one word: "Poletown." It's a city of neighborhoods, churches and parochial schools, of local grocery stores and tiny corner bars. It's a place of fierce traditions and loyalties, resistant to mayoral power. It's small-scale and human. What city is he building? Renaissance Center, Joe Louis, Riverfront, GM Poletown: big, ugly, brutal concrete projects which have no relation of scale to anything human. Young's Detroit is a place of mammoth construction with equally vast contract fortunes to be dispensed and a strangling indifference to everyday, street level life. Coleman Young, the old socialist, is building a Brave New World. And it isn't working. Humans don't live that way.[19]

Wylie recounts arriving in Poletown on a Saturday afternoon during the spring of 1981 to find three homes burning and an elderly woman standing on the street in tears because a gang of teenagers had just broken into her landlady's home. Those who refused to move "complained that they couldn't breathe because of the smoke and demolition dust that filled the air."[20]

Those who did move often died because of the trauma associated with the relocation. Those who moved but did not die immediately oftentimes did after a short period of time, partially because they were old anyway but partially because the uprooting was so painful and the soil they were replanted in was so socially and culturally impoverished. After moving to the safety of the suburbs, one former Poletown couple noticed that "nobody sits out on their porches." When the wife asked why, her husband explained it was because "they're watching TV."[21]

Father Joseph Karasiewicz was left in the less-than-enviable position of defending a parish which the archdiocese had already abandoned. He defended it in the name of a principle – "the principle that 'eminent domain' does not apply for private business."[22] By violating that principle, the courts and the city had established a "diabolic precedent,"[23] namely, that "any corporation will be able to destroy anything they please."[24] Defending this principle in court in front of liberal judges was to prove difficult as well for the same reasons. "How can I be concerned about the Immaculate Conception Church," Judge Feikens asked, "if the cardinal has already sold it?"[25] Dearden compounded the situation for Karasiewicz by lying about the methods he took to abandon the church.

On May 4, 1981, Dearden called Karasiewicz down to the chancery offices and told him that the parish would be suppressed and the church building abandoned on May 10. Six archdiocesan officials had already shown up at Immaculate Conception on April 30 to evict Karasiewicz, but he had refused to leave. Karasiewicz felt especially hurt because of the lack of consultation, both at the end of April and before. After the meeting Dearden stated that both parishes in Poletown had been consulted before they were sold, forcing Karasiewicz to say that Dearden was lying. Those responsible for the destruction of Poletown were worse than the Communists in Poland, according to Father Karasiewicz. In spite of all of the euphemisms which the powerful came up with to justify it, the destruction of Poletown was a " criminal act."[26] Reduced to its simplest moral terms, it involved "taking someone else's property against their will."[27] In other words, it was theft, even if the government whose duty it was to guard against such acts was perpetrating it.

Hoping to sway public opinion, the supporters of Immaculate Conception had a bulldozer towed to GM CEO Roger Smith's house on May 9 to demonstrate the enormity of what was happening to their homes by showing the incongruity of thinking that the same thing could happen to the home of the head of General Motors. One day later, on May 10, 1981 people gathered at the church to celebrate the last Mass there on the day decreed by the archdiocese as the parish's last day of existence. One of those attending the Mass was Joe Stroud, a reporter for the *Detroit Free Press*, whose editorial "Pain Is Real, But Can the Church Be Saved?" ran two days later. Stroud, like just about all of the fourth estate in Detroit, did not oppose the Poletown project, but attending Mass there on the last day of the parish, he found himself strangely "stirred by the sobbing of Polish women near me."[28] Dearden might have found the spectacle moving as well had he chosen to attend, but he spent May 10 at a local shopping mall blessing a Gucci store instead, begging for God's blessing "upon this enterprise, those who labor here, those whose craftsmanship is displayed here, those who will possess and enjoy these artistic creations."[29]

One person who was moved by the sobbing of the Polish women was Roger Smith. On May 14, Cardinal Dearden's last day in office, two days after reading Stroud's editorial, GM's CEO offered the corporation's first exception to the inexorable time-table that was the fundamental fact of life throughout the negotiations surrounding the construction of the plant. Confusing the church building with the community it symbolized, Smith attempted to solve the problem by offering to move the church to another location, but his offer was turned down at the last minute by Cardinal Dearden. "The prospect of relocating the church," Dearden stated at his own press conference, "does not solve the basic problem of a congregation limited in numbers. Immaculate Conception Parish no longer exists. For years, its membership has steadily declined. The Polish people who still reside in the area of the present church can readily be served by four existing Polish Catholic parishes within moderate distance from the project site."[30]

That the people in the parish felt differently became evident on May 11, when, after the official death of the parish one day before, they occupied the church basement and refused to leave, setting up a confrontation with the city that could have turned into a public-relations disaster for both Detroit and GM if the press had been less avid in supporting them. The only institution which came to the support of the church was the Ralph Nader organization and at the final Mass Karasiewicz commended them – even though none of them were Polish or Catholic – for their being motivated by "love and principle." On June 12, Karasiewicz met with Mother Teresa, who informed him that the church had already been saved and that in gratitude for this favor he should say the Memorare nine times to the Blessed Mother.

The church unfortunately had not been saved. In addition to that, the neighborhood was being burned to the ground one house at a time. During the first six months of 1981, there were 607 fires in Poletown, resulting in a grand total of twelve arrests, two of those for trying to set fire to the offices of the Turner Construction Company, the firm which the city had hired to demolish the neighborhood. On May 13, Pope John Paul II was shot in the middle of St. Peter's Square in Rome by a Turkish assassin with contacts with the KGB. John Edward Wojtijlo, who lived in Hamtramck and was on that city's council, came to Immaculate Conception Church to pray for his recovery and for the future of the church, which still had parishioners occupying its basement.

Their vigil, however, could not stop the carnage going on outside the church. The arsons continued to ravage the neighborhood throughout the month of June and were only interrupted by the bulldozers toppling the houses that had not yet been torched. As the stress associated with the arson and the looting increased, so did the casualties. One resident told one of the local papers that eight residents had died in the vicinity of Craig and Twombly alone. On the last Saturday in June, when firefighters arrived on the scene, they had their choice of putting out any one of the thirteen fires that were burning in Poletown that day. On June 28, there were eleven more fires to chose from.

Then the city decided that it had had enough. In the early morning hours, police attached one end of a chain to a tow truck and the other end to the side door leading to the sanctuary and ripped the door open, after which Detroit's Special Weapons Attack Team, accompanied by police dogs, swarmed into the church basement and dragged the last wailing Polish woman out of the church. The battle for Immaculate Conception Church was over. The Poles had lost, and GM and its lackeys in Detroit's city government had won. Six months later, when the site had been leveled and all trace of the people who had once lived in that neighborhood had been obliterated, there was one more casualty. After being forced out of his parish, Father Karasiewicz took up residence at St. Hyacinth's Parish, and it was there that the fifty-nine-year-old priest was found dead on the morning of December 14, 1981.

Detroit, the grim aftermath

By the time of his funeral, Detroit had a new cardinal archbishop, Edmund Szoka, a Pole, but by now no more beloved among Detroit's Polish Catholics than the Irishman Dearden had been. When Szoka walked down the aisle at St. Hyacinth's for Karasiewicz's funeral, the mourners turned their back to him as he passed by. Father Skalski, pastor of St. Hyacinth's, gave a sermon during which he praised Karasiewicz as someone who "tried to slow and stay the heavy hands of corporate, materialistic, economic objectives, masking themselves as the common good, while in actuality it would seem they were serving the rich."[31]

Three and a half years after Father Karasiewicz died, GM's Poletown plant finally opened for operation. Workers who had been with GM for some time noticed that the new plant brought with it new methods of operation. First, there were the robots. One year after the plant's opening, the robots still weren't functioning properly. In the paint shop, they often spray painted each other instead of the cars they were programmed to paint. One year after the plant opened, the automated guided vehicles didn't work either.

Failing to program its computers properly, GM tried to program its employees instead. That involved two weeks of "sensitivity training" for the plants employees, during which they "played psychological games to make us more outspoken and friendly."[32] As part of their efforts to make the employees at the Poletown plant more friendly, the sensitivity trainers played a "game," during which the players "tried to figure out, if you were in the middle of the ocean in a sinking boat, what you'd throw overboard . . . a pocket-knife, raft, etc."[33]

Actually, the purpose of the psychological game known as "Lifeboat" is to decide not *what* gets thrown overboard, but *who* gets thrown overboard. GM and the city of Detroit had already demonstrated the correct answer to that question by destroying an ethnic neighborhood to build the plant in the first place. Poletown was simply the logical conclusion to the policies which the government had been pursing for almost half a century, something that was already clear by the time Detroit's SWAT dragged the last wailing Polish lady from the basement of Immaculate Conception Church. The purpose of those policies was ultimately not better, more affordable housing but rather ever more refined and ever more brutal forms of social control, according to which the government and the agents it favored stripped its own citizens of their right to own property and their right to associate with the people they chose to be their neighbors. *Libido Dominandi* (the lust to dominate) is the inexorable law of empire, and the price which the ruling class was willing to pay to realize its goal of world domination was, ironically, the destruction of the very cities in which they lived.

Notes

1   Jeanie Wylie, *Poletown: Community Betrayed* (Urbana: University of Illinois Press, 1989), p. 133.
2   Ibid.
3   Ibid.
4   Ibid.
5   Ibid.

6 June Manning Thomas, *Redevelopment and Race* (Baltimore: The Johns Hopkins University Press, 1997), p. 164.

7 Ibid.

8 Ibid., p. 165.

9 Ibid.

10 Wylie, p. 60.

11 Ibid., p. 84.

12 Ibid., p. 105.

13 Ibid., p. 118.

14 Ibid., p. 117.

15 Ibid., p. ix.

16 Ibid., p. 79.

17 Ibid., p. 121.

18 Ibid., p. 207.

19 Ibid.

20 Ibid., p. xiv.

21 Ibid., p. 194.

22 Ibid., p. 134.

23 Ibid.

24 Ibid.

25 Ibid., p. 141.

26 Ibid., p. 182.

27 Ibid.

28 Ibid., p. 158.

29 Ibid., p. 150.

30 Ibid., p. 161.

31 Ibid., p. 200.

32 Ibid., p. 212.

33 Ibid.

"Pregnant with Death"

Brigid Clark graduated from Abington Friends School in June of 1983. Commemorating the event in his diary, Clark noted that his youngest child "values ideas" and "has good insights and judgment," but that now she "must move out of the shelter of suburban Quaker ways,"[1] a phrase which indicates that Clark had no idea of the sort of behavior the Friends were promoting at their schools.

Clarence Pickett joined Planned Parenthood in 1958. The Quakers were in the forefront of the sexual revolution in Philadelphia after having promoted it for the Rockefellers among coal miners in West Virginia during the 1930s and among Catholics working in sugar mills in Puerto Rico around the same time. Largely as a result of Martin Mullen's efforts at thwarting the Quaker desire to get the state of Pennsylvania involved in the sexual engineering of Philadelphia's black population, the AFSC met with Planned Parenthood to discuss what the two organizations could do to overcome Catholic opposition to their agenda. One of the things which flowed from Quaker involvement with Planned Parenthood was that Planned Parenthood was given control over sex education at Quaker schools, with results that were predictable, but which Clark was apparently unaware of, given his comments about Abington Friends being some sort of suburban shelter.

Two months after Brigid graduated from Abington Friends, Clark initiated a discussion of the Clark family's complex interaction with Roman Catholicism. Since Brigid never knew "the world in which her older sisters and brothers grew up, in which we tried to update Catholic ritual to build a family culture,"[2] the discussion must have taken on an abstract archeological quality, as if the family were sitting around discussing abandoned Mayan temples in the jungles of Central America. During the course of the discussion, Clark informed his youngest child that he and his wife "had been raised in a world of ritual that was latinized, pompous, [and] religiously rigid."[3] As a young married couple, the Clarks tried to reform their religion by grafting various "European Catholic folkways in modernized form on to Pentecost, Epiphany, Christmas, Easter Mass etc." but all those attempts ultimately failed because of "a cultural misfit. Americans are simply too informal, our families too averse to paternal direction to carry such ritual."[4]

As a result, the Clark family abandoned the practice of the Catholic faith around the time that Brigid was born. By "discarding" this "cultural posture," however, the Clarks found that the whole edifice of belief collapsed when they did. Tinkering with liturgical issues led the Clarks to question "the deeper issue of the acceptability of the formalized Church, the validity of Judaeo-Biblical palimpsests of Middle Eastern archeism [sic] and folk legend, and the way all that fitted with humanist philosophy and contemporary imperatives," and faced with a conflict between a faith which they were already portraying in archeological terms and "contemporary imperatives" of the sort that Clark needed to heed to move his career forward, the Clark family abandoned the Catholic faith and adopted in its place the mores of the ruling class in Philadelphia, principally by sending their youngest children to Quaker schools.[5]

In order to make this apostasy less apparent to both himself and his family, Clark adopted an Irish ethnocentrism that was completely inconsistent with choosing the Quakers to educate his children. Confronted with this combination of truculent nationalism and servile assimilationism, most of the Clark children simply decided that the world of ideas made no sense, and, as a result, they opted out of participating in it. Brigid was different in this regard, but that only meant that her father's attempts at guidance left her more confused than her siblings.

For one thing, Brigid, even after being subjected to toilet training in which she was taught to associate Cromwell with shit, was perplexed by her father's ethnocentrism. If he really believed it, one can imagine her thinking, why did he send me to Abington Friends? During the same year that she graduated from high school, Clark notes in his diary that "Josie and Brigid chided me for my interest in Irish things and claim I am exclusivist and ethnocentric."[6] Confronted with the charge, all that Clark can do is plead guilty. "I am ethnocentric," he wrote, because "you cannot have a cultural identity and not be partisan about it."[7] Shortly after that discussion, Clark mulled over purchasing more land in Sligo and eventually building a house there "to give this family some tendril to roots there"[8] in lieu of the religious roots he was not giving them in Philadelphia.

The Clarks undoubtedly discussed their loss of faith in the bantering tone that was typical of family gatherings, but Clark would later learn that Brigid found the religious issue troubling and perplexing in a way she did not feel able to express in conversations with her father. Just why she found his point of view perplexing is not difficult to understand. If Clark were as exclusivist and ethnocentric as he claimed, he should have sent his daughter to an Irish school. Cardinal Dougherty was an archdiocesan high school which still had a fairly large Irish population, and if that did not suit his taste there were boarding schools in Ireland. Clark chose Abington Friends, however, not out of ethnocentrism but rather out of the exact opposite motive, out of a desire to assimilate, because attending a Quaker school gave his daughter an advantage in being accepted at an Ivy League university, and in this respect Clark got exactly what he wanted.

In September of 1983, the Clarks "deposited Brigid in the fake-Gothic preserves of Yale University and bade her good luck in the semester."[9] Again Clark describes the situation in ways that his children must have found perplexing. If there were something ultimately "fake" about Yale, why was he so keen on having his daughter go there? There were equally ancient universities in Ireland. Brigid was being taught lessons in ambivalence that prevented the type of decisions that were necessary to the formation of character. Clark's character had been formed by a system of beliefs which he withheld from his children. Deprived of something that had served Clark well in his own life, they were left to shift as best they could.

In May of 1983, one month after Brigid received notice that she had been accepted at Yale, Clark's son Brian announced that he was going to marry the mother of his child. The wedding was to take place at Abington Friends Meeting on May 23. A milestone like a wedding makes the shortcomings of the ambivalent/ironic view of the world which Clark had adopted apparent. One of the reasons the Clark children avoided marriage was because of the fact that marriage, unlike cohabitation, is a ceremony that has to take place at a certain place as part of a certain tradition. Why the Clark children put off marriage can be attributed to a number of reasons. It was partially attributable to the *Zeitgeist* of sexual liberation prevalent at the time, but it was also attributable to the fact that in getting married, the Clark children would have to announce who they were. In the case of Conna, the oldest, the decision was first postponed by cohabitation but eventually when she decided on marriage, she got married in the Catholic Church. Brian, who was younger, was raised more under the Quaker influence, and so Clark shows neither surprise nor disapproval when Brian announces that he was going to get married under Quaker auspices. The decision was, among other things, indicative of the direction the family had taken when they cut loose from their Catholic moorings and decided to cast their lot, at least their educational lot, completely with the Quakers in 1971.

Brigid followed much the same trajectory. After graduating from Yale in May of 1987, she came to Clark and announced, in what was becoming something of a ritual for that generation, that she was planning to move in with Chris Noel, someone she had met at Yale. The announcement comes as no surprise to Clark. All he can do is "wish her happiness in liaison with Chris Noel,"[10] but no matter how much equanimity he summons to face the announcement, Clark can't help but note that things are different for his children than they were for him. "Young people now," he duly notes in his diary, eschew marriage in favor of "just going off together."[11] Life for the next generation of the Clark family now involves "no sacred ritual, no holy bonds"[12]; it is simply "a human agreement"[13] without lasting commitment in a life bereft of meaning as a result. Clark tries to be philosophical about the change, by claiming that in exchange for "the ceremonial dignity of plighted troth and wedding ritual," his children's generation enjoys "autonomy, self reliance, and what I believe to be a less occluded view of their relationships."[14] But the tenor of his diary entry bespeaks misgiving in spite of assuring himself that things are "different" now. He feels misgiving and foreboding because "the course of 'true love' is never smooth," and "the hazard of love" is "ever proved before trial."[15]

If Clark really believed this, he probably would have objected more strenuously to his daughter putting herself into what was a morally and psychologically untenable situation. But as in the fatal ambivalence he conveyed to his children by espousing Irish chauvinism and sending them to anglophile schools, so in the most basic facts of life, Clark had lost the courage of his convictions. Having abandoned his own moral and spiritual compass, he stayed his own course largely out of the habits he learned from the religion he abandoned, but the same psychic trajectory did not apply to the next generation, which was cast off onto a sea of uncertainty by parents who had lost the courage of their convictions and were only capable of ratifying the *Zeitgeist* as a result.

Once Brigid left for college, the Clarks were finished with the business of raising their children. Clark now had a comfortable salary for the first time unencumbered by the expenses associate with raising a large family, something which led to an equally comfortable life. The Clarks were able to travel more. They moved to a more expensive house closer to the city's largest park. Clark could indulge in hobbies like making furniture, and he could work on his final book "on the destruction of cities" at a leisurely pace. Nine years after he announced that he was writing it, he noted that he was sending it off to a publisher. By then the destruction of Philadelphia which he had helped orchestrate was continuing apace. "The neighborhoods suffer," Clark wrote after noting that "ten houses a day simply collapse in decay" in Philadelphia.[16] "We need," he concluded, "overhaul in drastic terms."[17]

Two months after Brigid went off to Yale, Clark announced in an anticlimactic way the culmination of black migration to the city of Philadelphia, before the fact. On November 7, 1983, he wrote in his diary that "Wilson Goode will be elected our first Black Mayor tomorrow."[18] Clark's use of the future tense is instructive of the fact that he knew it was going to happen before it actually happened. This is indicative of two facts: (1) black demographics coupled with the ethnic cleansing of the city's Catholics made the election of the city's first black mayor inevitable by 1983 and (2) the city's ruling class, seeing the handwriting on the wall, had anointed Goode as the successor to Bill Green, Jr., son of Bill Green, Sr., from whose hands Walter Phillips tried unsuccessfully to wrest control of the city.

What WASP political acumen could not do, black demographics could. The WASP ruling class had gone from being caliph to vizier, and it was only in that capacity – from behind the scenes, so to speak – that they could continue to exert influence on the city. Dennis Clark had reached the Irish ethnic phase of his life just in time to see the final eclipse of Irish political power in the city. Clark the interracialist should have rejoiced at the occasion, but by the time Wilson Goode became mayor, Clark no longer believed in interracialism. He was an ethnic partisan by that point in his life, aligned with a group that no longer had any political power in the city, largely because of his participation in the ethnic cleansing of Irish neighborhoods.

As some indication that the tide had turned for good, Martin Mullen finally lost his state-rep seat in Harrisburg in November of 1982, a fact not noted in Clark's diary. The advent of black political power in Philadelphia gives Clark little cause for rejoicing. All that Clark can see on the horizon in the wake of Goode's election is "low standards and no flair," something he terms "our local formula."[19] Goode's election causes Clark to wax nostalgic for the past. "Downtown urban renewal" under people like Ed Bacon, whom Clark criticized, may have destroyed large sections of the city, but "at least it moved things around."[20]

Wilson Goode would show that he, too, had the ability to move things around in Philadelphia. After opening Philadelphia up to extreme versions of racial patronage that brought the city to the brink of bankruptcy, Goode found that he had to confront one of the last outposts of urban guerrilla warfare of the sort that had been spinning out of control since the government got involved in sponsoring them in the 1960s. In this instance, the group was known as MOVE, a violent political sect which favored dreadlocks and disfavored public sanitation. All of its members took the surname Africa and during one violent confrontation at the sect's home in Powelton Village, a policeman was killed. The sect regrouped in West Philadelphia, not far from MBS, and when the police came to their door again six years later, another violent confrontation ensued. This time, the police, unable to dislodge the armed MOVE members from the bunker they had built on top of one of the West Philadelphia rowhouses they occupied, decided with Goode's approval to drop a bomb on their headquarters, resulting in one of the most devastating fires in the history of

Philadelphia. Wilson Goode, it turns out, could "move things around" too in a way remarkably similar in its ultimate effect to urban renewal.

By the time the flames died down several city blocks had been destroyed and a number of people, including children, were dead. The idea of peaceful integration leading to racial harmony died with them. Clark eventually wrote a novel about MOVE, but it never got published. Both the MOVE I and the MOVE II confrontations were important because they signaled the end of liberal illusion about racial harmony. After MOVE II, the liberals had to admit – to themselves, if to no one else – that racial harmony was an illusion, and that ethnicity and demographics were the ultimate political realities in the city.

Clark reacted to this shift by becoming more ethnic and quietly abandoning the ideas on racial justice which he had espoused as a young man. In their stead, he began to retreat into a Celtic fantasy world, becoming an advocate for an ethnic group that lived somewhere else and so was not involved in strife in Philadelphia. Once he made that move in his mind, his fantasies began to enlarge. In December of 1985, he confided to his diary that he longed "to shake off the constraints of working for the conservative Fels Fund so that I could throw my energy into fighting nuclear arms, ecological crimes, Nicaraguan victimization and censorship,"[21] but evidently not enough to give up his $42,500 salary. The incoherence of Clark's list is instructive, especially in comparison with the causes he espoused as a young man. The fantasies his disappointment spawned would have continued to enlarge, but reality, the ultimate reality, intruded into his life at around the time he turned 60.

In March of 1987, Clark was walking up a steep hill in Fairmount Park with his wife when he felt severe pains in his chest. One month later on April 6, Clark underwent angioplasty surgery to unclog the artery leading to his heart, an artery which was 99 percent blocked. During the time he spent recovering from the operation, Clark decided to retire from the Fels Fund at the end of June 1988. Four months after his operation, when he was just about to celebrate his total recovery, Clark mentioned difficulty urinating to his doctor, who announced after examining him, that Clark had prostate cancer, and would have to undergo both an operation in September of 1987 and weeks of radiation therapy thereafter. Having both heart disease and cancer made Clark feel as if he were in "the true American malady mainstream," but he was especially troubled by the fact that he had cancer, which made him feel as if he were "pregnant with death."[22]

Being "pregnant with death" had a number of meanings and the fact that Clark's illnesses did not prove conducive to thinking about the other three last things – judgment, heaven, and hell – give some indication that the death he bore within him had a spiritual dimension as well. Ever the glib Irishman, Clark noted during his recovery from surgery and radiation therapy that his family was "madly busy in anticipation of the Feast of Consumerism." "Ah, these Yule rites and superstitions," he noted in reference to Christmas, the celebration of Christ's birth.[23]

As if not to be deterred by his Irish glibness, the Almighty sent other deaths into Clark's life as if to remind him to be serious about his own. Three months later, Clark's younger sister Geraldine died on March 22, 1988, one day after her 58th birthday. "Gerry," Clark noted in his diary, because the distinction seemed important to him, "remained a believing Catholic."[24] However, unlike her brother, "she did not escape the world of

Philadelphia rowhouse respectability."[25] Deprived of any sense of finality because of his break with religion, all that Clark can note upon her death is that his sister was "very bright," but "did not have the GI bill to get herself to college," something Clark condemns as "a sad gender default by our government."[26]

If his sister's death was an implicit rebuke to Clark's lack of faith, his children were to rebuke him as well for his lack of secular cunning. Clark was caught in the middle. Three months after his sister's death, Brendan arrived with his two children and asked Clark, "Were you and Mom crazy?"[27] in reference to the fact that they had six children. It was an odd thing to say, especially coming from someone whose very existence resulted from that "craziness."

Caught between the two poles of his life – what he was and what he became – Clark is forced to explain himself once again. Clark pleaded innocent to the verdict of insanity because he and his wife "had been raised in an ethic that said, 'You are here to serve others.'"[28] If, however, that ethic were wrong, then Brendan Clark's question is completely justified. And being raised in the midst of the "Me Generation," Brendan was taught precisely that – that altruism and serving others – was crazy. If, on the other hand, the religious constellation of beliefs connected with and underpinning the command to serve others was not wrong, then why did Clark abandon it? Clark is forced to fall back on essentially consequentialist justifications for the belief system which structured his life so admirably but got abandoned nonetheless, to the puzzlement of his children. The ideal of service "fortified" Clark and his wife "greatly for the agitations of parenthood"[29] – even if it was based on Mediterranean or Semitic mythology. Ultimately, all that Clark can conclude is that "the theme of self-denial was as strong for us as the fulfillments of the 'me' generation to the youth of the '70s."[30] Once again, Clark lapsed into the historical relativism of the sort that turned all of his children off to the intellectual life.

All of them, except for Brigid, who, upon graduation from Yale, had taken a teaching post at Goddard College in Vermont and was, in addition, spending time at the McDowell writers' colony and networking with the other writers in Vermont. Brigid was the sole member of the next generation in the Clark family who took an interest in the Celtic lore and writing that motivated her father. Overburdened by a heavy teaching schedule and the responsibility for running the household details of her ménage with Chris Noel, Brigid had decided to give up teaching and devote herself full time to her writing when tragedy struck.

On January 28, 1992, she was killed in an automobile accident in Vermont. Prosperity was well on its way to lulling Dennis Clark to sleep at the end of his life, but the course of events, or whoever shapes them, had arranged for one final wake-up call to come to Dennis Clark before he died. If Clark could view the death of his sister with some equanimity, that was not the case when his daughter died. The event left him "disbelieving, shattered and undone."[31]

Still reeling from the phone call announcing their daughter's death, the Clarks rushed up to Vermont "to arrange for a swift funeral."[32] The arrangements included a memorial service at the Unitarian Church in Montpelier, at which there was "an outpouring of deep affection and tribute"[33] from Chris Noel, his sisters, and their friends. As part of his eulogy, Chris Noel announced that he and Brigid planned to be married in the fall. Their mutual friend Ben Kaplan announced that Brigid had asked him shortly before she died whether "his faith could offer something for her."[34] As his contribution to the services, Clark read "a couple of Irish folk tales."

Clark most probably was not pleased to learn that his daughter was thinking of converting to Judaism, not so much because of his passive/aggressive attitude toward his former employers at the Fels Fund as because it showed that the spiritual solutions (or lack thereof) which Clark had proposed as her father had been weighed and found wanting. Brigid, it turns out, wanted spiritual direction to her life after all. Deprived of it by Quaker schooling and a father who spent his psychic energy trying to justify his apostasy from Catholicism, Brigid sought it among her peers.

What Clark learned at the Unitarian memorial service was only the beginning of a series of ever-more-disconcerting revelations about what he did not know about his daughter's inner life. While going through Brigid's diaries and letters after her death, Clark learned that his daughter had had an affair with one of her teachers at Abington Friends. The affair had lasted from 1981, when Brigid was 16, until 1985, two years after she had graduated, but letters continued back and forth until 1991. Brigid had told her mother about the affair, but her mother had not informed Clark about it.

As a result, all of what he did not know about his daughter entered Clark's heart and mind at the same time that the grief over her death did. As a result of the affair, Brigid was seeing a psychiatrist because of depression. At the time of her death she was taking Prozac. Brigid was oppressed by the affair, but she was also distressed, in Clark's words, "by ambiguity in her ties to Chris Noel."[35] If she could be used this way by a figure of trust like a teacher, so her troubled reasoning went, why should she trust Chris Noel? They were not married after all. Technically, the two relationships were identical. The uncertainty which flowed from her current sexual relationship coupled with the sense of exploitation which flowed from her affair with her teacher coupled with the absence of spiritual direction in her life had caused Brigid to seek solace in therapy, where the therapist tried to alleviate the psychic pain with drugs. Clark felt that there may have been "a chemical basis to her depression,"[36] but the simple facts of the matter militate against that explanation.

The avidity with which Clark latches on to the chemical explanation is understandable because it lets him off the hook. Had he taken a less *laissez-faire* attitude toward her education, particularly in the realm of faith and morals, she probably would not have become involved in the relationships that were, according to her own testimony, the cause of her depression. Clark's first reaction upon hearing of the affair is pure atavistic Kensington bluster. "Had I known of the teacher's predation," he wrote in his diary, "I'd have taken a crowbar and broken his arms and legs, at least, at the time, the son of a bitch."[37] In lieu of doing that, Clark allowed his wife to bring the issue before the Friends Council on Education, which then planned to "insert warnings in faculty handbooks."[38] At the same time Clark blusters about breaking John Allen's arms and legs with a crowbar, he fulminates against the Catholic Church in Ireland for preventing a fourteen-year-old girl from leaving the country to get an abortion, so his feeling about the sexual exploitation of minors was distinctly local.

In order to deal better with his remorse, Clark wrote what amounted to an open letter to his remaining five children. In it he admitted that Brigid's death had made him "conscious of how distant" he was from her "inner life."[39] "Like many writing people," Clark continued, Brigid "tended to chew over things, magnify them, worry them."[40] Now Clark is worried that the same gulf may be separating him from his other children, if for no other reason than because "we're all such bantering types" and "not given to soulful exchanges."[41] Clark ends the letter by asking his children to "pardon the serious tone,"[42] but apart from a genuine attempt to express his love for his children, there is not much of substance that he takes away from her death. Certainly, there is no admission that the lack of direction in Brigid's life may have caused her unhappiness.

On February 16, two weeks after the Unitarian memorial service in Vermont, the Clark family, largely at the urging of Ann O'Callaghan, Clark's sister-in-law, participated in a Catholic memorial service at St. Malachy's Parish in Philadelphia. Mick Maloney, Philadelphia's premier Irish musician, canceled a concert in Ireland so that he could play at the service. As he had at other Clark family milestones, Father McNamee once again presided. His sermon at Brigid's service was more substantive and sober than the one he had given at Conna's ill-fated wedding. This time instead of mentioning Fidel Castro Father McNamee talked about Job. "Life," he told the assembly of 300 people who had gathered in Brigid's memory, "drags us to that necessary wisdom that his anguish brought to poor old Job: 'The Lord gives and the Lord takes away. Blessed be the name of the Lord.'"[43]

By focusing the sermon on Job, McNamee seemed to be addressing Dennis Clark more than anyone else in the congregation. Brigid had been given to him as a daughter and the same Lord who had given her had taken her away, and it was up to Clark to make sense of that chain of events from the only point of view that addressed such events coherently. "Hard to get there," Clark noted cryptically in his diary. "Perhaps the Eucharist," he continued, "being what it is can help us get there."[44] Was this Clark the protagonist writing about his own struggle to return to the faith he had denied his daughter, or was it simply Clark the scribe recording words he had heard in Father McNamee's sermon? Subsequent events indicate that the latter answer is more likely, but they should not obscure the fact that his daughter's death brought Clark closer to the faith he rejected than any other event in his life. If an event like this couldn't wake Clark from the dogmatic slumbers which secularism had led him into, then nothing could.

Clark never did get a crowbar, but he and his wife did take action against Allen in a "friendly" manner in a way that wrought more violence than someone as decrepit as Clark wielding a crowbar could. On May 13, 1992, Josepha Clark wrote a letter to Rod L. Kehl, Headmaster of The Benjamin School in North Palm Beach, Florida, informing him of the details of Allen's affair with her daughter Brigid. Allen fled to Florida after eighteen years at Abington Friends in 1988, probably because he felt that news of his sexual exploitation of the students there was going to get out eventually. Allen had also had an affair with another student at the school, and Brigid had made contact with her shortly before her death. Now the Clarks were in possession of incriminating, sexually explicit letters that Allen had written to their daughter, and they wanted the headmaster in Florida to be aware of Allen's "totally unethical and nonprofessional"[45] behavior.

The Clarks didn't propose any specific cause of action. In the end they didn't have to.

Six weeks after Josepha Clark wrote her letter, Allen committed suicide. His death brought closure but no resolution to Clark's lifelong association with the Quakers. Allen's death left Clark feeling "remorseful" but convinced nonetheless that they had followed the proper course of action. After his daughter's death, it is probably unlikely that Clark thanked God "that there were such people and such a tradition as that of the Friends" every time he passed a Friend's Meeting House. But a perusal of his subsequent diary entries made it just as self-evident that Clark failed to learn anything from the experience of his daughter's seduction under Quaker auspices as Abington Friends School or his own more complicated seduction at the hands of the same group.

In May of 1992, a little over three months after Brigid's death, Los Angeles erupted "in racial fury"[46] when a jury acquitted a number of policeman of any wrongdoing in the beating of Rodney King. Clark felt that the outcome was "entirely predictable."[47] The flames pouring out of 4,000 buildings in Los Angeles were traceable to "neglect, exploitation, out of control teenagers, many from single female headed homes, unemployed frustration, Reaganite cynicism, malign indifference, ignorance, black racism on white racism, blood feud on color TV, the rot under the consumer society"[48] – everything, in other words, except the policies which Clark strove to implement in Philadelphia.

In reaction to the policies which drove the Catholic ethnics out of the city of Philadelphia, Anthony Cardinal Bevilacqua announced in November of 1992, that he was planning to "close high schools and parishes around and in the city," a fact which prompts Clark to protest that "the social world of my youth is dissolving."[49] Those schools, according to Clark, were "our lifeboats in the urban storms,"[50] and now Bevilacqua was planning to close them down in spite of the fact that he had just raised $100 million from the city's Catholics.

Two weeks later, Clark attended yet another memorial service in honor of his daughter, this time one put on by the Abington Friends Meeting. Clark found it "a sad, but loving occasion."[51] But his feelings failed to address the role the Quakers played in the seduction of his daughter. Had they espoused the cause of sexual morality, the Quakers could have simply said that Allen had acted without their knowledge in spite of their beliefs. Now the best they could say because of their collaboration with Planned Parenthood and other groups in the subversion of that order was that Allen had acted out their beliefs without their knowledge. Clark didn't pursue the matter because at this point he didn't know what his beliefs were anymore. The fact that he attended their service indicates he accepted the Quakers' explanation of the seduction of his daughter, or anyone else's daughter, that was known as the sexual revolution, and that he was planning to leave it at that. The fact that the service was held by the Abington Meeting and not Abington Friends School indicated that Clark, insofar as he had any religious affiliation whatsoever by the end of his life, had become a Quaker himself. If nothing else, Clark's attendance at the memorial service the Abington Friends held for his daughter indicated that for the Irish assimilation and extinction were closely related terms.

By the last year of his life, Clark had become a personality in Irish circles in Philadelphia. As some indication of that fact, *Irish America Magazine* ran an article on "Philadelphia's Feisty Irishman" in their January/February 1993 issue. Clark, as ever, had some interesting things to say about technology and ethnicity and the need to "get unhooked from the automobile" to "break our addiction to this idiot mobility which has permitted people to move away from problems, rather than solve them."[52] But in general the neo-Irish ethnic movement of the '90s was as shallow if not as wide as the neo-ethnic movement of the 1970s.

Dennis Clark, we learn by reading further, grew up "with an Irish identity" because he was raised "in a predominantly Irish-American neighborhood."[53] As a result, the authors tell us, "he never lost touch with his roots"[54] – not even, we might add, while destroying the neighborhood his roots were rooted in. Rather than advert to that, Clark proposed what would have to be termed Irish Zionism as the ethnic wave of the future. With the potato famine, what Clark terms "the Irish Holocaust," now 150 years in the past, the Irish are in desperate need of something like the Holocaust which would be a "force driving to unite us the way the Jews do for Israel."[55]

Perhaps Clark had forgotten that the Irish already had a country. In fact, they had a country even when it was under British yoke, but it was not the country which got the Irish through those troubles. What got them through that period of time is precisely what Clark abandoned, namely, the Catholic faith. Clark mentions Catholicism in the same article in a way that had become predictable. Clark refers to the "cultural Catholicism" that held the nation together in the past as "a kind of Mediterranean voodoo."[56] That much was predictable, but then he added something new and interesting, almost in spite of himself. "This generation of Irish," he continued, referring to his children's generation, "has lost belief in the old twin pillars of church and state. But with no ready substitute, they are lost."[57] It was a caveat which was equally applicable to Clark's generation as well. By admitting that ethnicity was at its core something spiritual, Clark was inadvertently denying the validity of his own program of Irish Zionism while simultaneously affirming the fact that he was among the lost.

In early 1993, Clark visited his doctor, who in effect, told him "don't buy any two year subscriptions."[58] Knowing that the end was near, Clark was grateful for the "five fine years" he had had since his heart nearly froze up while he was walking out of the Wissahickon Valley. In spite of his illness, Philadelphia's Feisty Irishman traveled during the early months of 1993. Clark, however, did not travel to Ireland. He spent the last days of his life during which he was able to travel not in Sligo but at the Sonesta Hotel in New Orleans where he was "seeking desperately to avoid gluttony"[59] and in Miami at a hotel in the Art Deco district where he gazed down upon "a crowded expanse of dozing hermaphrodites"[60] at one of that city's gay beaches.

Dennis Clark died on September 17, 1993. Ann O'Callaghan, his sister-in-law, spent the last week of his life by his side. During that time, Clark, according to her testimony and in spite of her urging, did not request the last rites of the Catholic Church, and so, in accordance with his own wishes, he died without them.

Notes

1 Clark, Diary, 6/9/83.
2 Clark, Diary, 8/27/83.
3 Ibid.

4   Ibid.
5   Ibid.
6   Clark, Diary, 1/23/83.
7   Ibid.
8   Clark, Diary, 2/6/83.
9   Clark, Diary, 9/4/83.
10 Clark, Diary, 6/3/87.
11 Ibid.
12 Ibid.
13 Ibid.
14 Ibid.
15 Ibid.
16 Clark, Diary, 5/6/91.
17 Ibid.
18 Clark, Diary, 11/7/83.
19 Ibid.
20 Ibid.
21 Clark, Diary, 12/24/85.
22 Clark, Diary, 9/26/87.
23 Clark, Diary, 12/20/87.
24 Clark, Diary, 3/22/88.
25 Ibid.
26 Ibid.
27 Clark, Diary, 6/16/88.
28 Ibid.
29 Ibid.
30 Ibid.
31 Clark, Diary, 2/2/92.
32 Ibid.
33 Ibid.
34 Ibid.
35 Clark, Diary, 2/27/92.
36 Ibid.
37 Ibid.
38 Ibid.
39 Clark, Diary, 4/23/92.
40 Ibid.
41 Ibid.
42 Ibid.
43 Clark, Diary, 2/16/92.
44 Ibid.
45 Clark, Diary, 5/13/92.
46 Clark, Diary, 5/2/92.
47 Ibid.
48 Ibid.
49 Clark, Diary, 11/8/92.

50 Ibid.

51 Clark, Diary, 11/27/92.

52 Marybeth C. Phillips and Michael P. Toner, "Philadelphia's Feisty Irishman," *Irish America Magazine* (January/February 1993): 24.

53 Ibid.

54 Ibid.

55 Ibid.

56 Ibid.

57 Ibid.

58 Clark, Diary, no date.

59 Clark, Diary, no date.

60 Clark, Diary, no date.

Bibliography

Adelman, Bob, and Charles Johnson. *King: The Photobiography of Martin Luther King, Jr.* New York: Bob Adelman Books, 2000.

Alinsky, Saul. Saul Alinsky Papers, Archives, University of Illinois at Chicago, Chicago, IL.

Almblad Papers. Carl W. Almblad Collection, Wayne State University, Detroit, Michigan.

American Friends Service Committee, Community Relations Division, Housing folder, papers at the American Friends Service Committee Headquarters, Philadelphia, PA, 1958 through 1971.

American Friends Service Committee Family Planning Services for Medically Indigent Families in Philadelphia, American Friends Service Committee Archives, Philadelphia, PA, 1970.

American Friends Service Committee papers, Archives, University of Illinois at Chicago, Chicago, IL.

American Friends Service Committee, Race Relations File 1946 A-Z, American Friends Service Committee Archives, Philadelphia, PA.

Anderson, Martin. *The Federal Bulldozer: A Critical Analysis of Urban Renewal, 1949–1962.* Cambridge, Mass.: The MIT Press, 1964.

"An Appeal to Conscience," Editorial, *Detroit News* (June 25, 1963).

"Archbishop Says Birth Control Plan 'Dangerous,'" AP (December 18, 1965).

Bacon, Edmund N. *Design of Cities* New York: Viking Press, 1967.

——. Interview. 5/15/00.

——. Oral History. Walter M. Phillips oral history project Box 1, Temple University Urban Archives, Philadelphia, PA.

Baltzell, E. Digby. *Philadelphia Gentlemen: The Making of a National Upper Class.* New York: Free Press, 1958.

——. *The Protestant Establishment: Aristocracy and Caste in America.* New York: Random House, 1964.

——. *Puritan Boston and Quaker Philadelphia: Two Protestant Ethics and the Spirit of Class Authority and Leadership.* New York: The Free Press, 1979.

Baltzell, Martha Pickman. *Bridging Diversity: Confessions of a Yankee Catholic.* Kansas City: Sheed & Ward, 1997.

Barlett, Donald L., and James B. Steele. "Wall Collapses on Tucker Home," *The Philadelphia Inquirer* (September 5, 1971).

Barrett, Laurence. "Rebuff Kennedy on Plea to Curb Rights Protests," *Detroit News* (June 22, 1963).

Bauer, Catherine. "Can Cities Compete with Suburbia for Family Living?" *Architectural Forum* 105 (1956): 322.

Bauman, John F. *Public Housing, Race, and Renewal: Urban Planning in Philadelphia, 1920–1974.* Philadelphia: Temple University Press, 1987.

Becker, Gayle. "Delores Tucker Joins Radio," *The Evening Bulletin* (December 17, 1977).

Berman v. Parker, 75 S.Ct. 98.

Bird, Kai. *The Color of Truth: McGeorge Bundy and William Bundy: Brothers in Arms: A Biography.* New York: Simon & Schuster, 1998.

—————. *The Chairman: John J. McCloy and the Making of the American Establishment.* New York: Simon & Schuster, 1992.

Black, Forrest L. "Mullen Fights 'Subsidies' for Abortions," *The Evening Bulletin* (April 28, 1971).

—————. "Mullen Introduces Law to Outlaw All Abortions," *The Evening Bulletin* (April 28, 1971).

Blanshard, Brand. *The Church and the Polish Immigrant*, 1920 dissertation, no publisher, no city, copy in Widener Library at Harvard University.

Blanshard, Paul, *American Freedom and Catholic Power.* Boston: The Beacon Press, 1949.

—————. *Communism, Democracy, and Catholic Power.* Boston: The Beacon Press, 1951.

—————. *Personal and Controversial: An Autobiography.* Boston: The Beacon Press, 1973.

—————. "The Catholic Church and Education," *The Nation* (November 15, 1947): 525.

—————. "The Catholic Church in Medicine," *The Nation* (November 1, 1947): 466.

—————. "The Sexual Code of the Roman Church," *The Nation* (November 8, 1947): 496.

Bork, Robert H. *The Tempting of America* (New York: The Free Press, 1990).

Brown v. Board of Education of Topeka, Kansas, 75 S. Ct. 753.

Cantwell, Rev. David M. "Postscript on the Cicero Riot," *Commonweal* (September 14, 1951).

Capeci, Jr., Domenic J. *Race Relations in Wartime Detroit.* Philadelphia: Temple University Press, 1984.

Capeci, Jr., Domenic J., and Martha Wilkerson. *Layered Violence: The Detroit Rioters of 1943.* Jackson: University Press of Mississippi, 1991.

"Cardinal Stritch Assails Trumbull Park Violence," *Chicago Defender* (June 14, 1956).

Carlson, Allan, Interview on Gunnar Myrdal, 4/01.

Caro, Robert A. *The Power Broker: Robert Moses and the Fall of New York.* New York: Vintage Books, 1975.

"Catholics and Hollywood," *The Nation* 164 (February 15, 1947): 185.

"Cavanagh Urges All to Join in Rights Rally here Sunday," *Detroit News* (June 21, 1963).

Chase, Alston. "Harvard and the Making of the Unabomber," *The Atlantic Monthly* (June 2000): 41–65.

Chafets, Ze'ev. *Devil's Night and Other True Tales of Detroit*. New York: Random House, 1990.

"The Children's Choice." Film script (June 13, 1963). Clark, Diary, 9/13/63.

Citizens' Council on City Planning History of the Organization, URB 10, 1/1, Archives of the City of Philadelphia.

Clark, Brigid Maire. Autobiographical fragment. The Dennis Clark papers, University of Notre Dame Archives.

Clark, Dennis. *Cities in Crisis: The Christian Response*. New York: Sheed & Ward, Inc., 1960.

———. Diary, CCRK 1 Diary folder 1948–63, University of Notre Dame Archives; a full copy of the diary to Clark's death is at the Balch Institute, Philadelphia, PA.

———. *The Ghetto Game: Racial Conflicts in the City*. New York: Sheed & Ward, 1962.

———. *The Irish in Philadelphia: Ten Generations of Urban Experience*. Philadelphia: Temple University Press, 1973.

———. *The Irish Relations: Trials of an Immigrant Tradition*. East Brunswick, N.J.: Associated University Presses, Inc., 1982.

———. "Philadelphia: Still Closed," *Commonweal* (May 1, 1964).

———. Dennis Clark oral history, Walter M. Phillips Papers, Temple University Urban Archives.

———. The Dennis Clark papers. University of Notre Dame Archives.

Clark, Joseph Sill. Interview with Joseph S. Clark, 3/18/75, Walter M. Phillips oral history project, Temple University Urban Archives, Philadelphia, PA.

"Clearing Slums in Philadelphia," First Annual Report of the Philadelphia Housing Authority, 1939, City Archives, Philadelphia, PA.

Cleary, David M. "Sen. Clark Tells of Backing for Birth Control," *The Sunday Bulletin* (August 28, 1966).

Cleaver, Eldridge. *Soul on Ice*. New York: McGraw Hill, Ramparts Books, 1968).

Colaico, James A. *Martin Luther King, Jr.: Apostle of Militant Nonviolence*. New York: St. Martin's Press, 1988.

Committee of 70, Acc 144, Temple University Urban Archives, Philadelphia, PA.

Conquest, Robert. *The Nation Killers: The Soviet Deportation of Nationalities*. New York: The Macmillan Company, 1960.

Corbett, Paul. Interview, May 10, 2001.

Corr, John C. "Mullen Warns Shapp He Must Revise Position on Issues," *The Philadelphia Inquirer* (May 22, 1974).

————. "U.S. Funds Opposed for Catholic Schools," *The Philadelphia Inquirer* (July 28, 1966).

Crellin, Jack, and John M. Carlisle. "Cry for Freedom Rings out to Throng," *Detroit News* (June 24, 1963).

Cunningham, Jim. Interview, August 2000.

De Sade, Marquis. *Justine, Philosophy of the Bedroom, and Other Writings*. New York: Grove Press, 1965.

"Del Vayo – the Vatican and Democracy," *The Nation* 165 (July 12, 1947).

Delaney, Bob. Interview, July 2000.

Dershowitz, Alan M. *The Vanishing American Jew: In Search of Jewish Identity for the Next Century*. Boston: Little Brown and Company, 1997.

Descriptive Inventory of the Archives of the City and County of Philadelphia, Archives, City Planning Commission, City of Philadelphia, Philadelphia, PA.

"Detroiters Hail Lack of Violence in 'Freedom Walk,'" *Detroit Free Press* (June 25, 1963).

"Detroiters Poised for Bias march," *Detroit News* (June 23, 1963).

"Discrimination and Christian Conscience: A Statement Issued by the Catholic Bishops of the United States," November 14, 1958, *Pastoral Letters of the United States Catholic Bishops 1941–1961*. Washington, D.C.: National Conference of Catholic Bishops, 1983.

Divack, Alan. Interview, November 9, 2000.

Dolbeare, Cushing. Oral History. Walter M. Phillips oral history project 6/5/80, Temple University Urban Archives, Philadelphia, PA.

Dowdy, Earl B. "Cavanagh, Edwards Laud Police Handling of Rally," *Detroit News* (June 25, 1963).

DuBois, W.E.B., *The Philadelphia Negro*. New York: B. Blom, 1967.

Duff, Elizabeth. "Schools Are Blamed for Racial Tension," *The Philadelphia Inquirer*.

Dyson, Michael Eric. *I May Not Get There with You: The True Martin Luther King, Jr.* New York: Free Press, 2000.

Edwards, Sr., George Clifton. Papers, Box 13. Walter Reuther Library, Wayne State University, Detroit, Michigan.

Egan, Msgr. John. Interview, July 18, 2000.

Esposito, Virginia M., ed. *Conscience and Community: The Legacy of Paul Ylvisaker*. New York: Peter Lang, 1999.

Finkelstein, Norman. *The Holocaust Industry: Reflections on the Exploitation of Jewish Suffering*. London: Verso, 2000.

Flaherty, Hugh E. "U.S. Making Millions Available for Birth Control," *The Sunday Bulletin* (August 15, 1965).

Flynn, Raymond. Interview, June 9, 2000.

Frank, Richard. "Democratic Leaders Press Mullen to Drop Birth Control Fund Fight," *Evening Bulletin* (June 17, 1966).

Franklin, Benjamin. *Autobiography*, in *A Benjamin Franklin Reader*, ed. Nathan G. Goodman. New York: Thomas Y. Crowell Company, 1945.

Friends Suburban Housing Committee: Project Section, Community Relations Files 1956, Archives, American Friends Service Committee, Philadelphia, PA.

Fuller, Major-General J.F.C. *The Conduct of War 1789–1961*. New Brunswick, N.J.: Rutgers University Press, 1961.

Gans, Herbert J. *The Urban Villagers: Group and Class in the Life of Italian Americans.* New York: The Free Press of Glencoe, 1962.

Garrow, David J. *Bearing the Cross: Martin Luther King, Jr., and the Southern Christian Leadership Conference.* New York: William Morrow and Company, 1986.

Geschwender, James A. *Class, Race, and Worker Insurgency: The League of Revolutionary Black Workers.* Cambridge: Cambridge University Press, 1977.

Gill, Douglas. "Whitman Park Phantoms Picket Cavanaugh's Home," *The Evening Bulletin*, 5/20/71, p. 21, Temple University Urban Archives, Philadelphia, PA.

Gillon, Steven M. *Politics and Vision: The ADA and American Liberalism, 1947–1985.* New York: Oxford University Press, 1987.

Goddard, Stephen B. *Getting There: The Epic Struggle between Road and Rail in the American Century.* New York: Basic Books, 1994.

Goldstein, Paul. Interview, June 16, 2000.

"Greatest Freedom Walk: Leaders Hail City's Progress on in Rights," *Detroit News* (June 23, 1963).

Greenberg, Nancy. "Marty Mullen on Abortion: 'God has told me what I must do," *The Sunday Bulletin* (January 7, 1973).

Greer, George, and Eunice Greer. "Friends Suburban Housing: An Approach to Breaking Racial Barriers in teh Philadelphila Suburbs," *Friends Journal* (March 1959).

Gremly, William. "The Scandal of Cicero," *America* (August 25, 1951).

Hirsch, Arnold R. *Making the Second Ghetto: Race and Housing in Chicago 1940–1960* Cambridge: Cambridge University Press, 1983.

Hoeber, Frank W. Interview, May 2000.

Hunt, Michael. *Ideology and Foreign Policy* (New Haven and London: Yale University Press, 1987.

"An Important Message to the People of Pennsylvania concerning Family Planning," *The Philadelphia Inquirer* (June 29, 1966),

Issues, vol. VII, Nos. 11–12, November-December 1949, Temple University Urban Archives, Philadelphia, PA.

Jack, Homer A. "Chicago Has One More Chance," *The Nation* (September 13, 1947).

—————. "The New Chicago Fires," *The Nation* (November 22, 1947): 551.

Jackson, Kenneth T. *Crabgrass Frontier: The Suburbanization of the United States.* New York: Oxford University Press, 1985.

Jacobs, Jane. "The Need for Concentration," in *Classic Readings in Urban Planning*, ed, Jay M. Stein. New York: McGraw-Hill, Inc, 1995.

Johnson, Charles, and Bob Adelman. *King: The Photobiography of Martin Luther King, Jr.* (New York: Bob Adelman Books, 2000).

Jones, E. Michael. *John Cardinal Krol and the Cultural Revolution.* South Bend, Ind.: Fidelity Press, 1995.

—————. *Libido Dominandi: Sexual Liberation and Political Control.* South Bend, Ind.: St. Augustine's Press, 2000.

—————. *Living Machines* (San Francisco: Ignatius Press, 1995).

Joyce, Tom. "Kennedy Plan Stirs Congress to Rights Battle," *Detroit News* (June 20, 1963).

—————. "Specter of Coming Civil Rights Filibuster Haunts Capitol Hill," *Detroit News* (June 22, 1963).

Kaminski, Duke. "Fund Cutoff Threatened over Welfare Abortions," *The Evening Bulletin* (Decemer 21, 1971).

Kaplan, Morton A. "Letters," *Measure* (August/September 1995).

Katz, Adolph. "Old Houses must Come Down to Make Way for the New: Housing Refugees Not Eager to Go, But Most Feel Tearing Down Their Homes Is for the Best." *The Evening Bulletin,* 9/12/39. Richard Allen Homes Folder, Temple University Urban Archives, Philadelphia, PA.

Katz, Jon. "The Glorious Quest of Martin Mullen, a Lonely Crusader," *The Philadelphia Inquirer* (January 27, 1974).

Kaufman, Bill. "Does Anybody Stay in One Place Anymore?" *Family in America* 11, No. 4 (April 1997).

Kennedy, Lawrence W. *Planning the City upon a Hill: Boston since 1630.* Amherst: The University of Massachusetts Press, 1992.

Kitson, Major Frank. *Gangs and Counter-gangs.* London: Barrie and Rockliff, 1960.

Kleiner, Art. *The Age of Heretics: Heroes, Outlaws and the Forerunners of Corporate Change.* New York: Currency Doubleday, 1996.

Kohler, Saul. "Budget Periled as Democrats Vote to Bar Birth Control Funds," *The Philadelphia Inquirer* (July 26, 1966).

Kunstler, James Howard. *The Geography of Nowhere: The Rise and Decline of America's Man-Made Landscape.* New York: Simon & Schuster, 1993.

Lait, Jack, and Lee Mortimer. *Chicago Confidential.* New York: Crown Publishers, 1950.

Langdon, Philip. *A Better Place to Live: Reshaping the American Suburb.* Amherst: University of Massachusetts Press, 1994.

Lemann, Nicholas. *The Promised Land*. New York: A. A. Knopf, 1991.

Levine, Hillel, and Lawrence Harmon, *The Death of an American Jewish Community: A Tragedy of Good Intentions*. New York: The Free Press, 1992.

Lewis, David L. *King: A Critical Biography*. New York: Praeger, 1970.

Libros, Hal. *Hard-Core Liberals: a Sociological Analysis of the Philadelphia Americans for Democratic Action*. Cambridge, Mass.: Schenkman Publishing Co, 1975.

Liddell-Hart, B. H. *Strategy*. New York: Praeger, 1967.

Lincoln, Joseph L. "2 Kingsessing Killings Spark Racial Strife," *The Sunday Bulletin* (May 16 1971).

Lippmann, Walter. *Public Opinion* (New York: The Free Press, 1922, 1949).

Longstreth, Thatcher. *Main Line WASP: The Education of Thatcher Longstreth*. New York: W. W. Norton, 1990.

Lopez, Kathryn Jean, "Tocqueville Is Our National Psychoanalyst."

Lukacs, John. *Confessions of an Original Sinner*. South Bend, Ind.: St. Augustine's Press, 2000.

————. *Philadelphia: Patricians and Philistines, 1900–1950*. New York: Farrar Straus, Giroux, 1980.

————. Interview, June 9, 2000.

Lukas, J. Anthony. *Common Ground: A Turbulent Decade in the Lives of Three American Families*. New York: Alfred A. Knopf, 1985.

MacDonald, Michael Patrick. *All Souls: A Family Story from Southie*. Boston: Beacon Press, 1999.

Madden, Thomas J. "White Gang Is Resentful of 'Takeover' in Area," *The Philadelphia Inquirer* (May 16, 1971).

Mahl, Thomas. *Desperate Deception: British Covert Operations in the United States 1939–1944*. Washington, D.C.: Brassey's, 1998.

Maitin, Sam. Interview, July 31, 2000.

Mann, Jack. "Negroes Here Pledge More Demonstrations," *Detroit Free Press* (June 25, 1963).

McClory, Robert. *Turning Point: The Inside Story of the Papal Birth Control Commission, and How Humanae Vitae Changed the Life of Patty Crowley adn the Future of the Church*. New York: Crossroad, 1995.

McDermott, John, and Dennis Clark. "Helping the Panicked Neighborhood," reprinted from *Interracial Review* (August 1955).

McGreevy, John T. Interview, October 27, 2000.

————. *Parish Boundaries: The Catholic Encounter with Race in the Twentieth Century Urban North*. Chicago: University of Chicago Press, 1996

————. "Thinking on One's Own: Catholicism in the Amercan Intellectual Imagination, 1928–1960," *The Journal of American History* (June 1997).

McNally, Jay. Interview, July 26, 2000.

McNamee, Father Jack. Interview, May 2000.

McPherson, James Alan. "The Blackstone Rangers," in *Observations of Deviance,* ed. Jack D. Douglas. Washington, D.C.: University Press of America, 1970.

Meehan, Joseph J. "Changing Priest and Changing Parish: The Land of Jacob's Ladder," *Dimensions* (1975).

Meehan, Mary. "How Eugenics Birthed Population Control," *The Human Life Review* (Fall 1998).

Miller, Lawrence McK. *Witness for Humanity: A Biography of Clarence E. Pickett.* Wallingford, Penn.: Pendle Hill Publications, 1999.

Mitchell, Bob. Oral History, Walter M. Phillips Papers, Temple University Urban Archives, Philadelphia, PA.

Mollenkopf, John H. *The Contested City.* Princeton, N.J.: Princeton University Press, 1983.

Moore, Acel, and Gerald McKelvey. "Blacks Developing a 'Siege Mentality,'" *The Philadelphia Inquirer* (May 16, 1971).

Mullen, Martin. Martin Mullen Folder, Temple University Urban Archives, Philadelphia, PA.

"Mullen Battles Birth Control Paln, Promises Fight to Withhold Funds," *The Evening Bulletin* (December 19, 1965).

"Mullen Raps Clark on Birth Control," *Philadelphia Inquirer* (July 10, 1966).

"Mullen to Stump State for Gubernatorial Nod," *The Evening Bulletin* (January 3, 1974).

Mumford, Lewis. *The City in History. Its Origins, Its Transformations, and Its Prospects.* New York: Harcourt, Brace & World, Inc., 1961.

"Mrs. Tucker Denies All Ties with Husband's Business," *The Evening Bulletin* (September 5, 1971).

"Mrs. Tucker Speaks to Cheyney Students," *The Philadelphia Inquirer* (December 27, 1970).

Myrdal, Gunnar. *An American Dilemma: The Negro Problem and Modern Democracy.* New York: Harper & Row, 1962.

Nahaylo, Bohdan, and Victor Swoboda. *Soviet Disunion: A History of the Nationalities Problem in the USSR.* New York: The Free Press, 1990.

"The Negro Revolution," Editorial, *Detroit News* (June 23, 1963).

Newman, Barry. "West End Story: A Neighborhood Died, But One Bostonian Refuses to Let It Go," *The Wall Street Journal* (August 23, 2000).

Novak, Michael. *The Rise of the Unmeltable Ethnics: Politics and Culture in the '70s.* New York: the Macmillan Company, 1971.

Oates, Stephen B. *Let the Trumpet Sound: The Life of Martin Luther King, Jr.* New York: Harper & Row, 1982.

Odom, Maida. "Views from the Project," *Philadelphia Inquirer, Today Magazine* (November 23, 1980).

O'Callaghan, Ann. Interview, May 8, 2000.

"125,000 Walk Quietly in Record Rights Plea," *Detroit Free Press* (June 24, 1963).

"Parenthood Unit Asks State to Give Birth Control Funds," *The Evening Bulletin* (June 28, 1966).

Parks, Michael. "City Negroes Aim for Full Integration," *Detroit News* (June 25, 1963): 1.

Pastore, Anthony. Interview, May 10, 2001.

Peterson, David. "Race War 101: The Battle of Boston," *Culture Wars* (September 2001).

Petshek, Kirk. *The Challenge of Urban Reform: Policies and Programs in Philadelphia.* Philadelphia: Temple University Press, 1973.

Philadelphia City Planning Commission. General Report, 1951, Temple University Urban Archives, Philadelphia, PA.

Philadelphia City Planning Reports, Report for 1946, Temple University Urban Archives, Philadelphia, PA.

"Philadelphia Plans Again," The Better Philadelphia Exhibition, reprinted from *Architectural Forum,* December 1947, Temple University Urban Archives, Philadelphia, PA.

Phillips, Cabell. "GOP Loss Is Laid to the Big Cities: Party Analysis Says Urban Ethnic Groups Provided Victory for Kennedy," *New York Times* (February 26, 1961).

Phillips, Marybeth C., and Michael P. Toner. "Philadelphia's Feisty Irishman," *Irish America Magazine* (January/February 1993).

Phillips, Walter. The Walter M. Phillips Papers, Acc 527. Temple University Urban Archives, Philadelphia, PA.

Planned Parenthood ACC 315, 319, 413, 683, Box 3, Temple University Urban Archives, Philadelphia, PA.

Pohl, Otto J. *Ethnic Cleansing in the USSR, 1937–1949.* Westport, Conn.: Greenwood Press, 1999.

Polak, Maralyn Lois. "Martin Mullen: He's Never Met a Bad Woman," *The Philadelphia Inquirer* (October 22, 1978).

Quigley, Carroll. *Tragedy and Hope: A History of the World in Our Time.* New York: Macmillan, 1966.

Rafsky, William. William Rafsky Papers, Acc 355 Box 1 File 1-1,Temple University Urban Archives, Philadelphia, PA.

Regnery, Henry. *Memoirs of a Dissident Publisher.* New York: Harcourt Brace Jovanovich, 1979.

"Road Beyond the End of the Freedom March," Editorial, *Detroit Free Press* (June 25, 1963).

Rose, Mark H. *Interstate: Express Highway Politics 1939–1989.* Knoxville: University of Tennessee Press, 1979.

Rotella, Carlo. *October Cities: The Redevelopment of Urban Literature*. Berkeley: University of California Press, 1998.

Runkel, David. "Churches Aid Mullen 'Crusade' in Primary Battle with Shapp," *The Evening Bulletin* (April 23, 1974).

————. "Mullen Endorses Shapp," *The Evening Bulletin* (September 10, 1974).

————. "Phila's 10 'Most Wanted' Tax Delinquents Revealed," *The Philadelphia Inquirer* (March 18, 1980).

Sawher, Msgr. Clifford F.. *An Autobiography of a Grateful Priest*. Detroit: Assumption Grotto Press, 2001.

Sawyer, Henry W. III. Oral History, The Walter Phillips Oral History Project, Box 4, Temple University Urban Archives, Philadelphia, PA.

Schelter, Kathryn. Interview, May 5, 2000.

"Scranton Bars Halt in Birth Control Poilcy," *The Evening Bulletin* (July 27, 1966).

Simpson, Christopher. *Science of Coercion: Communication Research and Psychological Warfare 1945–1960*. New York: Oxford University Press, 1994.

Southern, David W. *Jobn LaFarge and the Limits of Catholic Interracialism, 1911–1963*. Baton Rouge: Louisiana State University Press, 1996.

Stalin, J.V. *Works*, vol. 2: 1907–1913. "Marxism and the National Question." Moscow: Foreign Languages Publishing House, 1953.

Steuteville, Robert. "Year of Growth for New Urbanism," *New Urban News* 3, No. 5 (September/October 1998).

Stinnett, Robert. *Day of Deceit: The Truth about FDR and Pearl Harbor* (New York: Simon & Schuster, 2001).

Stolberg, Mary M. *Bridging the River of Hatred: The Pioneering Efforts of Detroit Police Commissioner George Edwards*. Detroit: Wayne State University Press, 1998.

Sunstein, Emily W. *Mary Shelley: Romance and Reality*. Boston: Little, Brown & Co., 1989.

Tate, James H. J. Oral History, Walter M. Phillips Oral History Project, Temple University Urban Archives, Philadelphia, PA.

Taylor, Richard. Interview, May 2000.

Thomas, June Manning. *Redevelopment and Race*. Baltimore: The Johns Hopkins University Press, 1997.

Troxell, Eileen Dougherty. *A History of the Community of Saint Malachy*. Philadelphia.: no pub date.

Tucker, C. Delores. The C. Delores Tucker Folder, Temple University Urban Archives, Philadelphia, PA.

"Urban Renewal Midway," *The Evening Bulletin*, 3/12/62. Temple University Urban Archives, Philadelphia, PA.

Valentine, Steven R. *All Shall Live: Another Quaker Response to the Abortion Dilemma.* Richmond Ind.: Friends United Press, 1980.

Vereyser, Harry. Interview, 7/21/00.

Watson. John B. *Behaviorism.* Chicago: University of Chicago Press, 1930, 1958.

Weber, Michael. *Psychotechniken: die neuer Verfuerhrer* (Stein am Rhein: Christiana Verlag, 1997.

Who Shall Live? Man's Control over Birth and Death: A Report Prepared for the American Friends Service Committee. New York: Hill and Wang, 1970.

Whyte, William H. Jr. *The Organization Man.* New York: Simon & Schuster, 1956.

Williams, Vanessa. "Housing Officials See Obstacles to Replacing the High Rise Project," *Philadelphia Inquirer* (January 14, 1991).

Wirth, Louis. *Louis Wirth on Cities and Social Life.* Chicago: University of Chicago Press, 1964.

————. Papers, Archives, Regenstein Library, University of Chicago, Chicago, IL.

Wylie, Jeanie. *Poletown: Community Betrayed.* Urbana: University of Illinois Press, 1989.

Ylvisaker, Paul. *Conscience and Community: The Legacy of Paul Ylvisaker,* ed. Virginia M. Esposito. New York: Peter Lang, 1999.

————. Papers, Archives, Harvard University, Cambridge, MA.

Index